FEDERAL INCOME TAX

A STUDENT'S GUIDE
TO THE
INTERNAL REVENUE CODE

SIXTH EDITION

By

DOUGLAS A. KAHN
Paul G. Kauper Professor of L~
University of Michi~

JEFFREY H. K~
Larson Professor of ~
Florida State Universi~

FOUNDATION PRESS
2011

THOMSON REUTERS™

© 1990, 1992, 1994 FOUNDATION PRESS
© 1999 DOUGLAS A. KAHN
© 2005 FOUNDATION PRESS
© 2011 By THOMSON REUTERS/FOUNDATION PRESS
   1 New York Plaza, 34th Floor
   New York, NY 10004
   Phone Toll Free 1–877–888–1330
   Fax 646–424–5201
   foundation–press.com

Printed in the United States of America

ISBN 978–1–59941–377–8

Mat #40637319

To Edwin

In fond memory of the inspiration derived
from his life and work.

— DAK

To Mark Baccei, Patrick Geraghty, Liam Montgomery
and John Murnane

"Think where man's glory most begins and ends,
And say my glory was I had such friends." – W. Yeats

— JHK

PREFACE

Although the organization and structure of the book has been revised with this new edition, the goals of the book have not changed from previous editions. This book was written to meet the needs of the tax student who wishes to have a text to supplement the casebook or problem sets that are utilized in the student's course. It is designed to serve two functions.

One function is to provide an overview of the federal income tax laws so that the reader has a blueprint of the structure of the federal income tax system and accordingly is better able to see the role that specific provisions play in that scheme. To determine the meaning and scope of a specific statutory provision, it is useful to examine the provision in the context of the role that it plays in the overarching tax scheme. The authors believe that this book will be helpful to the reader's determination of how specific Code provisions fit within the Code's structure and will be a valuable aid to interpretation.

Another function of the book is to set forth concise, lucid explanations of the major principles of income taxation and significant specific income tax statutory provisions. If a text were written that discussed in detail all (or most) of the current income tax Code provisions, it would consist of a great many volumes. This single volume does not provide that type of coverage. Instead, the book focuses on the major principles that underlie the income tax system and examines those statutory provisions that the authors selected as of importance to tax students. Many of the statutory provisions that are included in this text are examined in detail. Others are described briefly, and the text merely explains the general manner in which they operate. In some instances, the authors have examined and critiqued the likely policy justifications for a statutory provision or for a common law tax doctrine.

Examples or illustrations of statutory provisions are provided throughout the book in order to help the reader understand how the tax provisions apply in various factual contexts. The extensive use of factual illustrations is a key feature of this book.

The authors wish to give special thanks to Tom Barnhill, Jesse Duddy, Alex Hargrove, Diane Liang, Alex Von Fricken and Megan Westcott for their research help in preparing the publication of this book. Thanks also to Diane Cochran, Valerie Horton and Mary McCormick for their work preparing the tables.

This book is up to date as of May 1, 2011.

Douglas A. Kahn
Paul G. Kauper Professor of Law
University of Michigan Law School

Jeffrey H. Kahn
Larson Professor of Law
Florida State University College of Law

v

TABLE OF CONTENTS

PART A. INCOME

PART B. TAX ACCOUNTING

PART C. ATTRIBUTION OF INCOME

PART D. DEDUCTIONS AND CREDITS

PART E. SALE OR EXCHANGE OF PROPERTY

PART F. AMT AND IRD

FEDERAL INCOME TAX

A STUDENT'S GUIDE
TO THE
INTERNAL REVENUE CODE

CHAPTER ONE

INTRODUCTION

¶ **1.0000. HISTORY.** The federal income tax was first adopted in the United States during the Civil War to meet the need for additional revenue. Both the North and the South adopted an income tax. The North's income tax was repealed shortly after the war, and the government of the South was dissolved.

In 1894, a federal income tax was again adopted by Congress. This tax was at a flat rate of two percent, but individual taxpayers (as contrasted to corporations) were granted a $4,000 exemption (in 2010, the current value of that amount is approximately $100,000). The validity of the tax was attacked on several grounds, including the assertion that an income tax is a direct tax and that the 1894 Act violated Article I, Section 9, Clause 4 of the Constitution since this "direct tax" was not apportioned among the states in proportion to population.

In the first decision in *Pollock v. Farmers' Loan & Trust Co.*,[1] the Supreme Court held six to two that a tax on rental income from realty was invalid as a direct tax that was not properly apportioned among the states. The Court also held, for a different reason, that a tax on municipal bond interest was unconstitutional. This latter holding was expressly overruled by the Court in *State of South Carolina v. Baker*.[2] Because the first opinion in *Pollock* left many vital questions unanswered, the parties sought and were granted a rehearing. In the second *Pollock* opinion,[3] the Court held five to four that a tax on income from realty or personalty was invalid as a direct tax. The Court further held that taxes on such income were integral elements of the revenue act which could not be separated from the other parts of the act and so the entire act was struck down.

In 1909, Congress adopted an income tax on the income of corporations. This tax was held to be valid by the Supreme Court in *Flint v. Stone Tracy Co.*[4] on the ground that it was a tax on the privilege of doing business and not a direct tax that had to be apportioned by state population.

---

1. 157 U.S. 429 (1895).
2. 485 U.S. 505 (1988).
3. 158 U.S. 601 (1895).
4. 220 U.S. 107 (1911).

At the same time that Congress passed the 1909 corporate tax, it proposed a constitutional amendment which was ratified by the states on February 25, 1913 as the Sixteenth Amendment. That amendment provides:

> The Congress shall have power to lay and collect taxes on incomes, from whatever source derived, without apportionment among the several states, and without regard to any census or enumeration.

Since ratification of the Sixteenth Amendment, courts have sustained the federal income tax laws against most constitutionally-based objections.

REVENUE ACTS

Shortly after the ratification of the Sixteenth Amendment, Congress passed the Revenue Act of 1913, which constituted an integrated federal income tax law. The 1913 Act imposed a normal tax of one percent (subject to certain exemptions) and a surtax of one percent to six percent on net income over $20,000. By its terms, the 1913 Act was effective for only a number of years after which it would lapse unless extended or unless a new revenue act was adopted. From 1913 to 1939, Congress passed revenue acts every two to three years, and each of those acts constituted a complete body of federal income tax law. The enactment of a new body of tax laws every few years proved to be inefficient, especially since many of the provisions of the expired acts were readopted in the new acts. In 1939, Congress codified the then existing tax laws as the Internal Revenue Code of 1939.

INTERNAL REVENUE CODE

With the adoption of the 1939 Code, a tax law remains in effect until repealed or amended. Amendments, additions, or deletions to provisions of the Code are made by congressional action; typically, Congress will amend a number of provisions within a single act rather than separately pass numerous acts changing individual sections of the Code. The acts amending provisions of the Code carry a variety of titles. Many are called "Revenue Acts" such as the Revenue Act of 1948 and the Revenue Act of 1978. Thus, a citation to a "Revenue Act" dated before 1939 refers to the entire body of federal tax law for that time; however, a "Revenue Act" subsequent to 1939 constitutes only a number of amendments to the Code. Examples of other names given to acts amending the Code are "Technical Amendments Act," "Tax Reduction and Simplification Act," "Taxpayer Relief Act," and "Jobs and Growth Tax Relief Reconciliation Act." The title "Tax Reform Act" is especially popular because it clearly designates the statutory changes as desirable; it is difficult to oppose a change labeled a "reform."

In 1954, Congress repealed the 1939 Code and adopted the Internal Revenue Code of 1954 in its place. The 1954 Code made substantive changes, but principally it was adopted to reorganize the Code into a more rational structure. The 1954 Code has been substantially altered over the years by congressional amendments. Until 1986, the title of the Code continued to be the "Internal Revenue Code of 1954." The Tax Reform Act of 1986 changed the title of the Code to the "Internal Revenue Code of 1986." References herein to the "§ " followed by a number are references to sections of the 1986 Code as amended at the time of this writing.

¶ 1.1000. RATE STRUCTURE. The federal income tax is imposed on taxable income rather than on gross receipts or gross income. In general, taxable income is equal to gross income less certain deductions.

The federal income tax is a graduated or progressive tax system (i.e., the rate structure was set so that the more dollars that a taxpayer earned in a taxable year, the higher was his rate of tax). Under a graduated or progressive tax structure, the tax rates increase in brackets so that while an additional dollar earned by a taxpayer may be taxed at a higher rate than the dollar earned just before it, the additional dollar earned will not increase the taxpayer's tax on the dollars previously earned.

The tax rate schedule that applies to an individual depends upon that individual's filing status—i.e., the status under which the individual filed a federal income tax return for that year. For example, separate tax rate schedules apply to: (1) a married couple who jointly file a return; (2) a married individual who files a separate return; (3) an unmarried individual who files a return as a "surviving spouse" (i.e., a person whose spouse died within the prior two years and where certain other requirements are met); (4) a "head of household," or (5) an unmarried individual who is not in either of the two prior categories. Different tax schedules are provided for each of the filing status categories listed above. A far more steeply progressive tax schedule is applied to estates and trusts. § 1(c). For convenience, in setting forth illustrations or examples of the application of the rate structure, we will use the rates applicable to a married couple who file a joint return.

The tax rate schedule for 2011 will expire at the end of 2012. The rate schedule for the year 2013 and thereafter may be different from the 2011 schedule. As noted in ¶ 1.1100, once a new schedule is established, the dollar amounts that comprise each tax bracket will be adjusted each subsequent year to reflect increases in the cost-of-living. § 1(f). To illustrate the manner in which tax rate schedules operate, we have set

forth below the nominal tax rate schedule for a taxable year beginning
in 2011 for married taxpayers who file a joint return.

Taxable Income	Tax Rate
Up to $17,000	10%
Over $17,000 but not over $69,000	15%
Over $69,000 but not over $139,350	25%
Over $139,350 but not over $212,300	28%
Over $212,300 but not over $379,150	33%
Over $379,150	35%

Tax rates can be viewed from several perspectives, each of which is
designated by a specific term. The schedule above shows the tax rates
that are applied to the dollar amounts in each tax bracket. The highest
tax rate that is applied to any of a taxpayer's taxable income is referred
to as the taxpayer's "marginal rate." For convenience, the word "taxpayer" sometimes is abbreviated as "TP" in this text. For example, if a
married TP filing a joint return had taxable income of $139,351 in 2011,
that TP's marginal rate for that year is 28%. The quotient obtained
from dividing a TP's tax liability for a given year by the TP's income for
that year is referred to as the TP's "average rate"—i.e., the percentage
of the TP's income that is payable as income tax. In calculating the
average rate, the "income" that is used sometimes is the TP's "taxable
income" and sometimes is the TP's "adjusted gross income."[5] For some
purposes, it is important to know a TP's marginal rate; and, for others,
the average rate is important.

While the *nominal* maximum marginal rate for 2010 income is 35%, the
effective marginal rate can be somewhat larger. There are several tax
provisions that, when an individual's income exceeds a specified figure,
reduce the amount of certain deductions that an individual otherwise
would be allowed. A reduction of an individual's allowable deductions
because he earned additional income is equivalent to increasing the
marginal tax rate on those additional dollars of income, and so the
actual maximum marginal rate for 2010 income can exceed 35%. Examples of deductions that are reduced or eliminated when a TP's income
rises above a specified amount are: the reduction of "miscellaneous
itemized deductions" (see § 67) and the floors provided for medical
expense deductions (§ 213(a)) and for personal casualty and theft losses
(§ 165(h)(2)(A)).

Another aspect of the current tax rates is that the Code establishes a
maximum marginal tax rate that can apply to an individual's net capital
gains. § 1(h). The meaning of "capital gains," and "net capital gains,"

---

5.   See ¶ **1.6310** for the meaning of those terms.

and the tax treatment of capital gains are described in Chapter **Twenty–Five**. For example, for the year 2010, the net capital gain of a TP, even one having a 35% marginal tax rate, may be taxed at a rate of only 15%—a very substantial savings in tax liability. Beginning in 2013, most net capital gains will be taxed at a maximum rate of 20% rather than the 15% rate that applies to 2011.[6]

Certain corporate dividends, although not treated as capital gains, may nevertheless qualify for capital gain rates. § 1(h)(11). That provision is scheduled to expire at the end of 2012.

¶ **1.1100. Indexing for Inflation.** The taxable income figures that delineate each tax bracket will be increased annually to reflect increases in the cost-of-living. § 1(f). In other words, the tax brackets are indexed for inflation. Before indexing was adopted, the tax rate structure was subject to "bracket creep." That is, inflation would reduce the purchasing power of the dollar figures that delineated each tax bracket, and consequently, over a period of years, a TP who earned more dollars because of inflation, but who earned the same (or even less) purchasing power as in prior years, would have a larger portion of his income taken from him as taxes. So, tax rates effectively were increased without Congress' passing any legislation. Indexing for inflation has eliminated that problem.

¶ **1.1200. Retroactive Increase in Tax.** A change in the tax law that results in an increase in the amount of a TP's tax liability can be made retroactive without violating the Constitution.[7]

¶ **1.1300. Internal Revenue Service.** The United States tax laws are administered by the Internal Revenue Service (sometimes referred to herein as the "Service" or the "IRS"), which is part of the Treasury Department and is headed by the Commissioner of Internal Revenue (referred to as the "Commissioner").

¶ **1.2000. SOURCES OF THE TAX LAW.**

¶ **1.2100. The Internal Revenue Code.** The most important source, of course, is the statutes which are contained in the Internal

---

6. As a consequence of an amendment adopted in 1997, there are several different tax rates applicable to different categories of capital gains. While some of the complexity engendered by the 1997 Act was removed by simplifying and liberalizing amendments adopted in 1998, there are still different rates for specified categories of capital gains; and the more complex treatment is scheduled to return for years after 2012.

7. *Reed v. United States*, 743 F.2d 481 (7th Cir. 1984). See also *United States v. Hemme*, 476 U.S. 558 (1986).

Revenue Code of 1986. Taxation is primarily a statutory subject, and one of the purposes of a course in that subject is to develop skills in statutory construction. A statute must be read with extreme care. Each word must be considered and weighed; even punctuation must be taken into account.

In construing a tax statute, it is helpful to examine the table of contents to the Internal Revenue Code and note where the section in question is listed. The organizational structure of the Internal Revenue Code may provide guidance to the construction of specific statutory language. In some circumstances, even the heading to a section may influence its construction.[8]

¶ **1.2110. Amendments.** As previously noted, from time to time Congress adds new sections to the Internal Revenue Code, deletes some sections, and amends others. Typically, a number of these changes are combined in one statutory act (e.g., the Tax Reform Act of 1969, the Tax Reform Act of 1976, the Revenue Act of 1978, the Economic Recovery Tax Act of 1981, and the Tax Reform Act of 1986).

¶ **1.2120. Legislative History.** The legislative history of the statutes included in the Code provide an important guide to their construction. Since 1939, the Committee Reports for each Act usually can be found in a volume of the Cumulative Bulletin[9] for the year in question. The Committee Reports for Acts adopted prior to 1939 are collected in one volume of the 1939 Cumulative Bulletin. In addition to the Reports, the Committee Hearings, the congressional debates and other historical material can be useful, but the Committee Reports will usually prove to be the major useful source.

For a number of years now, the staff of the Joint Committee on Taxation has published an explanation of most tax acts after their adoption. The explanations published by the Joint Committee Staff are sometimes referred to as the "Blue Book." Blue Books have been cited by courts and by the Commissioner as authoritative guides to the construction of the statutes discussed therein.[10]

8.   E.g., *House Jr. v. Commissioner*, 453 F.2d 982 (5th Cir. 1972).

9.   See ¶ **1.2300.**

10.   *Miller v. United States*, 65 F.3d 687 (8th Cir. 1995); *Holiday Village Shopping Center v. United States*, 773 F.2d 276 (11th Cir. 1985); and PLR 8550022.

In *Redlark v. Commissioner*,[11] the Ninth Circuit said, "While such post-enactment explanations cannot properly be described as 'legislative history,' they are at least instructive as to the reasonableness of an agency's interpretation of a facially ambiguous statute." The Supreme Court has characterized the Blue Book as a "compelling contemporary indication" of the meaning of a statutory provision.[12]

¶ 1.2200. Treasury Department Regulations. After the Internal Revenue Code, the most important primary source of tax law is the regulations promulgated by the Treasury Department. Most regulations are descriptive in form, often including examples to illustrate the operation of the statutory provision. Because of the increased activity of Congress in passing tax legislation on a virtually annual basis, the burden on Treasury to promulgate regulations has led to the use of a question and answer format in some instances. Such regulations are sometimes referred to as "Q and A regulations."

Regulations can be divided into three separate types: interpretative, legislative, and procedural.[13] The most common form is the interpretative regulation, which, as the name implies, construes and explains the statutes located in the Code. See § 7805. Interpretative regulations "clarify ambiguous terms in the statute or explain how a provision operates."[14] A second category is that of "legislative regulations." Certain statutes expressly delegate to the Secretary of Treasury the task of resolving by "legislative regulation" certain important matters that were omitted from the statute, and some statutes delegate the task of establishing the procedure for making an election authorized by the statute. E.g., § 453(d)(2). The Supreme Court stated that "if Congress has explicitly left a gap for the agency to fill, there is an express delegation of authority to the agency to elucidate a specific provision of the statute by regulation."[15] That type of regulation is legislative.[16]

---

11. 141 F.3d 936 (9th Cir. 1998), reversing, 106 T.C. 31 (1996).

12. *FPC v. Memphis Light, Gas & Water Div.*, 411 U.S. 458, 472 (1973).

13. See *Dunn v. Commissioner*, 615 F.2d 578 (2d Cir. 1980).

14. *Snowa v. Commissioner*, 123 F.3d 190 (4th Cir. 1997).

15. *Chevron U.S.A. v. Natural Res. Def. Council*, 467 U.S. 837, 843–844 (1984). For a discussion of the distinction between legislative and interpretative regulations, see Asimow, *Public Participation in the Adoption of Temporary Tax Regulations*, 44 The Tax Lawyer 343, 350–361 (1991).

16. *Redlark v. Commissioner*, 141 F.3d 936 (9th Cir. 1998).

A procedural regulation, which may also be either legislative or interpretative, deals with such matters as the time, place and manner of making elections, filing forms or statements, seeking administrative review of proposals.

The regulations for a specific statute are easily located. Since 1954, the income tax regulations have the prefix "1" and the number following the prefix is the number of the section of the Code under consideration. For example, a student seeking to examine a regulation construing § 105, would look at regulation § 1.105–1. The "–1" indicates that the regulation is the first in order promulgated under § 105. The regulations following Reg. § 1.105–1 are: §§ 1.105–2, 1.105–3, etc.

¶ **1.2210. Validity of Regulations.** Regulations are given "controlling weight unless they are arbitrary, capricious, or manifestly contrary to the statute."[17] "Only if the code has a meaning that is clear, unambiguous, and in conflict with a regulation does a court have the authority to reject the Commissioner's reasoned interpretation and invalidate the regulation."[18]

While regulations are entitled to great weight, a regulation may be held invalid by a court when it is inconsistent with the statutory language or when there is no statutory basis for the regulatory provision. When a statute may reasonably be construed to have any one of several alternative meanings, the selection of one such meaning in the regulations will be conclusive even if one or more of the alternative constructions were deemed preferable by the court.[19] A court will invalidate a regulation only if its construction is "unreasonable and inconsistent with the language, history, and purpose of the statute."[20]

The Supreme Court's decision in the *Chevron* case has set the standard for the deference to be given to regulations. Under

---

17. *Chevron U.S.A v. Natural Resources Defense Council, Inc.,* 467 U.S. 837, 844 (1984); *Mayo Foundation For Medical Education and Research v. United States,* ___ U.S. ___, 131 S.Ct. 704 (2011).

18. *Redlark v. Commissioner,* 141 F.3d 936, 939 (9th Cir. 1998).

19. *Atlantic Mut. Ins. Co. v. Commissioner,* 523 U.S. 382, 389 (1998); *Chevron U.S.A. v. Natural Resources Defense Counsel, Inc.,* 467 U.S. 837 (1984); *Fulman v. United States,* 434 U.S. 528 (1978).

20. *Estate of Bullard v. Commissioner,* 87 T.C. 261 (1986) (reviewed by the court). See also *Chevron U.S.A. v. Natural Resources Defense Counsel, Inc.,* 467 U.S. 837, 844 (1984); *Mayo Foundation For Medical Education and Research v. United States,* ___ U.S. ___, 131 S.Ct. 704 (2011).

Chevron, if a court determines, under customary statutory construction methods, that Congress had an intention as to the resolution of the precise question in dispute, the court should enforce that intention regardless of what the regulation may provide. However, if the court cannot determine the congressional intent for the precise question in dispute, then the regulation must be enforced unless it is inconsistent with the statute or goes beyond its scope. This rule for favoring the validity of a regulation is referred to as *"Chevron* deference." The often quoted language of *Chevron* that establishes a two-pronged test for determining whether to enforce a regulation is:

> When a court reviews an agency's construction of the statute which it administers, it is confronted with two questions. First, always, is the question whether Congress has directly spoken to the precise question at issue. If the intent of Congress is clear, that is the end of the matter; for the court, as well as the agency, must give effect to the unambiguously expressed intent of Congress. If, however, the court determines Congress has not expressly addressed the precise question at issue, the court does not simply impose its own construction on the statute, as would be necessary in the absence of an administrative interpretation. Rather, if the statute is silent or ambiguous with respect to the specific issue, the question for the court is whether the agency's answer is based on a permissible construction of the statute.[21]

Even when a regulation presents an unreasonable construction of a statute, it is doubtful that the Internal Revenue Service can repudiate its own regulation retroactively (i.e., a TP can generally act in reliance that the Service will accept the validity of a regulation). But see the concurring opinion of Justice Scalia in *United States v. Burke*[22] in which Justice Scalia said that an agency cannot be bound by its own regulation if that regulation is "contrary to law." Of course, if a statute is amended after the promulgation of a regulation, any statement in the regulation that is in conflict with the amendment will be invalidated and disregarded; and the Service is not obliged to follow that regulation.

In *Mayo Foundation*,[23] the Supreme Court held that both interpretative and legislative regulations are entitled to the same

---

21. *Chevron*, 467 U.S. at 842–843. See also *Mayo Foundation, supra* note 17.

22. 504 U.S. 229, 246 (1992).

23. *Supra* note 17.

Chevron deference. The *Mayo Foundation* decision has enhanced the scope and application of the *Chevron* deference rule as it applies to tax regulations. As a consequence of that case, it is expected that Treasury will become more aggressive in promulgating regulations to overturn adverse judicial decisions. In the authors' view, the *Mayo Foundation* rule does not apply to Proposed Regulations.

When a tax statute is re-adopted in essentially the same terms by a subsequent Congress, a court may assume that the subsequent Congress approved of the regulatory, judicial, or other administrative interpretations of the prior statutory provision.[24] That circumstance is referred to as "legislative re-enactment." It is not an absolute rule. In some cases, courts have required evidence that the subsequent Congress knew of the interpretation of the prior statute when they reenacted it.[25]

¶ **1.2220. Retroactive Application.** The general rule is that a regulation does not operate retroactively. There are exceptions, however. A regulation can apply to the earliest of (1) the date on which it was filed with the Federal Register, (2) if a final regulation, the date on which any proposed or temporary regulation to which the final regulation relates was filed with the Federal Register, or (3) the date on which any notice substantially describing the expected contents of any temporary, proposed, or final regulation was issued to the public. § 7805(b)(1). If a regulation is filed or issued within 18 months after enactment of the statutory provision to which the regulation relates, it can apply retroactively. The Secretary has discretion to apply a regulation retroactively to prevent an abuse. § 7805(b)(2), (3).

¶ **1.2230. Proposed and Temporary Regulations.** Before final regulations are promulgated, Treasury issues Proposed Regulations to inform the public of the position that the Treasury plans to take in its final regulations. The Proposed Regulations often are promulgated prior to Treasury's holding hearings or receiving comments from interested parties. In addition to Proposed Regulations, because of the quantity of tax legislation and the need for guidance by the public, Treasury often promulgates Temporary Regulations, which remain effective until replaced by

---

24. See *United States v. Correll*, 389 U.S. 299, 305–306 (1967); *Cottage Savings Assn. v. Commissioner*, 499 U.S. 554 (1991).

25. See *Swallows Holding Ltd. v. Commissioner*, 515 F.3d 162 (3d Cir. 2008).

the final regulations. Temporary regulations issued after November 20, 1988, will expire within three years of issuance, and any temporary regulation issued after that date must also be issued simultaneously as a proposed regulation. § 7805(e). Typically, there will be no hearings or comments prior to the promulgation of temporary regulations. Public comments on Proposed Regulations are invited before they become final regulations.[26]

¶ 1.2231. Significance of Proposed Regulations. The courts have held that Proposed Regulations are not entitled to receive the deference that is granted to final regulations.[27] The Tax Court has held in several decisions that Proposed Regulations "carry no more weight than a position advanced on brief by the" Commissioner.[28] However, even the Tax Court has said that Proposed Regulations "are not a complete nullity," and do give a "warning of things to come."[29]

¶ 1.2232. Significance of Temporary Regulations. Temporary Regulations are given the same deference and weight that is granted to final regulations.[30] Presumably, they are therefore entitled to *Chevron* deference. See **¶ 1.2210**.

¶ 1.2300. Revenue Rulings. In addition to the regulations, the Service publishes rulings indicating its interpretation of the tax law and its application of the tax laws to factual circumstances. Since 1954, these rulings have been published as "Revenue Rulings" which are cited as "Rev. Rul." Some Revenue Rulings are published as "Revenue Procedures" cited as "Rev. Proc." The Service also publishes "Notices" which are equivalent to Rulings.

The rulings and notices are published in a Bulletin called the "Internal Revenue Bulletin," cited as "I.R.B." The Internal Revenue

26. For a criticism of the current practice of issuing Temporary Regulations without first obtaining public comments, see Asimow, *Public Participation in the Adoption of Temporary Tax Regulations*, 44 The Tax Lawyer 343 (1991).

27. E.g., *Mearkle v. Commissioner*, 838 F.2d 880 (7th Cir. 1988). In the view of the authors, the *Mayo Foundation* rule applying *Chevron* deference to tax regulations does not apply to Proposed Regulations. See **¶ 1.2210**.

28. *Zinniel v. Commissioner*, 89 T.C. 357, 369 (1987); *F.W. Woolworth v. Commissioner*, 54 T.C. 1233, 1265–1266 (1970).

29. *Butka v. Commissioner*, 91 T.C. 110, 130 (1988), aff'd 886 F.2d 442 (D.C. Cir. 1989). See also, *Estate of Howard v. Commissioner*, 910 F.2d 633 (9th Cir. 1990).

30. *Nissho Iwai American Corp. v. Commissioner*, 89 T.C. 765, 776 (1987); *Truck & Equipment Corp. v. Commissioner*, 98 T.C. 141, 149 (1992); *Redlark v. Commissioner*, 141 F.3d 936 (9th Cir. 1998); *Miller v. United States*, 65 F.3d 687 (8th Cir. 1995).

Bulletins are published weekly; so fifty-two Bulletins are published each year (except that in 1993, as a cost cutting measure, the Service announced that it would publish only two Bulletins a month for the four months of June through September of that year). In any event, the Bulletins are accumulated semiannually in a bound volume called the "Cumulative Bulletin."

The Revenue Rulings are numbered by the year in which they are promulgated and by the order in which they were considered. Thus, Rev. Rul. 2000–11 refers to a ruling prepared in the year 2000 which has been numbered "11" (prior to 2000, only the last two digits of the year were used, e.g., Rev. Rul. 99–4). The Cumulative Bulletins (Cum. Bull. or C.B.) are also cited by the year involved. For example, 1958–2 Cum. Bull. 150 refers to page 150 of the second volume of the Cumulative Bulletin published in the year 1958. Accordingly, Rev. Rul. 70–11 is cited: Rev. Rul. 70–11, 1970–1 Cum. Bull. 229. Notices are numbered in the same manner as is employed for rulings; an example of a typical citation for a notice is: Notice 90–43, 1990–2 Cum. Bull. 336. If a citation is to an I.R.B. because, for example, the Bulletin has not yet been incorporated into a Cumulative Bulletin, the citation will give the date, number, and page of the I.R.B. For example, Ann. 93–82, 1993–22 I.R.B. 31 refers to the Announcement number 82 published in 1993 at page 31 of I.R.B. number 22.

In the interest of brevity, this text omits citations to Cum. Bulls. and I.R.B.'s and merely cites the Rev. Rul., Rev. Proc., or other item without directing the reader to the volume in which it is contained. The identity of the correct volume can be readily determined.

¶ 1.2310. **Acquiescences.** The Commissioner also publishes an acquiescence or nonacquiescence in certain (but not all) issues which the government lost in civil litigation. Prior to 1991, the Commissioner issued an acquiescence or nonacquiescence only with respect to Tax Court cases that were not decided by a Memorandum decision. Since 1991, the Commissioner has expanded the scope of its acquiescence/nonacquiescence policy to other civil tax cases, including Memorandum Decisions of the Tax Court, District Court, Court of Federal Claims decisions, and decisions of the Circuit Courts of Appeals.[31] An acquiescence (Acq.) or nonacquiescence (Nonacq.) is equivalent to a Rev. Rul. and is given about the same weight. The acquiescences and nonacquiescences are first published in the I.R.B. and then are accumulated and published in a Cumulative Bulletin.

---

31.   See 2007–1 Cum. Bull. xvii.

¶ **1.2320.** **Information Releases.** The Commissioner occasionally issues what amounts to a press release which is referred to as an "information release" (IR) and is published in the I.R.B. but not in the Cum. Bull. The Commissioner also issues, for informational purposes, General Litigation Bulletins which describe the decisions made in cases that involve related issues.

¶ **1.2330.** **Internal Memoranda.** As a consequence of a circuit court decision made under the Freedom of Information Act, the Commissioner is required to make available to the public most of the internal memoranda prepared by its staff.[32] The internal memoranda involved were General Counsel Memorandum (GCM), Actions on Decision (AOD), and Technical Memoranda (TM).

There are also documents known as Field Service Advice memoranda (FSAs) and Chief Counsel Advice memoranda (CCAs) that the National Office of the IRS issues to agents in local offices throughout the country. These advisory memoranda are required by statute to be made available to the public. § 6110(a), (b)(1)(A), (i).

¶ **1.2340.** **Significance.** Rev. Ruls., Acq. and Nonacq. are indicative of the viewpoint of the Service, but they are not entitled to great weight. The Service is not obligated to follow its published rulings or its long-standing administrative construction of the tax law, and they may be repudiated by the Service or by a court. E.g., *Dickman v. Commissioner*,[33] where the Supreme Court stated: "It is well established that the Commissioner may change an earlier interpretation of the law, even if such a change is made retroactive in effect ... This rule applies even though a TP may have relied to his detriment upon the Commissioner's prior position."[34] However, there is a question whether the government is barred from asserting a position in litigation that is at odds with a position taken in a published ruling that has not been withdrawn or modified. The Tax Court holds that the government is not permitted to make a contention in litigation that is contrary to a published ruling *unless* the IRS first withdraws or modifies the ruling.[35] It appears that the withdrawal or modification can be

---

32. See *Taxation with Representation Fund v. IRS*, 646 F.2d 666 (D.C. Cir. 1981).

33. 465 U.S. 330 (1984).

34. See also, *Dixon v. United States*, 381 U.S. 68, 72–75 (1965); and *Automobile Club of Michigan v. Commissioner*, 353 U.S. 180, 183–184 (1957).

35. *Phillips v. Commissioner,* 88 T.C. 529, 534 (1987) (reviewed by the court), rev'd on an unrelated issue, 851 F.2d 1492 (C.A.D.C., 1988); *Rauenhorst v. Commissioner*, 119 T.C. 157, 169–173 (2002).

made effective retroactively.

The Tax Court has stated on numerous occasions that a revenue ruling "is simply the contention of one of the parties to the litigation, and is entitled to no greater weight."[36] However, a number of circuit courts of appeals have not accepted the Tax Court's relegation of rulings to the scrap pile (except for the Tax Court's policy of preventing the government from contradicting its published rulings in litigation without first withdrawing or modifying them). While most appellate courts give little weight to rulings, they have attached some significance to them; and some appellate courts give considerable deference to rulings. For example, the Ninth Circuit stated that it would give weight to an established revenue ruling of long standing that fell within the Commissioner's "authority to implement the congressional mandate in some reasonable manner."[37] In *Ricards v. United States*,[38] the Ninth Circuit stated that while revenue rulings do "not have the force and effect of law," they "do constitute a body of experience and informed judgment to which courts may properly resort for guidance."[39] The Fifth Circuit said, "the Tax Court has long been fighting a losing battle with the various courts of appeals over the proper deference to which revenue rulings are due ... they are clearly less binding on the courts than treasury regulations or code provisions, but probably ... more so than the mere legal conclusions of the parties."[40] However, in a footnote to a subsequent portion of the Fifth Circuit's opinion, the court said that "the position of the Tax Court [on this issue] is not without some merit."[41] Also, in *Davis v. United States*,[42] the Supreme Court stated: "Although the Service's interpretive rulings do not have the force and effect of regulations [citation omitted], we give an agency's interpretations and practices considerable weight where they involve the contemporaneous construction of a statute and where they have been in long use." The Sixth Circuit went even further and said, "revenue rulings 'are entitled to great

---

36. E.g., *Estate of Lang v. Commissioner*, 64 T.C. 404 (1975). See also *Beyer v. Commissioner*, 92 T.C. 1304, 1311 (1989).

37. *Estate of Lang v. Commissioner*, 613 F.2d 770 (9th Cir. 1980).

38. 683 F.2d 1219 (9th Cir. 1981).

39. See also *Bob Jones University v. United States*, 461 U.S. 574 (1983); *Oetting v. United States*, 712 F.2d 358 (8th Cir. 1983).

40. *Estate of McLendon v. Commissioner*, 135 F.3d 1017 (5th Cir. 1998).

41. *Estate of McLendon v. Commissioner*, *supra*, fn. 12.

42. 495 U.S. 472 (1990).

deference and have been said to have the force of legal precedents unless unreasonable or inconsistent with the provisions of the Internal Revenue Code.' "[43]

In any event, it can be valuable for a TP to know the current position of the Service on an issue.

¶ **1.3000. LETTER RULINGS.** If, before embarking on a transaction, a TP wishes to know the position the Service will take as to the tax consequences of that transaction, the TP may request the Commissioner to rule in advance on that issue. The request for a ruling is made by sending a formal letter to the Commissioner according to procedures laid down by the Service.[44] The Service will not rule on certain questions (e.g., it generally will not rule on a question if it requires the resolution of a factual issue).[45] One important limitation is that the Service ordinarily will not issue a "comfort" ruling—that is, absent certain circumstances, it will not rule "with respect to an issue that is clearly and adequately addressed by statute, regulations, decisions of a court, revenue rulings, revenue procedures, notices, or other authority published in the Internal Revenue Bulletin."[46] Also, the Service will not rule on a "frivolous" issue.[47] The Service will not rule on alternative plans or hypothetical situations.[48] In its revenue procedures, the Service lists a number of specific areas in which it either will not rule or ordinarily will not rule.

If the Service is willing to rule, it does so in the form of a letter to the TP answering his question, and this letter is sometimes called a "letter ruling" or a "private letter ruling." As a matter of its practice, the Service will abide by its letter ruling but only as to the very TP who formally requested the ruling, only if the TP accurately stated all of the relevant facts in his request for the ruling, and only if the law is not changed after the ruling has been given.[49] If a TP wishes to have a more binding commitment from the Service, the TP can request the Service to enter into a "closing agreement." A closing agreement is a final agreement between the Service and a TP on a specific issue or liability. "It is

---

43. *The Progressive Corporation and Subsidiaries v. United States,* 970 F.2d 188, 194 (6th Cir. 1992).

44. See Rev. Proc. 2010–1.

45. See Rev. Proc. 2010–1 (Sec. 6) and Rev. Proc. 2010–3 (Sec. 4.02(1)).

46. Rev. Proc. 2010–1 (Sec. 6.11).

47. Rev. Proc. 2010–1 (Sec. 6.10).

48. Rev. Proc. 2010–1 (Sec. 6.12).

49. Rev. Proc. 2010–1 (Sec. 11).

final unless fraud, malfeasance, or a misrepresentation of a material fact can be shown."[50]

Except for certain information, including company name, which must be deleted, the Service must disclose its letter rulings (and other written determinations) to the public. § 6110. In this book, a letter ruling is cited as "PLR" or "Private Letter Ruling" followed by the number of that ruling. You will often see a letter ruling cited as "PLR" (i.e., "private letter ruling") even though there is very little privacy accorded to the ruling. Some of the letter rulings are deemed to be of such general interest that they are studied further by the Service and eventually serve as the basis for a published revenue ruling.

Upon receiving a request from a field office, the National Office of the Service will give advice or guidance to the field office in the form of an internal memorandum.[51] The advice will relate to technical and procedural questions and to the interpretation and proper application of the tax law. These advice memorandums are called "Technical Advice Memorandums" or "TAMs." The TAMs, in form and substance, are similar to Private Letter Rulings.

Both Private Letter Rulings and TAMs are identified by a nine-digit number, the first four digits of which designate the year in which it was promulgated (prior to 1999, only the last two digits of the year were used), the next two digits of which designate the week of that year in which it was promulgated, and the last three digits of which merely identify that PLR or TAM. For example, PLR 200038006 is a Private Letter Ruling that was promulgated in the 38th week of the year 2000, and is designated by the number 006.

While § 6110(k)(3) prohibits the use of written determinations, which term includes letter rulings, as precedents, the courts have occasionally referred to letter rulings as evidence of the interpretative position held by the Service during the period of time in which the rulings were in effect.[52]

¶ 1.3100. User Fees for Seeking a Ruling. Prior to 1988, the Service did not impose a charge for providing letter rulings or other statements of its views on issues posed by a TP. That is no longer true. Since February 1, 1988, a TP is required to pay a fee to the Service for requests for rulings, opinion letters, determination let-

---

50. Rev. Proc. 2010–1 (Sec. 2.02).

51. Rev. Proc. 2010–2.

52. E.g., *Rowan Cos., Inc. v. United States*, 452 U.S. 247, fn. 17 (1981).

ters, and for similar requests. See § 7528 and Rev. Proc. 2010–1 (Sec. 15). The 2010 fee schedule is set forth in Rev. Proc. 2010–1 (Appendix A). The fees range from a low of $150 to a high of $50,000. No fee is charged for certain items. The amount charged as a fee is determined by the category of the subject matter of the request. The fee is payable in advance and typically is not refundable unless the Service refuses to rule on the issues.[53]

¶ **1.3200. Transactional Tax Risk Insurance.** Some insurance companies offer to insure that a TP will obtain a desired tax consequence for a proposed transaction. Rather than to seek to obtain a ruling from the Service, a TP can purchase insurance to cover the risk of adverse tax consequences. The insurer will have its panel of tax experts screen a request for insurance coverage to evaluate the likelihood of the TP's prevailing on the issue and to determine whether the insurer should issue the policy.[54]

¶ **1.4000. TAX LITIGATION.** Tax disputes can be litigated in any one of three courts at the choice of the TP. He may select the Tax Court (previously known as the "Board of Tax Appeals"), a United States District Court, or the United States Court of Federal Claims. The Tax Court is authorized to have 19 active judges, who are appointed for a 15–year term, plus senior judges and special trial judges. § 7443. To bring suit in a District Court or the United States Court of Federal Claims, the TP must first pay the entire amount of his tax deficiency and then claim a refund from the Service. § 7422(a).[55] If any interest or penalty is owing on the deficiency, it is unsettled whether they must also be paid before a refund suit can be brought. The TP can petition for a redetermination of his tax deficiency in the Tax Court without first paying the deficiency. An appeal from the Tax Court or the District Court can be taken to a United States Court of Appeals for the appropriate circuit, and from there the losing party can seek certiorari to the United States Supreme Court. An appeal from the United States Court of Federal

---

53. Rev. Proc. 2010–1 (Sec. 15.10).

54. Kenneth A. Geary, "New Opportunities for Tax Lawyers: Insuring Tax Transactions," 104 Tax Notes 26 (July 5, 2004). If the insured collects on such a policy, will the proceeds payable to the insured be included in the insured's gross income? These policies typically provide a gross-up provision which the insured can purchase to provide additional coverage to pay for any income tax liability that the insured might incur from receiving the proceeds. One of the authors of this book has published an article concluding that the proceeds of a tax insurance policy are *not* includable in the insured's gross income. Jeffrey Kahn, "Hedging the IRS—A Policy Justification for Excluding Liability and Insurance Proceeds," 26 Yale Jour. on Regulation 1 (2009).

55. *Flora v. United States*, 357 U.S. 63 (1958), aff'd on rehearing, 362 U.S. 145 (1960).

Claims can be taken to the United States Court of Appeals for the Federal Circuit. Further review can be obtained only by certiorari to the Supreme Court.

While the Tax Court is located in Washington, D.C., its judges hold court in numerous cities throughout the United States.

¶ 1.4100. Review of Tax Court Decisions by the Entire Court. A Tax Court decision typically is made by a single Tax Court judge. However, the Chief Judge of the Tax Court has the authority to have a proposed decision of a judge reviewed by all of the active members of the Court. When a decision has been so reviewed, all of the active judges vote, and the decision is referred to as "reviewed by the court."

In an interview, a former Chief Judge of the Tax Court said that a decision of a single judge generally is selected by a Chief Judge for review by the entire court if: (1) it proposed to invalidate a regulation; (2) it conflicts with an opinion of a circuit court of appeals; or (3) it would reverse the effect of a prior Tax Court decision or opinion.[56]

¶ 1.4200. *Golsen* Rule. Will the Tax Court follow the precedent established by a circuit court of appeals decision if the case in question is appealable to that circuit court? Prior to 1970, the Tax Court took the position that, since it was a national court, it was not bound to follow the decision of a court of appeals to which an appeal from the case before the Tax Court would be taken.[57] This approach sometimes imposed a burden on the parties to an action by unnecessarily requiring them to appeal to obtain a decision of the court of appeals requiring the Tax Court to follow the appellate court's rule. Both parties incurred expenses and time in having to take that step. In a 1970 reviewed decision, the Tax Court decided the case of *Golsen v. Commissioner*.[58] In that decision, the Tax Court abandoned its prior practice and adopted the rule that, in deciding a case, it would henceforth apply the rule of the court of appeals to which an appeal in that case would lie. This rule of deference became known as the *Golsen* rule.

56. Daily Tax Report (DTR) No. 128 at p. G–2 (July 2, 1992).

57. See *Lawrence v. Commissioner*, 27 T.C. 713 (1957), rev'd on another issue, 258 F.2d 562 (9th Cir. 1958).

58. 54 T.C. 742 (1970) (reviewed by the court), aff'd 445 F.2d 985 (10th Cir. 1971).

¶ **1.4300. Memorandum Decisions of the Tax Court.** Tax Court opinions typically are published in an official reporter called the "United States Tax Court Reports" and cited as "T.C." The Chief Judge of the Tax Court can designate a judge's opinion as a "Memorandum Opinion," and those opinions are not published in the official publication. Memorandum Opinions are published by two unofficial publications that are readily available to the general public. At one time, Tax Court judges pretended to ignore Memorandum Opinions and would not cite them. That practice has changed, and Tax Court judges now do cite to Memorandum Opinions. However, a former Chief Judge of the Tax Court stated that Tax Court judges do not treat Memorandum Opinions as precedents to which stare decisis applies.[59]

¶ **1.4400. Board of Tax Appeals (BTA).** Originally, the Tax Court was known as the United States Board of Tax Appeals, whose decisions are cited as "BTA."

¶ **1.4500. Burden of Proof.** "Burden of proof" refers only to factual issues. Prior to the adoption of the Internal Revenue Service Restructuring and Reform Act of 1998, the burden of proof in tax cases, regardless of the forum in which the case was tried, was on the TP. There were some exceptions in which the burden was placed on the government for certain issues, but there were only a few statutory provisions for which that was true.

There are a few statutory provisions in which the burden of proof that the TP must carry is heavier than the usual one. E.g., § 533(a) requires a corporation to prove by "a preponderance of the evidence" that it did not have a tax avoidance purpose even though it had allowed its earnings to accumulate beyond its reasonable needs. While the 1998 Act significantly changed the general rules on burden of proof, it does not alter the burden that is placed on a party by a specific statutory provision (such as the provision mentioned above in § 533(a)). § 7491(a)(3).

The 1998 Act added § 7491 to the Code. This provision places the burden of proof in any tax case on the government if certain conditions are satisfied. The TP must first introduce credible evidence with respect to a factual issue that is relevant to the TP's liability for an income or transfer tax. The burden of proof then shifts to the government on that factual issue provided that the TP has complied with applicable statutory requirements to substantiate

59. Daily Tax Reports (DTR) No. 128 at p. G–2 (July 2, 1992).

certain expenditures (e.g., charitable gifts and travel and entertainment expenses) and provided that the TP has maintained records required by the Code and has cooperated with reasonable requests of the government for witnesses, information, documents, meetings, and interviews. § 7491(a). According to the legislative history, one element of the requirement of cooperating with the government is that the TP must have exhausted all administrative remedies (including appeal rights within the Service), but the exhaustion of remedies requirement does not require the TP to agree to an extension of the statutory period of limitations. As to corporations, partnerships, and trusts, they can avail themselves of this provision only if they satisfy certain net worth requirements (generally, the entity's net worth cannot exceed $7 million) and the entity cannot have more than 500 employees. § 7491(a)(2)(C). As to each of the conditions required for shifting the burden of proof to the government, the TP has the burden of proving that he has satisfied those conditions.

The government also has the burden of production with respect to the liability of an *individual* for a penalty, or an addition to tax, or any additional amount imposed by the Code. § 7491(c). Also, in certain circumstances where the government raised a new issue late in the proceedings, the burden of proof shifts to the government. That principle may still be applicable.

While the burden of proof applies only to factual issues, once the Commissioner has assessed a tax, the Commissioner's construction of a statute is entitled to a "legal presumption of correctness."[60] It is doubtful that the presumption of correctness is given much weight by the courts.

¶ 1.4600. **Recovery of Litigating Costs.** In certain (but not all) circumstances, a TP who prevails in litigation against the government can recover administrative and litigating costs from the government. This can include attorney fees, but there is a ceiling on the hourly rate that can be recovered.

¶ 1.5000. **CHECKLIST OF ISSUES.** In analyzing a tax problem, the following checklist of questions may be helpful in spotting relevant issues:

Does an item constitute income?

Does an item constitute a loss?

Is the income or loss realized?

---

60. *United States v. Fior D'Italia, Inc.,* 536 U.S. 238 (2002).

To whom was the income or loss realized?

When was the income or loss realized?

Was the income or loss "recognized" and, if so, when?

How is the income or loss characterized (e.g., capital gain or loss, section 1231 gain or loss, or ordinary income or loss)?

If a loss was recognized, is it deductible?

What items constitute tax deductions?

Are such tax deductions allowed?

When are such tax deductions allowed?

How is a tax deduction to be characterized (e.g., as an ordinary deduction or as a capital loss)?

Is a tax deduction an itemized or nonitemized deduction?

Is a tax deduction a "miscellaneous itemized deduction?"

What surtaxes are applicable?

What credits may be deducted from the tax bill (e.g., dependent care credit)?

¶ 1.6000.   ACCOUNTING FOR TAX PURPOSES.

¶ 1.6100.   **Accounting Period.** Income and deductions for tax purposes are determined for a taxable accounting period. Income and deductions are determined on an annual basis. See ¶ **1.6400**.

¶ **1.6110.   Election Period.** The taxable period is usually a calendar year, but a TP may be permitted to elect to report his income for a fiscal year which ends on the last day of any calendar month.

¶ **1.6120.   Short Year.** A taxable year may be a period less than 12 months; for example, where a TP dies prior to the close of his regular taxable year. §§ 441(b) and 443(a).

¶ **1.6130.   Variable Year.** In certain circumstances, a taxable year may be a period which varies between 52 and 53 weeks. § 441(f).

¶ **1.6200.   Method of Accounting.** The period in which a TP reports income or loss may depend upon the method of accounting used. If, as to one or more items, the method of accounting used by a TP does not "clearly reflect income," the TP can be required to report that item in a manner that does clearly reflect income. § 446(b).[61]

¶ 1.6210.   Cash Receipts and Disbursements Method. The standard method of tax reporting for individuals is based upon cash receipts. Under the cash receipts and disbursements method, income is reported when cash or its equivalent is actually or constructively received by the TP and expenses are generally deducted when actually paid. Treas. Reg. § 1.451–1. Certain corporate TPs are not permitted to use the cash receipts and disbursements method. The cash method also is prohibited to certain partnerships that have at least one partner that is a corporation, and tax shelter enterprises cannot use the cash method. § 448. Even for individual TPs, a TP usually cannot use the cash method if his business consists of the sale of inventories. § 471(a); Treas. Reg. § 1.446–1(c)(2)(i).

There are a few circumstances in which the Code requires a TP, even a TP who otherwise utilizes the cash method, to report certain types of income on what amounts to the accrual method. For example, if a corporate bond or other debt instrument is issued for a discount price (i.e., a price that is less than the principal of the debt (such as the face amount of a bond)), the amount of the discount may be treated as "original issue discount."[62] If so, the discount may have to be reported as income of the bondholder (or noteholder) over the term of the debt instrument even if payment will not be received in that year. § 1272.

¶ 1.6211.   Constructive Receipt. If a cash method TP has an unqualified vested right to receive immediate payment, the TP cannot escape the recognition of income therefrom by deferring the time that payment is to be made or by otherwise turning his back on the income. Such income is recognized at the time that the TP has the right to immediate payment, and the doctrine which causes that recognition of income is called "constructive receipt." Treas. Reg. § 1.451–2. However, if a cash method TP agrees to the deferral of payment *before his right to the payment has been earned*, subject to the requirements imposed by § 409A, the TP will not recognize income until the date on which the deferred payment or payments are

---

61.   See, e.g., *Ford Motor Co. v. Commissioner*, 71 F.3d 209 (6th Cir. 1995).

62.   Original issue discount is discussed in Chapter **Sixteen**.

to be made.[63] Similarly, an agreement to defer receipt of an income payment prior to the date on which the right to the payment becomes unconditional generally will not trigger the constructive receipt doctrine, and such income usually will not be recognized until the deferred payment is due.[64]

In 2004, Congress added § 409A to the Code to modify the constructive receipt doctrine's application to nonqualified deferred compensation arrangements. A deferred compensation plan is nonqualified if it is not covered by one of the statutory provisions that provide special beneficial treatment to certain deferred compensation benefits (i.e., it is not a qualified plan).[65] Section 409A establishes additional requirements for an employee to be allowed to defer compensation income. Section 409A does not cause income recognition if there is a substantial risk of forfeiture. § 409A(a)(1)(A).[66]

If a TP's control of the receipt of property is subject to substantial limitations or restrictions, the TP will not be treated as having constructively received the property. Treas. Reg. § 1.451–2(a).

¶ 1.6212. Economic Benefit. A cash method employee will recognize income on the employer's creation for the employee of a vested right to deferred compensation even though the employee will not receive the amount of the deferred compensation until some years later. Income will be recognized at the time that the employee's rights are established if the employee's interest has an ascertainable fair market value and if it provides the employee with an economic benefit that is the equivalent of the receipt of cash.[67] This principle is referred to as the "economic benefit" doctrine. A common circumstance in which this doctrine is applied occurs when an employer creates an obligation to provide an annuity for an employee to begin at a later date when the employee retires, and the employer funds its obligation so that the present value of employee's right to an annuity at a future date can be deter-

---

63. *Robinson v. Commissioner*, 44 T.C. 20 (1965).

64. *Martin v. Commissioner*, 96 T.C. 814 (1991).

65. See ¶ **3.7000.**

66. The operation of § 409A is discussed at ¶ **3.6100**.

67. See *Sproull v. Commissioner*, 16 T.C. 244 (1951), aff'd 194 F.2d 541 (6th Cir. 1952); *Goldsmith v. United States*, 586 F.2d 810 (Ct. Cl. 1978).

mined.[68]

While the economic benefit doctrine continues to be important, the provisions of § 83, which deal with an employee's or independent contractor's receipt of property or an interest in property as compensation for services, have preempted most of the subject matter of that doctrine.[69]

¶ 1.6220. Accrual Method. Under the accrual method, income or deductions are "realized" when the TP's right to receive payment or his obligation to make a payment becomes fixed and the amount is determinable with reasonable accuracy. The test for the proper date for the accrual of an expense is the "all events" test—i.e., the earliest date on which all of the events have occurred that determine the fact of liability and permit the determination of the amount of such liability with reasonable accuracy and for which economic performance has occurred with respect to the liability. Treas. Reg. § 1.461–1(a)(2)(i).[70] If only a portion of the amount of a liability can be determined and the other requirements are satisfied, the amount of the liability that can be determined with reasonable accuracy can be taken into account. Treas. Reg. § 1.461–1(a)(2)(ii).

Generally, the payment of a contested liability will accrue that liability even though the TP continues to contest it. § 461(f). Under § 461(h), subject to certain exceptions, a liability with respect to an item will not accrue under the "all events" test any earlier than the date on which economic performance with respect to that item occurs.

Even if the "all events" test is satisfied, an accrual method TP will be denied a deduction if its allowance would contravene the requirement of § 446(b) that a TP's reporting method must "clearly reflect income."[71]

¶ 1.6230. Other Methods. Various accounting methods may be developed to meet the special demands of a particular business.

---

68. See *United States v. Drescher*, 179 F.2d 863 (2d Cir. 1950).

69. Section 83 is discussed at ¶¶ **3.3000–3.3900**. The application of § 83 to property used to fund a nonqualified deferred compensation plan is modified by the 2004 adoption of § 409A. See ¶ **3.6100** for a discussion of that provision.

70. See *Charles Schwab Corp. and Subsidiaries v. Commissioner*, 107 T.C. 282, 291–296 (1996), aff'd 161 F.3d 1231 (9th Cir. 1998).

71. See, e.g., *Ford Motor Co. v. Commissioner*, 71 F.3d 209 (6th Cir. 1995).

For example, income from most construction, building, manufacturing, or installation contracts that are not completed within the
taxable year in which the contract was made (i.e., so-called "long-
term contracts") must be reported on the percentage-of-comple-
tion method. § 460. Generally, in the absence of a specific requirement, the Service will permit reporting based upon any fair,
good-faith accounting method.

¶ 1.6300.   Computation of Tax.

¶ 1.6310.   Method of Computation. The method of tax computation for an individual may be described as follows:

(a) Determine TP's *gross income*.

(b) Subtract the TP's *nonitemized deductions* (most of which are
listed in § 62(a)) in order to determine TP's *adjusted gross
income* (hereinafter AGI). [Note that the Code does establish a
few nonitemized deductions that are not listed in § 62. E.g.,
§ 71(f)(1)(B)].

(c) Subtract from AGI the TP's exemption deductions (explained
in Chapter **Eleven**) and subtract the greater of the TP's itemized
deductions or the TP's standard deduction (explained in Chapter
Ten). The resulting figure is the TP's taxable income.

(d) Apply tax rates to determine the normal tax. *Note:* Tax rates
change in stages so that not every dollar of income is taxed at the
same rate.

(e) Subtract *tax credits* and add *surtaxes* to arrive at liability or
refund. *Note:* In some instances, a tax credit is deducted before
adding any applicable surtax; in some instances, a tax credit is
deducted afterwards, depending upon the credit and surtax involved. Unless the surtax is computed as a percentage of the tax
liability (and no present surtax is so computed), it makes no
difference whether the credit is deducted before or after adding
the surtax.

¶ 1.6320. Illustration of Computation.

$50,200.00	(Gross Income for the Calendar Year 2003)
- $3,500.00	(§ 62(a) Deductions)
$46,700.00	(AGI)
- $10,500.00	(Exemptions plus Itemized Deductions)

$36,200.00	(Taxable Income)

$36,200.00	(Taxable Income)
$4,730.00	(Tax) [Tax on $36,200 taxable income using the tax rates applicable to married TPs filing a joint return]

$4,730.00	(Tax)
- $300.00	(Credits)

$4,430.00	(Total Tax Bill)

¶ **1.6330. Civil Penalties.** There are a large number of circumstances in which civil penalties are imposed on a TP either for failing to comply with a requirement (such as: failing to file a return or a required statement or failing to pay all of a tax that is due) or for providing misleading information. Several of those civil penalties are discussed below.

¶ **1.6331. Accuracy–Related Penalty.** Section 6662 of the Code imposes a penalty for the underpayment of a tax required to be shown on a return if the underpayment is attributable to one of seven circumstances described in that provision. This penalty does not apply to any portion of an underpayment for which a fraud penalty[72] is imposed. § 6662(b). An "underpayment" is the excess of the proper amount of tax that is owing over the amount shown to be owing on the return. § 6664(a). The underpayment is reduced by the amount of the unreported tax that was previously assessed or paid and is increased by any rebates to the TP. There are three exceptions to the accuracy-related penalty: the reasonable cause exception, the substantial authority exception, and the adequate disclosure exception. Those three are described below.

Reasonable Cause. Subject to an exception for a substantial overvaluation of gifts to a charity, no penalty will be imposed on any portion of an underpayment if there was reasonable cause for the TP's position and the TP acted in good faith. § 6664(c)(1). Another exception is that this provision does not apply to an underpayment arising from a transaction that either lacks economic substance (as defined in § 7701(*o*)) or fails the requirements of a similar rule. § 6664(c)(2). If a

---

72. See ¶ **1.6332.**

transaction is a "reportable transaction" as described in § 6707A(c), there are additional requirements for the reasonable cause exception to apply. § 6664(d).

Substantial Authority. One of the seven circumstances to which the accuracy-related penalty applies is an underpayment that is attributable to a TP's substantial "understatement" of the income tax that is owing. However, an understatement will not include any item for which there is or was substantial authority for the treatment accorded by the TP. § 6662(d)(2)(B)(i). In other words, such an item is treated, for purposes of determining a penalty, as if the item were correctly reported on the return. Treas. Reg. § 1.6662–4(d)(1). The substantial authority exception does not apply to the extent that the underpayment is attributable to a tax shelter—i.e., an entity or plan whose purpose is the avoidance or evasion of a federal income tax. § 6662(d)(2)(C)(ii).

The substantial authority standard is an objective standard that requires an analysis of the existing law and an application of the law to the applicable facts. The subjective belief of the TP is irrelevant to the availability of this exception. The types of authorities that can be utilized in determining whether substantial authority exists represent a wide variety of sources, including: proposed and Temporary Regulations, letter rulings, the Blue Book, legislative histories, and, of course, the Code, final regulations, and cases. Treas. Reg. § 1.6662–4(d)(3). While letter rulings are barred from being treated as precedents, they can be used to satisfy the substantial authority exception. All of the relevant authorities must be considered, and there is substantial authority only if "the weight of the authorities supporting the treatment is substantial in relation to the weight of the authorities supporting contrary treatment.... There may be substantial authority for more than one position with respect to the same item." Treas. Reg. § 1.6662–4(d)(3). Even if there are no interpretive authorities on point, a "position that is supported only by a well-reasoned construction of the applicable statutory provision" will constitute substantial authority. *Ibid.*

Adequate Disclosure and Reasonable Basis. That portion of an understatement of income tax that is attributable to an item with respect to which the relevant facts affecting its tax treatment are adequately disclosed in the return or in a statement attached to the return and for which there is a reasonable basis for the TP's treatment is treated as properly reported and therefore is not subject to a penalty. § 6662(d)(2)(B)(ii). The adequate disclosure and reasonable basis exception does not apply to tax shelter items. § 6662(d)(2)(C). The "reasonable basis" standard is a significantly higher standard than merely not being "frivolous" or "patently improper." The reasonable basis standard is *not* satisfied by a so-called "return position" that is merely arguable or merely a colorable claim. Treas. Reg. § 1.6662–3(b)(3)

The penalty imposed is 20% of the amount of underpayment that is attributable to a circumstance that is one of the seven listed in that provision. § 6662(a). If an underpayment is attributable to a "gross valuation misstatement," which term is defined below as it applies to most income tax property valuations, the penalty will be 40% of the portion of the underpayment that is attributable to that inaccurate valuation. § 6662(h). To the extent that an underpayment is attributable to one or more "nondisclosed noneconomic substance transactions," the penalty will be 40% of that amount of the underpayment. A nondisclosed noneconomic substance transaction is a transaction lacking economic substance for which the relevant facts affecting its tax treatment were not adequately disclosed in the return or a statement attached to the return. § 6662(i).

The seven circumstances to which, subject to the three exceptions discussed above, the accuracy-related penalty applies are:

(1) *Negligence or disregard of rules or regulations.* The term "negligence" refers to a failure to make a reasonable effort to comply with the Code or to take ordinary and reasonable care in preparing a tax return. Negligence can arise from the failure to keep adequate books or records or to substantiate items properly. Treas. Reg. § 1.6662–3(b)(1). The term "disregard" includes any careless, reckless, or intentional disregard of rules or regulations. § 6662(c). If a position taken by a TP is contrary to a regulation, the TP's position must be one that has a realistic possibility of being sustained. Treas. Reg. § 1.6662–3(b)(2).

(2) *Any substantial understatement of income tax.* An understatement of income tax for a taxable year is substantial if it exceeds the greater of: (i) 10% of the proper income tax for that year, or (ii) $5,000 ($10,000 for most corporations).

§ 6662(d)(1). For corporations, the threshold cannot exceed $10,000,000. An "understatement" is the excess of the proper amount that is required to be shown on the return over the amount actually shown on the return (less rebates). § 6662(d)(2). There are special provisions in § 6662A for understatements with respect to reportable and listed transactions as defined in § 6707A(c).

(3) *Any income tax substantial valuation misstatement.* As to property valuation, a misstatement on a return is substantial if the value or basis of any property that is claimed on the return is at least 150% of the actual value or basis of that property. § 6662(e)(1). There are specific rules concerning the price claimed for property or services in transactions between related organizations or businesses. A typical example of a misstatement of value is an overvaluation of property contributed to a charity. No penalty is imposed, however, unless the underpayment for that year that is attributable to substantial valuation misstatements exceeds $5,000 ($10,000 for most corporations). § 6662(e). As noted above, if there is a gross valuation misstatement, the penalty imposed is 40% of the underpayment attributable thereto—in other words, the penalty on that portion of an underpayment is doubled. The meaning of a "gross valuation misstatement" is set forth in § 6662(h).

(4) *Any substantial overstatement of pension liabilities.*

(5) *Any estate or gift tax substantial valuation understatement.*

(6) *Any disallowance of claimed tax benefits by reason of a transaction lacking economic substance (within the meaning of § 7701(o)) or failing to meet the requirements of any similar rule of law.*

(7) *Any undisclosed foreign financial asset understatement.*

The Code imposes additional reporting requirements and penalties for transactions connected to a tax shelter. See § 6700.

¶ 1.6332. Fraud Penalty. If any part of an underpayment is due to fraud, a penalty will be imposed that is equal to 75% of that amount of the underpayment that is due to fraud. If the Service succeeds in proving that any portion of an underpayment is attributable to fraud, then all of the underpayment will be deemed attributable to fraud except for the portion of the underpayment that the TP can prove by a preponderance of the evidence is not due to fraud—i.e., the burden of proof shifts to the TP once the government establishes fraud, and the "preponderance of the evidence" requirement makes that a somewhat heavier burden than is usual. § 6663.

¶ **1.6333.   Failure to File Return.** If a TP fails to file an income tax return on the required date and if the failure is not due to reasonable cause, a penalty will be imposed equal to 5% of the tax due for each month (or part thereof) that the return is not filed. The total penalty cannot exceed 25% of the tax due—i.e., the penalty applies only to the first five months of neglect to file. If the failure to file is attributable to fraud, the 5% monthly penalty is raised to 15%, and the maximum penalty is increased from 25% to 75%. There is a minimum penalty of the lesser of $135 or 100% of the tax due if the return is not filed within 60 days of the due date (including extensions of time). § 6651(a), (f). If no tax is due, there is no civil penalty for a failure to file. A *willful* failure to file a return is subject to a criminal penalty [§ 7203]; but if no tax is due, it is unlikely that the Service will prosecute. The penalty for a failure to file a return is the exclusive civil penalty for that failure. Neither the accuracy-related penalty nor the fraud penalty can apply to an underpayment due to a failure to file; but once the return is filed late, the accuracy-related penalty or the fraud penalty can apply to any underpayment attributable to an understatement in the late return. § 6664(b); Treas. Reg. § 1.6662–2(a).

¶ **1.6334.   Failure to Pay Tax.** If a TP fails to make a timely payment of an income tax that is shown to be owing on a tax return filed by the TP, a penalty is imposed in the amount of .5% of any unpaid tax for each month (or fraction thereof) in which an amount is unpaid. The penalties that can be imposed under this provision cannot exceed 25% in the aggregate. A similar penalty is applied if the TP fails to pay within 10 days after notice and demand for payment of any tax that is not shown on a return but which is due and owing; but then the monthly penalty will be 1%, instead of .5%. § 6651(a)(2), (3), (d). The penalties will not apply if there is reasonable cause for the delay.

¶ **1.6335.   Claim for Excessive Refund or Credit.** If a TP makes a claim for a refund or credit (other than an earned income credit) of an "excessive amount" (i.e., an amount that is greater than the amount that is allowable), a penalty is imposed equal to 20% of the excessive amount unless the TP had a reasonable basis for making the claim. The reasonable basis exception does not apply if the transaction in question lacked economic substance. § 6676.[73]

¶ 1.6336. Other Civil Penalties. The Code contains a great many civil penalties in addition to the several described above. For example, a TP who files a frivolous tax return or other submission is required to pay a $5,000 penalty in addition to any other penalties that might apply. § 6702. Some of those penalties are severe, and some are relatively minor. Some of the penalties described above are applied more stringently, and are subject to more restricted exceptions, when a transaction is connected to a tax shelter.

¶ 1.6337. Suspension of Penalty. A 1998 amendment provides that the imposition of certain penalties and additions to tax on an *individual* TP are suspended if the Service fails within a 36–month period to provide the individual with notice of the basis for the individual's liability and the amount thereof. § 6404(g). This provision does not apply if the individual did not file a timely tax return for the year in question. The suspension begins on the day after the close of the 36–month period and ends 21 days after proper notice is given to the individual. § 6404(g)(3).

¶ 1.6338. Statute of Limitations. Generally, the Service has three years from the date that a TP's return is filed to assess any tax. § 6501(a). However, if the TP omits from gross income an amount in excess of 25 percent of the amount of gross income reported on the return, the period is extended to six years. § 6501(e). This provision extending the period of limitations applies when income has been left out of the return; there is a question as to whether it also applies when the understatement of gross income is attributable to an overstatement of basis. In a final regulation promulgated in 2010, Treasury maintains that the extension of the period to six years can be triggered by an overstatement of basis.[74] The decisions of the Tax Court and three United States Courts of Appeals have rejected that construction, while the Seventh

---

73. See ¶ **1.9300** for a discussion of the "economic substance doctrine."
74. Treas. Reg. § 301.6501(e)–1(a)(1)(iii) adopted in T.D. 9511.

Circuit has embraced it.[75] The Supreme Court's 2011 decision in *Mayo Foundation, supra* n. 17, expanding the *Chevron* deference's application to tax regulations may influence courts to reverse that trend and validate the regulation.

There is no statute of limitations if the TP filed a "false return," willfully attempts to evade tax, or does not file any return at all. § 6501(c)(1)–(3).

¶ 1.6340.   Criminal Penalties. When a TP's failure to do a required act is willful or when fraud is involved, criminal penalties may apply. For example, if a person willfully attempts to evade or defeat any tax imposed by the Code, that person may be guilty of a felony which is punishable by a fine of up to $100,000 ($500,000 for a corporation) and by imprisonment for up to five years. § 7201. If a person willfully fails to file a return, pay a tax, or keep or supply required information, that person may be guilty of a misdemeanor, which is punishable by a fine of up to $25,000 and by imprisonment of up to one year. § 7203. The Code contains a number of criminal tax provisions.

¶ 1.6350.   Interest on Underpayments and Overpayments. In the event that a TP fails to make a timely payment of the correct amount of tax that is due, interest is charged on the underpayment from the date that payment was due. § 6601. If the TP pays the government more than the required tax, the government is required to pay interest on the overpayment from the date thereof. § 6611. As a consequence of a 1998 amendment, the interest rate for noncorporate TPs is the same for both overpayments and underpayments. § 6621(a).

For noncorporate TPs, the rate of interest payable by the government on an overpayment and the rate of interest payable by a noncorporate TP on an underpayment is equal to the "Federal short-term rate" plus three percentage points. § 6621(a). The Federal short-term rate is the average market yield (during a calendar month) of marketable obligations of the United States

---

75. *Intermountain Insurance Service of Vail, LLC v. Commissioner*, 134 T.C. No. 11 (2010); *Home Concrete & Supply, LLC v. United States*, 634 F.3d 249 (4th Cir. 2011); *Bakersfield Energy Partners, LP v. Comm'r*, 128 T.C. 207 (2007), aff'd 568 F.3d 767 (9th Cir. 2009); and *Salman Ranch Ltd. v. United States*, 573 F.3d 1362 (Fed. Cir. 2009) held that the overstatement of basis does not constitute an omission of gross income. See also *Colony, Inc. v. Commissioner*, 357 U.S. 28 (1958). Contra, *Beard v. Commissioner*, 633 F.3d 616 (7th Cir. 2011).

that have remaining periods to maturity of three years or less. § 1274(d)(1)(C). The Federal short-term rate is adjusted quarterly (the rate determined in the first month of a calendar quarter becomes the rate for the *following* calendar quarter), and so interest rates can change each quarter during a period in which an overpayment or underpayment is outstanding. § 6621(b).

An individual TP's liability for interest is suspended in the same manner as applies to penalties when the Service fails to provide timely notice to him as described in ¶ **1.6336**. § 6404(g).

¶ **1.6360. Interest on Penalties.** Interest does accumulate on a TP's obligation to pay a penalty. For most penalties, interest commences on the date that a notice and demand for payment is made, and no interest is payable if the penalty is paid within twenty-one days of the notice and demand. § 6601(e)(2)(A). However, for certain penalties, interest commences on the date on which the return for the taxable year in question was required to be filed. § 6601(e)(2)(B). The penalties for which interest commences with the due date of the return include: the fraud penalty, the accuracy-related penalty, and the penalty for failure to file a return. For suspension of an individual's liability for interest, see ¶ **1.6350**.

¶ **1.6400. Annual Accounting.** Income tax liability is determined for annual periods according to the facts as they existed at that time. This annual reporting requirement, based on the facts known at that time is necessary because of the administrative difficulties that a more open-ended approach would engender.[76] If a return was properly filed on the basis of facts and estimates available at that time, the TP cannot change the tax liability by filing an amended return after the filing deadline for the original period has passed unless the Commissioner accepts the amended return. The acceptance of the amended return is subject to the Commissioner's discretion.[77]

¶ **1.7000. CONCEPT OF INCOME.** The tax system is based upon the concept of "income." The Sixteenth Amendment grants Congress the authority to "lay and collect taxes on incomes, from whatever source derived, without apportionment among the several states, and without regard to any census or enumeration." The reference to "incomes" in

---

76. See, e.g., *Burnet v. Sanford & Brooks*, 282 U.S. 359, 365 (1931).

77. *Cameron v. Commissioner*, 105 T.C. 380, 386–387 (1995), aff'd *sub nom. Broadway v. Commissioner*, 111 F.3d 593 (8th Cir. 1997).

the Sixteenth Amendment has been construed to refer to gross income as distinguished from gross receipts or taxable income.

¶ 1.7100. Gross Income Generally. The general definition of gross income is set forth in § 61 which provides that: "Except as otherwise provided in this subtitle, gross income means all income from whatever source derived...." That circular definition is supplemented by numerous regulations and administrative and judicial determinations.

¶ 1.7110. Less Cost-of-Goods Sold. Gross income is equal to gross receipts less the cost-of-goods sold. For example, X sold a radio to Y for $50. X had paid $30 for the radio and $3 of his advertising and sales personnel expenses were attributable to the sale of the radio. X has gross receipts of $50, but his gross income is only $20. X had a net income of $17 after deducting his selling costs; the costs attributable to selling the radio are not deducted in determining gross income. However, in certain cases (such as the sale of stock), commissions and brokerage fees paid on a specific sale will reduce the amount realized by the TP on the sale and thus will reduce the TP's gross income.[78]

¶ 1.7120. Statutory Interpretation. The statutory language of § 61 provides only very broad guidelines for determining income. The statute, however, is supplemented by extensive regulations. In addition, part II of subchapter B lists items which are specifically included in gross income while part III of subchapter B lists items which are specifically excluded from gross income.

¶ 1.7130. Rule-of-Thumb Test: Increase in Net Worth. There is no single criterion for determining what is income for tax purposes, but it may be helpful to think of gross income as an increase in net worth. Gross income may arise from the receipt of money, services, property, or any other benefit having financial value. One popular definition of income is that income equals the amount of wealth accumulated plus the value of the personal consumption enjoyed by a TP during a taxable year. This is called the Haig–Simons definition.

¶ 1.7200. Realization of Income or Loss. A basic principle in tax law is that gain is not included in a TP's gross income until the gain is "realized." The word *realized* is a term of art that refers to a significant event that represents the severance of gain from the property that produced the gain. Realization also is required before a

---

78. See Chapter **Twenty–Four**.

loss incurred by a TP can be taken into account. In general, realization of gain or loss occurs when property either is converted into cash or is exchanged for other property differing materially either in kind or extent. Treas. Reg. § 1.1001–1(a). The difference in exchanged properties need not be great to be treated as "material."[79] As noted below, there are only a few exceptions to the principle that realization is a prerequisite to inclusion in income.

¶ 1.7210. **Illustration.** In Year One, X purchased stock for $100. By December, Year Two, the stock rose in value to $200. X enjoyed an economic (paper) gain on his stock in Year Two, but the gain was not realized in that year. In Year Three, X sold the stock for $500 cash; $100 of the $500 constitutes a return to X of the capital he had invested in the stock, and the remaining $400 is a realized gain which is included in X's gross income. The sale of the stock severed the gain from the capital stock which produced that gain. The result would be the same if in Year Three X transferred his stock to Y in exchange for stock of a different corporation owned by Y and having a fair market value of $500.

¶ 1.7220. **Constitutional Limitation.** The landmark case of *Eisner v. Macomber*[80] indicated that as a constitutional matter a gain *must* be realized by a TP before it can be taxed by the government. Although there is now substantial doubt as to the continuing vitality of that decision, the substance of the opinion has been incorporated in general policy not to tax gain before it has been realized. However, there are exceptions to that policy, and so realization is not required in a few circumstances. The most prominent exception is the "mark to market" requirement for dealers in securities. Section 465 requires dealers in securities to recognize gain or loss on the annual appreciation or depreciation of securities they hold as inventory. Another example is the requirement in § 1272 that the so-called "original issue discount" of certain debt instruments be accrued daily as interest income to the holder of the debt instrument even though it is not realized. The general rule is that realization will be required, and the few exceptions to that general rule rest on compelling policy considerations.

¶ 1.7300. **The Concept of Basis.** *Basis* is another vital term of art in tax law. It represents a concept of fundamental importance which must be fully mastered in any tax course.

---

79. See, e.g., *Cottage Savings Ass'n. v. Commissioner*, 499 U.S. 554 (1991).

80. 252 U.S. 189 (1920).

¶ **1.7310.** **Definition.** A TP's basis in property is his investment in that property for tax purposes. Basis is the maximum amount a TP can receive in payment for an asset *without* realizing a gain.

¶ **1.7320.** **Use of Basis.** The concept of basis is most frequently used in determining the amount of gain or loss realized on the sale, exchange, or other disposition of an asset. Basis may also be used for other purposes such as the determination of the amount of depreciation that is allowable for an asset used in a trade or business.

¶ **1.7321.** **Illustration 1.** *X* purchased unimproved land in Year One for $10,000 cash and made no improvements. In Year Three, the land had a value of $10,000 and *X* sold the land for $10,000 cash. Since *X* had a basis of $10,000 in the land, the $10,000 payment received by him in Year Three was a return of his capital, and *X* will not realize either a gain or a loss on the sale.

¶ **1.7322.** **Illustration 2.** *X* purchased unimproved land for $10,000 cash and made no improvements. Three years later, the land had a value of $8,000, and *X* sold the land for $8,000. *X* realized a loss of $2,000 on the sale since his investment in the land was $2,000 greater than the amount he realized on the sale. Whether *X* will be allowed a deduction for this loss depends upon statutory rules to be discussed later in this book.

¶ **1.7323.** **Illustration 3.** *X* purchased unimproved land for $10,000 cash and made no improvements. Three years later, the land had a value of $14,000, and *X* transferred the land to *Y* in exchange for stocks having a fair market value of $14,000. Thus, *X* received property having a value of $14,000 in exchange for land in which *X* had a basis of $10,000. Therefore, *X* realized a gain of $4,000 on the exchange.

¶ **1.7330.** **Determination of Basis.** There are several distinct methods of determining basis. Each method has application in special tax contexts.

¶ **1.7331.** **Cost Basis.** In most circumstances, a TP's initial basis in an asset will be equal to the actual amount of his investment (i.e., his cost). Thus, where a TP pays $500 cash for an automobile, his basis in the automobile is $500. If he subsequently sells the automobile for $600, he realizes a gain of $100 (amount received less the cost basis). If a TP owns unimproved land with a basis of $10,000 and a fair market value of $15,000, and he exchanges the land for corporate stock having a value of $15,000, he will realize a gain of $5,000 on the exchange. Moreover, he will have a basis of $15,000 in the stock he received since that amount represents his cost investment in the stock. The basis of property acquired in exchange for services performed by the TP is equal to the fair market value of the property on the date of acquisition.[81] The basis of property purchased subject to an encumbrance is determined in the manner stated at ¶ **24.1512**. The encumbrance will be a nonrecourse debt to the purchaser.

If a TP exchanges one item of property in kind (Item A) for another item of property (Item B) and if the exchange constitutes a taxable transaction, the Court of Claims held that the TP's basis in Item B is equal to the fair market value of Item B at the time of the exchange.[82] Thus, the critical element for determining the basis of property acquired in an arm's length exchange (as contrasted to a purchase for cash) is the fair market value of the *acquired* property; the value of the transferred property is not utilized.

¶ **1.7332. Transferred Basis.** In some circumstances, a TP's initial basis in an asset will be established by reference to someone else's basis (i.e., the basis of one person in an asset may be transferred to another who takes legal possession of the asset). For example, subject to an adjustment for gift taxes paid, the donee of a gift has the same basis in the donated property that the donor had. § 1015. Property, the basis of which is determined in whole or in part by reference to the basis that a transferor had in that property, is referred to as "transferred basis property." § 7701(a)(43).

¶ **1.7333. Exchanged Basis.** In some circumstances, a TP's basis in one asset may be transferred (in whole or in part) to another asset of the TP. The asset to which basis is transferred is referred to as "exchanged basis property." § 7701(a)(44).

---

81. See ¶¶ **3.1400–3.1430**.

82. *Philadelphia Park Amusement Co. v. United States*, 126 F.Supp. 184 (Ct. Cl. 1954). Note that the Court of Claims subsequently was absorbed into the United States Court of Appeals for the Federal Circuit.

¶ **1.7333–1. Illustration.** *X* owns all 100 outstanding shares of stock of Win All, Inc. Win All, Inc. declares a stock dividend of 100 shares of its stock to *X*. *X* realizes no gain on receiving the stock dividend [§ 305], but his basis in his original 100 shares of stock will be reallocated among the 200 shares of stock he holds after the stock dividend was distributed. § 307. The new 100 shares of stock that *X* received is exchanged basis property.

¶ **1.7334. Substituted Basis Property.** Transferred basis properties [¶ **1.7332**] and exchanged basis properties [¶ **1.7333**] are collectively referred to as "substituted basis property." § 7701(a)(42).

¶ **1.7335. Constructive Basis.** In some circumstances, a TP's basis in an asset is determined without regard to the amount invested in the asset by the TP or by anyone else. For example, except for the year 2010, when a TP acquires property from a decedent by inheritance or in some similar manner, the TP's basis usually will equal the fair market value of the asset at the decedent's death. § 1014.

¶ **1.7336. Adjusted Basis.** A TP's initial basis in an asset will be adjusted upward or downward to reflect subsequent events having tax significance. The basis of an asset at any given time is referred to as the *adjusted basis* of the asset. It is the adjusted basis of an asset that is used to determine the amount of a TP's gain or loss for tax purposes on the sale or disposition of the asset.

¶ **1.7336–1. Capital Improvement.** An upward adjustment of basis will be necessary when a TP makes a capital improvement to an asset. Thus, if a TP invests $5,000 in landscaping realty with an initial basis of $10,000, his basis for tax purposes is adjusted to $15,000.

¶ **1.7336–2. Recapture of Investment.** A downward adjustment to basis will be made when a TP *recaptures* part of his investment or when a TP becomes entitled to a tax benefit which is dependent upon his basis in the asset. Examples of such a benefit include a depreciation deduction and a partial loss caused by a casualty.

¶ **1.7336–2A. Illustration.** In Year One, *X* purchased a truck for $5,000 which he used in his business. *X* properly took a depreciation deduction of $1,000 on his tax return for Year One on account of his use of the truck, and accordingly his basis in the truck is reduced by $1,000. Then, on January 1, Year Two, X's truck was damaged when a tree limb fell on it. The *value* of X's truck before the accident was $3,600 and its value immediately afterwards was $3,400. Because of this casualty loss, X is entitled to a tax deduction of $200 and X's adjusted basis must be reduced by the corresponding amount. Thus, X's adjusted basis in the truck is reduced to $3,800 (i.e., $4,000 basis minus the $200 casualty loss).

¶ **1.7336–3. Mortgages and Liens.** The effect that mortgages and liens on property have on a TP's basis in the property, as well as the effect that the transfer or receipt of property subject to a lien has on the amount of gain or loss recognized on an exchange, are discussed at ¶ **24.1512**.

¶ **1.7400. The Concept of Recognition.** *Recognition* is another term of art in tax law. As noted above, a gain or loss or other income to a TP will not be taken into account for tax purposes until the gain, loss, or income is realized. However, even realized gain or loss will not be included in the computation of taxable income unless the realized gain, loss, or other income item is also *recognized*. Thus, realization is essential to taxability but not sufficient. The concept of recognition refines the question of when and how a particular gain or loss is to be taxed. Problems of recognition relate to specific tax law provisions governing certain transactions. In the absence of a special nonrecognition provision, income is recognized and taxable in the year that it is realized. § 1001(c). A "nonrecognition transaction" is a disposition of property in which gain or loss is not recognized in whole or in part. § 7701(a)(45).

¶ **1.7410. Effect of Nonrecognition.** A nonrecognition provision in the tax laws differs from a provision excluding an item of income from tax in that the latter *excludes* the item from *all* tax consequences while a nonrecognition provision typically only *defers* the tax consequences to a later date. It is useful to distinguish the concept of "nonrecognition" from the concept of "exclusion," but the reader should be aware that the term "nonrecognition" frequently is used to refer to exclusions as well as to tax-deferral provisions. See, e.g., § 267(d).

¶ **1.7420. Adjustment of Basis.** Tax deferral through a nonrecognition provision typically is accomplished by making an adjustment to a TP's basis in the property involved. The operation of several of these nonrecognition provisions will be examined in more detail later in this book.

¶ **1.7500. Deduction of a Recognized Loss.** In general, a loss is deductible only if a Code provision authorizes a deduction. So, a loss that is both realized and recognized will not necessarily be deductible; there must be a statute (or some tax principle) authorizing the deduction for one to be allowed. For example, if M sells her personal residence for $12,000 less than her basis, she realized and recognized a $12,000 loss; but M cannot deduct that loss from her income because there is no statute authorizing a deduction for a loss incurred on the sale of personally used property. See § 262.

¶ **1.8000. IMPUTED INCOME FROM PROPERTY OR SERVICES.** A TP's personal enjoyment of property that he owns provides him with the benefit of the use of that property. However, the benefit thus derived by the TP from the use of his own property is not included in his gross income. Similarly, a TP's performance of services for his own benefit (or for that of his immediate family) will benefit him by the value of those services, but such self-created benefits are excluded from gross income. Some examples of imputed income that are excluded from gross income are given below.

¶ **1.8100. Home Ownership.** X has $40,000 which she has invested at a ten percent rate of return. X wishes to reside in a house currently owned by Y. Y offers to sell the house to X for $40,000 or to rent it to X at an annual rental of $4,000. If X elects to rent the house, she can continue to collect $4,000 income on her investment; yet since that income is subject to tax, X cannot satisfy the full amount of the rent solely by paying over the after-tax income from her investment. X must make up the difference between the $4,000 income and the tax thereon from her capital or from other income sources. If, instead, X withdraws her $40,000 investment and purchases the house for cash, she will enjoy the benefit (or "income") of the $40,000 investment in her use of the house. Since X's use of the house does not increase her gross income, she can enjoy the benefit of living in the house by utilizing the "income" from the $40,000 that she invested in the house. If X decides to rent the house from Y, the income from her $40,000 investment will not be sufficient to pay the rent because that income is included in her gross income.

¶ **1.8200. Improvements.** A TP purchases wood worth $50 and uses it to construct a cabinet having a value of $460. While the TP has converted his services into $410 of value of property and thus has increased his net worth, none of the value added by his services is included in his gross income. Of course, the TP's basis in the cabinet is equal to his cost of $50.

¶ **1.8300. Services.** *B* shaves his face each morning. A barber would charge $15 for that service. *B* does not recognize gross income from the value of the service he performed for himself.

¶ **1.9000. SIGNIFICANCE OF STATE LAW AND FORM OF TRANSACTION.**

¶ **1.9100. State Law.** The rights and interests of persons in property typically are determined by local law; federal law rarely deals with such rights and interests. Federal tax law, therefore, looks to the applicable state law to determine the interests, rights, powers, duties and liability of parties, but the tax consequences of possessing those rights, powers, etc. are determined by federal law.[83] For example, whether a husband is obligated to make a payment to his divorced wife and the circumstances in which such obligation is terminated are determined by state law; whether payments having the characteristics established by state law are deductible as "alimony" for tax purposes is determined by federal tax law. In determining whether such payments qualify as "alimony" as that term is used in §§ 71 and 215(a), it is irrelevant whether the payments are characterized as "alimony" for state law purposes.

¶ **1.9200. Substance versus Form and Business Purpose.** When a transaction or a series of steps to a transaction have no economic significance and are designed solely to obtain favorable tax consequences, the tax law will recharacterize the transactions (or the steps) so as to reflect the economic substance of what was accomplished without regard to economically meaningless transactions or steps.[84] The substance versus form doctrine is not based on a statutory provision; rather it is a common law doctrine. While much of the tax law is comprised of statutes and regulations, there also are principles and doctrines that are established by court decisions. The substance versus form doctrine is one of those common law doctrines.

83.   *Morgan v. Commissioner*, 309 U.S. 78 (1940).

84.   See ¶¶ **1.9300, 26.4121**.

In some circumstances, the courts have required that a transaction have a valid business purpose to qualify for a tax treatment or for the transaction to be given effect.[85] The business purpose requirement is another example of a common law doctrine.

¶ 1.9300.   Economic Substance. In addition to the substance versus form and business purpose doctrines, the courts imposed a requirement, referred to as the "economic substance doctrine," that for a transaction to be taken into account for tax purposes, the transaction must make a meaningful change in the TP's economic position (apart from federal income tax consequences) and the TP must have had a substantial purpose (apart from federal income tax consequences) for engaging in the transactions. While that statement of the doctrine sets forth two separate conditions, the courts divided over the question of whether both of those conditions had to be satisfied and how they were applied. In 2010, Congress codified the economic substance doctrine when it adopted § 7701(o). In codifying the doctrine, Congress requires that both conditions must be satisfied. So, the statutory provision is more demanding than was the common law doctrine as applied by many of the courts. As noted in **¶ 1.6331**, if an underpayment is attributable to a transaction that lacks economic substance, a penalty equal to 20% of the underpayment is imposed. If the transaction was not disclosed, the penalty is doubled to equal 40% of the underpayment.

¶ 1.9400.   Estoppel of the Commissioner. While, in theory, equitable estoppel can be applied to prevent the Commissioner from asserting a position or imposing a tax, the courts are loathe to estop the Service and will do so only in rare circumstances.[86] In the absence of compelling features, "the policy in favor of efficient collection of the public revenues outweighs the policy of the estoppel doctrine in its usual context."[87] A necessary, but not sufficient, element to the successful imposition of the estoppel doctrine against the Commissioner is that the TP must establish that conduct of a government agent or entity reasonably induced detrimental reliance by a private party.[88]

---

85.   See, e.g., *Gregory v. Helvering*, 293 U.S. 465 (1935); *Estate of Kluener v. Commissioner*, 154 F.3d 630 (6th Cir. 1998).

86.   *Bennett v. Commissioner*, 1991 WL 107735 (4th Cir. 1991) (unpublished opinion).

87.   *Schuster v. Commissioner*, 312 F.2d 311, 317 (9th Cir. 1962).

88.   *Bennett v. Commissioner*, *supra*.

PART A
INCOME

CHAPTER TWO

FRINGE BENEFITS

¶ 2.0000. FRINGE BENEFITS. Of course, compensation paid for services, whether paid in cash or in some other form, is included in the service provider's gross income. Treas. Reg. § 1.61–2(a), (d). One might expect then that any economic benefit provided by an employer to an employee would be included in the employee's gross income. Economic benefits provided to, or on behalf of, an employee that are not part of the latter's wages are referred to as "fringe benefits." It was deemed inappropriate to tax certain fringe benefits for one or more of a variety of reasons—such as, the subjective nature of the value of the benefit to the employee raises difficult valuation issues, administrative difficulty of segregating the benefit from the function of the employee's work, or a wish for social policy reasons to induce employers to provide that benefit.

Because some fringe benefits are excluded from an employee's gross income, they have become an important means of compensating an employee. Fringe benefits include such items as free parking space, use of a company automobile, and reduced fares for air travel by an airline employee. A fringe benefit is included in an employee's gross income unless it is expressly excluded by statute. § 61(a)(1). Prior to 1984, some fringe benefits were excluded from gross income by the Code (e.g., group term life insurance coverage and furnishing of meals and lodging) and some were excluded by administrative practice of the Service. While the Tax Reform Act of 1984 extended the list of statutory nontaxable fringe benefits [e.g., §§ 132, 117(d)], the 1984 Act eliminated the availability of administrative exclusions from gross income. After 1984, a fringe benefit is included in the employee's gross income unless a *statutory* exclusion is available. Treas. Reg. § 1.61–21(a)(1). If a benefit is taxable, the TP will include in his gross income the difference between the fair market value of the benefit and the amount the employee paid (if any) for it.

Section 132 is a general provision that excludes from gross income eight separate types of fringe benefits, which are discussed at ¶¶ **2.2000–2.2800**. In addition, there are other Code sections that exclude specified fringe benefits from gross income. See, e.g., ¶ **2.5000** (group term life insurance).

¶ **2.1000. MEDICAL INSURANCE PAYMENTS.** An employer's contribution to an accident or health plan or to purchase medical insurance to compensate employees for personal injuries or illness of the employees, their spouses, and dependents, is excluded from the gross income of the employees. § 106. The tax consequences of receiving medical insurance benefits or health plan benefits are discussed in ¶¶ **19.7000–19.8513**.

¶ **2.2000. A GENERAL PROVISION FOR FRINGE BENEFITS.** Section 132 allows an employee to exclude from his gross income any fringe benefit which qualifies as a "no-additional-cost service," a "qualified employee discount," "a working condition fringe," a *"de minimis* fringe," a "qualified transportation fringe," a "qualified moving expense reimbursement," a "qualified retirement planning service," or "a qualified military base realignment and closure fringe." These are terms of art that are defined in § 132 and discussed below. Also, an employee's use of an "on-premises athletic facility" that is provided by his employer will not cause the employee to recognize gross income. § 132(j)(4).[1]

¶ **2.2100. No–Additional–Cost Service.** Services which are provided to, or on behalf of, an employee by his employer may qualify as no-additional-cost services if two requirements are met.

First, the services provided must be of the type offered by the employer to customers in the ordinary course of the line of business in which the employee performs substantial services. § 132(b)(1). Thus, if a corporate employer offers a free ride on the company's commercially operated passenger train to an employee who works as a waitress in a restaurant that her corporate employer owns and operates as a separate business, the benefit will not qualify as a no-additional-cost service because the employee is not working in the passenger train line of her employer's business. However, if free train service were offered by the employer to an accountant who deals with all areas of the corporation's business, the "same line of business" test would be satisfied. Treas. Reg. § 1.132–4(a)(1)(iv)(A). The "same line of business" requirement is discussed at ¶ **2.2240**.

Second, the employer must not incur a substantial additional cost (including foregone revenue) by providing such a benefit. § 132(b)(2). This determination is made without regard to any payment made by the employee for the service. Services that do not involve a substantial additional cost include services that would not be used if the

---

1. The requirements for qualifying an athletic facility for that exclusion are discussed in PLR 9029026.

employee did not utilize them, such as a vacant hotel room, an unoccupied seat on an airplane, train or other form of transportation. Treas. Reg. § 1.132–2(a)(2).

In certain circumstances, where several employers execute a written agreement to provide services to employees of both parties, the services furnished by one employer to an employee of the other employer can be covered by the "no-additional-cost" exception, provided that neither employer incurs any substantial additional cost (including foregone revenue) in providing such services. § 132(i). The exclusion from gross income of a no-additional-cost service is subject to the anti-discrimination rules [described at ¶ 2.2220] which prevent highly compensated employees from obtaining this exclusion if the employer's plan discriminates in favor of them.

As explained in ¶ 2.2230, some individuals who are not employees are treated as if they were employees for purposes of applying this provision.

¶ 2.2200. **Qualified Employee Discount.** Employers often offer property or services to an employee at a price lower than that charged to the employer's customers; the difference in such prices is referred to as an "employee discount." § 132(c)(3). Some or all of the value of an employee discount will be excluded from the gross income of the employee if the discount is offered on qualified property or service. § 132(c). To the extent that a discount is excluded from the employee's gross income, it is referred to as a "qualified employee discount." § 132(c)(1).

Property or services are qualified if they are offered for sale to customers in the ordinary course of the line of business in which the employee performs substantial services; however, qualified property does not include personal property that is held for investment and does not include any real property. § 132(c)(4). Thus, where a corporation owns and operates a department store chain and also owns and operates an automobile dealership as a separate business, a discount on the price of an automobile offered by the corporate employer to a sales clerk in its department store chain will not be a qualified employee discount. The "same line of business" requirement is discussed at ¶ 2.2240.

¶ 2.2210. **Limitation.** There are separate limitations that apply to discounts on qualified property and those that apply to discounts on qualified services. An employee discount on *qualified* *property* is excluded from a TP's gross income only to the extent that the discount does not exceed the "gross profit percentage" of the price charged to customers. § 132(c)(1)(A). The "gross profit percentage" is defined as the percent which the difference between the aggregate sales price of all property sold to customers in the line of business in which the employee is engaged and the aggregate cost of such property is of the aggregate sales price of such property. § 132(c)(2)(A). The gross profit percentage is determined by reference to the employer's sales experience over a representative period. § 132(c)(2)(B). An employee discount on *qualified services* is excluded to the extent that the discount does not exceed 20 percent of the price charged to the employer's customers for such services. § 132(c)(1)(B). To the extent that a qualified discount does not exceed the applicable limitation, it will be excluded from gross income and only the excess over the limitation is included in gross income.

¶ **2.2220. No Discrimination.** No-additional-cost services and qualified employee discounts will be excluded from the gross income of highly compensated employees only if they are offered to other employees on substantially the same terms. § 132(j)(1). That is, fringe benefit plans which discriminate in favor of highly compensated employees will disqualify those employees for treatment under § 132(a)(1) and (2). The employees who constitute the "highly compensated" classification are described in § 414(q). § 132(j)(6).

¶ **2.2230. Certain Individuals Treated as Employees.** Some individuals who are not actual current employees may receive free or discounted property or services from an employer and still qualify for exclusionary treatment under the no-additional-cost service and qualified employee discount provisions. For example, under these provisions, retired and disabled employees, spouses and dependent children of employees or of certain former or deceased employees are all treated as employees. § 132(h). For purposes of this provision, "dependent child" of an employee or deceased employee is specially defined by § 132(h)(2)(B). For air transportation, parents of an employee may receive free or discounted services. § 132(h)(3).

¶ **2.2240. Same Line of Business Requirement.** The exclusion from an employee's income for either a "no-additional-cost service" or a "qualified employee discount" fringe benefit is limited to property or services that are provided by the employer in the ordinary course of the same line of business in which the employee performs substantial services. The classification of a group of activities as a single line of business is determined by reference to categories established in the Enterprise Standard Industrial Classification Manual that is prepared by the U.S. Office of Management and Budget. A range of connected activities may be classified as a single line of business. For example, a general retail merchandise store is a single line of business, and so the retail sale of clothes, appliances, stationary, toys etc. at a department store are all part of a single line of business. A few other examples of a single line of business are: hotel and other lodging places, auto repair services and garages, and food stores. Treas. Reg. § 1.132–4(a)(2).

In certain circumstances, two or more lines of businesses conducted by an employer will be aggregated and treated as a single line of business. Treas. Reg. § 1.132–4(a)(3). For example:

(1) If it is uncommon in the industry of the employer for the several lines of businesses of the employer to be operated without the others, they will be treated as one line of business;

(2) If it is common for a substantial number of employees (other than those who work at the headquarters or main office of the employer) to perform substantial services for more than one line of business of the employer so that it is difficult to determine which employees perform substantial services for which business, then the several businesses in which the employees perform substantial services are treated as a single line of business.

If an employee performs services in more than one line of businesses that the employer conducts and if the businesses are not aggregated and treated as a single line of business, the employee can exclude no-additional-cost services and qualified employee discounts only in those lines of business for which the employee provides substantial services. Treas. Reg. § 1.132–4(a)(1)(iii). An employee who performs substantial services that benefit more than one line of an employer's business is treated as performing substantial services for each such line of business. If an employee of a minor line of an employer's business that is significantly interrelated with a major line of the employer's business performs substantial services that directly benefit both the minor and the major lines of business, the employee is treated as providing substantial services to both lines of business. Treas. Reg. § 1.132–

4(a)(1)(iv)(A). The following examples are drawn from Treas. Reg. § 1.132–4(a)(1)(iv)(B).

¶ 2.2241.   Illustration 1. *A* works for an employer who sells retail merchandise. *A* works in a department that provides repairs for purchased products of the employer. *A* is treated as providing substantial services to the retail merchandising line of business.

¶ 2.2242.   Illustration 2. *X* operates a hospital and a laundry service. While the laundry service handles the hospital's laundry, it also has gross receipts for laundry services provided to customers other than the hospital. *B* and *C* work for the laundry service. Approximately 40% of the work performed by *B* is in connection with servicing the laundry of the hospital. Since *B* performs substantial services that directly benefit the hospital's line of business, *B* is treated as providing substantial services to that line of business. *C* spends an insubstantial amount of work time dealing with the laundry services provided to the hospital; almost all of *C*'s time is spent on work for other customers. Since *C* does not perform substantial services that directly benefit the hospital line of business, *C* does not qualify for a no-additional-cost service or qualified employee discount from that business.

¶ 2.2300.   Working Condition Fringe. Property or services offered to an employee will not be included in an employee's gross income to the extent that the employee would be allowed a deduction for such items under §§ 162 or 167 (i.e., business expense deductions and depreciation deductions) had the employee paid for them himself. § 132(d). To qualify, the deduction must be allowable because the item would be an expense of conducting the trade or business of being an employee of the employer who provided the fringe. Treas. Reg. § 1.132–5(a)(2). Note that the anti-discrimination requirement of § 132(j)(1) [see ¶ 2.2220] does not apply to working condition fringe benefits.

For the possible application of the working condition fringe to educational or training assistance provided by an employer, see **¶ 2.7000.**

¶ 2.2400.   *De Minimis* Fringe. Where the value of the property or services provided to the employees is so small that accounting for them would be unreasonable or administratively impracticable, an employee will not be required to include such items in his gross income. § 132(e)(1). The value of the property or services is determined after taking into account the frequency with which those benefits are provided by the employer to his employees. Note that while the anti-discrimination requirements of § 132(j)(1) [see ¶ 2.2220] do not apply to *de minimis* fringe benefits, the special treatment accorded to eating facilities [¶ 2.2410] is subject to a similar anti-discrimination restriction.

¶ 2.2410. **Eating Facilities.** The operation of an eating facility by an employer may be treated as a *de minimis* fringe if the facility is located on or near the business premises of the employer and if the revenue derived from the facility normally equals or exceeds the direct cost of such operation. § 132(e)(2). The benefits of an eating facility will qualify as a *de minimis* fringe for highly compensated employees only if they are available on substantially the same terms to each member of a group of other employees which is defined under a reasonable, nondiscriminatory classification. § 132(e)(2).

Meals that are provided an employee on the business premises of the employer and for the convenience of the employer are excluded from the employee's gross income by § 119 [see ¶ 2.4000], which therefore can overlap with § 132(e)(2). These two statutory provisions are coordinated by the last sentence of § 132(e)(2). When an employee's meal is excluded from income by § 119, the employee is deemed to have paid for the meal; the constructive payment is equal to the direct operating cost of the facility that is attributable to that meal. That constructive payment can help to bring the meal within the requirement of § 132(e)(2) that the revenue from the facility at least equal the cost of operating the facility. The reason for constructing a payment lies in § 274(n) which limits the deduction for the cost of a meal to 50% of that cost. By treating the employee's meal as having been purchased by the employee, the employer can deduct 100 percent of the cost of providing that meal since § 274(n) will not apply to the employer. See § 274(n)(2)(B).

¶ 2.2500. **Qualified Transportation Fringe.** A qualified transportation fringe consists of any of the following four items:

(A) Qualified parking;

(B) Transportation in a commuter highway vehicle if such transportation is between the employee's residence and place of employment;

(C) Any transit pass; and

(D) Qualified bicycle commuting reimbursement. § 132(f).

There is a dollar ceiling on the monthly value of those four fringes that can be excluded. There is one ceiling on the amount of qualified parking that can be excluded in a month, and there is a different ceiling on the aggregate amount of transit passes and commuter transportation that can be excluded in a month. But, both of those ceilings are indexed to inflation; i.e., they increase when the cost of living rises. § 132(f)(2), (6). There is also an annual ceiling on the amount that can be excluded as a qualified bicycle commuting reimbursement, and that limitation amount is not indexed for inflation. § 132(f)(5)(F).

Although normally different amounts, the limitation for transit passes and commuter transportation are the same as the limitation for qualified parking for a month beginning after February 16, 2009, and before January 1, 2011. § 132(f)(2). For a taxable year beginning in 2010, the maximum monthly amount that can be excluded for those three categories is $230.[2] For the year 2011 and thereafter, the transit passes and commuter transportation limitation return to its regular limitation amount which is less than the qualified parking limitation.

The maximum amount of qualified bicycle commuting reimbursement that an employee may exclude as a qualified transportation fringe is determined by multiplying $20 (again, this amount is not indexed for inflation) times the number of months during the year in which the employee regularly used the bicycle for a substantial portion of the travel between the employee's residence and the place of employment. § 132(f)(5)(F). Thus, the maximum annual exclusion is $240. An employee will not be allowed to use the qualified bicycle commuting reimbursement provision if the employer provides the employee any other qualified transportation fringe. § 132(f)(5)(F)(iii)(II).

The qualified transportation fringe need not be furnished in kind to be excluded from income. An employer's cash reimbursement of an employee's cost also is excluded from income. § 132(f)(3). Also, a qualified transportation fringe is excludable even if the employee has

---

2. Rev. Proc. 2009–50.

a choice to either take that benefit or to receive additional compensation. § 132(f)(4).

The definitions of the four items that comprise the qualified transportation fringe and of other terms are set forth in § 132(f)(5). "Qualified parking" includes parking provided to an employee on or near the business premises of the employer and not near the employee's residence. § 132(f)(5)(C).

Note that there is no prohibition against providing a qualified transportation fringe that discriminates in favor of highly compensated employees.

¶ 2.2600. **Qualified Moving Expense Reimbursement.** The term "qualified moving expense reimbursement" means an amount received (directly or indirectly) by an individual from an employer as a reimbursement for (or payment of) expenses that would be deductible under § 217 as moving expenses if directly paid or incurred by the individual. Such amounts are excluded from the individual's gross income unless the individual had deducted the expense in a prior year. § 132(g). Any reimbursements or payments of an employee's moving expenses that are not excluded from income by § 132(g) are included in the employee's gross income under § 82. For example, since meals are not deductible under § 217, the receipt of a reimbursement or payment for meals will be included in income. §§ 82, 217(b)(1). The extent to which unreimbursed moving expenses are deductible under § 217 is discussed at ¶ **21.3400** *et seq.*

¶ 2.2700. **Qualified Retirement Planning Services.** In 2001, Congress added § 132(a)(7) and (m) to exclude "qualified retirement planning services." The term "qualified retirement planning services" means any retirement planning advice or information provided to an employee and his spouse by an employer maintaining a "qualified employer plan." § 132(m)(1). Note that while the antidiscrimination requirements of § 132(j)(1) [see ¶ **2.2220**] do not apply to qualified retirement planning benefits, the special treatment accorded to such services is subject to a similar anti-discrimination restriction. § 132(m)(2).

¶ 2.2800. **Qualified Military Base Realignment and Closure Fringe.** This provision allows an exclusion for certain compensation received by employees and members of the Armed Forces to offset losses attributable to the adverse effects on housing values that result from realignment or closing of a military base. § 132(a)(8), (n).

¶ **2.3000. REIMBURSED EXPENSES.** In general, if an employer reimburses an employee for personal expenses (or directly pays such personal expenses), the reimbursement (or direct payment) will be included in the employee's gross income. But, when an employee incurs an expense in the conduct of his employer's business, which expense qualifies as an allowable tax deduction of the employee, the employer's reimbursement or direct payment of such expense items will not constitute income to the employee provided that the employee is required to account (and does so) to the employer for all such expenses. Treas. Reg. §§ 1.62–2, 1.162–17(b) and 1.274–5(e)(2).[3] Some specific expense items are discussed in the following sections.

An employer may pay a per diem amount in lieu of reimbursing the employee's actual expenses and such amount will be considered substantiated if the per diem is equal to or below the appropriate Federal per diem rate.[4]

¶ **2.3100. Rationale.** It is worth noting that the reason that the Service will permit an employee to exclude from his gross income certain amounts of reimbursement that he receives from his employer for expenses that he incurred in the conduct of his employer's business solely for the employer's benefit is that such expenses are deductible under § 62(a)(2)(A) in determining the employee's adjusted gross income. In other words, those reimbursed expenses are nonitemized deductions. Thus, even if the employee elects not to itemize his deductions, those reimbursed expenses would be deductible and would wash out the income that the employee recognized on receiving the reimbursement. Since reimbursed expenses of an employee qualify as nonitemized deductions, the deduction of those expenses is not subject to the limitations that otherwise would be imposed by § 67 (a floor on miscellaneous itemized deductions) and § 68 (an overall limitation on itemized deductions that applies after 2012).

¶ **2.3200. Travel Expenses.** If an employee is required to travel while on his employer's business, the employer's reimbursement of the employee's actual travel expenses (including meals and lodging) will not be included in the employee's gross income. The employee must retain records and proof of expenditures in accordance with the requirements of § 274. Note that the provision in § 274(n)(1) limiting the deduction of meals to 50 percent of the cost does not apply to

3. See also Rev. Ruls. 76–71, 76–65, 76–62 and 77–351.

4. Rev. Proc. 2008–59.

an employee whose meal expenses (on travel status) are reimbursed by his employer, but the employer can deduct only 50 percent of the cost of the meal for which the employee was reimbursed. § 274(e)(3), (n)(1), (2)(A).

¶ 2.3300. **Expenses of Interviewing for a Job.** Although no deduction is allowable for the travel or other expenses incurred by a TP to interview for a job in a trade or business in which the TP was not previously engaged, if a prospective employer reimburses a TP for, or directly pays, the travel expenses incurred to interview for a job at the invitation of the prospective employer, the reimbursement and payments are excluded from the TP's gross income to the extent that they do not exceed the actual expenses.[5] The expenses to which this provision applies include the TP's round trip transportation costs and the costs of meals and lodging in the city at which the interview takes place. See ¶ **21.1475.**

¶ 2.3400. **Expenses Incurred on Behalf of Another in a Non-Employment Context.** The reimbursement of expenses incurred by a TP on behalf of a person or entity in a non-employment context is excluded from the TP's gross income. For example, the Service stated in Rev. Rul. 80–99 that when the expenses of a TP (who was a state employee) to attend and speak at a political fund-raising event were reimbursed by the political organization, the reimbursement was not included in the TP's gross income. See ¶ **21.1475.**

However, Treas. Reg. § 1.61–21(a)(3) states that a "fringe benefit provided in connection with the performance of services shall be considered to have been provided as compensation for such services." At one time, in audits, the Service raised the question as to whether the reimbursement of the expenses of a service provider who is not an employee nevertheless constitutes a fringe benefit that is taxable to the service provider to the extent not excluded by § 132. While this question was raised, the Service has not yet replaced or revoked Rev. Rul. 80–99, and the authors know of no instances in which the Service has actually adopted that approach and sought to collect taxes in reliance on it.

¶ 2.4000. **MEALS AND LODGING.** In the absence of a statutory exception, the fair market value of meals and lodging furnished to an employee as consideration for his services will be included in the employee's gross income. Treas. Reg. § 1.61–2(d)(3). The principal statu-

---

5. Rev. Rul. 63–77.

tory exclusion of meals and lodging is provided by § 119, the terms of which are described below. As noted in ¶ 2.2410, a statutory exclusion is granted for an employer's operation of an eating facility for his employees if the benefits to the employees qualify as a *de minimis* fringe under § 132(e)(2).

¶ 2.4100. **Exclusion of Meals and Lodging.** Under § 119, the value of meals and lodging furnished by an employer to an employee, his spouse and dependents are excluded from the employee's gross income if they were: (1) furnished for the convenience of the employer, and (2) furnished on the business premises of the employer. As to lodging, there is the additional requirement that the employee was required to accept the lodging as a condition of his employment so that the employee will be better able to perform his services (e.g., the requirement that a maintenance man for an apartment house live in one of the apartments is appropriate for his job since the employee must be available to tenants at any time of day or night). An employer's furnishing of necessary utilities to an employee as part of the furnishing of lodging to the employee can be excluded from the employee's gross income by § 119 as being within the exclusion for lodging.[6]

¶ 2.4200. **Meaning of Convenience of Employer.** Meals or lodging is "for the convenience of the employer" if there is a substantial noncompensatory purpose even if there is also a compensatory purpose. Treas. Reg. § 1.119–1(a)(2). If an employer provides meals on its business premises for its employees, and if the meals for more than half of the employees to whom meals are provided are provided for the convenience of the employer, then the meals provided to *all* of the employees are treated as provided for the convenience of the employer. § 119(b)(4). In other words, if more than half of the employees who are provided meals can exclude them under § 119, then all of the employees who are furnished those meals can exclude the value that they received thereby.

¶ 2.4210. **Illustration.** The Friendly National Bank allows its employees only 30 minutes for lunch. So that the employees can have lunch within that time, the bank operates a cafeteria and provides a free lunch for its employees. Most of the employees who eat lunch at the cafeteria are restricted to a 30–minute lunch period. Even though the employees are not required to eat in the cafeteria, the bank does provide lunch on its premises for a substantial noncompensatory reason. Since the meals provided to

---

6. Rev. Rul. 68–579; *Turner v. Commissioner*, 68 T.C. 48, 50 (1977).

more than half of the bank's employees who partake of it are furnished for a noncompensatory purpose, the president and other officers of the bank (whose lunch periods are not restricted) may also take their meals at the bank without incurring tax liability even though there is no noncompensatory purpose for the bank to furnish meals to that small minority. § 119(b)(4).

¶ 2.4300. Meaning of Business Premises. The term "business premises" refers to the place of employment of the employee. Thus, the business premises of a domestic servant's employer is the home in which the servant works. Treas. Reg. § 1.119–1(c)(1).

"Business premises" has been construed to mean "either (1) living quarters that constitute an integral part of the business property or (2) premises on which the company carries on some of its business activities."[7] The question of whether the furnishing of lodging that is physically separated from the business premises can qualify for the § 119 exclusion will depend upon whether the premises at which the employee resides is utilized in the conduct of the employer's business. This is a factual question the resolution of which depends upon a consideration of the employee's duties and of the nature of the employer's business.[8] In *Lindeman v. Commissioner,*[9] a house leased by the employer across the street from its business site for the use by an employee as the residence for himself and his family was held to be part of the employer's business premises. The employee had an office in his home and conducted some business there. In *Commissioner v. Anderson,*[10] a home provided to an employee several blocks from the business site was held not to be part of the business premises.[11] In PLR 8938014, the Commissioner held that lodging furnished to a hospital employee across the street from the hospital was not part of the business premises. However, the physical proximity of the lodging to the business site is not the important datum; it is the extent to which business of the employer is conducted at that site that is most important.

¶ 2.4400. Furnished in Kind. In order to be excluded from the

7. *Lindeman v. Commissioner,* 60 T.C. 609, 615 (1973), acq. See also, *Vanicek v. Commissioner,* 85 T.C. 731 (1985), acq; PLR 9801023.

8. Id.; PLR 8938014; and TAM 9404005.

9. 60 T.C. 609 (1973).

10. 371 F.2d 59 (6th Cir. 1966).

11. Cf. *Benninghoff v. Commissioner,* 71 T.C. 216 (1978), aff'd per curiam, 614 F.2d 398 (5th Cir. 1980).

employee's gross income, the meals and lodging must be actually furnished (furnished *in kind*) and not merely reimbursed or purchased. If the employer *reimburses* the employee for expenses in purchasing food or lodging rather than supplying them, the reimbursement may be taxed as gross income to the employee.[12]

¶ **2.4410. Furnishing of Groceries.** An unresolved question is whether an employer's furnishing of groceries to his employee will constitute the furnishing of meals in kind. In *Tougher v. Commissioner*,[13] the Tax Court held that groceries do not qualify as meals in kind. However, in a later case, by a 2–1 divided court, the Third Circuit rejected the *Tougher* position and excluded groceries furnished to a TP from his gross income under § 119.[14] The Service rejects the holding of the *Jacob* case and will allow an exclusion for groceries only when the case is within the jurisdiction of the Third Circuit.[15]

¶ **2.4420. Reimbursement for Employee's Meals Taken When Working Late.** When an employee works late at his employer's office and is reimbursed for his dinner at a downtown restaurant, the Service ruled in 1920 that the reimbursement will be excluded from gross income.[16] The question is whether, and to what extent, that exclusion from gross income is applicable today. Since it is a cash reimbursement for the cost of food that was not obtained on the business premises of the employer, it is clear that § 119 is inapplicable. As a consequence of the 1984 amendments, a fringe benefit is not excluded from an employee's gross income unless a statutory exclusion is applicable. Treas. Reg. § 1.61–21(a)(1). So, supper money will be included in an employee's gross income unless it fits within a statutory provision.

If reimbursed supper money is to be excluded from an employee's gross income, it most likely will have to qualify as a *"de minimis fringe"* benefit under § 132(a)(4).[17] The Joint Committee Staff's *General Explanation of the Revenue Provisions of the Deficit Reduction Act of 1984* states at p. 858 that a *"de minimis* fringe" includes "occasional supper money or taxi fare because of over-

---

12.   *Commissioner v. Kowalski*, 434 U.S. 77 (1977); Treas. Reg. § 1.119–1(e).

13.   51 T.C. 737 (1969), aff'd 441 F.2d 1148 (9th Cir. 1971).

14.   *Jacob v. United States*, 493 F.2d 1294 (3d Cir. 1974).

15.   PLR 9126063.

16.   OD 514, 2 Cum. Bull. 90 (1920).

17.   See TAM 9148001.

time work." See also Treas. Reg. § 1.132–6(d)(2). Typically, an employee will have to show that his reimbursements for meals are infrequent to exclude them. The Joint Committee Staff's *Explanation* also states at (p. 856) that reimbursed supper money will not qualify for exclusion as a "working condition fringe" under § 132(a)(3).

¶ **2.4500. Payment by Employee.** Where an employee is furnished meals or lodging and a fixed amount is deducted from the employee's salary as payment for the meals or lodging, the amount so deducted is excluded from the employee's gross income, and the fair market value of the furnished meals or lodging are either excluded from or included in gross income depending upon whether § 119 applies. Treas. Reg. § 1.119–1(a)(3).[18]

> ¶ **2.4510. Illustration.** *X* manages a motel for Sleepwell, Inc. *X* is required to live in a room at the motel. *X* receives a salary of $800 per month, and Sleepwell withholds $100 of that monthly salary as payment for the room. *X* will include only $700 per month in gross income, and the value of the room will be excluded from *X*'s gross income under § 119. If § 119 did not exclude the value of the room, the $100 withheld from *X* would be excluded from his gross income, but the rental value of the room would be included.

¶ **2.4600. Qualified Campus Lodging.** The value of lodging provided by an educational institution to an employee, his spouse, and any of his dependents may be excluded under § 119(a) if the conditions of that provision are satisfied. If § 119(a) does not apply, all or part of the cost of lodging provided to such persons at or near the campus of the educational institution nevertheless may be excluded from the employee's gross income under § 119(d), which excludes from gross income the value of "qualified campus lodging" furnished to an employee. A certain portion of the value of such lodging will be included in the employee's gross income to the extent that the amount of such portion exceeds the rent paid by the employee. § 119(d)(2).

¶ **2.5000. GROUP–TERM LIFE INSURANCE.** If an employer purchases group-term life insurance for its employees, the premium paid by the employer for a particular employee's coverage will be excluded from the employee's gross income to the extent that the premium does not

---

18. But see § 119(b)(3); *Cox v. Chaco*, 650 F.2d 174 (9th Cir. 1981).

exceed the cost (as determined under a schedule of premiums set forth in the Regulations rather than under the insurer's schedule) of $50,000 of insurance. § 79(a), (c). The premium paid by the employer in excess of the cost of $50,000 coverage is included in the employee's gross income. § 79. For the meaning of "group term life insurance," see Treas. Reg. § 1.79–1(a).[19] If a group term life insurance plan discriminates in favor of "key employees," either in terms of eligibility to participate or in terms of the type or amount of benefits, the exclusion from gross income will not apply to any key employee. § 79(d). The meaning of key employee is defined in § 416(i). § 79(d)(6).

¶ 2.6000.   **DEPENDENT CARE ASSISTANCE.** Dependent care assistance provided by an employer to its employees under a qualified program is excluded from the employee's income by § 129. There are two limitations on this exclusion. First, no more than $5,000 can be excluded in a taxable year. § 129(a)(2)(A). Second, there is an earned income limitation. If the employee is single, the exclusion cannot exceed the employee's earned income. If the employee is married, the exclusion cannot exceed the earned income of the *lower* earning spouse. § 129(b). If the lower earning spouse is a student or incapable of caring for himself, the spouse will be deemed to earn income of not less than a specified monthly amount. §§ 129(b)(2), 21(d)(2).

Dependent care assistance is the payment of, or provision of, services which, if paid by the employee, would qualify for so-called "employment-related expenses" under § 21. Section 21 grants a credit to TPs who have such expenses. That section, and how § 129 interacts with it, is discussed at ¶¶ **23.4000–23.4420**.

In order to qualify, the dependent care assistance program must meet certain requirements, including a prohibition against discrimination in favor of highly compensated employees. § 129(d).

¶ 2.7000.   **EDUCATIONAL ASSISTANCE PROGRAM.** Section 127 excludes from an employee's income certain educational assistance provided by the employer. The maximum amount of educational assistance that an employee can exclude in a calendar year is $5,250.

To qualify for the exclusion, the educational assistance must be provided pursuant to a written plan of the employer. The plan must specify the classification of employees who qualify for benefits, and that classification must not discriminate in favor of highly compensated employees

---

19.   See also Rev. Rul. 75–528.

[the meaning of "highly compensated employee" is set forth at § 414(q)]. § 127(b). If the plan is to qualify, eligible employees cannot be given the choice of receiving other remuneration in lieu of the educational assistance, and reasonable notification as to eligibility and terms of the program must be provided to all eligible employees. § 127(b)(4), (6).

The benefits that can be excluded from income under this provision are: (1) the payment by the employer of the employee's educational expenses, including (but not limited to) tuition, fees, books, supplies, and equipment, and (2) the provision by the employer of courses of instruction for the employee (including books, supplies and equipment). The statute does not permit the exclusion of certain expenses; for example, the statute does not exclude from income the payment or provision of: meals, lodging and transportation, and the payment or provision of tools or supplies which can be retained by the employee after the instruction is completed. Also, the statute does not exclude payments or provisions made with respect to education involving sports, games or hobbies. § 127(c)(1).

Certain self employed individuals can qualify for this exclusion. § 127(c)(2), (3). There is a ceiling on the percentage of the amount expended by an employer during a year on educational assistance that is allocated to the aggregate of individuals who are shareholders or owners of the employer (or their spouses and dependents) that have more than a 5 percent interest in the employer. § 127(b)(3).

To the extent that educational assistance does not qualify for exclusion under § 127, it will be included in the employee's gross income unless it can qualify for exclusion as a fringe benefit under § 132. The § 132 fringe benefit category that can apply to educational assistance in certain circumstances is the "working condition fringe." § 132(j)(8). See ¶ 2.2300.

¶ 2.8000.   QUALIFIED TUITION REDUCTION. The amount of an individual's "qualified tuition reduction" is excluded from his gross income. § 117(d). A "qualified tuition reduction" is the amount of reduction in tuition provided to an employee of an educational organization described in § 170(b)(1)(A)(ii) for education below the graduate level at the employer's or other qualified educational institution. The exclusion of tuition reduction not only applies to tuition reductions for the education of actual employees but also applies to such reductions for the education of any person who is treated as an employee under § 132(h) (such as an employee's spouse or dependent child). See ¶ 2.2230.

In PLR 9431017, the Service addressed the question of whether § 117(d) would apply if a university extended its tuition reduction policy to include a "domestic partner" of that employee. The Service ruled that § 117(d) will apply only if the state in which the employee resides recognizes the relationship of the employee and the domestic partner as a valid marital relationship. In that latter circumstance, the domestic partner will qualify as a spouse under § 132(h). Otherwise, § 117(d) will not apply and any tuition reduction afforded the domestic partner will constitute gross income to the employee.

A qualified tuition reduction that is provided with respect to a highly compensated employee will not be excluded from income unless such reductions are available to employees on a basis that does not discriminate in favor of highly compensated employees. § 117(d)(3). The term "highly compensated employee" is defined in § 414(q).

As discussed in detail in ¶ 2.8100, a qualified tuition reduction will be included in the student's gross income to the extent that the reduction represents payment for the student's services.

¶ 2.8100. **Teaching and Research Assistants.** The rule limiting the "qualified tuition reduction" exclusion to education below the graduate level does not apply to a graduate student at a qualified educational institution who is engaged in teaching or research activities for that institution. § 117(d)(5). Thus, qualified tuition reduction can be provided for graduate studies for such teaching and research assistants. However, to be excluded from a student's gross income, the reduction must comply with the requirement of § 117(c) that it does not represent a payment for the student's teaching or research services. The reduction will be a payment for services if the student is required to perform the services as a condition of receiving the reduction, and it does not matter in applying that provision if all candidates for the degree are required to perform such services. Prop. Reg. § 1.117–6(d)(1).

The principal standard for determining whether a tuition reduction was granted as compensation for a student's services is whether the services are primarily for the grantor's benefit rather than in furtherance of the student's education. If the services performed by the student are primarily for the benefit of the grantor, an amount of tuition deduction that is equal to the value of those services will be included in the student's gross income. Prop. Reg. § 1.117–6(d)(2), (3). If the grantor also made a cash payment to the student for the student's services, that payment will be taken into account in determining the amount of tuition reduction that constitutes compensation to the student for such services. Id. Since, in some cases, only a portion of a tuition reduction will constitute compensation to a student for services, it is possible for a tuition reduction to be divided into two portions: a compensatory portion that is included in the student's gross income, and a noncompensatory portion that is excluded from the student's gross income if it qualifies under § 117(d).

In determining the value of a student's services, the amount paid by the grantor for the same or similar services provided by comparable students who do not receive a tuition reduction or by non-student employees will be given considerable weight. Also, the amount paid by other educational organizations for similar services will be taken into account. Prop. Reg. § 1.117–6(d)(3).

¶ 2.9000. EMPLOYER–PROVIDED ADOPTION ASSISTANCE. An employee may exclude from income amounts paid under the employer's adoption assistance program for qualified adoption expenses in connection with the adoption of a child by an employee. § 137. For 2011, the total amount excludable is $13,360 (the limitation is adjusted each year for inflation).[20] See § 137(b)(1), (f). The amount excludable is phased out for TP's who have adjusted gross income that exceeds a certain amount (that amount is adjusted each year for inflation; in 2011, the phase-out begins when the TP has modified adjusted gross income in excess of $185,210).[21]

¶ 2.9000A. CAFETERIA PLANS. Section 125 provides that no amount shall be included in an employee's gross income solely because he is a participant in a cafeteria plan which provides choices among several plan benefits. § 125(a). A cafeteria plan is a plan where employee participants may choose among two or more benefits consisting of cash and qualified nontaxable benefits. § 125(d)(1). For example, a TP may elect to reduce his salary and receive nontaxable benefits instead. Without § 125, even TPs who chose to receive the nontaxable benefit would be subject to taxation under the doctrine of constructive receipt. Cafeteria plans are subject to nondiscrimination rules and only certain nontaxable benefits qualify. Among others, qualified benefits do not include the exclusion for § 132 fringe benefits and educational assistance programs. § 125(f).

---

20. Rev. Proc. 2010–40.

21. Id.

CHAPTER THREE

COMPENSATION FOR SERVICES

¶ 3.0000. COMPENSATION FOR SERVICES.

¶ 3.1000. AMOUNT AND TIMING OF INCOME.

Cash compensation for services rendered is income to the service provider when received or accrued. A bonus (including a holiday bonus), vacation pay, severance pay, and similar compensation payments are included in an employee's gross income. See Treas. Reg. § 1.61–2(a)(1). Compensation for services paid in some form other than cash ordinarily will be treated as income in the amount of the fair market value of the property or service received. Treas. Reg. § 1.61–2(d)(1).[1]

Instead of paying a service provider all of his compensation at the time the service was performed, the parties sometimes agree that a portion of the compensation will be deferred to be paid at a future date. Deferred future payments may be set to be made in installments or in a lump sum. Deferred payments may be made payable at specified dates or they can be made to begin after a specified occurrence such as an employee's retirement or death. The question is how the service provider's receipt of a right to payments at some future date will be treated for income tax purposes.

Should the service provider be taxed on the present value of the right to the future payment when he receives that right or should the income be deferred until some later date such as when the payment is actually made? For certain defined types of deferred compensation, the Code provides special rules that give favorable treatment as to when those deferred benefits will be taxable and as to how the amount to be taxed is determined.[2]

If it is necessary to determine the value of a right to a future dollar payment or of an obligation to make a payment at a future date, the concept of the "time value of money" comes into consideration.

---

1. But see ¶ 3.3000 *et seq.* for the special treatment accorded when the property given to the employee is subject to restrictions.

2. See ¶ 3.7000 *et seq.*

¶ **3.1100. Time Value of Money.** The value associated with the right to receive money at a future date depends upon both the amount of money to be paid and the time at which payment is to be made. That is, one dollar received by *X* today is worth more than one dollar to be received by *X* one year from now. Just how much more a current dollar is worth than the value of a dollar to be received one year from now depends upon what the market requires a lender to pay for the use of a dollar. Thus, if the current market interest rate is 10 percent simple interest, *X* would need to receive $1.10 one year from now to put her in the same position she would be in if she were to receive the one dollar today. Putting it another way, the present value of the right to receive $1.10 one year from now is $1. Similarly, an obligation to make a payment at a future date is a lesser liability than is an obligation to make that payment currently. If *X* is obligated to pay Y $1,000 two years from today and if the obligation is a deductible item, a grant to *X* of a current deduction of $1,000 would not account for the value to *X* of having the use of that $1,000 for two years prior to the time that payment must be made.

The value of the right to receive a specified amount at a future date is determined by discounting that amount to reflect the loss of potential income that the TP could have earned if the payment had not been deferred. Similarly, the amount of an obligation to make a payment in the future is discounted. This concept of taking into account the effect of the timing of receipts or payments is referred to as the "time value of money." The amount of discount depends upon the rate of return that is available and whether, and how frequently, the projected income is to be compounded. The tax law does not make a subjective determination as to what rate of return the TP in question could actually obtain. Instead, the Service provides a standardized rate based on the rate of return that certain federal obligations pay. Those standardized rates are updated monthly and are published.

¶ **3.1110. Increased Significance of Deferral.** Years ago, the time value of money was of less importance than today because interest rates were relatively low (three to four percent). In the interest of simplicity, the tax law typically ignored the benefits accruing to a TP because of time value. However, when market interest rates rose to double digits, the time value of money took on much greater significance and caused the Service to focus on this problem. Congress responded by enacting a number of provisions that require income reporting to reflect more accurately the economic reality of the value of the use of money.[3]

¶ 3.1200.   Tips. Tips and similar "gratuities" given for services are included in the recipient's gross income. Treas. Reg. § 1.61–2(a)(1). Indeed, tips are income even if the TP's receipt of such additional compensation violates state law.[4] Utilizing a formula grounded on an estimated amount of sales per hour worked and an estimated ratio of tips to sales (based on a discount of the percentage of tips on charged sales), the Service may determine that a food service employee had underreported tip income, and the Service may impose a negligence penalty on the employee.[5]

The Tax Court determined that a waitress can exclude from her gross income the amount of tips she received that she split with other waitresses and paid to her fellow workers (such as a busboy or a cook).[6] The TP also made payments to her employer for breakage and errors in taking a customer's order, but the court did not exclude those amounts from the TP's income. While the payments that the TP was required to make to her employer for breakage and improper reporting of orders are deductible expenses, they are itemized deductions and were disallowed because the TP used the standard deduction instead of itemizing.[7] The Tax Court did reject the Service's attempt to impose an accuracy-related penalty for the deficiency caused by the TP's excluding an amount for the payments to her employer.

To obtain greater compliance with the tax law by those receiving tips, in 1982 Congress amended § 6053 to impose reporting requirements on certain employers of persons who customarily receive tips for serving food and beverages to customers. In general, the requirement applies only to employers who operate a large food and beverage establishment. See § 6053(c)(4). If required to report, the employer must declare its gross receipts (including charged amounts) from the sale of food and beverages, exclusive of carry out sales and

---

3. One of those provisions is § 7872 which requires TPs to recognize the value associated with the use of money on the receipt of a loan bearing an inadequate interest rate. See Chapter **Sixteen**. Another example of this concern is the treatment of original issue discount that is described at ¶ **16.5000.**

4. *Killoran v. Commissioner*, 709 F.2d 31 (9th Cir. 1983).

5. See *McQuatters v. Commissioner*, 32 TCM 1122 (1973). The type of formula utilized in that case has been applied in subsequent cases and is referred to as the "McQuatters Formula."

6. *Brown v. Commissioner*, 72 T.C.M. 59 (1996).

7. Id. See Chapter **Ten**.

sales for which a substantial service charge is added, and it must allocate a portion of such gross receipts among the tipped employees to reflect the employer's estimate of the amount of their tips. The aggregate amount of tips so allocated among the employees must equal a specified percentage of the employer's gross receipts (as described above), usually eight percent but never less than two percent. § 6053(c)(3)(A), (C). This reporting requirement was adopted by Congress in response to an estimate by the Service that only sixteen percent of tips received by employees was being reported by them.

¶ 3.1300. **Services in Exchange for Services.** When two persons perform services for each other, and the performance of each person is intended as consideration for the performance of the other's service, the value of the service received is income to each recipient. Treas. Reg. § 1.61–2(d)(1). Where services are received in connection with the recipient's trade or business and the value of the payment made for those services (in whatever form made) is equal to or greater than $600, the person receiving the services is subject to the information reporting requirements imposed by §§ 6041(a) and 6041A(a).[8]

> ¶ 3.1310. **Illustration.** X, an attorney, drafted a will for Y, a doctor; and Y performed medical services for X. X and Y agreed not to bill each other since the value of services performed by each was about equal. X will realize income in an amount equal to the value of the medical services he received from Y; and Y will realize income equal to the value of the legal services he received from X.
>
> Even if the value of each of the services was greater than $600, the reporting requirements imposed on the recipients of services by §§ 6041 and 6041A would not apply. The medical services that X received were not an expense of X's business; and the legal services that Y received were not an expense of Y's business; and so those reporting provisions do not apply. Of course, each TP must report his income on his tax return.
>
> If the legal services that X performed had been the collection of a debt from a patient of the doctor, instead of the drafting of a will, the service would be an expense of the doctor's business, and so the reporting requirement would apply to the doctor in that case. The reporting requirement would not apply to the lawyer.

---

8. Rev. Rul. 85–101.

¶ **3.1400.** **Property in Kind.** Where payment for services is made in property (other than cash), the fair market value of the property is included in the service provider's gross income, and the service provider's basis in that property is equal to its fair market value. While the service provider could be either an employee or an independent contractor, for convenience we will refer to him as an employee. In effect, the employee is treated as if he had received for his services an amount of cash equal to the fair market value of the property he received and had then purchased that property from his employer for that cash amount.[9] The employer's constructive sale of the property to the employee can cause the employer to recognize a gain or loss.

¶ **3.1410.** **Illustration 1.** *X* is an employee of World Wide Widgets, Inc. World Wide gave *X* a holiday bonus of 100 shares of IBM stock having a market value of $500 per share. *X* will realize gross income of $50,000. *X*'s basis in the 100 shares will be $50,000. Note that World Wide is treated as having received payment of $50,000 for the IBM stock, and so World Wide can recognize a gain or loss on the transaction depending upon its basis in the IBM stock. In addition, World Wide may be allowed a business expense deduction of $50,000 for paying a bonus of that amount to its employee. The transaction is treated the same as it would have been if World Wide had paid X a cash bonus of $50,000, and X had then paid World Wide $50,000 to purchase the 100 shares of IBM stock.

¶ **3.1420.** **Illustration 2.** The same facts as those stated in ¶ **3.1410** except that X paid World Wide $10,000 cash for the receipt of the 100 shares of IBM stock. X is treated as if he received a $40,000 cash bonus, and had then paid World Wide $50,000 to purchase the 100 shares of IBM stock. X will have $40,000 of gross income, and World Wide may be allowed a $40,000 business expense deduction. X will have a $50,000 basis in the IBM stock. World Wide will be treated as having received $50,000 for the sale of the IBM stock and will recognize a gain or loss depending upon its basis in those shares.

¶ **3.1430.** **Illustration 3.** In Year One, World Wide gave *X* as a bonus 100 shares of World Wide's common stock having a value of $20 per share. Prior to that year, *X* owned no stock in World

---

9. For special rules concerning the furnishing of meals and lodging to an employee, see ¶ **2.4000** *et seq.*

Wide. *X* recognized gross income of $2,000, and X will have a basis of $2,000 in the World Wide stock. World Wide may be allowed to deduct $2,000 as a business expense. Although World Wide will be treated as having received $2,000 in payment for its stock, World Wide will not recognize a gain or loss because a corporation does not recognize gain or loss on selling its own stock. § 1032. Attempts to avoid or reduce the employee's taxable compensation by placing restrictions or conditions on property transferred for services (especially restrictions as to transferability and conditions creating a substantial risk of forfeiture) are covered by § 83.[10]

¶ 3.1500. Under Compensated Loan or Rental of Property in Kind. If an employer permits an employee to use an automobile that the employer owns for the personal use of the employee and if the employer fails to charge a fair rental for the automobile, the difference between the rental that the employee paid for the automobile (if any) and the fair rental value of the car will constitute gross income to the employee.[11] Similarly, an employee's use of other non-cash properties of his employer without charge or for an inadequate rental will cause the employee to recognize income.

If an employer loans cash to an employee for which no or inadequate interest is charged, § 7872 imposes tax consequences on both the employer and the employee.[12] There are exceptions to the application of § 7872 where the amounts involved are small.

The bargain element in an employer's rental to an employee can reasonably be viewed as a constructive receipt of rent by the employer and an immediate repayment to the employee as part of the employee's wages. Since the employee uses the rented property for personal purposes, no deduction is available to the employee for the constructive rental payment; and so the employee will have income and no offsetting deduction. While the constructive rental payment will constitute income to the employer, the income will be washed out by the deduction allowable to the employer for the constructive repayment to the employee as part of the latter's wages.

¶ 3.1600. Bargain Purchases. If an employee (or independent contractor) purchases property from his employer (or principal) for

10.   See ¶ **3.3000** *et seq.*

11.   See *Keeter v. Commissioner*, 36 T.C.M. 1018 (1977).

12.   See Chapter **Nine**.

less than the value of the property, the difference constitutes disguised compensation and is taxable. § 83.[13]

¶ **3.1610. Illustration 1. Disguised Compensation** X is an employee of Win All, Inc. X purchases Blackacre from Win All for $20,000, when the value of Blackacre is $35,000. The $15,000 "bargain" in X's purchase is disguised compensation and is included in X's gross income. X's basis in Blackacre is $35,000. Win All is treated as having received $35,000 for Blackacre and will compute its gain or loss accordingly. Win All also is treated as having paid $15,000 compensation to X, and that amount likely will qualify as a business expense deduction.[14]

¶ **3.1620. Illustration 2. Fringe Benefit Exception.** Y is an employee of Hudmaker's Department store. Y is employed as a salesperson in the store's toy department. The store permits all of its employees to purchase goods from the store at a ten percent discount. Y purchases a $200 washing machine for $180. The store's "gross profit percentage" (as defined in § 132(c)(2)) for the sale of all its goods to its customers in the normal course of business is forty percent. As a consequence of § 132(c) (a fringe benefit exception), Y will not realize any gross income because of making this bargain purchase.[15] Y's basis in the washing machine is $180.

¶ **3.1630. Illustration 3. Arm's Length Sale.** A owns Blackacre which has a value of $40,000. Because of financial problems, A needs to sell Blackacre quickly. B, an unrelated party, knows of A's financial distress. By shrewd bargaining, B purchases Blackacre from A for $35,000. Although B bought at a bargain price, the transaction was at arm's length and B will not realize income by making the bargain purchase. When the relationship between the purchaser and the seller does not suggest disguised compensation, no income will be realized. B's basis in Blackacre is $35,000.

¶ **3.2000. STOCK OPTIONS.** In the absence of a special statutory provision, when an employee of a corporation is granted an option to purchase the employer's capital stock at a favorable price, and the market value of the option can readily be determined, the employee will recognize gross income in an amount equal to the value of the option

---

13. But see § 132(c) and ¶¶ **2.2200–2.2242** and **3.4000–3.5000** for exceptions to this rule.

14. See ¶ **3.1420**.

15. See ¶¶ **2.2200–2.2242**.

over the amount (if any) that the employee paid for it. Treas. Reg. § 1.83–7(a). However, the Code does provide special tax treatment for options that satisfy certain statutory requirements. Those specially treated options are referred to as "statutory stock options," and they include so-called "incentive stock options" and options granted under an employee stock purchase plan.[16]

Stock options given to an employee that are not statutory stock options are referred to as either "nonstatutory stock options" or as "nonqualified stock options." The rules for the taxation of nonqualified stock options are set forth in § 83.[17]

¶ 3.2100. **Problems of Valuation.** In many circumstances, a nonqualified stock option will not have a "readily ascertainable fair market value" at the time that it is granted to an employee. In such cases, the employee will not be taxed when he acquires the option; the transaction is kept open for tax purposes. See § 83(e)(3); Treas. Reg. § 1.83–7(a). If the employee subsequently exercises the option, he will usually recognize gross income at that time in an amount equal to the difference between (1) the market value of the stock when purchased by the employee and (2) the sum of the amount paid for the stock by the employee plus any amount the employee paid to acquire the option. Treas. Reg. § 1.83–7(a). The price at which the stock can be purchased under the option is referred to as the "strike price."

If an employee sells or otherwise disposes of a nonqualified stock option to an unrelated person in an arm's length transaction, the tax treatment of that transaction is described in Treas. Reg. § 1.83–7(a). If the sale is not an arm's length transaction or is made to a related person, a different set of rules apply.

The Service generally prefers that a nonqualified stock option not be taxed when received and instead keep the transaction open and tax the transaction when the option is exercised or sold. To that end, the regulations provide strict criteria for determining whether an option has a "readily ascertainable fair market value;" and most nonqualified stock options will not meet those criteria.

If an option is actively traded on an established market, it will be deemed to have a readily ascertainable fair market value. Treas. Reg. § 1.83–7(b)(1). If an option is not actively traded on an established

16. See ¶¶ 3.4000–3.5000.
17. See ¶¶ 3.3000–3.3400.

market, it will not have a readily ascertainable fair market value unless *all* of the requirements set forth in Treas. Reg. § 1.83–7(b)(2) are satisfied.

¶ 3.2200. Deduction for Employer. An employer usually can deduct reasonable compensation paid to an employee as a business expense under § 162(a)(1). In regard to giving an employee a non-qualified stock option, the amount and timing of the employer's deduction will match the amount and timing of the income that the employee recognizes.[18]

¶ 3.3000. RESTRICTIONS ON ACQUIRED PROPERTY. The taxation of the receipt of property in payment for services is controlled by § 83. The same rules apply whether the service provider is an employee or an independent contractor; for convenience, we will refer to the service provider as an employee. The problem on which § 83 focuses arises when the property transferred as payment for services is subject to restrictions that would affect the property's value. Section 83 applies regardless of whether the property is transferred directly to the employee or to someone else because of services performed by the employee.

If property (including stock) that is acquired by an employee from his employer (whether or not acquired pursuant to an option) is subject to significant restrictions that affect the property's value, the time when the employee will be taxed and the extent to which the restriction will be taken into account in valuing the property are determined under special rules set out in § 83. In general, the value of the property less the consideration paid by the employee will be taken into account on the first date that the property is not subject to a substantial risk of forfeiture of the employee's interest (or on the first date that the employee's interest can be transferred by him so that the transferee is not subject to a substantial risk of forfeiture). § 83(a). Until the property becomes substantially vested, the transferor (rather than the transferee) continues to be treated as the owner of the property, and any income from the property that the transferee receives during that period (or right of the transferee to use the property during that period) is treated as compensation paid to the transferee. Treas. Reg. § 1.83–1(a)(1).

The application of § 83 to nonqualified deferred compensation plans was expanded by the 2004 adoption of § 409A. That provision is discussed at **¶ 3.6100**.

---

18. Cf. Treas. Reg. § 1.83–6(a). See **¶ 3.3500**.

¶ **3.3100.   Meaning of Property.** Section 83 applies to the receipt of "property" in connection with the performance of services. § 83(a). "Property" is defined in Treas. Reg. § 1.83–3(e) as including real and personal property other than cash. An "unfunded and unsecured promise to pay money or property in the future" is not property for purposes of § 83. Treas. Reg. § 1.83–3(e). Section 83 applies to such transfers of property regardless of whether made to the person who performed the services; but, for convenience, we will refer to the transferees as employees.

¶ **3.3200.   Lapse and Nonlapse Provisions.** When property acquired by an employee for services becomes taxable to the employee, the value of the property is determined by excluding all so-called "lapse restrictions" as if they were not present. § 83(a). A "nonlapse restriction" is a permanent limitation on the transferability of property which will require the holder of the property to sell or offer to sell the property at a price determined by a formula and which will continue to apply to and be enforced against the holder or any subsequent holder (other than the employer). A "lapse restriction" is a restriction other than a nonlapse restriction and includes, but is not limited to, a restriction that carries a substantial risk of forfeiture. Treas. Reg. § 1.83–3(h), (i).

¶ **3.3300.   Substantiality of Risk of Forfeiture.** For purposes of § 83, it is a factual question whether a risk of forfeiture is substantial, but the regulations do provide some guidance. For example, a risk of forfeiture is substantial when rights in transferred property are conditioned upon the future performance (or refraining from performance) of substantial services by any person. § 83(c)(1); Treas. Reg. § 1.83–3(c)(1).

If an employee is required to return the property to the employer on the occurrence of a condition, that *may* create a substantial risk of forfeiture depending upon the degree of likelihood that the condition will occur. For example, if the employee must return the property to the employer if the earnings of the employer do not increase, that will constitute a substantial risk of forfeiture; but if the employee must return the property only if the employee is discharged for cause or for committing a crime, that will not be considered a substantial risk of forfeiture. Treas. Reg. § 1.83–3(c)(2). If the employee is required to return the property if he accepts employment with a competitor of the employer (i.e., a covenant not to compete), that will not usually constitute a substantial risk of forfeiture, but particular facts may cause it to be so treated. Facts to be considered in such cases include: the age and health of the employee, the availability of other employment opportunities, the degree of the employee's skill, and the practice of the employer in enforcing such conditions. Id. If, on the required return of property pursuant to a restriction, the employer is required to pay the employee an amount equal to the fair market value of the property, the restriction will not constitute a substantial risk of forfeiture. Treas. Reg. § 1.83–3(c)(1). A requirement that a retiring employee return property received for services if he fails to render consulting services when requested will not constitute a substantial risk of forfeiture unless in fact he is expected to perform substantial consulting services. Id.

¶ 3.3400. **Election to be Taxed.** If § 83(a) otherwise prevents an employee from being taxed on the receipt of property, the employee has an election under § 83(b) to have the fair market value of such property (less any consideration paid by the employee to acquire it) included in his income at the time of his receipt. The value of the property for this purpose is determined by treating all lapse restrictions as nonexistent. § 83(b)(1)(A). If the election is made, the employee is treated as the owner of the property, and no additional amount is included in the employee's income when and if his interest in the property becomes substantially vested. On the other hand, if the property subsequently is forfeited, no deduction is allowable because of that forfeiture except that the employee can deduct the amount (if any) he paid the employer for the property. § 83(b)(1). The employee will recognize a (usually) capital loss but only for the amount, if any, he actually paid for the property. Treas. Reg. § 1.83–2(a).

Section 83(b) is a kind of tax gamble. If a TP makes that election, he must incur a tax liability at an earlier date than would otherwise be required. The TP will benefit from the election if the value of the property to be included in TP's income is significantly higher when the restriction terminates or is removed than the value that the property had at the time that the election was made.

Surprisingly, the Tax Court and the Ninth Circuit held that § 83 applies even if the employee pays consideration for the property equal to the property's fair market value. In *Alves v. Commissioner*,[19] the TP acquired stock from a corporation in connection with the TP's performance of services. Some of the acquired shares of stock were subject to restrictions which created a substantial risk of

---

19. 79 T.C. 864 (1982), aff'd 734 F.2d 478 (9th Cir. 1984).

forfeiture and some shares were not. The TP paid an amount for the stock that equaled the stocks' fair market value without any reduction in value because of the restrictions on some of TP's shares. The majority of the Tax Court and the Ninth Circuit held that the TP was subject to § 83(a) when the stock was sold or when the restrictions were removed (under § 83(a) the value of the stock at the time when the sale or restriction removal took place is compared to the consideration paid by the employee to determine the amount of income recognized by the employee). Because of the application of § 83(a), TP recognized ordinary income at those times. The TP could have prevented that consequence by making a timely election under § 83(b) to have the excess of the fair market value of the acquired stock at the date that TP acquired those shares over the amount that TP paid for such stock included in his gross income in the year that TP acquired the stock. Even though the amount of such excess would have been zero so that the election would not have caused TP to recognize any income, the election would have made § 83(a) inapplicable when the stock was sold or the restrictions were removed. Note that Treas. Reg. § 1.83–2(a) expressly authorizes a TP to make an election under § 83(b) even though the TP paid full value for the acquired property so that the TP's acquisition was not a bargain purchase. Consequently, when an employee purchases property (which is subject to a restriction that constitutes a substantial risk of forfeiture) from his employer at a price that constitutes fair value for the property without regard to the restriction, the employee should make a protective election under § 83(b).

¶ 3.3500. Employer's Deduction. If property becomes taxable to an employee under either § 83(a) or (b), and if the payment by the employer meets the requirements of §§ 162 or 212, the employer will be allowed a deduction for the amount included in the employee's income. § 83(h); Treas. Reg. § 1.83–6(a). No deduction is allowed under § 83(h) to the extent that the transfer constitutes a capital expenditure, a deferred expense or an amount properly included in the value of inventory, but the basis of the property to which the expenditure relates will be increased. Treas. Reg. § 1.83–6(a)(4). If a deduction is allowed and the property is subsequently forfeited, the employer is required to include in gross income in the taxable year of forfeiture the amount of the deduction that he previously took. Treas. Reg. § 1.83–6(c).

¶ 3.3600. Illustration 1. On March 5, Year One, *X* Corporation transferred 100 shares of its stock to *A*, an employee, as a bonus for

A's services. Any compensation paid to A for his services was deductible by the corporation under § 162(a)(1) as a business expense. The transfer was made subject to a condition that if *A* failed to remain in the employ of *X* for three years (other than a termination caused by *A*'s health or death), the 100 shares of *X* stock had to be returned to *X*. *A* was allowed to transfer the stock, but the condition that *A* remain in *X*'s employ for three years will apply to all subsequent transferees. At the time of the transfer to A, the fair market value of a share of *X*'s stock was $200, and so the value of the 100 shares that *A* received (without taking into account the restriction to which those shares were subject) was $20,000. Since *A* could not keep the stock unless he continued to provide services for *X* in the latter's employment for three years, and since he could not terminate that condition by transferring the stock to a third party, that condition is a lapse restriction and also constitutes a substantial risk of forfeiture. *A* did not make a § 83(b) election. *A* did not recognize income at the time that he received the stock in Year One because the substantial risk of forfeiture prevents the realization of that income.

At the end of the three-year period, A's interest in the stock will vest since the stock will no longer be subject to a risk of forfeiture. As shown in ¶ **3.3700**, A will be taxed when his interest in the stock vests at the end of the three-year period.

Although for property law purposes *A* is the owner of the 100 shares of *X* stock from the moment he receives them, for federal income tax purposes *A* is not treated as the owner of those shares until his interest vests. Consequently, any "dividends" paid on those shares to *A* by *X* during the three-year period when *A* is not considered the owner of those shares will not be treated as dividend income, but instead will be treated as compensation paid to *A* for his services. Treas. Reg. § 1.83–1(a)(1). The amount so included in *A*'s gross income as compensation will be deductible by *X* as a business expense.

¶ **3.3700. Illustration 2.** The same facts as those stated in ¶ **3.3600.** *A* continued in the employ of *X* for five years. The restriction on the 100 shares of *X* stock terminated on March 4, Year Four. At the date on which the restriction terminated, the fair market value of the stock is included in *A*'s income, and *A* thereafter is treated as the owner of those shares of stock for tax purposes. The fair market value of a share of *X* stock on March 4, Year Four, was $300, and so the value of the 100 shares that *A* held was $30,000. *A* must include $30,000 in his gross income. In the corporation's taxable year in which A recognized the $30,000 of gross income, the corporation will be allowed a deduction of $30,000 by § 83(h). Treas. Reg. § 1.83–6(a).

¶ **3.3800. Illustration 3.** The same facts as those stated in ¶ 3.3600. *A* died on June 23, Year Two. *A*'s death terminated the restriction and caused the then fair market value of the 100 shares of stock to be included in income. The income will be taxed to the estate of *A* as income in respect of a decedent. Treas. Reg. § 1.83–1(d).[20] In the corporation's taxable year in which the estate had income, the corporation will be allowed a deduction of a like amount.

¶ **3.3900. Illustration 4.** The same facts as those stated in ¶ 3.3600 except that *A* made a timely election under § 83(b) to recognize income when he received the 100 shares of *X* stock. *A* must include $20,000 in his gross income for Year One. *A* will be treated as the owner of the *X* stock for tax purposes, and so any dividends received by *A* will be treated as such for tax purposes. Neither *A* (nor his estate) will incur additional income taxes when the restriction terminates. In the corporation's taxable year in which *A* had gross income (Year One), the corporation will be allowed a deduction of a like amount.

If *A* leaves his employment within the prescribed three-year period and thereby forfeits the *X* stock, *A* will not be allowed a deduction for that forfeiture loss. In the event of that forfeiture, the corporation will include in its income for that year an amount equal to the deduction it took in Year One. Treas. Reg. § 1.83–6(c).

¶ **3.4000. INCENTIVE STOCK OPTIONS.** The receipt and exercise of certain stock options ("incentive stock options") are granted special tax treatment by §§ 421 and 422. An incentive stock option can be an option to purchase the stock of the TP's corporate employer or of a parent or subsidiary of a corporate employer. § 422(b). If the statutory requirements are satisfied, the employee will not recognize any income on receiving an incentive stock option or on exercising the option; and the employee's gain on a sale of the stock he acquired by exercising the option will be a capital gain. § 421(a).

However, for purposes of the Alternative Minimum Tax (AMT), the rules of § 83 will be applied to the exercise of the option unless the exercise of the option and the subsequent disposition of the stock occur

---

20. Income in respect of a decedent (IRD) is discussed at Chapter **Twenty–Nine**.

in the same year. Consequently, although the employee will not be subject to the regular income tax, he may incur a tax liability on exercising the option because of the application of the AMT.[21] In the discussion below of Incentive Stock Options, we will ignore the possibility that the AMT may cause some tax consequence.

¶ **3.4100. Receipt and Exercise of an Incentive Stock Option.** If an option qualifies as an incentive stock option, and if no sale or other disposition of the stock takes place within one year after the employee acquired the stock or within two years after the employee acquired the option, the employee will not recognize income either on the receipt, or on the exercise, of the option; and the employer will not be allowed a deduction for the bargain element in its sale of its stock to the TP. §§ 421(a), 422(a)(1). In addition, the employee must have been in the continuous employ of the corporation granting the option (or of a parent or subsidiary of that corporation) for the period beginning with the grant of the option and ending three months prior to the exercise of the option (unless the employee is disabled in which event the period ends one year prior to the exercise). § 422(a)(2), (c)(6). There are some exceptions to these holding and continuous employment rules. See e.g., § 422(c)(3). If either of those holding and continuous employment requirements are violated, the option will be treated as a nonqualified stock option to which § 83 will apply.[22] In addition to the benefit from excluding from gross income the bargain element in a TP's exercise of an incentive stock option, the TP's gain on a subsequent sale of the stock, which will often include that bargain element, will be a capital gain.

¶ **3.4200. Other Requirements.** In addition to the holding and continuous employment requirements, there are six other requirements that must be satisfied for an option to qualify as an incentive stock option. § 422(b). Among those other requirements, the option must be exercisable within ten years after the date on which the plan was adopted or the shareholders approved it, whichever is earlier; and the option price must be at least equal to the fair market value of the stock at the time that the option was granted. The option cannot be transferable other than by death, and, during the employee's life, must be exercisable only by the employee. If the terms of an option include a statement that it will not be treated as an incentive stock option, then it will not be treated as one. Id. There is no anti-discrimination requirement for an incentive stock option.

21. See ¶ 28.2290G.
22. See ¶ 3.3000.

An option will not be treated as an incentive stock option to the extent that a $100,000 limitation is exceeded. Under that limitation, the first time that an incentive stock option is exercisable, to the extent that the aggregate fair market value of the stock (determined at the time that the option was granted) that can be acquired by exercising incentive stock options in that taxable year exceeds $100,000, the options will not qualify. In determining the aggregate amount of stock that can be obtained by exercising options, all of the incentive stock option plans of the employer and of its parent and subsidiary corporations are taken into account. § 422(d).

¶ 3.5000. **EMPLOYEE STOCK PURCHASE PLAN OPTIONS.** An employee stock purchase plan (ESPP) is a plan to issue options to employees to purchase the employer's stock. The requirements of an ESPP are set forth in § 423(a) and (b). If all of the requirements are satisfied, § 421 applies and the employee does not recognize income on receiving or exercising the option. On the disposition of stock acquired from the exercise of the option, if certain conditions are satisfied, the employee may have capital gain treatment; but if those requirements are not satisfied, the employee will have ordinary income for all or part of his gain from the sale of the stock. § 423(c). Subject to a few exceptions, the plan must provide options to all the employees. § 423(b)(4). The Alternative Minimum Tax does not apply to ESPP options.

¶ 3.6000. **DEFERRED COMPENSATION.**

¶ 3.6100. **Nonqualified Plans.** A cash method TP does not report income until he has actually or constructively received cash or its equivalent.[23] Income is constructively received by a TP in the year that it is credited to his account, or set apart for him, or otherwise made available so that he has the unrestricted right to draw upon it. Treas. Reg. § 1.451–2(a). When a TP's right to draw funds is subject to substantial restrictions or a possibility of forfeiture, the TP will not be deemed to have constructively received the income until his control is unrestricted and free from significant contingencies. Id. Unless § 409A applies, a mere unsecured promise to pay a TP for services will not invoke the constructive receipt doctrine or constitute the equivalent of cash.[24] But if the promise is secured or if it is evidenced by a negotiable note, it likely will be treated as equivalent

---

23. See ¶¶ 1.6211–1.6212 for a discussion of the "constructive receipt" and "economic benefit" doctrines and their application to deferred compensation benefits.

24. Rev. Rul. 69–650; Rev. Rul. 60–31. See Treas. Reg. § 1.83–3(e).

to cash and be included in the TP's income. Even an unsecured nonnegotiable note is equivalent to cash if its fair market value is ascertainable.[25] If a note is received for services and if the note is subject to restrictions, § 83 will apply.

In 2004, Congress added § 409A to the Code to modify the constructive receipt doctrine's application to nonqualified deferred compensation arrangements. A deferred compensation plan is nonqualified if it is not covered by one of the statutory provisions that provide special beneficial treatment to certain deferred compensation benefits (i.e., it is not a qualified plan).[26] Section 409A does not cause income to be recognized if there is a substantial risk of forfeiture. § 409A(a)(1)(A). Section 409A places additional requirements for an employee to be allowed to defer compensation income. These additional requirements concern the dates on which distributions from the plan can be made and the dates on which the employee's election to defer can be made. If the requirements of § 409A are not met and if the employee did not report the deferred compensation as income when earned, the statute imposes interest plus a penalty equal to 20% of the unreported deferred income. § 409A(a)(1)(B). The statute does not apply to certain forms of compensation such as sick leave and disability pay. § 409A(d).

The principle under which a commitment to an employee becomes taxable if the value to the employee is ascertainable is called the "economic benefit" doctrine.[27] To some extent, the economic benefit doctrine (a judicially created principle) has been altered by § 83, which provides rules for the taxation of an employee or independent contractor who receives property or an interest in property in connection with the performance of services.[28]

The application of § 83 to the funding of a nonqualified deferred compensation plan is expanded by § 409A(b), which was adopted in 2004. The funding assets will be treated as transferred to the employee if they are foreign assets or later become foreign assets even if they are subject to the claims of the employer's creditors. § 409A(b)(1). Also, funding assets are treated as transferred to the employee on the date that a plan first provides that the assets will be restricted to providing deferred compensation benefits if there is a

25. See *Warren Jones v. Commissioner*, 524 F.2d 788 (9th Cir. 1975), rev'g 60 T.C. 663 (1973).

26. See ¶ **3.7000**.

27. See ¶ **1.6212**.

28. See ¶ **3.3000**.

change in the employer's financial health. § 409A(b)(2). This provision applies even if the assets are subject to the claims of the employer's creditors. The inclusion of that provision concerning the employer's creditors subjects so-called "rabbi trusts" to § 409A.[29]

A TP's right to a payment that is secured by an escrow deposit is covered by the economic benefit doctrine and is treated as a receipt of cash by the TP; if the TP is an employee or independent contractor, the transferred amount may be taxable under § 83. Treas. Reg. § 1.83–3(e). However, if the obligor, while contractually bound to deposit a specified amount in escrow, fails to make the deposit, there is no economic benefit or constructive receipt to the TP until funds are actually deposited in escrow.[30] If funds are deposited in the escrow account, but the account can be reached by creditors of the transferor (the employer), the escrow may qualify for the "rabbi trust" doctrine described in ¶ 3.6200 and therefore may not cause the employee to be taxed unless § 409A applies.[31]

> ¶ 3.6110. **Illustration 1.** *X*, a cash method TP, executed an employment contract with World Wide Widgets, Inc. under which World Wide agreed to pay *X* a salary of $80,000 per year; and to pay *X* or his estate—commencing with the termination of *X*'s employment or his retirement—$20,000 per year for a period of years equal to the number of years *X* worked for World Wide prior to his retirement or the termination of his employment. Thus, in effect, *X* receives an annual salary of $100,000 ($80,000 to be paid currently and $20,000 to be deferred). In fact, the salary is less than $100,000 since the deferred $20,000 payment should be discounted to determine its present value (i.e., the loss of present use of the funds has an economic value).[32] *X* must rely on World Wide's *unsecured* promise to make the deferred payments, and *X* must accept the risk that World Wide may not have the financial means of making those payments when they are due. World Wide's promise, which is not represented by notes, does not constitute the equivalence of cash; therefore, *X* will not include any of the deferred $20,000 payments in his gross income until they are actually paid to him.[33]

29. See ¶ 3.6200.

30. *Vaughn v. Commissioner*, 87 T.C. 164 (1986).

31. The circumstances and conditions in which the Commissioner will issue an advance ruling on the tax treatment of a proposed unfunded deferred compensation arrangement are set forth in Rev. Proc. 92–65, amplifying Rev. Proc. 71–19.

32. See ¶ 3.1100.

33. Rev. Rul. 60–31; Treas. Reg. § 1.83–3(e).

The delivery of a negotiable promissory note or check typically will be treated as a cash equivalent. Even the receipt of a nonnegotiable promissory note will be treated as the equivalent of cash if its value can be ascertained.

¶ 3.6120. Illustration 2. The same facts apply as ¶ **3.6110**, but World Wide secures its obligation to make the deferred payments to *X* or his estate by transferring an appropriate amount each year to an escrow fund held by a local bank. According to *X*'s employment contract, the bank, as escrow agent, is to make the deferred payments when due. Since *X* receives an ascertainable economic benefit each year when World Wide deposits a sum with the escrow agent, that benefit constitutes a cash equivalent and *X* must include the amount actually deposited in his gross income. This is an application of the economic benefit doctrine. Also, § 83 will apply to require *X* to recognize income. Treas. Reg. § 1.83–3(e). The distinction between this and the prior illustration rests on the secured or unsecured nature of the deferred compensation. To the extent that the payments are secured, the economic benefit to the employee is reasonably ascertainable and is sufficiently similar to a cash payment that those amounts are taxable. Unless interest on the sums deposited is payable to *X* either currently or at some future date, the amount of gross income recognized by *X* when World Wide deposits a sum in the escrow fund should be reduced to reflect the present value of that sum to *X*.

¶ 3.6130. Illustration 3. In Year One, Win All, Inc. paid the Friendly Insurance Company a $5,000 premium on an annuity policy for Win All's president, *X*. The policy provides a benefit payable to *X* or his estate upon his attaining his 65th birthday or upon his death. In Year One, *X* was 52 years old. The policy is to be held and owned by Win All until *X* reaches age 65 or dies, but Win All cannot cancel or assign the policy or change the beneficiary. The policy is not subject to the claims of Win All's creditors. *X* has received an economic benefit of $5,000 in Year One which he must report as gross income.[34] If the annuity policy were subject to the claims of Win All's creditors, the Service has ruled that its

---

34. *United States v. Drescher*, 179 F.2d 863 (2d Cir. 1950). See § 83.

purchase will not constitute income to X.[35]

¶ 3.6200. Rabbi Trust. *X* establishes a plan to provide monthly payments to its employee, *A*, to commence when *A* retires or to be payable to *A*'s estate if *A* dies before retirement. *A*'s interest in the deferred payments are vested. As previously noted, if *X* does not fund or otherwise provide security for the deferred payments, *A* will not be taxed until he receives payment. However, *X* funds the plan by transferring cash to an irrevocable trust (or an escrow account) which secures that the payments will be made. *A* cannot assign, transfer, or pledge his interest in the trust or escrow account. The trust assets (or escrow account) cannot be withdrawn by *X* (the employer) or distributed to it. The trust instrument (or escrow agreement) provides that the trust's assets (or escrow funds) are subject to the claims of general and judgment creditors of *X*, and that provision will permit *X*'s creditors to reach the trust's assets (or escrow funds) under local law.

In a number of letter rulings, the Commissioner has held that since creditors of *X* can obtain the trust's assets (or escrow funds) to satisfy the employer's debts, § 83 will not cause *A* to recognize income [§ 83 taxes an employee for the receipt of a beneficial interest in assets "which are transferred or set aside from the claims of creditors of the transferor," Treas. Reg. § 1.83–3(e)], and there will be no constructive receipt or economic benefit to *A*, who will not be taxed on the deferred amounts until paid.[36]

Most of those rulings predate the 2004 adoption of § 409A and so do not address the extent to which that section will apply to these types of plans (rabbi trust plans). These plans are subject to the exceptions created by § 409A(b) to treat certain transfers to fund a deferred compensation plan as having been made to the employee and so subject to § 83.[37]

Since one of the first rulings on the taxation of a trust of this kind involved a trust for a rabbi,[38] such trusts have become known as

---

35. Rev. Rul. 72–25.

36. E.g., PLR 8113107, PLR 8509023, PLR 200703012. See also, Rev. Rul. 72–25 holding that an employer's funding of a deferred compensation agreement with the purchase of an annuity did not cause the employee to recognize income when the employee had no interest in the annuity and it was subject to the claims of the employer's creditors. The Commissioner has approved such arrangements even when creditors of the employer can reach the trust's assets only if the employer becomes insolvent or bankrupt. E.g., PLR 9822030, PLR 8703061, and PLR 8844020.

37. See ¶ **3.6100**.

38. PLR 8113107.

"rabbi trusts."[39] They constitute one type of a nonqualified deferred compensation plan. An explanation for the Commissioner's approval of rabbi trusts is that the employer retains a significant reversionary interest in such trusts by his power to incur debts and thereby create creditors (and even insolvency) who can satisfy the employer's debts by taking the trust's assets. This power over the trust so intrudes upon the employee's security as to prevent the trust from providing an economic benefit of ascertainable value to the employee. Another explanation (and one adopted by the Commissioner in some of his rulings) is that the access of the employer's creditors to the trust's assets causes the employer to be treated as the owner of those assets under § 671 (the so-called grantor trust provision).

¶ 3.7000. QUALIFIED RETIREMENT PLANS. To encourage the establishment of retirement plans for employees, Congress has granted favorable tax treatment for deferred compensation plans that comply with a number of statutory requirements. As a result, qualified pension and profit-sharing programs have been widely adopted by employers. See §§ 401–404. In general, contributions made by an employer to a qualified pension or profit-sharing plan are deductible by the employer but are not included in the gross income of the employees who are beneficiaries of the plan, even though their interests are vested, until actually distributed to them from the fund. In addition, income earned by the fund is not taxed when earned. In effect, the tax on the employer's contributions and the income earned by the fund is deferred until payment is made to the beneficiary.

¶ 3.7100. Self–Employed. Self-employed persons can adopt a qualified deferred compensation plan for themselves under the so-called Keogh or HR–10 provisions. See § 401(c). The annual amount that can be contributed to a Keogh plan is much more limited than the amounts that can be contributed to ordinary employee plans. A self-employed individual may also qualify to use an Individual Retirement Arrangement, which defers a limited amount of income in certain circumstances.

¶ 3.7200. Individual Retirement Arrangements. There are four kinds of Individual Retirement Arrangements (IRAs)—individual retirement accounts, individual retirement annuities, individual retire-

---

39. Deferred compensation trusts that are not a rabbi trust are sometimes referred to as "secular trusts."

ment bonds, and Roth IRAs. Certain contributions to the first three types may be deductible, but contributions to a Roth IRA are not deductible. The amount that can be contributed annually to an IRA is severely limited. The income earned by an IRA (other than a Roth IRA) generally is not taxed until distributed, and the income earned by a Roth IRA may never be taxed.

¶ **3.8000. EMPLOYEE LIFE INSURANCE.** If an employer purchases insurance on the life of an employee and if the proceeds are payable to a beneficiary selected by the employee, the premium paid will be included in the employee's gross income. Treas. Reg. § 1.61–2(d)(2)(ii)(A).

¶ **3.8100. Illustration.** Win All, Inc. provides $20,000 individual term insurance coverage for its president, X, who named his wife as beneficiary. The annual premium for the policy is $200. Win All's payment of a $200 premium causes X to recognize $200 gross income.

¶ **3.8200. Group–Term Exception.** If an employer purchases group-term life insurance for its employees, the premium paid for a particular employee's coverage will be excluded from the employee's gross income to the extent that the premium does not exceed the cost (as determined under a standardized table prescribed by the Regulations) of $50,000 insurance. § 79(a), (c).[40]

---

40. See ¶ **2.4000**.

CHAPTER FOUR

DAMAGES AND LOSS RECOVERY

¶ **4.0000 DAMAGES AND LOSS RECOVERY.**

¶ **4.1000. COMPENSATORY DAMAGES.** The receipt of damages resulting from a claim (pursuant to a court judgment or a private settlement) calls into play special tax rules concerning compensatory damages. Note however that punitive damages are includable in gross income.[1] For example, two-thirds of the amount received under a treble damage award (e.g., for an antitrust claim) will constitute gross income to the recipient.

The tax treatment of compensatory damages must be divided into two categories—damages for harming or destroying property and damages for personal injuries suffered by an individual. The paragraph below briefly summarizes the current treatment of damages, and subsequent sections expand on this topic.

Damages for harming or destroying property will constitute realized income to the recipient to the extent that the amount of such damages exceeds the recipient's adjusted basis in the damaged or destroyed property. The realized income will be recognized (and therefore taxable) unless an amount equal to all or a portion of the damages is invested within a specified time period in property that permits the recipient to elect nonrecognition under § 1033. See ¶ **24.8000** *et seq.* To the extent that such damages do not exceed the TP's adjusted basis, they will not be included in gross income.

Damages received for a *physical* injury to one's person, or for a physical sickness, are excluded from income by § 104(a)(2). Damages received for a nonphysical injury to one's person generally are treated as income. To the extent that the TP is reimbursed for previously deducted medical expenses, receipt of the reimbursement will result in income recognition.

¶ **4.2000. DAMAGE CAUSED TO TANGIBLE PROPERTY.** Compensation received by a TP for damage caused to the TP's property will

---

1. *O'Gilvie v. United States*, 519 U.S. 79 (1996); *General American Investors Co. v. Commissioner*, 348 U.S. 434 (1955); and *Commissioner v. Glenshaw Glass Co.*, 348 U.S. 426 (1955). See also, § 104(a)(2).

be included in gross income only to the extent that the amount of the compensation exceeds the TP's adjusted basis in the damaged property. This is true regardless of whether the payor of the compensation is the person who caused the damage or is an insurer.

¶ **4.2100.** **Illustration 1.** *X* negligently collided with a car in which *Y* had a basis of $3,000. The car had a value of $2,500 before the collision and $1,500 after the collision. As a consequence of the collision, an antique vase which *Y* was transporting in his car was broken beyond repair. *Y* had a basis of $500 in the vase, which had a value of $1,200 prior to the accident. Because of limitations in § 165, no tax deduction was allowable to *Y* for the casualty loss he incurred.[2] Neither the car nor the vase was used by *Y* in his business.

X paid *Y* $1,000 compensation for the damage to *Y*'s car, and $1,200 compensation for having destroyed *Y*'s vase.

	Basis Before	Fair Market Value Before	After	Comp	Basis After	Tax Result
Car	$3,000	$2,500	$1,500	$1,000	$2,000	$0 Gain Realized
Vase	$500	$1,200	$0	$1,200	$0	$700 Gain Realized
Total	$3,500	$3,700	$1,500	$2,200	$2,000	$1,500 as recovery of capital

Y did not realize any gain from the $1,000 damages paid on the car, since the payment was less than his basis for the car. *Y*'s basis for his car is reduced by the amount recovered as damages (i.e., $1,000) to $2,000. However, *Y* will *realize* a gain of $700 ($1,200 compensation minus $500 basis) on the damages paid for the broken vase. This gain will be *recognized* unless a statutory provision for nonrecognition is applicable, such as § 1033. See ¶ **24.8000** *et seq.* The remaining $500 of recovery is excluded from income as a recovery of capital. *Y*'s basis in the vase is reduced to zero, and his basis in the car is reduced to $2,000.

¶ **4.2200.** **Illustration 2.** The same facts as those stated in ¶ **4.2100**, except that a portion of the casualty loss that *Y* incurred was deductible. As explained in Chapter **Eighteen**, for tax purposes, the amount of loss that *Y* sustained as a result of the collision is $1,500 (i.e., the difference between the values of each item before and after the collision but limited to the amount of *Y*'s basis in the item).

2.   See Chapter **Eighteen**.

At the time that Y filed his tax return for the year of the collision, there was no reasonable prospect that he would be reimbursed for any of the loss.[3] Because of limitations in § 165(h)(1), (2) on the amount that can be deducted for a casualty loss, Y was allowed a deduction of only $250 for the loss that he sustained. Y claimed a $250 deduction and obtained a tax benefit thereby.

Y's deduction of a $250 loss caused a reduction of Y's basis in the two damaged items. § 1016(a)(1). The reduction of basis is allocated between the car and the vase, presumably in proportion to the loss sustained on each item as determined for tax purposes. So, 2/3 of the $250 deduction ($167) reduces Y's basis in the car to $2,833; and 1/3 of the $250 deduction ($83) reduces Y's basis in the vase to $417. Since the vase no longer exists, its basis has no significance unless there is a subsequent recovery.

As stated in ¶ 4.2100, in a subsequent year, Y did obtain a recovery from X of $1,000 for the damage to Y's car and $1,200 of the damage to the vase. The $1,000 recovered for the damage to the car is less than Y's basis of $2,833; so Y does not recognize income from receiving that amount. Y's basis in the car is reduced to $1,833.

The $1,200 Y received for the vase exceeds Y's $417 basis by $783. Unless § 1033 applies, Y recognizes a gain of $783 and has a zero basis in the broken vase.

¶ 4.2300. **Illustration 3.** The same facts as those stated in ¶ 4.2100, except that Y's car was used in his business, and Y had a reasonable prospect of obtaining reimbursement. Because of the prospect of obtaining reimbursement, no deduction was allowable to Y for the loss he incurred, and he did not claim a deduction. Prior to receiving the payment from X, Y expended $900 in repairing the car, and Y claimed and was allowed a business expense deduction for that expense. As explained below, the Service maintains that the $900 repair cost must be capitalized, but the authors question the validity of the Service's position.

The amount of the $2,200 recovery that is included in Y's gross income is $700—the same amount that was included in ¶ 4.2100 and for the same reason. In the view of the authors, the deduction that Y obtained for repairing the car should have no effect on the tax treatment of the damages he received. The damage payment was not a reimbursement of the repairs he made, but rather was compensa-

---

3. Note that a TP cannot take a deduction for a casualty loss to the extent that he has a reasonable prospect of being reimbursed. ¶ **18.2510.**

tion for the loss he suffered when his property was damaged. The tax benefit rule does not apply. While the amount expended for repairs can be an indicator of the amount of casualty loss, the payment received from X is for the property loss itself and not a repair expense reimbursement.

The IRS maintains that the cost incurred in repairing a damaged item for which a casualty loss deduction was allowable (which loss will reduce the TP's basis in the damaged item under § 1016(a)(1)) is "in the nature of a replacement of the part of the property that was damaged," and therefore such a repair cost must be capitalized (i.e., added to the TP's basis) rather than deducted.[4] The Service's position on this issue is suspect and was questioned by a District Court in dictum in *Waldrip v. United States*.[5] The authors believe that the position adopted by the IRS in that ruling and proposed regulation is questionable, and so we treated the repair in this illustration as a deductible item. However, the Service likely will disallow the deduction, and a TP would have to litigate the issue. The outcome is far from certain.

¶ 4.2400. Recovery Not Required by Law. While early statements of the IRS as to the exclusion of compensatory recoveries indicated that a recipient must have had a legal right to the recovery to qualify for the exclusion,[6] the Service later repudiated its earlier stance in several General Counsel Memorandums.[7] Those General Counsel Memorandums dealt with the question of whether a receipt that was not obtained by legal right could be treated as compensation (or a prospect of compensation) that would prevent the deduction of a loss that was the source of the "compensatory" payment. The Service concluded that, for such treatment, compensatory payments need not be legally required to be made. A reasonable extension of that conclusion is that such receipts can qualify as compensatory payments for purposes of excluding them from income as well.

Accordingly, it appears that the current view of the Service is that there need only be a significant nexus between the loss and the payment for the latter to be treated as compensatory. There is no requirement that the recipient have had an enforceable right to the funds. It would seem to be sufficient if the purpose of the payment

---

4. Rev. Rul. 71–161; Prop. Reg. § 1.263(a)–3(e)(2), (g)(1). See **¶ 21.1444**.
5. 48 AFTR 2d 81–6031, fn.5 (N.D. Ga. 1981).
6. GCM 38032 (1979).
7. GCM 39228 (1984), GCM 39480 (1986), and GCM 39558 (1986).

was to redress a harm that the payor had caused, regardless of whether the payor had a legal obligation to make that payment.

Of course a compensatory payment must be distinguished from a gift, which is the product of detached and disinterested generosity. For example, if a payment is made because the payor feels a moral responsibility to mitigate the loss that his actions caused another, that would not be a gift, but would be a compensatory payment. To the extent that a payment is treated as a gift, then the entire amount of the gift is excluded from the payee's income by § 102.

¶ **4.2500. Recovery of Lost Dollars.** If X's error or wrongful action causes a loss of money to Y, if the loss is not deductible by Y, and if X reimburses Y for all or part of the dollars lost, will the reimbursement constitute gross income to Y? Just as damages received for injuries to property are excluded from income to the extent of the recipient's basis in the property, so are recoveries of lost dollars. They are treated as returns of capital and are not taxable. See *Clark v. Commissioner*.[8]

¶ **4.2510. Illustration 1.** X, a lawyer, gave bad advice to a client causing the client to pay $20,000 more in federal income tax than the client actually owed. By the time the error was discovered, the statute of limitation for amending the tax return had expired, so the client could not obtain a refund of his $20,000 overpayment. X then paid the client $20,000 to replace the $20,000 that the client had lost to the government because of X's error. The $20,000 that the client received from X is not included in the client's gross income. It is a recovery of capital.[9]

What if X's error did not rise to the level of malpractice and X had no legal obligation to compensate the client? The result to the client should be the same—i.e., the payment should be exempt from tax.[10] There are several reasons why X might wish to make that payment even if X had no legal obligation to do so. X might feel a moral responsibility for the loss and wish to make it right. X might have a selfish, business motive to make the payment to mute any criticism of his work that might circulate if the loss

8. 40 BTA 333 (1939), Acq. See also *Concord Instruments Corp. v. Commissioner*, 67 T.C.M. 3036 (1994); Rev. Rul. 57–47.

9. See *Clark v. Commissioner*, 40 BTA 333 (1939), Acq.

10. In *Clark*, the Tax Court described the lawyer's payment as having been made voluntarily, and the court held that the voluntariness did not affect the tax treatment of the payment.

were left unabated. Such motives are not detached and disinterested generosity, so the payment would not be a gift. However, the nexus between the payment and X's role in causing the loss makes it a compensatory payment. Accordingly, the replacement of dollars lost is equivalent to the replacement of basis lost through the destruction of property and is excluded from the client's income.

If X were legally liable for the excess $20,000 that the client paid to the IRS, and if X's insurance carrier paid $20,000, as a result of a settlement or court judgment, to the client to replace the lost dollars, neither the client nor X would have any income as a consequence of that payment.[11] In an article, one of the authors discussed the tax policy justification for this treatment.[12]

¶ 4.2520. Illustration 2. Z, a CPA firm, negligently caused Client to fail to take action necessary to qualify Client as a "regulated investment company" and thereby qualify for favorable tax treatment. Because of that error, Client became liable for higher income taxes than it otherwise would have incurred. As a result of the CPA's negligence, Client incurred penalties and interest on its tax liability. Z's insurance carrier reimbursed Client for the additional federal income tax Client incurred plus the associated penalties and interest that Client had to pay. Initially, relying on the *Clark* decision, the IRS ruled (in a Private Letter Ruling) that the payments received by Client were not income. Six years later, in 1997, the IRS revoked the earlier Private Letter Ruling and ruled that the payments are included in Client's gross income.[13] The Service distinguished the instant situation from *Clark* on the basis that in *Clark* and related precedents, the advisor's error caused the TP to pay the government a larger amount then the TP actually owed. In contrast, in the instant situation, the TP actually did owe the taxes that were collected and the interest and penalties for not paying it. The error was in failing to have Client take action that would have precluded those taxes; but, since the action was not taken, Client did owe the money in question. The Service then cited Treas. Reg. § 1.61–14(a) for the proposition that one person's payment of the income tax liability of another is income to the other unless

---

11. *Concord Instruments Corp. v. Commissioner*, 67 T.C.M. 3036 (1994).

12. See Jeffrey H. Kahn, *Hedging the IRS—A Policy Justification for Excluding Liability and Tax Insurance Proceeds*, 26 Yale J. on Reg. 1 (2009).

13. PLR 9743034 and PLR 9743035.

excluded by law. The Service concluded that the payments received by Client from the insurance carrier were income to the Client.

The Commissioner gave a similar ruling in PLR 9833007. Under the facts of that ruling, after winning a state lottery, the TP consulted attorneys for tax preparation advice. The attorneys failed to advise TP to pay the state income tax on his winning in the year in which he received the prize so that he could deduct that tax payment in computing his federal income tax. This failure caused TP to incur a higher federal income tax liability, and TP sought indemnification from the attorneys' malpractice insurer. The Commissioner ruled that any indemnification the TP obtained will be included in his gross income.

In the view of the authors, the position taken by the Service in the 1997 and 1998 Private Letter Rulings is wrong and cannot be sustained.[14] As to the 1997 rulings, regardless of whether the Client actually owed the taxes, Z's negligence caused the client to pay out a greater amount of taxes and associated costs than it otherwise would have incurred, and the payment that Client received was compensation for the loss that it suffered from that negligence. The compensatory replacement of lost dollars should be excluded from income. Of course, by not taking the action needed to qualify as a "regulated investment company," Client may have benefitted in some manner, such as saving some costs. But, that only goes to the question of the amount of damages and to the correct amount of compensatory payment that should be made. It should have no effect on the question of the taxability of Client's receipt of the compensatory payment. Similarly, an indemnification of a TP, as in the 1998 ruling, for the negligence of attorneys in failing to advise TP of a tax minimization step constitutes damages for lost capital in the form of a higher tax liability than was necessary.

¶ **4.3000. DAMAGE CAUSED TO INTANGIBLE PROPERTY.** Intangible assets (e.g., goodwill, trademarks, and copyrights) may be damaged by tortious conduct, such as defamation and infringement. Compensatory damages relating to such assets will consist of gross income only to the extent that the compensation exceeds the TP's basis in the intangible asset.

14. See *Concord Instruments Corp. v. Commissioner*, 67 T.C.M. 3036 (1994).

¶ **4.3100. Damage to Goodwill.** An unfair trade practice or a defamatory statement concerning the quality of a product or service of a business may cause damage to the "goodwill" of the business, for which the injured party may collect damages. "Goodwill" is an intangible asset that represents the potential that a business possesses to attract customers for its products or services. Following the general rule, compensation for damage to a TP's goodwill constitutes gross income to the extent that the compensation exceeds the TP's basis in his goodwill.

¶ **4.3200. Determining Basis in Goodwill.** In many instances, a TP will not have a basis in his goodwill. As a consequence, the entire compensatory payment will be included in his gross income. A TP usually will have a basis in his goodwill only when he has purchased the goodwill of another business. For example, if X purchased a going business from Y, a part of the purchase price may be allocated to goodwill. X will have an adjusted basis in the goodwill equal to the allocated part of the purchase price less amortization deductions previously allowed or allowable under § 197.

¶ **4.3300. Reimbursement for Lost Profits.** Reimbursement for profits lost by a TP due to some wrongful action by another will constitute gross income. There is no offset for basis. The distinction between compensation for damages inflicted on a TP's goodwill and compensation for lost profits is nebulous at best, inasmuch as the value of goodwill relates directly to its income producing quality. The trend in the cases is to favor the TP by finding that compensation was paid for damages caused to the TP's goodwill. This is so even though the value of the goodwill is determined by referring to the loss of profits suffered.[15] But see *Bresler v. Commissioner*[16] where the court held that a large portion of an antitrust settlement was for lost profits rather than for damage to goodwill. The court held in *Bresler* that the TP had the burden of proving that the corporation had suffered damage to its goodwill or that the settlement included a specific amount for damaged goodwill. The court would not accept the TP's contention that the settlement should be allocated according to the types of damage requested by the TP in the complaint. Only a relatively small amount of the settlement was treated as damages for goodwill. See also ¶¶ **4.3100 and 4.3200.**

A plausible distinction that might be employed is to treat compensation received for depriving the TP of the profit that the TP would

15. *Raytheon Production Corp. v. Commissioner*, 144 F.2d 110 (1st Cir. 1944).
16. 65 T.C. 182 (1975).

have earned under a specific contract as a substitute for that lost profit and so taxed as ordinary income. On the other hand, compensation received for damage done to a broad range of the TP's business (which thereby reduces its future profits from that portion of the business) should be characterized as a compensatory payment for the damage to the TP's goodwill.

Even if the TP has no basis in his goodwill (as often will be the case), so that all of the compensation will be included in TP's gross income regardless of whether characterized as paid for damage to goodwill or for lost profits, there is a tax consequence to the characterization of the payment. Compensation received for lost profits will be ordinary income to the TP. The income recognized from receiving compensation for damage to goodwill usually will be treated as gain under § 1231(a)(3)(A) which often will be treated as a long-term capital gain. See Chapter **Twenty–Six**.

¶ **4.3400.** **Illustration 1.** *ABC*, Inc. collected $100,000 compensatory damages from *XYZ*, Inc. for federal antitrust violations committed by the latter. The compensatory damages were measured by the amount of profits that *ABC* lost because of the unlawful activity of *XYZ*. It has been determined in many such cases that the lost profits are used only to measure the extent of the damage done to *ABC*'s goodwill. If *ABC* had a basis of $60,000 in its goodwill, it will realize income of $40,000 ($100,000 damages less $60,000 basis). Note that § 186 may provide some tax relief for *ABC* if the injury suffered by *ABC* as a consequence of the antitrust violation resulted in *ABC*'s having a net operating loss during the period in which such injuries were sustained (i.e., *ABC* may be permitted to reduce the amount of income it recognized from the receipt of the award for damages by the amount of such net operating losses that were not previously deducted).

¶ **4.3500.** **Illustration 2.** *X* breached a contract with *Y*. *Y* recovered $5,000 damages for profits lost because of *X*'s breach. The $5,000 damage payment will be included in *Y*'s gross income and will be fully taxable.

¶ **4.3600.** **Illustration 3.** *Z* filed a complaint with the National Labor Relations Board against a union for causing *Z*'s employer to fire him. *Z* recovered damages for lost wages. While such damages typically will not constitute wages for social security tax or unemployment tax purposes since they were not paid by or on behalf of *Z*'s employer, they do constitute gross income to *Z* for income tax purposes. Rev. Rul. 75–64. The damage payment relates entirely to lost earnings (equivalent to lost business profits) and thus will be treated as gross income.

¶ 4.4000. CHARACTERIZATION OF INSURANCE PROCEEDS.

The tax treatment of insurance proceeds collected upon the suffering of a loss may turn upon the nature of the risk that is insured. If the insurance proceeds are paid to compensate a TP for property loss or damage, the proceeds will not be taxable to the extent of the TP's basis in that property, and the TP's basis will be reduced accordingly. Any excess insurance proceeds will be treated as income to the TP, although the TP may be permitted to elect nonrecognition under § 1033 for part or all of his gain if he purchases qualified property within the statutory period.[17]

However, in *Marshall Foods, Inc. v. United States*,[18] the courts held that insurance proceeds received by a TP after a fire had damaged his business were paid to compensate the TP for a loss of income due to an interruption of his business, and therefore all the proceeds were deemed to be ordinary income to the TP. In other words, the court held that the proceeds were payable to compensate the TP for lost profits rather than as compensation for property damage. See also, Treas. Reg. § 1.1033(a)–2(c)(8).

In *Johnson v. Commissioner*,[19] the courts denied a loss deduction to a TP who had liquidated his partnership business for less than his basis because the TP had received life insurance proceeds from a policy insuring his partner's life and the court deemed the insurance to be compensation for the loss of value of the business due to the partner's death. The courts held that, while the TP realized a loss on the liquidation of the partnership, he was reimbursed for that loss by his receipt of the insurance proceeds, and so no deduction is allowable under § 165(a).

While the result reached in *Johnson* has pragmatic appeal, the decision is questionable. The authors doubt the wisdom of adopting a policy that requires an examination of the motive for acquiring insurance on the life of an employee or owner of a business as a condition to allowing a deduction for a business loss that is sustained after the insured's death.

17. See ¶ **24.8000** and following.

18. 393 F.Supp. 1097 (D.Minn. 1974), aff'd per curiam, 36 AFTR 2d 75–5095 (8th Cir. 1975).

19. 66 T.C. 897 (1976), aff'd per curiam by a divided court, 574 F.2d 189 (4th Cir. 1978).

Since *Johnson*, there has been no subsequent movement by the courts or the Service in that direction. For example, if a corporation purchases insurance on the life of a key employee,[20] it is unlikely that the corporation will be denied a deduction for operating losses incurred after the employee's death on the ground that it was compensated for those losses through its receipt of the insurance proceeds. The typical reason for purchasing such insurance is to protect the employer from the decline in revenue or rise in costs that will occur when the key employee dies, and the *Johnson* rationale would deny a deduction for losses incurred in those circumstances. If the corporation did not incur losses after the employee's death but merely incurred a reduction in its revenue, the *Johnson* doctrine would not apply; and so, even if the *Johnson* approach were adopted, the receipt of the insurance proceeds would have no tax consequence. It is questionable whether the result should be different when losses are incurred.

If a corporation did not incur losses after the insured employee's death but did incur increased expenses because of the loss of the employee's expertise, it is unlikely that a deduction will be denied for those additional business expenses. While the statutory provision for deducting a loss expressly provides in § 165(a) that no deduction will be allowed for a loss that is compensated by insurance, no similar provision is included in § 162 (the business expense deduction provision). However, if a business expense were reimbursed, either the expense would not be deductible or the reimbursement would be included in income. So, the tax status of such additional business costs is not much different from the status of business losses. The same question will control the tax issue—namely, whether the receipt of the life insurance proceeds constitutes a reimbursement of the additional expenses or losses that were incurred after the insured's death.

As yet, the *Johnson* approach has not been adopted by another court, and there is no sign of a trend in that direction. Perhaps, *Johnson* will remain an isolated and eccentric case.

¶ **4.4100. Illustration.** *B* owned a boat in which he had a basis of $10,000, and which had a value of $11,000. *B* had a casualty insurance policy on the boat. The boat was damaged by a fire, and *B* collected $2,000 from his insurer to compensate for the damage to his boat. No deduction was allowable for *B*'s loss since *B* was compensated. *B* did not recognize gross income on collecting the $2,000 insurance payment, but his basis in the boat was reduced to $8,000. If the

---

20. See § 101(j).

boat had been completely destroyed by the fire and *B* had collected $11,000 from his insurer, *B* would have realized a gain of $1,000; but if within a specified period of time he replaced the boat at a cost of more than $10,000, *B* could elect not to recognize all or part of the $1,000 gain under § 1033.[21]

¶ **4.4200.   Tax Insurance.** Uncertainty as to tax results is an ever present obstacle to business transaction. Private insurance companies have seen an opportunity to enter the market and provide a useful service which can reduce tax uncertainty obstruction to engage in promising endeavors. Some insurance companies now provide an insurance product to protect the insured against adverse tax consequences from proposed transactions.

However, if the adverse tax consequences arise (that is, the TP has additional tax liability) and the insurance company is contractually required to cover that liability, are the insurance proceeds that reimburse the insured for the additional tax liability included in the insured's gross income? If so, the insured might need to purchase additional coverage to pay for the tax incurred on receiving the proceeds.

Commentators have concluded that the proceeds are taxable, and insurance companies also appear to adopt that view since tax insurance generally includes gross-up provisions to cover the tax that might be imposed on the disbursement of the proceeds. Contrary to that general opinion, one of the authors argued that the tax insurance proceeds are not includable in the insured's gross income.[22]

¶ **4.5000.   DAMAGES RECEIVED ON ACCOUNT OF PERSONAL INJURIES.** Damages received as compensation for a personal *physical* injury or physical sickness is exempt from taxation, except for the recovery of previously deducted items. "The amount of any damages (other than punitive damages) received (whether by suit or agreement and whether as lump sums or periodic payments) on account of personal physical injuries or physical sickness ..." are excluded from gross income. § 104(a)(2). The personal injuries to which the statute refers are expressly limited to physical injuries. For example, while emotional harm and loss of reputation are personal injuries, they do not qualify as physical injuries. However, damages received for emotional distress are

---

21.   See § **24.8000** *et seq.*

22.   See Jeffrey H. Kahn, *Hedging the IRS—A Policy Justification for Excluding Liability and Tax Insurance Proceeds*, 26 Yale J. on Reg. 1 (2009).

excluded from income to the extent that either (1) the emotional distress is derived from a physical injury or physical sickness, (2) to the extent that the amount of such damages does not exceed the nondeducted medical expenses attributable to the emotional distress. § 104(a).

The scope of the § 104(a)(2) exclusion from income is very broad. Once that provision applies, even amounts compensating for lost wages are excludable from gross income.[23]

¶ 4.5100. Workers' Compensation Awards. Amounts received under a workers' compensation act as compensation for personal injuries or sickness are excluded from gross income. § 104(a)(1). The exclusion also applies to payments that are deemed similar in nature to workers' compensation. See PLR 200016012 where the Service excluded disability payments made to an injured police officer.[24] Note that amounts received under a workers' compensation act or similar provision are not required to be for a physical injury or sickness to be excluded from income. It is sufficient for the amount to be received for a personal injury or sickness, which may include emotional harm.

¶ 4.5200. Interest Received on an Award. When interest is paid to a TP on an award for compensatory damages, the interest represents compensation for the use of the TP's money; it is not compensation for the injury that the TP suffered. The TP must include the interest payment in gross income.[25] One might question whether prejudgment interest (i.e., interest for a period prior to the entry of a judgment) on an award for a physical injury should be excluded by § 104(a)(2) as being part of the plaintiff's loss from the physical injury. The courts have held that prejudgment interest is taxable and is not excluded from gross income by § 104.[26] Taxation is also imposed on payments similar to interest. For example, in *Francisco v. United States*,[27] the court held that a portion of a settlement was for "delay damages" which were similar to prejudgment interest and therefore taxable to the TP.

In *Rozpad*, the plaintiffs had obtained a judgment for a personal injury which included an award for prejudgment interest. During the

23. Rev. Rul. 85–97.

24. See also, Rev. Rul. 80–44, Rev. Rul. 85–105.

25. *Aames v. Commissioner*, 94 T.C. 189 (1990).

26. *Rozpad v. Commissioner*, 154 F.3d 1 (1st Cir. 1998); *Brabson v. United States*, 73 F.3d 1040 (10th Cir. 1996).

27. 267 F.3d 303 (3rd Cir. 2001).

appeal period, plaintiffs settled with defendants for a smaller amount than the judgment. The settlement was for a specified amount, which was stipulated to be without interest or costs. The First Circuit noted that when there is no indication of the amount of interest reflected in a judgment for or settlement of a physical injury claim, the courts will exclude the entire amount rather than speculate on the portion of the award or settlement that represents interest. But, when the amount of interest can be determined on a reasonable basis, it will be taxed. The court deemed the percentage of the trial judgment that constituted interest to be a reasonable allocation, and so the court applied the same percentage to plaintiffs' settlement. See ¶ **4.5800.** The portion of the settlement that the court found to be interest was held to be taxable.

¶ **4.5300.   Tort–Type Claims.** Treas. Reg. § 1.104–1(c) states that § 104(a)(2) excludes from gross income certain damages obtained pursuant to "tort or tort type rights." That requirement was endorsed by the Supreme Court. As a consequence of the 1996 amendment that limits the § 104(a)(2) exclusion to *physical* injuries, there is no longer a need to distinguish between tort and other (such as contract) claims since physical injuries will raise tort issues. Treasury has responded by issuing a proposed regulation in 2009 that eliminates the requirement that the damages be obtained under tort or tort type rights. Prop. Reg. § 1.104–1(c)(2). Although only proposed, a TP may apply this provision to damages awarded or agreed upon after September 13, 1995, and received after August 20, 1996. Prop. Reg. § 1.104–1(c)(3).

¶ **4.5400.   Physical and Nonphysical Personal Injuries.** An amendment to § 104, which was adopted as part of the Small Business Job Protection Act of 1996, limited the § 104(a)(2) exclusion from income to damages that are based on a claim that is attributable to a physical injury or physical sickness. See the penultimate sentence of § 104(a). The statute explicitly states that "emotional distress" does not constitute a physical injury or physical sickness, and the Conference Report to the 1996 Act states that "the term emotional distress includes physical symptoms (e.g.[,] insomnia, headaches, [and] stomach disorders) which may result from such emotional distress."[28] The statute does permit the exclusion of damages received on a claim for emotional distress to the extent that the amount of the damages do not exceed the amount of medical ex-

---

28. H. Rept. 104–586, p. 144, fn24 (104th Cong. 2d Sess. 1996).

penses attributable to that emotional distress that were not previously deducted.

The requirement that the medical expenses not have been previously deducted is stated in the first sentence of § 104(a). Note that if the reimbursed medical expenses had been deducted, the statute does not expressly require that the deduction have produced a tax benefit for the TP. The authors do not believe that a tax benefit requirement will be read into the statute.

Thus, if a TP has no physical injury within the meaning of the statute, damages received for a personal injury will be taxable except for the medical expense provision described above. Even if there are physical manifestations attributable to a nonphysical personal injury, damages will be taxable. The tax treatment of a TP who suffers a physical illness as a consequence of a nonphysical personal injury is discussed at ¶ **4.5500**. However, if the TP did suffer a physical injury, *any damages* that are based on a claim attributable to that physical injury are excluded from gross income. As previously noted, damages provided to compensate for lost wages or other income are excluded from gross income if the source of the claim is a physical injury. Moreover, damages for emotional distress and for consequences of that distress are excluded from income if the distress itself is the product of a physical injury.[29]

The key to the exclusion is that there has been a physical injury and that the damages received are attributable to that injury. The physical injury need not have occurred to the recipient of the damages. For example, the Conference Report states that damages received for the loss of consortium due to a physical injury to the TP's spouse are excluded from gross income by § 104(a)(2).[30] The IRS followed the Conference Report in an asbestos case in PLR 200121031. The treatment of damages received for a physical sickness is discussed at ¶ **4.5500**.

When a TP incurs only a very minor physical injury, but suffers substantial emotional distress, questions are likely to arise as to whether damages for that injury are excluded by the statute.

If the TP suffered a physical injury, will all damages arising out of the events in which the physical injury occurred be excluded? In the authors' view, for damages to be excluded, the injury being compensated must be a consequence of the physical injury. In *Commissioner*

---

29. H. Rept. 104–586, p. 144 (104th Cong. 2d Sess. 1996).

30. H. Rept. 104–586, p. 144 (104th Cong. 2d Sess. 1996).

v. Schleier,[31] the Supreme Court held that damages for violation of the Age Discrimination in Employment Act of 1967 were not excluded by the pre–1996 version of § 104(a)(2). While damages for all claims based on discrimination were made taxable by the 1996 amendment to § 104(a)(2), and that amendment resolves the issue decided in *Schleier*, the Supreme Court's analysis is likely to influence the construction of the post–1996 version of the statute. In *Schleier*, the Court held that damages must be attributable to a personal injury to be excluded from income—that is, the personal injury itself must be a source of the injury; it is not sufficient that the same acts that caused the personal injury also caused other injuries. It seems likely that the same approach will be applied to the requirement that the damages be attributable to a physical injury.

In PLR 200041022, the IRS provided some guidance to this issue. The facts of the ruling are that A was employed by C. C began sexually harassing A. Two dates are particularly important for purposes of the ruling. During the initial period, C physically touched A but did not cause any visible signs of bodily harm (e.g., cuts, bruises, etc.). Next, C assaulted A causing A to experience extreme pain (described by the ruling as the "First Pain Incident"). After that incident, A began to experience physical ailments, but doctors could not find anything wrong with her. At a later date, C again assaulted A, cutting and biting her (described by the ruling as the "First Physical Injury"). After A filed suit against C, A and C agreed to a settlement. The determination requested by the TP involved the question of whether the settlement proceeds were excluded under § 104(a)(2).

The IRS ruled that any damages allocable to events prior to the First Pain Incident were not received on account of a physical injury and therefore should be included in the TP's income. Any damages allocable to events beginning with the First Physical Injury were excluded from the TP's gross income under § 104(a)(2). However, the IRS refused to rule on damages allocable to events between the First Pain Incident and the First Physical Injury. The IRS stated that since the perception of pain is a factual matter, it could not rule whether the damages were excluded. This suggests that if the pain is of sufficient magnitude, a physical mark is not required in order to qualify for the exclusion under § 104(a)(2). The Service also refused to rule on the proper allocation of damages among the several periods and between compensatory and punitive damages.

---

31.   515 U.S. 323 (1995).

¶ **4.5410. Illustration 1.** *R* was an employee of *X* Corporation. *T* was *R*'s supervisor. Over the course of several years, *T* made lewd and improper statements to *R* and suggested that she would advance more rapidly in the company if she were to agree to a sexual relationship with him. *R* rejected these proposals. On one occasion, after *R* had again said "no" and turned to leave the room, *T* pinched her derriere. The pinch was hard enough to leave a bruise, but the bruise was minor and disappeared within a few days. Having had more than she could stand, *R* then sued *X* for allowing sexual harassment to take place. The suit was settled by *X*'s paying *R* $1,000,000 in damages. Will all or any part of those damages be excluded from *R*'s gross income by § 104(a)(2)? The answer to this is not yet settled. In the authors' view, the damages should be apportioned, and only damages directly attributable to the pinch should be excluded. While the pinch was one item in a pattern of harassment conduct, it was the only act that caused a physical injury. Most of *R*'s recovery is attributable to the emotional distress and humiliation that she suffered independently of the physical intrusion.[32] To the extent that *R* recovered damages for emotional distress arising from the pinch itself, those damages would be excluded.

The division of damages in such cases will be difficult to make, but not impossible; and equally difficult divisions have been required to be made in other areas of this same tax law.[33] If such an allocation is not required, then there are likely to be claims of some physical harm in many cases otherwise resting on emotional harm. An alternative or supplementary approach is to disregard minor physical injuries as de minimis.

¶ **4.5420. Illustration 2.** *G* is employed by *Z*. *Z* touches *G*'s breast, but does not bruise or otherwise injure *G*. Does that touching constitute a physical injury within the meaning of the statute? It would seem that the real harm suffered by *G* is essentially the same as that suffered by victims of discrimination or defamation, the damages from which are clearly taxable under the current version of § 104(a)(2). The source of *G*'s injury is a physical act, but her injury is the distress and humiliation of being treated in such a demeaning fashion. It does not appear to be a *physical injury*. It remains to be seen how the IRS and the

32. See, e.g., *Hansen v. Comm'r*, T.C. Memo. 2009–87.

33. See ¶ **4.5800.**

courts will deal with this issue. Even after PLR 200041022, it is by no means clear how it will be resolved.

¶ **4.5430. Illustration 3.** While attempting to cross a street, *N* is struck by an automobile and seriously injured. One of *N*'s legs had to be amputated, and *N* had permanent brain damage because of the injuries he suffered. *N* was unable to work for some months after his accident, and the work that he could do paid much less than he was earning before the accident. As a consequence of the accident, *N* became fearful of automobiles and had nightmares about his accident. His emotional distress caused him to have headaches. The insurance company for the driver of the car settled *N*'s claim for damages by paying *N* $5,000,000 as compensation for his injuries. The settlement allocated the damage payment among the following injuries: (1) Wages lost while *N* was unable to work, (2) Reduction of future income that *N* will suffer because of his injuries, (3) Reimbursement of *N*'s medical expenses, (4) Estimated future medical expenses that *N* will incur as a consequence of his injuries, (5) Emotional distress that *N* suffered, (6) Pain and suffering that *N* has had, and (7) Pain and suffering that *N* will likely have in the future because of the injuries. All of the $5,000,000 damages that *N* received is excluded from his gross income by § 104(a)(2). The only exception is that the damages allocated to medical expenses will be taxable to the extent that *N* previously took a tax deduction for those expenses.

¶ **4.5500. Damages for Physical Sickness.** In addition to excluding damages for personal physical injuries, § 104(a)(2) also excludes damages for a physical sickness. The scope of that provision is far from clear. It likely applies when an improper act or omission of another exposes a TP to an unhealthy substance that causes the TP to incur a physical sickness. For example, damages received for exposing an employee to noxious fumes that caused the employee to develop cancer are excluded from income under this provision.

As stated in the Conference Report to the 1996 Act, described in ¶ **4.5400**, the fact that emotional harm to a TP causes negative physical manifestations does not bring the damages for those consequences under the umbrella of the exclusion provided by § 104(a)(2). The Conference Report expressly mentions headaches and stomach disorders as consequences not covered by the statute. Those items might well be regarded as illnesses. The question of what types of physical sickness are covered by the statute and what types are not is unresolved.

In a recent Tax Court case, a TP was allowed to exclude under § 104(a)(2) damages received from her employer who had failed to act on her complaints about her work environment caused by conflicts with her superior over her assignments and her belief that he was embezzling funds that she had solicited for her employer. The stress and irritation caused to the TP by the employer's failure to act on her complaints aggravated her MS condition, and that was the source of the damages she received.[34] Since there was no physical contact with the TP, the court's decision to exclude those damages seems unduly generous, but there are other cases of this nature.[35]

It seems clear from the Conference Report that Congress did not wish to apply the income exclusion to illnesses flowing exclusively from acts that do not involve physical contact with the injured party. One might question whether damages for a physical illness should be excluded only if the illness is the product of a physical contact. The requirement for physical contact should be liberally construed. For example, exposure to noxious fumes should qualify as physical contact. The reader should be alert to the direction that case law takes in this area.

¶ 4.5600. **Damages for Victims of Discrimination or Defamation.** Prior to the 1996 amendment of § 104, damages for personal defamation were excluded from gross income, and damages for defamation of business reputation sometimes was. The treatment of damages for violation of statutes prohibiting employment discrimination was mixed. Damages for some types of discrimination were excluded while others were taxed. The determining factor was the type of remedy that the anti-discrimination provision provided. The 1996 amendment changed all that. Discrimination and defamation do not constitute physical injuries, even though the emotional distress that the victim suffers can lead to physical harm. The Conference Report on the 1996 amendment expressly states that, "the exclusion from gross income does not apply to any damages received ... based on a claim of employment discrimination or injury to reputation accompanied by a claim of emotional distress."[36]

¶ 4.5700. **Punitive Damages.** Prior to the 1996 amendment, there was considerable litigation over the question of whether punitive

---

34. *Domeny v. Commissioner*, 99 TCM 1047 (2010).

35. See Robert W. Wood, *Is Physical Sickness the New Emotional Disease?*, 126 Tax Notes 977 (2010).

36. H. Rept. 104–586, p. 144 (104th Cong. 2d Sess. 1996).

damages received in connection with a claim for compensatory damages for a personal injury were excluded from gross income by § 104(a)(2). Over the years, the Commissioner changed his position several times, and court decisions were mixed. In a 1989 amendment to § 104(a), Congress specified that punitive damages awarded when there was no physical injury was taxable, but Congress did not then address the question of whether punitive damages are excluded when there is a physical injury. The 1996 amendment resolved all doubts by making all punitive damages taxable, with one exception. The single exception applies to wrongful death damages in those states in which only punitive damages are permitted to be awarded for a wrongful death. In such a case, the punitive wrongful death award is excluded from income. The apparent reason for this exception is that the punitive award in such cases is a substitute for compensatory payments. This exception applies only if the state law providing only punitive damages for wrongful death was in effect on September 13, 1995. § 104(c).

The legislative history to the 1996 amendment makes clear that it operates prospectively only and is not intended to effect the construction of § 104 for years prior to the effective date of the amendment. How should punitive damages be treated if received before the amendment was effective? The confusion as to the pre–1996 treatment of punitive damages was resolved by the Supreme Court in *O'Gilvie v. United States*,[37] in which the Court held that punitive damages are included in gross income. Consequently, regardless of when received, except for certain wrongful death damages, punitive damages are included in gross income.

¶ 4.5800.   Allocation of Damages Between Punitive and Compensatory Elements. When a judgment is granted to a plaintiff in a suit in which punitive damages were sought for a physical injury, the court's verdict typically will state what amount of the award is compensatory damages and what amount is punitive; only the latter amount will be included in the plaintiff's gross income. When there has been no allocation by a court, a determination must be made as to the amount (if any) of damages that were received by a TP that constitute punitive damages. The allocation between compensatory and punitive damages is a question of fact on which the TP usually has the burden of proof.[38] Factors to be considered in making that

---

37.   519 U.S. 79 (1996).

38.   *Miller v. Commissioner*, 65 T.C.M. 1884 (1993), on remand from the Fourth Circuit's decision in *Commissioner v. Miller*, 914 F.2d 586 (4th Cir. 1990).

allocation include: the allegations made in the complaint, the defenses asserted, and the background of the litigation. The intent of the payor (if that can be determined) is a critical factor.[39]

If the parties settle their dispute by a payment of damages, the Commissioner may accept as determinative a reasonable allocation made in the settlement agreement of the amount of the damages that is compensatory and the amount that is punitive.[40] If no allocation is made in a settlement agreement, the payment often will be allocated between compensatory and punitive damages in the same ratio as those damages were requested in the plaintiff's complaint.[41]

In *Commissioner v. Miller*,[42] the Fourth Circuit remanded the case to the Tax Court to determine the proper allocation between compensatory and punitive damages of a lump sum settlement of two suits against the same party that was made after a jury verdict was issued in one of the plaintiff's suits. In *Miller*, the Fourth Circuit suggested several alternative methods of allocation which might be adopted, and the court indicated that an allocation agreed to by the parties to the suit might be accepted by the Tax Court. On remand, the Tax Court allocated the settlement between punitive and compensatory damages on the same ratio that the jury applied in the verdict of the first case (which case was included in the lump sum settlement).[43]

A reasonable allocation of damages that is made by a settlement agreement of the parties generally will be adopted by the courts to the extent that the "agreement is entered into by the parties in an adversarial context at arm's length and in good faith"[44] The difficulty with that principle is that a defendant rarely has anything at stake in the manner in which a damage payment is to be allocated among the

---

39. *Miller v. Commissioner*, 65 T.C.M. 1884 (1993), on remand from the Fourth Circuit's decision in *Commissioner v. Miller*, 914 F.2d 586 (4th Cir. 1990) and cases cited therein.

40. See *Matray v. Commissioner*, 56 T.C.M. 1107 (1989).

41. Rev. Rul. 85–98. But see *Bresler v. Commissioner*, [at ¶ **4.3300**] where the Tax Court rejected the contention that the antitrust settlement there involved should be allocated between lost profits and damaged goodwill according to the damages requested in the plaintiff's complaint. Also see *Francisco v. United States*, 267 F.3d 303 (3d Cir. 2001), where the allocation of "delay damages" to a lump sum settlement, which was executed after a jury verdict and while the case was on appeal, was made in the same proportion as was the delay damages in the jury's verdict.

42. 914 F.2d 586 (4th Cir. 1990).

43. *Miller v. Commissioner*, 65 T.C.M. 1884 (1993).

44. *Robinson v. Commissioner*, 102 T.C. 116 (1994); aff'd on that issue and rev'd on an unrelated issue, 70 F.3d 34 (5th Cir. 1995).

various claims that the plaintiff made. The allocation can affect the plaintiff's tax liability, but it often will have little or no effect on the defendant. So, the defendant might use the allocation issue as a bargaining chip to reduce the amount of damages payable, but it is difficult to see how an allocation can be "adversarial and at arm's length" when only one of the parties has anything at stake in the outcome. Nevertheless, courts and the IRS are likely to accept an allocation by the parties provided that the allocation is reasonable. There is considerable subjectivity in determining the proper allocation, and so a reasonable amount will lie within a wide range of permissible allocations. If an allocation made by the parties falls within that reasonable range, it likely will be accepted by the courts and by the Service. But, if the parties overreach and make an allocation that eliminates obviously significant items claimed by the plaintiff, the entire allocation will be ignored by the courts, who will then make their own determination of how the damages are to be allocated.[45]

In the *Robinson* case, cited above, the Tax Court declined to accept an allocation that was made in the judgement of a state court that resolved the issue in dispute. The Tax Court found that the state court judge had merely accepted the allocation given to the judge by the plaintiff (with no objection from the defendant) and had not made an independent determination. Applying the *Bosch* rule (referring to the rule established by the Supreme Court in *Commissioner v. Estate of Bosch*[46]) the Tax Court treated the state court's judgment as merely a datum to be weighed in determining the allocation (as contrasted to treating it as a binding determination). After weighing the state court's allocation, the Tax Court decided to make its own determination. Perhaps it is relevant to the Tax Court's decision in *Robinson* that the state court allocated 95% of the damages to items that were excluded from the plaintiff's income even though the plaintiff had substantial claims for items which would have been taxable to the plaintiff. The Fifth Circuit affirmed this aspect of the Tax Court's decision.[47]

---

45. See e.g., *Robinson v. Commissioner,* 102 T.C. 116 (1994); aff'd on that issue and rev'd on an unrelated issue, 70 F.3d 34 (5th Cir. 1995); *Rozpad v. Commissioner,* discussed at ¶ **4.5200**; *Delaney v. Commissioner,* 99 F.3d 20 (1st Cir. 1996); *Bagley v. Commissioner,* 121 F.3d 393 (8th Cir. 1997).

46. 387 U.S. 456 (1967).

47. 70 F.3d 34. See also, the similar treatment of TPs' efforts to avoid taxation on prejudgment interest that had been awarded in a judgement by subsequently settling the judgement for an undifferentiated lump sum. *Rozpad v. Commissioner,* discussed at ¶ **4.5200**, and *Delaney v. Commissioner,* 99 F.3d 20 (1st Cir. 1996).

¶ 4.5900. **Allocation of Lump Sum Award or Settlement Into Its Likely Component Parts.** In *Niles v. United States*,[48] the TP had received a jury award of $4,025,000 for personal injury. The defendant had appealed on the contention that the award was excessive. In successfully defending the amount of the award on appeal, the TP had presented a detailed hypothetical itemization of the amounts that might have made up the award, and the TP's itemization allocated $1,588,176 to future medical expenses. The Commissioner contended that the TP could not claim a medical expense deduction for medical expenses incurred after the award was made until the aggregate of such expenses exceeded $1,588,176 (the amount of the award that the TP allocated to future medical expenses in defending the size of the award). The Ninth Circuit held that no allocation is to be made where the award is a lump sum, and therefore the TP's subsequent medical expenses are deductible. The court reasoned that the TP's itemization was not evidence of what the jury intended to allocate for the TP's future medical expenses, and thus any allocation would be too speculative. Note that this decision is contrary to the Commissioner's holding in Rev. Rul. 79–427. In that ruling the Commissioner stated that it was proper to allocate some portion of the award to future medical expenses and that medical expenses may be deducted under § 213 only to the extent they exceed the allocated amount. See also Rev. Rul. 75–230, holding that a portion of a lump sum settlement of a negligence suit was attributable to medical expenses that the TP had previously deducted and so was included in TP's income. Also, note Rev. Rul. 75–232, denying a deduction for medical expenses to the extent that a prior settlement of a personal injury suit specifically allocated a portion of the amount paid to future medical expenses.

In cases where a TP has multiple claims, the damages for some of which would be excluded from gross income and for some of which would be included in gross income, a determination must be made as to the source of the damages collected by the TP. If the award of damages was made by a third party (e.g., a judge or a jury in a state court case), the Service is not obliged to accept that allocation but usually will do so unless the TP essentially dictated the allocations with no input from an adverse party.[49] If the allocation was dictated by the TP because the other party had no interest in the manner in which a sum was allocated and the state court simply accepted the

48. 710 F.2d 1391 (9th Cir. 1983).
49. See *Robinson v. Commissioner*, 70 F.3d 34 (5th Cir. 1995).

uncontested allocation, the Service and the courts will make their own determination of the proper allocation.[50]

¶ 4.5900A. Liquidated Damages. Some statutes provide for liquidated damages in cases involving a violation of certain rights or requirements. The legislative purpose for allowing liquidated damages sometimes is to provide compensation for injuries that are difficult to measure or prove and sometimes is to punish the wrongdoer and to deter violations. In some cases, both purposes may exist. If a liquidated damage provision is compensatory for a personal physical injury, then the receipt of such damage should be excluded from income under § 104(a)(2). If, instead, the purpose of a liquidated damage provision is punitive, it will be included in gross income. The determination of whether the function of a liquidated damage provision is compensatory or punitive can be difficult to make. The problem becomes even more difficult when (as is often the case) a liquidated damage provision serves both a compensatory and a punitive function. In that circumstance, should an allocation be made or should the liquidated damage be classified according to the principal purpose that it serves?

In several pre–1996 cases involving nonphysical injuries, the Tax Court held that the liquidated damages provided by the Age Discrimination in Employment Act (ADEA) when the violation of the Act is willful was not punitive.[51] The Supreme Court held in an unrelated case that the liquidated damages in that Act are punitive.[52] Since discrimination damages were made taxable by the 1996 amendment, it no longer matters that ADEA liquidated damages are punitive.

In the authors' view, if a liquidated damage is provided only when the tortfeasor's wrongful action was willful or egregious, it should be characterized as a punitive provision for tax purposes and dealt with accordingly. Unlike the case of the tort of malicious prosecution where malice is an element of *liability*, in the case of liquidated damages, the extent of the tortfeasor's bad behavior serves as the standard for the *amount* of damages to be awarded. In any event, the condition of willfulness or egregious behavior would seem to prevent the damage provision from being received "on account of" a personal physical injury as required by § 104(a)(2). The issue is not likely to

50. Id.

51. *Downey v. Commissioner (Downey I)*, 97 T.C. 150 (1991) (reviewed by the court); and *Downey v. Commissioner (Downey II)*, 100 T.C. 634 (1993) (reviewed by the court).

52. *Commissioner v. Schleier*, 515 U.S. 323 (1995).

arise *in* the post–1996 era since liquidated damages will not often occur when there is a physical injury.

¶ **4.6000. RATIONALE FOR EXCLUSION.** There is no definitive statement as to the reason for excluding physical personal injury damages from income. Before Congress enacted the exclusion, there were administrative and judicial determinations excluding the receipt of certain damages from income, and Congress codified that treatment when it adopted the antecedent to § 104(a)(2) in 1919. Neither Congress nor the courts have provided an explanation of the justification for the exclusion.

There have been suggestions from time to time as to the purpose of the exclusion. One suggestion is that the exclusion was adopted in order to reduce the size of damage awards. If damages were taxed to a plaintiff, a jury might increase the size of the award in order to increase the plaintiff's after-tax receipt to an amount that satisfies the jury's notion of fair compensation. However, it is highly unlikely that that consideration played a significant part in formulating the exclusion. If a damage award is properly classified as income, there is little reason to exclude it from income in order to reduce the burden on a tortfeasor. If the focus of Congress were on the size of damage awards, a more likely concern would be the tax consequence to a victim for recognizing a large amount of income in one taxable year due to the progressive rate structure of the income tax. A bunching of income could occur in such cases if the damages are paid in one lump sum. The proper cure for bunching is to provide income averaging for the receipt of such sums so that the victim can utilize lower tax rates for a larger portion of the damage award. An exemption of the entire amount of the award for such a purpose would be overkill and is not likely to have been the justification for the adoption of the rule. The rationale for the rule is likely to lie elsewhere.

The damages received by a victim because of a personal injury constitute an involuntary conversion of part of the victim's person. For example, if a victim recovers compensatory damages for the loss of an arm in an automobile accident, the measure of the amount of damages is a rough valuation of the personal and financial benefits that the victim could have enjoyed if he had retained the arm. In addition, the damages may compensate for pain and suffering and for out of pocket expenses incurred as a consequence of the injury. While an individual may use his arm to earn income, the arm is part of the individual's person as contrasted to items that the individual owns as property. So, the peculiar aspects of a damage award for a physical personal injury are the involuntariness of the conversion to cash and the personal, noncommercial nature of the item that was damaged. The taxation of an award for such a loss may conform to economic tax theory, but it would be harsh and grossly insensitive to the plight of a victim.

If a person's property is involuntarily converted, the victim usually can prevent the recognition of any gain realized on the conversion by purchasing property that is similar or related in service or use to the converted property. § 1033. There is no truly comparable means of reinvesting the proceeds received because of a physical injury. Since there is no effective device for deferring the income realized upon the receipt of damages for a physical injury, and since there are humanitarian reasons to feel concern for the plight of the victim, some form of tax relief is desirable. There is still a question whether the exclusion from income of the entire amount of such damages is too generous, but, to date, there has been no movement to substitute a different and less magnanimous provision.[53]

¶ **4.6100. Rationale for the Exclusion of Back Pay.** As previously noted, the amount of damages for a physical injury that represent compensation for back pay is excluded from the recipient's gross income. Since that amount represents an income item that would have been taxed to the recipient when received, why should the damage payment received in lieu thereof escape taxation? The same question might be asked as to why there is an exclusion for an award to compensate the TP for the loss of income that he might have earned in the future.

Frequently, the damages received for a personal injury, whether received pursuant to a settlement or to a jury's award, are obtained as an undifferentiated lump sum. The portion that represents back pay and the portion that represents the estimated loss of future income are not separately identified. If those amounts were to be treated differently for tax purposes than are damages for nonpecuniary losses, it would be necessary to determine how much of the award was attributable to lost income. Such treatment would impose a significant administrative burden on the TP and on the Service. While it would not be an insurmountable burden, it would be substantial. Perhaps, the wish to avoid having to make that determination is a factor in the decision to exclude such items from income.

---

53. For a more extensive discussion of a rationale for the exclusion of certain compensatory damages, see Douglas A. Kahn, *Compensatory and Punitive Damages for a Personal Injury: To Tax or Not to Tax?*, 2 Fla. Tax Rev. 327, 340–352 (1995).

In some cases, however, the amount of damages received for lost income (past and future) is separately identified. Why should those amounts not be taxed? If those amounts were taxed when separately identified but not when the damage is paid as an undifferentiated lump sum, the recipients of personal injury damages would be taxed differently depending upon the happenstance of whether the lost income item is separately identified. The extension of the exclusion to such cases may stem from an unwillingness to tax differently two sets of victims who received the same amount of damages but with different labels.

It is noteworthy that when Congress amended § 104(a) in 1996 to restrict the exclusion to damages for physical injuries, the Conference Report stated as one of its reasons for the amendment that the damages in nonphysical cases are generally for lost profits or wages that would have been taxed.[54] Why is it different when there is a physical injury? One difference is that the loss of wages or profits can be seen as merely a convenient indicator of the personal loss that the victim suffered. In other words, the victim receives compensation for the physical personal loss, and the resort to income reduction is just one means of attaching a monetary figure to a loss that cannot be valued as a commodity can.

¶ **4.7000. SALE OF PARTS OF TP'S BODY.** The exclusion from income provided by § 104(a)(2) applies only to *damages* received on account of a personal physical injury or illness. It has no application to payments received by a TP for the voluntary sale of a part of the TP's body, and such payments will be included in the gross income of the TP.[55]

When a TP voluntarily sells a body part, he has chosen to dispose of that part in a commercial transaction. One difference between a sale and a receipt of damages is that in the latter case the TP never had an opportunity to decide whether to commercialize the body part.

In *United States v. Garber*,[56] the TP had a rare type of blood that she was able to sell on a regular basis for a substantial profit of thousands of dollars per year. The TP failed to report to the Service her profit from

---

54. H. Rept. 104–586, p. 143 (104th Cong. 2d Sess. 1996).

55. Note that a provision of the National Organ Transplant Act [42 U.S.C. § 274e] prohibits the sale of human organs for use in human transplantation, but the statute does not prohibit the sale of a person's blood.

56. 607 F.2d 92 (5th Cir. 1979).

the sale of her blood, and she was convicted by a jury verdict of the crime of having willfully attempted to evade and defeat the income tax. Holding that § 104(a)(2) does not apply to the payment that the TP received for her blood, a divided panel of the Fifth Circuit affirmed her conviction;[57]but on a rehearing en banc, the Fifth Circuit reversed the conviction and remanded the case to the district court for further proceedings to determine whether the TP acted willfully.[58] The majority of the Fifth Circuit determined that since the question of the taxability of the sale of blood was a novel issue and since a defendant in a criminal case should be given great latitude in presenting her case, the district court erred in rejecting the TP's attempt to have a "tax expert" testify that the payments to the TP for her blood are excluded from gross income (the "expert" did not rely on § 104 for his conclusion). The majority also held that the district court erred in its instructions to the jury by indicating that the payments clearly were income to the TP who simply refused to pay the tax thereon. The majority did not resolve the question of whether the payments to the TP were gross income to her; they dealt instead with the question of whether there was sufficient doubt about the taxability to preclude a criminal prosecution for a willful act.

The majority did suggest as a possible ground for excluding such payments that since the TP could not prove that she had any basis in her blood, perhaps it should be assumed that her basis equaled the amount paid to her; but, the majority expressly refrained from resolving that question. The suggestion appears frivolous; there is authority for assuming that the properties exchanged in an arm's length exchange are of equal *value*, but there is no justification in reason or in precedent for assuming that the *basis* of property transferred is equal to the value of property received in exchange. In his concurring opinion in *Garber*, Judge Hill stated that the payments received by the TP were gross income to her; and the four dissenting judges in *Garber* reached the same conclusion.

In *Green v. Commissioner*,[59] the Tax Court held that payment received from the sale of blood is included in gross income. The TP in *Green* did not dispute the taxability of such payments; the issue she raised concerned the deductibility of certain expenses related to the sale of her blood. Nevertheless, the Tax Court passed on the issue of taxability.[60] In

57. *United States v. Garber*, 589 F.2d 843 (5th Cir. 1979).

58. *United States v. Garber*, 607 F.2d 92 (5th Cir. 1979).

59. 74 T.C. 1229 (1980).

60. 74 T.C. at p. 1233.

Lary v. United States,[61] the court denied a charitable deduction for a contribution of blood on the ground that the TP's sale of his blood at fair market value would have caused the TP to recognize ordinary income equal to the amount he would receive from such a sale. See ¶ **20.2300.**

¶ **4.8000. INSTALLMENT PAYMENTS OF DAMAGES.** When § 104(a)(2) applies to damages, it applies to periodic payments as well as to a lump sum payment. If a damage award is payable over a period of years, a portion of each installment payment represents interest to the recipient for the delay in receiving the money. In most installment sales, for example, when the installment payments do not provide for an adequate rate of interest, a portion of the installment payments is recharacterized as interest to reflect the unstated interest on the deferred payments. § 483. The installment payments of damages are exempted from any recharacterization, and the entire amount of the installment payments is excluded from gross income.

It is difficult to discern a reasonable policy justification for the exclusion of the interest element in periodic payments of damages. The administrative difficulty of setting an interest rate has not proved to be much of an obstacle in the other areas in which interest is imputed when the stated interest on deferred payments is inadequate. See, e.g., §§ 483, 1274. Perhaps, this is an excessive response to the concern for the plight of a victim of physical injury.

61. 787 F.2d 1538 (11th Cir. 1986).

CHAPTER FIVE

TAX BENEFIT RULE

¶ 5.0000. TAX BENEFIT RULE.

¶ 5.1000. GENERAL RULE OF INCLUSION.

If a TP deducted an item on his federal tax return and enjoyed a tax benefit thereby and in a subsequent year recovers all or part of that item, he will recognize gross income in the year the deducted item is recovered.[1] The rule has both an inclusionary and an exclusionary component; i.e., the recovery is included in the TP's gross income to the extent that the TP obtained a tax benefit from the prior year's deduction, and the recovery is excluded to the extent that the prior year's deduction did not provide a tax benefit.[2]

Hillsboro National Bank v. Commissioner[3] is a landmark decision for the tax benefit rule. The Supreme Court's decision in *Hillsboro* involved two consolidated cases, one of which was the *Bliss Dairy* case.[4] Since the principal holding in the Supreme Court's decision in *Hillsboro* dealt with the *Bliss Dairy* case, the Supreme Court's decision often is referred to by courts and commentators as the *"Bliss"* or *"Bliss Dairy"* case. In this text, the Supreme Court's decision is referred to as *"Hillsboro."*

For an item received in one year to be excluded from income under the tax benefit rule because it constitutes a recovery of an item that had been deducted in a prior year without obtaining a tax benefit, there must be a nexus between the prior year's deduction without tax benefit and the item that was received in the subsequent year.[5] The exclusion from income is allowed to the extent that the deductions that the company took in the prior year did not produce a tax benefit for the company.

---

1. *Dobson v. Commissioner*, 320 U.S. 489 (1943).

2. See *Hillsboro National Bank v. Commissioner*, 460 U.S. 370 (1983), pp. 380–381, fn. 12.

3. 460 U.S. 370 (1983).

4. See ¶¶ **5.2000** and **5.2100**.

5. See *Allstate Ins. Co. v. United States*, 936 F.2d 1271 (CAFC 1991) (excluding from gross income amounts obtained by an insurance company from the enforcement of subrogation rights the company acquired when it satisfied claims (and took deductions for those payments) in a prior year).

¶ **5.1100. Illustration 1.** In 2002, *X* loaned *Y* $10,000 in a business transaction. In 2005, *Y*'s $10,000 debt to *X* became worthless, and *X* deducted $10,000 from her 2005 tax return as a bad debt deduction under § 166. *X* enjoyed a tax benefit from the deduction. In 2009, *Y* paid *X* $3,000 as a partial payment on his $10,000 debt. Even though the $3,000 paid to *X* in 2009 was a partial return of a loan *X* had previously made and, therefore, was a return of *X*'s capital, the $3,000 is, nevertheless, included in *X*'s gross income since *X* had enjoyed a tax benefit by taking a deduction for the debt in 2005. Moreover, the $3,000 will be included in *X*'s gross income for 2009 even if *X* is in a higher (or a lower) marginal tax bracket in 2009 than she was in 2005 when she took the deduction.

¶ **5.1200. Illustration 2.** In Year One, *X* donated Blackacre (unimproved land) to the city of Flint, Michigan on condition that a library building be constructed on the land within ten years. *X*'s basis in Blackacre was $16,000. *X* deducted the value of Blackacre ($18,000) from his Year One tax return, and let us assume that deduction was properly allowed.[6] *X* obtained a tax benefit from the entire $18,000 deduction. In Year Seven, Blackacre is returned to *X* because the city decided not to build a library. The value of Blackacre in Year Seven was $22,000. *X* must include $18,000 of Blackacre's value in his gross income (it appears that the additional $4,000 in value of Blackacre is not included in *X*'s gross income since he never had a tax benefit for that portion of Blackacre). While there is no explicit authority as to the manner in which *X*'s basis in the recovered Blackacre is to be determined, it would seem that *X*'s basis in the recovered Blackacre would be $16,000—that is, *X*'s basis at the time of transfer will be reinstated.

If the value of Blackacre in Year Seven (when it was returned to *X*) had fallen to $14,000, it is unsettled whether *X* would be required to include only $14,000, or the full $18,000 deducted in Year One, in his gross income. It may be that *Hillsboro*[7] requires recognition of income in the amount for which a prior tax benefit was received regardless of the fair market value of the property at the time it was returned, but the authors doubt that *Hillsboro* will be applied in that manner. *Hillsboro* held that a subsequent event which is fundamentally inconsistent with a prior deduction requires recognition of income. The question here involves the extent of the inconsistency.

---

6. The question of deductibility turns on whether the possibility that the building would not be constructed is so remote as to be negligible. Treas. Reg. § 1.170A–1(e).

7. See ¶¶ **5.2000–5.2100.**

In footnote 37 of the *Hillsboro* decision, the Supreme Court noted that the TP in that case did not raise the question of whether the amount of income to be recognized by the TP because of the tax benefit rule should be less than the amount of deduction taken by the TP in a prior year; and so, the Court expressly refrained from addressing that issue. For a pre-*Hillsboro* decision that limits *X*'s income to the $14,000 value that Blackacre had when the city returned it to *X*, see *Rosen v. Commissioner*.[8] In a post-*Hillsboro* decision, the Tax Court followed *Rosen* and limited the TP's income on the return of property previously donated to a charity to the fair market value of the property when returned, but only *up to* the amount of charitable deduction previously taken.[9] Under the Tax Court's decision, only $14,000 is included in *X*'s income. Regardless of whether *X* is required to include $14,000 or $18,000 in his gross income, it is unclear what basis *X* will have in Blackacre—is *X*'s original $16,000 basis reinstated or is *X*'s basis equal to the amount included in his gross income?[10]

If only $14,000 is included in *X*'s gross income (in accordance with the decisions of the Tax Court and of the First Circuit), it might seem appropriate to reinstate *X*'s original basis of $16,000 reduced by the $4,000 of deduction that *X* obtained that was not recaptured when the property was returned. So, in that case, *X* would have a basis of $12,000 in Blackacre. On the other hand, the amount of deduction allowable for many charitable gifts does not depend upon the basis of the donated property; rather, the measure of the deduction is the fair market value of the donated property. The $4,000 of unrecovered deduction relates to a decline in value while the property was in the hands of the charity. That amount can be viewed as a kind of charitable contribution itself. In certain circumstances described in § 170(e), the amount of charitable deduction is limited to the TP's basis in the donated property; and if such property is recovered, perhaps the TP's basis in the recovered property should be reduced by any unrecaptured deduction. But, when the charitable deduction was not a type that is limited by the TP's basis, it seems to the authors that the TP should reinstate his original basis for the recovered property; in that case, there should be no reduction of basis because of an unrecaptured deduction.

¶ 5.2000.   ACTUAL RECOVERY vs. FUNDAMENTAL INCONSIS-

8.   611 F.2d 942 (1st Cir. 1980).

9.   *885 Investment Co. v. Commissioner*, 95 T.C. 156, 166 (1990).

10.   Cf. Treas. Reg. § 1.83–6(c).

TENCY. The question arose as to whether there has to be an actual physical recovery of a deducted item before the tax benefit rule can be applied. In *Tennessee–Carolina Transportation, Inc. v. Commissioner*,[11] the majority stated that "there need not be an actual physical 'recovery' of some tangible asset or sum in order to apply the tax benefit rule. The tax benefit rule should be applied flexibly in order to counteract the inflexibility of the annual accounting concept which is necessary for administration of the tax laws. The rule should apply whenever there is an actual recovery of a previously deducted amount or when there is some other event inconsistent with that prior deduction. . . . [An] inconsistency is enough to invoke the tax benefit rule." The Supreme Court subsequently adopted (in the *Hillsboro* case) a modified version of the view taken by the Sixth Circuit in the *Tennessee–Carolina* case.

In *Hillsboro National Bank v. Commissioner*,[12] the Supreme Court held that the tax benefit rule does not depend upon there being an actual recovery of the deducted item. While the Supreme Court held that an inconsistent subsequent event could trigger a tax benefit rule application, the Court held that only a certain type of inconsistent event did so. The test (under *Hillsboro*) is whether the subsequent event is *"fundamentally inconsistent* with the premise on which the deduction was initially based." (Emphasis added.) A subsequent event is fundamentally inconsistent with a deduction if it would have prevented the deduction from being allowable if it had occurred in the same year that the deductible event took place.

In *Hillsboro*, the Supreme Court said, "the tax benefit rule must be applied on a case-by-case basis. A Court must consider the facts and circumstances of each case in light of the purpose and function of the provision granting the deductions."[13]

One difficulty in applying the *Hillsboro* standard is that it requires an examination of the congressional purpose for granting the deduction to determine whether the subsequent event is "fundamentally inconsistent" with that purpose or with the factual assumptions on which the allowance of that deduction was based.[14]

11.   582 F.2d 378 (6th Cir. 1978), a 2–1 decision affirming a divided Tax Court decision.

12.   460 U.S. 370 (1983), reversing a Ninth Circuit decision in *Bliss Dairy v. United States*, 645 F.2d 19 (9th Cir. 1981).

13.   *Hillsboro, supra*, at 385–386.

14.   For examples of that difficulty, see *Byrd, Transferee v. Commissioner*, 87 T.C. 830 (1986), aff'd without opinion, 829 F.2d 1119 (4th Cir. 1987); *Rojas v. Commissioner*, 90 T.C. 1090 (1988) (reviewed by the court), aff'd 901 F.2d 810 (9th Cir. 1990). See also ¶¶ **5.2200–5.2400.**

The Court's approach in *Hillsboro* is that if a later event would have prevented the taking of a tax deduction if it had occurred in the same year as did the deductible item, then the tax benefit rule will apply to the later event. However, if the later event occurs in a context in which a nonrecognition provision prevents the recognition of income, a determination must be made as to which has priority—the nonrecognition provision or the tax benefit rule.[15]

The decision in *Hillsboro* gave the tax benefit rule priority over a nonrecognition provision that then applied to a corporation's liquidating distributions. But the court's opinion states that some nonrecognition provisions will prevail over the tax benefit rule, and a determination must be made in each such case as to which is to prevail. Id. The Court gave no guidance as to the standards to be employed in making that determination.

¶ 5.2100. Inconsistent Use of Expensed Goods. In some circumstances, the amount paid for the purchase of goods to be used in a business can be deducted in the year in which the purchase price is paid or accrued rather than capitalized. In such cases, the item is sometimes referred to as an "expensed" item, and the deduction is sometimes referred to as an "expense." The assumption underlying the expensing of an item is that the item will be utilized in the TP's business in a certain way. If subsequent events make clear that an expensed item will not be used in the assumed manner that underlay the granting of an expense deduction, will the tax benefit rule operate to require the TP to include in income that amount of deduction previously allowed as an expense? In other words, does the change in use of an expensed asset constitute an event that is fundamentally inconsistent with the expense deduction that the TP previously was allowed?

As previously noted, one of the two consolidated cases in the Supreme Court's *Hillsboro* decision was the *Bliss Dairy* case. *Bliss Dairy* involved a corporation that was in the dairy business and owned cattle for that purpose. The corporation purchased cattle feed and expensed the cost of that feed. An underlying assumption of permitting the corporation to expense the cost of the feed was that the feed would be consumed by the corporation's cattle over a period of time. Before all of the feed was eaten by the cattle, the corporation was liquidated and its assets, including the unused cattle feed, were distributed to the corporation's shareholders. Relying on the tax

---

15. *Hillsboro,* 460 U.S. at 386, n. 20.

benefit rule, the Commissioner contended that the previously expensed cost of the unused cattle feed is included in the liquidating
corporation's gross income since the liquidation erased the possibility
that the remaining feed would be used by the corporation. The
Supreme Court sustained the Commissioner's position and held that
the liquidating distribution of the feed was fundamentally inconsistent with the corporation's previous deduction of the cost of that feed
as an expense. As construed by the Supreme Court in *Hillsboro*, the
tax benefit rule can be viewed as a device to recapture a deduction
that was based on an assumption that certain events would occur if it
subsequently becomes clear that neither the assumed events nor any
comparable events will occur.

The *Hillsboro* decision did not include in the corporation's income
the cost of the feed that was eaten by the cattle prior to the
liquidation. If the cattle in *Bliss Dairy* had not been held for dairy
purposes but rather had been held for sale, would the cost of the feed
that was consumed by the unsold cattle also be subject to the tax
benefit rule? Consider the discussion below of two Tax Court cases
(and the Circuit Courts of Appeals decisions affirming those cases)
that dealt with that issue.

¶ 5.2200. **Expensed Cost of Having Purchased Unsold Inventory.** *Byrd, Transferee v. Commissioner*[16] involved a corporation
engaged in the plant nursery business. The corporation grew plants
for sale. The corporation deducted (i.e., expensed) the cost of purchasing young plants which the corporation would grow to maturity
and then sell. In the taxable year in question, the corporation was
liquidated and distributed its unsold plants as liquidating distributions. The Commissioner contended that the expensing of the young
plants was based on the assumption that the plants would be grown
to maturity and then sold. The liquidating distribution of the unsold
plants was fundamentally inconsistent with the allowance of an
expense deduction for the purchase of the plants, and so the liquidating corporation must include in income the amount of its unwarranted deduction for the purchase of those plants. Relying on the *Hillsboro* doctrine, the Tax Court sustained the Commissioner, and the
Fourth Circuit affirmed.

¶ 5.2300. **Expensed Costs of Maintaining and Cultivating Unsold Inventory.** In *Byrd*, the Commissioner did not raise the
question of whether the tax benefit rule should also have caused the

---

16.   See n.14, supra.

recapture of the costs that the corporation incurred and deducted for materials and supplies used to nurture the unsold plants. The Tax Court did not address that issue in *Byrd*. In a subsequent decision in *Rojas*, discussed below, the dissenting eight judges of the Tax Court expressed their view that the tax benefit rule would apply to the expenses for nurturing the unsold plants that the corporation in *Byrd* had deducted prior to its liquidation.[17] However, the majority of the Tax Court and the Ninth Circuit held that the tax benefit rule does not extend to those expenses.[18]

Rojas involved a corporation that was in the business of farming row crops. The corporation was liquidated and made liquidating distributions of harvested and unharvested crops. The Commissioner contended that, pursuant to the tax benefit rule, the previously deducted expenses that the corporation incurred for materials and services to cultivate those unsold crops (and for the seeds that grew into the crops) must be included in the corporation's income in the year of liquidation. The Commissioner relied on the *Hillsboro* doctrine. A majority of the Tax Court repudiated the Commissioner and held that the tax benefit rule did not apply. The court distinguished its earlier decision in *Byrd* on the ground that the expenses involved in *Byrd* were the expenses of purchasing the unsold plants, and so the purchased plants themselves were held by the corporation at the time of its liquidation. In *Rojas*, the materials and services for which the deductions were taken were consumed or used up by the time that the corporation liquidated. *Rojas* did not involve deductions for the cost of purchasing the unsold crops; it involved deductions for the cost of nurturing and growing those crops.[19] Eight Tax Court judges dissented in *Rojas*. The dissenting judges would have applied the tax benefit rule.

In affirming the Tax Court's majority, the Ninth Circuit stressed that the position adopted by the Commissioner would require a recapture of a portion of general and administrative overhead and maintenance costs whenever an uncontemplated event "frustrated the sale of any products which would otherwise have been completed and sold." The Ninth Circuit held that *Hillsboro* adopted a "limited

17. *Rojas v. Commissioner*, 90 T.C. 1090 (1988) (reviewed by the court), aff'd 901 F.2d 810 (9th Cir. 1990).

18. Id.

19. Note, however, that one of the previously deducted items was the cost of purchasing seeds, and the majority's failure to apply the tax benefit rule to that item might be inconsistent with *Byrd*'s application of the rule to the purchase of young plants.

rule," and the court refused to construe it as expansively as the Commissioner sought to do.[20]

¶ 5.2400. **Expensed Research Costs.** TP, who was engaged in the business of manufacture and sale of consumer products, engaged in extensive research and experiments to develop patented and unpatented technology to be used in its business. In a subsequent year, TP discontinued a product line and sold some of the patented and unpatented technology that it had developed from its research and experiments. TP had deducted the costs of the research and experimental work under § 174, which permits such costs to be expensed. In Rev. Rul. 85–186, the Service ruled that the sale of the technology was not fundamentally inconsistent with the purpose for allowing the costs of development to be expensed, and so the tax benefit rule did not apply.

¶ 5.2500. **Expenses Incurred in the Year in Which the Inconsistent Event Occurred.** In *Rojas*, the expenses which the Commissioner sought to recapture through the tax benefit rule were incurred in the same taxable year that the liquidation took place. The TPs contended that the tax benefit rule does not apply unless the inconsistent event occurs in a subsequent taxable year. Of course, an alternative approach would be to deny the deduction to the corporation since inconsistent events occurred in the same year. The Tax Court held that regardless of whether the deduction is denied or is recaptured by the tax benefit rule, the principle to be applied is the tax benefit principle.[21] As already noted, the Tax Court and the Ninth Circuit held in *Rojas* that the tax benefit principle did not apply to the expenses incurred in that case, and so the courts allowed the corporation to deduct those expenses.

¶ 5.2600. **Liquidation of a Corporation.** *Hillsboro, Byrd,* and *Rojas* all involved liquidating distributions of a corporation. At the time that the facts of those cases arose, the general rule, subject to certain exceptions such as the tax benefit rule, was that a liquidating corporation did not recognize income because of distributing appreciated assets to its shareholders. The Tax Reform Act of 1986 changed that general rule and amended § 336 to require a corporation (subject to a few exceptions) to recognize a gain equal to the amount of appreciation of any asset that it distributed in liquidation. As a consequence of that amendment, the application of the tax benefit

20. *Rojas v. Commissioner*, 901 F.2d 810, 813, n. 3 (9th Cir. 1990).
21. *Rojas,* 90 T.C. at 1099.

rule to most liquidating distributions likely is moot. Regardless of the application of that rule, the liquidating corporation will recognize a gain in an amount equal to the difference between the fair market value of a distributed asset and the corporation's adjusted basis in that asset. As to liquidating distributions, the tax benefit rule will be significant only in the unlikely event that the tax benefit rule is construed as requiring the recapture of previously deducted costs that exceed the fair market value of the distributed asset.[22]

¶ 5.3000. **EXCLUSION WHERE NO TAX BENEFIT.** If a TP deducted an item from his tax return but did not obtain a tax benefit for the entire amount of the deduction, the recapture of all or part of the item in a subsequent year will be excluded from the TP's gross income to the extent that he did not enjoy a tax benefit from the prior year's deduction. § 111. A tax benefit is obtained from a deduction if it was useful in reducing the TP's income tax for the year he claimed the deduction or for some other year to which the deduction was carried as a net operating loss or capital loss. If a deduction caused a net operating loss carryover (or a capital loss carryover) which, although unused, has not yet expired, it will be treated as having provided the TP with a tax benefit, and so the recovery of that amount will not be excluded from the TP's gross income. § 111(c). The provision in § 111 for an exclusion from gross income can apply to virtually any recaptured item that was previously deducted except for deductions allowed for depreciation, depletion, amortization, and amortizable bond premiums.

¶ 5.3100. **Illustration.** In Year One, X paid a property tax of $8,000 to the Commonwealth of Virginia. In Year One, X had a salary of $14,000 and had no other income. In his Year One tax return, he claimed deductions of: $1,000 for state income tax, $4,400 for interest payments on a home mortgage, $4,000 for personal exemptions. In addition, X claimed an $8,000 deduction for the payment of a property tax. Consequently, X's Year One return showed a net loss of $3,400. This was not a "net operating loss" which could be carried over to offset income in other years. X elected to deduct his itemized deductions in that year since his itemized deductions were greater in amount than his standard deduction. In Year Four, X received a refund of $4,500 from the Commonwealth of Virginia as a return of part of X's payment of the Year One property tax which had been redetermined. Although X had deducted the entire $8,000 payment from his Year One return, only $4,600 of it gave him a tax benefit (i.e., if X had deducted only $4,600 of the real

22. See ¶ 5.1200.

property tax, his tax bill for Year One would have been $0, so X got no tax benefit from the additional $3,400 of the property tax deduction). Therefore, under § 111, X will exclude $3,400 of the $4,500 refund he received in Year Four from his gross income, and only $1,100 of the refund is included in X's gross income.

The effect of the tax benefit rule as applied by § 111 is to cause X to be taxed on the same amount of income that would have been taxed if X had received the refund in Year One when he paid the property tax; but the *rate* of tax will be determined by X's Year Four income instead of by Year One. X received a refund of $4,500 in Year Four because it was determined that the correct amount of property tax that X owed in Year One was $3,500 instead of the $8,000 that X paid in that year. If X had paid a property tax of $3,500 in Year One, he would have reported taxable income of $1,100 in that year ($14,000 AGI minus deductions totaling $12,900 ($1,000 + $4,400 + $4,000 + $3,500)). Under § 11, X is taxed on the same $1,100 of income, but it is taxed in Year Four at X's marginal rate in that year.

¶ **5.3200. Standard Deduction.** In lieu of deducting itemized deductions (i.e., deductions other than exemption deductions and other than those deductions listed in § 62(a)) an individual TP can deduct a specified dollar amount referred to as the "standard deduction."[23] Thus, an individual has a minimum amount of deduction available regardless of the actual amount of his itemized deductions. Consequently, only the amount of an individual's itemized deductions that exceed his standard deduction can provide him with a tax benefit.[24]

¶ **5.3300. Illustration.** In Year One, Y, who was unmarried and had no dependents, properly deducted $5,000 for a state income tax payment. Y paid that amount of tax under protest because he claimed that his correct state tax liability was only $450. The $5,000 payment qualified as an itemized deduction. Y had no additional itemized deductions for that year. Y's only other deduction for that year was a personal exemption deduction of $2,000.[25] The personal exemption deduction is not an itemized deduction. Y's only gross income for that year was a salary of $23,000. Y had no nonitemized deductions. Y's standard deduction in that year was $3,000. Since his itemized deductions ($5,000) were greater than his standard deduc-

---

23.   See Chapter **Ten.** There are only a few nonitemized deductions that are not listed in § 62(a). See e.g., § 71(f)(1)(B).

24.   See Rev. Rul. 93–75; Rev. Rul. 92–91.

25.   See Chapter **Eleven.**

tion allowance ($3,000), Y elected to deduct his itemized deductions in lieu of taking a standard deduction. For Year One, Y reported taxable income of $16,000 (i.e., $23,000 adjusted gross income minus $7,000 itemized deductions and personal exemption).[26]

In Year Three, Y's state income tax liability for Year One was redetermined to be only $800 instead of the $5,000 that Y paid in Year One. Accordingly, in Year Three, the state refunded $4,200 of Y's Year One tax to him. Of that $4,200 refund, Y will exclude $2,200 from his gross income, and so only $2,000 will be included in his gross income. If Y had paid a state income tax of only $800 (the correct amount) in Year One, he would have used his $3,000 standard deduction in that year instead of deducting his itemized deductions. So, of the $5,000 state income tax deductions that he took in Year One, only $2,000 of that item reduced his tax liability since the remaining $3,000 was available to him as a standard deduction in any event. Accordingly, only the $2,000 of Y's refund that constituted a recovery of a deduction from which Y derived a tax benefit is included in Y's gross income.

Since Y elected to itemize his deduction for Year One under § 63(e), will Y be permitted to reverse that election and qualify for the standard deduction? Section 63(e)(3) authorizes a TP to change that election after the year in question in accordance with regulations. Treas. Reg. § 1.63–1 permits a TP to change an election from utilizing itemized deductions to the standard deduction and vice versa simply by recomputing the taxable income for the year for which the original election was made. The regulation does not expressly state that such a change of election can be made even after the statute of limitations for the earlier year has expired; but Treas. Reg. 1.63–1(b) states that a change of election does not affect the limitations period for claiming a credit or refund—thereby separating the period for claiming a refund from the period for changing the election. In the view of the authors, it would be unduly harsh to require a TP to abide by an election that was made for an amount of itemized deductions that effectively was reduced by the operation of the tax benefit rule. The failure to use the standard deduction is not comparable to the TP's failing to claim a deduction that was available when the return was filed. Rev. Rul. 93–75 and Rev. Rul. 92–91 provide support for the view that, in applying § 111, the standard

---

26. Note that Y's adjusted gross income was too small to invoke the § 68 limitation on itemized deductions. For the treatment of the recovery of an item the deduction of which had been reduced in a prior year because of § 68, see Rev. Rul. 93–75.

deduction can be used to compute the amount of tax benefit that the TP derived in the prior year.

¶ 5.4000.   GRATUITOUS RECOVERY. The Commissioner has maintained that a TP will recognize income on the recovery of a previously deducted item (for which a tax benefit was enjoyed) even though the recovery is obtained by a gift or other gratuitous transfer. In Rev. Rul. 76–316, the Commissioner ruled that an accrual method debtor was obliged to recognize gross income on the amount of interest it had previously accrued and deducted when the creditor gratuitously forgave the debt. The Tax Court and the Fifth Circuit, however, held that a TP's gratuitous recovery of an item will not constitute gross income to the TP even though the TP had previously deducted the item and obtained a tax benefit from that deduction.[27]

In *Hillsboro*,[28] the Supreme Court indicated its approval of the analysis used by the courts in *Putoma Corp. v. Commissioner*.[29] The Court noted that Congress has excluded gifts from the recapture rules of §§ 1245 and 1250, and the Court extrapolated from these exceptions a possibility that similar exceptions apply to the tax benefit rule.

In *Putoma*, a 50 percent shareholder of a corporation had sold property to the corporation and had received in payment an interest-bearing note of the corporation. The corporation reported its income on the accrual method of accounting and thus deducted the interest owing on its note at each due date even when it failed to make payment.[30] After a few years, the shareholder forgave the corporation its obligation to pay the interest then in default. A majority of the Tax Court held in *Putoma* that the cancellation of the corporation's debt did not cause the corporation to recognize income under either the tax benefit rule or the discharge of debt rule because the cancellation was made gratuitously (i.e., as a contribution to the corporation's capital which is exempt from tax by § 118). The Commissioner appealed only on the tax benefit rule issue, and a divided panel of the Fifth Circuit affirmed.

Congress responded to the *Putoma* decisions by amending § 108 to require a corporation to recognize income in certain circumstances

---

27.   *Putoma Corp. v. Commissioner*, 66 T.C. 652 (1976), aff'd 601 F.2d 734 (5th Cir. 1979).

28.   Discussed at ¶ **5.2000.**

29.   66 T.C. 652 (1976), aff'd 601 F.2d 734 (5th Cir. 1979).

30.   Note that § 267 did not bar the taking of such deductions since the shareholder did not own more than 50 percent of the corporation's stock.

where a debt of the corporation is canceled as a contribution to capital.[31] However, this statutory amendment deals only with contributions to capital. It seems unlikely that the spirit of the amendment will be extended to affect other types of gratuitous cancellations of debts such as gifts.[32]

¶ 5.5000. RECOVERY OF ERRONEOUSLY DEDUCTED ITEM.

Where a deduction for an expenditure was erroneously claimed and allowed and the TP later recovered the expenditure after the statute of limitations for amending the return had expired, the Tax Court held that the tax benefit rule did not apply.[33] The courts of appeals that have considered this issue have uniformly rejected the Tax Court's position and have held that the tax benefit rule applies without regard to whether the deduction in question was properly or erroneously taken.[34]

¶ 5.5100. Duty of Consistency.

While the Tax Court continues to adhere to its position that the tax benefit rule does not apply directly when the deduction was erroneously taken, the court applies another doctrine that, in many cases, reaches the same result by invoking the tax benefit rule through a more indirect route. The Tax Court has adopted a "duty of consistency" rule (or sometimes called a rule of "quasi estoppel") that prevents a TP from successfully asserting that a claimed deduction was erroneous.[35] If the TP is estopped from claiming that the prior treatment was incorrect, then the tax benefit rule will apply to the subsequent event. Since the application of the duty of consistency has the same result to the TP as a direct application of the tax benefit rule, courts of appeals have affirmed Tax Court decisions applying the duty of consistency rule; but they have done so on the ground that the tax benefit rule should be applied directly.[36]

The duty of consistency or quasi estoppel rule that the Tax Court

31. See ¶ **7.5000**.

32. See ¶ **7.6000**.

33. See *Canelo v. Commissioner*, 53 T.C. 217 (1969), aff'd on another ground, 447 F.2d 484 (9th Cir. 1971); *Hughes and Luce L.L.P. v. Commissioner*, 68 TCM 1169 (1994), aff'd on another ground, 70 F.3d 16 (5th Cir. 1995); *Davoli v. Commissioner*, 68 TCM 104 (1994).

34. See, e.g., *Hughes and Luce, L.L.P. v. Commissioner*, 70 F.3d 16 (5th Cir. 1995), cert. denied, 517 U.S. 1208 (1996); *Unvert v. Commissioner*, 656 F.2d 483 (9th Cir. 1981).

35. See, e.g., *Hughes and Luce, L.L.P. v. Commissioner*, 68 TCM 1169 (1994); *Davoli v. Commissioner*, 68 TCM 104 (1994).

36. See *Hughes and Luce L.L.P. v. Commissioner*, 70 F.3d 16 (5th Cir. 1995); *Unvert v. Commissioner*, 656 F.2d 483 (9th Cir. 1981).

applies is not as broad as a direct application of the tax benefit rule and so may not apply in some situations in which the tax benefit rule would. The duty of consistency arises (according to the Tax Court) when: (1) the TP made a representation or reported an item in one year; (2) the Commissioner acquiesced in or relied on that representation or report; and (3) the TP attempts to change that representation or treatment of the prior item in a later year after the statute of limitations for amending the earlier return has expired.[37] If all of the relevant facts were reported by the TP in his return, and reported correctly, but the TP came to the wrong conclusion as to the correct tax treatment of the item, the duty of consistency rule likely will not be applied by the Tax Court; whereas, a direct application of the tax benefit rule would cause the recognition of income to the TP. For example, in *885 Investment Co. v. Commissioner*,[38] the TP erroneously claimed a deduction for a contribution to a charity subject to a reversionary interest the possibility of occurrence of which was more than negligible. On the return of the property to the TP after the statute of limitations had run, the court applied the tax benefit rule because an appeal would lie to the Ninth Circuit which had previously rejected the erroneous deduction exception to that rule. The court followed the Ninth Circuit's view under the court's *Golsen* rule.[39] A reasonable inference from the court's opinion is that the court would not have applied the duty of consistency rule to that case if the court had not been constrained by the Ninth Circuit's position to follow the tax benefit rule. The question of the validity of the Tax Court's view that the tax benefit rule does not directly apply to erroneously taken deductions therefore is important, notwithstanding the court's adoption of the duty of consistency rule.

Whether the duty of consistency rule is needed or not, there is good justification for finding it valid. The purpose of having a statute of limitations for amending or challenging tax returns is to prevent a change of the items reported on the return once the time period has run. Once that period has run, the parties should not be allowed to challenge the accuracy of items on the return even for purposes of determining the tax treatment of events occurring subsequently. If that were not so, the accuracy of the tax return could be litigated in a subsequent year even though that would run counter to the purpose of the statute of limitations.[40]

37.   *Hughes and Luce L.L.P. v. Commissioner*, 70 F.3d 16 (5th Cir. 1995).

38.   95 T.C. 156 (1990).

39.   See *Golsen v. Commissioner*, discussed at ¶ **1.4200.**

40.   For a discussion of the duty of consistency rule in another context, see ¶ **26.4122.**

CHAPTER SIX

GIFTS AND INHERITANCES

¶ **6.0000. EXCLUSION FROM GROSS INCOME.** As previously noted, the Code expressly excludes certain items from gross income. For example, as discussed in Chapter **Two**, meals and lodging furnished for the convenience of an employer are excluded from income. § 119. Section 102(a) excludes from gross income gifts and inheritances. As used in this context, "inheritances" includes bequests and devises as well as property acquired from a decedent by intestacy. In this chapter, we will examine the scope of that exception, a rationale for it, and the determination of the basis that the recipient of the property acquires in it. We will first discuss gifts.

¶ **6.1000. TAXATION OF DONOR AND DONEE.** A donee will not recognize income on receiving a gift (other than a gift received by an employee from an employer). This is a statutory exclusion from income which is set forth in § 102(a). The tax law has provided an exclusion from income for gifts in every tax act that was passed since the adoption of the Sixteenth Amendment to the Constitution.

In 1986, Congress added § 102(c) to the Code requiring an employee to recognize income on receiving a gift from his employer.[1]

With one exception, a donor will not recognize a gain or loss on making a gift. There is no statutory provision immunizing the donor from recognizing gain or loss; it is a common law rule. The one exception to that rule is that under § 84 a donor of appreciated property to a political organization will recognize a gain in the amount of the appreciation. A donor can never recognize a loss on making a gift.

A gift sometimes is made by selling property at a bargain price. That type of transaction is referred to as a "part-sale, part-gift" or simply as a bargain sale.[2]

¶ 6.1100. Examples.

1. The scope of that exception is discussed at ¶ **6.4000**. The question of whether § 102(c) also applies to an inheritance from a deceased employer is discussed in ¶ **6.8500**.

2. The tax treatment of bargain sales is discussed at ¶¶ **6.7000–6.7310**.

¶ **6.1110.   Illustration 1.** X made a gift to Y of stocks having a fair market value of $100,000.Y is not an employee of X. X had a basis of $26,000 in the stocks. Y does not include any of the $100,000 value of the stocks in her gross income. § 102(a). X does not recognize a gain or loss on making the gift.

¶ **6.1120.   Illustration 2.** X made a gift of stocks having a basis of $58,000 and a fair market value of $100,000 to T in trust. The income of the trust is payable to Y for life; and, upon Y's death, the corpus of the trust is to be distributed to Z. Neither Y nor Z is an employee of X. Neither the trust, Y, nor Z will recognize any income because of the transfer of the property to the trust. However, during the term of the trust, income distributed from the trust to Y is not excluded from Y's gross income. Section 102(b) expressly prevents § 102(a) from applying to the income from donated property. The income distributed to Y will therefore be included in Y's gross income unless some other statutory provision excludes it.

Upon Y's death, the trust corpus will be distributed to Z. Z will not recognize any income from receiving the corpus of the trust. However, if any income earned by the trust in the trust's last taxable year is distributed to Z, Z will have to include that amount in income.

¶ **6.2000.   DEFINITION OF A GIFT.** A gift involves a transfer for which no or inadequate financial consideration was received. While inadequate consideration is a necessary condition for a transfer to be a gift, it is not sufficient. The definition of a gift was established by the Supreme Court in its decision in *Commissioner v. Duberstein,* 363 U.S. 278 (1960). The Supreme Court determined that the crucial factor for qualifying a transfer as a gift is the *intention* that the transferor had in making the transfer. To constitute a gift, the transfer must have been made for inadequate consideration and out of the transferor's "detached and disinterested generosity." If a transfer was made "out of affection, respect, admiration, charity, or like impulses," the transfer will be a gift; but if the transferor made the transfer as a consequence of "the constraining force of any moral or legal duty" or from 'the incentive of anticipated benefit," it will not qualify as a gift for income tax purposes.

¶ **6.2100.   Application of *Duberstein* Standard.** The phrase "detached and disinterested generosity" is universally quoted as the standard to be applied in determining whether a transferor had the requisite intention for there to have been a gift. Courts have stated that that phrase is the exclusive test for determining a gift. The reader should be aware that the phrase itself is not that helpful in resolving close questions as to whether a specific situation constitutes a gift. To apply that standard, it is necessary to understand what types of purposes for making a transfer are embraced within that phrase, and how those purposes interact with the facts of each situation. The Eighth Circuit expressed its doubts as to the usefulness of that phrase in *Goodwin v. United States*, 67 F.3d 149, 152, fn. 3 (8th Cir. 1995):

> Many courts nevertheless give talismanic weight to a phrase used more casually in the Duberstein opinion—that a transfer to be a gift must be the product of "detached and disinterested generosity." To decide close cases using this phrase requires careful analysis of what detached and disinterested means in different contexts. Thus, the phrase is more sound bite than talisman.

¶ 6.2110.   Term of Art. For tax purposes, a "gift" is a term of art whose definition does not turn upon the common law concept of gift. Moreover, the term has a different meaning in the income tax law than it does in the gift tax law.[3]

¶ 6.2120.   Factual Issue. The determination of a transferor's intent is a factual issue. *Commissioner v. Duberstein,* supra. Consequently, the standard of appellate review of a trial court's decision is limited.[4] Notwithstanding the factual characterization of the issue, appellate courts have been willing to reverse trial courts in a number of cases. The determination that a transfer is a gift can be described as a mixed question of fact and law or more accurately as an application of law to a set of facts. The standard of appellate review for such determinations is the same as the standard for pure factual findings.[5] Some courts, however, have treated the standard of review as being one for review of a legal issue.[6] That treatment is questionable, and those cases may be explained as being actually grounded on a very different rationale.[7]

---

   3. *Farid–Es–Sultaneh v. Commissioner*, 160 F.2d 812 (2nd Cir. 1947); *United States v. Davis*, 370 U.S. 65 (1962).

   4. See *United States v. Kaiser*, 363 U.S. 299 (1960).

   5. *Bausch & Lomb, Inc. v. Commissioner*, 933 F.2d 1084 (2nd Cir. 1991).

   6. E.g., *Olk v. United States*, 536 F.2d 876 (9th Cir. 1976).

   7. See ¶ **6.5000.**

¶ **6.2130. Exclusivity of Transferor's Intent.** In *Duberstein*, the Supreme Court stated that the transferor's intent is "the most critical consideration" in determining whether a transfer is a gift. Courts have taken that case to require that the transferor's intent be the exclusive determinant of gift treatment. There is reason to question whether there are circumstances in which the role of the transferee should be the controlling element. At this time, no court has been willing to adopt any standard other than the transferor's intent, but there are court decisions in which the role of the transferee may have influenced or even determined the outcome.[8]

¶ **6.2140. Mixed Intentions.** When the intentions of the transferor are mixed, the gift being made partly out of affection and partly out of the anticipation of economic benefit, the tax consequences turn on the dominant purpose of the transferor.[9]

¶ **6.2150. Tips and Gratuities for Services.** An individual can enjoy the services of another even though their relationship is not that of an employer and employee. For example, a diner can enjoy the services of a waiter. How should a voluntary payment to the service provider be treated? The payment is made in appreciation of the service and is a form of compensation to the service provider. In the *Duberstein* decision, the Court noted that a transfer made in return for services rendered is not a gift even if the transferor derived no economic benefit from it. The Court expressly stated that tips constitute gross income to the recipient.[10]

In some businesses (for example, the restaurant business), the employees' wages are lowered in anticipation of their receiving tips. In effect, the employer delegates to a customer the task of determining a portion of an employee's wage so that that portion of the employee's compensation can be adjusted according to the quality of the service the customer received. The tip is a part of the employee's compensation. The customers know that a tip is expected as part of the cost of their meal.

In a business in which there is no delegation of compensation to the customer, a customer's voluntary transfer to an employee might qualify as a gift. This can only be true if the employee does

8. That issue is discussed in ¶ **6.5000.**

9. *Commissioner v. Duberstein*, supra.

10. See also *Cracchiola v. Commissioner*, 643 F.2d 1383 (9th Cir. 1981).

not provide a service to the customer. For example, an athlete's performance does not constitute a service to a spectator, and so a spectator might be able to make a gift to the performer. That approach poses a question as to just what constitutes a service to a customer.[11]

Since tips are not always reported to the Service, the Service has designed a formula for estimating the amount of tips received by an individual; and, in *McQuatters v. Commissioner*, the Tax Court approved of the application of that formula.[12] In deference to that case, the formula is sometimes referred to as the "McQuatters Formula."[13]

¶ 6.3000. **RATIONALE FOR THE EXCLUSION.** Many commentators maintain that there is no policy justification for excluding gifts from the donee's income. They maintain that an addition to a person's wealth should be included in gross income regardless of the source of the addition. Why should someone who receives a gift be treated more advantageously by the tax law than someone who works hard to earn a wage? The authors wrote an article that responded to that contention and set forth a tax policy justification for the exclusion of gifts.[14] The following discussion is drawn from that article.

A commonly used definition of income for tax purposes is the so-called Haig–Simons formula that income equals the value of the TP's personal consumption during a year plus the amount of increase in the TP's wealth at the end of that year. Consumption refers to the preclusive use or destruction of societal goods or services. In other words, consumption relates to a TP's removing goods or services from the societal pool of resources and capturing those resources to the TP's use.

The significance of the Haig–Simons formula in this context is that it reflects the fact that income is inexorably tied to consumption. The income that a TP does not spend during the year and therefore accumulates for use at some future date represents the present value of consumption that will take place in the future. In effect, a TP is taxed

11. See the *Olk* case at **¶ 6.5000**.

12. *McQuatters v. Commissioner*, 32 TCM 1122 (1973).

13. Another formula that has been used is described in *Cracchiola v. Commissioner*, supra.

14. Douglas A. Kahn and Jeffrey H. Kahn, *"Gifts, Gafts, and Gefts"—The Income Tax Definition and Treatment of Private and Charitable "Gifts" and a Principled Policy Justification for the Exclusion of Gifts From Income*, 78 Notre Dame L. Rev. 441 (2003).

on the value of his current consumption in the taxable year plus the present value of future consumption. Of course, the TP himself may not be the one to use the income for consumption at a future date; it may be used by someone else. By taxing the accumulated wealth, rather than to wait until the actual consumption takes place, the tax law indicates its indifference as to who actually does the consuming.

The thrust of the foregoing characterization of the income tax is that once an income tax has been paid on accumulated wealth, there should not be a second imposition of an income tax when the accumulated wealth is used to obtain the consumption of an item or service. One tax—one consumption.

Instead of consuming an item or service himself, a TP might believe that he will obtain greater utility from having someone else consume it. The TP seeks the vicarious enjoyment of seeing or anticipating another's consumption. When a donor makes a gift to a donee, the donor does not thereby consume anything—i.e., the donor does not exhaust any societal asset or service. To the contrary, the purpose of the gift is to allow the donee to use the donated property for the donee's consumption. If the donee were required to pay an income tax on the receipt of the transfer, that would reduce the amount of consumption that could be obtained from the income on which the donor had already paid tax. It would impair the donor's capacity to have the accumulated wealth used by someone else. There would be two income taxes imposed even though there would be only a single consumption when the donee used the donated property.

The rationale for excluding gifts then is to allow the donor the greatest latitude in choosing how his wealth will be consumed. That principle points to excluding the gift. However, there is a conflicting principle that points to taxing the donee on the gift. That principle is that a person should be taxed on an addition to his wealth regardless of the source of the addition. The two principles are in conflict, and one must give way. Congress has chosen to give priority to the principle of allowing the donor a broader choice of how his income will be used for consumption. However, although no court has expressly adopted the view, there may be circumstances in which the principle of taxing the donee takes on greater weight and should be given priority.[15]

¶ 6.4000. GIFTS TO AN EMPLOYEE. Prior to 1986, there was considerable litigation concerning whether a transfer from an employer

15. See ¶ 6.5000.

to an employee qualified as a gift. In most circumstances, a transfer to an employee could not meet the detached and disinterested standard and so was included in the employee's gross income. But there were instances when such transfers were held to be gifts. For example, the Supreme Court's decision in *Duberstein* involved two companion cases. In one of those (the *Stanton* case), the TP received a gratuity from his employer upon his resignation. The Supreme Court reversed a Second Circuit decision treating the gratuity as income to the employee, but the Court remanded the case to the district court for additional findings. On remand, the district court held that the gratuity was a gift; and the Second Circuit affirmed.[16]

The issue arose most frequently when an employee received an award from his employer, or retired or died. On an employee's retirement, an employer sometimes gave him a severance payment. Typically, such payments would be included in the employee's gross income, but there were a few exceptions.[17]

On the death of an employee, an employer might make a payment to a member of the employee's family. Prior to 1986, the results in those death benefit cases were mixed. For example, in *Carter's Estate v. Commissioner*, a corporation's payment to the widow of a deceased employee was held to be a gift.[18] If it could be shown that the death benefit payment was made pursuant to an agreement with the employee for his services or was made pursuant to a past practice of paying death benefits, the payment would be included in the recipient's gross income.[19]

The adoption in 1986 of § 102(c) has made it very difficult to obtain gift treatment for severance and death benefit payments, and that provision is discussed below.

¶ 6.4100. Prizes and Awards. An employee can receive a prize or award for exemplary performance such as long or excellent service. In some cases, prior to 1986, the prize or award was excluded from income as a gift. Congress did not wish to leave open the possibility

16. *Stanton v. United States*, 186 F.Supp. 393 (D. N.Y., 1960), aff'd 287 F.2d 876 (2nd Cir. 1961).

17. See, e.g., *Stanton v. United States*, supra; and *Brimm v. Commissioner*, 27 TCM 1148 (1968).

18. *Carter's Estate v. Commissioner*, 453 F.2d 61 (2nd Cir. 1971).

19. See Bittker and Lokken, FEDERAL TAXATION OF INCOME, ESTATES AND GIFTS, ¶ 10.2.4 (3d ed., 1999).

that such prizes or awards could be excluded from the employee's gross income. Accordingly, in 1986, Congress added § 102(c) to the Code. That provision states that § 102(a) cannot apply to a transfer from an employer to, or for the benefit of, an employee. The focus of Congress in adopting that provision was on prizes and awards.[20] Since 1986, a prize or award to an employee will be included in the employee's gross income unless a statutory exception other than § 102(a) is applicable. E.g., § 74(c).

¶ 6.4200. **Post–1986 Gifts to An Employee**. While the legislative history to § 102(c) focuses on prizes and awards, the scope of the provision is much broader than that. On its face, the provision prevents gift treatment for any transfer to an employee. There are no exceptions listed in the provision. Nevertheless, there are good reasons to conclude that there are some circumstances in which a transfer to an employee can qualify as a gift. As a matter of policy, there is no reason to deny gift treatment for a gratuitous transfer when there are strong personal reasons for the transferor to have made the transfer as a gift merely because the transferee also happens to be an employee. For example, if G employs her daughter and if G gives her daughter a present on her birthday, the literal terms of § 102(c) would include the gift in the daughter's income. If the transfer is one that would otherwise be treated as a gift for tax purposes, it should not lose that characterization because the daughter is employed by G. Both the legislative history to § 102(c) and a proposed regulation state that there are circumstances in which the provision does not apply to a transfer to an employee.

When an employer transfers property to an employee, there is an inference that there are business reasons for making the transfer. The burden will be on the transferee to rebut that inference and show that the transfer was motivated by personal reasons. Only if the transferee can establish that there were personal reasons for the transfer that were not attributable to the employment relationship will the transfer be excluded from income as a gift.

The House Report for the 1986 Act, which added § 102(c), states:

> Of course, gifts between individuals made exclusively for personal reasons (such as birthday presents) that are wholly unrelated to an employment relationship are not includible in the recipient's gross income merely because the gift-giver is the employer of the recipient. A transfer between personal acquaintances will not be

20. H. Rept. 99–426, 99th Cong. 1st Sess. at 103–106 (Dec. 7 1985).

considered to have been made exclusively for personal reasons if reflecting any employment-related reason (e.g., gratitude for services rendered) or any anticipation of business benefit.[21]

In addition, Prop. Reg. § 1.102–1(f)(2) states:

> For purposes of section 102(c) extraordinary transfers to the natural objects of an employer's bounty will not be considered transfers to, or for the benefit of, an employee if the employee can show that the transfer was not made in recognition of the employer's employment. Accordingly, section 102(c) shall not apply to amounts transferred between related parties (e.g., father and son) if the purpose of the transfer can be substantially attributed to the familiar relationship of the parties and not to the circumstances of their employment.

There will be a relatively small number of circumstances in which a transfer to an employee will qualify as a gift. In most of the cases in which a transfer will be a gift, the parties will be related. Being related is not sufficient to qualify a transfer as a gift, it must be shown that the purpose of the transfer was not connected with the employment relationship. It does seem, moreover, that there are circumstances in which an employer and employee who are not formally related can have a personal relationship of such depth and closeness that a transfer to the employee could fall outside of the scope of § 102(c).

An employee will have a high burden of proof to escape the reach of § 102(c). Currently, there is no authoritative statement as to just what that burden might be. In the view of the authors, it will not be enough merely to show that the transferor had a personal reason to make the transfer. To avoid § 102(c), the authors believe that the transferee will have to prove that the transferor's personal reason was both necessary and sufficient for the making of the transfer. In other words, the transferor would not have made the transfer if he had not had that personal reason, and he would have made the transfer even if he did not have any other reasons to do so.

Even when § 102(c) applies, a transfer to an employee will be excluded from income if another statutory exception, such as the de minimis exception of § 132(e), applies.

¶ 6.4300. **Transfers from an Entity.** While there can be a personal relationship between an individual employer and an employee that permits a transfer to qualify as a gift, no such relationship can exist

---

21. H.Rept. 99–426, 99th Cong. 1st Sess. at 106, f.n. 5.

between a fictional entity, such as a corporation or a partnership, and its employee. While a senior officer or owner of the entity might have a personal relationship with an employee, it does not seem possible for the entity itself to have that relationship. Consequently, § 102(c) prevents a transfer from an employer that is an entity to an employee from qualifying as a gift.

¶ 6.4400. Severance Pay. One might question whether § 102(c) applies to a severance payment since the recipient is no longer an employee at the time that the payment is made. It would seem that the payment cannot be said to have been made to or for the benefit of an employee. Even if § 102(c) does not apply, the transferee would have a difficult hurdle to satisfy the *Duberstein* standard of detached and disinterested generosity. A payment on the retirement of an employee appears to be compensation for past services unless unusual circumstances exist. In any event, in the view of the authors (as explained below), § 102(c) does apply to the payment; and so it will be especially difficult for the employee to exclude it from income (i.e., he probably will have to show that a personal purpose was a necessary and sufficient reason for the employer's making the payment). If the employer is an entity, then no exception to § 102(c) can apply.[22]

In addition to its decision to tax employee awards and prizes as income, Congress chose a broad statute that reaches virtually all transfers that arise out of an employment relationship. It is likely that Congress adopted a bright line rule in order to minimize the subjective nature of the inquiry required in applying the *Duberstein* standard. It is highly unlikely that Congress intended to maintain the *Duberstein* standard for transfers to a retiring employee while utilizing a bright line test for active employees. The term "employee" should be construed to include a former employee when the transfer is made in respect of an employment relationship.

¶ 6.4500. Death Benefits. When an employer makes a payment to a spouse or other family member of a deceased employee, that death benefit could represent compensation for the deceased employee's past service. Moreover, the death benefit could provide an incentive for other employees to continue in the service of the employer and to work harder. On the other hand, if the employer had had a close personal relationship with the employee, and if the spouse or family member has financial needs, the payment could be motivated by

---

22. See ¶ **6.4300**.

sympathy and concern for the family. Before the adoption of § 102(c), the courts divided over the question whether death benefit payments were gifts—holding them to be gifts in some circumstances and income in others. Since 1986, there is a question as to whether § 102(c) applies to death benefits, and there has not yet been an authoritative resolution of that question.

For reasons mentioned in ¶ **6.4400** in connection with severance payments, it is likely that Congress intended § 102(c) to apply to death benefits. There were a number of death benefit cases prior to the 1986 Act, and the results were mixed. It seems unlikely that Congress would not have intended to have its bright line rule apply to those situations as well as to inter vivos transfers. Although a death benefit cannot be said to be made to or for the benefit of an employee, it is related to work performed by an employee and is made in respect of that employment. While one prominent treatise has concluded that § 102(c) does not apply to death benefits, the authors disagree.

¶ **6.5000. MODIFICATION OF *DUBERSTEIN* STANDARD.** The *Duberstein* standard of detached and disinterested generosity has been applied in determining a gift in all situations to which § 102(c) does not apply. No court or ruling has departed from the principle that a gift is determined by focusing on the intent of the transferor. There are circumstances, however, in which the role of the transferee should be determinative in precluding gift treatment even though the transferor had the requisite intention in making the transfer. While no court has formally adopted that approach, there are indications that it was the true source of a court's decision in a few cases. Take, for example, the decision of the Ninth Circuit in *Olk v. United States.*[23]

The TP in *Olk* was a craps dealer in several Los Vegas casinos. The patrons of the casinos used "tokes" (i.e., chips) to make their bets. A small percentage of patrons would give a portion of their winnings to the dealer. There was no custom that would pressure a patron to make such a "gift," and most patrons did not make them. Under the rules of the casinos, the tokes that a dealer received were required to be combined with tokes received by other dealers and then divided equally. The TP had a steady amount of receipts from this practice averaging about $30 a day. The question in litigation was whether the TP's receipt of these tokes constituted income to him or were gifts. In holding that the tokes

---

23.   536 F.2d 876 (9th Cir. 1976).

were gifts to the TP, the district court made a number of findings, one of which was that the patrons gave the tokes to the dealer out of detached and disinterested generosity. The Ninth Circuit treated that finding as an application of law to facts which the court characterized as a conclusion of law to which the "clearly erroneous" standard of review did not apply. Although the Ninth Circuit properly reversed the district court's decision, its stated rationale was flawed.[24] It appears that the Ninth Circuit's decision was significantly influenced by the fact that the receipt of the tokes was regarded by the dealers as a regular part of their compensation. The court said:

> Moreover, in applying the statute to the findings of fact, we are not permitted to ignore those findings which strongly suggest that tokes in the hands of the ultimate recipients are viewed as a receipt indistinguishable, except for erroneously anticipated tax differences, from wages. The regularity of the flow, the equal division of the receipts, and the daily amount received indicated that a dealer acting reasonably would come to regard such receipts as a form of compensation for his services. The manner in which a dealer may regard tokes is, of course, not the touchstone for determining whether the receipt is excludable from gross income. It is, however, a reasonable and relevant inference well-grounded in the findings of facts.[25]

While the Ninth Circuit reached the correct result in *Olk*, it might better have grounded its decision on the basis that when a transferee receives gratuitous transfers from strangers as a regular and anticipated element of his livelihood, the principle of taxing accretions to wealth takes on greater weight and should be given priority. The question of whether those circumstances warrant departing from the standard's exclusive reliance on the transferor's intention did not arise in *Duberstein* and so should not be deemed to be foreclosed by the decision in that case.

¶ 6.6000. BASIS OF GIFTS. For purposes of determining a donee's gain on the donee's subsequent disposition of donated property, the donee's original basis in the donated property is equal to the basis that the donor had at the time of the transfer. § 1015. For purposes of determining the donee's *loss* on a subsequent disposition of the donated property, the donee's original basis is the lesser of: (a) the donor's basis at the time of transfer or (b) the fair market value of the donated property on the date of transfer. § 1015(a). In the case of a bargain sale

24. See ¶ **6.2120**.

25. 536 F.2d at 879.

(i.e., a part gift-part sale), the basis that the purchaser-donee acquires in the property is described later.[26]

A gift may give rise to the imposition of a gift tax, but it will not necessarily do so. The gift tax law provides an annual exclusion and several deductions (e.g., marital and charitable deductions). In addition, there is a unified credit that effectively exempts another five million ($5,000,000) dollars from the tax.[27] §§ 2505(a), 2010(c). If there is a gift tax, its effect on the donee's basis is described below.

If a gift tax was paid on the transfer of an item, the donee's basis in that item will be increased by the portion of the gift tax that is attributable to the appreciated element of the property (the excess of the value of the property over the donor's basis). § 1015(d)(6). The basis cannot be increased to a figure that is greater than the fair market value of the property at the time of the gift. The portion of the gift tax that is attributable to the appreciated element of the donated property is determined by multiplying the gift tax by a fraction—the numerator of which is equal to the appreciated element of the gift and the denominator of which is equal to the amount of the gift. Treas. Reg. § 1.1015–5(c)(5), Ex. (1). For this purpose, the amount of a gift is equal to the fair market value of the donated item less any annual exclusion and gift tax deductions (i.e., marital and charitable deductions) attributable thereto. Treas. Reg. § 1.1015–5(c)(2).

Note that, for *gift tax* purposes, a donor is granted an exclusion for a specified amount of gifts the donor made during a calendar year to an individual. Each individual donee who received gifts from the donor in that year will qualify for the exclusion, but only gifts that do not constitute future interests can qualify. Currently, the amount of the exclusion is $13,000 per donee per year [the amount of exclusion effectively is increased if a gift *is treated* as having been made equally by a husband and wife]. For purposes of applying the basis adjustment rules, when more than one gift is made to the same donee in a calendar year, the exclusion is applied to the gifts in the order of time that they were made. Treas. Reg. § 1.1015–5(c)(2).

If a donor made more than one taxable gift in a calendar year, the gift tax on the aggregate amount of taxable gifts made that year is allocated among the several taxable gifts, according to the amount of each gift, to determine the tax on each donated item. See Treas. Reg. § 1.1015–5(c)(3), (5), Ex. (1). A "taxable gift" is defined in § 2503.

26. See ¶¶ **6.7200–6.7210**.

27. The five million dollar exemption is scheduled to expire in 2013.

A donor has the primary responsibility to pay any gift taxes, but donees are secondarily liable for such taxes if the donor fails to pay. The adjustment to basis that is provided for gift taxes paid on a gift applies regardless of whether the gift tax was paid by the donor or the donee. See Treas. Reg. § 1.1015–5(b)(2). If the donee pays the gift tax, that will reduce the amount of the gift and so will reduce the amount of the gift tax.

¶ **6.6100.   Illustration 1.** X gave Y 100 shares of Win All, Inc. stock having a fair market value of $10,000. X had a basis of $8,000 in the stock, and no gift tax was payable on the gift. Y's basis in the stock is $8,000—i.e., the same basis that X had. If Y subsequently sold the stock for $12,000, Y will realize a $4,000 gain on the sale. If Y sold the stock for $7,000, she will realize a $1,000 loss on the sale.

¶ **6.6200.   Illustration 2.** X gave Y 100 shares of Win All, Inc. stock having a fair market value of $8,000. X had a basis of $10,000 in the stock. No gift tax was payable on the gift. If Y subsequently sold the stock for $12,000, she will realize a $2,000 gain on the sale. If Y sold the stock for $7,000, Y's basis for purposes of computing loss will be $8,000 (the lower of X's basis or the fair market value of the gift at the date of transfer), and she will realize a $1,000 loss on the sale. Finally, if Y sold the stock for $9,000, Y will not realize a gain because her basis for computing gain was $10,000; and Y will not realize a loss because her basis for computing loss was $8,000. Consequently, Y will not realize either a gain or a loss.

¶ **6.6300.   Illustration 3.** X gave Y Blackacre which had a fair market value of $40,000. X had a basis of $22,000 in Blackacre, and X paid a gift tax of $3,000 on the transfer. No gift tax deductions were allowable for the gift, but $13,000 of the gift is excluded by virtue of the annual exclusion. Y's basis in Blackacre is the same as X's basis ($22,000) plus two-thirds (the fraction of the value of the gift representing the appreciated element) of the $3,000 gift tax paid. Y's basis in Blackacre, therefore, is $24,000.

Note that the appreciated element of the gift is determined without regard to the $13,000 annual gift tax exclusion, but the exclusion is taken into account in determining the amount of the gift, which therefore is $27,000. Treas. Reg. § 1.1015–5(c)(5), Ex. (1). So, the applicable fraction is:

$$\frac{\$18,000 \text{ (appreciation)}}{\$27,000 \text{ (taxable gift)}} \quad x \quad \$3,000 \text{ (gift tax)} = \$2,000 \text{ (added to basis)}$$

¶ **6.6400.   Illustration 4.** In Year One, *M* made a gift to *F* of Blackacre having a fair market value of $103,000, and *M* had a basis of $73,000 in Blackacre. In that same year, *M* made a gift to *G* of a painting having a fair market value of $73,000. *M* made no other gifts that year. *M* is allowed two $13,000 exclusions for gift tax purposes—one for the gift of Blackacre and one for the gift of the painting since the gifts were made to different donees. *M* was not allowed any deductions for those gifts, and she was not entitled to any credits (M had used up her unified credit by making gifts in prior years). The gift taxes for the two gifts totaled $55,500, and M paid that tax. *M* reported making a $103,000 gift to *F*; after deducting the $13,000 exclusion, she reported a taxable gift of $90,000. *M* also reported a $73,000 gift to *G*; after deducting the $13,000 exclusion, she reported a taxable gift of $60,000. So, the total of *M*'s taxable gifts for Year One was $150,000. The total gift tax on the two gifts was $55,500.

To determine *F*'s basis in Blackacre, it is first necessary to determine the amount of the $55,500 gift tax that is attributable to the gift of that item. The transfer of Blackacre constituted a taxable gift of $90,000 (after deducting the $13,000 annual exclusion). The total amount of taxable gifts made by *M* in that year was $150,000. So, the gift of Blackacre constitutes 90,000/150,000 or 60% of the taxable gifts made by *M* that year. Treas. Reg. § 1.1015–5(c)(3). Therefore, 60% of the $55,500 gift tax incurred by *M* is attributable to Blackacre—i.e., $33,300 of gift tax is attributable to Blackacre.

But, not all of the $33,300 gift tax that is attributable to the gift of Blackacre can be added to *F*'s basis in that property. Only the portion of the gift tax that is attributable to the appreciated element of Blackacre in the hands of *M* can be added to basis. The appreciated element of Blackacre at the time of the gift was $30,000—the value of Blackacre was $103,000 and *M* had a basis of $73,000 therein. But, the gift tax that *M* incurred is attributable to a taxable gift of only $90,000 (the extra $13,000 of value was excluded from gift taxation by the annual exclusion).The fraction of the $33,300 gift tax that is attributable to the appreciated element of Blackacre is the portion of the amount of taxable gift that was made because of the transfer of Blackacre that represents the amount of Blackacre's appreciation. Thus, the addition to Blackacre's basis is determined as follows:

$$\frac{\$30,000 \text{ (appreciation)}}{\$90,000 \text{ (taxable gift)}} \quad \text{x} \quad \$33,300 \text{ (gift tax for Blackacre)} =$$

$$\$11,100 \text{ (gift tax attributable to appreciation)}$$

F's basis in Blackacre equals the $73,000 basis that M had therein plus the $11,100 addition for the gift tax paid on account of the appreciated element of Blackacre. So, F obtains a basis of $84,100 in Blackacre. See Treas. Reg. § 1.1015–5(c)(5), Ex.(1).

¶ 6.7000. BARGAIN PURCHASES. When X (an individual) purchases property from Y and the consideration paid by X for the property is less than the property's value, the difference will constitute gross income to X in circumstances where the bargain price appears to be disguised compensation to X (e.g., where Y is X's employer). In that circumstance, the employer will recognize gain or loss on the difference between the fair market value of the property (not the bargain price paid by the employee) and the employer's basis in the property.[28]

In some cases (for example, where the two parties have a close familial relationship), the difference between the value and the purchase price will constitute a gift from Y to X. It is likely in such circumstances that Y deliberately sold the item for less than its value in order to transfer value to X for a donative purpose. If a bargain purchase constitutes a gift, it is sometimes referred to as a "part-gift, part-sale" transaction.

If there is no relationship between X and Y that indicates that the bargain element was either compensation or a gift to X (in other words, the exchange was an arms' length transaction), the bargain element has no tax consequence.

When the bargain element in a sale constitutes a gift to the purchaser, the donor-vendor will realize and recognize a gain only to the extent that the amount realized on the bargain sale exceeds the donor-vendor's basis in the property. Treas. Reg. § 1.1001–1(e)(1). In no circumstance, however, can a donor-vendor realize a loss on making a bargain sale. Even if the amount realized by a donor-vendor is less than his basis, and even if the fair market value of the transferred property also is less than the basis of the donor-vendor, no loss can be realized on a part-gift, part-sale transaction. Treas. Reg. § 1.1001–1(e).

In a part-gift, part-sale transaction, the basis of the donor-vendor is not apportioned between the part of the property that was sold and the part that was donated. Instead, the donor-vendor determines his gain by

28. See *International Freighting Corp. v. Commissioner*, 135 F.2d 310 (2nd Cir. 1943).

using the entirety of the basis of the transferred item. Treas. Reg. § 1.1001–1(e). There is one exception to that rule. If a bargain sale is made to a qualified charity, § 1011(b) requires that the basis in the property be divided between the part sold and the part donated. Treas. Reg. § 1.1011–2.

¶ 6.7100. Examples.

¶ 6.7110. Illustration 1. Intending to make a gift, *H* sold Blackacre to his son, *S*, for $20,000. Blackacre had a value of $50,000, and *H* had a basis of $65,000 therein. *H* will not realize a loss on the bargain sale. Treas. Reg. § 1.1001–1(e). *S* received a gift of $30,000 (less a $13,000 annual exclusion for gift tax purposes), which is the difference between the value of Blackacre ($50,000) and the purchase price paid by *S* ($20,000). No gift tax was payable on the gift.

The rules for determining *S*'s basis in the property are described below.[29] For the purpose of determining gain, *S* has a basis in Blackacre equal to the greater of the purchase price paid by *S* ($20,000) or the donor's basis ($65,000). Treas. Reg. § 1.1015–4. Thus, *S* will have a basis of $65,000 in Blackacre. For purposes of determining loss, *S* will have a basis of $50,000 in Blackacre since the value of the donated property ($50,000) was less than the donor's basis. If a gift tax had been paid on the transaction, *S*'s basis for gain or loss would be unchanged since there was no appreciated element to the transferred property.[30]

¶ 6.7120. Illustration 2. If *S* had paid $70,000 for Blackacre in Illustration 1 and if Blackacre had a value of $90,000 at the time of the "sale," *H* would recognize a $5,000 gain on the sale; *S* would receive a gift of $20,000 (less a $13,000 gift tax annual exclusion) and would have a basis of $70,000 in Blackacre for purposes of both gain and loss. If a gift tax had been paid on the transaction, *S*'s basis would be increased by the amount of that tax since all of the tax would be attributable to an appreciated element of the property.

¶ 6.7200. Basis of Purchaser–Donee in Bargain Purchase Situation. When the purchaser-donee of a bargain purchase arrange-

29. See ¶ 6.7200.
30. See ¶ 6.6000.

ment (part-gift and part-sale) pays less than the donor-vendor's basis, the purchaser-donee will assume the basis of the donor. Note, however, that the purchaser-donee's basis for purposes of determining *loss* cannot exceed the fair market value of the property at the date of transfer. When the purchaser-donee of a bargain purchase pays more than the donor-vendor's basis, then the purchaser-donee's basis equals the consideration he paid. Note also that the purchaser-donee's basis will be increased (but not above fair market value) by any gift tax paid on the appreciated element of the gift.[31]

¶ 6.7210. **Illustration.** In Year One, *M* had a basis of $30,000 in Greenacre which had a value of $60,000. In that year, intending to make a gift, *M* sold Greenacre to his daughter, *D*, for $25,000. *M* did not realize a loss on that bargain sale. Treas. Reg. § 1.1001–1(e). *M* reported having made a gift of $35,000 to *D*, and *M* paid a gift tax of $7,000 on that gift. Because of gifts made to *D* earlier that year, no annual exclusion was allowable for the bargain element of the transaction. *D*'s basis in Greenacre is equal to $30,000 (the donor's adjusted basis since that is greater than the $25,000 paid by *D*) plus the gift tax paid on the appreciated element of the donated property. At this writing, no regulation has yet been promulgated explaining how to determine the amount of gift tax paid on the appreciated element of property transferred pursuant to a part-gift, part-sale transaction. In the authors' opinion, the gift tax adjustment likely will be determined in the following manner:

The $25,000 paid to *M* did not cause *M* to recognize a gain because *M* offset $25,000 of his adjusted basis in Greenacre against the amount paid. *M*'s remaining $5,000 of basis in Greenacre should be allocated to the part-gift portion of the transaction. Since *M* had a basis of $5,000 in the $35,000 portion of Greenacre which constituted a gift to *D*, the appreciated element of the donated property is $30,000. Thus, 30,000/35,000 or 6/7 of the $7,000 gift tax is attributable to the appreciated element. *D*'s basis in Greenacre is $30,000 plus $6,000 of the gift tax payment which provides *D* with a total basis of $36,000.

¶ 6.8000. **INHERITED PROPERTY.** Property received by devise, bequest or inheritance is excluded from gross income by § 102(a). A testamentary transfer to an employee raises additional considerations,

31. In addition to the illustration at ¶ 6.7210, see the illustrations at ¶¶ 6.7110 and 6.7120.

and that situation is discussed later.[32]

¶ 6.8100. Settlement of a Claim for Inheritance. If an individual receives property in settlement of a claim against a decedent's estate that the individual is entitled to receive a share of the estate as a beneficiary, how should the tax law treat that settlement? If the individual's claim was litigated and the individual prevailed, the amount received by the individual would be treated as an inheritance. The amount received would be excluded from income by § 102(a) unless a bequest to that individual would have been taxable as compensation for past services. There is no reason to apply a different result if the parties settle the dispute rather than to litigate to judgment. If the settlement were not given the same treatment as would have been applied to a judgment in the litigation, it would deter settlements. Pursuant to the landmark Supreme Court decision in *Lyeth v. Hoey*,[33] a bona fide settlement is treated the same for tax purposes as would be a final judgement for the plaintiff. If it is determined that the settlement is based on a bona fide claim for an inheritance (other than a claim based on a promise to devise property if the promisee performed services), the amount received will be excluded from the individual's income.

TPs could try to abuse this rule by disguising a gift as a purported settlement of a testamentary dispute. They could thereby transfer property to someone who was omitted from the decedent's will and who does not have a valid claim. The omitted party could bring a claim, and the parties could "settle." To prevent that abuse, a court will examine the claim to see if it was bona fide.

¶ 6.8200. Income Earned from Inherited Property. While the inherited property itself will not be taxed, income attributable to an inherited asset will be included in gross income. § 102(b). Thus, the income from a testamentary trust will be included in the recipient's gross income unless it is excluded by some other statutory provision. For example, the interest from a state or municipal bond may be excluded from income under § 103.

¶ 6.8300. Income in Respect of a Decedent. Income earned by a decedent during his life but not recognized until after his death will be treated as gross income to the ultimate recipient of the income. For example, when *X* was entitled to a commission from his employer

---

32. See **¶ 6.8500**.

33. 305 U.S. 188 (1938).

at the time of his death, but the amount of the commission was not payable until a date after X's death, the commission will be included in the gross income of the person to whom it is paid. § 691. Such income is called "income in respect of a decedent."[34]

¶ 6.8400.   Basis of Property Acquired from a Decedent. Under § 1014(a), subject to a few exceptions, the basis of property that was included in a decedent's gross estate for tax purposes is equal to the fair market value of the property at the date of the decedent's death; or, if the decedent's executor elects the alternate estate tax valuation method under § 2032, the basis will equal the fair market value at the date that the property was valued for estate tax purposes under § 2032. If the executor made an election for certain real properties to be valued for estate tax purposes pursuant to the special valuation provided by § 2032A, the basis of such properties will be the same valuation figure as is used for estate tax purposes. § 1014(a)(3). If decedent's executor elects under § 2031(c) to reduce the value of land subject to a "qualified conservation easement," the basis of the excluded portion of the land will be the same basis that the decedent had in that portion. § 1014(a)(4).

There is a rebuttable presumption that the basis of property acquired from a decedent equals the value determined for that property for estate tax purposes. Treas. Reg. § 1.1014–3(a). Can a beneficiary rebut that presumption and establish that the property had a higher value at the valuation date than was determined for estate tax purposes? If the beneficiary had a role in determining the estate tax valuation, the beneficiary will be estopped from claiming a higher valuation in order to have a higher basis for the property. If the beneficiary had no role in determining the estate tax valuation, the beneficiary is not estopped from rebutting the presumption and establishing a higher basis.[35]

The basis rules of § 1014 apply to property acquired by the TP from a decedent in whose gross estate the property was included even if the TP had acquired the property from the decedent as a gift made by the decedent during his life. In such cases, the donee's original basis in the donated property would equal that of the donor, but the donee's basis would be changed under § 1014 as of the date of the decedent's death. If a donee sold, exchanged or otherwise disposed of the donated property prior to the donor's death, the death of the donor will not cause any adjustment to be made to the donee's basis,

---

34.   Income in respect of a decedent (IRD) is discussed in Chapter **Twenty–Nine.**

35.   TAM 199933001 (1999); *Shook v. United States*, 713 F.2d 662 (11th Cir. 1983).

and the determination of the donee's gain or loss on such disposition is not altered. § 1014(a).

Section 1014 basis rules apply to property in the hands of a person who either acquired that property from a decedent or "to whom the property passed from a decedent." § 1014(a). The definition of property acquired from or passed from a decedent is set forth at § 1014(b).

If a decedent died in the year 2010, basis will be determined differently. There is no estate tax applicable to a decedent who died in the year 2010, unless the decedent's estate elects to have the estate tax apply. The estate tax is applicable for estates of those who die after 2010. For decedents who die in the year 2010, the basis rules depend upon what election the decedent's estate makes. If the estate elects to be subject to the estate tax, the basis of the estate's property will be determined under § 1014. But if the estate elects to not be subject to the estate tax, then a modified carryover of the decedent's basis is applied by § 1022. That election does not apply to years after 2010, and § 1014 will apply after that year. We have omitted any discussion of § 1022 in this book.

¶ 6.8410. **Basis of Income in Respect of a Decedent.** Section 1014 does not apply to income in respect of a decedent. § 1014(c). Consequently, the basis of income in respect of a decedent is not changed by the decedent's death.[36]

¶ 6.8411. **Illustration.** In Year One, D purchased an interest-bearing United States bond for $70. No interest is payable on the bond until it is surrendered by the holder. D did not elect to include the appreciation of the bond's value as interest income over the term of the bond, and so the interest income from the bond is deferred until the bond is surrendered. D died in Year Five, and his executor did not elect the alternate valuation date. At that time, the bond could be surrendered for $100; and the bond had a value of $100, which is the amount included in D's gross estate for estate tax purposes. Thirty dollars of that amount is the right to receive income in respect of a decedent so that D's estate (and a transferee of the estate) will have a zero basis therein. The estate's basis in the bond (and the basis of the beneficiary to whom the bond is distributed from the estate) is $70—the fair market value (at the time

36.   Income in respect of a decedent is described in ¶ **6.8300**.

of D's death) of that portion of the bond that does not constitute the right to receive income in respect of a decedent.

¶ **6.8420. Property Acquired by Decedent As a Gift Within One Year of Death.** If appreciated property (i.e., property whose value exceeds its basis) was acquired by a decedent by gift within a year prior to the decedent's death and if such property (or the proceeds from the sale of such property by the decedent's estate or trust) passes from the decedent to the person who originally gave the property to the decedent or to the spouse of such person, the transferee's basis in the property will equal the basis that the decedent had therein immediately prior to his death. § 1014(e). The purpose of this provision is to prevent a step-up in basis of appreciated property by giving it to a dying person who bequeaths it back to the donor or donor's spouse.

¶ **6.8430. Penalty for Valuation Overstatement.** Under § 6662(e), the penalty imposed on a TP for underpaying his tax as a consequence of substantially overstating the value or adjusted basis of property (this is part of the "accuracy-related penalty") applies to a TP whose basis in property that is determined under § 1014 is substantially overstated because the value of the property at the applicable valuation date was overstated.[37] A substantial valuation overstatement occurs if the value or adjusted basis reported is 150 percent or more of the amount determined to be the correct value or adjusted basis, and if the resulting underpayment of tax is at least $5,000 ($10,000 for some corporations). § 6662(e)(1), (2). The penalty will not apply if the TP had a reasonable basis for the reported valuation and the claim was made in good faith. § 6664(c)(1). When the beneficiary of an estate adopted a basis equal to the value reported for the property on the decedent's estate tax return, the beneficiary's reliance on the estate tax return was not deemed a reasonable justification for the beneficiary's overstatement of value.[38]

¶ **6.8500. Testamentary Transfers to an Employee.** A deceased employer's bequest to an employee raises considerations that do not apply to inter vivos transfers. As noted in ¶ **6.8000,** a testamentary transfer of property usually is excluded from income by § 102(a). But what if the beneficiary had been an employee of the decedent? If the bequest is made in satisfaction of an agreement that property would be bequeathed if the employee performed services for the employer,

---

37. Rev. Rul. 85–75.

38. Rev. Rul. 85–75.

then the bequest should be included in the employee's income as compensation for past services.[39] In practice, it will be difficult for the Service to discover that a bequest was given in satisfaction of an agreement unless the decedent reneged on the agreement and caused the employee to claim against the estate.[40]

There is a question as to whether § 102(c) applies to testamentary transfers. The provision states that § 102(a) shall not apply to exclude from income a transfer by an employer to an employee. Since § 102(a) applies to both gifts and testamentary transfers, the language of § 102(c) does refer to testamentary transfers. The authors nevertheless have doubts that it applies to testamentary transfers, and no regulation or other authority addresses that question.

The title to § 102(c) is "**Employee gifts.**" While not a great amount of weight can be given to a title, it does suggest that the provision is limited to inter vivos transfers. There are some considerations that support that construction. Testamentary transfers that are not made pursuant to an agreement are more likely to have noncompensatory purposes than are inter vivos transfers. The decedent no longer has any reason to induce the employee (or other employees) to continue to provide services for him. It is more likely that the bequest is a product of the decedent's affection than to compensate for past services. In the absence of an agreement, a bequest will usually occur when there has been a close personal relationship with the beneficiary. For example, a household employee who works for a family for many years can come to be regarded as a kind of informal member of the family. It is not uncommon for a bequest to be made to such an employee. While there is no evidence in the legislative history as to Congress's intention, the authors deem it likely that the indirect reference in § 102(c) to testamentary transfers is attributable to an oversight and was not contemplated.

¶ **6.8600. Generation–Skipping Transfers.** In addition to estate and gift taxes, the Code imposes a tax (called a "generation-skipping tax") on certain transfers that pass to a person who is more than one generation removed from the transferor. § 2601 *et seq*. When that tax is imposed, the basis of the property that triggers the tax will be adjusted according to the terms of § 2654(a). The basis adjustment for certain types of generation-skipping transfers is the same as that applied by § 1014(a) for inherited property, and the basis adjustment

39. But see, *Roberts v. Commissioner*, 69 TCM 2409 (1995).

40. See ¶ **6.8100**.

for other types of generation-skipping transfers is similar to the adjustments made for gift taxes on donated property.[41]

¶ **6.9000. HOLDING PERIOD.** When a TP recognizes a gain or loss on the sale or exchange of an asset, the period of time in which the TP is deemed to have held the asset prior to disposing of it may be significant. A TP's "holding period" determines whether the gain or loss from the sale or exchange of a capital asset is a long-term or a short-term capital gain. In addition, a TP's holding period will determine whether gain or loss from certain involuntary conversions or from the sale or exchange of certain property used in a trade or business will be characterized under § 1231, which will affect the tax rate applicable to such gains and the treatment of such losses. The tax consequences of having long-term or short-term capital gain or of having gain or loss under § 1231 are discussed later in this work.[42]

Unless a special rule applies, a TP's holding period begins on the day after he acquired the property.[43] Section 1223 establishes holding period rules for a number of specific situations.

¶ **6.9100. Holding Period of Gifts.** A number of special holding period rules are set forth in § 1223. One of those rules provides that a person includes in his holding period the time in which the property was held by another person whose basis in the property determines, in whole or in part, the transferee's basis. § 1223(2). Specifically, § 1223(2) requires that "the property has ... the same basis in whole or in part in his hands [the transferee's] as it would have in the hands of such other person [the transferor's]."

As noted in ¶ **6.6000**, a donee's basis is equal to the donor's basis plus any gift tax paid on the appreciated element of the donated property. Even if a portion of a gift tax was added in determining the donee's basis, the donee's basis would still be in part the same basis that the donor had. So, a donee tacks on the holding period of the donor to determine how long the donee is deemed to have held the property. For example, G gave Blackacre to D, and G had held Blackacre for seven months and 10 days before making the gift. D's holding period for Blackacre will include the seven months and 10 days that D held it.

41. See ¶ ¶ **6.6000, 6.6300–6.6400**

42. See Chapters **Twenty–Four** and **Twenty–Five**.

43. Rev. Rul. 66–7 and Rev. Rul. 99–5.

¶ 6.9110. Holding Period of Purchaser–Donee from a Bargain Purchase. If, in a bargain purchase, the purchase price paid by a purchaser-donee is less than the donor-vendor's basis in the property, the purchaser-donee's basis will be equal to the donor-vendor's basis plus any gift tax paid on the appreciated element of the donated part of the transaction.[44] Since the purchaser-donee's basis will therefore be the same in whole or in part as the donor-vendor's basis, § 1223(2) applies. The holding period of the purchaser-donee, therefore, will include the period that the donor-vendor held the property.

If, in a bargain purchase, the purchase price paid by a purchaser-donee is greater than the basis of the donor-vendor, then the purchaser-donee's basis in the property will equal the amount that the purchaser-donee paid for it.[45] Does that mean that the purchaser-donee's basis is not the same in whole or in part as the donor-vendor's basis so that § 1223(2) will not apply? If so, the holding period of the purchaser-donee would not include the period that the donor-vendor held the property.

In *Citizens National Bank of Waco v. United States*, 417 F.2d 675 (5th Cir. 1969), the court held that § 1223(2) did apply, and so the purchaser-donee included in its holding period the time that the donor-vendor had held the property. The purchaser-donee in that case was a trust, and the court's holding may have been restricted to trusts because of the language in § 1015(b) concerning a trust's basis in property acquired in a bargain purchase. In a Technical Advice Memorandum issued by the Service some years after that decision, the Service rejected the court's holding and indicated that the service will not follow it.[46] The position of the Service is that the period that the donor-vendor held the property is not tacked to the holding period of the purchaser-donee if the purchase price exceeded the donor-vendor's basis.

¶ 6.9200. Holding Period of Inherited Property. Where the basis of property acquired from (or passing from) a decedent is determined under § 1014, the transferee will be treated as having held the property for more than one year, which is a sufficient period of time to qualify gain or loss from the sale of such property as long-term capital gain or loss or as § 1231 gain or loss. § 1223(9). So,

---

44. ¶ ¶ 6.7200–6.7210.

45. ¶ 6.7200.

46. TAM 7752001 (1977).

even if the transferee disposes of the property within one year of obtaining it, the transferee's gain or loss will either be long-term or § 1231 gain or loss.

As noted in ¶ **6.8400**, there is no estate tax for decedents who die in the year 2010 unless the estate elects to be subject to that tax; and the basis rules of § 1014 do not apply to the estates of decedents who died in that year and elected to not have the estate tax apply. Instead, a modified carryover of the decedent's basis is provided by § 1022. In such cases, it appears that the holding period of the decedent's property will be determined by § 1223(2) so that the holding period of the decedent will be tacked; but that has not yet been established. After the year 2010, § 1014 will again become applicable; and so the holding period rule described in the paragraph above will be applicable.

¶ **6.9000A.   POLITICAL CONTRIBUTIONS.** In general, contributions made to a political organization as dues or fees or proceeds from a fund-raising event will not constitute gross income to the political organization to the extent that such amounts are segregated for a proper political purpose, such as the attempt to influence the selection or election of an individual to a federal, state, or local office. § 527. If a politician uses contributed funds for personal use, the funds will be income to him unless he can prove that the donor intended the contribution to be an unrestricted gift within the meaning of *Commissioner v. Duberstein*.[47] The presumption is that political contributions are not intended to be unrestricted gifts, and the TP has the burden of proving otherwise.[48]

---

47.   See Rev. Proc. 68–19; *United States v. Pisani*, 773 F.2d 397 (2d Cir. 1985). *Duberstein* is discussed at ¶ **6.2000**.

48.   Rev. Proc. 68–19.

CHAPTER SEVEN

CANCELLATION OF DEBT

¶ 7.0000.   CANCELLATION OF DEBT.

¶ 7.1000.   TREATMENT OF THE RECEIPT OF LOANS, DEPOSITS, AND PREPAYMENTS.

¶ 7.1100.   Borrowed Funds. If a TP borrows $1,000 from a bank, his assets are increased by that amount; but since the TP's liabilities also are increased by $1,000, there is no increase in the TP's net worth. Even though the loan provides the TP with ready cash, it would be poor tax policy to tax the TP on the borrowed funds since they do not reflect an increase in his wealth. It also would be poor economic policy to discourage the obtaining of loans by taxing the debtor on the amount borrowed. At the very least, if loans were taxed, the debtor would have to be granted a deduction for repayments, which would unduly complicate the administration of the tax. While there is no statutory provision for exclusion, the courts and the Service uniformly have excluded borrowed funds from the debtor's gross income.[1] This exclusion is part of the common law of taxation. It is noteworthy that the exclusion of the loan from income is based on an assumption that the borrower will repay the borrowed amount at a future date.

¶ 7.1200.   Deposits. It has been settled for some time that a transferee of a deposit will not recognize income therefrom if the function of the deposit is to secure against damage to the transferee's property during the term of a lease or other contractual period or to secure the performance by the depositor of some contractually required act. Until a few years ago, the Commissioner maintained that a "deposit" is included in the gross income of a transferee upon receipt if it secures the depositor's obligation to pay for services or goods that the transferee is expected to provide. Rather than treating such transfers as a "deposit," the Commissioner treated them as advance payments for the services or goods.

This matter was resolved by the Supreme Court in its decision in

---

1.   See, e.g., *Commissioner v. Tufts*, 461 U.S. 300, 307 (1983).

Commissioner v. Indianapolis Power & Light Co.,[2] in which the Court rejected the Commissioner's position and provided guidelines for the characterization of such transfers. The Court held that the critical issue is whether the transferred funds constitute security for the performance of an act, or whether the transferred funds constitute a prepayment for services or goods to be received by the "depositor" at some future date. While the former is not income to the transferee, a prepayment (or advance payment) usually is included in the transferee's gross income upon receipt.[3]

Although the distinction between a deposit and a prepayment is not always easy to make, the Supreme Court provided helpful guidelines in *Indianapolis Power*. In *Indianapolis Power*, the TP was an electrical company (a utility) that required customers who failed to meet certain credit standards to deposit funds with the TP (the transferee). About 5% of the TP's customers were required to make that deposit. For some of the years involved, the TP paid no interest to the depositor for the first six months and then paid interest at a 3% rate. After a change of its practice, there were several years in which the TP paid no interest for the first twelve months of a deposit and then paid the depositor interest at a 6% rate. The deposited funds were commingled with the TP's own funds. The depositor was entitled to a return of the deposited funds upon satisfying any one of the following conditions: (1) the depositor subsequently satisfies a credit test; (2) the depositor makes timely payments either for nine consecutive months or ten out of twelve consecutive months; or (3) the depositor discontinues the use of the utility's electricity. The depositor was not obligated to purchase any electricity from the utility. When entitled to a refund of a deposit, the depositor could choose either to have the refund paid in cash or by check, or the depositor could elect to have the refund applied to future bills from the utility. If the depositor defaulted on the payment of a utility bill when the deposit was still in the hands of the TP, the TP had the right to use the deposit to pay the defaulted amount. Any deposit that was left unclaimed for seven years escheated to the State.

The Court held that the deposits that the TP received are not included in the TP's gross income. The Court acknowledged that the deposit gave an economic benefit to the TP since the TP had the use of the deposited funds at less than market interest rates. But, the Court held that a transferee's economic benefit is not sufficient to

---

2.   493 U.S. 203 (1990).

3.   For a limited exception to that rule of inclusion for certain TPs using the accrual method, see Rev. Proc. 2004–34.

characterize a transfer as an advance payment. To be so characterized, the transferee must have "complete dominion" over the transferred funds—i.e., the transferee must have some guarantee that it will be allowed to keep the funds.

¶ 7.1210. Deposit Treated As A Loan. The TP in *Indianapolis Power* paid no interest at all for some months on its use of the funds, and thereafter its interest payments were substantially below market rates. The benefit that the TP obtained thereby was the opportunity to use the deposited funds to produce income at a higher rate than the interest payable on the deposit. The Court deemed that opportunity comparable to what occurs in a typical loan setting—i.e., the borrower is able to produce more income with the borrowed funds than his interest payments. So, the Court held that the tax characterization of the transaction is not determined by the fact that the transferee obtains an economic benefit. The Court also held that the TP's commingling of the deposited funds with its own did not affect the characterization of the deposit; borrowed funds typically are commingled with the borrower's own funds.

The Court stressed that, while a prepayment can secure the payor's performance just as a deposit does, a prepayment does more than that. "It protects against the risk that the purchaser will back out of a deal before the seller performs." When a transfer is a prepayment, the transferee is assured that so long as it fulfills its part of the bargain, the transferred funds are its to keep. In the case of the utility, the TP could not retain the transferred funds permanently unless the depositor used its electricity (which the depositor was not required to do) and either elected to have the TP apply the deposited funds in payment therefor or defaulted on payment so that the TP was entitled to apply the deposit in payment of the defaulted amount. The Court stated:

> The individual who makes an advance payment retains no right to insist upon the return of the funds; so long as the recipient fulfills the terms of the bargain, the money is its to keep. The customer who submits a deposit to the utility, like the lender in the previous hypothetical, retains the right to insist upon repayment in cash; he may *choose* to apply the money to the purchase of electricity, but he assumes no obligation to do so, and the utility therefore acquires no

unfettered "dominion" over the money at the time of receipt. [Emphasis in original.][4]

¶ 7.1220. Tax Treatment of Loans With Inadequate Interest. When funds are borrowed at below market interest rates, there usually will be tax consequences to both the borrower and the lender, but not in all such cases.[5] The tax provision that imposes tax consequences on below market interest rate loans (§ 7872) was adopted in 1984, and the taxable years involved in the *Indianapolis Power* cases preceded that date. Under current law, the deposits that were the subject of that case would constitute a "compensation-related loan" within the meaning of § 7872(c)(1)(B)—i.e., the bargain element in the utility's cost of receiving the economic benefit of the loan would constitute partial consideration for the service that the utility provides to the depositors. As noted below, however, it is likely that the loans involved in the *Indianapolis Power* case would not have caused any tax consequences.

The Proposed Regulations treat a refundable deposit as a loan to the transferee unless the beneficial enjoyment derived from the deposited funds are retained by the transferor—for example, when the deposited funds are required to be held in escrow, to be returned to the depositor if there is no default, and *all* of the interest earned from the escrowed funds is payable to the transferor, the deposit will not be treated as a loan to the transferee. Prop. Reg. § 1.7872–2(b)(1)(iii). Under the facts that occurred in *Indianapolis Power*, the deposit in that case would constitute a loan to the transferee.

Therefore, if the facts of *Indianapolis Power* had occurred after the adoption of § 7872, Prop. Reg. § 1.7872–2(b)(1) would apply § 7872 to the utility company and to the depositors for the period during which the interest rate payable to the depositors (if any) was below a standardized rate of interest called the "applicable Federal rate." However, § 7872(c)(3) provides a *de minimis* exception under which that Code provision does not apply on any day on which the balance of the outstanding loans between the borrower and the lender does not exceed $10,000, provided that

---

4. For a criticism of the Supreme Court's decision, see Klein, *Tailor to the Emperor with No Clothes: The Supreme Court's Tax Rules for Deposits and Advance Payments*, 41 UCLA L. Rev. 1685 (1994).

5. See ¶ **9.4200** *et seq.*

tax avoidance was not a principal purpose of the interest arrangement. It is highly unlikely that any of a utility's depositors would deposit more than that amount, and so § 7872 usually will cause no tax consequences in such cases. But, in commercial settings in which a deposit of a large sum is made or in which a substantial amount of loans between the parties is outstanding, § 7872 may impose tax consequences.

¶ **7.1300. Prepayments.** The general rule is that the receipt of an advanced payment (a prepayment) for services or property must be included in income at the time of receipt. See Treas. Reg. § 1.61–8(b). This rule is subject to a limited exception for certain TPs using the accrual method.[6]

¶ **7.2000. DISCHARGE OF INDEBTEDNESS.** A creditor's discharge of a debtor's pecuniary obligation for less than the full amount that is due increases the debtor's net worth (or decreases the amount of his insolvency). The questions arise whether that increase in the debtor's net worth (or decrease in his insolvency) will cause the debtor to recognize income; and, if so, under what circumstances.

¶ **7.2100. Income to Debtor.** In its decision in *United States v. Kirby Lumber Co.*,[7] the Supreme Court established that the discharge of a debt can constitute income to the debtor. Prior to that decision, there was doubt as to whether a discharge of a debt could cause the debtor to realize income. The Supreme Court's decision that it can constitute income is codified in § 61(a)(12), which expressly includes in gross income the amount of a TP's discharge of indebtedness. A discharge, forgiveness, or cancellation of a debt refers to a creditor's cancellation of all or a portion of a debt without receiving adequate consideration. Several terms are used interchangeably to refer to the elimination or reduction of a debt for inadequate consideration—namely, it is referred to as: (1) discharge of indebtedness, (2) forgiveness of indebtedness or (3) cancellation of indebtedness.

In the title to this chapter, we have chosen to use the term "Cancellation of Debt," but we use that and other terms interchangeably throughout the book. The two most significant statutes that deal with this subject use the term "discharge of indebtedness." See §§ 61(a)(12), 108.

The *Kirby Lumber* decision rested on a net worth analysis—i.e., that the debtor's recognition of income was attributable to the fact that

6. See Rev. Proc. 2004–34.
7. 284 U.S. 1 (1931).

the debtor's net worth was increased. As discussed below, the authors contend that the net worth rationale is flawed and has caused courts to struggle with the application of the cancellation of debt doctrine in subsequent cases.[8]

For purposes of § 108 (the principal statutory provision that deals with discharge of indebtedness income), a "debt" refers to an indebtedness for which the TP is liable or which constitutes an encumbrance on property that the TP holds. § 108(d)(1). Should that statutory definition also be utilized in cases involving the application of a common law rule of discharge of indebtedness income as codified in § 61(a)(12)? See *Zarin v. Commissioner*,[9] in which the Third Circuit, while dividing 2–1 on that issue, held that the definition of debt in § 108(d)(1) also applies to § 61(a)(12).

After the *Kirby Lumber* decision, the courts began to define the circumstances in which a discharge of a debt will constitute income and those in which it will not. Thus, initially, the rules for determining income in this area were court-made; i.e., they were common law rules rather than statutory ones. Over time, Congress adopted statutory provisions some of which codified or modified the common law rules and some of which adopted new rules. The current tax rules for a cancellation of a debt are a mixture of statutory rules and common law rules.

¶ 7.2200. Statutory Rules. In 1939, Congress passed the antecedent of § 108, which was substantially modified in later years especially as a result of the amendments adopted as part of the Bankruptcy Tax Act of 1980 and of the 1986 Tax Reform Act (TRA). Prior to the 1980 amendments, the exclusive function of § 108 was to permit a debtor who *realized* income from a discharge of indebtedness to elect not to *recognize* that income in certain circumstances. If the election were made, the nonrecognition of income was balanced by adjustments required by § 1017 to the basis[10] of property held by the debtor. The 1980 amendments substantially expanded the scope of § 108 so that much (but not all) of what had been treated as unrealized income under the common law rules for a discharge of indebtedness was removed from the common law rules and subjected to special treatment in § 108 itself. The 1980 amendments continued

---

8. As discussed in ¶¶ **7.8000–7.8100.** The rationale that the authors believe to be the correct one is described at ¶ **7.8100.**

9. Discussed at ¶ **7.9000** *et seq.*

10. For the meaning of "basis," see ¶ **1.7300** *et seq.*

the prior law's authorization for a TP to elect nonrecognition of realized income in certain circumstances, but this election was terminated by the 1986 TRA. Thus, after 1986, income realized from a discharge of a debt will be recognized or not according to statutory or common law directions; with one minor exception for certain "qualified real property business indebtedness,"[11] the TP is not granted an election to prevent recognition.

Under the current state of the law, the determination of the income tax consequences of a discharge of indebtedness is determined to a greater extent by statutory rules than was previously so. However, there are a number of common law rules concerning discharge of indebtedness that were not codified or altered by the 1980 and 1986 amendments, and it appears that those common law rules continue to operate. Those common law rules are equally as important as the statutory provisions. Even where statutory rules apply, it is helpful in construing the statute to know the common law rules that were codified or altered by the statute. The discussion below will indicate whether the rules in question are statutory or common law principles.

¶ 7.2300. Distinguish Realization from Recognition and Exclusion from Nonrecognition. In analyzing a discharge of indebtedness, the student should first determine whether income is *realized*. If so, the student should then determine whether the income is recognized. If an item of realized income is not recognized, the student should then consider whether the item is excluded from income or whether it is nonrecognized under some type of deferral arrangement.[12] While it is not essential to make these distinctions, to do so should enhance the student's comprehension of the principles involved.

¶ 7.2310. Illustration 1: Satisfaction at Less than Face Amount. X loans $8,000 to Y who is not engaged in a farming business. Because of Y's subsequent financial difficulties, X accepts $6,000 in full satisfaction of Y's $8,000 debt even though Y is solvent. Y realizes and recognizes income of $2,000 (the amount of debt that was forgiven by X).

¶ 7.2320. Illustration 2: Redemption of Bonds. Win All, Inc. issued $1,000 face amount bonds for which it received $1,000 per

---

11. See ¶ **7.3500.**

12. The meaning of "realization," "recognition," and "exclusion" are discussed at ¶¶ **1.7200–1.7210,** and ¶¶ **1.7400–1.7410.**

bond. One year later, Win All purchased its own bonds on the open market for $950 per bond. At the time of purchase, Win All was solvent. Win All realized and recognized income of $50 per bond since that amount of its debt was, in effect, discharged.

¶ 7.2330. Illustration 3: Expiration of Period of Limitations. X loaned $10,000 to Y, who is not engaged in a farming business, in a bona fide transaction. Four years later, the statute of limitations for X's collection of the loan expired. The expiration of the limitations period provides Y with a valid defense to any claim that X might make for the repayment of the loan. The date on which a liability is terminated turns on the factual issue as to when the debtor no longer intends to pay the debt and the creditor can no longer reasonably expect payment.[13] The expiration of the statute of limitations does not necessarily terminate a debt since the debtor may nevertheless intend to repay it. In the absence of evidence that the debtor intends to repay, however, the expiration of the limitations period will constitute a discharge of the debt.[14] In the instant case, the expiration of the statute of limitations likely will be treated as a discharge of the $10,000 debt, and the rules governing discharge of indebtedness are applicable.

¶ 7.2340. Illustration 4: Prepayment of Mortgage Debt at a Discount. In the year 2014, X owned a personal residence which had a value of $125,000 and was subject to a mortgage debt, the outstanding balance of which was $45,000. X was solvent. The mortgage debt was owed to the Friendly National Bank. X had purchased the property 10 years earlier from Y, and so the mortgage debt was not a purchase money mortgage. The Bank offered to cancel the mortgage debt for a payment of $30,000. X accepted the Bank's offer and paid $30,000 to the Bank in full satisfaction of the debt. X will recognize gross income of $15,000 because the cancellation of the debt at a discount constitutes a discharge of indebtedness of that amount.[15]

If the mortgage debt had been discharged in 2012, X would not have recognized income because of § 108(a)(1)(E) since the debt was a qualified principal residence indebtedness.[16] In that case,

---

13. *Bear Mfg. Co. v. United States*, 430 F.2d 152 (7th Cir. 1970).

14. See *Estate of Bankhead v. Commissioner*, 60 T.C. 535 (1973).

15. *Michaels v. Commissioner*, 87 T.C. 1412 (1986).

16. § 108(h)(2). See ¶ **7.3700**. The provision for qualified principal residence indebtedness expires at the end of 2012.

X's basis in his residence would have been reduced by $15,000. § 108(h)(1).

¶ 7.2400. Acquisition of Debt by Person Related to the Debtor. Section 108(e)(4), which was added to the Code in 1980, treats an acquisition of a debt by a person who is related to the debtor as an acquisition by the debtor himself, and so the acquisition can give rise to discharge of indebtedness income if the price paid is less than the amount owing on the debt. The statute defines who are related persons for this purpose. For example: (1) the spouse, children, grandchildren, and parents of an individual (as well as spouses of the individual's children and grandchildren) are related to that individual [§ 108(e)(4)(B)]; (2) an individual and a corporation more than 50% of the value of whose stock is owned by that individual are related; and (3) a grantor or beneficiary of a trust is related to the fiduciary of that trust. The foregoing is only a short list of related persons. Section 108(e)(4) does not apply if the related party acquires the debt *from* a person who also is related to the debtor. Treas. Reg. § 1.108–2(b).

Presumably, the purpose of this provision is to prevent a debtor from circumventing the discharge of indebtedness rule by having the debt acquired by a person who is closely related to the debtor. While, in such a case, the debtor remains liable for the repayment of the entire debt, the amount of "repayment" that is in excess of the amount paid by the related person to purchase the debt in substance may represent a gift to the related person or a contribution to its capital.

The problem is that, although the debtor is treated as if he acquired the debt, the debt still is outstanding in the hands of the related party (the holder of the debt). How is the outstanding debt to be treated? What treatment is to be accorded to the debtor's subsequent actual satisfaction of the debt? If the related party sells the debt to a third person, how is that sale to be treated? These and other questions have been answered by Treasury in the regulation that it promulgated under § 108 on December 28, 1992. See Treas. Reg. § 1.108–2.

¶ 7.2410. Direct and Indirect Acquisition Of Debt. When a debt is acquired by a person who is related to the debtor, that is referred to as a "direct acquisition." What if a debt is acquired by an unrelated person (referred to as the "holder" of the debt) who subsequently becomes related to the debtor? If the holder acquired the debt in anticipation of becoming related to the debtor, that is referred to as an "indirect acquisition." Treas. Reg. § 1.108–2(c). The regulations provide criteria for determining whether a debt was acquired by a holder in anticipation of becoming related to the debtor, including safe harbors for excluding the holder from indirect acquisition treatment. The regulations also describe the tax consequences that flow from an indirect acquisition. Treas. Reg. § 1.108–2.

¶ 7.2500. **Spurious Discharge of a Debt.** As noted above, a discharge of a debt occurs only to the extent that the debt is canceled for inadequate consideration. If adequate consideration is given for the cancellation, the debt is satisfied (as contrasted to forgiven). A "spurious" discharge of indebtedness is a cancellation of a debt that appears superficially to be a discharge but in fact is made for valuable consideration. For example, if a debt were canceled in consideration of services performed for the creditor by the debtor or in payment for property acquired by the creditor from the debtor, the cancellation of the debt would not constitute a discharge covered by § 108 or by the common law rules governing discharge of indebtedness. Instead, the cancellation constitutes consideration paid for the services or the property received by the creditor—i.e., the debt was satisfied. The amount of such cancelled debt will constitute an amount realized by the debtor for the sale of services or property.[17]

In some cases, a debt may be canceled in part as consideration for value received by the creditor and in part as a discharge of a portion of the debt. Only the latter portion of the canceled debt is covered by § 108 and by the previously mentioned common law rules.

¶ 7.2600. **Student Loans.** The discharge of *certain* student loans will not cause the debtor to recognize gross income if the discharge is pursuant to a provision in the loan agreement that all or a portion of the debt would be canceled if the student worked for a specified period of time in certain professions for any of a broad class of employers. § 108(f). To qualify, the purpose of the loan must be to assist the student in attending a qualified educational institution, and the lender must be an entity that is one of those listed in § 108(f)(2).

¶ 7.2700. **Modification of the Terms of a Debt Instrument.** If the amount of principal required by a debt instrument to be paid to a

---

17. Treas. Reg. § 1.61–12(a). See ¶ **7.3620.**

creditor is reduced, then the reduction *may* cause discharge of indebtedness income to the debtor. But, regardless of whether the amount of principal that is payable is altered, what if other terms of the debt instrument are changed? For example, what if the interest rate or the maturity date is changed? Changes that do not lower the amount of principal payable by the debtor will not cause discharge of indebtedness income, but they may cause other tax consequences.

Treas. Reg. § 1.1001–1(a) states that an exchange of one item of property for another that differs *materially*, either in kind or in extent, will trigger realization of gain or loss. In *Cottage Savings Ass'n v. Commissioner*,[18] the Supreme Court sustained the validity of that regulation and adopted a very broad construction as to what constitutes a *material* difference in exchanged properties. In *Cottage Savings*, a TP was permitted to realize and recognize a loss on what amounted to an exchange of participating interests in 252 residential mortgages for participating interests in 305 different residential mortgages. While the mortgages were secured by different properties and had different obligors, they were economically equivalent interests. The Supreme Court held that to constitute materially different properties, it was necessary only that the exchanged properties "embody legally distinct entitlements."[19] The Court held that the differences in obligors and security for the two sets of mortgages were sufficient to satisfy that requirement.

In Treas. Reg. § 1.1001–3, expanding on the *Cottage Savings* decision, Treasury maintains that a substantial modification of a debt instrument represents an exchange of the old instrument for a new debt instrument and can trigger realization and recognition of a gain or loss. With one exception, a "modification" refers to any alteration of a legal right or obligation of the issuer or the holder of the debt instrument. Treas. Reg. § 1.1001–3(c). With some exceptions, a change of rights or obligations that occurs by reason of the terms of the debt instrument itself will not constitute a modification. Id. A modification will not result in there being a constructive exchange of debt instruments unless the modification is "substantial," and the regulation provides guidance as to what constitutes a "substantial" change.[20]

18.   499 U.S. 554 (1991).

19.   *Id.* at 566.

20.   See also, PLR 9819043 for examples of changes that were not deemed substantial. The exchange or modification of debt instruments is discussed at ¶¶ **24.1700–24.1710**.

¶ **7.3000. EXCLUSION OR NONRECOGNITION FROM IN-COME.** Some of the exclusions or nonrecognition of income from discharge of indebtedness are described below.

¶ **7.3100. Lost Deduction.** If a debtor would have been allowed an income tax deduction had the debtor paid a debt which instead was discharged (and so was never paid), the discharge of the debt is excluded from the debtor's income by § 108(e)(2). This exclusion from income was added by the 1980 amendments to § 108, and it constitutes a true exclusion in that there is no adjustment of basis or other tax attributes because of it.

¶ **7.3200. Rationale.** When a debtor recognizes income from the discharge of a debt, the substance of the transaction is that the debtor received from the creditor cash equal to the amount discharged and then returned that cash to the creditor in payment of the debt. Thus, while the debtor should recognize income for the amount of cash constructively received from the creditor, the debtor should be permitted a deduction to the extent that the payment of the debt would be deductible. If the payment of the debt would be fully deductible, the amount of the constructive deduction equals the income recognized by virtue of the discharge of the debt; and, so far as the debtor is concerned, the income and deduction from the transaction is a wash. For that reason, the Code excludes the discharge of deductible debts from the debtor's income and thereby reflects the fact that the debtor does not have any net income from the transaction.

What if the payment of the debt would be an itemized deduction, which deductions are subject to limitation on their deductibility? The statute, § 108(e)(2), requires only that the payment of the liability would give rise to a deduction, and the statute does not limit that provision to nonitemized deductions. The authors believe that the exclusion of § 108(e)(2) applies regardless of whether the deduction would be itemized or not. However, as of this writing, there is no definitive authority for the resolution of this question.

¶ **7.3300. Insolvency of Debtor.** Prior to the 1980 amendments to § 108, a debtor realized no income from the discharge of a debt if the debtor was insolvent immediately after the debt was discharged. Originally, this was a common law rule, but the current version is a statutory replacement of the common law. In this context, a person is insolvent if the total of his outstanding liabilities exceed the total value of his assets. In determining insolvency, there is authority that assets of the TP that are exempted by state (or federal) law from the claims of creditors (e.g., a homestead may be exempt) are not taken into account.[21] For example, in one case, the Tax Court ignored the exempted assets because those assets were not "freed" as a consequence of the discharge of a debt.[22]

If a debtor was insolvent before the debt was discharged but became solvent as a consequence of that discharge, under the common law rule, the debtor would realize income only to the extent of his solvency.[23] As noted below, that treatment continues to apply under the statutory replacement.

Under the common law (but not under current statutory law), no adjustment was made to the tax attributes of the debtor when a discharged debt was excluded from income because of insolvency. The common law rules were supplanted by the 1980 amendments of § 108 and § 1017 which were expanded to deal with the discharge of the debts of a bankrupt or insolvent debtor. § 108(e)(1). Some of those statutory rules are described below.

   ¶ 7.3310. Nonrecognition of Income. If a debt is discharged in a bankruptcy proceeding or if the debtor is insolvent immediately after the discharge occurs, the amount discharged is excluded from the debtor's income by § 108(a)(1)(A) and (B). If the debt was not discharged in a bankruptcy proceeding and if the debtor was insolvent before the discharge took place but becomes solvent by virtue of it, the debtor will recognize income to the extent of his solvency immediately after the discharge of the debt, provided that no other exception to income recognition is applicable. Section 108(a)(3) accomplishes that result by limiting the amount of discharge of a debt that is not recognized because of the insolvency exception to the amount by which the debtor was insolvent immediately prior to the discharge.

   The statute adopts the same meaning of insolvency as was used in the common law rule—namely, the excess of a debtor's liabilities over the fair market value of his assets. § 108(d)(3). In order to include contingent liabilities, such as guarantees, a TP must show, by a preponderance of the evidence, that he will be called

---

21. *Hunt v. Commissioner*, 58 T.C.M. 965 (1989).

22. Id. For the treatment of nonrecourse debts in determining a debtor's solvency, see ¶ **7.3330**.

23. *Lakeland Grocery Co. v. Commissioner*, 36 B.T.A. 289 (1937).

upon to pay the contingent obligation.[24] For this purpose, it is an all or nothing proposition. If the TP can carry the burden, he may count the entire face value of the liability in the § 108(a)(3) formula. If not, the contingent obligation is not counted as a liability of the TP.

The statutory rules depart from the common law approach by requiring adjustments in the amount of discharged debt that was excluded from the debtor's income because of his insolvency or bankruptcy to the favorable tax attributes of the debtor.[25] This treatment of requiring adjustments transforms the common law insolvency exception, which was a true exclusion from income, into a nonrecognition provision.

¶ 7.3320.   **Reason for the Insolvency Exception.** When a TP is insolvent, a creditor may agree to discharge all or part of a debt in order to permit the TP to obtain a "fresh start." A creditor might be motivated to do that in the hope of obtaining additional business from the debtor if the latter recovers and becomes successful, or the creditor may simply be able to obtain a greater return from a voluntary arrangement than he could obtain by imposing involuntary bankruptcy on the debtor. The purpose of the insolvency exception is to preserve a debtor's "fresh start" by relieving him of the burden of taxation that otherwise would be imposed on the discharge of his debt.[26] The imposition of a tax burden on the canceled debt of an insolvent debtor would simply increase the debtor's insolvency and therefore deter creditors from agreeing to debt reduction arrangements.[27] However, to the extent that the discharge of a debt renders the debtor solvent, the debtor has assets available to pay the tax on an equal amount of debt that was forgiven; and so, Congress has taxed the amount of discharged debt that increases a debtor's solvency.

24.   *Merkel v. Commissioner*, 192 F.3d 844 (9th Cir. 1999), *affirming* 109 T.C. 463 (1997).

25.   The adjustments will reduce positive tax attributes of the debtor in the manner described at ¶¶ **7.3400–7.3480**.

26.   H.R. Rep. No. 833, 96th Cong., 2d Sess. 7, 9 (1980); S. Rep. No. 1035, 96th Cong., 2d Sess. 8, 10 (1980).

27.   In the case of a discharge in a bankruptcy proceeding, there is no concern that taxing the discharge would deter creditors from agreeing to a reduction of the debt since the discharge is mandated by law. However, to tax the discharge would conflict with the policy underlying bankruptcy law to permit the bankrupt to wipe the slate clean and start anew. The exclusion from income is in deference to bankruptcy law's policy.

Instead of taxing the amount of discharged debt that increases a debtor's solvency, Congress could have chosen to tax the entire amount of the discharged debt, subject to the limitation that the tax imposed cannot exceed the amount by which the debtor became solvent. One can only speculate as to why that approach was not adopted. It would be somewhat more difficult to administer than the current treatment. Also, Congress may have wished to allow the debtor to remain solvent after payment of taxes since the motivation for a creditor to forgive some of the debt may have been to provide some solvency for the debtor, which solvency may be necessary to provide the debtor with a reasonable prospect of building a successful business.

¶ **7.3330. Nonrecourse Debts.** A nonrecourse debt is an indebtedness which is secured by property of the debtor, but for which the debtor has no personal obligation (i.e., if the debtor defaults, the creditor can collect only by levying on the security and cannot require any payments from the debtor). For the purposes of the discharge of indebtedness rules, a nonrecourse debt that is secured by a TP's property is treated as a debt of the TP. § 108(d)(1)(B). The discharge of a nonrecourse debt can cause recognition of discharge of indebtedness income, and this is so even when the amount of the nonrecourse debt exceeds the value of the property securing it.[28]

In determining whether and to what extent a debtor is insolvent, should the amount by which a nonrecourse debt exceeds the fair market value of the property that secures that debt (hereinafter, that portion of a nonrecourse debt is sometimes referred to as the "excess nonrecourse debt") be treated as a liability of the debtor? Since the creditor cannot collect the excess nonrecourse debt unless its security increases in value, that portion of the debt has no effect on the debtor's solvency and generally is ignored by the Commissioner in determining the extent to which a debtor is solvent or insolvent. However, if all or a portion of the excess nonrecourse debt itself is discharged, it would contravene the policy of the insolvency exception to ignore, in determining the extent of the debtor's insolvency, the amount of the liability that was discharged. Accordingly, the Commissioner has ruled that the excess of a nonrecourse debt over the fair market value of the security generally is ignored in determining the debtor's solvency;

---

28. Rev. Rul. 91–31.

but if all or a portion of the nonrecourse debt itself is discharged, the amount of such excess nonrecourse debt that is discharged will be counted as a liability of the debtor.[29]

¶ 7.3340. Illustration 1: Insolvent Before and After Discharge. *A* had assets with an aggregate value of $100,000, and *A*'s liabilities (none of which were nonrecourse debts) totaled $142,000. One of *A*'s creditors agreed to accept a $10,000 payment to cancel $50,000 of *A*'s liability. *A* was insolvent both before and after the discharge took place; after the discharge, *A* had assets of $90,000 and liabilities of $92,000. Although $40,000 of *A*'s liabilities was discharged, thus triggering realization of $40,000 of income, *A* did not *recognize* any income. § 108(a). Some of *A*'s tax attributes may be reduced as a consequence of that nonrecognition of income.[30]

¶ 7.3350. Illustration 2: Solvent After Discharge. The same facts as those stated in **¶ 7.3340** except that $60,000 of *A*'s liability was canceled for the $10,000 payment. As a consequence of the discharge, *A* realized income of $50,000, but he recognized income only to the extent that he became solvent. After the discharge, *A* had assets of $90,000 and liabilities of $82,000, and so he became solvent to the extent of $8,000. Therefore, *A* recognized income of $8,000. The remaining $42,000 of discharged debt does not cause income recognition, but can cause a reduction of tax attributes.

Stating it differently and in accord with statutory language, the amount of discharged debt ($50,000) that is not recognized as income cannot exceed the amount by which *A* was insolvent before the discharge took place ($42,000). So, $42,000 of the discharged debt is not recognized as income, and $8,000 is recognized.

¶ 7.3360. Illustration 3: Nonrecourse Debt that is Secured by Property with a Greater Value than the Amount of the Debt. *B* owns a building with a fair market value of $300,000. The building is subject to a mortgage in the amount of $250,000, and *B* has no personal liability to repay that mortgage debt (i.e., the mortgage debt is a nonrecourse debt).[31] None of B's debts are

---

29. Rev. Rul. 92–53.

30. See ¶ **7.3400** et. seq.

31. The meanings of "recourse debts" and "nonrecourse debts" are set forth in ¶¶ **24.1511–24.1511–1A.**

purchase-money debts. *B* owns other assets with a value of $80,000, and *B* is personally liable for debts (i.e., recourse debts) totaling $200,000. A creditor of *B* cancels $62,000 of *B*'s recourse debt for a payment of $12,000, and that constitutes a discharge of $50,000 of debt. Since the amount of *B*'s nonrecourse debt is less than the value of its security, it is treated as a liability for purposes of determining *B*'s insolvency. Therefore, immediately before the discharge, *B* was insolvent in the amount of $70,000. None of the discharged debt of $50,000 is included in *B*'s income, but it can reduce his tax attributes.

¶ 7.3370. Illustration 4: Nonrecourse Debt that is Greater in Amount than the Property Securing It. The same facts as those stated in **¶ 7.3360** except that: (1) the amount of the nonrecourse debt that is secured by the building is $450,000, and (2) the value of *B*'s other assets (i.e., assets other than the building) is $180,000. To the extent that the nonrecourse debt exceeds the $300,000 value of the building (it exceeds that value by $150,000), it is not treated as a liability of *B* for purposes of applying the insolvency exception. So, before the $50,000 discharge of *B*'s recourse debt took place, *B* had assets valued at $480,000, and his liabilities totaled $500,000 ($200,000 recourse debts and only $300,000 of the nonrecourse debt is counted as a liability). Since *B* was insolvent in the amount of $20,000 prior to the discharge of $50,000 of his recourse debts, $20,000 of that discharge is not included in his income, and only the remaining $30,000 constitutes recognized income.

¶ 7.3380. Illustration 5. Discharge of Nonrecourse Debt. The same facts as those stated in **¶ 7.3370** except that, in addition to the discharge of $50,000 of *B*'s recourse debts and on the same date, the creditor of the nonrecourse debt forgave $150,000 of that debt. Consequently, after that discharge of $150,000 of the nonrecourse debt, the outstanding balance of the nonrecourse debt ($300,000) equaled the fair market value of the building that secured it. The entire amount of the nonrecourse debt that was discharged was the portion of the debt that exceeded the value of the building that secured it. If the excess of the nonrecourse debt over the value of the security were not treated as a liability of *B*, the discharge of that amount would cause *B* to recognize income of $150,000 in addition to the $30,000 of income that *B* recognized because of the discharge of $50,000 of recourse debts. [If the $150,000 excess nonrecourse debt is ignored in determining *B*'s insolvency, *B* would have been insolvent in the amount of only

$20,000 prior to the discharge of $200,000 of debts ($50,000 recourse debts and $150,000 nonrecourse debts), and so *B* would recognize $180,000 of income from those discharges. But after the discharges were completed, *B* would have only $30,000 excess of asset value over his liabilities with which to pay the tax on that income—i.e., the total value of his assets would be $468,000, and the total amount of his liabilities would be $438,000. Clearly, to include $180,000 in *B*'s income would contravene the congressional policy to limit the amount of income recognized to the amount of net asset value that is available to pay the income tax. To prevent that from occurring, the Commissioner ruled in Rev. Rul. 92–53 that the amount of excess nonrecourse debt that is discharged is treated as a liability of the debtor. Accordingly, since the entire $150,000 excess nonrecourse debt was discharged, that entire amount is treated as a liability of *B*. The amount of *B*'s insolvency prior to the discharges, therefore, was $170,000; and so that amount of the $200,000 discharged debts is not recognized as income. Only the remaining $30,000 of discharged debts is recognized as income.

¶ 7.3400. Reduction of Tax Attributes. After the taxable income of the debtor for the year of discharge is determined [§ 108(b)(4)(A)], the amount of discharged debt that is excluded from the debtor's income because of insolvency, or bankruptcy, or as a qualified farm indebtedness, causes the following reductions of the debtor's tax attributes in the order indicated (subject to an election of the debtor to reduce his basis in depreciable property and in realty held for sale to customers in the ordinary course of business in lieu of the adjustments to other favorable tax attributes).[32] The discharge of a debt that is excluded from income because of insolvency, bankruptcy, or as a qualified farm indebtedness is referred to below as a "qualified discharged debt."

¶ 7.3410. Net Operating Loss. The debtor's net operating loss[33] for the taxable year and any net operating loss carryover to that taxable year are reduced dollar for dollar for the amount of qualified discharged debt that was excluded from income. § 108(b)(1), (2)(A), (3)(A). An adjustment is made first to any loss incurred in the taxable year and then any remaining adjustments

---

32. See **¶ 7.3480.**

33. The meaning of "net operating loss" and the operation of the rules for carrying forward and back that loss and deducting it in other taxable years are described briefly in **¶¶ 23.7000–23.7300.**

are applied to carryover losses incurred in prior years in the order of years in which they were incurred. § 108(b)(4)(B).

¶ 7.3420. General Business Credits. General business tax credits and credit carryovers to the taxable year (allowable under § 38) are reduced on a ratio of 33 1/3 cents for each $1 of qualified discharged debt that was excluded from income and was not applied as an adjustment to the debtor's net operating losses as described in ¶ **7.3410**. § 108(b)(2)(B), (3)(B).

¶ 7.3430. Minimum Tax Credit. The minimum tax credit[34] allowable under § 53(b) is reduced on the ratio of 33 1/3 cents for each $1 of qualified discharged debt that was excluded from income and that did not cause a reduction of the tax attributes listed above. § 108(b)(2)(C), (3)(B).

¶ 7.3440. Capital Loss. The debtor's capital loss for the taxable year and any capital loss carryover to such year is reduced dollar for dollar by any remainder of the qualified discharged debt that was excluded from income. § 108(b)(2)(D). An adjustment is made first to capital losses incurred in the taxable year and then any remaining adjustment is applied to carryover capital losses incurred in prior years in the order of years incurred. § 108(b)(4)(B).

¶ 7.3450. Basis of Property. The next tax attribute to be reduced (dollar for dollar) is the basis of property held by the debtor at the beginning of the taxable year following the year of the qualified discharge of debt. §§ 108(b)(2)(E), 1017(a).[35] If a TP has more than one type of property, the ordering in which basis reduction will take place is described in Treas. Reg. § 1.1017–1. Subject to those ordering rules, the property whose basis is to be reduced includes all of the debtor's property (except for certain "exempt property" of an individual [§§ 108(d)(10), 1017(c)]); it is *not* limited to depreciable property or to realty held for sale to customers. However, when a discharge occurs while the TP is insolvent or in a Title 11 case, § 1017(b)(2) provides a special rule for the reduction of basis pursuant to § 108(b)(2)(E); namely, the amount of reduction of basis cannot exceed the difference between the aggregate bases of the properties held by the debtor immedi-

---

34. The minimum tax credit is discussed at ¶ **28.6000**.

35. For the tax treatment of the subsequent disposition of property whose basis was reduced pursuant to § 1017 see ¶¶ **26.3200, 26.3231**.

ately after the discharge over the aggregate of the debtor's liabilities at that time.

¶ 7.3460. Passive Activity Loss and Credit Carryovers. The carryover under § 469(b) of an unused passive activity loss or credit is the next tax attribute to be reduced. § 108(b)(2)(F). The carryover of such losses is reduced dollar for dollar for any remainder of the excluded qualified discharged debt, but the carryover of a passive activity credit is reduced on a ratio of 33 1/3 cents for each dollar of remaining excluded qualified discharged debt. § 108(b)(3).

¶ 7.3470. Foreign Tax Credit. Finally, any remaining amount of the qualified discharged debt will reduce the debtor's foreign tax credit [§ 27] for the taxable year and the foreign tax credit carryover to that taxable year. § 108(b)(2)(G). This adjustment is made on the ratio of 33 1/3 cents for each $1 of remaining discharged debt. § 108(b)(3)(B).

¶ 7.3480. Election to Prevent Reduction of Net Operating Loss, Capital Loss, Credits and Credit Carryovers. In lieu of all or any portion of the adjustments to be made to the debtor's tax attributes, as described above, the debtor can elect instead to have reduced (dollar for dollar) the basis of depreciable property held by the debtor at the beginning of the taxable year following the year of discharge. § 108(b)(5). If this election is made, the reduction in basis is not limited to the difference between the aggregate bases and the aggregate liabilities of the properties held by the debtor immediately after discharge. § 1017(b)(2). The debtor is permitted to elect to treat as depreciable property certain realty which is held by the debtor for sale to customers in the ordinary course of the debtor's trade or business. § 1017(b)(3)(E). To the extent that the discharged debt reduces the debtor's basis in his depreciable property, that amount of the discharged debt will not affect the other tax attributes of the debtor. § 108(b)(5)(C).[36]

¶ 7.3490. Exclusion Versus Nonrecognition. As noted in ¶ 7.3100, the statutory exclusion from income of discharged debts of an insolvent or bankrupt debtor actually is a nonrecognition provision because of the adjustments that are required to be made to certain favorable tax attributes of the debtor. However, if the

36. For the tax treatment of the subsequent disposition of property whose basis has been reduced pursuant to § 1017, see ¶¶ **26.3200–26.3231.**

amount of the tax attributes of the debtor that can be reduced are less than the discharged debt, the debtor can nevertheless exclude all of the discharged debt from his income. To the extent that the amount of the discharged debt causes no adverse tax consequence to the debtor, the exclusion of that portion of the debt from the debtor's income constitutes a true exclusion as contrasted to a nonrecognition provision.

¶ 7.3500. **Qualified Farm Indebtedness and Qualified Real Property Business Indebtedness.** Subject to certain requirements, a TP does not recognize income from the discharge of a debt that constitutes "qualified farm indebtedness." § 108(a)(1)(C). A "qualified farm indebtedness" is a debt that was incurred directly in connection with the TP's operation of a farming business and which satisfies certain conditions specified in § 108(g). To the extent that income from a discharge of a qualified farm indebtedness is not recognized, the TP's tax attributes will be reduced in the identical manner that is described above[37] for the reduction of tax attributes due to nonrecognition granted for insolvency or bankruptcy. § 108(b).

A TP (other than a C corporation) also can elect not to recognize income from the discharge of so-called "qualified real property business indebtedness." § 108(a)(1)(D). Qualified real property business indebtedness refers to debt that was assumed or incurred by the TP in connection with real property used in a trade or business and that is secured by that real property and that meets certain other requirements. The term does not include qualified farm indebtedness, and the exclusion from income applies only if the TP elects it. The amount excluded from income will reduce the basis of depreciable real property of the TP. § 108(c)(1). No other tax attributes are reduced. Subject to other limits, this provision is applicable only to the extent that the principal of a debt is greater than the value of the realty securing it.

To the extent that the TP is insolvent, the insolvency exclusion takes precedence over both the qualified farm exclusion and the qualified real property business exclusion. § 108(a)(2)(B).

¶ 7.3600. **Purchase–Money Debt Reduction.** If the purchaser of property incurs a debt *to the seller* arising from the purchase of that property, a subsequent discharge of all or a portion of that debt

---

37. See ¶¶ 7.3400–7.3480.

which otherwise would have caused the debtor to realize income will not cause income to the debtor. Instead, the reduction of the debt will be treated as a reduction of the purchase price of the property and thus will reduce the purchaser's basis in that property. § 108(e)(5). This statutory provision is essentially a codification of the previously existing common law rule. This treatment of a discharge of a purchase-money debt does not apply to a discharge that takes place in a bankruptcy proceeding or when the debtor is insolvent; in those cases, the normal treatment of bankruptcy and insolvency discharges is applicable. § 108(e)(5)(B).

When property is purchased with the proceeds of a loan that was borrowed from a person other than the seller and is secured by the acquired property, a subsequent discharge of all or part of that nonrecourse debt (which does not involve a transfer of the property) will cause discharge of indebtedness income to the TP unless one of the statutory exceptions (such as insolvency) is applicable. Since the debt is not owed to the seller, § 108(e)(5) is inapplicable.[38] A statutory exception that might apply is § 108(a)(1)(E) for qualified principal residence indebtedness that is discharged prior to January 1, 2013.[39]

A debtor can have discharge of indebtedness income even if the amount of a nonrecourse debt that is discharged exceeds the fair market value of the property securing it. For the extent to which a nonrecourse debt is treated as a liability for the purpose of applying the insolvency exception, see ¶¶ **7.3330** and **7.3360** to **7.3380**.

> **¶ 7.3610. Illustration 1: Genuine Discharge.** *X* sells an apartment building to *Y* for $1,000,000. *Y* pays *X* $200,000 cash and assumes an outstanding first mortgage of $650,000. *Y* gives *X* his personal note for the $150,000 difference and secures the debt with a second mortgage on the building. Subsequently, a dispute arises between *Y* and *X* as to certain representations made by *X* as to the quality of the wiring in the building. In settlement of that dispute, *X* cancels $20,000 of *Y*'s personal obligation to him, thereby reducing *Y*'s debt to $130,000. At the time of the discharge, *Y* was solvent. The cancellation of part of *Y*'s debt constitutes a reduction of the purchase price for the building and does not constitute income to *Y*. § 108(e)(5).

> **¶ 7.3620. Illustration 2: Spurious Discharge.** The same facts apply as in ¶ **7.3610** except that there was no dispute concerning

---

38. See Rev. Rul. 91–31; *Preslar v. Commissioner*, 167 F.3d 1323 (10th Cir. 1999).

39. See ¶ **7.3700.**

the representations that X made. Instead, X canceled $20,000 of Y's debt to compensate Y for personal services that Y had performed for X. The cancellation of $20,000 of Y's debt is a spurious discharge[40] and is not covered by § 108. The cancellation of the debt will constitute income to Y as compensation for personal services.

¶ 7.3700. Home Mortgage Debt. Any discharge of qualified principal residence indebtedness that occurs prior to January 1, 2013, is excluded from the TP's income. § 108(a)(1)(E). Qualified principal residence indebtedness is acquisition indebtedness within the meaning of § 163(h)(3)(B) (the provision that allows a TP to deduct home mortgage interest)[41] except that § 108 increases the limitation amount to two million dollars. § 108(h)(2). Principal residence has the same meaning as when it is used in § 121 (the provision that allows a TP to exclude gain from the sale of a principal residence). Any amount excluded under this provision is applied to reduce (but not below zero) the basis that the TP has in the principal residence. § 108(h)(1).

This exclusion is useful in that it can apply to a discharge of a mortgage debt obtained from a third party in acquiring a principal residence whereas § 108(e)(5) would not apply to a discharge of that mortgage indebtedness since it is not a purchase money debt (i.e., the loan was not made to the TP by the seller of the property).[42]

¶ 7.4000. DISCHARGE AS A GIFT. A discharge of a debt might constitute a gift[43] and thus be exempted from income under § 102. The initial response of the Supreme Court was to treat a debt cancellation as a gift where a creditor collected the maximum amount that appeared feasible.[44] However, the Court changed its position and subsequently held that a discharge of a debt under such circumstances will yield gross income to the debtor.[45] Consequently, a discharge of a debt in a normal commercial setting is no longer likely to be treated as a nontaxable gift. Where the discharge is not in a commercial setting, as in the cancella-

40. The meaning of "spurious discharge" is set forth in **¶ 7.2500.** See Treas. Reg. § 1.61–12(a).

41. See Chapter **Sixteen.**

42. See ¶ **7.2340.**

43. For the definition of "gift" for income tax purposes, see Chapter **Six.**

44. *Helvering v. American Dental Co.*, 318 U.S. 322 (1943).

45. *Commissioner v. Jacobson*, 336 U.S. 28 (1949).

tion of a debt owed by one member of a family to another, the discharge may be construed as a gift.

¶ **7.5000.   CONTRIBUTION TO A CORPORATION'S CAPITAL.** A person's contribution to a corporation of which the person is a shareholder may constitute a contribution to the capital of the corporation and as such is excluded from the corporation's income by § 118. This exclusion of such contributions is similar in some respects to the exclusion of gifts from the income of a donee by § 102. Just as a discharge of indebtedness that constitutes a gift typically is excluded from the debtor's income, so one might expect the same treatment for a discharge of a corporation's debt to its shareholder where the discharge constitutes a contribution by the shareholder to the capital of the corporation. In many circumstances, such a discharge of a corporation's indebtedness will not cause income to the corporation.

A difficulty arises, however, where a corporation which reports its income on the accrual method has accrued and deducted an obligation to a cash method shareholder who has not included that item in his income because of his method of accounting (e.g., where a corporation has deducted accrued but unpaid salary to a cash method shareholder-employee). If the shareholder subsequently discharges the corporation's debt, there would be a windfall to the TPs unless either the corporation is required to recognize income (under a tax benefit concept)[46] or the shareholder is required to recognize income because of having essentially utilized his previously unpaid claim against the corporation as a contribution to the corporation's capital and thus derived an economic benefit from his claim. The Tax Court held, however, that neither the corporation nor the shareholder recognized income in such circumstance, and the Fifth Circuit affirmed the Tax Court's decision as to the corporation (the Government having failed to appeal the decision concerning the shareholder).[47] The congressional response to this problem is described below.[48]

¶ **7.5100.   Statutory Treatment.** Congress addressed this problem when it amended § 108 in 1980. In effect, § 108(e)(6) provides that a shareholder's discharge of a corporation's debt will not be excluded from the corporation's income under § 118 to the extent that the debt exceeds the shareholder's basis therein. Thus, to the extent that

46.   The tax benefit rule is described in Chapter **Five.**

47.   *Putoma Corp. v. Commissioner*, 66 T.C. 652 (1976), aff'd 601 F.2d 734 (5th Cir. 1979); see ¶ **14.2600.**

48.   See ¶¶ **7.5100–7.5200.**

the shareholder has not taken the debt into income or otherwise obtained a basis therein, the corporation will have a discharge of indebtedness which typically will be included in its gross income if it is solvent. Of course, if the corporation reports on the cash method so that it had not previously taken a deduction for the debt, and if a deduction would be allowable to the corporation on payment of the debt, the discharge of the debt will *not* cause the corporation to recognize income because of the exclusion in § 108(e)(2).

¶ 7.5200. Corporation's Satisfaction of Debt With Its Own Stock. When a corporation issues its own stock to a creditor in satisfaction of a debt, the corporation is treated as having satisfied the debt by the payment of an amount of cash equal to the fair market value of its stock. § 108(e)(8). So, the corporation will have discharge of indebtedness income to the extent of the difference between the principal amount of the debt and the value of the corporation's stock. However, if the distribution to the creditor is made in connection with a Title 11 case (i.e., a bankruptcy case), the debtor corporation will not recognize income because of the exception in § 108(a)(1)(A). Similarly, even if the distribution is not made in connection with a Title 11 case, if the debtor corporation is insolvent, it will not recognize discharge of indebtedness income to the extent of its insolvency. § 108(a)(1)(B), (3).[49] Of course, certain favorable tax attributes of the debtor corporation will be reduced by § 108(b) to the extent that the corporation's discharge of indebtedness income is not recognized.[50]

The same rules as those described above apply to a partnership's transfer of a capital or profits interest in the partnership to a creditor in satisfaction of a debt. § 108(e)(8). The partnership will have discharge of indebtedness income to the extent that the amount of the debt exceeds the fair market value of the interest that was transferred to the creditor.

If a corporation's debt is held by its shareholders in the same proportion as the corporation's stock is held, and if the stock distributed in cancellation of that debt is distributed pro rata to the corporation's shareholders, there is a question whether § 108(e)(8) will apply. The authors believe that, in such a case, the distribution should be treated as a stock dividend coupled with a cancellation of the corporation's debt. If so, the stock dividend usually will be

49. See ¶ **7.3310.**
50. See ¶ **7.3400** *et seq.*

excluded from the shareholder's income by § 305, and the cancellation of the corporation's debt will be determined by § 108(e)(6).[51]

A debt instrument of a corporation may be exchanged for stock of the same corporation pursuant to a conversion provision or to a recapitalization. There is a question whether § 108(e)(8) will apply to such an exchange.

¶ 7.6000. TAX BENEFIT RULE. When an accrual method TP is allowed a deduction for an accrued but unpaid expense, the subsequent discharge of that debt may cause the TP to recognize income under the tax benefit doctrine[52] even when the discharge would not otherwise have caused the debtor to recognize income because of the transactional view.[53] However, if the TP had not derived a tax benefit from all or part of the deduction previously allowed him, then all or a portion of the discharged debt will be excluded from the TP's gross income under § 111.[54] If the discharge of the TP's debt was gratuitous, there may be no income to the debtor even though the tax benefit rule would otherwise have caused the TP to recognize income from the recovery of the debt.[55] As noted in ¶ **7.5100**, in 1980 Congress dealt with this problem as it arises in connection with contributions to a corporation's capital. In so doing, Congress indicated in the legislative history to the 1980 amendments that it was acting in response to the *Putoma* decision which involved a contribution to capital. While a similar problem can arise where a cash method creditor makes a gift by discharging the deductible obligation of an accrual method debtor, Congress did not expressly deal with that problem. It remains to be seen whether the courts will extend the policy evidenced by § 108(e)(6) to gifts despite the failure of Congress to so provide.

¶ 7.7000. TRANSACTIONAL VIEW. In determining whether the amount of a discharged debt will be included in gross income, the courts should examine the entire transaction commencing with the creation of the debt, and the debtor will not be deemed to realize income unless it is apparent that the entire transaction resulted in a gain to him. This view is sometimes referred to as the "transactional view" or the "transac-

---

51. See ¶ **7.5100**.

52. See Chapter **Five**.

53. See ¶ **7.7000** for a discussion of the transactional view.

54. See Rev. Rul. 67–200.

55. Compare *Putoma Corp.* in ¶ **7.5000** excluding a gratuitous cancellation from income, with Rev. Rul. 76–316, where the Commissioner held that the tax benefit rule caused the debtor to recognize income even though the discharge was gratuitous.

tional approach." The courts have not uniformly embraced the transactional approach. Some courts have severely limited its application; but the authors believe that the better view, which has been adopted in a number of court decisions, is to apply the transactional rule liberally. There is little justification for placing a tax cost on what in effect is merely a renegotiation of the terms of a prior agreement. The transactional view permits parties to alter the terms of a prior agreement without incurring a tax cost unless the alteration constitutes a recovery of a previously enjoyed tax benefit.

The application of the transactional approach to prevent realization of discharge of indebtedness income should not require that there be an actual renegotiation of the terms of a contract. It should be sufficient that the consequences of the reduction of a debt be the same as those that would follow from a renegotiation of terms. Unless a discharged debt had previously provided the debtor with some tax benefit such as a tax deduction or an exclusion from gross income of an item that otherwise would have been included in income, the reduction or elimination of that debt merely places the debtor and creditor in the same position that they would have occupied at the time that the debt was created without changing the tax position of either party. For example, if in Year One, G contractually obligates herself to make a gift of $10,000 to her nephew, N, to be delivered to N in Year Four, and if in Year Four, N agrees to accept $6,000 in satisfaction of G's obligation, the position of G and N in Year Four is the same as it would have been if G had obligated herself in Year One to make a gift of only $6,000 to N. There is no reason to tax G differently from what she would have been taxed if she had originally committed to make a gift of $6,000. Since the incurrence of G's liability had no tax consequence, the reduction of that liability should not cause a tax liability.[56] Note that the transactional approach applies only to a genuine discharge of indebtedness; it does not apply to a spurious discharge of a debt.[57]

¶ 7.7100. Illustration 1: Charitable Pledges. X pledged to donate $1,000 to the Salvation Army, and under local law his pledge was a binding legal obligation. No deduction is allowed to an individual for making a charitable contribution until actual *payment* of the contribution is made. § 170(a)(1). X later reneged, and the Salvation Army agreed to accept $600 in full satisfaction of his pledge. The

56. See **¶ 7.8100** for a discussion of the authors' view of the rationale for the transactional approach.

57. Spurious discharge of debt is described in **¶ 7.2500**.

$400 debt of X that was forgiven by the Army is not income to X since the net effect was merely to reduce the charitable gift made by X from $1,000 to $600, and the $400 forgiveness represents no true gain for X.

Moreover, § 108(e)(2) may provide relief in this situation, even if the transactional view is not applied, if the $400 payment to the charity would have resulted in a charitable deduction under § 170. If so, since a charitable deduction is one of the itemized deductions that, for years after 2012, are subject to reduction by § 68, there could be a question as to whether the § 68 limitation is to be taken into account in applying § 108(e)(2), and, if so, how much of that § 68 reduction would be attributable to the charitable contribution. The application of the transactional view makes those questions moot.

¶ 7.7200.   Illustration 2: Cost of Inventory. X purchased 1,000 pairs of shoes from a company in England on credit for 2,000 pounds sterling; at the time of purchase, a pound equaled $3 in American currency. At the time X paid the English company, the pound had been devalued to $2 in American currency, allowing X to satisfy his contemplated $6,000 debt for $4,000. The $2,000 "savings" to X in dollars has been treated as income to X on the theory that X gained that amount on the transaction. Note that there is some judicial support, *English Shoes Ltd. v. Commissioner,*[58] for the contention that the entire "transaction" must be examined and that X may not be taxed unless the net effect of the purchase *and* sale of the shoes by X resulted in a gain. Thus, if X had sold the shoes at a loss, the amount of the loss must be deducted from the gain realized on the pound transaction.

It would appear that the court in *English Shoes* misconstrued the transactional approach. If a transactional approach were applied to the above facts, the effect of the devaluation would be to reduce X's basis in his inventory, thereby increasing his gain or decreasing his loss on the sale of the shoes. The application of the transactional approach should not depend upon whether X incurred a loss on the transaction. One consequence of the courts' failure to establish a conceptual structure for determining whether a forgiven debt consti- tutes gross income to a debtor is that some of the decisions in this area are irreconcilable.

----

58.   229 F.2d 957 (2d Cir. 1956).

¶ **7.7300. Severability of Credit.** In ¶ **7.7200**, the applicability of the transactional rule depends entirely upon whether the credit element of *X*'s purchase is severable from the purchase of the shoes or whether credit was such an integral part of the purchase that the reduction of the dollar amount of *X*'s debt should be treated as a reduction of the cost of purchasing the shoes. In the authors' view, the debt is so interwoven with the purchase of the shoes that the two are not severable for this purpose.

In Rev. Rul. 78–281, the TP borrowed foreign currency from a bank which the TP used to purchase a machine which it rented to a foreign customer. The foreign currency was devalued before the TP repaid the debt. The Commissioner ruled that the debt was severable from the purchase of the machine and so the TP's basis in the machine was the dollar value of the foreign currency it paid for the machine as of the date of purchase. The TP will recognize ordinary gain or loss on each installment payment to the bank in repayment of the loan. This circumstance differs from that involved in *English Shoes* in that the bank that loaned TP the foreign currency had no connection with the seller or with the purchase transaction.[59]

¶ **7.7400. Illustration 3: Payment from Third Party as Reduction of Purchase Price.** In a case that did not involve a discharge of indebtedness, the Tax Court adopted a position that is similar to the transactional approach. In *Freedom Newspapers, Inc. v. Commissioner*,[60] the court treated the receipt of a cash payment from a third party as a reduction of the purchase price paid for a newspaper business. The TP (a corporation) had been induced by a broker to purchase four newspapers, including one which the TP did not want, by the broker's promise to resell the unwanted newspaper or, if the broker failed to resell it, to pay $100,000 to the TP. The broker failed to resell the unwanted newspaper and therefore was required to pay $100,000 to the TP. This payment was made more than two years after the TP had purchased the four newspapers. Holding that the broker's guaranty was intimately tied to the purchase of the newspaper, the court treated the guaranty and the purchase of the newspaper as an integrated transaction. The Tax Court held that the $100,000 that the TP received from the broker constituted a reduction of the price it paid for the unwanted newspaper and did not constitute income to the TP but rather reduced its basis in that newspaper.

59. See ¶¶ **7.7400** and **7.7500.**

60. 36 T.C.M. 1755 (1977).

Since the broker's promise induced the TP to purchase the newspapers, perhaps the contractual arrangement between the broker and the TP can be said to be so integrally connected to the sale that the payment to the TP can be viewed as a reduction of the purchase price. In the authors' view, that analysis stretches the transactional approach beyond its proper boundary and the more proper analysis is described in *Preslar v. Commissioner*.[61]

However, the same result can be reached by a different route. Indeed, the Tax Court itself adopted an alternative holding that the $100,000 payment to the TP should be characterized as a return of capital under the *Arrowsmith* doctrine that a later payment or receipt is to be characterized according to earlier events to which the payment or receipt is intimately related.[62]

Rather than rely on a transactional view or on the *Arrowsmith* doctrine, the broker's payment pursuant to its guaranty can be viewed as similar to a damage or insurance payment and should be given the same tax treatment—i.e., such a payment is treated as a return of the property owner's capital and merely reduces its basis in the property in question. In this regard, consider the discussion below of the Commissioner's treatment of the discharge of a debt owed to a third party when the loan was made in connection with the purchase of property.

¶ 7.7500. **Third Party's Discharge of Debt as Reduction of Purchase Price.** A somewhat similar circumstance to the one that arose in *Freedom Newspapers* is the discharge of a portion of a nonrecourse debt that represents a loan that was made previously by a financial institution to permit the debtor to purchase realty from an unrelated party and which debt is secured by the purchased property. The typical reason that a financial institution will discharge a portion of such a debt is that the value of the property securing the debt has fallen below the balance of the nonrecourse debt that is outstanding. The discharge of the debt cannot qualify under § 108(e)(5) as a purchase price adjustment because the debt is not owed to the seller of the property. But can the discharge be excluded from the debtor's income under the common law transactional approach? In Rev. Rul. 92–99, the Commissioner rejected those

---

61. 167 F.3d 1323 (10th Cir. 1999). See ¶ **7.7500** for a discussion of *Preslar*.

62. See ¶ **25.4420** for a discussion of the Supreme Court's 1952 decision in *Arrowsmith* from which the doctrine of correlating the characterization of a payment or receipt with prior transactions sprung.

cases that permitted such a discharge to be treated as a reduction of purchase price, and the Commissioner ruled that the discharge of the debt constituted income to the debtor. Surprisingly, however, the Commissioner did state in that ruling:

> The Service will, however, treat a debt reduction in third-party lender cases as a purchase price adjustment to the extent that the debt reduction by the third party is based on an infirmity that clearly relates back to the original sale (e.g., the *seller's* inducement of a higher purchase price by misrepresentation of a material fact or by fraud). . . . No other debt reduction by a third party lender will be treated as a purchase price reduction. [Emphasis added.]

The concession made by the Commissioner in Rev. Rul. 92–99 appears to be unwarranted and overly generous. It is difficult to understand why a misrepresentation or fraud by the *seller* should change the characterization of a discharge of debt by a third party. A possible justification for the Commissioner's position may be that the third party would not cancel part of the debt because of the seller's fraud or misrepresentation unless the third party itself had been involved in the seller's original effort to sell the property to the TP. The authors are not persuaded by that approach. The third party's reduction of the nonrecourse debt is attributable to the reality that it cannot collect that amount because the security from which collection must be made is inadequate. It seems unlikely that the third party's decision to discharge the debt rests on whether the discovery that the value of the security is inadequate is caused by a revelation of the seller's fraud rather than on a decline in the real estate market. But, even if the third party's decision to reduce the debt were to rest on the seller's misrepresentations, that does not appear to tie the loan and the sale together so that the reduction of one can be said to change the price of the other. Only if the third party and the seller had acted in concert so that they were joint venturers should the loan and the sale be tied together as an integrated transaction.

In *Preslar v. Commissioner,*[63] the court stated that the purchase price reduction exclusion applies only to direct agreements between purchasers and sellers. Modifications by third parties alone will be treated under the normal discharge of indebtedness rules. Note, however, that certain third party debt reductions may qualify for

---

63. 167 F.3d 1323 (10th Cir. 1999).

exclusion treatment under § 108(a)(1)(C) and (D).[64] In addition, if the debt constitutes a qualified principal residence indebtedness and if it is reduced prior to January 1, 2013, its discharge may be excluded from income by § 108(a)(1)(E).[65]

¶ 7.8000.   OVERVIEW OF TRANSACTIONAL APPROACH. In the authors' view, the reason for the judicial confusion concerning the application of the transactional approach is that the Supreme Court's opinion in the landmark decision to include discharge of indebtedness in the debtor's income (*Kirby Lumber*[66]) rested on an erroneous rationale. The Supreme Court in *Kirby Lumber* emphasized that a reduction in a debtor's obligations increases his net worth, and this net worth approach has engendered confusion. While virtually every discharge of indebtedness will increase the debtor's net worth (except possibly for an insolvent debtor whose negative net worth is decreased), it is obvious that many such discharges should not cause the realization of income. As a consequence of the faulty rationale employed in *Kirby Lumber*, subsequent courts and Congress have struggled with the task of segregating those discharges that should be included in income from those that should not. The following rationale for the discharge of indebtedness rule, which has been suggested by several commentators, is more realistic than the net worth approach.

¶ 7.8100.   Suggested Rationale. When a person borrows money, he is not required to recognize income because his increase in assets is offset by a liability. Since it is assumed that he will satisfy the debt, the borrower recognizes no income by borrowing the funds. However, if it subsequently becomes clear that the debtor will not satisfy the debt, there no longer is a bar to including in income the amount previously borrowed by the debtor. Thus, when a debt is discharged, the realization of income should not be attributed to the increase in the debtor's net worth at that time but rather should be viewed as a removal of a bar to including a prior increase in the debtor's assets in his income. If a debt is not attributable to an increase in the debtor's assets or to the enjoyment of some tax benefit by him, there is little reason to treat the discharge of that debt as income to the debtor. It should be emphasized that the foregoing rationale is a theory of the authors and perhaps of a few commentators; it has not been adopted by any court. Note, however,

64.   See ¶ **7.3500.**

65.   See ¶ **7.3700.**

66.   See ¶ **7.2100.**

that this rationale is consistent with the Supreme Court's treatment of an analogous problem concerning the application of the tax benefit rule.[67]

¶ 7.8200. Effect of 1980 Amendment of § 108. As noted above, in 1980, Congress made significant modifications to § 108 some of which codified many of the common law rules concerning what constitutes a discharge of indebtedness. Except for the special treatment of the discharge of a purchase-money debt,[68] the amendments did not deal with the applicability of the transactional approach. One might question whether Congress intended the provisions of § 108 to be exclusive and so intended to repudiate common law rules that were not expressly codified. The authors believe that no such repudiation was intended and that the transactional approach is still alive and well. Note that when Congress wished to make an aspect of § 108 exclusive, it did so expressly. For example, in § 108(e)(1), Congress provided that there is no insolvency exception other than the insolvency provisions that are made in § 108 itself. Also, in Rev. Rul. 92–99, the Commissioner noted that the common law transactional rule continues to apply, although the Commissioner did not refer to it as the "transactional" rule or approach.

¶ 7.9000. DISCHARGE OF AN UNENFORCEABLE DEBT. The decision of a majority of the Tax Court and the reversal of that decision by a divided Third Circuit in *Zarin v. Commissioner*[69] are worthy of careful examination. *Zarin* involved the cancellation of gambling debts that were unenforceable under state law from the date that they were incurred by the TP. In an 11–8 decision, the Tax Court held that the TP recognized gross income to the extent that the gambling debt was canceled without consideration. In a 2–1 decision, the Third Circuit reversed and held the TP did not recognize any income. In view of the significance of this decision, the basic facts of *Zarin* are set forth below.

¶ 7.9100. The Facts of the *Zarin* case. The TP in *Zarin* was a compulsive gambler. A considerable amount of TP's gambling took place at a casino in a hotel (hereinafter referred to as "the Hotel") in Atlantic City. In 1978, TP was given a line of credit of $10,000 at the Hotel. Within a year and a half, TP's line of credit was increased to $200,000 even though the Hotel made no additional investigation of his credit worthiness.

---

67. See *Hillsboro National Bank v. Commissioner*, 460 U.S. 370 (1983).

68. See **¶ 7.3600.**

69. 92 T.C. 1084 (1989), rev'd 916 F.2d 110 (3d Cir. 1990).

Gambling at the Hotel's casino was done with chips provided by that casino. The chips could not be used outside of the casino for any purpose. TP's line of credit permitted him to obtain chips from the casino with which to gamble. TP obtained the chips by signing negotiable drafts commonly called "markers." The markers were held by the Hotel for a period of some 90 days after which they were redeemed by TP who gave the Hotel his personal check in the same amount.

In 1979, the New Jersey Casino Control Commission ordered the Hotel to cease and desist giving credit in excess of the properly approved credit limit, and all undeposited checks were ordered to be treated as credit provided to a patron. The complaints of credit abuse that led to the cease and desist order included 100 instances of abuse in providing excessive credit to TP and a gambling companion. In violation of that order, the Hotel subsequently substantially increased the credit that TP could draw upon to purchase chips.

By January, 1980, TP was gambling daily at the Hotel's casino for 12 to 16 hours per day. TP mostly played craps, and he was betting up to $15,000 on a roll. TP's gambling attracted other patrons of the casino to his table and induced many of them to increase the size of their bets. For that reason, TP was a valued patron of the Hotel's casino.

In April, 1980, for the acquisition of chips, TP delivered his personal checks and markers to the Hotel's casino in the aggregate amount of $3,435,000; those checks and markers were returned to the Hotel as having been drawn against insufficient funds. Under New Jersey law, gambling debts are enforceable only if certain conditions are satisfied. The Hotel sued TP for the unsatisfied amount, and the TP asserted a number of affirmative defenses. The suit was settled by TP's paying the Hotel $500,000 in cancellation of the $3,435,000 debt. A majority of the Tax Court held that TP thereby had discharge of indebtedness income in the amount of the difference of $2,935,000.

One of the issues in *Zarin* was whether the gambling debts that TP incurred were enforceable. The excessive credit granted by the Hotel to TP in contravention of a cease and desist order made the enforceability of those debts highly questionable. Because of the procedural framework in which the case arose, the Commissioner was held to have the burden of proof on that issue. Since the Commissioner could not meet its burden of proof, TP's gambling debts were deemed by the Tax Court and by the Third Circuit to be unenforceable at the time that they were incurred. The majority of the Tax Court held, and a majority of the Third Circuit disagreed, that the unenforceability of TP's debts was irrelevant to the question of whether he had recognized gross income from the discharge of a portion of those debts.

¶ 7.9200. Harsh Result In The Tax Court. The result reached by the Tax Court's majority is extremely harsh. The TP's debt to the Hotel represented gambling losses that he had incurred. The majority of the Tax Court took the position that TP's gambling losses were incurred in a different taxable year from the year in which the debt was canceled, and gambling losses can be deducted only from gambling winnings of the same taxable year. See Treas. Reg. § 1.165–10.

¶ 7.9300. Application of Transactional Approach. If the court had adopted a transactional approach, the TP would have prevailed. The TP did not purchase chips as an item of property. The chips were merely the tokens that were used to measure the amount of a patron's gambling winnings or losses. Indeed, the Tax Court's majority itself stated in their opinion that the chips were not property that the TP purchased but rather represented the "opportunity to gamble." The TP's gambling can be viewed as a service provided by the Hotel, and the credit provided to TP was therefore provided by the same person (the Hotel) that was providing the service which was the exclusive object to which the credit could be applied. On a transactional approach, the settlement of TP's debt for a lesser figure can be viewed as a reduction of the cost of the gambling service or as a reduction of TP's gambling losses. In other words, the credit accorded TP was so inextricably attached to the gambling activity that the cancellation of part of that debt cannot properly be treated as an event isolated from the gambling itself.

One court decision did not apply this approach. In *Rood v. Commissioner,*[70] the Tax Court held the cancellation of a gambling debt to be income to a TP where the debt was not disputed.

¶ 7.9400. The Third Circuit's Decision. In a 2–1 decision, the Third Circuit reversed the Tax Court and held that the TP did not recognize income.[71] The court rested its reversal on two independent grounds.

The court noted that § 108(d)(1) defines the term "indebtedness" of

---

70. T.C. Memo ¶ 96,248, *affirmed,* 122 F.3d 1078 (11th Cir. 1997).

71. *Zarin v. Commissioner,* 916 F.2d 110 (1990).

a TP as an indebtedness either: (1) for which the TP is liable, or (2) subject to which the TP holds property. While that provision expressly states that the definition applies only for purposes of that section, a majority of the Third Circuit held that § 108 is merely an elaboration of the general rule of inclusion in gross income that is set forth in § 61(a)(12), and so the majority held that the definition adopted in § 108(d)(1) was equally applicable for purposes of § 61(a)(12).[72] The majority agreed with the Tax Court's determination that TP's "debt" was unenforceable from the date that it was created, and so the court concluded that the TP was never liable for that "debt." The majority also held that since the gambling chips did not constitute property but rather were "nothing more than an accounting mechanism, or evidence of a debt, to facilitate gambling," TP did not hold property subject to an indebtedness. Consequently, neither of the alternative definitions of indebtedness provided by § 108(d)(1) was satisfied. The TP's "debt" did not constitute an "indebtedness" within the meaning of either § 108 or § 61(a)(12), and so the reduction of that "debt" did not cause discharge of indebtedness income.

This first ground on which the Third Circuit rested is highly questionable. If cash or property is acquired in a transaction that would otherwise be taxable to the recipient, it is the existence of an offsetting debt that prevents the recognition of income. If an unenforceable "debt" of a TP is not treated as a debt for discharge of indebtedness purposes, it should not constitute a debt for purposes of preventing income recognition from the TP's receipt of property. In such cases, the receipt of property should not be included in the recipient's income so long as the recipient acts in a manner that indicates his intention to pay the "debt." Once the facts indicate that the recipient does not intend to repay the debt, then the value of the property received earlier should be included in his gross income. Whether the inclusion of that item in income is the result of the discharge of indebtedness doctrine or of a comparable doctrine is of little moment (unless the TP is insolvent or falls within one of the other exceptions to the recognition of discharge of indebtedness income). The proper test for determining whether the TP recognized income when the "debt" was settled is whether the canceled "debt" had prevented the TP's recognition of income in a previous year— i.e., whether it represented property that the TP had received.

As an alternative ground for its decision for the TP, the majority held that the settlement of a disputed or contested liability does not

---

72. Judge Stapleton disagreed with the majority on this issue among others.

cause discharge of indebtedness income. In light of the dispute as to whether the casino could enforce the TP's debt, the court treated the *amount* of liability as being in dispute so that the settlement at a lower figure than demanded did not cause the TP to recognize income. The court's decision on this point might be seen as an application of the transactional approach which the authors proposed in ¶ **7.7000.** The court's analysis of a hypothetical circumstance that the court propounded to illustrate the operation of the contested liability rule appears to be an attempt to adopt a transactional approach. The court stated that if a TP (*F*) borrowed $10,000, then refused in good faith to repay, and if the debt was settled for $7,000, "the transaction would be treated as if the initial loan was $7,000" and *F* would recognize no income. While the hypothetical was poorly chosen, it does appear that the rule that the court had in mind is encompassed by a transactional approach.

If the court's disputed or contested liability rule is taken literally, it is of doubtful validity. The problem with that approach is the same as that noted above with the court's assertion that the cancellation of an unenforceable debt does not cause income recognition. The proper question to ask is whether the "debt" that was eliminated by the settlement had prevented the TP's recognition of income in a prior year.

A better explanation of the correct approach is set out in *Preslar v. Commissioner.*[73] In *Preslar*, the court noted that the problem with the *Zarin* approach is that it treated liquidated and unliquidated debt alike. The court held that in order for the contested liability doctrine to apply, the amount of the original debt must be unliquidated. That is, the IRS must be "unaware of the exact consideration initially exchanged in a transaction."

---

73. 167 F.3d 1323 (10th Cir. 1999).

CHAPTER EIGHT

CLAIM OF RIGHT AND ILLEGAL INCOME

¶ 8.0000.   CLAIM OF RIGHT AND ILLEGAL INCOME

¶ 8.1000.   ILLEGALLY OBTAINED INCOME. Income obtained by embezzlement or other illegal means is included in the wrongdoer's gross income even though he is obligated to return it when discovered.[1] In 1982, the Service estimated that the compliance rate for reporting illegal income is only five percent.[2]

¶ 8.1100.   Control as a Practical Matter. The issue of when illegally obtained income is to be taxed was addressed in *United States v. Dixon*.[3] In *Dixon*, the TP transferred funds from a client's account into his own account in 1975. The court held that the illegally obtained funds became income to the TP in the year in which the TP obtained "practical control" (control as a practical matter) over the funds.[4] Thus, the criminal conviction for willful tax evasion for 1976 was upheld, even though the TP received the funds in 1975, because "practical control" was not established until 1976.

¶ 8.1200.   Fraudulently Obtained Loans. In *Kreimer v. Commissioner*,[5] the TP obtained a loan by fraud. The court held that the taxation of such a loan depends upon whether the TP intended to repay the fraudulently obtained loan. If the TP did intend to repay the loan, the TP is treated as a borrower and will not be taxed on the borrowed funds. If there was no intention to repay the loan, the TP is treated as having received income and is therefore taxed on the loan. It appears to the authors that the "borrowed" funds should be

---

1.   Treas Reg. § 1.61–14(a). See also *James v. United States*, 366 U.S. 213 (1961); *United States v. Sullivan*, 274 U.S. 259 (1927). See ¶¶ **8.3000** and **8.4300.**

2.   S.Rept. 97–494, 97th Cong., 2d Sess. (July 12, 1982), page 251.

3.   698 F.2d 445 (11th Cir. 1983).

4.   Bank officials and the victim were suspicious of TP's intention to carry out his fiduciary responsibility with the funds, and their concerns were resolved in 1976, at which time TP first felt free to use the funds.

5.   47 T.C.M. 260 (1983) (appeal to 11th Cir. dismissed in 1984).

included in the TP's gross income regardless of his intention to repay; the lender's participation in the consensual recognition of the obligation to repay was obtained by fraud and so should be disregarded.

¶ 8.2000. INCOME RECEIVED BY ERROR. When property or funds are received under a mistake of fact or law, the property or funds are included in the gross income of the recipient notwithstanding that the recipient may be required to return the item to the payor when the error is discovered. The item is included in income under the so-called "claim of right" doctrine: The recipient acquired the property without a consensual recognition (express or implied) of an obligation to repay and without restriction as to his disposition of the property, at least until the error is discovered.

> **¶ 8.2100. Illustration.** In Year One, Win All, Inc. erroneously computed the bonus to be paid X, an employee. Accordingly, Win All over-paid X by $2,500. The error was discovered in Year Three, and X returned the $2,500. The $2,500 is included in the gross income of X for Year One, and X is entitled to a $2,500 deduction for Year Three when he repaid that amount of the bonus.[6] The repayment rules are discussed below.

¶ 8.3000. RETURN OF INCOME HELD UNDER A CLAIM OF RIGHT. When income is received because of a mistake of fact or law, the income is nevertheless included in the gross income of the recipient under the so-called "claim of right" doctrine. When the mistake or illegality is discovered and the TP returns the income to its rightful owner, the TP is granted a deduction.[7] The statutory basis for the deduction typically is § 165(c)(2). This deduction often will be an itemized deduction (it will be a nonitemized deduction in certain circumstances such as when the income was received in connection with the TP's self-employed business), but it is not subject to the 2% of AGI floor that applies to certain itemized deductions. § 67(b)(9). While § 67(b)(9) excludes from the 2% of AGI floor a deduction allowed under § 1341 for a return of an amount held under a claim of right, it appears likely to the authors that the exclusion will be construed as applying also to a deduction allowed under § 165 or common law tax rules (and not under § 1341) for the return of such amounts. When it is an itemized deduction, however, for years after 2012, it is subject to the reduction of itemized deductions that is imposed by § 68 when a TP's AGI exceeds a specified amount.

---

6. *United States v. Lewis*, 340 U.S. 590 (1951).

7. Rev. Rul. 65–254. See *Healy v. Commissioner*, 345 U.S. 278 (1953).

For an interesting case involving the deductibility of a TP's return to his victims of fraudulently obtained funds, see *Stephens v. Commissioner*, discussed at ¶ **18.1000**.

¶ **8.3100. Illustration.** *X* embezzled $2,000 from his employer *Y* in Year One. In Year Three, the theft was discovered, and in Year Four, *X* returned the $2,000 to *Y*. *X* must include the $2,000 of embezzled funds in his gross income for Year One, and *X* may deduct the $2,000 he returned to *Y* from *X*'s AGI for Year Four. This is an itemized deduction. While this deduction is not derived from § 1341, it nevertheless is likely that it will be excluded from the 2% of AGI floor by § 67(b)(9).

¶ **8.3200. Tax Bracket Differential.** If a TP who received income under the claim of right doctrine was in a higher marginal tax bracket when he received the gross income than when he returned it, the differential in tax rates will constitute a tax cost to the recipient. This cost is harsh when the income was received through an innocent error, particularly when the error was not made by the TP himself. Consequently, Congress has provided statutory relief. Note that if the TP was in a lower marginal tax bracket when he received the gross income item than when he returned it, the deduction allowable to the TP will provide him with a windfall. The amount of that windfall is mitigated by the fact that the TP lost the use of the money that he paid to the government as the tax on the claim of right income, and the TP earns no interest on that amount from the government. But, TP did have the use of the funds that were received under a claim of right until those funds were returned to the payor.

¶ **8.4000. STATUTORY RELIEF.** Under § 1341, when an item was included in a TP's gross income in a prior year because "it appeared that the TP had an unrestricted right to such item," and when the TP is entitled to a deduction of more than $3,000 in a later tax year because of the repayment of that item, the TP's income tax bill for the year of repayment will be computed by whichever of the following methods produces a smaller tax bill for the TP:

(1) the TP computes his tax in the normal manner by taking the repayment as a deduction (typically as an itemized deduction from his AGI) for that year; or

(2) the TP computes the tax without deducting any part of the repayment made in that year, and then the TP reduces his tax liability by the

amount of tax he paid in prior years because of the inclusion of the mistaken amount in his gross income at that time. In other words, the TP is granted a benefit equal to the value of the deduction at the marginal tax rates applicable to the TP when the item was included in his gross income. If the amount of such tax reduction exceeds the TP's current tax bill, the difference is refunded to the TP. § 1341(b)(1); Treas. Reg. § 1.1341–1(i). Thus, the tax reduction is a refundable tax credit.

¶ 8.4100. **Limitations.** The benefits of § 1341 are expressly withheld from certain items. For example, the amount of the allowable deduction must exceed $3,000. Also, the statutory relief does not apply to an item which was included in gross income by reason of the sale or other disposition of a TP's inventory or other items held for sale to customers in the ordinary course of his business. § 1341(b)(2). Perhaps the reason for this latter exclusion from § 1341 is that the deduction arises because of the TP's guarantee or because the customer returned the item. Those are common occurrences that likely take place repeatedly during each year, and it would be an administrative nuisance to make the calculations for each such occurrence. Finally, § 1341 does not apply to legal fees or other expenses incurred by a TP in contesting his obligation to repay an item previously included in income. Treas. Reg. § 1.1341–1(h).

¶ 8.4200. **Unrestricted Right.** The Commissioner has strictly construed the requirement in § 1341 that the item in question was included in the TP's gross income "because it appeared that the TP had an unrestricted right to such item." The Commissioner contends that the above language establishes a narrower test for § 1341 than the "claim of right" doctrine. Consequently, even though an item is included in a TP's gross income under the "claim of right" doctrine; if, from all the facts known at the time, it did not appear that the TP had an unrestricted right to the item, § 1341 will not apply.

¶ 8.4300. **Embezzled Funds and Other Funds Obtained By Intentional Wrongdoing.** Rev. Rul. 65–254 holds that the return of embezzled funds does not qualify for the relief granted by § 1341.[8] The embezzler is entitled to a deduction under § 165(c)(2), but under the Commissioner's view, the TP cannot enjoy the special relief afforded by § 1341 since in the year that he acquired the money he did not appear to have an unrestricted right to it. The Commission-

8. See also Rev. Rul. 68–153.

er's position has been sustained by the Tax Court,[9] by a district court,[10] and by the Sixth Circuit.[11] Those courts also held that the repayment of the embezzled funds (which exceeded TP's income for that year) could not qualify as a net operating loss carryover or carryback because embezzlement was not the TP's trade or business.[12]

The Commissioner's position was also sustained by the Fifth Circuit in *McKinney v. United States.*[13] In *McKinney*, the district court in Texas treated the rule requiring an embezzler to recognize income as separate and distinct from the claim of right doctrine, and so the court did not deal with the question of whether § 1341 covers all claim of right income. In affirming the district court, the Fifth Circuit said that it was not necessary to reach that question because the embezzler did not have an unrestricted right to the money and so § 1341 clearly did not apply.[14]

In a 1986 decision involving a TP who had received illegal kickbacks and salary while acting in a manner disloyal to his employer, a district court held that the TP's return of those funds did not qualify for § 1341 treatment because the TP had no bona fide claim of right to the funds.[15]

¶ 8.4400. Obligation to Repay. Similarly, the Commissioner maintains that § 1341 applies only if the TP *did not actually have an unrestricted right* to the item in the year of receipt, even though he appeared to have it. Therefore, if the TP's obligation to repay arises only because of an event that occurred *after* the year in which the TP received the item, the Commissioner contends that § 1341 is inapplicable because the TP did have an unrestricted right to the item in the year he received it.[16] The Commissioner's ruling on that issue (Rev. Rul. 67–437) dealt with a situation where the officers of a

---

9. *Yerkie v. Commissioner*, 67 T.C. 388 (1976).

10. *Hankins v. United States*, 403 F.Supp. 257 (N.D.Miss. 1975), aff'd by court order (5th Cir. 1975).

11. *Kraft v. United States*, 991 F.2d 292 (6th Cir. 1993).

12. See ¶ **23.7000.**

13. 574 F.2d 1240 (5th Cir. 1978).

14. See also *Kraft v. United States*, 991 F.2d 292 (6th Cir. 1993).

15. *Zadoff v. United States*, 638 F.Supp. 1240 (S.D.N.Y. 1986). See also, *Parks v. United States*, 945 F.Supp. 865 (W.D. Pa. 1996); and *Culley v. United States*, 222 F.3d 1331 (Fed. Cir. 2000).

16. Rev. Rul. 67–437.

corporation had received payments from the corporation that they were contractually obligated to return to the corporation if the payments were later determined to be nondeductible for the corporation. The Commissioner ruled that the repayments made by the officers pursuant to that contractual obligation did not qualify for § 1341 treatment.

The Commissioner's position on the treatment of returned funds pursuant to a condition imposed on the receipt of the funds was rejected by the Sixth Circuit in *Van Cleave v. United States*,[17] where the TP received a salary which he was contractually required to return to his corporate employer to the extent that it was subsequently determined to be excessively large and, therefore, partly nondeductible by the employer. The TP was a majority shareholder and president of the corporate employer. In holding that § 1341 applied to TP's repayment of part of the salary, the court indicated its belief that the TP did not have an unrestricted right to the excessive portion of the salary payment in the year of receipt. Thus, the subsequent determination was not an independent event, but was merely evidence establishing that the TP's salary was excessive.[18]

¶ 8.4500. **Validity.** The validity of Rev. Rul. 67–437 is very much in doubt. The *Van Cleave* decision rejected the Commissioner's position, and the Commissioner himself sometimes ignores or overlooks that issue in his rulings. For example, in Rev. Rul. 78–25, the *X* corporation sold its assets to *Y* and then liquidated. X's shareholder, *A*, reported a gain of more than $3,000 as a consequence of receiving liquidating distributions in excess of his basis in the *X* corporation's stock. Under the terms of *X*'s sale of its assets to *Y*, *X* and its shareholder, *A*, were required to fulfill certain subsequent conditions, and they failed to do so. *Y* sued *A* for the latter's failure to fulfill the required conditions. As a result, *A* paid *Y* an amount in excess of $3,000. The Commissioner ruled that the provisions of § 1341 are applicable to the payment that *A* made to *Y*.

¶ 8.4600. **Mathematical or Clerical Error.** In Rev. Rul. 68–153, the Commissioner ruled that § 1341 does not apply to the return of an overpayment received as a consequence of a clerical error or an error of computation. The rationale for that ruling is that on the basis of all facts known at the end of the year (at least when the facts are viewed correctly), it would not appear "that the TP had an

17.   718 F.2d 193 (6th Cir. 1983).
18.   See also Rev. Rul. 68–153 (Situation 3).

unrestricted right to such an item." The validity of this ruling has not been established. Indeed, if all of the Commissioner's rulings on § 1341 were valid, there would be precious few transactions to which § 1341 would apply.

¶ **8.4700.** **Net Operating Loss.** The computation under § 1341 is made somewhat more complicated when either the deduction of the returned item from the TP's gross income for the year of return, or the exclusion of the returned item from the TP's gross income for the year in which the item was received (or accrued), results in a net operating loss for such year. The method of computation is described in Treas. Reg. § 1.1341–1(d)(4)(iii), Ex. (5).

¶ **8.4800.** **Prompt Refund.** When a TP claims a refund based on § 1341, the Code provides that the claim will be examined and a refund paid within 90 days after the claim was filed. § 6411(d). The prompt refund made thereby is tentative and can be revised by the Commissioner at a later date after he has had more time to study the claim.

¶ **8.4900.** **Significance of § 1341.** The 1986 TRA reduced both income tax rates and the number of income tax brackets. While those rate and bracket changes reduced the significance of § 1341, much of the tax bracket significance was restored when Congress raised tax rates in 1993. While the tax rates have been reduced in recent years, thereby reducing the importance again, they are likely to be increased in a few years. In any event, even apart from tax bracket considerations, § 1341 retains considerable vitality. For example, if capital gain income is returned in a later year, § 1341 could be extremely helpful in avoiding the limitations on the deductibility of capital losses which might otherwise deny the TP a deduction. If § 1341 does not apply to such a repayment, the deduction may be classified as a capital loss in order to correlate the deduction with the type of income to which it relates. See ¶ **25.4420.**

CHAPTER NINE

ANNUITIES, LIFE INSURANCE, AND MISCELLANEOUS INCOME

¶ 9.0000. ANNUITIES, LIFE INSURANCE, AND MISCELLANEOUS INCOME

¶ 9.1000. ANNUITIES. An annuity is a contractual right to receive payments for a fixed term or for the life or lives of some person or persons. The contract under which these rights are obtained may be an annuity, endowment, or life insurance contract.

¶ 9.1100. Percentage of Annuity in Gross Income.

When a TP purchases a commercial annuity, each payment made to the TP (or to a surviving beneficiary of a joint annuity or a survivor's annuity) consists partly of a return of the TP's capital and partly of income earned on his investment in the annuity. A percentage of each annuity payment (the "exclusion ratio") is excluded from the TP's gross income, and the balance of the payment is included in gross income. § 72(b)(1). Once the aggregate amount of annuity payments that have been excluded from the TP's gross income equals the amount of the TP's investment in the annuity contract, all additional annuity payments will be included in the TP's gross income. § 72(b)(2).

¶ 9.1110. Exclusion Ratio.

The exclusion ratio is a fraction; the numerator is the TP's investment in the annuity contract; and the denominator is the TP's total expected return from the annuity over the period in which payments will be made (usually the period is for someone's life, the joint lives of several persons, or for a fixed term). When the period for payment is tied to the life of an individual, the regulations employ two different sets of tables for determining a TP's expected return—one set of tables applies for the portion of an annuity that is attributable to a pre–July 1, 1986, investment, and the second set of tables applies to the portion of an annuity that is attributable to a post–June 30, 1986, investment.[1]

---

1. If an annuity payment is received after June 30, 1986, the recipient can make an irrevocable election to have his expected return determined under the post–June 30, 1986,

¶ **9.1111. Illustration.** X purchased an annuity in 1990 which will pay her $10,000 per year, beginning with her 65th birthday in 2010, until she dies. The annuity is to be paid in monthly installments of a little more than $833. In 1990, X paid $120,000 for the annuity. X's expected return from the annuity is $200,000—i.e., $10,000 × 20 (the number of years of X's life expectancy under Table V in Treas. Reg. § 1.72–9, which is the applicable table for X in this circumstance). Using the cost ($120,000) as the numerator and the expected return ($200,000) as the denominator, the exclusion ratio is 120,-000/200,000; so 60% of each monthly payment is excluded from her gross income and 40% is included. Thus, X must include in her gross income $4,000 of each year's payments, which is the amount that represents income on her investment. A little more than $333 of each monthly payment will be included in her income. She will exclude $6,000 of each year's payments. This exclusion will apply to monthly payments made during the 20–year period beginning with the date on which the first monthly payment is made to X; so $500 of each monthly payment will be excluded from income. As shown in ¶ **9.1120**, the entirety of annuity payments made to X after her 85th birthday will be included in her gross income.

¶ **9.1112. Qualified Employer Retirement Plan.** For certain annuity plans for employees (referred to an "qualified employer retirement plans"), § 72(d) provides a simplified method for determining the amount of annuity payments that are a recovery of the employee's investment.[2]

¶ **9.1120. Termination of Exclusion Ratio.** The exclusion ratio will be used to exclude a percentage of annuity payments from gross income until the TP has recovered his investment. Thereafter, all of the subsequent annuity payments will be included in the TP's gross income. § 72(b)(2).

The effective date of the amendment limiting the exclusion to the TP's investment makes it applicable only if the "annuity starting date" is after 1986. The annuity starting date is the first day of the first period for which an amount is received as an annuity

tables regardless of when the investment was made. Treas. Reg. § 1.72–9. If no election is made, the TP will have separate computations made for the portions of annuity payments that are attributable to the two separate periods of investment.

2.   The simplified method is explained in Notice 98–2, 1998–1 Cum. Bull. 266, which also provides examples.

under the annuity contract. § 72(c)(4). Consequently, if the annuity starting date is on or before December 31, 1986, the exclusion ratio will apply to all payments made under the annuity contract, including payments made after the TP's investment has been recovered.

In the illustration above, when X attains her 85th birthday, she will have received $200,000 in total payments of which $120,000 will have been excluded from her gross income because it represents a return of her $120,000 cash investment. X will have recovered her entire cost investment by that time. Since X's annuity starting date is after December 31, 1986, all payments received by X after she has recovered her $120,000 investment will be included in her gross income.

¶ 9.1200. Deduction Allowable for Unrecovered Investment. If the payments under an annuity contract cease by reason of the annuitant's death and if at the time of such cessation there is an "unrecovered investment" in the annuity contract, the annuitant is granted an itemized deduction for the amount of the "unrecovered investment." § 72(b)(3). This deduction is taken on the annuitant's income tax return for his last taxable year. § 72(b)(3)(A). The deduction is not subject to the 2% of adjusted gross income floor that applies to certain itemized deductions referred to as "miscellaneous itemized deductions" [§ 67(b)(10)]; but, for years after 2012, the general limitation on itemized deductions that is imposed by § 68 does apply.

The "unrecovered investment" in an annuity contract is the difference between the amount of investment in the annuity contract as of the annuity starting date[3] and the aggregate amount of distributions made under the contract that were excluded from the recipient's gross income. § 72(b)(4). This provision allowing a deduction applies only if the annuity starting date was after December 31, 1986.[4]

¶ 9.1300. Employee Annuity. Prior to the enactment of the 1986 TRA, when part of the purchase price of an annuity contract was paid by the TP's employer and the amount was not included in the employee's gross income, a special rule applied in determining the employee's income from annuity distributions. If the total amount payable to the employee under the annuity contract in the first three

---

3. The "annuity starting date" is defined at **¶ 9.1120**.

4. Tax Reform Act of 1986, P.L. 99–514, § 1122(h)(1).

years (commencing with the date of the first annuity payment) was equal to or greater than the consideration contributed by the employee for the contract, then each annuity payment to the employee was excluded from gross income until the total amount excluded equals the total consideration paid by the employee. The full amount of all subsequent annuity payments was included in the employee's gross income. Treas. Reg. § 1.72–13. This special provision for certain employee annuities was repealed by the 1986 TRA. The repeal applies to employee annuities for which the "annuity starting date"[5] is after July 1, 1986.

Distributions from employee annuities that begin after July 1, 1986, are treated the same as those from a commercial annuity that was purchased by an annuitant, except for the availability of the simplified calculation that § 72(d) provides for "qualified employer retirement plans."[6]

¶ **9.1400. Private Annuity.** A private annuity is a contractual obligation of a person or organization not regularly in the business of selling annuity contracts. Typically, a private annuity will be purchased from a member of the annuitant's family or from a charitable organization. Some charitable organizations are so involved in providing annuities that they are treated the same as a commercial annuity company. Since the value of a private annuity contract may be speculative and the contract sometimes is purchased by the exchange of appreciated property, the tax rules that apply are more complex than those for commercial annuities.[7]

¶ **9.1500. Annuity Contract Not Held by a Natural Person.** The tax treatment that is provided by § 72 for payments received under an annuity contract applies only if the contract is owned by, or held on behalf of, a natural person. § 72(u). If an annuity contract is held by a fictional entity (such as a corporation), the holder of the contract will be required to report income from the contract in accordance with the normal application of its accounting method.

¶ **9.2000. LIFE INSURANCE.** A life insurance contract is defined in § 7702. The contract must be either a life insurance or endowment contract under local law and must satisfy one of two alternative tests—

---

5. The "annuity starting date" is defined at ¶ **9.1120**.

6. See ¶ **9.1112**.

7. To see the Service's current position, see Rev. Rul. 71–492, Rev. Rul. 69–74, and TAM 7008070450A (1970).

either (1) under the terms of the policy, the cash value of the policy will never exceed an amount determined under § 7702(b), or (2) the aggregate premiums for the policy do not at any time exceed a limitation established in § 7702(c) and the policy's death benefit will not be less than a specified multiple of the policy's cash surrender value. This definition is designed to prevent a mutual stock investment plan from passing as a life insurance contract by providing some minimum amount of death benefits in order to obtain the special tax treatment accorded to life insurance.

¶ 9.2100. **Lump–Sum Proceeds.** Generally, life insurance proceeds payable in a lump sum by reason of the death of the insured are not included in the gross income of the beneficiary. § 101(a)(1). One exception to that exclusion from income is where the person who originally acquired the policy from the insurer transfers it to someone else in a taxable exchange.[8] Even then, there are circumstances where the exclusion will apply.[9] If life insurance proceeds are to be paid in installments, a portion of the payments will be excluded and the rest will be included in income.

¶ 9.2200. **Life Insurance Proceeds Payable in Installments.** If life insurance proceeds are payable to a beneficiary in installments (regardless of whether the installments are in equal amounts) over a period of a life or a term of years, part of each payment represents a portion of the principal amount payable by reason of the insured's death, which amount is excludable from gross income under § 101(a)(1). The remaining part of each installment payment represents interest earned by that portion of the principal amount of the insurance proceeds that is held by the insurer. In essence, in such cases, the amount of the death benefit that is payable under the policy is not paid in a lump sum to the beneficiary, but instead is held by the insurer to fund the insurer's payment of an annuity to the beneficiary. The Code provides that the amount held by the insurer with respect to a beneficiary is to be prorated over the installment payments in the manner established by the regulations. § 101(d).

The proration of the amount held by the insurer with respect to a beneficiary is described in Treas. Reg. § 1.101–4 and –7. A portion of the amount held by the insurer is allocated to each installment

8.   See ¶ **9.2600**.

9.   An even narrower exception applies in certain circumstances to the proceeds of a so-called flexible premium contract that was issued prior to 1985. § 101(f).

payment in accordance with the percentage of the total amount of payments that each payment represents.[10]

The tax rules for determining the amount of installment payments that are excluded from gross income are similar to the rules that govern annuities. For example, when life insurance proceeds are to be paid in annual installments over the lifetime of a beneficiary, the amount held by the insurer will be divided by the life expectancy of the beneficiary, as determined by tables set forth in the regulations[11], and the resulting figure is excluded from each annual payment. Treas. Reg. § 1.101–7. In effect, a percentage of each installment that represents the amount held by the insurer will be excluded from the gross income of the beneficiary.

These proration rules apply only when the insurance proceeds are to be paid in installments. They do not apply if the insurance proceeds are left with the insurer who pays interest only to the beneficiary.[12]

¶ 9.2210. Amount Held By the Insurer With Respect to a Beneficiary. In the case of installment payments, the "amount held by the insurer with respect to a beneficiary" is the amount that is excluded from the beneficiary's gross income and is prorated among the installment payments. How is that amount determined? If a beneficiary has an option to receive a lump sum settlement on the insured's death, that lump sum will be deemed to be the "amount that was held by the insurer with respect to a beneficiary." Treas. Reg. § 1.101–4(b)(1). If no option for a lump sum settlement is available, the amount held by the insurer with respect to the beneficiary is the present value of the payments to be made to the beneficiary as determined by using the interest rate that the insurer uses in calculating the amount of the installment payments to be made to the beneficiary and by using mortality tables promulgated by Treasury. Treas. Reg. §§ 1.101–4(b)(1), 1.101–7.[13]

10. The manner in which the amount held by the insurer with respect to a beneficiary is determined is described in **¶ 9.2210**.

11. The mortality figures that the regulations employ are those in Treas. Reg. § 1.72–7(c)(1) and are utilized in the life expectancy tables that are set forth in Treas. Reg. § 1.72–9. Treas. Reg. § 1.101–7.

12. See **¶ 9.2500**.

13. The mortality figures that the regulations employ are those in Treas. Reg. § 1.72–7(c)(1) and are utilized in the life expectancy tables that are set forth in Treas. Reg. § 1.72–9. Treas. Reg. § 1.101–7.

¶ 9.2220. Termination of Exclusion. If a life insurance beneficiary who is entitled to payments for life outlives his life expectancy, the beneficiary will have excluded the amount held by the insurer when the life expectancy period is reached. Can the beneficiary continue to exclude the prorated amount from subsequent installment payments?

Prior to the adoption of the 1986 TRA, when installments were payable over the life of a beneficiary, the exclusion of a percentage of each installment payment continued to apply to installments received after the period of the beneficiary's life expectancy expired if the beneficiary outlived that period. Treas. Reg. § 1.101–4(c). Thus, the beneficiary could continue to exclude a fraction of the payments even after the beneficiary had already excluded an aggregate amount equal to the principal amount payable under the policy.

As noted in **¶ 9.1120**, the 1986 TRA changed the treatment of annuity payments under § 72 so that once an annuitant has recovered the amount invested in the contract, all subsequent payments are taxable to the recipient. While Congress made that change to the treatment of annuity payments received under § 72, it did not expressly change the treatment under § 101 of life insurance proceeds that are received in installments. Since the installment payments of life insurance proceeds over the life of a beneficiary constitute the payment of an annuity, the proration of the amount held by the insurer that is dictated by the regulations under § 101 are merely applications of the annuity provisions of § 72. The 1986 amendment of § 72 to the treatment of annuities therefore changed the treatment of installment payments made pursuant to a life insurance contract.

Section 72(a) states that that provision applies to amounts received as an annuity "under an annuity, endowment, or life insurance contract." Similarly, § 72(b), establishing the exclusion ratio, also refers to amounts received as an annuity under an annuity, endowment or life insurance contract. It is § 72(b)(2) that prohibits an annuitant from excluding from income more than the investment in the contract. It is clear that the addition to the Code of § 72(b)(2) applies to the proration of the death benefit under § 101 and that the amount held by the insurer with respect to the beneficiary constitutes the beneficiary's investment in the contract. Accordingly, once the beneficiary has excluded an amount equal to the death benefit, all subsequent installment payments will be included in the beneficiary's gross income.

¶ 9.2300. Illustration. F purchased a $100,000 life insurance policy on his life and named his son, S, as beneficiary. Upon maturity, the beneficiary has the option to take $100,000 as a lump sum settlement of the policy. Upon F's death, if S elected to receive the $100,000 proceeds in a lump sum, nothing would be included in S's gross income. Instead, S elected to leave the $100,000 with the insurer and to receive annual payments of $8,000 for the rest of his life. Under the applicable mortality tables set forth in the regulations, S had a life expectancy of 20 years. During the first 20 years that the $8,000 annual payments are made, S will exclude $1/20 \times$ $100,000 = $5,000$ of each annual payment, and the $3,000 balance of each annual payment will be included in S's gross income. Treas. Reg. § 1.101–4, and –7.

If S lives longer than his 20–year life expectancy, all $8,000 of each subsequent installment payment will be included in S's gross income.

¶ 9.2400. Cessation of Installment Payments Before the Entire Amount of the Death Benefit is Distributed. If the proceeds of a life insurance policy are left with the insurer to make installment payments for the life of a beneficiary and if all payments from the insurer are to cease upon the death of the beneficiary, the death of the beneficiary prior to the expiration of his life expectancy will leave undistributed some portion of the principal amount of the death benefit that was left with the insurer. Will the beneficiary or the beneficiary's estate be allowed a deduction for the unrecovered amount?

In the comparable circumstance where an annuitant for life dies prematurely, the 1986 TRA amended § 72 to grant an itemized deduction to the annuitant for his unrecovered investment. § 72(b)(3).[14] Prior to that amendment, no deduction was allowed. Similarly, no deduction was allowed for the unrecovered amount of insurance proceeds that were held by the insurer with respect to a beneficiary. For reasons discussed in **¶ 9.2220**, the 1986 amendment to the annuity provision applies to the installment payments made to a life insurance beneficiary receiving such payments for his life, and so an itemized deduction will be allowed to a beneficiary who does not attain his life expectancy.

---

14. See **¶ 9.1200**.

¶ 9.2500. Payment Only of Interest. If life insurance proceeds are held by the insurer under an agreement to pay interest only in contrast to making installment payments, the proceeds that are held by the insurer are excluded from the gross income of the beneficiary; but, the interest payments are included. § 101(c).

¶ 9.2600. Transfer for Value. If the original owner of a life insurance policy transfers the policy to another for valuable consideration, part of the insurance proceeds payable upon maturity of the policy may be taxable.[15] This treatment is sometimes referred to as the "transfer for value" rule.

¶ 9.2610. Permissible Transferees. The "transfer for value" rule does not apply if the transferee of the policy was the insured, a partner of the insured, a partnership in which the insured was a partner, or a corporation in which the insured was an officer or shareholder. § 101(a)(2)(B). Note that a transfer to a co-shareholder is *not* within this exception.

¶ 9.2620. Tax–Free Transfers. If the transferee of an insurance policy has the same basis in the policy, in whole or in part, as the transferor, the beneficiary's receipt of the insurance proceeds upon the insured's death are not income to the beneficiary unless the proceeds would have been taxable if there had been no transfer and the policy had continued to be held by the transferor. § 101(a)(2)(A). For example, if an insured were to make a gift of a policy insuring her life, the transfer for value rule will not apply.

¶ 9.2630. Amount Taxable. If the transfer of a life insurance policy was made for valuable consideration and if none of the above exceptions to the transfer for value rule are applicable, the beneficiary may exclude from gross income an amount of the proceeds equal to the consideration paid for the policy by the transferee plus the net premiums paid by the transferee (i.e., the beneficiary excludes an amount equal to his basis in the policy). The balance of the insurance proceeds will be included in the beneficiary's gross income.

¶ 9.2700. Illustrations.

¶ 9.2710. Illustration 1. H purchased a $100,000 face amount life insurance policy from the Reliable Insurance Co. insuring his life. H paid an annual premium of $5,000. H died after paying

15. The amount of the insurance proceeds that is taxable is described in ¶ **9.2630**.

premiums for three years, and the $100,000 proceeds were paid to H's wife, W, whom H had named as the beneficiary. Since H was the original owner of the policy and since he never transferred the policy to anyone, the $100,000 insurance proceeds are excluded from W's gross income.

¶ 9.2720. **Illustration 2.** Two years after *H* purchased the life insurance policy in the above illustration, H assigned the policy to Y who paid H $10,000 consideration for the purchase. Y was H's partner in a partnership which owned and operated a hardware business. Upon acquiring the policy, Y designated himself as beneficiary of the policy. Y paid one $5,000 premium before H died. After H's death, the insurer paid the $100,000 proceeds to Y as the beneficiary of the policy. Since, at the time that Y purchased the policy from H, Y was H's partner, the "transfer for value" rule is inapplicable. § 101(a)(2)(B). It would not matter if the partnership had terminated before H died since it is the relationship at the time of the transfer that controls. The $100,000 insurance proceeds that Y received are excluded from his gross income.

¶ 9.2730. **Illustration 3.** The same facts apply as in Illustration 2, except that Y was not a partner in a partnership with H. Instead, Y and H were shareholders in Y–H, Inc., a corporation which owned and operated a hardware business. Since Y is a purchaser for value and since co-shareholders are not exempted from the "transfer for value" rule, Y can exclude from his gross income only the $10,000 consideration he paid for the policy plus the $5,000 premium he paid. The remaining $85,000 of the proceeds is included in Y's gross income.

¶ 9.2800. **Terminally or Chronically Ill Insured.** If a policyholder surrenders the policy to the insurer, the amount the policyholder receives from the insurer that is in excess of his basis is included in his gross income. A very ill policyholder might need to collect on the policy before his death in order to have the cash to satisfy medical and similar expenses. Congress has provided tax relief for certain persons in that predicament.

If an insured is certified as being terminally ill or chronically ill, any amount received by him (or by another person who is the policyholder in certain circumstances) under the insurance contract will be treated as proceeds paid on the death of the insured and so may be excluded by § 101 from income. § 101(g). Also, if a policyholder of a policy on the life of a terminally or chronically ill insured sells any portion of the death benefit to a "viatical settlement provider," the amount received on the sale will be treated as if it were life insurance proceeds paid on the death of the insured. § 101(g)(2). A viatical settlement provider is a licensed person regularly engaged in the trade or business of purchasing, or taking assignment of, life insurance policies on the life of a terminally or chronically ill insured. § 101(g)(2)(B). If a state does not license viatical settlement providers, a person can qualify as such by satisfying requirements listed in § 101(g)(2). The terms, terminally and chronically ill individuals, are defined in § 101(g)(4)(A), (B).

¶ 9.3000.   MISCELLANEOUS INCLUSIONS IN GROSS INCOME.

¶ 9.3100.   Income of Child. Income earned by a child for the child's services is included in the child's gross income; it is *not* included in the parent's gross income even if the child's income is paid to the parent and is subject to the control of the parent. § 73(a). Note that a child's earned income for his services is not subject to the so-called "kiddie tax." § 1(g)(1), (4)(A).[16]

¶ 9.3200.   Prizes and Awards. In general, the fair market value of a prize or an award is gross income to the recipient. Quiz show and most contest prizes are taxable. However, there are several exceptions to this general rule. § 74.

¶ 9.3210.   Exception: Awards Transferred to Charities. A prize or award is excluded from gross income if: (a) the prize or award was given in recognition of religious, charitable, scientific, educational, artistic, literary or civic achievement; (b) the recipient did not take any action to enter the contest or proceeding; (c) the recipient is not required to render substantial future services as a condition to receiving the prize or award; and (d) the recipient assigns the prize or award to a governmental unit or tax-exempt charitable or like organization. § 74(b).

¶ 9.3211.   Effect of Transfer. If the exception described in ¶ 9.3210 applies, the prize or award is not included in the winner's gross income and no charitable deduction is allowed to the winner or to the payor.

¶ 9.3220.   Exception: Employee Achievement Awards. The 1986 Tax Reform Act provides an exclusion for employees who

---

16.   See Chapter **Fourteen.**

receive "achievement awards" that satisfy certain requirements. The fair market value of an achievement award is fully excludable from the employee's gross income only if the entire cost of the award is deductible by the employer. § 74(c). If part of the employer's cost is not deductible, then only part of the award is excluded from the employee's gross income. In such a case, the employee must include in his gross income the greater of: (1) the amount of the employer's cost that is nondeductible (but this amount cannot exceed the value of the award), or (2) the amount by which the value of the award exceeds the deduction allowable to the employer. § 74(c)(2).

The employer's cost for providing an "employee achievement award" typically will be a deductible business expense under § 162, but the amount of deduction allowable to the employer is restricted by § 274(j). Since the employee's exclusion of the award depends upon the amount of deduction allowable to the employer, this restriction on deductibility also affects the amount of the employee's exclusion.[17]

In appropriate circumstances, an employer's award to an employee will be excluded from the employee's gross income as a *de minimis* fringe benefit under § 132(e).[18]

¶ **9.3221. Employee Achievement Award Defined.** An "employee achievement award" is an item of tangible personal property that an employer transfers to an employee for "length of service achievement" or "safety achievement." The property must be awarded as part of a meaningful presentation, under conditions and circumstances that do not create a significant likelihood of the payment of disguised compensation. § 274(j)(3)(A). An example of facts that suggest disguised compensation is an employee award made at the time of annual salary adjustments as an apparent substitute for a previous program of awarding cash bonuses. Note that the award must consist of tangible personalty. An award of cash or a gift certificate will not qualify.

¶ **9.3222. Limitation on Length of Service Awards.** An employee cannot exclude an award given for length of service

---

17.   The operation of the § 274(j) limitation on the employer's deduction is described in ¶¶ 9.3224–9.3224–3.

18.   See ¶¶ 2.2400 and 9.3225.

if it is received during the employee's first five years of employment, or if the employee had previously received an award that year or during the past four years while working for that employer. § 274(j)(4)(B). For this purpose, previously made employee awards that were excludable by the employee as a *de minimis* fringe benefit under § 132(e) are disregarded.

¶ **9.3223.   Safety Achievement Awards.** All employees are eligible for this award except managers, administrators, clerical workers, and other professional employees. Once an employer has made safety awards during a taxable year to more than ten percent of the eligible employees, any subsequent safety awards made that year will be included in income. § 274(j)(4)(C).

¶ **9.3224.   Dollar Limitations on the Employer's Deduction.** The dollar amount of an employer's cost for an achievement award that can be deducted by the employer depends upon whether the award is a "qualified plan award." § 274(j)(2). As noted in ¶ **9.3220**, the amount excludable by the employee depends upon the amount of the employer's cost that is deductible.

¶ **9.3224–1.   Qualified Plan Award.** A qualified plan award is an employee achievement award provided under an established written plan of the employer that does not discriminate in favor of highly compensated employees. An employee achievement award will not constitute a qualified plan award if the *average* cost of all such awards that were made by the employer in that year exceeds $400. § 274(j)(3)(B).

¶ **9.3224–2.   Limitation   on   Non–Qualified   Plan Awards.** If an employee achievement award is not a qualified plan award, the maximum amount of cost that the employer can deduct for making such an award to an employee is $400. § 274(j)(2)(A). If in a taxable year an employer made to one employee more than one employee achievement award that were not qualified plan awards, the maximum deduction allowable for the aggregate cost of making such awards to that employee cannot exceed $400. § 274(j)(2)(A). You will recall that the amount of an award that an employee can exclude from income cannot exceed the amount of cost that the employer can deduct.

¶ **9.3224–3. Deduction for Qualified Plan Awards.** If an employer makes one or more "qualified plan awards"[19] to an employee in a taxable year, the maximum amount of deduction allowable for the aggregate cost of all employee achievement awards made to such employee (including employee achievement awards that are not "qualified plan awards") is $1,600. § 274(j)(2)(B).

¶ **9.3225. *De Minimis* Fringe Benefit.** In appropriate circumstances, an award to an employee will be excluded from the employee's gross income as a *de minimis* fringe benefit under § 132(e). Typically, this exception will apply only to an award of an item having a small value that is given to an employee who has not received a number of such awards. However, the Report of the Senate Finance Committee to the 1986 TRA stated that the *de minimis* fringe benefit exception ordinarily will apply to a traditional retirement gift presented to an employee on retirement after completing a lengthy service. If otherwise applicable, the *de minimis* fringe benefit exception can apply to such awards even if the employee achievement award exclusion of § 74(c) does not apply.[20]

¶ **9.3230. Exceptions: Scholarship.** Where the prize or award consists of a "qualified scholarship" under § 117, the amount received is excluded from the recipient's gross income. § 74(a). In general, a qualified scholarship is an amount received by an individual who is a candidate for a degree at an educational organization as a scholarship or fellowship grant to the extent that the amount is used for "qualified tuition and related expenses." § 117.[21]

¶ **9.3240. Fair Market Value.** If a prize or award is included in the recipient's gross income, the amount included is determined by reference to the fair market value of the property. Treas. Reg. § 1.74–1(a)(2). The fair market value of property is defined, for tax purposes, as "the price at which the property would change hands between a willing buyer and a willing seller, neither being under any compulsion to buy or to sell and both having reasonable knowledge of relevant facts." Treas. Reg. § 1.170A–1(c)(2).

---

19.   See ¶ **9.3224–1**.

20.   See Conference Report to the TRA 1986, H.R. Rept. 99–841, 99th Cong., 2d Sess. (1986) (Conf. Rep.), p. II–19; Senate Finance Committee's Report on TRA 1986, S.Rept. 99–313, 99th Cong., 2d Sess. (1986), pp. 53–54.

21.   See ¶ **9.3500** *et seq.*

One difficulty with this definition is that there is more than one market at which an item can be sold (e.g., retail market, wholesale market, private sale market) and a choice must be made as to the proper market to use.

The fair market value of an item is the cost of replacing it rather than the amount that could be realized on the liquidation of the item. So, it is necessary to determine the price that a member of the public would pay to purchase the item. Thus, if an item is generally obtainable by the public in the retail market, the fair market value of such an item is the price at which the item or a comparable item would be sold at retail. In *Anselmo v. Commissioner*,[22] the court affirmed the Tax Court's determination that the "public" for low quality unmounted gems is jewelry manufacturers and jewelry stores that create jewelry items, rather than the individual consumer. The fair market value therefore was determined by the wholesale rather than the retail market. In most cases, the retail market will control.

¶ 9.3300. **Medical Benefits.** The tax treatment of the receipt of medical benefits and the reimbursement of medical expenses is discussed in Chapter **Nineteen.**

¶ 9.3400. **Improvements Made by a Tenant on Lessor's Realty.**

¶ 9.3410. **Construction of the Improvement: Rent Substitute.** Where land is leased to a tenant who constructs an improvement on the land, the lessor does not recognize gross income thereby unless the improvement is intended as a rent substitute. Factors which would indicate that the tenant's improvement was intended as a rent substitute are: (a) a leasehold term which is significantly shorter than the useful life of the improvement, or (b) a leasehold term subject to the power of the lessor to terminate the lease at his option. In most circumstances, the tenant's construction of an improvement will not constitute income to the lessor at the time of construction.[23]

¶ 9.3420. **Termination of the Lease.** In *Helvering v. Bruun,*[24] the Supreme Court held that upon termination of a lease, the

---

22. 757 F.2d 1208 (11th Cir. 1985), aff'g 80 T.C. 872 (1983).
23. See *M.E. Blatt Co. v. United States*, 305 U.S. 267 (1938).
24. 309 U.S. 461 (1940).

lessor recognizes gross income in an amount equal to the fair market value of improvements previously constructed on the demised land by the tenant. Two years later, Congress adopted the antecedent of § 109 which specifically excludes the value of such improvements from the lessor's gross income upon termination of the lease unless the improvements represent a liquidation in kind of lease rentals. Treas. Reg. § 1.109–1(a).

Section 109 is a nonrecognition provision (not a complete exclusion) because the gain realized by the lessor on termination of the lease is deferred. Section 1019 prohibits any adjustments to the lessor's basis as a consequence of income which is realized on termination of a lease but is not recognized because of § 109. Thus, while the lessor does not recognize income on receiving the leasehold improvements, he does not acquire any basis for the improvements.

¶ 9.3421. **Illustration.** In Year One, L leased land in which he had a basis of $40,000 to T for 50 years at an annual rental of $4,000. T erected a building on the land at a cost of $100,000. Upon the expiration or termination of the lease, all improvements on the land will become the property of L. Twenty years later, L terminated the lease because of T's failure to pay rent, and L thereby acquired possession of the property including the building that T had constructed. The lease could not be terminated under its terms for any reason other than nonpayment of rent. At the time of termination, the fair market value of the building was $60,000. L did not recognize any gain on the termination of the lease. § 109. L's basis in the land is $40,000, and L's basis in the building is $0.

¶ 9.3500. **Qualified Scholarships.** Prior to 1954, scholarships were treated as a type of gift which usually were excluded from gross income. Since 1954, they have not been treated as gifts and have been dealt with in several Code provisions (e.g. §§ 117 and 127).[25] The most important of these provisions is § 117.

Section 117 excludes from gross income any amount received as a "qualified scholarship" by an individual who is a candidate for a degree at an "educational organization" as defined in § 170(b)(1)(A)(ii). A "qualified scholarship" is an amount received by an individual as a scholarship or fellowship grant to the extent that

---

25. Section 127 is discussed at ¶ **9.3560.**

the aggregate amount of scholarship and fellowship grants received by that individual do not exceed the amount of that individual's "qualified tuition and related expenses," which term is explained at ¶ 9.3510. There is no requirement that the funds received by a TP be traced to the payment of tuition and related expenses or that the scholarship grant require the TP to use the funds for that purpose. It is sufficient that the scholarship or grant does not prohibit such use or earmark the grant for a different use.[26] To the extent that the amount of scholarship or fellowship grant received by an individual exceeds his qualified tuition and related expenses, the excess is included in his gross income. Note that there are several credits and deductions allowed for qualified educational expenses.

¶ 9.3510. Qualified Tuition and Related Expenses. Qualified tuition and related expenses are limited to: (a) tuition and fees required for the enrollment or attendance of a student at an educational organization, and (b) fees, books, supplies, and equipment required for a course of instruction at the educational organization. § 117(b)(2). No exclusion is permitted for scholarship or grant money provided for room and board, allowances, or for expenses for travel, research, or clerical help. A recipient's record keeping requirements that must be satisfied to exclude a scholarship from the recipient's gross income are set forth in Prop. Reg. § 1.117–6(e). However, there is no requirement that the actual dollars of the grant be traced to a qualified expenditure. The TP merely needs to show that money was spent on qualified tuition and related expenses.[27] The grant need not specify that it is for tuition, but to the extent that it specifies that it is for room and board or other nonexcludable items, then the TP must include that amount in income. Prop. Reg. § 1.117–6(c)(1).

¶ 9.3520. Degree Candidates. The exclusion under § 117 applies only to degree candidates. A candidate for a degree includes students attending a primary or secondary school and students who are pursuing a degree at a college or a university. A candidate for a degree also includes a student, full or part-time, who receives a scholarship for study at an educational institution that: (a) provides an educational program that is acceptable for full credit towards a bachelor's or higher degree, or offers a program of training to prepare students for gainful employment in a

---

26. Conference Report on the Tax Reform Act of 1986, H. Rept. 99–841, 99th cong., 2d Sess. (1986), p. II–16; Prop. Reg. § 1.117–6(c)(1).

27. Id.

recognized occupation; (b) is authorized under Federal or State law to provide such a program; and (c) is accredited by a nationally recognized accreditation agency.[28]

¶ 9.3530. Payments for Teaching, Research or Other Services. Except for scholarships under two specific programs,[29] recipients of scholarships or fellowship grants are not permitted to exclude from their gross income that portion of a scholarship or grant representing payment for teaching, research or other services provided by the student. § 117(c)(1). Also, a qualified tuition reduction[30] will be included in the student's gross income to the extent that the reduction constitutes a payment for the student's services. § 117(c)(1).

¶ 9.3531. Athletic and Other Extracurricular Activity Scholarships. If a scholarship is granted by an educational institution because of a student's participation in a varsity sport or in some other extracurricular activity (such as a musical, dramatic or journalistic activity), a question might be raised as to whether the scholarship is granted for services rendered or to be rendered to the grantor institution. To date, the Service has not attempted to include such scholarships in a student's gross income. In several Tax Court cases involving the tax characterization of athletic scholarships, but not directly involving the taxability of such scholarships, the Commissioner agreed that an athletic scholarship can be excluded from the recipient's gross income under § 117.[31]

In Rev. Rul. 77–263, the Commissioner passed upon the exclusion from gross income of a one-year athletic scholarship that was awarded to an incoming freshman in anticipation of the student's participation in a varsity sport. The student was not required to participate in the sport; the scholarship could not be canceled in that year just because the student failed to participate in the sport; and the student was not required to undertake some other activity in lieu of participating in that sport. The Commissioner ruled that such an athletic scholarship is excluded from the student's gross income by § 117. A

---

28. General Explanation of the Tax Reform Act of 1986, prepared by the Staff of the Joint Committee on Taxation, 99th Cong., pp. 42–43 (1987); Prop. Reg. § 1.117–6(c)(4)(iii).

29. See § 117(c)(2).

30. See ¶ **9.3540.**

31. See, e.g., *Jolitz v. Commissioner*, 73 T. C. 732 (1980).

negative inference of the Commissioner's emphasis on the facts that the scholarship could not be canceled during that year because of the student's nonperformance in the sport and that no alternative service is required is that an athletic scholarship will be taxable to a student if the educational institution can cancel the scholarship in the event that the student fails to participate in the sport (or, even worse, if the institution can cancel the scholarship if the student's effort or performance in the sport is deemed to be sub-par).

The Service has not expressly addressed the question of whether such a scholarship will qualify for exclusion from gross income if the institution has no obligation to renew it for each of the student's subsequent years at the institution and if the institution has not, in fact, renewed such scholarships when a student voluntarily chose not to continue to participate in the sport or if the student's performance was deemed to be inadequate. While some athletic scholarships might fail such a test if it were adopted, for political reasons it does not seem likely that the Service will seek to tax athletic scholarships at this time or in the foreseeable future.

Of course, like all other scholarships, athletic scholarships will be taxable to the extent that they exceed qualified tuition and related expenses or if they are earmarked for nonexcludable items.[32]

¶ 9.3540. Qualified Tuition Reduction. The amount of an individual's "qualified tuition reduction" is excluded from his gross income. § 117(d). A "qualified tuition reduction" is the amount of reduction in tuition provided to an employee of an educational organization described in § 170(b)(1)(A)(ii) for education below the graduate level at the employer's or other qualified educational institution. The exclusion of tuition reduction not only applies to tuition reductions for the education of employees but also applies to such reductions for the education of any person who is treated as an employee under § 132(h) (such as an employee's spouse or dependent child).

In PLR 9431017, the Service addressed the question of whether § 117(d) would apply if a university extended its tuition reduction policy to include a "domestic partner" of an employee. The Service ruled that § 117(d) will apply to the domestic partner

---

32.   See ¶ **9.3510**.

only if the state in which the employee resides recognizes the relationship of the employee and the domestic partner as a valid marital relationship. In that latter circumstance, the Service ruled that the domestic partner will qualify as a spouse under § 132(h). That ruling preceded the congressional adoption of the Defense of Marriage Act in 1996. In light of that Act, domestic partners of the same sex cannot qualify for the exclusion even if the state recognizes them as married. The constitutionality of the Defense of Marriage Act has been challenged.

A qualified tuition reduction that is provided with respect to a highly compensated employee will not be excluded from income unless such reductions are available to employees on a basis that does not discriminate in favor of highly compensated employees. § 117(d)(3). The term "highly compensated employee" is defined in § 414(q).

As noted in ¶ **9.3530**, a qualified tuition reduction will be included in the student's gross income to the extent that the reduction represents payment for the student's services.

> **¶ 9.3541. Teaching and Research Assistants.** The rule limiting the "qualified tuition reduction" exclusion to education below the graduate level does not apply to a graduate student at a qualified educational institution who is engaged in teaching or research activities for that institution. § 117(d)(5). Thus, qualified tuition reduction can be provided for graduate studies for such teaching and research assistants. However, to be excluded from a student's gross income, the reduction must comply with the requirement of § 117(c) that it does not represent a payment for the student's teaching or research services.
>
> The principal standard for determining whether a tuition reduction was granted as compensation for a student's services is whether the services are primarily for the grantor's benefit rather than in furtherance of the student's education. If the services performed by the student are primarily for the benefit of the grantor, an amount of tuition reduction that is equal to the value of those services will be included in the student's gross income. Prop. Reg. § 1.117–6(d)(2), (3). If the grantor also made a cash payment to the student for the student's services, that payment will be taken into account in determining the amount of tuition reduction that constitutes compensa-

tion to the student for such services. *Id*. Since, in some cases, only a portion of a tuition reduction will constitute compensation to a student for services, it is possible for a tuition reduction to be divided into two portions: a compensatory portion that is included in the student's gross income, and a noncompensatory portion that is excluded from the student's gross income if it qualifies under § 117(d).

In determining the value of a student's services in order to determine how much of a tuition reduction is payment for those services, the amount paid by the grantor for the same or similar services provided by comparable students who do not receive a tuition reduction or by non-student employees will be given considerable weight. Also, the amount paid by other educational organizations for similar services of students or other employees will be taken into account. Prop. Reg. § 1.117–6(d)(3).

¶ **9.3550. Earned Income.** The amount of scholarships, and tuition reductions that are includable in a TP's gross income are considered earned income for the purpose of the standard deduction rule applicable to a TP who may be claimed as a dependent by another person.[33] For the limitations on a dependent's use of his standard deduction, see Chapter **Ten**. The dependent's earned income can positively affect the amount of basic standard deduction allowable under § 63(c)(5)(B).

¶ **9.3560. Educational Assistance Program.** Section 127 excludes from an employee's income certain educational assistance provided by the employer. The maximum amount of educational assistance that an employee can exclude in a calendar year is $5,250. § 127(a)(2).

To qualify for the exclusion, the educational assistance must be provided pursuant to a written plan of the employer. The plan must specify the classification of employees who qualify for benefits, and that classification must not discriminate in favor of highly compensated employees or their dependents [the meaning of "highly compensated employee" is set forth at § 414(q)]. § 127(b). The plan can benefit certain self-employed persons, subject to the anti-discrimination provision noted above.

---

33. Conference Report on the Tax Reform Act of 1986, H. Rept. 99–841, 99th Cong., 2d Sess. (1986), p. II–17; Prop. Reg. § 1.117–6(h).

§ 127(c)(2). Not more than 5% of the amount of such benefits can be paid or incurred during a year for individuals (and their spouses and dependents) who are significant shareholders or owners of the employer (i.e., an individual who on any day of the year owns more than 5% of the stock or the capital and profits interest in the employer is a significant shareholder or owner of the employer). § 127(b)(3). If the plan is to qualify, eligible employees cannot be given the choice of receiving other remuneration in lieu of the educational assistance, and reasonable notification as to eligibility and terms of the program must be provided to all eligible employees. § 127(b)(4), (6).

The benefits that can be excluded from income under this provision are: (1) the payment by the employer of the employee's educational expenses, including (but not limited to) tuition, fees, books, supplies, and equipment, and (2) the provision by the employer of courses of instruction for the employee (including books, supplies and equipment). The statute does not permit the exclusion of certain expenses; for example, the statute does not exclude from income the payment or provision of: meals, lodging and transportation, and the payment or provision of tools or supplies which can be retained by the employee after the instruction is completed. Also, the statute does not exclude payments or provisions made with respect to education involving sports, games or hobbies. § 127(c)(1).

To the extent that educational assistance does not qualify for exclusion under § 127, it will be included in the employee's gross income unless it can qualify for exclusion as a fringe benefit under § 132. One fringe benefit category that can apply to educational assistance in certain circumstances is the "working condition fringe." § 132(j)(8). In some circumstances, an employee's educational expenses may qualify as an itemized deduction as an employee business expense under § 162.

¶ 9.3570. **Tax Policy Justification for Scholarship Exclusion.** Congress has not made clear its rationale for excluding certain scholarships from gross income. Since educational expenses generally are not deductible (except for certain educational expenses that qualify as business expenses), there is even greater reason to question why certain scholarships are excluded. A variety of justifications have been suggested by commentators, and we will consider a few of those.

Many educational institutions (especially state schools) do not charge an amount for tuition that equals the value of the education that is purchased thereby. The tuition cost effectively is subsidized to the extent that it is less than market value. There has never even been a suggestion that a student should include in income the amount of subsidy he receives. It would be very difficult to measure the amount of that subsidy, but administrative difficulty is only one of the reasons that the bargain element in tuition is not taxed. For example, state universities typically charge nonresident students a higher tuition than they charge their resident students, and so the latter could be said to be subsidized at least to the extent of that difference in cost. Yet, resident students are not taxed on that subsidy. One reason for this may be a federal policy to encourage education. Another reason may be that a state's provision of goods or services in kind typically has not been taxed to the recipient. For example, the receipt of free secondary education and of police and fire protection services are not taxed. A state's subsidization of university education can be placed in the same category.

Given that the subsidy element in tuition charges is not taxable, the suggestion has been made that tuition reductions through scholarships also should be excluded. This is put on grounds of equity—that is, if the recipients of one type of educational subsidy are not taxed, the recipients of similar types of subsidies should be treated the same. While equity considerations are relevant, one should be cautious about the amount of weight to be accorded them. Often, the wish to provide comparable tax treatment for similar, but nevertheless different, items is not a sufficient reason by itself to warrant extending a favorable tax treatment. Assuming that a tuition reduction by a state school should be treated as a nontaxable grant of services by a state, there must still be a reason to extend that treatment to scholarships granted by private schools and by third parties.

One of several justifications offered by Professor Dodge is that tuition reductions (and a scholarship granted by an educational institution can be viewed as a tuition reduction to the extent that the amount of the scholarship does not exceed the student's tuition) is a type of price discrimination, and as such is not taxable.[34] Professor Dodge points out that when a TP purchases an airline ticket at a discount because of a special offering, he is

---

34. Dodge, *Scholarships Under the Income Tax*, 46 The Tax Lawyer 697 (1993).

not taxed on the difference between the special price that he obtained and the higher price paid by passengers who did not qualify for that bargain. He suggests that the price differential in tuition (even when that is accomplished through scholarships provided by the educational institution) should also be treated as a nontaxable bargain purchase.

But, there are important differences between an airline's price discrimination and a school's tuition reduction through the grant of scholarships. The former is provided by a carrier to increase its revenue by selling seats that otherwise would remain empty. That has not been the reason for providing scholarships. Typically, they are not designed to sell places in the school's student body that would go unclaimed if sold at the usual price. The price set for the airline passenger is set for revenue maximization purposes, and so the usual rule of treating an arms' length exchange as one of equal values should and does apply. The reason for providing a scholarship (and so a lower tuition cost) is not because business judgment dictates that price as the best that can be obtained; rather, the scholarship is provided as a means to accomplish some educational or political goal of the institution. Consequently, since the price of the student's education has been set to accomplish a goal of the institution rather than at the education's market value, the presumption of equality that adheres to an arm's length bargain is inapplicable.

For example, if the 1,000,000th customer to purchase a ticket on an airline was given a special bargain price as part of a goodwill campaign, the bargain element should be taxable income. A scholarship granted to a student is more like the latter circumstance than a commercial price discrimination.

It is tempting to treat a scholarship as similar or analogous to a gift, but the reasons for excluding gifts from a donee's gross income do not apply to scholarships, regardless of whether the grantor of the scholarship is the educational institution itself or some other entity. It is unlikely that the educational institution at which the student is attending has the requisite "detached and disinterested generosity" for granting the student a scholarship. When the scholarship is provided by a third party, the funds from which the scholarship is paid usually will have been obtained by a contribution for which a tax deduction was allowed, and so the justification for excluding a gift from income is not applicable to scholarship grants.

The best (and perhaps the only viable) justification for excluding certain scholarships from income may be the previously mentioned policy not to tax services received in kind from a state. While that policy apparently does not apply when the educational institution in question is not a state school, the same reasoning might be applicable there as well. A private college or university typically is a non-profit organization that serves a governmental function. The provision of services in kind (i.e., education) by such an entity is analogous to the provision of services directly by a governmental body. While there may be flaws in that analogy, when it is combined with the equitable consideration of giving the same tax treatment for subsidies to students that are granted by private, non-profit educational entities as is applied to subsidies that are granted by state institutions, and with the federal goal of encouraging education, the combined considerations may be sufficient to justify the exclusion. The same or similar considerations apply when the scholarship is granted by a third party, especially if the third party is a tax-exempt, non-profit organization.

¶ 9.3600. General Welfare Fund Distributions. Amounts received as distribution from a general welfare fund (typically a distribution made by a federal or state agency pursuant to a statute to provide help for needy persons in the interest of the general welfare) do not constitute gross income to the recipient.[35] Welfare funds obtained by fraud are included in the recipient's gross income.[36]

A welfare agency may wish to provide a welfare recipient with training that will make the person eligible for employment in a trade or it may wish to require recipients to perform services in order to inculcate work habits that will encourage them to find gainful employment. To accomplish those goals, the agency might require the recipient to perform services as a condition of receiving benefits. The payments may be based on an hourly wage for work performed. Should welfare benefits that are so conditioned be taxable or should they be excluded from income? As a policy matter, the answer would seem to depend upon whether the motivation for the employment was to obtain the benefit of the services performed or was to train the recipient to enable him to become employed. There is no reason to exclude from income welfare benefits for which no services are required but to tax them if services are required as part of the

35. See Rev. Rul. 73–87; Rev. Rul. 63–136; Notice 99–3.
36. Rev. Rul. 78–53.

rehabilitation of the recipient. The difficulty is to determine whether payments are given as a compensation for services performed or are welfare benefits that are tied to a training program. The Commissioner has imposed several requirements for qualifying such payments as welfare benefits.

The following requirements must be satisfied if the payments for a TP's services are to be excluded from income as welfare benefits. The TP's participation in the work program must be arranged and financed by a public agency that provides welfare benefits. The total amount of payments to the TP must not exceed the sum of the amount of welfare benefits that the TP would have received for his needs even if he could not work plus out of pocket expenses the TP incurs in performing the work. In other words, the number of hours worked must be only enough to provide the TP with an amount of pay that will provide subsistence for his needs and no more than that.[37]

¶ 9.3610. **Illustration 1.** J received welfare payments from a welfare agency of the State of Y that are sufficient to support J and his three children. The payments are excluded from J's gross income. The exclusion would apply even if J were required by the agency to perform work under a state welfare work relief program as a condition to receiving the payments, provided that the amount of pay J receives does not exceed the subsistence payment he would have received.

¶ 9.3620. **Illustration 2.** K purchased a house that is included as an historic building in the National Register of Historic Places. K plans to use the building as an office at which K will conduct his professional work. K applied for and received a grant from the state to restore the house. The grant was made pursuant to section 101 of the National Historic Preservation Act of 1966. In Rev. Rul. 80–330, the Commissioner held that the grant received by K is included in K's gross income. The Commissioner stated that the purpose of the grant was to preserve historically significant buildings as contrasted to a grant based on need which is made under a social benefit program to promote the general welfare.

¶ 9.3630. **Social Security Benefits.** Prior to 1984, the entire amount of payments received as Federal social security benefits were excluded from gross income. From 1984 to 1993, inclusive, a

---

37. Rev. Rul. 71–425, modifying Rev. Rul. 67–144. See also Notice 99–3.

portion of social security benefits, which could not exceed 50% of the benefits received, was included in income if the TP's modified income exceeded a specified figure. As a consequence of an amendment adopted as part of the Omnibus Budget Reconciliation Act of 1993, the amount of an individual's social security benefits that is included in gross income is now determined under a two-tier structure. The maximum amount of social security benefits that can be included in gross income is 85% of the benefits received in a taxable year, but the percentage can be smaller than that figure and can even be zero. § 86.

¶ 9.3631. **Definition of "Social Security Benefit."** For this purpose, a "social security benefit" refers to a monthly benefit received under Title II of the Social Security Act (which includes old age and survivors benefits) and to certain railroad retirement benefits.

¶ 9.3632. **Benefits From Another Country.** If a TP receives benefits under a social security program of a foreign country, all of those benefits are included in the TP's gross income.[38] The typical circumstance in which this occurs is when a citizen or former citizen of a foreign country becomes a resident of the United States and retires there.

¶ 9.3640. **Unemployment Benefits.** A TP's unemployment benefits are included in his gross income. § 85.

¶ 9.3700. **Rental Value of Parsonage.** The rental value of a home provided to a minister or a rental allowance actually used by the minister to rent a home, is excluded from the minister's gross income. § 107. While the statute refers to a "minister of the gospel," the provision is applied more broadly to include anyone performing similar duties for any religion. For example, the exclusion has been applied to a rabbi and a cantor.[39]

In one case, the Ninth Circuit questioned the constitutionality of this provision on the ground that it might constitute governmental support of religion. The case in which that question was raised was settled so that the question was not resolved.

38. Rev. Rul. 66–34.

39. See GCM 35898 (1974); PLR 8739009 (1987).

¶ **9.3800.   Receipt of Windfalls and Penalties.** In *Eisner v. Macomber*,[40] the Supreme Court quoted from an earlier case that "Income may be defined as the gain derived from capital, from labor, or from both combined." Since the receipt of a windfall or a penalty is not derived from capital or from labor, prior to 1955 several courts held that such receipts were outside the scope of the income tax. That view was repudiated and laid to rest by the Supreme Court in *Commissioner v. Glenshaw Glass Co.*,[41] where punitive damages were held to be included in gross income. In *Glenshaw*, the court stated that the definition of income employed in *Eisner v. Macomber* was useful to the analysis of that case but "was not meant to provide a touchstone to all future gross income questions."

¶ **9.4000.   INTEREST–FREE AND BELOW MARKET INTEREST RATE LOANS.** Prior to the Tax Reform Act of 1984, it was held by the Tax Court and seven Circuit Courts of Appeals that the recipient of a loan with a below-market interest rate did not receive income for the value of receiving such a loan even when there was a compensatory purpose for not requiring the borrower to pay adequate interest. Prior to the 1984 Act, no attempt was made to impose tax consequences on the lender for making such a loan.

The rationale for excluding the value of receiving a loan for which little or no interest was charged was that in such cases the borrower constructively received income of an amount equal to the present value of the use of the borrowed funds and constructively paid interest to the lender of a like amount. Since, prior to the adoption of § 163(h) as part of the Tax Reform Act of 1986, interest payments typically were deductible under § 163, the borrower's income and deduction were a wash, and the borrower had no net income from the transaction. However, there was a timing problem which prevented that construction of the transaction from being a wash. If the loan was for a term of years, the borrower received income in the year that the loan was made of an amount equal to the value of his right to use those funds for the entire term of the loan. Thus, in the year in which the loan was made, the borrower would recognize income of an amount equal to the entire value of the right to use the loaned funds over the term of the loan, and would be treated as making a payment of a like amount of interest to the lender in the same year. But, a portion (typically a large portion) of the constructive payment to the lender would constitute a prepayment of interest which cannot be deducted at the time of payment.[42] Deductions for the prepay-

---

40.   252 U.S. 189 (1920).

41.   348 U.S. 426 (1955).

42.   § 461(g).

ment of interest typically are allowed only in the subsequent years to which those deemed payments relate, but the borrower's income would be reported in the year that the loan was made. Thus, while the borrower would have an equal amount of income and deduction, the income would be recognized immediately and the deduction might be deferred for some years.

A number of courts felt that the borrower's income and deduction should be matched in the same year, and they accomplished that match by excluding from the determination of the borrower's taxable income the borrower's constructive income and his constructive interest deduction. The following discussion indicates the reason for the congressional decision to change the treatment of loans bearing below-market interest and explains the current treatment of such loans under § 7872.

¶ 9.4100.   **The Time Value of Money.** The value associated with the right to receive money depends upon both the amount of money to be paid and the time at which payment is to be made. That is, one dollar received by X today is worth more than one dollar to be received by X one year from now. Just how much more a current dollar is worth than the value of a dollar to be received one year from now depends upon what the market requires a lender to pay for the use of a dollar. The significance of the time value of money and the reason that Congress chose to address that issue are discussed at ¶¶ 3.1100–3.1110.

One of the areas that Congress addressed was the loan of money in which the amount of interest charged is less than the market rate. The Code provision that deals with that situation is § 7872. If inadequate interest is payable for a loan, that bargain element provides a financial benefit to the borrower, and that benefit should be taken into account for tax purposes. There also can be tax consequences to the lender for constructively making a payment to the borrower and receiving interest in return. The manner in which those benefits and payments are taken into account by § 7872 is discussed below.

¶ 9.4200.   **Loans to Which § 7872 Applies.** Section 7872 applies only to the following types of "below-market loans": gift loans, compensation-related loans (i.e., a loan between an employer and an employee or between an independent contractor and a person for whom he provides services), corporate-shareholder loans, tax avoidance loans, loans to a qualified continuing care facility, and any other below-market loan in which the interest arrangement has a significant effect on the federal tax liability of the lender or the borrower.[43] A "below-market loan" is either: a demand loan bearing interest at a rate that is less than the "applicable Federal rate,"[44] or a term loan in which the amount loaned exceeds the present value of all payments to be made under the loan. § 7872(e)(1). The meaning of "present value" is explained at ¶¶ **9.4810–9.4814**. For purposes of § 7872, the word "loan" is broadly defined.[45] For example, many refundable deposits are treated as loans.[46] A prepayment for services or property, an advance to an employee to defray anticipated expenses, and an advance or draw on a partner's share of partnership income may be excluded from the statutory reference to "loans" and so are not subject to § 7872.[47]

¶ 9.4300. Constructive Payment To Borrower. In general, § 7872 treats the lender of a below-market loan as making a constructive payment to the borrower of an amount equal to the foregone interest,[48] and this constructive payment will be treated as: a gift (in the case of a gratuitous transaction), a dividend (in the case of a loan from a corporation to its shareholder), paid compensation (in the case of a loan to a person providing services), or as some other payment characterization in accordance with the substance of the transaction. The constructive payment will be included in the borrower's gross income unless it is a gift or falls within some other exclusion from income. If an actual payment of the same character would have been deductible or amortizable by the lender (e.g., a payment for services rendered in connection with the lender's business), the amount of the constructive payment similarly will be deductible or amortizable by the lender. For most tax purposes, the parties will be treated as if the constructive payment had actually been made. For example, if a constructive payment from the lender to the borrower is treated as a gift, the lender may have gift tax consequences.

¶ 9.4400. Constructive Interest Payment to Lender. The same amount that the borrower is deemed to have received from the lender is deemed to have been repaid simultaneously by the borrower to the

---

43.   § 7872(c).

44.   The meaning of "applicable Federal rate" is discussed at ¶¶ **9.4814** and **16.5130**.

45.   Prop. Reg. § 1.7872–2.

46.   Prop. Reg. § 1.7872–2(b). See ¶ **7.1210**.

47.   Prop. Reg. § 1.7872–2(b)(3).

48.   See ¶ **9.4510–2** for the meaning of "foregone interest."

lender. Note that in certain circumstances concerning a gift loan between individuals, the amount of repayment to the lender may be less than the payment to the borrower.[49] This constructive repayment is treated as an actual payment of interest by the borrower to the lender. The constructive interest payment is included in the lender's gross income. The constructive interest payment may be deductible or amortizable by the borrower if an actual payment would qualify as an interest deduction. Note that as a consequence of amendments made by the 1986 TRA, many types of interest payments are nondeductible.[50]

If the constructive interest payment on a term loan can be deducted, the aggregate amount of the deduction will be allocated among the years of the loan's term as if the interest were "original issue discount"—i.e., the constructive interest will be compounded rather than simple interest, and so the amount of interest allocated to each successive year of the term will be greater than the interest allocated to the prior year.[51]

¶ 9.4500. **Definitions.** For the purposes of § 7872, a "gift loan" is a loan bearing below-market interest where the foregone interest qualifies as a gift.[52] A "gift loan" may be either a demand loan or a term loan. A "demand loan" is a loan which is payable in full at any time on the demand of the lender.[53] A "term loan" is any loan which is not a demand loan.[54] The market interest rate is set at the "applicable Federal rate."[55] A different applicable Federal rate is used for demand loans than is used for term loans.[56] The Federal short-term rate is used for demand loans, and the Federal rate for term loans depends upon the length of the term of the loan.

¶ 9.4510. **Gift Loans and Demand Loans.** If a gift or demand loan is a below-market loan, the foregone interest will be treated as having been transferred from the lender to the borrower and

---

49. See ¶ **9.4700**.

50. See Chapter **Sixteen**.

51. The operation of the original issue discount provision is discussed at ¶¶ **16.5000–16.5230**.

52. § 7872(f)(3).

53. § 7872(f)(5).

54. § 7872(f)(6).

55. The applicable Federal rate is described at ¶¶ **9.4814** and **16.5130**.

56. § 7872(f)(2).

retransferred from the borrower to the lender as an interest payment on the last day of the calendar year to which such foregone interest is attributable.[57] Note that both the transfer to the borrower and the retransfer to the lender are treated as having been made on the last day of that calendar year.[58] In appropriate circumstances, the recipient of a constructive transfer or retransfer will recognize income thereby and the deemed payor of a transfer or retransfer will qualify for a deduction, but there are many circumstances where a transfer or retransfer will not be deductible.

¶ **9.4510–1. Below–Market Loans.** In the case of a demand loan, a "below-market loan" is a loan for which the interest payable is at a rate less than the applicable Federal rate.[59] The applicable Federal rate for demand loans is the Federal short-term rate (compounded semiannually) in effect under § 1274(d) for the period for which the amount of the foregone interest is being determined.[60] For a term loan, a "below-market loan" is one where the amount loaned is greater than the present value of all payments due under the loan.[61]

¶ **9.4510–2.   Foregone Interest.** Foregone interest is defined as the difference between the amount of interest which would be payable in a given period under the applicable Federal rate and any interest actually payable on the loan during the same period.[62]

¶ **9.4600. *De Minimis* Exception for Gift Loans Between Individuals.** Section 7872 will not apply to a gift loan between two individuals on any day on which the aggregate amount of loans outstanding between the two individuals is not greater than $10,000.[63] However, this *de minimis* exception does not apply to a loan that is made for the purpose of purchasing or carrying an income-producing asset.[64]

57. § 7872(a).

58. § 7872(a)(2).

59. § 7872(e)(1)(A).

60. § 7872(f)(2)(B).

61. § 7872(e)(1)(B). For the meaning of "present value," see ¶¶ **9.4810** to **9.4814**.

62. § 7872(e)(2).

63. § 7872(c)(2)(A).

64. § 7872(c)(2)(B).

¶ 9.4700.   Retransferred Amount Limited to Net Investment Income. In the case of a gift loan between individuals, the amount treated as retransferred by the borrower to the lender for any year shall not exceed the borrower's net investment income for that year, unless one of the principal purposes for the interest arrangement is tax avoidance.[65] Simply stated, the net investment income is the excess of investment income over investment expenses.[66] This limitation will not apply on any day on which the aggregate amount of outstanding loans between the borrower and the lender exceeds $100,000.[67] If the net investment income for a borrower does not exceed $1,000, the net investment income will be treated as zero for that year.[68]

¶ 9.4800.   Treatment of Term Loans That Are Not Gift Loans. In the case of a below-market term loan that is not a gift loan, the lender will be treated as having transferred, and the borrower will be treated as having received, cash in an amount equal to the excess of the amount loaned over the present value of all payments required to be made under the terms of the loan.[69] This constructive cash payment from the lender to the borrower is deemed to take place on the date that the loan is made (or on a later date that § 7872 first becomes applicable to the loan).[70] In addition to this constructive payment of such excess amount from the lender to the borrower, the excess amount also will be treated as an original issue discount[71] (OID). This constructive OID is in addition to any other original issue discount (OID) arising under the terms of the loan.[72] The OID constitutes an interest payment from the borrower to the lender and so is income to the lender and, in certain (but not all) cases, may be deductible by the borrower. In general, OID is allocated to the term of the loan as if interest accrued daily at a fixed rate compounded semiannually. Thus, the amount of interest that is allocated to the later years of the loan's term is greater than the amount allocated to the earlier years. You will recall that a term loan is a below-market

65.   § 7872(d)(1)(A) and (B).

66.   See §§ 163(d)(4) and 7872(d)(1)(E).

67.   § 7872(d)(1)(D).

68.   § 7872(d)(1)(E)(ii).

69.   § 7872(b)(1).

70.   Id.

71.   The operation of the original issue discount provisions is discussed at ¶¶ **16.5000–16.5230**.

72.   § 7872(b)(2).

loan if the amount loaned exceeds the present value of all payments due under the loan.[73]

¶ **9.4810. Present Value.** The current value of the right to receive a dollar amount at a future date is referred to as the "present value" of that right. The present value of a right to receive a dollar in the future is the amount that when invested at a specified rate of interest would yield by the date on which the dollar payment will be received the amount of dollars to be received at that future date. For example, if $1 is invested for one year at 10% simple interest, the investor will have $1.10 at the end of that year. So, the present value of the right to receive $1.10 at the end of one year is $1 if the interest rate is 10% simple interest.

¶ **9.4811. Discount Rate.** A key factor in determining present value is the rate of interest that is used to arrive at the dollar figure that will produce the amount receivable at the time at which payment is due. The figure payable at the future date must be discounted to arrive at the present value of the right to receive that amount, and the discount is determined by the rate of interest that is utilized. This assumed interest rate is referred to as the "discount rate." The choice of the discount rate depends upon market conditions. The greater the risk of loss or that the lender will not collect the required payment, the higher the discount rate will be. That reflects the fact that the greater the risk to which an investor is subject, the higher will be the rate of return that the investor will demand as a condition of making that investment.

¶ **9.4812. Simple or Compounded Interest.** In addition to choosing a specified interest rate as the discount rate, it is also necessary to agree as to whether that interest rate will be a simple rate or a compounded rate. If a compounded interest rate is adopted, the frequency of compounding must be settled—i.e., daily, monthly, semiannually, annually or some other period.

¶ **9.4813. Computation of Present Value.** Once the discount rate is determined, the computation of present value is merely an application of mathematical principles. It is not necessary, however, to understand those principles or to be skilled in mathematics to make that computation. Numerous

73. § 7872(e)(1)(B).

tables are available which make the computation easy to make in most cases. For example, the following table provides the current value of the right to receive $1 at a specified future year where the discount rate is one of a number of alternative interest rates that are compounded annually.

Year	6%	7%	8%
1	.943	.935	.926
2	.890	.873	.857
3	.840	.816	.794
4	.792	.763	.735
5	747	.713	.681
6	705	.666	.630

Thus, referring to the table above, the current value of the right to receive one dollar six years from today, where the discount rate is eight percent compounded annually, is 63 cents. In other words, if 63 cents were invested for six years at an interest rate of eight percent compounded annually, it would produce an aggregate interest of 37 cents which, when added to the 63 cent investment, would provide the investor with one dollar at the end of that six-year period. If the amount to be received at the end of a six year period is greater than one dollar, the present value of that right (at a discount rate of eight percent compounded annually) is the product of multiplying .63 times the amount to be received in six years. For example, the present value of the right to receive $10,000 in six years, discounted at eight percent compounded annually, is $6,300 (i.e., .63 × $10,000). Similarly, the present value of the right to receive $10,000 in six years, discounted at six percent compounded annually, is $7,050 (i.e., .705 × $10,000).

¶ 9.4814. **Choosing the Discount Rate.** The discount rate that is chosen to determine the present value of a right to payment at a future date should reflect the rate of return that the market provides for investments involving similar risks. However, for tax purposes, it would be administratively infeasible for the Service to determine the extent of risk in a TP's right to a future payment and to determine the current market rate of return for investments with comparable risks. Instead of requiring ad hoc determinations, for purposes of applying § 7872 to term loans, Congress pegged the discount rate to the "applicable Federal rate" compounded semiannually. § 7872(f)(2)(A). The "applicable Federal rate" is the average market yield (during a one-month period) of marketable securities issued by the United States government.[74] There are separate rates for short-term, mid-term, and long-term United States securities, and the applicable rate will depend upon the length of the term of the loan—i.e., if payment is due within three years, the Federal short-term rate will be employed; if the term of the loan is greater than three years but no more than nine years, the Federal mid-term rate will be employed.[75] The applicable Federal rates are determined and published monthly by the Treasury Department; and so it is easy for a TP to determine the discount rate that is applicable at the time that a term loan is made to which § 7872 applies.

¶ 9.4815. *De Minimis* **Exception for Compensation–Related Loans and Corporation–Shareholder Loans.** Section 7872 will not apply to a compensation-related loan or a corporation-shareholder loan on any day on which the aggregate amount of outstanding loans between the borrower and the lender does not exceed $10,000 and the interest arrangement does not have as one of its principal purposes the avoidance of a federal tax.[76]

¶ 9.4816. Exception for Certain Loans to Qualified Continuing Care Facilities. Section 7872 will not apply to certain below-market loan to a "qualified continuing care facility"[77] pursuant to a contract that provides life-time care for the lender or the lender's spouse and that meets the conditions described in § 7872(g)(3). This exception applies to such below-market loans only to the extent that the aggregate amount of loans between the lender and the facility does not exceed $90,000. This exception applies to a calendar year only if either the lender or the lender's spouse is 65 years of age or older by the close of the year.[78]

74. §§ 7872(f)(2)(A), 1274(d)(1).

75. § 1274(d)(1).

76. § 7872(c)(3). However, if the loans are *term* loans, if the aggregate amount of such loans between a borrower and a lender that are outstanding exceeds $10,000 on any day, and if § 7872 applied to that day, a subsequent reduction of such loans to an amount of $10,000 or less will not excuse the parties from § 7872 for those subsequent days, and that provision will continue to apply to the loan. § 7872(f)(10).

77. Defined in § 7872(g)(4).

78. See § 7872(g).

¶ 9.4817. Exclusion of Certain Loans. Temporary regulation § 1.7872–5T lists several types of loans which will not be subject to § 7872—for example, loans made by a life insurance company to an insured under a loan right in the policy typically are excluded from § 7872. These loans are excluded because typically they have no significant effect on the tax liability of the borrower or the lender. However, if one of the principal purposes for the transaction is the avoidance of tax, the loan will be recharacterized as a tax avoidance loan under § 7872(c)(1)(D).[79]

79. Temp. Reg. § 1.7872–5T(a)(2).

PART B
TAX ACCOUNTING

CHAPTER TEN

ADJUSTED GROSS INCOME, ITEMIZED DEDUCTIONS, AND THE STANDARD DEDUCTION

¶ 10.0000. ROLE OF AGI AND STANDARD DEDUCTION IN DETERMINING TAXABLE INCOME. Taxable income is defined in § 63 as either (1) gross income minus allowable deductions other than the standard deduction or (2) "adjusted gross income" minus the standard deduction and the deduction for personal and dependent exemptions.

¶ 10.1000. CONCEPT OF ADJUSTED GROSS INCOME. Adjusted gross income (AGI) is the gross income of an individual less certain specified deductions, primarily those listed in § 62(a). There are only a few deductions that are not listed in § 62(a) that are allowed in determining AGI. E.g., §§ 71(f)(1)(B), 164(f), and 165(h)(5)(A). The deductions taken into account in determining AGI are called "nonitemized deductions," or "above the line deductions." All other deductions, except for the personal and dependent exemption deductions, are called "itemized deductions." Itemized deductions are sometimes referred to as "below the line deductions."

The AGI concept applies only to individuals and estates and trusts. AGI is applied to estates and trusts only for very special and limited purposes. § 67(e). Hereafter in this book, the term is used exclusively as it applies to individuals.

The legislative history to the predecessor of § 62 states that the purpose of the adjusted gross income concept is to create a standard of measurement of income that will provide figures that are as nearly equivalent as is practicable when the standard is applied to different types of TPs who derive their income from different sources.[1] The Ways and Means Committee, discussing the adoption of the concept, said that "adjusted gross income means gross income less business deductions." Although that purpose is frequently cited by the Service in ruling on whether specific items are to be taken into account in determining AGI, it has

---

1. S. Rep. No. 78–885, at 24–25 (1944).

very little predictive value. Many items are included in or excluded from the determination of AGI for political or financial reasons, and their treatment does not conform to the goal of having a standardized measurement of economic income. For example, subject to a few minor exceptions, the unreimbursed business expenses of an employee (other than moving expenses) cannot be deducted in determining the employee's AGI; even though, when the same expenses are incurred by a self-employed individual, they are deducted in determining AGI.[2]

¶ 10.1100. Function of AGI. An individual's adjusted gross income (AGI) serves a number of functions. One function is that AGI determines the deductions that are available to a TP who utilizes the standard deduction. **¶ 10.2000.** Another is that AGI serves as an element of the formulas that apply to determine the amount of certain expenditures or payments that are deductible. For example, the maximum amount of charitable contributions that an individual may deduct in a taxable year is a percentage of the individual's contribution base which is determined by reference to his AGI; an individual's deductions for medical care in a taxable year are limited to the excess of his medical care expenses over a percentage of the individual's AGI; and certain itemized deductions (including the unreimbursed business expenses of an employee) are characterized as "miscellaneous itemized deductions" and are deductible only to the extent that the aggregate of such deductions exceeds 2% of the TP's AGI. §§ 170(b)(1), 213(a), 67.[3]

> **¶ 10.1110. Miscellaneous Itemized Deductions.** "Itemized deductions" are deductions (other than the personal and dependent exemption deductions) that are not taken into account in determining AGI. **¶ 10.1000** In this book, the deductions that are taken into account in determining AGI are called nonitemized deductions. Those itemized deductions that are not listed in § 67(b) constitute a subcategory of itemized deductions that are called "miscellaneous itemized deductions." Miscellaneous itemized deductions are deductible only to the extent that the aggregate of those deductions in a taxable year exceeds 2% of the TP's AGI. If the alternative minimum tax[4] applies to a TP, no deduc-

2. The determination of whether an individual is an employee for tax purposes rests on the common law of agency. *Alford v. United States*, 116 F.3d 334 (8th Cir. 1997).

3. See *McKay v. Commissioner*, 102 T.C. 465, 493 (1994) (holding that the unreimbursed business expenses of an employee are subject to the 2% of AGI floor).

4. The AMT is discussed in Chapter **Twenty–Eight**.

tion is allowable for the TP's miscellaneous itemized deductions. § 56(b)(1)(A)(i).

¶ 10.1120. Overall Limitation on Itemized Deductions. In addition to the floor imposed on "miscellaneous itemized deductions," if an individual's AGI for a taxable year exceeds an "applicable amount"—i.e., for the year 2009, the applicable amount is $166,800 ($83,400 for a married TP who files a separate return) adjusted upward each year for any increase in the cost-of-living—then that individual's itemized deductions for that year are reduced by the *lesser* of: (1) 3% of the excess of the individual's AGI over the applicable amount, or (2) 80% of such itemized deductions that are otherwise allowable. § 68.[5] The § 68 limitation on the amount of an individual's allowable itemized deduction is referred to as the "overall limitation on itemized deduction." Section 68 does not apply to the following four deductions: medical expenses, investment interest (as defined in § 163(d)), personal casualty and theft losses, and wagering losses. § 68(c).

The overall limitation was reduced for the years 2006–2009. As the final part of that gradual phase-out, the § 68 limitation does not apply at all to the years 2010–2012.Unless Congress acts, the limitation of § 68 is scheduled to spring back in full force in the year 2013. § 68(f), (g), and section 901, Pub. Law 107–16 (the sunset provision), as extended by Pub. Law 111–312.

¶ 10.1200. Section 62 Deductions. AGI equals gross income minus the deductions listed in § 62(a) plus a few other deductions. See **¶ 10.1000.** The deductions taken into account in determining AGI, most of which are listed in § 62(a), are referred to in this book as "nonitemized deductions." Other than the exemption deductions, deductible items that are not deductible in determining AGI are referred to as "itemized deductions." The personal and dependent exemptions constitute a third category of deductions that is neither an itemized nor a nonitemized deduction.

A number of the deductions listed in § 62(a) (all of which are nonitemized deductions) are business expense deductions, but most of the unreimbursed business expenses of an employee (other than moving expenses) are excluded and so must be itemized. The business expenses of an employee qualify as nonitemized deductions to

---

5. Rev. Proc. 2008–66 (Sec. 3.11).

the extent that they are reimbursed by the TP's employer under a reimbursement or other expense allowance arrangement; thus, the income from the reimbursement and the deduction for the business expense will be a wash. A few designated employee expenses incurred in one of several specified businesses (for example, certain expenses of elementary school teachers) are nonitemized deductions. § 62(a)(2)(B)–(E). Also, the deduction allowed by § 217 for unreimbursed moving expenses (the expense of moving to a new locality because of a change in the TP's place of work) is a nonitemized deduction regardless of whether the TP is an employee or self-employed. § 62(a)(15). A few nonbusiness expense deductions qualify as nonitemized deductions. For example, deductible losses from the sale or exchange of property, and the deduction allowed under § 215 for alimony payments, are nonitemized deductions. Deductions are discussed at length later in this work. Note that § 62(a) does not make an expenditure deductible; rather, § 62(a) lists those items which are deductible under other Code provisions that are to be deducted from gross income in determining an individual's AGI.

An expense that falls within a specific statutory category for deduction may also constitute a business expense. For example, state taxes on realty are deductible under § 164 as a state and local real property tax. But, if the realty is used in the TP's business, the state tax will also constitute an expense of conducting that business and so is deductible under § 162. While a deduction for taxes under § 164 is an itemized deduction, a business expense deduction is a nonitemized deduction unless the business is that of being an employee. In cases where two Code provisions overlap, the courts and the Service have permitted TPs to use the more favorable provision.[6] Therefore, the payment or accrual of a state tax on realty that is used in a TP's self-employed business is treated as a nonitemized deduction. Temp. Reg. § 1.62–1T(d). Other business-related items are treated similarly if they are directly connected with the conduct of a business (other than an employee's business). Id.

The Service's position is that for an expense to qualify as a nonitemized business expense deduction, it must be directly, and not merely remotely, connected with the conduct of a trade or business (other than an employee's business). Temp. Reg. § 1.62–1T(d). The tax must be imposed on the business itself as contrasted to a tax on an individual who owns and conducts the business. To illustrate how the

---

6. *McNutt–Boyce Co. v. Commissioner*, 38 T.C. 462, 1962 WL 1124 (1962), aff'd per curiam, 324 F.2d 957 (5th Cir. 1963), Acq.; Rev. Rul. 92–29. See also, Temp. Reg. § 1.62–1T(d).

Service distinguishes a "direct" connection with a business from a "remote" one, the temporary regulation asserts that, while state property taxes imposed on realty used in a self-employed business are nonitemized deductions, state income taxes imposed on an individual's self-employed business income are itemized deductions. Id. The Service's position that the state income tax on an individual's business income is an itemized deduction was sustained by the Tax Court and the Fourth Circuit.[7]

¶ **10.2000. STANDARD DEDUCTION.** In lieu of taking itemized deductions, an individual TP can deduct a specified dollar amount which is referred to as the "standard deduction." Thus, where an individual TP elects to utilize the standard deduction, the TP will deduct his nonitemized deductions from his gross income in order to arrive at his AGI, and the TP will then deduct his standard deduction from his AGI. In addition, an individual TP who utilizes the standard deduction can deduct the amount (if any) of deductions permitted for the exemptions available to the TP. See Chapter **Eleven**. The nonitemized deductions and the exemption deductions are available to an individual regardless of whether he utilizes the standard deduction, but itemized deductions can be taken only if the TP does not use the standard deduction. If a TP does not utilize the standard deduction, or is not permitted to use a standard deduction, the TP is said to have "itemized" his deductions— i.e., the TP will deduct his itemized deductions in lieu of the standard deduction.

¶ **10.2100. Qualification for the Standard Deduction.** The standard deduction is available only to individuals. There is no standard deduction for corporate TPs or for trusts or estates. Not all individuals are permitted to utilize a standard deduction.

¶ **10.2110. Individuals Who Are Barred from Using the Standard Deduction.** Certain individuals are not eligible to use the standard deduction. § 63(c)(6). For example, a nonresident alien is not granted a standard deduction. If a married couple files separate returns, and if one spouse elects to "itemize" deductions, the other spouse is barred from using a standard deduction. § 63(c)(6)(A).

¶ **10.2120. Dependent's Use of Standard Deduction.** If an individual TP qualifies as a dependent exemption deduction for another person, the basic standard deduction [See ¶ **10.2210**]

7. *Tanner v. Commissioner*, 45 T.C. 145 (1965), aff'd per curiam, 363 F.2d 36 (4th Cir. 1966).

allowable to that TP *cannot exceed* the TP's earned income plus a specified amount (for 2011, the amount is $300) or a specified dollar amount (for 2011, the amount is $950), whichever is greater. § 63(c)(5).[8] Thus, in 2011, a dependent's basic standard deduction is available to reduce $300 of income plus the amount of income earned by that dependent from employment and from the active conduct of a trade or business. Alternatively, the dependent can deduct $950. These figures are increased annually to reflect changes in the cost of living. § 63(c)(4).

¶ **10.2121. Illustration 1.** *B* is an unmarried dependent child of *P* who is entitled to a dependent exemption deduction for *B*. In 2011, *B* had interest income (which is unearned income) of $400. *B* had no other income that year. *B* is not allowed a personal exemption deduction. § 151(d)(2). *B* is allowed a basic standard deduction of $950, and so *B* has $0 of taxable income in that year. § 63(c)(5).

¶ **10.2122. Illustration 2.** The same facts as those stated in ¶ **10.2121** except that *B* also had $600 of earned income in 2011. *B*'s basic standard deduction is limited to $950, and so *B*'s taxable income for 2011 is $50. As noted in Chapter **Fourteen**, even if *B* is under the age of 14, *B* will be taxed on that $50 at rates applicable to *B* himself without regard to the marginal tax bracket of *B*'s parents.

¶ **10.2123. Illustration 3.** The same facts as those stated in ¶ **10.2121** except that *B* also had earned income of $700 for 2011. *B* is allowed a basic standard deduction of $1,000 (*B*'s earned income plus $300) or $950, whichever is greater. So, *B*'s taxable income for 2011 is $100.

¶ **10.2124. Illustration 4.** The same facts as those stated in ¶ **10.2121** except that *B* also had earned income of $7,000 for 2011. While *B*'s basic standard deduction is limited to the greater of his earned income plus $300 or $950, it cannot exceed the amount that is allowable for TPs of his filing status. *B* is an unmarried TP, and the 2011 basic standard deduction for such a TP is $5,800. So, in 2011, *B* had gross income of $7,400 and a standard deduction of $5,800. *B*'s taxable income for that year is $1,600.

---

8. Rev. Proc. 2011–12 (Sec. 2.05).

¶ **10.2200. Amount of the Standard Deduction.** The standard deduction is divided into two separate parts: a "basic standard deduction," and an "additional standard deduction" for the aged and blind.

¶ **10.2210. Basic Standard Deduction.** The amount of the basic standard deduction depends upon the tax return filing status of the TP who is utilizing it. § 63(c)(2). For taxable years beginning in 2011, the basic standard deduction amounts are:

$11,600	joint return or surviving spouse
$8,500	head of household
$5,800	unmarried TP (other than surviving spouse or head of household)
$5,800	married TP filing separate return[9]

The amounts listed above are indexed annually (i.e., they are increased to reflect cost-of-living increases, if any). § 63(c)(4). Beginning in 2013, unless Congress acts, the joint return or surviving spouse standard deduction is scheduled to be 167% of the unmarried TP amount, rather than twice the amount as it currently is.

¶ **10.2220. Additional Standard Deduction.** Prior to the 1986 Act, an additional exemption deduction was granted for being aged or blind. This exemption was repealed by the 1986 TRA. In lieu of exemption deductions, Congress provides a TP an additional standard deduction allowance of a specified dollar amount for each of the following circumstances: the TP is 65 years of age or older; the TP is blind; the TP's spouse is 65 years of age or older and qualifies as an exemption of the TP under § 151(b); the TP's spouse is blind and qualifies as an exemption of the TP under § 151(b). §§ 63(c)(3), and 63(f). The personal exemption deductions are described in Chapter **Eleven**. The dollar amount for the additional standard deduction is indexed annually for inflation; for 2011, the dollar amount is $1,150.[10] If a TP has no spouse (and does not qualify as a "surviving spouse" as defined by § 2(a)), the additional standard deduction for being elderly or blind is a larger figure; for the year 2011, the amount of the deduction is $1,450, instead of the $1,150 amount that otherwise would be applicable. § 63(f)(3).[11]

9. Rev. Proc. 2011–12.

10. Rev. Proc. 2011–12.

11. Rev. Proc. 2011–12.

¶ **10.2300. Illustration.** In 2011, Mary Ryan, a 30–year–old un-married TP with no dependents and with good eyesight had the following income and deductible expenditures:

Income	*Deductible Expenditures*
$32,000—salary	$2,000—nonitemized deductions
$2,000—dividends	$1,800—itemized deductions
$800—interest	

$34,800—total

Mary's gross income is $34,800. Her AGI is $32,800—i.e., the differ-ence between her gross income ($34,800) and her nonitemized deduc-tions ($2,000). None of Mary's deductions is a miscellaneous itemized deduction. Mary's taxable income is determined as follows:

$32,800—AGI
($3,700)—personal exemption deduction
($5,800)—standard deduction

$23,300—taxable income

Mary will deduct a $5,800 basic standard deduction because that figure is greater than her itemized deductions which total only $1,800. Mary is not entitled to an additional standard deduction since she is neither aged nor blind.

¶ **10.2400. Illustration.** *H* was divorced from *Y* in Year One, and he married *Z* in Year Two. In October of Year Six, *H* and *Z* separated physically, but they were not divorced or legally separated in that year. Neither *H* nor *Z* has any children. *Z* filed a separate income tax return for Year Six, and she elected to deduct her itemized deduc-tions instead of taking a standard deduction. Because *Z* deducted her itemized deductions, *H* is not permitted to utilize a standard deduc-tion on his separate tax return for Year Six. § 63(c)(6)(A). The standard for determining whether a couple will be treated as married is determined at the close of a taxable year in accordance with § 7703. § 63(g).

¶ **10.2500. Illustration.** *R* is the unmarried 15–year–old daughter of *M*. *R* has good eyesight. *M* provides over one-half of *R*'s support, and *M* is entitled to a dependent exemption deduction for *R*.[12] In 2011, *R* had $4,000 of dividend and interest income from stocks and bonds that *R* had received as gifts from her grandparents two years

---

12. See Chapter **Eleven**.

earlier, and *R* earned $100 from her part-time employment as a babysitter. The only deductible expense that *R* had in 2011 was $300 in state income taxes. The deduction permitted for an individual's state income taxes is an itemized deduction (i.e., it is not included in the § 62(a) list), but it is not a miscellaneous itemized deduction. *R*'s taxable income is determined as follows:

4,100—gross income
($ 0)—§ 62(a) deductions

$4,100—AGI

$4,100
($950)—standard deduction
($ 0)—personal exemption

$3,150—taxable income

R is not allowed a personal exemption for 2011 because she qualifies as a dependent exemption deduction for *M*. § 151(d)(2). Also, because *R* qualifies as a dependent exemption deduction for *M*, the amount of *R*'s standard deduction is limited to $950. Since that amount is greater than *R*'s itemized deductions (which totaled only $300), *R* will utilize a $950 standard deduction in lieu of taking her itemized deduction.

CHAPTER ELEVEN

PERSONAL AND DEPENDENT EXEMPTION DEDUCTIONS

¶ 11.0000. EXEMPTIONS AND DEDUCTIONS IN GENERAL. Once the basic concepts relating to the determination of income are mastered, the student must develop a solid working knowledge of deductions. An exemption is merely one type of deduction that is available. There are *two classes* of exemptions—*personal* exemption deductions and *dependent* exemption deductions. Remember *deductions* are items which may be subtracted from gross income (or from adjusted gross income) as part of the calculation of taxable income; they are to be distinguished from *exclusions* which, as previously noted, relate to items which are not included in gross income in the first instance. The personal and dependent exemption deductions are described in this chapter. Most of the other tax deductions are described in subsequent chapters.

¶ 11.1000. DEDUCTIBLE FROM ADJUSTED GROSS INCOME (AGI). The amount of deduction allowable for an exemption is deducted from the AGI of an individual regardless of whether he utilizes a "standard deduction." The standard deduction is described at **¶¶ 10.2000–10.2500.** The exemptions do not constitute *itemized* deductions, and so their deduction does not affect the availability of the standard deduction. The exemptions are not deducted in determining AGI, and so do not affect the size of a TP's AGI, and they are not nonitemized deductions. Exemptions constitute a third category of deductions—they are neither itemized nor nonitemized. An exemption constitutes a statutorily prescribed amount of allowable deduction. As noted at **¶ 11.2000** *et seq.*, for years prior to 2010, the amount of an individual's deductions for exemptions was phased out if the individual's AGI exceeded a specified dollar amount.

¶ 11.1100. Corporations. In determining a corporation's regular tax liability, a corporation has no exemptions. If a corporation's tax liability is determined under the Alternative Minimum Tax system (§ 55), the corporation will have a $40,000 exemption, but that exemption is phased out if the corporation's Alternative Minimum

Taxable Income exceeds $150,000. § 55(d)(2), (3).[1]

¶ 11.1200. Types of Exemptions and the Exemption Amount.
There are two general types of exemptions available to an individual
TP: (a) *personal* (TP and spouse); and (b) *dependents*. An individual
is allowed a deduction of a specific dollar amount (an "exemption
amount") for each exemption to which he is entitled. The exemption
amount is increased annually to reflect increases in the cost-of-living;
that is, the exemption amount is tied to the cost-of-living index.
§ 151(d)(4). For the year 2011, the exemption amount is $3,700.[2]

For years prior to 2010, if a TP's AGI exceeded a specified amount,
the TP's exemption deductions were phased out.[3] This phaseout of
the deduction is scheduled to become operative for years following
2012.

¶ 11.1210. Personal Exemption. An individual is entitled to
one exemption for himself unless he is a dependent of another
person who is entitled to take a deduction for him as a dependent.
An individual who qualifies as a dependent exemption deduction
for another person is not allowed a personal exemption deduction
for himself or an exemption for his dependents. § 151(d)(2).

On a joint return, the exemptions of both spouses are deductible.
A married TP who files a separate return can take an exemption
for a spouse only if the spouse had no gross income and is not a
dependent of another person. § 151(b). The determination of
whether a TP's spouse had gross income or was the dependent of
another person is made in relation to the calendar year in which
the taxable year of the TP begins. § 151(b). The meaning of
"dependent" is explained at **¶¶ 11.1220–11.1243.**

¶ 11.1211. Marital Status of Taxpayer. Marital status is
determined on the last day of the taxable year. A TP who is
divorced or legally separated at that time is not treated as
married for tax purposes. If a TP's spouse dies during a
taxable year, an exemption can still be claimed for that year if
the marital status requirements were satisfied at the time of
death. § 7703(a)(1). In certain circumstances described in

---

1. Note that certain small corporations are not subject to the Alternative Minimum
Tax. § 55(e).

2. Rev. Proc. 2011–12 (Sec. 2.07).

3. ¶ 11.2000.

§ 7703(b), a married individual who lives apart from his or her spouse for the last six months of a taxable year and who maintains a household that is the principal abode of a child of the individual for more than one-half of the taxable year is treated as an unmarried individual. A "child" of an individual is a person related to the individual as described in § 152(f)(1). See ¶ 11.1231.

¶ 11.1211–1. **Legal Separation.** For a court decree to establish a legal separation, it "must expressly and affirmatively provide that the parties live apart in the future and, thereby, alter the original and normal marital relationship."[4] Whether a decree of separate maintenance will qualify as a decree of legal separation depends upon the local state law; in most circumstances, a decree of separate maintenance will not qualify.[5]

¶ 11.1211–2. **Validity of Divorce.** The standards for determining whether the validity of a divorce can be challenged in a tax proceeding and the tax consequences of obtaining a tax avoidance divorce (i.e., a divorce obtained for tax reasons when the parties plan to remarry promptly) are discussed at ¶¶ **15.8000–15.8300.**

¶ 11.1220. **Dependent Exemption Deduction.** The exemption deduction that is granted to a TP for having dependents is sometimes referred to as the "dependent exemption deduction." An individual TP is entitled to one exemption for each person who meets the definition of a "dependent" of that person. § 151(c). A "dependent" is defined as a person who is not excluded by one of the specific statutory exclusions described at ¶¶ **11.1240–11.1243** and who fits within one of two categories: (1) qualified children, and (2) qualified relatives. § 152(a). The meaning of those two terms is set forth below. The several statutory exclusions from dependent classification are described in ¶¶ **11.1240–11.1243.** Before examining those exclusions, we will define three relevant terms: "child," "qualified child," and "qualified relative." Unless one of the exclusions applies, a TP will have an exemption for each of the TP's qualified children and qualified relatives.

4. *Boettiger v. Commissioner*, 31 T.C. 477 (1958); *Capodanno v. Commissioner*, 69 T.C. 638, 647 (1978), aff'd, 602 F.2d 64 (3d Cir. 1979).

5. Compare *Capodanno v. Commissioner*, *supra* with *Legget v. Commissioner*, 329 F.2d 509 (2d Cir. 1964).

¶ 11.1230. Definition of "Child," "Qualified Child," and "Qualified Relative."

¶ **11.1231.   Child.** A child of an individual is a son, daughter, stepson or stepdaughter of that individual. § 152(f)(1)(A)(i). An individual who has been legally adopted by a person or who has been lawfully placed with a person for a lawful adoption is treated as a child of that person. § 152(f)(1)(B). An "eligible foster child" (defined in § 152(f)(1)(C)) of an individual is treated as a child of the individual. § 152(f)(1)(A)(ii).

This definition of a "child" is utilized in some other provisions of the Code. See e.g., § 7703(b)(1).

¶ **11.1232.   Qualifying Child.** A "qualifying child" with respect to a TP is defined in § 152(c) and includes persons whose relationship to the TP is not that of a "child" as the latter term is defined in ¶ **11.1231.** Since it refers to more than the children of the TP, perhaps Congress might have chosen a more appropriate term. Nevertheless, the term "qualifying child" is the one that is used.

The definition of a "qualifying child" is a uniform definition that is adopted in other provisions of the Code. It is not limited to the dependent exemption provision. The same term and definition, with some modifications, are used in the provisions for: the child tax credit (§ 24), the earned income credit (§ 32), the dependent care credit (§ 21(b)(1)(A)), and head of household filing status (§ 2(b)(1)(A)).

There are four categories of tests that an individual must satisfy to be a qualifying child. The individual must satisfy all four tests. Those four categories are: relationship, age, residency, and support.

(1) *Relationship Test.* To be a qualified child of a TP, an individual must be either: a child of the TP (as defined in ¶ **11.1231**), a descendant of such a child, a brother, sister, stepbrother, or stepsister of the TP, or a descendant of any such relative. § 152(c)(2).

(2) *Age Test.* To be a qualified child of a TP, the individual must be younger than TP. In addition, the individual must not have attained the age of 19 before the end of the calendar year in which the taxable year of the TP begins. As an alternative to the age 19 requirement, an individual will satisfy the age

test if, for at least five calendar months in the calendar year in which the TP's taxable year begins, the individual is a full-time student at an educational organization (or is pursuing a full-time course of institutional on-farm training); *and* if the individual has not attained the age of 24 before the end of the calendar year in which the TP's taxable year begins. If an individual is permanently and totally disabled at any time during the calendar year described above, the individual will satisfy the age test, regardless of the age of the individual. § 152(c)(3)(B).

(3) *Residence Test.* To be a qualified child of a TP, the individual must have the same principal place of abode as the TP for more than one-half of the TP's taxable year. § 152(c)(1)(B).

(4) *Support Test.* To be a qualified child of a TP, an individual must not have provided over half of the individual's own support for the calendar year in which the taxable year of the TP begins. § 152(c)(1)(D) In determining the percentage of support provided by an individual, a scholarship of the individual to study at an educational organization is not taken into account *if* the individual is a child of the TP and a full-time student.[6] § 152(f)(5). Note that there is no requirement that the TP have provided over half of the individual's support; it is sufficient that the individual did not provide over half of the individual's own support.

When an individual could qualify as a qualifying child of more than one TP, the Code provides a tie-breaking system to determine which TP will prevail. § 152(c)(4). An individual can be a qualifying child of only one person.

¶ 11.1233. **Qualifying Relative.** In addition to a qualifying child, a qualifying relative can provide a TP with a dependent exemption deduction. § 152(a)(2). There are four categories of tests that must be satisfied for an individual to be a qualifying relative of a TP. § 152(d)(1). The individual must satisfy all four tests. These four categories are: a relationship test, a gross income test, a support test, and a non-qualifying child test. Id.

---

6. The child must be a full-time student at an educational organization (or pursuing a full-time course of institutional on-farm training) for at least five calendar months of the TP's calendar year. § 152(f)(2).

(1) *Relationship Test.* To be a qualified relative of a TP, the individual must, with respect to the TP, be: (a) a child or descendant of a child (as defined in ¶ **11.1231**), (b) a brother, sister, stepbrother, or stepsister, (c) a son or daughter of a brother or sister, (d) the father or mother of the TP or an ancestor of either, (e) a brother or sister of the father or mother of the TP, (f) a stepfather or stepmother, (g) a son-in-law, daughter-in-law, father-in-law, mother-in-law, brother-in-law, or sister-in-law, (h) an individual (other than the TP's spouse) who for the taxable year has the same principal place of abode as the TP and is a member of the TP's household whose relationship with the TP does not violate local law. § 152(d)(2)(H), (f)(3).

(2) *Gross Income Test.* The individual's gross income for the calendar year in which the taxable year of the TP begins must be less than the exemption amount. § 152(d)(1)(B). For the year 2011, the exemption amount is $3,700. See ¶ **11.1200.** While, for years beginning after 2012, a TP's exemption amount may be reduced if the TP's AGI exceeds a threshold amount (See ¶ **11.2000**), the statute does not refer to any specific person's exemption amount, and therefore refers to the exemption amount for that taxable year without any reduction because of a person's AGI. The exemption amount changes yearly to reflect changes in the cost-of-living.

(3) *Support Test.* The TP must provide more than half of the individual's support in the calendar year in which the TP's taxable year begins. § 152(d)(1)(C). In determining the percentage of support provided to an individual by a TP, a scholarship of the individual to study at an educational organization is not taken into account *if* the individual is a child of the TP and a full-time student.[7] § 152(f)(5).

If no person contributed over one-half the support for an individual, but two or more persons together contributed more than half of that support, under certain conditions, the members of that group are permitted to designate one person from the group who will be deemed to have provided over one-half of the individual's support. § 152(d)(3). Such an agreement is called a "multiple support agreement."

---

7. The child must be a full-time student at an educational organization (or pursuing a full-time course of institutional on-farm training) for at least five calendar months of the calendar year in which the TP's taxable year begins. § 152(f)(2).

(4) *Non–Qualifying Child Test.* The individual must not be a qualifying child of the TP or of any other person in the taxable year. § 152(d)(1)(D). The term "qualifying child" is defined in ¶ **11.1232.**

¶ **11.1240. Exclusions from Dependent Classification.** There are three conditions that must be met for a qualifying child or a qualifying relative to be a dependent of a TP. If any of those three conditions is not satisfied, the individual will not be a dependent.

¶ **11.1241. Joint Return Exclusion.** An individual who files a joint return with his or her spouse cannot qualify as a dependent of any person. § 152(b)(2). So, one condition is that the individual did not file a joint return.

¶ **11.1242. Citizenship.** With one exception, an individual cannot qualify as a dependent unless the individual is either a citizen, national or resident of the United States, or a resident of a country that is contiguous to the United States. § 152(b)(3). The one exception to that requirement is that an adopted child of a United States citizen or national can qualify as a dependent if, for the adoptive parent's taxable year, the child has the same principal place of abode as the parent and is a member of the parent's household. Id.

¶ **11.1243. Ineligible Taxpayer.** If a TP qualifies as a dependent of someone for a taxable year, the TP is deemed not to have any dependents in that taxable year. § 152(b)(1). So, an individual who otherwise would have been a dependent of that TP will not be a dependent.

¶ **11.1250. Divorced or Separated Parents.** When a married couple with a young child or children divorce or separate, a question can arise as to which parent is entitled to claim a dependent exemption deduction for the children. If no special statutory provision applies, such a child typically will be a "qualified child" or a "qualified relative" of the parent who has custody of the child for more than one-half of the calendar year. But, what if the parents wish to have the dependent exemption deduction taken by the noncustodial parent (i.e., the parent who does not have custody of the child for more than one-half of the calendar year)? The Code permits the parents to elect to have the noncustodial parent qualify for the exemption deduction if the conditions specified in § 152(e)(2) are satisfied. This provision applies only if the child receives over half of his support during the calendar year from his parents and the parents are either: (1) divorced, or legally separated under a decree of divorce or separate maintenance, or separated under a written separation agreement, or live apart at all times during the last six months of the calendar year; and (2) the child is in the custody of one or both parents for more than one-half of the calendar year. § 151(e)(1). The operation of this provision is set forth in detail in Treas. Reg. § 1.152–4.

If a child can qualify a parent for a dependent exemption deduction only if the child is a qualifying relative (¶ **11.1233**), and if the obstacle to that qualification is that the support test of § 152(d)(1)(C) cannot be satisfied, the parents might be able to execute a "multiple support agreement" with another supporter of the child to qualify one of the parents for that deduction. See § 152(d)(3) and Treas. Reg. § 1.152–3. If a multiple support agreement applies to a child, regardless of whether the parents are a party to that agreement, then § 152(e) will not apply to that child. § 152(e)(5). In other words, the multiple support agreement has priority.

¶ **11.1260.   Old Age and Blindness Exemption.** Prior to 1987, an additional exemption was granted to a TP for old age and for blindness and for the old age and blindness of the TP's spouse. The 1986 TRA repealed that provision and substituted an additional standard deduction amount as described at ¶ **10.2220.**

¶ **11.2000.   PHASEOUT OF EXEMPTION AMOUNT IN CERTAIN YEARS.** As noted in ¶ **11.1200**, the amount of deduction for each exemption (personal and dependent) to which a TP is entitled is increased annually to reflect inflation. For the year 2011, the exemption amount is $3,700.[8]

For years prior to 2010 and after 2012, the amount of a TP's exemption deduction for a taxable year may be reduced if the TP's adjusted gross income (AGI) for that year exceeds a specified figure, which figure is referred to as the "threshold amount." This reduction of the exemption is referred to as a "phaseout." § 151(d)(3). The threshold amount is indexed to reflect inflation. § 151(d)(4). The amount of the reduction to each exemption deduction to which the TP would otherwise be entitled is equal to a percentage (called the "applicable percentage") of the

---

8.   Rev. Proc. 2011–12 (Sec. 2.07).

exemption amount that otherwise would apply. The applicable percentage is two percentage points for each $2,500 (or fraction thereof) by which the TP's AGI for that year exceeds his threshold amount. If the TP is a married person filing a separate return, the $2,500 figure is reduced to $1,250. The exemption amount cannot be reduced below zero. § 151(d)(3).

Only a fraction of the phaseout of an exemption deduction is applied for the years 2006–2009. As the final stage of that gradual reduction of the phaseout, the phaseout does not apply at all to the years 2010–2012. However, the phaseout is scheduled to spring back in full force in the year 2013.

¶ 11.2100. **Threshold Amount.** The threshold amounts for the year 2009[9] were as follows:

$250,200—joint return or surviving spouse

$208,500—head of household

$166,800—unmarried TP

$125,100—married TP filing a separate return

9. Since there is no phaseout for the years 2010–2012 (and since we don't know the 2013 numbers yet), we have listed the 2009 amounts.

CHAPTER TWELVE

INSTALLMENT METHOD

¶ **12.1000. SALES UNDER THE INSTALLMENT METHOD.** In the absence of a statutory provision, a cash method TP who sells property for a profit and receives as full or partial consideration a debt instrument of the purchaser that is payable in installments over a period of time usually would have to treat the fair market value of the debt instrument as an amount realized in the year of sale. In such cases, the TP would have to recognize the entire gain on the sale of the asset before the TP received the cash that he might need to pay the tax thereon. Sections 453–453B address this problem.

Section 453 provides that gain realized from the sale of property under an installment sales contract may be spread over the period in which payments are made if certain conditions are met. This method of reporting is available at the election of the TP on the sale of any type of property (other than properties and sales described in ¶¶ **12.1100–12.1300**) where at least one payment is to be made after the close of the taxable year in which the disposition occurred. § 453(b)(1). In such cases, the installment method will apply unless the TP affirmatively elects not to have it apply. § 453(d)(1).[1]

The installment method is not restricted to TPs who use the cash method. TPs who report their income on the accrual method can also use the installment method.

¶ **12.1100. Property Disqualified from Installment Treatment.** The installment method cannot be used for the sale of stocks and bonds that are traded on an established securities market, and the installment method also cannot be used for the sale of certain other properties of a kind that are regularly traded on an established market. § 453(k)(2). Because of § 453(b)(2), a so-called "dealer disposition" does not qualify for installment reporting under § 453. A

---

1. The election out of installment treatment must be made on or before the due date (including extensions of time) for filing the TP's return for the year in which the disposition occurs. A tardy election will rarely be permitted, and then only if the TP can show good cause. Temp. Reg. § 15A.453–1(d)(3)(ii).

"dealer disposition" is a disposition of: (1) real property which is held by the TP for sale to customers in the ordinary course of the TP's trade or business, or (2) personal property by a person who regularly sells or otherwise disposes of personal property of the same type on the installment plan. § 453(*l*)(1). A limited exception permits installment reporting for the disposition of property used or produced in the trade or business of farming and for the disposition of certain time share rights and residential lots. § 453(*l*)(2), (3). The installment method is not available for sales of personalty that would be included in the TP's inventory if on hand at the close of the taxable year. § 453(b)(2)(B). The installment method is not available for sales of personalty under a revolving credit plan. § 453(k)(1). A revolving credit plan is a plan under which customers of the TP who purchase personalty on credit have their debts accumulated into a single account for which the customer agrees to make payments each month of a part of his balance.

¶ 12.1200.   **Sale of Depreciable Property to or by a Controlled Entity.** The installment method is not available for sales of depreciable property between a person and a controlled entity, or between certain commonly controlled entities, or between a TP and a trust in which the TP or his spouse have a beneficial interest (other than a remote contingent interest). § 453(g). This exclusion does not apply if Federal income tax avoidance was not one of the principal purposes of making the disposition. § 453(g)(2).

¶ 12.1300.   **Recognition of Recapture Income.** When property, all or part of whose gain is subject to the recapture of depreciation provisions of §§ 1245 or 1250, is sold on an installment basis, the installment reporting rules do not apply to so much of the seller's gain as is subject to those recapture rules. The property's section 1245 or section 1250 recapture income must be recognized by the seller in the year of sale regardless of when the seller receives cash payments. § 453(i). The recapture of depreciation rules of §§ 1245 and 1250 are discussed at ¶¶ **26.3000–26.3330.**

¶ 12.1400.   **Contingent Selling Price.** Prior to the adoption of the Installment Sales Revision Act of 1980, the installment method did not apply if the selling price could not be determined with reasonable accuracy. The 1980 Act, however, permits the installment method to be used in cases where the gross profit, the total contract price, or both cannot be readily ascertained. § 453(j)(2). If the aggregate selling price of a sale or other disposition cannot be determined by the close of the taxable year in which the sale or disposition occurred, the transaction is referred to as a "contingent payment sale." The manner in which contingent payment sales are to be reported under the installment method is set forth in Temp. Reg. § 15A.453–1(c).

¶ **12.2000. NONDEALER DISPOSITIONS.** As noted in ¶ **12.1100**, the installment method of reporting is not available for "dealer dispositions." Several other exclusions from installment method reporting are described above. If a disposition of property qualifies for installment reporting, and if the amount of the sales price for the property exceeds $150,000, then two special rules may apply—one requiring the TP to make interest payments to the Service and one imposing special consequences if the installment obligation is pledged as security for a loan. § 453A. The interest and pledging rules that are imposed by § 453A are described below in ¶¶ **12.2100** and **12.2200**. These two special rules will not apply unless: (1) the installment obligation that the TP acquired in the disposition in question is outstanding at the close of the taxable year, and (2) the aggregate face amount of the installment obligations that the TP acquired in dispositions of property (in which the sales price exceeded $150,000) in that taxable year, and which amounts are outstanding at the close of the taxable year, exceeds $5,000,000. § 453A(b). These special rules do not apply to dispositions of certain farm property, residential lots, and timeshares; but other interest rules [§ 453(1), (3)] may apply to installment sales of residential lots and timeshares. § 453A(b)(3), (4).

¶ **12.2100. Interest Payments.** If an installment obligation that is subject to § 453A as described above is outstanding at the close of a taxable year, the TP is required to make an interest payment to the Service for the benefit the TP enjoys from having his tax liability deferred under the installment method of reporting. The rate of interest is the same rate as is imposed by § 6621(a)(2) on a TP for the underpayment of a tax liability. § 453A(c)(2)(B). The interest rate is applied against the "applicable percentage of the deferred tax liability" with respect to such obligation. The "deferred tax liability" for an installment obligation is the product of multiplying the unrecognized gain from the obligation as of the close of the taxable year times the maximum rate of tax applied by either §§ 1 or 11, whichever is appropriate, for that taxable year. § 453A(c)(3). The "applicable percentage" that is applied to the "deferred tax liability" is determined by dividing (1) the amount by which the aggregate face amount of all such installment obligations that are outstanding at the close of the taxable year exceeds $5,000,000 by (2) the aggregate face amount of all such installment obligations that is outstanding at the close of the taxable year.

¶ **12.2200. Pledges of Installment Obligations.** If an installment obligation that is subject to § 453A, as described in ¶ **12.2000**, is used as security to secure a loan, the net proceeds of the secured debt will be treated as a payment that was made on the installment obligation that serves as the security for the debt. § 453A(d). The amount of such constructive payment is subject to a ceiling based on the contract price as described in § 453A(d)(2). Of course, the constructive payment will cause the TP to recognize all or some portion of the gain that was deferred by using the installment method of reporting. See ¶ **12.5000**.

¶ **12.3000. INSTALLMENT SALE TO RELATED PARTY.** Prior to the adoption of the Installment Sales Revision Act of 1980, TPs were sometimes able to use the installment method as a tax avoidance device by selling an appreciated asset to a related party on an installment sale. The purchaser would acquire a basis in the asset equal to the purchase price and, thus, could promptly sell the asset to a third party for cash and recognize no income thereby. The income recognized by the original vendor (which was the source of the step-up in basis that the purchaser obtained) would be recognized in stages over a period of years. The 1980 Act closed that loophole. § 453(e).

Section 453(e) applies when two requirements are met:

(1) any person disposes of property to a related person, and

(2) before the payments are finalized on the first sale, the buyer disposes of the property.

If these two requirements are met, subject to certain limitations, the amount realized with respect to the second sale shall be treated as received by the original seller (i.e., the person who sold it to the related party) at the time of the second sale. § 453(e)(1), (3). Unless the property is marketable securities (in which case, there is no limitation), there is a two year limitation on the application of the provision (that is, the second disposition must take place within two years of the first disposition for the rule to apply). A TP may also avoid the application of this provision if he can show that neither the first nor second deposition had one of its principal purposes the avoidance of income tax. § 453(e)(7).

¶ **12.4000. DEFINITIONS.** The definition of the following terms is peculiar to the reporting of income under the installment method.

¶ **12.4100. Selling Price.** The selling price is the established purchase price for the property (i.e., the amount that the parties agree is to be paid for the property), but the selling price does not include interest payments. When mortgaged or encumbered property is sold and the purchaser either assumes the debt or takes the property subject to that mortgage or encumbrance, the selling price includes the amount of the mortgage or encumbering debt. Treas. Reg. § 1.453–4(c); Temp. Reg. § 15A.453–1(b)(2)(ii). If any interest is imputed to the transaction under §§ 483 or 1274, the imputed interest is excluded from the selling price; that is, the nominal price must be reduced by the amount that is treated as interest. Commissions or other selling expenses of the vendor do not reduce the selling price. Temp. Reg. § 15A.453–1(b)(2)(ii).

¶ 12.4200.   **Total Contract Price.** The total contract price is equal to the selling price except that if the property sold is subject to a "qualifying indebtedness" and the purchaser either assumes that debt or takes the property subject thereto, the total contract price includes only so much of that debt as exceeds the vendor's basis in the property. Temp. Reg. § 15A.453–1(b)(2)(iii). The term "qualifying indebtedness" is defined in Temp. Reg. § 15A.453–1(b)(2)(iv).

¶ 12.4300.   **Gross Profit.** The vendor's gross profit is equal to the difference between the selling price and the vendor's adjusted basis in the property. Generally, commissions plus other selling expenses are added to the vendor's adjusted basis in determining gross profit. Consequently, the gross profit effectively is reduced by commissions and other selling expenses of the vendor. Temp. Reg. § 15A.453–1(b)(2)(v).

¶ 12.4400.   **Payments.** For purposes of reporting gain on the installment method, payments include: cash or other property, marketable securities, *certain* assumptions of liabilities, evidences of indebtedness of the purchaser that are payable on demand, and evidences of indebtedness of a corporation or government that are readily tradable. Temp. Reg. § 15A.453–1(b)(3). In general, the seller's receipt of the purchaser's debt instrument is *not* a payment unless the debt is payable on demand or the debt is a readily tradable instrument of a corporation or a government. § 453(f)(3), (4); Temp. Reg. § 15A.453–1(e)(1). The amount (if any) by which the mortgage (or certain other encumbrances) on the property that are assumed or accepted by the purchaser exceeds the vendor's basis in the property constitutes a payment received in the year of sale. Otherwise, the purchaser's assumption or acceptance of a mortgage debt is not a payment.

¶ **12.5000.   INSTALLMENT REPORTING.** Where a sale qualifies for installment reporting and the vendor does not make a timely election under § 453(d) to exempt the sale from the installment method, the vendor will include in income for a taxable year only that proportion of the payments received (or deemed to have been received) in that year which equals the proportion of gross profit to the total contract price. Temp. Reg. § 15A.453–1(b)(2)(i). Interest payments are reported when received or deemed to have been received; interest is not included in the installment reporting of the vendor's profit.

¶ **12.5100.   Illustration.** In Year One, S purchased a house for $20,000 cash. S used the house as a summer residence, and she never rented it to anyone. In Year Six, S sold the house to B for $30,000, and she incurred no commissions or other selling expenses in that sale. B paid a $5,000 down payment in Year Six, and he gave S a mortgage to secure his debt for the remaining $25,000, which debt was to be satisfied over a 30–year period and bore adequate interest so that no interest was imputed to the transaction under §§ 483 or 1274. In addition to the down payment, B made payments totaling $1,000 against the principal of the debt during Year Six, and he made timely payments of his interest obligation. S did not elect out of the installment method; thus, § 453 is applicable. Under that method, S's gross profit is $10,000, which is the difference between her basis of $20,000 (since no improvements were made on the house and no depreciation was allowable) and the $30,000 selling price. S's contract price is $30,000. In this case, the contract price and the selling price are equal because the property was not transferred subject to an existing encumbrance. The proportion of gross profit to total contract price, one-third, will be applied to the $6,000 payments made in Year Six; thus, $1/3 \times \$6,000 = \$2,000$. S will report the $2,000 as gross income, and she will report one-third of all future principal payments as gross income. The character of the gross income that S recognizes from her receipt of the installment payments will be determined by the property that she sold. In this case, it appears that the income will be a long-term capital gain.

¶ **12.6000.   DISPOSITION OF INSTALLMENT OBLIGATION.** If an installment obligation is satisfied at less than its face value, if it is canceled or becomes unenforceable, or if it is distributed, transmitted, sold, or otherwise disposed of, gain or loss will be recognized in an amount equal to the difference between the basis of the obligation and: (a) the amount realized on a sale or exchange or satisfaction for less than face value; or (b) the fair market value of the installment obligation at the time of distribution, transmission, or disposition other than a sale or exchange. § 453B. Any gain or loss so recognized is treated as resulting from the sale or exchange of the property for which the installment obligation was received. If the obligor and obligee of a cancelled installment obligation (or one that becomes unenforceable) are related (within the meaning of § 453(f)(1)), the fair market value of the obligation is deemed to be no less than its face amount. § 453B(f)(2).

¶ 12.6100. Illustration. If in the illustration at ¶ 12.5100, in Year Seven, *S* made a gift to her son, *R*, of the debt owing to her from *B*, and if the value of *B*'s obligation at that date was $24,000 (the unpaid balance of the obligation), *S* would recognize a gain of $8,000 because of the disposition of the installment obligation. *S* had a basis of $16,000 in the obligation (the basis equals the difference between the face value of the obligation ($24,000) and the amount of income to be returned when it is paid in full ($8,000) [§ 453B(b)]), and consequently, she recognized $8,000 income on the disposition.

¶ 12.6200. Exceptions. A number of types of dispositions or transmissions of installment obligations are permitted to be made without causing the recognition of gain. For example, in general, transfers to a controlled corporation, transfers resulting from death, and, in many cases, transfers in liquidation of a controlled subsidiary corporation do not cause the transferor to recognize a gain. § 453B(c), (d); Treas. Reg. § 1.453–9(c)(2). A transfer of an installment obligation to a spouse or former spouse will not cause the transferor to recognize income if the transfer is one that is described in § 1041, but this exception does not apply if the transfer is made in trust. § 453B(g).

¶ 12.6300. Cancellation at Obligee's Death. When the terms of an installment obligation provide that it is to be canceled at the death of the obligee, the debt instrument is sometimes referred to as a "death-terminating installment note," and the sale for which such an instrument was received as partial or full payment is sometimes referred to as a "death-terminating installment sale." The Tax Court and the Eighth Circuit treated the cancellation of a death-terminating installment note upon the obligee's death as a disposition of the note (under § 453B(f)(1)) that triggers recognition of income to the obligee or to his estate (as described in ¶ 12.6000). The Tax Court held that it was the obligee himself who recognized the income, but the Eighth Circuit held that the income is recognized by the obligee's estate as "income in respect of a decedent" (IRD) under § 691(a)(5)(A)(iii).[2]

---

2. *Estate of Frane v. Commissioner*, 98 T.C. 341 (1992), aff'd in part and rev'd in part, 998 F.2d 567 (8th Cir. 1993). The concept of "income in respect of a decedent" is discussed in Chapter **Twenty–Nine**.

¶ **12.6400. Change of Terms of Installment Obligation.** As discussed in ¶¶ **24.1700–24.1720**, the regulations provide that a significant modification of the terms of a debt instrument will cause there to be a constructive exchange of the "old" debt instrument for a "new" debt, and that constructive exchange will cause the holder of the instrument to realize gain or loss. However, the preamble to T.D. 8675 (June 26, 1996) indicates that they do not apply to a modification of the terms of an installment obligation. See ¶ **24.1720**. Consequently, the regulations do not cause a modification of the terms of such an instrument to constitute a disposition of the instrument.

The question then is whether, apart from the regulations, a modification of the terms of an installment obligation will trigger a disposition of that instrument so that any deferred gain will be recognized. The cases and rulings on this issue to date have held that a change in the rate of interest, or the period for payment of such a debt, or even the identity of the obligor, does *not* constitute a disposition of the instrument and so does not trigger the recognition of deferred gain.[3]

The purpose of permitting installment reporting of the amounts received on an installment instrument that was acquired as part of the payment for the sale of an item is to defer the imposition of tax on the gain from the sale of the underlying item until the seller has cash in hand with which to pay the tax. If the seller disposes of the installment obligation, or if his rights in that instrument are terminated, there is no longer any justification to defer his recognition of the unrecognized gain from the original sale. In such cases, the tax on the remaining gain becomes payable when the seller's right to subsequent payments on the installment instrument cease. But, a modification of the amount of interest payable, or of the schedule on which payments are to be made, or a change of the identity of the obligor who will make the payments, does not change the conditions on which deferral of gain on installment sales is granted. Accordingly, such changes do not accelerate the seller's recognition of gain and consequent liability for payment of tax.[4]

---

3. *Rhombar v. Commissioner*, 47 T.C. 75, 86 (1966), Acq., aff'd on other grounds, 386 F.2d 510 (2d Cir. 1967); *Cunningham v. Commissioner*, 44 T.C. 103 (1965), Acq.; Rev. Rul. 82–122; Rev. Rul. 75–457; Rev. Rul. 74–157; Rev. Rul. 68–419; PLR 8932011; PLR 8710068.

4. Rev. Rul. 82–122.

CHAPTER THIRTEEN

JOINT RETURNS, HEAD OF HOUSEHOLD, AND SURVIVING SPOUSE

¶ 13.0000. JOINT RETURNS, HEAD OF HOUSEHOLD, AND SURVIVING SPOUSE.

¶ 13.1000. JOINT RETURN.

¶ 13.1100. Qualifications. A joint return may be filed by a husband and a wife even if one of them has no gross income. § 6013. A joint return is not permitted:

(a) unless a valid election is made [described in **¶ 13.1110**] if, at any time during the taxable year, either spouse is a nonresident alien;[1] or

(b) if the spouses have different tax years, with the exception that a joint return can be filed if the spouses' tax years begin on the same day but end on different days because of the death of one or both spouses and if the surviving spouse does not remarry before the close of the tax year.

¶ 13.1110. Election for Nonresident Alien. A joint return can be filed even though one spouse is a nonresident alien if the other spouse is a citizen or resident of the United States and if a proper election is made by both spouses under § 6013(g) or (h) to have the nonresident alien spouse treated as a resident of the United States for income tax purposes.

¶ 13.1120. Marital Status. The determination of whether a TP is married is made as of the last day of the TP's taxable year. However if a spouse dies before the close of the tax year, the status is determined as of the date of death. § 7703(a)(1). A TP

---

1. For the definition of "nonresident alien," see Treas. Reg. §§ 1.871–2 to 1.871–5.

who is legally separated from his spouse under a decree of divorce or separate maintenance is not considered to be married for purposes of filing a joint return. § 7703(a)(2). In certain circumstances, a married individual who maintains a household in which the individual and a dependent child reside, and whose spouse did not reside there during the last six months of the taxable year, is treated as unmarried. § 7703(b). For further discussion of marital status, see ¶¶ 15.8000–15.8300.

¶ 13.1130. **Change of Election.** In most (but not all) circumstances, a husband and wife may file a joint return for a tax year for which they had previously filed separate returns if they do so within three years after the last day for timely filing of the return for such year (without regard to extensions of time). § 6013(b). The situations when this election is not permitted are set forth in § 6013(b)(2). No election to change from a joint return to separate returns may be made after the due date of the return. Treas. Reg. § 1.6013–1(a)(1).

¶ 13.1140. **Joint Return with a Deceased Spouse.** In the case of the death of one or both spouses during the tax year, a joint return may be filed for the year of death. The decedent's executor or administrator makes the election except that the surviving spouse can file the joint return for the decedent if: (a) no return has previously been made for that year for the decedent; and (b) no executor or administrator has been appointed and none is appointed before the last day permitted for the timely filing of the return of the surviving spouse. If an executor or administrator is appointed subsequently, he may disaffirm the joint return at any time within one year after the last day for timely filing the return of the surviving spouse. § 6013(a)(3). When a joint return is filed for a deceased spouse, the taxable years of both spouses shall be treated as having ended on the closing date of the surviving spouse's tax year. § 6013(c).

¶ 13.1200. **Tax Computation for Joint Returns.**

¶ 13.1210. **Marriage Bonus and Marriage Penalty.** In some circumstances, a couple who marry and file a joint return will incur a lower tax than the combined tax that they would have paid if they were unmarried. This tax reduction obtained through marriage is sometimes referred to as a "marriage bonus." However, in some circumstances, a couple who marry will incur a greater tax than would have been incurred if they had remained unmarried. The added tax cost that arises because of their married state is sometimes referred to as a "marriage penalty." See ¶ **13.1400**. The focus of the critics of the marriage penalty has been on the manner in which the tax rate schedules can increase the aggregate tax burden of a married couple. The tax effect of a marriage (as a bonus or as a penalty) depends upon the amount of income that the couple have and upon how evenly or disproportionately their combined income is divided between them. Congress has mitigated some aspects of the marriage penalty. See ¶ **13.1400**.

¶ **13.1220. Combining Deductions.** One of the advantages of a joint return is that one spouse's excess of deductions over gross income can be used to reduce the gross income of the other spouse.

¶ **13.1230. Increase of Limitations on Deductions.** Some limitations on the amount that a TP can deduct for certain items are increased for married TPs who file a joint return. A number of dollar limitations on specified deductions are more restrictive for a married TP who files a separate return than for other TPs. For example, the limitation on the amount of a TP's net capital loss that can be deducted from ordinary income for a married TP who files a separate tax return is one-half the amount allowable for an unmarried individual. § 1211(b). Regardless of whether they file joint or separate returns, a husband and wife are treated as one person for purposes of applying some of the limitations on the amount of aggregate cost of business property that can be expensed under § 179. § 179(b)(4).

¶ **13.1240. Qualification for Tax Advantage.** Some tax advantages can be enjoyed by either married TP only if they file a joint return. For example, subject to the exception provided by § 21(e)(4), married TPs must file a joint return to obtain a credit for dependent care and household expenses; and a married individual must file a joint return to qualify for the earned income credit. §§ 21(e)(2), 32(d).

¶ **13.1300. Disadvantages of Joint Returns.**

¶ **13.1310. Joint and Several Liability.** Unless one of several exceptions applies, when a joint return is filed, each spouse is liable for the entire tax liability on their joint income, including any tax deficiency subsequently determined to be owing for that tax year. § 6013(d)(3). Prior to 1998, there were only limited exceptions to this joint and several liability of joint filers. In 1998,

Congress added § 6015 to the Code and greatly liberalized the extent to which a spouse can escape liability for a deficiency that is attributable to actions of the other spouse.

¶ 13.1320. Relief From Joint Liability. There are three provisions (all of which are set forth in § 6015) which allow relief to a spouse who filed a joint return and later finds that a deficiency is owing to the Service because of an item attributable to the other spouse. First, in general, all joint filers have the option of electing to be liable for tax deficiencies for that return (including interest and penalties) only to the extent that the deficiency would have been allocable to that filer if the filer had filed a separate return. § 6015(b). The conditions under which this election can be made and the limitations on the relief given are described in **¶ 13.1321**. This election is referred to as the "innocent spouse election." Second, when joint filers subsequently cease to be married, are legally separated, or have not lived together for at least 12 months, either can elect to limit that filer's liability for a deficiency on the joint return to the portion of the deficiency properly attributable to the electing filer. § 6015(c). The conditions for this election and the limitations on its application are set forth at **¶ 13.1322**. This election is sometimes referred to as the "separate liability election." Third, the Service is authorized to grant relief from liability to a joint filer, who does not qualify for either of the two elections noted above, if it would be inequitable to hold that person liable for any unpaid tax, deficiency, or a portion thereof. § 6015(f). The Service has provided guidance for TPs seeking equitable relief under § 6015(f) in Revenue Procedure 2003–61.

¶ 13.1321. Innocent Spouse Election. The election must be filed with the Service no later than the date two years after the day on which the Service began collection activities with respect to the electing filer. § 6015(b)(1)(E). The following conditions must be satisfied:

1.   There must be an understatement of tax on a joint return on which the electing party was a joint filer.

2.   The understatement must be attributable to erroneous items of the other joint filer.

3.   The electing individual establishes that, in signing the joint return, he "did not know, and had no reason to know," that there was an understatement.

4.   Taking into account all facts and circumstances, it would be inequitable to hold the electing filer liable for the deficiency attributable to the understatement.

In some circumstances, an electing party who does not qualify for full relief from such liability may be relieved of a portion of the liability. § 6015(b)(2).

¶ 13.1322.   Separate Liability Election. An election for immunity from liability for a joint return deficiency that is attributable to the other filer can be made by a joint filer who is no longer married to the other filer, or who is legally separated from the other filer, or who had not lived as a member of the same household as the other filer for the entire 12–month period ending on the date on which the election was made. § 6015(c)(3). Some of the conditions for this election are:

1.   The election must be made no later than 2 years after the Service has begun collection activities with respect to the electing filer.

2.   The election will not be effective to any part of the deficiency that is attributable to an item of which the electing filer had *actual knowledge* at the time of signing the return. Note that the absence of "actual knowledge" is a more lenient standard than the "did not know and had no reason to know" requirement that is employed in the innocent spouse election. The Service has the burden of proof on the question of whether the electing filer had actual knowledge of the item that is the source of the deficiency. Even if the electing filer had such actual knowledge, he can make the election if he can establish that he signed the return under duress. § 6015(c)(3)(C).

3.   The electing filer has the burden of proof on the issue of what portion of the deficiency is attributable to the other filer.

4.   If the nonelecting filer transferred property to the electing filer for the principal purpose of avoiding tax or the payment of tax, the amount of joint return deficiency for which the electing filer otherwise is liable is increased by the value of such transferred property. § 6015(c)(4).

5.   If the Service can establish that property was transferred between the joint filers as part of a fraudulent scheme of both

parties, the separate liability election is void. § 6015(c)(3)(A)(ii).

¶ **13.1330. Loss of Dependency Deduction.** If one spouse is a dependent of a TP (who is not the other spouse), the dependent's filing of a joint return will deny the dependency exemption to the TP. § 151(c)(2).

¶ **13.1340. Medical Deduction.** If both *H* and *W* have gross income and *H* has paid all of the medical expenses of the family, *H* will have a lower AGI if he files a separate return. Therefore, the limitation on allowable medical deductions will be reduced (only the excess over 7½% of AGI[2] is deductible). However, if *H* itemizes his deductions, *W* must do so also (i.e., *W* will not be allowed to use the standard deduction). § 63(c)(6)(A). Consequently, in most circumstances, the reduction of the medical expense limitation will not constitute a sufficient reason to file separate returns, but it can be a factor when other reasons exist.

¶ **13.1400. Marriage Penalty.** As noted in ¶ **13.1210**, while some couples enjoy a marriage bonus from their marriage, others incur a marriage penalty. The critics of the marriage penalty focus on the rate schedules, but another form of penalty is that the marriage may reduce the aggregate amount of certain deductions that would have been available to the couple if they did not marry. For example, the aggregate amount of cost of business property that can be expensed by a couple is halved if they are married. § 179(b)(4). Similarly, the aggregate amount of net capital loss that can be deducted from a couple's ordinary income is halved if they are married. § 1211(b).

Tax legislation has made two specific changes aimed at reducing the marriage penalty. First, the basic standard deduction for joint returns has been increased and is now twice the size of the standard deduction for single filers. See ¶ **10.2210**. Second, the maximum taxable income in the 15% income tax bracket for a joint return is twice the size of the maximum taxable income in the 15% bracket for a single filer. § 1(f)(8). However, those provisions are scheduled to expire after 2012. If Congress does not renew them, the standard deduction and the maximum figure for the 15% income tax bracket will be 167% of the applicable amounts for single TPs.

¶ **13.2000. SURVIVING SPOUSE.** A surviving spouse may use joint return rates to compute his or her tax liability for the two tax years

---

2. That figure is scheduled to increase to 10% of AGI for years beginning after 2012.

following the year of death of the decedent spouse. This is in addition to the privilege of filing a joint return for the year of death. § 1(a).

¶ 13.2100.   Definition. A surviving spouse is a TP:

(a) whose spouse died during either of the two tax years immediately preceding the taxable year;

(b) who maintains as his or her home a household which constitutes for the taxable year the principal place of abode of a dependent son, daughter, stepson or stepdaughter of the TP for whom the TP is entitled to an exemption; and

(c) who does not remarry before the close of the taxable year. § 2(a).

In addition, a TP will not qualify as a surviving spouse unless a joint return could have been filed with the deceased spouse for the tax year of the TP in which the spouse died. § 2(a)(2)(B).

¶ 13.2200.   Limited to Two Years. The effect of the surviving spouse provision is to extend the use of joint return rates for two years after the year of the decedent's death if the surviving spouse maintains an abode for a dependent child. The year of the decedent's death is not included in the surviving spouse provision because in that year the TP can elect to file a joint return with the deceased spouse. After the two-year period has expired, the TP may become eligible for head of household rates.

¶ 13.3000.   HEAD OF HOUSEHOLD. A "head of household" pays taxes at rates that are lower than those imposed on single TPs but higher than those imposed on married TPs filing a joint return. § 1(b).

¶ 13.3100.   Definition. A "head of household" is an individual who is neither married nor a surviving spouse entitled to joint return rates at the end of his tax year, and who either:

(a) maintains as his or her home a household which for more than one-half of the tax year is the principal place of abode, as a member of the household, of either:

(i) a "qualifying child" of the TP as defined in § 152(c) [see **¶ 11.1232**] with several modifications including that the child must not be married at the end of the TP's taxable year, and, unless the child was adopted, must be either a citizen of the United States or a resident of the United States or a contiguous country, or

(ii) any other person who is a dependent of the TP for whom the TP is entitled to an exemption for the tax year; or

(b) maintains a household (not necessarily the TP's home) which for the tax year constitutes the principal place of abode of the father or mother of the TP for whom the TP is entitled to a dependency exemption. § 2(b).

Note that except for a TP's father or mother, the other person must have his principal abode in the TP's home for the TP to qualify as a head of household. Also, except for a "qualifying child" of the TP, only dependents of a TP can qualify the TP for head of household treatment.

PART C

ATTRIBUTION OF INCOME

CHAPTER FOURTEEN

ANTICIPATORY ASSIGNMENT OF INCOME AND THE "KIDDIE TAX"

¶ **14.0000. ANTICIPATORY ASSIGNMENT OF INCOME AND THE KIDDIE TAX**

¶ **14.1000. SPLITTING OF INCOME.** Since the federal income tax has a progressive rate structure, the tax burden will be lighter if the same amount of income is divided among several TPs than if it is taxed to one TP.

¶ **14.1100. Illustration.** *X* earns an annual salary of $100,000 and has three minor children. If *X* could divide his salary equally among himself and his three children, there would be four TPs each reporting $25,000 income, rather than one TP with $100,000. While non-tax considerations may make such an arrangement undesirable, the tax advantages of splitting *X*'s income into four parts are obvious. In addition to utilizing lower marginal tax rates, it is possible in some cases that the parties could utilize the transferees personal exemptions and standard deductions.

¶ **14.1200. Devices.** A number of income splitting devices have been tried by TPs with varying degrees of success. While generally Congress and the Service have sought to prevent the successful splitting of income, Congress has expressly authorized income splitting in certain circumstances. For example, the alimony deduction [§ 215] is a congressionally blessed income splitting arrangement, and the special treatment provided for a husband and wife filing a joint return is another. The use of trusts or corporations as income spreading devices is not discussed in this work.

¶ **14.1300. Citizens of Community Property States.** When a married couple is domiciled in a state that has a community property system and when the spouses have not contracted out of that system, the income earned from the services of either spouse is divided equally between both spouses for income tax purposes.[1] Similarly, income produced by community property is divided equally between the two spouses.

Section 66 creates exceptions to the equal division rule for community income in certain circumstances where either (1) the spouses live apart for the entire calendar year, do not file a joint return, and do not transfer earned income from one to the other, or (2) one spouse treated the income as his and did not notify the other spouse of the nature and amount of the income.

Nine states have adopted a community property system: Arizona, California, Idaho, Louisiana, Nevada, New Mexico, Texas, Washington and Wisconsin. Wisconsin adopted a Marital Property Act which is treated as a form of a community property system. In five of those states, income from separate property is the income of the spouse who owns that property, but in the other four of those states (Idaho, Louisiana, Texas, and Wisconsin), income from most separate property is community income.[2]

Deductions for expenses incurred in connection with a community business or investment generally are divided equally between the spouses. Deductions for expenses incurred in connection with a separately owned business or investment generally are deductible by the spouse who is taxable on the income from that business or investment. Deductions for personal expenses, such as charitable contributions and medical expenses, are allocated equally between the two spouses if paid out of community funds; but if separate funds, were used to pay a personal expense, that expense is deductible by the spouse whose funds were used.[3]

Of course, if the spouses file a joint return, it will not matter how their income and deductions are allocated.

¶ 14.1400. Citizens of States Having a Marital Property Act. The Uniform Marital Property Act creates a new system of property rights that are similar to the rights granted by community property systems and has been treated as a form of a community property system. The Commissioner ruled in Rev. Rul. 87–13 that income from services performed by either spouse of a married couple who are domiciled in Wisconsin (a state that has adopted a version of the

---

1. *Poe v. Seaborn*, 282 U.S. 101 (1930).
2. IRS Pub. No. 555 at 5 (2007).
3. IRS Pub. No. 555 at 5 (2007).

Uniform Marital Property Act) is divided equally between the two spouses unless they had previously altered their property rights through a marital property agreement. Income earned by the spouses' property, whether marital or separate property, also is divided equally between the spouses. However, gain realized on the appreciation of a spouse's *individual* property is the income of that spouse alone unless the other spouse's uncompensated efforts produced the appreciation.

¶ 14.2000. DONATIVE ANTICIPATORY ASSIGNMENT OF INCOME.

¶ 14.2100. Assignment of Income from Services. If, without receiving a payment for it, a TP executes a valid contract assigning to another person all or a portion of the income the TP may earn at a future date from services previously performed by the TP or from services to be performed by the TP at a future date, the income is nevertheless taxed to the TP when paid.[4]

Of course, if an employee performs services in the course of his employment, the income produced by those services is taxed to the employer. The anticipatory assignment of income doctrine does not apply to cause an agent to be taxable on income produced by his effort for his principal.

¶ 14.2110. Illustration 1. Failed Income Splitting. In Year One, *X* contracted with *Y* that each of them was entitled to one-half of the income earned by the other. In Year Three, *X* earned a salary of $20,000, and, pursuant to his contract, *X* turned $10,000 over to *Y*. *X* must include the entire $20,000 salary in his gross income. The result would be the same if X had contracted with his employer that one-half of his wages were to belong to, and be paid to, Y by the employer. When the employer paid the wages to Y, they would be taxed to X.[5]

¶ 14.2120. Illustration 2. Termination of Doctrine on Death of Assignor. *Z* was employed as an agent of a life insurance company. When *Z* sells a life insurance policy to a customer, *Z* receives a portion of the initial premium paid by that customer as a commission. Moreover, *Z* is entitled to a percentage of each subsequent premium paid by that customer. The right of

4. *Lucas v. Earl*, 281 U.S. 111 (1930); *Helvering v. Eubank*, 311 U.S. 122 (1940).
5. See ¶ 14.2130.

Z to a percentage of future premiums is referred to as "renewal commissions." Z's right to renewal commissions can be assigned by Z to others or can be bequeathed by Z at her death. In Year One, Z retired and, as a gift, assigned to S, her son, all of her rights to renewal commissions. In Years Two, Three and Four, while Z was still living, S collected the renewal commissions for premiums paid on policies that Z had sold before her retirement. All of those commissions that were received by S while Z was alive are included in Z's gross income.[6] Z died on January 1, Year Five. The renewal commissions collected by S after that date are included in S's gross income. The anticipatory assignment of income doctrine ceases to apply when the assignor dies.

¶ 14.2130. **Services in Consideration of Payment to Third Parties.** When a TP agrees to perform services in consideration of a payment's being made to a third party, such as a charity, the TP must include the payment in his gross income. Treas. Reg. § 1.61–2(c). However, if the payment is made to a qualified charity, the TP may be entitled to a charitable deduction subject to the limitations imposed by § 170. The transaction is treated as if the TP had received the payment and then contributed the amount he received to the charity.

However, if the services are provided directly to a party (including a charity) under an arrangement in which no compensation is to be paid the TP, then the TP is merely providing his services without charge; and the TP does not recognize income. Treas. Reg. § 1.61–2(c).[7]

¶ 14.2131. **Illustration 1.** Michael, a prominent comedian, participates in a television special sponsored by a breakfast cereal manufacturer. Michael agreed to perform in consideration of the sponsor's paying $100,000 to the Trinity Church. Michael must include the $100,000 in his gross income. Michael will be treated as having received the $100,000 compensation and then donated $100,000 to the Trinity Church. He will be allowed a charitable deduction for that donation to the extent that a deduction is allowable under § 170. If Michael could demonstrate that he participated in the television special in his capacity as an agent or employee of the Trinity Church,

---

6. *Helvering v. Eubank*, 311 U.S. 122 (1940).

7. See also Rev. Rul. 68–503 and Rev. Rul. 71–33.

the $100,000 would not be taxed to him, but the burden of proof on that question is formidable.[8]

¶ 14.2132. Illustration 2. The Trinity Church produced a play in New York City, and *H*, a prominent actress, agreed to perform in the play without compensation. The Trinity Church earned a substantial income from the play largely because of the drawing attraction of *H* as an actress. *H*'s normal fee for her performance would be $100,000. *H* has no income from donating her services to the Trinity Church's enterprise.

¶ 14.2133. Illustration 3. In an unusual decision, *Teschner v. Commissioner*,[9] a majority of the Tax Court held that a TP who won an essay contest, the prize for which was an annuity of $1,500 payable to some person under the age of 17 to be named by the winner, did not have income in the value of the prize. The TP was older than 17 and therefore did not qualify as a potential recipient of the annuity. The court reasoned that under the terms of the contest the TP could not receive the prize and, therefore, did not make an anticipatory assignment to his seven-year-old daughter whom he named as the beneficiary of the prize. The Commissioner has issued a nonacquiescence in that decision. The decision of the Supreme Court in *United States v. Basye*[10] may well overrule *Teschner*. While *Bayse* can be distinguished from *Teschner*, the thrust of the Court's opinion in *Bayse* runs counter to the Tax Court decision.

¶ 14.2200. Assignment of Entirety of Property. Since most property is capable of producing income, the transfer of an entire property necessarily includes an assignment of the property's income potential. If all of the transferor's interest in the property is transferred, the transferor generally is not taxed on the income subsequently earned by the property.

To the extent that the donor's right to income from the property was matured at the time that the transfer of his entire interest was completed, the donor will be taxed on that income. The mere anticipation or expectation of future income will not cause the donor to be taxed. In determining whether the donor had a right to income at the

8. See ¶ **14.2380**.

9. 38 T.C. 1003 (1962).

10. 410 U.S. 441 (1973).

time of transfer, the courts use a realistic appraisal of the substance of the events rather than to permit the formal arrangements to control.[11]

¶ **14.2210. Illustration.** *X* owned an apartment development which produces an annual rental income of $90,000. *X* transferred the apartment development to his son, *S*, as an irrevocable gift. The rental income from the property earned after the gift will be taxed to *S* and not to *X*. However, when a TP transfers a property interest shortly before income was distributed on that property, the TP will be taxed on that income if the TP had a legal right to the income at the time that he transferred the underlying property. For example, if *X* transferred stocks the day before a previously declared dividend of $20,000 was payable, and where state law gave a stockholder a legal right to a dividend at the time that the dividend was declared, *X* will be taxed on the $20,000.[12] However, if state law did not give *X* a legal right to the dividend when it was declared, and if *X* gifted the stock after the dividend was declared but before he obtained a legal right to the dividend, *X* will not be taxed on the $20,000 dividend.[13]

¶ **14.2220. Completion of a Transaction.** In some circumstances, the steps towards producing income from the donated property may have reached such an advanced state by the time of the gift as to make the realization of that income almost an incidental end to a fait accompli. Examples of this have arisen where stock was gifted after the corporation had adopted a plan of liquidation or after a firm offer was made to acquire that stock, and significant steps had already taken place. In some such cases, applying the anticipatory assignment of income doctrine, the donor has been taxed on the gain recognized subsequently when the liquidation or purchase took place.[14]

¶ **14.2300. Assignment of Income Interest.** A difficult tax issue previously arose when a donor retained an underlying interest in property the income from which for a significant number of years was assigned by the donor to a donee. The question was whether the

11. *Ferguson v. Commissioner*, 108 T.C. 244 (1997).

12. See *Smith's Estate v. Commissioner*, 292 F.2d 478 (3d Cir. 1961).

13. *Caruth Corp. v. United States*, 865 F.2d 644 (5th Cir. 1989) (not taxing a dividend in a similar circumstance).

14. E.g., *Ferguson v. Commissioner*, 108 T.C. 244 (1997); *Hudspeth v. United States*, 471 F.2d 275 (8th Cir. 1972); *Kinsey v. Commissioner*, 477 F.2d 1058 (2d Cir. 1973).

number of years of income transferred by the TP had sufficient significance to warrant taxing the assigned income to someone other than the donor. It is virtually certain that changes to the rules concerning the taxation of trust income that were adopted as part of the Tax Reform Act of 1986 have simplified the application of the anticipatory assignment doctrine in this area. Since then, the anticipatory doctrine will apply to such transfers regardless of the number of years of income assigned to the donee. The reason for concluding that a change in the application of the anticipatory doctrine has taken place is explained below.[15]

¶ 14.2310. Illustration 1: Gift of Interest from Bonds. In 1981, *X* owned a corporate bond with coupons attached. The coupons represented interest to be paid on the bond at future dates, and the interest coupons could be transferred to third parties who could collect the interest when the coupons mature. In that year, *X* gave several unmatured coupons to *Y*, but *X* retained the bond and the remaining coupons. Prior to 1982, *X*'s attempt to divert the interest income, represented by coupons, from himself to *Y* would be unsuccessful for tax purposes because of the anticipatory assignment doctrine. The interest paid to *Y* when he surrenders the coupons was included in *X*'s gross income.[16] As a consequence of an amendment to the Code that was adopted in 1984, adding § 1286, the treatment of such gifts may now be somewhat different.[17] While it is possible that § 1286 applies only to purchases and so would not apply to the gift described in this illustration even if it were made after 1982, the authors believe that the statute does apply to gifts.

¶ 14.2311. Stripped Bonds and Coupons. The separation of all or part of the interest element of a bond from the right to the principal of the debt is referred to as stripping the bond. Such a bond is referred to as a "stripped bond," and the separated interest is referred to as a "stripped coupon." § 1286(e). While the practice of attaching actual coupons to bonds was discontinued some years ago, the Code continues to refer to the interest element in a bond as a coupon. § 1286(e)(5). If a bondholder disposes of a stripped coupon or a stripped bond after July 1, 1982, a number of tax consequences are imposed by § 1286. There is a question whether

15. See ¶ 14.2370.

16. *Helvering v. Horst*, 311 U.S. 112 (1940).

17. See ¶ 14.2311.

§ 1286 is invoked by making a gift of a stripped coupon (as contrasted to a sale), but the language of § 1286(b) applies to any disposition of a stripped coupon or bond. The following discussion is based on an assumption that § 1286 does apply to gifts.

Among other tax consequences, § 1286 will require the donor of a stripped coupon to (1) recognize income for any accrued interest on the bond and for any "accrued market discount" on the bond, determined at the time of the disposition, that was not previously recognized ["accrued market discount" applies to a bond that is purchased after its original issue and constitutes a portion of the difference between the bond's stated redemption price at maturity and the purchase price according to the portion of the remaining term of the bond in which it was held by the TP before disposing of the stripped coupons]; (2) increase the donor's basis by the accrued income and discount; (3) allocate the basis (as adjusted) between the items retained by the donor and the items that were transferred to the donee; and (4) the donor will be treated as having purchased the retained items for an amount equal to their redetermined basis and will thereby become subject to recognizing original issue discount income pursuant to § 1286(a). § 1286(b).

Section 1286(b) imposes similar consequences if a TP disposes of a stripped bond and retains the stripped coupons.

¶ 14.2320.   Illustration 2: Gift of Income Interest in Trust When Donor Retains a Reversionary Interest. *X* is the income beneficiary of a trust, the annual income from which is approximately $40,000. The income is payable to *X* for life, and the remainder is to be distributed to Z. In Year One, *X* assigned to *Y* the right to receive the income from the trust for a period of three years. *X*'s attempt to assign several years' income to *Y* while retaining his underlying interest in the trust (i.e., his right to income after the three-year period) will be unsuccessful for tax purposes. The income distributed to *Y* will be included in *X*'s gross income.[18]

¶ 14.2330.   Illustration 3: Gift of Entirety of Donor's Life Interest in a Trust. The same facts as those stated in ¶ 14.2320

---

18.   See *Harrison v. Schaffner*, 312 U.S. 579 (1941).

except that in Year One X gave to Y all of X's interest in the trust—i.e., the right to income from the trust for the rest of X's life. This assignment is successful for tax purposes and the income earned after the assignment is not taxed to X.[19] X did not retain any residuary interest in the trust after the interest given to Y expires. If there were accumulated income in the trust to which X had a right at the time of the transfer to Y, X would be taxed on that income when it is distributed from the trust to Y.

¶ 14.2340. Illustration 4. Gift of Entirety of Donor's Term Interest in a Trust. D died in Year One and bequeathed property to a testamentary trust in which A has an income interest for 20 years, and B has the remainder interest. In Year Two, A gave his entire interest in the trust to F. A did not reserve any reversionary interest in the property he gave to F. A will not be taxed on the trust income that is earned after the transfer and distributed to F. The tax consequence of the assignment is the same as the consequence of the assignment discussed in **¶ 14.2330**.

¶ 14.2350. Illustration 5. Gift of Donor's Remaining Term Interest in Trust Consisting of a Brief Period. The same facts as those stated in **¶ 14.2340** except that A did not give his remaining term interest in the trust to B until Year Nineteen when there was only one year remaining in A's term interest. Who will be taxed on the trust's income in that last year of the term when the trust distributes it to B? While A gave away all of the interest he had in the trust, it consisted of only one year's income. One might well be concerned that allowing A to escape the tax on the last year's income contravenes the spirit of the anticipatory assignment doctrine even though allowing it would seem to conform with the established rules. How the tax law will treat this transaction is an open question. The authors believe that the income will be taxed to A. If so, the question then is how long must the remaining term be for A to escape taxation on the subsequent income?

¶ 14.2360. Illustration 6. Gift of a Fraction of Donor's Income Interest or Gift of an Annuity for the Period of the Donor's Income Interest. The same facts apply as in **¶ 14.2320** except that X assigned to Y the right to one-fourth of the income from the trust for the remainder of X's life. While X retained a continuing interest in three-fourths of the trust, X has no residual

---

19. See *Blair v. Commissioner*, 300 U.S. 5 (1937).

interest in the one-fourth interest assigned to *Y* (i.e., *X* will have no interest in the one-fourth portion of the trust assigned to *Y* upon the expiration of that interest), and, consequently, the income subsequently paid to *Y* is not taxed to *X*. This assignment is distinguishable from the situation in ¶ **14.2320** where the donor assigned three years of income since in that case, the donor retained an interest in the future income of the entire trust.

In *Blair v. Commissioner*,[20] a life income beneficiary's assignment of a fixed annual dollar amount for the life of the transferor (i.e., an annuity for the life of the life income beneficiary of the trust) was held to be a successful assignment for tax purposes. The Court effectively treated the annuity interest as equivalent to a fractional share of the life income beneficiary's interest in the trust.

¶ **14.2370.** **Illustration 7: Gift of Term Interest for a Period of More Than Ten Years.** The same facts as in ¶ **14.2320** except that *X* assigned to *Y* the right to all the income from the trust for a period of 11 years, and X retained no power over the trust or to affect *Y*'s income interest during that period. While *X* retained a reversionary interest in the trust upon the expiration of the 11–year period, prior to the adoption of the Tax Reform Act of 1986 it was likely that the assigned interest would be deemed sufficiently significant that *X* would not be taxed on the income paid to *Y* during that 11–year period. Prior to the amendment of Subchapter J that was made by the Tax Reform Act of 1986, a transfer to a trust to pay income to a third party for more than ten years would ordinarily result in the trust's income being taxed to the third party even though the trust corpus reverts to the grantor when the more than ten-year period expires. Under the pre–1986 tax law, it, therefore, would be reasonable to allow a TP to assign successfully an income interest if the assignment is for a period of more than ten years. Under Rev. Rul. 55–38, a pre–1986 ruling, *X* would not recognize income during the 11–year period if the assignment of that 11–year interest were made by *X* prior to March 2, 1986. The Tax Reform Act of 1986 amended § 673 to provide that, for transfers made in trust after March 1, 1986 (subject to two minor exceptions), the income from the transferred property will be included in the grantor's gross income if the grantor retained a reversionary interest in either the

20. 300 U.S. 5 (1937).

corpus or income of the trust. Consequently, if *X* assigned the 11–year interest to *Y* after March 1, 1986, the income paid to *Y* should be included in *X*'s gross income. The common law anticipatory assignment of income rule should be modified to track the statutory provision for trust income.

¶ 14.2380.   Illustration 8: Income Earned by an Agent. A member of the faculty of a law school receives fees under the Criminal Justice Act for serving as the supervisory attorney for cases handled by the faculty member and by law students pursuant to a course in clinical law conducted by the faculty member. Pursuant to the faculty member's agreement with the law school, he endorses all such fees given to him over to the law school. The Commissioner has ruled that the faculty member's endorsement of the fees (and his agreement to endorse the fees) does not constitute an assignment of income, and the faculty member, therefore, is not required to include the fees in his gross income.[21] The faculty member was deemed to have acted as an agent of the law school in earning the fee. The Commissioner is not generous in determining whether a person performing services on behalf of a charitable organization was acting as an agent of the charity; strong evidence of an agency relationship will be required.[22]

In the instant problem, if the faculty member had not been treated as an agent, the fees would have been included in the faculty member's gross income, and he could then have treated the fees as having been contributed to a qualified charity. His deductions for those constructive contributions would be subject to the limitations (including the limitation on the maximum amount deductible) imposed on charitable deductions.[23] Even if the payment to the law school were deductible as a business expense, the deduction would be an employee business expense and so would be a miscellaneous itemized deduction that is subject to the 2% of AGI floor of § 67 and, for years after 2012, to the overall limitation of § 68.[24]

¶ 14.2400.   Conversion of Services to Property. As noted in **¶¶ 14.2100** and **14.2200**, the assignment of future income that is derived from the assignor's services is an anticipatory assignment of

---

21. Rev. Rul. 74–581.

22. E.g., *Schuster v. Commissioner*, 800 F.2d 672 (7th Cir. 1986).

23. See Chapter **Twenty**.

24. See Chapter **Ten**.

income, but the transfer of the donor's entire interest in an item of property does not cause the donor to be taxed on the income subsequently produced by the donated property. The question arises as to what extent can a person convert his services into property and successfully give away the property without being taxed on income produced by that property or from the sale of that property. In the case of renewal commissions, an insurance agent's right to receive a percentage of premiums paid in the future is treated as a kind of deferred compensation for the agent's services in selling the policy, and so the renewal commissions are taxed to the agent even when he has assigned the right to them to another.[25] However, when an artist paints a painting and then gives it to another who sells it, the income recognized on the donee's sale of that painting will be included in the donee's gross income and not in the gross income of the artist who painted it. The painter is deemed to have converted his effort into property which can be given away without triggering anticipatory assignment problems. Similarly, when an author gives away his copyright interest in a work he wrote, the author will not be taxed on the royalty income that the donee receives on the exploitation of that written work.[26]

¶ 14.2500. Taxation of Plaintiff on Portion of Taxable Award Paid to Taxpayer's Attorney Pursuant to Contingent Fee Arrangement. A TP seeks to enforce a claim for damages which will be taxable income to the TP if the TP prevails.[27] The TP employs an attorney to enforce the claim and to collect on it. The TP and the attorney agree to a contingent fee arrangement under which the attorney is entitled to a specified percentage of any amount collected on the claim. The claim is settled for $1,000,000 of which $400,000 is paid to the attorney pursuant to the contingent fee arrangement. The Supreme Court held that the entire amount of the award ($1,000,000), including the $400,000 that was paid to the attorney, is taxable to the TP under the anticipatory assignment of income doctrine.[28]

The *Banks* decision dealt with two cases that were consolidated in the Supreme Court. While the payment made to the attorney was deductible as an expense of collecting income (§ 212), it was treated

---

25. See ¶ 14.2120.

26. See Rev. Rul. 71–33, Rev. Rul. 54–599 and PLR 8444073.

27. See Chapter **Four** for a discussion of when tort damages are taxable or excludable from income.

28. *Commissioner v. Banks*, 543 U.S. 426 (2005).

as a miscellaneous itemized deduction at the time that the facts of the *Banks* case arose.[29] Consequently, the TP's deduction of the fees is subject to limitations imposed on miscellaneous itemized deductions, and is not deductible at all if the TP's tax liability is determined under the Alternative Minimum Tax system. The obvious inequity of this result led Congress to amend the Code prospectively while the cases were pending in the Supreme Court to make attorney fees and court costs nonitemized deductions when incurred in cases involving discrimination and a few comparable causes of action. § 62(a)(20), (e). A similar provision for the deduction of fees connected to a whistleblower case was added in 2006. § 62(a)(21). Those 2004 and 2006 amendments cured the problem for those TPs who subsequently litigate actions covered by those amendments, but it left the problem undisturbed for those not covered by those provisions.[30]

In *Banks*, the TPs contended that the contingent fee agreement with the attorney effected an assignment of a portion of each TP's claim to the attorney who therefore should be taxed on that portion of the award instead of the TP. Rejecting that contention, the Supreme Court held that the assignment of the claim was covered by the anticipatory assignment of income doctrine because of the control that each TP maintained over his claim (i.e., each TP had control as to whether to accept a settlement and over other major decisions concerning the prosecution of the claim). The TP's control over the asset that produced the income in question caused the TP to be taxed on that income. The Court also rejected a contention that the agreement between the TP and the attorney created a partnership or joint venture to enforce and collect the claim.

Although the Supreme Court in *Banks* declined to pass upon several issues raised for the first time in that Court, the decision in *Banks* likely is dispositive of the question of whether a TP is taxed on the portion of a taxable award that is payable to the attorney. The remedy for that harsh consequence lies with Congress to change the treatment accorded to deductions for expenses incurred in collecting income (as Congress did in 2004 and 2006 for a selected list of cases).

While the authors agree that the result reached by the Supreme Court in *Banks* is correct, notwithstanding the patent inequity of the

29. See Chapter **Ten**.

30. The nature and extent of these problems are discussed in Jeffery H. Kahn, *Beyond the Little Dutch Boy: An Argument for Structural Change in Tax Deduction Classification*, 80 Wash. L. Rev. 1 (2005). See Chapter **Ten** for an explanation of the different treatment accorded to itemized and nonitemized deductions.

result (the inequity is a product of faults in the Code's classification and treatment of certain deductions), we believe that the Court's analysis is questionable. The TP's assignment of a portion of the claim should have been characterized as an "anticipation of future income" event rather than as an anticipatory assignment of income.[31] In effect, the TP sold a portion of the claim to the attorney in exchange for the attorney's services. The taxation of that "sale" would then be deferred under § 83 until the attorney's interest vested which occurred when the case was finally settled. The result, however, under that approach would be approximately the same as the result that the court's approach reached.[32]

¶ 14.2600. Forgiveness of Debt. When a creditor forgives a debt the collection of which would have caused the creditor to recognize gross income, the forgiveness *may* constitute an assignment of income to the debtor—i.e., it may be treated as if the creditor had collected the debt and had subsequently turned over the cash proceeds to the debtor.

In *Commissioner v. Fender Sales, Inc.*,[33] the court held in a two to one decision that a corporation's distribution of equal shares of its own stock to its two equal shareholders in satisfaction of accrued but unpaid salaries owed to the shareholders for services rendered was gross income to the shareholders. The corporation had previously deducted the unpaid salaries when its obligation to pay them had accrued. In the view of the authors, the source of the shareholders' income should not have been the corporation's distribution of its stock (which in substance merely constituted a non-taxable stock dividend to them), but rather should have been the shareholders' forgiveness of the debt that the corporation owed them for accrued salary, which constituted an anticipatory assignment of income from the shareholders to the corporation. Contrary to the authors' view, when the court defined the amount of income recognized by a shareholder from the transaction, instead of referring to the amount of salary that was owed to a shareholder, the court said that a shareholder's income is the fair market value of the stock that the shareholder received. While the value of the stock a shareholder

31. The anticipation of future income rule is discussed in Chapter **Twenty–Seven**.

32. For a thorough discussion of this alternative approach, see Gregg D. Polsky, *A Correct Analysis of the Tax Treatment of Contingent Attorney's Fee Arrangements: Enough With the Fruit and Trees*, 37 Ga. L. Rev. 57 (2002).

33. 338 F.2d 924 (9th Cir. 1964).

received equaled the amount of salary owed to him, the fact that the court referred to the value of the stock suggests that it was taxing the shareholders on that item.[34]

The tax treatment of a shareholder who forgives a debt owed to him from the corporation was resolved by Congress in 1980 when it adopted § 108(e)(6).[35] For the current tax treatment of a corporation who distributes its stock to a creditor in satisfaction of its debt, see § 108(e)(8).

> **¶ 14.2610. Waiver of Statutory Fee.** When a fiduciary (such as a personal representative of a decedent's estate) becomes entitled to a fee set by statute for services performed, the Commissioner has ruled that the fiduciary's waiver of his right to that fee constitutes a gift to the debtor for gift tax purposes and constitutes an anticipatory assignment of income so that the fiduciary is taxed on the amount of the waived fee.[36] If the fiduciary waives the fee before performing any services or in certain cases within a reasonable time after commencing his fiduciary duties, the waiver will not constitute a gift or an anticipatory assignment of income.[37] The Commissioner's position has not been litigated.

¶ 14.2700. Family Partnerships.

> **¶ 14.2710. General.** A partnership pays no federal income tax. Instead, all of the tax items of the partnership (its income, deductions, credits, etc.) are allocated among the partners. Each partner treats his allocated share of a partnership tax item as if he personally had received the income or had incurred the expenditure for which the deduction or credit is allowed. § 702(b). In many cases, the tax items of a partnership are allocated among the partners according to the terms of the partnership agreement. § 704.

> **¶ 14.2720. Income Splitting.** The conduit attributes of a partnership make it a tempting device to split income among family

---

34. See Rev. Rul. 67–402, for a construction of the *Fender Sales* case that treats the distribution of stock to the shareholder as compensation rather than treating the shareholders' cancellation of the corporate debt as an assignment of income; see also *Putoma Corp. v. Commissioner*, 66 T.C. 652 (1976), aff'd, 601 F.2d 734 (5th Cir. 1979).

35. See Chapter **Seven** for a discussion of the tax consequences of a shareholder's cancellation of a debt owed to him by the corporation.

36. Rev. Rul. 64–225.

37. Rev. Rul. 56–472; and Rev. Rul. 66–167.

members. A TP could form a partnership in a trade or business with his children, seeking thereby to divide the partnership income among them. This device became an alternative to the irrevocable trust as an income splitting arrangement. Just as the judiciary and then Congress responded to such use of the trust device, so did they respond to the family partnership device.

¶ 14.2730. **Judicially Imposed Restriction.** Prior to 1951, the judicial decisions concerning family partnerships were somewhat checkered. In its landmark decision of *Commissioner v. Culbertson*,[38] the Supreme Court held that the test of the validity of income splitting by a family partnership was whether the parties formed and conducted the partnership in good faith—that is, whether they joined together with a business purpose for the present conduct of an enterprise. If a partner contributed no services to the enterprise, did not participate in management control, and did not contribute "original capital" to the enterprise, there was a strong (but not conclusive) presumption against his qualifying for partnership treatment. The judicial trend was to hold invalid for tax purposes a family partnership interest where the partner performed no vital services for the partnership and where the partner received his capital interest as a gift from a member of his family.

¶ 14.2740. **Statutory Resolution.** In 1951, Congress adopted the antecedent to § 704(e) in order to resolve the tax treatment of family partnerships and to reconcile the treatment of partnerships with general assignment of income principles. Under § 704(e), a person may successfully give a capital interest in a partnership to another (regardless of whether the donee performs services for the partnership) provided that capital is a material income-producing factor of the partnership's business. In that event, partnership income may be allocated to the donee partner, but a reasonable allocation of income must be made to the donor for any services that he performs for the partnership. Thus, a TP can use a family partnership to split income but only to the extent that the income is attributable to capital, and the TP must give that capital interest to the donee in order to qualify the allocation of the income from that capital for taxation to the donee.

A capital interest in a partnership means an interest in its assets as contrasted to a mere right to participate in the earnings of the

38. 337 U.S. 733 (1949).

partnership. Treas. Reg. § 1.704–1(e)(1)(v). These rules are similar to those adopted generally for the assignment of income.

The family partnership rules cannot be avoided by having a family member purport to "purchase" a partnership interest from another, and such purchased interests are treated as gifts for purposes of the family partnership statute unless it can be shown that the purchase was bona fide under criteria described in the regulations. § 704(e)(3); Treas. Reg. § 1.704–1(e)(4).

¶ 14.2750.   **Bona Fides.** A purported gift of a capital interest to a donee will not qualify the donee as a partner unless he is the real owner of such capital interest. The criteria for determining whether a donee is a bona fide partner are discussed in Treas. Reg. § 1.704–1(e)(2).

¶ 14.2760.   **Corporate Tax Parallel.** For a statutory provision applicable to Subchapter S corporations that parallels the treatment of family partnerships, see § 1366(e).

¶ 14.3000. TAXATION OF CHILD'S UNEARNED INCOME—KIDDIE TAX.

¶ 14.3100.   **Income Splitting with Minor Children.** Prior to the adoption of the Tax Reform Act of 1986, children (especially minor children) were a favored beneficiary of income splitting. A minor child typically has little or no earned income, and so the child will usually be in a low-income tax bracket. By transferring income-producing property to a minor child, the income thereafter produced by that property would generate much lower taxes than would be the case if the donor retained the property in which case the property's income would be taxed at the donor's marginal tax rate. The tax benefits were maximized if the child could utilize a personal exemption deduction and a standard deduction in determining his taxable income. While a tax benefit is still obtainable by transferring income-producing property to a child, the 1986 Act substantially reduced those benefits, especially for transfers to young children.

¶ 14.3110.   **Dependent's Deduction for Personal Exemption.** Typically, an individual TP is granted a deduction for a personal exemption (for the year 2011, the exemption amount is $3,700). However, as noted in Chapter **Eleven**, an individual who qualifies as a dependent exemption deduction for another person is not allowed a personal exemption deduction for himself. § 151(d)(2). Most young children will be supported by a living parent or parents and will qualify as a dependent exemption for that parent. Therefore, most young children will not be allowed a deduction for a personal exemption. So, if income is effectively shifted to such a child, the child cannot use an exemption deduction to reduce the amount of that income that is taxable. In some cases with older children (even with older children who are still minors), the child may not be a dependent of anyone and so can deduct a personal exemption for himself.

¶ 14.3120.   Dependent's Use of Standard Deduction. If an individual does not choose to itemize his deductions (i.e., he does not claim any itemized deductions), the individual will be allowed a standard deduction in lieu of his itemized deductions. The principal standard deduction is referred to as the "basic standard deduction." The amount of the basic standard deductions is set by the Code and then altered each year to reflect changes in the cost of living. For the year 2011, the basic standard deduction for an unmarried individual who is not a head of a household or a surviving spouse is $5,800. However, for certain individuals, the Code imposes a ceiling on the amount of standard deduction that is available for them. If an individual qualifies as a dependent exemption deduction for another person, the standard deduction allowable to that individual cannot *exceed* the greater of: (1) $300 (for the year 2011) plus the individual's earned income, or (2) a specified dollar amount which for the year 2011 is $950. § 63(c)(5).[39] In general, "earned income" refers to income earned by a person from his services (e.g., wages and fees) as contrasted to income earned from investments. In effect then, for the year 2011, while a dependent's standard deduction is available to reduce income earned by that dependent from his employment, it cannot reduce *more* than $950 of the dependent's passive income.[40] From year to year, the $300 and $950 figures mentioned above are increased to reflect changes in the cost of living. § 63(c)(4).

¶ 14.3200.   Kiddie Tax on Passive Income. Some of the passive income of a child who is under a specified age (usually 18) may be subjected to special tax treatment by § 1(g). For convenience, this special tax treatment of some of a child's passive income is sometimes referred to as a "kiddie tax." Note that the so-called "kiddie tax" is merely a special method for computing the tax on some of a

---

39.   Rev. Proc. 2011–12.

40.   See the illustration at ¶ **14.3300**.

child's passive income that provides a higher tax than does the normal method; it is not a surtax.

¶ 14.3210. Children Who Are Subject to the Kiddie Tax. The kiddie tax does not apply to a child who does not have at least one parent alive at the end of the taxable year; nor does it apply to a child who files a joint income tax return for a taxable year. § 1(g)(2). With one exception, the kiddie tax does not apply to a child who is 18 years old or older at the end of a taxable year. The one exception to that age requirement is that a child can be 18 years old or older (but never older than 23 years of age) if the earned income requirements of § 1(g)(2)(A)((ii)(II) are satisfied.

¶ 14.3220. Operation of the Kiddie Tax. Where applicable, the kiddie tax isolates a child's "net unearned income" from the child's other income and then computes the tax on the net unearned income at the same marginal rates as would have been applied if that amount had been included in the gross income of the child's parent or parents. The statute accomplishes this by defining the child's tax liability as the sum of the child's share of the "allocable parental tax" and the tax (at an unmarried TP's normal rates) on an amount equal to the difference between the child's taxable income and his net unearned income. § 1(g)(1). If the application of a separate kiddie tax causes a smaller tax liability on all of the child's income than would be imposed if all of the child's income were taxed at normal rates, then the kiddie tax will not apply; and the child's tax liability will be determined in the normal manner without any special treatment of unearned income. § 1(g)(1). In other words, if the normal application of the tax schedule yields a higher tax than the tax determined by using the kiddie tax, the higher tax is imposed. The definition of "net unearned income" and "allocable parental tax" and the operation of the kiddie tax are explained below.

¶ 14.3221. Earned Income. The "earned income" of a child is the income that the child earned as wages, salaries or professional fees, and other amounts received as compensation for personal services actually rendered by the child. §§ 1(g)(4)(A)(i), 911(d)(2). If the child is engaged as a self-employed person in the active conduct of a trade or business in which both capital and services are material income-producing factors, that portion of the child's self-employed income from the trade or business that represents reasonable compensation for the child's services (not to exceed 30% of the child's share of the net profits from the business) constitutes earned income. § 911(d)(2)(B).

¶ 14.3222. Net Unearned Income. The adjusted gross income of a child that is not "earned income," as defined in **¶ 14.3221**, is "unearned income." In general, unearned income refers to passive income produced by capital as contrasted to income derived from the child's services. Since the child's adjusted gross income (AGI) is used, the unearned income of a child will reflect that income's proportionate share of the child's nonitemized deductions (if any).

The "net unearned income" of a child is the child's unearned income reduced by the greater of (1) $1,900, or (2) the sum of $950 and the child's itemized deductions that are directly related to the production of the unearned income. § 1(g)(4)(A)(ii).[41] The $1,900 and $950 figures mentioned above are the figures for the year 2011.[42] For subsequent years, those figures will be changed to reflect changes in the cost of living. §§ 1(g)(4)(A), 63(c)(4), (5)(A). A child's net unearned income cannot exceed the child's taxable income. § 1(g)(4)(B).

¶ 14.3223. Amount of Child's Income that is Subject to Kiddie Tax. The kiddie tax operates only on a portion of a child's net unearned income. Thus, all of a child's earned income and some of his unearned income is excluded from the kiddie tax treatment. As stated in **¶ 14.3222**, for the year 2011, a *minimum* of $1,900 of a child's unearned income is excluded from the kiddie tax.

¶ 14.3224. Application of the Kiddie Tax. When the kiddie tax applies, the tax on the net unearned income of a child is determined by reference to the marginal income tax brackets of the child's parent. If only one parent is alive, reference is made to that parent's tax bracket. If both parents of the child are alive and file a joint tax return, reference is made to the parents' tax bracket for their joint return. If the parents are not married, reference is made to the tax bracket of the custodial parent of the child; if the parents are married but file separate returns, reference is made to the tax bracket of the

---

41. The meaning of the terms "itemized deductions" and "nonitemized deductions" is explained in Chapter **Ten**.

42. Rev. Proc. 2010–40 (Sec. 3.01).

parent with the highest amount of income. § 1(g)(5). According to the legislative history of the Tax Reform Act of 1986, in the case of a foster child, it is the income of the foster parent that determines the tax on the child's net unearned income.[43]

¶ **14.3225. Computation of the Child's Tax.** When the kiddie tax applies, the total amount of the child's tax liability for a taxable year is the sum of two partial taxes. The first partial tax is the amount of tax that is imposed by the normal tax schedule on an amount equal to the difference between the child's taxable income and the child's net unearned income for the year. Thus, this partial tax is the normal tax on all of the child's taxable income other than the child's net unearned income, which is isolated and subjected to a special partial tax computation referred to as the "child's share of the allocable parental tax" described in ¶ **14.3225–1**.

> ¶ **14.3225–1. Partial Tax on Net Unearned Income— The "Allocable Parental Tax."** The second partial tax imposed on a child is the specially computed tax on the child's net unearned income; this partial tax constitutes the "kiddie tax." The first step in computing this partial tax is to determine the parent or parents of the child whose income tax bracket will be employed.[44] Once the relevant parent has been determined, the next step is to add to that parent's taxable income for that year the net unearned incomes of all of the children of that parent whose incomes are subject to the kiddie tax and for whom that parent's income serves as the measuring standard. Using normal tax schedules, the amount of tax that would be imposed on the parent's reconstituted taxable income is then reduced by the amount of tax that is imposed on the parent's actual taxable income. The purpose of this computation is to determine the amount of additional tax that the parent would incur if the net unearned incomes of his children were included in the parent's income. This additional tax is referred to as the "allocable parental tax." The allocable parental tax is then allocated among the parent's children according to the proportion that each child's net unearned income bears to the total amount of net unearned incomes

---

43. S.Rept. 99–313, 99th Cong., 2d Sess. at p. 863 (1986).

44. The criteria for selecting that parent are described in ¶ **14.3224**.

that went into the computation of the allocable parental tax. § 1(g)(3).

¶ **14.3225–2. Total Tax Liability.** The amount of the allocable parental tax that is attributed to a child constitutes that child's second partial tax. This second partial tax is referred to as the "child's share of the allocable parental tax" or is sometimes colloquially referred to as the "kiddie tax." The child's total tax liability, then, is the sum of the two partial taxes—the partial tax on the child's taxable income other than his net unearned income[45] plus the child's share of the allocable parental tax.

¶ **14.3300. Illustration.** *D* is the only child of *F*, a widower who files a return as an unmarried individual. At the end of the year 2011, *D* was eleven years old. In 2011, *D* had no earned income; and *D* had $3,200 of interest income from bonds that *D*'s grandmother had given to *D* on her birth. *D*'s only deductible expense (other than the standard deduction) is a $200 state income tax payment that qualifies as an itemized deduction. *F* is entitled to a dependent exemption deduction for *D* since he provides her support. Regardless of whether *F* chooses to claim the dependent exemption deduction, the fact that he is entitled to take it is sufficient to disqualify *D* from having a personal exemption deduction for herself. § 151(d)(2). For the year 2011, *D* is allowed a standard deduction of $950. Since the standard deduction amount is greater than *D*'s itemized deductions ($200), *D* will use the $950 standard deduction. *F*'s taxable income for that year is $61,000.

Since D has no nonitemized deductions, her adjusted gross income is the same as her gross income of $3,200. *D* has taxable income of $2,250 after deducting her $950 standard deduction from her $3,200 of adjusted gross income. All of *D*'s income is unearned. After deducting from her $3,200 of adjusted gross unearned income the $1,900 of unearned income that is excluded from the kiddie tax by § 1(g)(4), *D* has $1,300 of net unearned income, which is the amount that is subject to the kiddie tax.

D's tax liability is comprised of two partial taxes. First, the partial tax on the $950 difference between *D*'s taxable income ($2,250) and *D*'s net unearned income ($1,300) is determined by applying the rates provided by the tax schedule for an unmarried individual, which is *D*'s filing status. This $950 of income is taxed at a 10% rate,

---

45. Described at ¶ **14.3225.**

which yields a partial tax of $95. The tax on the $1,300 of net unearned income that is subject to the kiddie tax is determined by adding $1,300 to F's taxable income and computing the additional tax that would be incurred by that addition. The additional tax is $325, and that amount constitutes the second partial tax on D's income. Note that the tax rates that apply to 2011 tax an additional $1,300 of taxable income to F at a 25% marginal rate. D's total tax liability for that year is $420 (the sum of the two partial taxes—$325 + $95). Note that if D's bonds were owned by her father, F, the $3,200 of interest income produced by those bonds would have been taxed to F at a 25% rate, causing an increased tax liability of $800. The tax reduction obtained by having the stocks owned by D, rather than by F, is $380 ($800 minus $420). The tax savings from splitting income to a young child may not be sufficient in many cases to warrant the effort of dividing the income.

¶ 14.3400. Election to Shift Child's Income to Parent. A parent might wish to dispense with the administrative task of filing a tax return for a young child. If specified requirements are satisfied, a parent can elect to have all of his child's income, less certain reductions, treated as the parent's income, and then the child has no income and need not file a tax return. § 1(g)(7). One of the requirements for this election is that all of the child's income for the taxable year consists of interest and dividends. This election is available only if the amount of the child's gross income falls within a stated dollar range; for the year 2011, the child's gross income must be greater than $950 and less than $9,500.[46] The amount of the child's gross income that is added to the parent's income is reduced by a figure determined under § 1(g)(7)(B).

---

46. Rev. Proc. 2010–40 (Sec. 3.01).

CHAPTER FIFTEEN

ALIMONY AND CHILD SUPPORT

¶ 15.1000. ALIMONY, SEPARATE MAINTENANCE, AND CHILD SUPPORT. The terms "alimony and separate maintenance" have a special meaning for tax purposes. An item that constitutes "alimony" for state law purposes will not necessarily constitute "alimony" for federal tax purposes, and vice versa.[1] As used herein, any reference to "alimony" will refer to alimony and separate maintenance as defined for federal income tax purposes. If a payment from a payor spouse to a spouse or former spouse qualifies as alimony for tax purposes, the payment will constitute ordinary income to the recipient and will be deductible by the payor. §§ 71(a), 215. The deduction allowable for such payments is taken from the payor's gross income in determining his adjusted gross income—that is, it is a nonitemized deduction.[2] § 62(a)(10). For convenience, we sometimes refer herein to the wife (W) as the recipient of such payments and to the husband (H) as the payor, but the same rules apply when the roles are reversed.

The Tax Reform Act of 1984 made extensive changes in the treatment of alimony through the amendment of § 71. For example, the requirements that previously existed that alimony payments be "periodic" and be made in discharge of a legal obligation arising out of a marital or family relationship were eliminated. The Tax Reform Act of 1986 (the 1986 TRA) made additional changes to § 71. The following discussion outlines the requirements under the current version of § 71. You should note that all the regulations to § 71 (including the temporary regulation), were promulgated prior to the adoption of the 1986 TRA, and so do not reflect the changes made by that Act.

¶ 15.2000. ALIMONY OR SEPARATE MAINTENANCE PAYMENT. The general rule under § 71(b)(1) is that payments are "alimony or separate maintenance payments" if they are *in cash* and received by or on behalf of a spouse under a "divorce or separation instrument" which does not designate the payments as not includable under § 71 and nondeductible under § 215. § 71(b)(1)(A), (B). Thus, if the parties do

---

1. E.g., *Human v. Commissioner*, 75 T.C.M. 1990 (1998).

2. See Chapter **Ten**.

not wish cash payments to be treated as alimony, they can elect "non-alimony" treatment by stating in the divorce or separation instrument that §§ 71 and 215 (the alimony provisions) do not apply. The term "divorce or separation instrument" is defined at ¶ **15.2700.** If *H* and *W* are legally separated under a decree of divorce or of separate mainte-nance, with one exception, they must not share the same household at the time the payments are made if the payments are to qualify as alimony. See ¶ **15.2400.** A payment will not qualify as alimony if the payor is obligated to make any such payment after the death of the payee spouse or to provide a substitute for such payments after the death of the payee spouse. ¶ **15.2500.** That requirement does not mean that a defaulted payment that was due before the payee's death cannot be paid after the payee died. The more likely construction of that requirement is that payment must become due prior to the payee's death. See ¶¶ **15.2500** and **15.2530**.

Note that §§ 71 and 215 do not apply to payments made between married TPs in a taxable year in which they elect to file a joint return. § 71(e).

¶ **15.2100.** **Payments of Property in Kind.** If *H* makes payments to *W* by giving her property in kind (i.e., property other than cash), such payments will not qualify as alimony. Temp. Reg. § 1.71–1T(b), A–5.

¶ **15.2200.** **Cash Paid to a Third Party Pursuant to a Divorce or Separation Instrument.** If the divorce or separation instrument provides for *H* to make a payment of cash to a third party which payment will inure to the benefit of *W*, that payment can qualify as alimony. However, any payments made to maintain property that is owned by *H* and used by *W* are not payments on behalf of *W* even if made pursuant to the terms of the divorce or separation instrument, and so such payments are not income to *W* under § 71. Premiums paid by *H* pursuant to the terms of the divorce or separation agreement for term or whole life insurance on *H*'s life will qualify as payments on behalf of *W* only if *W* is the owner of the policy. Temp. Reg. § 1.71–1T(b), A–6.

¶ **15.2300.** **Cash Paid to a Third Party at *W*'s Request or Ratification.** Cash payments made by *H* to a third party, even though not made pursuant to a divorce or separation instrument, can qualify as alimony if *W* makes a timely written request, consent, or ratification which expressly states that § 71 is to apply to that payment so that *W* will be taxed thereon. Temp. Reg. § 1.71–1T(b),

A–7. To be effective, *W*'s request, consent or ratification must be received by the payor spouse prior to the date of filing the payor spouse's first tax return for the taxable year in which the payment was made. Id. The regulation does not state that such a payment must be one that is made in substitution for an obligation to make a payment of a like amount that is required to be made to *W* pursuant to a divorce or separation instrument.

¶ 15.2400. Not Members of the Same Household. Generally, if spouses are legally separated under a decree of divorce or of separate maintenance and payment is made at a time when *H* and *W* are members of the same household, the payment cannot qualify as alimony. § 71(b)(1)(C). If, however, one spouse is preparing to leave the household when the payment is made and does in fact leave within one month after the date of payment, the spouses will not be treated as members of the same household. Temp. Reg. § 1.71–1T(b), A–9. Note that if the spouses are not separated under a decree of divorce or separate maintenance, a payment made pursuant to a written separation agreement or decree ordering support or maintenance for *W during* a divorce or separation proceeding can qualify as alimony even though the spouses are members of the same household. Id.[3]

¶ 15.2500. No Liability to Make Payments After Death of Payee Spouse. *H*'s liability to make payments to *W* must terminate upon *W*'s death. § 71(b)(1)(D). The termination of *H*'s obligation at *W*'s death may be a consequence either of a provision in the "divorce or separation instrument" or of the operation of local law. Prior to the 1986 amendment, there had to be a provision in the divorce or separation instrument terminating *H*'s liability on *W*'s death, but the 1986 TRA amendments changed that requirement so that it is sufficient if the liability is terminated either by local law or by the express terms of the divorce or separation instrument.

If the payor spouse's liability to make a payment will terminate if the payee spouse dies before it becomes payable, that will comply with the termination at death requirement. If the payor spouse fails to make a timely payment on the date that his liability becomes payable (i.e., all events have occurred to make the liability currently payable), the fact that the defaulted liability will not be terminated by the subsequent death of the payee spouse before actual payment is made does not violate the termination at death requirement. See

---

3. See *Venham v. Commissioner*, TC Memo ¶ 2000–165.

¶ **15.2530.** An obligation to make a payment, subject to termination on certain conditions such as death, can arise before the date on which the payment is to be made. In the view of the authors, the critical date for the termination at death requirement is the date on which the obligation first becomes *payable*; the death of the donee spouse before that date must terminate the obligation.

¶ **15.2510. Lump Sum Payment Required by Divorce or Separation Instrument.** Since the 1984 Act eliminated the requirement that a payment be "periodic" to qualify as alimony, there is nothing to prevent a lump sum payment required by a divorce or separation agreement from qualifying as alimony if the terms of § 71 are satisfied. However, the requirement (noted above) that the payor spouse's liability to make the payment must terminate on the payee spouse's death can be an obstacle. If neither local law nor the divorce or separation instrument provide that the liability to make the payment terminates if the payee spouse dies before the donor spouse is required to make the payment, the donor spouse's payment will not qualify as alimony because it will not comply with § 71(b)(1)(D). It does not matter whether the payee spouse actually does die before the liability was payable; the crucial factor is whether the death of the payee spouse before that date would have terminated the liability if it had occurred.

The decision of the Tax Court in *Webb v. Commissioner*[4] is worthy of note. In that case, *H* agreed in a written separation agreement with *W* to pay *W* a lump sum of $215,000, to be paid on the execution of the agreement. The parties executed the agreement, and *H* paid the $215,000 to *W* simultaneously with the signing of the agreement. The agreement created an obligation for *H* to pay *W* $215,000, and there was no provision in the agreement terminating that liability if *W* should die before payment was made. Consequently, if *W* had died after execution of the agreement but before the payment was made, her estate could have enforced the liability and required *H* to make the payment. The Tax Court held in *Webb* that the payment of the $215,000 did not qualify as alimony for tax purposes. It did not matter that payment was made simultaneous with the execution of the written separation agreement or that *W* actually was alive when the payment was made. The court deemed it determinative that the liability would

4. 60 TCM 1024 (1990).

be enforceable if payment had not been made before *W*'s death, regardless of when the payment was actually made.

In the authors' view, the Tax Court's decision in *Webb* is incorrect. The terms of the agreement made the liability payable on the execution of the agreement, and *W* had to be alive at that time or she could not have executed the agreement. The fact that the liability would be enforceable after *W*'s death if the payment were not timely made and if *W* died before the tardy payment took place appears to be irrelevant. The correct issue is whether *H*'s liability could be terminated by *W*'s death before it became payable, and it could not because the liability arose when *W* executed the agreement, and she had to be alive to do that. It should not matter that if *H* defaulted by failing to pay the sum at the time of execution when it was due, the defaulted liability could be enforced by *W*'s estate if she died before payment was made. However, *Webb* was cited with approval by the Service in a 1995 Technical Advice Memorandum.[5] But, as discussed in ¶ **15.2530**, the conclusions expressed in the 1995 Technical Advice Memorandum cannot be reconciled with the result in *Webb*.[6]

¶ **15.2520. Payment of Spouse's Legal Fees Pursuant to Divorce or Separation Instrument.** If a divorce or separation instrument requires *H* to pay the attorney fees that *W* incurred in the divorce or separation, can *H*'s payment of those fees qualify as alimony?[7] Unless the divorce or separation instrument, or local law, provides that *H*'s obligation to make that payment terminates on *W*'s death, the Service has concluded that the payments do not qualify as alimony because of the failure to comply with § 71(b)(1)(D).[8] The Service's view has been upheld in court.[9] If the parties wish to have the payments qualify as alimony, they could include a provision in the instrument that, after *W*'s death, *H* has no obligation to make any payments to *W* or to her attorney; and, even then, if W does not die, the payments would

---

5. TAM 9542001.

6. For a discussion of the proper treatment of a single payment, including the payment of a divorced spouse's legal or medical expenses, see Douglas A. Kahn, *Alimony Treatment for a Single Payment*, 125 Tax Notes 1211 (December 14, 2009).

7. Id.

8. TAM 9542001.

9. See *Berry v. Commissioner*, T.C. Memo ¶ 2000–373; *Sperling v. Commissioner*, 97 T.C.M. 1804 (2009).

be subject to the front-loading recapture rules of § 71(f).[10] Note that *H*'s liability to pay attorney fees would not become payable before *W*'s attorneys submitted their bill, and *W*'s death before the bill was submitted would not terminate *H*'s obligation.

¶ 15.2530. Late Payment of Defaulted Alimony. Consider the following illustration. *H* is required by a divorce decree to pay *W* $10,000 a month for so long as *W* lives. After paying on time for a year, *H* fails to make the required payments for three consecutive months and thus falls into arrears. *W* dies, and her estate demands that *H* pay the sum due for the three months in which he is in arrears. A court enforces that demand, and *H* makes the payments to *W*'s estate. This raises two questions. First, do the late payments themselves qualify as alimony? Second, while *H*'s liability to make payments for subsequent months ceases on *W*'s death, his obligation to make any payments that previously became due does not terminate on *W*'s death; the question thus arises as to whether that fact disqualifies all of the payments that *H* made (including those paid during *W*'s life)[11] from being treated as alimony. The answer to both is that the payments, including the late payments of the defaulted amount, can qualify as alimony for federal income tax purposes.

As noted in **¶ 15.2510**, the Tax Court held in *Webb* that even though a payor spouse's liability to make a lump sum payment became due at the time of the execution of the relevant instrument, the fact that payment could be enforced after the payee spouse's death prevented the lump sum payment from being alimony. If the same approach were applied to the monthly payments described in the paragraph above, it would render § 71 meaningless since virtually no obligation would qualify as alimony. Obviously, that cannot be. Accordingly, in TAM 9542001, the Service purported to distinguish the circumstance of the late payment of a defaulted item from that of the obligation to pay a lump sum or attorney fees. As to the situation presented in *Webb* (i.e., a lump sum payment was required to be made at the time of execution of the agreement), the Service's purported distinction is elusive at best; but the Service surely is correct that the right of a payee spouse's estate to enforce the payment of defaulted "alimony" does not prevent either prior "alimony" payments or the late payments themselves from qualifying as alimony for tax purposes.

10.   See ¶ **15.3000** *et seq.*

11.   See ¶ **15.2600**.

In the authors' view, the Service's conclusion that the enforceability of defaulted alimony payments does not violate the termination at death requirement is correct. However, the Service failed in its effort to disassociate that conclusion from the result reached by the Tax Court in *Webb*. The Service should repudiate the *Webb* decision and acknowledge that it is incorrect. Until it does so, a question can remain as to whether the crucial date for the wife's death to terminate a liability is the date (as the authors maintain is correct) on which the liability becomes *payable* rather than the date on which payment is actually made. It is inconceivable that the Service would retract its conclusion that the failure of a governing instrument or local law to terminate a defaulted liability, if the payee spouse dies before payment is made, does not violate the termination at death requirement of § 71(b)(1)(D).

¶ 15.2600. No Substitute Payments. *H* must not be required to make any payment (in cash or property) after *W*'s death that constitutes a substitute for payments that *H* was required to make during *W*'s life. § 71(b)(1)(D). Whether or not a payment made after *W*'s death constitutes a substitution for payments which terminate on *W*'s death depends upon all the facts and circumstances in the case, but provisions requiring initiation, increase, or acceleration of payments upon *W*'s death will indicate the use of substitute payments. Temp. Reg. § 1.71–1T(b), A–14. If *H* is obligated to make a substitute payment, then the payments for which the substitute is provided will not qualify as alimony; and of course, any such substitute payment also will not qualify. Temp. Reg. § 1.71–1T(b), A–13.

¶ 15.2610. Illustration. Under the terms of a divorce decree, *H* is obligated to make an annual cash payment to *W* of $40,000, terminating on the earlier of the expiration of ten years or *W*'s death. The decree also provides that at *W*'s death, if there are any living minor children of *H* and *W*, *H* will be obligated to make annual payments of $15,000 to a trust for the benefit of the children until the youngest child reaches the age of majority. At the time of the divorce, *H* and *W* had two children, ages 2 and 4. According to Treasury's regulations, these facts indicate that the $15,000 payments to be made to the trust after *W*'s death are a substitute for $15,000 of the $40,000 annual payment to be made to *W*. Thus, $15,000 of the $40,000 annual payments that are made to *W* will not qualify as alimony or separate maintenance payments. The remaining $25,000 of the $40,000 annual payments can qualify as alimony. Of course, payments made to the trust after *W*'s death will not qualify as alimony. Temp. Reg. § 1.71–1T(b), A–14, Ex. (1).

¶ **15.2700. Divorce or Separation Instrument.** The term "divorce or separation instrument" refers to divorce decrees, written separation agreements, and decrees for support. § 71(b)(2).

¶ **15.3000. FRONT–LOADING OF PAYMENTS—DEFINITIONS OF 1ST, 2ND AND 3RD, "POST–SEPARATION YEARS."** You will recall that the payor spouse is given a nonitemized deduction for alimony payments under §§ 215 and 62(a)(10). In the 1984 TRA, Congress restricted the extent to which alimony deductions could be concentrated in the early years of payment. Those restraints on the "front-loading" of alimony payments were substantially liberalized by amendments adopted as part of the 1986 TRA. Note that the changes made by the 1986 TRA are not reflected in the current regulations and Temporary Regulations. As amended, the sole restriction on such payments is a provision for recapturing certain alimony deductions granted to *H* for payments made in the first two years in which alimony is paid. Before considering that restriction, it is useful to define several terms that are employed in that provision. The term "1st post-separation year" refers to the first *calendar* year in which *H* makes a payment to *W* that qualifies as alimony under § 71. § 71(f)(6). The "2nd post-separation year" is the first calendar year following the 1st post-separation year; the "3rd post-separation year" is the first calendar year following the 2nd post-separation year. § 71(f)(6).

¶ **15.3100. Recapture Rules.** If the amount of alimony paid to *W* in the 2nd post-separation year is more than $15,000 greater than the amount of alimony paid to *W* in the 3rd post-separation year, a certain amount of the deduction granted to *H* for such payments in the 2nd post-separation year will be "recaptured" by requiring *H* to include that amount in his gross income for his taxable year that begins in the 3rd post-separation year. § 71(f)(1)(A). The amount so included in *H*'s gross income is called an "excess payment," which term is defined in ¶¶ **15.3400–15.3420.** If the amount of alimony paid to *W* in the 1st post-separation year is more than $15,000 greater than the *average* of the amount of alimony paid to *W* in the 2nd and 3rd post-separation years (after taking into account the excess alimony payment of the 2nd post-separation year that is recaptured), the "excess payment" for the 1st post-separation year also is recaptured in the taxable year of *H* that begins in the 3rd post-separation year. § 71(f)(3). The sum of the excess payments for the 1st post-separation year and the 2nd post-separation year is referred to as the "excess alimony payments." § 71(f)(2). The "excess alimony payments" (i.e., the sum of the excess payment for the 1st and 2nd post-separation years) is included in *H*'s gross income in his taxable year that begins in the 3rd post-separation year.

Note that the amount of alimony payments made in years subsequent to the 3rd post-separation year, or indeed whether any alimony payments are made after the 3rd year, has no effect on the recapture rules. The recapture rules relate only to the first three post-separation years.

¶ 15.3200. **Payee's Deduction of Recaptured Amount.** As stated above, the sum of the "excess payments" for the 1st and 2nd post-separation years are included in *H*'s gross income for his taxable year that begins in the 3rd post-separation year. The inclusion of that amount in *H*'s gross income essentially negates that amount of the deduction that *H* was allowed in the first two post-separation years. Since *H* is effectively denied a deduction for that amount, there is no reason for that amount to be treated as gross income to *W*. Yet, since the deductions that are recaptured by *H* represent alimony payments that previously were made to *W*, those payments were included in *W*'s gross income in the first two post-separation years. In order to wash-out that amount of gross income from *W*'s tax position, *W* is granted a deduction equal to the amount that *H* recaptured by including it in his gross income. § 71(f)(1)(B). This deduction is allowable to *W* in her taxable year that begins in the 3rd post-separation year; and it is taken from gross income in determining *W*'s adjusted gross income—i.e., it is a nonitemized deduction. § 71(f)(1)(B).

¶ 15.3300. **Taxable Year of Payor and Payee.** The taxable year of an individual typically is a calendar year. So, an individual's taxable year in which excess payments of the first two post-separation years are either to be included or deducted from gross income typically will be the 3rd post-separation year itself.

¶ 15.3400. **"Excess Alimony Payments."** The term "excess alimony payments" refers to the sum of a payor's excess payments for the 1st and 2nd post-separation years. § 71(f)(2). To determine that amount, it is necessary first to determine the "excess payments for the 2nd post-separation year," and then to determine the "excess payments for the 1st post-separation year."

¶ 15.3410. **Excess Payments for the Second Post–Separation Year.** Because of the manner in which the statutory formula operates, it is necessary to determine the excess payments for the second post-separation year before computing the excess payments for the first year. The "excess payment for the second post-separation year" is the excess of the amount of alimony *paid* by H in the second post-separation year over the sum of $15,000 and the amount of alimony paid by H in the third post-separation year. § 71(f)(4).

¶ 15.3420.   Excess Payments for the First Post–Separation Year. The excess payments for the first post-separation year is the excess of the amount of alimony paid by H in the first post-separation year over the sum of $15,000 and the average amount of alimony paid by H in the second and third post-separation years. In determining the average amount of alimony paid in the second and third post-separation years, the amount of alimony paid in the second post-separation year is reduced by an amount equal to the excess payments for the second post-separation year as determined in the manner described in **¶ 15.3410.** § 71(f)(3).

¶ 15.3430.   Illustration 1. H and W, who report their income on a calendar year basis, were divorced in Year One. The divorce decree requires H to make the following cash payments to W, all of which were made in a timely fashion: Year One, $50,500; Year Two, $42,000; Year Three, $10,000. Apart from the recapture rules, all of the requirements of § 71 are satisfied. Under § 215, in years One, Two and Three, H will deduct $50,500, $42,000, and $10,000 respectively. In each of those same years, W will include a like amount in her gross income. Since the first alimony payment was made in Year One, that year is the 1st post-separation year, and Years Two and Three are the 2nd and 3rd post-separation years respectively. In addition to the amounts of income and deductions described above, in Year Three H will be required to include $35,000 in his gross income, and W will be allowed to deduct $35,000, computed as follows:

Excess Payments in Second Post–Separation Year

Payment in Year 2	$42,000
Minus payment in Year 3 plus $15,000	(25,000)
Amount recaptured in Year 3 from Year 2 payment	$17,000

*Average Unrecaptured Payments Made
in Years Two and Three*

Payment in Year 3	10,000
Payment in Year 2 ($42,000) minus amount of Year 2 payment recaptured in Year 3 ($17,000)	25,000
Total for Years 2 and 3	$35,000
Average unrecaptured amount paid in Years 2 and 3 (1/2 × $35,000)	$17,500

Excess Payments in First Post–Separation Year

Payment in Year 1	$50,500
Minus the sum of $15,000 and the average unrecaptured payments made in Years 2 and 3 ($17,500)	(32,500)
Amount recaptured in Year 3 from Year 1 payment	$18,000
Excess alimony payments for Years 1 and 2 ($18,000 + $17,000)	$35,000

In summary, in Year Three, H will deduct the $10,000 alimony payment that he made to W in that year, and W will include $10,000 in her gross income. In addition, in that same year, H will include $35,000 in his gross income as the recapture of alimony deductions that he took in Years One and Two; and W will deduct $35,000 from her gross income in determining her AGI for Year Three. Note that it is irrelevant to the determination of H's recapture income (and of W's deduction) whether H made any alimony payments to W in years subsequent to Year Three.

¶ **15.3440. Illustration 2.** The facts are the same as those set forth in ¶ **15.3430** except that the amount of cash payments that H was required by the divorce decree to make, which payments were timely paid by H, were: Year One, $30,000; Year Two, $40,000; Year Three, $13,000. The amounts paid in those years will be included in W's gross income and deductible by H. In addition, H will include $12,000 in his gross income for Year Three, and W will deduct $12,000 from her gross income for that year, computed as follows:

Excess Payments in Second Post–Separation Year

Payment in Year 2	$40,000
Minus payment in Year 3 plus $15,000	(28,000)
Amounted recaptured in Year 3 from Year 2 payment	$12,000

Average Unrecaptured Payments Made in Years Two and Three

Payment in Year 3	$13,000
Payment in Year 2 ($40,000) minus amount of Year 2 payment recaptured in Year 3 ($12,000)	28,000
Total for Years 2 and 3	$41,000
Average unrecaptured amount paid in Years 2 and 3 (1/2 × $41,000)	$20,500

Excess Payments in First Post–Separation Year

Payment in Year 1	$30,000
Minus the sum of $15,000 and the average unrecaptured payments made in Years 2 and 3 ($20,500)	(35,500)
Amount recaptured in Year 3 from Year 1 payment	$0
Excess alimony payments for Years 1 and 2 ($0 + $12,000)	$12,000

¶ **15.3450. Illustration 3.** The facts are the same as those stated in ¶ **15.3430** except that the amount of cash payments that *H* was required by the decree to make, and which were timely paid, were: Year One, $30,000; Year Two, $40,000; Year Three, $3,000. The amount of deduction recaptured in Year Three (as gross income of *H* and as a deduction for *W*) is $26,500, computed as follows:

Excess Payments in Second Post–Separation Year

Payment in Year 2	$40,000

Minus payment in Year 3 plus $15,000	(18,000)
Amount recaptured in Year 3 from Year 2 payment	$22,000
Average Unrecaptured Payments Made in Years Two and Three	
Payment in Year 3	$3,000
Payment in Year 2 ($40,000) minus amount of Year 2 payment recaptured in Year 3 ($22,000)	18,000
Total for Years 2 and 3	$21,000
Average unrecaptured amount paid in Years 2 and 3 (1/2 × $21,000)	$10,500
Excess Payments in First Post–Separation Year	
Payment in Year 1	$30,000
Minus the sum of $15,000 and the average unrecaptured payments made in Years 2 and 3 ($10,500)	(25,500)
Amount recaptured in Year 3 from Year 1 payment	$4,500
Excess alimony payments for Years 1 and 2 ($4,500 + $22,000)	$26,500

¶ **15.3460. Exceptions to the Recapture Rules.** You will recall that the recapture rules apply where the amount of alimony *paid* in either the first or second post-separation year, or both, is significantly greater than the amount *paid* in the third post-separation year. There are certain circumstances in which smaller payments in the third post-separation year will not trigger a recapture because of statutory exceptions. For example, the recapture rules do not apply where the alimony payments terminate because of the death of either spouse or because of the payee spouse's remarriage. § 71(f)(5)(A). The recapture rules do not apply to payments received under a support decree. § 71(f)(5)(B). Another exception applies where payments may fluctuate because of certain external events. Payments made by *H* to *W* under an obligation to pay a "fixed portion or portions of the income from a business or property or from compensation for employment or self-employment," which obligation continues for a period of three years or more, are not subject to the recapture rules. § 71(f)(5)(C). Thus, a payor spouse whose payments fluctuate due to *certain* circumstances that are beyond his control will not be required to recapture income. However, the temporary regulation states that fluctuations caused by an external event that is beyond the payor's control will trigger recapture if the event is not one of those listed above. Temp. Reg. § 1.71–1T(d), A–25.

¶ **15.3500. Payments Made After Remarriage.** If the source of a spouse's obligation to pay alimony is a divorce decree, the local law of *some* states terminates that obligation upon the remarriage of the payee spouse. Nevertheless, a written separation agreement may require a payor spouse to continue making payments after the payee's remarriage. If the local statutes override the parties' separation agreement so that the payor has no legal obligation to make payments to the payee after the latter's remarriage, and if there is no subsequent written agreement requiring the payor to make payments, then any such payments made after remarriage will not qualify as alimony. The tax treatment of payments that do not qualify as alimony is discussed in ¶ **15.3510.**

However, if the payor has a continuing legal obligation under a divorce or separation instrument to make payments to the payee after remarriage, the payments will be alimony and so will be income to the payee and deductible by the payor, assuming all the requirements of § 71 have been met.[12] Thus, in *Blakey v. Commissioner,*[13] the Tax Court treated payments made after *W*'s remarriage as income to her and as deductible by *H* where the payments were required by a separation agreement that continued to be viable after *W*'s remarriage even though the agreement was approved in the parties' divorce decree. The agreement in *Blakey* was not incorporated into the divorce decree, but the Tax Court said that it would have reached the same result if the agreement had been incorporated. Under local law (Virginia) the contractual obligation to make payments to *W* after her remarriage was not superseded by the divorce

---

12. See *Spector v. Commissioner,* 71 TCM 3224 (1996); *Mass v. Commissioner,* 81 T.C. 112 (1983).

13. 78 T.C. 963 (1982).

decree and survived the termination of the court's jurisdiction.[14] The characterization of the payments by state law does not affect the tax law's characterization; even if state law does not label the post-remarriage payments as "alimony," they will be treated as alimony for tax purposes if they are required to be made.[15]

When payments are made pursuant to a separation agreement that is incorporated and merged into a divorce decree, and when the local law provides that a decree cannot require that alimony payments continue after the payee spouse's remarriage, payments made after a marriage do not qualify as alimony.[16] In such cases, the payor would have no legal obligation to make the payments which therefore would either be made voluntarily or under a mistaken belief of liability.

¶ 15.3510. **Treatment of Payments That Do Not Qualify as Alimony.** In Rev. Rul. 81–8, the Commissioner determined that payments made pursuant to a divorce decree after the remarriage of the payee spouse cannot qualify as alimony if, under local law, there is no legal obligation to make payments after that spouse's remarriage. However, the Commissioner further determined that the payments to such a remarried spouse constitute gross income under § 61, unless there is evidence that the payments are a gift (i.e., that they were made out of detached and disinterested generosity). Thus, under the Commissioner's ruling, the payor receives no deduction in such circumstances and, typically, the payee will recognize gross income. The ruling was amplified and superseded by Rev. Rul. 82–155, which treated such payments as income to W if paid by H's mistake but not income to W if H knew that he had no obligation to make the payment and intended to make a gift thereby. When H makes a payment for which he knows he is not obligated, it is likely that the payment will be a gift unless there is evidence that H had some compensatory purpose.

Rev. Rul. 82–155 was promulgated at a time when payment had

14. See also TAM 8642008 providing the same treatment on similar facts, except that the settlement agreement was incorporated (but not merged), into the divorce decree. In *Mass v. Commissioner*, 81 T.C. 112 (1983), a separation agreement was incorporated into the divorce decree, but it was not merged into the decree under state law. Thus, H's contractual obligation to pay continued after W's remarriage. The court held that the payments were alimony and so were includable in W's gross income under § 71 and deductible from H's gross income under § 215.

15. *Spector v. Commissioner*, 71 TCM 3224 (1996); TAM 8642008.

16. *Sherwood v. Commissioner*, 38 T.C.M. 660 (1979).

to be in discharge of a legal obligation arising out of a marital or family relationship to qualify as alimony. Although that requirement was eliminated by the 1984 TRA, the revenue ruling is still valid under current law. To qualify as alimony, a payment must be received under a divorce or separation instrument (§ 71(b)(1)(A)); if the payor has no legal obligation to make the payment, it will not satisfy that requirement.

¶ **15.3520. Modification of Agreement.** In *Hollander v. Commissioner,*[17] prior to their divorce, *H* and *W* executed an agreement settling their property interests and providing for annual payments to be made by *H* to *W* until *W* either died or remarried. They were divorced some three months later. Two years after the agreement had been executed, *W* informed *H* that she wished to remarry. *H* and *W* then executed an agreement which modified their first agreement by requiring *H* to make monthly payments to *W* after her remarriage. The Ninth Circuit held that the second agreement was incident to the prior divorce of *H* and *W*, and so the court held that the payments made by *H* to *W* after her remarriage constituted alimony.

If spouses who have been divorced for several years and have previously settled all legal obligations to each other voluntarily enter into a written agreement that requires *H* to make annual payments to *W*, can such payments qualify as alimony? The answer turns on whether the subsequent written agreement that *H* and *W* made several years after their divorce can qualify as a divorce or separation instrument as that term is defined in § 71(b)(2). Some authority may provide support for the construction that a subsequent written agreement can constitute a divorce and separation instrument.[18]

¶ **15.3600. Property Settlements.** Prior to the Tax Reform Act of 1984, the distinction between alimony payments and payments relating to a property settlement had important tax consequences. Property settlement payments were not covered under §§ 71 and 215. The 1984 Amendment's elimination of the requirements (previously applicable) that payments be periodic and that they be attributable to obligations arising out of the marital relationship has obviated the

---

17. 248 F.2d 523 (9th Cir. 1957).

18. See *Hollander v. Commissioner*, 248 F.2d 523 (9th Cir. 1957) and Temp. Reg. § 1.71–1T(b), A–7, discussed at ¶ **15.2300**. Also, cf., Temp. Reg. § 1.71–1T(b), A–8.

need to make the distinction between alimony and payments relating to a property settlement. A single cash payment to *W* can qualify as alimony under current law, subject to recapture rules if the payment is greater than $15,000, and subject to satisfying the termination at death requirement discussed at ¶¶ **15.2500** to **15.2530**.

In general, however, Congress chose to deny alimony treatment to payments that were likely to be a property settlement when it is administratively simple to identify them. To that end, some of the restrictions imposed by § 71 on qualifying for alimony are intended to deny alimony treatment for payments that are likely to be made pursuant to a property settlement. For example, any transfer of property in kind is excluded from alimony treatment. The apparent purpose of disqualifying cash payments from alimony treatment when such payments are to continue after *W*'s death, or when substitute payments are to be made upon *W*'s death, is that such payments are more likely to represent property settlements than support for *W*.

¶ 15.4000. TRANSFERS OF PROPERTY IN KIND. As noted in ¶ **15.2100**, a transfer of property in kind cannot qualify as alimony. The question arises as to whether a transfer of property in kind, made in connection with a marital split-up, might be treated as a taxable sale or exchange in which the transferor received the release of the transferee's marital rights. Under § 1041, a transfer to a spouse (or a former spouse if the transfer is made within one year after the marriage ceases, or if the transfer is related to the cessation of the marriage) will not cause the recognition of gain or loss to either the transferor or the transferee. In such cases, the transferee's basis in the transferred property is equal to the adjusted basis that the transferor had at the time that the transfer took place. Thus, the transferee is treated in the same manner as a donee of a gift except that the transferee's basis is not limited by the fair market value of the transferred property (as could apply to a gift where basis is determined by § 1015(a)). §§ 1015(e), 1041(b)(2). Note that a transfer to a nonresident alien will not qualify under § 1041 for nonrecognition of gain or loss. § 1041(d).

Transfers of property in trust for the benefit of a spouse (or former spouse) may also be covered by § 1041. However, a transfer in trust of an installment obligation can cause the transferor to recognize income. § 453B(g). Similarly, a transfer in trust can cause the transferor to recognize income if the sum of liabilities assumed or accepted by the trust exceeds the total adjusted basis of the transferred properties. § 1041(e).

¶ **15.4100.** **Related to the Cessation of Marriage.** A transfer to a former spouse is related to the cessation of the marriage if it is made pursuant to a divorce or separation instrument as defined in § 71(b)(2) or to an amendment or modification of such an instrument, and if the transfer occurs within six years after the end of the marriage. Temp. Reg. § 1.1041–1T(b).

A transfer by *H* to a third party will be treated as having been made to *W* if the transfer is made on behalf of *W* *and* if either: (1) the transfer is required by a divorce or separation instrument; (2) the transfer is pursuant to the written request of *W*; or (3) *H* receives from *W* a written consent or ratification of the transfer to the third party (which consent or ratification must state that the parties intend the transfer to qualify under § 1041 as a transfer to *W* and must be received by *H* prior to *H*'s filing of the first tax return for the year in which the transfer was made). Temp. Reg. § 1.1041–1T(c).

¶ **15.4200.** **Illustration 1.** *W* sold to her husband, *H*, 100 shares of stock of the *X* Corporation and Blackacre (unimproved land). The fair market value of the 100 shares of *X* stock was $10,000, and *H* paid that amount to *W* in cash. *W* had a basis of $16,000 in the 100 shares of stock. Although *W* realized a loss of $6,000 on that sale, none of her loss is recognized because of § 1041.

Two years later, *H* sold the 100 shares of *X* stock to *B*, an unrelated third party, for $12,000. *H* recognized a loss of $4,000 on that sale, and he is permitted to deduct that loss in determining his taxable income. *H*'s basis in the 100 shares of *X* stock was $16,000—the same basis that *W* had at the time of the sale to *H*. In determining his loss on the sale to *B*, *H*'s basis is not limited to the fair market value that the stocks had at the time that *W* transferred them to *H*. *H*'s holding period for the stock includes the time that *W* held the stock prior to selling it to *H*. § 1223(2). Note that the tax consequence to *H* of the sale to *B* would not be changed if two years earlier *W* had made a gift to *H* of the 100 shares of *X* stock instead of having sold those shares to *H*. Even if *H* had acquired the stock as a gift from *W*, § 1041 will override § 1015, and so *H*'s basis in the stock for loss purposes will not be limited to the stocks' value at the time that he acquired them. § 1015(e).

Consider the tax consequences on a different set of facts. The fair market value of Blackacre at the date of the sale to *H* was $30,000, and H paid W that amount in cash. W's basis in Blackacre was $18,000. So, W realized a gain of $12,000 on the sale, but she did not recognize any gain because of § 1041. H's basis in Blackacre is $18,000, the same basis that W had therein. H's holding period includes the time that W held Blackacre. § 1223(2).

¶ 15.4300.   Illustration 2. H and W each owned 100 shares of the outstanding stock of the Y Corporation. Y had 200 shares of stock outstanding, and so H and W each owned 50% of Y's stock.

H and W divorced. The divorce decree ordered the Y Corporation to redeem the 100 shares of Y stock that W held. The fair market value of those 100 shares of Y stock was $400,000, and W had a basis of $100,000 in those shares. Pursuant to the divorce decree, Y paid W $400,000 in redemption of her shares of Y stock. The Commissioner contended that W recognized a gain of $300,000 on that redemption. W contended that her transfer of her 100 shares of Y stock to Y was made on behalf of H pursuant to a divorce decree and so should be treated as a transfer to H himself. W therefore contended that the redemption of her Y stock was merely a circuitous sale to H, and thus that § 1041 precluded her recognition of any income from that "sale."[19] A majority of the Tax Court rejected W's contention in *Blatt v. Commissioner*[20] and held that she did recognize a gain from the redemption of her stock. The Tax Court distinguished and disapproved of a contrary decision by the Ninth Circuit.[21]

In an attempt to resolve the inconsistent standards used by the courts and avoid situations where the IRS was whipsawed (in that it could not tax either party), Treasury finalized Treas. Reg. § 1.1041–2. The regulations follow the primary and unconditional obligation standard. If H has a primary and unconditional obligation to purchase W's stock, then the transaction is treated as a constructive

19.   Note that if W's analysis is correct, then the amount paid by Y to W should be treated as a constructive distribution to H followed by a transfer from H to W; if so, H would have dividend income from the constructive distribution that was made to him.

20.   102 T.C. 77 (1994) (reviewed by the court).

21.   *Arnes v. United States*, 981 F.2d 456 (9th Cir. 1992). The *Arnes* case has an interesting follow up. After the wife prevailed in the 1992 Ninth Circuit case, the Service sought to tax the husband on the basis that the corporate distribution to the wife constituted a constructive dividend to the husband. In a decision reviewed by the court, a majority of the Tax Court held that there was no constructive dividend to the husband because he did not have a primary obligation to purchase W's stock. *Arnes v. Commissioner*, 102 T.C. 522 (1994). Consequently, neither Mr. nor Mrs. Arnes will recognize income from the redemption!

transfer of W's stock to H, followed by a redemption of that stock from H, followed by H's constructive transfer of the redemption proceeds to W (thus, W would not recognize any gain on the transaction). However, if H does not have such an obligation, W would be taxed under the normal redemption rules. Ultimately, the regulations provide H and W the ability to elect either treatment as long as they both agree and the elected treatment is expressed in the appropriate agreement. Treas. Reg. § 1.1041–2(c)(1) and (2).

¶ **15.5000. DIVORCE TRUSTS.** Prior to the Tax Reform Act of 1984 there were two alternative statutory provisions that applied to trusts which provided support for a former spouse, §§ 71 and 682. Trusts which were covered by § 71 are hereinafter referred to as "alimony trusts" and the other trusts are referred to as § 682 trusts. Since payments from an alimony trust met all of the requirements for alimony treatment under § 71, the income from an alimony trust was excludable from the gross income of the settlor (H) and the amount distributed to W was includable in her gross income. The income from a § 682 trust also is excludable from H's income, but the amount distributed to W from a § 682 trust will be includable in W's gross income only to the extent of the trust's income. Under the amended version of § 71, Congress eliminated alimony trusts and provides that such trusts are covered exclusively by § 682. Under § 682, the recipient of payments made out of a divorce trust is treated as a beneficiary of that trust. § 682(b). Thus, payments in excess of the trust's income will not be included in the recipient's gross income. No amount is included in the settlor's gross income. § 682(a).

¶ **15.6000. CHILD SUPPORT.** Any payment fixed in a divorce or separation instrument as payable for the support of children of H (the payor) will not be included in the gross income of W or deductible by H. §§ 71(c)(1), 215(b).

¶ **15.6100. Contingency Relating to a Child.** Payments which are to be reduced upon the happening of a specific contingency relating to a child, or at a time clearly associated with the happening of a contingency relating to a child, will be treated as payments fixed for child support to the extent of such reduction. § 71(c)(2)(A), (B). Reductions which are to occur when a child reaches a certain age, marries, or graduates from high school are examples of specific contingencies relating to a child. There are only two situations in which reductions will be presumed to be clearly associated with the happening of a contingency relating to a child of H. The first is where payments are to be reduced not more than six months before or after a child of *H* is to reach the age of 18, 21, or the local age of majority. The second is where payments are to be reduced on two or more occasions which occur not more than one year before or after a different child of *H* reaches a certain age between 18 and 24, inclusive. The certain age must be the same for each child but need not be a whole number of years. The presumption can be rebutted by a showing that the time for reduction was determined independently from any contingency relating to a child. Temp. Reg. § 1.71–1T(c).

¶ **15.6200. Illustration.** On May 1, 1986, *H* and *W* were divorced. Their two children, *X* (born February 10, 1976) and *Y* (born April 20, 1979), were 10 and 7, respectively. The divorce decree requires *H* to pay *W* $3,000 a month until July 1, 1996, at which time payments are to be reduced to $2,000 a month. On July 1, 2001, the payments are to be further reduced to $1,000 a month. On the date of the first reduction, *X* will be 20 years, 4 months, and 21 days old. On the date of the second reduction, *Y* will be 22 years, 2 months, and 11 days old. Each reduction is to occur not more than one year before or after a different child of *H* reaches any of the ages 21 years, 2 months, and 11 days through 21 years, 4 months, and 21 days. For example, the first reduction is within one year of the time *X* will reach the age of 21 years, 3 months; and the second reduction is within one year of the time *Y* will reach the age of 21 years, 3 months. Thus, the reductions will be presumed to be clearly associated with the happening of a contingency relating to a child. Unless the presumption is rebutted, $2,000 of the $3,000 in monthly payments will be treated as fixed for child support and so will not be deductible by *H* or includable in *W*'s gross income.

¶ **15.7000. INCOME SPLITTING.** *H* can claim a deduction from his gross income equal to the amount that is included in *W*'s gross income. § 215. This is a nonitemized deduction which is taken from gross income in determining adjusted gross income. § 62(a)(10). In effect, this permits *H* and *W* to split *H*'s income between them in a manner roughly similar to the splitting of income between spouses who file a joint return, except that *H* and *W* have more flexibility for tax planning. If only partial payment of a required amount is made, and if a provision has been made for child support, the amount paid is applied first to the nondeductible support of a minor child. § 71(a)(3).

¶ **15.8000. MARITAL STATUS.** A question may arise as to whether a man and woman who claim to have been married and later divorced will qualify as such for tax purposes. This question often turns on the validity of a divorce from a prior marriage. For example, *H* and *W–1* obtained a divorce decree in Year One; *H* married *W–2* in Year Two, and *H* and *W–2* obtained a divorce decree in Year Three pursuant to which *H* was obligated to pay *W–2* $200 a month for the rest of her life. For the $200 monthly payments to *W–2* to qualify as alimony, *W–2* must have been a lawful wife of *H* prior to their purported divorce, and *W–2* could not have been *H*'s lawful wife unless the divorce decree obtained by *W–1* was valid. The question of the validity of a prior divorce can arise in a variety of other tax contexts (e.g., the determination of whether either party to the putative divorce can file a joint return with a "second" spouse after a second marriage and whether gifts or bequests to a "second" spouse will qualify for the gift tax or estate tax marital deduction).

¶ **15.8100. Rule of Validation.** When spouses obtain a divorce decree, the Service will not challenge the validity of the decree so long as it has never been declared invalid by a court of competent jurisdiction; but if a state court, having jurisdiction of the parties or of the subject matter of the action, declares the prior divorce decree to be invalid, the Service generally will follow the later court decree and treat the divorce as invalid.[22] In so ruling, the Commissioner expressly rejected two decisions of the Second Circuit: *Borax v. Commissioner*[23] and *Wondsel v. Commissioner.*[24] In *Borax* and *Wondsel*, the Second Circuit held that the validity of a divorce for federal tax purposes was to be determined under a "rule of validation," which treats putative divorces as valid in all but a few cases. Under the "rule of validation," a divorce will be deemed invalid if declared so by a court of the jurisdiction that granted the divorce, but a declaration of invalidity by any other court would be disregarded. The purpose of this "rule of validation" was to promote certainty and uniformity which the court deemed to be important goals of the tax system.

¶ **15.8200. Status of the Rule of Validation.** As noted above, the Commissioner rejected the *Borax* and *Wondsel* "rule of validation."[25] The rule has fared badly in litigation since the Second Circuit adopted it in 1965. The Tax Court, the Ninth Circuit and the Seventh Circuit have rejected the rule of validation and essentially accepted the Commissioner's position.[26]

---

22. Rev. Rul. 67–442. See also Rev. Rul. 76–255.

23. 349 F.2d 666 (2d Cir. 1965).

24. 350 F.2d 339 (2d Cir. 1965).

25. Rev. Rul. 67–442.

26. See *Lee v. Commissioner*, 64 T.C. 552 (1975), aff'd 550 F.2d 1201 (9th Cir. 1977); and *Estate of Steffke v. Commissioner*, 64 T.C. 530 (1975), aff'd 538 F.2d 730 (7th Cir. 1976).

Even the Second Circuit has criticized the rule and apparently has retreated from its earlier decisions. In *Estate of Goldwater v. Commissioner*,[27] the Tax Court held that a divorce which was subsequently declared invalid by a state court of the state in which the spouse in question was domiciled (but not of the jurisdiction that granted the divorce) rendered the divorce invalid for federal estate tax purposes. Because an appeal in *Goldwater* would lie in the Second Circuit, the Tax Court deemed itself obligated to apply the law of the Second Circuit under its *Golsen* rule.[28] The Tax Court suggested that the "rule of validation" of the Second Circuit might apply only to income tax issues and not to estate tax questions. In affirming the Tax Court, the Second Circuit was somewhat critical of its earlier decisions in *Borax* and *Wondsel*, and the court did not rest its affirmance exclusively on the Tax Court's ground that the rule of validation applied only for income tax purposes.[29] In so doing, the Second Circuit distinguished an earlier decision of that court in the same calendar year which appeared to have adhered to the rule of validation—i.e., *Estate of Spalding v. Commissioner*.[30]

In *Spalding*, on a decedent's death, the issue arose as to whether she was validly married to her "husband" in light of a New York court's judgment that the decedent's husband's divorce from his first wife was invalid. The decedent lived and died a resident of California. The Tax Court held that the decedent was not validly married to her putative "husband," but the Second Circuit reversed the Tax Court. In *Goldwater*, the Second Circuit explained its reversal in *Spalding* as resting on the fact that the New York court's decree could not bind the decedent's estate since she had never been a resident of New York.

Thus, while the Second Circuit has not yet adopted the Commissioner's position, there is reason to question the extent to which that court will adhere to a strict rule of validation in the future. However, in a 1987 Tax Court decision that lay within the appeal jurisdiction of the Second Circuit, the Tax Court held that the "rule of validation" was the established rule of the Second Circuit, and the Tax Court followed that rule pursuant to its *Golsen* principle.[31]

---

27. 64 T.C. 540 (1975).

28. See *Golsen v. Commissioner*, 54 T.C. 742 (1970), aff'd 445 F.2d 985 (10th Cir. 1971).

29. *Estate of Goldwater v. Commissioner*, 539 F.2d 878 (2d Cir. 1976).

30. 537 F.2d 666 (2d Cir. 1976).

31. *Estate of Felt v. Commissioner*, 54 T.C.M. 528 (1987), appeal to 2d Cir. dismissed. The *Golsen* rule is discussed at ¶ 1.4200.

¶ **15.8300.** **Sham Divorces.** The Commissioner ruled in Rev. Rul. 76–255, that where a married couple obtained a divorce from a foreign jurisdiction, the motivation for which was tax reduction, and where the parties intended to remarry promptly and did so; the divorce will be disregarded for tax purposes even if it is a valid divorce under state law. The Fourth Circuit, in a 2–1 decision, adopted the Commissioner's view in *Boyter v. Commissioner*,[32] holding that whether a divorce should be considered a sham was a factual issue to be determined by the lower court.

32. 668 F.2d 1382 (4th Cir. 1981).

PART D
DEDUCTIONS AND CREDITS

CHAPTER SIXTEEN

INTEREST EXPENSE

¶ **16.0000.** **DEDUCTION FOR INTEREST EXPENSES.** Prior to the adoption of the 1986 TRA, subject to a few exceptions, most interest paid or accrued in a taxable year was deductible. Interest was deductible even though incurred in connection with the acquisition of property for personal, nonbusiness uses (e.g., interest on deferred payments for the purchase of household goods or for the purchase of a family car, interest on a home mortgage loan); but, subject to several exceptions,[1] the principal one being for so-called "qualified residence interest" (¶ **16.1420**), that is no longer so. Even under prior law, there were (and still are) provisions that deny deductions for interest connected with certain types of transactions; for example, interest incurred or continued to purchase or carry tax-exempt bonds is not deductible [§ 265(a)(2)], and interest payable on debts relating to certain life insurance coverage or to certain endowment or annuity contracts is nondeductible under § 264(a)(2) and (a)(4).

An interest payment (otherwise qualifying for a deduction) is deductible only if the TP has an unconditional and legally enforceable obligation to repay the underlying debt.[2] However, interest paid by a TP on a nonrecourse debt secured by property that the TP owns can qualify for an interest deduction so long as the debt is considered to be bona fide. See ¶ **16.2100.** Except for short-term consumer loans, the amount of interest for a taxable year that can be deducted cannot exceed the economic accrual of the interest obligation for that period.[3]

The principal Code provision granting a deduction for interest is § 163. When the only Code section under which an interest expense of an individual can be deducted is § 163, it constitutes an itemized deduction. However, if an interest expense is directly connected with the conduct of a trade or business (other than the business of being an employee), in which the TP materially participates, it can be deducted under § 162 as a business expense and so qualifies as a nonitemized deduction.[4]

---

1. One of those exceptions is for interest on certain education loans which, subject to limitations, is deductible. See ¶ **16.1300**.

2. *Linder v. Commissioner*, 68 T.C. 792 (1977).

3. Rev. Rul. 83–84; Rev. Proc. 83–40.

4. *Standing v. Commissioner*, 28 T.C. 789 (1957), aff'd, 259 F.2d 450 (4th Cir. 1958).The Service's nonacquiescence (1958–1 Cum. Bull. 7) in *Standing* was withdrawn in

Temporary Regulations provide that interest paid on a deficiency for a federal, state or local income tax and on indebtedness used to pay such taxes is nondeductible regardless of the source of the income that gave rise to the tax. See ¶ **16.1411**. As noted in that paragraph, five courts of appeals have denied a deduction for interest on an income tax deficiency.

While a deductible interest expense typically is an itemized deduction, it is excluded by § 67(b)(1) from the category of "miscellaneous itemized deductions." Consequently, interest expense deductions are not subject to the 2% of AGI floor that applies to many other itemized deductions. See ¶ **10.1110**. Since it is not a miscellaneous itemized deduction, a deductible interest expense is allowed in determining a TP's alternative minimum tax. See § 56(b)(1)(A)(i).

You will recall (¶ **10.1120**) that, for years after 2012, the aggregate itemized deductions of a TP for a taxable year are subject to an overall limitation imposed by § 68, which reduces the amount deductible according to a specified formula. Four itemized deductions are excluded from that overall limitation, and one of those exclusions is the deduction for *investment interest*. § 68(c)(2). Investment interest is described at ¶ **16.1220**.

Since interest that is directly connected with a self-employed trade or business (other than tax deficiency interest) is deductible as a nonitemized business expense, the only itemized interest deductions that will be subject to the overall limitation of § 68 when it becomes operative after 2012 are the qualified residence interest deduction (¶¶ **16.1420–16.1432**), interest on certain deferral of estate tax liability, interest on certain educational loans, and certain interest deductions that are taken into account under § 469 in determining the income or loss from a passive activity (¶ **16.1210**).

There are a number of provisions in § 163 denying a deduction for certain interest or limiting the amount of deduction. This chapter discusses many of those provisions, but it does not cover all of them.

¶ **16.1000. INTEREST INCURRED BY A NONCORPORATE TAXPAYER.** The 1986 TRA greatly expanded the circumstances in which interest incurred by a noncorporate TP is not deductible.

¶ **16.1100. Material Participation in Trade or Business.** When interest (other than income tax deficiency interest) is incurred in

1992–2 Cum. Bull. 1, which also substituted an acquiescence on other issues in that case, but made no reference to the treatment of interest. Since the Service concedes that similar statutory overlaps concerning the deductibility of state real estate taxes on realty that is used in a self-employed business permit such taxes to qualify as nonitemized deductions (¶ **10.1200**), the prospects for obtaining a like result for interest expenses connected with a self-employed business are favorable.

connection with an individual's conduct of a trade or business (other than the trade or business of providing services as an employee) in which the individual materially participates, the interest is deductible as a nonitemized deduction.[5] "Material participation" in an activity by an individual requires that the individual is engaged in that activity in a regular, continuous, and substantial basis.[6]

¶ 16.1200. Trades and Businesses in Which Taxpayer Does Not Materially Participate and Investments. When interest of a noncorporate TP is incurred in connection with an investment of the TP or with a trade or business (other than a passive activity) in which the TP does not materially participate, the deductibility of such interest is subject to several limitations. See ¶ **16.1220.** Such interest is referred to as "investment interest."[7] Interest incurred in connection with a "passive activity," as defined in § 469(c), is not treated as investment interest.[8] Qualified residence interest also is not treated as investment interest.[9]

¶ 16.1210. Passive Activities. Interest incurred by a noncorporate TP in connection with an investment is subject to the limitations described in ¶ **16.1220.** As noted above, interest incurred in connection with a passive activity, as defined in § 469(c), is not treated as investment interest. Such interest is subject to the limitations imposed by § 469 on losses incurred by a TP from passive activities.[10] Such passive activity interest will be aggregated with other deductions connected with passive activities and subjected to the limitations described in ¶ **18.9000** *et seq.*

Note that not all passive investments constitute a "passive activity" for purposes of § 469. For example, portfolio investments (including stocks and bonds) are excluded from the passive activity category,[11] and the interest incurred in connection with portfolio investments is treated as investment interest and is subject to the investment interest limitations. § 163(d)(5)(A)(i). Note also that the passive activity loss limitations of § 469 apply to person-

5. Such interest does not constitute "investment interest." § 163(d)(5), and (h)(2)(A).
6. §§ 163(d)(5)(C), 469(h)(1).
7. § 163(d)(3).
8. § 165(d)(3)(B)(ii).
9. § 165(d)(3)(B)(i).
10. See ¶ **18.9000** *et seq.*
11. § 469(e).

al service corporations and certain closely held corporations as well as to noncorporate TPs.[12]

¶ 16.1220.   Deduction of Investment Interest. "Investment interest" for a taxable year can be deducted only to the extent of the TP's "net investment income" for that year.[13] Net investment income is the excess of the TP's investment income over investment expenses other than interest expenses.[14] The excess of investment interest over net investment income that is not deductible in a current year is carried over and treated as investment interest incurred in the next taxable year.[15] If any of the carryover is not deductible in the next year because of the net investment income limitation, the unused carryover can be carried forward to subsequent years.

For purposes of the investment interest limitation, property held as an investment includes portfolio property (as described in § 469(e)(1)) and property held by a TP in connection with a trade or business that is not a passive activity and in which the TP does not materially participate.[16] Income and expenses from a passive activity that is covered by § 469 are not treated as investment income and expenses for purposes of § 163.[17] Investment interest does not include any "qualified residence interest," which is described at ¶¶ 16.1320–16.1332.[18]

Currently, qualified dividends are taxed at capital gains rates under § 1(h)(11). Such dividends are not included in investment income unless the TP elects under § 163(d)(4)(B) to treat them as investment income. Dividends for which that election is made are not treated as qualified dividends and so are taxed at ordinary income rates.[19]

Prior to 1993, investment income included the net gain recognized on the disposition of investment property. As a consequence of a 1993 amendment, the net gain from the disposition of

12.   ¶ 18.9160.
13.   § 163(d)(1).
14.   § 163(d)(4).
15.   § 163(d)(2).
16.   § 163(d)(5).
17.   § 163(d)(4)(D).
18.   § 163(d)(3)(B)(i).
19.   § 1(h)(11)(D)(i).

investment property is treated as investment income only to the extent that it is not a long-term capital gain.[20] However, a TP is provided with an election to treat all or part of the net gain from the disposition of investment property as investment income, and the amount of gain for which that election is made will be excluded from net capital gain and so will not qualify for the capital gains tax preferential rate.[21] In effect, a TP who wishes to have such long-term capital gain treated as investment income must elect to treat that gain as ordinary income.

As noted above, while the amount of a TP's investment interest that exceeds his net investment income for a taxable year is not deductible in that year, it can be carried over to the next year. But, what if the excess investment interest that is not deductible in a taxable year is greater than the TP's taxable income for that year? Should the TP be permitted to carry over that amount of the excess investment interest that exceeds his taxable income? If there were no limitation in § 163 on the deductibility of investment interest, the amount of TP's investment interest that exceeds his taxable income could not be deducted or carried over to another year; the excess interest expense would not create a net operating loss that could be carried over to subsequent years pursuant to § 172.[22] The carryover provision in § 163(d)(2) was intended to provide relief for a TP who was denied a deduction for investment interest because of the net investment interest limitation. If the carryover provision applies to investment interest in excess of taxable income, it will do far more than merely provide such relief; it will permit the carryover and ultimate deduction of an expense item that could never have been deducted by the TP if the net investment interest limitation had not been adopted. For this reason, initially, the Commissioner determined that the carryover provision of § 163(d) does not apply to investment interest in excess of the TP's taxable income for the year in which the interest expense was incurred.[23] While the Tax Court initially held for the Commissioner on this issue, the Fourth Circuit Court of Appeals reversed and held that the carryover of investment interest is not limited by the TP's taxable income.[24] In a subsequent case, a majority of the Tax Court overruled its earlier decision and

20. § 163(d)(4)(B)(ii).
21. §§ 1(h)(2), 163(d)(4)(B)(iii).
22. § 172(d)(4).
23. Rev. Rul. 86–70, revoked by Rev. Rul. 95–16.
24. *Beyer v. Commissioner*, 916 F.2d 153 (4th Cir. 1990), rev'g 92 T.C. 1304 (1989).

adopted the Fourth Circuit's view that the carryover of investment interest is not limited by the TP's taxable income.[25] After
losing three more Court of Appeals cases, the Service threw in the
towel and conceded that the carryover disallowed investment
interest is *not* limited by TP's taxable income for the year in
which the interest was paid or accrued.[26]

¶ 16.1300. Interest on Education Loans. As noted in **¶ 16.1400**,
with a few exceptions, interest on loans taken for purposes other
than business or investment are not deductible. One of those exceptions is for interest on certain loans taken to finance the payment of
higher education expenses. An individual is allowed a deduction for
interest paid on a ''qualified education loan'' for a student who is a
degree candidate carrying at least half the normal full-time work-
load.[27] To qualify, the student must be either the TP or a spouse or
dependent of the TP.[28] There is a dollar ceiling on the amount that
can be deducted in a taxable year. Currently, that ceiling is $2,500.[29]
That ceiling is reduced if the TP's modified adjusted gross income
exceeds a threshold figure.[30] For the year 2010, the threshold figure is
$60,000 ($120,000 if the TP files a joint return). For the year 2010, if
the TP's modified adjusted gross income equals or exceeds $75,000
($150,000 if a joint return is filed), then no deduction is allowed.[31] If
the TP is married at the end of the year, no deduction will be allowed
unless the TP and spouse file a joint return.[32]

The deduction for interest on education loans is an itemized deduction. It is not a miscellaneous itemized deduction. Section 67(b)(1)
excludes from miscellaneous itemized deductions interest that is
deductible under § 163. Section 163(a) provides that all interest paid
or accrued on an indebtedness is deductible. Section 163(h)(1) denies
a deduction for ''personal interest.'' Section 163(h)(2)(F) provides
that interest on educational loans that are deductible under § 221
are not treated as personal interest. Accordingly, the interest on
educational loans that is deductible under § 221 is also deductible

25. *Lenz v. Commissioner*, 101 T.C. 260 (1993) (reviewed by the court).

26. Rev. Rul. 95–16.

27. § 221.

28. § 221(d)(1)(A).

29. § 221(b).

30. Id.

31. Rev. Proc. 2011–12 (Sec. 2.08).

32. § 221(e)(2).

under § 163; and so that interest is not a miscellaneous itemized deduction.

For years after 2012, the deduction for interest on educational loans is subject to the overall limitation on itemized deductions imposed by § 68.

¶ 16.1400. Personal Interest. The 1986 TRA eliminated a deduction for interest of a noncorporate TP that is incurred in connection with most consumer purchases. Thus, interest on a personal loan taken out to finance the purchase of a family car or of household goods is no longer deductible. § 163(h)(1). Similarly, interest on income tax deficiencies or income tax payment extensions are not deductible. But see ¶ **16.1411.** A major exception to this denial of an interest deduction for consumer loans is that a deduction is allowed for "qualified residence interest."[33] Several additional exceptions are noted in ¶ **16.1410.**

Note that interest incurred on indebtedness property connected with a TP's trade or business, other than the business of being an employee, is deductible; but if the TP's business is that of an employee, no deduction will be allowed (i.e., such interest expense of an employee is treated as personal interest).[34] There is no justification for denying a deduction for interest on an employee's business debt, but Congress has done so.

¶ 16.1410. Exceptions. The denial of a deduction for personal interest does not apply to investment interest, which is subject to the limitations described in ¶ **16.1220,** nor to interest that is covered by § 469 as incident to a passive activity.[35] Nor does the denial apply to the deduction allowable under § 221 for interest on education loans.[36] Also, interest on certain deferrals of estate tax obligations, is deductible, but no deduction is allowable for an extension of time allowed under § 6166 for payment of estate tax in certain circumstances.[37] An important exception to the denial of a deduction for personal interest is that a deduction is allowed for

33. § 163(h)(2)(D). The term "qualified residence interest" is defined in ¶ **16.1420.**

34. § 163(h)(2)(A); *McKay v. Commissioner*, 102 T.C. 465 (1994), appeal vacated, 84 F.3d 433 (5th Cir. 1996).

35. § 163(h)(2)(C).

36. § 163(h)(2)(F); ¶ **16.1300.**

37. § 163(h)(2)(E), (k).

"qualified residence interest."[38]

¶ 16.1411. Interest on Tax Deficiency or Deferral Attributable to Self Employed Income. Prior to the Code's disallowance of a deduction for personal interest, which was added to the Code by the Tax Reform Act of 1986, the interest that an individual incurred on an income tax deficiency or an extension of time for payment of the tax was deductible. Typically, the deduction that was allowed an individual for such interest was an itemized deduction. However, if the income tax deficiency could be traced to the TP's self-employed business, the Tax Court and several Courts of Appeals treated the interest deduction as a nonitemized deduction on the ground that it was a business deduction under § 62(a)(1).[39] Such interest was also held to be a business deduction for purposes of computing the TP's net operating loss carryover.[40]

After the 1986 Act eliminated a deduction for personal interest, and thereby disallowed a deduction for interest on income tax deficiencies, the question arose as to whether the interest on an income tax deficiency that is traced to the conduct of a self-employed trade or business continues to be deductible as a business expense. The *Standing* and *Polk* line of cases,[41] while dealing with a different issue, did characterize such interest as a business expense, and therefore would seem to support allowing a deduction for post–1986 interest of that nature. However, in a Temporary Regulation promulgated in 1987, Treasury treated all such interest as nondeductible personal interest. The Temporary Regulation (Temp. Reg. § 1.163–9T(b)(2)(i)(A)) states that personal interest includes interest "paid on underpayments of individual Federal, State or local income taxes and on indebtedness used to pay such taxes, regardless of the source of the income generating the tax liability." The Temporary Regulation accords with a similar statement in the Blue Book for the Tax Reform act of 1986.[42] If

---

38. § 163(h)(2)(D). The meaning of "qualified residence interest" is described in ¶ 16.1420 *et seq.*

39. E.g., *Commissioner v. Standing*, 259 F.2d 450 (4th Cir. 1958), aff'ing 28 T.C. 789 (1957).

40. *Commissioner v. Polk*, 276 F.2d 601 (10th Cir. 1960), aff'ing 31 T.C. 412 (1958).

41. See ns. 39 and 40, supra.

42. Staff of the Joint Committee on Taxation, 99th Cong., 2d Sess., *General Explanation of the Tax Reform Act of 1986*, p. 266 (1987).

valid, and it has been sustained by five Courts of Appeals, the Temporary Regulation establishes that neither interest on such an income tax deficiency nor interest on a loan taken to obtain the funds to pay an income tax on self-employed business income can be deducted.

In *Redlark v. Commissioner*,[43] a majority of the Tax Court held that Temp. Reg. § 1.163–9T(b)(2)(i)(A) is invalid, and that interest on an income tax deficiency that can be traced to self-employed business income is deductible. In reversing the Tax Court, the Ninth Circuit deemed the language of the statute to be so broad and generalized that there was an implicit legislative delegation to the Commissioner to set the standards for what constitutes personal interest. The court therefore held that the Temporary Regulation is a permissible application and construction of the statute and must be sustained. Accordingly, the Ninth Circuit held that interest payable on an individual's income tax deficiency is not deductible regardless of the source of the deficiency.[44] Four other circuit courts of appeals came to the same conclusion that the Ninth Circuit reached, and held that such interest is not deductible.[45]

It is noteworthy that Temp. Reg. § 1.163–9T(b)(2)(iii)(A) provides that interest paid with respect to sales, excises, and similar taxes incurred in connection with a trade or business or an investment is not personal interest. Accordingly, such interest is deductible; but the interest incurred in connection with an investment is subject to the limitations on the deduction of investment interest described in ¶ **16.1220**.

¶ **16.1420. Deduction for Qualified Residence Interest.** Qualified residence interest is deductible as an itemized deduction, but it is not a miscellaneous itemized deduction.[46] It is, however, subject to the overall limitation on itemized deduction imposed by § 68 for years after 2012.

"Qualified residence interest" refers to interest on a debt that constitutes either an "acquisition indebtedness" or a "home

---

43.   106 T.C. 31 (1996) (reviewed by the court), rev'd 141 F.3d 936 (9th Cir. 1998).

44.   *Id.*

45.   *Kikalos v. Commissioner*, 190 F.3d 791 (7th Cir. 1999); *Allen v. United States*, 173 F.3d 533 (4th Cir. 1999); *McDonnell v. United States*, 180 F.3d 721 (6th Cir. 1999); *Miller v. United States*, 65 F.3d 687 (8th Cir. 1995).

46.   §§ 67(b)(1), 163(h)(2)(D).

equity indebtedness" with respect to a "qualified residence" of the TP.[47] A "qualified residence" is the principal residence of the TP (within the meaning of § 121), and one other residence which the TP selects.[48] As to the second residence, if the TP rents it for part of the year, for the property to be a qualified residence, the TP must use the property for personal purposes for longer than the greater of: (1) 14 days, or (2) ten percent of the number of days that it is rented.[49] If the TP does not rent the selected property at all during the year, it will be a qualified residence regardless of the amount of personal use to which the property is put.[50]

¶ 16.1430. **Qualified Residence Interest.** As noted above, qualified residence interest is interest on one or two types of indebtedness which is incurred with respect to a qualified residence—"acquisition indebtedness" and "home equity indebtedness."

¶ 16.1431. **Acquisition Indebtedness.** Acquisition indebtedness is a debt which was incurred in acquiring, constructing, or substantially improving a qualified residence of the TP and which is secured by such residence. The term also includes a debt, secured by the residence, which was incurred as the result of the refinancing of an acquisition indebtedness but only to the extent of the amount of the acquisition debt that was refinanced.[51] The aggregate amount of a TP's acquisition indebtedness for a given period cannot exceed $1,000,000 ($500,000 for a married TP who files a separate return); but this limitation does not apply to any indebtedness (hereinafter referred to as "pre-October 14, 1987 indebtedness") that was incurred on or before October 13, 1987, and that was secured by a qualified residence on October 13, 1987, and at all times thereafter until the interest is paid or accrued.[52] Interest paid or accrued on such pre-October 14, 1987 indebtedness, or (subject to time limitations) on a debt incurred to refinance

---

47. § 163(h)(3)(A).

48. § 163(h)(4)(A).

49. §§ 163(h)(4)(A)(i)(II), 280A(d)(1).

50. § 163(h)(4)(A)(iii).

51. § 163(h)(3)(B).

52. § 163(h)(3)(B)(ii), (D). Such pre-October 14, 1987 indebtedness is treated as acquisition indebtedness. Id.

such pre-October 14, 1987 indebtedness, is deductible. § 163(h)(3)(D). The $1,000,000 (or $500,000) limitation on the amount of post-October 13, 1987 indebtedness that can constitute acquisition indebtedness is reduced (but not below zero) by the amount of such pre-October 14, 1987 indebtedness of the TP. § 163(h)(3)(D)(ii). While not subject to the dollar ceiling of $1,000,000 (or $500,000), a TP's pre-October 14, 1987 indebtedness is treated as an acquisition indebtedness[53] and so can affect the amount of the dollar ceiling on home equity indebtedness and on post-October 13, 1987 acquisition indebtedness.[54]

¶ **16.1432. Home Equity Indebtedness.** Home equity indebtedness means a post-October 13, 1987 indebtedness (other than an acquisition indebtedness) that is secured by a qualified residence to the extent that the aggregate amount of such indebtedness does not exceed the difference between the fair market value of such qualified residence and the amount of the TP's acquisition indebtedness with respect to such residence. The aggregate amount that is treated as a TP's home equity indebtedness for any period cannot exceed $100,000 ($50,000 for a married TP who files a separate return).[55]

¶ **16.1500. Illustrations.**

¶ **16.1510. Illustration 1: Net Investment Income Limitation.** In Year One, B, a cash method individual, had interest income of $3,500 from corporate bonds that B owned. B had an outstanding debt of $30,000 which B had incurred in order to obtain part of the funds that he used to purchase the corporate bonds. The interest that B incurred and paid on that debt in Year One was $4,000. B had no other investment income or expenses in that year. B's taxable income for Year One was $40,000. B is permitted to deduct $3,500 of his interest expense (the amount equal to his net investment income) as an itemized deduction. The $500 of interest that cannot be deducted in Year One is carried forward and treated as an investment interest payment of $500 in Year Two. The $500 carryforward will be added to the investment interest that B paid in Year Two, and B can deduct

---

53. § 163(h)(3)(D)(i)(I).

54. See ¶ **16.1432**.

55. § 163(h)(3)(C).

the aggregate amount of Year Two investment interest only to the extent of *B*'s net investment income for Year Two.

¶ 16.1520.   Illustration 2: Interest on Consumer Loan. In Year One, *C*, a cash method individual, purchased an automobile for his personal use. *C* obtained a bank loan of $10,000 to purchase the automobile, and the loan was secured by the purchased vehicle. In Year One, *C* incurred and paid interest of $1,000 on the automobile loan. No part of the $1,000 interest payment is deductible. This is nondeductible personal interest.

¶ 16.1530.   Illustration 3. Interest on Loan for Employee's Business. The same facts as those stated in **¶ 16.1520**, except that the automobile that *C* purchased was exclusively used by *C* to travel on his route as a traveling salesman for his employer, a clothing manufacturer. Since the car is used in *C*'s trade or business of being an employee, the interest on the car loan is treated as personal interest that is nondeductible.[56]

¶ 16.1540.   Illustration 4. Home Equity Indebtedness. The same facts as those stated in **¶ 16.1520**, except that the loan for the automobile is secured by a mortgage on *C*'s personal residence, which has a fair market value of $110,000 and is subject to an acquisition indebtedness of $45,000. The $10,000 automobile loan is a home equity indebtedness, and so the interest payments on that debt constitute "qualified residence interest" and, therefore, are deductible.

¶ 16.1600.   Loan to Cash Method Taxpayer to Obtain Funds to Pay Interest on Another Loan from the Same Creditor. No deduction is allowed a cash method TP for interest paid on a loan (Loan #1) to the extent that the payment of the interest is derived from the proceeds of another loan (Loan #2) from the same lender. This is an application of the substance vs. form rule, and it applies when the court finds that the purpose of Loan #2 was to provide the funds to pay the interest on Loan #1. To deny the deduction, the court must determine that the interest payment on Loan #1 was derived from the proceeds of Loan #2, and that that was the purpose of undertaking Loan #2. In such a case, the form of the transaction is ignored. It is treated as a deferral of the interest due on Loan #1, and no deduction is allowable to a cash method TP for the accrual of unpaid interest. In effect, no payment has been made to the creditor;

---

56.   § 163(h)(2)(A).

instead, the amount of the debt owed to the creditor has been increased.[57]

Of course, a debtor can borrow from a third party to obtain the funds to pay the interest on a debt. The problem of deductibility arises when the debtor borrows from the same lender that made the original loan.

¶ **16.1610. Illustration.** *G*, a cash method individual, borrowed $100,000 from *L*. Simple interest of 8% is payable on the debt each year. At the end of the year, *G* borrows $8,000 from *L*, and gives *L* a note bearing 8% simple interest. Immediately afterwards, *G* pays $8,000 to *L* as the interest due on the $100,000 debt.

On those facts, it is likely that a court would find that the interest paid on the $100,000 debt was derived from the second loan made by *L*, and that the purpose of making that loan was to provide *G* with the funds to pay the interest. In that case, *L* will not be treated as having paid the interest, and no deduction will be allowed. It will be treated as if the interest accrued but was not paid.

¶ **16.2000. DEFINITION OF INTEREST.** Interest is the amount paid or accrued for the use of another's money. An interest deduction is allowed only for interest paid or accrued for the TP's use of money; no deduction is allowed for an interest payment made by a TP for money borrowed by someone else.[58]

¶ **16.2100. Illustration 1: Nonrecourse Debt.** A nonrecourse debt is one for which the debtor has no personal obligation to repay and which, upon default, the debtor can collect only by foreclosing on the property securing the debt. Individual *X* owns Blackacre (improved rental realty) which is subject to a mortgage of $50,000. *X* has no personal liability on the mortgage. If *X* makes an interest payment to the mortgagee of $4,000, his payment will be treated as interest for tax purposes if the underlying debt is bona fide.[59] A nonrecourse loan will be considered bona fide if it is reasonable to

57. *Davison v. Commissioner*, 107 T.C. 35 (1996), aff'd per curiam, 141 F.3d 403 (2d Cir. 1998). See also, *Battelstein v. IRS*, 631 F.2d 1182 (5th Cir. 1980) (en banc); *Wilkerson v. Commissioner*, 655 F.2d 980 (9th Cir. 1981); Ann. 83–130, 1983–32 IRB 30.

58. See *Secunda v. Commissioner*, 36 T.C.M. 763 (1977).

59. See Treas. Reg. § 1.163–1(b).

assume that the debt will be paid. For example, the debt will be bona fide if the underlying security bears a reasonable relationship to the amount of the purported indebtedness.[60] Assuming that X's debt is bona fide, the deductibility of the interest payment will depend upon the application of the passive activity loss limitation.[61]

¶ 16.2200.   Illustration 2: Interest on Another's Debt. X purchased Whiteacre from Y. X paid Y \$10,000 and assumed an outstanding mortgage of \$30,000. In addition, X assumed the obligation to pay \$1,000 defaulted interest on the mortgage obligation which Y had failed to pay. On X's subsequent payment of the \$1,000 of defaulted interest, X cannot treat that payment as interest because the payment is not made for money borrowed by X, but rather is made as part of the purchase price X paid to Y for the property.

¶ 16.2300.   Illustration 3: Interest on Tax Deficiency. Individual X owes an income tax deficiency of \$10,000 to the federal government. The income to which the income tax deficiency is attributable was not earned in a self-employed business. The interest payable on this tax deficiency is treated as personal interest, which is not deductible.[62] Even if the income to which the tax deficiency is attributable was earned in a self-employed business, five courts of appeals have sustained the Temporary Regulation's provision that the interest payment is not deductible.[63]

¶ 16.2400.   Illustration 4: Finder's Fee. Individual A desires to borrow \$1,000,000 for a business in which A materially participates as a self-employed person. B locates a lender who is willing to lend A the \$1,000,000. A pays B \$10,000 as a "finder's fee." The payment to B is not interest; it is made for B's services in locating an available source for a loan and is not a cost of the use of the money. However, since the loan is related to A's business, A can amortize the \$10,000 finder's fee payment over the term of the loan and deduct an aliquot (i.e., proportional) part of the fee each year as a business expense under § 162.

¶ 16.2500.   Penalty for Prepayment of Debt. Under the terms of some loans, a borrower is charged a fee (sometimes called a "prepayment penalty") if the borrower wishes to pay all or part of the

60.   Rev. Rul. 84–5; *Estate of Franklin v. Commissioner*, 544 F.2d 1045 (9th Cir. 1976), aff'g 64 T.C. 752 (1975).

61.   See § 469(c)(2).

62.   § 163(h).

63.   See ¶ **16.1411**.

principal before that payment becomes due (i.e., a prepayment of the principal). The "penalty" payable for such a prepayment is treated as interest for tax purposes.[64]

¶ **16.2600. Guarantor's Payment of Interest.** If, after a debtor's default, a TP who guaranteed the repayment of the debt fulfills his obligation by paying the creditors the amount due, including the unpaid interest, the TP will *not* be allowed an interest deduction for the interest payment. A guarantor is only secondarily liable for the debt, and the borrowed funds typically are used by the primary debtor rather than by the guarantor. The guarantor's interest payment is treated as a payment for another's use of money and so is not deductible as interest[65]. Whether the payment is deductible on some other ground will depend upon the circumstances under which the TP guaranteed the debt.

¶ **16.2700. Credit Card Annual Fee.** The annual fee paid for the use of a credit card is not interest.[66]

¶ **16.3000. ASCERTAINING PORTION OF CARRYING CHARGES FOR CERTAIN INSTALLMENT PURCHASES THAT CONSTITUTE INTEREST.** If personal property or educational services are purchased under an installment contract which states carrying charges separately, but for which the interest charge cannot be ascertained, then payments equal to six percent of the average unpaid balance of the contract during the taxable year are treated as interest. § 163(b)(1). The amount treated as interest, however, cannot exceed the aggregate carrying charges attributable to that year. § 163(b)(2). Whether such interest is deductible depends upon whether the purchased personal property or educational services is connected with the TP's business (other than the business of being an employee) or investment. Personal interest is not deductible.

¶ **16.4000. INADEQUATE INTEREST.** In certain cases where the stated interest payable on deferred purchase payments or on a loan of cash is less than market rates, the Code imputes interest payments of a sufficient amount to raise the interest rate to a reasonable figure.[67] The deductibility of such imputed interest is determined by the rules applicable to an actual payment of interest.

64. Rev. Rul. 57–198; PLR 199951037; PLR 199951038.

65. *Rushing v. Commissioner*, 58 T.C. 996 (1972), Acq.

66. Rev. Rul. 2004–52.

67. Inadequate interest on a deferred purchase payment is discussed in ¶ **16.4100**. The treatment of inadequate interest on a loan is discussed at ¶ **16.4200**.

¶ **16.4100. Deferred Purchase Payments.** If a contract of sale allows deferred payments for a period of greater than one year, payments made more than six months after the sale may be treated under § 483 as including *unstated interest*, which may be deductible by the buyer-debtor if the interest qualifies for a deduction and is included as ordinary income to the creditor-vendor. The total unstated interest is equal to the excess of the total payments to be made over the present value of those payments. The present value is computed by using a discount rate that is equal to the applicable Federal rate as determined by reference to § 1274(d).[68] In many cases, the discount rate will be limited to a maximum rate of nine percent compounded semiannually.[69] In certain cases where land is sold on a deferred payment arrangement between family members, the maximum discount rate is six percent compounded semiannually.[70]

The total unstated interest is apportioned among the payments that are due to be made more than six months after the sale in a similar manner to that employed in determining original issue discount (OID); that is, the interest allocated to a payment reflects the interest accrued to that date on a compounded basis.[71]

In many cases when a debt instrument is given as partial or full consideration for property in kind, the OID rules of §§ 1272–1274 are applicable to the debt instrument.[72] In those cases, §§ 1272–1274 take priority and § 483 does not apply. § 483(d)(1). As noted in ¶ **16.5300**, when a debt instrument is received as partial or full payment for property in kind, in some circumstances the provisions of § 483 will apply; in others, the OID rules of §§ 1272–1274 will apply, and, in some cases, neither will apply.

¶ **16.4110. Exceptions.** As to the purchaser of personalty or of educational services in which carrying charges are separately stated and to which § 163(b) applies,[73] § 163(b) takes priority over § 483.[74] As noted in ¶ **16.4100**, in most cases, § 483 will not apply to a debt instrument to which the OID rules of § 1272

---

68. § 483(b). See ¶ **16.5130**.

69. § 1274A.

70. ¶ **16.4110**.

71. See ¶¶ **16.5000** and **16.5200**.

72. ¶ **16.5300**.

73. See ¶ **16.3000**.

74. § 483(d)(3).

apply.[75] Section 483 does not apply in certain other circumstances described in § 483(d), including a sale or exchange in which the sale price does not exceed $3,000. Neither § 483 nor the OID rules of §§ 1272–1274 apply to the *obligor* on a debt instrument given as consideration for the purchase of personal use property.[76]

If an individual sells land under a deferred payment contract to a member of his family (as defined in § 267(c)(4)), the imputed interest rate cannot exceed six percent compounded semiannually. This maximum rate limitation does not apply if one of the parties to the transaction is a nonresident alien.[77] For any one calendar year, the aggregate amount of sales price between two related individuals that can qualify for this maximum rate limitation is $500,000.[78]

¶ **16.4200.   Loans Bearing Inadequate Interest.** When a loan, which is made without a discount, either bears no interest or bears below-market-rate interest, the OID rules do not apply, but it is clear that an item of value has been passed by the lender to the borrower. The reason that inadequate interest is charged to the borrower may be compensatory or it may be donative. In any event, in many (but not all) such circumstances, Congress has chosen to recharacterize the transaction by constructing a transfer to the borrower of all or a part of the amount by which the stated interest (if any) is inadequate (as compared with market rate interest) and by constructing an interest payment from the borrower to the lender.[79] The market rate interest is determined by reference to the "applicable Federal rate."[80] The constructive transfers and interest payments that are deemed to have been made under § 7872 can cause income tax consequences and (in certain cases) gift tax consequences.[81]

¶ **16.5000.   ORIGINAL ISSUE DISCOUNT.**[82] A debt instrument is

75.   § 483(d)(1).

76.   § 1275(b)(1).

77.   § 483(e)(4).

78.   § 483(e)(3).

79.   § 7872.

80.   § 7872(f). The meaning of "applicable Federal rate" is described at ¶¶ **9.4814** and **16.5130**.

81.   See ¶ **9.4200** *et seq.* for a discussion of § 7872 and of the timing problems that can arise under that provision.

82.   For an excellent treatment of the function of present value and the operation of the OID rules, see Posin, *The Time Value of Money in Corporate Takeovers*, 21 Conn.L.Rev. 49, 53–62 (1988).

sometimes issued at a discount price; that is, the issue price is less than the amount of principal that is payable by the debtor over the term of the debt. The amount of such discount is called "original issue discount" or "OID."[83] There is a *de minimis* exception: if the original issue discount is less than the product of multiplying 1/4 of 1 percent of the stated redemption price at maturity times the number of complete years to maturity; then the debt will be treated as not having any original issue discount.[84]

The OID represents additional interest that effectively is payable by the debtor over the period of the loan. The period of the loan is divided into "accrual periods," each of which typically is a six-month period.[85] The tax law allocates a portion of the OID to each day of each accrual period and treats the amount so allocated as interest received by the creditor and paid by the debtor. With a few exceptions, this imputation of interest payments is made regardless of the method of accounting employed by the creditor and by the debtor.

The interest so allocated is included in the creditor's gross income and, in proper circumstances, is deductible by the debtor.[86] The deductibility of such interest depends upon the debtor's use of the loan proceeds.

Certain debt instruments are excluded from OID treatment: tax-exempt obligations, United States savings bonds, short-term debts, (i.e., debts with a term period of one year or less [but note that the discount on a short-term debt may have to be accrued and recognized by the holder under § 1281]), and certain nonbusiness loans between natural persons if the aggregate amount of loans between those persons does not exceed $10,000.[87]

Note that interest (including OID) of a cash-method debtor on a short-term debt is deductible only when paid.[88] Also, if the obligor of a debt instrument having OID is on the cash method and if the debt is incurred in connection with personal use property, the obligor cannot deduct interest until paid;[89] this provision will apply primarily to qualified

83. § 1273(a)(1).

84. § 1273(a)(3).

85. § 1272(a)(5).

86. §§ 163(e), 1272(a).

87. § 1272(a)(2).

88. § 163(e)(2)(C).

89. § 1275(b)(2).

residence interest in view of the current law's disallowance of a deduction for most personal interest.

¶ **16.5100. Definitions of Terms.** OID is defined as the difference between the "stated redemption price at maturity" of a debt instrument and the issue price.[90] A debt instrument refers to a bond, debenture, note, certificate, or other evidence of indebtedness.[91] The term "debt instrument" does not include certain annuity contracts.[92]

¶ **16.5110. Stated Redemption Price at Maturity.** The "stated redemption price at maturity" is the *total* amount payable on a debt instrument over the term of the debt. It includes interest payments other than payments that are based on a fixed rate and are payable unconditionally during the term of the loan at fixed periodic intervals of no greater than one year.[93]

¶ **16.5120. Issue Price.** A debt instrument's "issue price" depends upon whether the debt instrument was publicly offered and upon whether it was issued in exchange for cash, property, or services. For purposes of the OID rules, any reference to "property" is deemed to refer to property, services, and the right to use property; but it does not refer to cash.[94]

If a publicly offered debt instrument is issued for cash, the issue price is the price at which the debt instrument was first offered to the public at a price at which a substantial amount of such debt instruments were sold.[95] If a debt instrument which is not publicly offered is issued for cash, the issue price of each such debt instrument is the price paid by the first buyer of that debt instrument.[96]

If a debt instrument is issued for "property," and if the debt instrument either is part of an issue that is traded on an established securities market or is issued in exchange for stocks or securities that are so traded or (in certain cases) is issued in exchange for other "property" of a kind that is regularly traded

90. § 1273(a)(1).
91. § 1275(a)(1).
92. § 1275(a)(1)(B).
93. § 1273(a)(2).
94. § 1273(b)(5).
95. § 1273(b)(1).
96. § 1273(b)(2).

on an established market, then the issue price of such debt instrument is equal to the fair market value of the "property" for which the debt instrument was issued.[97] In all other cases when a debt instrument is issued for "property," if the stated interest payable under the debt instrument provides an interest rate that is equal to or greater than the "applicable Federal rate," compounded semiannually, the issue price will equal the stated redemption price at maturity, and so, there will be no OID.[98] However, in such cases when the debt instrument does not provide an adequate interest rate, the Commissioner will impute the issue price under § 1274. With one minor exception, this imputed issue price is the sum of the present values of *all* payments due under the debt instrument.[99] The present value of a payment is determined as of the date of the sale or exchange by applying a discount rate equal to the "applicable Federal rate" compounded semiannually.[100]

As previously noted, the significance of the "issue price" is that OID is equal to the difference between the "stated redemption price at maturity" and the "issue price." Thus, the smaller the issue price, the greater that the OID can be.

¶ 16.5130.   **Applicable Federal Rate.** The "applicable Federal rate," which is used as the discount rate, is determined and published monthly by the Treasury Department on the basis of the average market yields of market obligations of the United States.[101] There are separate Federal rates for short-term, mid-term and long-term debt instruments.[102]

The applicable Federal rate is sometimes used to impute the issue price of a debt. As noted in ¶ **16.5120**, the Commissioner will impute the issue price of a debt by discounting the payments to be made only if: (1) the debt is given as partial or full payment for "property" (as specially defined in ¶ **16.5120**), and (2) there is not adequate stated interest. Even then, there are a number of exceptions set forth in §§ 1274(c)(3), and 1273(b)(3), which will bar the application of this discount method.

97.   § 1273(b)(3).

98.   §§ 1273(b)(4), 1274.

99.   § 1274(b)(1).

100.   § 1274(b)(2).

101.   § 1274(d)(1)(C).

102.   § 1274(d).

When the issue price is imputed under § 1274, the discount rate is the applicable Federal rate (compounded semiannually) at the date of sale or exchange of the property for which the debt instrument is issued.[103] In the case of sales and leaseback transactions, the discount rate for imputing the issue price of a debt instrument is 110 percent of the applicable Federal rate.[104] In certain sales or exchanges, the discount rate cannot exceed nine percent compounded semiannually.[105]

¶ 16.5140. *De Minimis* Exception. If the amount of OID for a debt instrument is so small that it does not warrant making periodic allocations of interest accruals, it would be an administrative nuisance to require that treatment. The Code responds to that concern for administrative convenience by establishing a *de minimis* rule under which a relatively small amount of OID is disregarded. Specifically, the Code provides that if the amount of OID for a debt instrument is less than the product of multiplying the number of complete years to the instrument's maturity times one-fourth of one percent of the stated redemption price at maturity, then the amount of OID will be treated as zero.[106] The figure, as so computed, that constitutes the ceiling on the *de minimis* rule is referred to as the "*de minimis* amount."[107]

¶ 16.5150. Illustrations.

¶ 16.5151. *De Minimis* Rule. A debt instrument that provides for a payment of $100 after 10 years is issued for $98. Before applying the *de minimis* rule, the OID is $2—the difference between the stated redemption price at maturity ($100) and the issue price ($98). One-fourth of one percent of the $100 stated redemption price at maturity is 25 cents. Multiplying 25 cents times the number of complete years to maturity (10) provides a $2.50 ceiling for the *de minimis* rule—i.e., $2.50 is the *de minimis* amount.[108] Since the OID for the instrument is less than $2.50, it is treated as zero. If the debt instrument had been issued for $97.50 or less, the OID

103. § 1274(b)(2).
104. § 1274(e).
105. § 1274A.
106. § 1273(a)(3).
107. Treas. Reg. § 1.1273–1(d)(2).
108. § 1273(a)(3).

would not have been less than the *de minimis* amount, and so the OID would not be treated as zero.

¶ 16.5152. Issue Price When Debt or Property is Traded on an Established Securities Market. *R* Corporation exchanged its bond (a debt instrument) for 50 shares of the stock of the *X* Corporation. The fair market value of the 50 shares of *X*'s stock is $10,000. If either the *X* stock is traded on an established securities market or the *R* bond is part of an issue a portion of which is traded on an established securities market, the issue price of the *R* bond will be $10,000 since that is the fair market value of the property for which the bond was issued.[109]

¶ 16.5153. Imputed Issue Price. In Year One, *C* transferred a truck with a fair market value of $8,500 to *H* in exchange for a debt instrument issued by *H* that was not traded on an established securities market. The principal amount of the debt instrument is $10,000 to be paid in a lump sum in 5 years. The debt instrument provides for 5% interest to be paid semiannually. The applicable Federal rate for mid-term securities at that time was 10%. The issue price of the debt instrument is the sum of the present values of the interest payments and the present value of the $10,000 amount payable at maturity. The present value of each payment is determined by discounting that payment at 10% compounded semiannually, determined as of the date on which the exchange took place.

In determining the stated redemption price at maturity of *H*'s debt instrument, the 5% interest payments are excluded since they are based on a fixed rate and are payable unconditionally during the term of the loan at fixed periodic intervals of no greater than one year. So, the stated redemption price at maturity is $10,000. In contrast, the issue price of *H*'s debt instrument includes the present values of the interest payments. Consequently, the OID equals the difference between $10,000 (the stated redemption price at maturity) and the sum of the present value of the $10,000 required payment plus the present values of the interest payments that are required to be made over the 5–year term of the debt instrument.

109. § 1273(b)(3).

¶ **16.5200. Accrual and Allocation of OID.** Once the amount of OID is determined, that amount is allocated among the accrual periods for the term of the debt instrument. The OID is allocated on a daily basis for each such accrual period (typically a six-month period). In general, the daily amount of OID is determined by treating the debt instrument as earning interest at a fixed rate, compounded semiannually, so that the amount of annual interest increases over the term of the debt instrument. The portion of OID that is allocated to a taxable year is included in the creditor's gross income for that year and is treated as paid or accrued by the debtor in that year. The deductibility of interest allocated to a debtor is determined by the rules described at ¶¶ **16.0000–16.1500**. In effect, the creditor and debtor are placed on the accrual method for purposes of reporting OID regardless of whether they otherwise report their income on that method.[110]

¶ **16.5210. Yield to Maturity.** The fixed rate which is used to determine the daily OID allocations is the "yield to maturity" of the debt instrument (i.e., the rate that if applied to the issue price and compounded semiannually would provide by the maturity date an amount equal to the OID).[111]

¶ **16.5220. Computation of OID.** The daily allocation of OID typically is determined separately for each six-month period (the accrual period) in the term of the debt. If the debt instrument does not provide for an acceleration of the payment of principal, the method of computing the daily allocation of OID for each six-month period in the term of the debt is to multiply the fixed rate (the yield to maturity) times the "adjusted issue price" (the issue price plus previously accrued OID) as determined at the beginning of the six-month period and then allocate the resulting figure (less interest paid in that six-month period) on a daily basis within that six-month period.[112] If the debt instrument permits prepayments of principal or certain other accelerations of principal payments, § 1272(a)(6) adopts a more complex formula for determining the daily portion of OID.

¶ **16.5230. Adjustment to Creditor's Basis.** A creditor's basis in a debt instrument is increased by the amount of OID that is

110. But see, §§ 163(e)(2)(C), 1275(b)(2) discussed at ¶ **16.5000**.

111. § 1272(a)(3).

112. § 1272(a)(3)–(5).

included in his gross income.[113]

¶ 16.5300. Sale or Exchange of Property. As indicated in ¶ 16.5120, the § 1272 OID principles are not restricted to debt instruments that are acquired for cash. Sections 1272 and 1274 OID rules can also apply to debt instruments acquired in connection with the sale or exchange of property or services. The § 1272 and § 1274 OID rules, therefore, overlap with the treatment of deferred payment sales in § 483. While the treatment of § 1272 and § 1274 OID rules is similar to the treatment under § 483 of deferred payment sales, there are differences—for example, the amount of unstated interest is computed differently for purposes of §§ 1272 and 1274 than it is for purposes of § 483 deferred payment sales, and (more importantly) a cash method TP will include interest under § 483 in income when received as contrasted to the treatment of OID by § 1272 which requires that the interest be taken into income as it accrues. The Code excludes certain sales or exchanges of property from the imputed issue price rules of § 1274; for example, exclusions are provided for: debt instruments received for the sale of a principal residence; certain sales of land between family members; the sale by an individual, estate or testamentary trust of a farm for less than $1,000,000; certain sales of patents; and the sale of property for which the aggregate consideration does not exceed $250,000.[114] The imputed issue price rules do not apply if none of the payments on the debt instrument are due to be made more than six months after the sale or exchange of the property for which the instrument was given.[115] In many sales in which one of the exceptions to § 1274 applies, the deferred payment rules of § 483 will apply; however, there are a few types of transactions that are exempt from both § 1274 and § 483. For example, when a TP gives his personal note as consideration for the purchase of personal use property, neither § 483 nor § 1274 will apply to the TP (the *obligor*).[116]

¶ 16.5400. Subsequent Holder of Debt Instrument. The OID rules not only apply to the original holder of the debt instrument, but also apply to any subsequent holder. So, if a TP purchases a debt instrument from the holder of that instrument and if there was OID when that instrument was issued, the OID will continue to be

113. § 1272(d)(2).
114. § 1274(c)(3).
115. § 1274(c)(1).
116. § 1275(b).

allocated to the purchaser on a daily basis.[117] However, if the amount paid by the purchaser for the debt instrument is greater than the sum of the issue price of the instrument and the aggregate OID previously included in the gross income of any holder, the daily OID allocation that is treated as income to that purchaser will be reduced by an allocated portion of that excess (the purchaser's "acquisition premium").[118] A holder will not recognize any OID as income if he purchased the debt instrument at a premium (i.e., if he paid more for the debt instrument than its stated redemption price at maturity).[119]

The sale of a debt instrument (for a premium or otherwise) has no effect on the amount of *deduction* that continues to be allowable to the issuer; only the holder's income can be affected.

¶ 16.5500. Characterization of Gain from the Retirement, Sale or Exchange of A Debt Instrument. Amounts received on retirement of a debt instrument are treated as having been received in exchange therefor.[120] In the absence of an explicit provision to the contrary, the gain recognized on a sale or exchange of a debt instrument usually will constitute a capital gain since the instrument usually will be a capital asset. Exceptions to capital gains treatment are set forth in § 1271.

In general, § 1271(a)(2) characterizes the gain from the sale or exchange of debt instruments as ordinary income to the extent that the gain represents previously unreported OID. This provision does not apply to a debt instrument if there was no intention by the issuer to call the debt instrument before maturity.[121] An intention to call an instrument before maturity means that there was an understanding between the issuer and the original purchaser that the issuer will redeem the instrument before maturity.[122] This provision does not apply if the holder of the debt instrument purchased it at a premium, nor does it apply to tax-exempt obligations.[123] However, the gain recognized on the sale or exchange of short-term government obligations will cause ordinary income to the extent that the gain

117. As described at ¶¶ **16.5200–16.5230**.

118. § 1272(a)(7).

119. § 1272(c)(1).

120. § 1271(a)(1).

121. § 1271(a)(2)(A).

122. Treas. Reg. §§ 1.1271–1(a)(1), 1.1232–3(b)(4)(i).

123. § 1271(a)(2)(B).

represents the ratable share of acquisition discount.[124]

Acquisition discount is the excess of the stated redemption price at maturity over the TP's basis in the debt instrument.[125] The ratable share of that discount is determined by comparing the number of days the TP held the debt instrument to the number of days in the period from the TP's acquisition of the instrument to its maturity.[126]

¶ 16.6000. **MARKET DISCOUNT.** Section 1276 requires that any gain on the disposition of a "market discount bond" that was acquired in the marketplace (i.e., it was not acquired from the issuer) shall be treated as ordinary income to the extent that the gain is attributable to accrued "market discount." A "market discount bond" is a bond having a market discount except: obligations payable in no more than one year; United States savings bonds; tax-exempt obligations such as debts of a local government; installment obligations; and a few other exceptions.[127] The term "bond" refers to any bond, debenture, note, certificate of indebtedness, or other evidence of debt.[128]

"Market discount" is equal to an excess of the stated redemption price at maturity over the TP's basis when the obligation was acquired.[129] If the purchased bond had original issue discount, a "revised issue price" (i.e., issue price plus OID recognized prior to the purchase in question) will be used in determining market discount in lieu of using the stated redemption price at maturity.[130]

Unless the TP elects otherwise, the "accrued market discount" will be determined by first allocating the market discount ratably to each day over the period that begins with the TP's acquisition of the bond and ends on the date that the bond matures, and second, multiplying that daily accrued discount times the number of days that the TP held the bond.[131] In lieu of a ratable daily allocation of market discount, the TP can elect under § 1276(b)(2) to determine accrued market discount by applying a constant interest rate, compounded semiannually, to the TP's basis in the bond. If the bond's principal can be paid in more than one

124. § 1271(a)(3)(A).
125. § 1271(a)(3)(C).
126. § 1271(a)(3)(D).
127. § 1278(a)(1).
128. § 1278(a)(3).
129. § 1278(a)(2).
130. § 1278(a)(2)(B), (4).
131. § 1276(b)(1).

payment, accrued market discount is determined in a manner set forth in regulations.[132]

The holder of a market discount bond can elect under § 1278(b) to accrue and recognize a portion of the market discount each year that he holds the bond, and if that election is made, the provisions of § 1276 will not cause ordinary income on the sale of the bond.[133] Also, if that election is made, TP's basis in the bond will be increased by the amounts included in his gross income.[134] If made, the election will apply to all market discount bonds that were acquired by the TP in the taxable year in which the election was made, and the election will apply to subsequent taxable years until revoked by the TP with the consent of the Secretary (or his delegate).[135]

¶ 16.6100. **Partial Principal Payments.** If a distribution of a portion of the principal of a market discount bond is made to the holder of the bond, the distributee will recognize ordinary income to the extent that the amount of the distribution does not exceed the accrued market discount on the bond.[136] In such an event, the amount of the bond's accrued market discount will be reduced by the amount of the distribution that is treated as ordinary income to the holder of the bond.[137] This latter provision prevents the holder of the bond from being taxed twice on the same amount of discount.

¶ 16.6200. **Stripped Bonds or Coupons.** If the holder of a bond separates some of the interest coupons from the bond and then disposes of either the bond or the stripped coupons, the transferor must recognize interest income as provided in § 1286. For this provision to apply, it is not necessary that the bond actually contain coupons, which are rarely found on bonds currently. For purposes of that statute, the right to receive interest on a bond is treated as a "coupon."[138] So the statute can apply to a circumstance where the interest element of a bond has been separated from the right to repayment of the principal.

132. § 1276(b)(3).
133. § 1278(b)(1)(A).
134. § 1278(b)(4).
135. § 1278(b)(2), (3).
136. § 1276(a)(3)(A).
137. § 1276(a)(3)(B).
138. § 1286(e)(5).

¶ 16.7000. DENIAL OF DEDUCTION. In addition to the denial of deductions described at **¶¶ 16.1200–16.1600**, deductions are disallowed from certain kinds of interest payments, such as:

(a) interest on a debt incurred to purchase a single premium life insurance policy;[139]

(b) interest on debts incurred in connection with a plan to systematically borrow part or all of the annual increments in a life insurance policy's cash value (or of the increments in cash value of an annuity or endowment contract);[140]

(c) interest on debts incurred in connection with the purchase or *holding* of an obligation when the income from the obligation is wholly exempt from federal income tax (e.g., interest on a loan used to purchase municipal bonds which provide tax-free income).[141]

¶ 16.7100. Construction Period Interest. Interest paid or accrued by a TP on an indebtedness incurred or continued for the purposes of constructing or producing tangible property (or for the purchase of certain property to be held for sale to customers) must be capitalized and added to the basis of such property (or added to the inventory costs of produced or purchased inventory).[142] As to produced or constructed property, this provision applies only to interest paid or incurred during the production period which is allocable to produced property that either: (a) is real property, (b) is property with a class life (as determined by § 168) of at least 20 years, (c) has an estimated production period exceeding two years, or (d) has an estimated production period exceeding one year and a cost exceeding $1,000,000.[143] This capitalization requirement does not apply to the production of property for the TP's personal use; for example, the interest connected with the construction of a personal residence for the TP is not capitalized.[144]

¶ 16.8000. PREPAID INTEREST. A prepayment of interest (that is otherwise deductible) made by an accrual-method TP must be amortized over the period of the loan. A cash-method TP also must capitalize a

---

139. § 264(a)(2).

140. § 264(a)(3). There are some exceptions to this rule.

141. § 265(a)(2).

142. § 263A.

143. § 263A(f).

144. § 263A(c)(1).

prepaid interest payment and amortize that amount.[145] Thus, a cash-method TP effectively is put on the accrual method for purposes of deducting prepaid interest payments. Prepaid interest must be allocated ratably over the period of the loan.[146]

¶ **16.8100. "Points"—Current Deduction.** Section 461(g)(2) permits a current deduction in certain cases for "points" paid by a cash method TP *in connection with* a loan incurred for the purchase or improvement of the TP's principal residence and secured thereby. "Points" are dollar obligations that are imposed by the lender on the borrower (typically at the closing of the loan) in lieu of charging a higher annual interest rate. Each "point" is equal to 1% of the total amount loaned. The payment of points is currently deductible if incurred in connection with a loan for the purchase or improvement of the TP's principal residence (and secured by such residence) if the use of points and the amount charged are in accord with the established practice in that community. To be deductible, the points must be charged for the loan; if payment is for appraisal fees, title fees, inspection fees, attorney fees, or property taxes, it will not be deductible regardless of how the parties attempt to characterize the payment.[147] This provision for a current deduction constitutes an exception to the general rule that prepaid interest must be amortized.

¶ **16.8200. Safe Harbor for the Current Deduction of Points.** In Rev. Proc. 94–27, the Service provided a safe harbor for a cash method TP to obtain a current deduction for the payment of points for a loan undertaken in connection with the acquisition of the TP's principal residence. This safe harbor provision does not apply to points incurred in connection with the *improvement* of a principal residence. To come within this safe harbor provision, all of the following conditions must be satisfied:

(1) The Uniform Settlement Statement that is prescribed by the Real Estate Settlement Procedures Act of 1974 must clearly designate the amount of points that are incurred in connection with the indebtedness.

(2) The amount of points must be stated as a percentage of the indebtedness.

145. § 461(g).

146. *Zidanic v. Commissioner*, 79 T.C. 651 (1982).

147. Rev. Proc. 94–27.

(3) The amount of points must conform to an established business practice for charging points for loans for the acquisition of personal residences in the area in which the residence is located, and the amount of points must not exceed the amount generally charged in that area.

(4) The points must be paid in connection with the acquisition of the TP's principal residence and must be secured by it.

(5) The points must be paid directly by the TP. If a TP who purchases a principal residence uses the cash method of accounting, points paid by the seller of the residence (including points charged to the seller) will be treated as paid directly by the TP provided that the TP excludes the seller-paid points from his purchase price for the residence in computing his basis in the residence.

Rev. Proc. 94–27 1994 specifies a number of circumstances in which the safe harbor will not apply. For example, it does not apply to points paid for a refinancing loan, a home equity loan, or a line of credit even when such loans are secured by the personal residence. It does not apply to a loan obtained in order to make improvements to TP's residence. It also does not apply to points paid for a loan to acquire property that is not the TP's principal residence, such as a second home, vacation property, and investment or trade or business property.

The failure to come within the protection of the safe harbor does not necessarily mean that the payment of points is not deductible.

¶ 16.8300. "Points" Paid on Refinancing a Home Mortgage. In Rev. Rul. 87–22, the Commissioner announced that points paid on the refinancing of a home mortgage (at least to the extent that the amount of the "new" refinanced mortgage does not exceed the balance of the "old" mortgage at the time of refinancing) is not protected by § 461(g)(2) since the loan is not incurred for the purchase or improvement of the TP's home. Since the Commissioner determined that the exception provided by § 461(g)(2) does not apply to refinanced loans, he held that the points paid for refinancing home mortgages must be amortized over the period of the loan. Rev. Proc. 87–15. A majority of the Tax Court sustained the Commissioner's position in *Huntsman v. Commissioner*,[148] but because of the special facts of that case (described below), the Eighth Circuit Court of

---

148. 91 T.C. 917 (1988) (divided decision).

Appeals reversed.[149]

Huntsman involved the refinancing of a short-term "bridge loan" (i.e., an acquisition loan to purchase TP's principal residence that was taken for a short period during which the borrower seeks to obtain permanent financing) which was secured by a first mortgage on TP's principal residence plus a second mortgage taken one year later to make home improvements. The first mortgage acquisition loan was repayable in full in three years (i.e., it was a so-called balloon loan). A little more than two and one-half years later, TP obtained permanent financing (a 30–year variable rate mortgage) and used the proceeds to pay off the bridge loan and the home improvement loan. The TP paid the lender three points (amounting to $4,440) for making the permanent financing loan. The question in *Huntsman* was whether TP's payment of points for the permanent refinancing could be deducted in the year of payment or whether it must be amortized over the 30–year period of that loan. The Tax Court held that the points must be amortized. In reversing the Tax Court, the Eighth Circuit stressed that the refinancing of the bridge and home improvement loans were made *in connection with* the purchase or improvement of the TP's principal residence since the TP's obvious expectation at the time he obtained a three-year bridge loan was to replace it with permanent financing. The court's opinion suggests that the fact that the refinanced loan was a short-term bridge loan was critical to its decision. It is doubtful that the Eighth Circuit would allow a current deduction for points paid for the refinancing of a long-term acquisition loan. In an AOD (CC–1991–02) promulgated on February 11, 1991, the Service stated that while it would not seek Supreme Court review of the Eighth Circuit's decision in *Huntsman* because there is no conflict among the circuit courts, the Service will not follow that decision in jurisdictions outside of the Eighth Circuit.

¶ 16.8400. Unamortized Loan Costs Deductible on Taxpayer's Death. In Rev. Rul. 86–67, the Commissioner stated that unamortized loan costs (which include unamortized interest prepayments) that exist at a TP's death can be deducted in the decedent's final return. The TP's death ends the period during which he can benefit from the loan.

¶ 16.9000. SHAM TRANSACTIONS. The interest deduction has played a prominent role in a number of tax reduction schemes. Many

149.   905 F.2d 1182 (8th Cir. 1990).

such plans consist of mere paper transactions in which bookkeeping entries are made but very little of substance occurs. In most of those cases, courts have disallowed the claimed interest deduction.[150] Several cases have suggested that even where a loan transaction was not a sham, if the TP's sole motive in taking the loan was tax-oriented, the deduction might be denied. E.g., *Goldstein v. Commissioner.*[151] The *Goldstein* approach is related to the "economic substance" doctrine. See ¶ **16.9100** below. While the subsequent congressional adoption of restrictions on deductibility of interest paid on loans incurred in connection with an investment[152] would seem to cast doubt on the continuing vitality of the *Goldstein* approach, the case has been cited with approval.[153]

¶ **16.9100.   Economic Substance.** In addition to the profit motive, substance versus form, and business purpose requirements, the courts imposed a requirement referred to as the "economic substance doctrine" that for a transaction to be taken into account for tax purposes, the transaction must (1) make a meaningful change in the TP's economic position (apart from tax consequences) and (2) the TP must have had a substantial purpose (apart from tax consequences) for engaging in the transaction. While that statement of the doctrine sets forth two separate conditions, the courts divided over the question of whether both of those conditions had to be satisfied and how they were to be applied. In 2010, Congress codified the economic substance doctrine by adopting § 7701(*o*). In its codification of the doctrine, Congress requires that both conditions must be satisfied. In addition, the statute provides that state and local tax benefits and financial accounting benefits that a transaction provides are not taken into account in determining whether the transaction satisfies the economic substance requirement. To the extent that a TP relies on a showing of a potential profit to satisfy the above requirements, the Code establishes a standard for determining whether that item can be taken into account. § 7701(*o*)(2)(A).

---

150.   E.g., *Knetsch v. United States*, 364 U.S. 361 (1960).

151.   364 F.2d 734 (2d Cir. 1966).

152.   See § 163(d).

153.   See *Sheldon v. Commissioner*, 94 T.C. 738 (1990) (reviewed by the court).

CHAPTER SEVENTEEN

STATE AND LOCAL TAXES

¶ **17.0000. DEDUCTION FOR PAYMENT OF TAXES.** Except for the generation-skipping tax that is imposed by § 2601 on certain income distributions and for the environmental tax imposed by § 59A, payments of federal taxes (e.g., federal income, estate or gift taxes, or federal excise taxes) are not deductible.[1] Some state and local taxes and foreign taxes are deductible.[2] One-half of the self-employment social security tax paid by a *self-employed* TP is deductible as a nonitemized deduction.[3] Payments of *some* federal taxes that constitute business expenses or income producing expenses are deductible under §§ 162 or 212.[4] For example, the payment of the social security and employment taxes imposed on an employer in carrying on a trade or business is deductible.[5]

¶ **17.1000. DEDUCTIBLE TAXES.** Even when not connected with a trade or business, state and local income taxes and real and personal property taxes are deductible as are foreign income and real property taxes.[6] In addition, state, local, and foreign taxes incurred in connection with a trade or business or a profit-seeking venture are deductible even if such taxes are not listed in § 164(a)(1)–(6).

However, no deduction is permitted for a transfer or stamp tax that is paid or accrued in connection with the acquisition or disposition of property.[7] If such a transfer or stamp tax is paid or accrued in connection with the acquisition of property, the tax is added to the TP's basis in the property; if such a tax is paid in connection with the sale or other disposition of property, the tax is deducted from the amount realized by the TP on making that disposition.[8]

1. § 164(a).
2. *Id.*
3. § 164(f).
4. See Treas. Reg. § 1.164–2(f).
5. Rev. Rul. 2007–12, *Eastman Kodak Co. v. United States,* 534 F.2d 252 (Ct. Cl. 1976), Acq.
6. § 164(a).
7. § 164(a).
8. Id.

For many years, state and local sales taxes were deductible, but that provision for a deduction was deleted by the Tax Reform Act of 1986 ("1986 TRA"). For the years after that deletion and prior to 2004, state and local sales taxes were not deductible.

In the American Jobs Creation Act of 2004, Congress amended § 164 to permit a TP to elect either to take a deduction for state and local income taxes or instead to deduct state or local sales taxes.[9] This provision for an election was initially scheduled to terminate after a few years but has been extended several times since then. Currently, under the Tax Relief Unemployment Insurance Reauthorization and Job Creation Act of 2010, the election and its accompanying provisions remain applicable for the period beginning after December 31, 2003 and before January 1, 2012.[10] The motivation for granting that option was to permit a deduction for the payment of state taxes to citizens of states that do not have an income tax and derive their revenue primarily from sales taxes.

If a TP elects to deduct pre–2012 state and local sales taxes, the TP has an option of either deducting the actual taxes paid, or the TP can use the tax stated in tables the IRS provides, which tables are based on the average amount of sales taxes paid by persons in that state whose filing status, adjusted gross income, and number of dependents is similar to the TP's.[11]

If the TP elects to use the tables, for the purchase of certain items designated by the IRS, such as an automobile or boat, the TP can add a deduction for the actual state and local sales tax the TP paid.[12] That provision permits a TP to use the tables for his aggregate small purchases, and still get a deduction for the tax actually paid for large ticket items such as an automobile.

This provision for an election to deduct state and local sales taxes terminates in 2012; so, as currently written, the provision applies only for taxes paid or accrued in the years 2004 to 2011.

Taxes assessed against realty for local benefits of a kind tending to increase the value of the assessed property are not deductible.[13] To the

---

9. § 164(b)(5).

10. § 164(b)(5)(I).

11. § 164(b)(5)(H).

12. § 164(b)(5)(H)(i)(I).

13. § 164(c)(1). This provision refers to assessments for adding streets, sidewalks and similar improvements "imposed because of and measured by some benefit inuring directly to the property against which the assessment is levied...." Treas. Reg. § 1.164–4(a).

extent that such taxes are for the purpose of maintenance or repair or for the purpose of meeting interest charges, they can be deducted.[14] The burden is on the TP to show the amount of the tax that is allocable to such purposes. The TP may be able to capitalize the nondeductible portion of such taxes, and, if the property whose value is increased is used in a trade or business and is depreciable, the TP can depreciate that portion of the tax.[15]

Estimated state income tax payments are deductible in the year made if the TP is on the cash method and made the payment in good faith. If the TP had no reasonable basis at the time of payment to believe that any additional tax liability will be incurred for the next taxable year, the estimated tax payment is not deductible.[16] The federal environmental tax on corporate TPs and the generation-skipping tax (GST) imposed on certain income distributions are deductible. § 164(a)(4), (5). For the allocation of real estate taxes for the year in which the realty is sold, see **¶ 17.3000**.

As noted in **¶¶ 10.1200** and **17.4000**, a state tax that is deductible only under § 164 will usually be an itemized deduction; but it will not be a miscellaneous itemized deduction.[17] Unless connected with a business, such taxes are not deductible in determining the Alternative Minimum Tax.[18] However, a state tax on property used in a trade or business will also qualify as a business expense deduction under § 162, and so will be a nonitemized deduction if the TP is self-employed. When qualifying as a nonitemized deduction, the tax is deductible in determining the Alternative Minimum Tax.[19] The state *income* tax on an individual's business income will be an itemized deduction, regardless of whether the TP is self-employed or an employee.[20]

¶ 17.1100.   Definition of "Tax." The question sometimes arises as to whether a payment required to be made to a state (or to a foreign government) should be treated as a "tax" for federal income tax purposes. A "tax" has been defined (for Federal income tax purposes) as an enforced contribution, exacted pursuant to legislative authority

---

14.   § 164(c)(1); Treas. Reg. § 1.164–4.(b)(1); GCM 37927.

15.   Rev. Rul. 73–188.

16.   Rev. Rul. 82–208.

17.   § 67(b)(2).

18.   § 56(b)(1)(A)(ii). The Alternative Minimum Tax is discussed at Chapter **Twenty-Eight**.

19.   § 56(b)(1)(A).

20.   See **¶ 10.1200**.

in the exercise of the taking power, and imposed and collected for the purpose of raising revenue to be used for public or governmental purposes and not as a payment for some special privilege granted or service rendered.[21]

The Service contends that there is a federal standard for determining whether an expenditure qualifies as a tax under § 164 regardless of whether state law characterizes the payment as a tax. However, the Service's attempts to deny a deduction for payments of a percentage of a dollar amount of wages which are *required* to be made by Rhode Island and California employees to a state disability fund were unsuccessful.[22] The Tax Court treated the payments as a state income tax for which a deduction is allowed by § 164. The Service has conceded this issue and now allows a deduction for such required payments.[23] Contributions of employers or employees to *voluntary* plans to provide disability benefits are not taxes within the meaning of § 164.

A New York law attempted to make tenants personally liable for real estate taxes imposed on the demised property so that the tenants could qualify a portion of their rent for an income tax deduction. In Rev. Rul. 79–180, the Commissioner determined that, in fact, the realty taxes were not imposed on tenants, whose only liability was to pay their rent; therefore no deduction is allowed to the tenants.

¶ **17.2000.   TAXES NOT DEDUCTIBLE.** Death and gift taxes (other than generation-skipping state and federal taxes imposed on certain income distributions)[24] are not deductible whether imposed by the federal or state government.[25] The payment or accrual of state and local sales taxes that are not connected with the conduct of a trade or business or a profit-seeking activity is not deductible except for when TP elects to deduct in lieu of deducting state and local income taxes, as discussed above.[26] Federal income taxes and an employee's social security taxes are not deductible.[27] The non-deductibility of taxes assessed against realty for local benefits of a kind tending to increase the value of the assessed

21. See Rev. Rul. 61–152.

22. *McGowan v. Commissioner*, 67 T.C. 599 (1976); *Trujillo v. Commissioner*, 68 T.C. 670 (1977).

23. Rev. Ruls. 81–191 through 81–194.

24. § 164(a)(4), (b)(4).

25. § 275.

26. See ¶ **17.1000**.

27. § 275(a)(1).

property is discussed at ¶ **17.1000**. The apportionment of realty taxes between a buyer and a seller is discussed at ¶ **17.3000**.

¶ **17.2100. Capitalization of Taxes Allocable to the Production of Commercial Realty.** The direct cost of producing or constructing tangible property are capitalized and added to the basis of the produced property. § 263A. Prior to the adoption of the 1986 TRA, which added § 263A to the Code, some of the indirect costs incurred in producing property were currently deductible and some were required to be capitalized. The 1986 TRA amended the Code to require that most of the indirect costs of producing property must be capitalized. The indirect costs that are required to be capitalized include taxes which are allocable to the produced property.[28] So, real property taxes incurred with respect to realty on which a commercial building is being constructed will not be deductible but instead will be added to the TP's basis in the building and deducted as part of the depreciation allowance for that building. Only taxes incurred or paid during the construction period (the period beginning with the date on which construction begins and ending with the date that the constructed property is ready to be placed in service) will have to be capitalized. If the building that the TP constructs is for the personal use (as contrasted to an investment or business use) of the TP (e.g., the construction of a personal residence), the capitalization requirements do not apply; in such cases, real estate taxes are currently deductible.[29]

¶ **17.2200. Tax Imposed on Another.** A person cannot deduct under § 164 a payment of a tax which was imposed on someone else. So, if a TP purchases realty which is encumbered by a lien for unpaid real property taxes which had accrued prior to the TP's purchase of the realty, the TP's subsequent payment of the overdue taxes constitutes part of the cost of the property to the TP and is not deductible by him.[30] To the extent that a real estate tax for the year of sale is allocated to the buyer under § 164(d) [see ¶ **17.3000**], it is treated as a tax imposed on the buyer and is deductible by him.

¶ **17.3000. APPORTIONMENT OF REAL ESTATE TAX.** Upon the sale of real property, the real property tax for the real property tax year of sale will be allocated between the buyer and seller according to the

28. § 263A(a)(2)(B).

29. § 263A(c)(1).

30. *Reinhardt v. Commissioner*, 75 T.C. 47 (1980).

number of days of that taxable year during which each held the property.[31]

¶ 17.3100.   Illustration: Method of Apportionment. *D*, a cash-method TP, sold Blackacre to *B,* a cash-method TP, on February 28, Year One, which was not a leap year. On July 15, of that year, the State of *X* assessed a real property tax of $1,000 on Blackacre for that calendar year. *B* paid the tax on January 10, Year Two. *D* is entitled to an income tax deduction for Year One equal to 58/365 x $1,000 since *D* is deemed to have held Blackacre until one day prior to the day of sale. *B* is entitled to a deduction of 307/365 x $1,000 in Year Two.

¶ 17.4000.   ITEMIZED DEDUCTIONS. For a tax payment (or accrual) to qualify as a nonitemized deduction, the expense must be directly, and not merely remotely, connected with a trade or business; and the TP's business must not be that of being an employee. State or local property taxes imposed on realty that is used in a trade or business (other than the trade or business of being an employee) constitute nonitemized deductions, but state or local taxes imposed on an individual's *income* are an itemized deduction even when the individual's income is derived from the conduct of a self-employed trade or business.[32]

Thus, most state and local taxes that are deductible will be itemized deductions. Even when treated as an itemized deduction, such taxes are *not* subject to the 2% of AGI floor on the deduction of miscellaneous itemized deductions because taxes that are deductible under § 164 are excluded from that limitation by § 67(b)(2). However, if an individual's taxes are treated as itemized deductions, they are included with other itemized deductions of the TP and, for years beginning after 2012, are subject to the overall limitation on itemized deductions that is imposed by § 68 when an individual's AGI exceeds a specified amount.[33]

Employee business expenses that are not reimbursed by the employer are miscellaneous itemized deductions and are subject to the 2% of AGI floor.[34] If an employee incurs state taxes in connection with his business of being an employee, those taxes qualify for deduction under both §§ 164 and 162. If taken under § 164, the deduction is not a miscellane-

31.   § 164(d).

32.   See ¶ **10.1200**.

33.   See ¶ **10.1120**. Section 68 currently is not operative but is scheduled to apply to years beginning after 2012.

34.   See ¶ **10.1100**.

ous itemized deduction, and so is not subject to the 2% of AGI floor that applies to individual TPs. But, if the deduction is taken as a business expense under § 162, it will be a miscellaneous itemized deduction. The question is which of those two provisions takes priority, or is the TP allowed to choose? When both §§ 162 and 164 have applied to the tax expense of a self-employed TP, the courts and the IRS have allowed the TP to use § 162 so that the item would be a nonitemized deduction. That benefitted the TPs in those cases. In the instant situation, the TP would be benefitted if the deduction is characterized by § 164 so that it is not subject to the 2% of AGI floor. The authors believe that since the deduction is allowable by § 164, the exception in § 67(b)(2) is applicable, and the tax is not subject to the 2% of AGI floor.

¶ **17.5000. ALTERNATIVE MINIMUM TAX.** As noted in ¶ **17.4000**, a tax deductible under § 164 is excluded from the list of miscellaneous itemized deductions, and so is not subject to the 2% of AGI floor; but for years beginning after 2012 such taxes are subject to the overall limitation on an individual's itemized deductions imposed by § 68. With only three exceptions, taxes deductible under § 164 cannot be deducted in determining an individual's Alternative Minimum Tax.[35] One of the exceptions is that a tax which can be deducted as a nonitemized deduction will be allowed in determining the Alternative Minimum Tax.[36] The other two exceptions are that the deduction for the generation-skipping tax imposed on income distributions and the deduction for the environmental tax imposed by § 59A are allowed in determining the Alternative Minimum Tax.[37] All other deductible state and local and foreign taxes are disallowed in determining the Alternative Minimum Tax.

The disallowance of a deduction for most taxes in determining the Alternative Minimum Tax applies only to individual TPs. Similarly, the limitations on the deduction of miscellaneous itemized deductions and the overall limitation on itemized deductions[38] do not apply to corporate TPs.

The Alternative Minimum Tax is discussed in Chapter **Twenty–Eight**. An individual TP must compute both his regular income tax liability and his Alternative Minimum Tax liability, and then the individual TP must

35. § 56(b)(1)(A)(ii).

36. See ¶ **17.1000**.

37. §§ 56(b)(1)(A), 164(a)(4), (5).

38. Imposed by §§ 67 and 68.

pay whichever of those two is greater. The scope of the Alternative Minimum Tax is expanding, and a significant percentage of individual TPs pay that tax rather than the regular tax. This expansion of the scope of the Alternative Minimum Tax greatly increases the significance of the denial of a deduction for most taxes in determining an individual's Alternative Minimum Tax liability.

CHAPTER EIGHTEEN

LOSSES

¶ **18.0000. DEDUCTION OF LOSSES.** A corporation or other business entity typically is allowed a deduction for its losses since such losses are *presumed* to be incurred in connection with business activities.[1] An *individual* is allowed a deduction for a loss incurred by him only if the loss was incurred in connection with: (a) the individual's trade or business, (b) a transaction entered into for profit, or (c) a casualty or a theft of the individual's property.[2] No deduction is allowed a TP for a loss to the extent that the TP is compensated by insurance or otherwise.[3]

¶ **18.1000. DENIAL OF DEDUCTION ON PUBLIC POLICY GROUNDS.** The Commissioner maintains that no deduction will be allowed for a loss incurred as a consequence of a theft or as an incident of a trade or business or of a transaction for profit if the loss was incurred in connection with an illegal activity of the TP. The Commissioner contends that a deduction must be denied in such cases to prevent a frustration of public policy.[4] Despite the fact that claimed deductions for *business expenses* cannot be denied on public policy grounds,[5] the Tax Court has sustained the Commissioner's position that the public policy exception does apply to *losses* for which a deduction is sought under § 165 and accordingly has denied claims for theft and casualty loss deductions arising out of illegal transactions.[6]

It is not sufficient for nondeductibility that an expenditure merely bears a relationship to an illegal act; "the test for nondeductibility always is the severity and immediacy of the frustration" of a sharply defined national or state policy that would result if a deduction were allowed.[7] In this connection, it is noteworthy that the Tax Court has held that a loss

1. § 165(a).

2. § 165(c).

3. § 165(a).

4. Rev. Rul. 77–126.

5. Treas. Reg. § 1.162–1(a).

6. See ¶¶ **21.5400** and **21.5500**.

7. *Tank Truck Rentals v. Commissioner*, 356 U.S. 30, 35 (1958); GCM 37985 (1979). See *Commissioner v. Tellier*, 383 U.S. 687 (1966).

incurred in conducting an illegal business (i.e., the confiscation by the government of a truck, horse trailer, and marijuana owned by a marijuana dealer), if it could be deducted at all, could be deducted only under § 165 as a loss, and, based on public policy considerations, the court disallowed the deduction.[8] In that case, the court rejected the TP's attempt to claim the loss as a business expense deduction under § 162 (which is not subject to the public policy exception)[9] because the loss provision is the more specific statutory direction.

The decisions of the Tax Court and the Court of Appeals for the Second Circuit in *Stephens v. Commissioner*,[10] are worth noting. *Stephens* involved a TP who had been convicted of fraud and conspiracy in violation of federal statutes and who had been sentenced to prison plus several relatively small fines on each of five counts. One of the prison terms was suspended and TP placed on probation on condition that TP make restitution to his victim. The court chose that device to pressure the TP to draw on funds in a Bermuda bank account that only the TP could reach. The amount of restitution was $1 million, of which about $530,000 had been obtained by fraud, and the rest was interest. The TP had paid income tax on the $530,000 of fraudulently obtained funds.

TP sought to deduct the restitution payment of the $530,000 fraudulently obtained funds under § 165(c)(2) as a loss incurred in a transaction entered into for a profit. Section 162(f) prohibits the allowance of a business expense deduction under § 162(a) for the payment of a fine or similar penalty to a government for a violation of a law. While the Tax Court noted that § 162(f) does not apply to a deduction claimed under § 165, the court held that the congressional policy that underlies the adoption of § 162(f) should be applied to deny a deduction under § 165 for a fine or similar penalty of a type that would preclude a § 162 deduction. In other words, the Tax Court adopted a public policy limitation on the deductibility of losses under § 165, and the court incorporated the terms of § 162(f) into that public policy limitation.

The Tax Court held that the TP in *Stephens* is not allowed a deduction for the restitution payments he made because, having been ordered in lieu of a prison term, the payments constituted a fine or similar penalty. Of course, the payments were made to a private person, and § 162(f) applies only to payments to a "government." The Tax Court held that § 162(f) does not require that the payment be made directly to a

8. *Holt v. Commissioner*, 69 T.C. 75 (1977), aff'd per curiam, 611 F.2d 1160 (5th Cir. 1980). See also *Santilli v. Commissioner*, 69 T.C.M. 2974 (1995).

9. See ¶¶ **21.5000–21.5500**.

10. 93 T.C. 108 (1989), rev'd 905 F.2d 667 (2d Cir. 1990).

government; it is sufficient that the origin of the TP's liability to make the payment is his criminal violation and that the payment satisfies a criminal penalty otherwise imposed on the TP.[11]

In reversing the Tax Court's decision in *Stephens*, the Second Circuit held that the restitution payments are deductible by the TP under § 165(c)(2).[12] The Second Circuit concurred with the Tax Court's view that the policy underlying § 162(f) should be imposed as a limitation on § 165 as well. However, the Court of Appeals determined that the restitution payments made to the victim were compensatory in nature, not punitive. The Second Circuit distinguished *Waldman*[13] on the basis that restitution was the only penalty imposed in that case, and distinguished *Bailey*[14] on the basis that the payment in that case originally was imposed as a fine and subsequently was applied to claims for restitution, and was deemed by the Sixth Circuit to have retained its status as a penalty. The Second Circuit did not say whether it would follow *Waldman* or *Bailey* in like circumstances.

The Second Circuit also held that § 162(f) applies only to payments to a government and that the policy incorporated into § 165 is similarly limited. The Second Circuit held that the policy of § 162(f) that is incorporated into § 165 as a public policy limitation does not apply to the TP's restitution payment to his victim since the victim is a private person, not a government.

Finally, the Second Circuit held that no national or state policy would be frustrated by allowing the deduction that the TP claimed, and so the general terms of the public policy limitation on § 165 deductions are inapplicable. This position of the Second Circuit is in conflict with the view expressed by the Tax Court and the Sixth Circuit.[15]

Perhaps the most important aspect of the *Stephens* decisions is that both the Tax Court and the Second Circuit Court of Appeals accepted the view that there are public policy limitations on deductions claimed under § 165, albeit they disagreed as to how one of those public policy limitations was to be construed. The Commissioner contends that the

11. See also *Waldman v. Commissioner*, 88 T.C. 1384 (1987), aff'd in a one-sentence order, 850 F.2d 611 (9th Cir. 1988); and *Bailey v. Commissioner*, 756 F.2d 44 (6th Cir. 1985).

12. *Stephens v. Commissioner*, 905 F.2d 667 (2d Cir. 1990).

13. *Waldman v. Commissioner, supra* n. 11.

14. *Bailey v. Commissioner, supra* n. 11.

15. For a contrary view, treating as a fine or penalty a restitution payment made to a non-governmental party pursuant to a criminal preceding, see *Kraft v. United States*, 991 F.2d 292 (6th Cir. 1993); and *Waldman v. Commissioner, supra* n. 11.

public policy limitation on deductions applies to every Code section except §§ 61, 162, 212, and 471.[16] Thus, the Commissioner contends that the public policy limitation applies to limit deductions claimed under § 165, and the courts have adopted that view.

Casualty loss deductions also have been denied on public policy grounds. For example, no deduction will be allowed for fire damage that is attributable to a deliberate act of arson by the TP even when the spread of the fire was not intended or anticipated by the TP. In *Blackman v. Commissioner*,[17] the TP deliberately set fire to his wife's clothes (apparently as an act of spite), and the fire spread and caused substantial damage to the house and to its contents. In denying the TP a casualty loss deduction, the Tax Court relied on the public policy limitation as one of two alternative grounds for its decision. See also, ¶ **18.2300**.

¶ **18.2000. CASUALTY AND THEFT LOSSES.** Section 165(c)(3) allows a deduction for a loss of property arising from a fire, storm, shipwreck, or other casualty or from theft even though the property was used for purely personal purposes and was not used in connection with a business or profit-seeking activity. When the damaged or stolen property was neither business nor investment property, the loss is sometimes referred to as a personal casualty or theft loss. The deductibility of personal casualty and theft losses is subject to restrictions described at ¶¶ **18.2500–18.2551**. A deduction is allowed under the casualty or theft loss provision only for damage or loss suffered by the TP on property owned by him; no deduction is allowed under that provision for a TP's liability for damages caused by the TP to the property of another.[18]

A personal casualty or theft loss deduction will be allowed only to the extent of the loss in value of the damaged or stolen property; and, as we shall see, the amount allowed may be even less than that. No deduction is allowed for out-of-pocket costs incurred in connection with a personal casualty or theft loss. For example, no deduction is allowed for the additional living expenses incurred as a consequence of the unavailability of a damaged residence. Some expenses of this type, such as repairs of damaged property, can be used as a measurement of the amount of decline in value that the damaged property suffered.[19]

It is worth noting that § 123 excludes from gross income the amounts received by a TP, pursuant to an insurance contract, to reimburse the

16. GCM 36665 (1976); GCM 36962 (1976).

17. 88 T.C. 677 (1987), aff'd without published opinion, 867 F.2d 605 (1st Cir. 1988).

18. See, e.g., *Miller v. Commissioner*, 34 T.C.M. 528 (1975).

19. See ¶ **18.2410**.

TP for the extra living costs incurred for the TP and his household while his residence is unavailable for occupancy because of a casualty (or because of the threat of a casualty). The amount of such insurance reimbursements that is excluded is limited to the excess of the actual living expenses incurred during the unavailability of the residence over the amount of living expenses that would have been normal for the TP and his household to incur if the residence were occupied. Note that the Code excludes the reimbursement of such expenses from income even though, if not reimbursed and therefore borne by the TP, the expenses would not be deductible. As previously noted, a reimbursement of a nondeductible expense is not always given parallel tax treatment to the treatment that would have been accorded to the expense if unreimbursed—such reimbursements sometimes are excluded from gross income even though the expenditure is nondeductible.[20]

Subject to specific exceptions such as the denial of a deduction for the payment of a fine, if a TP incurs a loss of property which is used in a business or profit-seeking venture, he is entitled to a deduction for the amount of that loss whether or not it was caused by a casualty or theft.[21] Similarly, a TP may be permitted to deduct as a business expense under § 162 the amount he paid to another for damages that TP caused if his liability was incurred in the course of his trade or business.[22]

Casualty and theft losses incurred by an individual with respect to property that was used in a business or profit-seeking venture are deductible under § 165(c)(1) or § 165(c)(2) rather than § 165(c)(3). Unless expressly mentioned otherwise, any reference hereafter to a casualty or theft loss refers to a loss incurred with respect to property that an individual had used exclusively for personal purposes.

¶ 18.2100. Illustration: No Deduction for Loss Incurred on Condemnation of Residence. *X*'s personal residence was condemned by the city which paid *X* $20,000 as compensation. *X* had a basis of $25,000 in the property, so he realized a $5,000 loss. The loss does not constitute a casualty or theft loss, and, since the residence was not property held in a trade or business or in a profit-seeking venture, *X* is *not* entitled to a deduction.

¶ 18.2110. Rationale. The exhaustion of personally used property through ordinary use or deterioration constitutes personal

20. See, e.g., ¶ **21.1475** discussing the treatment of reimbursements received by a TP to interview for a job.

21. See Rev. Rul. 90–61; Rev. Rul. 87–59.

22. See, *Miller v. Commissioner, supra* n. 18.

consumption. While personal consumption does reduce a TP's wealth, it does not affect his "ability to pay" for the purpose of determining his tax under a progressive rate structure. A TP cannot reduce his share of the nation's tax burden merely by consuming his wealth. However, when a TP's wealth is reduced as a consequence of some sudden outside force, such as a storm or fire, his "ability to pay" taxes is affected in a way that is different from the decline in wealth caused by normal deterioration. Even though the item damaged or lost by a casualty or theft was purchased by the TP for his consumption, the loss that the TP suffered does not reflect his consumption of the item, but rather reflects a loss caused by external forces. Consequently, subject to substantial dollar limitations, Congress has granted a deduction for losses caused by a casualty or by theft to reflect the decline in the TP's "ability to pay." Indeed, a deduction is allowed even if the TP's negligence was a factor in causing the casualty or in allowing the theft to occur since his carelessness does not constitute a personal consumption of the item.[23]

Of course, if a TP deliberately set fire to an item or wantonly sat by and permitted a fire to destroy it, that would constitute a personal consumption of the item, and no deduction will be allowed for such a loss. Such a loss would not be "unexpected," which is one of the requirements for qualifying as a casualty.[24]

¶ 18.2200.   **Definition of Casualty.** In § 165(c)(3), Congress provides a casualty loss deduction for losses arising from fire, storm, shipwreck or "other casualty." The Commissioner and the courts have made their determination as to whether a loss was caused by an "other casualty" on the basis of whether the nature of the event that caused the loss is analogous to one of the three types of casualties named in the statute (i.e., fire, storm, and shipwreck). The Commissioner maintains that an event is an "other casualty" only if it is of a "sudden, unexpected and unusual nature."[25] The Commissioner defines those terms as follows: "To be 'sudden' the event must be swift and precipitous and not gradual or progressive. To be 'unexpected'

23.   Treas. Reg. § 1.165–7(a)(3)(i). For the effect of a TP's negligence on the deductibility of a loss, see ¶ **18.2300**.

24.   See ¶ **18.2200**. In *Blackman v. Commissioner*, 88 T.C. 677 (1987), aff'd without published opinion, 867 F.2d 605 (1st Cir. 1988), the courts denied the TP's claim for a casualty loss for fire damage when the TP started the fire and either intentionally or out of gross negligence allowed it to spread.

25.   Rev. Rul. 72–592.

the event must be one that is ordinarily unanticipated that occurs without the intent of the one who suffers the loss. To be 'unusual' the event must be one that is extraordinary and nonrecurring, one that does not commonly occur during the activity in which the taxpayer was engaged when the destruction or damage occurred, and one that does not commonly occur in the ordinary course of day-to-day living of the taxpayer"

The "unexpected" and "unusual" standards are sufficiently similar that, in the authors' view, they could be combined into a single standard of foreseeability—that is, the event causing the loss must not be one that could or should have been anticipated. The manner in which the foreseeability of an event should be weighed in determining the deductibility of losses is discussed at ¶¶ **18.2211–18.2213.**

¶ **18.2210. Requirement That a Loss Be Sudden.** A loss incurred as the consequence of a gradual deterioration of an asset is attributable to the consumption or use of that asset, and so such losses are not treated a casualty. For example, damage caused by rust or by moths is not deductible. While the courts have divided on the issue, the Commissioner maintains that termite damage is not a casualty because the damage is the result of a gradual deterioration caused by a steadily operating cause.[26]

In *Short v. Commissioner*,[27] the TPs' residence was damaged due to a severe drought. The TPs first noticed the damage to their home in 1981. The damage progressed and became more of a problem in 1982. TPs claimed a casualty loss deduction for the year 1982. The Tax Court denied the claim for a deduction because the loss was not sudden; it resulted from progressive deterioration. The court acknowledged that a drought can constitute a casualty under appropriate circumstances, but not when there is a substantial time lag between the drought and the damage. The court suggested that the TPs might have had a stronger case if they had claimed a loss deduction in 1981 when they first noticed some damage since that would have been a shorter time after the drought occurred. For the treatment of the loss of plants, shrubs, and trees because of a drought, see ¶ **18.2214**.

In one case, the death of trees caused by an insect-carrying

26. Rev. Rul. 63–232.
27. 55 T.C.M. 54 (1988).

disease was held not to be a casualty.[28] Yet in a 1979 ruling,[29] the Commissioner allowed a deduction when ornamental trees died five to ten days after a massive beetle attack occurred in an area where such attacks are unusual.

¶ 18.2211. The Application of the Foreseeability Standard. As previously noted, the Commissioner's requirements that the event causing a loss be unexpected and unusual actually constitutes a single standard of foreseeability. Let us consider how rigidly this requirement of nonforeseeability is applied.

If, for personal use, a TP purchases an asset that he knows is likely to be destroyed in a few years by a regularly recurring event, the destruction of the item can be regarded as part of the cost of the TP's consumption for the period of time that he used it. The extent to which foreseeability will prevent the deduction of a loss is unclear. A deduction will not be denied merely because a TP knew that damage or loss had a statistical probability. For example, the likelihood that a TP who regularly drives an automobile in a large metropolitan area will someday suffer collision damage may be high, but that probability will not preclude the TP from deducting such a loss when it is incurred.[30]

The Tax Court has held that foreseeability of damage is merely one factor to be weighed to determine whether a deduction will be allowed.[31]

¶ 18.2212. Weighing Foreseeability. It is difficult to determine what weight should be accorded to the foreseeability of an event that causes a loss. Foreseeability does not appear to have influenced the congressional decision to allow a deduction for losses caused by the three categories of events that are expressly named in § 165(c)(3). There are areas of the United States where severe storms are common occurrences, and yet Congress expressly provided for the deductibility of storm damage. As noted in ¶ 18.2211, the regulations permit a

---

28. *Maher v. Commissioner*, 680 F.2d 91 (11th Cir. 1982).

29. Rev. Rul. 79–174.

30. Treas. Reg. § 1.165–7(a)(3).

31. E.g., *Heyn v. Commissioner*, 46 T.C. 302 (1966), Acq., allowing a casualty loss deduction for a landslide caused by an excavation.

deduction for damage to an automobile resulting from a collision regardless of the statistical probability that such damage will occur. Automobile collisions are deemed to be sufficiently analogous to shipwrecks (which are expressly named in the statute) to be deductible. Perhaps, the standard *should be* that foreseeability will preclude casualty characterization whenever the likelihood of the TP's suffering such a loss, viewed at the time that the property was first put to use by the TP, was so high that the TP took (or should have taken) that probable loss into account as a cost of the intended personal use of the property.[32]

¶ 18.2213. Examples of the Commissioner's Application of the Foreseeability Requirement. In PLR 8247060, the Commissioner denied a deduction for the damage incurred when the engine to TP's automobile froze during an extremely cold period. There was some indication that the amount of anti-freeze in the car was insufficient. The Commissioner held that the damage did not result from a casualty because below freezing temperatures are not so unusual in the middle Atlantic states where the TP resided as to make the occurrence of those temperatures an unanticipated event.

In PLR 8227010, the Commissioner denied a deduction for the damage to TP's uninsured automobile which was incurred in an automobile race. TP had been racing cars as a competitive amateur sport for some years prior to the loss in question. The Commissioner reasoned that collisions are not unusual in automobile races, and so TP's loss was not so unexpected as to permit casualty characterization.

¶ 18.2214. The Treatment of Droughts. The criteria for distinguishing a deductible casualty loss from a nondeductible loss is based on whether the event that caused the loss is one that is associated with the normal exhaustion of the item that was damaged or destroyed. The treatment accorded to losses incurred when ornamental trees or shrubs are killed by a drought is instructive in determining what constitutes a casualty.

If a TP, who lives in an area where droughts are unusual, purchases shrubbery and trees to landscape his home, he may

32. See Rev. Rul. 90–61.

be aware that a drought could destroy them, but he likely does not expect that a drought will occur. If a drought does occur and destroys his shrubbery and trees, the TP will wish to claim a casualty loss deduction.

The Commissioner asserts that damage caused to property through "progressive deterioration" is not a casualty loss. The Commissioner contends that the destruction of ornamental trees and shrubs because of a drought will not usually qualify as a casualty because the drought typically kills gradually over a long period of time.[33] In Rev. Rul. 77–490, the Commissioner modified his position somewhat by acknowledging that a drought loss can constitute a casualty in certain circumstances which he did not identify.

In a 1981 case,[34] the Tax Court allowed a casualty loss deduction for a loss of ornamental plants and shrubs because of a severe drought that took place in California. The death of the plants and shrubs took place over a three-to four-month period, and the court held that it was swift and unusual and therefore not a consequence of gradual deterioration.[35]

In Rev. Rul. 90–61, an abnormal drought caused the death of tree seedlings that had been planted for use in TP's lumber business. The Commissioner allowed the TP a deduction under § 165(a) for the loss of the seedlings even though the Commissioner determined that the loss did not constitute a casualty because it lacked suddenness. Since the loss occurred in connection with TP's trade or business, it was deductible as a business loss under § 165(c)(1). The Commissioner concluded that, while the loss was not a casualty, it did not need to be one to qualify as a business loss, and so the loss qualified as a business loss deduction.

Since this loss was a business deduction under § 165(c)(1), there is no requirement that it qualify as a casualty or that it have been unexpected or unusual. Nevertheless, casualty classification can be significant because it may affect the characterization of the loss as ordinary or capital; if the loss qualifies as a casualty, it is excluded from § 1231 treatment by § 1231(a)(4)(C). The Commissioner ruled that the loss was not

---

33. Rev. Rul. 66–303; Rev. Rul. 76–521. See also Rev. Rul. 90–61.

34. *Ruecker v. Commissioner*, 41 T.C.M. 1587 (1981).

35. See also, *Short v. Commissioner* at ¶ **18.2210**.

a casualty and so was subject to § 1231 treatment. The operation of § 1231 is discussed at Chapter **Twenty–Six**.

¶ 18.2215. Damage to or Destruction of Property Contrasted with Losing Property. As noted at ¶ **18.2110**, the fact that the damage to a TP's property was attributable to the negligence of the TP will not bar a deduction. But, the courts have drawn a line between events, on the one hand, when carelessness caused the loss of property and, on the other hand, when carelessness resulted in property of the TP's being damaged or destroyed because of the introduction of a sudden destructive force. For example, a deduction was denied when a TP placed a diamond ring in tissue paper and her husband then mistakenly disposed of the tissue paper, with the ring inside, down a toilet.[36] On the other hand, when a TP placed her diamond ring in a waterglass next to the sink and her husband then poured the contents of the glass down the drain and activated the garbage disposal which damaged the ring so severely as to render it worthless, the Tax Court allowed a casualty loss deduction.[37]

If property is lost as a consequence of the introduction of a sudden force, a deduction may be allowed. For example, a TP was allowed a casualty loss deduction for a diamond that was lost when her husband accidentally slammed a car door on the TP's hand, breaking the prongs of the setting for the diamond and dislodging the stone, which was never found despite a diligent search.[38]

¶ 18.2216. Timing of Deduction. A casualty loss deduction is taken in the taxable year that the casualty loss was incurred unless there exists a reasonable prospect for reimbursement; in the latter situation, the loss deduction is taken in the year in which the prospect for reimbursement ceases to exist.[39] One exception to that general rule occurs when the President declares an area a disaster area under the Disaster Relief and Emergency Assistance Act. In that event, under § 165(i), a TP

---

36. *Keenan v. Bowers*, 91 F.Supp. 771 (E.D.S.C. 1950).

37. *Carpenter v. Commissioner*, 25 T.C.M. 1186 (1966).

38. *White v. Commissioner*, 48 T.C. 430 (1967), Acq.

39. See ¶¶ **18.2510** and **18.2550**.

may be permitted to elect to deduct the loss in the taxable year prior to the year in which the disaster occurred.

¶ 18.2217.   Itemized or Nonitemized Deduction. The deduction allowable for a casualty or theft loss of property used by the TP for nonbusiness, personal purposes will be an itemized deduction, except that it will be a nonitemized deduction to the extent that the TP has a "personal casualty gain"[40] in that taxable year.[41]

When a casualty or theft loss of personally used property is an itemized deduction, it will not be a "miscellaneous itemized deduction" and so is not subject to the 2% of AGI floor and is not subject to the overall limitation on itemized deductions that applies to years after 2012.[42]

¶ 18.2220.   Caveat. There are commentators who contend that casualty and theft losses of personally used property are personal consumptions and so no deduction should be allowed for them. Regardless of the merits of that view, Congress has allowed a deduction, but it sometimes is difficult to determine whether an event is covered by the statutory provision. The best guide for making that determination is to ascertain the likely congressional purpose for allowing a deduction and to examine the event in the light of that likely purpose. It should be noted that in recent years the detractors of the deduction have influenced Congress to limit severely the amount that can be deducted for losses incurred in connection with personally used property.[43]

¶ 18.2230.   Judicial Construction. The courts have adopted a mechanistic approach in their construction of the term "casualty." They have looked to the three events specifically mentioned in the statute (fire, storm, and shipwreck) and have identified common characteristics of those events to be that they are sudden and unanticipated. The courts then require that an event which is not one of the three enumerated in the statute be sudden and unanticipated in order to qualify for the deduction. Since such events typically will not constitute personal consumptions, that distinction generally works well. However, it should not be ap-

---

40.   A "personal casualty gain" is defined at **¶ 18.2531**).

41.   See **¶ 18.2532**.

42.   §§ 67(b)(3), 68(c)(3).

43.   See **¶¶ 18.2530–18.2540**.

plied so mechanically that the courts lose sight of the reason that sudden and unanticipated events are deductible. Otherwise, a court may resolve such questions as to whether termite damage constitutes a casualty on the basis of the time elapsed before the damage was discovered. The proper question to be asked is whether termite damage constitutes an anticipatable deterioration (similar to rust) or whether it constitutes an external force which a person would not expect to occur, even though such person recognizes the possibility that that event might occur.

¶ **18.2300. TP's Negligence.** A casualty loss deduction will not be allowed if the casualty was caused by the "willful act or willful negligence" of the TP or someone acting on his behalf.[44] "Willful negligence" is defined in a law dictionary as a "reckless disregard of the safety or the rights of others" or a "willful determination not to perform a known duty."[45] It refers to an even more aggravated form of negligence than gross negligence. However, in a 1987 decision,[46] the Tax Court stated that a TP's gross negligence would bar a casualty loss deduction.

Other than cases of willful or perhaps gross negligence, a TP's negligence will not bar him from deducting the casualty loss that he suffered thereby. A TP's deliberate destruction of his own property will not qualify as a deductible casualty loss.[47]

¶ **18.2400. Computation of Amount of Deductible Loss.**

¶ **18.2410. Alternate Methods.** Once there has been a casualty loss, it is necessary to determine the amount of the loss as the first step in determining the amount of deduction that is allowable. The allowable deduction is dependent upon, but not necessarily equal to, the amount of the casualty loss.

The amount of a casualty loss is the lesser of: (a) the difference between the fair market value[48] of the damaged property immediately before and immediately after the casualty, or (b) the adjusted basis of the damaged property.[49] In many instances, the cost of

44. Treas. Reg. § 1.165–7(a)(3)(i).

45. Black's Law Dictionary 1186 (4th ed. 1968).

46. *Blackman v. Commissioner*, 88 T.C. 677 (1987), aff'd without published opinion, 867 F.2d 605 (1st Cir. 1988).

47. See ¶ **18.1000.**

48. The meaning of "fair market value," is explained at ¶ **9.3240**.

49. Treas. Reg. § 1.165–7(b)(1).

repairs will be accepted as evidence of the decline in value caused by the casualty.[50] The cost of removing debris that was a product of a casualty is included in the determination of the cost of repairing the damage.[51]

¶ 18.2411. Replacement Cost. When an item is completely destroyed, the TP can establish the fair market value immediately before the event by establishing the replacement cost of the destroyed item and then reducing that replacement cost by a depreciation allowance for the time that the item was held by the TP.[52] This replacement cost minus depreciation method is used principally for evaluating the loss to household goods. It is worth emphasizing that the amount of loss incurred is not necessarily the amount which may be deducted.[53]

¶ 18.2412. No Replacement Is Available. In a 1982 decision,[54] the Tax Court adopted a modified version of the replacement cost method in valuing the amount of loss suffered because of the destruction of mature trees on land on which a residence was situated. Essentially, to measure the amount of loss, the court used the replacement cost (which included the cost of removing the trunks of the old trees) of the tallest trees available, although the only available trees were shorter than the trees that were lost. In addition, the court included in its measurement of the loss a small amount for the decline in the fair market value of the property that would result from replacing the destroyed trees with shorter ones; it appears that the court may have simply plucked a figure out of the air to represent this estimated decline in fair market value.

¶ 18.2420. Business Property. If the damaged property is used in a trade or business, the amount of the casualty loss will be determined in the same manner as is used to determine the amount of casualty loss suffered by nonbusiness property;[55] except that if such business property is totally destroyed, the amount of loss is the adjusted basis of the destroyed property irrespective of

50.   Treas. Reg. § 1.165–7(a)(2)(ii), and see *Turecamo v. Commissioner*, 64 T.C. 720, 730 (1975), aff'd, 554 F.2d 564 (2d Cir. 1977).

51.   Rev. Rul. 71–161.

52.   *Pfalzgraf v. Commissioner*, 67 T.C. 784 (1977), Acq.

53.   See ¶ **18.2500** and following.

54.   *Zardo v. Commissioner*, 43 T.C.M. 626 (1982).

55.   See ¶ **18.2410**.

whether the adjusted basis was greater or lesser than the value of the damaged property prior to the casualty.[56]

¶ **18.2421. Illustration 1: Partial Loss.** *X*'s automobile was damaged in a collision. *X*'s negligence caused the accident, but *X* was not grossly negligent. The value of *X*'s automobile immediately before the accident was $2,200, and the value immediately after the accident was $1,500. *X* had a basis of $2,500 in the car. *X* had no insurance coverage and no prospect of being reimbursed for his loss. Whether *X*'s car is used by him solely for personal purposes or in his trade or business, the amount of his casualty loss is $700 ($2,200 value before the accident minus $1,500 value after the accident), since the difference in value before and after the accident was a lesser amount than *X*'s adjusted basis. You will recall that the amount of loss incurred is not necessarily the amount that can be deducted because there are limitations on the amount of deduction that is allowable.[57]

¶ **18.2422. Illustration 2: Complete Destruction When Basis Exceeds Value.** Assume the same facts as in ¶ **18.2421** except that *X*'s car was completely destroyed by the collision and had no salvage value. If *X* used the car for personal purposes, the amount of his loss would be $2,200 ($2,200 value before the accident minus the $0 value afterwards), but if *X* used his car for business purposes, the amount of his loss would be $2,500 (the adjusted basis of the car).

¶ **18.2423. Illustration 3: Complete Destruction When Value Exceeds Basis.** The same facts apply as those stated in ¶ **18.2422** except that *X*'s adjusted basis in the car was only $2,000. Whether the car was used for business or personal purposes, the amount of *X*'s loss is $2,000 since the adjusted basis of the car is less than the decline in value.

¶ **18.2424. Application to Business Property.** On its terms, the casualty loss deduction provided by § 165(c)(3) does not apply to business property. The statute refers to "losses of property not connected with a trade or business." However, business property losses clearly are deductible. For an individual, such losses are deductible under § 165(c)(1) as a loss

---

56. Treas Reg. § 1.165–7(b)(1)(ii).

57. The limitations on the amount of deduction permitted for a casualty or theft loss are discussed at ¶ **18.2500** *et seq.*

incurred in a trade or business; for a corporate TP, such losses are deductible under § 165(a). Since a casualty or theft constitutes an event of sufficient significance to warrant recognition of the loss incurred, the treatment of casualty losses on business property is discussed in the same regulations that deal with casualty losses on nonbusiness property, and there is every reason to consider them together. However, the consolidated consideration of business and nonbusiness properties should not obscure the fact that a deduction is allowed for those two types of properties under quite different statutory provisions. It is for this reason, for example, that the limitations on the deduction of casualty losses that are imposed by § 165(h) do not apply to losses suffered with respect to business property.

Note, however, that it can matter whether a loss from damage to business property constitutes a casualty since that can determine whether § 1231 applies, which, in turn can determine the character of the loss as ordinary or capital. If the loss is a casualty, it may be excluded from § 1231 treatment by § 1231(a)(4)(C). The operation of § 1231 is discussed at Chapter **Twenty–Six**.

¶ **18.2500. Limitations on Deduction.** The amount of casualty and theft losses that can be deducted is subject to three limitations—two of which apply only to losses incurred with regard to personally used property and one of which (the prospect of reimbursement limitation) applies to losses incurred with regard to all properties regardless of use. The three limitations are: (1) the prospect of reimbursement [¶¶ **18.2510–18.2515**], (2) the $100 floor [¶¶ **18.2520–18.2521**], and (3) the ten percent of AGI floor [¶¶ **18.2530–18.2534**].

¶ **18.2510. Prospect of Reimbursement.** A loss is deductible in the taxable year in which it was "sustained."[58] A casualty or theft loss is not sustained and, therefore, cannot be deducted in a taxable year to the extent that, at the end of the year, there is a reasonable prospect of the TP's being reimbursed by the wrongdoer or by an insurer.[59] If, at the end of a taxable year, there is a

---

58. Treas. Reg. § 1.165–1(d)(1).

59. Treas. Reg. § 1.165–1(d)(2). For an example of the application of the reasonable prospect of reimbursement principle to prevent the deduction of a theft loss, see *Jeppsen v. Commissioner*, 128 F.3d 1410 (10th Cir. 1997).

reasonable prospect of reimbursement for only a portion of a casualty or theft loss, the remaining portion for which no reimbursement is anticipated is deemed to have been sustained in that taxable year. Any amount of casualty or theft loss that was treated as not being sustained in a taxable year because of a prospect of reimbursement will be treated as having been sustained in the first subsequent taxable year at the end of which it can be determined with reasonable certainty that reimbursement will not be obtained.[60]

The prospect of reimbursement limitation is based on the provision in § 165(a) that limits the deduction under that section to a loss that is "not compensated for by insurance or otherwise." This limitation applies to all types of losses regardless of whether they are incurred in connection with a trade or business or with personally used property.

¶ 18.2511. Refusal to Seek Reimbursement from Insurer. Prior to 1986, a majority of the Tax Court and the Sixth and Eleventh Circuit Courts of Appeals held that when a TP chooses not to obtain reimbursement from an insurer for a casualty or theft loss which was covered by insurance, the loss is nevertheless sustained and deductible by the TP.[61] The amendments made by the Tax Reform Act of 1986 repudiated that position. An individual TP's loss on personally used property that is covered by insurance cannot be included in the TP's casualty or theft losses unless the TP files a timely insurance claim.[62] Note, however, that the statute applies only to a failure to enforce an insurance claim. If a TP fails to pursue a claim against a tortfeasor, that may not prevent a deduction, especially in light of the uncertainties of success in litigation and in collection. The deductibility may rest on a weighing of the risks of litigation against the amount of the claim.

60. Treas. Reg. § 1.165–1(d)(2)(ii).

61. *Hills v. Commissioner*, 691 F.2d 997 (11th Cir. 1982) (divided decision), aff'g 76 T.C. 484 (1981) (reviewed by court); *Miller v. Commissioner*, 733 F.2d 399 (6th Cir. 1984) (en banc divided decision).

62. § 165(h)(4)(E). In this connection, note *Campbell v. Commissioner*, 54 T.C.M. 632 (1987), where the Tax Court denied a claim for a deduction for a business loss to the extent that the TP's loss was covered by insurance even though the TP did not claim reimbursement from the insurer.

¶ **18.2512. Effect of Suing for Recovery.** The question of whether a reasonable prospect of recovery exists is a question of fact to be determined from all the existing facts and circumstances.[63] If a TP files suit to recover a loss (whether the suit is filed before or shortly after claiming a deduction for that loss), the filing of the suit raises a presumption that the TP believed that he had a reasonable prospect of recovering the loss which, therefore, would not be deductible.[64] To obtain a deduction for the loss prior to a settlement of the suit, the TP has the burden of showing that no reasonable prospect of recovery exists despite the TP's prosecution of the suit. An example of a successful claim for a deduction in such a situation is a 1991 decision of the Tax Court allowing a casualty loss deduction for damage to TP's home that was caused by a contractor's negligence even though TP had obtained a judgment against the contractor and was continuing to attempt to collect on that judgment.[65] The court determined that TP's prospects for collecting on the judgment were slim at best.

¶ **18.2513. Insurance as an Indirect Reimbursement.** When a TP collects insurance proceeds (such as fire insurance or life insurance) on the occurrence of an event, a question may arise as to whether the insurance reimburses the TP for a loss suffered by him and so prevents the TP from taking a deduction for that loss. In *Johnson v. Commissioner*,[66] the TP collected life insurance proceeds on the death of his partner pursuant to a policy the TP had acquired to insure his partner's life. The TP then liquidated the partnership business and received an amount that was less than his basis. The Tax Court held that the loss realized on that liquidation was reimbursed by the life insurance proceeds, which the court determined was purchased to protect against a decline in value of the business caused by the partner's death. The court disallowed the deduction claimed by the TP for the loss

63. Treas. Reg. § 1.165–1(d)(2)(i).

64. *Dawn v. Commissioner*, 675 F.2d 1077 (9th Cir. 1982); *Gale v. Commissioner*, 41 T.C. 269 (1963); *Lapin v. Commissioner*, 60 T.C.M. 59 (1990), aff'd 956 F.2d 1167 (9th Cir. 1992); but see the dictum in *Parmelee Transportation Co. v. United States*, 351 F.2d 619 (Ct. Cl. 1965).

65. *Marx v. Commissioner*, 62 T.C.M. 1370 (1991).

66. 66 T.C. 897 (1976), aff'd per curiam by a divided court, 574 F.2d 189 (4th Cir. 1978).

incurred on the liquidation, and a divided court of appeals affirmed. This issue is discussed at ¶ 4.4000 in which the authors suggest that there are reasons to doubt that the *Johnson* decision will be followed, and, to date, it has not been.

¶ 18.2514.   **Subsequent Recovery.** The fact that a TP who took a loss deduction recovers all or part of that loss in a subsequent year does not prove that there was a reasonable prospect of recovery in the year in which the loss was incurred. If there was no reasonable prospect in the year of loss, a subsequent recovery by the TP of a previously deducted item will usually be treated as income to him in that year under the tax benefit rule.[67]

As an administrative matter, requiring that a recovery be included in income in the year of recovery is preferable to requiring that the prior year be kept open so that an amended return would have to be filed deleting the casualty or theft deduction. The position adopted by the tax law to include the recovery in income conforms with the annual accounting concept and is easier to administer.

¶ 18.2515.   **Inventory.** A theft loss to the inventory of a TP's business has been held to be deductible without regard to the likelihood that the TP will be reimbursed for the loss.[68] This is because the deduction is allowed under § 471 (as a downward adjustment of closing inventory) rather than under § 165 (as a theft loss).[69] The Tax Court determined that there are good policy reasons not to apply the "prospect of reimbursement" limitation to inventory adjustments even if caused by a theft.[70] Of course if a deduction is allowed, a subsequent reimbursement (such as the receipt of insurance funds) will be included in the TP's gross income.[71]

---

67.   Treas. Reg. § 1.165–1(d)(2)(iii). See Chapter **Five** for a discussion of the tax benefit rule. See also, Rev. Rul. 71–161 allowing a casualty loss deduction for an item for which an unexpected reimbursement was received in a subsequent year; *Montgomery v. Commissioner*, 65 T.C. 511 (1975) where the court held that a TP's collection of insurance proceeds on a claim for hurricane damage to a building was gross income to the TP who had taken a casualty loss deduction in an earlier year.

68.   *National Home Products, Inc. v. Commissioner*, 71 T.C. 501 (1979).

69.   Treas. Reg. § 1.165–7(a)(4).

70.   *National Home Products, Inc. v. Commissioner*, *supra*, n. 68.

71.   Id.

¶ **18.2520. $100 Floor.** A second limitation on deductibility, the $100 floor, applies only to casualty and theft losses that an individual incurred with regard to personally used property. If damaged or stolen property was not used in the TP's trade or business or in an income-producing activity, the amount of loss incurred in connection with one casualty or theft can be deducted only to the extent that the amount exceeds $100.[72] The $100 floor applies to the total amount of loss incurred in a casualty or theft; it does not apply to each item that was damaged or stolen in a single casualty or theft.

¶ **18.2521. Illustration.** In Year One, *F*'s house was burgled, and the thief stole $25,000 in cash from *F*'s safe. Later that year, *F*'s automobile was totally destroyed in an accidental collision. In that same collision, a rare vase that *F* was transporting in the automobile also was destroyed. At the time of the accident, *F* had a basis of $15,000 in the automobile and a basis of $6,000 in the vase. Immediately before the collision occurred, the fair market value of the automobile was $10,000, and the value of the vase was $18,000. Neither the automobile nor the vase were insured, and both items were worthless after the collision. *F* had no prospect of receiving reimbursement for any of these losses. *F*'s adjusted gross income for Year One was $100,000. None of the items that were stolen or destroyed were used in *F*'s trade or business or in a profit-seeking venture. In determining the amount of deduction allowable to *F* for the loss of his car and vase, we will ignore the "10% of AGI" floor for a net casualty loss[73] because the large amount of theft loss that *F* suffered in that year is itself sufficient to satisfy that floor. The amount of loss sustained by *F* because of the collision is $16,000 (i.e., $10,000 from the destruction of the automobile, and $6,000 from the destruction of the vase). The $100 floor is applied against the entire $16,000 loss since both items were destroyed in the same casualty; the floor is not applied separately to each of the two items destroyed in that casualty. Consequently, without regard to the 10% of AGI floor for a net casualty loss, *F* is entitled to deduct $15,900 because of the damage caused by the collision. Note that an additional $100 floor will apply to the $25,000 theft loss that *F* suffered when his house was burgled because that loss was incurred in a separate incident.

72. § 165(h)(1).

73. For a discussion of the 10% floor, see ¶ **18.2530**.

¶ **18.2530. The Ten Percent of AGI Floor for a Net Casualty Loss.** The third and final limitation on an individual's deduction of casualty and theft losses applies only to personally used property. This third limitation is comprised of two distinct parts, each of which is discussed separately below.

¶ **18.2531. Definitions.** Before examining this third limitation, it is useful to define several terms. A "personal casualty gain" is the gain recognized by a TP from the involuntary conversion of personally used property which occurred as a consequence of a fire, storm, shipwreck, or other casualty, or from theft. A personal casualty gain can arise from a reimbursement from an insurer or from the person causing the loss. A "personal casualty loss" is the amount of loss to personally used property that the TP sustained by reason of fire, storm, shipwreck, or other casualty, or from theft. In determining a TP's "personal casualty loss," the $100 floor[74] for each separate casualty and theft is deducted.[75] The excess of a TP's aggregate personal casualty losses for a taxable year over the TP's aggregate personal casualty gains for such year are referred to as the TP's "net casualty loss" for that year. Note that personal casualty gains and losses include theft gains and losses.

¶ **18.2532. Effect of Personal Casualty Gains on Treatment of Personal Casualty Losses.** A TP's aggregate personal casualty losses for a taxable year (which amount, you will recall, reflects a reduction for the $100 floor) are deductible to the extent of the TP's aggregate personal casualty gains for that year; and to that extent, such losses are not subject to the 10% of AGI limitation.[76] To the extent that a TP's aggregate personal casualty losses for a taxable year exceed the TP's aggregate personal casualty gains for that year, the excess is subject to the 10% of AGI limitation.

The presence of personal casualty gains also can effect the treatment of personal casualty losses as itemized or nonitemized deductions.[77] If there is a net casualty loss[78] in a taxable

---

74. That floor is described at ¶ **18.2520**.

75. § 165(h)(3)(B). The characterization of such gains and losses is discussed at ¶ **18.2534**.

76. § 165(h)(2).

77. See ¶ **18.2217**.

year, the amount of personal casualty losses (which figure reflects the reduction for the $100 floor) that does not exceed the TP's personal casualty gains for that year are treated as nonitemized deductions.[79] The excess of personal casualty losses over personal casualty gains (if any) will be an itemized deduction, but will not be a miscellaneous itemized deduction.[80] If there is *not* a net casualty loss in a taxable year, all personal casualty gains and losses will be treated as gains and losses from the sale of capital assets; and so the losses will be nonitemized deductions.[81]

¶ **18.2533.   The 10% of AGI Floor.** As stated above, if the TP's aggregate personal casualty losses for a taxable year exceed the TP's aggregate personal casualty gains for that year, the excess is referred to as the "net casualty loss" for that year.[82] A TP's net casualty loss for a taxable year can be deducted only to the extent that that amount exceeds 10% of the TP's AGI for that year. § 165(h)(2)(A)(ii). To the extent that a net casualty loss is deductible, it will be an itemized deduction. See ¶ **18.2217**.

¶ **18.2534.   Characterization   of   Personal   Casualty Gains and Losses.** If a TP's aggregate personal casualty gains for a taxable year exceed the TP's aggregate personal casualty losses for that year, all such gains and losses will be treated as capital gains and capital losses respectively.[83] If a TP's aggregate personal casualty gains do not exceed the TP's personal casualty losses for a taxable year, the losses will be ordinary and the gains also will be ordinary since they are not included in § 1231 by § 1231(a)(3)(A) and (B) and since there will have been no sale or exchange as required by § 1222.[84]

¶ **18.2535.   Illustration 1.** In Year One, *J* had adjusted gross income (AGI) of $150,000.[85] In that year, she had $40,000 of

---

78.   That term is defined in ¶ **18.2531**.

79.   § 165(h)(5)(A).

80.   § 67(b)(3).

81.   §§ 165(h)(2)(B), 62(a)(3).

82.   See ¶ **18.2531**.

83.   § 165(h)(2)(B).

84.   Capital gains and losses are discussed in Chapter **Twenty–Five**, and section 1231 gains and losses are discussed in Chapter **Twenty–Six**.

85.   Note that TP's AGI will reflect the amount of her personal casualty losses that constitute nonitemized deductions, which in this Illustration equals the entire $32,000 of her personal casualty losses.

personal casualty gains and $32,000 of personal casualty losses (after taking off the $100 floor). *J* is allowed to deduct the entire $32,000 of her personal casualty loss. Since she can deduct her personal casualty losses to the extent of her personal casualty gains, and since those gains exceed her losses, the 10% of AGI floor is inapplicable. All of her personal casualty gains and losses are treated as capital gains and losses. The $32,000 of personal casualty losses are a nonitemized deduction.[86]

¶ **18.2536.   Illustration 2.** The same facts as those stated in Illustration 1 except that, after taking off the $100 floor, *J*'s personal casualty losses for that year were $62,000. In that case, *J* is allowed a $47,000 deduction for the losses she suffered. She can deduct $40,000 because she had that amount of personal casualty gains, and she can deduct the $7,000 excess of her net casualty loss ($22,000) over the 10% of AGI floor ($15,000). The remaining $15,000 of her personal casualty loss is not deductible. Since her personal casualty losses exceed her personal casualty gains, both will be treated as ordinary. However, $40,000 of *J*'s deduction (the amount that equals *J*'s personal casualty gain) is a nonitemized deduction, and the remaining $7,000 of *J*'s deduction is an itemized deduction.

¶ **18.2537.   Illustration 3.** The same facts as those stated in Illustration 1 except that, after applying the $100 floor, *J*'s personal casualty losses for that year were $52,000. In that case, *J* will be allowed to deduct only $40,000 of her losses— i.e., the amount that is equal to her personal casualty gains. Since her net casualty loss ($12,000) is less than the 10% of AGI floor ($15,000), no amount of her net casualty loss is deductible. Both her deductible casualty losses and her casualty gains are treated as ordinary. *J*'s deduction will be a nonitemized deduction.

¶ **18.2540.   Separate Application.** With one exception, the floors of $100 per casualty and theft and of 10% of AGI for a net casualty loss apply separately to each TP. Thus, if John and Ralph were joint owners of a recreational motorboat that was destroyed by fire, and if they had no other losses or personal casualty gains in that year, John can deduct only the amount of his loss in excess of the sum of $100 plus 10% of John's AGI for

86.   §§ 165(h)(2)(B), 62(a)(3).

that taxable year, and Ralph's deduction is subject to the floor of $100 plus 10% of Ralph's AGI. The one exception to this separate treatment is that a husband and wife *who file a joint return* will be treated as a single individual, and so the deduction for the properties of a husband and wife (whether co-owned or separately owned) that were damaged or stolen in the same event will be subjected to a single $100 floor.[87] Of course, the spouses' loss in excess of their $100 floor will be aggregated with the spouses' other personal casualty losses for that year, and the aggregate amount will be deductible only to the extent of their aggregate personal casualty gains plus the excess of their net casualty loss over 10% of their combined AGI.

¶ 18.2550.   Reimbursement Prospects. As noted in **¶ 18.2510**, a property loss incurred by a TP from a casualty or theft is deemed not to have been sustained in the year of the casualty or theft to the extent that the TP has a reasonable prospect of reimbursement. In such event, the loss will be treated as having been sustained in a subsequent year when it is determined with reasonable certainty that all or some part of the hoped-for reimbursement will not be received.[88] It appears that the floor of 10% of AGI for the deduction of a net casualty loss that was incurred by an individual in a year in which a reasonable prospect of reimbursement existed and that is deemed to have been sustained in a later year in which the prospect of reimbursement is negated will be measured by the individual's AGI in the later year.

¶ 18.2551.   Illustration: Effect of Reimbursement Prospect on the AGI Floor. In Year One, X had AGI of $20,000; thus 10% of X's AGI for that year is $2,000. In that year, Y became intoxicated while a guest in X's home, and Y negligently set fire to and thereby totally destroyed a painting that X had recently purchased. X's basis in the painting was $5,600 and that was its value immediately prior to its destruction. The painting was not insured.

X claimed reimbursement from Y. Because of Y's poor financial condition, X agreed in Year One to a settlement with Y under which Y would pay $4,000 for the damage he caused. This payment was to be made in installments to commence in Year Two. In his tax return for Year One, X reported a loss of

87.   § 165(h)(5)(B).

88.   Treas. Reg. § 1.165–1(d)(2).

$1,600 since there was no reasonable prospect of recovering that portion of his $5,600 loss. *X* had no other losses or personal casualty gains in that year. The deductibility of the $1,600 loss sustained in Year One is subject to a $100 floor.[89] The remaining $1,500 of the sustained loss is not deductible because it is less than $2,000 (10% of *X*'s AGI). So, *X* is not entitled to a casualty loss deduction in Year One.

Y never made any of the payments to *X* that were required by the settlement agreement. In Year Three, *X* determined that he could not collect anything from *Y*, and *X* abandoned his claim for the $4,000 that *Y* had agreed to pay. *X* had AGI of $45,000 in Year Three; 10% of that figure is $4,500.

In his tax return for Year Three, *X* reported that he sustained a $4,000 loss as a consequence of it having become clear in that year that *X* would not receive any reimbursement for the destruction of his painting.[90] *X* sustained no other losses and had no personal casualty gains in Year Three. The $4,000 loss that *X* sustained in Year Three is not subject to the $100 floor since the $100 limitation for the destruction of the painting had been applied in Year One (i.e., the deduction of the casualty loss is subject to a single $100 limitation even though the loss is deemed to have been sustained in two separate years.)[91]

The remaining question is how should the 10% of AGI floor be applied? While the result is extremely harsh, it appears likely that the deduction of *X*'s loss will be subject to two AGI floors—$2,000 for the loss sustained in Year One and $4,500 for the loss sustained in Year Three. If so, none of the loss sustained by *X* can be deducted.

¶ 18.2600. Table of Deductible Casualty and Theft Losses. The following tables show the amount of loss that an individual TP may deduct as a consequence of a casualty where: there is no reasonable prospect of reimbursement, the TP sustained no other losses and had no personal casualty gains in that year, and the TP had AGI of $20,000 in that year. In these tables, references to "casualty" losses includes both casualty and theft losses. In Table I, the damaged property was held for personal use, and in Table II, it was held for business use.

89. Treas. Reg. § 1.165–7(b)(4)(ii).
90. Treas. Reg. § 1.165–1(d)(2).
91. Treas. Reg. § 1.165–7(b)(4)(ii).

TABLE I—PROPERTY HELD FOR PERSONAL USE

a Basis	b FMV	c Salvage	d Casualty Loss
8,000	6,000	2,000	1,900
8,000	12,000	2,000	5,900
8,000	6,000	–0–	3,900
8,000	12,000	–0–	5,900

TABLE II—PROPERTY HELD FOR BUSINESS USE

a Basis	b FMV	c Salvage	d Casualty Loss
8,000	6,000	2,000	4,000
8,000	12,000	2,000	8,000
8,000	6,000	–0–	8,000
8,000	12,000	–0–	8,000

(a) TP's adjusted basis in the damaged property.

(b) Fair market value of the damaged property immediately before the casualty.

(c) Fair market value of the damaged property immediately after the casualty occurred.

(d) Amount deductible under § 165 because of the casualty.

¶ **18.2700. Adjustment to Basis.** When a TP claims a deduction for a casualty loss, the TP's basis in the property will be reduced by the amount of the deduction. Section 1016(a)(1) requires that basis be adjusted for a loss "properly chargeable to capital account." A reasonable construction of that provision would not reduce a TP's basis for a casualty loss to the extent that the loss is nondeductible because of a floor or other limitation.[92] To the extent that a deduction was allowable but the TP failed to take the deduction on the TP's tax return, it is unclear whether the TP's basis should be reduced. There is little authority on this issue, but there is a mild suggestion in Treas. Reg. § 1.165–1(c)(1) that basis is reduced only for casualty losses that are actually "claimed" as deductions by the TP.

However, in Rev. Rul. 71–161, the Commissioner said that in the case of property damaged or destroyed by a casualty, basis "must be reduced by the amount of *allowable* loss deduction under section 165 of the Code." (Emphasis added.) Rev. Rul 71–161 further states that basis must also be reduced by the amount of insurance or other compensation "received or *recoverable* (i.e., there exists a claim for

---

92. See e.g., Rev. Rul. 71–161.

reimbursement with respect to which there is a reasonable prospect of recovery).'' (Emphasis added.) Both of those statements in the ruling are open to question in that they call for a reduction of basis that can exceed the amount of deduction that was allowed. Under that ruling, the TP's basis will be increased by the amount expended by the TP in repairing the damaged property.

¶ **18.2710. Costs of Repairing Business Property.** If a deduction is allowed (or allowable) for damage suffered by business property because of a casualty, will the cost of repairing that property also be deductible as a business expense? The Service maintains that to the extent that the repairs are merely replacing the damaged property, they must be capitalized.[93]

In the view of the authors, the Service's position is questionable. The deductibility of the repair should not be affected by the allowance of a deduction for the damage suffered by the property. The Service's position to the contrary is based on the principle that an event should not provide duplicate deductions. To the extent that a deduction is allowed for a casualty loss, the Service's ruling considers an allowance of a deduction for the cost of replacing the damaged parts of the property as a duplication of the deduction already allowed. Of course, if the replacement is one that would be required to be capitalized in any event (even when there had been no preceding casualty), then it should be capitalized in this circumstance as well. But if the "replacement" or other repair otherwise qualifies as a deductible "repair" of business property,[94] then the cost should be deductible. As discussed in ¶ **18.2711**, the allowance of a deduction for the costs of repairs does not constitute a duplication of deduction for the damage suffered. In this regard, a District Court has stated that the Service's assertion in Rev. Rul 71–161 that, in such circumstances, the repair should be capitalized is a "dubious proposition."[95]

Section 263(a)(2) denies a deduction for an amount expended in restoring or in making good the exhaustion thereof for which an allowance is or has been made in the form of a deduction for depreciation, amortization, or depletion.[96] In the authors' view,

---

93. Rev. Rul. 71–161; GCM 34438 (1971).

94. See ¶ **21.1440** *et seq.*

95. *Waldrip v. United States*, 48 AFTR2d 81–6031, n.5 (N.D. Ga. 1981).

96. Treas. Reg. § 1.263(a)–1(a)(2).

this provision is not applicable in determining the deductibility of a repair of an item for which a casualty loss deduction was allowed. On its terms, the statute is limited to restoration of the exhaustion of an asset's life for which depreciation or other amortization deductions were taken. Such a restoration would lengthen the life of the property beyond that which it had after the exhaustion took place. The provision has no application to the restoration of a loss incurred because of a casualty.

Moreover, the description of a repair in Treas. Reg. § 1.162–4 supports the construction of § 263(a)(2) that the latter applies only to expenditures that lengthen the life of the property. That regulation recognizes that a repair in the nature of a *replacement* must be capitalized, only if the item "appreciably prolongs the life of the property." If the expense appreciably prolongs the life of the repaired property beyond the life it would have had if the repair had not become necessary, it would not be a "repair" for tax purposes. So, if the expense constitutes a true repair, as defined for tax purposes, § 263(a)(2) will not apply.

If the Service's position for capitalization of expenses incurred to repair a deductible loss caused by a casualty were adopted, a question can arise as to the proper treatment of the costs of repairs that exceed the amount of deduction that was allowable for the casualty loss. This problem did not arise in Rev. Rul. 71–161 because the cost of repairs (and debris removal) in that case exactly matched the amount of deduction allowed for the casualty (a hurricane).[97] They matched exactly because the TP in that ruling elected to use the cost of repairs (and debris removal) as the measure of the amount of loss caused by the hurricane. Since it was business property and the TP had a sufficient basis, the entire amount of the loss was deductible. The problem with the cost of repairs being greater than the amount of the deduction allowed for damage to business property arises only when the loss in value due to the casualty is greater than the TP's basis in the property. If that does occur, it seems that, even under the Service's position, the amount of repair cost in excess of the casualty loss deduction should be deductible.

¶ 18.2711. **Double Deduction.** As noted above, the Service has ruled that the cost of repairing damaged business property for which a casualty deduction is allowable cannot be deducted as a business expense because the allowance of one deduction

---

97. See Treas. Reg. § 1.165–7(b)(1).

for the loss suffered and a second deduction for the cost of repairs would contravene the prohibition in Treas. Reg. § 1.161–1 that "double deductions are not permitted." In the authors' view, that regulatory prohibition is not applicable. A reasonable construction of the regulation is that a single item of loss or expense cannot be deducted twice. In the question in point, there are two separate items involved albeit both are the result of a single casualty (i.e., the first item is a decline in value of the damaged property and the second item is the expenditure of cash to repair that property).

There is no tax windfall in allowing both deductions since the casualty deduction causes a reduction of the TP's basis in the damaged property, and the repair constitutes a cash outlay. While, as is the case with all repairs, the cash outlay will increase the value of the damaged property by curing the damage, it will not increase the TP's basis unless the policy that the Commissioner adopted in Rev. Rul. 71–161 is validated.

¶ 18.2712. **Costs of Repairing Personally Used Property.** On the other hand, when personally used property is damaged by a casualty for which a deduction is allowed in part, what should be the tax consequence of the cost of making repairs to that property? The cost of repairs is not deductible since it is neither a business nor a profit oriented expense. If the authors are correct in asserting (contrary to the Service's ruling) that the cost of repairing business property should not be capitalized, will that preclude capitalizing the cost of repairing personally used property? As a policy matter, it would seem desirable to retain the basis of the damaged property to the extent that an amount is expended on repairs. In other words, the optimum treatment would seem to be to reduce the basis of the damaged property by the difference between the amount of deduction that was *allowed* and the amount expended in repairing the property. However desirable that result may be, there is no statutory or other authority for that treatment. It is likely, therefore, that the repair will have no effect on the TP's basis unless the position adopted in Rev. Rul. 71–161 is adopted.

¶ 18.2720. **Cost of Removal of Business Property.** When business property (other than a building) ceases to be used in the business, the adjusted basis of the property and the cost of removing it from its location, are deductible as a business loss.[98] The loss deduction is allowed regardless of whether the retired property was depreciable.[99]

¶ 18.2730. Cost of Removal of Business Property Pursuant to a Replacement. If an item used in a business is removed to make way for a replacement, the general rule is that the cost of removal is attributed to the discarded item and is allowed as a business loss deduction.[100] The deduction is allowable regardless of whether the item was depreciable. One exception to this general rule is that the cost of demolishing a building must be added to the basis of the land, but that is a special statutory provision.[101]

If a component of a depreciable asset is removed and replaced, the deduction of the cost of removal depends upon whether the cost of the component is a deductible repair or a capitalized improvement.[102]

¶ 18.2800. Theft Losses. A theft loss is deemed to have been sustained in the year that the TP *discovers* the loss.[103] The amount of a theft loss is determined in the same manner as the amount of a casualty loss, but the value of the property immediately after the theft is treated as zero.[104] The amount deductible is subject to the same restrictions as are imposed on casualty losses (i.e., the $100 floor, the 10% of AGI floor on a net casualty loss, and the prospect of reimbursement rules apply also to theft losses of personally used property).

¶ 18.2810. Illustration: Inconsistent Treatment. *X*, an employee of *Y*, embezzled $10,000 from *Y* in Year One. For the purpose of hiding her embezzlement, *X* altered *Y*'s books to reflect a cost of *Y*'s inventory that was $10,000 greater than the actual amount paid to purchase that inventory. Ignorant of the falsification of his books, *Y* claimed and was allowed a cost of

---

98. Rev. Rul. 2000–7.

99. Treas. Reg. §§ 1.165–2(c), 1.167(a)–8, and Rev. Rul. 2000–7.

100. Rev. Rul. 2000–7.

101. § 280B. See ¶ **18.9000A.**

102. Rev. Rul. 2000–7. See ¶ **21.1440.**

103. § 165(e).

104. Treas. Reg. § 1.165–8(c).

goods sold for Year One that was based on the falsified books and that resulted in *Y*'s reporting taxable income for Year One that was understated by $10,000. In Year Six (after the statute of limitations had run on *Y*'s tax return for Year One), *Y* discovered *X*'s embezzlement and became aware of the fact that the cost of his inventory for Year One was $10,000 less than the amount he had reported to the Service. There was no prospect that *Y* could obtain reimbursement of the $10,000 that *X* stole. On his tax return for Year Six, the year in which *Y* first discovered the embezzlement, *Y* claimed a theft loss deduction of $10,000. Since the loss was claimed under § 165(c)(1) as a business loss, none of the floors that apply to § 165(c)(3) is applicable. In a similar situation, the Commissioner contended that no theft loss deduction should be allowed to *Y* because *Y* had already obtained the benefit of reduced taxable income in Year One, and to permit a deduction in Year Six would allow a double reduction of taxable income. A majority of the Tax Court, however, allowed a TP a theft loss deduction in such a situation. *B.C. Cook & Sons, Inc. v. Commissioner.*[105]

In *Cook*, the Tax Court concluded that the Commissioner's only remedy, if any, was to assess a deficiency for Year One if either the statute of limitations for that year was open or if the defense of the statute of limitations was barred by the mitigation provisions of §§ 1311–1315. The Tax Court's decision in *Cook* was repudiated by a district court decision[106] which disallowed the claim for a theft loss deduction. Indeed, Judge Dawson, who wrote the majority opinion in the 1972 *Cook* decision, stated in his concurring opinion in a subsequent (1975) related *Cook* case that he had changed his mind and now believed that he had erred in the first *Cook* case when he allowed the TP a theft loss.[107]

¶ 18.2820. Definition of Theft. For tax purposes, "theft" covers any criminal appropriation of another's property to the benefit of the taker, including theft by swindling, false pretenses and any other guile. Whether a theft occurs depends upon the law of

---

105. 59 T.C. 516 (1972).

106. *Stahl Speciality Co. v. United States*, 551 F.Supp. 1237 (W.D.Mo. 1982).

107. *B.C. Cook & Sons, Inc. v. Commissioner*, 65 T.C. 422 (1975), Nonacq., aff'd, 584 F.2d 53 (5th Cir. 1978), in which the courts held that the mitigation statutes do not apply to this circumstance and so the Commissioner was barred by the statute of limitations from assessing a deficiency for Year One. The Commissioner nonacquiesced in the Tax Court's decision.

the jurisdiction where it was sustained, but the exact nature and nomenclature of the crime (e.g., larceny, embezzlement, or obtaining money under false pretenses) is of little importance so long as it amounts to theft.[108]

¶ 18.2821. **Illustration: Importance of State Law Definition of Theft.** The Tax Court held that X's loss from the purchase on the open market of stocks of the Equity Funding Corporation (Equity), which purchase was made in reliance on false statements issued by Equity, did not qualify as a theft loss because, under the applicable state law, Equity's fraud did not constitute a "theft" since Equity did not acquire any of X's assets through its fraudulent statements. However, X's loss on other Equity stocks, which he had purchased directly from Equity pursuant to a stock option plan for Equity's employees, did qualify as a theft loss deduction subject to the requirement that there be no reasonable prospect of reimbursement.[109]

¶ 18.3000. **PROOF THAT CASUALTY OR THEFT OCCURRED.** While proof that an item of the TP has mysteriously disappeared is not sufficient to establish that a casualty or theft loss occurred, it is not necessary for the TP to identify the specific event that caused the loss. To qualify for a casualty or theft loss deduction, a TP need only present evidence sufficient to support a reasonable inference that the loss was due to a casualty or theft.

In a 1981 Tax Court memorandum decision,[110] the testimony of an expert witness that it was improbable that a diamond stone would fall out of its setting unless a substantial force were applied to the ring was held to be sufficient evidence to establish that a casualty loss had occurred even though the TP could not identify the precise event that dislodged the missing diamond from the setting. The court allowed the TP a deduction for the loss of her diamond stone. However, in a 1982 Tax Court memorandum decision, a TP was not allowed a deduction for household goods that disappeared during the process of moving because the TP was unable to prove the cause of the disappearance.[111]

In an earlier Tax Court decision in which the Commissioner acquiesced, a TP was granted a theft loss deduction even though she could not prove

---

108. Rev. Rul. 77–18.

109. *De Fusco v. Commissioner*, 38 T.C.M. 920 (1979).

110. *Kielts v. Commissioner*, 42 T.C.M. 238 (1981).

111. *Owens v. Commissioner*, 45 T.C.M. 156 (1982).

who committed the theft or precisely when it occurred.[112] The TP did prove that a number of valuable items in her house were gone and that there was some evidence that the house had been entered during her extended absence. The court suggested that while several items might disappear from a house without explanation, it was highly unlikely that a large number of valuable personal items would be mislaid or otherwise disappear without the involvement of some outside agency. The Tax Court deemed it sufficient for granting the deduction that a reasonable inference from the TP's evidence is that a theft, rather than a mere mysterious disappearance, had occurred. Had the facts pointed to no more than a mysterious disappearance, no deduction would have been allowed.

¶ 18.4000. **NET OPERATING LOSS.** When a TP's deductions exceed his gross income, his deductions for casualty and theft losses may be included in computing his *net operating loss* which may be carried back or forward and deducted from gross income recognized in other taxable years.[113]

¶ 18.5000. **WAGERING LOSSES.** Gambling losses sustained in a taxable year are deductible only to the extent that the TP had gambling winnings in that same year.[114] Thus, if a TP lost $5,000 at a race track but won $1,000 in a poker game in the same year, he may deduct $1,000 of his loss. Similarly, if in that year the TP had instead won $8,000 in a poker game, he would have to pay taxes only on his net winnings of $3,000. If a TP had $10,000 in gambling winnings in Year One and $6,000 in gambling losses in Year Two, the TP would include all $10,000 of his winnings in his gross income for Year One, and the TP would not be allowed any deduction for his $6,000 gambling loss in Year Two.

¶ 18.6000. **RESIDENCE AND OTHER NON-INCOME PRODUCING PROPERTY.** No deduction is allowed for a loss recognized on the sale of a TP's personal residence or on the sale of any other personal (non-income) property.[115] The fact that no provision of the Code grants a deduction for such losses is sufficient to deny a deduction; in addition, § 262 has been cited as authority for denying a deduction.

¶ 18.7000. **CONVERSION TO BUSINESS PROPERTY.** If a TP converts his personal residence or other property, formerly used by him

---

112. *Jacobson v. Commissioner*, 73 T.C. 610 (1979), Acq.

113. § 172(d)(4)(C); see ¶¶ 23.7000–23.7300.

114. § 165(d), and Treas. Reg. § 1.165–10.

115. Treas. Reg. § 1.165–9(a).

for personal purposes, into a business or income-producing property, a loss recognized on the TP's subsequent sale of the converted property will be deductible. The actual rental of a residence may constitute such a conversion, but the mere unsuccessful offering for rent will not likely qualify as a conversion for *this* purpose.[116] In determining the amount of *loss* so recognized by a TP, the TP's basis at the time of conversion is the lower of: (a) his adjusted basis at that date; or (b) the fair market value of the property at that date.[117] The TP's basis at the time of conversion (as so computed) is then further adjusted for depreciation or other appropriate items incurred after the date of conversion.[118]

The above method for determining the TP's basis at the time of sale is only for purposes of measuring the TP's recognized *loss* (if any) on the sale. The normal rules for determining basis are used in measuring the TP's gain (if any) on the sale.

¶ 18.8000.   AT RISK LIMITATION. The extent to which deductions (otherwise allowable) that arise in connection with the conduct of a single trade or business or investment activity are disallowed or deferred because they exceed the amount of the TP's investment in that activity is set forth in § 465 (the "at risk" limitation provision). Section 465 applies only to "losses" as defined in § 465(d), which adopts a different meaning for the term "loss" than that which is used in § 165. For purposes of the "at risk" limitation, a loss from an activity is the excess of the TP's deductions (otherwise allowable) that are attributable to that activity over the TP's income from that activity. The treatment of such losses (including the restriction on their deductibility, the carryover provision, and the recapture of previously deducted losses) is discussed below.

The at risk provision applies to individuals and to certain closely held corporations.[119] Note that the § 465 at risk limitation applies only to deductions that produce a loss; it does not limit credits. However, comparable at risk rules are applied by other Code provisions to certain credits.[120]

116. See ¶ 21.1370.

117. Treas. Reg. § 1.165–9(b).

118. Cf., Treas. Reg. § 1.165–7(a)(5) for a similar rule when converted property is damaged in a casualty.

119. § 465(a).

120. See, e.g., §§ 49 and 42(k).

Prior to the adoption of the 1986 TRA, the "at risk" limitation provision did not apply to real estate investments. The 1986 TRA extended the "at risk" limitation to real estate investments, but the application to realty is more limited than it is to other types of activities.[121]

¶ **18.8100. Separately Identified Activities.** If § 465 is applicable to a TP, the TP's various business interests and investments (including the TP's share of such interests held by a partnership or an S corporation) must be divided so that each activity is separately identified. For example, each oil and gas property of a TP will be treated as a single activity. Similarly, each film or video tape that the TP holds for the purpose of exploitation constitutes a separate activity.[122] In a small number of cases, all the activities in a specific category can be aggregated and treated as a single activity.[123] A few categories of activities that cannot be aggregated are set forth in § 465(c)(2)(A), but the categorization of most activities has been left to the Commissioner to accomplish by way of regulation.[124]

¶ **18.8110. Safe Harbors.** Except for those activities that the Treasury singles out in regulations to be treated as separate activities, the Code provides that all of the TP's activities which constitute a trade or business and in which the TP actively participates in its management are aggregated and treated as a single activity.[125] As we shall see, the significance of aggregating several actively conducted trades or businesses into a single activity is that losses incurred in one such trade or business can then be deducted against income earned in another such trade or business without regard to the amount that the TP has at risk.

¶ **18.8120. Partnerships and S Corporations.** Trades or businesses conducted by a partnership or by an S corporation will be aggregated and treated as a single activity if at least 65% of the losses for the taxable year of such a partnership or S corporation are allocable to persons who actively participate in the management of the business.[126] Also, certain designated activities of a

121. See ¶¶ **18.8230–18.8234.**

122. § 465(c)(2); Prop. Reg. § 1.465–42.

123. § 465(c)(2)(B), (3)(B), (C).

124. § 465(c)(3)(C). See Temp. Reg. § 1.465–1T for the aggregation of certain (but not all) activities of a partnership or an S corporation.

125. § 465(c)(3)(B).

126. § 465(c)(3)(B)(ii).

partnership or S corporation can be aggregated and treated as a single activity.[127]

¶ **18.8200. Limitation on Deductions.** Section 465 limits the extent to which deductions incurred in one activity can be offset against income earned from a different activity. This provision imposes no restrictions on the extent to which deductions incurred in an activity can be utilized to reduce income earned from that same activity.[128] Thus, the TP's income from the activity is determined as of the end of the TP's taxable year;[129] and the TP's deductions that arise from that activity for that taxable year are allowable to the extent that they do not exceed such income. When the deductions (otherwise allowable) for one taxable year from one activity exceed the income for that year from the same activity, the excess is termed a "loss."[130] Note that as used in § 465, the term "loss" has a different meaning than the same term has in § 165. Such losses are often referred to as a "section 465(d) loss."[131]

Since a TP is denied a deduction only for "losses," a deduction is allowed to the extent that deductions (including carryover losses) from an activity do not exceed the income received or accrued from that activity. The amount of section 465(d) loss from an activity is deductible by the TP for that taxable year only to the extent that the TP is "at risk" for such activity at the end of the taxable year.[132]

  ¶ **18.8210. Carryover of Nondeductible Losses.** When a TP is precluded by § 465 from deducting all or a portion of a loss from an activity for a taxable year, the undeducted section 465(d) loss is carried over to the next taxable year and treated as if it were a deductible item incurred in that year.[133] Thus, to the extent that the TP has net income from that activity (regardless of the character of that income (i.e., ordinary, capital gain etc.)) in the next year, the carryover loss can then be deducted.[134] Similarly,

127. See Temp. Reg. § 1.465–1T.

128. See § 465(d).

129. Unless the income is earned by a separate entity, such as an S corporation, in which event it is the end of the taxable year of the entity that is the point of reference.

130. Id.

131. Prop. Reg. § 1.465–11(a)(1).

132. § 465(a).

133. § 465(a)(2).

134. See Prop. Reg. § 1.465–2(b).

the carryover can be deducted in the next year to the extent of the amount that the TP is at risk with regard to that activity at the end of such year. The amount of loss (including deductions from a carryover of section 465(d) losses) that is not deductible in the next year because of § 465 will be carried forward and treated as a deduction incurred in the next succeeding year. So, a loss that is nondeductible because of § 465 can be carried forward to future years until fully deducted or until the TP ceases to exist. A section 465(d) loss that is carried over is sometimes referred to as a "suspended section 465(d) loss."

¶ 18.8220. Gain Recognized on the Disposition of an Activity. The income received or accrued from an activity includes gain recognized on the disposition of that activity or of an interest in that activity.[135] Consequently, any deductions incurred in any activity in the year of its disposition and any suspended section 465(d) losses from that activity carried over to that year can be deducted to the extent that the TP recognized a gain on the disposition.[136]

¶ 18.8230. Real Property. The holding of real property pursuant to a trade or business or profit-seeking activity is a separate activity to which the at risk limitations of § 465 apply. Prior to the adoption of the 1986 TRA, the holding of real property was excluded from the at risk rules. While the 1986 Act expanded the at risk rules of § 465 to apply to the holding of real estate, Congress provided a more generous scheme for real estate holdings for determining what constitutes being at risk than is provided for other types of activities.[137] For purposes of determining whether the special rules for calculating the extent to which a TP is at risk with regard to the holding of real property apply, the activity of holding real property includes the holding of personal property and the providing of services that are incidental to making real property available as living accommodations.[138] For this purpose, the activity of holding real property does not include the holding of mineral property.[139]

¶ 18.8231. Liberal Definition of "At Risk." The special treatment accorded to holding real property is that the amount

135. Prop. Regs. §§ 1.465–12, 1.465–66.

136. See Prop. Regs. § 1.465–12(b), Ex.

137. ¶¶ 18.8231–18.8234.

138. § 465(b)(6)(E)(i).

139. § 465(b)(6)(E)(ii).

at which a TP is at risk includes certain nonrecourse debts which are secured by real property used in that activity. The nonrecourse debts which qualify for inclusion in the amount for which the TP is at risk are referred to as "qualified nonrecourse financing."[140]

¶ 18.8232. **Qualified Nonrecourse Financing.** "Qualified nonrecourse financing" is financing:

(a) which is secured by real property used in the holding of a real property activity;

(b) which is borrowed by the TP with respect to the activity of holding real property;

(c) which is borrowed from a "qualified person,"[141] or from a federal, state or local government, or is guaranteed by a federal, state or local government;

(d) except when regulations provide otherwise, for which no person is personally liable for repayment [to the extent that the TP himself is personally liable, the debt is a recourse debt which is included in the amount for which the TP is at risk];

(e) which is not a convertible debt.[142]

¶ 18.8233. **Qualified Person.** A nonrecourse debt will qualify for at risk treatment only if the amount was borrowed from (or guaranteed by) a federal, state or local government or if the amount was borrowed from a "qualified person." A qualified person is any person who is actively and regularly engaged in the business of lending money and who is not:

(a) a person related to the TP;

(b) a person from whom the TP acquired the property (or a person related to such person); or

(c) a person who receives a fee with respect to such property (or a person related to such person).[143]

Financing from a person related to the TP is permitted if the lender is actively and regularly engaged in the business of

---

140. § 465(b)(6)(A).

141. See ¶ **18.8233.**

142. § 465(b)(6)(B).

143. §§ 465(b)(6)(D)(i), 49(a)(1)(D)(iv).

lending money and if the terms of the financing are commercially reasonable and are on substantially the same terms as those involving unrelated parties.[144] As used in the Code, the term "person" includes corporations, partnerships, associations, and trusts as well as individuals.[145]

¶ **18.8234. Related Person.** For purposes of § 465(b), a person is related to another person (and is therefore referred to as a "related person") if the related person bears a relationship to the other that is specified in §§ 267(b) or 707(b)(1), except that in applying those two provisions "10 percent" is substituted for "50 percent" wherever the latter appears.[146] In addition, a person is related to another if both are engaged in trades or business under common control.[147]

¶ **18.8240. Basis.** If a deductible item would otherwise have reduced a TP's basis, the fact that the at risk limitation prevents the deduction of that item will not prevent the reduction of the TP's basis.[148] The at risk limitation rules have no effect on the determination of basis.

¶ **18.8300. Computation of At Risk Amount.** The amounts for which the TP is deemed to be at risk for an activity are described in § 465(b). A number of the adjustments that are made in computing the TP's at risk amount are described in ¶¶ **18.8310–18.8320**.

¶ **18.8310. Additions to the At Risk Amount.** The following additions are made to the at risk amount:

(a) the amount of money and the adjusted basis of property in kind that are contributed by the TP to the activity will increase the TP's at risk amount. If the contributed funds were borrowed by the TP, the adjustment is determined as described below in (c). If property that the TP contributed in kind is encumbered, the increase to TP's at risk amount will nevertheless equal the adjusted basis of the property if the TP is personally liable for repayment of the debt; but if the TP is not personally liable, *no more* than the excess of TP's basis

---

144. § 465(b)(6)(D)(ii).

145. § 7701(a)(1).

146. § 465(b)(3)(C).

147. § 465(b)(3)(C)(ii).

148. Prop. Reg. § 1.465–1(e).

over the encumbrance will increase that at risk amount (and in certain circumstances the amount of increase will be less than that figure).[149] A subsequent reduction of the encumbrance will increase the at risk amount if TP was not personally liable on the debt but will not increase the at risk amount if the TP was personally liable.[150]

(b) The TP's share of income from the activity (including tax-exempt income) in excess of the TP's share of allowable deductions from the activity for the taxable year will increase the TP's at risk amount.[151]

(c) Amounts borrowed by the TP for use in or contribution to the activity will increase the TP's at risk amount to the extent that the TP either is personally liable for the repayment of the debt or has pledged property (other than property which is used in such activity) as security for the repayment of the debt. Such pledged property will permit the inclusion of borrowed funds in the TP's at risk computation only to the extent of the fair market value of the TP's interest in the pledged property. Certain borrowed funds are excluded from the at risk computation; for example, funds borrowed by the TP from a person who has an interest (other than an interest as a creditor) in the activity, or from a person related to someone (other than the TP) who has an interest in the activity, are disregarded.[152] The exception for funds borrowed from a person who has an interest in the activity does not apply to a loan made by a shareholder to a corporation.[153]

(d) Repayment of loans by the TP will increase the TP's at risk amount to the extent that the debt had previously prevented an increase in the TP's at risk amount for contributions that he had made to the activity.[154]

(e) Notwithstanding the above, transactions which are designed to avoid the reach of § 465 and which do not normally occur in commercial practice will be disregarded.[155] Similarly, where a TP who appears to be at risk for an amount is

149. Prop. Reg. § 1.465–23(a).

150. Prop. Regs. §§ 1.465–23(a)(2)(ii), 1.465–24(b)(1), 1.465–25(b)(2)(i).

151. Prop. Reg. § 1.465–22(c).

152. § 465(b)(3).

153. § 465(b)(3)(B)(ii).

154. Prop. Reg. § 1.465–25(b)(2).

155. Prop. Regs. §§ 1.465–1(b), 1.465–4.

insulated through guarantees, nonrecourse financing, and the like, the amount purportedly at risk is not taken into account.[156]

¶ 18.8320. Reduction of At Risk Amount. The following reductions are made to the at risk amount:

(a) To the extent that the TP's share of a section 465(d) loss from an activity (i.e., a section 465(d) loss is the excess of deductions from the activity over its income) is allowable as a deduction because of the amount at which the TP is at risk for such activity, the amount at which the TP is at risk will be reduced by the amount of such deduction that is thereby allowable.[157] A TP's at risk amount is reduced by the amount allowable as a deduction under § 465 even when the deduction is disallowed by the Passive Activity Loss Limitation (PAL) Rules of § 469—i.e., the disallowance of a deduction by § 469 has no affect on the determination of the TP's at risk amount. A TP's at risk amount is also reduced by the TP's share of nondeductible expenses that relate to the production of tax exempt receipts for the activity.[158]

(b) Money withdrawn by a TP from an activity will reduce the at risk amount of the TP.[159] The TP's at risk amount will be reduced by the excess of the adjusted basis of property in kind which is withdrawn from the activity by or on behalf of the TP over any liabilities to which the property is subject and for the payment of which the TP is not liable.[160]

¶ 18.8400. Recapture of Loss Deduction. When a TP deducts a section 465(d) loss from an activity by virtue of the TP's at risk position in that activity, the TP should not be permitted, without tax consequences, to reduce his risk in the activity in a subsequent year to the extent that the reduction in risk would have prevented the deduction of past section 465(d) losses had the loss and the risk reduction occurred in the same year. Section 465(e) deals with that problem by requiring the TP to recapture such prior deductions by

156. § 465(b)(4).

157. § 465(b)(5).

158. Prop. Reg. § 1.465–22(c)(2).

159. Prop. Reg. § 1.465–22(b).

160. Prop. Reg. § 1.465–23(c).

including a like amount in his gross income for the taxable year in which the reduction of his at risk amount occurred. For carryover purposes, the amount so included in the TP's gross income is treated as a deduction incurred in that activity in the next succeeding taxable year.[161] Thus, if the TP subsequently earns sufficient income from the activity or obtains an increase in his at risk position, the recaptured loss can be deducted at that time.[162]

¶ 18.8410. **Computation of Amount of Recapture of Section 465(d) Losses.** The recapture of previously deducted section 465(d) losses is accomplished in the manner described below after making an annual determination of the amount that a TP is at risk in an activity; this determination (you may recall) reflects a reduction for the deductible losses from that activity and the money and property withdrawn from that activity.[163] If, at the end of a taxable year, the amount that the TP has at risk is a negative amount (i.e., the net amount deducted from the TP's at risk amount for the year exceeds the amount at which the TP was at risk at the beginning of the year), the TP shall include in his gross income an amount equal to the negative figure.[164] However, the amount so included in the TP's gross income shall not exceed the amount of section 465(d) losses from that activity that were allowable as deductions in prior years reduced by the amounts previously included in the TP's gross income as a recapture of previously deducted losses from that activity.[165]

¶ 18.8420. **Illustration: Operation of Recapture Rule.** *B* invests $5,000 in a business activity in Year One. The activity incurs a section 465(d) loss in Year One of which *B*'s share is $2,400. *B* is allowed a deduction for the loss, and *B* then has $2,600 at risk at the beginning of Year Two. In Year Two, the activity earns a profit of which *B*'s share is $300. In July of Year Two, *B* receives a cash distribution of $3,500 from the activity. *B*'s at risk position at the end of Year Two is $2,600 plus $300 minus $3,500 = a negative ($600). *B* is required to include the negative at risk amount of ($600) in his gross income for Year Two. *B*'s aggregate loss deductions for prior years ($2,400) less

161. § 465(e)(1)(B).

162. The operation of this recapture rule is described and illustrated in ¶¶ **18.8410** and **18.8420**.

163. See ¶¶ **18.8310** and **18.8320**.

164. § 465(e)(1).

165. § 465(e)(2).

the amount of loss previously recaptured ($0) is greater than the ($600) negative figure, and thus that amount of income is recognized. At the beginning of Year Three, *B*'s at risk amount will be zero since the ($600) negative figure is increased by the $600 of income recognized by *B* in Year Two. *B* will carry forward a $600 deduction to Year Three (i.e., the $600 of income recognized as a recapture of previously taken deductions is treated as a deduction incurred in that activity in the next year). In Year Three, without regard to the $600 carryover deduction, the activity earns a profit of which *B*'s share is $200. *B* will deduct $200 of his carryforward deduction in Year Three and carry forward the remaining $400 deduction to Year Four.

¶ 18.8500. Interaction with Passive Activity Losses and Credits. The "at risk" limitations of § 465 are applied first without regard to the limitations on passive activity losses ("PAL") imposed by § 469.[166] The PAL rules apply only to losses that otherwise would be deductible after applying the § 465 limitations. If a section 465(d) loss is allowable under the at risk rules but is disallowed under the PAL rules of § 469, the amount at which the TP is at risk is nevertheless reduced by the loss for which a deduction was denied by the PAL rules.

¶ 18.8600. Donative Transfer of Entire Interest in Activity with Suspended Section 465(d) Loss. Prop. Reg. § 1.465–67 deals with the treatment of a transfer of a transferor's entire interest in an activity (or the entity conducting the activity) with suspended section 465(d) losses if the basis of the transferee in the transferred interest is determined in whole or in part by the basis of the transferor. This covers gifts as well as some nonrecognition exchanges.[167]

A suspended section 465(d) loss that is not deductible prior to the transfer cannot be deducted thereafter. However, the amount of suspended section 465(d) loss is added to the transferor's basis in the transferred interest, which can cause an increase in the transferee's basis in that interest.[168]

¶ 18.8700. Donative Transfer of Entire Interest in Activity in Which Transferor Has A Positive Amount At Risk. Prop. Reg. § 1.465–68 deals with the treatment of a transfer of a transferor's

---

166. See ¶¶ **18.9000–18.9520**.

167. If the transferor recognizes any gain on the transfer, see ¶ **18.8220**.

168. Prop. Reg. § 1.465–67.

entire interest in an activity (or the entity conducting the activity) in which the transferor has a positive amount at risk if the basis of the transferee in the transferred interest is determined in whole or in part by the basis of the transferor. In that case, the transferee will include in his amount at risk the sum of: (1) the amount at which the transferor was at risk, plus (2) the amount of gift tax (if any) paid on the transfer that increased the transferee's basis under § 1015(d). In other words, the transferee inherits the transferor's at risk account and adds to that account the amount of increase in basis allowed by § 1015(d) for gift tax payment. There is a limitation on the at risk amount that the transferee can obtain by this provision. The at risk amount that the transferee obtains from this provision cannot exceed the difference between the transferee's basis and the amount that the transferee paid the transferor (including in the payment the acceptance of any liabilities encumbering the transferred property).[169]

¶ **18.8800. Transfer of An Interest In An Activity By Reason of Death.** Prop. Reg. § 1.465–69 deals with the treatment of the passing of an interest in an activity by death. If, at the close of a taxable year in which the decedent died, the decedent's amount at risk in an activity in which he held an interest is a positive figure, that amount is added to the successor's amount at risk. In addition, a successor will increase his amount at risk in the activity by the amount of increase in basis that the successor has in the interest over the decedent's basis because of § 1014. In other words, any step-up in basis caused by § 1014 is added to the successor's amount at risk.

¶ **18.9000. LIMITATIONS ON THE DEDUCTIBILITY OF LOSS-ES AND CREDITS GENERATED BY A PASSIVE ACTIVITY.** In the 1986 TRA, Congress adopted a number of provisions to eliminate (or at least to minimize) tax shelter investments. One of the most important of those anti-shelter provisions is the adoption of § 469 which limits the amount of loss deductions and credits that can be utilized when arising out of a "passive activity." For convenience, we will sometimes refer to these limitations on passive activity losses and credits as a "PAL" (i.e., a passive activity limitation). While aimed at tax shelters, the PAL provision also reaches other investments.

In general, subject to some exceptions, the losses arising out of a passive activity can be deducted only from the income produced by that activity or by other passive activities. Similarly, certain tax credits (other than

169. Prop. Reg. § 1.465–68(c).

the foreign tax credit) arising out of a passive activity can be utilized only to reduce income taxes incurred as a consequence of income produced by passive activities.

If an item of a passive activity is one that reduces a TP's basis in a property interest, the TP's basis will be so reduced even if no deduction is allowable for the item because of the § 469 PAL rules.[170] In other words, § 469 can deny or defer a deduction or credit, but it will not prevent the reduction of basis that the loss or deduction otherwise requires.

Keep in mind that the purpose of the PAL is to match deductions and credits from passive activities with the income from such activities. The aim of the provision is to prevent an acceleration of deductions and credits so that they are obtained in a year prior to the year in which the income from that activity is recognized. The concern is with the *timing* of deductions and credits rather than with the question of whether the TP will ever incur the expenditure or loss for which the deduction or credit is allowed. The PAL was adopted to deal with a gap in the tax law that arose because of the time value of money—i.e., if a TP's deduction in one year is offset by an equal amount of income in a later year, which income arose because of the deduction that was previously allowed, the TP will benefit (even if both the income and the deduction are subject to the same marginal tax rate) because of the time value of money. So, the aim of the PAL is different from the aim of the at risk rules, which are designed to insure that a TP will bear the loss or expenditure for which a deduction is allowed.

Except for closely held corporations, the passive activity loss of a TP for a taxable year is the amount by which the "passive activity deductions" exceed the "passive activity gross income" for that year.[171] Those terms are discussed at ¶¶ **18.9142 and 18.9143**.

¶ **18.9100. Division of Investment and Business Activities Into Three Categories.** The "PAL" provision divides a TP's investment and business activities into three separate categories. Those three categories are described at ¶¶ **18.9110 to 18.9130**.

¶ **18.9110. Passive Activity Category.** The passive activity category, which is defined in ¶ **18.9200**, constitutes one of those three categories.

---

170.   See Temp. Reg. § 1.469–1T(d)(1).

171.   Temp. Reg. § 1.469–2T(b)(1).

¶ 18.9120.   Portfolio Activity. A second category can be characterized as a "portfolio" activity. While the Code does not employ the term "portfolio," it is convenient to designate the activities that comprise the second category with a term that reasonably describes them; and the term "portfolio" is used in the regulations[172] and the committee reports. A portfolio activity includes investments that produce: interest, dividends, annuities, or royalties (other than royalties derived in the ordinary course of a trade or business).[173] In addition, gain or loss attributable to the disposition of portfolio property or of any property held for investment is treated as gain or loss from a portfolio activity. For this purpose, an interest in a passive activity is not an investment.[174] For convenience, we will refer to income arising out of a portfolio activity as "portfolio income."

¶ 18.9130.   Third Category and Material Participation. Any activity that is not a passive activity or a portfolio activity[175] is in the third category. Thus, the third category includes investment activities that are not portfolio investments, and it includes a trade or business activity. For this purpose, a trade or business activity is a profit-oriented activity or an activity connected with a trade or business.[176] However, an activity cannot qualify for the trade or business category unless the TP "materially participates" in the conduct of that activity—i.e., the TP is involved in the operations of the activity on a basis that is: "regular, continuous, and substantial."[177] In determining whether a TP materially participates in an activity, the participation of the TP's spouse is taken into account.[178] The seven tests for determining whether a person materially participates in an activity are set forth in Temp. Reg. § 1.469–5T. According to that temporary regulation, an individual materially participates in an activity for a taxable year if (and only if) any one of the following seven tests is satisfied:

(1) the individual participates in the activity for more than 500 hours during the taxable year;

172.   E.g., Temp. Reg. § 1.469–2T(c)(3)(i)

173.   § 469(e)(1).

174.   § 469(e)(1)(A).

175.   See ¶ 18.9120.

176.   § 469(c)(6).

177.   §§ 469(c)(1), 469(h)(1).

178.   § 469(h)(5).

(2) the individual's participation in the activity constitutes substantially all of the participation in the activity that takes place that taxable year;

(3) the individual participates in the activity for more than 100 hours that taxable year, and the individual's participation for that year is not less than that of any other individual;

(4) the activity is a "significant participation activity" (as that term is defined in Temp. Reg. § 1.469–5T(c) and see ¶ 18.9141) of the individual for that taxable year, and the individual's aggregate participation in all significant participation activities for that year exceeds 500 hours.

(5) the individual materially participated in the activity for any five taxable years (that need not be consecutive) during the ten taxable years that immediately precede the taxable year;

(6) the activity is a personal service activity and the individual materially participated in the activity for any three taxable years (that need not be consecutive) preceding the taxable year; or

(7) based on all the facts and circumstances the individual participates in the activity on a regular, continuous, and substantial basis during the taxable year.

¶ 18.9140.   Significance of Division Into Categories. The purpose of the PAL provisions is to isolate the income, deductions and most of the credits arising from certain passive activities so that the deductions and credits from such activities can be used only to reduce the income or tax liability from the same or other passive activities. The first step to accomplish that purpose is to define "passive activity" and then to divide all activities into passive and non-passive categories and to permit the deductions and credits from passive activities to be taken only against the income (or income tax) incurred from passive activities. That discourages the making of investments in activities for the purpose of creating tax deductions and credits that otherwise could be utilized to lower the TP's tax liability from income-producing activities.

But Congress determined that the division of activities into only two categories (passive and non-passive) would not be adequate to accomplish its goal. Certain types of passive activities typically produce income rather than a net loss—for example, an investment in stocks and bonds will usually produce dividend and interest income. If the investment in such income-producing properties were treated as a passive activity, the losses produced by tax shelter investments could then be utilized to reduce or eliminate the income tax that otherwise would be incurred on the income-producing passive investments. If that were permitted, there would still be an incentive to invest in tax shelters. To prevent that, Congress carved a third category (generally referred to as a "portfolio activity") out of the passive activity category, and the income, deductions, and credits generated by portfolio activities are treated the same as those generated by other non-passive activities. Thus, the losses and credits generated by the narrowed category of passive activities cannot be offset against the income generated by portfolio activities. In addition, certain types of income that otherwise would be classified as passive activity income instead are recharacterized by the regulations as non-passive.[179]

¶ 18.9141. Recharacterization of Passive Income. Temporary Regulations list six types of passive activities the gross income from which can be recharacterized as non-passive.[180] This provision can apply only to a TP's gross income for a year to the extent that it is attributable to all or a portion of the TP's "net passive income" from one or more of the six types of passive activities that are listed in the Temporary Regulations. While it is *gross* income that is recharacterized, the amount of gross income that is so treated is measured by all or a portion of the TP's net passive income from an activity for that year. If an activity, which is one of the six types listed in the Temporary Regulations, produces a "net passive loss" for a year, that activity will not cause any gross income to be recharacterized, but its net passive loss may cause a *reduction* of the amount of gross income that is attributable to the TP's net passive income from an activity that is recharacterized.[181] A TP's "net passive income" from an activity for a taxable year is the amount by which the TP's passive activity gross income (as specially determined) exceeds the TP's passive activity deductions from the activity for that year. Conversely, the

179. See Temp. Reg. § 1.469–2T(f).
180. Temp. Reg. § 1.469–2T(f)(2)–(7).
181. See Temp. Reg. § 1.469–2T(f)(2).

TP's "net passive loss" from an activity for a taxable year is the amount by which the TP's passive activity deductions from the activity exceed the TP's passive activity gross income (as specially determined) from the activity for that year.[182]

Five of the six passive activities that are listed in the temporary regulations are:

(1) a trade or business activity in which the TP is a "significant" participant but not a "material" participant [the terms "significant" and "material" participation in a trade or business activity are defined in Temp. Reg. § 1.469–5T; an individual significantly participates in a trade or business activity if the individual participates in the activity for more than 100 hours during the year and if the individual does not materially participate in the activity];

(2) the rental of nondepreciable property [this provision for the recharacterization of net passive income applies if less than 30 percent of the unadjusted basis of the properties leased to TP's customers is depreciable under § 167];

(3) a passive equity-financed lending activity;

(4) the rental of certain properties incidental to development activity;

(5) the rental of property to a nonpassive activity.

¶ **18.9142. Passive Activity Deductions—Exclusion of Certain Deductions.** "Passive activity deductions" are defined in Temp. Reg. § 1.469–2T(d). In determining the amount of passive activity deductions of an activity, certain deductions are disregarded. The types of deductions to be disregarded are set forth at Temp. Reg. § 1.469–2T(d)(2)–(6). A few examples of excluded deductions are: charitable contributions; casualty and theft losses; state, local or foreign tax payments or accruals; a miscellaneous itemized deduction as determined by § 67(b); a carryover or carryback of a net operating loss; and an expense that is allocable to portfolio income.

¶ **18.9143. Passive Activity Gross Income.** This term is defined at Temp. Reg. § 1.469–2T(c). In general, income from

---

182. Temp. Reg. § 1.469–2T(f)(9)(i), (ii). The meanings of the terms "passive activity deductions" and "passive activity gross income" are explained at ¶¶ **18.9142** and **18.9143**.

a passive activity, including the gain recognized on the disposition of an interest in a passive activity and gain recognized on the disposition of property used in a passive activity, will be included in the TP's passive activity gross income. However, the temporary regulation cited above excludes certain items of income from passive activities from the TP's passive activity gross income. Some of the exclusions are listed in Temp. Reg. § 1.469–2T(c)(7).

¶ 18.9150. Carryover of Disallowed Losses and Credits. The losses and credits from a passive activity that are disallowed to a TP by PAL can be carried forward to the immediately succeeding taxable year and treated as if they were incurred in that year.[183] Such carryover losses and credits are subject to PAL restrictions in the year to which they are carried.

¶ 18.9151. Taxable Disposition of a Passive Activity. The typical attribute of a tax shelter activity was that the deductions and credits from that investment were concentrated in the early term of the activity. This often resulted in the TP's recognition of substantial income from that activity in its later years. Consequently, most tax shelters operated as a deferral of tax obligations. A tax deferral is of benefit to an investor principally because of the time value of money. The PAL restricts the benefit to be derived from such deferrals by deferring the tax benefit from net losses and credits that are attributable to passive activity investments until such activities produce taxable income. Thus, such losses and credits are held in abeyance to be matched with the income from those activities that effectively was deferred by preferential tax treatment.

When a TP disposes of his entire interest in a passive activity in a taxable transaction (i.e., a transaction in which all realized gain or loss is recognized), any deferred gain from that activity will then be recognized. Consequently, any remaining carryover losses that are attributable to *that* activity can be deducted in the year of such taxable disposition unless the sale or other disposition is made to certain persons who are related to the TP.[184] A disposition does not permit the allowance of carryover credits.

183. § 469(b); Treas. Reg. § 1.469–1(f)(4).

184. § 469(g).

If the sale of TP's interest in a passive activity is made on an installment basis, then the TP's carryover losses from that activity are deductible on an installment basis.[185]

If a carryover loss is greater than the gain that the TP recognized on the disposition of his interest in the passive activity, it demonstrates that, to the extent of such difference, the activity resulted in a real economic loss. Therefore, there is no reason to continue any further the deferral of the carryover losses from that activity. So, in such cases, the entire amount of a TP's carryover losses from a passive activity are allowed to be deducted in the year of such taxable disposition.[186] Of course, this provision requires that where losses of several passive activities are deferred, it is necessary to allocate the carryovers among the several activities that produced them so that the carryovers attributable to any single activity can be identified.

When carryover losses are deducted in a year of disposition of that activity, the deduction is applied in the following order:

(1) income or gain from that passive activity (including gain from the disposition of the property),

(2) income or gain from other passive activities,

(3) any other income or gain.

In certain circumstances noted below, a disposition of an interest in property that was used in a passive activity at the time of disposition is given special treatment.

¶ 18.9151A. The Twelve–Month Rule. As noted above, it is advantageous for a TP to have passive income since that permits the TP to utilize passive losses and credits that otherwise would be deferred. A TP who has held a nonpassive activity for some years might seek to convert that activity to a passive one shortly before selling it so that the gain recognized on the sale would constitute passive income since the characterization of the gain from a disposition of property usually is made according to the use of the property at the time of disposition. To restrain that manipulation, the regulations provide that when a TP disposes of an interest in property that had been used in more than one activity in the twelve-

185. § 469(g)(3).

186. § 469(g).

month period that ends on the date of the disposition, the amount realized from the disposition and the adjusted basis of the property must be allocated among the several activities according to the number of days of use in each activity during such twelve-month period. The gain or loss determined to be from a non-passive activity will be treated as non-passive income or loss.[187]

However, in lieu of that allocation, the TP may elect to allocate the disposed-of interest entirely to the activity in which the property was predominantly used during that twelve-month period *if* the value of the disposed-of interest does not exceed the lesser of (1) $10,000, or (2) 10% of the sum of the fair market values of such interest and of all other properties used in that activity during the twelve-month period.[188]

¶ 18.9151B. Substantially Appreciated Property. In addition to the twelve-month rule, the regulations impose an even more extensive restriction on gain recognized from the sale of substantially appreciated property (SAP). Substantially appreciated property (SAP) is defined as property which has a fair market value that is greater than 120% of the adjusted basis of such property.[189] All of the gain recognized from the disposition of substantially appreciated property is treated as non-passive income unless the property was used in a passive activity either (1) for the entire 24–month period ending on the date of disposition, or (2) for a time equal to 20% of the period during which the TP held such property.[190]

¶ 18.9152. Transfers at Death or by Gift. When the TP dies before disposing of his interest in a passive activity, the unused carryover losses from that activity can be deducted in the year of the TP's death, but only to the extent that such unused losses exceed the step-up in basis (if any) that the transferee of such interest obtained because of the TP's death (i.e., the excess, if any, of the transferee's basis over the basis that the TP had at the time of his death is a "step-up" in

187.   Temp. Reg. § 1.469–2T(c)(2)(ii).

188.   Id.

189.   Treas. Reg. § 1.469–2(c)(2)(iii)(C).

190.   Treas. Reg. § 1.469–2(c)(2)(iii)(A).

basis).[191] The amount of such carryover loss that is equal to the transferee's step-up in basis can never be deducted. Any unused carryover of tax credits that were disallowed by § 469 will be lost on the TP's death.

If a TP makes a gift of an interest in a passive activity, the unused carryover loss from that activity (and probably any net loss incurred by the TP from that activity in the year of disposition) can never be deducted; but that unused loss is added to the donee's basis in the transferred interest.[192] If the basis acquired by the donee is greater than the fair market value of the property at the date that the gift was made, § 1015(a) limits the donee's basis to such fair market value for the purpose of determining a *loss* recognized by the donee on a subsequent disposition. It appears that an addition to the donee's basis that is attributable to the donor's unused passive losses is subject to that limitation for the purpose of determining any loss recognized by the donee on a subsequent disposition.

That addition to the donee's basis merely reinstates some of the donor's basis that had previously been reduced by a passive activity loss that was not deductible. If the donor had retained that basis (i.e., if it had not been reduced by the passive activity loss), the donee's loss basis in the transferred asset would have been limited to the property's fair market value at the time of the gift, and there is no reason not to apply that same limitation to the addition to basis that the donee obtains by § 469(j)(6).

¶ 18.9153. **Former Passive Activity.** An activity is a "former passive activity" in a taxable year if, with respect to the TP, the activity is not a passive activity for the taxable year, but was a passive activity for any prior taxable year.[193] The unused deductions from passive activity years can be taken against the income from the activity in the current taxable year, and the unused credits from passive activity years can be offset against the regular tax liability from the activity in the current taxable year (after utilization of carryover deductions from that activity). Any excess deductions and credits continue

---

191. § 469(g)(2).

192. § 469(j)(6).

193. § 469(f)(3).

to be treated as arising from a passive activity.[194] If the activity produces portfolio income in the current taxable year, it would seem that the carryover losses and credits from prior passive activity years should not be permitted to offset such portfolio income or the tax liability therefrom; but the literal language of § 469(f)(1) makes no exception for portfolio income.

¶ 18.9160. Persons Subject to Passive Activity Limitations. The passive activity provisions apply to individuals, estates, trusts, personal service corporations, and certain closely-held corporations.[195] The passive activity limitations operate more generously for certain closely-held corporations than they do for other TPs.[196]

¶ 18.9200. Definition of "Passive Activity." A passive activity is an activity (other than a portfolio activity) which involves the conduct of a trade or business (which, for this purpose, includes a profit-orientated investment) in which the TP does not materially participate.[197] The meaning of "material participation" is explained in **¶ 18.9130**. Except as provided otherwise by regulation, a TP will not be deemed to materially participate in an activity in which he has only a limited partnership interest.[198] Temp. Reg. § 1.469–5T(e)(2) explains the circumstances in which a limited partner will be treated as having materially participated in an activity. Note that the regulation distinguishes between "material participation" and "significant participation."[199] A working interest in oil or gas property (other than an interest in an entity in which the TP's liability is limited) generally will *not* be treated as a passive activity regardless of whether the TP materially participated in that activity.[200]

¶ 18.9210. Rental Activity. Prior to the amendments made by the Omnibus Budget Reconciliation Act of 1993 (OBRA), a "rental activity" was treated as a passive activity even if the TP materially participated in the conduct of that activity.[201] Even after the

---

194. § 469(f)(1).

195. § 469(a)(2).

196. § 469(e)(2).

197. § 469(c)(1).

198. § 469(h)(2). The definition of a limited partnership interest is set forth in Temp. Reg. § 1.469–5T(e)(3). A member's interest in an LLC that is treated for tax purposes as a partnership will be treated as a limited partnership interest.

199. See ¶ 18.9141.

200. § 469(c)(3), (4).

201. § 469(c)(2), (4); Temp. Reg. § 1.469–1T(e)(1)(ii).

1993 amendment, this continues to be true for all rental activities other than rental real estate activities. The definition of "rental activity" is explained below.

As a consequence of the 1993 amendments, while the rental activities of many TPs will continue to be treated as passive activities, the rental real estate activities of many (but not all) of those who materially participate in a real property trade or business will not be treated as a passive activity.[202] The requirements for the exclusion of a rental real estate activity from passive activity classification are explained at ¶ 18.9212. This provision has no affect as to whether a limited partner materially participates in the business of the entity.[203]

¶ 18.9211. **Definition of "Rental Activity."** Subject to specified exceptions listed below, a "rental activity" is one where payments are received principally for the use of tangible property.[204] According to the regulations, an activity is a rental activity for the taxable year if (1) during the year, tangible property held in connection with the activity is used by customers or is held for use by customers, and (2) gross income or (in the case of property held for use by customers) anticipated gross income attributable to the conduct of the activity represents (or will represent) amounts paid or to be paid principally for the use of such tangible property.[205]

¶ 18.9211–1. **Exclusions From Rental Activity.** The regulations contain a number of exceptions which preclude certain activities that involve the rental of tangible property from qualifying as "rental activities" for purposes of PAL.[206] According to the regulations, an activity involving the use of tangible property is not a rental activity for a taxable year if for that taxable year any one of the following six conditions exists:

(1) The average period of customer use for such property is seven days or less;

---

202. § 469(c)(7).

203. § 469(c)(7)(A).

204. § 469(j)(8).

205. Temp. Reg. § 1.469–1T(e)(3)(i).

206. Temp. Reg. § 1.469–1T(e)(3)(ii).

(2) The average period of customer use for such property is 30 days or less, and "significant personal services" (i.e., services performed by individuals of a type described in Temp. Reg. § 1.469–1T(e)(3)(iv)) are provided by or on behalf of the owner of the property in connection with its rental;

(3) "Extraordinary personal services" (as defined by Temp. Reg. § 1.469–1T(e)(3)(v)) are provided by or on behalf of the owner in connection with the rental regardless of the average period of customer use;

(4) The rental of such property is incidental to a non-rental activity of the TP as determined by Temp. Reg. § 1.469–1T(e)(3)(vi);

(5) The TP customarily makes such property available during defined business hours for nonexclusive use by various customers (this exception is probably designed to exclude facilities such as a golf course or a health club whose customers will normally be invitees or licensees rather than tenants or lessees); or

(6) The TP provides tangible property for use by a partnership, S corporation or joint venture (which conducts an activity other than a rental activity) in which the TP owns an interest.[207]

¶ 18.9211–2. **Exception for Certain Losses and Credits from Rental Real Estate Activity.** If the exclusion from passive activity characterization described at ¶ 18.9212 is applicable to an individual, then § 469 will not apply to that individual's share of losses and credits from a rental real estate activity. But, if that exclusion is not applicable to an individual, and if the individual's AGI is not too large, a certain amount of losses and credits from a rental real estate activity *may* be excluded from the § 469 limitation.

If a *natural person* who has AGI that is less than $150,000 "actively" participates in one or more rental real estate activities, that person will be permitted to deduct a certain amount of the net loss (not more than $25,000) from those activities against any of his income (i.e., the PAL of § 469

---

207. Temp. Reg. § 1.469–1T(e)(3)(vii).

does not apply to that amount of loss).[208] No regulations defining active participation have been promulgated as yet, but there are some guidelines.

A TP cannot qualify as an active participant in an activity unless the aggregate value of the interests in that activity held by the TP and his spouse is ten percent or more of the value of all the interests in that activity.[209] In determining whether a TP actively participates in a rental activity, the participation of the TP's spouse is taken into account.[210]

Except as provided otherwise in Temp. Reg. § 1.469–5T(e)(2), a person whose only interest in a rental activity is a limited partnership interest is not an "active" participant in that activity.[211]

The maximum amount of loss from rental real estate activities that a TP can deduct under the active participant exception is $25,000, and that figure is reduced by 50 percent of the excess of the TP's modified AGI over $100,000.[212] For this purpose, there are a number of modifications to a TP's AGI; for example, it is modified by excluding deductions for passive activity losses, interest on education loans, qualified tuition payments, and for IRA contributions; and by including the income, that is otherwise excluded by § 135, from the redemption of U.S. Savings bonds used to pay higher education costs, the amounts received by an employee to help pay for adoption expenses; and by excluding social security income.[213]

¶ 18.9211–2A. Low Income Housing and Rehabilitation Credits. A passive activity may generate tax credits, and such credits are subject to the § 469 limitations.[214] Special rules apply if the credits are generated by a rental real estate activity and are otherwise available to a natural person who "actively" participated in the activity.

208. § 469(i).

209. § 469(i)(6)(A).

210. § 469(i)(6)(D).

211. § 469(i)(6)(C).

212. § 469(i)(3)(A).

213. § 469(i)(3)(F).

214. § 469(a).

When tax credits are attributable to a rental real estate activity, the amount of such credits that exceeds the amount of income tax attributable to passive activities is allowable to the extent that such excess credit does not exceed the "deduction equivalent" of $25,000.[215] Except for two tax credits and one deduction, the $25,000 amount is phased out when the individual's modified AGI exceeds $100,000 (the same phase-out provision that is described in ¶ **18.9211–2**).[216]

The two tax credits that receive special treatment insofar as the phase-out is concerned are: (1) the tax credit for new construction and rehabilitation of low income housing [§ 42] and (2) the tax credit for certain expenses toward rehabilitating historic and certain other buildings [§ 47]. For credits allowed by § 42, there is no reduction of the $25,000 amount.[217] For credits allowed by § 47, the $25,000 amount is reduced by 50 percent of the excess of the TP's modified AGI over $200,000 (as contrasted to the usual $100,000 figure).[218] One other important difference in those two credit allowances from the allowance of loss deductions from such a rental real estate activity is that the §§ 42 and 47 credits are allowable to a natural person who owns an interest in such a rental real estate activity regardless of whether that person "actively" participated in the activity.[219]

The deduction that receives special treatment in this regard is the commercial revitalization deduction. The portion of the passive activity loss that is attributable to a commercial revitalization deduction under § 1400I is allowable without regard to whether the TP "actively" participated in the activity and is not subject to the phaseout provision.[220]

¶ 18.9212. Special Rules for a TP Who Materially Participates in a Real Property Trade or Business. Under

---

215. § 469(i)(1), (2). The meaning of a deduction equivalent is defined in § 469(j)(5).

216. § 469(i)(3)(A).

217. § 469(i)(3)(D).

218. § 469(i)(3)(B).

219. § 469(i)(6)(B).

220. § 469(i)(3)(C), (6)(B).

§ 469(c)(7), the automatic classification of rental activities as passive activities does not apply to rental real estate activities if the following two requirements are satisfied:

(1) more than one-half of the personal services performed by the TP in trades or businesses is performed in "real property trades or businesses" in which the TP materially participates. The meaning of material participation in a trade or business is explained at ¶ **18.9130**, which definition is applicable to this provision; and so the participation of spouses in a real estate trade or business are combined to determine whether either spouse materially participated; and

(2) the TP performs more than 750 hours of services during the taxable year in real property trades or businesses in which the TP materially participates.

While the participation of spouses can be combined in determining material participation of either spouse, they cannot be combined for the purposes of the other requirements. So, each person's own performance of service must satisfy the 750–hour requirement and the more-than-one-half of TP's services requirement.[221]

The term "real property trade or business" means any real property development, redevelopment, construction, reconstruction, acquisition, conversion, rental, operation, management, leasing, or brokerage trade or business.[222]

Personal services that are performed as an employee do not qualify as services performed in a real property trade or business unless the employee has more than a 5% ownership interest in the employer.[223]

As to corporate TPs, if the TP is a closely held C corporation, it will qualify for the exclusion from passive activity characterization if more than 50% of the corporation's gross receipts are derived from a real estate trade or business in which the corporation materially participates.[224] The meaning of material participation for a closely held C corporation is defined in § 469(h)(4).

---

221. § 469(c)(7)(B).

222. § 469(c)(7)(C).

223. § 469(c)(7)(D)(ii).

224. § 469(c)(7)(D)(i).

If the requirements of this provision are satisfied, then any rental real estate activity of the TP is not treated as a passive activity. This provision is applied by treating each rental real estate activity of the TP as a separate activity unless the TP elects to treat all such interests as one activity.[225]

¶ 18.9220. Earned Income. A TP's earned income (that is, income earned by the TP from his services) is not treated as passive activity income.[226]

¶ 18.9300. Regulatory Exclusion From Passive Activity Category. Those TPs that have passive activity investments that generate losses might seek passive activity investments that generate taxable income so that they can utilize their loss deductions from their passive activity investments. To that end, TPs might structure a new investment in a manner that would cause the income therefrom to constitute passive activity income. To prevent an abusive use of such arrangements, Congress has given Treasury broad authority to exclude certain types of income from the passive activity category when it is necessary to do so to prevent a frustration of the congressional purpose in adopting the passive activity limitations.[227]

¶ 18.9400. Interaction with At Risk Rules. The at risk rules[228] are applied first, and any deduction that would be permitted after applying the at risk rules will then be subject to the passive activity limitation imposed by § 469.[229]

¶ 18.9500. Operation of the PAL. The following examples illustrate the operation of the PAL.

¶ 18.9510. Illustration 1. *X*, a natural person, has interests in two passive activities—PA–1 and PA–2. In Year One, *X* has salary income of $170,000, and *X* has a net loss of $30,000 from PA–1 and a net loss of $20,000 from PA–2. A deduction of those losses is not barred by the at risk rules. *X* also has dividend income of $8,000 from publicly held stocks that *X* owns. *X* is not permitted to deduct any amount for the losses incurred by his interest in

225. § 469(c)(7)(A).

226. § 469(e)(3).

227. § 469(*l*). Treasury exercised that authority by promulgating Temp. Reg. § 1.469–2T(f), which is discussed at ¶¶ **18.9141** and **18.9143**.

228. § 465. See ¶ **18.8000** *et seq.*

229. Temp. Reg. § 1.469–2T(d)(6).

PA–1 and PA–2. Those losses are carried forward and treated as having been incurred in X's next taxable year.

¶ **18.9520. Illustration 2.** The facts are the same as those stated in ¶ **18.9510**. In Year Two, X had salary income of $180,000, and he had dividend income of $9,500. X had a loss of $8,000 from PA–2. A deduction of that loss is not barred by the at risk rules. In Year two, X sold his interest in PA–1 for a recognized gain of $18,000. X had no other income or loss from PA–1 in that year. X can deduct from his gain on the sale of PA–1 $18,000 of his $30,000 carryover loss from PA–1. This washes out that gain. X can deduct the $12,000 balance of PA–1 carryover loss from his salary and dividend income. The $8,000 loss that X incurred with respect to PA–2 is not deductible in that year. For Year Three, X has a carryover loss from his PA–2 investment of $28,000 (i.e., $20,000 from Year One and an additional $8,000 from Year Two).

¶ **18.9000A. DEMOLITION OF STRUCTURE.** When a TP razes a building that he owns and uses in a trade or business or in a profit-seeking venture, he incurs expenses in demolishing the building (or other structure) and may have an unrecovered basis in the demolished structure (i.e., a basis that has not been recovered through depreciation or other deductions). Since the building (or other structure) was used in the TP's business or profit venture, should he be permitted a deduction for the expenses of razing the structure and for his remaining adjusted basis in the structure? At one time, a deduction would be allowed unless the TP had purchased the property with the intention of razing it (for example, so that a more efficient building might be constructed on the lot in its place). In such cases, the cost of razing the building and all or much of the unrecovered basis was not deductible and instead was added to the TP's basis in the underlying land.

The current rule, which is set forth at § 280B, prohibits a deduction for the cost of demolishing a structure and denies a deduction for any unrecovered basis regardless of what purpose the TP had when he acquired the property. Any amount of the expenses of demolishing the structure and of the unrecovered basis of the structure that would have been deductible if it were not for § 280B, will instead be added to the TP's basis in the land. One aspect of this provision is that it eliminates what had been a difficult factual issue to resolve—namely, what intention a TP had when he acquired improved realty and subsequently demolished the structure.

CHAPTER NINETEEN

MEDICAL EXPENSES

¶ 19.0000. MEDICAL EXPENSES. Expenses *paid* for the medical care of a TP, his spouse, and dependents are deductible subject to certain limitations described below. § 213(a). The term "dependent" in this provision adopts the definition of that term in § 152 (the provision for a dependent exemption deduction) except that several of the requirements that are imposed by § 152 are deleted. § 213(a). For example, for medical expense deduction purposes, there is no limitation on the amount of gross income that a dependent can have, whereas for exemption deduction purposes, there is a strict limitation. See § 152(d)(1)(B). Because of those deletions, an individual can be a TP's dependent for purposes of the medical expense deduction even though the individual does not qualify for a dependent exemption deduction for the TP.

A medical expense must have actually been paid to be deductible, and the TP must not have been reimbursed for it. So, an individual using the accrual method nevertheless would have to have paid an accrued medical expense to be eligible to deduct it. For timing purposes, the expense is deductible in the year it was paid regardless of when it was incurred. Treas. Reg. § 1.213–1(a)(1).

Typically, in other areas of the tax law, a capital expenditure incurred in connection with an activity whose expenses are deductible, cannot be deducted when paid or accrued. Instead, while there are exceptions, such expenditures are amortized over a period of time. That is not the case for medical expenditures. A capital expenditure that is made primarily for a medical reason is deductible when paid.[1] Treas. Reg. § 1.213–1(e)(1)(iii).

As with other deductions, a TP cannot deduct a medical expense to the extent that he was reimbursed or compensated for it. The tax consequences of a TP's having his medical expenses paid or reimbursed by an insurer, employer or other person are discussed at **¶ 19.8000** *et seq.*

Section 21 allows a TP a credit in certain circumstances for a portion of the cost of dependent care services incurred to permit the TP to be employed. It is possible for a medical expense paid for a dependent to qualify for a credit

---

1. The application of this rule and its restrictions are discussed at **¶ 19.5000**.

under § 21 as well as a deduction under § 213; but the TP must choose
which provision to use. A TP cannot take a deduction under § 213 for any
amount of a dependent's medical expense for which the TP takes a credit
under § 21. § 213(e).

The amount of medical expenses that can be deducted in a taxable year is
subject to a floor so that only the aggregate amount of such expenses that
exceeds that floor can be deducted.[2]

¶ 19.1000.   DEFINITION OF MEDICAL CARE. For purposes of
§ 213, "medical care" refers to amounts paid for the "diagnosis, cure,
mitigation, treatment, or prevention of a disease, or for the purpose of
affecting any structure or function of the body." An expenditure that is
merely beneficial to the general health of an individual (as contrasted to
an expense designed to alleviate or cure a specific illness) is not an
expenditure for medical care.

As discussed below, transportation costs incurred primarily for and
essential to the medical purposes described above constitute medical
care expenses.[3] Subject to requirements described below, premiums paid
on certain medical insurance coverage qualify for a deduction.[4]

Amounts paid for the care (including personal care services), treatment,
mitigation, and rehabilitation of a "chronically ill individual" (and,
subject to a ceiling, the premiums for insurance to cover such costs)
constitute medical care expenses. §§ 213(d)(1)(C),(D), (10), 7702B(c). A
"chronically ill individual" is defined in § 7702B(c)(2) as including an
individual who has been certified by a licensed health care practitioner
as being unable to perform (without substantial assistance) at least two
activities of daily living for a 90–day period due to a loss of functional
capacity. The term also includes an individual who requires substantial
supervision to protect from threats to health and safety due to severe
cognitive impairment. This provision, which was added to the Code in
1996, will provide a deduction for the cost of personal care services for
individuals who are unable to care for themselves because of Alzheimer's or dementia.

¶ 19.1100.   Medicine and Drugs. Not every expenditure that constitutes a medical care expense is deductible. For example, the costs

2.   The amount of that floor and its operation are discussed at ¶¶ **19.2000–19.2230**.

3.   ¶¶ **19.1400–19.1420**.

4.   ¶ **19.1600**.

of medicines and drugs are medical care expenses.[5] The regulations state that "medicines and drugs" refer to items that are legally procured and generally accepted as falling within the category of medicines and drugs, regardless of whether they can be obtained only with a prescription. Treas. Reg. § 1.213–1(e)(2). The term does not include toothpaste, hand lotions and similar items. But, the statute does not allow a deduction for all medicines and drugs. The cost of insulin is deductible. The only other costs for medicines and drugs that are deductible are those for "prescribed drugs." § 213(b). A "prescribed drug" is a drug or "biological" which can be obtained only with a physician's prescription. § 213(d)(3). A "biological" is described in Blackstone's *Pocket Medical Dictionary* as a biological product such as a serum or vaccine.

If a drug can be obtained without a physician's prescription (i.e., an over-the-counter drug), its cost is not deductible even if a physician prescribed it.[6]

¶ 19.1110.   Reimbursement of Cost of Medicine or Drugs. While the cost of nonprescription drugs is not deductible, it is significant that they nevertheless are classified as medical care expenses. In addition to § 213, there are other Code provisions that apply to medical care expenses. For example, § 105(b) excludes from an employee's gross income reimbursements of medical care expenses that an employee received from a health insurance plan funded by the employee's employer.[7] In Rev. Rul. 2003–102, the Commissioner ruled that an employer's reimbursements of an employee's cost of purchasing nonprescription drugs was a reimbursement of medical care costs that is excluded from the employee's gross income under § 105(b) even though those expenses would not have been deductible under § 213 if they had not been reimbursed. Congress partially negated that ruling by amendments made to the Code in 2010.

For taxable years beginning after 2010, a reimbursement from an employer-provided medical plan or insurance policy of the cost of a medicine or drug will not be excluded from the TP's gross income unless it was prescribed by a physician. § 106(f). With one exception, this amendment brings the requirements for excluding

5. Rev. Rul. 2003–102.

6. Rev. Rul. 2003–58.

7. See ¶ **19.8511**.

a reimbursement of a medicine or drug expense from income in line with the requirements for deducting the cost of such items. The one exception is that the medicine or drug need only be prescribed by a physician for the exclusion to apply whereas the item must not be obtainable without a prescription for the deduction to apply. The exclusion provision is more liberal in that it allows the reimbursement of an over-the-counter medicine or drug to be excluded if the item was prescribed by a physician.

Similar restrictions on the exclusion of reimbursements for the cost of medicines and drugs were added to the provisions concerning Archer MSA plans and Health Savings Accounts. §§ 220(d)(2)(A) and 223(d)(2)(A).

Note that the restriction on the exclusion of reimbursements of expenses for nonprescribed medicines and drugs does not apply to benefits received under an insurance policy that was purchased by the TP with his own funds. Benefits from a self-purchased insurance policy are excluded from income under § 104(a)(3) and are not subject to the § 106(f) restriction.

¶ **19.1200. Personal Expenditure.** The line between a medical expense and a personal expense which relates in part to a physical or mental condition is sometimes difficult to draw. For example, in Rev. Rul. 75–319, the Commissioner ruled that the expenses incurred by a husband and wife for marriage counseling services performed by a clergyman associated with a counseling center were personal, nondeductible expenses. The ruling stressed that the expense was not incurred for the prevention or alleviation of a physical or mental defect or illness, but rather to help improve the TP's marriage. However, in that same year, the Commissioner ruled that the fees paid by a husband and wife for psychiatric treatment for their "sexual inadequacy and incompatibility" were deductible medical expenses.[8]

¶ **19.1210. Cosmetic Surgery.** The definition of "medical care" in § 213(d)(1)(A) includes an expense paid for "the purpose of affecting any structure or function of the body." One might have thought that a deduction for medical care would be confined, as a regulation provides, "strictly to expenses incurred primarily for the prevention or alleviation of a physical or mental defect or illness." Treas. Reg. § 1.213–1(e)(1)(ii). To the contrary, the Service expanded the scope of the deduction to cover the expense for

8. Rev. Rul. 75–187.

any operation that was designed to affect the structure or function of a body.

In Rev. Rul. 76–332, the Commissioner ruled that an expense incurred for cosmetic plastic surgery (a face lift) for the purpose of improving the TP's personal appearance was deductible. The face lift operation had not been recommended by a physician, and the TP was not suffering from a mental disorder. The Commissioner determined in Rev. Rul. 76–332 that since the face lift operation affected a structure of the human body, it constituted medical care. The Commissioner cited with approval his earlier ruling on the deductibility of a vasectomy, abortion, and similar operations.[9] In Rev. Rul. 82–111, the Commissioner sustained the deductibility of expenses incurred for a cosmetic hair transplant and for hair removal by electrolysis, but denied a deduction for the cost of tattooing and for the cost of having a TP's ear pierced.

Both Rev. Rul. 76–332 and Rev. Rul. 82–111 were vitiated by an amendment adopted as part of the Omnibus Budget Reconciliation Act of 1990. As amended, § 213(d)(9) expressly precludes a medical expense deduction for cosmetic surgery (or similar procedures) unless the surgery or other procedure is necessary to ameliorate a deformity attributable to "a congenital abnormality, a personal injury resulting from an accident or trauma, or disfiguring disease." "Cosmetic surgery" is defined in § 213(d)(9)(B) as a "procedure which is directed at improving the patient's appearance and does not meaningfully promote the proper function of the body or prevent or treat illness or disease."

¶ 19.1211. **Gender Reassignment Surgery.** In 2006, the Service released a Chief Counsel Advice holding that the expense of gender reassignment surgery would not qualify for a deduction under § 213.[10] While noting that the issue of whether gender reassignment surgery involves the treatment of a disease is controversial, the Service suggested that since Congress disallows most deductions for change of appearance (such as cosmetic surgery), no deduction should be allowed for such treatment.

In 2010, the Tax Court disagreed with the Service and held that such expenses were deductible under § 213.[11] The court

---

9. See ¶ **19.1900**.

10. ILM 200603025.

11. *O'Donnabhain v. Commissioner*, 134 T.C. No. 4 (Feb. 2, 2010).

held that "gender identity disorder" is a disease within the meaning of § 213 and thus TP's hormone therapy and sex reassignment surgery qualified as treatment of a disease rather than as cosmetic surgery. The court denied a medical deduction for TP's breast augmentation surgery but noted that, in some cases, the expense of such surgery may qualify if required to meet the "social gender role."

¶ 19.1220. Religious Cure. The question has arisen as to whether expenses incurred in seeking a cure of a disease or illness from a religious source constitutes a medical expense. A treatment need not be administered or proscribed by a licensed medical doctor to qualify as a medical deduction.[12] For example, a TP's transportation costs of attending meetings of an Alcoholics Anonymous Club are deductible.[13] The amount paid for services rendered by an authorized Christian Science practitioner qualifies as a medical expense.[14]

The expense of taking a child suffering with a malignant tumor to the Shrine of Our Lady of Lourdes in Lourdes, France was held to be primarily for the purposes of spiritual help rather than to alleviate a physical defect and so was nondeductible.[15]

Similarly, the expenses of a trip by the TP's wife to Samoa (her original homeland) for the purpose of being treated for a stroke by native "doctors" were held to be nondeductible.[16] The wife's condition had been diagnosed as hopeless by her doctors in California where she lived. The Samoan "doctors" had no medical school training, and their treatment consisted of prayers to the spirits, herbs and massages. They gave the same treatment to all persons regardless of the nature of the illness. The Tax Court determined that the TP probably did not have a "reasonable expectation" that the Samoan trip would cure his wife, and that the trip was a "last resort." The relevance of those two determinations is unclear, but perhaps they influenced the court's view as to the bona fides of the purported medical purpose of the trip as contrasted to making a final visit to the wife's homeland. Al-

---

12. See ¶ **19.1240**.

13. Rev. Rul. 63–273.

14. Rev. Rul. 55–261.

15. *Ring v. Commissioner*, 23 T.C. 950 (1955) (reviewed by the court).

16. *Tautolo v. Commissioner*, 34 TCM 1198 (1975).

though the court did not address that subject, it may have been the actual rationale for the result the court reached.

¶ **19.1230.** **Divided Purpose.** Frequently, in medical expense cases, the medical purpose for incurring the expense is clear. If, however, the TP claims a medical reason for incurring an expense that would normally be a personal item, the TP may obtain a medical expense deduction only if he can satisfy a heavy burden of proof to show that it was undertaken primarily for a medical reason. The Tax Court has held that, in such cases, the TP's burden is to prove that he would not have incurred the expense but for the medical care need, and that the expenditure was an essential element of the treatment for the TP's illness.[17] In one case,[18] the court said,

> Certain treatments are inherently medical in nature (i.e., surgery), and TPs have little difficulty convincing the Commissioner or courts that such procedures fit within the section 213 definition. Other treatments ... are more commonly recognized as nonmedical procedures intended for an individual's general well-being. In those instances where a normally nonmedical procedure is claimed as a basis for a medical deduction, the burden is on such TPs to show that the procedure comes within the requirements of the statute.

In accord with that view, the Tax Court denied a TP a medical deduction for the cost of divorcing his wife even though his marriage impaired his mental health and his psychiatrist recommended the divorce as vital to his treatment. The court held that the TP had not met his burden of proving that he would not have obtained a divorce if he had not been ill.[19] Similarly, the Tax Court denied a deduction for the amounts spent on shopping excursions recommended by the TP's psychiatrist.[20] The court stated that to qualify for a deduction, there must be a direct or proximate relation between the expense and the diagnosis, cure, mitigation, treatment or prevention of a disease.

While the cost of the construction of a swimming pool to meet the medical needs of a TP or his dependent generally is deductible,

---

17. *O'Donnabhain v. Commissioner*, 134 T.C. No. 4 (2010); *Jacobs v. Commissioner*, 62 T.C. 813 (1974). See also Rev. Rul. 87–106.

18. *Huff v. Commissioner*, 69 T.C.M. 2551 (1995).

19. *Jacobs v. Commissioner*, 62 T.C. 813 (1974).

20. *Rabb v. Commissioner*, 31 T.C.M. 476 (1972).

subject to the limitations discussed in ¶ **19.5000**, no deduction will be allowed unless the principal reason for constructing the pool was medical care.[21] The TP will have a heavy burden of proof in such cases.

A doctor's instruction to undertake an expenditure of this type is a significant factor in meeting the burden of proving that it was done for a medical reason.[22] Indeed, in some cases of this nature, a doctor's recommendation may be necessary, albeit not sufficient, to qualify the expenditure for a deduction. A doctor's opinion is sometimes necessary to prove that a disease exists or that a typically personal expenditure constitutes a treatment for a disease.[23] A doctor's opinion is not always required and sometimes is merely one among several factors to be weighed. In Info 2001–0155, the Service said,

> Among the objective factors that indicate that an otherwise personal expense is for medical care are the taxpayer's motive or purpose, recommendation by a physician, linkage between the treatment and the illness, treatment effectiveness, and proximity in time to the onset or recurrence of a disease.

In Rev. Rul. 87–106, the Commissioner stated that while capital expenditures incurred for medical reasons are currently deductible as medical expenses,[24] the amount of such expenditures that are incurred for non-medical reasons (such as architectural and aesthetic compatibility with the TP's residence) is not deductible.[25] The Commissioner has stated that he will not provide an advance ruling on the question of whether a proposed capital expenditure for an item that is ordinarily used for personal purposes is primarily intended for a medical purpose.[26]

¶ **19.1240. Doctor's Instruction.** An expense need not have been incurred on the advice of a medical doctor to qualify as a deductible medical expense. The nature of the services rendered controls the determination of whether it is medical care; the

---

21. Compare *Evanoff v. Commissioner*, 44 T.C.M. 1394 (1982) (no deduction) with *Ferris v. Commissioner*, 582 F.2d 1112 (7th Cir. 1978) (discussed in ¶ **19.5300**) (deduction for part of the cost).

22. See ¶ **19.2140**.

23. Info. 2001–0155 (June 29, 2001).

24. See ¶ **19.5000**.

25. See also *Ferris v. Commissioner*, 582 F.2d 1112 (7th Cir. 1978) and ¶ **19.5300**.

26. Rev. Proc. 2010–3, Sec. 3.01(26). But see ¶ **19.5000**.

determination does not rest on the experience, title, and qualification of the person rendering the service.[27] However, when the purposes for making an expenditure may have had personal as well as medical reasons, a doctor's instruction (while not conclusive) will be a significant factor in finding that the primary purpose of the expenditure was to serve a medical need.[28]

In Info 2001–0155 (June 29, 2001), the Service stated that a doctor's opinion is sometimes necessary to show that a disease is present or that a typically personal expenditure constitutes a treatment for a disease. For example, in Rev. Rul. 2002–19, the Service suggests that one of the conditions for deducting the cost of a weight loss program is that a physician have diagnosed that the TP is suffering from obesity or from some other disease that requires weight loss for treatment.[29] The Internal Revenue Code itself explicitly requires that to qualify an individual's long-term care expenses for a deduction under § 213(d)(1)(C), the individual must be certified by a licensed health care practitioner to satisfy certain conditions specified in § 7702B(c)(2).[30]

In Rev. Rul. 76–80, the Commissioner held that a TP could not deduct the cost of purchasing a special type of vacuum cleaner that would alleviate the TP's allergy to household dust by removing dust from the air. Although use of an air cleaner had been recommended to the TP by his physician, the physician had not suggested using this type of vacuum cleaner as an air cleaner. Relying in part on the fact that no medical recommendation had been made to the TP to purchase the machine, the Commissioner ruled that there was "no evidence, such as a medical prescription, that the vacuum cleaner was purchased primarily for medical care."

¶ 19.1300. **Illegal Expenditures.** The regulations deny a deduction for medical care expenditures that are illegal. Treas. Reg. § 1.213–1(e)(1)(ii). In Rev. Rul. 97–9, the Service ruled that even though a TP's purchase of marijuana pursuant to a physician's prescription was legal under the local state law, it nevertheless was nondeductible because it violated the Federal Control Substance Act,

27. *Brown v. Commissioner*, 62 T.C. 551 (1974), aff'd per curiam, 523 F.2d 365 (8th Cir. 1975); *Tautolo v. Commissioner*, 34 T.C.M. 1198 (1975).

28. See ¶ **19.1230**.

29. See ¶ **19.1820**.

30. See ¶ **19.1000**.

which lists marijuana as a controlled substance.[31] However, in October, 2009, the United States Department of Justice announced that it would not prosecute for the use of marijuana for medical purposes if the use were legal under applicable state law. In light of that announcement, the question arises as to whether the Service might reconsider its position on the nondeductibility of the cost of marijuana in those circumstances.

¶ **19.1400.   Transportation.** Medical expenses include the cost of transportation incurred primarily for and essential to medical care. § 213(d)(1)(B). "Transportation costs," the cost of transporting a person from one location to another, must be distinguished from the broader term "travel expenses." While travel expenses include transportation costs, they also include living expenses (meals and lodging) incurred at the new location.[32]

The Commissioner ruled in Rev. Rul. 78–266 that child care expenses incurred to permit a patient to visit a physician for medical treatment are personal, nondeductible expenses. The Commissioner did not treat the child care expenses as part of the cost of visiting the doctor.[33]

¶ **19.1410.   No Deduction For Depreciation.** The statute permits a deduction only for expenses "paid" during the taxable year. When a TP uses his own vehicle for transportation for medical care purposes, the Commissioner contends (and the courts have held) that the TP cannot claim a medical expense deduction for depreciation of the vehicle so used because the Commissioner asserts that a depreciation allowance is not an amount paid.[34] In *Commissioner v. Idaho Power Co.*,[35] the Supreme Court treated a depreciation allowance on equipment being used by the TP in the construction of a capital asset to be used in the TP's business as an amount paid for the construction of the capital asset and, therefore, a nondeductible capital expenditure. It might appear that a depreciation allowance on a vehicle being

---

31.   21 U.S.C. § 812(c).

32.   The extent to which medical travel expenses are deductible is discussed at ¶¶ **19.1700–19.1730**.

33.   See *Ochs v. Commissioner*, 195 F.2d 692 (2d Cir. 1952). See also, *Estate of Levine v. Commissioner*, 43 T.C.M. 259 (1982), aff'd 729 F.2d 1441 (2d Cir. 1983).

34.   See Rev. Proc. 64–15 citing *Gordon v. Commissioner*, 37 T.C. 986 (1962).

35.   418 U.S. 1 (1974).

used for medical care purposes similarly should be treated as an amount paid for medical care and thus be deductible. However, in a split decision, the Tenth Circuit denied a claim for a medical expense deduction for the depreciation of a vehicle which was so used.[36] The Tenth Circuit did not deem *Idaho Power* to be controlling.[37] Of course, the transportation costs actually paid by the TP in using his own vehicle (e.g., gas, parking fees and tolls) for a medical purpose are deductible.

¶ 19.1420. Standard Mileage Allowance. If a TP uses his own car as a means of transportation for medical purposes, in lieu of itemizing his actual transportation expense, the TP may elect the optional standard mileage rate which, for the year 2010, is 16.5 cents per mile. The optional mileage allowance can be taken in lieu of deducting operating expenses (including gas and oil). However, parking fees and tolls are not reflected in the mileage allowance, and so can be deducted separately.[38] The mileage allowance does not reflect any amount for depreciation of the vehicle since depreciation is not allowed as a medical care deduction—i.e., it is not an amount *paid*.[39]

¶ 19.1500. Payment with Borrowed Funds. While a medical expense must actually be paid to be deductible, the timing of the deductibility of the payment of a medical expense does not turn upon whether the TP used his own funds or whether he used borrowed funds. If a TP used borrowed funds, the expense is allowed as a deduction in the taxable year that the payment was made rather than in the year that the TP repaid the loan.[40]

¶ 19.1510. Credit Cards. If a TP uses a bank's credit card to pay a medical expense, he creates a creditor-debtor relationship between the payee and the bank, and he retains no control over that relationship. The use of the credit card is equivalent to the payment of the medical expense with borrowed funds, and so the deduction is allowable in the year in which the credit card charge is made rather than in the year in which the TP repays the bank.[41]

---

36. *Weary v. United States*, 510 F.2d 435 (10th Cir. 1975).

37. Accord, *Henderson v. Commissioner*, 80 T.C.M. 517 (2000); *Pfersching v. Commissioner*, 46 T.C.M. 424 (1983); and *Elwood v. Commissioner*, 72 T.C. 264 (1979).

38. Rev. Proc. 2009–54.

39. See ¶ **19.1410**. See also Rev. Proc. 2010–51 (Sec. 5.03).

40. *Granan v. Commissioner*, 55 T.C. 753 (1971).

41. Rev. Rul. 78–39.

¶ **19.1600. Insurance Premiums.** Premiums for medical insurance are included in a TP's allowable medical expenses. If an insurance policy provides for coverage other than medical care insurance (e.g., a lump sum payment for loss of life or limb), only the amount of the premium which is attributable to the medical care insurance is deductible. Even that amount cannot be deducted unless the insurance company provides an explicit statement of the amount of the premium that is paid for medical care and unless the amount charged by the insurance company for medical care is not an unreasonably large portion of the entire premium. § 213(d)(6). Premiums paid for insurance to cover the cost of medical care for a "chronically ill individual" (such as the cost of care for a person suffering from Alzheimer's or dementia) qualify as deductible medical care expenses, subject to a dollar ceiling. § 213(d)(1)(D), (10).[42]

¶ **19.1610. Disability Insurance.** Premiums paid to provide specified amounts of payments to the insured in the event that the insured becomes disabled are not deductible as medical care expenses. Treas. Reg. § 1.213–1(e)(4). If the purpose of the insurance is to protect the existence of a sole proprietorship that the insured owns and operates from the harm that the business would suffer because of the loss of the individual's services, the premiums *might* then be deductible under § 162 as business expenses. Note that the payments that an individual receives from an insurer pursuant to a disability insurance policy are excluded from the individual's gross income by § 104(a)(3).

¶ **19.1620. Premiums Paid by Self–Employed Individual.** The premiums paid by a self-employed person for medical insurance to cover himself, his spouse and dependents are deductible as business expenses under § 162(*l*). The insurance must be provided pursuant to a plan for the trade or business in which the TP is self-employed. The dollar amount that is deductible cannot exceed the individual's "earned income" from the trade or business with respect to which the plan providing the medical care coverage is provided. § 162(*l*)(2)(A). The deduction is not available for the payment of a premium for any month in which the TP is eligible to participate in a subsidized health plan maintained by an employer of the TP or his spouse. § 162(*l*)(2)(B). Any amount of premium deductible for a self-employed TP under § 162(*l*) cannot be taken as a medical care expense under § 213. § 162(*l*)(3). The

---

42. See ¶ **19.1000**.

deduction is not allowed in determining the social security tax on a TP's self-employed income. § 162(*l*)(4).

¶ **19.1700.** **Travel Expenses.** "Travel expenses" refer to all of the expenses incurred in making a trip including: the transportation costs, the costs of meals and lodging, and other expenses incurred at the new location. As noted in ¶ **19.1400**, transportation costs incurred primarily for and essential to medical care are deductible. However, subject to several exceptions,[43] other travel expenses (including the cost of meals and lodging) are not deductible.[44] Treas. Reg. § 1.213–1(e)(1)(iv).

¶ **19.1710.** **Institutional Care.** The cost of in-patient hospital care, including the cost of meals and lodging that are provided to an in-patient, are treated as deductible medical expenses. Treas. Reg. § 1.213–1(e)(1)(v). Similarly, expenses (including meals and lodging) incurred while residing in an institution that is not a hospital are deductible medical care expenses if the principal reason for residing at that institution is to receive medical care. Treas. Reg. § 1.213–1(e)(1)(v). It appears likely that the costs of meals received in connection with such medical care will not be subjected to the 50% of cost limitation of § 274(n), and so will not have to be separately identified and segregated from the other institutional costs.

Whether medical care is the principal reason for a person's residing at an institution is a question of fact the determination of which rests on an examination of the condition of the person in question and of the services received by that person at the institution. For example, the cost of institutional care for a mentally ill person who is unsafe when left alone is deductible. Treas. Reg. § 1.213–1(e)(1)(v)(a).

A frequently litigated issue is whether the cost of a child's attending a private boarding school is deductible when the child suffers with physical or emotional disorders. In general, when a child with emotional problems is boarded at a school because that school provides a strictly ordered environment, but provides no special services for the child's disorder, no deduction will be allowed for the expense of boarding the child even if the child's doctor recommends that the child be sent to such a school. However, when a boarding school caters to a specific illness or

43. The exceptions are described in ¶¶ **19.1710** and **19.1720**.

44. See *Commissioner v. Bilder*, 369 U.S. 499 (1962).

infirmity of a child, all the expenses (including meals, lodging, and educational costs) of the child's boarding and matriculation at that school are deductible. For example, in PLR 8401024, the Commissioner allowed a medical expense deduction for the costs of having a child who suffered with dyslexia attend a school for handicapped students with special learning disabilities. The school provided the services of a number of professional specialists who deal with various aspects of the handicaps of those with learning disabilities. Since the determination of deductibility rests on factual issues, there has been considerable litigation concerning various types of boarding school experiences, and the Commissioner has had mixed success in litigating this issue.

¶ **19.1711. Primary Purpose Not Medical.** When the primary purpose of a person's residing at an institution is something other than to receive medical care, then only the cost of actual medical care received by such person is deductible. In such cases, none of the costs of meals and lodging are deductible. Treas. Reg. § 1.213–1(e)(1)(v)(b).

¶ **19.1720. Limited Deduction for Lodging Expenses.** In general, unless an individual resides in an institution,[45] lodging expenses incurred while away from home for medical care purposes are not deductible. There is a limited exception to that general rule. Amounts paid for lodging while away from home primarily for and essential to medical care are deductible if: (1) the medical care is provided by a physician in a licensed hospital or in a medical care facility that is related to, or the equivalent of, a licensed hospital; (2) the lodging is not lavish or extravagant; and (3) there is no significant element of personal pleasure, recreation, or vacation in the travel away from home. § 213(d)(2). The amount deductible for lodging under this provision cannot exceed $50 per night for each individual. § 213(d)(2). For a deduction to be allowed under § 213(d)(2), the *primary* purpose of the TP must be to receive treatment from a physician. If a physician's treatment is merely an incidental purpose of the TP, and the primary purpose is to alleviate a health problem by staying in a locality with a favorable climate, no deduction for lodging will be allowed.[46]

¶ **19.1730. Illustration: Travel Expenses.** X suffers from an asthmatic condition and a heart condition. X's doctor recom-

45. See ¶ **19.1710**.

46. *Polyak v. Commissioner*, 94 T.C. 337 (1990).

mended that X reside in Arizona for the months of August and September each year since those months are the worst periods for X's asthmatic attacks and the climate in Arizona will mitigate X's attacks. X followed his doctor's advice and went to Arizona for those two months. While residing in Arizona, X did not visit a doctor or receive any treatment. X spent the following sums:

(a) X paid the doctor a fee of $200.

(b) On August 1–3, X drove from New York to Phoenix in his automobile, and X expended $80 for gas and oil while traveling on the road.

(c) In addition, X spent $150 for food and lodging while traveling on the road.

(d) While living in Arizona, X spent $2,000 on lodging and $1,200 on food.

(e) X returned to New York in October, and his return expenses were $85 for gas and oil and $175 for food and lodging.

Subject to the limitation as to the amount of medical expenses that can be deducted, X's $200 payment to his doctor is a deductible medical expense. Since X went to Arizona to mitigate a specific medical condition rather than merely to benefit his general health, X's $165 costs for gas and oil in driving to Arizona and back are also deductible medical expenses. In lieu of that amount, X could deduct a standard mileage allowance.[47] X is not allowed any depreciation deduction for the use of his car. The $2,000 spent for lodging and the $1,200 spent for food while in Arizona are not deductible because food and lodging while living away from home for medical purposes are not treated as medical expenses unless one of the exceptions described at ¶¶ **19.1710** and **19.1720** is applicable. Neither of those exceptions applies to the instant facts.

It is probable that the $325 that X expended on food and lodging in transit to and from Phoenix qualify as deductible medical care expenses. While the Service contends that food and lodging expenses incurred in transit to a place being visited for medical care purposes are not deductible, the Tax Court and the Sixth Circuit have allowed a deduction for such expenses.[48] If the expense of meals obtained on travel status is determined to be deductible,

---

47. See ¶ **19.1420**.

48. *Montgomery v. Commissioner*, 51 T.C. 410 (1968), aff'd 428 F.2d 243 (6th Cir. 1970). Accord *Pfersching v. Commissioner*, 46 T.C.M. 424 (1983).

only 50% of the cost of such meals can qualify for a deduction. § 274(n).

¶ 19.1800. Specific Illness. In general, an expense incurred to improve the general health of a TP will not be deductible. Instead, the expense must either relate to a specific illness or it must be incurred for the purpose of affecting a structure or function of the body. Treas. Reg. § 1.213–1(e)(1)(ii). Notwithstanding that general rule, it is likely that fees paid to a doctor for any medical services, including an annual check-up, will be deductible even though the services are not attributable to a specific illness.[49] Of course, if the treatment is one that does not qualify for a deduction, such as cosmetic surgery, the doctor's fee will not be deductible.

In GCM 37115 (1977), the Commissioner stated that for an expense to qualify for a medical care deduction, it must either be for the purpose of affecting a structure or function of the body, or: "(1) the taxpayer must show the present existence or the imminent probability of a mental or physical disease, defect, or illness;" and "(2) the expense must be for goods or services directly or proximately related to the diagnosis, cure, mitigation, treatment or prevention of the disease."

¶ 19.1810. Illustration: Luxury Vacation. Y, who was feeling rundown, visited his doctor. Y's doctor advised him to take a cruise as a rest cure, and Y did so. The cost of the cruise is not a deductible medical expense since it was not incurred in connection with a specific illness, but rather was for the general good health of the TP. Treas. Reg. § 1.213–1(e)(1)(ii) and (iv).

¶ 19.1820. Weight Reduction and Stop–Smoking Programs. In Rev. Ruls. 79–151 and 79–162, the Commissioner ruled that the cost of participation, pursuant to a doctor's recommendation, for general health improvement purposes in either a weight reduction or stop-smoking program is not deductible. However, the Commissioner subsequently revised his position on those issues.

In Rev. Rul. 2002–19, the Commissioner accepted that obesity itself is a disease.[50] Consequently, the ruling concluded that the

---

49. See *Murray v. Commissioner*, 43 T.C.M. 1377 (1982).

50. The medical standard that is used to determine whether a person is obese is referred to as the "Body Mass Index" or "BMI." The BMI is the product of the person's weight in pounds times a specified figure divided by the person's height in inches.

cost of a weight loss program by a person who has been diagnosed as obese by a physician is a medical care expense. Even if the person is not obese, if he suffers from a disease (such as hypertension) for which a physician has directed him to lose weight, the cost of participating in a weight loss program is a medical expense. The Commissioner distinguished Rev. Rul. 79–151 because the TP in that latter ruling did not suffer from a specific disease, and participated in the weight loss program merely to improve his general health and appearance.

However, the 2002 ruling held that the TPs could not deduct the cost of reduced-calorie diet food because those foods substitute for the foods the TPs would normally have had and because they satisfy the TPs' nutritional needs.[51] In an earlier pronouncement, in Info 2001–0155 (June 29, 2001), the Service indicated that to the extent that a special diet for weight loss exceeds the cost of the TP's regular diet, the additional cost is a medical care expense. The latter position accords with the Tax Court's view.[52] Even if the Service adopts that view, the TP's burden to show that there is an additional cost and the amount thereof will be very difficult to meet. If a deduction is allowed for the additional cost of meals, only 50% of that additional cost will be deductible. § 274(n).

As to smoking, Rev. Rul. 99–28 revoked Rev. Rul. 79–162. In Rev. Rul. 99–28, the Service acknowledged that scientific studies had determined that nicotine is addictive and is harmful to the health of the smoker. The Service determined that the cost of treatment for an addiction to a harmful substance is a medical care expense. The Service held that one of the TPs who was the subject of that ruling could deduct as medical care expenses the cost of participating in a smoking-cessation program even though the TP had no specific disease and even though a doctor had not instructed the TP to cease smoking. Another TP, who was also the subject of that ruling, was allowed to deduct as medical care expenses the cost of prescription drugs to alleviate the effects of nicotine withdrawal.

However, the cost of nicotine gum and nicotine patches were held not to be deductible because they contain a drug (other than insulin) and do not require a prescription from a physician. The

51. See ¶ 19.6000.
52. Id.

cost of a drug (other than insulin) that can be obtained without a
physician's prescription is disallowed as a deduction by § 213(b).[53]

¶ 19.1900. Abortion. The Commissioner has ruled that the cost of
a legal abortion or vasectomy is a medical expense. Rev. Rul. 73–201.
See also Rev. Rul. 73–603, allowing a deduction for the cost of a legal
operation to render a woman incapable of bearing children. Such
expenses are incurred for the purpose of affecting a structure or
function of the body and so were held to be deductible.

¶ 19.2000. LIMITATIONS ON MEDICAL EXPENSE DEDUCTIONS.

Once the amount of medical care expenses is determined, it is
necessary to determine the extent to which the expenses are deductible.
For example, as previously noted,[54] the medical expense of purchasing
nonprescription drugs is not deductible. As a basic rule, it should be
remembered that no deduction is permitted for expenses for which the
TP has been compensated by insurance or otherwise. The amount of
uncompensated medical care expenses that can be deducted by a TP in a
taxable year is subject to a "floor" so that only the excess of such
expenses over the "floor" can be deducted. § 213(a). The "floor" is
described below.

¶ 19.2100. Amount Deductible. Medical care expenses of a TP
are deductible only to the extent that the aggregate amount of such
expenses for the TP's taxable year exceeds a specified percentage of
the TP's adjusted gross income (AGI) for that year. § 213(a). The
percentage of AGI that constitutes the floor currently is 7.5%, but
that figure is scheduled to increase to 10% of AGI for years beginning
after 2012.

Thus, for a year beginning prior to 2013, no deduction is allowed for
an amount of medical care expenses that is equal to 7.5% of the TP's
AGI for that year, and that amount is the "floor" for the medical
care expense deduction. Only the amount of medical expenses for
that year that exceeds 7.5% of the TP's AGI is deductible.

For a year beginning after 2012, the floor is 10% of the TP's AGI.
However, the increase to 10% of AGI does not apply in a taxable year
ending before January 1, 2017, to a TP who has attained the age of
65 prior to the end of that year or whose spouse has attained the age
of 65. § 213(f). For such a TP, the 7.5% of AGI floor will apply
instead of the 10% floor.

---

53. See **¶ 19.1100**.

54. Id.

Medical care expense deductions are itemized deductions, and so are allowed only if the TP elects to itemize his deductions. They are not miscellaneous itemized deductions, and so are not subject to the 2% of AGI limitation, and are not subject to the overall limitation that § 68 imposes on most itemized deductions for years beginning after 2012.[55]

Note that for the purpose of determining a TP's Alternative Minimum Tax, the floor for the deduction of medical expenses is 10% of the TP's AGI.[56] Once the scheduled 10% of AGI floor applies to a TP for regular tax purposes, that provision in the Alternative Minimum Tax will become inconsequential.

¶ **19.2200. Illustrations of Computation.** In each of the following illustrations assume that X has AGI of $15,000 for the year 2011. Thus, 7.5% of X's AGI for that year is $1,125. Assume also that the Alternative Minimum Tax is not applicable to the TP that year.

¶ **19.2210. Illustration 1.** In 2011, X's only medical care expense is the $800 premium he paid for medical insurance covering X, his wife, and their two dependent children. The premium payment qualifies as a medical care expense. The premium payment ($800) plus other medical care expenses ($0) is less than 7.5% of X's AGI ($1,125), so no deduction will be allowed.

¶ **19.2220. Illustration 2.** The same facts as in ¶ **19.2210** except that in 2011, X also expended $240 on medicines for his wife and his dependent son, and X was not compensated for those expenses. Of the amount expended by X on medicines, $50 was spent on cough medicine, aspirin, salves for muscle aches and similar items all of which can be purchased at a pharmacy without a physician's prescription. The remaining $190 was spent on drugs prescribed by X's doctor and which can be obtained only with a physician's prescription. Only the $190 spent on drugs for which a prescription was required qualify as a medical care expense. Since X's total medical care expense of $990 ($800 for insurance premiums plus $190 for prescribed drugs) is less than 7.5% of X's AGI ($1,125), no deduction is allowed.

¶ **19.2230. Illustration 3.** The same facts as in ¶ **19.2220** except that in 2011, X also paid a dentist $285 for dental work performed on X's dependent daughter. This payment qualifies as

55. See ¶ **19.3000**.
56. See ¶ **28.2240**.

a medical care expense. X's medical expenses for 2011 total $1,275 ($800 for insurance premiums plus $190 for prescribed drugs plus $285 dental expenses). This figure exceeds 7.5% of X's AGI ($1,125) by $150, and so X is allowed an itemized deduction of $150 for medical care expenses. This deduction is not subject to the 2% of AGI floor on miscellaneous itemized deductions.

Note that if X had had those expenses in 2013, and if both X and his wife are younger than 65, the floor would have been 10% of X's AGI, which equals $1,500. In that case, X's medical expenses would be less than the floor, and X would not be allowed any medical expense deduction for that year.

¶ 19.3000. **ITEMIZED DEDUCTION.** The medical expense deduction is an itemized deduction, but it is not a miscellaneous itemized deduction and so is not subject to the 2% of AGI floor. § 67(b)(5). The medical expense deduction is not subject to the overall limitation on itemized deduction that applies for years subsequent to 2012 when an individual's AGI exceeds a specified figure. § 68(c)(1). As previously stated,[57] medical expenses for a taxable year are deductible only to the extent that they exceed a percentage of TP's AGI (currently 7.5% and scheduled to rise to 10%), and so there is no reason to apply any additional limitations or floors.

¶ 19.4000. **BUSINESS EXPENSE.** An expense for services or goods which mitigate a TP's illness or physical defect may also be appropriate and helpful to the TP's conduct of his trade or business. For example, a handicapped TP who has to travel on business may need to have a helper accompany him to enable him to perform his duties. The helper's performance both mitigates the TP's illness and enables him to earn his income. The question may arise as to whether such an expense is deductible as a medical expense under § 213 or as a business expense under § 162. A "medical" business expense is not subject to the limitations on deductibility such as the percentage of AGI floor that applies to medical expenses.[58] The Commissioner has ruled that for such an expense to qualify as a business expense deduction (rather than as a medical expense) all three of the following elements must be present: (1) the nature of the TP's work clearly requires that he incur the expenses to satisfactorily perform such work; (2) the goods or services purchased by such expense are clearly not required or used, other than incidental-

---

57. ¶ 19.2100.

58. An unreimbursed employee "medical" business expense is subject to the same limitations as all other unreimbursed employee expenses. See §§ 62(a)(1), 67(a), 68(a).

ly, in the conduct of the TP's personal activities; and (3) the Code and regulations are otherwise silent as to the treatment of such an expense.[59]

¶ 19.5000. CAPITAL ACQUISITION FOR MEDICAL CARE. Although capital expenditures typically are not currently deductible for federal income tax purposes (they may be amortized in appropriate cases), capital acquisitions or improvements made primarily for medical care purposes are currently deductible medical expenses[60] if the purchased asset does not constitute a permanent improvement or betterment of property. Thus, the costs of purchasing eye glasses, a seeing eye dog, artificial teeth and limbs, a wheelchair, and crutches are currently deductible medical care expenses. Treas. Reg. § 1.213–1(e)(1)(iii). Such expenses are deducted (subject to the usual floor and limitations) in the year paid and are not amortized over the useful life of the asset.

When a capital acquisition that was made primarily for medical care purposes constitutes an improvement or a betterment of the TP's property, only the difference between the cost of the asset and the increase in value of the improved property as a consequence of the acquisition is a medical care expense.[61]

Since 1982,[62] the Commissioner has stated that he will not provide advance rulings on the factual question of whether a capital expenditure for an item that ordinarily would be used for personal, living, or family purposes (such as a swimming pool) was primarily motivated by medical care objectives.[63] Despite that asserted refusal to rule, in 1983 the Commissioner ruled that a TP was entitled to a medical care expense deduction for the amount by which the TP's cost of adding a swimming pool to his property exceeded the increase in value of the TP's property resulting from that addition.[64] The TP's purpose in adding the pool was to comply with his physician's instruction that TP swim several times a day as a treatment for osteoarthritis.

Also, in Rev. Rul. 87–106, the Commissioner listed thirteen specific expenditures which will qualify as a medical expense if made for the primary purpose of accommodating a personal residence to the handi-

---

59. Rev. Ruls. 75–316, 75–317. The provision in § 162(*l*) allowing a business expense deduction for certain medical insurance premiums paid by a self-employed person is discussed at ¶ **19.1620**.

60. Subject to the floor discussed at ¶ **19.2100**.

61. Rev. Rul. 83–33.

62. Rev. Proc. 82–65.

63. Rev. Proc. 2010–3 (Sec. 3.01(26)).

64. Rev. Rul. 83–33.

capped condition of the TP, his spouse, or one of his dependents. The ruling expressly states that the list is not intended to preclude a deduction for other such expenditures. The listed expenditures are considered by the Commissioner to be ones that generally do not increase the value of the residence, and so the entire amount of the listed expenditures is a deductible medical expense.

If part of a capital expenditure that otherwise qualifies as a medical care expense is made for a non-medical purpose, that portion of the expenditure will not be deductible. For example, if in constructing a swimming pool for a medical purpose, the TP expends an additional amount to make the pool more attractive so that it will not detract from the architectural and aesthetic splendor of the home, the additional amount is not a deductible expense.[65]

¶ 19.5100. Illustration 1: Improvement of Taxpayer's Property. X has a heart condition, and her doctor advised her to construct a bathroom on the first floor of her two-story home so that X will not have to climb the stairs more than once a day. X has the bathroom constructed at a cost of $5,000 for the primary purpose of protecting her health. The value of X's home is increased by $3,000 as a consequence of making the improvement; $2,000 of X's cost constitutes a deductible medical care expense (subject to the floor limitation).

¶ 19.5200. Illustration 2: Improvement of Rented Property. The same facts as those stated in **¶ 19.5100** except that X rents her two-story home from Y (an unrelated party), and X nevertheless builds the bathroom (with Y's permission) at a cost of $5,000. Since no property of X was improved by the expenditure, the entire $5,000 cost is a medical care expense.[66]

¶ 19.5300. Excessive Costs. If a TP constructs or purchases a facility that is more lavish than is needed for medical purposes, the additional cost incurred above that needed to construct or purchase a functionally adequate facility may not qualify as a medical expense. In *Ferris v. Commissioner*,[67] a TP constructed a swimming pool that was needed for medical purposes. The TP spent over $190,000 to construct the pool so that it was architecturally and aesthetically compatible with the TP's luxury home. The Court held that the

65. See ¶ **19.5300**.

66. Rev. Rul. 70–395.

67. 582 F.2d 1112 (7th Cir. 1978).

additional cost incurred to achieve that compatibility was not incurred primarily for medical purposes and so did not qualify for a medical expense deduction.[68]

¶ 19.5400. Illustration 3: Accommodation to Handicap. A TP cannot walk and is confined to a wheelchair. To accommodate his home to his handicap, TP incurred expenses to: (1) construct entrance and exit ramps to the residence; (2) widen interior doorways; (3) lower kitchen cabinets and equipment; and (4) install handrails throughout the house. All of those expenses qualify as medical expenses.[69]

¶ 19.6000. SPECIALLY PREPARED FOOD. The Commissioner contends that the cost of obtaining food or beverage which is prepared specially for medical reasons is not deductible if the food or beverage is taken as a substitute for food or beverage normally consumed by the TP and satisfies his nutritional requirements.[70] In those rulings, the Commissioner did not expressly discuss whether the TP could deduct, as a medical expense, the additional cost of obtaining specially prepared foods over the cost that he otherwise would have incurred for his food. The Tax Court has consistently held that the excess cost is deductible if the TP can prove that the special diet is needed for medical purposes and can prove the amount of extra cost incurred to have that diet. By way of analogy, the Commissioner has allowed a medical expense deduction for the extra cost incurred on obtaining a braille text book for a blind child over the cost of a regular printed edition.[71] Perhaps the Commissioner has not authorized a deduction for the excess cost of food because of the administrative difficulty of determining what amount the TP would have expended for his food if he did not need the special diet. But see Info 2001–0155 (June 29, 2001) in which the Service said that the excess of the cost of special meals required for medical reasons over the cost that the TP would have incurred for regular meals is deductible as a medical expense. The burden of the TP to prove the amount of the excess cost is difficult to satisfy.

The TPs who have litigated this issue have had mixed results. While the Tax Court consistently holds that the excess cost of such meals is a deductible medical expense, the TPs often have foundered on failing to meet the burden of proving the amount of the excess cost, if any.

68. See also Rev. Rul. 87–106.
69. Rev. Rul. 87–106.
70. Rev. Rul. 55–261; Rev. Rul. 2002–19.
71. Rev. Rul. 75–318.

Compare *Cohn v. Commissioner*,[72] (allowing a deduction for the additional cost of having a restaurant prepare salt-free food so as to comply with a salt-free diet) with *Harris v. Commissioner*,[73] (denying a deduction for the cost of specially prepared food for a diabetic); *Huff v. Commissioner*,[74] (denying a deduction for the cost of vitamins and food supplements): *Massa v. Comissioner*,[75] (denying a deduction to a TP with Crohn's disease for the cost of a special diet because, among other reasons, the TP failed to prove any excess cost).

In *Randolph v. Commissioner*,[76] the Tax Court allowed a medical expense deduction for the additional cost incurred by the TP in obtaining chemically uncontaminated food where the TP was allergic to a variety of chemicals found in pesticides and herbicides. The Court determined the amount deductible by comparing the TP's cost for the organic (uncontaminated) food he obtained with statistics showing the average price of similar contaminated food in the Chicago area. Accord, *Von Kalb v. Commissioner*,[77] allowing a deduction for the additional cost of a high-protein diet required by the TP for medical reasons. In *Van Kalb*, the TP was allowed to deduct the additional amount she spent on groceries to meet her special dietary needs, but she was not allowed to deduct any portion of the amount she spent at restaurants for meals. The TP's evidence of an additional cost for meals was provided by comparing the cost of her groceries to those of her friends.

To qualify for a deduction, a TP must prove: (1) that he has a specific medical condition that requires a special diet, and (2) the actual amount of the additional cost incurred because of that dietary need.[78] This is a difficult burden to meet, especially as to the requirement of showing the additional cost incurred. Generally, when a TP has prevailed, the court has applied the *Cohan* rule that allows a court to make an estimate of an amount that cannot be established with precision.[79]

If the additional cost of specially prepared food can qualify as a medical expense, only 50% of that additional cost is deductible. § 274(n).

72.   38 T.C. 387 (1962), Nonacq.

73.   46 T.C. 672 (1966).

74.   69 T.C.M. 2551 (1995).

75.   77 T.C.M. 1484 (1999), aff'd 208 F.3d 226 (10th Cir. 2000).

76.   67 T.C. 481 (1976).

77.   37 T.C.M. 1511 (1978).

78.   *Nehus v. Commissioner*, 68 T.C.M. 1503 (1994), aff'd without opinion, 108 F.3d 338 (9th Cir. 1997).

79.   *Cohan v. Commissioner*, 39 F.2d 540 (2d Cir. 1930).

¶ **19.7000. HEALTH SAVINGS ACCOUNTS.** Many health coverage plans provided by employers for their employees have low deductible features so that the employee will bear only a small amount of any medical expense incurred. That circumstance gives the employee little incentive to make a cost benefit calculation when determining whether to undergo a medical procedure. This leads to expensive expenditures for unnecessary medical procedures.

In an effort to remedy that situation, in 1997, Congress adopted § 220 to provide special tax treatment for "Medical Savings Accounts." In general, this provision permitted an employee who was a participant in a high deductible medical plan provided by his employer to deduct contributions to a fund which would be available to pay for medical expenses not covered by the employer's plan. The amount deductible is subject to a dollar limitation. To the extent that the funds in the Account are used to pay for qualified medical services, they are not taxable to the employee. The purpose of this provision and of its replacement provisions is to encourage employers to use high deductible insurance plans and to provide tax relief for employees to fill in the gap in their insurance coverage with their own funds. Since the employees will be using their own funds to pay for medical services, it is expected that they will be more prudent in their purchase of those services.

The name of Medical Savings Accounts was changed in the year 2000 to "Archer MSAs." § 220. The Archer MSA's provision was replaced in the year 2003 by the "Health Savings Accounts" provision, which is set forth in § 223. While there are differences between the Health Savings Accounts and the Archer MSAs, the general operation of the two is similar. The Archer MSAs provision continues to apply to those who previously set up those accounts. § 220(i). If an employee wishes to establish a new account, to qualify for a beneficial tax treatment, the new account must be established as a Health Savings Account under § 223.

¶ **19.8000. REIMBURSED EXPENSES.** The medical expenses of many TPs are paid wholly or partly by insurance that is purchased by the TP himself or by his employer on his behalf. In general, when a TP's medical costs are paid by such insurance or directly paid by the TP's employer, the TP will not recognize gross income unless the TP had previously taken a deduction for those expenses. Note that there is no floor or dollar limitation as to the amount that can be so excluded from a TP's gross income.

¶ **19.8100. Medical Insurance.** When a TP purchases a medical or accident insurance policy with his own funds, any benefits (including reimbursements) received by him under the policy because of an accident or illness will generally be excluded from the TP's gross income. § 104(a)(3). Even if the TP had previously deducted the payment of premiums for the policy, that will not prevent the exclusion of the benefits from gross income. There is no requirement that the benefits from the policy be a reimbursement for expenses borne by the TP; the statute requires only that the benefits be provided for a personal injury or sickness. However, medical benefits will be included in the TP's gross income to the extent that they constitute reimbursements of medical expenses that had previously been deducted by the TP. § 104(a); Treas. Reg. § 1.213–1(g).

¶ 19.8110.   **Insurance Speculation.** A practice arose of engaging in so-called "insurance speculation," in which multiple medical insurance policies are purchased by a TP who hopes to become ill enough to require hospitalization so that he can reap a profit from collecting payments on all of his policies. Some hospitalization insurance plans provide for payments to the insured without regard to other coverage the insured may have, and so it is possible to earn a profit from an illness. If a TP who engages in insurance speculation is legitimately hospitalized for an illness, current law does not cause any of the insurance proceeds collected by the TP to be included in his income—i.e., there is no limitation in § 104(a)(3) that restricts the exclusion from income to the amount of expenses actually borne by the TP. However, in such cases, a question can arise as to whether the TP's illness was bona fide. It is possible for an insurance speculator to conspire with a doctor to receive a diagnosis of illness and an order for hospitalization; if that is found to have occurred, none of the insurance payments received by the TP will be excluded from income.

In *Dodge v. Commissioner*,[80] the TP had collected from a number of medical insurance policies that had been purchased as part of an insurance speculation program. The Tax Court held that TP can exclude the insurance proceeds only if the claims made on the policies were legitimate and only if the claims related to actual injuries or sickness of the TP. The court further held that the TP has the burden of proof on those issues, and that TP's burden is not satisfied by the fact that the insurance companies honored the TP's claims. The court held that the circumstantial evidence in that case raised serious questions concerning the legitimacy of

80.   96 T.C. 172 (1991).

taxpayer's "alleged injuries and sickness." The court found that the testimony given by taxpayer and by his doctor lacked credibility. The court was not convinced that the insurance proceeds "related to actual, legitimate personal injuries or sickness." The court held that the insurance proceeds are included in TP's gross income.

¶ 19.8200. Disability Insurance. When a TP purchases a disability insurance policy with his own funds, any disability benefits received by him under the policy are excluded from his gross income. § 104(a)(3). That exclusion is an aspect of the fact that § 104(a)(3) does not require that the benefits from the policy be a reimbursement of expenses. Disability benefits received by a TP under an insurance policy are included in gross income if the premiums were paid by the employer since § 104(a)(3) does not apply then.[81]

¶ 19.8300. Workmen's Compensation Benefits. Generally, any amount received by a TP under a workmen's compensation act as compensation for personal injuries or sickness will be excluded from gross income. § 104(a)(1). However, to the extent that such compensation constitutes a reimbursement of medical expenses that were previously deducted by the TP, the payments will be included in gross income.

¶ 19.8400. Premiums Paid By Employer for Medical Insurance. Premiums paid by an employer for accident or health insurance to compensate employees for personal injuries or sickness generally are excluded from the gross income of the employees. § 106. Similarly, amounts paid by an employer to fund an accident or health plan for employees is excluded from the employees' gross income. In such cases, if the employees are to be taxed at all, it will be when they receive benefits from the plan; and, as shown below, even then the benefits usually are excluded from an employee's gross income.

For certain kinds of plans, there are limitations on the amount of the employer's payment or contribution that can be excluded from the employee's income. For example, the amount of contribution to a HSA or an Archer MSA plan for an employee that is excluded from the employee's income is subject to a ceiling. § 106(b)(1). There is no exclusion from income for employer-provided coverage of long-term care services if the coverage is provided through a flexible spending or similar arrangement. § 106(c).

---

81. Rev. Rul. 73–155.

There are no anti-discrimination requirements as a condition to the exclusion of an employer's payment of insurance premiums or contributions to an accident and health plan. Consequently, insofar as premium payments are concerned, the insurance coverage can discriminate in favor of high-salaried employees.

¶ 19.8500. Employee Health and Accident Plans. When an employer provides a health or accident plan for an employee, or when an employer pays the premiums on an accident or medical insurance policy covering an employee and the employee's family (which premium payments were not included in the employee's income), the tax consequences from receiving benefits under that plan or policy depend upon the nature of the benefits.

¶ 19.8510. Benefits Attributable to Employer. If an employee receives health or accident benefits directly from an employer or from a third party who was compensated by the employer to provide those benefits (and the compensation was not included in the employee's gross income), the extent of the exclusion of the benefits in the employee's income is determined by the provisions of § 105. See §§ 104(a)(3), 105. The statute provides that such benefits will be included in the employee's income unless certain statutory requirements are satisfied. § 105(a). Despite the ominous tone of that provision, most benefits will comply with the requirements and so are excluded.

One of the requirements that must be met is that the benefit must either be paid pursuant to an insurance policy or the benefit must be payable under an accident or health plan that was previously adopted by the employer. § 105(e). The plan can be informal; it need not be written nor need the employee have the right to enforce the benefits provided by the plan. However, if the employee has no enforceable right to the benefits, then, at the time of the employee's illness or injury, the employee must have been included within the plan and the employee must have had actual or constructive knowledge of the plan (i.e., information about the plan was reasonably available to the employee). Treas. Reg. § 1.105–5(a).

While the requirement that the benefit to the employee be made pursuant either to insurance or to an accident or health plan is a *sine qua non* for excluding such a benefit from the employee's income, it is not sufficient. The additional requirements that must be met depend upon the nature of the benefit received.

These additional requirements are described below.[82]

Note that a self-employed person will not be treated as an "employee" for purposes of § 105, and so no health or accident benefits received by a self-employed person can be excluded from income under that section. § 105(g). However, under proper circumstances, the benefits may be excluded by § 104(a)(3), which is a more expansive provision than § 105.

¶ 19.8511. Reimbursement or Payment of Medical Expenses. Amounts paid under an employee health or accident plan, or under an employer-paid insurance policy, will be excluded from the employee's gross income to the extent that such payments are made in satisfaction of, or to reimburse the employee for, undeducted medical care costs that were incurred by the employee for the medical care of the employee, the employee's spouse or dependents. § 105(b). For purposes of this provision, a "dependent" is defined in § 152 (the dependent exemption provision), but some of the restrictions in § 152 do not apply.[83] § 105(b).

The requirement that the benefit be a reimbursement means that only amounts paid for medical care expenses that were actually borne by the employee are excluded from income. This requirement prevents the collection of multiple benefits from several insurance policies for the same expense, and so precludes the use of employer-provided insurance in an insurance speculation scheme.[84]

For purposes of § 105(b), the term "medical care costs" is defined in § 213(d) and is not subject to the limitation on the deduction of medicines and drugs in § 213(b).[85] However, an amendment to the Code that was adopted in 2010 imposes a restriction on the reimbursement of medicine and drugs that can be excluded from the employee's income. Under § 106(f), a reimbursement of a medicine or drug is excluded from income only if the medicine or drug was prescribed by a physician or is insulin. The medicine or drug need not be one that can only be obtained by prescription. So, the reimbursement for the cost of

82. ¶¶ **19.8511—19.8513**.

83. See ¶ **19.0000**.

84. See ¶ **19.8110**.

85. Rev. Rul. 2003–102.

an over-the-counter drug or medicine will be excluded provided that it was prescribed by a physician.[86] Dietary supplements (e.g., vitamins) are not medical care expenses, and so the reimbursement of their cost will be included in the employee's income.[87]

If such payments reimburse an employee for medical expenses that the employee had deducted on his income tax return for a prior year, the reimbursement will be included in the employee's gross income to the extent that the prior deductions were allowed to the employee. § 105(b).

¶ 19.8512. **Anti-discrimination Requirement.** If the reimbursement or payment of medical expenses of a type described above are made from a plan of which the employer is a self-insurer, then such payments to or for the benefit of a so-called "highly compensated individual" are subject to certain anti-discrimination requirements. § 105(h). In addition to benefits, the selection of participants in the plan must not discriminate in favor of highly compensated individuals, and the statute describes what participation is required to satisfy that requirement.

A self-insured plan includes any plan for which reimbursement is not provided by an accident or health insurance policy. § 105(h)(6). See Treas. Reg. § 1.105–11(b). A "highly compensated individual" is an individual who either: (1) is one of the five highest paid officers of the employer, (2) after applying certain stock attribution rules, owns more than 10% of the stock of a corporate employer, or (3) is among the highest paid 25% of all employees. § 105(h)(5). The exclusion of certain employees is not taken into account. For example, employees who have not completed 3 years of service, or who have not attained the age of 25, or who are part-time or seasonal employees can be excluded. § 105(h)(3)(B).

A reimbursement or payment from a self-insured plan to a highly compensated individual will not be fully excluded from the employee's income unless the self-insured plan does not discriminate in favor of highly compensated individuals. If the self-insured plan does so discriminate, then the payments or reimbursements made to a highly compensated individual can

---

86. See ¶ **19.1110**.

87. Rev. Rul. 2003–102.

be excluded only to the extent that they do not exceed the benefits that are payable under the plan for employees who are not highly compensated. In other words, to the extent that a highly compensated individual receives benefits in excess of what would be payable to a less compensated employee, the excess cannot be excluded. The manner in which the excess amount is determined is described in § 105(h)(7) and in Treas. Reg. § 1.105–11(e). Note that a reimbursement for routine medical diagnostic procedures for the employee (not for his dependent) is not subject to the anti-discrimination requirements. Treas. Reg. § 1.105–11(g). Note also that if a plan is discriminatory, that will have no effect on the exclusion of benefits provided to or for the benefit of employees who are not highly compensated individuals. Finally, note that if medical reimbursements are paid under an insurance policy the premiums for which were paid by the employer, the anti-discrimination requirements are inapplicable since the payments or reimbursements are not made under a self-insured plan.

¶ 19.8513. **Payments Unrelated to Medical Expenses and to Absence From Work.** Gross income does not include amounts received under an employee accident or health plan (or an employer paid insurance policy) to the extent that such amounts constitute compensation for permanent loss (or the loss of use) of a member or function of the body, or the permanent disfigurement of the employee, his spouse, or his dependent. § 105(c). To qualify for this exclusion the compensation must be computed by reference to the injury sustained and without regard to the period of the employee's absence from work. The meaning of § 105(c) is explored in *Watts v. United States*.[88] In *Watts*, the TP was prevented from continuing work due to severe hypertension. In denying the TP an exclusion, the court held that the TP had to show a permanent loss (or loss of the use) of a member or function of the body or a permanent disfigurement for § 105(c) to be applicable. For a similar view, note Rev. Rul. 63–181, where a lump sum disability payment to a TP suffering from terminal cancer that totally and permanently disabled him was excluded from gross income under § 105(c). The Commissioner ruled that the disability was so acute as to constitute a permanent loss (or loss of the use) of a member or function of the TP's body.

88. 703 F.2d 346 (9th Cir. 1983).

The payment involved must not be determined by reference to the period of the employee's absence from work. Note that the exclusion of payments described in this paragraph is *not* subject to any anti-discrimination requirements.

CHAPTER TWENTY

CHARITABLE CONTRIBUTIONS

¶ **20.0000.** **CHARITABLE CONTRIBUTIONS IN GENERAL.** Under § 170, contributions or gifts of cash or other property to, or for the use of, qualified charitable organizations may be deductible from the donor's AGI as an itemized deduction. The meaning of "gift" or "contribution" is discussed in ¶ **20.1100.** As noted there, in this context, the two words are synonymous and are used interchangeably.

Only gifts of property are deductible; a contribution of services is not deductible.[1] Unless specifically provided otherwise, the amount of a charitable gift or contribution is equal to the fair market value of the donated property at the time of the contribution. The special treatment accorded to gifts to a charity of appreciated property (i.e., property whose value exceeds its basis) is discussed at ¶¶ **20.2300–20.2434–2.** The meaning of "fair market value" is discussed at ¶ **9.3240.** In *Anselmo v. Commissioner,*[2] the court affirmed the Tax Court's determination that the value of a contributed item of property is the price of such item in the market in which items of that type are most commonly sold to the public. The court also concluded that in determining fair market value, the choice of the relevant market is a question of fact. See Treas. Reg. § 1.170A–1(c)(2).

Note that the deductibility of contributions to an organization is determined by § 170. The tax exempt status of an organization (i.e., whether it is taxable on its income) is determined by other sections of the Code—principally § 501.

¶ **20.1000.** **DEFINITION OF CHARITABLE CONTRIBUTION.** As defined in § 170(c), a charitable contribution means a contribution or gift which is paid to or for the use of:

(a) a state, a United States' possession, any political subdivision of any of the foregoing, the United States, or the District of Columbia, provided that the contribution or gift is made exclusively for public purposes;

1. Treas. Reg. § 1.170A–1(g). See ¶ **20.5200.**
2. 757 F.2d 1208 (11th Cir. 1985).

(b) a corporation, trust, community chest, fund, or foundation

(i) created or organized in the United States or any possession of the United States, or under the law of the United States, or of any state or possession of the United States or of the District of Columbia;

(ii) organized and operated exclusively for religious, charitable, scientific, literary, or educational purposes, or to foster national or international amateur sports competition (but if it is not a "qualified amateur sports organization" as defined in § 501(j), only if no part of its activities involve the provision of athletic facilities or equipment), or for the prevention of cruelty to children or animals;

(iii) no part of the earnings of which inures to the benefit of any private individual or shareholder;

(iv) no substantial part of the activities of which is attempting to influence legislation, but certain charities will be permitted a greater amount of lobbying and lobbying-type expenses if the charity makes a valid election under § 501(h); and

(v) which does not participate or intervene in any political campaign on behalf of, or in opposition to, any candidate for public office; and

(c) certain other organizations (e.g., veterans organizations, fraternal lodges, non-profit cemeteries) listed in § 170(c)(3), (4), and (5).

¶ 20.1100. Contribution or Gift. A "contribution" or "gift" to a charity is a payment of cash or property without adequate consideration and made for the purpose of conferring a benefit on the charity.[3] For purposes of the deduction, the words "contribution" and "gift" are synonymous, and are used interchangeably.[4] Since the meanings of the two words are the same, we will focus on the meaning of the word "gift."

In determining whether an uncompensated transfer to an individual is excluded by § 102 from the transferee's gross income as a gift, the definition of a "gift" was established by the Supreme Court's decision in *Commissioner v. Duberstein*.[5] Under the *Duberstein* rule, the principal characteristic of a private gift is that it was made by the

---

3. *Mason v. United States*, 513 F.2d 25 (7th Cir. 1975).

4. *DeJong v. Commissioner*, 309 F.2d 373, 376 (9th Cir. 1962).

5. 363 U.S. 278 (1960).

transferor out of "detached and disinterested generosity."[6] The courts are divided as to whether the same standard is to be applied in determining whether a transfer to a charity constitutes a gift for charitable deduction purposes. Some courts have applied the *Duberstein* standard, and others have rejected it.[7] While the Supreme Court has not expressly passed on this issue, its opinions in *United States v. American Bar Endowment*,[8] and, *Hernandez v. Commissioner*,[9] suggest that the Court does not favor the use of the *Duberstein* standard for this purpose. Indeed, the Ninth Circuit, which adopted the *Duberstein* standard in the *DeJong* case, subsequently held that that standard is not applicable when the transferor to the charity is a corporation.[10]

If the *Duberstein* standard is inapplicable, what then is the standard for determining a charitable gift? The standard is whether the transferor received a substantial *quid pro quo* flowing from the transfer. In *Hernandez v. Commissioner*,[11] the Supreme Court said that gifts are "payments made with no expectation of a financial return commensurate with the amount of the gift." The cumulative benefits, both direct and indirect, that the transferor received are taken into account, but only benefits that have financial significance are considered. In other words, psychic benefits, such as enjoying the pleasure derived from making the gift, are ignored. Also, the benefits that the transferor shared with other members of the general public are ignored. For example, a gift to a theater company that allows it to perform for the general public is not treated as a benefit to the transferor merely because he can enjoy their performances along with other members of the public.

Indirect benefits are taken into account. An example of an indirect benefit is found in *Singer Company v. United States*.[12] In that case, Singer sold sewing machines at a significant discount to a number of charities. The question was whether the company could take a

---

6. Id. at 285. See ¶¶ **6.2000–6.2140**.

7. Compare, *DeJong v. Commissioner*, 309 F.2d 373, 377–379 (9th Cir. 1962); *Fausner v. Commissioner*, 55 T.C. 620 (1971) (adopting the *Duberstein* standard) with *Crosby Valve & Gage Co. v. Commissioner*, 380 F.2d 146 (1st Cir. 1967). But see, *Singer Co. v. United States*, 449 F.2d 413, 422 (Ct. Cl. 1971) (rejecting that standard).

8. 477 U.S. 105 (1986).

9. 490 U.S. 680 (1989).

10. *United States v. Transamerica Corp.*, 392 F.2d 522, 524 (9th Cir. 1968).

11. 490 U.S. 680, 690 (1989).

12. 449 F.2d 413, 424 (Ct. Cl. 1971).

charitable deduction for the amount of the discount.[13] The court allowed the company a deduction for the discount it gave on the sale of sewing machines to certain charities (such as churches, the Red Cross, and hospitals), but denied a deduction for the discounts given to schools. The court held that Singer obtained an indirect benefit from its bargain sales to the schools in that many of the pupils who used the sewing machines would become attached to them and would constitute a pool of potential future customers.

The determination of whether a transferor has received a substantial benefit is made by examining "the external features of the transaction" rather than by conducting "imprecise inquiries into the motivations" of the transferor.[14] The receipt of religious benefits in exchange for a transfer poses special issues which are discussed at ¶ **20.1210**.

¶ **20.1200. Dual Payments.** A deduction may be allowed for a transfer to a charity even though the transferor receives consideration for the transfer if the value of the property transferred to the charity is greater than the value of the consideration received. A transfer of that nature is called a "dual payment."[15] The transfer is partly a sale or purchase and partly a contribution to the charity. The dual payment transaction is similar to the part-gift, part-sale transaction that applies to a bargain sale to an individual for a donative purpose as described in ¶¶ **6.7000–6.7120**. Of course, the amount of the charitable deduction for a dual payment is the amount by which the value transferred to the charity exceeds the value of the consideration received. If the TP transferred appreciated property to the charity, the statutory limitations on the amount of deduction permitted for contributions of appreciated property will apply.[16]

A donor to a charity might receive a relatively small benefit from the contribution. It would be administratively impractical to take into account every miniscule benefit that accompanies a contribution. Consequently, the Service has agreed to ignore benefits received by a donor that are "insubstantial." This is a kind of *de minimis* rule. The standards for determining what benefits are substantial are discussed at ¶ **20.1300**.

---

13. When property is transferred to a charity for less than adequate consideration, the transaction is referred to as a "dual payment," and that type of transaction is discussed at ¶ **20.1200**.

14. *Hernandez v. Commissioner*, 490 U.S. 680, 691 (1989).

15. See *United States v. American Bar Endowment*, 477 U.S. 105, 119 (1986).

16. See ¶¶ **20.2300, 20.2400–20.2434**.

For a transfer to a charity for substantial consideration to qualify as a dual payment for which a charitable deduction is allowable, a two-pronged test must be satisfied. First, the transfer to the charity will be deductible only to the extent that it exceeds the market value of the benefits received in return. Second, the transferor must have intended to transfer that excess to the charity as a gift—that is, the transferor deliberately transferred excess value to the charity for the purpose of making a gift. This two-pronged test was first stated in Rev. Rul. 67–246, and it was expressly adopted by the Supreme Court in *United States v. American Bar Endowment.*[17] If a TP fails either of those two prongs, no deduction will be allowable. The TP has the burden of proving that the transfer satisfies both prongs. While the second prong raises a subjective issue, resting on the transferor's intent, the Supreme Court has emphasized that the determination of that issue should be made exclusively on the basis of identifiable external facts.[18]

It can be difficult to apply both of those prongs when the benefits received are ones that are not purchased in a commercial market. This problem is especially difficult to resolve when the benefits received are religious services.[19]

As noted above, a donor's receipt of a benefit from making a gift to a charity will be ignored if the benefit is insubstantial.

¶ **20.1210. Intangible Religious Benefits.** In *Hernandez v. Commissioner,*[20] the Supreme Court rejected the contention that the receipt of intangible religious benefits is to be ignored in determining whether a payment to a religious organization is deductible. The Court refused to adopt a blanket exception for intangible religious benefits. The *Hernandez* case involved religious benefits provided by the Church of Scientology for a stated fee.

The Church of Scientology treats the human spirit by providing "auditing" and "training" sessions to its members, which constitute one-on-one counseling and the education of a member by a person known as an "auditor." The auditing process is part of the religious teaching and practice of the organization. It is intended

---

17. 477 U.S. 105, 117–119 (1986). See also, Treas. Reg. § 1.70A–1(h)(1).

18. *Hernandez v. Commissioner,* 490 U.S. 680, 691 (1989).

19. The receipt of intangible religious benefits is discussed at ¶ **20.1210**.

20. 490 U.S. 680 (1989).

to identify the spiritual difficulty of the member and to help the member deal with that difficulty. The organization sets fixed fees for these auditing sessions, the amount of which varied with the length and sophistication of the sessions. These fixed fees were referred to by the organization as a "price" or "fixed contribution." The prices were set forth in schedules promulgated by the organization.

In a 1978 ruling, the Commissioner determined that the fees paid by Church of Scientology members for auditing were not deductible as charitable contributions.[21] For purposes of considering the merits of that ruling, it can be assumed that the Church of Scientology qualifies as a religious organization. The 1978 ruling was inconsistent with the long-standing practice of the Service to allow a charitable deduction for fixed payments where the quid pro quo for the payment was exclusively a religious benefit. For example, the Service ruled in 1970 that "pew rents, building fund assessments and periodic dues paid to a church" are deductible contributions.[22] The 1970 ruling superseded and was merely a restatement of the published position taken by the Service more than 50 years earlier.[23] While no other rulings were promulgated, there is every reason to believe that the Service allowed deductions for set fees to attend Jewish services at High Holy Days, and tithes paid by Mormons and for similar fees.

The question of deductibility of auditing fees came to a head when the issue reached the Supreme Court in *Hernandez v. Commissioner*.[24] In a 5–2 decision, the Court held that the fees were not deductible. The Court rejected the TP's contention that the receipt of an intangible religious benefit does not constitute consideration that precludes a charitable deduction for a payment to the charity. As pointed out by the dissents in *Hernandez*, a problem with treating religious benefits, especially intangible religious benefits, as consideration in dual payment cases is that those benefits are not bought and sold in a commercial market, and there is no reasonable means to determine their dollar value.

In commercial transactions, if a fee is expressly set for a service, and if the parties are at arms' length, the tax law treats the value of the service as equal to the amount of the fee. But, it is doubtful

---

21. Rev. Rul. 78–189, *obsoleted by* Rev. Rul. 93–73.

22. Rev. Rul. 70–47.

23. A.R.M. 2, 1 Cum. Bull. 150 (1919).

24. 490 U.S. 680 (1989).

that that approach is appropriate for determining the value of a religious service for which a set fee is paid. Even though the religious organization established a specified fee for the service, the transaction is not at arms' length because the TP may have donative motives for agreeing to pay the amount of that fee—i.e., the TP may be willing to pay the stated amount because part or all of it represents a gift to the organization. It is difficult to determine how much of the fee is a gift and how much of the fee (if any) is paid in order to receive the service. The difficulty of characterizing payments ostensibly made for religious services is similar to the problem of characterizing a "contribution" that a TP makes to a college when the "contribution" entitles the TP to purchase tickets to athletic events. As we shall see, Congress expressly allows a TP to deduct 80% of that contribution.[25]

A similar issue arises when a charity auctions items or services that were donated to the charity for that purpose. The bidders in such auctions typically are people who have reasons to make a contribution to the charity. The successful bid often is significantly higher than the value of the item or service purchased. This could be treated as a dual payment,[26] in which the excess payment over the value of the item constitutes a charitable gift. The value of the item or service should not be deemed to be equal to the amount of the successful bid. In other words, the price agreed upon by the buyer and seller is not determinative of the value of the item or service. While the commercial value of the purchased item or service can often be determined because it is sold on the commercial market, this is not always the case. For example, if the bidder purchased the opportunity to have dinner with a prominent author, how is the value of that opportunity to be determined? The point is that the amount paid by the bidder is not a reliable indicator of the actual value. However, a TP who makes a purchase at such an auction will have a difficult burden to establish that the two-pronged requirements of the dual payment circumstance are satisfied.[27] Perhaps, the presence of a celebrity will not be taken into account and only the value of the meal will be considered.

In *Hernandez*, the TP raised on appeal for the first time the contention that the Service's position on auditing fees was discriminatory in that the Service allowed deductions for fees

25. § 170(*l*). See ¶ **20.1240**.

26. See ¶ **20.1200**.

27. Id.

charged by other religious groups. The Court held that the record before it was inadequate for the Court to resolve the issue of whether there was an administrative inconsistency and whether that should bar the government from denying a deduction in that case. The two dissenters in *Hernandez* emphasized the administrative inconsistency of the Service's positions.

A TP is not entitled to receive a benefit contrary to the tax law merely because that treatment was erroneously accorded to another by the Service at some time in the past.[28] However, if the Service has consistently allowed a benefit to one class of TPs, there is support for the view that the benefit cannot then be denied to a similarly situated person unless the current denial of the benefit is the consequence of a change of position by the Service.[29]

The question of administrative inconsistency in the Service's treatment of the Church of Scientology was subsequently raised by the TPs in *Powell v. United States*.[30]

The TPs' claim that the Service wrongly disallowed their deduction for payment to the Church of Scientology had been dismissed by the district court. The Court of Appeals held that the claim of administrative inconsistency made a valid cause of action if factually established, and so the court vacated the district court's order and remanded the case to the district court. The Service then backed away from its victory in *Hernandez*; and, in a nonpublic agreement with the Church of Scientology, the Service agreed to allow members of that church to deduct fees paid for auditing and training sessions. In that same year, the Service issued Rev. Rul. 93–73 in which it declared obsolete its earlier Revenue Ruling 78–189 which had stated that no charitable contribution deduction will be allowed for payments to the Church of Scientology for auditing and similar services. The 1993 ruling does not include any discussion as to what position the Service now takes on this issue; it merely revokes the 1978 ruling as obsolete. The meaning of obsoleting a ruling is described by the Service in its Cumulative Bulletins. In 2008–1 Cum. Bull. iii, the Service states as follows:

---

28. *Mid–Continent Supply Co. v. Commissioner*, 571 F.2d 1371 (5th Cir. 1978).

29. *Powell v. United States*, 945 F.2d 374 (11th Cir. 1991). Cf., *Church of Scientology Flag Service Org. v. City of Clearwater*, 2 F.3d 1514 (11th Cir. 1993). But see, *Sklar v. Commissioner*, 282 F.3d 610 (9th Cir. 2002).

30. 945 F.2d 374 (11th Cir. 1991).

Obsoleted describes a previously published ruling that is not considered determinative with respect to future transactions.

The term is most commonly used in a ruling that lists previously published rulings that are obsoleted because of changes in law or regulations. A ruling may also be obsoleted because the substance has been included in regulations that were adopted subsequently.

The Service has not said why its 1978 ruling is now obsolete. After all, the Supreme Court sustained the ruling in the *Hernandez* case. But, in *Hernandez*, the Court declined to pass on the question of whether the 1978 ruling was inconsistent with the administrative position that the Service has taken with respect to other religious organizations; and the Eleventh Circuit subsequently held that the Service is not permitted to treat one religion differently from others.[31] It would appear that the Service might have come to recognize the inconsistency in its positions and had decided not to apply the *Hernandez* principle to payments to any religious organization for religious benefits. That possibility has been negated by the position the government took in a subsequent litigation. In a 2008 decision, the Ninth Circuit rejected the TP's contention that a payment to a religious organization for a purely religious benefit is deductible.[32]

If the Service's agreement with the Church of Scientology were extended to other religions, it would raises questions as to the treatment of fees paid to attend a parochial school providing both religious and secular education or for solely religious education such as a fee to attend Sunday school. That issue is discussed next.

¶ 20.1220. Tuition or Fees for Religious and Secular Education. The question arose whether a "contribution" to a religious organization that operates a school in which the TP's child attends, and for which no or inadequate tuition is charged, can qualify for a charitable deduction, and, if so, in what amount? In *DeJong v. Commissioner*,[33] which preceded *Hernandez* by some 27 years, the TPs claimed a charitable deduction for contributions to a religious organization that owned and operated a grammar and high school at which two of the TP's children attended. The school charged no tuition, and raised most of its funds by solicit-

---

31. *Powell v. United States*, 945 F.2d 374 (11th Cir. 1991).

32. *Sklar v. Commissioner*, 549 F.3d 1252 (9th Cir. 2008).

33. 309 F.2d 373 (9th Cir. 1962).

ing contributions from parents of enrolled students. The TPs contributed $1,075 to the school, and the Service allowed all but $400 of it as a charitable deduction. The Service treated $400 as the value of the two children's education, and denied a deduction for that amount. The Tax Court and the Ninth Circuit upheld the Service's denial of that deduction. The courts and the Service treated the claimed "contribution" as a dual payment, only part of which is deductible.[34]

A related question is whether the payment of tuition to a parochial school that provides both secular and religious education can be allocated between the secular and religious benefits the children receive, and a deduction allowed for the payment for the religious portion of the education. Two recent cases involving this situation were brought by the same persons against the Commissioner.[35] For convenience, we will refer to those two cases as *Sklar I* and *Sklar II* respectively.

The TPs in both *Sklar* cases were Orthadox Jews who sent their children to Jewish parochial schools. The students devoted 55% of their time in school to religious education. The TPs claimed a deduction for 55% of the tuition they paid to the schools on the ground that it was paid for religious education. In both cases, the Ninth Circuit affirmed the Tax Court's decision denying any deduction to the TPs.

In *Sklar I*, while the court discussed several issues, its holding rested on the ground that the TPs did not meet their burden of proving that the benefit of the secular part of the students' education had a market value that was less than the amount of their tuition. The court held that the value of the secular education was to be determined by reference to tuition paid to private schools rather than to the zero cost of a public school education In other words, the court held that the TPs failed to satisfy their burden to show that the contribution met the first prong of the two-pronged test for deducting part of a dual payment.[36]

While the court's opinion in *Sklar I* suggests that it would not allow a deduction for the cost of religious education, the court did not pass on that issue. It was not necessary for the court to reach

---

34. See ¶ **20.1200** for a discussion of dual payments.

35. *Sklar v. Commissioner*, 282 F.3d 610 (9th Cir. 2002); *Sklar v. Commissioner*, 549 F.3d 1252 (9th Cir. 2008).

36. See ¶ **20.1200**.

that issue since the TPs failed to satisfy the two-pronged test for dual payments.

Even if it were decided to allow a deduction for the cost of religious education, a question would arise whether there are not secular aspects of that education. For example, history and languages can be part of a religious education. How can those subjects be distinguished from secular education just because they are taught in the context of religious training?[37]

The TPs in *Sklar I* also raised the issue of administrative inconsistency. They contended that the Service's agreement to allow the members of the Church of Scientology to deduct the fees paid for religious education (that is, auditing and training) made it unconstitutional for the Service to deny a deduction for the cost of religious training provided by other religions. The holding in *Sklar* avoided that issue by finding that the TPs had failed to establish the value of the secular education that their children received. However, the language of the majority opinion in that case, and of the concurring opinion of Judge Silverman, indicates that the court would reject the TPs' contention if the court were subsequently to reach that issue; and the court did reject it in *Sklar II*. Instead of expanding the Service's concession to other religions, the court in *Sklar II* indicated that it would hold unconstitutional the Service's allowance of a deduction to members of the Church of Scientology as violating the Establishment clause.

In the subsequent *Sklar II* case, the Sklars produced evidence showing the cost of private school education in their area.[38] That evidence failed to sway either the Tax Court or the Ninth Circuit, both of whom denied the claim for a deduction. The evidence showed that the tuition that the Sklars paid was greater than some private schools and less than others. The Sklars therefore failed to show that the value of the secular education their children received was less than the tuition they paid, and so they failed to satisfy the first prong of the dual payment requirements.

¶ **20.1230. Tickets as Compensation.** If a TP who makes a contribution to a charity receives tickets to a performance as a

---

37. For more discussion of these issues, see Douglas A. Kahn and Jeffrey H. Kahn, *"Gifts, Gafts and Gefts"—The Income Tax Definition and Treatment of Private and Charitable "Gifts" and a Principled Policy Justification for the Exclusion of Gifts from Income,* 78 Notre Dame L. Rev. 441, 495–524 (2003).

38. *Sklar v. Commissioner*, 549 F.3d 1252, 1264 (9th Cir. 2008).

consequence of making the contribution, part of the "contribution" will be treated as a payment for the tickets. It does not
matter whether the TP uses the tickets to attend the performance; it is sufficient if he retains the tickets, rather than refusing
them or promptly returning them. Rev. Rul. 67–246.

In that same ruling, the Commissioner urged charities to indicate
the amount of payment to the charity that constitutes a payment
for the ticket or other benefit and the amount that is a gift, in
their solicitations and on any ticket, receipt or other evidence of
payment that they give to donors. As to the circumstances in
which a charitable donee is *required* to provide such information
to a donor, see ¶ **20.9300**.

¶ **20.1240. Contributions to Colleges that Entitle the TP
to Purchase Tickets to Athletic Events.** If a TP makes a
payment to a college or university and, as a result, receives the
right to purchase preferred or difficult-to-obtain tickets to athletic
events in a stadium of that school, and if the payments otherwise
would have qualified as charitable contributions, 80% of the
amount paid by the TP will qualify as a charitable contribution.[39]
If any portion of the TP's payment is for the purchase of tickets
(as contrasted to obtaining a right to purchase tickets), that
portion must be separated and treated as a straight purchase.
Only 80% of the remaining portion of the payment is deductible.[40]

¶ **20.1300.   Substantial Benefit to Donor.** If the benefits received
or expected to be received by a donor from a gift to a charitable
organization are substantial, no deduction will be allowed unless the
TP can prove that the value of the benefit received is less than the
value of the donated property and that the TP made the gift with the
knowledge of that difference.[41] A "substantial" benefit is one that is
greater than those benefits that accrue to the general public. *Ottawa
Silica Co. v. United States.*[42]

In *Ottawa Silica*, a deduction was denied for a gift of land to a city
for the construction and placement of a high school. The construction

---

39. § 170(*l*).

40. Id.

41. *Stubbs v. United States*, 428 F.2d 885 (9th Cir. 1970); *Dowell v. United States*, 553
F.2d 1233 (10th Cir. 1977). See ¶ **20.1200** for the treatment and qualification of "dual
payments."

42. 699 F.2d 1124 (Fed. Cir. 1983).

of a high school on that land would increase the value of other land that the TP owned in that area, and the court deemed that there was a sufficient benefit to preclude a deduction. The benefit to the TP in that case might be classified as "indirect" in that it was not something transferred to the TP by the donee. It is clear that the benefit to a transferor need not be direct to warrant denying a charitable deduction. The Federal Circuit's view on that question is that the benefit need only flow from the donee's use of property even though no direct compensation is paid to the donor.[43] If the monetary value of the substantial benefit received by the TP is less than the value of the property transferred to the charity, the difference in value will be deductible as a charitable contribution if the external features of the transaction demonstrate that the TP knew of that difference and nevertheless effected the transaction for the purpose of conferring a benefit on the charity.

The Commissioner has recognized that in many cases the value of a benefit given to a donor is very small in comparison with the amount of the donor's contribution. For administrative reasons, there is good cause to ignore such benefits when they are inconsequential. Accordingly, in a 1990 Revenue Procedure,[44] the Commissioner determined that if the fair market value of the benefits that a donor receives for making a contribution to a charity is insubstantial, then those benefits will be ignored, and the entire amount of the contribution will qualify for a charitable deduction. In that 1990 Revenue Procedure, the Commissioner set forth several safe harbors, subject to indexing for inflation, in which a benefit from a charity will be deemed to be insubstantial. For example, for the year 2011, if a donor's payment to a charity occurs pursuant to a fund-raising campaign in which the charity informs its donors of the amount of their contributions that are deductible and if the fair market value of all the benefits received by a donor because of the contribution is no more than either 2% of the payment made by the donor or $97, whichever is less, the benefit received by that donor will be treated as insubstantial.[45] The dollar figures in the 1990 Revenue Procedure have been changed from time to time to reflect increases in the cost-of-living.

¶ 20.1400. **Gift Subject to Contingency.** If a gift to a charity is subject to a contingency that will deprive the charity of the donated

---

43. See also *Singer Co. v. United States*, 449 F.2d 413, 422–423 (Ct. Cl. 1971).

44. Rev. Proc. 90–12.

45. Rev. Proc. 90–12, as modified by Rev. Proc. 2010–40 (Sec. 3.16).

property if it occurs, the question arises whether any charitable deduction will be allowed for that gift. A deduction will be allowed for such a gift only if the likelihood that the contingency will occur is "so remote as to be negligible."[46] The language "so remote as to be negligible" has been construed to mean "a chance which persons generally would disregard as so highly improbable that it might be ignored with reasonable safety in undertaking a serious business transaction."[47]

¶ 20.1500. Reward Money. The Commissioner ruled that a contribution by the parents of a murder victim of reward money to the police department for information leading to the conviction of the murderer is a contribution to a political subdivision for exclusively public purposes and is deductible pursuant to § 170.[48]

¶ 20.1600. Indirect Payment for Lobbying. As a consequence of the amendments made in 1993, no deduction is allowed to a business for expenses incurred to lobby for legislation or rules of a benefit to the TP's business. Congress feared that TPs might circumvent that restriction by utilizing a tax-exempt entity as a conduit to pay for the lobbying activities. To prevent a TP from obtaining a deduction for contributions to a tax-exempt organization which pays for lobbying of a business interest to the TP, Congress adopted § 170(f)(9).

¶ 20.1700. Nondeductibility of Depreciation Allowances. No charitable deduction is allowed for a taxable year unless actual payment to the charity was made in that year (subject to an exception for *corporate* donors that report on the accrual method). TPs are not allowed a charitable deduction for depreciation allowances for property used for charitable purposes because depreciation does not constitute a "payment."[49] As noted in connection with the medical expense deduction in **¶ 19.1410**, one might question whether the Supreme Court's decision in the *Idaho Power*[50] case will cause depreciation allowances to be treated as a payment, but it is virtually certain that *Idaho Power* will not be so extended.[51]

46. Treas. Reg. § 1.170A–1(e).

47. *885 Investment Co. v. Commissioner*, 95 T.C. 156, 161 (1990), quoting from, *United States v. Dean*, 224 F.2d 26, 29 (1st Cir. 1955).

48. Rev. Rul. 81–307.

49. *Orr v. United States*, 343 F.2d 553 (5th Cir. 1965). See also, Rev Proc. 2010–40 (Sec. 5.03).

50. *Commissioner v. Idaho Power*, 418 U.S. 1 (1974).

51. Note also § 170(f)(3) denying a deduction for a TP's contribution to a charity of the right to use property. See **¶ 20.4420**.

¶ **20.1710. Travel Expenses.** Subject to limitations described below, travel expenses (including the cost of meals[52] and lodging while away from home) that are incurred and paid by a TP for a charitable purpose, and for which personal pleasure, recreation, or vacation was not a significant element, are deductible. If a TP has a vehicle for personal use, some of the costs of operating that vehicle for a specific charitable use are deductible subject to limitations described below.

No deduction is allowed for depreciation of a vehicle that is used by the TP for a charitable purpose.[53] As to other costs of operating the vehicle, the TP has a choice. The TP may either deduct the actual expenses incurred in operating the vehicle (e.g., gas and oil) or the TP may elect to use the optional standard mileage rate which for the year 2011 was fourteen cents per mile.[54] The mileage allowance does not reflect depreciation since depreciation deductions are not permitted for the charitable use of an asset.[55] Interest expenses relating to the purchase of the automobile and state and local property taxes on the vehicle do not qualify as charitable contributions, but the taxes may qualify for an itemized deduction under § 164.[56] If a TP elects to use the mileage allowance, the TP can also deduct his actual costs for parking fees and tolls in addition to the allowance.[57]

A deduction is not allowed for a travel expense unless there is no significant element of personal pleasure, recreation, or vacation involved.[58] If the TP's allowable travel expenses include meals that the TP purchased while on travel status, only 50% of the cost of such meals is deductible.[59]

¶ **20.1720. Expenses to Free TP in Order to Permit TP to Perform Services for a Charity.** The Commissioner denied a deduction for a TP's cost of child care for young children that

52. As noted below, only 50% of the cost of meals is deductible. § 274(n)(1).

53. See ¶ **20.1700**.

54. § 170(i); Rev. Proc. 2010–51 (Sec. 5.01); and Notice 2010–88.

55. Rev. Proc. 2010–51 (Sec. 5.03).

56. Rev. Proc. 2010–51 (Sec. 5.04). Interest payable on a loan to purchase the vehicle will not be deductible under § 163 if the vehicle is used for personal, nonbusiness purposes. See Chapter **Sixteen**.

57. Rev. Proc. 2010–51 (Sec. 5.04).

58. § 170(j).

59. § 274(n)(1).

were incurred in order to free the TP to perform gratuitous services for a qualified charity.[60] For costs of performing services for a charity to be deductible, the costs must be "nonpersonal and directly connected with and solely attributable to the rendition of such services."[61]

¶ 20.1800. Borrowed Funds and Credit Card Payments. A contribution is deemed made when the payment is made to the charity regardless of whether the donor used his own funds or borrowed funds. If a contribution is made to a charity through the use of a bank credit card, the contribution is deemed to have been made at the time that the charge was made rather than when the donor repaid the sum to the bank.[62]

¶ 20.2000.   LIMITATIONS ON AMOUNT OF DEDUCTION.

¶ 20.2100.   Percentage Limitation on an Individual's Charitable Deduction. There is a limitation on the maximum amount of charitable gifts that can be deducted in a taxable year. There is a different limitation for individuals than the one provided for corporations. In this book we will focus primarily on charitable gifts by individuals.

The limitation on the maximum amount of deduction that will be allowed an individual for charitable contributions turns upon the nature of the charitable donee and the nature of the gift. The limitation is expressed in the statute as a percentage of the TP's "contribution base." If the amount of an individual's charitable gifts exceeds the maximum limitation, the excess amount usually can be carried forward to a specified number of subsequent years. The scope and operation of the carryover provisions are described later in this chapter.[63] There is no carryback of unused charitable deductions to prior years.

¶ 20.2110.   Definition of Contribution Base. The term "contribution base" refers to a TP's adjusted gross income (AGI) computed without taking into account any net operating loss that

---

60.   Rev. Rul. 73–597. For a denial of a medical expense deduction for a similar situation involving medical expenses, see Ochs v. *Commissioner*, 195 F.2d 692 (2d Cir. 1952); Rev. Rul. 78–266.

61.   Id.

62.   Rev. Rul. 78–38. Compare **¶ 19.1500** and **¶ 19.1510** for a discussion of the use of borrowed funds or a credit card to pay a medical expense.

63.   See ¶¶ **20.2200–20.2240** and ¶¶ **20.2432–20.2434–2**.

the TP may incur in a subsequent year that will be *carried back* to the taxable year and deducted from the TP's gross income for that year.[64] In other words, a TP's contribution base equals his AGI computed without regard to any net operating loss *carryback* authorized by § 172.

¶ 20.2120. Maximum Limitation on Gifts to "A" Charities. Gifts or contributions (other than gifts of appreciated capital gain property) of an amount up to 50 percent of the TP's contribution base are deductible provided that the gifts or contributions are made *to* (but not "for the use of") a qualified charitable organization that is one of the types listed in § 170(b)(1)(A).[65] Examples of such organizations are: churches, educational organizations, hospitals, medical care institutions, and organizations that are substantially supported by the public or the government and that perform a charitable or educational function. The donee organizations to which the 50% of contribution base limitation applies are defined in § 170(b)(1)(A) and are hereafter referred to as "A" charities. A qualified charitable organization that does not constitute an "A" charity is referred to as a "B" charity. "B" charities are comprised principally of posts or organizations for war veterans and of certain, but not all, private foundations.

There are special requirements that must be met before a gift of a partial interest in property can qualify for a charitable deduction.[66] If a gift of a partial interest in property is deductible, the question then arises as to whether the deduction qualifies for the 50% limitation.

A gift in trust, the income or an annuity from which is payable to an "A" charity, does not qualify as a gift *to* the "A" charity, but rather is a gift for the use of the "A" charity; therefore, the gift of the income or annuity interest does not qualify for the 50% limitation.[67] However, a gift of a remainder interest in a trust to an "A" charity will qualify for the 50% limitation if specified conditions are satisfied.[68] A remainder interest in tangible personal property is subject to a special limitation.[69]

---

64. § 170(b)(1)(G).

65. Treas. Reg. § 1.170A–8(b).

66. Those requirements are discussed at ¶¶ **20.4000–20.4540**.

67. The extent to which the gift of an income or annuity interest can be deducted at all is discussed in ¶ **20.4100**.

68. Treas. Reg. § 1.170A–8(a)(2). Those conditions are described in ¶ **20.4200**.

69. See § 170(a)(3). See ¶ **20.4500**.

¶ **20.2130.   Limitation on Charitable Gifts Not Made to an "A" Charity.** Any charitable contribution or gift (other than a gift of appreciated capital gain property) which does not qualify for the 50% of contribution base limitation (i.e., a gift to a "B" charity or a gift for the use of an "A" or "B" charity) is subject to a maximum limitation of whichever is less—either: (a) 30% of the TP's contribution base, or (b) the difference between 50% of the TP's contribution base and the amount of deduction allowed to the TP for the tax year for contributions to "A" charities (determined without regard to the special limits[70] on the amount of deduction allowable for gifts to "A" charities of certain appreciated capital gain property.)[71] For convenience, we will sometimes refer to this limitation as the "30% limitation." As noted above, gifts *for the use of* a charity (whether an "A" or "B" charity) are subject to the 30% limitation. Stating the 30% limitation differently, the TP can deduct an amount up to 30% of his contribution base provided that his total amount of charitable deductions for the taxable year (including gifts to both "A" and "B" charities) cannot exceed 50% of the TP's contribution base. When a gift of appreciated property is made to an "A" charity, the determination of the limitation on gifts made to a "B" charity involves additional considerations.[72]

¶ **20.2131.   Illustration 1: Fifty Percent Limitation.** *X*, an individual, has $60,000 AGI and contribution base in Year One. *X* gave $30,000 cash to Zion Lutheran Church, an "A" charity, and $2,000 cash to a private foundation which constitutes a "B" charity. *X* can deduct the $30,000 he gave the church since that complies with the 50% limitation on gifts to "A" charities, but *X* cannot deduct any part of the $2,000 contributed to the private foundation since his total deductions for the year cannot exceed 50% of his contribution base. However, the $2,000 contribution to the "B" charity is carried over to *X*'s next five taxable years and deducted in the earliest year allowable under the limitations provided in § 170(b)(1)(B).[73] In many cases, a TP's contribution base will equal his AGI since it is only when he is entitled to a net

---

70. These limits are discussed at ¶¶ **20.2430–20.2432–1**.

71. § 170(b)(1)(B).

72. These are discussed in the Illustrations at ¶ **20.2432–2** and ¶ **20.2434–2**.

73. See ¶ **20.2200**.

operating loss carryback deduction in that year that any modification of AGI must be made in computing the contribution base.

¶ 20.2132. Illustration 2: Thirty Percent Limitation. In Year One, *X*, an individual, had $60,000 AGI and contribution base. *X* gave $5,000 cash to a church, and he gave $20,000 cash to a private foundation which constitutes a "B" charity. *X* can deduct the $5,000 given to the church, but *X* can deduct only $18,000 of the amount given to the foundation in that year (i.e., 30% of the TP's contribution base ($60,000) = $18,000). *X* will carry over the remaining $2,000.[74]

¶ 20.2133. Maximum Limitation on Deductions for a Corporation's Charitable Gifts. The amount of charitable deductions for a taxable year that a corporate TP can deduct is limited to 10% of the corporation's taxable income for that year computed with certain modifications.[75] For corporate donors, no distinction is made for gifts to "A" or "B" charities.

¶ 20.2140. Religious Purpose of an Organization. There are tax advantages for an organization to qualify as a church or a religious organization in addition to its qualifying for the 50% of contribution base limitation. There has been litigation over the question of whether an organization qualifies as religious.

In *Church of the Chosen People v. United States*,[76] the court applied the three-part test, which was set forth in a prior Third Circuit non-tax case,[77] in holding that the TP did not qualify as a religious organization. The court denied tax-exempt status to the TP. The test that the court adopted focuses on the following questions: (a) whether the organization's beliefs address fundamental and ultimate questions concerning the human condition, (b) whether the beliefs are comprehensive in nature and constitute an entire system of belief instead of merely an isolated teaching, and (c) whether the beliefs are manifested in external forms. "The Gay Imperative," the plaintiff's only major doctrine in *Church of the Chosen People*, failed that standard because it was neither comprehensive in nature nor manifested in external

74. Id.

75. § 170(b)(2).

76. 548 F.Supp. 1247 (D.Minn. 1982).

77. *Africa v. Commonwealth of Pennsylvania*, 662 F.2d 1025 (3d Cir. 1981).

forms in ways analogous to other religions. Although not mentioned in its opinion, perhaps the district court was influenced by
the fact that the "church" was also known by the name "Demi-
god Socko Pantheon."

¶ 20.2150.   Qualification as a Church. There can be tax advantages for a religious organization to qualify as a church. For
example, a church is not required to give notice to the Service
that it is not a private foundation.[78] A church is an "A" charity;
whereas, a religious organization that is not a church sometimes
can be a "B" charity.[79]

Not every religious organization qualifies as a "church."[80] In a
speech, a former Commissioner listed fourteen criteria that the
Service utilizes in determining whether a religious organization is
a church; and the Tax Court listed those criteria in *First Church
of In Theo v. Commissioner*.[81] While the Tax Court did not adopt
those criteria, it found them helpful and gave them some weight.
The court held that the TP was not a church and instead was a
private foundation. The Commissioner's fourteen criteria were
listed and utilized by the Tax Court and the Eighth Circuit in
Spiritual Outreach Society v. Commissioner.[82]

While it is useful for a religious organization to qualify as a
church, it is not necessary for it to do so to qualify contributions
made to it for a charitable deduction.[83] However, if the religious
organization is not a church, it may constitute a "B" charity
which is subject to a more restrictive limitation on the amount of
an individual's contribution to it that are deductible.

The contributions to certain charitable organizations ("A" charities), of which churches are included, are given favored tax status
in that the maximum amount of an individual's contributions to
those organization that are deductible is greater than the maximum amount allowable for contributions to qualified charities
that are not "A" charities.[84] If certain conditions are satisfied, a

78.   See ¶ 20.9A000.

79.   The distinction between "A" and "B" charities and the significance of the two
classifications are described in ¶ 20.2120.

80.   *Chapman v. Commissioner*, 48 T.C. 358, 363 (1967).

81.   56 T.C.M. 1045 (1989).

82.   58 T.C.M. 1284 (1990), aff'd 927 F.2d 335 (8th Cir. 1991).

83.   § 170(c)(2)(B).

84.   See ¶¶ 20.2120–20.2130.

religious organization that is not a church nevertheless will qualify as an "A" charity, and so an individual's contributions to it will qualify for the same maximum limitation that applies to gifts made to churches. A religious organization that is not a church will constitute an "A" charity if the organization either: (1) receives a substantial part of its support in the form of contributions from the general public, or (2) qualifies as a private foundation of the type that is described in § 170(b)(1)(F).[85] If not, the amount of an individual's contributions to that organization that can be deducted will be more restricted than are contributions to a church.

¶ 20.2200. **Carryover of Unused Deduction.** Under § 170(d), when an individual makes a charitable contribution to "A" charities in excess of the maximum limitation of 50% of the TP's contribution base, the excess may be carried over to the TP's next five taxable years and deducted in the earliest year allowable under the 50% limitation applicable to that year. An individual also is allowed a five-year carryover for gifts made to "B" charities in excess of the amount allowed as a deduction for that year.[86] Similarly, an individual is granted a five-year carryover for gifts made *for the use of* an "A" or "B" charity in excess of the amount allowed as a deduction. The carryover of gifts to or for the use of a "B" charity or for the use of an "A" charity are treated as gifts to a "B" charity in each of the five subsequent years to which the contribution is carried.

¶ 20.2210. **Illustration 1: Computation of Amount of Carryover.** *X* is an individual. In each of *X*'s taxable years One through Four, *X* had AGI and a contribution base of $40,000. In Year One, *X* gave $22,000 cash to one "A" charity, $10,000 cash to a second "A" charity, and $4,000 cash to a "B" charity. *X* can deduct only $20,000 of the $32,000 he gave to "A" charities. None of the $4,000 that he gave to a "B" charity is deductible in Year One. *X* may carry forward for five years the difference between his gifts to "A" charities ($32,000) and 50% of his contribution base ($20,000) (i.e., *X* can carry forward $12,000). *X* also receives a carryover of his $4,000 gift to the "B" charity.

¶ 20.2220. **Illustration 2: Limitation on Use of Carryover.** The same facts apply as in ¶ 20.2210. In Year Two, *X* gives $15,000 to an "A" charity. In that year, *X* will use $5,000 of his

---

85. § 170(b)(1)(A)(vi), (vii).
86. § 170(b)(1)(B).

carryover of contributions to "A" charities, and so his charitable deductions will total $20,000 (i.e., X will use his carryover contribution to the extent of the difference between 50% of his contribution base in Year Two ($20,000) and the amount actually contributed to "A" charities in that year ($15,000)). Thus, X has $7,000 of his carryover charitable gifts to "A" charities remaining after Year Two. X also has a $4,000 carryover remaining from the contribution that he made to a "B" charity in Year One since he cannot use any of that carryover in Year Two.

¶ **20.2230. Illustration 3: Effect of Carryover Deduction on Gifts to "B" Charities.** The same facts apply as in ¶ **20.2220**. In Year Three, X gave $14,000 to an "A" charity and $5,000 to a "B" charity. X must use $6,000 of his "A" charity carryover in Year Three (50% of X's contribution base ($20,000) minus the $14,000 contributed to an "A" charity). Thus, X deducts $20,000 in Year Three and carries forward $1,000 of unused "A" charity carryover from his Year One deduction. He also carries forward $4,000 in unused carryover from his Year One contribution to a "B" charity and $5,000 from his unused contribution to a "B" charity in Year Three.

¶ **20.2240. Illustration 4: Use of Carryover Deduction.** The same facts apply as in ¶ **20.2230**. In Year Four, X gave $4,000 to an "A" charity. X will use his $1,000 remaining carryover from contributions that he made to "A" charities in Year One, and he will also use all $9,000 of his carryovers from contributions that he made to "B" charities in Years One and Three. Thus, X will deduct a charitable contribution of $14,000 in Year Four. X has no further carryover deductions after Year Four.

¶ **20.2300. Gifts of Appreciated Property That Is Not Capital Gain Property.** When a donor gives property to a charitable organization and the donor would have recognized ordinary income or short-term capital gain had he sold the donated property for its fair market value, the amount of the charitable contribution will be reduced by the amount of gain which the donor *would have* recognized as ordinary income or as short-term capital gain had he sold the property for its value.[87] Different limitations are imposed when a TP makes a gift to a charity of appreciated property (property whose value is greater than its basis) the gain from the sale of which would have been taxed to him as either long-term capital gain or as gain

---

87. § 170(e)(1)(A).

under § 1231 (such property is called "capital gain property").[88] A contribution of appreciated tangible personal property to or for the use of a charity and a transfer of appreciated property of any kind (other than certain publicly traded stock) to or for the use of certain private foundations are subject to special limitations that apply regardless of whether the donated property is capital gain property.[89]

In certain limited circumstances, § 170(e)(3) allows a corporation a deduction for a portion of the appreciated element of a *corporation's* inventory (or certain other ordinary income property) which the corporation contributes to certain qualified charities. A similar deduction is allowed for the corporate contribution of certain scientific equipment or apparatus that was constructed by the corporation, provided that the original use of the property is by the charitable donee which must be an institution of higher learning that uses the property for research, experimentation or research training and provided that other statutory requirements are satisfied.[90]

¶ 20.2310. Illustration 1: Property with Zero Basis. *X* wrote a novel. Before publication, *X* assigned the copyright to the book to a qualified charity. *X* had no basis in the copyright, and the value of the copyright was $25,000. If *X* had sold the copyright for its value ($25,000), *X* would have recognized a $25,000 gain, none of which would have been long-term capital gain or § 1231 gain.[91] Consequently, the amount given by *X* to the charity is deemed to be the value of the copyright ($25,000) *reduced* by the amount of ordinary income that *X* would have recognized if he had sold the copyright for its value ($25,000). Thus, *X* is treated as having made a charitable gift of zero dollars.

¶ 20.2320. Illustration 2: Property with Dollar Basis. *X* is an art dealer who purchases and sells paintings. In Year One, *X* bought a painting for $25,000. By Year Three, the painting had a value of $40,000. If *X* had sold it for its value, *X* would have recognized a gain of $15,000, none of which would have been long-term capital gain or § 1231 gain since *X* held the painting for sale to his customers. *X* donated the painting to an art museum that was a publicly supported organization.[92] The museum retained the

88. See ¶ **20.2400** *et seq.*

89. See ¶¶ **20.2410** and **20.2420**.

90. § 170(e)(4).

91. See §§ 1221(a)(3) and 1231(b)(1)(C).

92. While the gift was of tangible personal property, since the donee was publicly supported and will use the donated painting in connection with its charitable purpose,

painting in its collection and did not sell it. The amount of X's contribution is the value of the painting ($40,000) *reduced* by the ordinary income that X would have recognized if he had sold the painting ($15,000). For charitable deduction purposes, X made a gift of $25,000 to the charity.

¶ 20.2330. Illustration 3: Appreciation is Partially Capital Gain and Partially Ordinary Income. X owned depreciable equipment which he gave to a qualified public charity that used the equipment in conducting its charitable function and did not sell it.[93] The value of the equipment at the time of the gift was $30,000 and X had an adjusted basis of $15,000 therein. If X had sold the equipment for its value instead of making a gift of it, he would have recognized ordinary income of $5,000 (depreciation recapture under § 1245) and X's remaining gain of $10,000 would have constituted a gain under § 1231. X is deemed to have made a gift of $25,000—that is, $30,000 minus $5,000 (the amount of X's potential gain that would not have been treated as long-term capital gain or as an § 1231 gain)—subject to the limitations on gifts of capital gain property described in ¶ **20.2430**.

¶ 20.2340. Illustration 4: Installment Obligation. Y made a gift of an installment obligation[94] to a qualified charity. Since Y is required to recognize as gross income, at the time of donation, the difference between the value of the obligation and Y's basis therein,[95] the gift is not treated as a gift of appreciated property and the special limitations on such gifts are not applicable.[96]

¶ 20.2400. Gift of Capital Gain Property. When a TP makes a gift or contribution to a qualified charity of appreciated property, the sale of which at fair market value would have caused the TP to recognize long-term capital gain,[97] or gain under § 1231, the charitable deduction will be subject to the restrictions described in ¶¶ **20.2410–20.2434–2**. For convenience, appreciated property, the

instead of selling it, the special limitation imposed by § 170(e)(1)(B), which is described in ¶ **20.2410**, is not applicable.

93. Note that the special limitation imposed by § 170(e)(1)(B) on certain gifts of tangible personalty does not apply. See ¶ **20.2410**.

94. The installment method of reporting is described in Chapter **Twelve**.

95. § 453B.

96. See Rev. Rul. 74–336.

97. Self-created musical compositions (or copyrights for such compositions) which qualify as capital assets pursuant to an election made under § 1221(b)(3) are not treated as capital assets for purposes of § 170. § 170(e)(1)(A).

sale of which at fair market value would produce a long-term capital gain or § 1231 gain is sometimes referred to as "capital gain property."[98] For the treatment of a gift or contribution of appreciated property, the sale of which at fair market value would have caused the TP to recognize ordinary income or a short term capital gain, see ¶¶ **20.2300–20.2340**.

¶ **20.2410. Tangible Personal Property.** When a TP gives appreciated *tangible personal property* to or for the use of a qualified charity (regardless of whether the donee is an "A" charity or a "B" charity), the amount of the charitable contribution is limited to the donor's adjusted basis in the donated property. § 170(e)(1)(B)(i). This limitation is not applicable if the donee's use of the donated property is related to its charitable function or purpose.[99] In addition if the donee is a private foundation that is treated as a "B" charity, an identical limitation *may* be required by § 170(e)(1)(B)(ii).[100] The same treatment applies to the contribution of patents, certain copyrights, a trademark, and similar intangible properties.[101]

¶ **20.2411. Illustration 1: Limitation on Amount of Gift.** Since Year One, *X* (an individual) owned a painting by Titian in which he had a basis of $30,000. X was not a dealer in paintings and held the Titian for his personal use. In Year Twelve, *X* gave the painting to the Zion Lutheran Church, an "A" charity. The value of the painting at the time of the gift was $50,000. If *X* had sold the painting for its value, he would have recognized a $20,000 long-term capital gain. Unless it can be demonstrated that the church's use of the painting is related to its charitable function, *X* will be deemed to have made a charitable contribution of only $30,000 (i.e., the amount of *X*'s gift is limited to his adjusted basis in the donated painting).

¶ **20.2412. Illustration 2: Donee's Use of Property in Conduct of Charitable Function.** The same facts apply as in ¶ **20.2411** except that *X* gave the painting to the Corcoran Art Museum, a publicly supported organization that qualifies

---

98. Id.

99. Unless the charity complies with a certification requirement, to be excluded from this limitation, the charity must not have disposed of the tangible personal property before the end of the taxable year when it was donated. § 170(e)(1)(B)(i)(II).

100. See ¶ 20.2420.

101. § 170(e)(1)(B)(iii).

as an "A" charity. Since the museum's use of the painting is clearly related to its educational purposes, X is deemed to have made a contribution of $50,000 (the fair market value of the painting). However, because the painting is appreciated capital gain property, the amount deductible by X will be subject to the limitations established in § 170(b)(1)(C) discussed in ¶ 20.2430.

¶ 20.2420. Gifts to Certain Private Foundations. The amount of charitable contribution that is made by making a gift of appreciated property to or for the use of certain private foundations described in § 170(e)(1)(B)(ii) is equal to the donor's adjusted basis in the donated property.[102] Note that there are some special exceptions to this rule; for example, contributions of "qualified appreciated stock" are not subject to the limitation described above.[103] In general, the "qualified appreciated stock" exception permits a deduction for the full value of a gift to a private foundation of stocks that are listed on a securities market.[104] Of course, if this exception applies, the special percentage limitations on gifts of appreciated property will apply to the gift.[105]

¶ 20.2430. Gifts of Capital Gain Property. When a TP makes a gift to an "A" charity of "capital gain property" (i.e., property the sale of which at fair market value would cause the TP to recognize a long-term capital gain or a § 1231 gain), § 170(b)(1)(C) establishes a separate percentage of contribution base limitation. This limitation on gifts of "capital gain property" applies only if the special limitation of § 170(e)(1)(B) is not applicable.[106] For example, if the amount of a gift to a charity of tangible personal property is limited by § 170(e)(1)(B)(i) to the donor's basis in the donated property, then the special percentage of contribution base limitations imposed by § 170(b)(1)(C) is inapplicable.

---

102. § 170(e)(1)(B)(ii).

103. § 170(e)(5).

104. Stock of a corporation will not constitute "qualified appreciated stock" if the aggregate amount of stock of such corporation that has been contributed by the TP (and by certain persons related to the TP) to private foundations described in § 170(e)(1)(B)(ii) exceeds ten percent (in value) of such corporation's outstanding stock. Id.

105. See ¶¶ 20.2430–20.2433.

106. § 170(b)(1)(C)(i). The special limitation of § 170(e)(1)(B) is described at ¶¶ 20.2410–20.2420.

¶ **20.2431. Thirty Percent Limitation.** When a TP makes a contribution of "capital gain property"[107] to an "A" charity, the maximum amount of such contributions that may be included in the TP's charitable deductions for that year is an amount equal to 30% of the TP's contribution base. As noted above, this 30% limitation does not apply to a gift if the amount of that gift is limited by § 170(e)(1)(B) to the donor's basis in the donated property.[108]

¶ **20.2432. Carryover of Excess Contributions.** The amount of a TP's contributions of capital gain property to "A" charities that is in excess of the 30% limitation may be carried forward by the TP to the next five taxable years, and the carryforward deduction in each of those years is subjected to the 30% of contribution base limitation.

¶ **20.2432–1. Illustration 1: Operation of Thirty Percent Limitation and Carryover.** In Year One, *X* (an individual) had AGI and a contribution base of $80,000. In Year One, *X* gave Blackacre, land valued at $50,000, to the Zion Baptist Church, an "A" charity. *X* had a basis of $46,000 in Blackacre. Because Blackacre was "capital gain property," *X* can use only $24,000 of his gift (30% of his contribution base of $80,000) as a charitable contribution. This is so even though the appreciated value of Blackacre over *X*'s basis was relatively small in comparison with Blackacre's total value; it is sufficient that there is any appreciation in value. But X could utilize the election described at ¶ **20.2434**. *X* carries forward $26,000 (the difference between Blackacre's value ($50,000) and $24,000 (30% of *X*'s contribution base)) for the next five years.

In Year Two, *X* had a contribution base of $70,000, and he gave $5,000 cash to the Salvation Army, an "A" charity. In Year Two, *X* will deduct $5,000 for the cash gift to the Salvation Army, and he will deduct $21,000 as a carryover from his Year One gift—i.e., *X* has a carryover of $26,000 which is subject to the 30% limitation so that 30% of $70,000 = $21,000 and, therefore, only that amount of the carryover can be deducted in Year Two.

In Year Three, *X* had a contribution base of $62,000, and *X* gave $30,000 cash to the Red Cross, an "A" charity. While

---

107. See ¶ **20.2400** for the meaning of "capital gain property" in this context.

108. § 170(b)(1)(C)(i).

X had an unused carryover of $5,000 from Year One ($21,000 of the $26,000 carryover was used in Year Two), he can deduct only $1,000 of it in Year Three because the amount of *X*'s actual contributions in that year was only $1,000 less than 50% of *X*'s contribution base. Thus, *X* deducts the $30,000 contribution to the Red Cross, and he deducts $1,000 of his carryover.

In Year Four, *X* made no gifts and had a contribution base of $40,000. *X* can deduct the $4,000 unused balance of his carryover from Year One in Year Four.

¶ 20.2432–2. Illustration 2: Effect that Gift of Capital Gain Property to an "A" Charity Has on Deductibility of a Cash Gift to a "B" Charity. The same facts apply as in ¶ 20.2432–1 except that in Year One, *X* also gave $3,000 cash to a "B" charity. *X* is not allowed any deduction in Year One for his $3,000 gift to the "B" charity because the amount he gave to the "A" charity (the church), computed without regard to the 30% limitation, exceeded 50% of his contribution base.[109] However, *X* is permitted to carry forward the $3,000 contribution that he made to the "B" charity.

¶ 20.2433. Gifts of Capital Gain Property to "B" Charities. A contribution base limitation also applies to charitable gifts of "capital gain property" to a "B" charity. The deduction for such gifts is subject to both a 20% limitation on gifts of "capital gain property" to "B" charities and a 30% limitation on gifts of "capital gain property" to both "A" and "B" charities.[110] Stated another way, the donor of "capital gain property" to "B" charities may deduct the lesser of: (a) 20% of the TP's contribution base, or (b) the difference between 30% of the TP's contribution base and the amount of deduction allowed for that tax year for contributions of "capital gain property" to "A" charities. It is unclear whether the application of the 30% limitation requires that gifts of capital gain property to an "A" charity are to be taken into account if the TP elects to exclude such gifts from the 30% limitation as described in ¶ 20.2434. It is likely that such gifts will not be taken into account in that circumstance.

---

109. § 170(b)(1)(B)(ii).

110. § 170(b)(1)(D)(i).

The significance of imposing a separate 30% limitation on gifts to "B" charities lies in situations where the donor made gifts of capital gain property to "A" charities in the same year so that the amount allowed for the gift to the "B" charity is less under the 30% limitation than the amount allowed under the 20% limitation. The amount of a TP's contribution of "capital gain property" to a "B" charity that exceeds these percentage limitations may be carried forward to the next five taxable years and such carryforward deduction will be subject to the same percentage limitations.[111]

Most "B" charities will be private foundations; the principal exception is veterans' posts or organizations which typically will be "B" charities. Since a gift of many types of capital gain property to a "B" charity (other than a veterans' post or organization) will be limited by § 170(e)(1)(B) to the donor's adjusted basis in the donated property, it is surprising that Congress further restricted such gifts by imposing the 20% and 30% limitations.

¶ 20.2434. Election to Reduce Amount of Gift. If, for a taxable year, a TP does not wish to have his contributions to "A" charities of capital gain properties subjected to the 30% limitation provision, the TP can elect to be exempted from the 30% limitation provision for that year. To so elect, the TP must elect to have *all* his contributions of capital gain properties in that taxable year (including gifts to both "A" and "B" charities) covered by the limitations imposed by § 170(e)(1). Thus, if a TP makes that election, in lieu of the 30% of contribution base limitation, the amount of the TP's gifts of capital gain properties will be restricted to the TP's basis in those properties.[112] The principal use of this election is likely to be in situations where the amount of appreciation of donated capital gain property is relatively small.

¶ 20.2434–1. Illustration 1: Acceleration of Timing of Deduction. *X* (an individual) had a contribution base of $60,000 in Year One. In Year One, *X* donated Blackacre

111. § 170(b)(1)(D)(ii).

112. § 170(b)(1)(C)(iii). If a TP makes this election for a taxable year, the computation of any carryforward charitable deductions to that taxable year which are traceable to a contribution of capital gain property in a prior tax year will be made as if the TP had also made this election in the prior tax year. § 170(b)(1)(D)(ii).

(land) to Temple Beth El, an "A" charity. *X* had a basis of $29,500 in Blackacre which had a value of $30,000. If *X* made no election, *X* would deduct $18,000 as a charitable gift in Year One and carry over $12,000 for a five-year period. Instead, *X* can elect to treat the gift under § 170(e)(1)(B) so that the amount of the gift is limited to *X*'s basis in Blackacre. Thus, under the election, *X* would deduct a charitable contribution of $29,500 in Year One, and *X* would have no carryover deductions.

¶ 20.2434–2. Illustration 2: Effect on Gifts to "B" Charities. *Y* (an individual) had a contribution base of $60,000 in Year One. In Year One, *Y* donated Blackacre (land) to the American Red Cross, an "A" charity. *Y* had a basis of $14,000 in Blackacre which had a fair market value of $16,000. In Year One, *Y* also gave Whiteacre (land) to a publicly supported veterans' organization, which is a "B" charity. Note that the special limitation imposed by § 170(e)(1)(B)(ii) does not apply to a "B" charity unless it is a private foundation. *Y* had a basis of $7,000 in Whiteacre, which had a value of $10,000. If *Y* made no election, she could deduct $18,000 as a charitable deduction for that year, and she would have a carryover of $8,000 from her contribution of Whiteacre to the veterans' organization (which carryover is subject to the 20% and 30% limitations described in § 170(b)(1)(D)).

If, instead, *Y* elects to treat the gifts that she made that year under § 170(e)(1)(B), she can deduct $14,000 for the gift to the "A" charity and $7,000 for the gift to the "B" charity for a total deduction of $21,000 for that year. In that case, *Y* will have no carryover of unused contributions. Note that the 20% and 30% limitations of § 170(b)(1)(D) apply to *Y*'s gift of Whiteacre to the veterans' fund even though *Y*'s election required that the amount of that gift be limited to *Y*'s basis in Whiteacre. In this case, however, neither the 20% nor the 30% limitation restricted the amount of *Y*'s deduction. In allowing a deduction of $7,000 for the gift of Whiteacre to the veterans' organization, the authors assume that the 30% limitation that is imposed by § 170(b)(1)(D) will be applied without taking into account *Y*'s gifts of capital gain property to an "A" charity since the TP's election to reduce the amount of all of her gifts of capital gain property exempted the gift to "A" charities from the 30% limitation that is imposed by § 170(b)(1)(C). If the authors' construction of § 170(b)(1)(D) is correct, the 30% limitation will never apply to gifts of capital gain property to "B" charities if an election is made under § 170(b)(1)(C)(iii) since in such cases the 20% limitation will always be smaller than the 30% limitation.

¶ 20.3000. BARGAIN SALES. As noted in ¶ 20.1200, when a TP sells property to a qualified charity for less than the property's value and when the TP intended to confer a benefit on the charity, the transaction is a dual payment—that is a part-sale and part-gift transaction. For purposes of determining the TP's gain, if any, on the receipt of a payment from the charity, the TP must allocate to the part of the property sold only that portion of his adjusted basis in the property which bears the same ratio to his adjusted basis as the amount realized bears to the fair market value of the transferred property.[113] The remaining basis is allocated to the contributed portion of the property. Any limitation under § 170(e)(1) on the amount of charitable contribution that is attributable to a gift of appreciated property is determined by reference to the amount of the TP's basis that is allocated to the contributed portion of the property.[114]

¶ 20.3100. Illustration: Allocation of Basis. X (an individual) owned Blackacre with a value of $40,000, and X had an adjusted basis of $10,000 in Blackacre. If X were to sell Blackacre for its fair market value, X would recognize a long-term capital gain of $30,000. For the purposes of conferring a $10,000 benefit on University Y, X sold Blackacre to University Y for $30,000. X made a charitable gift of $10,000 to Y. X received $30,000 consideration for that part of Blackacre that he sold to Y. As shown below, X must allocate $7,500 of his $10,000 adjusted basis in Blackacre to the portion of Blackacre that he sold.

$$\frac{\$30,000 \text{ amount realized}}{\$40,000 \text{ value of Blackacre}} \times \$10,000 \text{ adj. basis} = \$7,500$$

Thus, X recognized a gain of $22,500 ($30,000 amount realized minus $7,500 allocated basis), and X is entitled to a charitable contribution of $10,000. All of the limitations noted in ¶¶ 20.2430–20.2434–2

113. § 1011(b).

114. See *Estate of Bullard v. Commissioner*, 87 T.C. 261 (1986) (reviewed by the court).

apply to the portion donated (i.e., the $10,000 donation constituted appreciated property since X had a basis of only $2,500 therein). In this case, since none of the limitations of § 170(e)(1) applies, only the percentage of contribution base limitation is applicable.

¶ 20.4000. GIFTS OF PARTIAL INTEREST IN PROPERTY. When a TP gives a charity less than his entire interest in an item of property, or gives a charity a partial interest in a trust, which constitutes less than the TP's entire interest, the Code imposes special conditions on deductibility. Moreover, if the charitable gift is a partial interest in *appreciated property*, the donor's basis in that property must be apportioned between the contributed portion and the non-contributed portion of that property for the purpose of applying the rules concerning charitable gifts of appreciated property that are described in **¶¶ 20.2300, 20.2400**, and **20.2410**. See also § 170(e)(2) and Treas. Reg. § 1.170A–4(c)(1).

¶ 20.4100. Gifts of an Income Interest in a Trust. Under § 170(f)(2)(B), subject to the exception for the situation where all of the beneficiaries of the trust are charities,[115] no deduction is allowed for a gift of property to a trust in which the charity has an income interest unless:

(a) the charity's interest in the trust is either a guaranteed annuity interest or a fixed percentage of the value of the trust property valued and distributed annually (this latter interest is a form of unitrust); *and*

(b) the income earned by the trust is included in the TP's gross income under § 671 (the grantor trust provision).

As previously noted, a deductible gift of an income (or annuity or unitrust) interest in a trust does not qualify for the 50% limitation provision but, instead, (if deductible at all) is subject to the same percentage limitations that apply to gifts made to a "B" charity irrespective of whether the beneficiary of the trust is an "A" or a "B" charity. If a donor receives an income tax deduction for a gift in trust of an annuity interest to a charity and if, in a subsequent year prior to the termination of the charity's interest, the donor ceases to be taxed under § 671 on the income earned by the trust (e.g., when the donor dies before possession passes to the remainderman), then on such subsequent date the donor shall be treated as having received an amount of income equal to the amount of deduction

---

115. See ¶ 20.4300.

previously allowed the donor for the charitable gift *reduced by* the discounted value of all income earned by the trust and taxed to the donor prior to his ceasing to be taxed on the trust's income.[116]

¶ 20.4200. Gifts of Remainder Interests in a Trust. Under § 170(f)(2)(A), no deduction is allowed for a gift to a trust in which a charity has a remainder interest unless the trust is a charitable remainder annuity trust, a charitable remainder unitrust or a pooled income fund.[117] If a deductible gift of a remainder interest is made to an "A" charity, the gift will qualify for the 50% limitation.[118] If the donor has retained the power to change the recipient of the remainder interest from an "A" charity to a "B" charity, the 30% limitation on gifts to "B" charities will apply.[119]

¶ 20.4210. Charitable Remainder Annuity Trust. A charitable remainder annuity trust is a trust from which a sum certain (which must be no less than 5% nor more than 50% of the initial value of all the property transferred to the trust) is payable at least annually to beneficiaries, at least one of whom is not a qualified charity, for a term of no more than 20 years or for the life or lives of such individual beneficiaries and, upon termination of the payments, the trust assets must be transferred to, or for the use of, a qualified charity. No payment (other than the fixed annuity payments) may be made to non-charitable beneficiaries.[120]

¶ 20.4220. Charitable Remainder Unitrust. A charitable remainder unitrust is a trust from which a fixed percentage (which must not be less than 5% nor more than 50%) of the net value of the trust's assets (valued annually) is payable at least annually to beneficiaries, at least one of whom is not a qualified charity, for a term of no more than 20 years or for the life or lives of individual beneficiaries and, upon termination of those payments, the trust assets must be transferred to, or for the use of, a qualified charity. The trust instrument may provide, in lieu of the percentage payment described above, for a distribution of the trust income to the income beneficiaries in any year in which the trust income is less than the percentage payment and for the distribution of annual trust income in excess of the percentage payment

116. § 170(f)(2)(B); and Treas. Reg. § 1.170A–6(c)(4).
117. Those three types of trusts are described at **¶¶ 20.4210–20.4230**.
118. Treas. Reg. § 1.170A–8.
119. See Rev. Rul. 79–368.
120. § 664(d)(1).

to the extent that the aggregate payments in prior trust years were less than the aggregate amount of percentage payments required for those years, but no other amounts may be distributed to the income beneficiaries.[121]

¶ **20.4230.   Pooled Income Fund.** Generally, a pooled income fund is a fund maintained by a public charity to which a person can transfer property. The charity places the property in an investment pool and pays the donor (or his beneficiary) an aliquot share of the income for life. The charity maintains the investment pool and possesses the remainder interest therein.[122]

¶ **20.4300.   Exceptions for Gifts of Complete Interests.** If a TP makes a gift to a trust all the beneficiaries of which are qualified charities, then the limitations in ¶¶ **20.4100–20.4200** are not applicable, and the entire amount donated by the TP constitutes a charitable gift.[123]

¶ **20.4400.   Contributions Not Made in Trust of Partial Interest in Property.** When a TP contributes less than his entire interest in property (other than a transfer made in trust) to a qualified charity, the TP is not allowed a charitable deduction for the gift unless the gift would have qualified for a deduction under § 170(f)(2) if the gift had been made in trust.[124] If the gift of a partial interest in property constitutes the entirety of the TP's interest, a deduction is allowed. Treas. Reg. § 1.170A–7(a)(2).

¶ **20.4410.   Exceptions.** The restriction on gifts of a partial interest in property does not apply to the gift of a legal (i.e., non-trust) remainder interest in a personal residence or farm nor does it apply to the gift of an undivided portion of the TP's entire interest in an item or property.[125] To qualify as a gift of an undivided portion of an interest in property, the charity must be given the right, as a tenant in common with the donor, to

121.   § 664(d)(2) and (3).

122.   § 642(c)(5).

123.   § 170(f)(2)(D).

124.   § 170(f)(3)(A). The requirements for deducting a gift of a partial interest in a trust are described in ¶¶ **20.4100–20.4300**.

125.   § 170(f)(3)(B)(i) and (ii). In a 1987 ruling, the Commissioner held that the restriction on gifts of partial interests does not apply to a gift of a portion of a legal remainder interest in a personal residence or farm. Rev. Rul. 87–37, revoking Rev. Rul. 76–544.

possession, dominion and control of the property for a portion of each year appropriate to its interest in such property.[126]

A deduction is allowed to a TP for granting to an "A" charity, with respect to realty, either: (a) the entire interest of the donor other than a qualified mineral interest, (b) a restriction in perpetuity on the use which may be made of the realty (i.e., a permanent easement), or (c) a remainder interest in the realty, if the grant is made exclusively for "conservation purposes" (as defined in the statute).[127] Such a contribution is referred to as a "qualified conservation contribution."

¶ 20.4420. Illustration: Uncompensated Lease of Property. *X* (an individual) owns improved Blackacre having a rental value of $3,000 per year. In Year One, *X* contributes the use of Blackacre to his local church for a period of one year. Since *X* has given only a portion of his interest in Blackacre to the church, and the church's right to use the property (akin to an income interest) would not have qualified for a deduction under § 170(f)(2)(B) if the gift had been made in trust since the church did not receive an annuity or unitrust interest, § 170(f)(3) prohibits *X* from deducting the rental value of the property.

¶ 20.4500. Contribution of a Future Interest in Tangible Personalty. The contribution to a charity of a future interest in tangible personalty will not be treated as complete until all intervening interests in the property either expire or are possessed by persons other than the donor or persons standing in a relationship to the donor described in § 267(b) or § 707(b).[128] When the specified intervening interests expire or terminate, the gift will then be complete; and the determination of the qualification of the gift for a charitable deduction will be made on the basis of the facts that exist at that time.

A gift of an undivided interest in property (such as a painting) to a charity that grants the donee charity the right to the property for a portion of each year does not constitute a gift of a future interest.[129]

---

126. Treas. Reg. § 1.170A–7(b)(1). See *Winokur v. Commissioner*, 90 T.C. 733 (1988), Acq.

127. § 170(f)(3)(B)(iii), (h).

128. § 170(a)(3).

129. *Winokur v. Commissioner*, 90 T.C. 733 (1988).

However, such gifts are subject to additional restrictions and consequences that are imposed by § 170(*o*).

¶ 20.4510.   Illustration 1: Retention of Possession by Donor. Mary owned a valuable painting by Monet. In Year One, Mary gave a remainder interest in the painting to the Phillips Art Museum, a publicly supported organization that qualifies as an "A" charity. Mary retained the right to possess the painting for ten years, after which time possession passes to the museum. Mary is not deemed to have made a gift in Year One. In Year Eleven, when Mary's possessory interest expires, Mary is treated as having made a gift of the painting to the museum.

¶ 20.4520.   Illustration 2: Donation of Possessory Interest to a Related Party. The same facts apply as in ¶ 20.4510 except that in Year One Mary gave her son, Randolph, the possession of the painting for ten years, and then the possession of the painting passes to the museum. Since Randolph is within the group of relatives of Mary described in § 267, Mary is not deemed to have made a gift of the painting until Randolph's possessory interest expires.

¶ 20.4530.   Illustration 3: Donation of Possessory Interest to a Nonrelated Party. The same facts apply as in ¶ 20.4510 except that in Year One, Mary gave her son, Randolph, possession of the painting for five years, then the right to possession passes to Mary's close friend, Alice, for five years, and then possession passes to the museum. Mary is not deemed to have made a gift in Year One. In Year Six, when possession passes to Alice, who is not within the list of Mary's relatives stated in § 267(b), Mary is deemed to have made a gift of the remainder interest to the museum. However, § 170(f)(3) will deny Mary a charitable deduction for making the gift, since the charity's remainder interest (viewed as of Year Six) was not a charitable remainder annuity trust or unitrust, nor was it a pooled income fund.[130] In this case, Mary will never be allowed a charitable deduction.

¶ 20.4540.   Illustration 4: Restrictions on Donee's Use of Property. Robert made a gift to a museum of a rare book collection. Under the terms of the gift, the museum is required to store the books in a locked room, Robert retained the right for life to full access to the collection, and Robert retained for life the

---

130.   See Rev. Rul. 73–610.

right to deny access to the collection to any person seeking to use the books. Robert's gift likely will be treated as a gift of a future interest in tangible personalty in which Robert retained an intervening interest, and so Robert is not entitled to a charitable deduction.[131]

¶ 20.5000. CONTRIBUTION OF SERVICES. A charitable deduction is allowed only for contributions of property. The value of a contribution of personal services is not deductible.[132] In *Grant v. Commissioner*,[133] a negligence penalty (currently imposed by § 6662 as part of the accuracy-related penalty) was imposed on an attorney who claimed a deduction for the fair market value of services contributed to a charity. The court held that the regulation disallowing such a deduction[134] was valid. The Service has narrowly construed the meaning of property.

¶ 20.5100. Donation of Blood to a Charity. A donor's contribution of blood is generally treated as a contribution of a service and therefore is not deductible. In *Lary v. United States*,[135] the court held that a donation of blood was not deductible regardless of whether it was characterized as the performance of a service or the contribution of property. Even if the blood donation is treated as a contribution of property, the TP has the burden of proving the amount of his basis in his blood; only the amount of TP's basis in his donated blood is deductible. If TP had sold the donated blood for its fair market value, any amount received in excess of basis would be ordinary income, and, therefore, the excess of the value of TP's donated blood over TP's basis is nondeductible under § 170(e)(1)(A). It is highly unlikely that a TP can prove that he has any basis in his blood.

¶ 20.5200. Expenses Incurred in Providing Services. While a TP's contributions of services to a charity are not deductible, the unreimbursed, out-of-pocket expenses incurred by the TP in connection with providing those services are deductible. For example, subject to limitations described in ¶ 20.1710, a TP's expenditures for uniforms, transportation, and travel away from home that are necessary to the rendition of gratuitous services by the TP for a qualified charity are deductible.[136] However, a TP is not permitted to deduct

---

131. See Rev. Rul. 77–225; and Treas. Reg. § 1.170A–7(b)(1)(i).

132. Treas. Reg. § 1.170A–1(g).

133. 84 T.C. 809 (1985), aff'd without opinion, 800 F.2d 260 (4th Cir. 1986).

134. Treas. Reg. § 1.170A–1(g).

135. 787 F.2d 1538 (11th Cir. 1986).

136. Treas. Reg. § 1.170A–1(g).

expenses that the TP paid on behalf of another person in connection with the latter's performance of services for a charity.[137] The Commissioner has ruled that child care expenses incurred to free the TP to perform services for a charity are personal, nondeductible expenses.[138] As to travel expenses, § 170(j) prohibits a deduction unless there is no significant element of pleasure, recreation or vacation in the travel.

¶ **20.5210. Payment of Expenses of Other Persons Performing Services for a Charity.** As noted in ¶ **20.5200**, the unreimbursed expenses incurred and paid by a person in connection with that person's performance of services for a charity are deductible. But, what if a person who does not perform services for a charity pays the expenses incurred by another person in connection with the latter's performance of services for the charity? In *Davis v. United States*,[139] the Supreme Court held that no deduction will be permitted for paying the expenses of another when the payor is not himself providing services to the charity. As part of its holding in *Davis*, the Court held that the payment of another's expenses does not constitute a contribution "for the use of" the charity as that phrase is used in § 170 because that phrase refers to contributions made in trust for a charity.

¶ **20.6000. ASSIGNMENT OF INCOME.** A TP may assign to a charity income from services performed by the TP or income earned by property owned by the TP. The usual anticipatory assignment of income rules[140] apply equally to gifts to a charity. If a gift is treated as an anticipatory assignment of income, the income will be included in the TP's gross income. TP will be allowed a charitable deduction, but the amount of that deduction will be subject to the percentage limitations imposed on charitable deductions.

¶ **20.7000. PUBLIC POLICY EXCLUSIONS FROM EXEMPT STATUS.** The Supreme Court has held that an organization having an

---

137. ¶ 20.5210.

138. Rev. Rul. 73–597. The same approach has been taken in connection with a claim for a medical expense deduction for child care expenses incurred to free a parent to receive medical care. The Service and several courts have denied deductions for such expenses. ¶ 19.1400.

139. 495 U.S. 472 (1990). In that case, the payments were made directly to two missionaries by their parents. While the payments were used by the missionaries to defray their expenses and were intended for that use, there were no explicit restrictions as to how they used the funds.

140. See Chapter **Fourteen**.

exempt purpose specified in § 501(c)(3) may, nevertheless, be denied exempt status because the organization practices racial discrimination. In *Green v. Connally*, the district court construed the word "charitable" in § 501(c)(3) as incorporating a public policy limitation defined by federal public policy against racial discrimination in education; and the Supreme Court affirmed per curiam.[141] The Supreme Court subsequently affirmed decisions in two cases where tax-exempt status was denied to private educational institutions whose racially discriminatory policies were based on asserted religious beliefs.[142] The Supreme Court based its denial of tax-exempt status on statutory construction and public policy grounds, stating that "to warrant exemption under § 501(c)(3), an institution must fall within a category specified in that section and must demonstrably serve and be in harmony with the public interest."[143] The question remains open as to whether this denial can be extended to groups which discriminate on bases other than race (e.g., gender or religion).

Failing to qualify for tax-exempt status means that gifts to those organizations will not qualify for a charitable deduction.

¶ **20.8000. ITEMIZED DEDUCTION.** The charitable deduction is not listed in § 62(a), and so constitutes an itemized deduction. The 2% of AGI floor does not apply to charitable deductions. § 67(b)(4). Charitable contributions are subject to the overall limitation on the deduction of itemized deductions that is imposed by § 68 for years subsequent to 2012 when an individual's AGI exceeds a specified amount.[144]

¶ **20.9000. OVERVALUATION.** There is evidence that TPs sometimes overvalue the property donated to a charity and thereby overstate the amount deductible. Congress has imposed reporting and verification requirements to minimize that abuse.

¶ **20.9100. Substantiation Requirements.** For a charitable contribution of $250 or more, no deduction will be allowed unless the TP obtains from the donee a contemporaneous written acknowledgement

---

141. 330 F.Supp. 1150 (D.D.C. 1971), aff'd per curiam sub nom., *Coit v. Green*, 404 U.S. 997 (1971).

142. *Bob Jones University v. United States*, 639 F.2d 147 (4th Cir. 1980), aff'd, 461 U.S. 574 (1983); *Goldsboro Christian Schools, Inc. v. United States*, 644 F.2d 879 (4th Cir. 1981), aff'd sub nom., *Bob Jones University v. United States*, 461 U.S. 574 (1983). See also, Rev. Rul. 71–447.

143. *Bob Jones University v. United States*, 461 U.S. at p. 592.

144. See ¶ **10.1120**.

of the gift.[145] The written acknowledgement must include:

(1) a statement of the amount of cash contributed and a description of any non-cash property that was contributed (but there is no requirement that the acknowledgement state the value of the donated non-cash property); and

(2) a statement as to whether the donee provided any goods and services in consideration, in whole or in part, of the donation, and a description of the goods or services provided to the donor and a good faith estimate of the value of those goods or services [however, if the only consideration provided to the donor was an "intangible religious benefit" that generally is not sold commercially, it need not be valued and the donee charity need only include a statement of the nature of the religious benefit].

The requirement of a contemporaneous written acknowledgement is waived if the donee organization files a return that conforms with requirements established by the Service in regulations.[146]

The Service is authorized to promulgate regulations that will describe circumstances in which the substantiation requirement need not be satisfied.

¶ 20.9200. Information Required. If a TP makes a contribution to a charity for which a deduction of more than $500 is claimed, no deduction will be allowed unless the information and substantiation requirements described below are satisfied.[147] The deduction will not be denied if the failure to comply is due to reasonable cause and not to willful neglect. Id.

(1) The TP must include with the return for the taxable year in which the contribution was made a description of the contributed property and such other information as the Service may require.

(2) If the value of donated property exceeds $5,000, the TP is required to obtain a qualified appraisal and is required to include on his return information about the property and about the qualified appraisal. This requirement does not apply if the contributed property is cash, publicly traded securities, inventory-type property, patents, copyrights, trademarks and similar property, or a vehicle for which information is required by the provision described at

---

145. § 170(f)(8).

146. § 170(f)(8)(D).

147. § 170(f)(11)(A).

¶ 20.9400.[148]

(3) If the value of the donated property is $500,000 or more, the TP is required to attach the qualified appraisal to his return. This requirement does not apply if the contributed property is cash, publicly traded securities, inventory-type property, patents, copyrights, trademarks and similar properties, or a vehicle for which information is required by the provision described at **¶ 20.9400.**[149]

In applying the dollar thresholds for the above reporting and appraisal requirements, all similar donated properties, whether donated to one or more donees, are aggregated.[150]

If a TP contributes property (other than publicly traded securities) to a charity, the claimed value of which (plus the value of similar items donated by the donor to one or more charitable donees) exceeds $5,000, and if the charitable donee sells, exchanges or otherwise disposes of that property within three years after its receipt, the donee is required to file a return with the Service. The information to be disclosed on that return includes an identification of the donor and a statement of the amount received by the donee on its disposition of the donated property.[151] The donee is required to send a copy of that return to the donor.[152]

¶ 20.9300. Disclosure of Information. In addition to the substantiation and reporting requirements, the Code imposes a disclosure requirement on the donee organization when the amount transferred to the donee exceeds $75 and the donor received partial consideration for the transfer.[153] The more than $75 figure applies to the amount transferred to the donee without reduction for the amount of any partial consideration that the donor received from the donee. This disclosure requirement does not apply to a contribution to a religious organization in return for which the transferor receives an intangible religious benefit that generally is not sold commercially outside of a donative context.

Specifically, the donee is required to provide the donor with a written statement that:

148. § 170(f)(11)(A), (C).
149. § 170(f)(11)(A), (D).
150. § 170(f)(11)(F).
151. § 6050L(a).
152. § 6050L(c).
153. § 6115.

(1) explains that the contribution is deductible only to the extent of the excess of the value of the contribution over the value of any goods and services furnished to the donor in return; and

(2) provides the donor with a good faith estimate of the value of the goods and services that the donor received.

If the donee fails to comply with those disclosure requirements, a penalty may be imposed on the donee.[154]

When the item or benefit received by a donor is of insubstantial value, the charitable donee may inform the donor that the donor's contribution is fully deductible. The Service has provided guidelines for the determination of whether an item or benefit is of insubstantial value.

¶ 20.9400. **Donation of a Vehicle.** The Service has evidence that the donation of automobiles to charities has been a major source of overvaluations. To deter that practice, in the American Jobs Creation Act of 2004, Congress added § 170(f)(12) to the Code, which applies to the donation of certain vehicles (including automobiles, boats and aircrafts).[155] If the claimed value of the vehicle exceeds $500, a number of substantiation, reporting and certification requirements are imposed on the donor and the donee. If the charity sells the vehicle (which had a claimed value greater than $500) without making any material improvement or without there having been a significant intervening use by the charity, the donor cannot take a deduction for the donation that is greater than the gross proceeds that the donee received.[156]

¶ 20.9500. **Penalty For Overvaluation.** If a TP has an underpayment of income tax for a taxable year that is attributable to a significant overstatement of the value of property contributed in kind to a charity (i.e., the TP overvalued the contributed property and thereby obtained a greater charitable deduction than was proper), a penalty may be imposed on the TP under § 6662. This penalty is part of the accuracy-related penalty that is described at ¶ **1.6331**.

¶ 20.9A000. **ADVANCE NOTICE REQUIREMENT.** Section 508 requires *most* organizations seeking tax-exempt status under § 501(c)(3) to notify the Secretary that they are applying for such status. What

---

154. § 6714.

155. The provision does not apply to the donation of inventory-type property. § 170(f)(12)(E).

156. § 170(f)(12)(A)(ii).

significance does that requirement have for the resolution of whether a contribution to an organization described in § 170(c)(2) qualifies for a deduction? While the statute does not expressly require notification by § 170(c)(2) organizations, most § 170(c)(2) organizations also are § 501(c)(3) organizations.

If a § 501(c)(3) organization fails to give timely notice to the Service that it is not a private foundation, it will be presumed to be a private foundation.[157] The classification of an organization as a private foundation may affect the amount of deduction allowable for contributions to that organization.[158] Organizations that are not required to notify the Secretary are listed in § 508(c) and Treas. Reg. § 1.508–1(a)(3). For example, churches are excluded from this requirement.[159]

¶ 20.9B000. **DECLARATORY JUDGMENT.** The Code permits an organization to obtain a declaratory judgment as to whether it is a qualified charitable organization under §§ 501(c)(3) or 170(c)(2) and as to certain similar questions.[160] The organization can seek the declaratory judgment only after the Service has either rejected the organization's claim or has failed to make a determination of the claim within 270 days.

The petition for declaratory judgment can be brought in either the Tax Court, the United States Court of Federal Claims, or the United States District Court for the District of Columbia at the option of the organization. No judgment will be issued until the organization has exhausted its administrative remedies as defined in § 7428(b)(2). A court's declaratory judgment under this provision is reviewable in the same manner as a final judgment or decree of that court.

To mitigate the drying up of contributions to an organization whose administrative ruling of charitable status was revoked by the Service, § 7428(c) permits an *individual* to deduct up to $1,000 of contributions made by him and his spouse to an organization whose administrative ruling of qualification as a § 170(c)(2) organization was revoked by the Service if the organization has filed a timely petition for a declaratory judgment of that issue. Such contributions made after the notice of the Service's revocation of its determination of charitable status was published and prior to a court's final determination that the organization

157. § 508(b).
158. See, e.g., § 170(b)(1)(B), (D), (e)(1)(B)(ii).
159. § 508(c)(1)(A).
160. § 7428.

does not qualify for § 170(c)(2) status will be deductible. This provision for a deduction of up to $1,000 will not apply to an individual who is wholly or partly responsible for the circumstances that constituted the basis of the revocation.[161]

¶ **20.9B100.   Scope of Review.** In a 1978 decision,[162] the Tax Court examined the scope of the declaratory judgment proceeding that is authorized by § 7428. Essentially, the proceeding is a review of the administrative determination of the Service rather than a de novo determination of the charitable status of the petitioner. Typically, the court's determination will be made on the administrative record, and only in rare circumstances will the court allow additional evidence to be introduced.

161. § 7428(c)(3).

162. *Houston Lawyer Referral Service, Inc. v. Commissioner*, 69 T.C. 570 (1978).

CHAPTER TWENTY–ONE

BUSINESS AND NONBUSINESS EXPENSES

¶ 21.0000. BUSINESS AND NONBUSINESS EXPENSES. The federal income tax is imposed on taxable income (i.e., gross income reduced by allowable deductions). The most common and important deductions are the expenses of conducting a trade or business or other profit-seeking venture. Business-related expenses are usually deductible under the general rule of § 162, but some business-related expenses are deductible under more specific provisions of the Code (e.g., business bad debts under § 166). A deduction may be authorized by more than one section of the Code, but no more than one deduction is allowed for a single item. See Treas. Reg. § 1.161–1. No deduction is allowed for an expense for which the TP has the right or an expectation of being reimbursed.[1]

¶ 21.1000. ORDINARY EXPENSES: GENERAL. Section 162 grants a deduction for the *ordinary and necessary* expenses of conducting a trade or business. An expense is deductible under § 162 if:

(a) the TP is engaged in a "trade or business" (e.g., a "gentleman farmer" who operates a farm as a hobby rather than as a business is not engaged in the trade or business of farming);

(b) the expense was paid or incurred in connection with the conduct of the trade or business; and

(c) the expense was "ordinary and necessary" [a term of art explained at ¶¶ **21.1500–21.1522**].

¶ 21.1100. Trade or Business. The term "trade or business" is not defined in either the Code or the Regulations and has no precise single definition. An individual may be engaged in more than one trade or business at the same time. The term "trade or business" is used in a number of Code sections, but it has a more restricted meaning in § 162 than it does in most other sections in which it is

---

1. Rev. Rul. 80–348. See *Campbell v. Commissioner*, 54 T.C.M. 632 (1987), where the Tax Court denied a business loss deduction to the extent that the loss was covered by insurance even though the TP did not claim reimbursement from the insurer.

employed. For example, in *Snow v. Commissioner*,[2] the Supreme Court held that the term "trade or business" as used in § 174 (providing a current deduction for research and experimental expenses) has a broader scope than that term has when used in § 162.

In general, for purposes of § 162, a "trade or business" is an activity entered into for the purpose of making a profit and with the expectation that the activity ultimately will produce a profit. It is sufficient if the TP contemplates eventually turning a profit; he need not expect a profit at the outset—i.e., it is permissible to anticipate start-up losses.[3] The test is whether the TP's expectation of a profit is bona fide; it need not be a reasonable expectation.[4] A consistent history of losses over a number of years does not establish conclusively that a venture was not entered into for profit, but it is evidence of that possibility. In the view of the authors, the provision in § 7701(*o*)(2)(A) as to how profit potential is to be determined in applying the economic substance doctrine does not affect the rules described above.

While a profit motive is essential to qualify for a business expense deduction, it is not sufficient. The "taxpayer must be involved in the activity with continuity and regularity and . . . the taxpayer's primary purpose for engaging in the activity must be for income or profit. A sporadic activity, a hobby or an amusement diversion does not qualify."[5] If the activity is not a trade or business, the expense may qualify as a deduction under § 212 if the activity is profit-motivated.[6]

An exception to the profit motive requirement is that under § 7701(a)(26), the performance of the functions of a public office constitutes a trade or business regardless of whether the TP is compensated for his services.[7]

¶ 21.1110. Substance Versus Form and Business Purpose. When a transaction or a series of steps to a transaction have no economic significance and are designed solely to obtain favorable tax consequences, the tax law will recharacterize the transactions

---

2. 416 U.S. 500 (1974).

3. *Nickerson v. Commissioner*, 700 F.2d 402 (7th Cir. 1983).

4. *Churchman v. Commissioner*, 68 T.C. 696 (1977); *Dreicer v. Commissioner*, 78 T.C. 642 (1982).

5. *Commissioner v. Groetzinger*, 480 U.S. 23 (1987).

6. See **¶ 21.1200**.

7. *Frank v. United States*, 577 F.2d 93 (9th Cir. 1978).

(or the steps) so as to reflect the economic substance of what was accomplished without regard to economically meaningless transactions or steps. The substance versus form doctrine is not based on a statutory provision; rather it is a common law doctrine.

The courts have also required that a transaction have a valid business purpose to qualify for a tax treatment.[8]

¶ 21.1120. **Economic Substance.** In addition to the profit motive, substance versus form, and business purpose requirements, the courts imposed a requirement referred to as the "economic substance doctrine" that for a transaction to be taken into account for tax purposes, the transaction must (1) make a meaningful change in the TP's economic position (apart from tax consequences) and (2) the TP must have had a substantial purpose (apart from tax consequences) for engaging in the transaction. While that statement of the doctrine sets forth two separate conditions, the courts divided over the question of whether both of those conditions had to be satisfied and how they were to be applied. In 2010, Congress codified the economic substance doctrine by adopting § 7701(o). In its codification of the doctrine, Congress requires that both conditions must be satisfied. In addition, the statute provides that state and local tax benefits and financial accounting benefits that a transaction provides are not taken into account in determining whether the transaction satisfies the economic substance requirement. To the extent that a TP relies on a showing of a potential profit to satisfy the above requirements, the Code establishes a standard for determining whether that item can be taken into account. § 7701(o)(2)(A). So the statutory provision is more demanding that was the common law provision as applied by many of the courts.

As noted in ¶ **1.6331**, if an underpayment of the federal income tax is attributable to a transaction that lacks economic substance, a penalty equal to 20% of the underpayment is imposed. If the TP failed to disclose the transaction, the penalty is doubled to 40% of the underpayment. § 6662.

¶ 21.1130. **Facts and Circumstances Test.** As a consequence of a statement made by Justice Frankfurter in his concurring opinion in a 1940 Supreme Court decision, a question arose as to

---

8. See e.g., *Gregory v. Helvering*, 293 U.S. 465 (1935).

whether an activity could qualify as a trade or business only if it constituted the offering of goods or services. This issue arose primarily in the context of whether a professional gambler could be engaged in the trade or business of gambling. The issue was laid to rest by the Supreme Court's repudiation in *Commissioner v. Groetzinger*,[9] of the notion that there is a requirement that goods or services be offered. In *Groetzinger*, after the TP lost his job in sales and market research, he turned to parimutuel wagering, primarily on greyhound racing. In the year 1978, he went to racing tracks six days a week for 48 weeks. TP gambled only on his own account; he made no bets for others, nor did he sell tips or function as a bookie. TP spent a substantial amount of time studying racing forms and similar materials. He devoted 60 to 80 hours per week on these gambling-related endeavors. In 1978, TP had gross winnings of $70,000 on his gambling; but he lost $72,032 so he had a net loss for that year of $2,032. The Commissioner contended that TP's gambling activity did not constitute a trade or business and so, under the state of the law as it existed at that time, a portion of TP's gambling losses constituted a tax preference item that caused the TP to incur an alternative minimum tax liability. The Supreme Court held that TP was in the trade or business of gambling and so incurred no alternative minimum tax liability. The Court repudiated the suggestion that an activity must offer goods or services to constitute a trade or business. Rather than draw a bright line for classification as a trade or business, the Court determined that the facts and circumstances of each case must be examined. The activity must be profit-motivated, and the TP must have a bona fide expectation of earning a profit (but a reasonable expectation is not required). Also, the TP must be involved in the activity with regularity and continuity.

As to a gambling activity, note that gambling losses are deductible only to the extent of gambling winnings in the same taxable year. § 165(d).

¶ 21.1140.   Stock Investment Activity and Rental Realty Activity.

¶ 21.1141.   Stocks and Securities Investment Activity.
Investing in stocks and securities does not constitute a trade or business even when the investment activity is extensive and

---

9.   480 U.S. 23 (1987).

involves many dollars.[10] However, investing in stocks and securities must be distinguished from "trading" or "dealing" in them, which are described below and are treated quite differently. Salaries, fees and other expenses incurred in connection with stock investments are not deductible under § 162 as business expenses. While such expenses usually will be deductible under § 212, they will be treated as miscellaneous itemized deductions under § 67(b) and can be deducted only to the extent that the aggregate of such items exceeds 2% of the TP's AGI. Moreover, if the alternative minimum tax (AMT) applies to the TP, no deduction is allowed for any of those expenses. § 56(b)(1)(A)(i). If the AMT does not apply to the TP, for years after 2012, the deduction for those expenses is also subject to the overall limitation on itemized deductions that is imposed by § 68 when an individual's AGI exceeds a specified amount. Note, however, that investment interest [defined in § 163(d)(3)] that is deductible is not subject to the 2% of AGI floor or the § 68 limitation on itemized deductions and is not disallowed by the alternative minimum tax system. §§ 67(b)(1), 68(c)(2).

There are three categories of persons who purchase stocks and securities—investors, traders and dealers.[11] If a person who buys and sells stocks and securities qualifies as a "trader," as contrasted to an investor, the trader's activity will constitute a trade or business.[12] A "trader" in stocks or securities is one who buys and sells stocks or securities frequently "in an endeavor to catch the swings in the daily market movements and profit thereby on a short term basis."[13] To qualify, the TP must engage in such market transactions almost daily for a substantial and continuous period which generally must exceed one taxable year.[14]

While the expenses of a trader in stocks are deductible business expenses under § 162, the trader's gains and losses from

---

10. *Higgins v. Commissioner*, 312 U.S. 212 (1941).

11. *Chen v. Commissioner*, TC Memo 2004–132 (2004).

12. See *Commissioner v. Groetzinger*, 480 U.S. 23 (1987); *Moller v. United States*, 721 F.2d 810 (Fed. Cir. 1983).

13. *Moller v. United States*, 721 F.2d 810 (Fed. Cir. 1983); *Mayer v. United States*, 32 Fed. Cl. 149 (Fed. Cl. 1994); *Purvis v. Commissioner*, 530 F.2d 1332, 1334 (9th Cir. 1976); *Chen v. Commissioner*, TC Memo 2004–132 (2004).

14. *Chen v. Commissioner*, TC Memo 2004–132 (2004).

the sale of those stocks will be capital gains and losses since a trader does not sell to "customers" as required by § 1221(a)(1).[15]

A "dealer" in stocks and securities is described in ¶ 25.4230. The expenses of a dealer will also be business expenses. The gains or losses of a dealer on the sale of stocks and securities will be ordinary income and loss because a dealer does sell to customers in the ordinary course of a trade or business.

¶ **21.1142. Rental of Real Estate.** The question has arisen whether the rental of realty that the TP owns constitutes a trade or business. Before the adoption in 1942 of the antecedents to §§ 212 and 167(a)(2), that question was of considerable significance since the expenses of operating the realty and depreciation deductions for a leased building would be allowable only if the rental activity constituted a trade or business. In the context of deductions, the question is much less significant now since not only will such expenses and depreciation be allowable by §§ 212 and 167(a)(2), they will be nonitemized deductions under § 62(a)(4). However, the issue is still important because the determination of the character of a gain or loss on the sale of the realty will depend upon whether the realty was used in a trade or business rather than merely held as an investment. That issue is of particular importance if the TP recognizes a loss on the sale of the realty. A gain or loss recognized on the sale of rented realty will be a capital gain or loss if the rental activity was not a trade or business, but will be characterized by § 1231 if the rental activity constituted a trade or business. § 1231(b)(1). A § 1231 loss often qualifies as an ordinary loss, which typically is more useful to a TP than is a capital loss. § 1231(a)(2).[16]

The standard for determining whether rental realty was used in a trade or business has changed over the years. Initially, the Service and the Tax Court treated the mere rental of improved realty as a trade or business, but imposed greater requirements if the rental realty was not improved. The courts and the Service no longer use a different standard for improved and unimproved rental realty. In both cases, the test for determining whether the rental activity constitutes a trade or

---

15. See ¶ **25.4230**.

16. See ¶ **26.2000** *et seq.* for a discussion of the operation of § 1231.

business turns on the degree of activity of the TP in the conduct of that activity. If the TP does not manage the property or incur costs and effort in advertising and renting it (for example, if the property is rented under a net lease in which the lessor does little more than collect the net rent), the property likely will be treated as an investment rather than as part of a trade or business.[17]

Section 280A imposes special limitations on the amount that can be deducted for the rental of a dwelling unit if the TP uses all or part of the unit for personal purposes at any time during the taxable year.[18]

¶ 21.1150.   Time When Business Commences. It is important to determine when a TP commences the conduct of a trade or business since the expenses incurred prior to that date may not be deductible. A TP is first deemed to be carrying on a business at the time that the facts show that there has been sufficient progress that the TP will almost certainly engage in a profit-seeking activity. In *Aboussie v. United States*,[19] the court denied a deduction for the premium paid by a limited partnership for mortgage insurance in connection with a housing project which the partnership was constructing. In the year in question, the construction had barely begun, and so the court determined that considerable uncertainty existed at that time as to whether and when the project would produce profits.

¶ 21.1160.   Interruption of Business. If a TP ceases to conduct a business for a period of time, the question can arise as to whether the TP remains in the business for the period of time that he is inactive. If the hiatus is relatively brief and was intended to be temporary, the TP will continue to be in the same business.[20] If the TP ceases to conduct a business for an indefinite period, the TP will be deemed to no longer be in that business.[21]

¶ 21.1170.   Activity Not Engaged in for Profit. There have been many "hobby" cases concerning the deductibility of expenses incurred in activities such as farming, the owning and

---

17.   TAM 8350008. See *Curphey v. Commissioner*, 73 T.C. 766 (1980).

18.   The operation of those limitations is discussed at ¶¶ **21.1190–21.1196**.

19.   779 F.2d 424 (8th Cir. 1985).

20.   *Furner v. Commissioner*, 393 F.2d 292 (7th Cir. 1968).

21.   *Damron v. Commissioner*, 46 T.C.M. 903 (1983).

racing of horses, the writing of books. The results have been mixed but largely turn on factual findings as to the TP's motive.

The Tax Reform Act of 1969 (the 1969 TRA) added § 183 to the Code which deals with the deductibility of expenses incurred in connection with an "activity not engaged in for profit." Section 183 does not affect the deductibility of expenses which are deductible without regard to whether they are incurred in connection with a profit-seeking activity (such as state income and property taxes), but it does *limit* the deductibility of other expenses of non profit-seeking activities. Since § 183(c) defines an "activity not engaged in for profit" as one whose expenses are not allowable as deductions under §§ 162, 212(1) or (2), on its face the language of § 183 would not seem to impose a significant limitation on deductibility (i.e., if such expenses do not qualify under § 162 or § 212, they would likely not be deductible in any event). Presumably, the congressional purpose for adopting § 183 was to restrict the deduction of expenses connected with activities which lie in a marginal zone which might be characterized as either personal or income-related depending upon factual findings. Therefore, courts may narrow their construction of the applicability of § 162 or § 212 as a consequence of the 1969 adoption of § 183. See *Jasionowski v. Commissioner*,[22] stating that § 183 "has clearly placed a gloss on post–1969 judicial profit-motive inquiries."

¶ 21.1171. Determining "Profit–Making Activity." In Treas. Reg. § 1.183–2(b), the Treasury lists nine factors to be taken into account in determining whether an activity is engaged in for profit.[23] The Tax Reform Act of 1976 (the 1976 TRA) adopted a specific provision [§ 280A] dealing with the deductibility of expenses incurred in connection with the rental or other business use of realty that the TP or certain related parties occupied as a personal residence for part of the taxable year.[24]

¶ 21.1172. Presumption. If a venture nets a profit in three or more of the five consecutive years ending with the taxable year in question, § 183(d) establishes a rebuttable presump-

---

22. 66 T.C. 312 (1976).

23. For an example of a court's use of those factors, see *Burger v. Commissioner*, 809 F.2d 355 (7th Cir. 1987).

24. The provision is discussed at **¶¶ 21.1190–21.1196** and **¶¶ 21.1530–21.1536**.

tion that the venture is a profit-seeking venture. If the activity is the breeding, training, racing, or showing of horses, the period is two or more of seven consecutive years. A failure to qualify for the presumption does not create a negative inference that the activity was not profit-seeking. In *Churchman v. Commissioner*,[25] the court held that an artist was engaged in an activity for profit even though she failed to earn a profit in any of the six years in which she had engaged in artistic activities. The court felt that the loss years were a less significant factor for an artist than for most trades because an artist often has to endure a long period of economic loss before achieving the public acclaim that leads to a profit. The court was influenced by the extensive efforts made by the TP to market her works so that her activity went beyond the creative stage and indicated a strong profit motive.

¶ 21.1180. Net Income from Non–Profit Activity. Prior to the 1986 adoption of limitations on the amount of deduction allowable for itemized deductions, even when a venture did not qualify as a profit-seeking activity, only the net income from the venture was taxed. § 183. In determining the net income from such an activity, expenses connected with the activity which are deductible without regard to whether the activity constituted a profit venture (e.g., state income and property taxes, and casualty losses) are deducted first, and other expenses of the activity are deductible only to the extent of the balance. § 183(b). By definition, expenses which are deductible under § 183 are not business expenses and, therefore, must be itemized; that is, they are not deducted in determining AGI.[26] Also, those expenses are miscellaneous itemized deductions, the deductibility of which is subject to the 2% of AGI floor imposed by § 67(a), and are not deductible at all in the alternative minimum tax system. Therefore, even when the income earned from a hobby exactly equals the expenses incurred in conducting the hobby, a TP may have a net income from the activity because the amount of deduction allowable for those expenses may be less than the amount of income from the activity. These expenses also are subject to the § 68 overall limitation on the amount of itemized deductions that can be deducted.[27]

25.   68 T.C. 696 (1977).

26.   Rev. Rul. 75–14; Rev. Rul. 76–287.

27.   See ¶¶ 10.1110–10.1120.

¶ **21.1181.** **Illustration 1: Hobby Expenses.** *X*, a successful chemist, is a talented and enthusiastic chess player who plays in four to six chess tournaments a year. In Year One, *X* won $350 in prizes from such tournaments. During the year, he incurred travel expenses of $650 in the course of his chess activities. Although *X* is not engaged in chess as a trade or business (it is a hobby), he may, nevertheless, treat $350 of his expenses, the amount of his winnings, as an itemized deduction (subject to the 2% of AGI floor), and he will receive no tax allowance for the $300 expenses he incurred in excess of his winnings. If Year One is after 2012, and if *X*'s AGI exceeds a specified amount, his expenses that are otherwise deductible are subject to the limitation imposed by § 68. If X's tax is determined under the alternative minimum tax system, none of X's expenses is deductible. § 56(b)(1)(A)(i).

¶ **21.1182.** **Illustration 2: Non Profit–Seeking Deductions.** The same facts apply as in ¶ **21.1181** except that *X* won $365 and incurred $350 travel expenses. *X* paid $35 in state income taxes on his winnings. *X* had no other expenses in connection with this hobby. The $35 state tax expense is not a miscellaneous itemized deduction because of § 67(b)(2), and, therefore, that expense is not subject to the 2% of AGI floor. Assuming that the § 68 limitation is inapplicable, *X* netted $330 (gross income minus state tax) from the venture without taking the travel expenses into account. Therefore, *X* may treat only $330 of his travel expenses as a miscellaneous itemized deduction.

¶ **21.1190.** **Rental of a Dwelling Unit Also Used for Personal Purposes.** The 1976 TRA added § 280A to the Code which (among other provisions) imposes restrictions on the deductibility of expenses incurred by a TP in connection with the rental of a dwelling unit to another, or in connection with other business use of a dwelling unit, if the TP is deemed to have used the dwelling unit for personal purposes at any time during the taxable year. This part of this Chapter focuses on the limitations on deductions connected with the rental of a dwelling unit. For the limitations imposed on the deduction of expenses incurred in the business use of a dwelling, see ¶¶ **21.1530–21.1536.**

If a dwelling unit is rented for fewer than 15 days in a taxable year, a kind of *de minimus* rule, which is described in ¶ **21.1193**, is applied.

A TP is deemed to have used a dwelling unit for personal purposes for a day if for any part of that day the unit is used: (a) for personal purposes by the TP or by another person who owns an interest in the unit or by certain members of the TP's family (or the family of such other person); or (b) by any individual under a swap arrangement which enables the TP to use some other dwelling unit; or (c) by any person (other than certain employees of the TP) who rents the unit for less than a fair rental on such day. § 280A(d)(2). As a consequence of a 1981 amendment to § 280A, a TP is permitted to rent a dwelling unit to anyone who does not have an interest in the unit, including a member of the TP's family, for use by the tenant as the tenant's principal residence provided that the tenant pays a fair rental to the TP. § 280A(d)(3)(A). In addition, a TP can rent a dwelling unit to a person having an interest in the unit if the rental is fair and is made pursuant to a "shared equity financing agreement" as defined in § 280A(d)(3)(C).

Section 280A applies only to individuals and to so-called S corporations (a corporation that has validly elected to be taxed under certain specified provisions of the Code). In the case of an S corporation, the personal use of the unit would be made by any shareholder of the corporation. § 280A(f)(2).

Section 280A has no effect whatsoever on the deductibility of expenses which are allowable without regard to whether the activity is profit-seeking (e.g., casualty losses and state income taxes)—such deductible expenses are sometimes referred to in this book as "non profit-seeking deductions." § 280A(b).

¶ 21.1191. Allocation of Expenses. When a TP is deemed to have used a dwelling unit for personal purposes on any day during the taxable year, the amount of expenses incurred in connection with the dwelling unit (other than non profit-seeking deductions) must be allocated between the period of time in which the dwelling unit (or a portion thereof) was rented at a fair value and the period of time that the unit (or a portion thereof) was otherwise actually used. The amount deductible (other than non profit-seeking deductions) cannot exceed the amount of expenses so allocated to the fair rental use of the property. § 280A(e); Prop. Reg. § 1.280A–3(c). The allocation of expenses described above is made according to the ratio of the number of days in the year that the dwelling was actually rented to the number of days that it was actually used for any purpose (including rental of the property); the days in which the unit was neither rented nor used for any other purpose are not taken into account in making this allocation. Prop. Reg. § 1.280A–3(c)(1), (d)(3) and (4), Ex.[28]

¶ 21.1192. "Gross Income from Rental Limitation." In addition to the allocation requirement described in **¶ 21.1191**, § 280A imposes an additional limitation on deductibility (which is similar to the limitations imposed under § 183)[29] if the TP is deemed to have used the dwelling unit for personal purposes during that taxable year for the *greater* of (a) 14 days; or (b) 10% of the number of days during such taxable year in which the unit was rented at a fair rental. § 280A(c)(5), (d)(1). For the purpose of determining whether the 10% of rental days provision applies, any day on which a unit is deemed to have been used by the TP for personal purposes will not constitute a day on which it was rented for fair value.[30] In such cases, the deductions allocated to the fair rental use of the unit (other than non profit-seeking deductions) are deductible only to the extent that the gross income from rental use for that taxable year exceeds the amount of non profit-seeking deductions which are allocable to the period of fair rental use for that year. § 280A(c)(5). The "gross income from rental use" (i.e., the "gross rental income") equals the gross receipts from rentals reduced by the expenses of obtaining tenants such as realtor's fees and advertising expenses. Prop. Reg. § 1.280A–3(d)(2). The reference to non profit-seeking deductions in this text is to deductions (such as mortgage interest on a principal residence and state property taxes) that are deductible regardless of whether connected to an income activity. The amount of deduction that is disallowed by this provision is carried over to the next taxable year of the TP and treated as a deduction in that year, subject to the same limitations. § 280A(c)(5).

If the limitations of § 280A disallow part of the TP's deductions, but allow part of them, which of the TP's deductions are

---

28. See also *Bolton v. Commissioner*, 77 T.C. 104 (1981), aff'd 694 F.2d 556 (9th Cir. 1982). For a discussion of the standards employed in determining whether the rental for a unit was for fair value, see *Razavi v. Commissioner*, 74 F.3d 125 (6th Cir. 1996).

29. Those limitations are described at **¶ 21.1180**.

30. In contrast, for other purposes of applying § 280A, a day on which a unit is both rented and used for personal purposes can still be counted as a day on which the unit is rented for a fair rental. Prop. Reg. § 1.280A–3(c)(1).

to be disallowed and which permitted? The Proposed Regulations set forth an order of priority for allowing the deductions. Prop. Reg. § 1.280A–3(d)(3). The order is described in the illustration at ¶ **21.1192–3**.

¶ **21.1192–1. Allocation of Non Profit–Seeking Deductions.** One reason that the amount of nonprofit-seeking oriented deductions that are allocated to the period of rental use is important is because the profit-seeking deductions allowable for that period cannot exceed the difference between the gross rental income and such non profit-seeking deductions. According to the Tenth and Ninth Circuits and the Tax Court, the amount of non profit-seeking deductions that are allocable to the period of rental use is the fraction of such deductions that reflects the fraction of the entire taxable year that is comprised of days of fair rental use.[31] Thus, according to the courts, unlike the allocation of profit related expenses (which allocation[32] is made by comparing the days in which the unit is rented with the days that it is actually used for any purpose), the allocation of non profit-seeking deductions is made by comparing rental days with the total number of days in the taxable year including days in which the unit is neither rented nor otherwise used.

In its Proposed Regulations, Treasury determined that non profit-seeking deductions are to be allocated to the period of rental use in the same manner that other expenses are allocated—i.e., Treasury would allocate such expenses according to the percentage of days of *use* of the unit that the number of fair rental days constitutes. Prop. Reg. § 1.280A–3(d)(3), (4), Ex. As noted above, in *Bolton* and in *McKinney*, the Tax Court and the Ninth and Tenth Circuits adopted a different formula for that allocation; and the courts' formula is more favorable to TPs. In those cases, the Tenth and Ninth Circuits expressly noted the contrary Proposed Regulation and repudiated it as an invalid interpretation by Treasury.

31. *Bolton v. Commissioner,* 694 F.2d 556 (9th Cir. 1982), aff'ing 77 T.C. 104 (1981); *McKinney v. Commissioner,* 732 F.2d 414 (10th Cir. 1983).

32. The method of allocation is described in ¶ **21.1191**.

¶ 21.1192–2.   Exception for Rental of Principal Residence for Consecutive Period of Twelve–Months. If a TP rents his entire principal residence for an entire taxable year, there will be no limitations on his deductions because of § 280A; but it is possible for § 183 to apply in certain circumstances. If a TP rented his principal residence for a 12–month period (or more) that straddled two taxable years and if no statutory relief were provided, TP's use of the property as his residence for part of each of those two taxable years could cause § 280A to apply to the deductions available for each year. However, the statute does provide partial relief. If the TP's personal use of the property is as his principal residence, § 280A(d)(4) provides that the "gross income from rental" limitation on deductions described in ¶ **21.1192** is not applicable if the TP rents (or holds for rent) the property for a fair rent for a consecutive period of at least 12 months (or a lesser period if the property is sold or exchanged at the end of the period). In such an event, the TP will not be treated as using the property for personal purposes for any day in those two taxable years that the TP used the property as his principal residence. This exception does not, however, prevent the limitation on deductions caused by the allocation of expenses described at ¶ **21.1191**; it precludes only the application of the limitation of deduction for "gross income from rental" rules [§ 280A(c)(5)] that are described at ¶ **21.1192**.

¶ 21.1192–3.   Illustration. X owns a vacation residence in Northern Michigan, and the property is not subject to a mortgage. In Year One, which was not a leap year, X and her family (i.e., her husband and children) occupied and used the residence for a total of 90 days; the residence was rented at a fair rental to unrelated parties for a total of 180 days, and the residence was unused and unoccupied for the remaining 95 days of that year. The rent that X received for the residence in that year was $2,600, and X expended $100 in advertising costs to rent the property. Therefore, the gross rental income that X received was $2,500. In that year, X incurred and paid a property tax of $1,000 because of her ownership of the residence. The portion of the property tax that is allocable to the rental of the residence qualifies as a nonitemized deduction [§ 62(a)(4)]; however, the portion of the property tax that is attributable to the non-rental period is treated as an itemized deduction. In addition, X incurred and paid $5,000 of expenses for repairs of the residence, and only that portion of those expenses that is allocable to the rental period can be deducted (i.e., those expenses can be deducted only to the extent that they can be attributed to a profit-seeking activity). So, only the portion of those expenses that can be allocated to the rental of the residence is deductible, and even then the amount of deduction is limited by the provisions of § 280A. The amount of depreciation deduction allowable for the use of the residence *during the rental period* is $1,000, but the deductibility of the depreciation allowance also is subject to the limitations of § 280A.

The Proposed Regulations provide an order of priority for the deduction of the expenses connected to the rental use of the residence. Prop. Reg. § 1.280A–3(d)(3). First, the expenses attributable to that period that are deductible without regard to their connection to a profit-seeking activity (such as mortgage interest and state taxes) are taken into account. Second, the profit-seeking deductions (other than those that cause an adjustment to basis such as depreciation deductions) are taken into account. Lastly, the deductions attributable to the rental use that do cause an adjustment to basis (such as depreciation deductions) are taken into account.

The only expense of X that can be deducted without regard to whether it is connected to a profit-seeking activity is the state property tax. The Proposed Regulations clearly include property taxes in this category. It is noteworthy, however, that while the property tax is a deductible item regardless of whether it is connected with a rental activity, only that portion of the property tax that is attributable to the rental use of the property is a nonitemized deduction. The question then is how much of the $1,000 property tax is attributable to the rental period. If the allocation described in the Proposed Regulations is adopted, the allocation is made by comparing the portion of the rental period (180 days) to the portion of the year that the residence is used for any purpose (270 days). On that method of allocation, 180/270 x $1,000 = $667 is allocated to the rental period. However, holdings of the Tax Court and the Ninth and Tenth Circuit Courts of Appeals suggest that the allocation should be made by comparing the number of days of the rental period (180 days) to the total number of days in that year (365 days).[33] On that method of allocation, 180/365 x $1,000 = $493 is allocated to the rental period. We will use the method of allocation that was adopted by the Tax Court and by the two Circuit Courts, and so we will allocate $493 of the property tax to the rental income. That leaves $2,007 of gross rental income that can be offset by the other deductions.

The next item to be deducted is the portion of the $5,000 of expenses for repairs that are allocable to the leasing of the residence. As to those expenses, there is no dispute over the correct method of allocation. The number of days of rental use (180) are to be compared to the number of days of total use (270). § 280A(e). So, 180/270 x $5,000 = $3,333 is allocated to the rental use of the property. The $1,667 of those expenses that is disallowed as a deduction because of this allocation is not carried over; it is never deducted. But, even as to the $3,333 that is allocated to the rental period, the amount that can be deducted is limited by § 280A(c)(5) to the amount of gross rental income ($2,500) less the non profit-seeking deductions that are attributable to the rental period ($493), and so only $2,007 of the $3,333 of allocated deduction can be deducted in Year One. The remaining $1,326 of disallowed deduction is carried over to Year Two and deductible then, subject to the same limitations. § 280A(c)(5).

Finally, since after taking the allowable deductions described above, there is no more gross rental income left, the $1,000 of depreciation deduction that is allocated to the rental period is not allowed because of the § 280A(c)(5) limitation. The $1,000 of depreciation is carried over to Year Two and can be deducted in that year, subject to the same limitations.

¶ 21.1193. Rental for a Brief Period. If a dwelling unit which is deemed to have been used by the TP as a residence in

---

33. While those courts were dealing with an issue of deductibility, they were not dealing with a question of the extent to which a deductible expense was a nonitemized deduction.

a taxable year is rented for fewer than 15 days of that year, no deductions (other than non profit-seeking deductions) will be allowed for expenses incurred in connection with the rental of that unit, but the rent received by the TP will be excluded from his gross income. § 280A(g).

¶ 21.1194.   Coordination with § 183. Although the consequences of § 280A are similar to those imposed by § 183, the applicability of the two sections turns on quite different standards. While the application of § 183 rests on the profitability of a venture, § 280A turns more upon the number of days in which the TP uses the dwelling unit for personal purposes, albeit one of the limitations that § 280A imposes does turn on profitability. § 280A(c)(5). If § 280A is applicable to the rental of a dwelling unit for a taxable year, then § 183 does not apply. See § 280A(f)(3).

¶ 21.1195.   Temporary Rental of Residence. In adopting the provisions of § 280A that are applicable to a TP's rental of a dwelling unit, Congress apparently was taking aim at the rental of a "vacation home" during all or part of the year that the TP does not use it. However, the actual language of § 280A is broader than that and will apply to a TP who is away from his residence for a part of a taxable year and rents it to another for that period. Thus, if Professor *X* at Duke University teaches at the University of Virginia for the fall semester as a visiting professor, Professor *X* will be subject to § 280A if he rents his home in Durham, North Carolina to another for that fall semester.

¶ 21.1196.   Nonitemized Deductions. Expenses incurred in connection with rental property that are deductible under § 212 are nonitemized deductions. § 62(a)(4). Section 280A operates as a limitation on the amount of otherwise allowable deductions that can be taken; it does not change the character of the deductions that are allowed. Consequently, such expenses (to the extent allowed) are not subject to the 2% of AGI floor that applies to miscellaneous itemized deductions.

¶ 21.1200.   Nonbusiness Expenses. Expenses incurred by an individual TP in connection with a profit-seeking venture which is not a "trade or business" may be deducted. Section 212 authorizes a deduction for "ordinary and necessary" expenses paid or incurred: (a) for the production or collection of income; (b) for the management, conservation or maintenance of income-producing property; or

(c) in connection with the determination, collection or refund of any tax. Such deductions are sometimes called "nonbusiness expense deductions," and they are to be distinguished from personal expense deductions such as medical expenses. Note, however, that many (but not all) items that are deductible under § 212 will constitute miscellaneous itemized deductions under § 67(b) and so will be subject to the 2% of AGI floor imposed by § 67(a), and will not be deductible at all if the alternative minimum tax is applicable. For years after 2012, such expenses also are subject to the limitation on itemized deductions that is imposed by § 68 when an individual's AGI exceeds a specified amount.[34]

¶ **21.1210. Compared with "Trade or Business" Expense.** For an expense to be deductible under § 212(1) or § 212(2), it must meet the same requirements that a trade or business expense must meet to qualify under § 162 except that it will not be connected with a "trade or business." Thus, the expense must be "ordinary and necessary" and cannot constitute a capital outlay. For the meaning of "ordinary and necessary" see **¶¶ 21.1500–21.1522.** A deduction for a payment claimed under § 212 will be disallowed if the payment is of a type for which a deduction would be disallowed under § 162(c), (f), or (g) if the deduction were claimed as a business expense (i.e., certain bribes, kickbacks, illegal payments, fines, and treble damages are not deductible). Treas. Reg. § 1.212–1(p).

¶ **21.1220. Illustration 1: Expenses of Seeking Alimony.** *W* seeks a divorce and alimony from *H*, and she thereby incurs $2,000 in legal fees. Since alimony is includable in gross income, that portion of W's expenses that was incurred in seeking alimony is deductible as an expense for the production of income. Treas. Reg. § 1.262–1(b)(7).[35] This deduction will constitute a miscellaneous itemized deduction that is subject to the 2% of AGI floor and to the overall limitation on itemized deductions imposed by § 68.[36] However, the portion of *W*'s legal fees incurred in obtaining the divorce is not deductible; only the portion of the fees attributable to establishing her right to alimony and to the collection of the alimony is deductible. It is necessary therefore to allocate the legal fees on a reasonable basis between the work performed in seeking a divorce and that performed in seeking alimony. If the

---

34. See **¶¶ 10.1110–10.1120.**

35. See *Hesse v. Commissioner*, 60 T.C. 685 (1973).

36. See **¶¶ 10.1110–10.1120.**

amount of legal expenses that were incurred for seeking alimony cannot be separately determined, no deduction is allowed.[37]

Note that even though W's establishment of her right to alimony creates a right to receive income over a period of years, the cost of establishing her right to that income is currently deductible, rather than capitalized.[38]

¶ 21.1230. Illustration 2: Expenses Incurred in Seeking Damages. Since punitive damages are included in the recipient's gross income,[39] the expenses incurred in seeking punitive damages, whether or not the TP's suit is successful, are deductible under § 212(1), subject to the 2% of AGI floor and to the overall limitation on itemized deductions imposed by § 68.[40] If the TP's tax is determined under the alternative minimum tax system, no deduction is allowable for those expenses. § 56(b)(1)(A).

If a TP seeks compensatory damages and if receipt of those damages would be excludable from the TP's gross income (and that will not always be the case), only the portion of a TP's expenses that are attributable to seeking punitive damages is deductible. The allocation of the TP's expenses may be made by using the proportion of punitive damages obtained by the TP to the total amount of damages awarded to the TP (or obtained by settlement). If a TP loses his suit for damages or if the TP obtains a lump sum settlement without apportionment between compensatory and punitive damages, the portion of the TP's expenses that is attributable to seeking punitive damages is still deductible. Typically, the apportionment of expenses in such cases is made by using the proportion of punitive damages claimed in the TP's complaint to the entire amount claimed in TP's complaint.[41] Of course, if the receipt of compensatory damages would be taxable to the TP (as is true, for example, of compensatory damages for defamation), then all of the TP's expenses in seeking damages (compensatory and punitive) are deductible.

¶ 21.1231. Costs Incurred in Discrimination Suits. The question arose as to the proper treatment of legal fees received

37. See Rev. Rul. 72–545. *Munn v. United States*, 455 F.2d 1028 (Ct. Cl. 1972).

38. See **¶ 21.1400** *et seq.* for a discussion of the requirements of capitalization.

39. See § 104(a)(2).

40. See **¶¶ 10.1110–10.1120.** The deductions are miscellaneous itemized deductions.

41. Rev. Rul. 85–98.

under a contingent fee arrangement in suits in which the damages sought were included in the plaintiff's taxable income. The Government contends that the entire amount of the plaintiff's award, including the amount paid to the attorney under the contingent fee arrangement, is taxable to the plaintiff. While the fee paid to the attorney is deductible, in the absence of a statutory exception, it constitutes a miscellaneous itemized deduction, and so is subject to the limitations imposed on those deductions. Much worse, the size of the fees typically will be large enough to cause the TP to be taxed under the alternative minimum tax system, and no deduction at all is allowed for miscellaneous itemized deductions under that system. This is a harsh result, and there were even a few cases where a TP who won a sizeable award ended up having a large deficit after paying the attorney fees and the taxes on the entire award.

TPs litigated the issue of whether they were taxed on the portion of the award that was payable to the attorney under a contingent fee arrangement; but, in *Banks,* the Supreme Court held that the entire amount of the award is taxable to the plaintiff, and so resolved the issue for the government (albeit two issues raised in amicus briefs were left open by the Court).[42]

While the *Banks* case was still pending in the Supreme Court, Congress addressed part of this problem by amending § 62 to provide that attorney fees and court costs incurred in an action for damages under certain specified statutes involving some type of discrimination or whistleblowing protection are nonitemized deductions. § 62(a)(20). Since nonitemized deductions are not subject to any of the limitations imposed on itemized deductions, the inclusion of the attorney's fee in income and the allowance of a nonitemized deduction for the fee is a wash. While the amendment covers all attorney fees, whether contingent fees or not, it reaches only fees and costs incurred in discrimination and whistleblowing suits, and leaves the problem intact for plaintiffs in other suits. The problem of the treatment and classification of certain deductions is much larger than the discrimination and whistleblowing suits problem on which Congress focused exclusively, and

---

42. *Commissioner v. Banks,* 543 U.S. 426 (2005). The *Banks* decision is discussed in more detail at ¶ **14.2500**.

some reform is needed.[43]

¶ 21.1240. Illustration 3: Expenses Incurred in Management of Income–Producing Property. *X* owns a portfolio of common stocks which is managed by a bank. The bank's fees are deductible by *X* (subject to the 2% of AGI floor and to the § 68 overall limitation on itemized deductions) as expenses of managing, conserving or maintaining income-producing property. The deductions are miscellaneous itemized deductions. Similarly, trustee fees and commissions are usually deductible under § 212(2), but also typically are classified as miscellaneous itemized deductions. For an exception to that classification, see **¶ 21.1250**.

¶ 21.1250. Expenses Paid or Incurred In the Adminstration of an Estate or Trust. Expenses paid or incurred in the administration of an estate or trust are deductible under § 212 as expenses to produce income and for the conservation of income-producing property. The deductions of an estate or trust that are not protected by § 67(e) constitute miscellaneous itemized deductions and so are subject to the 2% of AGI floor and other limitations that apply to such deductions.[44] Section 67(e) characterizes several deductions of an estate or trust as nonitemized deductions which are not subject to any of those limitations. One of those nonitemized deductions is the expenses paid or incurred in the administration of a trust or estate, but only if the expenses "would not have been incurred if the property were not held in such trust or estate." Consequently, the expenses of administering a trust or estate will be miscellaneous itemized deductions unless the expense is one that would not have been incurred by a person who is not an estate or trust. A dispute arose as to the construction of that requirement. Does it mean that the expense must be one that could not possibly be incurred by anyone other than a trust or estate or alternatively does it mean that the expense is one that is not customarily incurred by persons who are not a trust or estate? A unanimous Supreme Court decision resolved that issue by holding that it is sufficient to comply with the requirement to show that a trust or estate's administration expense was a type that would not customarily be incurred by a

---

43. For a discussion of those issues, see Jeffrey H. Kahn, *Beyond the Little Dutch Boy: An Argument for Structural Change in Tax Deduction Classification*, 80 Was. L. Rev. 1 (2005).

44. See *Knight v. Commissioner*, 552 U.S. 181 (2008).

person who was not a trust or estate.[45]

¶ 21.1260. Expenses Incurred in Reducing Taxpayer's Obligation to Pay Deductible Expenses. When a TP incurs an expense to reduce the extent to which he is obligated to make payments that are deductible in determining taxable income, the expense is incurred to obtain a result that will increase the TP's taxable income. That is, a reduction of the TP's deductions will increase the amount of his taxable income. The question arises as to whether such expenses can be deducted under § 212(1) as expenses incurred for the "production of income." In *Hunter v. United States*,[46] the Second Circuit denied a deduction to a TP for attorney fees incurred in defending against his wife's suit for alimony (the payment of alimony is deductible under § 215). The court held that § 212(1) applies to expenses incurred for the production of *gross* income. It is not sufficient to seek to increase taxable income.

¶ 21.1270. Tax–Related Expenses. Section 212(3) grants a deduction for expenses incurred in connection with tax counseling or the preparation of a tax return or a claim for a tax refund or redetermination.[47] This is a miscellaneous itemized deduction that is subject both to the 2% of AGI floor and to the limitation imposed by § 68.[48] However, the cost of having prepared that portion of a tax return that relates to the TP's conduct of a self-employed trade or business is a nonitemized deduction and so is exempt from the limitations and ceiling imposed on certain itemized deductions.[49] Similarly, the expenses incurred in resolving asserted tax deficiencies relating to the TP's trade or business are nonitemized deductions.[50]

It appears that the personal or perhaps even the capital nature of a transaction that caused the imposition of a tax will not affect the deductibility of expenses incurred in determining or reporting that tax.[51] There is a question whether expenses incurred in obtaining tax advice incident to a decision concerning the acquisi-

---

45. Id.

46. 219 F.2d 69 (2d Cir. 1955).

47. See ¶ 21.1360.

48. See ¶¶ 10.1110–10.1120.

49. Rev. Rul. 92–29.

50. Rev. Rul. 92–29.

51. See *Sharples v. United States*, 533 F.2d 550 (Ct. Cl. 1976).

tion or disposition of an asset are deductible under § 212(3). Compare *Honodel v. Commissioner*[52] (holding such expenses to be nondeductible because they are not "ordinary and necessary") with *Collins v. Commissioner*[53] (allowing a deduction for the cost of tax advice incident to the acquisition of an asset).

The apparent purpose of § 212(3) is to provide a deduction for the cost that a TP incurs in dealing with the complexity of the tax laws. It would not seem to matter in what context the tax issue arose since it is the complexity of the tax law that is the focus of the deduction. Indeed, the case that stimulated the adoption of the antecedent of § 212(3) was the denial of a deduction for expenses incurred in litigating a gift tax issue, and the personal nature of the gift did not prevent Congress from acting to allow a deduction for those expenses.[54]

¶ **21.1300. Personal Expenses.** No deduction is permitted for personal, living, or family expenses. § 262.

¶ **21.1310. Mixed Purposes.** A TP's motives for incurring an expense may be mixed (i.e., he may have both business and personal motives). Generally, if the purpose of the TP is a significant factor in characterizing an expense, the *primary* purpose of the TP is decisive although the issue is not free of doubt.[55] As noted below, a TP's purpose in incurring an expense will not control the tax treatment of it; instead, it is the nature of the transaction which led to the expenditure that usually controls the tax treatment.

¶ **21.1320. Deductibility Determined from the Source of the Obligation or from the Immediate Objective of the Expense.** A TP may incur an expense for what appears on its face to be a personal or family purpose, but the TP may contend that his actual purpose was connected with his business or investment activities. If the source of the TP's obligation is personal (such as a marital relationship) no deduction will be allowed.

¶ **21.1321. Illustration: Defense of Divorce Suit.** *H* was sued for divorce by *W*, and he incurred legal expenses in

---

52. 722 F.2d 1462 (9th Cir. 1984), aff'g 76 T.C. 351 (1981).

53. 54 T.C. 1656, 1666 (1970), Acq.

54. See Treas. Reg. § 1.212–1(*l*).

55. See *Shiosaki v. Commissioner*, 475 F.2d 770 (9th Cir. 1973).

defending the suit. *H* contended that his purpose in defending the suit was not to bar the divorce but rather to retain his controlling interest in the corporation which employed him. Consequently, *H* claimed his expenses to be deductible under § 212(2) as having been incurred for the conservation of income-producing property. However, the Supreme Court held that the origin and character of a divorce action is personal and family-oriented and accordingly disallowed the claimed deduction. *United States v. Gilmore.*[56]

It is unsettled whether the portion of *H*'s expenses that is attributable to an effort to retain his ownership of stock is a capital expenditure to be added to *H*'s basis in those stocks. While this issue was expressly left open by the Supreme Court in its *Gilmore* decision, the tenor of that decision suggests that no addition to basis should be allowed. But see the district court decision on remand in *Gilmore*[57] (allowing *H* to increase his basis); *Serianni v. Commissioner*[58] (allowing *W* to increase her basis in certain stocks by a portion of legal fees incurred in a divorce action to establish her equity interest in those stocks).[59]

¶ 21.1330. Immediate Objective Controls Characterization. A TP's immediate objective for incurring an expense may be personal, but his reason for engaging in the activity may be grounded on business considerations. For example, a TP might contend that his ultimate purpose in defending an action against himself for assault and battery was to protect his job which he would lose if he were unsuccessful in defending the action. The proper test for deductibility is whether the origin of the action for assault and battery was personal, and, if so, no deduction should be allowed the TP regardless of his motives for defending the suit.[60] Similarly, a TP may incur an expenditure of a capital nature and claim a deduction on the ground that the ultimate purpose of the expenditure was to accomplish a current business objective. His ultimate motivation should not matter. This ap-

---

56. 372 U.S. 39 (1963).

57. *Gilmore v. United States,* 245 F.Supp. 383 (N.D. Cal. 1965).

58. 80 T.C. 1090 (1983).

59. See ¶ 21.1350.

60. E.g., *Michaels v. Commissioner,* 32 AFTR 2d 73–5859 (9th Cir. 1973), aff'g 30 T.C.M. 834 (1971).

proach to characterizing expenditures is sometimes referred to as the "origin test."

In general, TPs have been unsuccessful in making that contention, and the courts characterize such expenditures according to the immediate objectives of the TP rather than on his ultimate purpose. In *Woodward v. Commissioner*,[61] and *United States v. Hilton Hotels*,[62] the Supreme Court held that the payments there in question (appraisal costs to determine the value of stock held by minority shareholders) were nondeductible capital expenditures and that the ultimate purpose of the TP for acquiring the stock of the minority shareholders did not make the expenditures deductible.

The origin test does not prevent an item from being divided into its parts each of which is characterized separately and receives the appropriate tax treatment.[63]

¶ 21.1340. The Origin Test. The Supreme Court's adoption in *Gilmore*[64] of the "origin" test for determining whether an expense is personal or business-oriented is a useful test in certain circumstances. Thus, if X negligently operated his automobile and thereby injured Y, the deductibility of the damages X paid to Y will turn upon whether X was operating his car for personal purposes or in pursuit of his business. But not all expenses which have a personal origin should be nondeductible. For example, if a divorced wife sues her ex-husband for defaulted alimony, her legal fees are deductible even though the source or origin of her claim is her former marital relationship—that is, the alimony she will collect will be gross income to her and so she should be permitted to deduct the cost of obtaining it. Treas. Reg. § 1.262–1(b)(7).[65] Similarly, a plaintiff who obtains damages for libel of his personal reputation will be permitted to deduct his legal fees. See **¶ 21.1230.** While the origin of such actions may be personal, the immediate objective of the suit is to obtain gross income for the

61. 397 U.S. 572 (1970).

62. 397 U.S. 580 (1970).

63. See e.g. *Boagni v. Commissioner*, 59 T.C. 708 (1973), Acq.; *Dye v. United States*, 121 F.3d 1399 (10th Cir. 1997).

64. n. 56 supra.

65. *Wild v. Commissioner*, 42 T.C. 706 (1964), Acq.; *Hesse v. Commissioner*, 60 T.C. 685 (1973), Acq., aff'd without a written opinion, 511 F.2d 1393 (3d Cir. 1975). See also *Nickell v. Commissioner*, 831 F.2d 1265 (6th Cir. 1987).

TP, and so the TP's net income can properly be determined only by reducing the gross income so acquired by the amount expended in obtaining it. Allowing this deduction appears to conform with the congressional purpose for adopting § 212(1).

¶ 21.1341. **Proper Use of the Origin Test.** The proper operation of the origin test has not yet been resolved. The Tax Court has adopted a view of the operation of the origin test that is especially appealing. The Tax Court stated in *Boagni v. Commissioner*,[66]

> Quite plainly, the "origin-of-the-claim" rule does not contemplate a mechanical search for the first in the chain of events which led to the litigation but, rather, requires an examination of all the facts. The inquiry is directed to the ascertainment of the "kind of transaction" out of which the litigation arose [(citation omitted)]. Consideration must be given to the issues involved, the nature and objective of the litigation, the defenses asserted, the purposes for which the claimed deductions were expended, the background of the litigation, and all facts pertinent to the controversy.

The above statement has been quoted with approval in a number of subsequent Tax Court decisions.[67]

The Tax Court's articulation of the origin test was criticized and rejected by the Ninth Circuit in *Keller Street Development Co. v. Commissioner*.[68] The Ninth Circuit in *Keller Street* stated that the *Boagni* description of the origin test was actually a description of the "primary purpose of the litigation" test, which the Ninth Circuit noted had been rejected by the Supreme Court. The Ninth Circuit held that the proper application of the origin test is a two-step process: first, the transaction from which the taxable event "proximately resulted" must be identified (e.g., the event that prompted the cause of action and was the basis of the suit), second, the transaction that was identified in the first step must be characterized. Note that the Ninth Circuit did agree with the Tax Court that the origin test does not rest on a determination of the first in a

---

66.   59 T.C. 708, 713 (1973), Acq.

67.   E.g., *Mosby v. Commissioner*, 86 T.C. 190 (1986); *Lucas v. Commissioner*, 79 T.C. 1 (1982); *Duntley v. Commissioner,* 54 T.C.M. 1138 (1987); *Colvin v. Commissioner*, TC Memo ¶ 2004–67 (2004); *Melcher v. Commissioner*, TC Memo 2009–210 (2009); *Santa Fe Pacific Gold v. Commissioner*, 132 T.C.240 (2009).

68.   688 F.2d 675 (9th Cir. 1982).

chain of events that led to the litigation; instead, the court seems to rely on the character of the event that has the closest nexus to the litigation.

The authors have the following suggestions as to how the rule should operate.

¶ 21.1341–1. Business Deductions. In general, it is appropriate to use the origin test to determine whether an expenditure or loss qualifies as a business expense or business loss. A business expense deduction (or business loss deduction) should not be allowed for an expenditure unless the transaction in question has business origins or is attributable to a previous change of purpose from a personal to a business activity (such as a permanent conversion of a personal residence to rental property).

Even in respect to business expenses, the origin test is not always useful. For example, if *H* and *W* are seeking a divorce, and *W* telephones business clients of *H* and makes defamatory statements concerning *H*'s professional skills, the expenses that *H* incurs in obtaining an injunction prohibiting *W* from contacting *H*'s clients should be deductible notwithstanding the fact that the origin of the problem is the marriage of *H* and *W*. It is necessary to determine whether the expense is more closely related to *H*'s business than it is to his personal life since the expense relates to both parts of *H*'s life. This is an example of why it is not appropriate in applying the test simply to determine the first of a chain of events that led to the expenditure.

¶ 21.1341–2. Nonbusiness Deductions. Despite the fact that the *Gilmore* case itself[69] involved a question of the availability of § 212, the origin test is less helpful in distinguishing a personal expenditure from a nonbusiness expense deduction item under § 212 and in distinguishing business and nonbusiness deduction items from a capital expenditure. The test for determining whether § 212 applies should rest more on the character of the expenditure than on its origin. The character of an expenditure rests on a number of surrounding factors of which its origin is merely one. If the expenditure is directly related to the

69. n. 56 supra.

production of gross income, a deduction should be allowed regardless of the origin of the TP's claim to that income item. The nexus between the expenditure and the collection of the income typically will be so immediate that there will be little or no uncertainty as to whether the expenditure is more closely attributable to the income production than to the activity from which the income claim was derived. Thus, a spouse's expenses to collect alimony are deductible. On the other hand, if an expenditure which has personal origins also relates to the conservation of income-producing property, it usually will be difficult to determine whether the expenditure should be treated as part of the cost of the personal activity or whether it is more closely attributable to the cost of retaining the income-producing property. The test for deductibility or capitalization of such expenditures could have been made to turn on the primary purpose of the TP in making the expenditure as determined subjectively for each TP. The administrative difficulty of applying a subjective test is so great that the Supreme Court rejected the primary purpose test and instead adopted the origin test.

¶ 21.1341–3. **Summary.** In summary, the origin test may be useful in determining whether an expenditure qualifies as a business expense or as an expense of maintaining or conserving income-producing property, but it is not useful in determining whether an expenditure qualifies as one for the production of income. An expenditure to produce income bears such a proximate relationship to the income that there is not the uncertainty of purpose that exists for expenditures which satisfy personal goals.

¶ 21.1341–4. **Applying the Origin Test to Capital Expenditures.** Courts have applied the origin test to determine whether an expenditure is to be treated as capital or ordinary.[70] The authors doubt that the distant origin of an activity is an appropriate determinant of whether an expenditure is a capital item. Instead, the inquiry might better focus on a number of considerations such as the immediate objective of the expenditure (as determined from objective facts rather than from the view of the subjective

---

70. E.g., *Anchor Coupling Co. v. United States*, 427 F.2d 429 (7th Cir. 1970); *Entwicklungs und Finanzierungs A.G. v. Commissioner*, 68 T.C. 749 (1977).

goal of the TP) and the character of the transaction. The origin of a transaction is an important input in determining the nature of the expenditure, but it ought not be the exclusive criterion. The origin test can work perfectly well to differentiate capital expenditures provided that a related group of transactions can be separated so that the origin of each separate transaction is used to characterize the events. This separation of related transactions is difficult to do, and the courts have often failed to do so properly. Because of the difficulty of applying the origin test alone, the authors believe that several criteria, such as the immediate objective and character of the expenditure, should be employed together with a consideration of the origin of the activity. These several criteria should merely be factors to help the court reach the ultimate issue of whether an expenditure is more closely related to a capital transaction or to an ordinary business or profit-seeking transaction.

Consider the tax treatment of commissions and fees incurred to facilitate the sale of a parcel of real estate. Unless incurred by a dealer in real estate, those expenses must be capitalized and either offset against the amount realized on the sale or taken as a loss deduction if the property fails to be sold. On the other hand, if the owner of the real estate is a dealer in real estate, the commissions and fees are nonitemized deductible business expenses when paid or incurred. Prop. Reg. § 1.263(a)–1(d). The origin of those expenses for a TP who deals in real estate is the ordinary conduct of his trade or business which consists of buying and selling real estate. If the TP actually sells the realty in the same taxable year that he incurred the expenses, then the tax consequences of treating the expenses as nonitemized deductions will be identical to capitalizing them and using them to offset the amount realized on the sale. But if the TP sells the realty in a different taxable year than the one in which he incurred the expenses, the tax consequences of the two alternative treatments will be quite different.

¶ 21.1341–5. Illustration 1: Expense Arising from Acquisition of a Capital Asset. *X* was engaged in a manufacturing business. *X* sought to acquire a trademark from *Y* to use in *X*'s business. The cost of acquiring the trademark is a capital expenditure. In bidding for the trademark, X made derogatory comments about Z, a competitor of X, who also was bidding to acquire the trademark. Z learned of the comments made by X, and Z sued X for defamation. X settled the suit by paying Z $100,000 damages. Was the origin of X's expenditure the capital acquisition of a trademark or was the origin the ordinary conduct of X's business? The origin test, in and of itself, provides little guidance. Perhaps a better way to frame the question is whether the acquisition of capital assets is an integral part of X's business so that expenses incurred while so engaged are business expenses unless they have a closer nexus to the immediate acquisition of the asset than they do to X's general business activity. In the authors' view, this type of expenditure should be allowed as a business expense.

¶ 21.1341–6. Illustration 2: Expense Arising from Acquisition of a Capital Asset. The same facts apply as in **¶ 21.1341–5** except that X succeeded in purchasing the trademark from Y. Y subsequently filed suit against X for having made misrepresentations. X paid Y $10,000 damages to settle the suit. X was certain that he would prevail in the suit, but he settled in order to terminate the adverse publicity that the suit had generated. The origin test has been employed in similar cases to characterize X's payment as a capital expenditure. But, is the origin of X's payment his fear of adverse publicity or the representations that he made to induce Y to sell? The courts have resolved that question by focusing on the origin of Y's suit rather than on X's reason for making the payment. In effect, the courts look to the immediate objective of the payment—to settle the suit brought by Y—and they will not look at X's subjective motives for settling the dispute.[71]

¶ 21.1341–7. Illustration 3: Mixed Business and Personal Objectives. Prior to completing his medical school education, W executed an agreement with the Navy under which he received a Naval reserve commission and a deferment from active duty until completion of residency training in his specialty. Upon completing his residency, W sought administrative and judicial relief from the order to

---

71.   See Rev. Rul. 73–146, and TAM 200126008.

report to active duty, but the effort was unsuccessful. *W* incurred $1,000 in legal fees in his attempt to avoid active duty. While *W* could have earned more income from the private practice of medicine than from serving on active duty in the Navy, the desire to avoid Navy duty rests at least as much on personal considerations as on financial ones. The personal considerations are so integral to *W*'s decision that they cannot readily be separated from *W*'s financial concerns (indeed it is likely that the personal considerations are dominant). The analysis of the nature of the transaction should be made from the objective facts and should not be based on a subjective evaluation of *W*'s actual thought process. No deduction should be allowed. On similar facts, the Tax Court utilized the origin test and held that the origin of *W*'s expenditure was to obtain a deferral from active duty, which is a personal matter, and so the Court denied *W*'s claim for a deduction.[72]

¶ 21.1341–8. Illustration 4: Distinguishing Purposes of Closely Held Corporation from Purposes of Its Shareholder. *W* sued *H* for divorce and *W* named as additional defendants three corporations whose stock was either owned by *H* or by a corporation owned by him. *W* sought to restrain the business activities of the corporations and to gain control of them. The defendants successfully resisted *W*'s action, and they incurred legal fees and expenses of approximately $1,300,000. On its motion, the divorce court ordered that the legal fees and expenses be incurred one-fourth by each defendant. The Commissioner denied a deduction to the corporations for their payment of their share of the fees and expenses. In *Dolese v. United States*,[73] the Tenth Circuit allowed the corporations a deduction only for that part of their fees and expenses that was attributable to freeing the corporations from the restraint on conducting their business activities and for that part of their fees and expenses that was incurred in resisting *W*'s effort to take over control of the corporations since the takeover could be injurious to the well-being of the corporations. The balance of the fees and expenses paid by the corporations were not only nondeductible; they also

72. *West v. Commissioner*, 71 T.C. 532 (1979).

73. 605 F.2d 1146 (10th Cir. 1979).

were treated as a constructive dividend to *H* and taxable to him.

¶ 21.1341–9. Illustration 5: Difficulty of Identifying Origin. *H* and *W* owned all of the stock of the *X* Corporation, and *H* served as its president. *H* loaned a car belonging to the corporation to his son, *S*, and *S* negligently injured *B*, an unrelated party, in an automobile accident. *B* sued *H*, *W*, *S*, and *X* for more than $4,000,000. As a consequence of *B*'s filing suit, the bank froze *X*'s credit line and demanded security for an outstanding note, and *X* suffered other financial threats. *X* settled the suit with *B* by having *X*'s insurer pay *B* over $100,000, and *X* paid *B* over $50,000 from funds *X* borrowed from its bank. *X*'s counsel advised *X* that if the suit went to trial, the company likely would be found liable for having negligently allowed *S* to use the car. In a divided decision of the Fourth Circuit in *Kopp's Co. v. United States*,[74] the majority of the court held that the settlement payments and legal fees paid by *X* are deductible business expenses. In dissenting, Judge Ervin stressed that the origin of the suit was *H*'s loan of the company car to *S*, which was a personal (i.e., nonbusiness) transaction. Judge Ervin did not believe that the corporation was liable for damages and he felt that even if *X* were so liable and had business reasons to settle the suit, the personal origin of the suit prevents the corporation from qualifying for a deduction.

¶ 21.1341–10. Illustration 6: Multiple Disputes. *A*, who was in the business of mining coal, mined and removed coal from two tracts of land owned by *F*. After several years, *F* brought suit against *A*. *F* claimed in his complaint that *A* had not paid *F* royalties that were due for coal taken from one of the tracts pursuant to a lease between the parties. *F* requested a judgment for the unpaid royalties. *F* also claimed that there was no lease between the parties for mining the second tract, and so *A* was a trespasser as to its mining operations on that tract. *F* sought compensatory and punitive damages for the trespass and taking of coal from the second tract. *A* raised several defenses in his answer, one of which was that the parties had made a valid oral lease which permitted *A* to mine the

---

74.   636 F.2d 59 (4th Cir. 1980).

second tract. The parties arrived at an out-of-court settlement of their dispute. *A* sought to deduct the legal fees that he incurred in that litigation. In a somewhat similar case, the Tax Court held that the origin of *F*'s suit against *A* was partly a claim for royalties under a lease and partly a claim for trespass, and that *A*'s defense was partly to resist the claim for royalties and partly to defend his title to the oral leasehold of the second tract. The portion of the fee for resisting the royalty claim is deductible as a business expense, and the portion allocable to defending *A*'s title to the leasehold is a nondeductible capital expenditure.[75] The court allocated the fee on a 50%–50% basis between those two disputes.[76]

¶ **21.1342.** **Misuse of the Origin Test.** Whatever may be the merits of the origin test, it has confused some courts and led them into making extraordinary decisions. For example, in *Brown v. United States*,[77] the TP, her sister and her brother were shareholders of a corporation. The brother offered to purchase the stock of the TP and her sister. The TP became suspicious over the terms of the offer—particularly as mention was made of another corporation (wholly owned by the brother) which did business with the family corporation. The TP and her sister consulted an attorney who, after an investigation, informed them that the brother's corporation had acquired the most valuable assets and operations of the family corporation in transactions which constituted a fraud upon the TP and her sister as shareholders of the family corporation. The brother refused to divulge any information about his wholly owned corporation, and so the TP and her sister brought a shareholder derivative suit. This suit was settled favorably for the TP and her sister who thereby exchanged their stock holdings for debentures of the family corporation at a value 80% greater than the offer made for their stock by the brother. In addition, the settlement increased the TP's annual income from the family corporation eightfold and guaranteed the TP and her sister seats on the board of directors. The TP sought to deduct her legal fees. The Sixth Circuit reversed a district court judgment allowing the deduction. The Sixth

---

75. See ¶¶ **21.1460–21.1461**.

76. *Frazee McCall Joint Venture v. Commissioner*, 60 T.C.M. 1466 (1990). Expenses incurred in defending title to property are capital expenses. Prop. Reg. § 1.263(a)–2(d)(2).

77. 526 F.2d 135 (6th Cir. 1975).

Circuit held that the origin of the TP's suit was to determine the value of her stock so that she could properly respond to her brother's offer and so no deduction is allowable for the legal fees, which were capital expenditures.[78]

¶ 21.1350. Capital Expenditures in Defending a Divorce Action. In several cases subsequent to the Supreme Court's decision in *Gilmore*,[79] expenses for seeking or defending a divorce action were treated as capital expenditures and were added to the TP's basis in the property he wished to protect or obtain.[80] Those cases appear to be inconsistent with the thrust of the Supreme Court's decision in *Gilmore*, but the issue is unsettled.

¶ 21.1360. Tax Advice Incident to a Divorce. The former Court of Claims (which is now incorporated into the United States Court of Appeals for the Federal Circuit) held that the expenses of obtaining tax advice incident to a divorce proceeding are deductible under § 212(3);[81] and the Commissioner conceded this issue in Rev. Rul. 72–545, provided that a reasonable basis exists for determining the amount of TP's legal fee that is allocable to tax advice.

A contrary view was suggested by the opinions of three dissenting judges and two concurring judges in the Tax Court's decision in *Merians v. Commissioner*,[82] where those five judges maintained that a fee for tax advice that was given in connection with estate planning is not deductible under § 212(3), albeit the fee *might* be deductible in certain cases under § 212(2) as a conservation of income-producing property. Those opinions imply that the deductibility of the cost of tax advice depends upon the underlying transaction to which the tax advice relates. The Commissioner conceded by stipulation in *Merians* that such fees are deductible under § 212(3). The majority of the Tax Court accepted that stipulation and therefore did not discuss the wisdom of the Commissioner's concession. The comments of the five concurring

---

78. For another peculiar application of the origin test, see the divided decision of the Seventh Circuit in *Fischer v. United States*, 490 F.2d 218 (7th Cir. 1973).

79. n. 56, supra.

80. *Gilmore v. United States*, 245 F.Supp. 383 (N.D. Cal. 1965); *George v. United States*, 434 F.2d 1336 (Ct. Cl. 1970).

81. *George v. United States*, 434 F.2d 1336 (Ct. Cl. 1970); *Munn v. United States*, 455 F.2d 1028 (Ct. Cl. 1972).

82. 60 T.C. 187 (1973), Acq.

and dissenting judges on this issue were largely dictum and were not adopted in the majority's opinion. Subsequent court decisions also have not adopted the dictum of the five concurring and dissenting judges. For example, in a subsequent decision, the Tax Court allowed a deduction for the portion of the legal fees incurred in a divorce proceeding that is allocable to tax advice.[83] In *Goldaper*, the Service did not contest the deductibility of such fees but contended that no part of the lawyer's services was allocable to tax advice. The court allocated a portion of the fee to tax advice and allowed a deduction.

¶ 21.1370. Conversion of Residence. When a TP moves out of his personal residence and converts it to an income-seeking activity, he can thereafter deduct the costs of maintaining and repairing the property as well as a depreciation allowance. Treas. Regs. §§ 1.212–1(h) and 1.167(g)–1. In the taxable year in which the TP moved out, the amount of such deductions may be subject to the limitations imposed by § 280A.[84]

The question arises as to what action of a TP is sufficient to constitute a conversion to an income-producing activity. Merely attempting to sell an unwanted prior residence will not usually qualify as a conversion to an income-producing activity. Actually renting the property usually will suffice.[85] However, a temporary renting of a former residence whole trying to sell the property likely will not be sufficient to constitute a conversion; the rental activity is merely an effort to reduce costs while endeavoring to sell the property.[86] Regardless of whether actually rented, a bona fide offering of a former residence for rent (or offering it for rent or sale at the option of the tenant/purchaser) typically will be sufficient to constitute a conversion.[87] Note, however, that a mere offering to rent will not be a sufficient conversion to permit the TP to deduct a loss recognized on the subsequent sale of the property even though it is a sufficient conversion for purposes of allowing the deduction of maintenance costs and depreciation.[88]

---

83. *Goldaper v. Commissioner*, 36 T.C.M. 1381 (1977).

84. See ¶ **21.1190**.

85. E.g., *Bolaris v. Commissioner*, 776 F.2d 1428 (9th Cir. 1985).

86. *Saunders v. Commissioner*, TC Memo 2002–143 (2002).

87. See *Robinson v. Commissioner*, 2 T.C. 305 (1943).

88. See Chapter **Eighteen**.

When the former residence is offered only for sale by the TP (and not for rent), a deduction will not be permitted for maintenance costs in most cases; but in certain circumstances, a deduction will be allowed.[89] In *Smith*, the Tax Court suggested that merely holding for sale is sufficient to effect a conversion, but later cases repudiated that view. In *Newcombe v. Commissioner*,[90] the Tax Court reconsidered this issue in a case where, immediately after moving out, the TP had offered a former residence for sale at a price in excess of its then market value but not in excess of the TP's basis in the property. The court disallowed the TP's claim for a deduction for maintenance costs and depreciation; the case was reviewed by the entire court and there were no dissents. The majority opinion held that a number of factors must be examined to determine whether a formerly occupied residence has been converted into "property held for the production of income." If the residence is offered for sale only (and not for rent), it will be treated as converted if the TP can show that he intended to hold the property until he could sell it for more than its basis and for more than its value at the date of "conversion" (post-conversion appreciation). If the property is offered for sale (even at a price in excess of its then value) immediately or shortly after the TP moves out, that will ordinarily be strong evidence that he is not holding it for post-conversion appreciation. The larger asking price could merely be a bargaining ploy. The critical issue is the purpose or intention of the TP.

In *Newcombe*, the majority found that the TP did not in fact hold the property for post-conversion appreciation. While the court noted that its decision in *Smith v. Commissioner, supra* had reached a contrary result, it disapproved of that earlier decision and stated that the *Smith* case had "little precedential value."

Seven Tax Court judges in *Newcombe* concurred with the result reached by the majority opinion. The seven concurring judges stated, however, that property need only be held for post-conversion appreciation to qualify as property held for the production of income; they disagreed with the statement in the majority opinion that the property must also be held for sale at a price in excess of the TP's basis.

"Whether an individual holds property for the production of income is a question of fact, and depends on the purpose or

---

89. See *Smith v. Commissioner*, 26 T.C.M. 149 (1967), aff'd per curiam, 397 F.2d 804 (9th Cir. 1968); and *Lowry v. United States*, 384 F.Supp. 257 (D. N.H. 1974).

90. 54 T.C. 1298 (1970).

intention of the individual, as gleaned from all of the facts and circumstances of the particular case."[91] In *Newcombe*, the court listed five factors to be considered in making that determination, and those five factors have been adopted in subsequent Tax Court cases.[92] The five factors are:

(1) the length of time the house was occupied by the TP as a residence

(2) whether the TP permanently abandoned personal use of the house

(3) the character of the property (recreational or otherwise)

(4) whether the house was offered for rent

(5) whether it was offered for sale.

Newcombe has been cited with approval in subsequent cases.[93]

The question of whether a personal residence has been converted arises where the property was previously used by the TP as a residence. If the TP seeks to sell an inherited or purchased residence that was not so used by the TP, there is no question of a conversion; and maintenance expenses and depreciation deductions will be allowed.[94]

¶ 21.1380. Statutory Restrictions. Section 274 prohibits a deduction for certain entertainment and travel expenses which otherwise might be deductible as business expenses or as nonbusiness expenses under § 212. Some expenses are disallowed only if the TP fails to comply with a requirement of substantiation [§ 274(d)] but some are disallowed regardless of substantiation— for example, the cost of attending a convention or seminar that is held on a cruise ship is nondeductible under § 274(h)(2) unless certain special requirements are satisfied. Typically, no deduction will be allowed for an expense for a facility (such as a yacht, hunting lodge, swimming pool, or tennis court) which is used in conjunction with an activity of a type that is generally associated with an entertainment, amusement or recreational activity. § 274(a)(1). No deduction will be allowed for dues paid or incurred for membership in a club organized for business, pleasure, recreation or other social purpose. § 274(a)(3).

91. *Grant v. Commissioner*, 84 T.C. 809, 825 (1985).

92. E.g., *Saunders v. Commissioner*, n. 86, supra.

93. E.g., *Quinn v. Commissioner*, 65 T.C. 523 (1975).

94. E.g., *Mitchell v. Commissioner*, 47 T.C. 120 (1966).

¶ 21.1390. 50 Percent Limitation on Deduction of Entertainment and Meal Expenses. Subject to limited exceptions listed in § 274(n)(2), because of § 274(n)(1), a TP can deduct only 50% of his unreimbursed entertainment and meal expenses that are otherwise deductible. A more liberal deduction allowance is provided for meals consumed while away from home by employees in certain transportation industries. § 274(n)(3).

> **¶ 21.1391. Illustration.** *D* conducts seminars for a fee. The price for each attendee includes food and beverages provided at the seminar. *F* who attends a seminar for business purposes is entitled to deduct the fee that he paid to *D*, other than any reduction of that deduction required by § 274(n). The expenses that *D* incurred in presenting the seminar, including the expenses incurred in providing food and beverages, are deductible business expenses. The reduction imposed by § 274(n)(1) does not apply to *D* because he is selling the food and beverages for full consideration in money or money's worth. § 274(e)(8), (n)(2)(A). However, *F* will have to determine the amount of the fee he paid that is attributable to food and beverages, and *F* can deduct only 50% of that amount. It would be helpful to the attendees' determination of their deduction if *D* would provide a statement of the amount of the fee that is attributable to food and beverages, but such an allocation is not binding on the government, nor is it required.[95] If *F* were an employee who was reimbursed by his employer for the fee he paid to *D*, the entire amount would be deductible by *F* [and thus would wash out the income that *F* recognized because of the reimbursement], but the employer could deduct only 50% of the amount of the reimbursement that is attributable to the payment for food and beverages.

¶ 21.1390A. Limitation on Deduction for Executive Compensation. There is a ceiling on the amount of deduction that is allowable for compensation paid or incurred to certain executive employees of a publicly held corporation. For this purpose, a "publicly held corporation" is a corporation issuing a class of common equity securities that is required to be registered under Section 12 of the Securities Exchange Act of 1934. § 162(m)(2). The maximum amount of deduction allowable for compensation to a covered employee is $1,000,000. § 162(m)(1). A covered employee is: the chief executive officer of a publicly held corporation

95. See PLR 9029015.

(or a person acting in that capacity), or an employee whose compensation for that year must be reported under the Securities Exchange Act to the corporation's shareholders because the employee is one of the publicly held corporation's four highest compensated officers (other than the chief executive) for that year. § 162(m)(3). The $1,000,000 ceiling applies to the deduction for all remuneration provided to a covered employee except that certain designated types of compensation are excluded and so are not subject to the $1,000,000 ceiling. For purposes of applying the $1,000,000 limitation, the following items are not treated as compensation of the covered employee [§ 162(m)(4)]:

(1) commissions payable solely because of income generated by the covered employee;

(2) remuneration received because of the attainment of one or more performance goals if certain outside director and shareholder approval requirements are satisfied;

(3) payments made to a tax qualified retirement plan;

(4) amounts that are excluded from the covered employee's gross income (such as excludable fringe benefits and employer-provided medical insurance coverage); and

(5) remuneration paid pursuant to certain binding contracts that were in effect on February 17, 1993.

The deduction for an employer's expenses in entertaining certain individuals (generally, officers, directors and owners) is limited to the amount that such persons include in their income. § 274(e)(2).

¶ 21.1400. Capital Expenditures. A capital expenditure cannot be deducted in the year in which it is paid or accrued. Instead, it must be capitalized. See Prop. Reg. § 1.263(a)–1. One of the goals of the income tax system is to match expenditures with the income that they produce. When an expenditure produces an income stream that will be received over a period of years, a current deduction of that expenditure would provide a distorted picture of the income actually earned each year. That is, the income reported in the year of the expenditure would be too low, and the income reported in the years in which the income stream is received would be too high. If, instead, the expenditure is capitalized and then amortized over the period in which the income stream is received, there would be a closer matching of income and expenses and a more accurate portrayal of the TP's yearly income.

However, matching of income and expenses is only one of the goals of the tax system. When that goal comes into conflict with others, a decision must be made as to which will take priority. It is for that reason that not all expenditures that produce a future income stream are capitalized. A principal reason for not capitalizing a particular expenditure is that it would impose a greater administrative burden then the benefit of matching would provide. It is essentially a cost-benefit analysis. As Judge Posner stated, "If one really takes seriously the concept of a capital expenditure as anything that yields income, actual or imputed, beyond the period (conventionally one year) in which the expenditure is made, the result will be to force the capitalization of virtually every business expense. It is a result courts naturally shy away from. The administrative costs of conceptual rigor are too great."[96] The determination of which expenditures are capitalized and which are currently deductible can be difficult to make and therefore has led to a significant amount of litigation, the holdings of which cannot always be reconciled.

The difference in consequence between an expense and a capital expenditure is the timing of the recovery of the TP's cost. An expense is deducted in the year paid or accrued. A capital expenditure (if deductible at all) must be amortized over a period of time; if not amortizable, it is taken into account upon the disposition of the asset or the dissolution of the enterprise.[97]

Generally, a current deduction is not allowed for an amount spent for the acquisition, creation, or improvement of an asset which will be used or enjoyed by the TP over a period of more than 12 months. §§ 161, 263. But see ¶ **21.1410** for discussion of an exception for the acquisition of an item having a small cost or a short useful life. Typically, if the useful life of a business item is 12 months or less, the cost is deducted currently even when the item will be used in two taxable years.[98] There also are statutory exceptions providing that a specified amount of certain expenses can be "expensed" (i.e., deducted immediately instead of being amortized). See, e.g., §§ 179, 195(b), 709(b) and ¶ **22A.2000**.

In its 1971 decision in *Commissioner v. Lincoln Savings & Loan Ass'n*,[99] the Supreme Court appeared to have suggested that an expenditure was not a capital expenditure unless it created or en-

---

96. *Encyclopaedia Britannica, Inc. v. Commissioner*, 685 F.2d 212 (7th Cir. 1982).

97. See *FMR Corp.and Subsidiaries v. Commissioner*, 110 T.C. 402 (1998).

98. Rev. Ruls. 69–560 and 73–357.

99. 403 U.S. 345 (1971).

hanced a separate and distinct asset. The Supreme Court subsequently repudiated that suggestion in *Indopco, Inc. v. Commissioner*.[100] *Indopco* involved the question of the deductibility of expenses incurred in connection with a friendly corporate acquisition. The expenses in question were the fees paid to an investment banking company to determine the value of a corporate target's stock and the fees paid to a law firm to conduct the acquisition and to obtain favorable tax treatment for the target's shareholders. The TPs contended that the fees were deductible business expenses rather than nondeductible capital expenditures. The Supreme Court held that the expenses were capital expenditures and therefore were not deductible.

The Supreme Court held that *Lincoln Savings* holds only that expenditures that serve to create or enhance a separate and distinct asset should be capitalized; it does not stand for the view that expenditures that do not create or enhance a separate asset cannot be capital expenditures. In other words, the creation or enhancement of a separate and distinct asset is a "sufficient but not a necessary condition to classification as a capital expenditure." The courts have not established standards for determining whether a separate and distinct asset has been created.[101]

In Prop. Reg. § 1.263(a)–3(d)(2), Treasury defined what constitutes a separate unit of property. In general, a functional interdependent standard is used; but special rules apply for buildings and certain other assets. Functionally interdependent components of property are treated as a single item of property. A component is functionally interdependent with another if the placing of one in service is dependent on the placing of the other in service. Prop. Reg. § 1.263(a)–3(d)(2)(iii)(A).

It is worth emphasizing that the creation or enhancement of a separate and distinct asset is still a relevant datum. While such creation or enhancement is not a necessary condition of finding that an expenditure is to be capitalized, it is a sufficient condition.[102]

In *PNC Bancorp. v. Commissioner*,[103] the Tax Court held that a bank's loan origination fees must be capitalized and amortized because each loan that was consummated was a separate and distinct asset. The principal business of the bank was to accept deposits and

100. 503 U.S. 79 (1992).

101. *FMR Corp. and Subsidiaries v. Commissioner*, 110 T.C. 402 (1998).

102. See e.g., Prop. Reg. § 1.263(a)–2(a).

103. 110 T.C. 349 (1998), rev'd 212 F.3d 822 (3d Cir. 2000).

to make loans. The "loan origination fees" for which the court denied a deduction included amounts paid to third parties for appraisals and reports on property offered as security for a proposed loan, credit reports on the borrower, salaries and fringe benefits paid to the bank's employees for evaluating the borrower's financial status, evaluating collateral and other security arrangements, negotiating the terms of a loan, processing loan documents, and closing the loan transaction. In the view of the Tax Court, the recurring nature of those expenses did not save them from capital expenditure characterization because the court deemed each loan to be a separate and distinct asset that was created by those expenses.

The Third Circuit reversed the Tax Court and authorized the bank to deduct currently the loan origination fees.[104] The court held that while the fees were associated with a capital asset, they did not create that asset. Mere association of an expenditure with an asset is not a reason to require capitalization of the expenditure. In reaching its decision, the court appeared to have been influenced by the "recurring, routine, day-to-day" nature of the expenses in question. See *Encyclopaedia Britannica, Inc. v. Commissioner*, supra, where the court stated, "The distinction between recurring and nonrecurring business expenses provides a very crude but perhaps serviceable demarcation between those capital expenditures that can feasibly be capitalized and those that cannot be."

The Eighth Circuit's decision in *Wells Fargo & Co. v. Commissioner*,[105] may point the way to a proper application of the capitalization doctrine and may explain the result reached by the Third Circuit in the *PNC Bancorp* case. *Wells Fargo* dealt with the question of whether a portion of salaries paid to regular officers of the corporate TP should be capitalized because that portion of their salary is allocable to services the officers provided in exploring and negotiating a friendly consolidation with another corporation. The Tax Court had held that a portion of the officers' salaries had to be capitalized. The Eighth Circuit reversed the Tax Court and held that they were currently deductible. The court noted that the officers were regularly employed by the corporation and were not employed for the purpose of assisting with the proposed consolidation. There is a suggestion in the opinion that if the officers had been hired to work on the consolidation or if their compensation had been raised because of their work on the consolidation, their salaries (or the additional compensation they received) might then have had to be capitalized.

---

104. *PNC Bancorp v. Commissioner*, 212 F.3d 822 (3d Cir. 2000).
105. 224 F.3d 874 (8th Cir. 2000).

The court stated, "payments made by an employer are deductible when they are made to employees, are compensatory in nature, and are directly related to the employment relationship (and only indirectly related to the capital transaction, which provides the long-term benefit)." Referring to the "origin of the claim" doctrine, the court held that the origin of the expenditure was the regular employment of the officers; and their assignment to the consolidation issue was incidental to their work.

If on every occasion in which an employee, whose normal work does not require capitalization of his salary, engages in a task that will produce a long-term benefit to the employer, a portion of the employee's salary would have to be allocated to that task and capitalized, that would impose a significant administrative burden on the employer and on the IRS. In that case, the benefit of better matching of income and expenses may not be sufficient to justify imposing that burden. On the other hand, if an employee spends all of his working time on a project that leads to the creation of an item, and if the period during which his time is spent on that project is significant, it would not be that difficult to determine how much of his salary is allocable to the item. Similarly, if an employee's salary is raised when he begins working on a project and is reduced when he completes the project, it is reasonable to conclude that the additional salary is payment for working on that special project, and therefore to allocate that amount of his salary to that project and to capitalize that amount if the project produces an identifiable income stream over a period of time.

In § 263A, Congress has imposed the burden of allocation of costs for producing or purchasing certain specified properties. There is reason to question whether it would be appropriate to extend that allocation burden to properties not listed in that statute.

The Supreme Court noted in *Indopco* that the distinction between a current expense and a capital expenditure is one of degree and not of kind. The test is whether the expenditure will produce substantial benefits into the future. The Court conceded that not all future benefits (i.e., benefits that extend beyond the taxable year in which the expenditure occurred) are of sufficient significance to warrant capital expenditure treatment. The mere presence of an incidental future benefit will not be enough. It is necessary to weigh both the extent of the benefit and the length of time in the future that it will continue. This weighing process rests on a judgment that cannot be reduced to a quantifiable standard.[106]

---

106. See *FMR Corp. and Subsidiaries v. Commissioner*, 110 T.C. 402 (1998).

The Service has repeatedly suggested (e.g., Notice 96–7) that the *Indopco* decision does not change the tax rules relating to capitalization of expenses and merely eliminates the confusion that temporarily existed because of language in the *Lincoln Savings* decision. However, *Indopco* has placed a gloss on the capital expenditure issue that has tilted the decisions on that issue away from expense treatment.[107]

Subsequent to the *Indopco* decision, there have been numerous examples of a current deduction's being allowed for an expenditure that creates benefits that will be enjoyed in the future. For example, the expenses of so-called institutional advertising generally are deductible. Treas. Reg. § 1.162–20(a)(2) provides that the cost of institutional or goodwill advertising that keeps the TP's name before the public generally is deductible.[108] In Rev. Rul. 92–80, the Commissioner held that the *Indopco* decision did not affect the deductibility of advertising costs, which continue to be currently deductible. However, in the *RJR Nabisco* case, the Commissioner contended that while the expenses of executing an advertising campaign are currently deductible, the expenses of creating or developing an advertising campaign must be segregated and capitalized. The Tax Court held that no distinction was proper and that all advertising expenses are currently deductible so long as the benefits resulting from the advertising campaign "are among the traditional benefits associated with ordinary business advertising."[109]

In holding that *Indopco* did not change the rule that incidental repairs of business assets are deductible expenses "even though they may have some future benefit," the Commissioner stated in Rev. Rul. 94–12 as follows:

> The *Indopco* decision clarifies that the creation or enhancement of a separate and distinct asset is not a prerequisite to capitalization. That clarification does not, however, change the fundamental legal principles for determining whether a particular expenditure can be deducted or must be capitalized. With respect to expenditures that produce benefits both in the current year and in future years, the determination of whether such expenditures must be capitalized requires a careful examination of all the facts.

107. Id.

108. See *RJR Nabisco Inc.and Consolidated Subsidiaries v. Commissioner*, TC Memo 98–252 (1998).

109. Id.

In Rev. Rul. 94–77, the Commissioner allowed a deduction for severance pay made to employees in connection with a business downsizing even though that may produce future benefits through lower operating costs. In Rev. Rul. 96–62, the Commissioner confirmed that *Indopco* has no effect on the deductibility of the cost of training new employees, and that such expenses generally are deductible.

¶ 21.1410. Small Cost and Short Period Exceptions. If the cost of an item to be used in a trade or business that otherwise would have to be capitalized is too small to warrant amortizing it over a period of years, it may be deducted currently. See Treas. Reg. § 1.162–12(a) permitting a current deduction for the cost of inexpensive ordinary farm tools such as shovels and rakes. While that regulation relates to farm tools, the small cost exception is applied universally. When the cost of an item is deducted currently, the deduction is referred to as "expensing" the cost.

In *Sharon v. Commissioner*,[110] the Tax Court held that a $25 bar examination fee paid to obtain a license to practice law in New York that the TP had capitalized and amortized could have been deducted currently because of the small size of the fee, but a bar examination fee in the hundreds of dollars paid by the TP to obtain a California license to practice law was sufficiently large to require amortization. The amortization of those capitalized amounts was to be spread over the period of the TP's life expectancy. See also *Kohen v. Commissioner*,[111] allowing a current deduction for a $90 bar application fee even though it was a capital expenditure.

As previously noted, there also is a short period exception to capitalization. Typically, if the useful life[112] of a purchased item is 12 months or less, the cost of the item can be deducted currently (i.e., expensed) even when the life of the item falls into two taxable years.[113] For example, if in November, Year One, X purchased tires for a truck used in his business, and if the tires had a useful life of ten months in X's business, X can deduct the cost of the tires in Year One even though 80% of its use will occur in

---

110. 66 T.C. 515 (1976), aff'd 591 F.2d 1273 (9th Cir. 1978).

111. 44 T.C.M. 1518 (1982).

112. The economic useful life of an asset refers to the period over which the property may reasonably be expected to be useful in the TP's trade or business rather than to the physical life of the asset. See Prop. Reg. § 1.162–3(d)(2).

113. Rev. Rul. 69–560 and Rev. Rul. 73–357.

Year Two. If the tires had a useful life to X of thirteen months (i.e., greater than one-year), then X would have to amortize the cost.[114]

There is a question as to whether the 12–month rule will apply if only a very small part of the useful life of the asset will occur during the taxable year in which the cost was paid. For example, if Y purchased tires with an 8–month useful life on December 30, Year One, should Y be prohibited from expensing the cost of those tires in Year One? The Tax Court suggested that approach for prepaid expenses on the authority of § 446(b) to require that the TP's method of accounting accurately reflect his income.[115] It is unsettled whether that approach is valid and whether it will be extended to the acquisition of tangible assets. It is noteworthy that in Proposed Regulations that were promulgated in 2008 concerning the deductibility of materials and supplies, the Proposed Regulations authorize the expensing of the costs of incidental materials and supplies under certain conditions, one of which is that a current deduction will not prevent a clear reflection of the TP's taxable income. Prop. Reg. § 1.162–3(a)(2).

The small cost and short period exceptions are reflected in Prop. Reg. § 1.162–3(d)(1)(ii) and (iii). See also, Prop. Reg. § 1.263(a)–2(d)(4).

¶ 21.1420. Allocation to Year of Use. Capital expenditures are not "ordinary" expenses under § 162, and so cannot be deducted under that section. Also, § 263 expressly denies a deduction for such expenditures. Section 263A generally requires the capitalization of direct and indirect costs of tangible and certain intangible properties that were produced or improved by the TP or purchased for resale. See ¶ 21.1453. If the benefits of the expenditure will not last indefinitely (or if a statute expressly provides for amortization), the portion of a capital expenditure which is allocable to the years of use may be deductible in those years under rules of amortization or depreciation discussed later in this work.[116]

¶ 21.1421. Illustration 1: Purchase of Tangible Property. X paid $50,000 to purchase a machine which he expects to use in his business for ten years. The purchase price is a

---

114. FSA 200122002 (2001).

115. See ¶ 21.1431.

116. See Chapter **Twenty–Two**.

capital expenditure and is not currently deductible. Since the machine will be used over a ten-year period, part of the cost will be deductible in each of those years.

¶ 21.1422. Illustration 2: Purchase of Intangible Property. On January 1, Year One, *Y* paid $1,000 for a five-year term fire insurance policy to cover the building used in his business. The payment is a capital expenditure and is not currently deductible, but *Y* will be able to deduct $200 each year of the five-year term.

¶ 21.1423. Illustration 3: Purchase of Property with an Inexhaustible Life. *Z* purchased unimproved land for $50,000 to be used in his business. The payment is a capital expenditure, and none of it is deductible since land is not an exhaustible asset.

¶ 21.1424. Illustration 4: Use of Depreciable Property in Constructing an Asset. *X*, a public utility, used various items of equipment (such as cars, trucks, trailers, and radio equipment) in constructing new tangible assets. *X* contended that it could depreciate the cost of such items over their useful lives and take a current deduction for the depreciation allowance in each year. The Commissioner contended that the depreciation allowance for such items could not be deducted currently, but instead must be added to the cost basis of the asset which was constructed with the equipment. In *Commissioner v. Idaho Power Co.*,[117] the Supreme Court concurred with the Commissioner and treated the depreciation allowance as an amount paid for the construction of the new assets that therefore must be added to the basis of those newly constructed assets instead of being deducted currently. The same treatment will be accorded to an accelerated cost recovery system (MACRS) allowance for the equipment under § 168.[118]

> **¶ 24.1424–1. Wages.** The amount of wages paid to employees for their work in constructing or acquiring a capital asset, which is owned by the employer, is not a deductible expense but rather is a capital expenditure to be included in the employer's basis in the constructed or acquired property.[119] For a discussion of whether a portion of wages

117. 418 U.S. 1 (1974).

118. See Chapter **Twenty–Two**.

119. See *Commissioner v. Idaho Power Co.*, 418 U.S. 1 (1974). For an example of the treatment of the payment of wages as a capital expenditure for the construction of improvements on realty, see *Chevy Chase Motor Co. v. Commissioner*, 36 T.C.M. 942 (1977).

paid to an employee who devotes part of his working time to the creation of income that will be received over some years, see ¶ **21.1400**.

¶ 21.1430. Prepaid Expenses and the Cost of Currently Consumable Assets. A prepayment of expenses to be incurred in the future is essentially the same as purchasing an asset to be used in the future. The question of whether a prepaid expense is currently deductible or must be amortized over the period to which it relates hinges on whether the TP has purchased a separate item and on the length of time of the prepayment. Similarly, the deductibility of the cost of acquiring an asset that will be used up over a period of 12 months or less rests on the same issue.[120]

However, when a cash method TP seeks to deduct in the year of payment a prepaid expense (the benefit from which will be enjoyed in two taxable years), the resolution of the issue often depends on whether the Commissioner can require the allocation of the expense between the taxable years to which it relates on the basis of the Commissioner's authority under § 446(b) to require that the TP's method of accounting accurately reflects the TP's income.

¶ 21.1431. Determining the Propriety of Expensing Prepayments or the Cost of Consumable Assets. As previously noted, the Supreme Court's *Indopco* decision stressed that the duration and extent of benefits obtained from an expenditure must be weighed to determine whether it must be capitalized. In *Zaninovich v. Commissioner*,[121] the Ninth Circuit adopted a mechanical rule that where a payment of a business expense by a cash method TP relates to a period of 12 months or less, the payment is currently deductible in the taxable year in which the payment is made and need not be capitalized. The Ninth Circuit, reversing a Tax Court decision, allowed a deduction for the prepayment of rent for a 12–month period even though 11 of those months lay in the taxable year following the year in which the payment was made.[122] For the treatment of the prepayment of interest on a loan, which treatment is dictated by § 461(g), see Chapter **Sixteen.**

---

120.   See ¶ **21.1410**.
121.   616 F.2d 429 (9th Cir. 1980), rev'g 69 T.C. 605 (1978).
122.   Id.

¶ 21.1440.   Capital Expenditure Versus Repairs. One of the difficult factual issues in tax law is to distinguish a repair from a capital expenditure. A capital expenditure must be capitalized and so cannot be deducted in full in the year occurred. On the other hand, the cost of repairs on business property or property held for profit is a currently deductible expense. The regulations define a repair as "incidental repairs which neither materially add to the value of the property nor appreciably prolong its life, but keep it in an ordinary, efficient operating condition." Treas. Reg. § 1.162–4. Routine maintenance of a unit of property is not an improvement and so can be expensed.[123] Prop. Reg. § 1.263(a)–3(e)(1). In contrast, a capital expenditure adds to the value of the property and frequently prolongs its life. Capitalization is also required when the expenditure makes the item adaptable for a different use.[124]

The determination of whether a repair materially adds to the value of an asset is made by comparing the value of the asset after the repair is made with the value it had before the repair became necessary. *Plainfield–Union Water Co. v. Commissioner.*[125] In Rev. Rul. 94–38, the Service adopted the position on the definition of a repair that the Tax Court had formulated in the *Plainfield-Union Water* case—namely, that the proper test of whether value was added is to compare the status of the asset after the expenditure with the status it had before the condition arose that necessitated the expenditure. In that ruling, the Service said that its nonacquiescence in the *Plainfield-Union* case was on other grounds.

In 2008, Treasury promulgated Proposed Regulations that provide much greater detail for making the distinction between a deductible repair and a capital expenditure. Prop. Regs. §§ 1.162–3 and 1.263(a)–3. When finalized, the Proposed Regulations will answer many of the questions that can arise in this area.

¶ 21.1441.   Caveat. It is far easier to state the distinction between repairs and capital expenditures than to apply it in

---

123.   Prop. Reg. § 1.263(a)–3(e)(1). The Proposed Regulation lists items that do not constitute routine maintenance including: (1) the replacement of a component for which the TP had taken a loss deduction (other than a casualty loss), (2) the repair of damage to a unit whose basis had been reduced because of a casualty loss; (3) expenses incurred to restore a unit to former efficient condition after it had deteriorated to a state of disrepair and was no longer functional for its intended use. Prop. Reg. § 1.263(a)–3(e)(2).

124.   TAM 9315004; Prop. Reg. § 1.263(a)–3(h).

125.   39 T.C. 333, 338 (1962), Nonacq. See also, *Jacks v. Commissioner*, 55 T.C.M. 968 (1988).

practice. The 2008 Proposed Regulations will be of significant assistance.

¶ 21.1442. Major Renovations. When expenditures are incurred in connection with a plan of capital improvement such as a major renovation of an apartment building, all such expenditures are capitalized even though some portions of them would have been deductible if incurred separately.[126]

¶ 21.1443. The *Indopco* Decision Has No Effect on the Deductibility of Repairs. As discussed in ¶ 21.1400, the Supreme Court held in its *Indopco* decision that the creation or enhancement of a separate and distinct asset is not a prerequisite to treating an item as a capital expenditure. In Rev. Rul. 94–12, the Commissioner ruled that the *Indopco* decision has no effect on the determination of the deductibility of incidental repairs. The standards for deducting repairs were not altered by the Supreme Court's decision.

¶ 21.1444. Repair of Damage Caused by a Casualty. In Rev. Rul. 71–161, the Commissioner said the repair of damage caused by a casualty for which a loss deduction had been allowed was in the nature of a replacement and so must be capitalized.[127] It seems likely that the Commissioner's position is based on the principle that there should not be more than one tax deduction for the same event. See Treas. Reg. § 1.161–1. As discussed in Chapter **Eighteen**, the allowance of a deduction for the amount expended on repairing damage does not constitute a duplication of the deduction allowed because of the loss suffered from the casualty. One deduction is for the decline in value of property caused by a casualty, and the other is due to the amount of money expended in repairing the damage. There is dictum in a District Court decision stating that the Service's view that such repairs must be capitalized is a "dubious proposition."[128] In the Proposed Regulations promulgated in 2008, Treasury has incorporated its position on such repairs. The Proposed Regulation explicitly denies a deduction for the cost of restoring damaged property and

---

126. *Ruttenberg v. Commissioner*, 52 T.C.M. 370 (1986). See *United States v. Wehrli*, 400 F.2d 686 (10th Cir. 1968).

127. See also, GCM 34438 (1971).

128. *Waldrip v. United States*, 48 AFTR2d 81–6031 (N.D. Ga. 1981).

requires that those costs be capitalized. Prop. Reg. § 1.263(a)–3(e)(2), (g)(1).

¶ 21.1445. Environmental Clean–Up Costs. *X* purchased uncontaminated land. *X* conducted a manufacturing business that discharged hazardous waste on to the land. *X* incurred expenses to clean-up the land and free it of contamination. *X* also incurred continuing expenses to keep the land free of subsequent contamination. The Service initially ruled that all of those expenses are currently deductible under § 162, and are not capital expenditures under § 263. Rev. Rul. 94–38. Subsequently, the Service revised its position. While agreeing that the expenditures do not fall within § 263, the Service determined that the expenses were costs of the manufacturing of inventory, and so the costs are capitalized under § 263A and added to inventory costs. Rev. Rul. 2004–18.

X also constructed groundwater treatment facilities (including wells, pipes, pumps, and other equipment) to extract, treat and monitor contaminated groundwater. *X* expects to operate these groundwater facilities for 8 years. The cost of constructing those facilities must be capitalized under § 263 and cannot be deducted as a current expense. Rev. Rul. 94–38.

If the land that *X* purchased had been contaminated when he purchased it, would *X* be allowed a deduction for cleaning-up the land and freeing it from contamination or would those costs be capitalized as part of the cost of acquiring the land? If *X* knew of the contamination at the time that *X* purchased the land, then clearly the cost of cleaning-up should be capitalized. The purchase price paid for the land should have reflected the costs that the buyer would have to incur to put the land into useable condition, and so the costs incurred to accomplish that are part of the cost of acquiring the land in useable condition. But, what if *X* were unaware of the contamination at the time of purchase? In that case, the purchase price of the land probably did not reflect those costs since they were not anticipated at the time. The question of deductibility in that case is unclear. The authors believe that, in those circumstances, a case can be made for treating the costs of cleaning-up as a repair, but the issue is far from settled.

¶ 21.1446. Materials and Supplies. The cost of incidental materials and supplies that meet certain requirements is deductible when paid so long as the deduction does not prevent the accurate reporting of a TP's income. Amounts paid for non-incidental materials and supplies are deducted when the materials and supplies are used and consumed in the TP's business. Prop. Reg. § 1.162–3(a). The Proposed Regulation defines what is meant by "materials and supplies."

¶ 21.1447. Developing or Purchasing Software. In Rev. Rul. 69–21, the Service ruled that the development of software is sufficiently akin to research and experimental expenditures (albeit it is not such an expenditure) that the expenses incurred in developing software should be given similarly liberal cost recovery treatment. Accordingly, a TP who develops software can treat its expenses as currently deductible provided that it has not previously treated such development costs differently (*i.e.*, by amortizing them). Alternatively, a TP can choose to amortize such development costs over a period of 5 years (or less if TP can show a shorter useful life). Amortization will be required if the TP had previously elected to amortize such expenses.

On the other hand, if a TP purchases software (as contrasted to developing it himself), the cost must be capitalized and can be amortized over a 5–year period (or shorter if the software has a shorter useful life). Rev. Rul. 69–21, and Rev. Proc. 97–50. In some circumstances, such as where a TP pays a consulting firm to develop software for the TP, there will be a question whether the TP developed the software (and hired an expert to do the work) or whether the TP purchased the software. See TAM 8614004. The tax consequences can be quite different. The criteria for distinguishing developed software from purchased software are explained in Jeffrey Kahn's article, *Deducting Year 2000 Costs*,[129] That article also discusses: (1) the tax treatment of the costs of fixing the software program problems faced by many TPs because of a failure in programs to anticipate the arrival of the Year 2000, and (2) the possibility that in certain (but not all) cases, the cost of purchasing software to cure the Year 2000 problem might be currently deductible as a repair.

¶ 21.1450. Expenses Incurred In Connection With the Purchase or Sale of an Asset. When an expenditure is incurred

---

129.   79 Tax Notes 1621 (June 22, 1998).

in connection with the acquisition or sale of an asset, it is a capital expenditure that either is added to the basis of the asset or is subtracted from the amount realized on the sale. Whether an expense that is related to a sale or purchase is to be treated as a deduction, or instead is to be treated either as part of the acquisition cost of an asset or as an offset to the amount realized on the sale of an asset, is sometimes a difficult issue.[130]

¶ 21.1451. Start–Up Expenses of Beginning a Trade or Business. Section 162 allows a deduction for the ordinary and necessary expenses of carrying on a trade or business. In order to be deductible, the expenses must relate to a trade or business that was functioning at the time that the expense was incurred.[131] Unless expressly authorized by statute, start-up or pre-opening expenditures of a new trade or business are not deductible under § 162. See **¶ 21.1451–2** for a discussion of the special statutory provision dealing with those expenditures.

If an existing trade or business investigated whether to expand its business (for example, by opening a branch) and how to go about doing so, the pre-opening expenditures incurred in connection with that expansion are on a different footing than are the pre-opening expenditures of investigating whether to venture into a different trade or business from the one it is currently conducting. In the expansion situation, the expenditure is incurred in connection with a trade or business that is functioning at the time the expenditure is incurred, and so that obstacle is not present. Let us now consider how the pre-opening expenditures will be treated in each of those situations.

¶ 21.1451–1. Expanding a Business. The expenditures connected with a business can be divided into five stages: (a) expenses incurred in making an investigation to determine whether to enter a business and, if so, which business to acquire (these are referred to as investigatory expenses); (b) expenses incurred in attempting to purchase a specific business; (c) expenses incurred in preparing to commence business operations; (d) expenses incurred in the current conduct of the business; and (e) expenses incurred in

---

130. See ¶ 21.1341–5.

131. *Hardy v. Commissioner*, 93 T.C. 684, 687 (1989) (reviewed by the court).

terminating the business. Expenses incurred in the latter two stages (i.e., (d) and (e)) typically are deductible. Investigatory expenses (i.e., stage (a)) are deductible if they are ordinary and necessary and connected to the expansion of an already on-going business.[132]

The test for determining whether an expense is an investigatory expense is the "whether" and "which" test. So long as the TP is seeking to determine *whether* to enter a business or *which* business to acquire, the expenses are investigatory.[133]*Wells Fargo* allowed a deduction for investigatory expenses of one bank to explore whether to combine with another bank and, if so, which bank. Once a TP focuses on a specific business to acquire, the expenses to acquire that business are capitalized. Thus, the expenses in stage (b) are capitalized. In *Wells Fargo*, once the TP had focused on the specific bank it considered combining with, the expenses thereafter were capitalized. The expenses incurred in stage (c) also are capitalized.

In *FMR Corp. and Subsidiaries v. Commissioner*,[134] the Tax Court denied a deduction (or any amortization) for the TP's expenses of creating regulated investment companies, which TP then advised and managed, even though that was a recurring activity in the conduct of TP's business. The court held that *Indopco* had cut the ground out from cases that had held that expansion expenses of an existing business are deductible. Instead, the court held that, regardless of whether an expenditure is attributable to an expansion of a business, the proper test for its deductibility is whether either (1) a separate and distinct asset was created, or (2) future benefits of substantial duration and extent will be obtained. In other words, the expense must meet the "ordinary and necessary" requirement that applies to both § 162 (business expenses) and § 212 (nonbusiness expenses). Relying on the second standard, the Tax Court held that the expenses must be capitalized. The court did not allow amortization because the TP could not prove an ascertainable useful life.

132. *Wells Fargo & Co. v. Commissioner*, 224 F.3d 874 (8th Cir. 2000).
133. Id.; Rev. Rul. 99–23.
134. 110 T.C. 402 (1998).

Investigatory expenses incurred in connection with a new trade or business (i.e., not incurred in expanding a trade or business already conducted by the TP) are capitalized. The statutory relief provided for such investigatory expenses is described in ¶ **21.1451–2**.

¶ 21.1451–2. Congressional Action. In 1980, Congress added § 195 to the Code, and in 1984 Congress significantly amended that provision and amended it again in 2004. This provision authorizes a TP to elect to take a current deduction for $5,000 of "start-up expenses," which amount is reduced by the extent to which the TP's start-up expenses for that year exceed $50,000. The remaining start-up expenses can be amortized over a 180–month period (i.e., 15 years). This deduction and amortization provision applies only if the TP elects it under § 195(b).

"Start-up expenditures" include an amount paid in connection with investigating the creation or acquisition of an active trade or business. The start-up expenses that can be deducted or amortized are only the investigatory expenses (i.e., the expenses incurred during the "whether" and "which" period. Rev. Rul. 99–23). The amortization of start-up expenditures commences with the month in which the active trade or business begins. Section 195(a) expressly bars a deduction for start-up expenditures except to the extent allowed by that section; therefore, such expenses must either be deducted or amortized under a § 195(b) election or cannot be deducted at all. The election is available to a TP only as to that amount of the expenditure which, if it had been paid or incurred in connection with the expansion of an existing trade or business in the same field, would be allowed as a current deduction in the year paid or incurred. § 195(c)(1)(B). Thus, it would seem that § 195 applies only to the ordinary and necessary costs of investigating whether to enter into a new business and which business to acquire.

The holding of *Wells Fargo* permitting the current deductibility of an expenditure for the investigation of expanding an existing business is buttressed by the apparent congressional assumption in adopting § 195 that such expenses are usually deductible.[135] Once the investigation of the TP goes beyond the "whether and which" period, and focuses on the acquisition of a specific business, the expenses connected with acquiring that business or getting it started will be capitalized. However, the Tax Court's view is that § 195 did not change the standard for the deductibility of expansion expenses; and, given the *Indopco* standard, only expansion expenses that do not create a separate and distinct asset or provide future benefits of substantial duration and extent are deductible.

Deductions for interest, taxes, and research and experimental expenses are excluded from § 195, and so are deductible, or not, without regard to that provision. § 195(c)(1).

¶ 21.1451–3. **Date on Which Active Trade or Business Begins.** The date on which an active trade or business begins plays an important role in the deductibility of expenses. One function of that date is that expenses incurred afterwards can be deducted currently under § 162 as business expenses. Expenses incurred prior to that date will be capitalized, except for certain investigatory expenses for the expansion of an existing business. If a TP elects to amortize his start-up expenses under § 195(b), then the month in which the active trade or business begins will also serve as the date on which the amortization deductions commence.

Unfortunately, the date on which an active trade or business is deemed to begin is a question of fact which can be difficult to determine. Even the standard to be applied in determining that date is not settled. The Commissioner has adopted the standard employed by the Fourth Circuit in *Richmond Television Corporation v. United States.*[136] The *Richmond Television* case, which arose prior to the adoption of § 195, dealt with the question of the deductibility of start-up expenditures as business expenses under § 162. In the first *Richmond Television* case, the court stated that a TP does not begin a trade or business "until such time as

135. See also, H. Rept. 96–1278 on the Miscellaneous Revenue Act of 1980, at 11 (1980), 1980–2 Cum. Bull. 709, 712–713,

136. 345 F.2d 901 (4th Cir.), vacated and remanded per curiam on other grounds, 382 U.S. 68 (1965), original holding on this issue reaffirmed., 354 F.2d 410 (4th Cir. 1965).

the business has begun to function as a going concern and performed those activities for which it was organized." The Commissioner has adopted this "going concern" standard in applying § 195.[137] A more liberal standard for determining the beginning of a business was suggested by the Senate Finance Committee's Report[138]on the Miscellaneous Revenue Act of 1980 (which was the Act in which § 195 was first adopted), but the Commissioner expressly rejected that suggestion in the letter rulings cited above. In any event, when a TP purchases a going business, the TP is deemed to begin the business at the date of acquisition. § 195(c)(2)(B).

¶ 21.1451–4. **Nonbusiness Expenses.** Prior to the 1984 adoption of § 195, there was a question whether start-up expenditures of a noncorporate TP to investigate a profit-seeking activity could be deducted under § 212 as a non-business expense. This issue may have been resolved by the addition of § 195(a) to the Code in 1984. That provision expressly denies a deduction for start-up expenditures (as defined in that provision) other than those permitted by § 195 itself, and that makes the deduction and amortization election provided by § 195(b) the exclusive means of obtaining any deduction for such expenditures.[139] Because § 195 applies only to the start-up expenses of a trade or business or an activity performed in anticipation of becoming a trade or business, it will not preclude deductions for start-up expenses of a profit-seeking activity unless the exclusivity of that provision is extended to § 212 expenses.

¶ 21.1452. **Abandoned Project.** If, after investigating the financial prospects of entering a business in which the TP is not then engaged and after making preparations to commence business activities, the TP then abandons the project before beginning operations, the question arises as to whether the expenses incurred in the preliminary preparation and investigation are deductible under § 165 as a loss incurred in a transaction entered into for a profit. The deductibility of such expenses may turn on how much the TP had done before

---

137. E.g. TAM 9331001, PLR 9027002; PLR 9047032, and Rev. Rul. 81–150.

138. S. Rept. No. 1036, 96th Cong. 2d Sess. 14 (1980).

139. *Hardy v. Commissioner*, 93 T.C. 684 (1989) (reviewed by the court).

abandoning the project. No deduction is allowable for the loss under § 165(c)(1) since the TP never commenced a trade or business. A deduction will be allowed for the loss under § 165(c)(2) if the TP's actions were sufficient to constitute a "transaction" entered into for profit. If the TP merely investigates whether to engage in a business and does not focus on a particular business, he may not have been sufficiently committed to the venture to characterize it as a transaction for profit, and, consequently, he may be denied a deduction for his expenses.[140] However, if the TP takes significant steps in preparation of entering the business so that it goes beyond a general search and has focused on the acquisition of specific assets and if the TP then abandons the project, he will be allowed a deduction. Rev. Ruls. 57–418, 71–191 as explained in Rev. Rul. 79–346.

Note that § 195 will not be of any help to the TP since the $5,000 deduction provided by that provision is available for the taxable year in which the active trade or business begins, and the amortization of investigatory expenses there authorized commences with the month in which the active trade or business begins.

In *Larsen v. Commissioner*,[141] the Tax Court allowed a geologist to deduct under § 165 the cost incurred in unsuccessfully attempting to acquire oil and gas leases for certain properties. The Commissioner contended that these expenses were not deductible because at the same time that the TP was unsuccessfully seeking the leases in question, the TP was also successfully seeking oil and gas leases on other properties, and therefore the Commissioner contended that the costs in question should be treated as part of the capital expended in acquiring the leases on the other property. The Tax Court held that each lease was a separate transaction and allowed the TP a current deduction for the abandoned projects.

¶ 21.1453. Expenses of Producing Property—the Uniform Capitalization Rule. Subject to certain exceptions, a TP's direct and indirect costs of producing real property or tangible personal property are required to be capitalized (if the produced property is not inventory) or included in inventory

---

140. See Rev. Rul. 57–418; *Frank v. Commissioner*, 20 T.C. 511 (1953).

141. 66 T.C. 478 (1976), Acq.

costs (if the produced property is inventory). § 263A. For the purposes of this statutory provision, tangible property includes books, films, sound recordings, video tapes and similar properties. § 263A(b). In certain circumstances, the cost of the TP's purchasing inventory or inventory-type property to be resold by the TP must either be capitalized or included in inventory costs. § 263A(b)(2). For the treatment of expenses incurred by an author in producing a book (including the expenses incurred in research), see ¶ **21.1490A**.

¶ **21.1460.   Defense or Perfection of Title.** Expenditures incurred by a TP in acquiring title to property or in defending or perfecting title to property are capital expenditures. Prop. Reg. § 1.263(a)–2(d)(2).[142]

¶ **21.1461.   Illustration: Dispute Over Title.** *D* and *E* owned 1,000 shares of IBM common stock as joint tenants with rights of survivorship. *D* had purchased the IBM stock with his own funds. *E* was *D*'s housekeeper. *D* died and *E* claimed ownership of the stock as a surviving joint tenant. *D*'s heir, *X*, sued for the stock, claiming that *D* held the IBM stock jointly with *E* as a convenience, that *D* did not intend that the stock would become *E*'s property upon *D*'s death, and that *X*, as *D*'s heir, was entitled to the stock. *E*'s legal fees incurred in the successful defense of the suit are capital expenditures.[143] The fees were incurred by *E* to retain ownership of the stock as contrasted to maintenance or repairs to keep an item in operating condition. The expenses incurred by *X* in unsuccessfully prosecuting the suit are not deductible.

¶ **21.1462.   Protection of Goodwill.** While the cost of purchasing goodwill (for example where goodwill is sold as part of a going business) is a nondeductible capital expenditure (which may be amortizable under § 197), an expense incurred in protecting the TP's existing goodwill is currently deductible. For example, in Rev. Rul. 76–203, a moving and storage company was allowed a deduction for compensation it voluntarily paid to customers whose uninsured goods were destroyed in a fire that consumed the TP's warehouse.

142.   See ¶ **21.1341–10**.

143.   See *Woodward v. Commissioner*, 397 U.S. 572 (1970), and *United States v. Hilton Hotels*, 397 U.S. 580 (1970).

¶ 21.1470. Expense of Seeking or Obtaining Employment.
Treas. Reg. § 1.212–1(f) provides that the expenses "of seeking
employment or in placing oneself in a position to begin rendering
personal services for compensation" are not deductible under
§ 212. Presumably this is because they constitute capital expenditures of entering a business in contrast to an expense of conducting an existing business activity. While in Rev. Rul. 60–223, the
Service initially ruled that the fee paid to an employment agency
for actually placing the TP in a job is deductible; it revoked that
ruling in Rev. Rul. 75–120 and adopted a different approach,
which is described in ¶ **21.1473.**

¶ 21.1471. Taxpayer Already in the Business. At first,
the Tax Court appeared reluctant to grant a deduction for a
fee (or other expense) paid to an employment agency to locate
a job opportunity (as contrasted to actually securing the TP in
a new job). *Louis v. Commissioner.*[144] In *Louis*, the Tax Court
restricted Rev. Rul. 60–223[145] to allow a deduction only for fees
paid to an employment agency "for having secured employment" for the TP, and the court held that the ruling did not
cover a fee to an employment agency which is payable for
seeking a job for the TP where no job was actually secured for
him. The court did not expressly approve of Rev. Rul. 60–223;
rather, the court held that even if that ruling was valid, it was
of no help to the TP. In subsequent holdings, even though a
TP did not obtain a job, the court allowed a deduction for such
expenses when the TP was already established in his trade and
was seeking a position in the same trade. The fee is deductible
in such cases under § 162 as having been made incident to the
TP's conduct of his business of being an employee in that
same trade.[146] It is now settled that the deductibility of an
employment agency's fee does not depend upon whether the
agency obtains an employment offer for the TP.[147] The Commissioner's current position is explained at ¶ **21.1473.**

**¶ 21.1472. The Expense of Obtaining or Retaining a
Political Office.** A state court judge was permitted to deduct

---

144. 25 T.C.M. 1047 (1966).

145. ¶ **21.1470.**

146. *Primuth v. Commissioner*, 54 T.C. 374 (1970); *Motto v. Commissioner*, 54 T.C.
558 (1970).

147. *Cremona v. Commissioner*, 58 T.C. 219 (1972), Acq.; *Black v. Commissioner*, 60
T.C. 108 (1973).

his expenses of defending a misconduct charge brought against him. The judge's defense of his right to his office is distinguishable from expenses of seeking reelection which constitute nondeductible expenses. Rev. Ruls. 74–394; 75–120. The fees and costs of a political campaign (including a campaign for a judicial office) are not deductible.[148] No deduction is allowable regardless of whether the TP is seeking election to a new position or reelection to a position already held by the TP. One reason for the disallowance of an incumbent's campaign expenses is to prevent the tax law from tilting the availability of financial resources in favor of an incumbent. Similarly, the costs incurred in obtaining or securing a political appointment are not deductible even if the TP has made a career of public service.[149]

¶ 21.1473. **The Commissioner's View.** In Rev. Rul. 75–120, the Commissioner revoked his earlier rulings on this subject, and ruled that expenses incurred by an employee in seeking new employment in the employee's trade or business are deductible under § 162 irrespective of whether the employee actually secures a new position. However, to be deductible, the employee must be seeking new employment in the same trade or business in which he is already established. If the employee seeks employment in a new trade or business, his expenses of seeking that employment (including a fee to an employment agency) will *not* be deductible irrespective of whether the TP actually obtains and accepts a new job. If a TP is unemployed at the time he seeks employment, his trade or business will consist of the services he performed for his past employer if there is substantial continuity between his last employment and the seeking of a new job (i.e., the time lag cannot be too great). When deductible under Rev. Rul. 75–120, a TP's *unreimbursed* costs are miscellaneous itemized deductions and so are subject to the 2% of AGI floor imposed by § 67(a) and to the reduction of itemized deductions imposed by § 68.

If the TP's expenses are reimbursed by the prospective em-

---

148. *McDonald v. Commissioner*, 323 U.S. 57 (1944); *Nichols v. Commissioner*, 511 F.2d 618 (5th Cir. 1975).

149. *Estate of Rockefeller v. Commissioner*, 83 T.C. 368 (1984) denying a deduction for costs incurred in connection with investigations and congressional hearings on the confirmation of the TP's nomination to be Vice–President of the United States.

ployer, the reimbursement is excluded from the TP's income.[150]

In Rev. Rul. 75–120, the Commissioner expressly notes that the expenses of a political campaign are not deductible. Thus, notwithstanding the rule that the expenses of seeking employment in the TP's established line of business are deductible, the expenses of a campaign for election or reelection to a public office (including a judicial office) are not deductible. The reason for this is explained in ¶ **21.1472.**

¶ **21.1474. Administrative Feasibility.** The view adopted by the Commissioner in Rev. Rul. 75–120 is more consistent with the regulations than was Rev. Rul. 60–223, which was revoked. However, there can be substantial administrative burdens in determining what constitutes a *new* trade or business, and it remains to be seen how liberally the Commissioner or the courts will apply the requirement that an employee be seeking a job in the same trade or business. In Rev. Rul. 78–93, a TP who had been engaged in the full-time practice of law and who also was a part-time lecturer at a law school incurred expenses for career counseling which led to the TP's obtaining a position as a full-time assistant professor on the faculty of a law school. The Commissioner ruled that the TP had been engaged in two trades or businesses and so the full-time law faculty position was not a new trade or business for the TP. The Commissioner allowed a deduction for the TP's expenses.

¶ **21.1475. Reimbursed Expenses for Interviewing for a Job.** As noted above, a TP's expenses in interviewing for a job in a new trade or business are not deductible. But if the prospective employer reimburses the TP or pays those expenses directly, and if the employer had invited the employee to interview, the reimbursements and direct payments are excluded from the TP's gross income. Rev. Rul. 63–77. The types of reimbursed expenses that can be excluded from gross income include the TP's transportation costs and the cost of meals and lodging for the TP's stay in the city where the interview takes place. In one sense, the TP provides a service to the prospective employer by coming to that person's place of business to allow the prospective employer to interview the TP.

Similarly, the Commissioner ruled that reimbursements of

150.   See ¶ **21.1475.**

travel expenses made by a political organization to an appointed state government employee to permit the latter to attend and address a political fund raising event is excluded from the employee's gross income. Rev. Rul. 80–99. In that ruling, the Commissioner stated, "it is also a well-established position of the Internal Revenue Service that reimbursements for expenses incurred by a TP on behalf of another in a nonemployment context are not includible in the TP's income."

¶ 21.1480. Deductibility of Capital Expenditures. Capital expenditures are not currently deductible—that is, the item cannot be expensed. However, a capital expense often may be amortized and deducted by the TP over the period of years during which it is estimated the TP will use the asset or improvement for which the expenditure was incurred. This deduction will be permitted only if the asset or improvement is held in connection with a "trade or business" or a profit-seeking venture.

¶ 21.1481. Depreciation and Amortization. In some cases, the TP's deduction of a capital expenditure is taken as depreciation under §§ 167 or 168.[151] The term "depreciation" includes deductions allowable under the accelerated cost recovery system (MACRS) provided by § 168. In other cases, in lieu of depreciation, the deduction will be taken as amortization, possibly under §§ 162 or 212, or as some other form of amortization that is expressly authorized by a statutory provision. Amortization is sometimes provided for items that otherwise could not be depreciated—for example, § 197 allows the amortization of the capitalized costs of goodwill when purchased as part of the purchase of a going business.

Depreciation itself is a form of amortization which is given a special designation. Depreciation is simply amortization that is allowed as a deduction by §§ 167 or 168. In tax parlance, the word "amortization" often is used to designate amortization deductions that do not qualify as depreciation.

¶ 21.1482. Illustration 1: Allocation of Cost Between Depreciable and Nondepreciable Items. *X* paid $60,000 for the purchase of improved Blackacre. Of that price, $10,000 was paid for the land, and $50,000 was paid for a small apartment house situated on the land. *X* can take depreciation

151. Those provisions are discussed in Chapter **Twenty–Two**.

deductions for the $50,000 he paid for the building. However, since the useful life of the land will never terminate, *X* is not permitted any deduction for the cost of the land.

¶ 21.1483. Illustration 2: Depreciation of an Intangible Asset. On January 1, *X* paid $3,000 for a five-year fire insurance policy insuring the building used in his business. *X* can amortize the $3,000 payment over the five-year useful life of the insurance protection he bought. Consequently, *X* can deduct $600 in that year and in each of the four succeeding years as a depreciation deduction under § 167.

¶ 21.1490.   Uniforms. An employee's cost of the acquisition and maintenance of a uniform is deductible if the uniform is required by the employer, is not readily adaptable to general use so that it could be used in place of regular clothing, and is not so used. Rev. Rul. 70–474. Where allowed, the cost of a uniform is currently deductible and need not be depreciated over the useful life of the garment.[152] A current deduction is allowed pursuant to the "small cost" exception to the treatment of capital expenditures.[153]

¶ 21.1491. Itemized Deduction. If deductible at all, an employee's expense of purchasing a uniform is a miscellaneous itemized deduction (as contrasted to a § 62 deduction) unless the TP's employer reimburses him for the expense. If a TP is reimbursed by his employer, the expense of purchasing the uniform (if deductible at all) is deductible under § 62(a) from the TP's gross income (i.e., it is a nonitemized deduction), thereby washing out the income that the TP recognized on receiving the reimbursement. § 62(a)(2)(A); Rev. Rul. 72–110. If not reimbursed, the cost constitutes a miscellaneous itemized deduction that is subject to the 2% of AGI floor imposed by § 67 and to the reduction of itemized deductions required by § 68.

¶ 21.1492. Test for Determining "Adaptable to General Use." The question has arisen as to whether the determination that a type of clothing that an employee is required to purchase and wear is adaptable to general use by the employee outside of his work turns on the standards and tastes of the community (the so-called "objective" approach) or whether it

---

152. *Mortrud v. Commissioner*, 44 T.C. 208 (1965); *Loinaz v. Commissioner*, 34 T.C.M. 71, 77, n.2 (1975).

153. See ¶ **21.1410**.

turns on the individual standards and tastes of the employee (the "subjective" approach). The Tax Court adopted the subjective approach. In *Pevsner v. Commissioner*,[154] the court allowed the TP to deduct the cost of Yves St. Laurent clothes that she bought to wear in her work as manager of a boutique selling only women's clothes designed by Yves St. Laurent. The TP was expected to wear such clothes at work, but the court found that it would be inappropriate and out of keeping with the TP's lifestyle for her to wear the clothes outside of her work (the TP preferred a more conservative style of dress). The Fifth Circuit reversed the Tax Court in *Pevsner*. Applying an objective standard, the court denied a deduction to the TP for the cost of her clothes.[155] If an objective approach is adopted, a question remains as to the identification of the community whose standards and tastes are to be adopted.

¶ 21.1490A. Books, Films, Plays, Photographs, Sound Recordings, Fine Art Products, and Similar Properties. Prior to the adoption of the Technical and Miscellaneous Revenue Act of 1988, the uniform capitalization rule imposed by § 263A[156] required the expenses of an author in producing a book to be capitalized as part of the cost of producing the book. Similarly, the cost of producing a film, video tape, dramatic work or other artistic property had to be capitalized. In many cases, such capitalized costs could have been recovered by the artist or author over the recovery period of the asset if it were depreciable by its creator. Note that the special provision in § 174 for the deduction of research and experimental expenditures does not apply to research performed in connection with literary or historical projects. Treas. Reg. § 1.174–2(a)(1).

However, as a consequence of the 1988 amendment adding subsection (h) to § 263A, many of the expenses of authors, photographers and artists are exempt from the capitalization requirements of that section and so can be taken as current deductions. The exemption from the uniform capitalization statute applies only to a "qualified creative expense," which is defined in § 263A(h)(2) as an expense:

---

154. 38 T.C.M. 1210 (1979), rev'd 628 F.2d 467 (5th Cir. 1980). See also *Yeomans v. Commissioner*, 30 T.C. 757 (1958), Nonacq.

155. *Pevsner v. Commissioner*, 628 F.2d 467 (5th Cir. 1980).

156. See ¶ 21.1453.

(1) that is paid or incurred by an individual in the trade or business (other than as an employee) of being a writer, photographer, or artist [in certain circumstances, the term can also apply to the qualified expenses of a personal service corporation substantially all of whose stock is owned by such an individual (§ 263A(h)(3)(D))]; and

(2) that, in the absence of § 263A, would be allowable as a deduction.

The statutory exclusion does not apply to certain expenses; it does not apply to expenses relating to printing, photographic plates, motion picture films, video tapes and similar items.

The exclusion from § 263A of certain creative expenses does not necessarily make them currently deductible. It removes one obstacle to taking them as current deductions, but they must also pass muster as not being capital expenditures under § 263.[157] The likelihood, however, is that such expenses will not be required to be capitalized, and the exclusion from § 263A is some evidence that Congress intended a more liberal treatment of the expenses of those involved in artistic professions.

The exclusion applies to the qualified creative expenses of three broad categories of professions: writers, photographers, and artists. Those three categories are defined in § 263A(h)(3) as follows.

Writer. A writer is an individual whose personal efforts create (or may reasonably be expected to create) a literary manuscript, a musical composition (including the accompanying words), or a dance score.

Photographer. A photographer is an individual whose personal efforts create (or may reasonable be expected to create) a photograph or a photographic negative or transparency.

Artist. An artist is an individual whose personal efforts create (or may reasonably be expected to create) a picture, painting, sculpture, statue, etching, drawing, cartoon, graphic design, or original print edition.[158]

¶ **21.1500. Ordinary and Necessary.** Only expenses that are "ordinary and necessary" are deductible as business expenses under

---

157. See *Encyclopaedia Britannica v. Commissioner*, 685 F.2d 212 (7th Cir. 1982).

158. In determining whether an expense is paid or incurred in the trade or business of being an artist, the following criteria shall be taken into account: (1) the originality and uniqueness of the item created (or to be created), and (2) the predominance of aesthetic value over utilitarian value of the item. § 263A(h)(3)(C)(ii).

§ 162 or as expenses incurred in connection with profit-seeking ventures under § 212. The term "ordinary" and the term "necessary" have been construed as having separate independent significance.

¶ **21.1510. Necessary Defined.** Of the two terms, the requirement that the expense be "necessary" has proved to be less of an obstacle than the requirement that the expense be "ordinary." A "necessary" expense is merely one that is "appropriate and helpful" to the TP's conduct of his trade or business or profit-seeking venture.[159] Thus, the judicial construction of that requirement has been more modest than the term "necessary" might suggest.

¶ **21.1511. Failure to Seek Reimbursement.** If an employee pays for an item for which he is entitled to be reimbursed by his employer and if the employee fails to seek reimbursement, the employee cannot deduct his payment of the item because the expense was not "necessary."[160]

¶ **21.1520. Ordinary Defined.** The term "ordinary" has been given several different constructions. In the landmark case of *Welch v. Helvering*,[161] Justice Cardozo defined the term "ordinary" as requiring that the expense not be unique in the experience of the group or community of which the TP is a member. In many subsequent cases (for example, the *United Draperies* case),[162] courts have applied Cardozo's definition In other cases, the courts have indicated that the term "ordinary" merely distinguishes a capital expenditure, which sometimes may be amortized or depreciated, from a current expense which is to be deducted when paid or accrued.[163] The latter view—a more sensible con-

---

159. *Welch v. Helvering*, 290 U.S. 111 (1933); *Commissioner v. Tellier*, 383 U.S. 687 (1966).

160. *Lucas v. Commissioner*, 79 T.C. 1 (1982); *Boser v. Commissioner*, 77 T.C. 1124 (1981), Acq., aff'd without published opinion (9th Cir. 1983); but see, *Heineman v. Commissioner*, 82 T.C. 538, 545 (1984), allowing a deduction for costs incurred by an executive for which he did not seek reimbursement but for which no plan existed providing him with a right of reimbursement.

161. 290 U.S. 111 (1933); cf., *Brenner v. Commissioner*, 62 T.C. 878 (1974).

162. *United Draperies, Inc. v. Commissioner*, 340 F.2d 936 (7th Cir. 1964) (disallowing a deduction for lawful "kickbacks").

163. *Commissioner v. Tellier*, 383 U.S. 687 (1966); and *Commissioner v. Lincoln Savings and Loan Ass'n*, 403 U.S. 345 (1971).

struction of the statute—has been gaining favor with the Service and with the courts.[164]

In two cases from the 1980s, the Tax Court and the Sixth Circuit allowed TPs to deduct "kickbacks" that were legal to make.[165] In a subsequent Sixth Circuit case, a divided panel denied a deduction for kickbacks that were legal to make; the court held that the kickbacks were not "necessary" because the majority of the court thought that the TP could have obtained its business without making the kickbacks.[166] That latter decision is unusual (and of doubtful validity) because courts typically do not second guess the business judgment of a TP.

In *Trebilcock v. Commissioner*,[167] the court denied a deduction for a salary paid to a minister to consult with the TP and his employees concerning their spiritual, personal, and business problems. The minister had no expertise in business matters, and his advice came through prayer to God. The court held that even the portion of the minister's salary that was attributable to his business advice was nondeductible because the TP failed to prove that such expenses were "ordinary" in the TP's type of business.

¶ **21.1521.   Current View.** In *Conley v. Commissioner*,[168] the TP had controlled a corporation which owned and operated a public relations business. The business was unsuccessful and the corporation became insolvent. The TP then obtained employment with several large public relations firms. To preserve his reputation in the public relations field, the TP used his own funds to pay debts of the insolvent corporation, including the corporation's obligation for unpaid federal social security and withholding taxes and for state unemployment taxes due on account of its employees. The Tax Court held that the TP's payments of the corporation's debts were made for the purpose of protecting his own reputation in the public relations field

---

164. See Treas. Reg. § 1.162–1(a); *FMR Corp. and Subsidiaries v. Commissioner*, 110 T.C. 402 (1998); and Rev. Rul. 74–323.

165. *Brizell v. Commissioner*, 93 T.C. 151 (1989); *Raymond Bertolini Trucking Co. v. Commissioner*, 736 F.2d 1120 (6th Cir. 1984).

166. *Car–Ron Asphalt Paving Co. v. Commissioner*, 758 F.2d 1132 (6th Cir. 1985). See also *Diamond v. Commissioner*, 56 T.C. 530, 542–3 (1971), aff'd, 492 F.2d 286 (7th Cir. 1974) following and approving of the *United Draperies* approach.

167. 64 T.C. 852 (1975), aff'd by court order, 557 F.2d 1226 (6th Cir. 1977).

168. 36 T.C.M. 1644 (1977).

and therefore are deductible under §§ 162, 165 or 212.[169] However, the court held that the TP's payment of the corporation's liability for federal and state taxes was not deductible because to allow a deduction would "frustrate a well-defined public policy."

The holding in the *Conley* case is at odds with the Supreme Court's decision in *Welch v. Helvering*[170] to disallow a deduction for a TP's payment of his prior employer's debts, but the *Welch* decision justifiably has been subjected to criticism. The Tax Court's resort to public policy as a ground for denying the TP a deduction for the payment of the corporation's tax liabilities is questionable.[171] If the TP's payments of the corporation's debts are otherwise deductible as having been made to protect his reputation, the corporation's benefit from the TP's use of his funds should not affect the determination of TP's right to a deduction.

¶ 21.1522. Roles of the Term "Ordinary." The Seventh Circuit stated that the term "ordinary" has two different uses: (1) "to prevent the deduction of certain expenses that are not normally incurred in the type of business in which the TP is engaged ('ordinary' in this sense blends imperceptibly into 'necessary')," and (2) "to clarify the distinction between expenses that are immediately deductible and expenses that must first be capitalized."[172]

¶ 21.1530. Office in Home. Prior to the 1976 TRA, a TP who maintained an office in his personal residence was sometimes permitted to deduct an aliquot share of his rent or to depreciate the portion of his house that was dedicated to office use, but the case law on this question (particularly for employees) was unsettled.[173] The 1976 Act resolved much of this issue by adopting § 280A which established severe restrictions on the deductibility of the cost of a home office. Under that provision, no deduction is allowed for the business use of all or part of a dwelling unit which

---

169. See also, *Lohrke v. Commissioner*, 48 T.C. 679, 684–689 (1967).

170. n. 151, supra.

171. See ¶ **21.5000**.

172. *Encyclopaedia Britannica v. Commissioner*, 685 F.2d 212 (7th Cir. 1982).

173. Compare *Newi v. Commissioner*, 432 F.2d 998 (2d Cir. 1970); and *Green, Jr. v. Commissioner*, 59 T.C. 456 (1972) with *Bodzin v. Commissioner*, 509 F.2d 679 (4th Cir. 1975).

was used by the TP for personal purposes for more than 14 days of that taxable year unless one of the exceptions described below is applicable. For the limitations on the deductibility of expenses incurred in renting a dwelling to a tenant, see ¶¶ **21.1190–21.1196.**

¶ **21.1531.   Exceptions.** A deduction for a home office will be allowed where a portion of the dwelling unit is *exclusively used* on a regular basis: (a) as the principal place of business for *any* trade or business of the TP; or (b) as a place of business which is used by patients, clients, or customers in meeting or dealing with the TP in the normal course of his trade or business. A deduction will also be allowed for the maintenance of a separate structure, which is not attached to the dwelling unit, in connection with the TP's trade or business. § 280A(c). If a home office is also used for personal, nonbusiness purposes, no deduction will be allowed.[174] A home office need not be used exclusively for only one business of the TP for home office expenses to be deductible; but if the TP uses the home office for more than one business, then no deduction for home office expenses will be allowed unless the use for *each* of those businesses qualifies under § 280A(c). If any one of the businesses fails to qualify, no deduction will be allowed for any of the expenses.[175]

If a deduction is allowable under § 280A for the use of a home office, the amount of the deduction is limited by § 280A(c)(5) to the difference between the gross income for that year from such use and the sum of the non profit-seeking deductions allocable to such use (see ¶ **21.1190**) and the deductions of that trade or business that are not allocable to the home office use. Any deduction disallowed by this provision is carried over to the next year. § 280A(c)(5).

¶ **21.1532.   Principal Place of Business.** There can be only one principal place of business for each trade or business conducted by a TP. When a TP conducts a trade or business in more than one location (one of which is the TP's home), there was some controversy as to the standard to be employed in determining which location was the *principal* place of that

174. *Langer v. Commissioner*, 63 T.C.M. 1900 (1992), aff'd 989 F.2d 294 (8th Cir. 1993).

175. *Hamacher v. Commissioner*, 94 T.C. 348, 356–357 (1990).

business. The Supreme Court initially resolved that dispute in *Commissioner v. Soliman*,[176] but the Court's standard would have denied a deduction for home office use to thousands of small business owners. Dissatisfied with that consequence, Congress responded in the 1997 Act by amending § 280A(c)(1) so as to reverse the result reached in *Soliman* in certain specified circumstances. If those specified circumstances do not exist, the standard adopted by the Supreme Court in *Soliman* is applicable.

Before examining the 1997 amendment, let us put it in context by considering the history of the litigation over this issue. The Tax Court took the view that the determination of the principal place of the TP's business does not rest exclusively on a comparison of the number of hours spent at each location. Initially, the test that the Tax Court employed in determining whether the TP's home office constitutes the TP's principal place of business rested on whether the home office was the "focal point" of the TP's conduct of that trade or business.[177] In general, the "focal point" of a TP's business is the place where goods or services are provided to customers or where income is earned. Two Circuit Courts of Appeals (the Second and the Seventh) repudiated the "focal point" standard.[178]

With six judges dissenting, the Tax Court abandoned its "focal point" test in *Soliman v. Commissioner*.[179] In place of the "focal point" test, the Tax Court adopted a "facts and circumstances" test. The relative amount of time spent at the home office was only one factor to be taken into account. Other factors mentioned by the court are: the business exigencies for having a home office, whether the functions performed in the home office are essential to the conduct of the business, whether the office is suitable for those functions, and the appropriateness of the furnishings of the office.

The TP in *Soliman* was an anesthesiologist who administered to patients at three hospitals. None of the hospitals provided him with an office. TP dedicated one room of his apartment

---

176. 506 U.S. 168 (1993).

177. *Baie v. Commissioner*, 74 T.C. 105 (1980).

178. *Weissman v. Commissioner*, 751 F.2d 512 (2d Cir. 1984); *Meiers v. Commissioner*, 782 F.2d 75 (7th Cir. 1986); *Cadwallader v. Commissioner*, 919 F.2d 1273 (7th Cir. 1990).

179. 94 T.C. 20 (1990) (reviewed by the court), aff'd by a divided court, 935 F.2d 52 (4th Cir. 1991), reversed, 506 U.S. 168 (1993).

exclusively for use as an office at which he performed numerous administrative functions (including maintaining medical records for his patients and billing and collections) and worked on his continuing medical education requirements. The office did not satisfy the "focal point" test that the Tax Court had used up to that time. Applying a more flexible "facts and circumstances" test, the Tax Court allowed deductions for the home office expenses. In a 2–1 decision, the Fourth Circuit affirmed. The court emphasized that: (1) the home office was essential to TP's business, (2) he spent a substantial amount of time there, and (3) there was no other location available for the performance of the office functions of TP's business.

In reversing the decisions of the Tax Court and the Fourth Circuit, the Supreme Court held that no deduction will be allowed for a home office unless that office is the most important, consequential and influential place at which the TP conducts his business.[180] There is no set formula for making that determination; instead, it rests on an inquiry into the facts of each case. However, the Court did identify two considerations that it termed "primary" and to be given the greatest amount of weight in making this determination: namely, (1) the relative importance of the activities performed at each location, and (2) the amount of time spent at each place.

Under the Supreme Court's *Soliman* standard, the analysis begins with an objective examination of the type of business which the TP conducts. In order to determine which functions that are performed at different locations are the most important, the nature of the TP's business must be understood. Most businesses will have a pattern in which certain functions are more significant than others.

The Supreme Court rejected the notion that the fact that the function conducted at the TP's home office is an important element of the TP's business is sufficient to authorize a deduction for his home office expenses. The determination of deductibility rests on a comparison of the relative importance of the functions conducted at the several locations at which the TP works. If all of the functions conducted by the TP are necessary to the business, only the location of the most important of those is the principal place of the TP's business. The Court noted that some businesses have no principal place of business. If so, no deduction can be allowed for home office

---

180. *Commissioner v. Soliman*, 506 U.S. 168 (1993).

expenses. The home office does not become the principal place of business by default.

In the Taxpayer Relief Act of 1997, Congress added the last sentence to § 280A(c)(1). This amendment creates a special exception to the *Soliman* standard for determining principal place of business and provides a home office deduction for many small business owners who otherwise would not qualify. The standard established by the Supreme Court in *Soliman* is applicable if the special exception created by the 1997 amendment does not apply.

The amendment provides that the principal place of business includes a place which is used by the TP for the administrative or management activities of a trade or business of the TP if there is no other fixed location of that trade or business where the TP conducts substantial administrative or management activities for such trade or business. Section 280(c)(1) (last sentence). The legislative history to the amendment suggests that if the TP does perform some administrative work at another fixed location, that will not prevent the application of the special exception *if* the administrative work done at the other location is insubstantial (i.e, minimal paperwork).

There is no requirement, in order for a home office to qualify as a principal place of business, that a TP perform any management or administrative tasks there; but, if the TP does so and does not perform substantial administrative tasks at any other fixed location of that business, that alone will be sufficient to qualify the home office as the principal place of that business, provided that the other requirements of § 280A (such as the requirement of exclusive use) are satisfied. Had this provision been applicable at the time that the facts of *Soliman* took place, the TP in *Soliman* would have qualified for a home office deduction. Many TPs (e.g., doctors, salespeople, and teachers) have no principal place of business, and conduct management and administrative functions of their businesses from an office in their home dedicated exclusively to that function. The Supreme Court's *Soliman* decision would have prevented most of those people from obtaining a deduction for their home office, but the 1997 amendment will allow a deduction subject to the limitations otherwise imposed by § 280A.

¶ **21.1532–1.   Illustration 1: Others Perform Administrative Tasks Too.** *B* is a self-employed surgeon. She performs operations at the *X* hospital. While some administrative tasks are performed by *B*'s secretary in an office at the hospital, *B* has a room in her home that is used exclusively for *B*'s conducting administrative tasks, such as billing and maintaining medical records of her patients. One-fourth of the administrative work for *B*'s medical practice is performed by the secretary at a room in the hospital, and the remaining 75% is performed by *B* in her home office. Although most of *B*'s work (meeting patients and performing surgery) is performed outside her home, and although a significant portion (25%) of the administrative work is done by another person at the hospital, the home office will qualify as a principal place of *B*'s medical practice. § 280A(c)(1). The expenses of the home office will be deductible.

¶ **21.1532–2.   Illustration 2: Taxpayer Carries Out Minor Administrative Duties at Another Fixed Location.** The same facts as those stated in **Illustration 1** except that *B* has no secretary and so she does the 25% of the administrative work at the room at the hospital as well as the 75% of the administrative work that she does in her home office. The home office will not qualify as the principal place of *B*'s medical business, and so no deduction is allowable for home office expenses. The fact that *B* does more than a minimal amount of administrative work at a fixed location of her medical business (the room at the hospital) will prevent the special qualification of the last sentence of § 280A(c)(1) from applying. In the absence of the operation of that special provision, the work that *B* performs at home likely will not satisfy the requirement that the home office be the most important, consequential, and influential place at which *B* conducts her business. When the special provision does not apply, the standard for determining whether a home office is the principal place of business is the standard established by the Supreme Court in *Soliman*. In other words, the 1997 amendment can be seen as creating a special exception to the *Soliman* standard, but otherwise *Soliman* is controlling.

¶ 21.1533. Place of Business Used by Patients, Clients, or Customers in Meeting or Dealing with the Taxpayer. In lieu of qualifying as the principal place of TP's business, a home office can satisfy § 280A by being the place where patients, clients or customers meet or deal with the TP in the normal course of TP's trade or business. § 280A(c)(1)(B). The use by such persons must be substantial and integral to the TP's business. Prop. Reg. § 1.280A–2(c).

In *Green v. Commissioner*,[181] the TP, an account executive for a real estate management firm, maintained a home office at which the TP received numerous telephone calls on a regular basis from his clients. These telephone calls were a regular part of the conduct of the TP's business. Only rarely did a client come to the TP's home and meet with him in person. The TP's employer provided the TP with an office at which he spent approximately 20% of his eight-hour workday. Because the TP was difficult to reach during the day, he received numerous phone calls from his clients in the evening, and he maintained a room in his house exclusively as his office. In a sharply divided decision, the Tax Court held that the phone conversations with clients was sufficient, on the facts of that case, to qualify as a "meeting or dealing" with clients. Seven judges dissented on the ground that "meeting or dealing" requires that the client be physically present at the home office. The Ninth Circuit reversed the majority's decision on the same ground as that asserted by the dissenting Tax Court judges.[182]

¶ 21.1534. Employee's Home Office. If the TP is an employee, no deduction will be allowed for a home office (even if one or more of the conditions described above are satisfied) unless the exclusive use of the home office is for the convenience of the TP's employer. § 280A(c)(1). In *Cadwallader v. Commissioner*,[183] the court held that when an employee is provided by his employer with adequate facilities to perform his work, he cannot obtain a deduction for a home office because he chooses to perform work there. The home office is then for the convenience of the employee and not for the

---

181. 78 T.C. 428 (1982), rev'd 707 F.2d 404 (9th Cir. 1983).
182. Id.
183. 919 F.2d 1273 (7th Cir. 1990).

employer as required by the statute. In *Cadwallader*, the
Seventh Circuit denied a deduction for home office expenses to
a professor of psychology at a State university, even though
the professor did most of his writing and research at that
home office, since the university provided the professor with
an adequate office on campus. The court stated that if the
university (the TP's employer) had failed to provide him with
adequate office facilities for his research and writing, and if
the TP had used the home office exclusively and regularly to
do his research and writing, the TP would then have been
entitled to deduct his home office expenses. If that latter
situation had existed (and it did not in that case), it would
have indicated that the employer expected the professor to
outfit an office for his use, and so the TP's use of the home
office would then have been for the convenience of the employer.

¶ 21.1535. **Storage Use.** In certain cases, a deduction may
be allowed for the cost of maintaining space in a dwelling unit
to store inventory of the TP for use in the TP's trade or
business, but only if the dwelling unit is the sole fixed location
of the trade or business. § 280A(c)(2).

¶ 21.1536. **Limitation on Deductions.** Of course, § 280A
does not prevent a TP from deducting expenses attributable to
the home office space which are deductible without regard to
whether the space is employed in an income-seeking activity
(e.g., real estate taxes). Such expenses are hereinafter referred
to as "non profit-seeking deductions." If none of the exceptions to § 280A is applicable, no deduction (other than non
profit-seeking deductions) will be allowed for the use of a home
office. If one or more of the exceptions is applicable, then
§ 280A(c)(5) limits the amount of deduction allowed for the
use of the office for the taxable year to the excess of the TP's
gross income for the taxable year from the use of the home
office over the sum of: (1) the deductions for that year allocable to the use of the office which are allowable whether or not
the office was so used and (2) the deductions for that year
allocable to the trade or business in which the home office use
occurs but which are not allocable to the home office use. Any
expenses of the home office that are not deductible in a taxable
year because of this limitation are carried over and treated as
deductions allocable to such home use in the succeeding taxable year. § 280A(c)(5).

¶ **21.1600. Unreasonably Large Expenses.** If an otherwise deductible expense is unreasonably large (i.e., an expense which is greater than the normal payment for such services or benefits), the unreasonable portion of the expense will not be allowed as a business deduction. For example, *ABC*, Inc. pays an annual salary of $300,000 to *X*, its sole shareholder, for his services as president. A reasonable salary, based on salaries paid to persons performing comparable services, would be $180,000. Therefore, $120,000 of the salary paid to *X* is not deductible since it was not an ordinary and necessary expense.[184] The question of whether a payment is unreasonably large does not arise if the transaction is between two persons acting at arm's length.

In the case of a payment for services between people who are not at arm's length, the question arises as to how to determine what amount of compensation is reasonable. One could examine what is paid in the market for comparable services. It sometimes is difficult to determine what services are comparable. Courts have designed multi-factor tests looking at such items as the service provider's qualifications and the nature and scope of the service provider's work.[185] In an interesting decision, Judge Posner characterized those tests as unhelpful and proposed the use of a single "independent investor" test.[186]

¶ **21.1700. Bribes, Illegal Kickbacks, and Other Illegal Payments.**

¶ **21.1710. Payments to Government Officials.** No deduction is allowed for a bribe or kickback to an official or employee of any government or governmental agency if the payment is unlawful. In addition, if a payment is made to an official or employee of a foreign government, and if the payment is unlawful under the Foreign Corrupt Practices Act of 1977, the payment is not deductible. § 162(c)(1). The statute imposes a heavy burden of proof on the Service on the issue of whether the bribe, kickback or payment was illegal.

¶ **21.1720. Other Bribes and Kickbacks.** No deduction is allowed for other bribes, kickbacks and payments (i.e., those made

---

184. See Treas. Reg. § 1.162–8.

185. See e.g., *Edwin's Inc. v. United States*, 501 F.2d 675 (7th Cir. 1974).

186. *Exacto Spring Corporation v. Commissioner*, 196 F.3d 833 (7th Cir. 1999). See also, *Menard, Inc. v. Commissioner*, 560 F.3d 620 (7th Cir. 2009).

to persons other than government officials or employees), if they are illegal under the law of the United States, or under any state law which is generally enforced, if such law subjects the payor to a criminal penalty or to the loss of license or privilege to engage in a trade or business. The Service bears a heavy burden of proof on the question of whether a bribe, kickback or payment is illegal. § 162(c)(2). In addition, no deduction is permitted for a kickback, rebate, or bribe made by a person providing services or supplies under a medicare or medicaid program if the payment is made in connection with the furnishing of such services or supplies. § 162(c)(3).

¶ 21.1730. Illegal Payments. As noted in **¶ 21.1720**, § 162(c)(2) denies a TP a deduction for any payment that is illegal under a federal or state law which is generally enforced and which subjects the payor to a criminal penalty or the loss of a license or privilege to engage in a trade or business. A "state law which is generally enforced" refers to a statute of a state or the District of Columbia unless either the statute is never enforced or the only persons charged with violations thereof are either infamous or those whose violations are extraordinarily flagrant. Treas. Reg. § 1.162–18(b)(3). It would appear that § 162(c)(2) overturns the holding in *Commissioner v. Sullivan.*[187] The *Sullivan* case is discussed at ¶ **21.5100**.

¶ 21.1731. No Penalty. When an employment agency specified gender in an advertisement, which made the ad illegal under the Civil Rights Act of 1964, the agency nevertheless was permitted to deduct the cost of the advertisement as a business expense. Since the Civil Rights Act did not impose a penalty for such violations, § 162(c) is inapplicable. Since 1969, there has not been a public policy exception to prevent the deduction of a business expense under § 162; the statutory exclusions to § 162 are the exclusive exclusions. Treas. Reg. § 1.162–1(a). See Rev. Rul. 74–323.

¶ 21.1732. Applications of Illegal Payment Rule. For some interesting applications of the provisions of § 162(c) denying a deduction for illegal expenses, see Rev. Rul. 82–149; *Max Sobel Wholesale Liquors v. Commissioner*[188] In *Sobel*, in violation of state law providing for minimum prices, the TP (a wholesale liquor dealer) secretly transferred extra liquor to its

187. 356 U.S. 27 (1958).
188. 69 T.C. 477 (1977), aff'd, 630 F.2d 670 (9th Cir. 1980).

customers. The Tax Court and the Ninth Circuit held that those transfers were a reduction of the purchase price for the liquor sold and so were not deductible expenses which would have been denied by § 162(c).[189] This holding (permitting a reduction of purchase price) applies to rebates between a buyer and seller. The Tax Court and the Ninth Circuit have declined to extend that holding to rebates made by an agent to a buyer.[190]

While, as noted above, there are no non-statutory exceptions to the deduction of business expenses under § 162, there are cases holding that public policy can be applied to prevent the deduction of a loss even though no statutory exception is applicable. The question of whether public policy considerations can bar the taking of a deduction under § 165 for a *loss* incurred in an illegal transaction is considered at ¶¶ **21.5400** and **21.5500** and in Chapter **Eighteen**.

¶ 21.1800.   Miscellaneous.

¶ 21.1810.   Lobbying Expenses. Even prior to the adoption of the Omnibus Budget Reconciliation Act of 1993, most lobbying expenses could not be deducted. There were some important exceptions. The 1993 amendments deny deductions for virtually all lobbying expenses except for lobbying with a local council or similar governing body. § 162(e).

¶ 21.1820.   Fines and Penalties. No deduction is allowed for the payment of a fine or similar penalty to a government because of a violation of the law. § 162(f). For the tax treatment of the payment of expenses which are illegal to make, see ¶¶ **21.1730** and **21.5000–21.5200**.

¶ 21.1821.   Illustration: Characterization of a Fine. The TP, a public school teacher, engaged in a strike that was illegal under state law. The applicable state law provided that a teacher who is found to have participated in a strike will have withheld from her pay an amount equal to twice the teacher's daily pay for each day (or part thereof) that the teacher was absent from school in violation of the state law. Had the TP not been on strike, she would have received $1,509 pay for the

---

189.   See also Rev. Rul. 82–149.

190.   See *Alex v. Commissioner*, 628 F.2d 1222 (9th Cir. 1980), aff'g 70 T.C. 322 (1978) (a divided decision).

days that she was absent. The school district did not pay the TP the $1,509 wages for those days, and the district withheld an additional $1,509 from her subsequent salary payments for work performed after the strike was discontinued. The Tax Court held[191] that the $1,509 that was withheld from the TP because she did not work on those days was not included in her gross income; but the additional $1,509 which was withheld as a penalty for her illegal strike constitutes gross income to the TP and because of § 162(f) is not deductible by her. The TP is deemed to have received the $1,509 for work performed subsequent to the strike and then to have paid that amount to the state as a fine for her illegal activity.

¶ 21.1822. **Deductible Civil Penalty.** For a civil penalty to fall within the § 162(f) bar against deductibility, it must be one which punishes or deters the TP who pays the penalty. If the "penalty" is remedial in nature (e.g., if it constitutes a provision for liquidated damages), the payment will not be subject to § 162(f) and will be deductible if it otherwise qualifies as a business expense or some other deductible expense. In *Middle Atlantic Distributors, Inc. v. Commissioner,*[192] the federal government sued the TP to recover, under 19 U.S.C. § 1592, the value of liquor fraudulently withdrawn from the TP's warehouse and, contrary to United States customs law, introduced into commerce in the United States. The suit was settled for less than 20% of the amount claimed, and the Tax Court allowed the TP a deduction for the amount paid by the TP in settling the suit. The court determined that 19 U.S.C. § 1592, on which the suit was brought against the TP, is both remedial and punitive in its nature. Consequently, the court looked to the intention of the parties in settling the suit to characterize the payment as remedial or punitive. Since the TP's offer to settle and the settlement agreement itself referred to the settlement as an amount representing liquidated damages, the court concluded that the settlement payment was remedial and, therefore, was a deductible business expense.

¶ 21.1823. **Purpose of Penalty.** The Commissioner will examine the purpose of requiring a payment that is characterized as a "penalty" to determine whether it is truly intended

191. *Tucker v. Commissioner*, 69 T.C. 675 (1978). See Rev. Rul. 76–130.
192. 72 T.C. 1136 (1979).

as a punitive measure. For example, in Rev. Rul. 88–46, the Commissioner allowed a deduction for the payment of a "nonconformance penalty" imposed by the Environmental Protection Agency under the Clean Air Act on a manufacturer of trucks for failing to conform to emission standards established under that Act. The Commissioner determined that the purpose of the "penalty" was to prevent nonconforming manufacturers from gaining a competitive advantage over conforming manufacturers who incurred higher costs in order to meet the emission standards.

¶ 21.1824. Restitution Payments. A TP's repayment to a third party of funds improperly or unlawfully obtained from the third party usually will not be a "penalty" to the TP even if the restitution was made pursuant to a court order. If the TP's receipt of the funds caused him to recognize gross income, the repayment of the funds to the victim usually will be deductible by the TP. However, in several Tax Court cases, restitution payments that were ordered to be made by a court as an alternative to a jail term were characterized as "penalties," and so the Tax Court found that the payments were not deductible by the TP. The fact that the payments were made to private individuals did not preclude their being characterized as penalties by the Tax Court. It was deemed sufficient that the State exercised control over the disposition of the penalty; the payment need not be made directly to the State.

The Tax Court and the Ninth Circuit held that the test for penalty characterization is the origin of the liability rather than the identity of the payee.[193] The Tax Court concluded that the purpose of ordering the TPs in those cases to make monetary restitution to their victims was to punish the TPs since the restitution payments were ordered as an alternative to a prison term. In *Waldman*,[194] the courts applied § 162(f) to deny a deduction. In *Stephens*,[195] the Tax Court applied the congressional policy exemplified by § 162(f) to deny a deduction claimed under § 165(c)(2) as a loss incurred in a profit transaction. The Second Circuit reversed the Tax Court's

---

193. *Waldman v. Commissioner*, 88 T.C. 1384, 1389 (1987), aff'd by court order, 850 F.2d 611 (9th Cir. 1988); *Stephens v. Commissioner*, 93 T.C. 108 (1989), rev'd, 905 F.2d 667 (2d Cir. 1990).

194. n. 193, supra.

195. Id.

decision in *Stephens* and allowed a deduction.[196] The decisions of the Tax Court and of the Second Circuit in *Stephens* are discussed in Chapter **Eighteen**.

¶ 21.1830. Treble Damages Under the Antitrust Laws. If a TP is convicted of a criminal violation of the antitrust laws or if his plea of guilty or nolo contendere to such a charge is accepted, then the TP cannot deduct two-thirds of any amount paid by him on a judgment under (or in settlement of an action brought under) Section Four of the Clayton Act on account of such violation or related violation. § 162(g).

¶ 21.1840. Contributions to Charitable Organizations. No deduction is allowed under § 162 for a contribution or gift that would have been deductible under § 170 as a charitable contribution if it were not for the percentage, dollar, or timing limitations set forth in that section. § 162(b). The genesis of this limitation is described in *Marquis v. Commissioner*.[197] The limitation imposed by § 162(b) applies only to a contribution or gift—i.e., to a payment for which there was no expectation of financial return commensurate with the payment.[198] If a payment to a charitable organization is made with the expectation of receiving a quid pro quo for it, the payment is not a contribution or gift and so can qualify as a business expense under § 162 if the requirements of that provision are satisfied.

¶ 21.2000. CREDIT FOR CHILD AND DEPENDENT CARE AND HOUSEHOLD EXPENSES. The expenses of a working parent or parents for the care of a child (or other dependent) while the parent is at work are not deductible as a business (or nonbusiness) expense. While the expense of caring for children may be a necessary cost of freeing the parent from the home so that he can earn income, it also is an expense arising out of personal, family obligations. The cost of child care is analogous to commuting expenses which are not deductible even though a TP is not able to earn gross income unless he travels from his residence to his place of work.

The business overtones of those expenses and of related household expenses were sufficiently compelling, however, to induce Congress to provide tax relief in some circumstances. For taxable years beginning

---

196. Id.

197. 49 T.C. 695, 698–701 (1968).

198. *Marquis v. Commissioner*, n. 197, supra; Rev. Rul. 77–124; and Rev. Rul. 72–314.

prior to 1976, § 214 allowed a limited amount of deduction for such expenses, but that provision was repealed by the 1976 TRA. The 1976 Act substituted a tax credit for the deduction that had previously been allowed and altered some of the requirements for qualifying for the tax relief. Section 21 grants a nonrefundable credit that can equal as much as 35%[199] of so-called "employment-related expenses"[200] to an individual who qualifies under the statute.

The percentage of employment-related expenses that qualify for the credit is reduced by one percentage point for each $2,000 (or fraction thereof) by which the TP's AGI for that year exceeds $15,000;[201] but in no event shall the percentage be less than 20%. § 21(a).

Note that dependent care assistance provided by an employer to its employees is excluded from the employee's gross income by § 129. While no more than $5,000 can be excluded in a taxable year, the amount excluded is not subject to any reduction because of the size of the TP's AGI. To qualify under § 129, the employer's plan for providing such benefits cannot discriminate in favor of highly compensated employees or their dependents. § 129(d)(2).

¶ 21.2100. **Qualifying Individuals.** Section 21 grants a credit to an individual for whom there is at least one "qualifying individual." A "qualifying individual" is a person who is either (1) a dependent[202] of the TP (as defined in § 152(a)(1)) who has not attained the age of 13 years, or (2) a dependent (as defined in § 152 with some modifications) or spouse of the TP who is physically or mentally incapable of caring for himself and who has the same place of abode as the TP for more than one-half of the taxable year. The statute provides a special rule for treating certain children of divorced or separated parents as qualifying individuals with respect to one of the parents. § 21(e)(5).

¶ 21.2200. **Employment–Related Expenses.** A qualified TP is allowed a credit equal to 20% to 35%[203] of the amount paid for household services and for expenses for the care of a "qualifying individual" if such expenses are incurred to permit the TP to be

---

199. Under a sunset provision, for years beginning after 2012, that 35% maximum percentage will be reduced to 30% unless Congress acts to change it.

200. Employment-related expenses are defined at ¶ **21.2200**.

201. Under a sunset provision, for years beginning after 2012, that $15,000 figure will be reduced to $10,000.

202. The term "dependent," is defined at ¶¶ **11.1220–11.1243**.

203. See n. 199, supra.

gainfully employed during a period for which there is at least one qualifying individual with respect to the TP. These expenses are referred to as "employment-related expenses." Such expenses for services performed outside the TP's household are taken into account only if incurred on behalf of a dependent of the TP who is under the age of 13, or on behalf of a qualifying individual who spends at least eight hours each day in the TP's household. If the outside care is provided by a dependent care center (as defined by § 21(b)(2)(D)), expenses are taken into account only if the center complies with all rules and regulations of a state or local government unit. § 21(b)(2)(C).

¶ 21.2300.   **Limitations on Credit.**

¶ 21.2310.   **Dollar Limit.** The amount of employment-related expenses incurred in a taxable year, which is taken into account under § 21, cannot exceed $3,000 if the TP has only one qualifying individual for that year or $6,000 if the TP has two or more qualifying individuals.[204] § 21(c). Those dollar figures are reduced by the amount of dependent care assistance that the TP receives from his employer that is excluded from the TP's gross income by § 129. *Id.* Thus, if in the year 2010, a TP has AGI of $15,000 or less and received no dependent care assistance from an employer, the maximum credit allowable for that taxable year is 35% x $3,000 = $1,050 for one qualifying individual and 35% x $6,000 = $2,100 if there is more than one qualifying individual.

If instead a TP had AGI of $22,000 for the 2010 taxable year, the maximum credit for one qualifying individual is 31% x $3,000 = $930; and the maximum credit for more than one qualifying individual is 31% x $6,000 = $1,860.[205]

¶ 21.2320.   **Earned Income Limitation.** The amount of a TP's employment-related expenses which are taken into account under § 21 cannot exceed: (1) the "earned income" of the TP if the TP is not married at the end of the taxable year, or (2) if the TP is married at the end of the taxable year, the *lesser* of the TP's earned income and the earned income of the TP's spouse for that

---

204.   Under a sunset provision, for taxable years beginning after 2012, the $3.000 figure will be reduced to $2,400, and the $6,000 figure will be reduced to $4,800.

205.   See ¶ 21.2000. The $22,000 figure is $7,000 greater than the $15,000 ceiling that applies to 2010. That $7,000 figure constitutes 3 steps of $2,000 plus a fraction of a fourth step. So, the 35% rate is reduced by 4 percentage points to a 31% rate.

year. § 21(d). However, for each month that one (and only one) of the spouses was either a full-time student at an educational institution or was physically or mentally incapable of caring for himself, the statute treats such spouse as having earned income of no less than either $250 or $500 depending upon whether there is only one qualifying individual or whether there is more than one. § 21(d). Under a sunset provision, for taxable years beginning after 2012, the monthly $250 and $500 figures are scheduled to be reduced to $200 and $400 respectively.

¶ 21.2330. **Payments to Dependents.** Section 21(e)(6) prohibits a credit for amounts paid by a TP to a person for whom a dependent exemption deduction[206] under § 151(c) is allowable either to the TP or his spouse. No credit is allowable for payments made to a child of the TP (as defined at ¶ **11.1231**) who has not attained the age of 19 by the close of the taxable year regardless of whether the child qualifies the TP for a dependent exemption. § 21(e)(6)(B).

¶ 21.2340. **Married Taxpayers.** If a TP is married at the close of a taxable year, no credit will be allowed under § 21 for that year unless the TP and his spouse file a joint return. § 21(e)(2). An individual who is separated from his spouse under a decree of separate maintenance or divorce is considered unmarried. § 21(e)(3). A married TP is treated as unmarried for a taxable year if he: (1) filed a separate tax return for that year; (2) maintained as his home a household which was the principal place of abode of a qualifying individual; (3) the TP's spouse was not a member of that household at any time during the last six months of such taxable year; and (4) the TP furnished over one-half the cost of maintaining the household during the taxable year. § 21(e)(4).

¶ 21.3000. **TRAVEL EXPENSES.**

¶ 21.3100. **General.** Traveling expenses (including reasonable amounts expended for meals and lodging) while away from "home" in the pursuit of a trade or business are deductible under § 162(a)(2). If the TP is self-employed, the deductions are nonitemized deductions; but only 50% of the cost of meals is deductible. § 274(n).

If the TP is an employee and if the expenses are not reimbursed, the deductions will constitute miscellaneous itemized deductions that are

---

206. See ¶ **11.1220**.

subject to the 2% of AGI floor and also are subject to the reduction of itemized deductions imposed by § 68.[207] In addition, if an employee's expenses for meals are not reimbursed, subject to a few narrow exceptions, only 50% of the cost of those meals is allowable as an itemized deduction (the remaining 50% is disallowed). § 274(n). The 50% of meals' cost that constitutes an itemized deduction is then added to other miscellaneous itemized deductions and subjected to the 2% of AGI floor and to the reduction of itemized deductions imposed by § 68. If the employee's expenses are reimbursed by his employer, then the entire amount of such expenses is deductible as a nonitemized deduction. § 62(a)(2)(A). In that case, the 2% of AGI floor does not apply, and the employee can deduct 100% of the cost of his meals; but the employer can deduct only 50% of the amount of cost of the employee's meals that he reimbursed.

Note that for employees engaged in the transportation industry, a higher percentage of the cost of their meals that are consumed while "away from home"[208] is deductible. § 274(n)(3).

¶ 21.3110. **Conditions to be Satisfied.** The Supreme Court held in the *Flowers* case[209] that a TP must satisfy three conditions to become entitled to deduct a travel expense under § 162(a)(2):

(a) the expense must be reasonable and appropriate;

(b) the expense must be incurred while away from home; and

(c) the expense must arise out of the exigencies of the TP's business (i.e., there must be a direct connection between the expenditure and the conduct of the TP's business).

¶ 21.3111. **Substantiation.** Section 274(d) imposes requirements as to record keeping and substantiation that a TP must maintain to qualify for a deduction for travel expenses which are otherwise deductible under §§ 162 or 212.[210] If the TP is an employee who is reimbursed by his employer for travel expenses, the substantiation requirement will be satisfied if the employee is provided with a per diem allowance that does not

207. See ¶¶ 10.1110–10.1120.

208. The meaning of the term "away from home" has been the subject of litigation. See ¶ 21.3200.

209. *Commissioner v. Flowers*, 326 U.S. 465 (1946).

210. See Notice 95–50.

exceed certain guidelines.[211]

¶ **21.3112. Standard Mileage Allowance.** Instead of maintaining records for the use of an automobile for business travel, the Service permits the TP to use a standard mileage allowance. This allowance represents the operating costs of the vehicle (e.g., depreciation of the vehicle, gasoline, oil, maintenance and tires). Parking fees and tolls are not included in the mileage allowance and can be deducted separately. The mileage allowance for business use in 2011 is 51¢ per mile. Notice 2010–88. The amount of the mileage allowance is revised periodically. The Service publishes a notice designating the amount of the mileage allowance that is to be treated as depreciation that reduces the TP's basis in the automobile. Rev. Proc. 2010–51 (Sec. 4.04).

¶ **21.3120. "Transportation Costs" Distinguished.** It should be noted that the cost of *transportation*, unlike meals and lodging, may be deducted either under the general language of § 162(a) as an ordinary business expense or under § 162(a)(2) as part of a traveling expense. The general provision of § 162(a) does *not* require that the expense be incurred away from the TP's home. Also note that the term "transportation" is a narrower concept than the terms "travel expense" or "traveling expense" in that the latter include both transportation costs and the expenses of meals and lodging; whereas the term "transportation costs" does not include meals and lodging costs.

¶ **21.3130. Deduction of the Cost of Meals That Are Not Incurred as Travel Expenses.** It is possible in certain cases for 50% of the cost of meals to be deductible under the general language of § 162(a) as an ordinary business expense even when the meals are not part of a travel expense. For example, the cost of a business entertainment that is deductible can include the cost of 50% of the TP's meal. See § 274(a), (k). Fifty percent of the cost of meals taken during a business discussion or pursuant to a business program can be deductible. Treas. Reg. § 1.274–2(f)(2). Apart from entertainment expenses and business meetings, there are only a few circumstances when the cost of a meal that is not part of a travel expense can be deducted. In a divided decision, the Eighth Circuit permitted state troopers who were required by

211. See Rev. Proc. 97–59.

their employer to take their meals at public restaurants adjacent to the highways they patrolled to deduct the cost of those meals.[212]

¶ 21.3140. Travel Expense of Individual Accompanying Taxpayer. Under § 274(m)(3), the travel expenses of a spouse, dependent, or other individual accompanying the TP (or accompanying an officer or employee of the TP) on business travel are not deductible unless:

> (1) the spouse, dependent or other individual is an employee of the TP [the Statement of Managers in the Conference Report to the 1993 Reconciliation Act describes this condition as requiring that the spouse, dependent or other individual be a bona fide employee of the person paying or reimbursing the expenses];
>
> (2) the travel of the spouse, dependent, or other individual must be for a bona fide business purpose; and
>
> (3) such expenses must otherwise be deductible by the spouse, dependent, or other individual.

The denial of travel expense deductions for such persons does not apply to moving expenses that are deductible under § 217.[213]

¶ 21.3200. Away From Home: General. Since § 162(a)(2) is available only for expenses incurred by the TP while away from "home," it is necessary to locate the TP's "home." The Service maintains that for purposes of § 162(a)(2), a TP's "home" is the location of the TP's regular, or principal (if more than one regular) place of business rather than the location of the TP's residence. Rev. Rul. 99–7. The Tax Court and at least five Circuit Courts of Appeals concur with the government's view, but the Second Circuit has held that a TP's home is his residence.[214]

---

212. *Christey v. United States*, 841 F.2d 809 (8th Cir. 1988). See also *Sibla v. Commissioner*, 611 F.2d 1260 (9th Cir. 1980).

213. See ¶¶ 21.3400–21.3430.

214. Compare *Six v. United States*, 450 F.2d 66 (2d Cir. 1971); *Rosenspan v. United States*, 438 F.2d 905 (2d Cir.); and the concurring opinion of Judge Keeton in *Hantzis v. Commissioner*, 638 F.2d 248 (1st Cir. 1981) with *Coombs v. Commissioner*, 608 F.2d 1269 (9th Cir. 1979); *Michel Jr. v. Commissioner*, 629 F.2d 1071 (5th Cir. 1980); *Weiberg v. Commissioner*, 639 F.2d 434 (8th Cir. 1981); *Andrews v. Commissioner*, 931 F.2d 132 (1st Cir. 1991).

The *Andrews* case involved an interesting factual situation. The TP had two seasonal businesses—one in Massachusetts and one in Florida. He had a residence in both states. Each year, TP and his wife lived in Massachusetts during the season for that business, and

The Sixth Circuit also adopted the "principal place of business" test and held that, when the TP has two business localities, the determination of the location of a TP's principal place of business rests on a weighing of three factors: (a) the length of time spent in each locality; (b) the degree of TP's business activity in each locality; and (c) the relative portion of income derived from each locality.[215]

In several cases, the courts of appeals have eschewed the need to determine a TP's home and instead have rested their decision on the question of whether there was a business reason for the TP to maintain his home in one locality while working in another locality. If not, no deduction was allowed.[216]

Despite those cases, if the job at the other locality is temporary and if the TP's residence is an abode in a real and substantial sense [see ¶ 21.3250], there should not be a requirement of a business reason to live in one locality and work in the other. However, if there is no business reason for the TP to reside where he does, it will be difficult to establish that the TP lives in an abode in a real and substantial sense as that term has been defined. In a recent decision, Judge Posner criticized the temporary job exception and stated that it does not work well.[217]

¶ 21.3210.   Military Assignment. In *Commissioner v. Stidger*,[218] the Supreme Court held that the "home" of a military officer who was assigned to a post in Japan was his post abroad rather than the state of California where his wife and children resided.

he lived in Florida for the season of the Florida business. The Tax Court held that the TP's home was his principal place of business, and his home when he lived in each residence was at his principal place of business at that time. So, the Tax Court denied the TP any travel expense deduction because it held that he was never away from home. The First Circuit reversed and held that only one of the residences was the TP's home, and so he could deduct his travel expenses at the other residence. The court emphasized that it was business exigencies that caused the TP to maintain two residences, and so his expenses at one should be deductible. The court left it to the Tax Court to decide which of TP's two residences was in his principal place of business. The TP will be allowed to deduct his expenses in living at the other residence. In considering factors to decide which of the two places was the TP's principal place of business, the court suggested that the amount of time spent at each is an important factor.

215. *Markey v. Commissioner*, 490 F.2d 1249, 1255 (6th Cir. 1974). See also *Andrews v. Commissioner*, n. 214, supra.

216. *Hantzis v. Commissioner, supra*; *Wilbert v. Commissioner*, 553 F.3d 544 (7th Cir. 2009); *Daly v. Commissioner*, 662 F.2d 253 (4th Cir. 1981) (a divided en banc decision).

217. *Wilbert v. Commissioner*, n. 216 supra.

218. 386 U.S. 287 (1967).

The Court relied heavily on the special position of the military with particular emphasis on the tax-free allowance Congress has granted military personnel to provide them subsistence and quarters.

> ¶ **21.3211.** *Stidger* **and Non–Military Taxpayers.** In *Stidger*, the Supreme Court expressly declined to resolve the question of what constitutes the tax home of non-military TPs. However, there is language in *Stidger* which refers with apparent approval to the Service's position that a TP's home for tax purposes is his principal place of business, and, therefore, *Stidger* has been cited in support of that position.[219] But in rejecting the Service's construction of "home," the Second Circuit treated the decision in *Stidger* as *sui generis* for military personnel.[220]

¶ **21.3220.** **Overnight or "Sleep or Rest" Rules.** The Service maintains that travel "away from home" refers only to travel where the TP is away for a sufficient period of time to reasonably require sleep or rest. The application of this rule (sometimes referred to as the "overnight rule" and sometimes as the "sleep or rest rule") is explained in Rev. Rul. 75–168. As to the deductibility of meals, in the *Correll* case, the Supreme Court sustained the government's "overnight rule" and denied a deduction for meals where the TP was not away from home for a sufficient period to require sleep.[221] You will recall that even if meals are deductible, only 50% of the cost of the meals can qualify for a deduction (a larger percentage for employees working in the transportation industry).[222]

Several courts have applied the overnight test to deny a deduction for transportation expenses, rather than limiting that rule to the cost of meals.[223] Note, however, that in *some* cases, notwithstanding the inapplicability of § 162(a)(2), a TP can deduct his cost of transportation for non-overnight trips under the general provision of § 162(a) which is not subject to the overnight rule. Rev. Rul.

---

219. See *Sanders v. Commissioner*, 439 F.2d 296 (9th Cir. 1971).

220. *Six v. United States*, n. 214, supra.

221. *United States v. Correll*, 389 U.S. 299 (1967).

222. See ¶ **21.3100**.

223. E.g., *Turner v. Commissioner*, 56 T.C. 27 (1971) (reviewed by the entire court but vacated and remanded by the Second Circuit on the government's motion); and *Sanders v. Commissioner*, n. 219, supra.

90–23 as modified by Rev. Rul. 99–7. See ¶ **21.3312–4B** for a discussion of the policy considerations underlying the overnight rule.

¶ 21.3221. Transportation Between Residence and Work Location (Commuting Expense). In the absence of one of several exceptions, a TP's transportation cost of travelling between his residence and a work location is a nondeductible commuting expense. Treas. Reg. §§ 1.162–2(e), 1.262–1(b)(5). While the TP could not earn income if he did not travel to his place of work, the expense also has personal, nonbusiness elements in that the TP chose his place of residence for personal reasons, and a commuting expense is as much a cost of getting to and from the residence as it is to get to and from the work location. Rather than divide the expenses into business and nonbusiness portions, the tax law denies a deduction for all of the costs.

There are important exceptions to the nondeductibility of commuting expenses. These exceptions are set forth in Rev. Rul. 99–7. In examining these exceptions, keep in mind that a deduction is allowed for the TP's transportation costs in travelling from one work site to another work site regardless of whether the two work sites are part of the same employment or whether they are sites of different employments with different employers. Rev. Rul. 55–109. There is no personal element in travelling from one work location to another. However, if one of the work sites is also the TP's residence, there is some personal element to the travel, and so a special set of rules have been designed for that situation.

(1) If the TP's principal place of business, as determined under § 280A(c)(1)(A), is located in his residence, the TP can deduct the daily transportation cost incurred in going between the residence and another work location in the same trade or business, regardless of whether the other work location is regular or temporary, and regardless of whether the other work location is within or outside the metropolitan area in which the TP resides. Rev. Rul. 99–7. This is merely an application of the rule that the transportation costs of travelling between work locations are deductible. It would seem, although omitted from the ruling, that where the residence is the TP's principal place of business, a TP can deduct the daily transportation costs of travelling between his residence and a

work location for a different business than the one conducted as his residence. There is no personal element in making that trip.

(2) If the TP has at least one *regular* work location (i.e, a regular place of business) away from his residence, the transportation cost of going between his residence and a *temporary* work location in the same trade or business is deductible, regardless of whether the temporary work location is within or outside of the metropolitan area in which the TP resides. Rev. Rul. 99–7. The meaning of a "temporary job" is discussed at ¶ **21.3312.**

(3) Even if a TP does not conduct any business at his residence, the TP can deduct the transportation costs of going between his residence and a temporary work location that lies *outside* the metropolitan area in which the TP lives and normally works. If the temporary work location is within the metropolitan area in which the TP lives, no deduction will be allowed for the transportation costs unless either of the exceptions in (1) and (2) above is applicable. Rev. Rul. 99–7. The meaning of a "temporary job" is discussed at ¶ **21.3312.**

As to the meaning of the term "regular place of business," which term is used in Rev. Rul. 99–7, the Tax Court held in *Walker v. Commissioner*[224] that the term is broader than the "principal place of business" standard. In *Walker*, the TP (a professional tree cutter) worked seven hours a week at his residence, maintained a workshop there, stored his tools there, and was contacted there for employment at temporary job sites. The court held that his residence was a "regular place of business," but not a "principal place of business." In PLR 9806007, the Service ruled that a work location at which the TP spent 25% to 27% of his working days was a regular place of business. While the Service has stated it will not follow the *Walker* decision, that rejection does not refer to the portion of the *Walker* decision that determined the meaning of a "regular place of business." See Rev. Rul. 99–7.

¶ **21.3230. Major and Minor Post.** When a TP has a principal place of business in one location and a minor post in another location, he may deduct the round-trip expenses incurred in traveling to his minor post, including (if he complied with the

---

224. 101 T.C. 537 (1993).

overnight rule) the cost of his meals and lodging. Of course, if unreimbursed, only 50% of the cost of meals is deductible, and (unless reimbursed) the travel expenses of an employee are subject to the 2% of AGI floor and the reduction of itemized deductions imposed by § 68. §§ 67(b), 274(n).

¶ 21.3231. Expenses at Temporary or Minor Post. The Commissioner ruled in Rev. Rul. 63–145 that a TP who is residing at a temporary or minor post can deduct the cost of commuting from his lodging to his place of business at that temporary or minor post provided that such costs are reasonable in amount and incurred away from home (i.e., the area in which TP's principal place of business is located) in the pursuit of his business. The Commissioner also ruled in Rev. Rul. 63–145 that the TP can deduct his laundry and dry cleaning expenses while away from home on business. Other incidental expenses that can be deducted are tips for baggage handlers and for waiters. See Rev. Proc. 93–50, Sec. 3.02(3). Even if the TP does not remain overnight at his minor post, he can usually deduct under § 162(a) his cost of round-trip transportation between his principal and minor post [see ¶ 21.3221]; but since the TP is not "away from home" if he fails to remain overnight, he cannot deduct any part of the cost of his meals or other living expenses. Rev. Rul. 55–109.

¶ 21.3232. Illustration. A TP is employed in Detroit for nine months of the year, but he is required by his employer to work in Dallas for three months of the year. TP is not reimbursed by his employer for his expenses in travelling to Dallas or living there. Dallas is the TP's minor post, and the TP can deduct his cost of transportation from Detroit to Dallas and return. Since the TP satisfied the overnight rule, he can also deduct his reasonable costs of meals (subject to the 50% limitation described at ¶ 21.3100) and lodging while living and working in Dallas, and he can deduct the cost of commuting from his lodging in Dallas to his Dallas office. These deductions are allowable even though the TP is required to work for three months of each year in Dallas (i.e., the trip to the minor post is a recurring one). Rev. Rul. 75–432. Unless reimbursed by his employer, the travel expenses of an employee constitute miscellaneous itemized deductions which are subject to the 2% of AGI floor imposed by § 67 and the overall limitation on itemized deductions imposed by § 68.

¶ **21.3233. Travel Among Multiple Jobs.** When a TP works at several jobs on the same day, his transportation cost of traveling from one job site to the other is a deductible business expense. Rev. Rul. 55–109. While the TP may not be away from home and so § 162(a)(2) is inapplicable, the expenses are deductible under the general provision of § 162(a).

In PLR 8023052, the TP held three jobs. There was no indication in the ruling that the TP's residence could qualify as a principal place of business. The Commissioner ruled that no deduction is allowed for the cost of the TP's transporting himself to the first job of the day, but the costs of transporting himself from the first job to the second and from the second job to the third are deductible. The letter ruling suggests that the transportation costs incurred in going from the third job to the TP's home at the end of work may be deductible if the third job lies outside the general locality of the TP's customary employment; otherwise, those costs are not deductible. In light of Rev. Rul. 99–7, it would seem that regardless of the distance between the third job's work location and the TP's residence, no deduction will be allowed for the cost of returning to the residence unless the third job was temporary.

¶ **21.3234. Office in Residence as Minor Post.** When a TP maintains an office in his residence so that he may work there in the evening or on the weekends and the home office does not qualify as the principal place of business, the TP *cannot* deduct the cost of going between his home and the downtown office at which he works during the day.[225] The downtown office is not a temporary job site. The primary purpose of such transportation costs is personal rather than business-oriented, and therefore no deduction is allowed. In effect, such expenses do not satisfy the "exigencies of the business" requisite.[226] However, the Commissioner and the Tax Court have held that if the TP's home office is his *principal* place of business, the TP's round-trip expenses of going from his home office to other work locations may be deductible.[227]

---

225.   *Green, Jr. v. Commissioner*, 59 T.C. 456 (1972); *Mazzotta v. Commissioner*, 57 T.C. 427 (1971), aff'd per curiam, 465 F.2d 1399 (2d Cir. 1972); and *Matteson v. Commissioner*, 514 F.2d 43 (8th Cir. 1975). See ¶ **21.3221**.

226.   See ¶ **21.3110**.

227.   Rev. Rul. 94–47; *Wisconsin Psychiatric Services, Ltd. v. Commissioner*, 76 T.C. 839, 849–850 (1981); *Curphey v. Commissioner*, 73 T.C. 766 (1980).

¶ **21.3240. Boundaries of a Taxpayer's "Home."** The Service has held that a TP's home includes the general geographic area in which his principal place of business is located and is not restricted to city limits or to other political divisions. Rev. Rul. 55–109. Presumably, if a TP's home is deemed to be his place of residence, it would include the general geographical area in which he resides.

¶ **21.3250. No Principal or Regular Place of Business but a Regular Place of Abode.** If a TP who is in a trade or business has no principal or regular place of business, but does have a regular place of abode in a real and substantial sense, then his residence may qualify as his tax home, and he may be "away from home" when he is at work on a temporary job *in a different vicinity*. Rev. Rul. 73–529. However, if the temporary job is located within the metropolitan area in which the TP's regular place of abode is located, then no deduction is allowable for the transportation costs of going to and returning from the temporary job. Rev. Rul. 99–7. The significance of classifying an abode as the TP's home is that the TP might then be able to qualify travel expenses away from that home for the § 162(a)(2) deduction.

The Commissioner has listed three criteria which the Service will employ in determining whether an abode is sufficiently substantial to constitute a home: (1) whether the TP performs a portion of his business in the vicinity of the abode and resides at the abode on such occasions; (2) whether the TP incurs double living expenses when away from the abode on business; and (3) whether the TP either (a) has not abandoned the vicinity of his historical place of lodging, (b) has a spouse or lineal descendant residing at the abode, or (c) uses the abode frequently for his lodging. Rev. Rul. 73–529. If a TP satisfies all three criteria and has no principal or regular place of business, the Service will treat the abode as his home. If he satisfies only two of the criteria, the Service *may* treat the abode as his home but will not necessarily do so; if he fails to satisfy two of the criteria, the Service will treat him as an itinerant. See ¶ **21.3260**.

Even if a TP's abode is treated as his tax home, the TP may founder on the exigencies of the business requisite[228] or on the overnight rule[229] and thus lose his claim for a deduction under

---

228. See *Hantzis v. Commissioner*, 638 F.2d 248 (1st Cir. 1981); *Tucker v. Commissioner*, 55 T.C. 783 (1971).

229. See *Turner v. Commissioner*, 56 T.C. 27 (1971).

§ 162(a)(2).[230] Transportation costs to a temporary job sometimes can be deducted under the general provision of § 162(a).

While the Service has not revoked any of its rulings on this subject, it is possible, but unlikely, that the Service will no longer be willing to treat an abode, however substantial, as a TP's home. That is, the Service may no longer apply that approach in light of those cases holding that there is no deduction unless the TP has a business reason for remaining in the residence.[231] Instead of rejecting the abode rule, the Service is more likely to take a narrow view of what constitutes an abode in a real and substantial sense.

¶ 21.3260. No Principal or Regular Place of Business and No Permanent Residence. If a TP has no principal or regular place of business and also has no regular place of abode in a real and substantial sense, he has *no tax home* and, therefore, can have no traveling expenses under § 162(a)(2) for expenses incurred away from home.[232] However, in certain cases, a TP's costs of transporting himself (but not his family and not his food and lodging expenses) may be deductible under § 162(a) as an ordinary business expense. For example, the costs of the TP's going from one work location to another are deductible. Since such a TP has no permanent residence, his food and lodging expenses do not constitute extraordinary expenses caused by the exigencies of his trade or business.

¶ 21.3270. Temporary Jobs. Even if the Commissioner's interpretation of "home" is adopted, a TP who leaves the location of his principal place of business in order to travel to a temporary job for a sufficient time to require sleep or rest is deemed to be away from home.[233] Of course, if the Commissioner's interpretation of "home" is rejected, as one Circuit Court has done, a TP who travels to a temporary job is away from home if he is away from his place of residence; but that view has been rejected by a

---

230. See *Daly v. Commissioner*, 662 F.2d 253 (4th Cir. 1981) (en banc).

231. See *Wilbert v. Commissioner*, n.216, supra.

232. Rev. Rul. 75–432; *James v. United States*, 308 F.2d 204 (9th Cir. 1962); *Brandl v. Commissioner*, 513 F.2d 697 (6th Cir. 1975); *Deamer v. Commissioner*, 752 F.2d 337, 339 (8th Cir. 1985); and *Rosenspan v. United States*, 438 F.2d 905 (2d Cir. 1971) (denying deductions to a traveling salesman who had no permanent residence and who traveled throughout the year). See also *Barone v. Commissioner*, 85 T.C. 462 (1985); and *Yeates v. Commissioner*, 873 F.2d 1159 (8th Cir. 1989).

233. See *Six v. United States*, 450 F.2d 66 (2d Cir. 1971); Rev. Rul. 75–432.

number of courts. To obtain a deduction, the TP must also satisfy the requirement that his travel expenses are within the exigencies of his business. The application of the temporary job exception to the "exigencies" requirement is discussed at ¶ **21.3312.** The distinction between a temporary job and a job of indefinite duration is discussed at ¶ **21.3312–1.**

> ¶ **21.3271.** **Summer Employment of a Student.** In *Hantzis v. Commissioner,*[234] the First Circuit denied a deduction for transportation costs between Boston and New York City and living expenses in New York City for a Harvard law student who worked as a legal assistant in a New York law firm for her summer employment. The TP's husband remained in Boston because his work as a university professor required him to teach in Boston that summer. The TP claimed that she was away from her home in Boston when she lived in New York at a temporary job. The First Circuit, in reversing the Tax Court's determination that a deduction was allowable, held that a TP is not away from home unless the TP can demonstrate a business reason both for having a location in the place she claims as home as well as in the place where she is working. The TP had no *business* reason for maintaining a home in Boston. While the court did not rest its decision on the TP's failure to satisfy the exigencies of the business requirement, its construction of the "away from home" requirement resembles the exigencies of the business requirement. In general, the courts and the Service have resisted claims for deductions for temporary summer jobs of students.

¶ **21.3300.** **Exigencies of the Business.**

> ¶ **21.3310.** **Commuting Expenses.** The cost of a TP's transportation from his residence to his business office and the cost of returning to his residence is normally a nondeductible expense. Treas. Reg. §§ 1.162–2(e), 1.262–1(b)(5). While the TP could not earn gross income if he did not make the trip from his residence, the expense also has overtones of personal, nonbusiness considerations in that the TP chose his place of residence for personal reasons. There are a few instances where commuting-type expenses are deductible (e.g., the cost of commuting to a place of business while the TP is living at a temporary or minor post). Other examples are set forth in ¶ **21.3221.**

---

234. n. 228, supra.

¶ **21.3311. Transportation of Tools.** If a TP drives from his residence to his place of work and if he carries tools or heavy objects with him in his car, the question arises as to whether he will be allowed to deduct his transportation expense under § 162(a) as an ordinary business expense of transporting the tools even though the expense is not deductible as a traveling expense under § 162(a)(2).

¶ **21.3311–1. Requisites for Deduction.** The Commissioner initially adopted the position in Rev. Rul. 63–100, which was later revoked, that a TP will be permitted a deduction in such cases only if: (1) the tools or other objects are too heavy or too bulky to be carried with the TP by an alternate method of transportation; and (2) the TP would not have driven to work *but for* the need to transport his tools or other objects.

¶ **21.3311–2. The *Fausner* Decision.** Two Circuit Courts of Appeals (the Second and the Seventh Circuits) rejected the reasoning of Rev. Rul. 63–100 and allowed a TP, who would have driven to work even if there were no need to transport his tools, nevertheless to deduct a portion of his commuting costs. In *Fausner v. Commissioner*,[235] the Fifth Circuit declined to follow the lead of those two Circuits Courts.

The TP in *Fausner* was a commercial airline pilot who drove his automobile 84 miles round trip from home to his place of employment, and the TP claimed a deduction for the expenses of driving that distance because he carried a flight-kit bag and an overnight bag in his automobile. The TP admitted that he would have driven to work even if it were not necessary to carry the bags since no public transportation was available. In a per curiam opinion, the Fifth Circuit denied the TP a deduction. The court stated: "Since the record shows that Fausner would have driven his car to and from his place of employment anyway, we cannot find that he is entitled to what would amount to special relief which would distinguish him from other TPs because of the mere fortuity that he placed the bags he was required to carry in the trunk of his commuting vehicle." The court also stressed that there was no evidence that the TP

---

235.   472 F.2d 561 (5th Cir.), aff'd 413 U.S. 838 (1973).

incurred any additional expenses in carrying the bags over his nondeductible commuting expenses (which he would have incurred in any event).

¶ 21.3311–3. The Supreme Court's Decision. The Supreme Court granted certiorari in *Fausner* and summarily (without oral argument or briefs) affirmed the Fifth Circuit's decision.[236] In a brief per curiam opinion, the Court noted that the TP would have driven to work in any event, and the Court stated: "Additional expenses may at any time be incurred for transporting job-required tools and materials to and from work. [The Court here cited Rev. Rul. 63–100 which had propounded the *but for* text described at **¶ 21.3311–1.**] Then an allocation of costs between 'personal' and 'business' expenses may be feasible. But no such allocation can be made here."

¶ 21.3311–4. The Commissioner's Revised Position. In Rev. Rul. 75–380, the Commissioner revoked Rev. Rul. 63–100, rejected the *but for* test, and adopted an entirely new standard. The Commissioner's current position, as expressed in that ruling, is that a TP cannot deduct the cost of commuting to work even if he would not have driven but for the need to transport bulky or heavy tools. A TP will be allowed a deduction for any additional expense he incurs in transporting the tools over his commuting expense. Thus, if the TP rented a trailer in which to carry the tools, the additional cost of renting the trailer will be deductible, but the cost of driving to work in his car (to which the trailer is attached) will not be deductible. Rev. Rul. 75–380. The Commissioner contends in Rev. Rul. 75–380 that this "additional expense" standard was the one adopted by the Supreme Court and by the Fifth Circuit in *Fausner*. Despite making this contention in Rev. Rul. 75–380, in litigating subsequent cases, the Commissioner has applied the *but for* test.[237]

---

236. *Fausner v. Commissioner*, 413 U.S. 838 (1973).

237. See *Fausner v. Commissioner*, 38 T.C.M. 1365 (1979); and see **¶ 21.3311–5.** For an interesting controversy concerning the operation of the *but for* test, see *McCabe v. Commissioner*, 76 T.C. 876 (1981), aff'd by a divided court, 688 F.2d 102 (2d Cir. 1982).

¶ 21.3311–5. Litigation Position of the Commissioner. In *Grayson v. Commissioner,*[238] and in *Randazzo v. Commissioner,*[239] the Tax Court stated that the Commissioner conceded in his briefs in those cases that a TP can deduct his expenses of driving his car from his home to work and back where the TP would have used public transportation had it not been for the need of transporting his tools, which he kept in the trunk of his car. The concession of the Commissioner is inconsistent with Rev. Rul. 75–380, and instead follows the *but for* test. The Commissioner's concession apparently was made also in *Radocy v. Commissioner.*[240]

Notwithstanding the Commissioner's concession, the Tax Court denied the TP's claims for a deduction in *Randazzo* and in *Radocy* because the court believed that the TPs in those cases would have driven their cars to work even if they did not have to transport their tools. However, in the *Grayson* case, the court allowed the TP to deduct the transportation costs. The court accepted the TP's contention that he would not have used his car but for the need to transport his tools even though the TP would have had to "hitchhike" part of the distance to and from work if he did not use his own car.

¶ 21.3311–6. Future Treatment. It is by no means certain that Rev. Rul. 75–380 will be followed by courts in future litigation.[241] There is language in the *Fausner* opinions to support the Commissioner's position, but the opinions could more readily be construed to support the *but for* test, especially since both the Fifth Circuit and the Supreme Court took pains to point out that Fausner would have driven to work in any event and since the Supreme Court cited with apparent approval Rev. Rul. 63–100 (which promulgated the *but for* test). Moreover, the fact that the Supreme Court's decision was a summary affirmance and that the opinions of both courts were merely brief per curiam opinions makes it less plausible that either of those courts intended to promulgate an entirely new

238. 36 T.C.M. 1201 (1977).

239. 36 T.C.M. 1199 (1977).

240. 36 T.C.M. 1129 (1977).

241. But see *Coker v. Commissioner*, 487 F.2d 593 (2d Cir. 1973).

standard for deductibility. The revised position of the Commissioner [Rev. Rul. 75–380] may not have great practical significance because few TPs (if any) would be able to meet the *but for* standard if it were made applicable.

¶ 21.3312. Temporary Job Exception. When a TP travels from his residence to a temporary post of duty or to a place of employment where his job is temporary, there is an administratively created exception to the requirement that traveling expenses under § 162(a)(2) be incurred for the exigencies of business. In such cases, if the requirements laid down in Rev. Rul. 99–7 are satisfied [see **¶ 21.3221**], or possibly if the TP has a regular place of abode in a real and substantial sense [**¶ 21.3250**], the TP's cost of transportation to the job location and back are deductible under § 162(a)(2).[242] The TP's costs of meals and lodging while living at the temporary post also are deductible if the "sleep or rest" requirement is satisfied.[243]

The rationale for this rule is that where a TP accepts a job in a different location, it is reasonable to expect him to move his residence to that location. If he fails to do so, that is a personal decision the cost of which is not a business expense. However, if the job is of short duration, it is not reasonable to expect him to move his family and belongings there. Consequently, in such cases, the additional costs borne by the TP should be treated as business expenses.

As previously noted, in a recent case, the Seventh Circuit criticized the temporary job exception rule and inferred that the court would not apply it.[244]

Note that when a TP is away from home in the pursuit of a trade or business, the fact that the TP rents out his residence for all or part of the period that he is away will not preclude the TP from deducting his travel expenses under § 162(a)(2). § 280A(f)(4). That approach is generous and seems inconsistent with the likely purpose of allowing a deduction for travel expenses to provide relief for a TP who incurs double living expenses because of the demands of his business.

---

242. *Peurifoy v. Commissioner*, 358 U.S. 59 (1958); *Six v. United States*, 450 F.2d 66 (2d Cir. 1971).

243. See *Six v. United States*, n. 242, supra.

244. *Wilbert v. Commissioner*, n. 216, supra.

¶ 21.3312–1. **Meaning of Temporary.** If a TP realistically anticipates that he will be away from his abode for less than one year and if, in fact, he is away for less than one year, the job will qualify as temporary. As a consequence of a 1992 amendment to § 162(a), the literal terms of the statute would seem to require that if a TP's period of employment away from home lasts for more than one year, regardless of how short a time the TP had anticipated that the away-from-home employment would last, the employment will not qualify as "temporary," and therefore the TP's travel expenses will not be deductible. § 162(a) (last sentence). However, in several rulings that were promulgated in 1993 and 1999, the statutory amendment has been construed more liberally than the explicit language would suggest.

First, the Commissioner discussed the operation of the 1992 amendment in Notice 93–29. While the statutory language bars temporary job treatment when the period of employment away from home exceeds one year, the Commissioner described the rule in Notice 93–29 as barring temporary job treatment when "the taxpayer's period of employment away from home *in a single location* lasts for more than one year." [Emphasis added.] The limiting language "in a single location" is consistent with the Conference Report to the amending Act. One question that needs to be resolved is whether the rule will apply when the TP is employed away from home for more than one year at two or more different jobs for different employers but at the same location. In Notice 93–29, the Commissioner stated that the Service intends to publish further guidance on the 1–year rule and requested comments from the public on that rule.

In a subsequent ruling, Rev. Rul. 93–86, which was essentially repeated in Rev. Rul. 99–7, the Commissioner again addressed the meaning of the 1992 amendment. According to those rulings:

> (1) If employment away from home in a single location is expected to last for more than one year, or if there is no realistic expectation that the employment will last for one year or less, the employment will be treated as indefinite (and so does not qualify for the travel expense

deduction) even if the employment actually lasts for less than one year.

(2) If employment away from home in a single location is realistically expected to last for one year or less, but at some later date it becomes realistic to expect the employment to last for more than one year, the employment will be treated as temporary (in the absence of facts and circumstances indicating otherwise) until the date that the TP's realistic expectation changed, and it will be treated as not temporary from that date forward.

¶ 21.3312–2. Travel to Nearest Habitable Community. If the general area of a TP's permanent employment is not a habitable community for the TP (e.g., where a civilian employee works at a large military base which prohibits civilians from living on the base), the question has arisen as to whether the TP can claim a deduction for the expense of the round-trip transportation between the nearest habitable community and the place of employment.

¶ 21.3312–2A. Illustration. Jones is employed at an AEC plant in Neutron, Arizona. The nearest habitable community is Proton, Arizona, which is 50 miles from Neutron. Jones resides in Electron, Arizona, which is 60 miles from Neutron and 10 miles from Proton. Jones seeks to deduct the transportation cost of traveling the 100 mile round-trip distance between Neutron and Proton each work day. Jones contends that while the cost of the 20 miles he travels round-trip between Electron and Proton is incurred as a consequence of his personal decision to live in Electron and therefore is not deductible, the transportation cost of the 100 miles he travels round-trip between Proton and Neutron is incurred as a consequence of the exigencies of his business and therefore is deductible.

¶ 21.3312–2B. Justification for the Deduction. There is considerable justification for granting a deduction to TPs in the position of Jones in the illustration above. The transportation cost of traveling round-trip from Proton to Neutron is little different from the cost of transportation to different offices of an employment after first reporting to work at one such office, which costs are clearly deductible. The Ninth Circuit initially allowed a TP a deduction for transportation costs between his work post and the nearest habitable community;[245] but the court subsequently overruled that decision in *Sanders v. Commissioner*[246] and held that such costs are not deductible. The decision in *Sanders* rests heavily on the Supreme Court's decision in *Correll*[247] that for purposes of claiming a deduction for meals, a TP is not away from home under § 162(a)(2) unless his trip extends overnight (i.e., the Court extended *Correll* to bar a deduction for transportation costs).

¶ 21.3313.   Commuting Combined With Tour of Duty. In *Pollei v. Commissioner*,[248] the Tenth Circuit allowed a deduction to city police captains for the cost of driving from their residence to police headquarters and return because the captains were required by the police department to be on duty during such commuting trips as part of a cost-cutting program. The court determined that the tour of duty requirement was imposed upon the TPs and was bona fide. The Service noted its fear that a decision for the TPs in *Pollei* might open the floodgates in that many employers would adopt a tour of duty requirement. The Tenth Circuit suggested in dictum that there would not be many cases in which commuting expenses would qualify for a deduction because most TPs would not be able to demonstrate that their tour of duty requirement was imposed on them involuntarily and that their work requirement was of sufficient amount to warrant a deduction.

¶ 21.3400.   Moving Expenses. A TP's unreimbursed expenses in moving from his former residence to the location of a new place of work which is at least 50 miles further from his former residence than was his former place of work (or if none, at least 50 miles from his former residence), is a deductible expense if the conditions established in § 217 are satisfied. In general, these conditions are that the TP must either: (a) be a full-time employee in the new location for at least 39 weeks during the 12–month period following his arrival; or (b) during the 24–month period following his arrival, be a full-time employee or perform services as a self-employed

---

245. *Wright v. Hartsell*, 305 F.2d 221 (9th Cir. 1962).

246. 439 F.2d 296 (9th Cir. 1971).

247. ¶ 21.3220.

248. 877 F.2d 838 (10th Cir. 1989), rev'g 87 T.C. 869 (1986).

individual on a full-time basis for at least 78 weeks, of which not less than 39 weeks were performed during the 12–month period described above. § 217(c)(2). If the TP fails to satisfy either of the above conditions because of his death, disability, discharge (other than for willful misconduct), or transfer by his employer, he will nevertheless be permitted the deduction. However, the premature discharge or transfer of a TP will not excuse the TP's failure to satisfy the work period requirements unless his employment was one in which he could reasonably have been expected to comply with those requirements. § 217(d)(1); Treas. Reg. § 1.217–2(d)(1).

To qualify for the deduction, the move must bear a reasonable proximity both in time and place to the commencement of work at the new principal place of business. Generally, if the moving expense occurred within one year of the TP's commencement of work at the new location, that condition will be satisfied. Treas. Reg. § 1.217–2(a)(3)(i).

¶ 21.3410. **Deductible Items.** The expenses deductible under § 217 include: (a) the cost of traveling, including lodging, incurred by the TP and members of his household in moving from the former location to the new one; and (b) the cost of moving the household goods and personal effects of the TP and the members of his household. § 217(b)(1). The moving expenses of a person other than the TP will be deductible only if such person has both the old residence and the new residence as his principal place of abode and is a member of the TP's household. § 217(b)(2). No deduction will be allowed for the cost of meals (including meals taken while travelling from the old to the new location). § 217(b)(1).

¶ 21.3411. **Deductions for Relocation Expenses.** Prior to 1994, deductions were allowed, subject to a dollar limitation, for the cost of traveling to the new job location to search for a new residence and for the cost of meals and lodging incurred while occupying temporary quarters at the new job location for any 30 consecutive day period after the TP obtained employment. Also, prior to 1994, the TP could deduct certain expenditures, subject to a dollar limitation, incurred in connection with the sale of the TP's former residence, the purchase of a new residence, the settlement of a lease on the TP's prior residence, or the acquisition of a lease for the TP's new residence. None of those expenses are now deductible. The provision for deducting those items was deleted from the Code by the Omnibus Budget Reconciliation Act of 1993.

¶ 21.3412. **Nonitemized Deduction.** Unreimbursed moving expenses that are deductible under § 217 are nonitemized deductions. § 62(a)(15).

¶ 21.3420. **Reimbursement by Employer.** A reimbursement of an employee's moving expenses by his employer is excluded from the employee's gross income to the extent that the reimbursed expense would have been deductible by the employee under § 217 if he had not been reimbursed. § 132(a)(6), (g).

¶ 21.3430. **Members of the Armed Forces.** Section 217(g) provides special (and liberal) rules for the treatment of the expenses of a member of the Armed Forces on active duty who moves pursuant to a military order and incident to a permanent change of station.

¶ 21.3440. **Foreign Moves.** If a TP moves to a new principal place of work outside of the United States, storing expenses are included in the deductible expenses. § 217(h). If an individual who was working and residing outside of the United States retires or dies, special liberal provisions apply for moving that person and his belongings to a residence in the United States.§ 217(i).

¶ 21.3450. **Standard Mileage Allowance.** If a TP utilizes an automobile to drive from his old location to his new place of business, the TP may elect to utilize a standard mileage allowance to determine the costs of operating the vehicle in that move. The current mileage allowance for moving expenses under § 217 is 19¢ a mile. Notice 2010–88. Parking fees and tolls are not included in the mileage allowance and can be deducted separately. The amount of the mileage allowance is revised periodically.

¶ 21.4000. **EDUCATION EXPENSES.**

¶ 21.4100. **Deductible Expenses.** Except as noted otherwise in ¶ 21.4200, educational expenses are deductible business expenses, even though the education may lead to a degree, if the education either: (1) maintains or improves skills required of the TP in his employment or other trade or business, or (2) satisfies a requirement imposed by the TP's employer, or by some law or regulation, as a condition of the TP's retention of an established employment relationship, status, or rate of compensation. Treas. Reg. § 1.162–5(a).

¶ **21.4200. Nondeductible Education Expenses.** Even though an education expense complies with one of the requirements established in ¶ **21.4100**, it will not be deductible: (1) if the education in question is essential to satisfy the minimum educational requirements for qualification in the TP's employment or other trade or business, or (2) if the education will lead to qualifying the TP for a new trade or business regardless of whether the TP intends to enter the new trade or business. Treas. Reg. § 1.162–5(b).

¶ **21.4210. Illustration 1: Continuing Professional Education Courses.** *X*, a licensed attorney practicing in Washington, D.C., spends two weeks in New York City to attend a course on new developments in federal taxation. *X* is maintaining and improving his skills as an attorney. Consequently, *X*'s costs of attending the course, including the cost of his transportation and of his lodging and 50% of his meals while living in New York City are deductible. If, while in New York City, X also engaged in a significant amount of personal activities such as sightseeing, X will have to apportion his living expenses between the time spent on educational pursuits and the time spent on personal activities. Only the living expenses allocated to the former are deductible. X will be allowed to deduct all of the transportation costs incurred in going to New York City and returning. See Treas. Reg. § 1.162–5(e)(2), Ex. (1).

If X spent six weeks in New York City of which only two weeks were devoted to the course, his primary purpose for making the trip would likely be deemed to have been to take a vacation rather than to obtain the education. In that case, none of X's transportation costs would be deductible. X would still be allowed to deduct his cost of lodging and 50% of the cost of his meals for the two weeks in which he was engaged in the course. The balance of his expenses for lodging and meals would not be deductible. Treas. Reg. § 1.162–5(e)(2), Ex. (2).

¶ **21.4220. Illustration 2: Law School Course.** *Y*, a licensed CPA, attends night law school and acquires a law degree. *Y* took the law courses to improve his skills as an accountant, and he has no intention of leaving his profession to practice law. Since the law degree satisfies the minimum educational requirement for becoming an attorney, *Y* cannot deduct his educational expenses regardless of the fact that he does not intend to enter the legal profession.[249]

¶ 21.4230. Illustration 3: University Courses. *Z* became an ordained minister at the age of 19. *Z* subsequently entered college and earned a bachelor's degree. The Tax Court and the Tenth Circuit permitted *Z* to deduct the expenses of his attending college because *Z*'s college education aided him in serving his congregation and did not qualify him for a new profession.[250]

There are some other cases in which a TP has been allowed to deduct the expenses incurred in obtaining a degree. The Tax Court and the Ninth Circuit allowed a high school teacher to deduct the expenses of obtaining a Ph.D. degree.[251] In *Toner v. Commissioner*,[252] the Third Circuit allowed a parochial school teacher to deduct the cost of taking college courses towards earning a bachelor's degree where the requirements for teaching at the parochial school were satisfied by a high school education. While in *Toner,* a bachelor's degree was a minimum requirement for qualifying to teach in public schools, the Third Circuit determined that that did not qualify TP for a new trade or business because, under the special regulatory treatment accorded to teachers, all types of teaching are considered to involve the same general kind of work.[253]

The reader should not assume that it is customary for a TP to be allowed to deduct the cost of obtaining a college or advanced degree. In most cases, the expenses of obtaining a college or advanced degree will not be deductible because they will satisfy the minimum educational requirements of a new trade or business.[254] See, e.g., *Davis v. Commissioner*,[255] (expenses of a Ph.D. program were nondeductible); *Browne v. Commissioner*,[256] (expenses of obtaining a bachelor's degree were nondeductible); *Link v. Commissioner*,[257] (summer employment was not sufficient to

249. *O'Donnell v. Commissioner*, 62 T.C. 781 (1974).

250. *Glasgow v. Commissioner*, 486 F.2d 1045 (10th Cir. 1973); aff'g 31 T.C.M. 310 (1972).

251. *Ford v. Commissioner*, 487 F.2d 1025 (9th Cir. 1973), aff'g 56 T.C. 1300 (1971).

252. 623 F.2d 315 (3d Cir. 1980).

253. See ¶ **21.4260**.

254. See ¶ **21.4250**.

255. 65 T.C. 1014 (1976).

256. 73 T.C. 723 (1980).

257. 90 T.C. 460 (1988), aff'd 869 F.2d 1491 (6th Cir. 1989).

establish TP in a trade or business, and so cost of obtaining MBA degree was not deductible); and *Robinson v. Commissioner*,[258] (no deduction for cost of four-year degree program at a university nursing school).

¶ 21.4240.   Bar Review Courses. In *Sharon v. Commissioner*,[259] a majority of the Tax Court allowed the TP to amortize over his life expectancy the cost of obtaining a license to practice law in New York, the subsequent cost of his obtaining admission to the bar of the state of California, and the subsequent cost of obtaining admission to the bar of the Supreme Court of the United States. The Court included the cost of the TP's traveling from California to Washington to be present for his admission to the Supreme Court's bar (as required by the Court's rules) in the TP's amortizable cost of obtaining admission to the bar. However, the Tax Court held that the TP's cost of his college and law school education and the cost of a New York bar review course and a California bar review course were nondeductible educational expenses and could not be deducted or added to the amortizable cost of the TP's obtaining a license to practice law in either of those states.

A majority of the Tax Court deemed the TP's admission to the California bar as acquiring a new trade or business even though the TP was already an attorney licensed in New York. Consequently, the majority held that the California bar review expenses were incurred to meet the minimum educational requirements of that trade or business. See Treas. Reg. § 1.162–5(b)(2)(iii), Ex. (3). On appeal, the Ninth Circuit affirmed the Tax Court's decision to deny a deduction for the expenses of TP's college and law school education and of his two bar review courses. The court said that the "allocation of those expenses between the nondeductible personal component and any deductible capital component would not be feasible."[260]

¶ 21.4250.   Common Sense Standard. The Tax Court stated that it will apply a common sense test for resolving education expense cases where the TP obtains a degree (i.e., it will make a factual comparison of the type of activities performed by persons

258.   78 T.C. 550 (1982).

259.   66 T.C. 515 (1976), aff'd 591 F.2d 1273 (9th Cir. 1978).

260.   *Sharon v. Commissioner*, 591 F.2d 1273 (9th Cir. 1978).

with such a degree with the type of activities performed without such a degree).[261] For example, in *Robinson v. Commissioner*,[262] a licensed practical nurse was denied a deduction for the costs of a four–year university degree program at the University of Minnesota School of Nursing, which degree allowed TP to take an examination to qualify as a registered nurse.

¶ **21.4260. Teachers.** The Commissioner and the courts are more liberal in permitting a deduction for educational expenses of teachers than for other professions or trades. For example, Treas. Reg. § 1.162–5(b)(3)(i) states that "all teaching and related duties shall be considered to involve the same general type of work." Thus, courses taken by a classroom teacher to qualify as a principal are not courses to qualify for a new trade or business and so typically are deductible. The Commissioner ruled in Rev. Rul. 71–58 that a TP who held a permanent teaching certificate in State *A* and who had been employed as a secondary teacher in that state could deduct the cost of courses that she took in order to satisfy the teaching certificate requirements of State *B* to which she had moved. The Commissioner ruled that the change of employers and location was merely a change of duties in the same general type of work as a classroom teacher and did not constitute a change to a new trade or business. Similarly, in *Laurano v. Commissioner*,[263] the Tax Court allowed a Canadian citizen, who was certified to teach in Toronto, Canada and who had moved to New Jersey, to deduct the cost of several courses that she took in order to obtain certification to teach in New Jersey. The court distinguished its treatment of lawyers in *Sharon v. Commissioner*,[264] on the ground that Treas. Reg. § 1.162–5(b)(3)(i) expressly adopted a liberal construction of the trade or business requirement for teachers.[265]

¶ **21.4270.   Previously Engaged in a Trade or Business.** An educational deduction will not be deductible unless it is in furtherance of a trade or business in which the TP is already engaged. The Tax Court's decision in *Wassenaar v. Commission-*

261.   *Glenn v. Commissioner*, 62 T.C. 270 (1974).

262.   78 T.C. 550 (1982).

263.   69 T.C. 723 (1978), Acq.

264.   n. 259, supra.

265.   For a similar comment as to the regulations' liberal treatment of teachers, see *Toner v. Commissioner*, n. 252, supra.

er,[266] provides an interesting application of that requirement. In *Wassenaar*, the TP graduated from Wayne State University Law School in Detroit, Michigan, and, without first obtaining a job in the legal profession, he went to New York City and enrolled in the LL.M. program in taxation at New York University (NYU). The TP received the LL.M. degree after one academic year and then returned to Detroit to join a law firm. In the summer before his graduation from Wayne State, the TP had clerked for a law firm for which he was compensated. In addition, the TP had served as a member of the board of editors of the Wayne State Law Review for two years for which he received compensation. The TP passed the Michigan bar examination before enrolling at NYU, but he was not formally admitted to the bar until after he graduated from NYU. The Tax Court held that although the TP was qualified to practice law when he enrolled at NYU, he had not yet engaged in the practice of law. The court acknowledged that the TP had performed work of a legal nature before attending NYU, but the court held that it did not constitute the practice of law. The court noted that since the TP was not formally admitted to the bar until after receiving his LL.M., he was not authorized to practice law before that date. The court also noted that the TP's attendance at NYU constituted an essentially uninterrupted continuation of his legal education. Accordingly, the court denied the TP's claim for a business expense deduction for the expenses incurred in attending NYU. If the TP had first practiced law (even for a brief period) before enrolling at NYU, he likely would have qualified for a deduction.[267]

¶ 21.4300. **Travel As Education.** Travel itself may educate a TP by improving his skills in his profession or trade. For example, travel to France would improve the skills of a French teacher. An amendment to the Code made by the 1986 TRA denies a deduction for travel *as a form of education*. § 274(m)(2). The cost of travel that is not itself educational but is merely the means of reaching a place where the TP will receive a business-related education continues to be deductible subject to the limitations on the deductibility of employee expenses and on the deductibility of meals.

¶ 21.5000. **FRUSTRATION OF PUBLIC POLICY.** Prior to 1970, an expense would not qualify as "necessary" under § 162 if allowance of

---

266. 72 T.C. 1195 (1979). See also *Kohen v. Commissioner*, 44 T.C.M. 1518 (1982).

267. PLR 9112003. But cf., *Link v. Commissioner*, n. 257, supra; *Johnson v. United States*, 332 F.Supp. 906 (E.D.La. 1971).

the deduction would frustrate a sharply defined national or state policy (i.e., such an expenditure would not be "appropriate and helpful").[268] The national or state policies involved had to be evidenced by some governmental declaration and not merely by the mores of the community.[269] However, the regulations state that an expense paid or incurred after December 30, 1969, which would otherwise be allowable as a business deduction, will *not* be disallowed as a deduction solely because it violated "a sharply defined public policy." Treas. Reg. § 1.162–1(a). Thus, such an expense will be disallowed only if deduction is barred by a specific statutory provision. See Rev. Rul. 74–323[270] But see, *Conley v. Commissioner*,[271] where the Tax Court used public policy as a reason for disallowing a deduction for an individual's payment of a corporation's tax liabilities.[272] For the treatment of fines and penalties, see ¶ **21.1820.**

¶ **21.5100. Illegal Under State Law.** In *Tank Truck Rentals*,[273] the Supreme Court noted that if the expenditure in question is illegal under state law, "the frustration of state policy is most complete and direct." However, in *Commissioner v. Sullivan*,[274] decided the same day as *Tank Truck Rentals*, the Court allowed a deduction for salaries and rent paid by an Illinois bookmaker even though the payment of rent for the use of a bookmaking establishment was itself illegal under Illinois law. As noted in ¶ **21.1730**, the *Sullivan* case apparently was overturned by the 1969 and 1971 congressional amendments to § 162(c)(2).

¶ **21.5200. Reconciliation.** The *Sullivan* case might be reconciled with *Tank Truck Rentals* on the basis that the payment of rent for premises is a normal expense of most legal businesses and therefore to disallow the deduction in *Sullivan* would in effect constitute imposing a discriminatorily higher tax on the TP merely because he was engaged in an illegal business. Since the Government taxes illegally obtained income, it would ill behoove it to deny deductions for expenses that are so comparable to deductible expenses of legitimate business enterprises. Nevertheless, such expenses are disallowed as deductions by § 162(c)(2) which renders the *Sullivan* case a virtual nullity.

268. *Tank Truck Rentals, Inc. v. Commissioner*, 356 U.S. 30 (1958).

269. *Lilly v. Commissioner*, 343 U.S. 90 (1952).

270. The ruling is discussed at ¶ **21.1731.**

271. 36 T.C.M. 1644 (1977).

272. See ¶ **21.1521.**

273. n. 268, supra.

274. 356 U.S. 27 (1958).

¶ 21.5300. **Expenses to Defend Criminal Action.** If a TP has a criminal action brought against him because of activities connected with his business (e.g., an antitrust violation), his legal expenses in defending that criminal action are deductible under § 162, regardless of whether he is convicted or acquitted.[275] The rationale for allowing a deduction for such expenses is that the origin of the expense arose in a business setting. See Rev. Rul. 68–662.

¶ 21.5310. **Illustration 1: Defending Tax Fraud Charges.** In Rev. Rul. 68–662, a TP, who was an officer of a corporation with the responsibility of filing the corporation's tax returns, embezzled corporate income and did not report the amounts on either the corporation's tax return or on his own return. The TP was indicted on two criminal counts—one for filing a false corporate tax return and one for filing a false return of his own. The TP was convicted on both counts. The Commissioner allowed the TP to deduct his legal fees for litigating count one under § 162 because the charge of filing a false corporate return arose out of his duty as an employee to file that return. The fees for litigating the second count were held to be deductible under § 212(3).

¶ 21.5320. **Illustration 2: Resisting Forfeiture of an Asset.** TP, a corporation, incurred legal fees in an unsuccessful effort to resist the government's forfeiture of its car when TP's president and sole shareholder had been caught carrying marijuana in the car. The Tax Court held that the TP's legal fees were nondeductible capital expenditures to defend the TP's title to the car, and so the amount of the fees were added to TP's basis in the car.[276] The deductibility of the fees therefore depends upon whether the TP is allowed a deduction for the loss it suffered on the forfeiture of its car; and that issue is discussed at ¶ 21.5500.

¶ 21.5400. **Theft Loss from Illegal Transaction.** In many instances, a "confidence" scheme is designed to steal from a victim by inducing the victim to engage in an illegal transaction. For example, in *Mazzei v. Commissioner*,[277] the TP was induced to give $20,000 cash to several persons who were to put the bills through a little black box that they represented would create identical bills. Instead, they stole TP's money. The majority of the Tax Court denied the TP's claim for a theft loss deduction on the ground that it is against

---

275. *Commissioner v. Tellier*, 383 U.S. 687 (1966).

276. *Holmes Enterprises, Inc. v. Commissioner*, 69 T.C. 114 (1977).

277. 61 T.C. 497 (1974). See also *Richey v. Commissioner*, 33 T.C. 272 (1959).

public policy to permit a deduction for a loss suffered by one who was engaged in a counterfeiting scheme, albeit the TP was a somewhat naive participant. Five judges dissented in the *Mazzei* case because they felt that the deduction would not frustrate public policy as the frustration doctrine was defined in the *Tank Truck Rentals* and *Sullivan* cases.[278] Moreover, the dissenters pointed out that while the exclusivity of the exclusions from deductibility of illegal expenses stated in § 162(c) operates directly only as to § 162 business expense deductions, the legislative history of that provision "does seem to call for judicial restraint in other areas where Congress has not specifically limited deductions."[279] In Rev. Rul. 81–24 the Commissioner ruled that the frustration of public policy doctrine continues to be applicable to deny a claim for a deduction for a loss under § 165.[280]

¶ 21.5500. Loss Deductions That Contravene Public Policy. As noted at **¶ 21.5000**, an expense that would otherwise be deductible under § 162 (or under § 212) will not be disallowed as a deduction solely because it contravenes "a sharply defined public policy." Treas. Reg. § 1.162–1(a). The question arises as to whether a deduction otherwise allowable under § 165 for a loss can be disallowed because the grant of a deduction would contravene public policy—that is, are only §§ 162 and 212 deductions immune from the public policy exception? As noted in **¶ 21.5400**, the Tax Court has disallowed a theft loss deduction for reasons of public policy, and the Commissioner maintains that the frustration of public policy doctrine is applicable to § 165. In *Blackman v. Commissioner*,[281] the Tax Court disallowed a claim for a casualty loss deduction for the destruction of TP's home by a fire that the TP started when he put his wife's clothes on the stove, set them on fire and left the house. The Court held that the TP was at least grossly negligent and that it would contravene public policy to allow him a deduction. In *Holmes Enterprises, Inc. v. Commissioner*,[282] the sole shareholder and president of the TP (a corporation) was caught carrying marijuana in an automobile owned by the TP. The automobile was seized by the United States and forfeited to it. Although the car was used by the TP for business purposes, the Tax Court denied the TP a loss deduction for the forfeiture under § 165 because the deduction would

278. Those cases are discussed at **¶ ¶ 21.5000–21.5200**.

279. 61 T.C. at 506.

280. See **¶ 21.5500**. See also *Stephens v. Commissioner*, discussed in Chapter **Eighteen**; and GCM 36963 (1976).

281. 88 T.C. 677 (1987).

282. 69 T.C. 114 (1977).

frustrate a sharply defined national policy against the possession and sale of marijuana.[283] The forfeiture of an automobile to a government because the automobile was used to transport contraband might be characterized as a fine or penalty for which no deduction is allowable under § 162(f). Although that issue was one of several urged by the government in *Holmes Enterprises*, the court chose to rely on the frustration of public policy for its decision. See also *Stephens v. Commissioner*,[284] in which both the Tax Court and the Second Circuit agreed that the public policy limitation does apply to deductions claimed under § 165, although they disagreed as to how the public policy limitation is to be construed.

283. Accord, *Holt v. Commissioner*, 69 T.C. 75 (1977), aff'd per curiam, 611 F.2d 1160 (5th Cir. 1980).

284. 93 T.C. 108 (1989), rev'd 905 F.2d 667 (2d Cir. 1990).

CHAPTER TWENTY–TWO

DEPRECIATION AND AMORTIZATION

¶ 22.0000. COST RECOVERY.

¶ 22.1000. GENERAL. This chapter deals with the manner in which deductions for capital expenditures are determined. When a TP incurs a current expense in connection with his trade or business, he usually will be allowed to deduct that expense during the tax year in which he pays or accrues it. For example, the cost that a retail business incurs in advertising for the sale of its goods is a current deduction. However, as previously explained, the cost of purchasing an asset to be used for more than 12 months is usually not currently deductible. The TP has not actually spent the dollars he paid for such an asset, but rather has converted them into a different type of property. For example, if *A* buys a computer at a cost of $2,000 in Year One and if *A* expects to use the computer in his business for five years, he cannot deduct the $2,000 cost of the computer in Year One since he acquired an asset of like value. But see **¶ 22A.2000** for discussion of a provision allowing a TP to deduct currently the cost of a business asset (referred to as "expensing" the cost) subject to a dollar limitation on the amount that can be deducted in a taxable year.[1]

Nonetheless, *A*'s computer will not last forever. Each year, a portion of the useful life of the computer will be exhausted until, after five years, the computer is no longer useful in A's business. In effect, each year that *A* uses the computer, *A* uses up a portion of the $2,000 purchase price. An accurate measurement of *A*'s net income for any one of those years will include a deduction of some amount to represent the portion of the $2,000 cost that is properly allocable to that year. The allocation of the cost of an asset over the years in which the asset is employed in a profit-seeking activity can be accomplished by a depreciation allowance or by some other method of amortizing the cost of the asset. Depreciation and amortization, therefore, are methods for deducting (and thereby "recovering") a capital expenditure over the period of time (the "recovery period") to which the expenditure relates.

---

1. This provision for expensing a limited amount of cost is designed to encourage small businesses to modernize their equipment.

¶ 22.1100. Meaning of Depreciation. Depreciation is an allocation of the cost or basis of property (tangible or intangible) among
the years of its use in a trade or business or for the production of
income. To qualify for a depreciation deduction, the property must be
used in a trade or business or for the production of income. This
requires the TP to demonstrate that he had "an actual and honest
objective of making a profit" from the activity in which the property
is used. The test is subjective. The TP's expectation of a profit need
not be reasonable on an objective standard, but it must be bona fide.[2]

While business expenses must be "ordinary and necessary" to be
deductible under § 162 (see ¶ 10.1500), a majority of the Tax Court
held that there is no such requirement for allowing depreciation
deductions under § 168 (and so also under § 167).[3] The depreciable
item need only be used in the TP's trade or business or for production of income. The use need not meet the "ordinary and necessary"
standard; nor need the amount of the depreciation deduction be
reasonable when considered in light of the income to be produced.[4]

A depreciation deduction is allowed under § 167 (and § 168) for the
exhaustion, wear and tear, and obsolescence of qualified property
that was placed in service by the TP. The deduction is determined by
reference to the asset's basis. The deduction is distributed over a
recovery period. Unless the depreciation is taken under § 168, the
"recovery period" is equal to the "useful life" of the asset. Useful life
is described in ¶ 22.3100. When depreciation is taken under § 168,
the recovery period is set differently and does not depend upon the
asset's useful life.

No depreciation deduction is allowable for inventory or for property
held for sale to the TP's customers in the ordinary course of
business.[5]

For tax purposes, "depreciation" refers to the deduction allowable
under §§ 167 or § 168 for the amortization of the TP's basis.
Depreciation is merely a special type of amortization; it is an amortization deduction that is authorized by either of those two sections of
the Code—§§ 167 or 168. A deduction taken under either of those
two Code sections is referred to as "depreciation." An amortization

2. *Beck v. Commissioner*, 85 T.C. 557, 569 (1985).
3. *Noyce v. Commissioner*, 97 T.C. 670, 689–691 (1991) (reviewed by the court).
4. Id.
5. Treas. Reg. § 1.167(a)–2; and Rev. Rul. 89–25.

deduction allowable under any other section of the Code (for example, §§ 169, 197, and 248) is referred to as "amortization." The operation of the amortization deduction provisions requires that the allocation of basis be spread evenly over the recovery period, but depreciation deductions are not always so restricted.

¶ 22.1110. Accelerated Cost Recovery System (ACRS). The depreciation of most (but not all) tangible property, real or personal, is determined by § 168. The depreciation methods established by § 168 are referred to as the accelerated cost recovery system or "ACRS." ACRS is merely a type of depreciation that a TP is required to use for most tangible property. § 168(a). The methods of depreciation that are employed by the current modified version of ACRS are described in **¶ 22A.0000** *et seq.*

¶ 22.1111. Modified Accelerated Cost Recovery System (MACRS). The original version of ACRS applies to tangible property that was placed in service between 1981 and 1986. Substantial modifications were made to ACRS in 1986, and the modified version of that system is referred to as the "Modified Accelerated Cost Recovery System" or simply as "MACRS." MACRS applies to tangible property that was placed in service after 1986. In this text, the authors discusses only the modified version of ACRS (i.e., the current version), and so all references hereafter to the system will be to "MACRS."

¶ 22.1112. Continuing Significance of § 167. Section 167 applies to intangible property and to tangible property that was placed in service by the TP prior to 1981. There are a few circumstances in which the depreciation of tangible property that is placed in service after 1980 is determined by § 167,[6] but most such properties will be depreciated under MACRS or amortized under a specific statutory provision.[7] Properties for which depreciation is precluded (such as undeveloped land and inventory) are not depreciable under MACRS.

Note that § 168(a) states that the depreciation of tangible property provided by § 167 is to be determined by using § 168. In other words, the MACRS system is itself a system of depreciation that is incorporated into § 167. For convenience of distinction, in this work a reference to MACRS refers to

6. See **¶ 22A.3100**.
7. MACRS is discussed at **¶ 22A.3000** *et seq.*

depreciation under § 168, and a reference to depreciation under § 167 usually refers to depreciation allowable under a method other than the MACRS system.

¶ 22.1120.   Sufficiency of Interest. A question may arise as to whether the nominal owner of property has a substantial enough interest in the property to entitle him to a depreciation deduction. In *Frank Lyon Co. v. United States*,[8] the Court sustained a TP's claim for depreciation deductions for a building that the TP owned under a sale and leaseback arrangement (i.e., the TP purchased the building from the tenant while the building was under construction and then, after the building was completed, rented the building to the tenant on a net lease basis so that the tenant thereafter occupied and used the building). It is arguable that the substantive role of the nominal owner in this type of transaction is merely that of a mortgagee and that the nominal tenant is actually the owner of the property. The Court held that the sale and leaseback arrangement was not a sham and that, in substance, the TP was the owner of the building.

¶ 22.1200.   Depreciation as a Capital Expenditure. Typically a depreciation or amortization allowance is deductible in the year to which the allowance is attributable. However, if depreciable equipment is used to construct any asset, the depreciation allowance for the equipment is treated as a capital expenditure and, thus, is added to the TP's basis in the constructed asset; the amount so added to the TP's basis in the constructed asset may be depreciated over that asset's recovery period.[9]

¶ 22.1210.   Starting Date for Depreciation. Depreciation of an asset first becomes allowable when the asset is placed in service; this occurs when the asset is placed "in a condition or state of readiness and availability."[10]

¶ 22.1300.   Depreciable Property.

¶ 22.1310.   Tangible Property. Prior to the adoption of ACRS in 1981, tangible property used in a trade or business or held for the production of income which had a *determinable useful life* could be depreciated. The requirements for depreciating tangible

---

8.   435 U.S. 561 (1978).

9.   *Commissioner v. Idaho Power Co.*, 418 U.S. 1 (1974). See § 263A.

   10.   Rev. Rul. 76–238. See Rev. Rul. 76–428; and *Cooper v. Commissioner*, 542 F.2d 599 (2d Cir. 1976).

property under ACRS or MACRS are the same except that, according to a majority of the Tax Court and two Circuit Courts of Appeals, there is no requirement that the property have a determinable useful life. ¶ 22A.3110. Instead, tangible property that is used in a trade or business or held for the production of income can be depreciated under ACRS or MACRS if the property can be shown to be subject to wear and tear, exhaustion or obsolescence. For example, while land is tangible property, it is not subject to exhaustion, wear and tear, or obsolescence; so it cannot be depreciated.[11]

¶ 22.1320. Intangible Property. Intangible property used in a trade or business or held for the production of income which has a *determinable useful life* may be depreciated on a straight line basis. Treas. Reg. § 1.167(a)–3. Intangible property is not covered by MACRS. § 168(a). Instead of utilizing straight line depreciation, certain types of intangible property (e.g., movies and television films) can be depreciated on an income-forecast method.[12] Certain intangible properties can be amortized under specific Code provisions. For example, § 197 permits the amortization of purchased goodwill, going concern value, and similar intangibles over a 15–year period.[13]

¶ 22.1321. Goodwill and Similar Intangible Properties. Prior to the adoption of the Omnibus Budget Reconciliation Act of 1993, the general rule was that goodwill and some similar intangible properties could not be depreciated or amortized because there was no ascertainable limit to their useful life. However, when a TP was able to segregate an intangible item from goodwill and demonstrate that the item had an ascertainable useful life, the cost of the item could be depreciated on a straight line basis.[14] The uncertainty of the application of the doctrine permitting the amortization of some (but not all) intangibles that were similar to, if not part of, goodwill generated friction between TPs and the Service and had an adverse effect on negotiations for the purchase of a going

---

11. Treas. Reg. § 1.167(a)–2. See ¶ **22.4000**.

12. § 167(g); *Schneider v. Commissioner*, 65 T.C. 18, 32 (1975); Rev. Rul. 60–358. See ¶ **22.3370**.

13. See ¶ **22.1321**.

14. The most prominent example of this was the Supreme Court's decision in *Newark Morning Ledger Co. v. United States*, 507 U.S. 546 (1993) to allow the amortization of the paid subscription lists of several newspapers that the TP had purchased.

business. There were many related areas that generated disputes and led to somewhat artificial distinctions. For example, the payment made by a purchaser of a business for the seller's covenant not to compete could be amortized, but a similar payment to protect the goodwill that the purchaser sought to acquire could not be amortized. In an effort to bring certainty and predictability to this area, Congress added § 197 to the Code.

As a consequence of that amendment, a TP is permitted to amortize a purchased "amortizable section 197 intangible" over a 15–year period, beginning with the month in which the intangible was acquired. Some of the items that are amortizable under § 197 would have been depreciable under § 167, if § 197 had not been adopted. When § 197 is applicable to an intangible item, it is the exclusive source of amortization of that item; no depreciation or amortization of such an intangible will be permitted other than that provided by § 197. § 197(b).

Subject to a number of specifically described exceptions, the following items are an incomplete list of section 197 intangibles:

(1) goodwill,[15]

(2) going concern value,[16]

(3) the labor force of the acquired business,

(4) business books and records, operating systems, and any other information base,

(5) patents, copyrights, computer software, formulas, processes, knowhow and similar items,

(6) licenses, permits, and other rights granted by a governmental unit or agency,

(7) a covenant not to compete obtained in connection with the acquisition of an interest in a trade or business or a substantial portion thereof, and

(8) a franchise, trademark, or trade name. § 197(d).

15. Goodwill is the value of a trade or business that is attributable to the expectancy of continued customer patronage, whether due to the name or reputation of a trade or business or any other factor.

16. Going concern value is the additional element of value of a trade or business that attaches to property by reason of its existence as an integral part of a going concern.

There are a number of items that are excluded from section 197 intangibles notwithstanding their inclusion in the above list. § 197(e). Certain computer software is excluded as is an interest in land or in a lease of tangible property. Certain properties that were not acquired in connection with the acquisition of a trade or business (or a substantial portion thereof) are excluded from section 197; such properties include: patents and copyrights, and an interest in a film, video tape, book or similar property. § 197(e)(4). So, if an interest in a patent or copyright is acquired separately and not as part of an acquisition of a trade or business, § 197 will not apply. Section 197 does not apply to any property acquired by reason of someone's death so that the property's basis is determined under § 1014. § 197(f)(9)(D). Also, any interest in a partnership, trust or estate, or corporation cannot be amortized under § 197. § 197(e)(1).

In some cases, as in the case of a patent or copyright, the cost of an excluded item can be depreciated or amortized under § 167 or under some other Code provision. Treas. Reg. § 1.167(a)–14(c)(4). In some cases, the exclusion from § 197 means that no deduction for depreciation or amortization will be allowed.

A section 197 intangible is amortizable under that provision if: (1) it is held in connection with a trade or business or a profit-seeking activity, and (2) either was acquired after August 10, 1993, or (if the TP so elects) was acquired after July 25, 1991. If an intangible is self-created by a TP, there are additional limitations on whether it can qualify for amortization. § 197(c)(2). A self-created intangible is not excluded from § 197 if it is one of the following properties: (1) a franchise, trademark or trade name, (2) a license, permit or other right obtained from a governmental unit or agency, or (3) a covenant not to compete that was created in connection with an acquisition of an interest in a trade or business. Other self-created properties will be excluded unless they were created in connection with a transaction involving the acquisition of assets constituting a trade or business or a substantial portion thereof.

In general, if an amortizable section 197 intangible that was acquired in a transaction (or series of related transactions) is sold for a loss or becomes worthless, and if one or more other amortizable section 197 intangibles that were acquired in the same transaction (or series of transactions) are retained, no loss will be recognized; and the TP's adjusted basis in the retained amortizable section 197 intangibles will be increased by the amount of loss that was disallowed. § 197(f)(1).

¶ 22.1330. **Inventory or Stock in Trade.** Inventory, stock in trade, and property held for sale to customers in the ordinary course of business cannot be depreciated.[17]

¶ 22.2000. **IMPORTANCE OF DISTINCTION BETWEEN DE-PRECIATION AND AMORTIZATION.** The distinction between amortization and depreciation [see ¶ 22.1100] is important principally because amortization deductions must be spread evenly over the useful life of the property; on the other hand, some tangible property may be depreciated under methods which concentrate the deductions in the earlier years of the property's life. Amortization is similar to the straight line method of depreciation.

¶ 22.2100. **Shortened Amortization Period.** In certain circumstances defined by statute, an asset or expenditure may be amortized over a specific period of time that typically is far shorter than the asset's useful life. For example, the expenses of organizing a corporation may be amortized by the corporation over a 180–month period. § 248. In some cases, up to $5,000 of the organizational expenses can be deducted immediately (i.e., expensed). Id. However, *some* items that are required to be amortized under § 197 will be amortized over a longer period by that provision than would have been the case if § 197 did not apply.

¶ 22.3000. **ELEMENTS OF A DEPRECIATION DEDUCTION.** Since depreciation is a method of allocating the adjusted basis of an asset to the years in which it is used, the first element to be determined is the adjusted basis of the depreciable asset. Unless MACRS is applicable, once the adjusted basis of the depreciable asset is known, the TP must determine the expected useful life of the asset, the salvage value of the asset, and the method of depreciation to be employed. As we will see, when MACRS is applicable, the determination of depreciation is simpler.

¶ 22.3100. **Useful Life.** The estimated useful life of an asset is the length of time, determined at the date of acquisition, that the TP expects to use the asset. For example, if a TP buys a new business car and sells his old car every two years, the new car has an estimated useful life of two years. It is the estimated "useful life" to

---

17. Treas. Reg. § 1.167(a)–2; Rev. Rul. 89–25.

the TP in his business that controls, not the estimated physical life of the property.[18] To adopt a life that is shorter than the asset's physical life, the TP had to show the actual experience with such assets in his trade or business or the experience with similar assets in the type of trade or business that the TP conducts.[19]

¶ **22.3110.** **No Exhaustible Life.** Some assets, such as unimproved land, have no exhaustible "useful life" and, therefore, cannot be amortized or depreciated in the absence of a specific statutory provision. Some such assets, for example, goodwill, are permitted in certain circumstances to be amortized over a specified period of time by an explicit Code provision. See ¶ **22.1321.**

¶ **22.3120.** **General Asset Accounts or Multiple Asset Accounts.** At their election, many businesses do not compute depreciation separately for each business asset. The depreciation of a single asset is sometimes referred to as depreciation under a "single asset account method." Instead, the assets acquired in a taxable year are divided into broad categories; the assets in each category are lumped together into one account; and the cumulative total of the bases of the assets in each account is depreciated at a single rate and method over a single recovery period This method of depreciating assets is sometimes referred to as a "general asset account method" or as a "multiple asset account method." All of the assets that comprise a general asset account will have been acquired in the same taxable year. Treas. Reg. § 1.168(i)–1(c)(2)(i)(E). General asset accounts can be used for properties that are depreciated under MACRS. § 168(i)(4). Under MACRS, the types of properties that qualify for general asset treatment are more extensive than was permitted under the pre–1981 version of depreciation. Under MACRS, the manner in which depreciation is determined in a general asset account and the treatment of dispositions of property held in such an account are described in Treas. Reg. § 1.168(i)–1.

¶ **22.3130.** **Conclusive Guidelines.** In order to reduce conflict over the useful life of an asset, the Treasury adopted a regulation that established a range of "useful lives" within which a TP could select the life he preferred. For the first several years of the TP's use of the asset, the TP's selection was conclusive. This method, called "asset depreciation range" or "ADR," was elective if the TP used the General Asset Account method. The mid-point of the

---

18. *Massey Motors, Inc. v. United States,* 364 U.S. 92 (1960).

19. *Honodel v. Commissioner,* 722 F.2d 1462 (9th Cir. 1984).

range of recovery periods that applied to a class of assets under ADR was referred to as the "class life" of those assets.

The ADR plan stirred considerable controversy, but it was codified by Congress in the Revenue Act of 1971. The ADR system was replaced by ACRS (and later by MACRS) when § 168 was adopted in 1981. As will be seen in ¶ 22A.3411, an updated version of the class lives that were adopted under the ADR plan are utilized in § 168 to determine the MACRS recovery period of many assets. The MACRS recovery period is not necessarily equal to the ADR class life, but it often is determined by reference to that class life.

¶ 22.3140. Depreciation or Amortization of a Term Interest. Section 167(e) denies a depreciation or amortization deduction for a term interest in property if the remainder interest is held by a person who is related to the person who holds the term interest. A related person is a person bearing a relationship to the TP that is described in § 267(b) or (e). § 167(e)(5)(B). The basis in the term interest of the person holding that interest is reduced by the amount of depreciation disallowed as a deduction by that provision, and (subject to several exceptions)[20] the remainderman's basis in the remainder interest is increased by a like amount. § 167(e)(3), 4(A).

Section 167(e) does not apply to a term interest that was acquired by gift, bequest, or inheritance. § 167(e)(2)(A). In such a case, § 273 precludes any deduction for depreciation or amortization of such a term interest regardless of the identity of the remainderman; and when § 273 applies, no adjustment to basis is made because of the disallowed depreciation.

Sections 167(e) and 273 deny a deduction only for the depreciation or amortization of a TP's basis in a term interest; those provisions do not prevent the TP from deducting depreciation or amortization of underlying property to which the term interest relates to the extent that such depreciation or amortization is allocated to the TP under § 167(d). See ¶ 24.1410.

¶ 22.3141. Illustration. The Y trust held a commercial building. A had a term interest in the trust, and S had the

---

20.   The exceptions arise when the term interest is held by a tax-exempt organization, a nonresident alien, or a foreign corporation. § 167(e)(4)(A).

remainder interest. On January 1, Year One, *A* sold his 10–year term income interest in the trust to *B* for $40,000, *B* is the brother of *S*, and so they are related persons for purposes of § 167(e). The trust is entitled to $2,000 of depreciation for the use of the building in Year One. That $2,000 of depreciation is allocated between *B* (the income beneficiary) and the trust according to § 167(d); but, in this case, all of the $2,000 of depreciation will be allocated to *B*. Section 167(e) does not deny *B* a deduction for the depreciation of the building that is allocated to him.

B has a $40,000 basis in his term interest, part of which is being exhausted every year. If there were no § 167(e), *B* would be allowed to amortize his basis over the 10–year term and deduct $4,000 in Year One. Section 167(e) prevents *B* from deducting any depreciation or amortization for his $40,000 basis. *B*'s basis nevertheless is reduced by the disallowed depreciation or amortization deduction. The $4,000 of depreciation or amortization that reduced *B*'s basis in his term interest is added to *S*'s basis in her remainder interest in the trust. § 167(e)(3).

¶ **22.3200. Salvage Value.** The salvage value of an asset is an estimate (made at the time of acquisition) of what the resale value of the asset will be at the end of its estimated useful life. It should be emphasized that salvage value is an *estimate*; it is not recomputed each year that the market value of the asset fluctuates. As noted in ¶ **22A.3300**, salvage value is ignored in determining depreciation under MACRS.

¶ **22.3300. Methods of Depreciation.** The *method* selected by the TP determines the rates at which the asset will be depreciated. Prior to 1981, for certain (but not all) kinds of property, any method which provided a "reasonable allowance" of depreciation was acceptable if the total depreciation taken during the first two-thirds of the useful life of the property would not exceed the amount that would have been taken had the double declining balance method been used. ¶ **22.3360.** Three methods of depreciation that *were* specifically permitted by the Code, and were the most commonly used, are straight line, declining balance, and sum of the years-digits. The sum-of-the-years digits method is no longer permitted, and is discussed here to provide background information as to the development of the depreciation rules. However, there are other reasonable methods of depreciation that are still allowed (e.g., the units of production method, and the "income forecast" method). § 167(g). When the latter two methods (units of production and income forecast) are permitted, they can be utilized in lieu of MACRS. § 168(f)(1). The declining balance and straight line methods are employed by MACRS.

¶ **22.3310.   Units of Production Method.** The units of production method measures the life of the asset in terms of its production capacity and allocates depreciation according to the units produced.

¶ **22.3311.   Illustration.** *X* purchased a machine for $10,000 which is estimated to be capable of producing 1,000,000 widgets during its *economic* life. During Year One, the machine produces 220,000 widgets. Assuming no salvage value, the depreciation deduction for Year One under the units of production method is $2,200 (220,000 × $10,000 ÷ 1,000,000).

¶ **22.3320.   Straight Line Method.** Prior to MACRS, the straight line method measured the annual depreciation deduction for an asset by deducting the asset's salvage value from the original basis of the asset and dividing the difference by the estimated useful life of the property. MACRS (or ACRS) utilizes the same method for calculating straight line depreciation except that salvage value is ignored.

¶ **22.3321.   Illustration.** On January 1, 1970, *X* purchased a desk for his office for $5,000. Its estimated "useful life" is ten years at the end of which its value is expected to be $500. *X* can deduct $450 depreciation each year for ten years ($5,000 − $500 ÷ 10). Dividing the number of years (ten) into 100% produces the straight line rate (10%). The straight line rate times the difference between the asset's original basis and its salvage value equals the depreciation to be taken each year. Note that salvage value is ignored when depreciation is taken under MACRS.

¶ **22.3330.   Declining Balance Method.** The declining balance method measures depreciation by applying a fixed percentage to the property's adjusted basis as of the beginning of the tax year for which the depreciation is claimed. Since the adjusted basis will be lower each year, this method is called "declining balance." Salvage value is disregarded in making this computation.

¶ **22.3331. Salvage Value Disregarded.** Even before MACRS was adopted, salvage value was not taken into account in computing declining balance depreciation because the application of a fixed percentage to a declining amount leaves a residue of undepreciated basis, usually equal to between ten and thirteen percent of the original basis, when the asset's "useful life" has expired. Thus, the method of depreciation itself has a salvage value built into the annual computations.

¶ **22.3332. Minimum Useful Life.** With very few exceptions, under the pre-MACRS system, the declining balance method could be employed only if the depreciable asset had a useful life of at least three years.[21]

¶ **22.3333. New Property.** Prior to MACRS, declining balance, other than 150 percent declining balance, could be used only if the TP was the first person to use the depreciable asset or if the TP built or constructed the asset. One hundred fifty percent declining balance depreciation could be deducted for used *personal* property having a useful life of at least three years. In determining the depreciation of personal properties under MACRS, it is irrelevant whether the property is new or used. The declining balance method was available only to a limited extent for realty acquired between 1969 and 1986; for realty acquired after 1986, the declining balance method is not available.

¶ **22.3333–1. Illustration.** In 1970 (a pre-MACRS year), *X* purchased a second-hand desk with a useful life of six years for use in his business office. *X* could elect to use either the straight line or the 150 percent declining balance method of depreciation, but *X* could not use the double declining balance method or the sum of the years-digits method, which were limited to new property. As we will see later in this chapter, if the desk had been purchased in a year to which MACRS applies, the TP could have depreciated it on the double declining balance method.

¶ **22.3334. Rate of Depreciation.** The percentage to be applied against the declining balance is a multiple of the straight line rate. For example, 150 percent declining balance on a ten-year life asset is one and one-half times the straight

---

21. Rev. Rul. 67–248; and see *Holder Driv–Ur–Self, Inc. v. Commissioner*, 43 T.C. 202 (1964).

line rate of 10% or a 15% rate, and double declining balance is twice the straight line rate or a 20% rate.

¶ 22.3334–1. **Illustration.** On January 1, 1971, a TP purchased new office furniture for $20,000 which had an estimated life of eight years and a salvage value of $3,500. The TP elected to use the double declining balance method (also known as the 200 percent declining balance method). The straight line rate for an 8–year period is 12.5% (i.e., 100/8 = 12.5%). Consequently, the double declining balance rate is 2 × 12.5% = 25%. There was no half-year or mid-quarter convention at that time; so, since TP purchased the furniture on the first day of the year, TP was allowed the entire year's depreciation for 1971. The amount of depreciation allowable to TP for each of the first three years of his use of the furniture is set forth below.

1.   The TP's depreciation for 1971 is computed as follows: 25% of $20,000 = $5,000 depreciation in 1971. Note that salvage value is ignored in applying the declining balance method.

2.   The depreciation for 1972 is calculated as follows: 25% × $15,000 (i.e., $20,000 original basis minus $5,000 depreciation taken) = $3,750 depreciation for 1972. Note that the 25% rate remains the same in each year that depreciation is taken.

3.   The depreciation for 1973 is calculated as follows: 25% × $11,250 (i.e., $20,000 − $5,000 − $3,750) = $2,812.50 depreciation for 1973.

¶ **22.3340.   Sum-of-the-Years-Digits   Method.** Since   this method is no longer permitted, it is explained here only to provide the student with background into the development of the depreciation deduction.

The sum-of-the-years-digits method measures depreciation by applying a fraction with a constant denominator but a declining numerator to the original basis of the asset less salvage value. The numerator of this fraction is the number of remaining years of the asset's "useful life" and the denominator is the sum of the digits representing each year of the asset's "useful life." Note that this method is not available for property placed in service after 1980.

¶ **22.3341. Illustration.** On January 1, 1971, X purchased a new machine for use in her business. X paid $11,000 for the machine which has a "useful life" of ten years and a salvage value of $1,000. Thus, X will use $11,000 − $1,000 salvage = $10,000 as her depreciable basis.

1. In 1971, the first year, the rate of depreciation will be 10 (remaining useful life) ÷ (10 + 9 + 8 + 7 + 6 + 5 + 4 + 3 + 2 + 1) = 10/55, and the amount of deductions allowed X will be 10/55 × $10,000 = $1,818.

2. In 1972, X will deduct 9 ÷ (10 + 9 + 8 + 7 + 6 + 5 + 4 + 3 + 2 + 1) = 9/55 × $10,000 = $1,636.

3. In each subsequent year, the rate will be 8/55, 7/55, 6/55, 5/55, etc.

¶ **22.3342. Required Useful Life.** The sum-of-the-years-digits method was available only for depreciating assets having a "useful life" of at least three years. It is not available for real property acquired after 1969, and it is not available for any property acquired after 1980.

¶ **22.3343. New Property.** The sum-of-the-years-digits method was available only for new property (i.e., property first put to use by the TP or property built or constructed by the TP).

¶ **22.3350. Accelerated Methods.** Both declining balance and sum-of-the-years-digits are accelerated methods of depreciation (i.e., a greater amount of the asset's basis is deducted in the earlier years of the asset's life than in its later years).

¶ **22.3360. Other Methods of Depreciation.** In addition to declining balance and sum-of-the-years-digits, prior to 1981, a TP could elect to use any other consistent method of depreciation which would provide aggregate depreciation deductions during the first two-thirds of the asset's full life that did not exceed the amount of depreciation that would have been allowed to the TP during that period under the double declining balance method. This provision applied only to personalty with a "useful life" of at least three years and which the TP either built or purchased new, and to some, but not to all, realty. This flexibility is not available for property placed in service after 1980.

¶ **22.3370. Income Forecast Method.** The rights that a TP has in motion picture films, video tapes, and certain other properties have a limited useful life and can be depreciated as intangible property. As with many intangible properties, the rights in such properties would be depreciated on the straight line method. Because the flow of income from such properties is greatly uneven (for some films, virtually all of the income will be produced in the first one or two years of the film's exploitation, whereas some films will continue to produce income for many years), straight line depreciation does not provide an accurate allocation of the cost of acquiring or creating the film to the years of its exploitation. Consequently, the Commissioner permits a TP to utilize an income forecast method for depreciating such properties, and that method was codified by Congress when it added § 167(g) to the Code in 1996.[22] The types of properties which can be depreciated on the income forecast method are listed in § 167(g)(6) and include (in addition to films and video tapes) books, copyrights, sound recordings, theatrical productions, and patents. Prop. Reg. § 1.167(n)–5(a). This method cannot be used for an asset which is amortizable under § 197. § 167(g)(6); Prop. Reg. § 1.167(n)–5(b).

The income forecast method permits a TP to depreciate certain assets over an 11–year period in a manner that conforms each year's deduction to the proportion of income that is derived from the asset that year. The income forecast method requires the TP to make an estimate (i.e., a forecast) of the amount of income that his interest in the property will produce over the first 11 years of its exploitation. Each year, the TP can take a depreciation deduction equal to a fraction of his original basis in the property; the fraction for a year's depreciation is determined by making the actual income from the property for that year the numerator and by making the denominator equal to the total amount of income that is estimated will be derived from the property over the first 11 years of its exploitation. The estimate of the total amount of income that constitutes the denominator of the fraction is calculated again in a year in which information becomes available indicating that the forecasted income is inaccurate. Prop. Reg. § 1.167(n)–3(c). The basis of the property, against which the fraction is applied, remains the same without reduction for depreciation, but the basis can be recalculated to reflect additions to basis for amounts expended after the property was put into service. Prop. Reg. § 1.167(n)–2(b).

---

22. See Rev. Rul. 95–52; Rev. Rul. 60–358, as amplified by Rev. Rul. 64–273, and Rev. Rul. 79–285. *Citizens & Southern Corp. v. Commissioner*, 91 T.C. 463, 512–513 (1988), aff'd without opinion, 900 F.2d 266 (11th Cir. 1990).

If a TP has any basis remaining in the asset at the beginning of the 11th taxable year of its exploitation, the TP can deduct all of the remaining basis in that taxable year. § 167(g)(1)(C). So-called "look-back" rules can cause a TP to receive or pay interest if the depreciation taken under the income forecast method proves excessive or inadequate in some years. § 167(g)(2)–(4).

¶ 22.4000. **LAND.** Undeveloped land cannot be depreciated or amortized because it has no ascertainable useful life. Treas. Reg. § 1.167(a)–2. If improved realty is acquired, only the improvements can be depreciated. It is therefore necessary to allocate the TP's basis between the land and the improvements, and no depreciation is allowed for the land.

¶ 22.4100. **Illustration.** A TP paid $400,000 for improved real estate. The purchase price must be allocated according to fair market values at the time of TP's acquisition between the land, which is not depreciable, and the improvement, which is depreciable. Thus, if at the time that the TP purchases the property, the fair market value of the building on the land was $350,000 and the fair market value of the land was $50,000, the TP can depreciate only his $350,000 basis in the building.

¶ 22.5000. **DEPRECIATION OF IMPROVED REAL ESTATE.** While land is not depreciable, having no exhaustible life, real estate improvements are depreciable. Prior to the Tax Reform Act of 1969, the rules for depreciating personalty also applied to realty, but subsequent to the 1969 Act, real estate had to be considered separately and depreciated under a different set of rules. Realty placed in service after 1980 is depreciated under ACRS or MACRS, the current provisions of which are described later in this chapter.

¶ 22.6000. **ADJUSTMENT TO BASIS.** The basis of depreciable property is reduced by the amount of depreciation claimed by a TP on his tax return (the amount "allowed") that actually provided the TP with a tax benefit. § 1016(a)(2). The depreciation so claimed is called the depreciation "allowed" to the TP, and the amount allowed reduces basis only to the extent that it provided the TP with a tax benefit. In no event will basis be reduced by less than the amount of depreciation deduction that is "allowable" under the method of depreciation elected by the TP. § 1016(a)(2). The amount of *allowable* deduction reduces the TP's basis without regard to whether the *allowable* deduction would have provided a tax benefit to the TP.

As to personal property that is depreciable under MACRS but for which the TP failed to claim any depreciation deduction, prior to 1990 the allowable depreciation that reduced the TP's basis *usually* would be determined under the declining balance method. Prop. Reg. § 1.1016–3(a)(3). As a consequence of the amendment of § 1016(a)(2) by Section 11812(b)(10) of the Omnibus Budget Reconciliation Act of 1990, the allowable depreciation will be determined by employing the straight line method of depreciation. The 1990 amendment changed the second sentence of § 1016(a)(2) to require the use of the "straight line method" when the TP failed to adopt a method of depreciation, and the amendment is made applicable to property placed in service after November 5, 1990.

¶ **22.6100.   Mileage Allowance for Use of Automobile.** In lieu of calculating the costs of operating an automobile for business use, a TP can elect to use an optional mileage allowance of a specified number of cents per mile. See ¶ **21.3112**. The Service will provide a notice of the amount of mileage allowance that represents depreciation which reduces the TP's adjusted basis for the automobile. Rev. Proc. 2010–51(Sec. 4.04).

¶ **22.7000.   RECAPTURE OF DEPRECIATION.** The extent to which depreciation deductions may be "recaptured" when the TP disposes of the depreciable property is discussed later in this work. See §§ 1245 and 1250 discussed in Chapter **Twenty–Six**.

¶ **22.8000.   DEPRECIATION IN THE YEAR OF SALE.** When a depreciable asset that was not depreciated under MACRS is sold or otherwise disposed of during a tax year, depreciation may be deducted for the portion of the tax year prior to the sale or other disposition. Such depreciation may be deducted regardless of whether the TP's adjusted basis in the asset, after adjusting for depreciation deducted in the year of sale, is lower than the price for which the TP sold the asset.[23] Depreciation is also allowed for part of the year in which an asset that was depreciated under MACRS is sold or otherwise disposed of; the manner in which such depreciation is determined is explained at ¶¶ **22A.3490–22A.3491**.

¶ **22.9000.   RETIREMENT OR ABANDONMENT OF A DEPRECIABLE ASSET.** If a TP ceases to use a depreciable asset in the TP's trade or business, whether by retirement of the asset or by its abandonment, and if the TP does not sell or exchange the asset, the TP usually

---

23. *Fribourg Navigation Co., Inc. v. Commissioner*, 383 U.S. 272 (1966).

will be allowed a loss deduction for the difference between the asset's adjusted basis and its salvage value. Salvage will be ignored in the case of an abandonment. Treas. Reg. § 1.167(a)–8.

¶ 22A.0000. MODIFIED ACCELERATED COST RECOVERY SYSTEM (MACRS).

¶ 22A.1000. GENERAL. As noted in ¶ 22.1110, for most tangible property placed in service after 1980, depreciation is determined under a method set forth in § 168 and referred to as the accelerated cost recovery system (ACRS) or, for years after 1986, as the modified accelerated cost recovery system (MACRS). MACRS is merely one type of a depreciation system. The manner in which MACRS operates and the types of properties to which it applies are discussed in this chapter. As noted at ¶ 22.1112, § 168(a) states that the depreciation of tangible property that is provided by § 167(a) is to be determined by using § 168 (i.e., by using MACRS). Treas. Reg. § 1.168(a)–1(a) states, "The allowance for depreciation under section 168 constitutes the amount allowable under section 167(a)." Thus, a deduction allowable under MACRS is properly referred to as depreciation. For example, the reference in the title to § 179 to "depreciable" business assets includes assets the cost of which is recoverable under MACRS. Properties which are precluded from depreciation (such as undeveloped land) cannot be depreciated under MACRS.

¶ 22A.1100. Choice of Single Asset Account Depreciation or the General Asset Account Method. Under MACRS, a TP can choose to depreciate each asset separately or to combine assets and depreciate them on a General Asset Account method.[24]

¶ 22A.2000. EXPENSING THE COST OF CERTAIN DEPRECIABLE BUSINESS ASSETS. When the cost of an item can be deducted in full in the year paid or incurred, as contrasted to amortizing the cost over a period of time, that treatment of the cost is called "expensing." In other words, if a cost is "expensed," it is deducted when paid or incurred and is not depreciated or otherwise amortized.

Before examining MACRS, it is useful to consider the special deduction allowable under § 179 for the cost of purchasing certain tangible depreciable property that is used in a trade or business. Section 179 permits a TP who purchases so-called "section 179 property" to elect to deduct all or part of the cost of purchasing that property as a current expense in the taxable year in which the property is placed in service. § 179(a).

---

24. The General Asset Account method is discussed at ¶ 22.3120.

There is a ceiling on the total amount of cost that can be deducted in a taxable year, and that total amount is reduced if the aggregate cost of section 179 property for the year exceeds a threshold figure.

This deduction is sometimes referred to as "bonus depreciation," even though it is a misnomer to refer to an expensed item as a kind of depreciation. Any amount of the cost that is deducted under § 179 will not be included in the TP's basis in that asset. § 179(a); Treas. Reg. § 1.179–1(f)(1). The TP's remaining basis is depreciable under the normal rules of depreciation. So, in the year of acquisition of the property, the TP gets both bonus depreciation and regular depreciation for the asset.

The maximum amount[25] that can be deducted under § 179 in a taxable year beginning in the year 2008 or 2009 is $250,000, but that amount is reduced (not below zero) by the amount by which the cost of section 179 property that was placed in service in that year exceeds $800,000. § 179(b)(1), (2). For a taxable year beginning in the year 2010 or 2011, the maximum amount that can be deducted under § 179 is $500,000, and that amount is reduced (but not below zero) by the amount by which the cost of § 179 property that was placed in service that year exceeds two million dollars. Those two figures are reduced to $125,000 and $500,000 respectively for a taxable year beginning in 2012.[26] For a taxable year beginning after 2012, those two figures are scheduled to be reduced to $25,000 and $200,000 respectively. § 179(b)(1), (2).

The maximum amount that can be deducted under § 179 by a TP in a taxable year cannot exceed the aggregate taxable income that the TP derived that year from the active conduct of trades or businesses. § 179(b)(3). For this purpose, taxable income is determined by aggregating the net incomes or losses for that year of all trades or businesses that are actively conducted by the TP. Treas. Reg. § 1.179–2(c)(1). The taxable income from a trade or business is computed by excluding deductions allowable under § 179 and certain other deductions (e.g., net operating loss carryovers and carrybacks) listed in Treas. Reg. § 1.179–2(c)(1).

---

25. The Omnibus Budget Reconciliation Act of 1993 amended the Code to provide for certain geographic areas to be designated as "empowerment zones" and "enterprise communities." §§ 1391–1397(F). One of the benefits granted to businesses that operate in an empowerment zone is that the amount that can be expensed under § 179 for qualified businesses in such a zone is substantially increased. § 1397A.

26. For a taxable year beginning in 2012, those two figures will be increased by an adjustment for inflation. § 179(b)(6).

In general, the active conduct of a trade or business means "meaningful" participation in the management or operations of the trade or business. Treas. Reg. § 1.179–2(c)(6)(ii). Any amount that is disallowed as a deduction because of this taxable income limitation is carried forward and treated as a cost of section 179 property in the next year (and so may be deductible in that year or, if not, can be carried forward again). § 179(b)(3). If section 179 property is sold or if it is transferred in a transaction in which some or all of the gain or loss is not recognized, immediately prior to that sale or transfer, the adjusted basis of the asset is increased by any outstanding carryover of unused deduction with respect to the property. This provision also applies to transfers at death. Treas. Reg. § 1.179–3(f)(1).

If a TP is married and files a separate return, the maximum cost of section 179 properties that can be deducted by both parties is determined by treating the TP and his spouse as one person except that the "taxable income" limitation described above is applied separately to each party. The maximum amount of section 179 cost that is then determined to be deductible is allocated between the TP and the spouse equally unless they elect otherwise. § 179(b)(4).

The TP's election to take a deduction under § 179 must specify the items whose cost is to be expensed and must specify the amount of cost of each such item that is to be deducted. Once made, the election can be revoked only with the permission of the Commissioner, which will be granted only in extraordinary circumstances. § 179(c)(2); Treas. Reg. § 1.179–5(b). However, an election made with respect to a taxable year beginning in the period 2003 to 2012 can be revoked by the TP unilaterally; but, once made, that revocation cannot be retracted. § 179(c)(2). The meaning of the "cost" of property is specially defined in § 179(d)(3) to exclude any substituted basis of that property.

The types of property that constitute section 179 property are tangible property[27] to which MACRS applies and which is section 1245 property[28] (as defined in § 1245(a)(3)) and which is "purchased" for use in the active conduct of a trade or business. § 179(d)(1). The meaning of "purchase" is specially defined in § 179(d)(2), which employs a narrower definition than is customarily applied to that term. Section 179 does not apply to buildings or to their structural components since those properties do not qualify as section 1245 property. § 1245(a)(3)(B).

---

27. For years beginning after 2002 and before 2013, section 179 property includes certain computer software that was purchased and placed in service for use in the active conduct of a trade or business. § 179(d)(1)(A)(ii).

28. See ¶ 26.3220.

¶ **22A.2100.   Recapture of Deduction.** If "at any time" an item of section 179 property is not used predominantly in the TP's trade or business, part of the deduction that the TP obtained under § 179 for that item is recaptured by requiring the TP to include that amount in his gross income. § 179(d)(10). The Blue Book for the 1986 TRA states that the reference in § 179(d)(10) to "any time" is limited to any time prior to the expiration of the recovery period for the depreciation of that asset.[29] The regulations have adopted that construction and so limit recapture to the recovery period. Treas. Reg. § 1.179–1(e)(1). The "recovery period" of an asset is explained at ¶ **22A.3430.**

The amount recaptured is the excess of the amount expensed under § 179 (regardless of whether that deduction provided TP with a tax benefit) over the amount of additional depreciation that would have been allowable under § 168 for the period preceding the event causing the recapture if § 179 had not been elected and thereby reduced the depreciable basis of the section 179 property. Treas. Reg. § 1.179–1(e)(1). In most circumstances where section 179 property is sold, § 1245 will apply to the disposition and cause recapture of all or some of the expensed deduction. § 1245(a)(1)–(3). See ¶ **26.3000** *et seq.* The recapture provision of § 179(d)(10) does not apply when § 1245(a) applies. Treas. Reg. § 1.179–1(e)(3).

In addition to the section 179 bonus depreciation, all or a portion of the costs of certain specified properties that are placed in service in the period 2008 to 2012 inclusive can be deducted in that year under § 168(k).

¶ **22A.2110.   Basis Adjustment.** If § 179(d)(10) recapture applies, the amount that is recaptured under that provision is added to the adjusted basis of the section 179 property immediately before the event that caused the recapture. Treas. Reg. § 1.179–1(e)(3). This prevents double taxation of the recaptured amount.

If a § 179 deduction is taken for a luxury automobile (or for certain "listed property"), special limitations on the amount of deduction that is allowable will apply. § 280F(d)(1). In that case, for purposes of applying the limitation, the § 179 deduction for that year is treated as a § 168 deduction, and so the total of the §§ 168 and 179 deductions for that year are subject to the § 280F limitations. Treas. Reg. § 1.280F–2T(b)(4), (e), Examples (4)–(7).

---

29.   General Explanation of the Tax Reform Act of 1986, prepared by the Staff of the Joint Committee on Taxation (1986) at p. 110.

If the cost of a "sport utility vehicle" (as defined in § 179(b)(5)(B)) is not subject to § 280F, the cost of that vehicle that is taken into account under § 179 cannot exceed $25,000. § 179(b)(5).

¶ 22A.2200. Estates and Trusts. The bonus depreciation deduction is not available to a TP that is an estate or trust. § 179(d)(4).

¶ 22A.2300. Illustration. *B*, an unmarried individual, reports his income on a calendar year basis. In 2005 (when the maximum amount of § 179 deduction that can be allowed is $105,000), *B* purchased both a machine (at a cost of $112,000) and a truck (at a cost of $20,000) for use in his business. *B* made no other purchases in 2005. *B* had taxable income of $240,000 from the active conduct of his business in 2005. Both the truck and the machine were placed in service in 2005. *B* can make any one of the following elections under § 179. *B* can elect to deduct:

(a) $20,000 of the cost of purchasing the truck, and no expense deduction for the cost of purchasing the machine; or

(b) $20,000 of the cost of purchasing the truck, and $85,000 of the cost of the machine; or

(c) $105,000 of the cost of purchasing the machine, and no expense deduction for the cost of the truck; or

(d) $92,500 of the cost of the machine and $12,500 of the cost of the truck; or

(e) $91,500 of the cost of the machine and $13,500 of the cost of the truck; or

(f) some other combination of the costs of the two items so long as the total cost taken as a deduction does not exceed $105,000.

B's election must specify each item selected and the amount of cost of that item to be deducted under § 179. This specification is required so that the adjusted basis of the assets can be determined and so *B*'s regular depreciation deductions of the asset can be determined. Note that B is not required to utilize the bonus depreciation deduction and can elect to use only part of it or none.

¶ 22A.3000. MACRS (THE MODIFIED ACCELERATED COST RECOVERY SYSTEM). MACRS is a system of depreciation that utilizes straight line and declining balance methods of depreciation. The straight line and declining balance methods of depreciation are described at ¶¶ 22.3320–22.3330 and ¶¶ 22.3334–22.3334–1. The initial system that was adopted in 1981 was known as ACRS, but after it was modified in 1986, it came to be referred to as MACRS to distinguish the amended version from the original system. ACRS was adopted by Congress in 1981 and has been modified several times since then; the modifications adopted as part of the 1986 Tax Reform Act are especially significant, and since that modification was made the system has been referred to as MACRS. The current operation of MACRS is explained below. Some of the salient distinctions between MACRS and prior systems of depreciation are that MACRS:

- does not take salvage value into account for any purpose;

- adopts a statutorily specified period of time over which the adjusted basis of property is recovered (in contrast to prior systems of depreciation which typically used a recovery period that was based on the property's useful life);

- makes no distinction between new and used property (the depreciation of used property under MACRS is not subject to special restrictions and is determined the same as it is for new property);

- utilizes the half-year or mid-quarter convention for personalty and the mid-month convention for buildings;

- and generally (for personalty) provides a greater acceleration of recovery of cost than was provided by the depreciation systems that were used prior to 1981.

For guidelines to the application of MACRS, see Rev. Proc. 87–57.

¶ 22A.3100. MACRS Property. The only property that is depreciable under MACRS is tangible property, real or personal, of a character subject to the allowance for depreciation that either is used in a trade or business or otherwise is held for the production of income. §§ 167(a), 168(a). Neither MACRS nor ACRS applies to any property that was placed in service by the TP prior to 1981. MACRS does not apply to intangible property. Even some tangible properties that are placed in service after 1980 are excluded from MACRS—for example, certain public utility property, sound recordings, films and video tapes are excluded. § 168(f). MACRS also does not apply to tangible property that the TP elects to exclude from MACRS if the property is properly depreciated by the TP on the units of production method of depreciation[30] or (subject to one exception) on some other method of depreciation that is not determined by reference to a term of years. § 168(f)(1). One example of a method available in lieu of MACRS is the standard mileage rate that is permitted for determining the deduction for the business use of an automobile.[31]

¶ 22A.3110. Determinable Useful Life. Prior to the adoption of ACRS in 1981, the period over which depreciation could be taken was the useful life of the asset.[32] Because of that requirement, an asset could not be depreciated unless the TP could show that it had a determinable useful life. See Rev. Rul. 68–232. When Congress adopted ACRS, it eliminated useful life as the measure of an asset's recovery period. **¶ 22A.3000.** Instead, the recovery period for depreciation under ACRS or MACRS is a statutorily established period, and it does not depend upon the actual life of the asset.

The Service maintains that, notwithstanding the elimination of useful life in determining the amount of depreciation for a given year, there remains a requirement that a tangible asset cannot be depreciated under ACRS or MACRS unless the TP can show that the asset has a determinable useful life. The Service maintains that the statement in § 168(a) that that section is a special application of § 167(a) depreciation of tangible property means that the requirement of § 167 that the asset have a determinable useful life applies also to MACRS.

The Service litigated this issue in two separate cases, and lost both. A majority of the Tax Court and the Second and Third Circuit Courts of Appeals held that there is no requirement that an asset have a determinable useful life to be depreciated under ACRS or MACRS. *Simon v. Commissioner*;[33] *Liddle v. Commissioner*.[34] The courts held that it is sufficient that the asset be subject to exhaustion, wear and tear, or obsolescence.

In *Simon*, the items in question were 19th Century violin bows. The TPs were highly skilled professional musicians that used the

30. See ¶¶ **22.3310–22.3311**.

31. See Notice 2010–88.

32. See ¶¶ **22.3000–22.3100**.

33. 103 T.C. 247 (1994) (reviewed by the court), Nonacq., aff'd 68 F.3d 41 (2d Cir. 1995)

34. 103 T.C. 285 (1994) (reviewed by the court), Nonacq., aff'd 65 F.3d 329 (3d Cir. 1995).

bows in their performances. The TPs produced evidence that the use of the bows did cause wear and tear to the bows and that the bows would lose their capacity to produce excellent sound after extended use. However, the bows were also collectible items that were valuable without regard to their capacity to produce outstanding music. Consequently, the value of the bows rose while the TPs used them because of their value as collectibles. The Tax Court and the Second Circuit Court of Appeals held that the bows could be depreciated under ACRS (because of the years involved in the suit, ACRS was the applicable statutory system). Since the bows suffered wear and tear and exhaustion in the use to which the TPs put them, they qualified for depreciation as 5–year property.[35] On a similar set of facts, the Tax Court and the Third Circuit Court of Appeals reached the same result in *Liddle*.

The Commissioner nonacquiesced in both the *Simon* and the *Liddle* decisions. The Commissioner has stated that the Service will litigate this issue in other circuits when the opportunity arises.[36]

¶ **22A.3111.   Works of Art.** A valuable painting by a master does not have a determinable useful life. Rev. Rul. 68–232. In *Clinger v. Commissioner*,[37] the Tax Court held that a painting, which was hung in the TP's place of business for a business purpose, was not depreciable under ACRS (§ 168) because it does not have a determinable useful life. The court also denied TP's claim for an expense deduction under § 179.

As noted above, in several subsequent decisions that were reviewed by the entire court and affirmed by two Circuit Courts of Appeals, the Tax Court held that there is no requirement in ACRS or MACRS that an asset must have a determinable useful life. See § **22A.3110.** However, even under those decisions, a TP must show that the asset to be depreciated under MACRS is subject to exhaustion, wear and tear, or obsolescence.[38] In *Simon* and *Liddle*, there was evidence that the musical instruments in those cases were suffering wear and year and exhaustion. That may not be true when dealing

---

35.   See ¶ **22A.3410** for the classifications of MACRS property.

36.   AOD 1996–009.

37.   60 T.C.M. 598 (1990).

38.   *Simon* and *Liddle*, ¶ **22A.3110.**

with a fine painting. Generally, the TP will have the burden of proof on that issue. See ¶ **1.4500.**

It should be noted that not every painting constitutes a fine work of art. If a painting does not qualify as an artistic achievement, it may be no more than a wall decoration; and, as such, can be depreciated if used in a business office (the same as any office furnishing).

¶ 22A.3200.   Adjusted Basis. Since MACRS utilizes the straight line and declining balance methods of depreciation, deductions are determined by reference to the adjusted basis of the property. See § 167(c).

¶ 22A.3300.   Salvage Value. Salvage value is not taken into account in determining depreciation under MACRS regardless of whether depreciation is determined under the straight line or declining balance method. §§ 168(b)(4), (g)(2)(A). The elimination of salvage value as a factor in determining depreciation is one of the important changes that was made by the congressional adoption of ACRS and MACRS.

¶ 22A.3400.   Determination of the Amount of Depreciation. To determine the amount of depreciation that is allowable for an item of MACRS property, it is necessary first to determine the classification of the property in question and then to determine three factors: "the applicable depreciation method," "the applicable recovery period," and "the applicable convention." § 168(a).

¶ 22A.3410.   Classification of Property. The current version of MACRS divides MACRS properties into six classifications: three-year property, five-year property, seven-year property, ten-year property, fifteen-year property, and twenty-year property. § 168(e)(1). In addition, MACRS provides specified recovery periods for residential rental property, nonresidential real property, water utility property, and railroad grading or tunnel bore. § 168(c)(1).

¶ 22A.3411.   Use of ADR Class Lives. With some exceptions, the MACRS classification of an asset is determined by reference to its class life under a method for determining the recovery period for depreciating properties that was available prior to 1981; this method was called "asset depreciation range" or "ADR." ADR is described at ¶ **22.3130.** Under ADR, a TP could elect to use a recovery period that fell within a range of years that was provided for broad categories of properties. The mid-point of the range of years for each class of property is referred to as the "class life" for that property. Thus, properties that had a depreciation range under ADR of from four to six years are said to have a class life of five years.

The class life of an asset under ADR is established by the Commissioner's publication of a Revenue Procedure that sets class lives for broad categories of properties. For example, the class life for office furniture, fixtures and equipment is ten years. While ADR is not available for assets placed into service after 1980, an updated version of the ADR class lives is used to determine the classification of many categories of assets under MACRS. For that reason, the Commissioner continues to update the lists of ADR class lives. See § 168(i)(1) which provides that for MACRS purposes "class life" means the class life of an asset under ADR as that system was established by statute as of January 1, 1986. The current list of ADR class lives is set forth in Rev. Proc. 87–56 (as modified by Rev. Proc. 88–22).

Rev. Proc. 87–56 (as modified) not only sets forth the current ADR class lives of categories of assets, the Revenue Procedure also sets forth the recovery period for each category for general MACRS depreciation purposes and the recovery period for each category for purposes of the MACRS alternative depreciation system. See ¶ **22A.3460.** For example, office furniture, fixtures and equipment are listed in the Revenue Procedure as having a recovery period of seven years for the purpose of the general depreciation allowance provided by MACRS, and such assets have a recovery period of ten years for the purpose of the alternative MACRS depreciation allowance set forth at § 168(g). Rev. Proc. 87–56.

Since the Revenue Procedure provides the recovery periods of assets for both regular MACRS depreciation and alternative MACRS depreciation purposes, a TP can use those tables to compute the proper depreciation allowance, and the TP does not need to know the asset's class life (albeit the Revenue Procedure also sets forth the asset's class life). However, the reader should be alert to the possibility that Congress will change the recovery period for an item by amending the statute and that change will not be reflected in the Revenue Procedure. For example, late in 1988, Congress changed the recovery period for nonresidential buildings from 31.5 to its current period of 39 years. Both Rev. Proc. 87–56 and its modification in Rev. Proc. 88–22 were promulgated prior to that statutory change, and therefore do not reflect it.

¶ 22A.3412. Classification by Class Life. Many types of property are classified into MACRS categories by reference to their class lives. § 168(e)(1). As noted in **¶ 22A.3413**, a number of items of property are classified by specific provisions in § 168 itself; but, in the absence of a specific provision, the class life of the asset will control its classification. For example, unless specifically provided for in § 168, an asset that has a class life of four years or less is classified as three-year property, and an asset that has a class life of more than four years but less than ten years is classified as five-year property. § 168(e)(1). Most personal properties that do not have a class life (i.e., they are not included in the ADR list) are classified as seven-year property. § 168(e)(3)(C).

¶ 22A.3413. Classification by Specific Provision in § 168. A number of items of property are classified by a specific provision in § 168 itself without regard to the item's class life. § 168(e)(3). For example, a race horse that is more than two years old when placed in service and any horse (other than a race horse) that is more than twelve years old when placed in service is treated as three-year property. § 168(e)(3)(A). In addition, if a dealer holds consumer property that the dealer will lease to individuals under a "rent-to-own contract," the property is three-year property. § 168(e)(3)(A)(iii). A rent-to-own contract is a lease with an option to purchase that meets the requirements of § 168(i)(14), and there are numerous requirements. Some of the requirements are (1) that the tenant is not obligated to make all of the serial payments under the lease, but if he does so, the property passes to the tenant; (2) that the tenant can terminate its rental obligation at anytime by returning the property in good working order to the dealer; and (3) that a substantial portion of the contracts that the dealer makes are terminated by the tenant's returning the property to the dealer.

The five-year property category includes any automobile or light purpose truck, any property used in connection with research and experimentation, and any "qualified technological equipment." § 168(e)(3)(B). The term "qualified technological equipment" is defined in § 168(i)(2) to include *inter alia* computers and peripheral equipment, but the term does not include typewriters, calculators, adding machines, copiers, and several other items listed in § 168(i)(2)(B)(iv). The treatment of buildings is described later in this chapter.

Note that the tables in Rev. Proc. 87–56 [see ¶ **22A.3411**] that set forth the recovery period of categories of assets for the purpose of applying the MACRS general and alternative depreciation systems incorporates the recovery periods established for certain assets by § 168 itself. For example, the Revenue Procedure lists that the recovery period of automobiles and taxis for general depreciation purposes is five years even though the class life of such assets is listed as three years.

¶ **22A.3414.   Monitoring of MACRS Categories.** Congress instructed the Treasury to monitor and analyze the actual experience of TPs in using depreciable assets. § 168(i)(1). Initially, Congress also authorized Treasury to modify class lives or assigned recovery periods when Treasury's study of the experience that TPs have had with such assets warranted a change in the recovery period, but this authority was withdrawn by Congress in its amendment of § 168(i)(1) in the Technical and Miscellaneous Revenue Act (TAMRA) of 1988. Perhaps, if the studies of experience that Treasury reports to Congress indicate that a class life or a recovery period is unrealistic, Congress will alter it.

¶ **22A.3415.   Buildings.** Most depreciable buildings will be classified either as residential rental property or as nonresidential real property. "Residential rental property" is a building or structure 80% or more of the gross rental income from which for the taxable year is rental income from dwelling units; but the term does not include hotels, motels or any other establishments more than 50% of whose units are used on a transient basis. § 168(e)(2)(A). "Nonresidential real property" refers to buildings (and certain other real properties) that are not residential rental property and that have a class life of 27.5 years or more. § 168(e)(2)(B), (i)(12). The recovery period for such properties is 27.5 years for residential rental property and 39 years for nonresidential real property.

¶ **22A.3416.   Change in Use.** Congress authorized Treasury to promulgate regulations for the determination of depreciation deductions of an asset whose property status is changed even though the asset continues to be held by the same TP. § 168(i)(5). For the depreciation of an asset that is converted from personal use to business or income-producing use or vice versa, see ¶¶ **22A.3500–22A.3600.** For the determination of depreciation when the recovery period or depreciation method of a MACRS asset changes, see Treas. Reg. § 1.168(i)–4(d).

¶ 22A.3417. Short Taxable Year. A short taxable year is a taxable year of less than 12 months. The manner in which depreciation is determined for a TP's short taxable year is described in Rev. Proc. 89–15.

¶ 22A.3420. Combination of Declining Balance and Straight Line Depreciation. While the declining balance method of depreciation provides a more accelerated rate of recovery than does the straight line method, there is a point in time during the recovery period of an asset being depreciated on the declining balance method when the recovery for the remaining years of that period will be decelerated if the TP continues to use the declining balance method. The maximum acceleration of recovery is obtained by using the declining balance method to depreciate the asset in the early years of its recovery period and then, at some point, to switch to the straight line method to depreciate the remaining adjusted basis of the asset. The change to the straight line method is made by amortizing the adjusted basis of the property at the beginning of the year over the remaining time of the asset's recovery period. Where declining balance is used under MACRS, the statute provides that the depreciation will switch to straight line at the beginning of the first taxable year that the straight line method will produce a larger allowance than would the continued use of the declining balance method. § 168(b)(1).

¶ 22A.3421. Straight Line Method Required for Certain Properties. Most buildings and their structural components placed in service after 1986 must be depreciated on the straight line method. § 168(b)(3). Any addition to or improvement of a building also will be depreciated on the straight line method. § 168(i)(6). Other properties that are required to be depreciated on the straight line method are: (1) railroad grading or tunnel bore, (2) tree or vine bearing fruit or nuts, (3) water utility property, (4) qualified leasehold improvement property (described in § 168(e)(6)), and (5) qualified restaurant property (as described in § 168(e)(7)). § 168(b)(3). As noted in ¶ **22A.3460,** property depreciated under the Alternative Depreciation System is depreciated on the straight line method.

¶ 22A.3422. Method for Depreciating 15–Year and 20–Year Property. The 150 percent declining balance method is used to depreciate 15–year and 20–year property and property used in a farming business.[39] As stated in ¶ **22A.3420,** the depreciation method for such properties will change to straight line in the first year that straight line will produce a larger allowance than does the 150 percent declining balance. Instead of using the declining balance method, a TP can elect to use straight line depreciation.

¶ 22A.3423. Method for Depreciating Other Properties. Unless the TP elects otherwise, all other classifications of properties (e.g., three-year and five-year properties) are depreciated on the 200 percent declining balance method (i.e., the double declining balance method), switching to the straight line method in the optimum year. § 168(b)(1).

¶ 22A.3424. Election to Use the Straight Line or 150 Percent Declining Balance Method. When a TP otherwise would have depreciated an asset on the declining balance method, the TP can elect instead to depreciate that asset on the straight line method. § 168(b)(3)(D), (5). Similarly, when a TP otherwise would have depreciated an asset on the 200 percent declining balance method, the TP can elect to depreciate that asset on the 150 percent declining balance method (or, as noted above, on the straight line method). § 168(b)(3)(D), (5). The election can be made for one or more classes of property, but, once made, it is irrevocable and applies to all items of property in the selected class that are placed in service in the taxable year for which the election is made. § 168(b)(5). An election is made for one taxable year at a time and need not be made again in the next taxable year. When an election is made under § 168(b)(5) to employ either the straight line or the 150 percent declining balance method of depreciation, the recovery period for the assets that are subject to that election is the same as it would have been if no election had been made.

---

39. § 168(b)(2). In addition, certain electric meters and grid systems are depreciated on the 150 percent declining balance method unless the TP elects straight line depreciation. § 168(b)(2)(C).

¶ **22A.3424–1. Illustration.** In Year One, *X* purchased and placed into service in his business: three items of seven-year property, two items of three-year property, six items of five-year property, and an apartment house that constitutes residential rental property. The apartment house is depreciated by *X* on the straight line method over a 27.5–year recovery period. § 168(b)(3), (c). The other items of property that *X* acquired in that year can be depreciated on the double declining balance method. Instead, *X* elected to depreciate the items of property that are classified as seven-year property on the straight line method. Because of that election, all three items of seven-year property will be depreciated on the straight line method; the election cannot be made on an asset by asset basis. However, since *X* made no election for the other two classifications of properties, the three-year and five-year properties will be depreciated on the double declining balance method. In Year Two, *X* purchased and placed in service two items of seven-year property. Unless *X* makes another election, those items of seven-year property will be depreciated on the double declining balance method.

¶ **22A.3425. Straight Line Under the Alternative System.** As shown in ¶ **22A.3460**, an alternative system of depreciation is required to be used for certain properties. This alternative system can be elected by the TP for assets that are not required to be depreciated under that system.

If applicable, the alternative system requires that the assets subject to that system be depreciated on the straight line method over a recovery period that often (but not always) is longer than that employed by MACRS for assets that are not subject to the alternative system.

If the TP elects the alternative system for a building, the election can be made on an asset by asset basis. For other assets, the election must be made for all assets in the same classification. § 168(g)(7). Once made, the election to use the alternative system of depreciation is irrevocable for that classification of assets for that taxable year. § 168(g)(7). The difference between making an election under the alternative system and making it under § 168(b)(5) is that the former may require the use of a longer recovery period than does the latter; both elections require the use of the straight line method.

¶ 22A.3430. Applicable Recovery Period. The recovery period is the period over which the asset is to be depreciated. The recovery period of an asset is determined by the MACRS classification of the asset. § 168(c). Except for buildings, water utility property, railroad gradings and tunnel bores, the recovery period for an item of property is the same as the years used in classifying the property. For example, the recovery period for three-year property is three years; the recovery period for five-year property is five years; and so forth. The recovery period for residential rental property is 27.5 years, and the recovery period for nonresidential real property is 39 years. § 168(c). The recovery period for railroad gradings and tunnel bores is 50 years. Certain qualified property that is used predominantly in the active conduct of a trade or business within an Indian reservation is given a substantially shorter recovery period than otherwise would apply. § 168(j). The reader should be alert to the fact that Congress tends to change these recovery periods from time to time—especially as to buildings.

¶ 22A.3431. Alternative System. As noted in **¶ 22A.3460**, certain assets are required to be depreciated under an alternative system of depreciation that is set forth in § 168(g). The alternative system also can be elected by the TP for classifications of property or for individual buildings.

¶ 22A.3432. Typically, the recovery period for assets depreciated under the alternative system is longer than the periods provided under the normal method. For example, buildings will be depreciated over a 40–year recovery period under the alternative method, as contrasted to the 27.5–year period and 39–year period that are used in § 168(c). The recovery period under the alternative system sometimes is the same as the period under the normal method, but it is never less.

¶ 22A.3440. Applicable Convention. Depreciable property can be purchased or disposed of at various times throughout a taxable year. The question can arise as to the amount of depreciation that can be deducted for an asset in the year that it is placed into service or sold. See Rev. Proc. 89–15. MACRS adopts several conventions which are used to determine the percentage of the year for which depreciation is allowable for such an asset. For buildings (and structural components), the "mid-month convention" is used. § 168(d)(2). For other MACRS properties, the "half-year convention" is used unless the aggregate bases of such properties (other than buildings, railroad gradings, tunnel bores, and property which is placed in service and disposed of in the same taxable year) that were placed in service in the last quarter of the taxable year is greater than 40% of the aggregate bases of all such properties that were placed in service in that taxable year. § 168(d)(1), (3). In the latter case, "the mid-quarter convention" is used for all such properties that were placed in service in that taxable year. The mid-quarter convention does not apply to: nonresidential real property, residential rental property, railroad gradings, tunnel bores, and property placed in service and disposed of in the same taxable year; and such properties are not taken into account in applying the more than 40% of aggregate bases computation to determine whether the mid-quarter convention applies to other properties.

¶ 22A.3441. **Mid–Month Convention.** The mid-month convention applies to most buildings. When a building that is subject to the mid-month convention is placed in service in a calendar month, it is treated as having been placed in service in the middle of that month. When a building that is subject to the mid-month convention is disposed of in a calendar month, it is treated as having been disposed of in the middle of that month. § 168(d)(4)(B).

¶ 22A.3442. **Half–Year Convention.** When property that is subject to the half-year convention is placed in service during a taxable year, it is treated as having been placed in service on the mid-point of such taxable year. When such property is disposed of in a taxable year, it is treated as having been disposed of on the mid-point of such taxable year. § 168(d)(4)(A). If the half-year convention applied to the property when it was first placed into service, it will also apply to the property in the year of its disposition. Treas. Reg. § 1.168(d)–1(c).

¶ 22A.3443. **Mid–Quarter Convention.** When property that is subject to the mid-quarter convention is placed in service in a quarter of a taxable year, it is treated as having been placed in service on the mid-point of such quarter. When such property is disposed of in a quarter of a subsequent taxable year, it is treated as having been disposed of on the mid-point of such quarter. § 168(d)(4)(C). If the mid-quarter convention applied to the property when it was first placed into service, it will also apply to the property in the year of its disposition. Treas. Reg. § 1.168(d)–1(c).

¶ 22A.3450. Illustrations. All of the properties in the following examples are tangible properties that are used by the TP in his business, are subject to wear and tear and exhaustion, and so are depreciable under MACRS. All of the properties were purchased and placed into service after the year 1986. All of the parties in the following examples report their income on a calendar year basis and are unmarried.

¶ 22A.3451. Illustration 1. On January 5, Year One, X purchased and placed into service a light general use truck. X made no other purchases that year. X paid $25,000 for the truck. X elected to expense $10,000 of that cost under § 179. The $10,000 of cost that X expensed is not charged to capital account [§ 179(a)] and so is not part of X's basis in the truck. X, therefore, has an adjusted basis of $15,000 to depreciate under MACRS. Since the truck is five-year property,[40] and since TP did not elect otherwise, it is to be depreciated on the double declining balance method over a five-year recovery period, using a half-year convention. Accordingly, the depreciation deduction for Year One is $3,000—i.e., 40% of $15,000 for one-half a year. The straight line rate for a five-year recovery period is 20%, and so the double declining balance rate is 40%. Because of the half-year convention, the property is treated as having been placed in service in the middle of Year One (notwithstanding that it was actually placed in service in the first month of the year), and so depreciation is allowable for only one-half of that year. The total amount of deductions allowable to X for Year One because of the truck is $13,000 – $10,000 deduction under § 179 and $3,000 of depreciation deduction.

¶ 22A.3452. Illustration 2. The same facts as those stated in ¶ 22A.3451. On April 24, Year Two, X sold the truck to an unrelated party for its fair market value. Since the half-year convention applied to the truck when it was first put into service, the half-year convention will also apply to the truck in the year in which is sold. Under the half-year convention, X is treated as having sold the truck at the mid-point of Year Two. Accordingly, X is allowed a depreciation deduction of $2,400

---

40. § 168(e)(3)(B)(i).

for Year Two—i.e., 40% of the truck's $12,000 adjusted basis for a half of a year.

Since under § 1245(a) the sale of the truck will be subject to recapture of previously deducted depreciation and amortization, (and a previously deducted expense under § 179 is treated as an amortization deduction that can be recaptured by § 1245), the recapture provision of § 179(d)(10) is preempted and does not apply. Treas. Reg. § 1.179–1(e)(3).

¶ 22A.3453. Illustration 3. On February 8, Year One, Y purchased and placed into service a computer. Y paid $40,000 for the computer. On April 10, Year One, Y purchased and placed into service a factory building that qualified as nonresidential real property. Y paid $100,000 for the building. Y leases the land on which the factory is situated on a 50–year lease. On September 16, Year One, Y purchased and placed into service an automobile. Y paid $10,000 for that automobile. On October 3, Year One, Y purchased and placed into service a light general purpose truck. Y paid $35,000 for the truck. Y elected not to expense under § 179 any of the cost of the properties that he purchased in that year. Consequently, Y obtained no deduction under § 179. Y made no other purchases in that year, and Y did not dispose of any property in that year.

The building is depreciated over a period of 39 years on the straight line method so the depreciation for the building for an entire year would be $100,000/39 = $2,564. Under the mid-month convention, Y is treated as having placed the building in service in the mid-point of April; thus, Y is allowed depreciation for only 8.5 months. The depreciation for Year One, therefore, is 8.5/12 × $2,564 = $1,816.

The depreciation of the other assets placed in service in Year One (the personalty) will be determined under the double declining balance method over a five-year recovery period. Usually, the half-year convention would be used for such properties, but, in this case, the mid-quarter convention must be used. Exclusive of the building, Y's aggregate bases for properties placed in service in Year One is $85,000. Two of those properties—the computer and the automobile—were purchased in the first and third quarters of the year respectively. The truck was purchased in the fourth quarter of that year. Since Y's basis in the truck ($35,000) represents more than 40% of Y's aggregate bases ($85,000) in all the depreciable assets (other than the building) that he placed in service that year, the mid-quarter convention must be used for all those assets. Note that if Y were to dispose of one of those three items in a subsequent year during the recovery period of that item, the mid-quarter convention would apply to the item in the year of its disposition since the mid-quarter convention applied to it when it was first placed in service.

The computer was placed in service in the first quarter, and so it is deemed to have been placed into service in the mid-point of that quarter. Y's depreciation for the computer for Year One is 40% × $40,000 × 10.5/12 = $14,000. The depreciation for the automobile is 40% × $10,000 × 4.5/12 = $1,500. The depreciation for the truck is 40% × $35,000 × 1.5/12 = $1750. Note that the limitation on the amount of depreciation deduction allowable for a passenger automobile that is imposed by § 280F(a)(1) does not apply in the instant case because the amount of depreciation for the automobile is lower than the statutory ceiling.

¶ 22A.3454.   **Illustration 4.** The same facts as those stated in ¶ 22A.3453. On July 3, Year Two, Y sold the computer that he had acquired in Year One. Y purchased a new computer and placed it in service in September of Year Two. Y made no other purchases or dispositions in that year. The depreciation for the new computer that Y purchased is determined under the half-year convention. However, since the depreciation for Y's old computer was determined under the mid-quarter convention in the year that it was placed in service, the depreciation for the year that Y disposes of that computer also will be determined under the mid-quarter convention. § 168(d)(3)(A), (4)(C). The computer was sold in the third quarter, and Y had an adjusted basis of $26,000 in the computer at the beginning of the year. Y's depreciation for that computer for Year Two is 40% × $26,000 × 7.5/12 = $6,500.

¶ 22A.3460.   **Alternative Depreciation System.** Certain properties that are subject to MACRS are required to be depreciated on an alternative system that is set forth in § 168(g). The alternative system utilizes only the straight line method of depreciation and provides recovery periods that often are longer (and never are shorter) than those provided by § 168(c). The recovery period for buildings is 40 years and the recovery period for property which has no class life (i.e., it is not listed in the ADR lists) is 12 years. All other properties have a recovery period equal to their class life, which typically is determined by the ADR lists.[41] However, the statute provides a special class life for a number of specified properties, and that class life then becomes the recovery period for such properties. § 168(g)(3). For example, the class life for municipal sewers is 50 years. § 168(g)(3)(B). Some of these special class lives provide the same recovery period as is provided by the ordinary version of MACRS. For example, the recovery period for automobiles, light general purpose trucks, and qualified technological equipment is five years under both ordinary MACRS and under the alternative system. 168(e)(3)(B), 168(g)(3)(C), (D). The recovery periods for categories of assets for the purpose of the alternative depreciation system are set forth in Rev. Proc. 87–56.

¶ 22A.3461. **Properties for Which the Alternative System is Required.** The properties for which the alternative depreciation system must be used are listed in § 168(g)(1)(A)–(D). They include among others: tangible property used predominantly outside the United States in that taxable year, property which was financed by tax-exempt bonds, and certain properties that are leased to a tax-exempt entity.

In addition, if certain specified properties (referred to as "listed properties") are used only partly for a business purpose and if the business use constitutes 50% or less of the TP's use, the depreciation for the portion of the property that is employed in the business is determined under the alternative depreciation system. § 280F(b)(1), (3). The "listed properties" are described in § 280F(d)(4). Subject to certain exceptions, they include passenger automobiles, other transportation means, and computers. An employee's use of listed property in connection with his employment is not treated as a business use of that property unless such use is for the convenience of the employer and is required as a condition of employment. § 280F(d)(3)(A).

¶ 22A.3462. **Election.** When an item of property is not required to be depreciated on the alternative system, the TP can elect to use that system. § 168(g)(7). For buildings, this

---

41. See Rev. Proc. 87–56, at ¶ **22A.3411**; § 168(g)(2)(C).

election can be made on a building by building basis; for other properties, the election must be made for an entire MACRS classification of property. The election is made for a single taxable year. If another election is desired for the next year, it must be made anew. Once made, the election is irrevocable.

¶ 22A.3463. **Corporations' Earnings and Profits.** The alternative depreciation system serves an important function in measuring the amount of corporate distributions to shareholders that are treated as dividend income to the shareholders. A "dividend" from a corporation is a distribution made by the corporation on account of its outstanding stock to the extent that the distribution is made out of the corporation's "earnings and profits." §§ 301(c)(1), 316(a). "Earnings and profits" is a term of art that refers to the accumulated earnings of the corporation as measured in a special manner so as to more accurately represent economic reality. The depreciation deductions for computing a corporation's earnings and profits is determined by using the alternative system of depreciation regardless of whether the corporation's depreciation was determined for taxable income purposes under either the ordinary MACRS or the alternative system. § 312(k)(3).

¶ 22A.3464. **Minimum Tax.** As noted in ¶ **28.2211**, the alternative minimum tax that is imposed by § 55 uses the 150 percent declining balance method for many properties.

¶ 22A.3470. **Optional Tables.** In Rev. Proc. 87–57, the Commissioner has provided tables that set forth the amount of depreciation deduction allowable in each year of an item's recovery period under various depreciation methods, recovery periods, and conventions. The depreciation for a year is determined by multiplying the appropriate percentage listed in the table times the *unadjusted* basis of the asset. The TP is given the option to use these tables. The tables include depreciation schedules for the alternative depreciation system and for the alternative minimum tax as well as for the ordinary MACRS depreciation system. Note that the tables in the Revenue Procedure for the ordinary MACRS depreciation of a nonresidential building are no longer applicable because they do not reflect the 1988 expansion of the recovery period for such properties to 39 years.

¶ 22A.3480. **Luxury Automobiles.** Section 280F imposes dollar ceilings on the amount of annual depreciation deductions and rental deductions that are allowable for the business use of passenger automobiles. For this purpose, the expense deduction allowed by § 179 is treated as depreciation and so is subject (along with actual depreciation) to those ceilings. § 280F(d)(1).

¶ 22A.3490. Disposition of MACRS Property. When MACRS property is sold in a taxable transaction, the depreciation allowable to the seller in the year of disposition turns on the convention that is applicable to that property (i.e., half-year, midquarter, or mid-month). See **¶ 22A.3440.** The convention that applies to the property is the same as the convention that was applied to the property when it was first placed into service or use. Treas. Reg. § 1.168(d)–1(c). However, if MACRS property is disposed of in the same taxable year that it was acquired, no depreciation is allowable to the TP. See Treas. Reg. § 1.168(i)–4(c). The buyer will commence depreciating the purchased property by referring to his basis in the property and by using his applicable method, convention, and recovery period.

¶ 22A.3491. Disposition of MACRS Property in a Nonrecognition Transaction. When MACRS property is disposed of in a nonrecognition transaction of a type listed in § 168(i)(7)(B), the transferee steps into the shoes of the transferor and continues to depreciate the property as if he were the transferor. Prop. Reg. § 1.168–5(b). The types of transactions to which this provision applies include certain transfers between a partnership and a partner, and between a corporation and a shareholder. This provision applies only to so much of the transferee's basis in the MACRS asset as does not exceed the transferor's basis. Prop. Reg. § 1.168–5(b)(1). To the extent that the transferee's basis in the MACRS asset exceeds the transferor's, the transferee can depreciate that excess amount of the basis as if it were newly purchased property. Prop. Reg. § 1.168–5(b)(7). To the extent that the transferee's basis does not exceed the transferor's basis, and if the transferor and transferee use the same taxable year, the depreciation allowance for the year of disposition is allocated between the transferor and the transferee in proportion to their holding period in that year (utilizing only whole months). See Prop. Reg. § 1.168–5(b)(4).

If a TP makes a gift of MACRS property to a donee who holds the property for a business or income-producing use, the Proposed Regulations apply the same treatment for determining the donee's depreciation of the property, and the allocation of depreciation for the year in which the gift was made, as the one described above for certain nonrecognition transactions between partnerships and partners and between corporations and shareholders. Prop. Reg. § 1.168–5(f)(3).

If a TP acquires MACRS property in exchange for MACRS property that the TP held, and if the exchange is a like-kind transaction to which § 1031 applies, the method for depreciating the newly acquired property is set forth in Notice 2000–4.[42] For so much of the basis of the acquired MACRS property as does not exceed the basis of the MACRS property transferred by the TP, the TP will be allowed the same depreciation deductions as would have been allowable for the transferred property if the exchange had not taken place. If the TP's basis in the acquired MACRS property exceeds the basis that the TP had in the transferred property, that excess amount of TP's basis is depreciable as newly purchased MACRS property under whatever method TP chooses that is permitted by the MACRS rules. See also, Prop. Reg. § 1.168–5(f)(2).

If MACRS property of a TP is involuntarily converted, and if the TP reinvests some or all of the proceeds of the conversion in MACRS property that qualifies some or all of the TP's gain from the conversion for nonrecognition under § 1033, the method for depreciating the newly acquired property is set forth in Notice 2000–4.[43] For so much of the basis of the acquired MACRS property as does not exceed the basis of the converted MACRS property, the TP will be allowed the same depreciation deductions as would have been allowable for the converted property if the conversion had not taken place. If the TP's basis in the acquired MACRS property exceeds the basis that the TP had in the converted property, that excess amount of TP's basis is depreciable as newly purchased MACRS property under whatever method TP chooses that is permitted by the MACRS rules. It would seem that the depreciation for the converted property in the year of conversion and for the replacement property in the year of replacement will apply only to the portion of those years in which the property is in the service or use of the TP. See, Prop. Reg. § 1.168–5(f)(1).

42. 2000–1 C.B. 313. See Chapter **Twenty–Four** for a discussion of the operation of § 1031.

43. 2000–1 C.B. 313. See Chapter **Twenty–Four** for a discussion of the operation of § 1033.

¶ 22A.3500. Conversion of Property From Personal To Business or Income–Producing Use. If property that was held for personal use is converted to business or income-producing use in a taxable year, the property will be depreciable as if it were first placed in service on the date of the conversion. Treas. Reg. § 1.168(i)–4(b). The basis to be used in beginning to depreciate the property is the *lesser* of its adjusted basis or its fair market value at the time of conversion. Id. Note that if the TP's personal use of certain properties comprises 50% or more of a taxable year, the limitations on depreciation deductions imposed by § 280F may apply to that year. See ¶ 22A.3461.

¶ 22A.3510. Illustration. In Year One, G purchased an automobile for $20,000 for her personal use. On March 12, Year Three, G began to use the automobile exclusively in her business which is conducted by her as a self-employed person. The conversion of the automobile from personal to business use makes the automobile depreciable under MACRS. G's basis in the automobile at the time of conversion was still $20,000, but the fair market value of the automobile at that date was $12,000. G can depreciate the automobile under MACRS in Year Three and thereafter, but she must use the lower fair market value of $12,000 as the basis to be depreciated. Unless G purchased other MACRS property for her business that required use of the mid-quarter convention, G will use the half-year convention for the Year Three's depreciation for the automobile. G can use whatever method of depreciation and recovery period that MACRS would permit for newly acquired property.

¶ 22A.3600. Conversion of Property From Business or Income–Producing Use To Personal Use. If MACRS property that was used in a business or income-producing activity is converted to personal use, it will be treated as a disposition of the property. Treas. Reg. § 1.168(i)–4(c). A fraction of the depreciation that would have been allowable for use of the property in the year of conversion if no conversion had occurred is allowable to the TP. The fraction is equal to the percentage of the whole months in that year that the TP is deemed to have used the MACRS property for business or income-producing purposes, utilizing the applicable convention to determine the number of months that the property was so used. Id. The conversion of the property does not cause the TP to recognize gain or loss; nor is there any recapture of depreciation under §§ 1245 or 1250. Id. However, §§ 1245 or 1250 will apply to a subsequent disposition of the converted property. Id. No depreciation is allowed for MACRS property that is placed in service and then disposed of in the same taxable year. Id.

Note that if the TP's personal use of certain properties comprises 50% or more of a taxable year, the limitations on depreciation deductions imposed by § 280F may apply to that year. See ¶ **22A.3461**. Note also that if the TP had expensed any of the cost of the property under § 179 when he purchased it, the conversion may cause the TP to recapture some of that deduction under § 179(d)(10). See ¶ **22A.2100**.

CHAPTER TWENTY-THREE

MISCELLANEOUS CREDITS AND DEDUCTIONS

¶ 23.0000. MISCELLANEOUS CREDITS AND DEDUCTIONS.

¶ 23.1000. CREDITS AND DEDUCTIONS IN GENERAL. A tax credit is deducted from a TP's tax liability in contrast to a tax deduction which is deducted from either the TP's gross income or his adjusted gross income (AGI). Thus, each dollar of tax credit allowed a TP is a full dollar of benefit to him, while the dollar of benefit of a deduction depends upon the TP's marginal tax bracket. Some tax credits provide a refund for a TP whose tax liability is less than the amount of his credit while others do not. For some credits, an unused credit can be carried back or forward to other taxable years and utilized in those years. See, e.g., § 39.

¶ 23.1100. Examples of Tax Credits and Deductions. Several examples of tax credits include the nonrefundable dependent care credit, the refundable earned income credit, and the Hope and Lifetime Learning Credits. The credit for the return of income held under a claim of right is discussed in Chapter **Eight**. The two miscellaneous deductions discussed in this chapter are net operating losses and depletion.

¶ 23.2000. INVESTMENT TAX CREDIT. The regular investment credit, which was repealed by the Tax Reform Act of 1986, allowed a TP a credit for an investment in certain qualified tangible personal property used in the TP's trade or business. The amount of investment credit allowed for such purposes was a percentage, generally ten percent, of the *basis* of *new* property or of the *cost* of *used* property placed in service in the TP's business during the taxable year.

While the former regular investment credit has been eliminated, an investment credit is still permitted for a few specified expenses. § 38(a)(2), (b)(1). Section 38 provides for a business tax credit, which is comprised of some 35 credits of which an investment tax credit is one. The current investment credit is comprised of several separate credits including the rehabilitation credit and the energy credit. § 46. See §§ 47 (the rehabilitation credit) and 48 (the energy credit).

The basis of the property with respect to which an investment credit was allowed will be reduced by all or a portion of the amount of that credit. § 50(c). A reduction of basis under that provision is treated as depreciation deduction for purposes of applying the recapture of depreciation rules of §§ 1245 and 1250. § 50(c)(4).

Any unused business tax credit, including the investment tax credit, can be carried back one year and carried forward for twenty years. § 39(a). The credit is carried to earliest years first. § 39(a)(2).

¶ 23.3000. EARNED INCOME CREDIT. A refundable credit, referred to as the "earned income credit" is provided for the purpose of reducing the tax burden of certain low income individuals who earn income from providing services. § 32. An individual who is eligible to receive the credit is referred to as an "eligible individual."[1] The credit is available only to those eligible individuals who have "earned income" and whose total income for that year is below stated boundaries. To that end, if the amount of an eligible individual's adjusted gross income (or the amount of the individual's earned income if that is greater) for a taxable year exceeds a specified figure, the credit is phased out by a specified percentage of that excess. § 32(a). In general, an individual's "earned income" refers to income produced by the individual's services or work as contrasted to income produced from investments or otherwise from capital.[2]

The credit is disallowed if the TP's aggregate amount of "disqualified income" for a taxable year exceeds a specified figure, which figure is adjusted annually for cost-of-living increases. § 32(i), (j). For the year 2011, the specified figure is $3,150.[3] Disqualified income refers to certain types of investment income including dividends, interest (both taxable and tax-exempt), net capital gains, and the net passive activity income as defined in § 469. § 32(i)(2).

¶ 23.3100. Determination of Credit. An "eligible individual"[4] who has a sufficiently low amount of adjusted gross income is allowed a refundable credit for a percentage of his "earned income."[5] The percentage that is applied to the eligible individual's earned

---

1. See ¶ **23.3130** for the requirements to qualify as an eligible individual.
2. See ¶ **23.3120.**
3. Rev. Proc. 2011–12, Sec. 2.04(2).
4. See ¶ **23.3130** for a definition of eligible individual.
5. See ¶ **23.3120.** for a definition of "earned income."

income to determine the amount of credit is referred to as the "credit percentage." The amount of the credit percentage depends upon the number of "qualifying children"[6] that the eligible individual has in that year. In most years, there are three categories for applying credit percentages; they are for eligible individuals with one qualifying child, two or more qualifying children or no qualifying child. For the years 2009 through 2012, a fourth category was added for eligible individuals with three or more qualifying children. For the year 2011, the credit percentage that is applicable for an eligible individual is: 34% if the eligible individual has one qualifying child, 40% if the individual has two qualifying children, 45% if the eligible individual has three or more qualifying children, and 7.65% if the individual has no qualifying child.[7] § 32(b)(1)(A), (3)(A) as amended Section 101(c) of Public Law 111–312.

The statute imposes a ceiling on the amount of an eligible individual's earned income that can be used to establish the amount of the individual's earned income credit. § 32(a)(1). In other words, the amount of an individual's earned income that can be multiplied times the credit percentage is limited to a maximum figure. This maximum figure is referred to as the "earned income amount." The earned income amount depends upon the number of qualifying children that the eligible individual has in that year.[8]

The amount of an individual's credit is reduced by a percentage (referred to as the "phaseout percentage") of the excess of the individual's adjusted gross income (or earned income if that is greater) over a specified amount. § 32(a). The specified amount is referred to as the "phaseout amount." The amounts of the phaseout percentage and of the phaseout amount depend upon the number of qualifying children that the individual has in that taxable year.[9] Note that the dollar figure of the phaseout amount for each such year will be increased to reflect changes in the cost of living (i.e., the figures will be indexed to reflect inflation). § 32(j).

Since there is a ceiling on the amount of earned income that can be used to establish an earned income credit (the earned income amount), that results in there being a ceiling on the amount of credit

6. See ¶ 23.3140 for a definition of a qualifying child.

7. See ¶ 23.3150.

8. The earned income amounts for different categories of eligible individuals are set forth in ¶ 23.3110.

9. The schedule of the phaseout percentages and the phaseout amounts for different categories of eligible individuals is set forth in ¶ 23.3160.

that an eligible individual can obtain in a taxable year. For example, for the year 2011, the *maximum* amount of earned income credit that an eligible individual with one qualifying child can obtain is $3,094—i.e., the product of multiplying 34% (the credit percentage for that category) times $9,100 (the earned income amount for that category).

¶ 23.3110. Earned Income Amount. As noted above, the "earned income amount" is the maximum amount of earned income that can be used to determine an individual's earned income credit. While there normally are three categories of eligible individuals for the schedule of earned income amounts, for the years 2009 through 2012, there are four categories. The scheduled dollar figures for the earned income amount is indexed for inflation. § 32(j).

For a taxable year beginning in 2011, the earned income amounts for the four categories of eligible individuals and the maximum amount of credit such individuals can have are as follows:[10]

Eligible Individual	Earned Income Amount	Maximum Credit
No Qualifying Child	$6,070	$464
One Qualifying Child	$9,100	$3,094
Two Qualifying Children	$12,780	$5,112
Three or More Qualifying Children	$12,780	$5,751

¶ 23.3120. Earned Income. The term "earned income" means wages, salaries, tips, other employee compensation, and a TP's net earnings from self-employment (as defined in § 1402) less one-half of the self-employment tax imposed by § 1401. § 32(c)(2). A number of items are excluded from earned income. For example, earned income is determined without regard to community property laws, and no amount received as a pension or annuity is taken into account. § 32(c)(2)(B). Also, earned income does not include unemployment compensation and workmen's compensation; and it is reduced by any net loss from self employment. Treas. Reg. § 1.32–2(c)(2).

¶ 23.3130. Eligible Individual. An individual who has at least one qualifying child[11] is an "eligible individual" for that taxable

---

10.   Rev. Proc. 2011–12, Sec. 2.04(1).

11.   See ¶ 23.3140 for a definition of the term "qualifying child."

year. § 32(c)(1)(A). An individual who does not have a qualifying child for the taxable year will nevertheless qualify as an eligible individual if the following three requirements are satisfied:

(1) the individual's principal place of abode was in the United States for more than one-half of the taxable year,

(2) before the close of the taxable year, the individual (or the individual's spouse) attained his or her 25th birthday but did not attain 65 years of age, and

(3) the individual does not qualify under § 151 as a dependent exemption deduction[12] for another TP for that year. § 32(c)(1).

Note that in the third requirement listed above, it is the individual's *qualification* for a dependent exemption deduction that precludes that individual, who has no qualified children, from being an eligible individual; it does not matter for this purpose whether the other TP claimed such a deduction on account of the individual.

Certain persons are precluded from qualifying as an eligible individual. See § 32(c)(1)(B), (C), and (D). For example, an individual who is a qualifying child of another TP for a calendar year that begins within the individual's taxable year cannot qualify as an eligible individual for his taxable year.

¶ 23.3140.   **Qualifying Child.** Since 2005, the Code has provided a uniform definition[13] of the term "qualifying child" for several Code provisions including the earned income credit. A qualifying child is defined in § 152(c), but the earned income credit provision makes several modifications to that uniform definition. § 32(c)(3).

The uniform definition of a qualified child is much broader than that term would indicate. It includes a child of the TP and a descendant of that child; and it also includes a brother, sister, stepbrother and stepsister of the TP and descendants of those relatives. There are additional requirements that must be met to be a qualified child. One of those requirements is that the "child" must either (1) have not attained the age of 19 years by the close of the year, (2) be a student (as defined in § 152(f)(2)) who has not attained the age of 24 before the close of the year, or (3) be

---

12.   See Chapter **Eleven** for the meaning of that term.

13.   See Chapter **Eleven** for a description of that uniform definition.

totally and permanently disabled at any time during that year. § 152(c)(3). In addition, there is a residence requirement and a support requirement, but those two requirements are modified or eliminated by § 32(c)(3) for purposes of the determining the earned income credit.

For purposes of the earned income credit, the uniform definition is modified as follows:

(1) there is no requirement that the "child" not have provided over one-half of his support (i.e., the "support test" of § 152(c)(1)(D) does not apply).

(2) the special rules for children of divorced parents (§ 152(e)) do not apply,

(3) the requirement in § 152(c)(1)(B) that the individual occupy the same principal place of abode as the TP for one-half of the year is satisfied only if that abode is in the United States (however, the principal place of abode of a member of the Armed Forces is treated as being in the United States for any period during which that person is stationed outside of the United States while serving on extended duty),

(4) an individual who is married at the end of a taxable year cannot be a qualifying child of the TP unless the TP is entitled to a dependent exemption deduction for that individual under § 151 (or would be entitled to a deduction if it were not for § 152(e)).

¶ **23.3150. Credit Percentage.** As previously stated, the percentage that is multiplied times an individual's earned income in order to arrive at the earned income credit is referred to as the "credit percentage." The amount of the credit percentage depends upon the number of qualifying children that the eligible individual has in that taxable year, and it depends upon the year for which the credit is utilized. While normally there are three categories of eligible individuals for applying the schedule of credit percentages, for the years 2009 through 2012, there are four categories. The following schedule sets forth the credit percentages for a years beginning in 2011 for the four categories of eligible individuals for that year (§ 32(b)(1)(A), (3)(A)).

Eligible Individual.	**Credit Percentage**
No qualifying child	7.65%
One qualifying child	34%
Two qualifying children	40%
Three or more qualifying children	45%

¶ 23.3160. **Phaseout of Credit.** An individual's earned income credit is phased out when the individual's adjusted gross income (or earned income if greater) for that taxable year exceeds a threshold figure. The threshold figure is referred to as the "phaseout amount." § 32(a)(2)(B). The phaseout of the credit is accomplished by reducing the earned income credit by the product of multiplying a specified percentage (referred to as the "phaseout percentage") times the excess of the individual's adjusted gross income (or earned income if greater) over the phaseout amount. The phaseout amounts are set by schedules and are indexed for inflation. The amounts of the phaseout percentage are determined by a statutory schedule that establishes those figures according to the number of qualified children that the eligible individual has. § 32(b)(1). The schedule contains three categories of eligible individuals.

In the years 2009 through 2012, there is an increase in the phaseout amount for married TPs who file a joint income tax return. § 32(c)(2)(B), (3)(B) as amended by Section 103(c) of Public Law 111–312. The following schedule sets forth the phaseout percentages and amounts for a year beginning in 2011 for the three categories of eligible individuals who do not file a joint tax return.

Eligible Individual	Phaseout Percentage	Phaseout Amount
No qualified child	7.65	$7,590
One qualified child	15.98	$16,690
Two or more qualified children	21.06	$16,690

The phaseout amounts for a TP filing as a Head of Household or as a Surviving Spouse are the same as those for a single TP. For the years 2009 through 2012, the phaseout amount for married TPs who file a joint income tax return is a little more than $5,000 greater than the phaseout amount for other TPs. § 32(b)(2)(B), (3)(B) as amended by Section 103(c) of Public Law 111–132. The additional amount for married TPs who file jointly is scheduled to expire in the year 2013.

¶ 23.3170. **Illustration.** In order to demonstrate how the credit operates, the determinations in this illustration are made without using tables provided by the Service for that purpose. See § 32(f). The calculations can be made much more easily by using the tables. Since the illustration takes place in 2010, the earned income amount and phaseout amount are slightly less than the 2011 figures listed above.

In 2010, B, a widow, had two children—a five-year old daughter and a two-year old son, both of whom live in B's home in the United States. Since B has qualified children, she is an eligible individual. In 2010, B had earned income of \$14,000, and she had adjusted gross income of \$17,000. B's disqualified income does not exceed the \$3,100 limitation so she does not violate that requirement.

Let us first calculate the credit (we will refer to as the "tentative credit") without taking into account the phaseout provisions. Before taking the phaseout into account, B has a tentative earned income credit of \$5,036. The tentative credit is determined by multiplying 40% (the applicable credit percentage) times \$12,590 (the earned income amount). Although B had earned income of \$14,000, the maximum amount that can be used in determining her credit is the earned income amount, which in this case is set at \$12,590.

The \$5,036 tentative credit is then reduced by the product of multiplying 21.06% (the phaseout percentage) times \$550 (i.e., the excess of \$17,000 (the greater of B's adjusted gross income and her earned income) over the statutory phaseout amount of \$16,450). Since 21.06% times \$550 = \$116 (rounded off), B's earned income credit for the year 2010 is \$4,920 (the difference between her tentative credit of \$5,036 and the \$116 phaseout reduction).

¶ 23.3200. **Refundable Credit.** Since the earned income credit is refundable, if the amount of an individual's credit exceeds the amount of that individual's tax liability, the excess will be refunded to the individual. § 6401(b)(1).

¶ 23.3300. **Married Individual.** If an eligible individual is married, the individual will not be allowed an earned income credit for a taxable year unless the individual files a joint income tax return for that taxable year. § 32(d). In certain circumstances described in § 7703(b), an individual who actually is married nevertheless is treated for tax purposes as an unmarried individual.[14]

¶ 23.3400. **Tables Provided by the Service.** To facilitate the computation of the earned income credit, § 32(f) requires the Service

14. See Chapter **Twelve**.

to provide tables which are to be used in determining the amount of an eligible individual's credit.

¶ 23.3500. Advance Receipt of A Portion of an Individual's Credit. An employee who has at least one qualifying child can require his employer to make an advance payment to him of a specified part of the earned income credit for which the employee likely will qualify at the end of the year. Such payments are not treated as additional compensation to the employee; instead, they are treated as if they were made out of withholding or FICA taxes that otherwise would be payable by the employer on behalf of the employee. § 3507.

¶ 23.4000. CREDIT FOR DEPENDENT AND CHILD CARE AND HOUSEHOLD SERVICES. If a TP has a young child that cannot be left unattended or has a dependent who is unable to care for himself, the TP cannot leave that individual to earn income unless he obtains the services of someone to take care of that person while the TP is away earning income. The question arose as to whether a TP in that situation can deduct the cost of caring for the child or dependent as a business expense since the TP could not be free to earn business income if he did not incur the expense of providing care for that individual. The courts rejected that contention and held that no deduction is allowable.[15]

While the expense of caring for such an individual is a necessary cost of freeing the TP from that burden so he can earn income, it also is an expense incurred to satisfy a personal obligation of the TP. It is a kind of hybrid expenditure—partly connected to business and partly to personal obligations.[16] Such costs are analogous to commuting expenses which are not deductible[17] even though a TP is not able to earn income unless he travels from his residence to his place of work.

The business overtones of those expenses and of related household expenses were sufficiently compelling, however, to induce Congress to provide tax relief in certain circumstances. For taxable years prior to 1976, the Code allowed a limited amount of deduction for such expenses, but that provision was repealed by the 1976 TRA. In place of that deduction, the 1976 Act substituted a nonrefundable tax credit, which is set forth in § 21. The credit is allowed only to an individual who meets specified requirements.

---

15. E.g., *Smith v. Commissioner*, 40 B.T.A. 1038 (1939), aff'd per curiam, 113 F.2d 114 (2d Cir. 1940).

16. See § 262 denying a deduction for "personal, living, or family expenses."

17. Treas. Reg. §§ 1.162–2(e), 1.262–1(b)(5).

One requirement is that if a TP is married at the close of a taxable year, no credit will be allowed unless the TP and his spouse file a joint income tax return. § 21(e)(2). Under certain circumstances, married TPs who are separated are treated as if they are not married for purposes of this provision. § 21(e)(3), (4).

If the amount of the credit exceeds the TP's tax liability, the excess is not refundable and cannot be carried to any other year.

¶ 23.4100. **Qualifying Individual.** The nonrefundable credit is allowed only to a TP for whom there is at least one "qualifying individual." A "qualifying individual" is a person who is either (1) a "qualified child" of the TP as defined in § 152(a)(1) who has not attained the age of 13 years, or (2) a dependent of the TP, as defined in § 152 with modifications, or a spouse of the TP. For a spouse or dependent of the TP (other than a qualified child) to be a qualifying individual, he must be physically or mentally incapable of caring for himself and must have the same place of abode as the TP for more than one-half of the taxable year. § 21(b)(1).

The reference to a "qualified child" in § 152 has a much broader scope than that term would indicate. It not only includes a child of the TP; it also includes descendants of such a child; and it also includes a brother, sister, stepbrother, or stepsister of the TP and a descendant of any such relative. § 152(c)(2). In addition, the "child" must meet other requirements including the requirements (1) that the "child" must have the same place of abode as the TP for more than one-half of the taxable year, (2) that the "child" must not have provided over one-half of his own support for the calendar year in which the TP's taxable year begins, and (3) that the "child" must either (i) have not attained the age of 19 years by the close of the year, (ii) be a student who has not attained the age of 24 before the close of the year, or (iii) be totally and permanently disabled at any time during that year. § 152(c)(1), (3).

The "dependent" defined in § 152 refers to either a "qualifying child" or a "qualifying relative" of the TP. A "qualifying relative" must have a relationship to the TP within one of the categories listed in § 152(d)(2), and those relationships include all of the relationships that comprise the "qualified child" category as well as a number of other relationships. Consequently, an individual could be both a qualifying child and a qualifying relative of a TP, or the individual could fall within only one of those categories. There are additional requirements for being a qualified relative, but some of those requirements do not apply for purposes of determining whether a person is a qualifying individual under § 21. § 21(b)(1)(B). For example, for purposes of § 21, there is no requirement that the individual's gross income cannot exceed a specified amount. See §§ 21(b)(1)(B), and 152(d)(1)(B).

¶ 23.4200. Amount of the Credit. The credit is a percentage of the so-called "employment-related expenses," the meaning of which term is explained below,[18] of a TP who qualifies for the credit. The percentage figure ranges from 20% to 35%, depending upon the size of the TP's AGI. The general figure is 35%, but that figure is reduced by one percentage point for each $2,000 (or fraction thereof) by which the TP's AGI for that year exceeds $15,000. However, the percentage figure cannot be less than 20% so that is the minimum figure. The 35% figure and the $15,000 figure are scheduled to be reduced to 30% and $10,000 respectively for years beginning after 2012.

¶ 23.4300. Employment–Related Expenses. Employment-related expenses are the expenses incurred for household services and for the care of a qualifying individual if such expenses are incurred to permit the TP to be gainfully employed during a period for which there is at least one qualifying individual with respect to the TP. § 21(b)(2). Such expenses incurred for services outside the TP's household are taken into account only if incurred on behalf of a qualifying child who is under the age of 13 or on behalf of a qualifying relative who regularly spends at least eight hours each day in the TP's household. § 21(b)(2)(B). Expenses of outside care are included if provided at a "dependent care center" as defined in § 21(b)(2)(C) and (D). Expenses incurred for a qualifying individual to attend a camp are not included unless the individual spends overnight in the camp. § 21(b)(2)(A).

Expenses incurred for dependent care services are not counted if the person performing the services either (1) qualifies for a dependent exemption deduction for the TP or his spouse, or (2) is a child of the TP who is under the age of 19 years at the end of the year. § 21(e)(6).

There are limitations on the amount of employment-related expenses that can be taken into account. There are specified dollar limitations, and those dollar amounts will be reduced in certain circumstances. Those limitations are described below.

18. See ¶ 23.4300.

¶ 23.4400. Limitations on Employment–Related Expenses Taken Into Account.

¶ 23.4410. Dollar Limit. The amount of employment-related expenses incurred in a taxable year that is taken into account under § 21 cannot exceed $3,000 if the TP has only one qualifying individual for that year, or $6,000 if the TP has more than one qualifying individual for that year. § 21(c). Those dollar figures are subject to reduction in several circumstances described below.

Note that dependent care assistance provided by an employer to an employee is excluded from the employee's gross income by § 129 if the conditions of that provision are satisfied. The maximum amount of such assistance that the employee can exclude from income is $5,000, and that amount is not subject to any reduction because of the size of the employee's AGI. The dollar limits on employment-related expenses described above are reduced, dollar-for-dollar, for the value of dependent care assistance that the TP received from his employer and excluded from gross income under § 129. § 21(c).

¶ 23.4420. Earned Income Limitation. The amount of a TP's employment-related expenses that are taken into account under § 21 cannot exceed: (1) the "earned income" of the TP for that year if the TP is not married at the end of the taxable year, or (2) if the TP is married at the end of the taxable year, the *lesser* of the TP's earned income for that year and the earned income of the TP's spouse for that year. "Earned income" has the same meaning as it has in § 32(c).[19] Treas. Reg. § 1.21–2(b)(3).

If no relief were provided, that provision would prevent any credit to a married couple where one of the spouses is a full-time student who therefore has no earned income. Similarly, if the spouse is a qualifying individual, the spouse may very well have no earned income. To mitigate that hardship, the Code provides that a spouse who is a full-time student at an educational institution or is a qualifying individual is deemed to have earned income for that year of no less than a specified dollar amount. § 21(d). For the years 2011 and 2012, the minimum dollar amount is $250 if there is only one qualifying individual, and $500 if there is more than one qualifying individual. Unless Congress acts, those figures are scheduled to be reduced to $200 and $400 respectively for taxable years beginning after 2012.

---

19. For the definition used by § 32(c), see ¶ **23.3120**.

¶ 23.4500. Illustrations.

¶ 23.4510. Illustration 1. In 2011, G is not married and has a five-year old child who is a qualifying individual. In that year, G has AGI of $15,000, all of which is earned income. G received no dependent care assistance from his employer. G has child care expenses of $4,000 all of which were incurred to permit G to be employed. The maximum amount of employment-related expenses that G can take into account is $3,000 since he has only one qualifying individual. Since G's AGI does not exceed $15,000, there is no reduction of the percentage applied in determining his credit. G is allowed a credit equal to 35% x $3,000 = $1,050. Since the child is under the age of 13 and is a qualifying child, it does not matter whether the child care was performed in G's household or outside of it.

¶ 23.4520. Illustration 2. The same facts as those stated in **¶ 23.4510** except that G had two young children under the age of 6 years, both of whom are qualifying individuals. The total amount of child care expenses were $4,000, and G incurred household cleaning expenses of $1,000. All of those expenses were incurred to permit G to be employed. G's total employment-related expenses are $5,000. The dollar limit on those expenses that can be taken into account is greater than that amount (i.e., it is $6,000). So, G is allowed a credit of 35% x $5,000 = $1,750. If the amount of that credit exceeds G's tax liability, the excess amount is not refundable and cannot be carried to any other year.

¶ 23.4530. Illustration 3. The same facts as those stated in **¶ 23.4520** except that G's AGI for that year was $26,000. The percentage that is multiplied times G's employment-related expenses of $5,000 is reduced one percentage point for each $2,000, or part thereof, that the TP's AGI exceeds $15,000. As to G's AGI, there are five separate $2,000 increments above $15,000 plus another $1,000, which is part of a sixth increment. Consequently, the 35% percentage figure is reduced by six percentage points to 29%. The credit amount then is 29% × $5,000 = $1,450.

¶ 23.5000. HOPE CREDIT (AMERICAN OPPORTUNITY TAX CREDIT) AND LIFETIME LEARNING CREDIT. The Code provides two separate credits for qualified higher education costs.

For the years 2011 and 2012, the Hope Scholarship Credit, currently referred to as the American Opportunity Tax Credit (AOTC), provides a credit for a percentage of the qualified tuition and related expenses of an eligible student for the first four years of postsecondary education. § 25A(i). The credit equals 100% of $2,000 of such expenses and 25% of the next $2,000 of such expenses. So, the maximum credit for a year is $2,500. The credit is available for only four years. If the TP's AGI exceeds a figure determined under a formula, the amount of the credit is reduced. § 25A(i)(4). If the credit exceeds the TP's tax liability, with some exceptions, a portion of the credit is refundable.

For years after 2012, the amount of the Hope credit will be lower, it will not be refundable, and it can be taken for only two years. The AGI reduction provision will kick in at a lower figure, but those figures will be indexed for inflation. The amount of the credit will be 100% of $1,000 of qualified expenses, and 50% of the next $1,000; but those $1,000 figures also will be indexed for inflation. § 25A(h)

The Lifetime Learning Credit provides a credit equal to 20% of qualified tuition and related expenses for education that was incurred in a taxable year subject to a ceiling of $10,000 of expenses per year. Consequently, the maximum amount of the credit for one year is $2,000 per TP (i.e., it does not depend on the number of eligible students in the TP's family). § 25A(c). The amount of the credit is phased out for TPs with an AGI above a specified amount, and those phase-out figures are indexed for inflation. § 25A(d), (h).

¶ **23.6000. OTHER CREDITS.** The Code provides credits for a variety of expenses (e.g., an adoption credit [§ 23]; a child tax credit [§ 24]; a credit for increasing research activities [§ 41]; a credit for the acquisition, rehabilitation, or construction of low-income housing [§ 42]; and a credit for the elderly and for the permanently and totally disabled [§ 22].)

¶ **23.7000. NET OPERATING LOSS CARRYOVER AND CARRYBACK.** Because income and deductions are reported annually, in the absence of a statutory exception, a TP cannot use a deduction allowable in one tax year to offset income reportable in another tax year.[20] This principle falls under the so-called "annual accounting" rule. To mitigate the harshness of the annual accounting rule, Congress permits a carryover and a carryback of a "net operating loss" to other tax years when the loss can be deducted. § 172. This puts the tax treatment of businesses that have fluctuating income on a par with businesses that have stable income. In general, subject to a few exceptions, a net operating loss (NOL) can be carried back for two years prior to the year of loss and

---

20. *Burnet v. Sanford & Brooks Co.*, 282 U.S. 359 (1931).

carried forward for twenty years after the loss was incurred. Thus, the loss is deductible over a span of twenty-three years.

¶ 23.7100. Computation. A net operating loss for a taxable year is computed by determining the TP's taxable income for that year with certain modifications described in § 172(d). For example, applying § 172(d), the deduction for exemptions under § 151 is disallowed, and, with certain exceptions, nonbusiness deductions can be used to reduce only nonbusiness income. The net operating loss will usually be less than the loss a TP shows on his return in computing his taxable income because of the modifications required by § 172(d).

¶ 23.7200. Types of Losses Deductible. Generally, a net operating loss, which may be carried over to offset income of other years, includes:

(a) losses from the operation of a business;

(b) losses from sales, exchanges or involuntary conversions of assets used in a trade or business;

(c) casualty and theft losses on property *not* used in a trade or business allowed under § 165(c)(2) or (3).

¶ 23.7300. Chronology of Carryover. Subject to a few exceptions, a net operating loss is carried back two years and forward twenty years from the year that the loss was incurred. § 172(b)(1)(A). It must be carried first to the second preceding year, and any loss not offset against income is applied to reduce income of the subsequent years in chronological order. However, a TP can elect not to carry back a net operating loss, and if the TP so elects, the TP will only carry forward such loss for twenty years. § 172(b)(3).

¶ 23.8000. DEPLETION. The owner of a natural deposit or other wasting asset (e.g., oil, gas, minerals, gravel, timber) is entitled to a depletion deduction to offset his capital investment against the income from the sale or use of the asset. § 611.

¶ 23.8100. Depletable Property. Most natural deposits and certain other wasting assets, such as timber, are depletable.

¶ 23.8200. Economic Interest. A TP must have an "economic interest" in a depletable asset to be permitted a depletion deduction. Treas. Reg. § 1.611–1(b). "Economic interest" is a term of art defined in Treas. Reg. § 1.611–1(b). Generally, one has an economic interest if he must look to the extraction of the mineral or severance of the timber to recover his capital investment.[21]

¶ **23.8300.** **Methods of Depletion.** There are two methods of determining a deduction for depletion; the cost depletion method, and the percentage depletion method. The bulk of the political controversy over depletion allowances focuses on percentage depletion.

¶ **23.8310.** **Cost Depletion.** The cost depletion method is similar to the units of production method of depreciation.[22] The cost depletion method allocates a portion of the TP's cost or other basis for a wasting asset to the units of that asset sold or consumed during a tax year. The allocation is made by dividing the TP's adjusted basis in the asset at the beginning of the tax year by the estimated number of recoverable units (tons of ore, barrels of oil, board feet of timber, etc.) remaining as of the beginning of the tax year. The cost of each unit sold or consumed during the tax year is deducted from the income from the deposit or extract. Treas. Reg. § 1.611–2(a). The estimated number of recoverable units includes units that have been extracted from the property but which were not sold prior to the beginning of the tax year. Under the cost depletion method, the aggregate depletion deducted by a TP cannot exceed the TP's investment in the asset (i.e., his cost or other basis).

¶ **23.8311.** **Illustration 1.** In Year One, *X* purchased a deposit for $1,000,000 and determined that the number of recoverable units was 100,000 tons. *X* mined 30,000 tons in Year One, but *X* sold only 20,000 tons and stored the remaining 10,000 tons. *X*'s cost depletion for Year One is:

$$\frac{\$1,000,000 \text{ adjusted basis}}{100,000 \text{ recoverable units}} \times 20,000 \text{ units sold} = \$200,000 \text{ depletion deduction}$$

¶ **23.8312.** **Illustration 2.** In Year Two, *X* discovered that the number of remaining recoverable units in the deposit was 200,000 tons, including the 10,000 tons mined but unsold but excluding the 20,000 tons sold in Year One. *X* sold the 10,000 remaining units from its Year One activity, but *X* did not mine or sell any additional units in Year Two. *X*'s depletion allowance for Year Two is:

21. *Commissioner v. Southwest Exploration Co.*, 350 U.S. 308 (1956).

22. See Chapter **Twenty–Two**.

$$\frac{\$800{,}000 \text{ adjusted basis as of } 1/1/02}{200{,}000 \text{ recoverable units}} \times 10{,}000 \text{ units sold} = \$40{,}000 \text{ depreciation deduction}$$

¶ 23.8320. Percentage Depletion. Percentage depletion provides a deduction equal to a specified percentage of the TP's *gross* income from the depletable property during the tax year, but the deduction cannot exceed 50% of the taxable income from the property computed without the depletion allowance. The percentage of taxable income limitation is 100% for oil and gas properties. If the percentage depletion allowance in any year is less than the cost depletion allowance, the TP may use the cost depletion method for that year. § 613(a).

¶ 23.8321. Percentage Based on Type of Deposit. The percentage of gross income that may be deducted as a percentage depletion allowance depends upon the kind of deposit (e.g., the depletion percentage for sulphur and uranium is 22% of gross income; for gold and silver, 15%; and for gravel, peat and sand, only 5%). § 613(b). Percentage depletion is available only for those natural deposits listed in §§ 613(b) and 613A. Timber is not subject to percentage depletion.

With certain exceptions (particularly for small producers), there is no percentage depletion for oil and gas. § 613A(a), (c). Even for small producers, the percentage allowed for oil and gas depletion was scaled down for 1984 and subsequent years. § 613A(c). However, percentage depletion at 22% is allowed for regulated natural gas and natural gas sold under fixed contract. § 613A(b)(1).

¶ 23.8330. Cumulative Depletion Deduction Allowed in Excess of Taxpayer's Basis. Since percentage depletion is a percentage of gross income from the property, it is not limited to recovery of actual basis. The cumulative depletion deductions taken by a TP under the percentage depletion method may exceed the TP's capital investment in the asset. In this very important respect, percentage depletion is quite unlike depreciation, amortization, or even cost depletion.

PART E
SALE OR EXCHANGE OF PROPERTY

CHAPTER TWENTY–FOUR

REALIZATION AND RECOGNITION

¶ 24.1000. **REALIZATION OF GAIN OR LOSS ON THE DISPO-SITION OF PROPERTY.** A basic principle of tax law is that gain or loss is not included in or deducted from the gross income of a TP until it is "realized." While there are a few special circumstances in which unrealized income is included in gross income, realization typically is required, and the realization principle is a basic tenet of the tax law. The word *realized* is a term of art that refers to a significant event that represents the severance of gain from the property that produced the gain. See ¶¶ **1.7200–1.7220.**

The gain realized from the sale or other disposition of property is the excess of the amount realized over the TP's adjusted basis [the term "basis" is explained at ¶¶ **1.7300–1.7336–3**] in the property sold or otherwise transferred by him. If the TP's adjusted basis in the property exceeds the amount realized by him, then the difference is the amount of loss realized by the TP on the sale or other disposition. § 1001(a).

A realized gain or loss will be "recognized" by the TP for tax purposes unless a section of the Code (e.g., § 1031 for exchanges of certain kinds of property) provides that gain or loss will not be recognized. § 1001(c).[1]

It should be noted also that a recognized loss is not deductible from gross income unless some section of the Code authorizes a deduction (e.g., § 165 authorizes a deduction of many types of losses).

¶ 24.1100. **Recovery of Cost.** When a TP has an investment (or "basis") in property, only the amount realized in excess of his investment can constitute a gain. While there is no dispositive authority on the question, there is a view that the Constitution prohibits the taxation of a TP's recovery of his capital because such a tax would be a direct tax on his property and, therefore, invalid unless apportioned among the states by population. In effect, this view construes the term "income" in the Sixteenth Amendment as referring to gross income as contrasted to gross receipts. The Su-

---

1. Several such nonrecognition provisions are discussed in this chapter.

preme Court's decision in *Stanton v. Baltic Mining Co.*[2] (a case dealing with the depletion deduction allowable to a mining corporation) raises questions concerning the viability of that construction.

In *Baltic Mining*, the applicable income tax law permitted only a 5% depletion allowance on the sale of the ore in question, and the TP's actual cost for the ore was greater than the amount of deduction it obtained from the 5% depletion allowance. The TP objected that it should be permitted to deduct its actual cost of the ore since the application of the inadequate depletion allowance resulted in its being taxed on receipts that were merely a return of its capital investment and such a tax is an unconstitutional direct tax on its property.

The Court sustained the application of the income tax to the TP's receipts less the depletion allowance even though that allowance was inadequate to provide the TP a recovery of its capital. The language of the Court's opinion is less than illuminating—the Court even suggested that the tax is an excise tax (and therefore an indirect tax) on the privilege of conducting a mining operation—but the decision does not repudiate the view that a TP normally must be permitted to recover his cost. *Baltic Mining* can be explained on the ground that the allocation of the cost of a mine to the tons of ores mined and sold requires an estimate of the number of tons in the mine and this estimate is often too speculative to be reliable. When the determination of the cost of a ton of ore is so speculative, it is permissible for Congress to establish a specific depletion rate which is a reasonable rate on the basis of industry-wide experience even though a predetermined rate will produce hardships in some cases and windfalls in others. The interests of administrative convenience can preclude individual determinations of cost where the established rate is reasonable for the industry as a whole.[3]

> **¶ 24.1110. Gain Attributable to Inflation.** In many cases, much or all of the gain that is recognized by a TP on the sale of an asset is attributable to inflation and does not reflect an increase in true economic value. In other words, on the sale of an asset, a TP's receipt of more dollars than that initially expended for the asset some years earlier may be attributable to the declining value of a dollar during that period; that is, the purchas-

---

2.   240 U.S. 103 (1916).

   3.   *Penn Mutual Indemnity v. Commissioner*, 32 T.C. 653 (1959), aff'd, 277 F.2d 16 (3d Cir. 1960).

ing power of a dollar decreased so that the larger number of dollars that the TP received does not represent any greater purchasing power than the smaller number of dollars that the TP had initially invested in the asset. In *Hellermann v. Commissioner*,[4] the Tax Court held that gain due solely to inflation nevertheless constitutes income within the meaning of the Sixteenth Amendment; thus, the federal tax on such income is constitutional. Congress can establish the dollar as a unit of legal value independent of the purchasing power that a dollar might possess.

From time to time, proposals are made to adjust a TP's basis in property to reflect changes in the cost of living. If adopted, such proposals would preclude the imposition of an income tax on appreciation that is attributable to inflation. To date, no such proposal has been adopted.

¶ 24.1200. Cost Reflecting Unlawful Expenditure. Prior to the Tax Reform Act of 1969, business expenses were sometimes held to be nondeductible on the ground that the allowance of a deduction would frustrate public policy. In 1969, Congress expressly disallowed deductions for certain business expenses (e.g., illegal expenses). That statutory disallowance was intended to be exclusive; hence, the public policy exception no longer applies to business expenses (or profit-oriented expenses under § 212) that are not expressly barred by statute.[5] It is possible that the public policy exception continues to apply to deductions allowed for losses and for nonbusiness and nonprofit oriented expenses.[6]

In any event, in the absence of a statutory provision, the public policy exception generally will not apply to bar a TP from recovering his cost of an item on its disposition even though the cost represents an unlawful expenditure.[7] However, the availability of such costs as an offset to an amount realized may be barred by statute. In this regard, note that Treas. Reg. § 1.471–3(d) provides that the "cost" of an item "shall not include an amount which is of a type for which a deduction would be disallowed under section 162(c), (f) or (g) and the regulations thereunder in the case of a business expense."

4. 77 T.C. 1361 (1981).

5. See Treas. Reg. § 1.162–1(a) and ¶ **21.5000**.

6. *Mazzei v. Commissioner*, 61 T.C. 497 (1974); *Conley v. Commissioner*, 36 T.C.M. 1644 (1977); *Lincoln v. Commissioner*, 50 T.C.M. 185 (1985); see ¶¶ **18.1000, 21.5400** and **21.5500**.

7. *Sullenger v. Commissioner*, 11 T.C. 1076 (1948).

¶ **24.1300. Part–Gift, Part–Sale.** When a TP sells property for less than its value and the difference constitutes a gift to the purchaser (and not merely an arm's length bargain), the TP cannot realize a loss on the sale. Treas. Reg. § 1.1001–1(e). If the amount paid exceeds the TP's basis in the transferred property, the TP will recognize a gain in the amount of such excess. Treas. Reg. § 1.1001–1(e). Unless the part-gift, part-sale is made to a qualified charity, the TP's entire basis is allocated to the amount realized in determining his gain. If the part-gift, part-sale is made to a qualified charity, the TP's basis must be allocated between the portion that was sold and the portion that was given away. § 1011(b); see ¶¶ **20.3000–20.3100.**

¶ **24.1310. Illustration.** *X* sold Blackacre to his son, *S*, for $10,000. *X* had a basis of $30,000 in Blackacre, and the value of Blackacre at the time of sale was $25,000. The $15,000 difference between the value of Blackacre and the amount paid by *S* constitutes a gift to *S*. Even though *X* received an amount which was $20,000 less than his basis in Blackacre, *X* did not realize a loss on the sale.

¶ **24.1320. Disguised Sales.** In appropriate circumstances, a transfer for which no direct consideration is paid by the transferee nevertheless may be treated as part-gift, part-sale. For example, consider the transfer of encumbered property [discussed at ¶¶ **24.1510–24.1520**], and consider a transfer made subject to the transferee's payment of the gift tax [discussed at ¶ **24.1550**].

¶ **24.1400. Sale of a Term Interest.**

¶ **24.1410. Disregard of Basis.** When a TP sells or otherwise disposes of a "term interest in property" that the TP had acquired from a spouse or by gift or inheritance, then the TP's gain (or loss) is determined without allocating to the TP any part of the uniform basis of the property as determined under §§ 1014 (inheritance), 1015 (gifts), or 1041 (transfer from a spouse or former spouse). In determining the gain from such a sale, the TP's basis in the term interest will be zero. § 1001(e). The effect of this provision is to treat the entire proceeds received from the sale of certain term interests as income to the vendor. The significance of this provision is noted in an illustration at ¶ **27.3320.**

Note that § 273 prohibits a depreciation or amortization deduction for a term interest that was acquired by gift, bequest or inheritance. Also, § 167(e) precludes a depreciation or amortization deduction for a TP's term interest for any period during which the remainder interest in such property is held (directly or indirectly) by a person related to the TP (i.e., a person bearing a relationship to the TP described in § 267(b) or (e)). When § 167(e) applies, the disallowed depreciation or amortization deduction nevertheless reduces the TP's basis in his term interest. § 167(e)(3)(A). With a few exceptions, the amount of the disallowed deduction that reduces the TP's basis in the term interest will be added to the remainderman's basis in his interest. § 167(e)(3)(B), (4)(A). The overlap of §§ 167 and 273 is cured by granting priority to § 273; hence, § 167(e) does not apply to a term interest if § 273 is applicable. § 167(e)(2)(A). Note also that §§ 273 and 167(e) prevent only the depreciation of the TP's term interest; if the underlying property to which the term interest relates is depreciable, part (or all) of that depreciation deduction may be allocated to the TP under § 167(d) and deducted by the TP. Any such allocated deduction will reduce the TP's basis.

¶ 24.1420. **Definition of "Term Interest."** A "term interest in property" means: (a) a life interest in property; (b) an interest in property for a term of years; or (c) an income interest in a trust. § 1001(e)(2).

¶ 24.1430. **Exception.** The TP is entitled to use his basis in a term interest in property if the sale or disposition of the term interest is part of a transaction in which the entire interest in the property is transferred (e.g., both the income and remainder interests are transferred). § 1001(e)(3). It appears that for the exception to apply, the transfers of the income and remainder interest must be part of an integrated transaction. While the statute is not entirely clear, it seems that the income and remainder interest could be transferred to different persons so long as the transfers were made pursuant to an integrated plan.

¶ 24.1440. **Illustration 1.** X died on January 1, Year One, and bequeathed 1,000 shares of Win All, Inc. stock in trust, the income from which is to be paid to X's 48–year–old widow, W, for her life, and upon W's death, the trust corpus is to be distributed to X's daughter, D. The value of the 1,000 shares of Win All, Inc. stock at X's death was $500,000, and X's executor did not elect the alternate valuation date. The basis of the stock is $500,000 (its value at the time of X's death). W's basis in her income interest in the trust under § 1014 is determined by utilizing tables provided by the Service that allocate the $500,000 basis of the stock between the life income beneficiary (*W*) and the remainderman (*D*). Assume that the tables initially allocate $430,000 of the stocks basis to *W* and $70,000 to *D*. Although *W*'s life interest (a term interest) has an exhaustible life, *W* is not permitted any deduction for depreciation or amortization of her basis. § 273. On February 1, Year One, *W* sold her income interest in the trust to her nephew, *N*, for its fair market value of $400,000. *W*'s basis in the income interest is disregarded, and *W* recognized a gain of $400,000 on the sale. Treas. Reg. § 1.1014–5(c), Ex. (1). *N* has a basis of $400,000 in the income interest that he purchased, and *N* can amortize and deduct that basis over the period of *W*'s life expectancy.

¶ **24.1450. Illustration 2.** The same facts apply as in ¶ **24.1440** except that on February 1, Year One, *D* sold her remainder interest in the trust to *N* for $75,000. Thus, in effect, *W* and *D* joined together to transfer the entire interest in the trust to *N*. Consequently, assuming that the sales made by *W* and *D* were integrated parts of a unified transaction, *W*'s basis is not disregarded, and she recognized a loss of $30,000 ($430,000 basis minus $400,000 amount realized). § 1001(e)(3).[8] *D* recognized a gain of $5,000.

¶ **24.1500. Amount Realized.** The amount realized from a sale or other disposition of property is the sum of the money received plus the fair market value of any property (other than money) received. Treas. Reg. § 1.1001–1(a).

¶ **24.1510. Encumbered Property.** When encumbered property is transferred, the amount realized by the transferor includes the amount of the encumbrances on the property plus any personal obligation of the transferor that is assumed by the transferee. *Crane v. Commissioner*.[9] This rule is part of the so-called "*Crane* doctrine," which doctrine is sometimes referred to as the "*Tufts* doctrine" instead of *Crane*. The *Crane* doctrine applies when the debt that constitutes the encumbrance on the property is a nonrecourse debt. In the case of a nonrecourse debt, the fair market value of the encumbered property is not relevant to a determination of the tax consequences of a transfer, including a transfer to the creditor. The treatment of a transfer subject to a nonrecourse debt when the fair market value of the encumbered property is less than the outstanding debt is described at

---

8. See *McAllister v. Commissioner*, 157 F.2d 235 (2d Cir. 1946).

9. 331 U.S. 1 (1947).

¶ **16.1511.** The treatment of a transfer of encumbered property when the debt is a recourse debt is described at ¶¶ **16.1511–1– 16.1511–3.**

¶ **24.1511. Nonrecourse Debt in Excess of Value.** A nonrecourse debt is one for which the debtor has no personal liability to repay and for which, upon default, the creditor can collect only by foreclosing on the property securing the debt. When encumbered property is transferred and the amount of nonrecourse debt secured by the encumbrance is greater than the fair market value of the property, the question arises as to whether the amount realized by the transferor under the *Crane* doctrine includes the excess of the debt over the property's value. In an often cited footnote in the *Crane* case (fn. 37), the Supreme Court suggested *in dictum* that the excess of nonrecourse debt over the fair market value will not be included in the amount realized by the transferor. In a case decided a few years after *Crane*, this suggestion was rejected by the Tax Court. The Commissioner also rejected it in Rev. Rul. 76–111. Treas. Reg. § 1.1001–2(b), promulgated in 1980, repudiates fn. 37 and treats the amount realized by the TP as including the entire debt even if the fair market value of the transferred property is less than the debt. See also Treas. Reg. § 1.1001–2(c), Ex. (7). The Supreme Court laid this issue to rest in 1983 when the Court repudiated fn. 37 and held that the entire amount of the debt is included in the transferor's gross income regardless of the value of the transferred property. *Commissioner v. Tufts.*[10] For this purpose, it makes no difference whether the encumbered property is transferred to the creditor or to a third party. The *Tufts* application of the *Crane* doctrine principle has been codified in several recent statutory provisions; e.g., §§ 311(b)(2), 336(b), 7701(g). But see § 752(c).

¶ **24.1511–1. Recourse Debt in Excess of Value— Transfer to Creditor Who Cancels Debt.** A recourse debt is a debt which the debtor is personally liable to repay. If a TP holds property that is encumbered by a recourse debt of a greater amount than the value of the property, and if the TP transfers the property to the creditor, the tax consequence of that transfer depends upon whether it is made in partial or in full satisfaction of the debt. If the

10. 461 U.S. 300 (1983).

creditor agrees to cancel the debt in exchange for receiving the property even though the property's value is less than the amount of the debt, then the transaction is divided into two parts for purposes of applying the tax rules. First, the difference between the amount of the recourse debt and the value of the property is treated as a cancellation of indebtedness, which will be included in the TP's gross income under § 108 as ordinary income unless one of the exceptions to § 108 is applicable. Treas. Reg. § 1.1001–2(a)(2), (c), Ex. (8). The balance of the recourse debt is treated as the amount realized on the disposition of the encumbered property; the difference between the amount realized and the TP's adjusted basis in the property will constitute a gain or loss, which typically will be either a capital gain or loss or a section 1231 gain or loss. *Id.*

¶ **24.1511–1A. Illustration.** *F*, who is solvent, holds Blackacre (unimproved land). *F*'s basis in Blackacre is $25,000. Blackacre is encumbered by a $45,000 mortgage for which *F* has a personal liability (i.e., the mortgage debt is a recourse debt). The fair market value of Blackacre is $40,000. *F* transfers Blackacre to the mortgagee who agrees to cancel the mortgage. The mortgagee, who is a bank, was not the person who had sold Blackacre to *F*. *F* has $5,000 of cancellation of indebtedness income. The exception to income treatment provided by § 108(e)(5) is inapplicable since the mortgagee was not the person who sold the property to *F*, and the insolvency exception is inapposite.

In addition, *F* received $40,000 as the amount realized on the disposition of Blackacre, and so *F* recognized a gain of $15,000 on that disposition. Treas. Reg. § 1.1001–2(c), Ex. (8). The gain likely is a capital gain.

¶ **24.1511–1B. Rationale for Different Treatment of Recourse and Nonrecourse Debts.** As noted above, when property that is encumbered by a nonrecourse debt is transferred to the creditor, the entire amount of the debt is treated as an amount realized by the transferor even when the amount of the debt is greater than the value of the transferred property. However, if the debt is a recourse debt and if the debt is greater than the value of the property, then if the creditor cancels the debt, the difference between the amount of the debt and the value of the property constitutes a cancellation of indebtedness. What justification is there for this difference in treatment?

If a loan is made to a TP on a nonrecourse basis, the lender implicitly agrees to accept the encumbered property as full payment for the outstanding balance of the debt if the debtor does not satisfy the debt in cash or other property. In effect, the creditor has contractually given the debtor the option of "selling" the encumbered property to the creditor in satisfaction of the unpaid balance of the debt. A transfer of property in satisfaction of a debt is treated as a sale of the property. ¶ 24.3000. The debtor effectively has a put to sell the property to the creditor at any time for the then balance of the debt. The amount realized by the debtor on that "sale" of the property is equal to the outstanding balance of the debt.

On the other hand, when the debt is a recourse debt, the creditor has not consented at the time of the loan to accept the underlying property as payment for the outstanding debt. To the contrary, the creditor has retained the right to collect from the debtor any deficiency in the payment received that results from an inadequacy in the value of the encumbered property. So, if the creditor agrees to forego his right to collect the deficiency from the debtor, that constitutes a forgiveness by the creditor of that portion of the debt. The regulation reflects the reality that the creditor does forgive a portion of the debt when he chooses not to enforce his right to require the debtor to make-up the unpaid portion of the debt.

¶ 24.1511–2. Recourse Debt in Excess of Value of Property—Transfer to Creditor Who Does Not Cancel Debt. If the creditor who acquires the encumbered property does not cancel the recourse debt, the excess of that debt over the value of the property is not satisfied by the transfer. The debtor continues to be personally liable to the creditor for the repayment of the unsatisfied amount. There is no reason to assume that the debtor will not repay that amount. While the authors know of no authoritative resolution of this issue, it appears to the authors that there is no cancellation of indebtedness in that circumstance. The amount of the debt equal to the property's fair market value should be treated as the amount realized on the disposition of the property, and the balance of the debt remains outstanding, albeit no longer secured by any property.

¶ 24.1511–3. Recourse Debt in Excess of Value of Property—Transfer to Third Party Who Assumes the Debt. If the debtor transfers the encumbered property to a third party who assumes personal liability for the recourse debt, the debtor remains secondarily liable for the debt if there is a default at a time when the value of the property is inadequate to satisfy the debt. One possible treatment of this transaction, which however was rejected by the regulations, would be to limit the amount realized by the debtor to the fair market value of the property. That approach would be of consequence only if the fair market value of the property was less than the debt at the time of the transfer and it is unlikely that that circumstance will arise frequently. Instead, Treas. Reg. § 1.1001–2(a)(4)(ii) treats the debtor as having been discharged of the entire recourse debt in such cases.[11] The treatment mandated by the regulation avoids administrative difficulties that would be encountered if there were no immediate tax consequence for the excess debt since the matter would then have to be kept open until it could be determined whether the third party, the debtor or neither will actually pay the excess amount of the debt. It is much simpler administratively to assume that the third party will pay the entire debt since he assumed personal liability to do so. Consequently, it appears that the entire amount of the recourse debt will be included in the amount realized by the debtor on the disposition of the property. The debtor and the third party are dealing at arms' length, and they have arrived at an agreement under which the purchaser is willing to undertake personal liability for the entire debt as payment for the property, and so the parties should be deemed to have treated the property as having a value equal to the debt.

---

11. The regulation does not raise the possibility that the fair market value of the property might be less than the debt but it makes no exception for that circumstance.

¶ 24.1512. Transfer Subject to a Nonrecourse Liability That Was Incurred on TP's Acquisition of the Transferred Property. If a TP incurs a nonrecourse liability by reason of the acquisition of property, the TP's basis in the property typically will reflect that liability; that is, the likelihood that the TP will satisfy the liability is deemed sufficient to treat the TP as having paid the amount as part of the cost of the property. Where the liability is included in the TP's basis, the TP's transfer of the property, subject to the unpaid balance of that liability, presents a situation where it is clear that the TP will not satisfy that amount of the liability which will be paid by the transferee or by some other party. The inclusion of the balance of the liability in the amount realized by the TP is required by the fact that the TP previously enjoyed a tax benefit from that liability in having obtained an increased basis in the property on the assumption that the TP would eventually pay that amount to the creditor. The failure of the TP to make that payment (as evidenced by the transfer of the property) causes the liability to be included in the amount realized under an approach that is similar to the tax benefit rule. See Chapter **Five.** If any part of a liability incurred on the acquisition of property was not taken into account in determining the TP's basis in that property (e.g., where a TP inherits realty subject to a mortgage that is greater than the value of the property), the unpaid balance of that part of the liability will not be included in the amount realized by the TP on transferring the property. Treas. Reg. § 1.1001–2(a)(3).

¶ 24.1512–1. Illustration 1. M died owning Blackacre having a fair market value of $100,000 and subject to a mortgage of $115,000. M's executor did not elect the alternate valuation date. M devised Blackacre to D who took the property subject to the mortgage. While it is not settled, it is likely that D's basis in Blackacre will be $100,000 (the fair market value at M's death). Cf., Treas. Reg. § 1.1001–2(c), Ex. (8); Rev. Rul. 80–42. Two years later, D transfers Blackacre to X (an unrelated party) for $5,000 cash, and X took the property subject to the mortgage, the outstanding balance of which was still $115,000. Assuming that the authors correctly determined that D's initial basis in Blackacre was $100,000, only $100,000 of the outstanding debt will be included in the amount realized by *D* plus, of course, the $5,000 cash that *D* received.

¶ 24.1512–2. Illustration 2. The same facts apply as in **¶ 24.1512–1** except that *D* made payments on the principal of the mortgage before transferring it to *X* so that, at the time of transfer, the unpaid balance was $105,000. In this circumstance, the result is unclear. Should the amount excluded from the amount that *D* realized be $15,000, or $5,000, or should it be 15,000/115,000 x $105,000? Should the $10,000 that *D* previously paid on the principal of the mortgage be added to her basis so that only $5,000 of the debt taken over by *X* will be excluded from the amount realized by *D*?

¶ 24.1512–3. Illustration 3. HUD, a government agency, insured a mortgage on realty purchased by the TP. After TP's default, HUD acquired the mortgage. HUD then paid the real estate taxes when they became due, and HUD charged TP for interest payments on the mortgage debt. TP did not make any payments to HUD, and the latter added to the principal of TP's mortgage debt the taxes that HUD had paid and the interest that was owing to HUD. These additions amounted to advances of funds by HUD to TP. The mortgage debt was a nonrecourse debt. TP accrued the property tax and interest obligations and deducted the accrued items from its gross income. Subsequently, TP defaulted on the debt, and HUD took title to the encumbered realty. At that time, the value of the realty was less than the amount of the nonrecourse debt. The entire amount of the debt, including the amounts representing advancements made by HUD to TP, constitute an amount realized by TP. Even though the advancements were not included in TP's basis, they are included in his amount realized.[12]

¶ 24.1513. Insolvent Transferor. The solvency or insolvency of a transferor does not affect the amount realized by the transferor under the *Crane* doctrine. In *Estate of Delman v. Commissioner*,[13] property acquired through a nonrecourse debt was repossessed by the seller, and the purchaser was insolvent both before and after the repossession. The Tax Court held

---

12. See *Allan v. Commissioner*, 856 F.2d 1169 (8th Cir. 1988); **¶ 24.2220**.

13. 73 T.C. 15 (1979).

that the repossession constituted a sale or exchange under the *Crane* doctrine; thus, the forgiveness of indebtedness rules of § 108 and of the common law doctrine enunciated by the Supreme Court in *Kirby Lumber*[14] are inapplicable. The unpaid balance of the nonrecourse debt constituted an amount realized by the purchaser and caused the recognition of gain to the extent that the balance of the debt exceeded the purchaser's basis in the repossessed property.

¶ 24.1514. Gift of Property Subject to Nonrecourse Debt. A question has arisen as to whether a transfer of property subject to a nonrecourse debt will cause the debt to be an amount realized by the transferor if no other consideration was paid. In other words, for a sale or exchange to occur under the *Crane* doctrine, is it sufficient that the TP is treated as having realized an amount under *Crane* or must the TP have intended to sell or exchange the property as contrasted to making a gift? While this issue usually will arise only when the liability in question exceeds the TP's basis, when such a transfer is made to a qualified charity, the allocation of basis required by § 1011(b) may cause the recognition of gain by the TP in some circumstances (even in some circumstances where the transferor's basis in the transferred property is greater than the outstanding liability) regardless of the fact that the transfer was intended to be a gift.[15] The treatment of such donative transfers to a charitable donee is discussed in Rev. Rul. 81–163.[16]

A somewhat similar type of problem arises when a gift is made on condition that the donee pay any gift taxes imposed on the donor for making the gift (the so-called "net gift" transaction). The nature of this problem and the Supreme Court's resolution of it are discussed at ¶ **24.1550.**

¶ 24.1515. Transfer in Trust for Spouse or Former Spouse. In general, no gain or loss is recognized on a transfer of property, outright or in trust, to or for a spouse (or a former spouse if incident to a divorce). § 1041; ¶¶ **15.4000–15.4300.** This nonrecognition provision applies to such transfers regard-

---

14. See ¶ **7.2100.**

15. See *Estate of Levine v. Commissioner*, 634 F.2d 12 (2d Cir. 1980), aff'g 72 T.C. 780 (1979).

16. See ¶¶ **20.3000–20.3100.**

less of whether made gratuitously or as part of a sale or exchange. One exception to this provision is that gain will be recognized on a transferor of property in trust for a spouse (or former spouse) to the extent that the sum of the liabilities assumed or accepted by the trust exceed the transferor's basis in the transferred property. § 1041(e). A second exception arises when the transfer is made in trust and the transferred property is an installment obligation. § 453B(g).

¶ 24.1520. Illustration. *X* sold Blackacre to *Y*. At the time of sale, Blackacre was subject to a mortgage, the outstanding balance of which was $30,000. *X* had no personal obligation to satisfy that $30,000 mortgage. *X*'s adjusted basis in Blackacre at the time of sale was $38,000. In payment for Blackacre, *Y* paid *X* $15,000 cash, and *Y* took Blackacre subject to the outstanding $30,000 mortgage. The amount realized by *X* on the sale was $45,000 ($15,000 cash plus the $30,000 mortgage), and, consequently, *X* realized a gain of $7,000 ($45,000 amount realized minus $38,000 basis). It should be noted that *Y*'s basis in Blackacre immediately after purchasing it is $45,000 ($15,000 cash paid plus the $30,000 mortgage).

¶ 24.1530. Expenses of Sale. Certain expenses of selling property (such as commissions and brokerage fees) are not deductible expenses but instead reduce the amount realized on the sale and thereby reduce the gain realized (or increase the loss realized) on the sale. Treas. Reg. § 1.263(a)–2(e). But see **¶ 1.7110**.

¶ 24.1540. Selling Commissions. Selling commissions, such as brokerage fees on the sale of stock, constitute a selling expense and, thus, typically reduce the amount realized on the sale; except for "dealers" in securities, such commissions are not treated as a deductible expense. Treas. Reg. § 1.263(a)–2(e).

¶ 24.1550. Transfer Subject to Gift Tax (Net Gifts). If a donor makes a gift on which a gift tax is payable, the donor is primarily liable for the payment of the gift tax. If the donor fails to pay the gift tax, the donee is obligated to make that payment. If a donor makes a gift subject to a condition that the donee pay the gift tax on that transfer, the payment of the gift tax by the donee satisfies a legal obligation of the donor and so is treated as consideration paid by the donee to the donor. Such transactions are sometimes referred to as "net gift" transactions—i.e., the amount of the gift is the "net" of the value of the transferred property reduced by the amount of gift tax paid by the donee.

While the initial court decisions were contrary, it is now settled that the gift tax paid by a donee in a net gift transaction constitutes consideration received by the donor for income tax purposes.[17] Consequently, the donor will recognize income to the extent (if any) that the gift tax paid by the donee exceeds the donor's adjusted basis in the transferred property.

¶ 24.1551. Illustration. R transferred Blackacre (unimproved land) to her daughter, L. At that time, the fair market value of Blackacre was $100,000, and R had an adjusted basis of $12,000 in Blackacre. The transfer was made subject to the condition that L pay any gift tax imposed on the transfer. The gift tax was $20,000, and L paid the tax. R recognized a gain of $8,000 on this transaction.

¶ 24.1552. Computation of Donor's Gain. The amount of a donor's gain from a net gift transaction is equal to the difference between the gift tax on the transaction and the donor's basis in the transferred property. In a net gift transaction, the gift tax on the transaction is determined by applying the applicable gift tax rate to the amount of the gift—i.e., the difference between the fair market value of the transferred property and the amount of the gift tax imposed on the transaction. The difficulty is that the amount of the donor's gift and the amount of the gift tax imposed on the transaction are mutually dependent figures. There is an algebraic formula for determining those two figures, and so it is possible to ascertain the amount of the gift tax on the transaction and accordingly to determine the amount of gain realized by the donor.

¶ 24.1553. Donee's Basis. A net gift transaction is one type of a part-sale, part-gift transaction. A transferee's basis in property acquired in a part-sale, part-gift transaction is equal to the greater of: (1) the amount of consideration paid by the transferee or (2) the adjusted basis of the transferor in the transferred property. Treas. Reg. § 1.1015–4(a); **¶ 6.7200.** In the circumstance where the gift tax on the transaction is greater than the donor's adjusted basis in the transferred property (and so, the donor recognized a gain), the donee's basis in the transferred property is at least equal to the amount of consideration paid by the donee (i.e., the donee's payment of the gift tax is the consideration paid by the donee).

---

17. *Diedrich v. Commissioner*, 457 U.S. 191 (1982).

In addition, the amount of gift tax paid on the *appreciated* element of the transferred property is added to the basis that the donee otherwise would have in the transferred property, and the sum is the amount of the donee's basis. § 1015(d)(6); Treas. Reg. § 1.1015–4(a); **¶¶ 6.6000, 6.7210.** While the increase to a donee's basis cannot raise it to an amount in excess of the fair market value of the transferred property, the addition to a donee's basis of the gift tax paid on a net gift will never cause the donee's basis to exceed the fair market value of the transferred property; and so that limitation has no effect on a net gift transaction. In the situation where the gift tax is greater than the donor's basis, then the entire amount of the gift to the donee is a gift of appreciated property, and so the entire amount of the gift tax payment is an adjustment to the donee's basis. Thus, when the gift tax is greater than the donor's basis, the donee's basis in the transferred property will be an amount equal to double the gift tax imposed on the transaction.

¶ 24.1554. Illustration. *X* made a gift of unimproved Blackacre to *Y*, subject to *Y*'s payment of any gift tax imposed on the transaction. The fair market value of Blackacre was $450,000, and *X* had a basis of $50,000 in that property. The gift tax on the transaction was $120,000, and *Y* paid that amount. *X* recognized a gain of $70,000 on the part-sale, part-gift transaction. *Y*'s basis in Blackacre is equal to the sum of the consideration paid by *Y* ($120,000) and the gift tax imposed on the gift portion of the transaction (i.e., $120,000). Thus, *Y*'s basis in Blackacre is $240,000.

¶ 24.1560. Receipt of Property with Unascertainable Value. The amount realized by a transferor on an exchange of property is measured by the fair market value of the property received by the transferor in exchange. If the property received is of a type that is not traded on a market, it may be necessary to value it by estimating what a hypothetical buyer would pay for the item and what a hypothetical seller would charge for the item if both the buyer and the seller were in possession of all relevant facts and were under no compulsion to buy or to sell. However, if the property received is one which cannot be readily valued and is one on which self-liquidating payments will be made over a period of time (for example, a second mortgage on realty when the amount that will actually be collected from the debtor is uncertain), it may not be necessary to close the transaction when the transferor receives the right to such payments. If so, in such cases, rather than close the transaction when the transferor receives the instrument representing the right to the liquidating payments, and so to value the instrument that the transferor received on the basis of speculation as to the amount that will actually be collected by the transferor, the transaction will instead be left open so that no gain will be recognized by the transferor until the amount collected by him under the instrument exceeds his unrecaptured basis in the property transferred by him. In such cases, after recovering his basis, all subsequent payments received by the transferor will be included in the transferor's gross income. This method of reporting gain is sometimes called the "cost recovery method." *Burnet v. Logan*[18] is the landmark case on keeping a transaction open when the value of the property received is not ascertainable because there is no market for it.[19]

¶ **24.1561. Installment Sale Treatment.** The Installment Sales Revision Act of 1980 amended § 453 to permit installment reporting of gain from sales when the amount payable is subject to contingencies. § 453(j)(2). The Senate Finance Committee's report on the 1980 Act states that as a consequence of so extending installment reporting treatment, the cost recovery method should be allowed only in "extraordinary cases involving sales for a contingent price when the purchaser's obligation cannot reasonably be ascertained."[20]

¶ **24.1562. Illustration.** *L* owned 6 and 1/4% of the stock of the A & H Iron Co. (A & H), a publicly held corporation. A & H owned a 12% interest in a 97–year lease to mine iron ore from the *M* mine. The lease agreement did not establish any maximum or minimum tonnage to be mined per year, and the actual tons of iron ore that were allocated to A & H varied from year to year. *L* had a basis of $250,000 in her shares of A & H stock. In Year One, the shareholders of A & H sold their shares to the *Y* Corporation for a cash payment plus the right to 60 cents for every ton of ore thereafter acquired either by *Y* or by A & H under the lease agreement to mine *M*. For her shares, *L* received $140,000 cash and the right to 6 and 1/4%

18. 283 U.S. 404 (1931).

19. See also *McShain v. Commissioner*, 71 T.C. 998 (1979); but see *Warren Jones Co. v. Commissioner*, 524 F.2d 788 (9th Cir. 1975).

20. For a detailed discussion of the installment method of reporting gain, see Chapter **Twelve**.

of the 60 cents per ton payments to be paid by *Y* for each ton of ore it or A & H acquires under the lease. The government treated the sale by the shareholders as a closed transaction. The government estimated the amount of iron ore in the *M* mine, and it calculated the present value of *L*'s right to 6 and 1/4% of 60 cents times A & H's 12% share of the iron ore contained in the *M* mine. The government treated the sum of the cash paid to *L* plus the present value of her right to a share of the iron ore payments as the amount realized by her on the sale. However, in *Burnet v. Logan*[21] on similar facts, the Supreme Court held that "it was impossible to determine with fair certainty the market value" of the agreement by *Y* to pay 60 cents per ton, and, consequently, the Court held that the transaction was to remain open until the payments were completed. The Court held that *L* did not recognize any gain until the cash payments to her (including the initial cash payment) exceeded her basis. Once the payments to *L* exceed her basis, every dollar received by her thereafter will constitute a gain to *L* from the sale of her A & H stock. Note, however, that a portion of *all* payments received more than six months after the sale *may* be treated as interest on the deferred amount and so taxable as ordinary income. See § 483.

¶ **24.1563. Extraordinary Circumstances.** In an exchange of property, the property received typically will have an ascertainable fair market value, and it is only in extraordinary circumstances that the property cannot be valued so that the cost recovery rule is employed. Treas. Reg. § 1.1001–1(a).[22] This is especially true in light of the expansion of § 453 by the 1980 Act as indicated in ¶ **24.1561.** In *Tribune Publishing Co. v. United States*,[23] the Ninth Circuit held that the cost recovery method of *Burnet v. Logan* does not apply when it is clear that the TP realized a gain on the exchange even though the amount of that gain is uncertain. According to the Ninth Circuit, it is only where it is uncertain that the TP had any gain that the cost recovery method can apply. However, apart from the applicability of the cost recovery method, a difficult question remains as to whether a purchaser's bare unsecured nonnegotiable promise to pay money to the seller is the

---

21. See ¶ **24.1560.**

22. See also Rev. Rul. 58–402. But compare *Dorsey v. Commissioner*, 49 T.C. 606 (1968) where the Tax Court rejected the general thrust of the Revenue Ruling.

23. 836 F.2d 1176 (9th Cir. 1988).

equivalent of cash as required by the cash receipts and disbursements method for reporting the seller's gain.[24]

¶ 24.1600. Material Differences in Exchanged Properties. Treas. Reg. § 1.1001–1(a) states that an exchange of one item of property for another that differs *materially*, either in kind or in extent, will trigger realization of gain or loss. In *Cottage Savings Assoc. v. Commissioner*,[25] the Supreme Court sustained the validity of that regulatory provision and adopted a very broad construction as to what constitutes a *material* difference in exchanged properties. In *Cottage Savings*, a TP was permitted to realize and recognize a loss on what amounted to an exchange of participating interests in 252 residential mortgages for participating interests in 305 different residential mortgages. While the mortgages were secured by different properties and had different obligors, they were economically equivalent interests. The Supreme Court held that to constitute materially different properties, it was necessary only that the exchanged properties "embody legally distinct entitlements." The Court held that the differences in obligors and security for the two sets of mortgages were sufficient to satisfy that requirement.

¶ 24.1700. The Treatment of the Modification of A Debt Instrument as an Exchange of Properties. As noted in **¶ 24.1600**, an exchange of debt instruments will trigger a realization and recognition of gain or loss if the exchanged instruments differ materially either in kind or in extent. The Supreme Court's decision in *Cottage Savings*[26] gave a very broad construction to what constitutes a "material" difference. So, if *A* who holds a debt instrument of *B* transfers that instrument to *B* in exchange for a new debt instrument of *B* with materially different terms, the exchange will cause *A* to realize gain or loss on the exchange. That realized gain or loss will be recognized unless the exchange qualifies for nonrecognition under some statutory provision.

Instead of a holder and debtor's exchanging one debt instrument for another, the parties can simply modify the terms of the debt instrument that the holder possesses. Of course, if the modification of a debt results in reducing the amount of the debtor's obligation, that *may* trigger cancellation of indebtedness income to the debtor under § 108.[27] Regardless of whether the debtor recognized cancellation of

---

24. See *Warren Jones Co. v. Commissioner* in **¶ 24.1560**.

25. 499 U.S. 554 (1991).

26. See **¶ 24.1600**.

27. See **¶ 7.2000** *et seq.*

indebtedness income, there is a question as to whether the modification of the terms of a debt instrument will be treated as the exchange of one debt instrument for a new debt instrument so as to trigger realization of gain or loss by the holder of the debt instrument.

¶ **24.1710.   Significant Modification.** According to the regulations, a "significant modification" of a debt instrument is treated as an exchange of the original instrument for a new instrument that differs materially either in kind or in extent. Treas. Reg. § 1.1001–3(b). In other words, a significant modification of a debt will cause the holder of the debt to realize gain or loss. The regulation provides guidance for determining what constitutes a modification and whether a modification is significant for this purpose.

Modification. In general, a modification means any change of a legal right or obligation of the holder or issuer of a debt instrument regardless of whether the alteration is evidenced by an amendment of the instrument, or by the conduct of the parties, or otherwise. Treas. Reg. § 1.1001–3(c)(1). Certain changes in a debt instrument that are described in Treas. Reg. § 1.1001–3(c)(2) are not treated as a modification. For example, an alteration of rights or obligations that occurs pursuant to the original terms of the debt instrument does not constitute a modification; but if the alteration occurs because of one party's exercise or waiver of a right pursuant to a power granted by the terms of the original instrument, the alteration will be treated as a modification unless that party had the *unilateral* power to exercise or waive the right.

Significant. The regulation lists a number of changes to a debt instrument some of which constitute a substantial modification and some of which do not. Treas. Reg. § 1.1001–3(e)(1)–(6). If a modification of a debt instrument is not one of the types included within that regulatory list, the test of whether that modification is "significant" turns upon the facts and circumstances of each such instance. Treas. Reg. § 1.1001–3(e)(1). A few of the items that the regulation specifically categorizes as either significant or not are noted below.

(1) *Yield.* A change in the yield that a debt instrument provides (i.e., its effective interest rate) will be significant only if the resulting yield varies from the prior rate by more than a specified percentage. Treas. Reg. § 1.1001–3(e)(2).

(2) Timing or amount of payments. Some changes in the timing or amount of payments are significant and some are not. For example, the regulation provides a safe harbor for an insignificant change of timing when the deferred payments are payable no later than the lesser of five years or 50% of the original term of the instrument. Treas. Reg. § 1.1001–3(e)(3)(ii). Also, deferrals of de minimis payments are ignored. *Id.*

(3) Change of obligor. A change of the obligor of a debt instrument will usually be a significant modification, but in some circumstances it will not be. Treas. Reg. § 1.1001–3(e)(4). For example, a change in the obligor of a nonrecourse debt is not significant. The addition of a co-obligor on a debt instrument is not significant unless its purpose is to circumvent other rules concerning a change of obligors. *Id.*

(4) Change of security. A change in the collateral securing a recourse debt is a significant modification if it results in a "change in payment expectations" [defined below]. A change in the collateral securing a nonrecourse debt usually will be significant; however, a change of collateral will not be significant if the items of collateral are either fungible or of a type where the particular units pledged do not alter the nature of the secured interest (e.g., government securities or securities of the same type and rating). Treas. Reg. § 1.1001–3(e)(4)(iv)(B). The subordination of a debt instrument to other debt of the issuer is a significant modification if it results in a change of payment expectations. Treas. Reg. § 1.1001–3(e)(4)(v). For this purpose, a "change in payment expectations" occurs if there is either a substantial enhancement or impairment of the obligor's capacity to meet the payment obligation of the debt instrument. Treas. Reg. § 1.1001–3(e)(4)(vi).

(5) Changes in the nature of the instrument. A change of a debt instrument to property that is not debt for federal tax purposes is significant. Also, with some exceptions, a modification is significant if it changes a recourse debt instrument to a nonrecourse debt instrument or vice versa. Treas. Reg. § 1.1001–3(e)(5).

(6) Multiple changes. If a number of changes are made simultaneously to a debt instrument, no one of which would have constituted a significant modification, the cumulative effect of the several changes will not constitute a significant modifica-

tion. Each change is examined separately, and only if one of them is significant will the modification cause a deemed exchange of debt instruments.

But when a number of changes to a debt instrument are made over a period of time and when, while no one of those changes was significant, they would have constituted a significant modification if they had taken place at the same time, the cumulative effect will be taken into account and the changes will be treated as a significant modification. For example, if several changes were made over a period of a few years to the maturity date of a debt instrument and if the final maturity date would have been a significant modification if all of the changes had been made at one time, the changes will constitute a significant modification. Treas. Reg. § 1.1001–3(f)(3).

¶ **24.1720. Installment Instruments.** The regulation does not apply to an installment debt instrument and does not affect the issue of whether modifications to such an instrument cause there to be a taxable disposition of it.[28] At this writing, the cases and rulings indicate that changes in the terms of an installment obligation do not cause a disposition of that instrument. See ¶ **12.6400.**

¶ **24.2000. BASIS.**

¶ **24.2100. General.** The adjusted basis of purchased property generally is determined under § 1012. When a TP acquires encumbered property, the basis problems are somewhat more difficult.

¶ **24.2200. Encumbered Property.** When a TP purchases property subject to an encumbrance, the encumbrance is treated as part of the TP's purchase price and accordingly is included in the TP's basis. For this purpose, it does *not* matter whether the TP has a personal obligation to pay the debt underlying the encumbrance on the property. Similarly, a TP's basis in property includes the amount of debt undertaken by the TP as part of the TP's payment for the property. Thus, the amount of a nonrecourse promissory note issued by the TP to the seller is included in the TP's basis if the transaction is bona fide.[29] A nonrecourse debt or note is a debt which the debtor has no personal liability to repay; thus, the creditor can enforce the debt only by foreclosing on the property securing the debt.

---

28.   Preamble to T.D. 8675 (June 26, 1996).

29.   *Siegel v. Commissioner*, 78 T.C. 659 (1982).

In their casebook on federal income taxation, Professors Gunn and Ward state that there are two exceptions to the general rule that includes an encumbrance in the purchaser's basis: (1) a mortgage so greatly in excess of the property's value that the purchaser is unlikely to pay it off usually will not be included in the purchaser's basis (the "reasonable security" approach), and (2) "contingent and indefinite" obligations of the purchaser are not included in basis.[30]

¶ 24.2210.   **Illustration 1.** *X* purchased Blackacre from *Y*. Blackacre was subject to a mortgage of $35,000. *X* paid *Y* $25,000 cash, and *X* took Blackacre subject to the mortgage. *X* did not *assume* the mortgage or otherwise undertake a personal obligation to pay the $35,000 debt. *X* is treated as having paid *Y* $60,000 ($25,000 cash plus the $35,000 mortgage), and, thus, *X* has a basis of $60,000 in Blackacre.

¶ 24.2220.   **Illustration 2.** *Z* owns Blackacre which has a value of $70,000, and a basis to *Z* of $15,000. *Z* acquired Blackacre in Year One. In Year Thirty, *Z* borrowed $30,000 from the Friendly National Bank and secured the loan by a mortgage on Blackacre. *Z* has no personal obligation to repay the loan, and the Bank's sole recourse on default is to foreclose on its mortgage. *Z* does not recognize a gain by borrowing the $30,000 even though the amount of the loan exceeds his basis, and *Z*'s basis in Blackacre is not affected by the mortgage since it is not a purchase-money mortgage.[31] In Year Thirty–Two, *Z* sold Blackacre to *D* for $40,000 cash, and *D* took Blackacre subject to the $30,000 mortgage. *Z*'s amount realized on the sale is $70,000 ($40,000 cash plus $30,000 mortgage), and since *Z*'s basis in Blackacre was $15,000, *Z* realized a gain of $55,000.

¶ 24.2300.   **Allocation of Basis.**

¶ 24.2310.   **General.** When a part of a larger property is sold, an equitable portion of the TP's basis in the larger property is allocated to the part that was sold, and the TP's gain or loss is computed accordingly. Treas. Reg. § 1.61–6(a). The equitable apportionment of basis is made according to the respective values of the several parts of the property, usually determined as of the

---

30.   Gunn and Ward, *Federal Income Taxation* (West Pub. Co., 6th ed. 2006), p. 543–44 (and cases cited therein).

31.   See *Woodsam Assoc., Inc. v. Commissioner*, 198 F.2d 357 (2d Cir. 1952).

date that the TP acquired the property.[32]

¶ **24.2311. Illustration.** *X* purchased unimproved Blackacre, a 20 acre tract, in Year One at a cost of $80,000. In Year One, the front ten acres of the tract were three times as valuable as the rear ten acres, but *X* purchased the entire 20 acres as a single tract. In Year Thirty–One, *X* divided Blackacre into two tracts of ten acres each, and *X* sold the rear ten acres to *Y* for $50,000. By Year Thirty–One, the front ten acres of the tract were only twice as valuable as the rear ten acres. *X*'s basis in Blackacre ($80,000) must be allocated equitably between the front ten acres and the rear ten acres according to their respective values at the date that *X* purchased Blackacre (i.e., in Year One). Thus, one-fourth of the $80,000 basis ($20,000) is allocated to the rear ten acres, and *X* realized a gain of $30,000 ($50,000 amount realized minus $20,000 basis) on the sale in Year Thirty–One.

¶ **24.2320. Sale of Stocks.** When a TP acquired stock in a corporation on different dates or at different prices, the TP's sale of some of the shares of the stock will be treated as the sale of the earliest stock acquired by him unless the actual shares sold are identified. Treas. Reg. § 1.1012–1(c)(1). In other words, unless the shares of stock sold by the TP are identified, the stock is deemed to have been sold on a first-in, first-out (FIFO) basis. Identification of shares of stock can be accomplished by delivering to the transferee the actual certificates of the stock sold or, if the stock is held in the custody of a broker, by instructing the broker to sell specific shares. A written confirmation of that instruction from the broker within a reasonable time will be an acceptable identification. Treas. Reg. § 1.1012–1(c)(3). Other means of identification are discussed in Treas. Reg. § 1.1012–1(c).

¶ **24.2330. No Means of Allocations.** If a TP sells a part of property and no reasonable allocation of the TP's basis in the property can be determined, the amount realized will reduce the basis of the property and no gain will be recognized if the TP has sufficient basis. If the TP's basis is reduced to zero, any excess received will be gain. See *Inaja Land Co. v. Commissioner.*[33] However, it will be a rare case where no allocation of basis can be determined.[34] The holding in *Inaja* rests on the analogous doctrine

---

32. See *Fairfield Plaza, Inc. v. Commissioner*, 39 T.C. 706 (1963), Acq.

33. 9 T.C. 727 (1947), Acq.

34. See *Gladden v. Commissioner*, 262 F.3d 851 (9th Cir. 2001) (for purpose of allocating basis to expected water rights on land, Ninth Circuit remanded case to determine

established in *Burnet v. Logan*[35] that in an exchange, the receipt of self-liquidating property that cannot be valued may cause the transaction to be kept open until the transferor collects the payments to be made on such property.

¶ **24.2331. Illustration.** TP operated a private fishing club on the bank of a river. The TP had a basis of $61,000 in the land on which the club was operated. The city of Los Angeles diverted polluted waters into the river abutting the fishing club and, thereby, greatly harmed the TP's use of its property as a fishing preserve. The TP collected a net of $49,000 from the city in release of all claims the TP had against the city. In *Inaja*,[36] the Tax Court held that the payment was received for a right of way or easement and for damage to the TP's riparian rights, and that a portion of the TP's $61,000 basis in the land should be allocated to the interests in the land for which the payment was received and only that portion constitutes the TP's basis. However, the Court found that no apportionment could be made with reasonable accuracy, and, therefore, for purposes of determining the TP's gain, the Court permitted the TP to use his entire $61,000 basis in the land to offset the payment received. Thus, the TP realized no gain or loss from the payment made by the city. Thereafter, the TP's adjusted basis in the land was $12,000 ($61,000 minus $49,-000).

¶ **24.3000.   SETTLEMENT OF OBLIGATION.** The transfer of property in full or partial settlement of a pecuniary obligation is treated as a sale or exchange of the property.[37] This principle has been extended to cover the transfer of property by a decedent's executor to satisfy a pecuniary bequest made in the decedent's will and to cover a transfer of property by a trustee to satisfy a pecuniary gift. Treas. Reg. § 1.661(a)–2(f).[38] The satisfaction of pecuniary bequests with appreciated property will cause the estate to recognize a gain to the extent that the value of the property exceeds its estate tax value (i.e., its value at the date of the decedent's death or alternate valuation date). Similarly, the satisfaction

whether comparisons could be made to purchases without expectation of water rights, in which case the premium attributable to the expectation of water rights would be its basis).

35. See ¶¶ **24.1560–24.1562**.

36. See ¶ **24.2330**.

37. *United States v. Davis*, 370 U.S. 65 (1962). Cf., *Commissioner v. Keystone Consolidated Indus.*, 508 U.S. 152 (1993).

38. See also *Kenan v. Commissioner*, 114 F.2d 217 (2d Cir. 1940) and Rev. Rul. 82–4.

of a pecuniary bequest with depreciated property (i.e., property whose basis exceeds its fair market value) will cause the estate to recognize a loss. Note that § 267(b)(13) does not disallow a deduction for the estate's loss.

¶ **24.3100.   Illustration 1.** *D* died owning stock which had a value of $75,000 at *D*'s death, and *D*'s executor did not elect to use the alternate valuation date. Consequently, under § 1014, the estate's basis in the stock is $75,000. *D*'s will bequeathed $100,000 to *X*. A year later, the value of the stock had increased to $100,000. *D*'s executor distributed the stock to *X* in satisfaction of the $100,000 pecuniary bequest. The distribution is treated as a taxable exchange of stock for *X*'s claim to $100,000, and *D*'s estate will recognize a gain of $25,000.

¶ **24.3200.   Illustration 2.** *D*'s will bequeathed to *B* properties from *D*'s probate estate, to be chosen by *D*'s executor, having an aggregate fair market value of a specified amount. The distribution of such assets from *D*'s estate to *B* is the satisfaction of a pecuniary bequest that causes the estate to recognize a gain or loss. Rev. Rul. 86–105.

¶ **24.4000.   MARITAL TRANSFERS.** Prior to 1984, when one spouse transferred property to the other in consideration of the release of marital rights (e.g., dower and the right to a forced share), the transfer was treated as a taxable exchange to the transferor spouse who realized a gain or loss in an amount equal to the difference between the value of the transferred property and its basis.[39] Since 1984, no gain or loss is recognized on a transfer of property (other than an installment obligation transferred in trust) outright or in trust to or for the benefit of a spouse. § 1041. This provision applies to sales or exchanges of property as well as to gratuitous transfers. This provision also applies to transfers made to a former spouse incident to a divorce. The operation of § 1041 is described at ¶ **15.4000.** However, when property is transferred to a trust for a spouse (or former spouse) and when the amount of liabilities assumed or accepted by the trust exceeds the transferor's basis in the property, the transferor will recognize a gain in the amount of that excess.[40]

¶ **24.5000.   GIFTS OF APPRECIATED PROPERTY TO A POLITICAL ORGANIZATION.** If a person transfers appreciated property (i.e., property whose value is greater than the transferor's basis therein)

---

39. *United States v. Davis*, 370 U.S. 65 (1962).

40. See ¶ **24.1515.**

to a political organization, the transferor will recognize a gain to the extent that the property's value exceeds his basis. § 84.

¶ **24.5100. Item by Item Determination.** The language of § 84 suggests that it applies separately to each item of property transferred by a donor to a political organization. If so, a donor who transfers one appreciated asset and one depreciated asset to a political organization will be required to recognize a gain on the appreciated asset but will not be permitted to recognize a loss on the depreciated asset (i.e., a depreciated asset is an asset whose value is less than the transferor's basis therein).[41]

¶ **24.6000. RECOGNITION OF GAIN OR LOSS ON THE DISPOSITION OF PROPERTY.**

¶ **24.6100. General.** Any gain or loss that is *realized* on the disposition of property will also be *recognized* (i.e., taken into account for tax purposes) unless a statutory provision establishes that the gain or loss will not be recognized. § 1001(c). It should be emphasized, however, that a recognized *loss* is not deductible unless some section of the Code grants a deduction for it.

¶ **24.6110. Illustration.** *X* sold his personal home to *Y* for $40,000. *X* had a basis of $50,000 in his home. *X* recognized a loss of $10,000, but the loss is not deductible because it will not qualify under any provision of the Code that authorizes a deduction. A deduction for a loss that is recognized from the sale of a personal residence likely is explicitly disallowed by § 262 (denying a deduction for "personal, living, or family expenses"), but no deduction would be allowable even if § 262 were deemed to be inapplicable.

¶ **24.6200. Nonrecognition of Gain or Loss on Certain Exchanges of Property.**

¶ **24.6210. General.** In the absence of a statutory provision of nonrecognition, the exchange of one property for another that differs materially from the one transferred will constitute a taxable exchange in which gain or loss will be both realized and recognized. There are a number of statutory provisions either requiring or permitting nonrecognition of gain or loss for certain kinds of exchanges. Several of those provisions are described in this chapter.

---

41. Cf., *Morris Investment Corp. v. Commissioner*, 156 F.2d 748 (3d Cir. 1946); and Rev. Rul. 76–377.

¶ **24.6220. Illustration.** *A* owns 100 shares of stock of World Wide, Inc. having a fair market value of $10,000 and a basis of $6,000. *B* owns 200 shares of stock of Planet, Inc. having a value of $10,000 and a basis of $12,000. *A* and *B* exchange their stock holdings so that *A* acquires *B*'s 200 shares of Planet, Inc., and *B* acquires *A*'s 100 shares of World Wide, Inc. Since the stocks of separate corporations are materially different, *A* realized and recognized a gain of $4,000 on the exchange and *B* realized and recognized a loss of $2,000.

¶ **24.7000. EXCHANGES OF LIKE-KIND PROPERTY.** Section 1031 precludes recognition of gain or loss when property held for productive use in a trade or business or for investment is exchanged solely for property "of a like kind" to be held either for productive use in a trade or business or for investment. The requirement that the exchanged properties be held either for productive use in a trade or business or as an investment is satisfied when property held for productive use in a trade or business is exchanged for property to be held as an investment and vice versa. Treas. Reg. § 1.1031(a)–1(a). An exchange of property on which neither gain nor loss is recognized is sometimes referred to as a "tax-free exchange."

In connection with deferred exchanges that qualify for § 1031 treatment (see ¶ **24.7150–24.7155**), the property that a TP transfers in a like kind exchange is referred to as the "relinquished property," and the property that the TP acquired in the transaction is referred to as the "replacement property." See Treas. Reg. § 1.1031(k)–1(a). That same terminology is useful to describe the property in any type of § 1031 exchange.

¶ **24.7100. Like Kind.** The term "like kind" refers to the nature or character of the property; it does not refer to its grade or quality. Treas. Reg. § 1.1031(a)–1(b). Thus, an exchange of improved real property for unimproved realty constitutes an exchange of like kind. *Id.* Realty located outside the United States is not of like kind to realty located in the United States. § 1031(h)(1). Also, personal property "used predominantly within the United States and personal property used predominantly outside the United States are not property of like kind." § 1031(h)(2). The standards for determining the location of predominant use are set forth in § 1031(h)(2).

The regulations treat a leasehold interest in realty for a term of 30 years or more as property that is of like kind to a fee interest in realty. Treas. Reg. § 1.1031(a)–1(c). In *Jordan Marsh Co. v. Commis-*

sioner,[42] a TP had realized a loss on a sale of realty that it owned. As part of the plan of the transaction, the TP immediately had leased back from the buyer the realty that it had sold. The TP's lease was for a term of a little more than 30 years, and the TP had an option to renew the lease for an additional 30 years if the TP constructed buildings on the property. The price at which the property was sold equaled the fair market value of the property, and the rental payments under the lease were fair rents for the property. The Commissioner contended that the purported sale and leaseback was actually a like-kind exchange to which § 1031 applied so that no loss was recognized by the TP on the purported sale. The court held that § 1031 did not apply and allowed the TP to recognize its loss from the sale. If the purchase price of the property had been significantly less than its value and if the rental payments had not been a fair rate, there is a possibility that the transaction might have been treated as a disguised loan to the purported seller; in which event, the TP would have been denied a loss deduction.

Certain types of properties that are listed in § 1031(a)(2) are excluded from the nonrecognition that is otherwise mandated by that section of the Code. Thus, § 1031 is *not* applicable to exchanges of stock in trade, property held primarily for sale, stocks, bonds, notes, other securities or evidences of debt or interest, partnership interests, certificates of trust, or choses in action. § 1031(a)(2).

Prior to the Tax Reform Act of 1984, exchanges of partnership interests were not specifically excluded from § 1031 nonrecognition. The exclusion was adopted because of the belief that partnership interests typically represent investments similar to other items already excluded from like-kind treatment. Court decisions prior to 1984 had limited § 1031 treatment to exchanges of interests in partnerships holding similar underlying assets, but there was concern that this limitation might prove inadequate to deal with potential tax shelter abuse and administrative burdens.

The application of the § 1031(a)(2) exclusion from § 1031 nonrecognition treatment turns upon the substance of the TP's interest as contrasted to the formal designation provided for that interest. For example in Rev. Rul. 92–105, the Commissioner treated a TP's interest in an Illinois land trust as an interest in the realty that was held in the trust. The TP had created the land trust and transferred to it Blackacre (real property that the TP held as an investment). Under Illinois law, the TP (as the beneficiary of the trust) had the exclusive control over and power to manage the realty, and the TP

42. 269 F.2d 453 (2d Cir. 1959).

had the exclusive right to receive rents or other earnings or proceeds from the property. The TP (as beneficiary) was required to file all tax returns, pay all taxes and other liabilities with respect to the realty. The trustee's only responsibility was to hold the title to the property and to transfer the title at the direction of the TP. TP transferred his interest in the Illinois land trust to a third party in exchange for Whiteacre, which TP then held as an investment. The Commissioner determined in Rev. Rul. 92–105 that the nominal "trustee" of the land trust was merely an agent of the TP, and so TP's purported transfer of his interest in the land trust was actually a transfer of Blackacre itself. The Commissioner held that the exchange qualified for nonrecognition as a § 1031 like-kind exchange.

¶ 24.7110. **Personal Properties.** Treas. Reg. § 1.1031(a)–2, provides a detailed statement of the manner in which the like-kind standard is to be applied to exchanges of personal property. As noted above, the like-kind standard for exchanges of realty is quite liberal—realties constitute like-kind properties regardless of whether they are improved or unimproved and regardless of the functional use to which the different items of realty are put. The only exception is an exchange of realty located in the United States for foreign realty. The standard for personal properties is more restricted. Personal properties are divided into three broad categories—(1) depreciable tangible personal property, (2) intangible personal property, and (3) nondepreciable tangible personal property. A like-kind exchange of personal properties must be of properties that fit within the same broad category, but that alone is not sufficient. The types of exchanges within each of those three categories that qualify as like-kind exchanges for purposes of § 1031 are discussed below. Note that personal property predominantly used in the United States is *not* of like kind to personal property predominantly used outside the United States. § 1031(h)(2).

¶ 24.7111. **Depreciable Tangible Personal Property.** Many types of depreciable tangible personal properties are classified into so-called "General Asset Classes" for the purpose of determining the recovery period to be used in depreciating those assets under the Modified Accelerated Cost Recovery System (MACRS) that is applied by § 168. The Asset Class into which a type of property is catalogued determines the item's "class life," which in turn controls the recovery period for depreciating that asset. See ¶ **22A.3411.** Currently, the classification of assets into General Asset Classes is established by Rev. Proc. 87–56. Those classifications may be modified from time to time in the future.

Treas. Reg. § 1.1031(a)–2(b)(1) states that depreciable tangible personal properties that are listed in the same General Asset Class are treated as like-kind property for purposes of § 1031. The General Asset Classes to which this provision applies are the asset classes 00.11 through 00.28 and 00.4 of Rev. Proc. 87–56. For example, asset class 00.11 includes office furniture, fixtures, and equipment that is not a structural component of a building. This class includes such items as desks, files, safes, and communications equipment (other than communications equipment that is listed in another asset class). Asset class 00.21 includes certain airplanes and all helicopters. Asset class 00.22 includes automobiles and taxis. Asset class 00.23 lists only buses. Asset class 00.241 includes light general purpose trucks (i.e., the unloaded weight of the truck is less than 13,000 pounds). Asset class 00.242 includes heavy general-purpose trucks.

So, if an office desk were exchanged for an office safe, that would be a like-kind exchange since the two items are included in the same asset class in Rev. Proc. 87–56. However, if a helicopter were exchanged for a heavy general purpose truck, that exchange will not be one of like-kind property because the two assets are listed in different asset classes and are not otherwise of like kind.

The same-class provision is merely a safe harbor for like-kind treatment. It is not a requirement. So, an exchange of tangible personal properties that are listed in different asset classes may nevertheless qualify for § 1031 treatment if the assets are of like kind. Treas. Reg. § 1.1031(a)–2 states that, "[i]n determining whether exchanged properties are of a like kind, no inference is to be drawn from the fact that the properties are not of a like class."

Certain tangible personal property assets are classified into "Product Classes" in the *Standard Industrial Classification Manual* sometimes referred to as the "SIC Manual," which is provided by the Executive Office of the President, Office of the Management and Budget. The assets listed in the SIC Manual are classified into one of the Product Classes that are listed in that Manual. Some types of assets that are classified in the

Asset Classes of Rev. Proc. 87–56 also are included within one of the Product Classes listed in the SIC Manual. In such cases, for purposes of applying this safe harbor provision to § 1031, the item's Product Class is ignored; only the Asset Class of the item is taken into account. Some types of assets that are omitted from Rev. Proc. 87–56's list of Asset Classes are included in the list of Product Classes in the SIC Manual. For those items, the Product Class category is used in the same manner as the Asset Class categories. In other words, if the assets that are exchanged are not included in an Asset Class but are included in the same Product Class, the exchange will be treated as a like-kind exchange. Treas. Reg. § 1.1031(a)–2(b).

The Asset Classes list of Rev. Proc. 87–56 and the Product Classes list of the SIC Manual may be modified from time to time in the future. Unless otherwise provided, the Service will follow the modified versions of those documents once they become effective, but a TP is permitted to use the unmodified version for exchanges that occur within one year after a modification becomes effective. The Commissioner is authorized not to accept a modification in whole or in part. Treas. Reg. § 1.1031(a)–2(b)(4), (5).

¶ 24.7112. Intangible Personal Property. The standard employed for applying § 1031 to exchanges of intangible personal property rests solely on whether the properties are of like kind. No safe harbor standard (such as a like-class standard) is provided for those properties. The like-kind standard is applied to such properties by examining the nature or character of the rights involved (e.g., patents or copyrights) and by examining the nature or character of the underlying property to which the intangible property relates. Treas. Reg. § 1.1031(a)–2(c)(1).

¶ 24.7112–1. Illustration 1. Copyrights on Novels. *B* exchanges a copyright on a novel for a copyright on a different novel. This is a like-kind exchange. Treas. Reg. § 1.1031(a)–2(c)(3), Ex. (1).

¶ 24.7112–2. Illustration 2. Copyrights on Novels and Songs. *C* exchanges a copyright on a novel for a copyright on a song. The regulation states that this is not a like-kind exchange. Treas. Reg. § 1.1031(a)–2(c)(3), Ex. (2).

¶ 24.7112–3. Goodwill or Going Concern Value. The regulation states that the goodwill or going concern value of one business is not of like kind to the goodwill or going concern value of another business. Treas. Reg. § 1.1031(a)–2(c)(2).

¶ 24.7112–4. FCC Licenses to Broadcast. H exchanged an FCC radio license for an FCC television license. The nature of the licenses (rather than the nature of the business in which they are used) controls whether the properties are of like kind. The Commissioner ruled that this is a like kind exchange and qualifies for § 1031 treatment.[43]

¶ 24.7113. Nondepreciable Tangible Personal Property. The standard employed for the exchange of such properties is the like-kind standard. No safe harbor standard (such as a like-class standard) is provided for those properties. Treas. Reg. § 1.1031(a)–2(c)(1).

¶ 24.7120. Mandatory Nonrecognition. The nonrecognition established in § 1031 is mandatory (i.e., the TP *cannot elect* to recognize a gain or loss realized in an exchange described in that section), but the strict requirements for qualifying for § 1031 treatment make it possible to plan an exchange so that § 1031 does not apply. For example, if property is received by a TP more than 180 days after the date the TP transfers his property (or after the due date of the TP's return for that year), it will not qualify as like-kind property. § 1031(a)(3)(B). Also, the property to be received by the TP in the transfer must be identified on or before the date 45 days after the TP transfers the property he relinquished in the exchange. § 1031(a)(3)(A). The operation of these time limit requirements is discussed at **¶ 24.7153.** A TP who wishes to recognize a gain or loss could deliberately violate one of the requisites of § 1031. In most cases, however, the deliberate violation of the time limits will not be a practical means of avoiding the nonrecognition rules because the transferor will be unwilling to defer the identification or receipt of the acquired property.

¶ 24.7130. Property Acquired for Purpose of Exchanging It for Other Property. If *X* acquired property for the sole purpose of exchanging it with *Y* for property of a like kind, the

---

43. TAM 200035005.

Commissioner contends that the transaction will not qualify for nonrecognition as to X since, arguably, he did not hold the property either for investment or for productive use in a trade or business. Rev. Rul. 77–297; Rev. Rul. 75–291; but see ¶ **24.7170.** The Commissioner's position is questionable; but even if § 1031 does not apply to X in such cases, Y can enjoy nonrecognition under § 1031 even though Y participated in the plan for X to acquire the property he subsequently exchanged with Y. Regardless, Y held the property that he transferred for investment purposes.[44] Indeed, Y will qualify for § 1031 treatment even if the property that Y received in the exchange was not acquired by X until after the date that Y had transferred his property to X, provided that the time restrictions discussed in ¶ **24.7153** are satisfied.

¶ **24.7140.   Multiple Party Exchanges.** A swap of properties can qualify under § 1031 even though more than two parties are involved and a prearrangement is made for the purchase of some of the property to be exchanged.[45] In *Garcia v. Commissioner,*[46] the transaction involved three properties, four parties, and various escrow agreements. TP's property was sold as a part of the transaction, but TP received only like kind property in the exchange, and so the transaction, which took place over some time, was treated as an § 1031 exchange as to the TP. The facts of the *Garcia* case arose prior to the 1984 amendments to § 1031 that established time limits for the identification and receipt of property acquired in an exchange for the exchange to qualify for nonrecognition under § 1031. See ¶ **24.7153** for a discussion of the conditions that must be satisfied when there is a deferred exchange.

¶ **24.7141.   Illustration.** X, who owned Blackacre, wished to exchange Blackacre for Whiteacre, which was owned by *M. M* was not interested in exchanging Whiteacre for other property, but she was willing to sell it for cash. Z wanted to purchase Blackacre from X, but X preferred a swap in order to preclude the recognition of gain. X informed Z that he would sell

44.   E.g., *Biggs v. Commissioner*, 632 F.2d 1171 (5th Cir. 1980), aff'g 69 T.C. 905 (1978); Rev. Rul. 77–297; Rev. Rul. 90–34.

45.   E.g., *Biggs v. Commissioner*, in ¶ **24.7130**; *Barker v. Commissioner*, 74 T.C. 555 (1980); *Starker v. United States*, 602 F.2d 1341 (9th Cir. 1979); Rev. Rul. 90–34; Rev. Proc. 2000–37; Treas. Reg. § 1.1031(k)–1(g)(4). See *Garcia v. Commissioner*, 80 T.C. 491 (1983), Acq., for a liberal application of § 1031 in a multi-party exchange.

46.   Supra, note 45.

Blackacre to *Z* through a multiple step transaction using a fourth party, *Y*, and escrow arrangements. Under the agreement that was reached, *Y* would purchase Whiteacre from *M*, transfer it to *X* in exchange for Blackacre and some cash, and then sell Blackacre to *Z* for cash. All of the transfers took place simultaneously, and all of the cash was paid into escrow and then distributed. The consideration paid by *Y* for Whiteacre came partly from the cash *Y* received from *Z* for Blackacre, partly from the proceeds of a new mortgage taken out on Whiteacre by *X*, and the rest from part of the cash paid by *X* in connection with his exchange of Blackacre for Whiteacre. In a similar situation, the Tax Court held in *Barker v. Commissioner*[47] that § 1031 prevents *X* from recognizing any gain on the transaction. The Court applied § 1031 to a four-party transaction although the purchases and exchanges were prearranged. See also Rev. Rul. 90–34; and Treas. Reg. § 1.1031(k)–1.

¶ 24.7150. Deferred Exchanges—The *Starker* Principle. A deferred exchange is one where the relinquished property is transferred before the replacement property is acquired, or vice versa. In the mid 1980s, two cases (the *Starker* cases), involving the same set of facts, permitted a deferred exchange to qualify for § 1031 nonrecognition even though the replacement property was identified and acquired some years after the relinquished property was transferred. Perhaps the several *Starker* decisions provide the most liberal construction of § 1031 to date. While the holding of the *Starker* cases has been restricted by the time limitations adopted as part of the 1984 amendments to § 1031 (described at **¶ 24.7153**) and perhaps by the conditions laid down in Treas. Reg. § 1.1031(k)–1, the principles established by the *Starker* cases continue to be viable (subject to the time restrictions adopted in 1984), and so those cases are worth exploring.

In *Starker*, the TPs transferred land, having a value in excess of $1,500,000, to a corporation. In consideration of the transfer, the corporation agreed to acquire realty selected by the TPs and to deed it to them. The corporation established a "credit account" of over $1,500,000 for the TPs; as each parcel that was selected by the TPs was purchased by the corporation and deeded over, the balance of the credit account was to be reduced accordingly. The unused balance of the credit account was to be increased by 6% each year. After five years had elapsed, any credit balance remaining was to be paid to the TPs in cash.

47. Supra, note 45.

¶ **24.7151.** *Starker I.* In the first of two cases (*Starker I*), a district court held that the two Starkers involved in that suit did not recognize gain on the transaction because the realty selected by them and transferred to them from the corporation (the replacement property) was covered by § 1031.[48] Those two Starkers had only a small portion of the land that was transferred; hence, relatively small amounts were involved. The Service voluntarily caused its appeal in that case to be dismissed.

¶ **24.7152.** *Starker II and Starker III.* The Service then contended that T.J. Starker, who had owned the major share of the transferred land, recognized gain on the transaction because § 1031 is inapplicable. In the second district court case (*Starker II*), the same judge who had decided *Starker I* changed his mind and held for the Service.[49] On appeal, the Ninth Circuit reversed the lower court decision in what is referred to as *Starker III*.[50] *Starker II* and *Starker III* involved the receipt of twelve parcels of property by the TP from the corporation: nine of the parcels were deeded directly to the TP (T.J. Starker); two of the parcels (at the TP's direction) were deeded directly to the TP's daughter (one of these parcels was used by the daughter as her residence); and title to the last parcel was not acquired by the corporation which, instead, acquired contract rights to purchase the property and transferred those contract rights to the TP. In *Starker III*, the Ninth Circuit held that the decision in *Starker I* controlled the disposition of the issue in *Starker III* as to the treatment of the nine parcels deeded to the TP. The court applied collateral estoppel and held that § 1031 covered the TP's receipt of those parcels. However, the court held that collateral estoppel did not apply to the remaining three parcels.

As to the two parcels that were deeded directly to the TP's daughter, the court held that § 1031 was inapplicable because title was not acquired by the TP himself.[51] However, regarding the contract rights that the TP received from the corporation to purchase the twelfth parcel, the Ninth Circuit, approving of

---

48. *Starker v. United States*, 35 AFTR2d 75–1550 (D.Or. 1975).

49. *Starker v. United States*, 432 F.Supp. 864 (D.Or. 1977).

50. *Starker v. United States*, 602 F.2d 1341 (9th Cir. 1979).

51. A contrary view of the transaction might have treated it as a constructive transfer of the two parcels to the TP who then gifted them to his daughters.

the reasoning in *Starker I*, held that § 1031 provided nonrecognition. The Ninth Circuit required the TP to recognize interest income for the 6% growth factor. The increase in the TP's account was treated as interest income by the court.

¶ 24.7153. Deferred Exchanges—Time Limitations. Congress believed that the decisions of *Starker* and similar cases, suggesting that there was no limit to the time that like-kind exchanges can be kept open, were too liberal.[52] To remedy this, Congress amended § 1031 to bar like-kind treatment for the receipt of property that the TP received more than 180 days after the TP transferred his property or that the TP received after the due date (including extensions) for filing a return for the year in which the TP transferred his property. § 1031(a)(3)(B). The 1984 amendments also barred like-kind treatment for property that the TP received in exchange if the replacement property was not identified as property to be transferred to the TP within 45 days of the date that the TP relinquished his property. § 1031(a)(3)(A). While the 1984 amendments expressly bar § 1031 treatment when an exchange fails to comply with the time limit requirements for identification and receipt of property, a deferred exchange can qualify for § 1031 treatment when the time limitations of § 1031(a)(3) are satisfied.

The conditions under which a deferred exchange will qualify for § 1031 nonrecognition treatment are set forth in Treas. Reg. § 1.1031(k)–1. One of the conditions imposed by that regulation (in addition to the time limitations) is that either: (1) no more than three properties be acquired in the exchange (the three-property rule), or (2) any number of properties can be acquired provided that their aggregate fair market value at the end of the identification period does not exceed 200% of the aggregate fair market value of the properties that the TP relinquished (which value is to be determined at the date that they were transferred by the TP)—the 200% rule. Treas. Reg. § 1.1031(k)–1(c)(4)(i).[53] The treatment of exchanges of multiple properties is described at ¶ **24.7400**.

52. See General Explanation of the Revenue Provisions of the Tax Reform Act of 1984, prepared by the staff of the Joint Committee on Taxation, pp. 244–245.

53. See Handler, *Final Regs. on Deferred Like–Kind Exchanges Provide Additional Clarifications*, 75 J.Tax. 10 (1991).

Apart from the time restrictions, a TP who utilizes a deferred exchange arrangement must take care not to have constructive or actual receipt of cash or other property that would be treated as boot. See § **24.7200** for the meaning of "boot." The regulations provide a safe harbor for TPs to follow and be assured that they will not be deemed to have received cash or other boot. Treas. Reg. § 1.1031(k)–1(g).

¶ 24.7154. Acquisition Directly from Third Party. In Rev. Rul. 90–34, the TP transferred unencumbered Blackacre directly to *Y* who thereby became obligated to purchase property to be identified by the TP within the permitted time period and then transfer the property to the TP within the required period. The TP made a timely identification of Whiteacre held by *Z*, and *Y* dutifully purchased Whiteacre and had *Z* transfer title to Whiteacre directly to the TP. Thus, *Y* never held title to Whiteacre. The Commissioner ruled that there is no requirement in § 1031 that *Y* obtain title to the property that the TP acquired; it is only required that the TP acquire like-kind property in exchange for the property he transferred. The Commissioner held that § 1031 applied to the TP's exchange so that he recognized no gain or loss.

¶ 24.7155. Reverse–Starker Transactions. A reverse-Starker transaction is where the replacement property is acquired before the relinquished property is transferred. One method for accomplishing this is to "park" the replacement property with an accommodation party who holds the replacement property until the ultimate transferee of the relinquished property is determined. Once that is determined, the TP transfers the relinquished property to the accommodation party in exchange for the replacement property; and the accommodation party transfers the relinquished property to the ultimate transferee in exchange for cash. The accommodation party receives a fee for the service. Other methods have been adopted, including other "parking" methods. For example, the accommodation party can promptly exchange the replacement property for the relinquished property, and then hold the relinquished property (as parked property) until it is purchased from the accommodation party by the ultimate transferee. These parking arrangement will not qualify for a § 1031 exchange treatment unless certain conditions are satisfied, including that the accommodation party, even though acting as an agent of the TP, will be treated as the beneficial owner of the parked property for federal income tax purposes; and so income from the parked property will be treated as income of the accommodation party. In Rev. Proc. 2000–37, the Service set forth a set of conditions, the satisfaction of which provide a safe harbor for TPs who wish their reverse-Starker transaction to qualify for § 1031 treatment.

¶ 24.7160. Momentary Ownership of Acquired Property. If a TP, who acquired property in a like-kind exchange, promptly transfers the acquired property to a corporation controlled by the TP, the Commissioner maintains that the TP will not qualify for nonrecognition under § 1031 on the like-kind exchange since the TP did not hold the acquired property for investment or for productive use in his trade or business. Rev. Rul. 75–292.[54] However, in *Magneson v. Commissioner*,[55] the courts allowed nonrecognition of gain where a TP acquired property in a like-kind exchange and immediately transferred the acquired property to a partnership in exchange for a partnership interest. The Ninth Circuit held that the TP did not discontinue his holding of the acquired property but merely changed the form of his holding. While the position of the Commissioner in Rev. Rul. 75–292 has not yet been repudiated by the courts, its validity has been placed in doubt by the *Magneson, Bolker,* and *Maloney v. Commissioner* decisions, discussed at **¶ 24.7170.**

¶ 24.7170. Momentary Ownership of Property Prior to the Exchange. In Rev. Rul. 77–297, the Commissioner ruled that if *A* purchased property for the purpose of transferring it to *B* in a like-kind exchange, the exchange will not qualify for § 1031 treatment as to *A* because he did not hold the transferred property as an investment for use in his business (the Commissioner further held that § 1031 could apply to *B* in that transaction). See **¶ 24.7130.** The Commissioner's view was adopted by the District Court for the Central District of Illinois.[56] Nevertheless, several decisions of the Tax Court and the Ninth Circuit on analogous issues cast serious doubts on the validity of the Commissioner's view.

54. See also *Regals Realty Co. v. Commissioner*, 43 B.T.A. 194 (1940), aff'd 127 F.2d 931 (2d Cir. 1942).

55. 753 F.2d 1490 (9th Cir. 1985), aff'g 81 T.C. 767 (1983).

56. *Barker v. United States*, 668 F.Supp. 1199 (C.D.Ill. 1987).

In Rev. Rul. 77–337, the Commissioner denied § 1031 treatment to a TP who promptly transferred property that he had acquired on the liquidation of a corporation in exchange for property of a like kind. In *Bolker v. Commissioner*,[57] the Ninth Circuit allowed § 1031 nonrecognition for a like-kind exchange by a TP who transferred property that he had received three months earlier from the liquidation of a corporation. While the court distinguished Rev. Rul. 77–337 on the ground that the intent to transfer the liquidated property in that ruling was formed before the liquidation took place, the court was critical of that ruling (and similar rulings) and apparently rejected the Commissioner's view. The rationale for the court's allowing § 1031 treatment to the TP is expressed in the following quotation from the Ninth Circuit's *Bolker* decision:

> [W]e hold that if a taxpayer owns property which he does not intend to liquidate or to hold for personal pursuits, he is "holding" that property "for productive use in trade or business or for investment" within the meaning of § 1031(a). Under this formulation, the intent to exchange property for like-kind property satisfies the holding requirement, because it is *not* an intent to liquidate the investment or to use it for personal pursuits.

The corporate liquidation that took place in *Bolker* was accomplished pursuant to a special tax provision (§ 333) that provided partial or full nonrecognition of gain to the corporation's shareholders, and this tax provision was repealed in 1986. It is unclear whether the special tax nature of the liquidation was a factor in the court's decision in *Bolker*.

In a subsequent Tax Court case, the court allowed § 1031 treatment for a like-kind exchange made by a corporation less than one month prior to liquidating pursuant to the now-repealed § 333.[58] In *Maloney v. Commissioner*,[59] the Tax Court emphasized the special nature of the now defunct § 333 liquidation. While the disposition in *Maloney* was made of property shortly after it was acquired in a like-kind exchange, the policy for allowing momentary ownership applies equally to the question of whether it is permissible under § 1031 for a TP to exchange property that was obtained by the TP just before making the exchange.

57.   760 F.2d 1039 (9th Cir. 1985).

58.   *Maloney v. Commissioner*, 93 T.C. 89 (1989).

59.   Id.

In *Magneson v. Commission*,[60] the Ninth Circuit and the Tax Court allowed nonrecognition of gain for a like-kind exchange where the TP promptly transferred the acquired property to a partnership in exchange for a partnership interest. While that case involved the momentary holding of property acquired in a § 1031 exchange, it does provide support for the position that the momentary holding of property before exchanging it for like-kind property does not disqualify the exchange for § 1031 treatment.

In light of the *Bolker, Maloney,* and *Magneson* decisions, and notwithstanding the District Court's decision in *Barker*, the Commissioner's position is very much in doubt. It appears to be an overly restrictive reading of a provision that has otherwise been liberally construed.

¶ 24.7180. Exchanges With a Related Person. If a like-kind nonrecognition exchange takes place between "related persons," and if within two years after the date of the last transfer that was incident to that exchange either party disposes of like-kind property that that person acquired in the exchange, then gain or loss realized by both parties from the exchange will be recognized— i.e., the nonrecognition treatment of § 1031 becomes inapplicable. § 1031(f). There are three types of disposition of acquired like-kind property that do *not* cause the loss of § 1031 nonrecognition treatment for the original exchange—i.e., a disposition of such acquired property within the proscribed two-year period will not cause recognition of gain or loss if the disposition takes place: (1) after the death of either of the parties, (2) as a consequence of a compulsory or involuntary conversion if the like-kind exchange occurred before the threat or imminence of the conversion arose, or (3) it is established that neither the exchange nor the disposition had as one of its principal purposes the avoidance of Federal income tax. § 1031(f). In certain circumstances described below, the two-year period of § 1031(f) will be extended. Persons are related for this purpose if they have a relationship described in either § 267(b) or § 707(b)(1). § 1031(f)(3).

The proscribed two-year period of § 1031(f) for the disposition of acquired like-kind property is extended as to any such property for the period that the holder of that property did not bear a risk of loss or whose risk of loss with respect to that property was substantially diminished because of a contractual arrangement

60. See ¶ 17.3160.

such as a put, a short sale, or the holding of another party of a right to acquire the property. § 1031(g).

The evil at which this provision is aimed can occur when a high income tax bracket TP transfers appreciated property to a relative who is in a low income tax bracket pursuant to a § 1031 exchange in which the low bracket relative promptly sells the appreciated property. The § 1031 exchange could be a device to allow the shifting of the gain from a sale of the property to a low bracket TP and thereby reduce the tax burden on that sale. This provision is aimed at blocking that device.

¶ **24.7200.   Boot.** In tax parlance, when persons exchange property, the gain or loss from which is not recognized (e.g., exchanges of like-kind property under § 1031) and, in addition to the property that is permitted to be exchanged tax-free, one or more of the transferors also transfers cash or other property that is not permitted to be exchanged tax-free, the cash or other property is referred to as "boot." Thus, a TP may receive property which is permitted to be exchanged for the property he transferred under the nonrecognition statute, and he may also receive cash or other property to boot. Some commentators and courts use the term "boot" to refer exclusively to *cash* received in a nonrecognition-type transaction and refer to other nonqualified property as "other property."

¶ **24.7210.   Effect of Boot on Recognition of Gain.** A very few nonrecognition statutes provide that the receipt of boot by a TP will cause him to recognize all realized gain from the exchange. The more typical nonrecognition statute, as exemplified by § 1031, provides that a TP's receipt of boot causes him to recognize any realized gain on the exchange only to the extent of the boot received. § 1031(b).

¶ **24.7211.   Illustration.** *X* owned unimproved Blackacre which had a value of $50,000 and a basis of $10,000. *Y* owned unimproved Whiteacre which had a value of $40,000 and a basis of $20,000. *X* transferred Blackacre to *Y* in exchange for Whiteacre plus $10,000 cash. The $10,000 cash that *X* received constituted boot to him. *X realized* a gain of $40,000 on the exchange, but he *recognized* a gain of only $10,000 (i.e., *X recognized* his realized gain up to the extent of the boot he received). *Y realized* a gain of $20,000; but since *Y* did not receive any boot, *Y* did not *recognize* any gain at all.

X's transfer of Blackacre for like-kind property plus cash constitutes an exchange of multiple properties. While Treas. Reg. § 1.1031(j)–1 sets forth the manner in which a multiple-properties exchange is to be treated under § 1031, that regulation is aimed primarily where both parties to the exchange transferred multiple properties. However, the regulation also can apply to the less complex circumstance in which one party transfers only one asset and receives in exchange two or more assets, some of which are of like kind and some of which are not. In that less complex situation (which is presented by this illustration), the application of § 1031 can readily be determined without resorting to Treas. Reg. § 1.1031(j)–1.

The operation of that regulation (Treas. Reg. § 1.1031(j)–1) is complex. The basic scheme is that in multiple asset exchanges those properties that are of like kind are matched to the extent of their equal values, and the amount that is matched does not cause the recognition of gain or loss. Any excess value is treated as boot. Because the authors believe that students will not need to know exactly how that regulation operates, it is not discussed in detail in this work

¶ 24.7220. Liabilities as Boot. When property which is subject to a mortgage or other encumbrance is transferred in a § 1031 exchange (i.e., the encumbrance represents a nonrecourse debt), the amount of the encumbrance is treated as boot received by the transferor. Treas. Reg. § 1.1031(b)–1(c). This rule conforms with the *Crane* doctrine.[61] If the transferor received in exchange property which was subject to a mortgage, the mortgages are offset for purposes of determining his boot. Treas. Reg. § 1.1031(b)–1(c). As a result of a 1999 amendment, a nonrecourse liability will be taken into account only if it is "assumed" by the transferee as that term is specially (and unusually) defined in § 357(d). § 1031(d). With one minor exception, a nonrecourse liability (a debt for which there is no personal liability to repay) that secures property is deemed to have been assumed by the transferee who took the property subject to that liability. § 357(d)(1)(B). In the illustrations that follow, when property is transferred subject to a liability, the transferee is deemed to have assumed that liability for purposes of § 1031.

¶ 24.7221. Illustration 1. *X* owned unimproved Blackacre having a value of $100,000 and subject to a mortgage of

61. Discussed in ¶¶ 24.1510–24.1550.

$60,000. *X* had a basis of $70,000 in Blackacre. *Y* owned unimproved Whiteacre having a value of $120,000 and subject to a mortgage of $80,000. *Y* had a basis of $85,000 in White-acre. *X* and *Y* exchanged Blackacre for Whiteacre and each took subject to the existing mortgages on the properties. *X* *realized* a gain of $30,000, but under § 1031, *X* did not *recognize* any gain at all since the mortgage on Whiteacre which he accepted ($80,000) was greater than the mortgage on Blackacre ($60,000) which he disposed of and, thus, *X* did not receive any boot. *Y* *realized* a gain of $35,000 on the exchange, but *Y* *recognized* a gain of only $20,000—i.e., the mortgage on Whiteacre ($80,000) transferred by *Y* was $20,000 greater than the mortgage on Blackacre ($60,000) which *Y* received and that difference constitutes boot to *Y*.

The gain *realized* by *X* and *Y* is computed as follows:

(a) Gain realized by *X*:

Amount *realized* by *X*

Value of Whiteacre	120,000
Release of Mortgage on Blackacre	60,000
	180,000

Less

Basis of Blackacre	70,000
Mortgage on Whiteacre (assumed)	80,000
	150,000

Gain *realized*	30,000

(b) Gain *realized* by *Y*:

Amount *realized* by *Y*

Value of Blackacre	100,000
Release of Mortgage on Whiteacre	80,000
	180,000

Less

Basis of Whiteacre	85,000
Mortgage on Blackacre (assumed)	60,000
	145,000

Gain *realized*:	35,000

¶ **24.7222. Illustration 2.** The same facts as in ¶ **24.7221**, except that the value of Whiteacre was only $110,000, and, therefore, in addition to exchanging the real properties, *Y* paid *X* $10,000 cash. *X realized* a gain of $30,000, and he *recognized* a gain of $10,000 (i.e., the $10,000 cash paid to *X* is boot to him and, according to Treas. Reg. § 1.1031(d)–2, Ex. (2), the $20,000 excess of mortgage accepted by *X* cannot be used to offset the cash he received in determining his boot). [Note that Treas. Reg. § 1.1031(j)–1 will provide the same result if the procedures established in that regulation are applied.] *Y* realized a gain of $25,000:

Amount *realized* by *Y*		
	Value of Blackacre	100,000
	Release of Mortgage on Whiteacre	80,000
		180,000
Less		
	Basis of Whiteacre	85,000
	Mortgage on Blackacre (assumed)	60,000
	Cash paid	10,000
		155,000
Gain *realized* by *Y*		25,000

Y recognized a gain of only $10,000 since the mortgage on Whiteacre transferred by *Y* is reduced by both the mortgage on Blackacre and the $10,000 cash paid by *Y*, and therefore *Y* received boot of only $10,000.

¶ **24.7230. Effect of Receipt of Boot on Recognition of Loss.** No loss can be recognized in an exchange of property of like kind under § 1031 even if the TP also receives boot in the exchange. § 1031(c). Note, however, that a TP will recognize a loss in a § 1031 exchange if the TP transfers depreciated boot to the transferee. See ¶ **24.7320**.

¶ **24.7300. Basis of Property Received in a § 1031 Exchange.** The basis of property acquired by a TP in a tax-free exchange under § 1031 is the same as the TP's basis in the property transferred by him reduced by any *money* received by the TP on the exchange and increased or decreased by any gain or loss *recognized* by the TP on the exchange. § 1031(d). In addition, the TP's basis in the property acquired by him is increased by the amount of money given by the TP to the transferee as partial payment for the acquired property, and the TP's basis in the acquired property is also increased by the amount of any mortgage to which such acquired property is subject. If the TP transferred property to the transferee subject to a mortgage, the amount of that mortgage is treated as money received by the TP and accordingly reduces the TP's basis in the property acquired by him.[62] If the TP received boot other than money, then a portion of the basis so determined in an amount equal to the value of the boot is allocated to the boot property, and the balance of the basis is allocated to the like-kind property.

¶ 24.7310. Illustration 1. X owned unimproved Blackacre having a value of $80,000 and a basis to X of $55,000. X transferred Blackacre to Y in exchange for unimproved Whiteacre which had a value of $80,000. There were no encumbrances on either Blackacre or Whiteacre. X realized a gain of $25,000 on the exchange, but he did not recognize any gain because of § 1031. X's basis in Whiteacre is equal to the basis he had in Blackacre since X received no boot and recognized no gain on the exchange. Thus, X has a basis of $55,000 in Whiteacre.

¶ 24.7320. Illustration 2. X owned unimproved Blackacre having a value of $100,000, and subject to a mortgage of $40,000. X had a basis of $55,000 in Blackacre. Y owned unimproved Whiteacre having a value of $90,000 and subject to a mortgage of $34,000. Y had a basis of $40,000 in Whiteacre. Y also owned 100 shares of Win All stock having a value of $4,000, and Y had a basis of $8,000 therein. X transferred Blackacre to Y in exchange for Whiteacre and the 100 shares of Win All stock. Both parties took the realty subject to existing mortgages. X realized a gain of $45,000, but X recognized a gain of only $10,000 (i.e., his boot was the $4,000 value of the Win All stock plus the $6,000 excess of the mortgage on Blackacre over the mortgage on Whiteacre). X's basis is computed as follows:

55,000	Basis in Blackacre
+ 10,000	Gain recognized
+ 34,000	Mortgage on Whiteacre received
- 40,000	Mortgage on Blackacre transferred
$ 59,000	Basis in Whiteacre and Win All stock.

$4,000 of this basis is allocated to the 100 shares of Win All stock, and the remaining $55,000 is allocated to Whiteacre.

---

62. See ¶ **24.7220** where it is stated that for purposes of this provision, with one minor exception, a transferee's taking property subject to a nonrecourse liability is treated as an assumption of that liability.

As for Y, he did not recognize any gain or loss on his transfer of Whiteacre since he did not receive any boot in exchange—the mortgage on Whiteacre ($34,000) was offset by the $40,000 mortgage to which Blackacre was subject. However, Y also transferred Win All stock in exchange for a part of Blackacre and since that was not a like-kind exchange, Y recognized a loss of $4,000 on the stock (i.e., Y received $4,000 value of Blackacre in exchange for his Win All stock in which he had a basis of $8,000). Y's basis in Blackacre is computed as follows:

40,000	Basis in Whiteacre
+ 8,000	Basis in Win All stock
+40,000	Mortgage on Blackacre
- 4,000	Loss *recognized* by Y
- 34,000	Mortgage on Whiteacre
$ 50,000	Y's basis in Blackacre.

¶ 24.7330. Overview. The *modus operandi* of a nonrecognition provision is that any realized gain or loss for which nonrecognition treatment has been granted is merely deferred. See **¶¶ 1.7421–1.7423.** To provide for this deferral, the basis of certain properties of the TP must reflect the realized but unrecognized gain or loss; and in the context of § 1031, it is the TP's basis in the like-kind property he acquired in the exchange that will reflect the unrecognized gain or loss (since the TP's basis in boot received in kind will equal its fair market value, none of the unrecognized gain or loss will be reflected in the boot). Thus, an easy method of checking whether you have correctly computed the basis of property acquired in a nonrecognition exchange is to determine the difference between the property's basis and its fair market value and that difference should equal the amount of unrecognized gain or loss. For example, in **¶ 24.7320**, X realized a gain of $45,000 of which only $10,000 was recognized; consequently, X's basis in Whiteacre (the replacement property he acquired) should reflect the unrecognized gain of $35,000. Whiteacre's value was $90,000, so to reflect a $35,000 gain on Whiteacre's sale, X's basis in Whiteacre must be $55,000; and that is the basis applied to Whiteacre by § 1031(d).

¶ 24.7400. Multiple Properties. Not all exchanges of like-kind properties are transacted as a simple exchange of one item of property (encumbered or not) for another item of like-kind property, perhaps with an addition of an item of boot. In some circumstances, the parties will exchange a number of different properties, some of which are of like kind to one or more of the properties received in the exchange and some of which are not. Multiple properties exchanges can occur when a going business is acquired in an exchange, but this type of transaction is not limited to circumstances when a going business is involved. In such complex exchanges (in which the overall exchange is at arms' length and of equal value on both sides), when a TP receives like-kind properties that have a greater aggregate value than the properties of like kind that the TP transferred, the excess value will be consideration for other properties transferred by the TP. Conversely, if the aggregate value of the like-kind properties that the TP transferred is greater than the aggregate value of the like-kind properties that the TP received, the TP will have received boot consideration to make up that difference. Of course, in making those comparisons of value, the effect of encumbrances or other liabilities must be taken into account. The regulations provide a system for dealing with these complex exchanges in Treas. Reg. § 1.1031(j)–1, but we will not describe the workings of that regulation in this text because it is not likely to be assigned in a basic tax course due to its complexity.

¶ **24.8000.   INVOLUNTARY CONVERSIONS.** When property is involuntarily converted into money as a result of its destruction in whole or in part, theft, seizure, requisition, condemnation, or threat of imminence thereof, the TP *may elect* to avoid recognition of the gain of the conversion if he acquires replacement property within a statutory period. § 1033. A loss sustained because of an involuntary conversion is recognized; § 1033 does not apply to losses. The loss may or may not be deductible; it must first qualify under § 165.

¶ **24.8100.   Elective.** When property is converted into money or dissimilar property, the TP may elect whether or not to recognize a gain if § 1033 applies. However, if the property is converted directly into other property similar or related in service or use to the converted property (a rare occurrence), then § 1033 is mandatory and prohibits the recognition of gain. Only conversions into money are discussed because that is the more typical occurrence.

¶ **24.8200.   Requirements.** If during the statutory period, for the purpose of replacing the converted property, the TP purchases other property similar or related in service or use to the converted property (or purchases stock in the acquisition of control of a corporation owning such other property), at the election of the TP, the TP will recognize gain on the conversion of his property into money only to the extent that the *amount realized* by him on the conversion exceeds the cost of such replacement property or stock. Thus, if an electing TP's cost of replacement property equals or exceeds the amount that the TP realized from the involuntary conversion of similar or related property, none of the TP's gain will be recognized; if the amount realized by the TP exceeds his cost of replacement property, the electing TP will recognize that amount of his realized *gain* that equals the excess of his amount realized over his replacement cost.

¶ **24.8210. Statutory Period.** The statutory period for purchasing the replacement property begins with the date of disposition of the converted property or the earliest date of threat or imminence of requisition or condemnation of the converted property and ends two years after the close of the TP's first taxable year in which any part of the gain from the conversion was realized; however, this period may be extended by a district director upon application by the TP. Treas. Reg. § 1.1033(a)–2(c)(3).

¶ **24.8220. Election.** The election not to recognize gain under § 1033 is made on the TP's tax return for the year or years in which the TP realized a gain from the conversion. Treas. Reg. § 1.1033(a)–2(c)(2). A failure by the TP to report the gain realized from such a conversion on the TP's tax return for the year in which the gain was realized is treated as an election not to recognize gain under § 1033. Treas. Reg. § 1.1033(a)–2(c)(2).

¶ **24.8230. Similar or Related in Service or Use.** The similarity required for replacements of converted property is greater than that required of "like-kind" property to qualify for a tax-free exchange under § 1031. For example, improved real estate is not similar or related in service or use to unimproved real estate. Treas. Reg. § 1.1033(a)–2(c)(9). For real property held for business use or investment which is involuntarily converted as a result of its seizure, requisition, condemnation, or threat or imminence thereof, the statute employs a "like-kind" standard for replacement rather than a standard of similar or related in service or use, provided that the replacement property is to be held for business use or for investment. § 1033(g). This special rule for the involuntary conversion of certain realty also grants the TP an additional year's time to replace the converted realty. § 1033(g)(4).

¶ **24.8231. Investment in a Partnership.** In *MHS Co. v. Commissioner*,[63] the TP invested the cash proceeds of a condemnation sale of its realty in a joint venture which was formed to acquire and improve other realty. Under local law and Federal tax law, the joint venture constituted a partnership. The Tax Court and the Sixth Circuit held that the TP's purchase of a partnership interest did not qualify as a like-kind replacement under § 1033(g) because a partnership interest is characterized as personal property by the local state law and personalty is not of a like kind to realty.[64] Note that while § 1033(a)(2)(A) permits a TP to purchase a *controlling* interest in a corporation owning property that is similar or related in service or use to the converted property in lieu of acquiring such property directly, that provision does not apply for purposes of § 1033(g). § 1033(g)(2).

¶ **24.8300. Residence.** An involuntary conversion of a TP's personal residence is covered by § 1033. Note that the exclusion of gain from the sale of a residence that is allowed in certain circumstances by § 121 can apply to gain from an involuntary conversion and can apply in addition to the nonrecognition provided by § 1033. § 121(d)(5). See ¶ **24.9110–24.9120.** If a TP's *principal* residence or any of its contents are compulsorily or involuntarily converted as a result of a "presidentially declared disaster," the provisions of § 1033 are greatly liberalized for such properties by § 1033(h).

¶ **24.8400. Basis.** The basis of property purchased in replacement of converted property which caused the nonrecognition of at least part of the gain realized on the conversion is the cost of the replacement property less the amount of realized gain that was not recognized. § 1033(b). If several properties are purchased in replacement of the converted property, the basis so determined is allocated among those properties according to their respective costs.

¶ **24.8410. Illustration.** *X* owned a ship having a value of $140,000 and a basis of $80,000. *X*'s ship was completely destroyed by fire on October 4, Year One, and *X* collected $140,000 insurance proceeds on account of his loss. On January 4, Year Two, *X* purchased a new ship at a cost of $125,000. *X* elected nonrecognition under § 1033. *X* realized a gain of $60,000 on the conversion of his ship, but he recognized a gain of only $15,000. The difference between the amount realized ($140,000) and the cost of the replacement ship ($125,000) establishes a ceiling on

63. 35 T.C.M. 733 (1976), aff'd per curiam 575 F.2d 1177 (6th Cir. 1978).

64. See also, Rev. Rul. 55–351.

the amount of gain that X will recognize. X's basis in the new ship is its cost ($125,000) less the unrecognized gain on the old ship. Of the $60,000 gain realized on the old ship only $15,000 was recognized and $45,000 went unrecognized. Thus, X's basis in the new ship is $80,000 ($125,000 − $45,000 = $80,000).

¶ 24.9000. OTHER NONRECOGNITION PROVISIONS. There are a number of nonrecognition provisions in addition to the two already discussed. A few of these provisions are noted in ¶ 24.9200.

¶ 24.9100. Sale of Residence. Prior to 1997, § 1034 provided nonrecognition for gain realized on the sale of a principal residence to the extent that, within a specified time period, the proceeds of the sale were reinvested in acquiring another principal residence. Section 1034 was repealed in 1997.

Another provision of the pre–1997 version of the Code (§ 121) excluded from gross income a specified amount of gain recognized on the sale of a residence if the TP was at least 55 years of age at the time of the sale. That exclusion applied only once in the lifetime of a TP. The Taxpayer Relief Act of 1997 greatly liberalized § 121 by increasing the amount of gain from the sale of a principal residence that will be excluded from gross income, and by expanding the scope of that provision. The current terms and application of the § 121 exclusion are described below.

The § 121 exclusion applies to gain from the sale of property if during the 5–year period preceding the sale or exchange, the TP had both used and owned the property as the TP's principal residence for a time or times aggregating at least 2 years. § 121(a). For convenience, we will refer to those two requirements as the "2–year use requirement" and the "2–year ownership requirement" respectively. In certain specified circumstances, periods of ownership and use by other parties or of other properties are tacked onto the TP's ownership and use period. See § 121(d)(3), (5)(C), (g).

There is no limit on the number of times that a TP can sell a principal residence and use the exclusion of § 121, but the full exclusion can be taken only once every two years. § 121(b)(3). In other words, if a TP sells a principal residence within two years of the date on which he sold a prior principal residence for which a § 121 exclusion was allowed, the second sale will not qualify for the full amount of the § 121 exclusion. However, as described below, a TP who sells a principal residence because of certain external circumstances, can qualify for an exclusion of a lesser maximum amount even though the TP fails to satisfy the 2–year use and ownership requirements and even though the TP had utilized § 121 for a sale of another residence within two years prior to the current sale or exchange. § 121(c).

If the terms of § 121 are satisfied, the exclusion will apply unless the TP elects not to have it apply. § 121(f). A TP might elect not to have § 121 apply to a sale in order to obtain a larger exclusion for a sale of a principal residence that the TP contemplates making within two years after the first sale. It seems unlikely that this will occur often.

The maximum amount of *gain* that can be excluded under § 121 is $250,000. § 121(b)(1). The maximum amount of gain that can be excluded is increased to $500,000 for married TPs who file a joint return for the year in which the sale or exchange took place, provided that the following three requirements are satisfied:

(1) either spouse meets the 2–year *ownership* requirement,

(2) both spouses meet the 2–year *use* requirement, and

(3) neither spouse utilized § 121 for the sale or exchange of an earlier principal residence within two years of the date on which the current sale or exchange took place.

If the husband and wife fail to satisfy all of the requirements listed above, the terms and limitations of § 121 are applied to each spouse separately as if they were not married. § 121(b)(2)(B). Thus, either spouse may qualify for an exclusion of up to $250,000 if that spouse qualifies for § 121 treatment. For this purpose, each spouse is treated as owning the property during the period that the other spouse owned it. § 121(b)(2)(B). This latter provision liberalizes the application of the 2–year ownership requirement, but does not affect the 2–year use requirement.

If a TP or a married couple fail to satisfy the 2–year use or ownership requirement or if they sell a principal residence within two years of having applied § 121 to a prior sale, of if they fail to satisfy all or any combination of those restrictions, the TP or married couple nevertheless can qualify for an exclusion of a lesser maximum amount if the current sale or exchange is due to a change in place of employment, health or (to the extent provided in regulations) unforeseen circumstances. § 121(c). The maximum amount that can be excluded under § 121(c) is a fraction of the maximum amount that could have been excluded if the three requirements mentioned above had been satisfied—i.e., a fraction of either $250,000 or $500,000 depending upon whether the qualified party is one TP or a married couple. The denominator of the fraction is 2 years. The numerator is the shorter of: (1) the aggregate periods during the 5–year period ending on the date of sale or exchange in which the property was owned and used by the TP as TP's principal residence, or (2) the period between the last date on which the TP used § 121 and the date of the current sale or exchange. § 121(c)(1).

¶ 24.9110. **Interface of §§ 121 and 1033.** The destruction, theft, seizure, requisition, or condemnation of a principal residence is treated as a sale of that property to which § 121 can apply. If a principal residence is involuntarily converted and if the TP qualifies for and elects nonrecognition of gain under § 1033, both the § 121 exclusion of gain and the § 1033 nonrecognition can be utilized. The amount of gain excluded by § 121 is taken first. Then, the amount realized on the sale is reduced by the amount of gain excluded by § 121. Only the balance remaining need be reinvested in another residence to qualify for § 1033 treatment. § 121(d)(5). In other words, for purposes of applying § 1033, the amount realized on the conversion of the principal residence is the actual amount realized reduced by the amount of gain excluded by § 121.

¶ 24.9120. **Basis.** The difference between a nonrecognition provision and an exclusion is that in the former the unrecognized gain or loss is reflected in the TP's basis and therefore in a sense is merely deferred while an exclusion permanently removes all tax consequences from the transaction. Section 121 grants an exclusion of a specified maximum amount of gain, but § 1033 is a nonrecognition provision, and consequently the unrecognized gain from § 1033 is reflected in the TP's basis in the new property. § 1033(b).

¶ 24.9200. **Other Sales or Exchanges.** Gain or loss from certain exchanges of insurance policies [§ 1035], United States obligations [§ 1037], and from certain reacquisitions of real property [§ 1038] is not recognized. A considerable number of nonrecognition provisions operate in the corporate tax law area (e.g., transfers to a controlled corporation [§ 351], certain exchanges pursuant to a reorganization [§§ 354 and 361], certain exchanges (or receipt of stock) pursuant to a corporate division [§ 355], exchange of certain stock of the same corporation [§ 1036], and others). The partnership tax area also contains nonrecognition provisions (e.g., nonrecognition of gain or loss on contribution or property to a partnership in exchange for a partnership interest. § 721).

¶ 24A.1000. DISALLOWANCE OF LOSS DEDUCTION FOR CERTAIN SALES OR EXCHANGES.

¶ 24A.1100.   **Sales Between Related Parties.** Section 267 denies a loss deduction to a TP where the loss resulted from a sale or exchange to a person who is deemed to be related to the TP under the terms of § 267(b). For example, to list a few of the parties to which § 267 applies, no deduction is allowed for a loss recognized on a sale or exchange between: (1) a TP and certain members of his family (e.g., his ancestors, descendants, and brothers and sisters) listed in § 267(c)(4); (2) an individual and a corporation when more than 50% of the value of the stock is owned by the individual; (3) a grantor and a fiduciary of a trust; (4) except in the case of an exchange resulting from a distribution from an estate in satisfaction of a pecuniary bequest, a personal representative of an estate and a beneficiary of that estate. § 267(b). Section 267 does not apply to transfers between spouses or former spouses under § 1041(a); such transfers are controlled exclusively by § 1041. § 267(g).

  ¶ 24A.1110.   **Transferee's Gain on Subsequent Sale.** Where the purchaser of property from a vendor who recognized a loss on the sale but was disallowed a deduction under § 267 subsequently sells or exchanges the property (or other property whose basis in his hands is determined by reference to the original property), any gain realized by the purchaser on the subsequent sale will be recognized only to the extent that it exceeds the amount of loss deduction disallowed to the original vendor under § 267. § 267(d). This provision applies only to realized gain; it does not serve to increase the TP's loss deduction if the property is subsequently sold at a loss. Also, this exclusion of gain provision applies only to sales or exchanges made by the *original purchaser*.

  ¶ 24A.1120.   **Illustration.** X had a basis of $10,000 in Blackacre (unimproved land) which he held for investment purposes. X sold Blackacre to his brother Y for its value of $7,000. X recognized a loss of $3,000, but he was barred from taking a tax deduction for the loss by § 267. Y's basis in Blackacre is $7,000—the amount that Y paid X to purchase it.

    ¶ 24A.1121.   **Illustration 1.** Y subsequently sold Blackacre for $11,000. Y realized a gain of $4,000, but only $1,000 of the gain is recognized because § 267(d) precludes recognition of Y's gain to the extent that X's loss was disallowed under that section.

¶ **24A.1122. Illustration 2.** *Y* subsequently sold Blackacre for $6,000. *Y* realized a loss of $1,000, and he may deduct that amount if he held Blackacre as an investment. Section 267(d) has no application.

¶ **24A.1123. Illustration 3.** *Y* gave Blackacre to his son *S*. As the donee of a gift, *S*'s basis in Blackacre is $7,000—the same basis that *Y* had in the property. § 1015(a). *S* subsequently sold Blackacre for $11,000. *S* recognized a gain of $4,000 on the sale. § 267(d) applies only to a sale by *Y* (the original transferee) and, therefore, has no effect on the amount of gain recognized by *S*.

¶ **24A.1130. Sales Between Two Related Trusts.** No deduction is allowed for a loss recognized by a trust on a sale to another trust if the same person is the grantor of both trusts. § 267(b)(5). Two trusts with a common income beneficiary, but with different grantors and contingent beneficiaries, were allowed to deduct losses from sales to each other in *Joseph E. Widener Trust v. Commissioner.*[65] The Tax Court said that § 267 was inapplicable and a deduction could be denied only if the sale were not bona fide.

¶ **24A.1200. Denial of Certain Deductions.** Section 267(a)(2) denies a TP a deduction for certain expenses or interest owing to persons related to the TP until such time as the item is included in the income of the related person. This provision applies primarily to accrual method TPs who accrue interest or expenses owing and unpaid to related persons who report their income on the cash receipts and disbursements method. In such cases, the accrual TP's deduction is deferred until the item is paid so that it is included in the related person's income.

¶ **24A.1300. Wash Sales.** No deduction is allowed for a loss sustained by a TP on the sale or other disposition of stock or securities when, within 30 days before or 30 days after the sale (i.e., a 61–day period), the TP acquired by purchase (or a taxable exchange) or contracted to acquire substantially identical stock or securities. § 1091. A contract or option to acquire or sell stock or securities will itself constitute "stock or securities" except to the extent that regulations provide otherwise. § 1091(a). A sale or disposition that falls within § 1091 is sometimes called a "wash sale." The denial of a deduction for such a "wash sale" does not apply: (1) to a corporation

---

65. 80 T.C. 304 (1983), Acq.

that is a dealer in stocks and securities and sustained a loss on the disposition of stocks and securities in the ordinary course of its business, or (2) to a noncorporate TP if the disposition of the stocks and securities is made in connection with the TP's trade or business. Treas. Reg. § 1.1091–1(a).

¶ 24A.1310. Forbidden Period. The 61–day period in which the purchase of substantially identical stock or securities will deny the TP a loss deduction is the period beginning 30 days prior to the sale or other disposition and ending 30 days after the sale or other disposition.

¶ 24A.1320. Basis of Purchased Stocks or Securities. If a loss deduction is disallowed because the sale or disposition constituted a "wash sale," the TP's basis in the purchased stocks or securities is equal to the TP's basis in the stock or securities disposed of in the wash sale increased or decreased by the difference between the selling price of the loss stock or securities and the purchase price for the newly acquired stock or securities. § 1091(d). Since basis is adjusted under § 1091, that section is actually a nonrecognition provision (i.e., a deferral of the loss rather than a permanent disallowance). The holding period of the purchased stock or securities includes the holding period of the stock or securities whose disposition triggered the § 1091 nonrecognition or loss. § 1223(3).

¶ 24A.1330. Matching Stocks or Securities Sold with Those Acquired. When more than one loss of such stock or securities is sustained in a taxable year, § 1091 is applied in accordance with the order in which the dispositions took place. When the amount of stock or securities acquired within the 61–day period is less than the amount disposed of, the acquired shares of stock or securities are matched in the order of their acquisition with an equal number of shares of stock or securities that were disposed of. When the amount of stock or securities that were acquired within the 61–day period is not less than the amount that were disposed of, the disposed shares of stock or securities are matched with an equal number of acquired stock or securities in accordance with the order of the latter's acquisition. Treas. Reg. § 1.1091–1(b), (c) and (d). This matching device is used to determine the identity of the shares of stocks or securities sold or otherwise disposed of for which no loss deduction is allowed and to determine the basis of the newly acquired shares of stocks or securities.

¶ 24A.1340. Illustrations.

¶ 24A.1341. Illustration 1. *X* and *Y* are not related. *X* owned 100 shares of Win All, Inc. common stock in which he had a basis of $10,000. On February 6, Year One, *X* sold the 100 shares of Win All stock to *Y* for $6,500—their fair market value. On March 2, Year One, *X* purchased 100 shares of Win All common stock from his broker for $6,700. *X* cannot deduct the $3,500 loss he sustained on the February sale because the transaction constitutes a wash sale under § 1091. *X*'s basis in the 100 shares purchased on March 2 is $10,200 (i.e., the $10,000 basis in his old stock plus the $200 difference between what he paid for his new stock and the selling price of his old stock).

¶ 24A.1342. Illustration 2. The same facts apply as in **¶ 24A.1341** except that on March 2, Year One, *X* paid only $6,250 for the 100 shares of Win All stock he bought on that date. Section 1091 bars *X* from taking a loss deduction for the February sale. X's basis in the 100 shares of stock purchased on March 2 is $9,750 (i.e., the $10,000 basis in his old stock minus the $250 difference in the payment he received for his old stock and the price he paid for the new stock).

¶ 24A.1343. Illustration 3. In Year One, *X* purchased 100 shares of common stock in Widget, Inc. for $5,000 (i.e., $50 per share of stock). On August 10, Year Ten, *X* purchased an additional 200 shares of Widget's common stock for $6,000 (i.e., $30 per share of stock). On September 2, Year Ten, *X* sold to an unrelated person for $3,000 (i.e., $30 per share of stock) the 100 shares of Widget's stock that he had purchased in Year One. *X* realized a loss of $2,000 on that sale, but *X* cannot deduct any of that loss because he had purchased substantially identical stock within the 61–day period and therefore the sale was a wash sale. *X* has a basis of $5,000 in 100 of the shares of Widget stock he acquired in Year Ten, and he will have a basis of $3,000 in the other 100 shares that he purchased in that year. Since the order of time of acquisition probably cannot be determined, it is possible that *X* will have a basis of $8,000 in his 200 shares of Widget stock to be allocated equally among the shares (i.e., $40 per share).

CHAPTER TWENTY–FIVE

CAPITAL GAINS AND LOSSES

¶ 25.0000. CAPITAL GAINS AND LOSSES.

¶ 25.1000. GENERAL. Current tax law provides preferential treatment in the form of a ceiling on the applicable tax rate that is applied to "net capital gains." The excess (if any) of a TP's net long-term capital gain over his net short-term capital loss for a taxable year is characterized as a "net capital gain."[1] Any gain or loss that is not treated as a capital gain or loss is referred to as "ordinary income" or as "ordinary loss." §§ 64 and 65.

The Code provides a ceiling on the maximum tax rate that can be applied to an individual's net capital gain, and we will refer to that ceiling as the maximum rate. In 2011, the maximum marginal rate on an individual's taxable income is 35%; but net capital gains cannot be taxed at that high a rate. The maximum rate on an individual's net capital gain typically is 15%. § 1(a)–(d), (h), (i)(2). For years beginning after 2012, there will be an increase in the ordinary rates that apply to taxable income, and there will be an increase to some of the maximum rate ceilings that apply to net capital gains. For years beginning after 2012, the maximum marginal rate that can apply to an individual's taxable income is scheduled to be 39.6%, and the most typical maximum rate that can apply to an individual's net capital gains is 20%.

As we will see, for the year 2011, there are four different maximum rates that apply to different types of capital gains, but the maximum rate that will apply most frequently is the 15% rate. For years beginning after 2012, unless Congress acts to change the rules, there will be six different maximum rates for net capital gains, and the rate that will apply most frequently is a 20% rate.

Currently, there is no preferential tax treatment for a *corporation's* net capital gains.

---

1. See ¶ **25.2300**.

¶ 25.2000. TAX TREATMENT OF CAPITAL GAINS AND LOSSES.

¶ 25.2100. Groupings of Long-and Short–Term Gains and Losses.

Capital gains and losses are separated into two groups: long-term gains and long-term losses are placed into one group, and short-term gains and short-term losses are placed into a different group. A capital gain or loss that is recognized on the sale or exchange of a capital asset is long-term if the TP had held the asset for more than one year, and such a gain or loss is short-term if the TP had held the asset for one year or less. § 1222(1)–(4). A capital gain or loss generally is the gain or loss recognized on the sale or exchange of a capital asset. A "sale or exchange" is a term of art that has a specific meaning in the Code.[2] The definition of "capital asset" is set forth in § 1221 and is discussed later in this chapter.[3]

¶ 25.2200. Netting of Gains and Losses.

A TP's long-term capital gains and *deductible* long-term capital losses are netted to determine the "net long-term capital gain" or the "net long-term capital loss." § 1222(7), (8). The TP's short-term capital gains and *deductible* short-term capital losses are netted to determine the "net short-term capital gain" or the "net short-term capital loss." § 1222(5), (6).

¶ 25.2300. Net Capital Gain.

After completing the preliminary grouping and netting process described in ¶ 25.2200, the TP's net long-term capital gain (if any) for the taxable year is reduced by the TP's net short-term capital loss (if any) for that taxable year. The excess of net long-term capital gain over net short-term capital loss is referred to as a "net capital gain." § 1222(11). It is only a noncorporate TP's net capital gain that qualifies for a maximum rate.

A TP is granted an election to exclude from net capital gain (and therefore treat as ordinary income) all or part of the net gain from the disposition of property held as an investment. §§ 1(h)(2), 163(d)(4)(B)(iii). That election will qualify the net gain from the disposition of such property as "investment income" from which "investment interest" can be deducted. § 163(d)(4)(B)(iii).[4]

¶ 25.2310. Significance of Tax Rate Ceiling.

For 2011, the maximum marginal tax rate that can be imposed on an individual's taxable income is 35%. § 1(i)(2).That maximum tax rate is scheduled to increase to 39.6% for years after 2012. Even if an

2.   See ¶¶ **25.5000–25.5300.**
3.   See ¶ **25.3000** *et seq.*
4.   See ¶ **16.1220.**

individual's taxable income places him in the maximum marginal tax bracket (35% for 2011 and 39.6% for years after 2012), the maximum marginal tax rate that can be imposed on most types of that individual's net capital gain is 15% for the year 2011 and 20% for years after 2012. § 1(h)(1)(C). You can see that there is a significant advantage to having income classified as a capital gain. As we will see, in 2011, there are four different maximum rates that can apply to net capital gains depending upon the nature of the long-term gains that comprise the TP's net capital gain. For years after 2012, there will be six different rates.

¶ 25.2320. Application of the Maximum Tax Rates to Net Capital Gains. For the year 2011, the four highest marginal tax rates that apply to an individual's taxable income are: 25%, 28%, 33%, and 35%. For years beginning after 2012, those four rates are scheduled to be 28%, 31%, 35%, and 39.6% respectively.

An individual's net capital gain will qualify for a ceiling on the rate of tax that can be imposed. A capital gains rate can be viewed as an alternative rate to the normal tax rate structure. Instead, since none of the several capital gains rates will apply to a capital gain to the extent that the normal rate that would be applicable to that gain is smaller, a capital gain's rate can be viewed as a maximum rate. In this text, the capital gains tax is described as the maximum tax rate that can be applied to certain types of net capital gains.

The maximum rates on net capital gains apply for purposes of both the regular income tax and the alternative minimum tax. §§ 1(h), 55(b)(3).[5]

The first step in applying the capital gains rates is to divide the noncorporate TP's capital gains and losses into two separate categories—long-term and short-term. The long-term capital gains and losses are aggregated to arrive at the net long-term capital gain or loss, and short-term capital gains and losses are aggregated to arrive at the net short-term capital gain or loss. Only if there is a net long-term capital gain that is greater than a net short-term capital loss (if any) for that year will the maximum rate limitations for net capital gains apply. As previously noted, the excess of net long-term capital gain over net short-term capital loss (if any) is referred to as the "net capital gain." The

---

5. The alternative minimum tax is discussed in Chapter **Twenty–Eight**.

limitation on maximum rates apply to an individual's net capital gain.

¶ **25.2321.   Treatment of Capital Gains.** Prior to the 1997 and 1998 amendments to the Code, the task of determining the tax on capital gains was largely completed once the net capital gain for the year was computed. As a consequence of those amendments, it is no longer sufficient to determine the net capital gain. The current version of the Code applies different maximum rates to several categories of net capital gain, and so the TP's long-term capital gains and losses must be divided into subcategories. In 2011, the several maximum rates for net capital gain are (reading from top to bottom) 28%, 25%, 15%, and 0%. For years beginning after 2012, the 15% rate is scheduled to be increased to 20%, and the 0% rate is increased to 10%. So, for years after 2012, the maximum tax rates for net capital gains will be (reading from top to bottom) 28%, 25%, 20%, and 10%.

For convenience, properties the gain from which would be taxed at one of those maximum rates will sometimes be referred to herein as property in a category designated by the maximum rate for that property. Since the post–2012 rates will soon become applicable, we will use the post–2012 rates to designate the categories of property. So, property that is subject to a 28% maximum rate is referred to as 28% category property. Similarly, property subject to one of the other maximum rates (using post–2012 rates) are referred to as 25% category property, 20% category property, and 10% category property respectively.

Beginning in 2013, there will be two more maximum rates. If 20% category or 10% category property was held by the TP for more than five years before disposing of it, there will be a 2 percentage point reduction of the maximum rate applicable to the aggregate gain of such property. Consequently, for property held for more than five years, the maximum rate for the aggregate gain on the disposition of such 10% category property in a taxable year after 2012 will be 8%, and the maximum rate for the aggregate gain recognized on the disposition of such 20% category property will be 18%. In this book, we will not make reference to those 8% and 18% properties as being in a separate category. Moreover, we will not give any further discussion to the 8% and 18% rules.

Keep in mind that the rates applicable to net capital gains are *maximum* rates. If the normal marginal rate (under the tax rate schedule) that would be applied to any amount of a TP's net capital gain is less than the maximum capital gain rate, the lower normal rate is applied to that amount of the gain.

For convenience, let us refer to a TP's taxable income that is not part of the net capital gain as "ordinary income." The amount of tax on the TP's ordinary income is determined by applying the rates from the regular tax schedule to that income. § 1(h)(1)(A). The application of the regular tax rate schedule is applied to taxable income after excluding the net capital gain, and so applies first to the TP's ordinary income. Thus, the TP's net capital gain is placed in the marginal tax bracket for taxable income immediately above the TP's ordinary income. This stacking maximizes the benefit of providing a ceiling on the tax rate applicable to net capital gains since a TP's lower tax rates will be applied first to the ordinary income.

While other maximum rates apply in circumstances described below, the maximum tax rate that most frequently will be applied to a net capital gain is 20% for years after 2012. § 1(h)(1)(C). As noted above, we will refer to property subject to that rate as "20% category property." If all or a portion of a net capital gain from 20% category property would be taxed under the normal tax rate schedule at less than a 20% rate, then the maximum 20% rate for such net capital gains would be of no benefit to the TP for that amount of his gain. To remedy that problem, the maximum rate for such gains is reduced to 10%. Such property that is subject to a 10% maximum rate is referred to herein as "10% category property."

The first ordinary tax rate above a 20% rate is 28% in years following 2012. If any portion of the net capital gain from property in the 20% category would be taxed at less than a 28% rate for post–2012 years by the regular tax rate schedule, then that amount of the gain will be subject to a maximum rate of 10%. § 1(h)(1)(B).

However, there are three subcategories of net capital gain that do not qualify for either the 20% or the 10% maximum rates and so the gains and losses from the sale or exchange of properties in those subcategories must be separately determined. The portion of the net capital gain that is not within any of those three subcategories and is not so-called "qualified dividend income"[6] is referred to as the "adjusted net capital gain." § 1(h)(3). Adjusted net capital gain is segregated from the other capital gains because different maximum rates apply to the other capital gains.

Before examining the three subcategories of capital gains and the rates that are applied to them, let us consider an illustration of how the mechanics of the tax system operates when the TP has a net capital gain. This illustration omits some of the complexity of the mechanics of the provision because it does not contain any of the subcategories of capital gains, and because the marginal rate on the TP's ordinary income exceeds the 25% rate bracket.

¶ 25.2322.   Illustration. For the year 2010, *F*, an unmarried individual who is neither a head of household nor a surviving spouse, had taxable income of $140,000, of which $30,000 was a net capital gain. None of *F*'s capital gains or losses were derived from 28% or 25% category items. F had no carryover losses to that year.

To determine *F*'s tax, first reduce his taxable income by his $30,000 net capital gain, and then compute the tax on the resulting figure of $110,000. The entire amount of *F*'s net capital gain is taken out because the resulting figure of $110,000 is greater than the amount of *F*'s taxable income that, under the 2010 normal rate schedule, is taxed at a rate below 25% (i.e., $34,000 of *F*'s 2010 taxable income is taxed at a rate below 25%). Note that if the year involved were after 2012, the dividing line would be whether the TP's ordinary income exceeded the amount that is taxed at a rate that is below 28%. The fact that the TP's ordinary income exceeded those figures means that there is no capital gains that would have been taxed under the normal tax schedule at a rate that is less then the maximum capital gain rate.

You will recall that capital gains are stacked on top of the TP's ordinary income to determine what ordinary rates would apply to it. The first partial tax is the tax at normal rates on $110,000; the tax on that amount is $24,509. The second partial tax is equal to 15% of $30,000 (the amount of *F*'s net capital gain which was excluded from the first computation),

---

6.   "Qualified dividend income" is described in ¶ **25.6300**.

which provides a partial tax of \$4,500. All of *F*'s net capital gain qualified for the maximum 15% rate since *F* had no 28% or 25% category gain. Note that if the year involved were after 2012, the maximum rate would be 20%. The total tax due then is the sum of the two partial taxes. The tax due is \$29,009 (\$24,509 + \$4,500).

If no maximum rate had been provided for net capital gains, the tax on *F*'s \$140,000 of taxable income would have been \$32,909. The maximum rate limitation reduced *F*'s tax bill by \$3,900 (the difference between the \$32,909 tax that he would have incurred and the \$29,009 tax that he actually incurred).

¶ **25.2323. The 25% and 28% Category Properties.** There are three categories of capital gain and loss that have to be identified and separated from the rest. Two of those subcategories, collectibles and "section 1202 gain," are taxed at a maximum rate of 28% and therefore comprise the 28% category property. Let us examine the collectibles and section 1202 gain subcategories separately.

¶ **25.2323–1. Collectibles.** The gain and loss from the sale or exchange of a "collectible" that is a capital asset that has been held for more than one year must be separated from other capital gains and losses. § 1(h)(5). Only gains that are included in gross income and losses that are taken into account in computing taxable income are included in this separate calculation. § 1(h)(5)(A). A gain or loss from the sale or exchange of collectibles that qualify for this treatment (i.e., capital assets held for more than one year) is referred to as "collectibles gain" and "collectibles loss" respectively. § 1(h)(5)(A). Collectibles gain also includes the gain from the sale of an interest in a partnership, S corporation, or trust that is attributable to unrealized appreciation of collectibles held by that organization. § 1(h)(5)(B). A "collectible" includes works of art, antiques, rugs, gems, alcoholic beverages, stamps, and coins (but certain coins are excluded). §§ 1(h)(5)(A), 408(m). The gains and losses from the sale or exchange of collectibles that were capital assets that had not been held for more than one year are short-term capital gains and losses and are not included in the collectibles gains or the collectibles losses.

The collectibles gains are combined with the "section 1202 gain" (described below), and the sum is then reduced by collectibles losses and capital losses.[7] The maximum tax rate on the net of collectibles gains and section 1202 gain reduced by collectibles losses and capital losses is 28%.

¶ 25.2323–2. Section 1202 Gain. Section 1202 excludes from income a percentage of the gain recognized by a noncorporate TP on the sale or exchange of so-called "qualified small business stock" that had been held for more than 5 years.[8] There is a ceiling on the amount of exclusion that is allowable. § 1202(b)(1). See **¶ 25.8200**. The amount of gain from the sale or exchange of qualified small business stock that is included in TP's income (usually 50% of the gain, but only 25% of the gain is included for the sale of qualified stock acquired after February 17, 2009, and before January 1, 2011) is included with the gain from collectibles in the 28% category and so is taxed at a maximum rate of 28%. § 1(h)(4), (7). Hereafter, we will refer to the exclusion as 50% even though it can be as high as 75% in some circumstances.

There is a ceiling on the amount of gain that is eligible for the percentage exclusion provided by § 1202. We refer to the gain from the sale or exchange of qualified small business stock that exceeds the ceiling of eligible gain as "ineligible gain," and an individual's ineligible gain is not included in the 28% category.[9] The amount of § 1202 income that is included in the 28% category (the eligible gain) is referred to as "section 1202 gain." § 1(h)(7). Thus, if the ceiling on the amount of § 1202 exclusion does not apply, only 50% of the gain from the sale of such qualified small business stock is taxed, and the rate of tax on that amount cannot exceed 28%. The net effect is that the eligible gain from the disposition of such qualified small business stock is taxed at a maximum rate of 14%.

The collectibles gain and the section 1202 gain are added together and comprise the gains in the 28% category. The

---

7. The manner in which capital losses are allocated among the several categories of capital gains is described in **¶ 25.2413**.

8. See **¶ 25.8000** *et seq.*

9. See **¶¶ 25.8200–25.8240**.

accumulated gain is then reduced by the sum of: collectibles loss, net short-term capital loss, and long-term capital loss carried over to that year. § 1(h)(4). In addition, if the aggregate losses in the 20% category exceed the aggregate gains in the 20% category, the excess loss is allocated to the 28% category and included with the deductions in that category.[10] For convenience, the sum of the losses in the 28% category is sometimes referred to herein as the "28% category losses." After deducting the 28% category losses, if the net figure is a gain, it is taxed at a maximum rate of 28%. As explained in ¶ **25.2413**, if after deducting the 28% category losses the net figure is a loss, that loss is deducted from lower rate categories of net capital gains in descending order of the rate category.[11]

¶ **25.2323–3. Unrecaptured Section 1250 Gain.** The third subcategory is gain from the disposition or involuntary conversion of section 1250 property (primarily buildings and their structural components) that has been held for more than one year, but only to the extent that such gain is treated as a long-term capital gain.[12] To the extent that such gain that qualifies for treatment as long-term capital gain is attributable to depreciation adjustments that were made to the property's basis, the tax on the gain is limited to a maximum rate of 25%. § 1(h)(1)(D), (6). This is the only type of gain that is subject to the 25% maximum rate, and therefore is the only gain included in the 25% category. This type of gain is referred to as "unrecaptured section 1250 gain." § 1(h)(6).

If the 28% category losses exceed the 28% category gains, the excess losses will reduce the unrecaptured section 1250 gain that is subject to the 25% maximum tax rate. § 1(h)(6)(A)(ii). If the losses allocated to the 25% category exceed gains in that category, the excess is allocated first to the 20% category, and any excess remaining from that

10. Notice 97–59.

11. § 1(h)(6). See also Notice 97–59.

12. The extent to which the gain from the sale or exchange or involuntary conversion of depreciable property will be treated as a long-term capital gain is set forth primarily in § 1231 and is explained in Chapter **Twenty–Six**. "Section 1250 property" is defined in § 1250(c).

category is then allocated to the 10% category.[13]

As explained in Chapter **Twenty–Six**, the gains and losses from the disposition or conversion of certain properties (sometimes called "section 1231 property," which includes real property used in a trade or business) are aggregated. A gain or loss from such a disposition or conversion is referred to as a "section 1231 gain" or a "section 1231 loss." § 1231(a)(3). If, after aggregating the sections 1231 gains and losses for a taxable year, there is a net gain, it is referred to as a "net section 1231 gain"; and if there is a net loss, it is referred to as a "net section 1231 loss." § 1231(c)(3), (4). A TP's unrecaptured section 1250 gain, which qualifies for the 25% maximum rate, cannot exceed the TP's net section 1231 gain for that year. § 1(h)(6)(B).

If there is a net section 1231 gain, all of the section 1231 gains and losses are treated as long-term capital gains and losses; but if there is a net section 1231 loss, all of the section 1231 gains and losses are treated as ordinary income and ordinary loss.[14] However, if a TP has a net section 1231 gain within five years of having had a net section 1231 loss, the ordinary loss treatment accorded to that prior year's net section 1231 loss is "recaptured" by treating a comparable amount of the current year's net section 1231 gain as ordinary income. § 1231(c).[15] If part of the net section 1231 gain in the current year is comprised of unrecaptured section 1250 gain, and if there is a recapture under § 1231(c) of part of the net section 1231 gain because of a prior year's net section 1231 loss, the question is how the recapture (which constitutes ordinary income treatment) is to be allocated among the several section 1231 gain items. The amount of such recapture that is allocated to the unrecaptured section 1250 gain will cause it to be treated as ordinary income to that extent, and so that amount will no longer qualify as unrecaptured section 1250 gain and will not qualify for the 25% maximum rate. The 1998 amendment to the Code states that the manner in which the recaptured net section 1231 gain is to be allocated among the section 1231 gain items can be determined by Treasury in the promulgation of either forms or

13.   See Notice 97–59.

14.   See ¶ **26.2200**.

15.   See ¶ **26.2221**.

regulations. § 1(h)(8). In Notice 97–59, which was promulgated prior to the adoption of the 1998 amendments, the IRS provided that any recaptured ordinary income under § 1231(c) is to be allocated first to section 1231 gain in the 28% category, second any remaining ordinary income is allocated to section 1231 gain in the 25% category, and finally any remaining ordinary income is allocated to section 1231 gain in the 20% category. The Service has not changed its approach.

¶ 25.2324. **Additional Tax Rate.** A TP's net capital gains are included in his adjusted gross income. Therefore, those tax deductions and credits that are reduced when a TP's adjusted gross income (AGI) exceeds a specified figure are affected by a TP's net capital gains. A few examples of tax benefits that are so reduced are: the 2% of AGI floor on miscellaneous itemized deductions, the percentage of AGI floor on medical expense deductions, the reduction of itemized deductions under § 68 when a TP's AGI exceeds a specified figure, the phaseout of the personal exemptions under § 151(d), the 10% of AGI floor on the deduction of net personal casualty losses under § 165(h)(2), and the reduction of the credit available for dependent care services that is mandated by § 21(a)(2). The *effective* rate on a net capital gain therefore can exceed the nominal rate listed in the Code when the gain causes a reduction of deductions or credits.

¶ 25.2330. **Significance of Groupings.** The existence of any preference for net capital gains makes it necessary to group long-term and short-term capital gains and losses separately so that the amount of net capital gain can be determined. Apart from the preferential treatment of net capital gains of noncorporate TPs, there are independent reasons to group long-term and short-term capital gains separately. One reason is that there are some provisions in the Code that treat long-term capital gain differently from other income. For example, in general, a gift of appreciated property to a qualified charity is treated more favorably if the sale of that property would have produced a long-term capital gain than would be the case if the sale would have produced short-term capital gain or ordinary income. See § 170(b)(1)(C), (D), (e)(1)(A). In addition to the difference in the treatment of capital gains, it is necessary to distinguish capital gains and losses from ordinary income and losses because of the limitations that Congress imposes on the deductibility of capital losses.[16]

¶ 25.2400. Limitation on Capital Loss Deductions: General. Capital losses are deductible only if a provision of the Code specifically authorizes the deduction. Typically, if deductible, the statutory authorization is under § 165, but that section is not exclusive. For example, § 166(d) allows a deduction for a nonbusiness bad debt as a short-term capital loss. If deductible, a capital loss will be a nonitemized deduction. § 62(a)(3).

If permitted under a Code provision, a capital loss is subject to the limitation on deductibility of capital losses imposed by § 1211. The following discussion describes the limitations contained in § 1211 upon capital losses otherwise deductible under § 165 or under some other Code provision and how those losses are allocated among the several categories of net capital gains. Since a deductible capital loss is a nonitemized deduction, § 1211 contains the only limitation on the deduction of capital losses.

¶ 25.2410. Deductible from Capital Gains. A TP's capital losses which are otherwise deductible may be deducted from his capital gains. § 1211. For this purpose, it is irrelevant whether the losses or gains are short-term or long-term; as previously noted in describing the groupings procedure,[17] a capital loss is first deducted from the capital gains of like term (long-term or short-term) and only the excess loss (if any) is deducted from the net gain, if any, of the other term.

If, after allocating the capital losses to all of the capital gains, there is an excess of capital loss remaining, a noncorporate TP may deduct his excess capital loss against up to $3,000 of his ordinary income. § 1211(b).[18] The excess capital loss, which is not deductible because of the limitations of § 1211, may be carried over to other years under the provisions of § 1212 described later in this chapter.[19]

---

16. See ¶¶ **25.2400–25.2430**.

17. The allocation of capital losses among the four categories of net capital gains is described in ¶ **25.2413**.

18. See ¶ **25.2420**.

19. See ¶¶ **25.2430–25.2432**.

¶ **25.2411. Illustration 1.** In 2011, X, an individual, had a long-term capital gain of $20,000, a long-term capital loss of $5,000 and a short-term capital loss of $10,000. X had ordinary income of $100,000. All of X's capital gains and losses were recognized from the sale of corporate stock so that, apart from § 1211 limitations, the losses are deductible under § 165(c)(2). X deducts his $5,000 long-term capital loss from his $20,000 of long-term capital gain, providing him with a net long-term capital gain of $15,000. Since X had no short-term capital gain, his $10,000 short-term capital loss constitutes a $10,000 net short-term capital loss. His net capital gain is the excess of his net long-term capital gain ($15,000) over his net short-term capital loss of $10,000. Thus, X has a net capital gain of $5,000. Since X had no 25% or 28% category income, his net capital gain qualifies for the 15% maximum rate that applies in 2011.

¶ **25.2412. Illustration 2.** In Year One, individual Y had the following gains and losses from the sale of corporate stock: $20,000 short-term capital gain; $8,000 short-term capital loss; $10,000 long-term capital loss. Y may offset his $18,000 of capital losses against its $20,000 of short-term capital gain. Y first deducts his $8,000 short-term capital loss from his $20,000 of short-term capital gain, and that provides Y with a net short-term capital gain of $12,000. Y then deducts his $10,000 net long-term capital loss from his $12,000 net short-term capital gain, leaving a remaining short-term capital gain of $2,000. Note that since Y had no long-term capital gains, his $10,000 long-term capital loss constituted a net long-term capital loss of that same amount. Y has a net short-term capital gain of $2,000 in excess of his net long-term capital loss. There are no maximum limitations on the rates for a short-term capital gain, and so that $2,000 gain will be included in Y's ordinary income and taxed at ordinary rates.

¶ **25.2413. Allocation of Capital Losses.** Let us now look at how capital losses are allocated among the four capital gain categories. The first step is to divide into separate computational baskets long-term and short-term capital gains and losses and to compute the net gain or loss for each separate basket. If there is no net capital gain (i.e., if there is no excess of net long-term capital gain over net short-term capital loss), then no maximum tax rates are applicable. However, if there is a net capital gain, certain items must be carved out of that figure and the tax thereon is limited by specified maximum rates.[20]

Short-term capital losses for a taxable year (including short-term losses carried to that year under § 1212) are deducted first from short-term capital gains. If the aggregate short-term capital losses exceed the aggregate short-term capital gains (which means that there is a net short-term capital loss for that year), the net short-term capital loss is applied first to reduce any net long-term capital gain in the 28% category. If there is a net loss in the 28% category, that loss is then allocated to the 25% category, and then any unused loss is allocated to the lower categories in descending order.

The operating principle is that gains and losses in each net long-term category are netted. If there is a net loss in any category, that loss is applied to the highest rate category that has a net gain; and any resulting excess loss in that category is applied to lower rate categories in descending order. As noted above, short-term capital losses are deducted first from short-term capital gains, and any resulting net short-term capital loss is allocated first to the 28% category. The operation of this approach is described more specifically below.

The long-term capital gains in the 28% category (i.e., collectibles gain and section 1202 gain) are reduced by the sum of: (1) collectibles loss, (2) net short-term capital loss, (3) long-term capital losses carried to that year under § 1212, and (4) net losses from the 20% category. § 1(h)(4), and Notice 97–59. If there is a net loss in the 28% category, it is applied in descending order to the next highest categories that have a net gain—i.e., first to gains in the 25% category, and then to gains in the 20% category. If there is a net loss in any of the other categories, that excess loss is applied first to the highest rate category (the 28% category) and then in descending order to the next highest rate categories.[21] For example, if a TP's losses in the 20% category exceed the gains in that category, the excess loss will be deducted from gains in the TP's 28% category; and if there is a net loss in the 28% category, that net loss will be deducted from gains in the TP's 25% category and so on.

20. See ¶¶ 25.2321–25.2323–3.
21. Notice 97–59.

Any long-term capital loss remaining after applying it to the four categories is deducted from the TP's net short-term capital gain (if any). For a noncorporate TP, if there is a net loss remaining after applying the losses to all four categories and to the net short-term capital gain, $3,000 of that loss can be deducted.[22] Any remaining loss is carried forward and treated as described in ¶ **25.2430**.

¶ **25.2420. Deductible from Ordinary Income.** Where the aggregate capital losses of a noncorporate TP exceed his capital gains for that year, the TP can deduct the excess against up to $3,000 of his ordinary income. § 1211(b). A corporate TP is not permitted to deduct its excess capital losses against any of its ordinary income. In the case of a married TP who files a separate tax return, such an excess loss can be deducted from no more than $1,500 of ordinary income. The deductibility of such excess capital losses is the same whether the excess is attributable to a short-term loss or a long-term loss. To the extent that a capital loss is not deductible because of the limitations of § 1211 (e.g., the amount of an individual's capital losses that exceeds the sum of his capital gains plus $3,000 of his ordinary income is not deductible because of § 1211), the nondeductible amount can be carried forward to subsequent years under the provisions of § 1212.[23]

¶ **25.2421. Illustration.** In Year One, X, an unmarried individual, had taxable income of $38,000 before taking into account her capital gains and losses. In that year, X had a short-term capital gain of $8,000, and X had a long-term capital loss of $17,000. All of X's capital gains and losses were from the sale of corporate stock, and so, subject to the § 1211 limitations, her losses were deductible under § 165(c)(2). Under § 1211(b), X can deduct $8,000 of her long-term capital loss since that is the amount of her short-term capital gain for that year. X can also deduct an additional $3,000 of her net loss. So, X is permitted to deduct a total of $11,000 of her long-term capital loss, and the remaining $6,000 of that loss cannot be deducted from her Year One income. The nondeductible $6,000 of X's loss can be carried over and deducted in subsequent years.

22. ¶ **25.2420**.
23. Described at ¶ **25.2430**.

¶ **25.2430. Carryover of Capital Loss.** A noncorporate TP's excess capital loss for a tax year (i.e., capital losses that are not used to reduce the TP's income for that year because of the limitations of § 1211) is carried forward to the TP's succeeding tax year and is treated as if it were actually recognized in that succeeding year. § 1212(b). Thus, if any of the carryover loss cannot be deducted in the next taxable year because of § 1211 limitations, it will be carried forward to the next year and so on. A carryforward capital loss has the same character (long-term or short-term) as it had when the loss was incurred. § 1212(b)(1).

A carryforward long-term capital loss is first applied to the TP's 28% category in the carryover year. § 1(h)(4)(B). If there is a net loss in the 28% category, the excess loss is applied to the other categories in descending order as described in ¶ **25.2413**.

A carryforward short-term capital loss is first applied to the TP's short-term capital gains for the carryover year, and any excess of short-term capital loss for that year (i.e., the net short-term capital loss) is deducted from long-term capital gains in the same manner that long-term capital loss carryovers are allocated. See the paragraph above and ¶ **25.2413**.

The effect of the carryover provision is to permit a noncorporate TP to carry forward capital losses for an indefinite number of years until the loss is absorbed or until the TP dies. With one minor exception (§ 1212(c)), a capital loss of a noncorporate TP can only be carried forward; it cannot be carried back to prior years

¶ **25.2431. Priority of Allocation to Ordinary Income.** If a noncorporate TP has both a net short-term capital loss and a net long-term capital loss in the same year, a question can arise as to the order in which those two net losses should be used as a deduction against $3,000 of the TP's ordinary income. This question arises only for the purpose of determining the characterization of the TP's losses that are carried forward to subsequent years. In these circumstances, the TP's net short-term capital loss will be deducted first. Only to the extent that the amount of the net short-term capital loss is inadequate to obtain the full $3,000 deduction will the net long-term loss be deductible from ordinary income. § 1212(b)(2).

¶ **25.2432. Unclaimed Carryover Loss Deduction.** In Rev. Rul. 76–177, the Commissioner ruled that to the extent that a carryover capital loss could have been deducted in a subsequent year, that amount of the carryover loss was used up in that year even though the TP failed to claim a deduction for it.

¶ **25.3000. DEFINITION OF "CAPITAL ASSET."** Section 1222 defines capital gains or losses as the gain or loss from the "sale or exchange of a capital asset."

¶ **25.3100. Statutory Definition.** Section 1221 defines a capital asset as "property held by the TP (whether or not connected with his trade or business)," excluding an enumerated list of eight categories of property, four of which are discussed below. It would seem that any property that is not described within the eight excluded categories would be a capital asset, but the construction of that provision has had a somewhat checkered history.

Despite the broad statutory definition of a capital asset as all property other than a list of specified exceptions, the Supreme Court initially determined that the statute encompasses only those kinds of properties that the Court believed Congress intended to qualify for the special capital gains tax treatment, but the Court subsequently retreated from that view.[24]

¶ **25.3200. Meaning of the Term "Property."** While the term "property" in § 1221 would appear on its face to cover most rights that a TP might be able to sell, the courts have excluded some interests from that term.

¶ **25.3210. Compensatory Payment For the Use of Property.** Where the TP, a motor common carrier, received compensation from the government for the temporary requisition of the TP's facilities during World War II, the Supreme Court held that although an interest of the TP was taken by the government within the meaning of the compensatory requirements of the Fifth Amendment, the taken interest did not constitute property within the meaning of § 1221.[25] In effect, the Court treated the compensatory payments to the TP as rent for the use of property. Similarly, the Service has ruled that a TP's collection of insurance for the loss of the use of a production facility when it is was destroyed by fire constitutes ordinary income to the TP.[26]

24. Compare *Corn Products Refining Co. v. Commissioner*, 350 U.S. 46 (1955), with *Arkansas Best Corp. v. Commissioner*, 485 U.S. 212 (1988). See also ¶¶ **25.4200–25.4220**.

25. *Commissioner v. Gillette Motor Transport, Inc.*, 364 U.S. 130 (1960).

26. Rev. Rul. 74–444. While the facility was § 1231 property rather than a capital asset, the principle is the same.

¶ **25.3220. Relinquishment of Personal Rights.** Any right that a TP might have in her deceased husband's life story was held not to be property within the meaning of § 1221; and, consequently, the payment received by the TP from a moving picture company for the relinquishment of those rights was ordinary income to the TP.[27]

¶ **25.3230. Validity of Narrow Construction of the Term "Property."** As the paragraphs above reflect, the courts have adopted the view that certain items, which in other settings are considered to be "property," are denied capital asset characterization because they do not qualify as "property" for purposes of § 1221. The Supreme Court's decision in the *Arkansas Best* case (at ¶ **25.4220**) rejected the view that the term "capital asset" could be construed by courts to exclude property that is not excluded by one of the statutory exceptions set forth in § 1221. However, the Court expressly approved of the view that the term "property" has a narrower meaning in § 1221 than it has in other contexts, and the Court expressed its approval of several such cases including the *Gillette Motor* decision (at ¶ **25.3210**).[28]

¶ **25.3300. Statutory Exclusions.** Section 1221 lists eight categories of property which are excluded from the term "capital asset." Four of those categories are discussed below.

¶ **25.3310. Property Held Primarily for Sale to Customers in the Ordinary Course of the Taxpayer's Trade or Business.** The most litigated of the statutory exclusions is § 1221(a)(1), which excludes a TP's stock in trade, inventory, or property held by the TP primarily for sale to customers in the ordinary course of his trade or business. Most of the litigation concerning § 1221 deals with the construction of the phrase "property held ... primarily for sale to customers...."

In *Case v. United States*,[29] the court listed eight factors to use in deciding whether property was held primarily for sale. They are:

(1) The purpose for which the property was acquired

---

27. *Miller v. Commissioner*, 299 F.2d 706 (2d Cir. 1962); see also Rev. Rul. 65–261.

28. *Arkansas Best Corp.*, 485 U.S. at 217, n.5.

29. 633 F.2d 1240 (6th Cir. 1980).

(2) The purpose for which the property was held

(3) The extent of improvements made to the property

(4) The frequency, number, and continuity of sales

(5) The nature and substantiality of the transactions

(6) The nature and extent of the TP's dealings with similar property

(7) The extent of advertising to promote sales

(8) Whether or not the property was listed for sale either directly or through brokers

The court did not indicate what relative weight should be given to each of those eight factors.

¶ 25.3311. Taxpayer's Purpose. The term "primarily" refers to the purpose of the TP for holding the property *at the time of sale*. The term "primarily" does not refer to the TP's purpose for the entire period he held the property. For example, if a TP held land for ten years as an investment and then held it for sale to customers for one month prior to selling it, the purpose at the time of sale controls. The TP's prior dealings are significant only as evidence of his purpose at the time of sale. Most TPs hold property primarily for sale at the time of the sale.[30] Thus, the majority of cases in this area focus on the question of whether the property was held primarily for sale *to customers in the ordinary course of the TP's trade or business*.

¶ 25.3312. Customers. A TP who buys and sells large numbers of stocks and securities but who deals through a stock broker does not hold such stocks and securities for sale to customers—i.e., the TP makes no sales to a "customer."[31] Indeed, the term "customers" was incorporated into § 1221 to preclude ordinary loss treatment for the sale of most stocks and securities. Congress feared that if an ordinary loss were recognized on the sale of stock, the federal revenue might be reduced severely in a year in which stock prices dipped. Consequently, except for a few statutory exceptions for certain specially defined types of stock [e.g., §§ 306 and 1244], gain or

30. But cf. ¶¶ **25.3314–25.3314–3A**.

31. *Van Suetendael v. Commissioner*, 3 T.C.M. 987 (1944), aff'd 152 F.2d 654 (2d Cir. 1945).

loss from the sale of stock usually constitutes capital gain or loss.

¶ 25.3313. Ordinary Course of Trade or Business. Property is not within the "primarily for sale" exception unless the property is held for sale to customers in the ordinary course of the TP's trade or business. It is necessary to distinguish a sale of an investment that the owner wishes to liquidate from a sale that is part of an operating trade or business. The degree of activity in which the TP engages is an important factor in making that distinction.

¶ 25.3313–1. Illustration 1. *X* purchased Blackacre as an investment in 1958. In 1990, *X* decided to sell Blackacre. *X* listed Blackacre for sale and after a few months sold it to *Y* for a gain of $30,000. *X* does not trade in real property as a business. While, at the time of sale, *X* was holding Blackacre for sale, he was not holding it for sale to customers in the ordinary course of his trade or business. Consequently, he recognized a long-term capital gain of $30,000 on the sale. If *X* had subdivided Blackacre into 100 lots and sold the lots to separate purchasers, his activity in selling multiple lots may constitute a trade or business so that § 1221(a)(1) would apply to exclude the land from the definition of capital asset. That is, *X*'s multiple sales of lots may cause purchasers to be "customers," and *X*'s activity in subdividing lots and selling them may place *X* in the trade or business of selling realty.[32] Even in that latter circumstance, *X* may qualify for relief affording capital gains treatment for much of the gain recognized from the sale of lots under certain circumstances described in § 1237.[33]

¶ 25.3313–2. Illustration 2. *X* regularly buys and sells real estate in the course of her business. *X* purchased Blackacre as an investment. After five years, *X* sold Blackacre to *Y*. Blackacre will be treated as a capital asset if *X* can satisfy her heavy burden of proving that she held Blackacre as an investment even though she held other realty for sale to customers in her business.

---

32. *Mauldin v. Commissioner*, 195 F.2d 714 (10th Cir. 1952); see also **¶ 25.3314–2A**.

33. See **¶ 25.3350**.

¶ **25.3314. Definition of "Primarily."** The meaning of the term "primarily" is important if a TP holds property both for sale to customers in the ordinary course of business and for another purpose or purposes. To exclude the property under § 1221(a)(1), is it sufficient that the TP's intent to sell was a significant but not the dominant purpose for holding the property? After several courts of appeals divided on that question, the Supreme Court, in *Malat v. Riddell*,[34] held that the exclusion applies only if the TP's purpose to sell the property to customers in the ordinary course of his business was his dominant purpose. So, the word "primarily" means "of first importance" or "principally."

¶ **25.3314–1. Dual Purpose.** The *Malat* rule's significance arises in a dual purpose case (e.g., a situation where a TP held property either for sale or for rent at the option of the customer). While the *Malat* case itself was not a dual purpose case, the Court characterized it as such. As noted below, the dual purpose situation will arise more frequently in connection with depreciable or real property used in a business, which will not be a capital asset but *may* be a § 1231 asset. See ¶ **26.2000**.

¶ **25.3314–1A. Illustration.** For the past three years, *R* has held a number of unimproved lots that she had purchased and that she offers either for lease or for sale at the option of the buyer or lessee, whichever the case may be. During that three-year period, *R* has leased 28 lots, and she has sold 14 lots. *R* has no preference as to whether a lot is sold or leased. In February of this year, *K* (an unrelated party) elected to purchase one of the lots (Blackacre) from *R* pursuant to her continuing offer either to rent or to sell. *R* recognized a profit on that sale. *R*'s gain will be a capital gain unless the property is deemed to have been held primarily for sale to customers in the ordinary course of *R*'s business or unless the property is excluded from capital asset treatment by § 1221(a)(2) as real property used in a trade or business. While the property almost certainly is excluded by § 1221(a)(2), for the sake of examining the dual purpose doctrine, let us assume that § 1221(a)(2) is inapplicable. Let us also assume that the number of *R*'s sales of

---

34. 383 U.S. 569 (1966).

realty over the three-year period and the manner in which she has conducted her real estate activities would be sufficient to place her in the business of selling realty to customers in the ordinary course of a trade or business. The question, then, is whether, under the *Malat* rule, R's dual purpose for holding Blackacre will preclude the taxation of her gain as ordinary income on the ground that she did not hold the property *primarily* for sale. While it appears that *Malat* would grant capital gain treatment to R (again, assuming unrealistically that § 1221(a)(2) is inapplicable), it is difficult to see why someone who regularly sells property to customers should enjoy capital gains treatment merely because that person also regularly rents such property to customers and is indifferent as to which takes place. One answer may be that dual purpose property will not qualify for capital asset characterization because it will always be depreciable or real property used in a trade or business, which is excluded from capital asset treatment by § 1221(a)(2). If so, while such property may then appear to qualify for treatment under § 1231, which can give rise to capital gain treatment, the gain from the sale of such property likely will be denied § 1231 treatment for the reasons described at ¶¶ **26.2141–26.2152**.

¶ **25.3314–2. Change of Purpose.** A TP may purchase property for one purpose and subsequently change his purpose for holding the property. The crucial issue is the TP's purpose *at the time of sale*.

¶ **25.3314–2A. Illustration 1.** X purchased a large tract of land for the purpose of going into the cattle business. X intended to use the land to graze cattle that he planned to purchase. However, because of adverse influences on the cattle business, X never purchased any cattle and, consequently, never entered the cattle business. X held the land for 18 years, and then he subdivided it into lots and promoted the sale of the lots. While X's original purpose was to use the land in a business, he changed his purpose before he sold the lots, and his dominant purpose at the time of sale was to sell to customers. X's activities in subdividing the land into salable units, clearing the lots, preparing them for sale, advertising the lots, and soliciting sales, combined with the number of his sales, were deemed sufficient to make the sale of lots a business activity of *X* so that his gain was not capital gain by virtue of § 1221(a)(1).[35] As noted in ¶ **25.3350,** § 1237 may provide some relief for a TP in this circumstance.

¶ 25.3314–2B. Illustration 2. A TP is in the business of selling television sets. He decides to liquidate his business, and so he sells his entire inventory of television sets to another dealer. Inventory is excluded from capital assets under § 1221(a)(1). The courts have not been receptive to a contention that the TP changed his purpose for holding the television sets before the liquidating sale and that he was not holding them for sale *to customers* at that time. Since "inventory" is expressly excluded by § 1221(a)(1), the courts seem unwilling to regard the television sets as having lost their characteristic as inventory even though the TP is liquidating his business.[36]

Surprisingly, the prospects of establishing a change of purpose for holding land are better than is the case for inventory. Land held for sale to customers in the ordinary course of a trade or business is not "inventory" and that formalistic distinction may well enhance the prospects of establishing that a TP changed his purpose so that he held the land for investment immediately prior to the sale. In this regard, compare the Fifth Circuit's *Ridgewood Land Co., Inc. v. Commissioner,*[37] granting capital gains treatment to land sold under a condemnation order even though prior to condemnation the land had been held for sale to customers, with the Third Circuit's *Juleo, Inc. v. Commissioner,*[38] and Ninth Circuit's *McManus v. Commissioner,*[39] holding that land sold under a condemnation order in similar circumstances retained its characteristic of property held for

---

35. *Mauldin v. Commissioner*, 195 F.2d 714 (10th Cir. 1952); see also *Biedenharn Realty Co., Inc. v. United States*, 526 F.2d 409 (5th Cir. 1976).

36. See *Williams v. McGowan*, 152 F.2d 570 (2d Cir. 1945); *Grace Bros., Inc. v. Commissioner*, 173 F.2d 170 (9th Cir. 1949).

37. 477 F.2d 135 (5th Cir. 1973).

38. 483 F.2d 47 (3d Cir.1973).

39. 583 F.2d 443 (9th Cir. 1978).

sale to customers and accordingly that the gain there-from was ordinary income. The Third and Ninth Circuits held that the condemnation sale was merely the means by which the sale was effected, but the Fifth Circuit held that the condemnation of the land converted it to investment property because the TP could no longer hold it for sale to customers. The Sixth Circuit, in *Case v. United States*,[40] held that a condemnation of land is one of the factors to be weighed in determining capital asset characterization, but it is only one factor and not conclusive.

¶ **25.3314–3. Undecided Purpose.** A TP may purchase property for the purpose of either renting it, developing it, or selling it, depending upon the market circumstances. For example, a TP may purchase land for the purpose of either subdividing it into lots and selling the lots or developing apartment units on the land and leasing the units, depending upon which appears more profitable at the time that the TP makes his election. This is a different situation from that described as a "dual purpose." In the dual purpose situation, the TP leaves the decision to buy or to rent to the "purchaser," but in the instant circumstances, the TP himself will decide subsequently how he will use the property. This type of situation might better be described as an "undecided purpose" as it is more closely analogous to a change of purpose than to a dual purpose. Thus, it would appear that the proper test in an undecided purpose case should be the purpose of the TP at the time of sale. Since the TP will likely be holding the property for sale at that time, capital asset classification should turn on whether the TP is holding the property for sale *to customers in the ordinary course of a trade or business*.

¶ **25.3314–3A. Treatment in the Courts.** However, in *Malat v. Riddell* [¶ **25.3314**], the TP had an undecided purpose, and the Supreme Court characterized it as a dual purpose and treated it accordingly. As Professor Bernstein observed in his excellent article *Primarily for Sale: A Semantic Snare*,[41] the Court was probably led astray by the error of counsel and the lower courts in

---

40. 633 F.2d 1240 (6th Cir. 1980).

41. 20 Stan. L.Rev. 1093 (1965).

characterizing the issue as a dual purpose case, and it is possible that *Malat* will not be applied to subsequent, undecided purpose cases. This, however, is speculative, and the *Malat* decision has not yet been so restricted.[42]

¶ 25.3315. Appellate Review. What is the correct standard for appellate review of a trial court's determination that property was or was not held by a TP primarily for sale to customers in the ordinary course of the TP's trade or business? If the trial court employed proper legal principles, is its determination a finding of fact to be sustained unless clearly erroneous? The Circuit Courts of Appeal are divided as to whether such determinations are a resolution of an issue of law and reviewable as such, or whether such determinations are factual findings which are subject to the clearly erroneous standard of review.[43] The Fifth Circuit subsequently rejected its prior position on this issue; and, basing its decision on a non-tax Supreme Court decision, held that the trial court's determination is one of fact and reviewable under the clearly erroneous standard.[44]

¶ 25.3320. Real Property Used in a Trade or Business and Depreciable Property Used in a Trade or Business. Section 1221(a)(2) excludes from the category of "capital assets": (a) real property used in a trade or business; and (b) property used in a trade or business of a character which is subject to the allowance for depreciation under § 167. While such properties will not qualify as capital assets, the gain or loss on the sale or exchange of such properties may qualify for the special tax treatment afforded by § 1231.[45] Note that except for a holding period requirement, the language of § 1231 includes within its rules the exact properties excluded from the definition of capital assets by § 1221(a)(2).

---

42. See *Hollywood Baseball Ass'n v. Commissioner*, 423 F.2d 494 (9th Cir. 1970); *Gamble v. Commissioner*, 68 T.C. 800 (1977). In *Gamble*, the Tax Court applied *Malat* to an undecided purpose case and held that a sale qualified for § 1231 treatment.

43. Compare *Biedenharn Realty Co., Inc. v. United States*, 526 F.2d 409, n. 25 (5th Cir. 1976) (treating this as an issue of law), with *Gartrell v. United States*, 619 F.2d 1150 (6th Cir. 1980) (treating as a factual issue).

44. *Byram v. United States*, 705 F.2d 1418 (5th Cir. 1983). See also *Jersey Land & Development Corp. v. United States*, 539 F.2d 311 (3d Cir. 1976), in which the court rejected the clearly erroneous standard.

45. Discussed at Chapter **Twenty–Six**.

¶ **25.3321. Illustration 1.** *X* operated an insurance broker-age business at a building which *X* owned. *X* depreciated the building on the straight-line method. *X* subsequently sold the building and the land on which it is situated to *Y*. Since the realty was used in *X*'s business, it does not qualify as a capital asset, but any gain or loss recognized by *X* on the sale will be granted special treatment under § 1231 if *X* had held the realty for more than one year. If § 1231 characterizes the gain from the sale of the realty as a long-term capital gain, the amount of such gain that is attributable to adjustments made to TP's basis in the building because of depreciation deductions will be "unrecaptured section 1250 gain" for which the maximum tax rate is 25%.[46]

¶ **25.3322. Illustration 2.** *X* used an automobile exclusively for business purposes. The automobile, therefore, was a depreciable asset. *X* sold the automobile and recognized a loss on the sale. The automobile is not a capital asset, but will be treated as a § 1231 asset if held for more than one year.

¶ **25.3323. Illustration 3. Goodwill.** *X* sold his hardware business to *Y*, and *Y* paid $10,000 for the goodwill of the business. At the time of the sale, *X* had owned its goodwill for more than one year.

For many years, goodwill and going concern value were treated as capital assets. While they were used in a trade or business, they were not of a character that is subject to depreciation. However, when Congress added § 197 to the Code in 1993, goodwill, going concern value and similar intangibles that are purchased as part of the acquisition of a going business became amortizable and are treated by § 197(f)(7) as property which is of a character subject to the allowance for depreciation. The characterization of goodwill as property subject to the allowance for depreciation applies only to goodwill that is amortizable under § 197. Goodwill that is self-created by the efforts of a TP is not amortizable and so continues to be a capital asset. Only goodwill that is purchased can be amortized. So, while the gain or loss recognized on the sale of goodwill purchased before August 11, 1993, will still be treated as capital gain or loss, the gain or loss recognized on the sale of goodwill that was purchased after August 10, 1993, as part

---

46. See ¶ 25.2323–3.

of the acquisition of a going business, will be treated as § 1231 income or loss except to the extent that the § 1245 recapture of depreciation rule causes the recognition of ordinary income. Treas. Reg. § 1.197–2(g)(8).[47]

¶ 25.3324. Illustration 4. Rental Real Property. A sold to B realty which A had rented to a tenant at a fair rental for use by the tenant as a single family residence. A recognized a gain on the sale. A had bought the property five years earlier for the purpose of renting it, and she held it for rent until she sold it to B. A never occupied the premises herself, and continuously rented it to unrelated tenants except for two short periods of vacancy between tenants. The question is whether A is deemed to have held the property in a trade or business or did she hold it as an investment? If A's rental activity constitutes the conduct of a trade or business, the property is not a capital asset since it will be realty that is held in a trade or business. The gain on the sale will constitute § 1231 gain.[48] However, if A's rental activity does not constitute the conduct of a trade or business, the realty will be a capital asset, and A's gain on the sale will be a long-term capital gain.[49] If A managed the property, maintained it, advertised for tenants when there was a vacancy, and collected the rent herself or through an agent; that activity likely will be sufficient to classify A as having been in the trade or business of renting the property.

¶ 25.3330. Copyrights, Literary Compositions, and Similar Properties. Section 1221(a)(3) excludes from capital assets a copyright; a literary, musical, or artistic composition; a letter or memorandum; or similar property held by a TP:

(a) whose personal efforts created the property; or

(b) in the case of a letter, memorandum, or similar property, if the property was prepared or produced for the TP; or

(c) if the TP acquired the property in such a manner that his basis in the property is determined in whole or in part by reference to the basis that a person described in (a) or (b) above had in the property.

As a consequence of a 2005 amendment, at the election of the TP, this exclusion from capital asset characterization as well as the

47. See Chapter **Twenty–Six**.

48. See ¶ **26.1100**.

49. The criteria for resolving that issue are discussed at ¶ **21.1142**.

property primarily held for sale exclusion will not apply to a musical composition or a copyright to a musical work that is sold or exchanged after May 17, 2006, if sold by the person who created the composition or acquired it in accordance with (c) above. § 1221(b)(3). Consequently, if the election is made, such a sale may qualify for capital gain treatment. However, such a copyright that is depreciable and used in a trade or business will be excluded from capital asset characterization by § 1221(a)(2). See ¶ 26.2141.

¶ 25.3331. **Patents.** While the Code excludes a copyright held by its creator from the definition of capital assets (other than a copyright for a musical work), no exclusion is made for a patent held by an inventor. This omission is deliberate, and the gain or loss from the sale of a patent will be a capital gain or loss unless the patent is excluded from capital assets under some other specific exception (e.g., if the TP is a professional inventor who is in the business of selling patents to customers). Even a professional inventor can enjoy capital gains treatment if the specific conditions of § 1235 (dealing with the sale of patents) are satisfied. Care should be taken that the patent will be treated as sold and not merely licensed since income from a license is ordinary income. However, for income tax purposes, an *exclusive* license to exploit an invention that is not limited to a time period that is less than the remaining life of the patent is treated as a sale and thus may qualify for capital gains treatment. If a TP wishes to qualify for the special relief accorded by § 1235 to the sale of a patent, the TP must transfer *all substantial rights* (or an undivided fraction of those rights) to the patent. For example, a restriction as to geographic use within the country of issuance will preclude the application of that special relief provision. Treas. Reg. § 1.1235–2(b). Except for musical composers, a writer or artist (professional or amateur) receives no comparable relief to that provided for inventors by § 1235.

¶ 25.3340. **Accounts Receivable.** Accounts or notes receivable acquired in the ordinary course of business from services rendered or from the sale of inventory or of property held for sale to customers in the ordinary course of business are not capital assets. § 1221(a)(4). Thus, gain recognized from the sale of such receivables will be ordinary income rather than capital gain.

¶ 25.3350. Real Property Subdivided for Sale. As previously noted, if a TP who otherwise is not in the business of selling realty to customers subdivides a tract of land into a number of lots or parcels and then sells the lots or parcels in a series of individual transactions, the number of such sales and the extent of the TP's commercial activity in marketing the lots (or parcels) may cause the TP to be treated as engaged in the business of selling realty to customers. If no statutory relief were afforded, the TP's profits from those sales would be treated as ordinary income. However, Congress has provided relief in § 1237.

If the requirements of § 1237 are satisfied, all or part of a TP's gain from the sale of such a lot (or parcel) will qualify for capital gain treatment. The requirements are as follows:

(1) The tract (or any part thereof) was not previously held by the TP primarily for sale to customers in the ordinary course of a trade or business (determined after applying § 1237),

(2) In the taxable year in which the sale of the lot or parcel occurred, the TP did not hold any other realty (i.e., realty other than the tract) primarily for sale to customers in the ordinary course of a trade or business,

(3) No substantial improvements that would enhance the value of the sold lot (or parcel) were made by the TP (or by certain other persons described in the statute) on the tract either while the TP held the property or pursuant to a contract of sale of the property,

(4) Unless acquired by the TP by inheritance or devise, the lot (or parcel) was held by the TP for at least 5 years before the sale.

If the total number of lots (or parcels) of the same tract that were sold by a TP within the coverage of § 1237 is five or fewer, then all of the TP's gain from such sales will be a capital gain. If a TP sells more than five lots (or parcels) of the same tract, then a portion of the TP's gain will be treated as ordinary income. § 1237(b)(1). The imposition of ordinary income treatment for a portion of the TP's gain applies only to gain recognized from the sale of such lots (or parcels) in and after the first taxable year in which the TP sold the sixth lot (or parcel). The amount of gain from the sale of any such lot (or parcel) that is treated as ordinary income is equal to 5% of the selling price of that lot (or parcel).

The provisions of § 1237 do not apply to the sale of a lot or parcel unless the gain that a TP recognizes from that sale would be treated as gain from property held primarily for sale to customers in the ordinary course of business, and the exclusive reason for that treatment must be because of the TP's activity in subdividing the tract and selling the lots or parcels. If the gain would be treated as ordinary income for some other reason, then § 1237 is inapplicable.

Of course, § 1237 is merely a safe harbor. If the gain from the sale of a lot or parcel would be treated as a capital gain in the absence of § 1237, then the latter section will not apply and the gain will be so treated. Thus, the 5% of selling price exception to capital gain treatment will be inapplicable.

¶ 25.4000. JUDICIAL EXCEPTIONS TO CAPITAL GAINS TREATMENT.

¶ 25.4100. Anticipation of Ordinary Income. The anticipation of income doctrine is discussed at Chapter **Twenty-Seven**. The following is a very brief and incomplete summary of the purpose of that doctrine.

When a TP receives an amount from the sale of a property interest which amount represents an anticipation of ordinary income to be earned by the property (i.e., the amount realized is received in lieu of ordinary income), the amount realized by the TP is characterized as ordinary income. Thus, where a landlord receives a payment from his tenant to terminate the tenant's lease, the amount received by the landlord is a substitute for rent and is treated as ordinary income.[50] As discussed in Chapter **Twenty-Seven**, although the "in lieu of ordinary income" test is often cited by the courts, it is of little or no use in distinguishing transactions that are subject to the anticipation of income doctrine from those that are not.[51]

¶ 25.4200. *Corn Products* Doctrine. In *Corn Products Refining Co. v. Commissioner*,[52] the Supreme Court denied capital gain and loss treatment for gains and losses recognized by the TP from the sale of corn futures which the TP had purchased to insure that its

---

50. *Hort v. Commissioner*, 313 U.S. 28 (1941); see also Treas. Reg. § 1.61–8(b).

51. To see the application of this doctrine, the reader should turn to Chapter **Twenty-Seven**.

52. 350 U.S. 46 (1955).

cost of acquiring corn to be used in the manufacture of starch, syrup and other products would not exceed a specified amount (i.e., the amount payable for the delivery of corn under the futures contract). The corn futures were purchased by the TP as a "hedge" against a rise in the price of corn. As we shall see, there is very little viability left to the *Corn Products* doctrine, and it appears likely that the doctrine is completely defunct.[53] Note that, as a consequence of a statutory amendment, gain or loss from a hedging transaction that is identified as such within a specified time period will be ordinary income or loss. § 1221(a)(7), Treas. Reg. § 1.1221–2.

¶ 25.4210. Rationale. While, in *Corn Products*, the Court conceded that the corn futures were not excluded from capital assets by any of the statutory exclusions, it determined that Congress did not intend to provide capital gain and loss treatment to profits and losses arising from the everyday operations of a TP's business. Since the purchase and sale of corn futures was integrally related to the TP's business, the gains and losses were treated as ordinary gain and loss. This doctrine is frequently referred to as the *"Corn Products* doctrine." While the reasoning of the Court in *Corn Products* has been repudiated, hedging transactions may nevertheless result in ordinary income or loss. The treatment of hedging transaction is set forth in Treas. Reg. § 1.1221–2.

¶ 25.4220. Repudiation of the Doctrine. The significance and scope of the *Corn Products* doctrine was substantially reduced by the Supreme Court's decision in *Arkansas Best Corp. v. Commissioner*.[54] In *Arkansas Best*, the Supreme Court did not purport to overrule the *Corn Products* case, but the Court so narrowed the holding of *Corn Products* as to repudiate much of the *Corn Products* doctrine that had previously been thought to have been established. In *Arkansas Best*, the Supreme Court rejected the notion that there are exceptions to the capital asset characterization of § 1221 apart from those statutory exceptions expressly stated in § 1221 itself (or in another Code provision). After *Arkansas Best*, the general rule is that the motive of the TP when acquiring an asset is not relevant in determining the character of gain or loss recognized on the disposition of the asset.[55] The Supreme Court limited the *Corn Products* holding to a determina-

53. But, compare **¶ 25.4220** with **¶ 25.4230**.

54. 485 U.S. 212 (1988). But see **¶ 25.4230**.

55. See *First Chicago Corporation and Affiliated Corporations v. Commissioner*, 69 T.C.M. 2089 (1995).

tion that the "inventory" exception set forth in § 1221(a)(1) applies to gain or loss incurred on a "hedging" transaction that was designed to limit the cost of inventory that the TP would acquire for its business. Several courts have construed *Arkansas Best* as authorizing an expansive construction of the explicit statutory exceptions in § 1221 to the term "capital assets."

¶ 25.4230. Corporate Stock. Corporate stock usually constitutes a capital asset so that the sale or exchange of that stock will produce capital gain or loss. Purchasers of stock fall into one of three categories—investors, traders, and dealers.[56] Most purchasers are investors, and their gains and losses on the sale of stock typically will be capital gains and losses. There are several statutory exceptions that mandate ordinary gain or loss treatment in special circumstances. See §§ 306, 1244.

A "trader" is a person who buys and sells stock almost daily for a substantial and continuous period that generally must exceed a single taxable year. However, a trader does not sell to "customers" as required by § 1221(a)(1), and so the gains and losses recognized by a trader are capital gains and losses even though a trader does qualify as engaged in a trade or business of buying and selling stock.[57]

A "dealer" is a person who acts very much as a merchant who buys wholesale and sells to customers in a retail market. A dealer purchases stocks in the hope of selling them for a profit not because of a rise in value of the stocks but because the purchasers are willing to pay more than the dealer's cost. In effect, the dealer is a middle man who makes a market for the sale of the stocks.[58] A dealer's gains and losses on the sale of stock is ordinary income and loss since he sells to customers in the ordinary course of his trade or business. § 1221(a)(1).

In a number of cases that were decided prior to the *Arkansas Best* decision (at ¶ **25.4220**), courts held that the gain or loss recognized from the sale of corporate stock which had been purchased for a business purpose, as contrasted to an investment or trading purpose, was ordinary gain or loss (actually, only cases involving a loss would arise because a TP who had a gain on such sales was

---

56. *Chen v. Commissioner*, TC Memo 2004–132 (2004); *see also* ¶ **21.1141**.

57. See ¶ **21.1141**; *see also Chen v. Commissioner*, RIA TC Memo 2004–132 (2004).

58. See *King v. Commissioner*, 89 T.C. 445, 458–459 (1987).

not likely to point out that the stock had been acquired for a business purpose).[59] *Arkansas Best* repudiated that position.

While the business or investment motive of the TP is no longer a factor in determining capital or ordinary treatment, one aspect of that pre-*Arkansas Best* doctrine (the "source of supply" principle) may still be valid. One of the more common circumstances in which ordinary loss treatment was allowed was where stock of a corporation was purchased in order to give the purchaser access to assets of the target corporation which the purchaser needed for its inventory (the so-called ·"source of supply" context).[60] The Supreme Court's decision in *Arkansas Best may* have vitiated the doctrines laid down in those decisions, but the Claims Court has stated in an opinion that the "source of supply" principle continues to be viable in the post-*Arkansas Best* period.[61]

In *Circle K Corporation v. United States*,[62] a 1991 opinion passing on a summary judgment motion, the Claims Court[63] relying on *Corn Products*, held that the loss recognized on the sale of corporate stock which had been purchased to protect the TP's inventory source was an ordinary loss. The Claims Court held that the *Corn Products* doctrine required ordinary loss treatment and that *Arkansas Best* had not overruled that aspect of *Corn Products*. The court agreed that *Arkansas Best* had repudiated the construction of the *Corn Products* doctrine that looked to the motive of the TP in having acquired an asset, but the court maintained that the Supreme Court did not repudiate the doctrine that a loss should be ordinary when there was a substantially close connection between the TP's acquisition of the stock and the conduct of TP's business so that it fairly can be characterized as an integral part of TP's inventory-purchase system. The *Circle K* case was subsequently dismissed, and no decision was entered in the case.[64]

¶ 25.4300. Sale of Right to Personal Services or Contract

59. See, e.g., *Campbell Taggart v. United States*, 744 F.2d 442 (5th Cir. 1984).

60. See *Booth Newspapers, Inc. v. United States*, 303 F.2d 916 (Ct. Cl. 1962).

61. *Circle K Corporation v. United States*, 68 AFTR 2d 91–5462 (Cl. Ct. 1991).

62. 68 AFTR 2d 91–5462 (Cl. Ct. 1991).

63. Note that the name of the Claims Court has been changed to the "Court of Federal Claims."

64. See Field Service Advisory (FSA), 1997 WL 33106654 (April 17, 1997) also stating that the opinion in *Circle K* is erroneous.

Rights. This subject often raises issues under the Anticipation of Income doctrine, which is discussed at Chapter **Twenty-Seven**.

¶ **25.4310. Personal Services.** When a TP has a right to future income as consideration for services performed, the TP's gain from the sale of his right to such income will usually be treated as ordinary income.[65] The cases on this issue often rely on the "in lieu of" test—that the payment was received as a substitute for, or in lieu of, ordinary income payments such as wages.

¶ **25.4320. Contract Rights.** While there is a division of authority, a TP's gain from the sale of contract rights, other than a tenant's sale of his leasehold interest, will often be treated as ordinary income.[66] The courts rest their characterization of the gain as ordinary income either on the "in lieu of" test or on the ground that there was no "sale or exchange" as required by § 1222.[67] The decisions in this area cannot be harmonized under any general principles. A better view would not preclude capital gain treatment for the sale of all contract rights, but instead would rest upon the nature of the contract rights involved in the sale.

¶ **25.4321. Illustration.** In *Commissioner v. Ferrer*,[68] the TP had executed a contract with an author for the TP to produce the author's play. The contract granted the TP the exclusive right to produce the play, the right to prevent the disposition of motion picture rights before a certain date, and, if a motion picture was produced, the TP was entitled to a percentage of the proceeds from the picture. The TP made advance payments to the author in consideration of this agreement, and, consequently, the TP had an investment in his contract rights. The TP released the author from this contract in consideration of specified payments from a company that wished to produce the work as a motion picture. The court treated the "release" as a sale and held that the TP was entitled to capital gains on the sale of a capital asset, with the exception that the portion of the payment attributable to the release of the TP's right to a percentage of the movie proceeds was treated as ordinary income because it was received "in lieu of" license fees.

---

65. See *Bellamy v. Commissioner*, 43 T.C. 487 (1965).

66. See *Commissioner v. Pittston Co.*, 252 F.2d 344 (2d Cir. 1958).

67. The "sale or exchange" requirement is discussed at ¶ **25.5000**.

68. 304 F.2d 125 (2d Cir. 1962).

¶ **25.4322. Characterizing Payment.** Thus, *Ferrer* indicates that capital gain treatment should not rest on the artificial distinction between a release and a sale. The payment received by the TP should be characterized according to what was actually sold; and, where appropriate, the gain should be treated in part as capital gain and in part as ordinary income.

¶ **25.4323. Illustration.** *X* leased premises to a tenant, *Y*, who wished to modify the premises for its own special uses as a TV studio. *Y* was obliged under the lease to restore the premises to their original condition upon the termination of the lease. *Y* became concerned, after several years of rising costs, about the cost of making such restorations at a future date. To protect itself against rising future costs, *Y* paid *X* $125,000 in consideration of *X*'s releasing *Y* from its obligation to restore the premises. The Tax Court in *Sirbo Holdings, Inc. v. Commissioner*[69] held that the payment constituted ordinary income to *X*; after expressing some doubts in an earlier appeal, the Second Circuit affirmed the Tax Court's decision.[70]

¶ **25.4330. Leasehold Interest.** A tenant's sale or release of his leasehold interest in property will usually be treated as a capital transaction.[71] Indeed, § 1241 eliminates any "sale or exchange" problems from release cases by providing that any amount received by a lessee for cancellation of a lease is considered as an amount received "in exchange" for the lease.

¶ **25.4400. Correlation with Prior Transactions.** A gain or loss (or an expenditure) may be characterized as ordinary or capital, whichever is appropriate, in order to correlate the current year's tax consequences with the tax consequences imposed on prior transactions that are related to the current year's gain, loss, or expenditure.

¶ **25.4410. Illustration 1.** *X*, a bank, deducted overdue notes as business bad debts, which are fully deductible from ordinary income. Subsequently, the debtors became able to make payments on the overdue notes, and *X* then sold the notes to a third party for about 40% of the unpaid balance of the notes. The payment received by *X* on the sale of the notes was treated as ordinary income. Since the substance of the transaction was to reduce the

---

69.   61 T.C. 723 (1974).

70.   509 F.2d 1220 (2d Cir. 1975).

71.   *Metropolitan Bldg. Co. v. Commissioner*, 282 F.2d 592 (9th Cir. 1960).

amount of the debts that was actually uncollectible, and since *X* had deducted the full amount against ordinary income, the payment received in the subsequent year should be treated as ordinary income.[72]

¶ **25.4420.   Illustration 2.** On the liquidation of a corporation, a shareholder (the TP) recognized a long-term capital gain on the difference between the amount he received in liquidation of his corporate stock and his basis in his stock. § 331. In a subsequent year, a judgment was obtained against the corporation. The TP and other shareholders were required to pay the judgment as transferees of the corporation's assets. The TP claimed an ordinary deduction for the payment, but the Supreme Court, in *Arrowsmith v. Commissioner*,[73] held that the tax consequence of the payment must be correlated with the treatment of the liquidating distributions that the TP had received in the earlier year. The Court held that the net effect of the TP's payment was to reduce the amount that he received from the corporation as a liquidating distribution, and, since those distributions had been treated as long-term capital gain to the TP, his payback must be treated as a capital loss.[74] Note that § 1341 may provide relief for a TP in this circumstance.[75]

¶ **25.4430.   Insider Stock Profits.** As a result of a settlement or of a judgment, an officer or director of a corporation is required to return to the corporation the "profits" the officer or director recognized on the sale of stock because there either was or may have been a violation of § 16(b) of the Securities Exchange Act of 1934. As used in this context, the term "profits" has a special meaning; namely, it refers to the difference between the price at which the TP sold stock and the price that he subsequently paid when he purchased stock of the same corporation. The question is whether the TP's payment to the corporation, pursuant to the settlement or judgment, should be treated as a capital loss in order to correlate the payment with the treatment of the taxable gain which the TP recognized when he sold the stock. The Tax Court has held that the payment to the corporation is not integrally related to the gain earned by the TP on the sale of his stock; thus, the payment should be treated as an ordinary busi-

---

72. *Merchants National Bank v. Commissioner*, 199 F.2d 657 (5th Cir. 1952).

73. 344 U.S. 6 (1952).

74. *Arrowsmith v. Commissioner*, 344 U.S. 6 (1952).

75. Rev. Rul. 78–25. See also ¶ **8.4000.**

ness expense deduction. However, four circuit courts of appeal have rejected the Tax Court's view and have held that the payment is a capital loss to the TP.[76]

¶ 25.4440. Correlation with a § 1231 Loss. In Year One, a TP recognized losses on the sale of depreciable properties used in his business. Since the TP had no gain under § 1231 that year, the TP deducted the losses as ordinary losses under § 1231.[77] In Year Seven, the TP was reimbursed by *X* for the losses the TP had recognized in Year One; the reimbursement was paid to the TP as part of the settlement of the TP's claim against *X* for an antitrust offense. The reimbursement constitutes gross income to the TP under the tax benefit rule. The question is: Should the reimbursement be treated as a gain under § 1231 (which *may* be treated as a long-term capital gain) or should the reimbursement be treated as ordinary income since the losses recognized in Year One were allowed as ordinary losses? In *Bresler v. Commissioner*,[78] a similar reimbursement was treated as ordinary income. What would be the tax treatment of the reimbursement if part of the Year One loss had been "recaptured" under § 1231(c) by characterizing a subsequent net section 1231 gain as ordinary income? If the *Bresler* position is adopted, it would seem that the amount of Year One loss that was recaptured should be treated as if it had been a capital loss. But there is another reason to treat a subsequent gain as a § 1231 gain rather than to correlate it with the nominal characterization of the prior year's § 1231 loss. The actual effect of a § 1231 loss or gain can be different from its nominal characterization.[79] In some cases, therefore, reliance on the nominal characterization can be inappropriate.

¶ 25.5000. SALE OR EXCHANGE. Section 1222 defines long-term and short-term capital gains and losses as gain or loss "from the sale or exchange of a capital asset" held for a specified period (more than one year for a long-term gain or loss, and one year or less for a short-term gain or loss). The term "sale or exchange" has been construed as a term of art establishing an additional requirement for obtaining capital gain

---

76. See *Anderson v. Commissioner*, 480 F.2d 1304 (7th Cir. 1973), rev'g 56 T.C. 1370 (1971); *Mitchell v. Commissioner*, 428 F.2d 259 (6th Cir. 1970), rev'g 52 T.C. 170 (1969); *Cummings v. Commissioner*, 506 F.2d 449 (2d Cir. 1974); *Brown v. Commissioner*, 529 F.2d 609 (10th Cir. 1976).

77. See ¶ **26.1100**.

78. 65 T.C. 182 (1975).

79. See ¶¶ **26.2237–26.2267–3**.

or loss treatment. A "sale or exchange" of an asset is a narrower concept than a "disposition" of an asset. There are statutory provisions characterizing certain specific transactions as a "sale or exchange" so that the capital gain or § 1231 provisions may apply to those situations. See, e.g., §§ 1234A, 1241 (cancellation of a lease), and 1271(a)(1) (retirement of a debt instrument).

¶ **25.5100. Involuntary Conversion.** The amount received by a TP on a forced sale of his property under a foreclosure proceeding or under a condemnation proceeding is held to be received from an actual sale of the property which meets the requirements of § 1222.[80] However, an amount received by a TP as insurance proceeds for damage to his property is not received pursuant to a sale or exchange. The problem that some involuntary conversions do not constitute a sale or exchange has been dealt with in several specific sections of the Code. The gain or loss from most involuntary conversions, whether or not treated as a sale or exchange, will be determined either under § 1231 [discussed in ¶ **26.2100**] or under § 165(h).

¶ **25.5110.   Abandonment.** When a TP abandons property, the loss does not result from a sale or exchange. This creates an artificial distinction between abandoning property for an ordinary loss and selling it in a foreclosure proceeding which may result in a capital loss.

¶ **25.5200.   Bootstrap Sales.** When a TP sells income-producing property for a set price and when the buyer makes no down payment on the purchase and has no *personal obligation* to pay the purchase price but is obligated to pay the purchase price only out of the earnings (if any) from the purchased property, the transaction is sometimes referred to as a "bootstrap sale." In one case involving a bootstrap sale to a charity, the government contended that the transaction was not a sale or exchange under § 1222 but rather was akin to a joint venture in which the seller continued to share in the profits of the property. The Supreme Court, however, rejected the government's contention in *Commissioner v. Clay B. Brown*,[81] where the lower court had found that the price for which the stock was sold was a reasonable price.

Kraut v. Commissioner[82] involved a transaction similar to the one in

---

80.   See *Helvering v. Hammel*, 311 U.S. 504 (1941).

81.   380 U.S. 563 (1965).

82.   62 T.C. 420 (1974), aff'd 527 F.2d 1014 (2d Cir. 1975).

Clay Brown except that the value of the business that was purported to have been sold was significantly less than the amount paid to the sellers.

In *Kraut,* the two shareholders of a corporation sold their stock to a religious tax-exempt organization. At the time of the sale, a religious organization was not subject to the tax on unrelated business income. The shareholders had only a nominal amount of basis in their stock. As compensation for the sale, the shareholders were to receive 75% of the profits of the business subject to a minimum and maximum figure. The buyer had no obligation to pay anything other than profits from the business; in the event of a default, the sellers sole remedy was to enforce their security interest in the assets of the business. The principal tangible assets used in the business were leased so that the business owned little of value. The business had been conducted by the husbands of the two shareholders. The husbands were retained by the buyer as employees of the business and continued to operate it.

The business operated successfully for several years but then became unprofitable and was terminated. The aggregate net amount that each of the sellers received from the buyer as their share of profits exceeded $600,000, and they both reported that amount as a capital gain. The Commissioner determined that the actual value of the stock was less than $169,000. The Commissioner allowed capital gain treatment for the amount that each shareholder received that was equal to the value of her stock. The Commissioner treated the rest of the payments to the sellers as ordinary income. This resulted in only a small portion of the payments qualifying for capital gains treatment.

The Tax Court determined that the entire transaction was not a bona fide sale. It is likely that if the Commissioner had treated all of the payments as ordinary income, the Tax Court would have sustained that determination. But the Commissioner had allowed capital gain treatment for a portion of the payments, and the Tax Court was unwilling to disturb that determination. The Service asked the court to allow it to change its determination, but the court denied that request. The TPs attempted to prove that the stock had a higher value than the Commissioner's determination. The court held that they failed to establish a higher value. While the Tax Court made no finding as to the actual value of the stock, the court indicated that it felt that the Commissioner's determination was too generous to the TPs. The court sustained the Commissioner's determination as to capital gains and ordinary income treatment.

The Second Circuit affirmed the Tax Court's decision. It is not clear whether the Second Circuit would have sustained a determination that all of the proceeds received by the sellers were ordinary income since that issue was not presented to the court. But the allowance of capital gain treatment for an amount equal to the value of the stock was consistent with an earlier Second Circuit decision.[83]

¶ 25.5300.   Cancellation of Lease or Distributor's Agreement. Amounts received by a lessee for his agreement to cancel the lease are treated as amounts received for the lessee's exchange of the lease and so comply with the "sale or exchange" requirement. § 1241. The gain recognized by the lessee may therefore qualify for capital gain treatment if other requirements are satisfied. Since a leasehold interest in realty is treated as personal property, a disposition of the lease does not come within the exception from capital asset qualification in § 1221(a)(2) for realty used in a trade or business. The same provision for an exchange also applies to a distributor of goods who receives payment for the cancellation of the distributor's agreement (but only if the distributor has a substantial capital investment in the distributorship). § 1241.

¶ 25.6000.   STATUTORY CHARACTERIZATION OF CERTAIN TRANSACTIONS. Certain transactions are characterized as capital or ordinary by specific statutory provisions. Two of those provisions are listed below. Other provisions include the rules on recapture of previously claimed deductions in §§ 1245, 1250, and 1252, and the recognition of ordinary loss on the sale of certain stock covered by § 1244. Some other statutory provisions are § 1235 (sale or exchange of patents), § 1237 (real property subdivided for sale), § 1256 (Section 1256 contracts), and § 1258 (conversion transactions).

¶ 25.6100.   Bad Debt Deduction. A nonbusiness bad debt deduction is treated as a short-term capital loss by § 166(d).

¶ 25.6200.   Worthless Security. A worthless security is treated as if it were sold for zero at the end of the tax year in which it becomes worthless and, thus, will usually be treated as a long-term capital loss. § 165(g).

¶ 25.6300.   Qualified Dividend Income. Most dividends from domestic corporations (and from certain foreign corporations) will be taxed at capital gain rates. § 1(h)(11). For year beginning after 2012, such dividends will qualify for a maximum tax rate of 20%, or even

---

83.   See *Berenson v. Commissioner*, 507 F.2d 262 (2d Cir. 1974).

10% if the TP is in a low tax bracket. While the dividend is taxed at capital gain rates, it is not treated as a capital gain. Consequently, capital losses cannot be deducted from dividend income except to the extent of the $3,000 of excess capital losses that can be deducted from non-capital gain income.[84] While most dividends from domestic corporations will qualify for the capital gain tax treatment, there are some exceptions. For example, the capital gain tax treatment will not apply if the stock on which the dividend was paid was held by the shareholder for less than a specified period of time. § 1(h)(11)(B)(iii).

¶ 25.7000.   HOLDING PERIOD. A TP's holding period of a capital asset determines whether a gain or loss on the sale or exchange of the asset will be long-term or short-term. A long-term gain or loss is recognized on the sale or exchange of an asset held for more than one year. A short-term gain or loss is recognized on the sale or exchange of an asset held for one year or less. § 1222. For taxable years beginning after 2012, if 20% category property or 10% category property was held for more than five years before it was sold or exchanged, the maximum tax rate for that sale or exchange will be reduced by 2 percentage points. The TP's holding period is also important in determining whether a gain or loss recognized on the sale or exchange or involuntary conversion of an asset will be included in the § 1231 hotchpot [discussed in ¶ 26.2200].

¶ 25.7100.   Tacking. A TP's holding period for an asset is determined under § 1223. In some circumstances, the previous holding period of one person in property may be "tacked" on to the period of a TP who subsequently holds the same property. If a transferee's basis in transferred property is determined in whole or in part by reference to the transferor's basis, the transferor's holding period is tacked on to the transferee's holding period. § 1223(2).

¶ 25.7110.   Illustration. After holding Blackacre for twelve months, X gave Blackacre to Y as a gift, and Y sold Blackacre one month later. Y's basis in Blackacre is determined by reference to the basis that X had in the property. § 1015. X's twelve-month holding period is tacked on to Y's holding period so that Y is deemed to have held Blackacre for thirteen months when he sold it. § 1223(2).

¶ 25.7120.   Tacking in Tax–Free or Partially Tax–Free Exchanges. In some circumstances, a TP's holding period for one property may be tacked to the holding period of another property

84.   See ¶ 25.2410.

acquired in an exchange in which the TP's basis in the acquired property is the same basis, in whole or in part, as the basis that the TP had in the property he transferred in the exchange. To qualify for tacking, the property transferred by TP in the exchange must have been either a capital asset or property described in § 1231 in the hands of the TP. § 1223(1).

¶ 25.7121. **Illustration 1.** *X* held Blackacre (unimproved land) as an investment for ten years and then exchanged Blackacre for Whiteacre (unimproved land) which *X* also held as an investment. *X* realized a substantial gain on the exchange, but under § 1031 no gain is recognized. *X* sold Whiteacre three months later. Presumably, Blackacre was either a capital asset or a § 1231 asset in *X*'s hands. *X*'s ten-year holding period for Blackacre is tacked on to his period of holding Whiteacre. § 1223(1).

¶ 25.7122. **Illustration 2.** *X* held Blackacre as an investment for eight years and then exchanged it for Whiteacre (unimproved land) plus $5,000 cash. *X* also held Whiteacre as an investment. Blackacre qualified as a capital asset of *X*'s. *X* realized a substantial gain on the exchange, but under § 1031 *X* recognized only $5,000 of that gain (the amount of "boot" received by *X*). *X* sold Whiteacre three months later. X's basis in Whiteacre is determined in part by his basis in Blackacre. Consequently, *X*'s eight-year holding period for Blackacre is tacked on to his holding period of Whiteacre. § 1223(1).

¶ 25.7123. **Constructive Holding Period.** Property acquired by a TP from a decedent who died after 2010 and whose basis in the property is determined by § 1014 will be treated as having been held by the TP for more than one year when disposed of by the TP. § 1223(9).

¶ 25.8000. **GAIN FROM QUALIFIED SMALL BUSINESS STOCK.**

¶ 25.8100. **Exclusion from Gross Income.** In 1993, Congress adopted a provision to provide tax relief for gains recognized from the sale or exchange of stock of certain small corporations referred to as "qualified small businesses." When this provision is applicable, a percentage of the gain from the sale or exchange of such stock will be excluded from the TP's gross income. § 1202(a). For such stock that was acquired after February 17, 2009, and before January 1, 2011, the percentage of gain that is excluded is 75%. For such stock acquired after 2010 or before February 18, 2009, the percentage of gain that is excluded generally is 50%.

The purpose of this relief provision is to facilitate the raising of capital by small, newly incorporated businesses by reducing the tax burden on a shareholder's disposition of original issue stock in certain circumstances described below. The availability of tax relief on the disposition of such stock will provide an inducement to invest in new ventures. In order to qualify for the percentage exclusion from gross income, the stock must have been held by the shareholder for more than 5 years, it must have been acquired as part of an original issue after August 10, 1993, and only noncorporate shareholders can obtain the exclusion (i.e., a sale of such stock by a corporate shareholder will not qualify for the percentage exclusion). § 1202(a), (c).[85]

¶ 25.8200. Limitation on Amount of Exclusion. The gain that qualifies for application of the percentage exclusion is called "eligible gain." The maximum amount of "eligible gain" from a disposition of qualified stock that a noncorporate shareholder can take into account in applying the percentage exclusion is the *greater* of: (1) $10,000,000 ($5,000,000 for a married TP filing a separate return) reduced by the aggregate amount of eligible gain that the shareholder had taken into account in prior years because of dispositions of qualified stock of the same corporation, or (2) 10 times the shareholder's aggregate adjusted basis in the qualified stock of that corporation that the shareholder disposed of in that taxable year. § 1202(b)(1). In making that calculation of basis, no additions to basis occurring after the stock was originally issued are taken into account. The amount of gain that otherwise would be qualified for the percentage exclusion if it were not for having exceeded the dollar limitation described above is sometimes referred to herein as "ineligible gain."

> **¶ 25.8210. Eligible Gain.** "Eligible gain" means gain from the sale or exchange of "qualified small business stock" (**¶ 25.8400**) that had been held for more than five years. § 1202(b)(2).

> **¶ 25.8220. Treatment of Ineligible Gain.** Any gain recognized by the TP in excess of the limitation described above (i.e., ineligible gain) typically will be treated as a long-term capital gain. Such gain typically will qualify for the 20% maximum rate (15% rate for 2011) for net capital gain.

---

85. Additional requirements are noted in **¶ 25.8400**.

¶ **25.8230. Alternative Minimum Tax.** Seven percent of the amount that is excluded from gross income by § 1202(a) is treated as an alternative minimum tax preference item and so may cause the TP to be subject to the alternative minimum tax. § 57(a)(7); see also Chapter **Twenty-Eight**.

¶ **25.8240. Section 1202 Gain.** The amount of eligible gain that is not excluded from income by the percentage exclusion allowed by § 1202(a) is classified as "section 1202 gain" and is included in the group of long-term capital gains that receive a 28% maximum tax rate.[86] In effect, this means that the portion of eligible gain that is not excluded from gross income by § 1202(a) is taxed at a 28% maximum rate rather than the more typical 20% (or 15% for 2011) maximum rate.

¶ **25.8300. Qualified Small Business.** A "qualified small business" is a domestic corporation (certain types of corporations are precluded from qualifying, for example, an S corporation (sometimes called a tax-option corporation), cannot qualify) whose aggregate gross assets (or those of a predecessor corporation) did not exceed $50,000,000 at any time during the period between August 10, 1993, and the time immediately after the issuance of the qualified stock. In addition, the corporation must agree to make such reports to the Service and to its shareholders as the Service may require. § 1202(d). For this purpose, the corporations comprising a parent-subsidiary chain as defined in § 1202(d)(3) are treated as a single corporation. The "aggregate gross assets" of a corporation (or of a parent-subsidiary chain) refers to the cash and aggregate basis of its non-cash assets, except that for this purpose the basis of a contributed asset is deemed to be equal to the value that that asset had at the time of contribution. § 1202(d)(2). An asset whose basis is determined in whole or in part by reference to the basis of a contributed asset will be treated as if it were that contributed asset in applying the latter rule.

¶ **25.8400. Qualified Small Business Stock.** "Qualified small business stock" is defined in § 1202(c). To be qualified small business stock:

(1) the stock must be acquired by the shareholder after August 10, 1993, and at its original issuance (directly or through an underwriter) in exchange for money, other property (other than stock) or as compensation for services (other than services as an underwriter);

---

86. See ¶ 25.2323–2.

(2) the issuing corporation must be a qualified small business (¶ **25.8300**) at the date of issuance;

(3) during substantially all of the shareholder's holding period for such stock, the corporation either (i) meets the "active business" requirements of § 1202(e), or (ii) was a "specialized small business investment company" as defined in § 1202(c)(2)(B).

CHAPTER TWENTY–SIX

QUASI-CAPITAL ASSETS, RECAPTURE OF DEPRECIATION, AND SALE OF A BUSINESS

¶ 26.0000.   QUASI–CAPITAL ASSETS, RECAPTURE OF DEPRECIATION, AND SALE OF A BUSINESS.

¶ 26.1000.   **BACKGROUND: PROPERTY USED IN TRADE OR BUSINESS.** As noted in ¶ **25.3320**, real property or depreciable property used in a trade or business is excluded from the definition of capital assets by § 1221(a)(2). During World War II, many such properties were involuntarily converted by government requisition, condemnation, or, in the case of some ship owners, by the destruction of the ships by foreign powers. In addition, plants and equipment were sold to the federal government. From 1938 to 1942, any gain recognized by the TP from such conversions or sales was ordinary income. In the case of an involuntary conversion, the TP could defer the gain under the antecedent to § 1033 by reinvesting the proceeds in property similar or related in service or use. During the war, however, there frequently were no replacement properties available.

¶ **26.1100.   Congressional Relief.** To relieve the TP's plight, Congress adopted the antecedent to § 1231 in 1942. Under § 1231, the recognized gains and losses from sales or exchanges of property used in a trade or business and the recognized gains and losses from involuntary conversions of certain capital assets and property used in a trade or business are netted. Each such gain or loss is referred to as a "section 1231 gain" or a "section 1231 loss." § 1231(a)(3). Subject to several exceptions described later in this chapter, if the netting computation results in a net gain (referred to as a "net section 1231 gain"), all such gains and losses are treated as long-term capital gains and long-term capital losses.[1] If the net figure is a loss (referred to as a "net section 1231 loss"), or if the net is zero, all such gains and losses are treated as ordinary income and loss. The effect of this netting procedure (referred to as a "hotchpot") is that section 1231

---

1.   But see ¶ **26.2221**.

gains and losses are offset against each other; and if there is a net loss, the net figure is given ordinary loss treatment, but if there is a net gain, the net figure is given long-term capital gain treatment except to the extent that the recapture provision of § 1231(c) [¶ **26.2221**] applies. In making this comparison of recognized gains and losses (the "hotchpot"), only gains that are included in gross income and losses that are deductible (without regard to the limitation in § 1211 on the deductibility of capital losses) are taken into account. § 1231(a)(4).

If a net section 1231 loss did not qualify as an ordinary deduction, a businessman would have a disincentive against selling a depreciable asset for a loss since he could retain it and continue to claim ordinary deductions for the asset's depreciation. Because of the "hotchpot" formula that is utilized in § 1231, and because a net section 1231 gain may be treated as ordinary income to the extent that the TP had net section 1231 losses in any of the preceding five taxable years [¶ **26.2221**], it is a mistake to refer to a gain from the sale of depreciable property as a long-term capital gain. Such a gain should be thought of as a "section 1231 gain," which may or may not be treated as a long-term capital gain depending upon the TP's other section 1231 gains and losses during the tax year and during the preceding five years. Another reason for not thinking of section 1231 gains and losses as capital or ordinary is explained at ¶ **26.2237**. The operation of § 1231 and the recapture of depreciation provisions are discussed in this chapter.

As a consequence of statutory amendments made in 1997 and 1998, even when a net section 1231 gain qualifies for long-term capital gain treatment, the amount of such gain that is attributable to depreciation adjustments to the basis of depreciable realty (primarily buildings and their structural components) that was involuntarily converted or disposed of must be segregated. Such gain is referred to as the "unrecaptured section 1250 gain," and the maximum tax rate applicable to such gain is 25% instead of the more typical 20% rate.[2] Note that currently the more typical net capital gain rate is 15%, but, in referring to tax rates in this chapter, we will use the tax rates applicable to post–2012 years.

As shown in ¶¶ **26.2237–26.2237–3**, even when the hotchpot results in all of the section gains and losses for that year being characterized as long-term capital gains and losses, it may be a mistake to conclude that a specific section 1231 gain item will be given long-term capital

2.   See ¶¶ **25.2323–3** and **26.2214**.

gain effect. Conversely, even when all section 1231 gains and losses for a taxable year are characterized as ordinary, it may be a mistake to conclude that a specific section 1231 loss item will have the effect of an ordinary loss.

¶ 26.2000. SECTION 1231.

¶ 26.2100. Transactions Included in § 1231. Section 1231 applies (1) to the gain or loss recognized on the sale or exchange of "property used in the trade or business"; and (2) to the gain or loss recognized from the involuntary conversion (as a result of destruction in whole or in part, theft or seizure, or an exercise of the power of requisition or condemnation, or the threat or imminence thereof) of "property used in the trade or business" and of capital assets held by the TP for more than one year and held in connection either with a trade or business or with a transaction entered into for profit. Note that gains and losses from the involuntary conversion by casualty or theft of capital assets that are not held in connection with a trade or business or with a transaction entered into for profit are dealt with in § 165(h).[3] One important consequence of including the involuntary conversion of certain capital assets in § 1231 is that the gains from such conversions may thereby qualify for long-term capital gain treatment even if the conversion did not constitute a sale and exchange. Note that if the aggregate of gains and losses from involuntary conversions by casualty and theft that are otherwise included in § 1231 is a net loss, then the gains and losses from such conversions are excluded from § 1231 treatment.[4]

The term "property used in the trade or business" is a term of art that is explained in ¶¶ **26.2140–26.2152.** As you can see from that explanation, a capital asset that is used in connection with a trade or business is separate and distinct from "property used in the trade or business" since the latter phrase refers only to business property that is either real property or property of a character which is subject to depreciation under § 167, neither of which can be a capital asset because of § 1221(a)(2).

¶ 26.2110. Involuntary Conversion of Capital Assets. An involuntary conversion includes a loss from a casualty or theft even though no compensation is received. Note that the gain or

3. See ¶¶ **18.2531–18.2537.**
4. See ¶ **26.2213.**

loss on a *capital asset* falls under § 1231 only if it results from an involuntary conversion and only if the asset is held in connection with a trade or business or profit-seeking transaction for more than one year. In certain circumstances, even the gains and losses from the involuntary conversions of such capital assets are excluded from § 1231.[5]

¶ 26.2120. Illustration 1. *X*'s personal residence is destroyed by fire and *X* collects $40,000 insurance proceeds. *X* does not reinvest the proceeds in realty. *X* had owned her home for ten years and had a basis of $30,000 in it. From the receipt of the proceeds, *X* recognized a gain of $10,000 which will not be characterized as a section 1231 gain because the residence was not held in connection with a trade or business or a profit-seeking transaction. The treatment of the gain is dealt with in § 165(h).[6]

¶ 26.2130. Illustration 2. *X* owned land which he had used in his business for two years. *X* sold the land for a $4,000 gain. *X*'s gain is a section 1231 gain.

¶ 26.2140. Definition of "Property Used in the Trade or Business." "Property used in the trade or business" is a term of art in tax law meaning real property and depreciable property held by the TP for more than one year and used in the TP's trade or business; however, this definition is subject to some statutory qualifications. § 1231(b). In this context, "depreciable property" is property of a character which is subject to the allowance for depreciation under § 167. Id.

> **¶ 26.2141. Exclusion of Specified Properties.** Section 1231(b)(1) expressly excludes from "property used in the trade or business": (a) the TP's inventory; (b) property held by the TP primarily for sale to customers in the ordinary course of his trade or business; (c) a copyright, a literary, musical, or artistic composition, a letter or memorandum, or similar property that is held by a TP who created that property or who is described in § 1221(a)(3);[7] and (d) a United States government publication received from the government without charge or for a price less than that at which the publication is sold to the general public.

5. See ¶ **26.2213**.

6. See ¶¶ **18.2531–18.2537**.

7. See ¶ **25.3330**.

The exclusion of a copyright literary, musical or artistic composition etc. mirrors the same exclusion from the definition of a capital asset set forth in § 1221(a)(3). A 2005 amendment of § 1221 provides a TP with an election to remove musical compositions and copyrights for musical works from the list of excluded properties in § 1221(a)(3) and to insulate it from the exception for property primarily held for sale to customers in the ordinary course of a trade or business. § 1221(b)(3).[8] Section 1231 does not provide a comparable election.

¶ 26.2142. **Primarily For Sale Exclusion.** The exclusion of property held by the TP primarily for sale to customers in the ordinary course of his trade or business is identical to the exclusion from capital assets established in § 1221(a)(1), and it should be construed in the same manner. The Supreme Court's decision in *Malat v. Riddell*[9] that the word "primarily" refers to the TP's dominant purpose is also applicable to § 1231(b)(1)(B).[10]

The First Circuit has held that the function of the word "primarily" in § 1231 is to distinguish (a) sales in liquidation of an asset which is of no further use to the TP in his business (which sales may come within § 1231), from (b) sales made in the ordinary course of business of an asset that, if not sold, would still be useful in the TP's business. The latter sales are excluded from § 1231 treatment by the "primarily for sale" exception even though such sales are made infrequently and even though the TP preferred to rent the asset rather than to sell it.[11] The "primarily for sale" condition is satisfied in such cases because: (1) the sale is made in the ordinary course of TP's business, and (2) at the time of the sale, the TP holds the property primarily for sale (regardless of what purpose the TP had prior to that time). In essence, this construction of the

---

8. See ¶ **25.3330**.

9. Discussed in ¶ **25.3314**.

10. *Hollywood Baseball Ass'n v. Commissioner*, 423 F.2d 494 (9th Cir. 1970); *Gamble v. Commissioner*, 68 T.C. 800 (1977).

11. *International Shoe Machine Corp. v. United States*, 491 F.2d 157 (1st Cir. 1974). See also *Honeywell Inc. v. Commissioner*, 87 T.C. 624, 633 (1986); *Recordak Corp. v. United States*, 325 F.2d 460 (Ct. Cls. 1963).

word "primarily" was adopted by the Commissioner in Rev. Rul. 80–37.[12]

¶ 26.2150. *Corn Products* Doctrine. There was a question whether, in addition to the statutory exclusions listed in § 1231(b), sales which are integrally related to the normal conduct of a TP's business should be excluded under the judicial exception established by the Supreme Court in *Corn Products Refining Co. v. Commissioner*.[13] The virtual demise of the *Corn Products* doctrine makes that question moot. The *Corn Products* doctrine[14] was established in denying capital gain and loss treatment under § 1222. The Ninth Circuit held that the *Corn Products* doctrine also applied to § 1231.[15] The application of *Corn Products* to § 1231 would be one means of preventing gain from the sale of property held for a dual purpose from being treated as a long-term capital gain. An alternative ground for denying § 1231 treatment to such sales was stated in *International Shoe Machine v. United States*[16] and was adopted by the Commissioner in Rev. Rul. 80–37.[17] In view of the Supreme Court's repudiation in *Arkansas Best Corp. v. Commissioner*[18] of much of the *Corn Products* doctrine (or at least of the doctrine that the *Corn Products* case previously had been thought to have established),[19] the tax treatment of such sales likely will be controlled exclusively by the *International Shoe Machine* approach.

¶ 26.2151. Illustration 1. *X* offered typewriters for sale or for rent. *X* actually preferred to rent the typewriters because his profit margin was greater on rentals than on sales, but *X* was required by his distributor to offer the typewriters for sale as well. *X* sold relatively few typewriters; only 8% of his annual profit is attributable to sales, while 92% is attributable to rental income. *X* holds the typewriters for a dual purpose; but even if his dominant purpose is to rent rather than to sell, *X*'s sales are an integral part of his business. In view of the

---

12. See also TAM 8621003 and TAM 9448004.

13. 350 U.S. 46 (1955).

14. Discussed at ¶¶ **25.4200–25.4230**.

15. *Hollywood Baseball Ass'n v. Commissioner*, 423 F.2d 494 (9th Cir. 1970).

16. 491 F.2d 157 (1st Cir. 1974).

17. See ¶ **26.2142**.

18. 485 U.S. 212 (1988).

19. See ¶¶ **25.4200–25.4230**.

Supreme Court's decision in the *Arkansas Best* case,[20] the *Corn Products* doctrine either no longer exists or has been so substantially narrowed that it will not affect the characterization of *X*'s gain. Under similar facts, the First Circuit held, in the *International Shoe Machine* case, that the gain from such sales constituted ordinary income for the reasons stated in ¶ **26.2142**.[21] While not citing the case, the Commissioner adopted the *International Shoe Machine* approach in Rev. Rul. 80–37.[22]

¶ **26.2152. Illustration 2.** *Y* manufactured and sold steel cable. *Y* delivered the cable to its customers on steel reels which *Y* owned. *Y* took depreciation deductions for the steel reels. *Y*'s customers were required to pay a deposit on the steel reels. If a customer did not return the reel within one year, title to the reel passed to the customer, and *Y* retained the deposit. Most customers did return the reels. The question was whether *Y*'s gain on the reels which were not returned was ordinary income or a section 1231 gain. In Rev. Rul. 75–34, the Commissioner ruled that *Y*'s gain on the sale of the reels which were not returned was section 1231 gain except to the extent that the recapture of depreciation rules (§ 1245) applied. It is difficult to reconcile this 1975 ruling with the *International Shoe Machine* case and with Rev. Rul. 80–37.[23] It seems likely that the Commissioner will not adhere to the view taken in Rev. Rul. 75–34.

¶ **26.2200. How § 1231 Applies to Gain and Losses.** The recognized section 1231 gains and the recognized section 1231 losses are netted. If the result is a net gain, both gains and losses are treated as long-term capital gains and losses (subject to the "recapture" rules described at ¶ **26.2221**). If the result is a net loss, both gains and losses are treated as ordinary gains and losses.

The practical effect of this "hotchpot" procedure is that a net section 1231 gain is treated as a long-term capital gain and a net section 1231 loss is an ordinary loss deduction. However, because of the recapture rules described at ¶ **26.2221**, all or part of a net section 1231 gain may be treated as ordinary income.

20. See ¶ **26.2150**.
21. But see ¶ **26.2152**.
22. See also TAM 8621003.
23. See ¶ **26.2142**.

¶ 26.2210.   Computation of the Hotchpot.

¶ 26.2211.   Gains and Losses Included. Gains are included only to the extent they are included in the TP's gross income. Losses are included only to the extent they are otherwise deductible. § 1231(a)(4)(A). For this purpose, the limitation on deducting capital losses established in § 1211 is ignored.

¶ 26.2212.   Gains Excluded. Gains are excluded from § 1231 to the extent that such gains are treated as ordinary income because they represent a recapture of deductions under, for example, §§ 1245, 1250, 1252, or 291(a)(1).

¶ 26.2213.   Gains and Losses from Certain Involuntary Conversions. Recognized gains and losses from involuntary conversions arising from fire, storm, shipwreck, or other casualty, or from theft of property used in the trade or business or of a capital asset held for more than one year in connection with a trade or business or profit-seeking transaction are excluded from § 1231 *if,* for the taxable year, the losses from such involuntary conversions exceed the gains therefrom. § 1231(a)(4)(C). However, if such losses do not exceed such gains for the taxable year, then both are included in § 1231. Thus, there is a second "hotchpot" of gains and losses from the involuntary conversions of such properties. This rule is designed to give a TP an ordinary deduction for casualty and theft losses (in excess of gains from such sources) under § 165 rather than offsetting the loss against other section 1231 gains that might otherwise be treated as a long-term capital gain.

Note that the types of involuntary conversions that are included in the second hotchpot do not include some of the involuntary conversions that are subject to § 1231 treatment. Specifically, gain or loss from the condemnation, requisition, or threat or imminence thereof, are not included in the second hotchpot.

¶ 26.2214.   Unrecaptured Section 1250 Gain. As previously noted in ¶ 26.1100, the gain from the disposition or conversion of certain depreciated realty (primarily buildings and their structural components) that is attributable to depreciation adjustments to basis and that qualifies as a long-term capital gain is referred to as "unrecaptured section 1250 gain." The maximum tax rate on such gain is 25% instead of the more typical 20% rate for post–2012 years. § 1(h)(1)(D), (7).[24]

¶ 26.2215.   Goodwill and Going Concern Value. Prior to an amendment to the Code in 1993, gain or loss from the sale of goodwill or going concern value was treated as capital gain or loss. As a result of that amendment, they now are sometimes treated as capital gain or loss and sometimes treated as section 1231 gain or loss. The current treatment of those items is discussed at **¶ 25.3323**.

¶ 26.2220.   Net Section 1231 Gain and Net Section 1231 Loss. A "net section 1231 gain" is the excess of the aggregate section 1231 gains for a taxable year over the aggregate section 1231 losses for that year. § 1231(c)(3). A "net section 1231 loss" is the excess of the aggregate section 1231 losses for the taxable year over the aggregate section 1231 gains for that year. § 1231(c)(4).

¶ 26.2221.   Recapture of Net Section 1231 Losses. If in a taxable year a TP has a greater amount of section 1231 losses than he has section 1231 gains, the gains and losses are treated as ordinary. The effect of this hotchpot treatment is to characterize the net section 1231 loss (i.e., the excess of the aggregate of section 1231 losses for that year over the aggregate of section 1231 gains for that year) as an ordinary loss. This ordinary loss treatment for a net section 1231 loss is recaptured to the extent that the TP has a net section 1231 gain in any of the succeeding five years. § 1231(c). The recapture is accomplished by treating a net section 1231 gain for a taxable year as ordinary income to the extent that the TP had net section 1231 losses in any of the preceding five years that had not previously been recaptured (a so-called "non-recaptured net section 1231 loss").

¶ 26.2222.   Allocation of Recapture. For post–2012 years, there are four different maximum tax rates that apply to net capital gains (28%, 25%, 20% and 10%).[25] When a TP has a net section 1231 gain, part of which will be treated as ordinary income because of the § 1231(c) recapture rule, the question

---

24.   See ¶ 25.2323–3.

25.   See ¶ 25.2321 for a discussion of maximum rates on net capital gains, including a 2 percentage point reduction from the 20% and 10% rates for property held for more than 5 years.

arises as to which of the underlying section 1231 gains is to be treated as ordinary income. Some section 1231 gains may qualify for a 20% maximum tax rate, some (the unrecaptured section 1250 gain) for a 25% rate, and perhaps some for a 28% maximum rate. Currently, it does not seem possible for a § 1231 gain to be within the 28% category. The amount that is recharacterized as ordinary income under the § 1231(c) recapture rule will not qualify for a maximum rate limitation. A 1998 amendment authorized Treasury to determine by forms or regulation the manner in which such recaptured income is to be allocated. § 1(h)(8). In Notice 97–59, which was promulgated prior to the 1998 amendment, the Commissioner stated that the recaptured ordinary income is to be allocated first to 28% category section 1231 gain, then any remaining recapture ordinary income to 25% category section 1231 gain, and any remaining recapture ordinary income to 20% category gain.[26] It is likely that this same approach will be applied to section 1231 gains under the 1998 amended version of the Code as well.

¶ 26.2230. Illustrations: Operation of § 1231. All properties referred to in the following examples were held by the TP for more than one year. All years referred to in the following examples are taxable years that began after the year 1984. In the following examples, there were no events having significance for § 1231 purposes other than the events mentioned in the examples.

¶ 26.2231. Illustration 1. In Year One, X recognized a gain of $10,000 from the sale of land that he used in his business, and X recognized a loss of $4,000 from the sale of depreciable property used in his business. X had no net section 1231 loss in any of the five years preceding Year One. Since X's section 1231 gains for Year One exceed his section 1231 losses for that year, the gain from the sale of the land is treated as a long-term capital gain and the loss from the sale of the depreciable property is treated as a long-term capital loss. The effect of this characterization is to net the section 1231 gains and losses and to treat the net gain (referred to as the "net section 1231 gain") as a long-term capital gain. For the significance of qualifying as long-term capital gain, see **¶ 25.2321.**

26.   See ¶ 25.2323–3.

¶ **26.2232. Illustration 2.** The same facts apply as those stated in ¶ **26.2231**, except that, in Year One, X had a valuable sculpture stolen from his office and an automobile that X owned and used in his business was destroyed by fire. As a work of art, the sculpture was not a depreciable asset. Instead, the sculpture was a capital asset that was used in connection with X's business; and the automobile was "property used in the trade or business." X had a basis of $4,000 in the sculpture which had a value of $10,000 and was uninsured. X's basis in the automobile was $2,000. X collected $3,000 on his insurance coverage for the car. X is entitled to a $4,000 theft deduction for the sculpture [§ 165(c)(1)], and he recognized a $1,000 gain from the insurance proceeds that he received for his car. X did not elect under § 1033 not to recognize the gain from the conversion of his car. While the theft loss and the gain on the involuntary conversion of the car otherwise would have been included in § 1231, they will be excluded by § 1231(a)(4)(C) because X's losses from such conversions are greater than his gains from such conversions. X is allowed an ordinary deduction of $4,000 for the theft of the sculpture, and he recognizes ordinary income of $1,000 from the receipt of the insurance proceeds.[27] X's $10,000 gain from the sale of land will be a long-term capital gain, and X's $4,000 loss from the sale of depreciable property will be a long-term capital loss.

¶ **26.2233. Illustration 3.** The same facts as those stated in ¶ **26.2232**, except that, in Year One, a painting that X held for personal purposes and kept in his residence was destroyed by fire. X had a basis of $30,000 in that painting, and he collected $38,000 insurance proceeds to compensate for that loss. X recognized a gain of $8,000 from the conversion of that painting, and he did not elect under § 1033 not to recognize that gain. The $8,000 gain is not included in § 1231. X's painting is a capital asset, but it is not held in connection with a trade or business or a profit-seeking transaction. The $8,000 gain is treated as long-term capital gain by § 165(h)(2)(B). The tax consequences of the other events that occurred to X in Year One are the same as was described in ¶ **26.2232**.

¶ **26.2234. Illustration 4.** In Year One, Y recognized a $30,000 loss on the sale of an apartment building that Y had

---

27. The gain that X recognized by receiving insurance proceeds for the conversion of his car does not arise from a "sale or exchange" and so does not qualify for capital gain characterization under § 1222.

owned and operated as a business. In that same year, *Y* received $3,000 insurance proceeds because of the loss of a valuable painting that was destroyed by a fire in *Y*'s office. The painting was a capital asset that was used in connection with *Y*'s business since it had been hung on *Y*'s office wall as a decoration and was a nondepreciable work of art. *Y* had a basis of $1,000 in the painting, and so he recognized a gain of $2,000 from his collection of the insurance proceeds. Since *Y* had no losses from involuntary conversions in Year One, his gain from the conversion of his painting is included in § 1231. *Y*'s section 1231 loss for Year One ($30,000) exceeds his section 1231 gain for that year ($2,000), and so both gain and loss will be treated as ordinary. The effect of this characterization is to net the gain from the painting against the loss from the sale of the apartment building and to treat the excess loss, referred to as the net section 1231 loss, as an ordinary loss. Thus, *Y* had a net section 1231 loss of $28,000 in Year One.

¶ 26.2235. Illustration 5. The same facts as those stated in **¶ 26.2234**. In Year Two, *Y* had no section 1231 gains or losses. In Year Three, *Y* had a $10,000 section 1231 gain and a $6,000 section 1231 loss. If there was no recapture rule, that gain and loss would be treated as long-term capital gain and long-term capital loss. § 1231(a)(1). Y has a net section 1231 gain of $4,000. The recapture rule causes that $4,000 of net section 1231 gain to be characterized as ordinary income. § 1231(c). The net section 1231 gain for Year Three is treated as ordinary income to the extent that *Y* has an unrecaptured net section 1231 loss (referred to in the statute as a "non-recaptured net section 1231 loss") from the five years prior to Year Three. In Year One, two years prior to Year Three, *Y* had a net section 1231 loss of $28,000, and none of that loss was recaptured in the intervening year between Years One and Three. Therefore, all of *Y*'s $4,000 net section 1231 gain for Year Three is treated as ordinary income. That constitutes a recapture of $4,000 of the net section 1231 loss that *Y* had in Year One. After Year Three, *Y* has a non-recaptured net section 1231 loss from Year One of $24,000. Because of the treatment of the $4,000 of net section 1231 gain as ordinary income, Y's remaining section 1231 gain of $6,000 exactly equals Y's section 1231 loss for that year. Since Y's section 1231 gains do not exceed Y's section 1231 losses, the remaining $6,000 section 1231 gain and the $6,000 section 1231 loss will be treated as ordinary gain and ordinary loss. § 1231(a)(2). It would not matter if the $6,000 gain and loss were both treated as long-term capital gain and loss since they would sill offset each other.

¶ 26.2236.   Illustration 6. The same facts as those stated in **¶ 26.2235.** *Y* had no section 1231 gains or losses in Years Four and Five. In Year Six, *Y* had a net section 1231 gain of $42,000. In that year, *Y* had a non-recaptured net section 1231 loss of $24,000 from Year One which is within the five-year period preceding Year Six. Therefore, $24,000 of *Y*'s net section 1231 gain for Year Six is treated as ordinary income, and the remaining $18,000 of his net section 1231 gain is treated as a long-term capital gain.

¶ 26.2237.   Section 1231 Gains and Losses As Capital or Ordinary. If an individual were to consider selling an asset for a section 1231 gain or loss, how should he evaluate the tax treatment that the gain or loss will receive? Under what circumstances should he expect the gain or loss to be treated as a long-term capital gain or loss and under what circumstances should he consider the gain or loss to be ordinary? The predicted tax treatment may well influence the decision whether to sell or hold the property.

The first line of prediction is to look at the hotchpot for that year. If, after selling the item for a loss, there will be a net section 1231 loss that year, the individual might conclude that his loss will have ordinary loss treatment. Conversely, if the item will be sold for a gain and if there will be a net section 1231 gain that year, and if there will be no recapture under § 1231(c), the individual might conclude that his gain on the sale of the item will be treated as a long-term capital gain. In fact, the determination of the effective treatment of a gain or loss can be more complicated than merely considering the hotchpot; and the failure to take another consideration into account could lead to the individual's making a mistake in deciding to sell the item.

In some circumstances, a gain or loss from the sale of the item in question may change the hotchpot so that what would have been a net section 1231 gain will become a net section 1231 loss or vice versa. In evaluating the tax consequence of a contemplated sale, the TP should take into consideration whether the addition of that gain or loss to the hotchpot will cause a gain that would have been treated as capital to be treated as ordinary gain or whether a loss that would have been treated as ordinary will be changed to a capital loss. If either of those changes will take place, the actual effect of the gain or loss will be different from its nominal characterization.

¶ **26.2237–1. Illustration 1.** In December of Year One, X is contemplating the sale of land for a section 1231 gain of $40,000. Earlier in that year, X had a section 1231 loss of $25,000. X had no other section 1231 transactions that year, and X would not have any recapture under § 1231(c) for a net section 1231 gain that year. If X were to make the December sale, both the $40,000 gain on that sale and the $25,000 prior loss will be treated as long-term capital gain and loss respectively. However, it would be a mistake for X to conclude that he will have long-term capital gain treatment for his $40,000 gain if he makes the December sale. He should take into account that a $25,000 loss will be changed from an ordinary deduction to a capital loss. In other words, that $25,000 loss that otherwise would have reduced X's ordinary income will instead reduce a capital gain. In effect, $25,000 of X's $40,000 gain from the December sale will be given the same tax treatment as it would have if it were an ordinary gain.

¶ **26.2237–2. Illustration 2.** The same facts as those stated in ¶ **26.2237–1,** except that X also had a $28,000 section 1231 gain in Year One. Consequently, even without making the December sale, X's section 1231 gain of $28,000 exceeds his section 1231 loss of $25,000. In deciding whether to sell in December, X knows that he already has a net section 1231 gain for that year. Consequently, if he sells in December, he will not change the character of any other section 1231 gain or loss he has that year. X can then properly conclude that his $40,000 gain on the December sale will not only nominally be characterized as a long-term capital gain, but will also have that same effect.

¶ **26.2237–3. Illustration 3.** In December of Year One, Y is contemplating the sale of an item for a section 1231 loss of $35,000. Earlier that year, Y had a section 1231 gain of $15,000, and Y had no other section 1231 transactions that year. Y did not have a net section 1231 loss in any prior year. If Y does not make the December sale, the $15,000 section 1231 gain will be treated as a long-term capital gain. If Y does make the December sale, both the $35,000 loss and the $15,000 prior gain will be treated as ordinary. Since the December sale will convert a $15,000 gain from long-term capital to ordinary, the consequence of making the sale is that $15,000 of the loss that Y recognizes will have the same effect as if it were a capital loss. Only the remaining $20,000 will have an ordinary loss effect.

¶ 26.3000. **RECAPTURE OF DEPRECIATION: GENERAL.** The statutory scheme which allowed a deduction against ordinary income for depreciation of business property, yet permitted the gain from the sale of such property to be treated as a section 1231 gain, was regarded by some as a system that effectively authorized the conversion of an ordinary income deduction into a long-term capital gain. The availability of accelerated depreciation methods (including MACRS) and of the expense deduction (so-called "bonus depreciation") under § 179 aggravates this problem.

¶ 26.3100. **Illustration of Purported Abuse of Trading a Capital Gain for Ordinary Deductions.** On January 1, 1960, X purchased a new truck to be used in his business at a cost of $5,000. The truck had a useful life of five years. X elected to use the double declining balance method of depreciation and accordingly took a depreciation deduction of $2,000 on his 1960 tax return (the half-year convention does not apply since the year involved precedes the adoption of the accelerated cost recovery system). On January 1, 1961, X sold the truck to Y for $4,000. Since X's adjusted basis in the truck was $3,000 ($5,000 cost minus $2,000 depreciation), X recognized a section 1231 gain of $1,000 on the sale. X had no section 1231 losses in 1961, so the $1,000 gain recognized on the sale of the truck would be treated as a long-term capital gain. But X realized a $1,000 gain only because he had taken a $2,000 depreciation deduction. The net effect of this rule is that X deducted $1,000 from ordinary income at the cost of a $1,000 long-term capital gain only $500 of which was subject to tax under the tax treatment of long-term capital gain at that time.

¶ 26.3110. **Statutory Imposition of Recapture.** The Treasury characterized the $1,000 gain in ¶ 26.3100 as a "recapture" of the depreciation that the TP had previously deducted and urged Congress to tax such gain as ordinary income. The government sought a statutory rule that would correlate the tax characterization of the TP's gain with the tax characterization of the depreciation deductions that were effectively recouped when the property was sold.[28] Beginning with the year 1962, Congress added several sections to the Code that recapture some or all of the ordinary deductions that would otherwise have created section 1231 gains. The recapture provisions have been expanded and modified by Congress since the provision was first adopted in 1962.

In addition to the recapture provisions, gain from sale or exchange of certain types of non-capital assets between persons of specified relationships is treated as ordinary income. For example, any gain recognized on the sale or exchange of depreciable property between certain related parties is treated as ordinary income by § 1239. The characterization as ordinary income is not restricted to depreciation recapture; *all* of the gain is treated as ordinary income. Similarly, § 707(b)(2) treats as ordinary income any gain recognized on the *sale or exchange* of property that is not a capital asset in the hands of the transferee if the gain is from a sale or exchange between a partnership and either (1) persons owning more than 50% interest in the partnership, or (2) another partnership, a majority of whose ownership is held by the same persons as hold the ownership of the transferor partnership.

¶ **26.3200.   Section 1245: In General.** Section 1245 provides that gain realized from the disposition of depreciable personal property and a very narrow category of certain depreciable tangible realty will be treated as ordinary income to the extent that the gain is attributable to adjustments to basis caused by deductions previously allowed for depreciation or amortization of the property. Gain will be treated as ordinary income to the extent that the gain arises because of adjustments for depreciation or amortization reflected in the TP's adjusted basis. Note that this recapture rule will apply to the amortization deductions allowable under § 197 for goodwill, going concern value and other intangible properties. Certain other adjustments to basis (i.e., an adjustment caused by a § 179 expense deduction and an adjustment caused by §§ 108 and 1017 because of the nonrecognition of income realized from a discharge of indebtedness) can cause ordinary income recognition under § 1245 on the disposition of the asset. §§ 1017(d), 1245(a)(2)(C).

---

28.   For a criticism of the Treasury's characterization of such gain as a "recapture" of depreciation, see Douglas Kahn, *Accelerated Depreciation—Tax Expenditure or Proper Allowance for Measuring Net Income?*, 78 MICH. L.REV. 1, 43–53 (1979).

¶ 26.3210. Priority of Recapture of Depreciation Deductions. While § 1245 causes the recapture of certain kinds of amortization deductions as well as depreciation deductions, hereafter reference will be made primarily to depreciation deductions. However, the reader should keep in mind that amortization deductions are included in the discussion.

Section 1245 recaptures depreciation not only on sales and exchanges but also on other dispositions of depreciable property unless exempted by an express provision in § 1245 itself. Section 1245 takes priority over any other section of the Code. Consequently, a disposition of property may cause a TP to recognize ordinary income under § 1245 even though another section of the Code provides that no gain will be recognized. A disposition of § 1245 property can cause the recognition of income unless it is a type of disposition that is excluded from income recognition by § 1245(b); an exclusion is available only to the extent that that provision so provides.[29]

¶ 26.3220. Section 1245 Property. Property, the disposition of which is subject to so-called recapture of depreciation under § 1245, is referred to as section 1245 property. The types of property that are so characterized, and therefore are subject to § 1245, are properties of a character subject to the allowance for depreciation under § 167 that are either:

(a) personal property (tangible or intangible);

(b) certain real property (other than a building or its structural components) which is either depreciable property or for which certain amortization deductions are allowed; or

(c) any property which otherwise is not section 1245 property or section 1250 property will be treated as section 1245 property if the basis of such property was reduced under § 1017 because of the TP's nonrecognition of income caused by a discharge of indebtedness. § 1017(d)(1).

Several types of properties (e.g., a single-purpose agricultural or horticultural structure) are subject to § 1245 by specific provisions in that section (§ 1245(a)(3)(D), (E), and (F)).

Thus, section 1245 property applies to all depreciable or amortizable personalty. Section 1245 property does not include buildings

---

29. See ¶ 26.3240.

or their structural components. But section 1245 property does include certain depreciable or amortizable realty other than a building or its structural components.[30]

¶ 26.3230. Computation of Ordinary Income. In general, on the disposition of section 1245 property, the amount recaptured is either the depreciation claimed or the gain, whichever is the lesser amount. For this purpose, "gain" refers to the amount of appreciation of the asset (the excess of its value over the TP's basis). The technical terms of the statute state that the TP will recognize ordinary income in the amount by which the TP's adjusted basis is exceeded by the lower of either: (a) the TP's "recomputed basis" (defined below); or (b) either (1) the amount realized by the TP in the case of a sale or exchange, or (2) the fair market value of the property in the case of other dispositions.

¶ 26.3231. Recomputed Basis. A TP's recomputed basis equals the TP's adjusted basis plus any deductions allowed or allowable to the TP or to any other person (e.g., a donor) for depreciation or amortization to the extent that such deductions are reflected in the TP's adjusted basis. The adjustments to the basis of an asset that are taken into account include: depreciation allowable under §§ 167 or 168 (MACRS), the amount of expense deduction taken under § 179,[31] and the amount of reduction of basis of the asset caused by §§ 108 and 1017 because of the nonrecognition of income realized from a discharge of indebtedness. §§ 1245(a)(2) and 1017(d)(1)(B). If the TP can prove that the amount of such deductions that was *allowed* (i.e., the amount claimed as deductions on a federal tax return and permitted to be deducted) is less than the amount of such deductions that was allowable, then only the amount allowed is used in determining recomputed basis. § 1245(a)(2)(B).[32]

---

30. Note that the disposition of a building that was placed in service between 1981 and 1986, and that was depreciated on some method other than the straight-line method, may be subjected to recapture of depreciation under § 1245. **¶ 26.3310.** Also note that a *corporation* will recapture a percentage (usually 20%) of the amount of depreciation or amortization that the corporation would have been required to recapture under § 1245 upon its disposition of a building if § 1245 had been applicable to the disposition of the building. § 291(a)(1). See **¶ 26.3330.**

31. See Chapter **Twenty–Two**.

32. Note that there are special rules for determining the recomputed basis of player contracts on the sale or exchange of a franchise to conduct a sports enterprise. § 1245(a)(4).

¶ **26.3231–1.   Illustration 1.** On January 14, Year One, *X* purchased a truck for use in his business at a cost of $5,000. The truck was five-year property. X depreciated the truck on the 200% declining balance method and used the half-year convention. *X* did not expense any of the cost of the truck under § 179. *X* properly claimed a depreciation deduction of $1,000 for the truck for Year One. On February 5, Year Two, *X* sold the truck for $4,100. *X* properly claimed a depreciation deduction of $800 for the truck for Year Two. *X*'s adjusted basis in the truck was $3,200, and *X*'s recomputed basis was $5,000 ($3,200 of adjusted basis plus $1,800 of adjustment to basis attributable to depreciation). Since the amount realized by *X* ($4,100) is less than his recomputed basis ($5,000), the difference ($900) between the amount realized and the adjusted basis constitutes ordinary income to *X*. Thus, *X* recognized a gain of $900, all of which is treated as ordinary income.

¶ **26.3231–2.   Illustration 2.** The same facts apply as in ¶ **26.3231–1**, except that *X* sold the truck for $2,500. The amount realized by *X* is less than his recomputed basis and is also less than *X*'s adjusted basis ($3,200). Consequently, *X* has no § 1245 gain from the sale. *X* recognized a section 1231 loss of $700.

¶ **26.3231–3.   Illustration 3.** The same facts apply as in ¶ **26.3231–1**, except that *X* sold the truck for $6,000. *X*'s recomputed basis ($5,000) is less than the amount realized ($6,000). The difference between *X*'s recomputed basis ($5,000) and his adjusted basis ($3,200) constitutes ordinary income under § 1245. Thus, *X* recognized a gain of $2,800 on the sale—$1,800 of which constitutes ordinary income and the remaining $1,000 of which constitutes a section 1231 gain. Stating it differently, if *X* had not been entitled to any depreciation deductions for the truck (and if none had been allowed), *X* would have had a $5,000 basis in the truck when he sold it, and so *X* would have recognized a gain of only $1,000—the appreciation in value which took place after he acquired the truck. Yet, because of the depreciation allowable to *X*, he had a basis of only $3,200 when he sold the truck, and therefore, he recognized a gain of $2,800 on the sale—$1,800 of which gain would not have been recognized but for the depreciation adjustments to his basis and $1,000 of which would have been recognized in any event. The $1,800 of *X*'s gain which is attributable to his depreciation allowance is treated as ordinary income and the remaining $1,000 of *X*'s gain is treated as section 1231 gain.

¶ 26.3231–4. **Illustration 4.** The same facts apply as in ¶ 26.3231–1, except that on January 1, Year Two, *X* gave the truck to his son, *S*, who then used the truck in his business. *X* did not recognize any gain under § 1245 when he disposed of the truck because gifts are specifically excluded from recapture treatment by § 1245(b)(1). Assume that *X* is not entitled to any depreciation deduction for Year Two, and all of the depreciation deductions for the use of the truck in Year Two is allocable to *S*. Prop. Reg. § 1.168–5(f)(3) (providing for the apportionment of annual depreciation between a donor and a donee). *S* properly deducted $1,600 depreciation for the truck in Year Two. On January 15, Year Three, *S* sold the truck for $5,500. Under § 1015, *S*'s adjusted basis when he received the truck in Year Two was equal to his father's adjusted basis of $4,000. *S* properly took a depreciation deduction of $480 for Year Three. After taking depreciation deductions for Years Two and Three that totaled $2,080, *S*'s adjusted basis was $1,920 at the time of the sale. *S*'s recomputed basis was $5,000 (i.e., $1,920 adjusted basis plus $2,080 depreciation allowed to *S* plus $1,000 depreciation allowed to *X* since *X*'s depreciation deduction is reflected in *S*'s adjusted basis). The amount of § 1245 recapture is determined by the recomputed basis ($5,000) since that is a lesser figure than the amount realized on the sale ($5,500). Thus, the difference between *S*'s recomputed basis ($5,000) and his adjusted basis ($1,920) is ordinary income. Accordingly, *S* recognized $3,080 ordinary income and $500 section 1231 gain from the sale.

¶ 26.3240. **Exceptions to § 1245.** You will recall that § 1245 overrides other provisions of the Code and can cause the recognition of income on a disposition that otherwise is covered by a nonrecognition provision of the Code. § 1245(a)(1), (d). However, certain dispositions are excluded (in whole or in part) from § 1245 by the provisions of § 1245(b). Unless a transfer or disposition is listed in § 1245(b), recapture will occur. Some of the transactions to which § 1245(a) does not apply are: (a) gifts; (b) transfers at death (other than income in respect of a decedent in certain circumstances); (c) certain tax-free transactions (i.e., certain transactions upon which gain or loss is not recognized because of a statutory provision), but only those tax-free exchanges that are listed in § 1245(b)(3) are excluded; (d) "like-kind" exchanges and involuntary conversions, to the extent that gain is not recognized under § 1031 or § 1033, ordinarily are not dispositions that require recapture, but if property which is not section 1245 property is acquired by the TP in the transaction, then § 1245 will apply to the extent of the value of such non-section 1245 property.

¶ 26.3300. **Recapture of Depreciation Taken on Buildings.** As noted above, § 1245 does not apply to a disposition of a building, its structural components, or to many other types of realty. In 1964, two years after § 1245 was adopted, Congress enacted § 1250 to recapture a portion of the depreciation that was allowed on real property (other than the limited types of realty that were covered by § 1245). Section 1250 applies to "section 1250 property" which is defined as real property that is of a character subject to depreciation and is not included within the terms of § 1245. As originally adopted, § 1250 was far gentler on real property than § 1245 is on personalty. The recapture rules of § 1250 were broadened by Congress in the years following its adoption. Since those changes were prospective, it is necessary to determine the status of § 1250 at the time that an item of section 1250 property was first placed into service by the TP to determine the consequences of disposing of that item. In most of the years of its applicability, for realty held longer than one year, § 1250 required a recapture of no more depreciation than the excess of the depreciation deductions allowed to the TP over the amount of depreciation that was allowable under the straight-line method over the same period of use. This excess amount of depreciation is referred to as the "additional depreciation." In certain circumstances only a portion of the additional depreciation would be recaptured. This limitation of recapture to all or part of the additional depreciation applies only if the TP's holding period of the section 1250 property is greater than one year. § 1250(b)(1). Note that if realty is not held for more than one year, the gain or loss on its disposition will not qualify for § 1231 treatment and so all of the gain or loss on the disposition will be ordinary.

¶ 26.3310. **Recapture for the Disposition of Buildings That were Placed into Service Between 1981 and 1986.** Most buildings other than residential rental property that were placed into service after 1980 and before 1987, and that were depreciated on a method other than the straight-line method, are subjected to the recapture rules of § 1245 rather than those of § 1250. Thus, on the disposition of such a building that was depreciated on an accelerated method, all of the allowed depreciation (and not just the additional amount of depreciation) is subject to recapture.

¶ 26.3320. **Current Treatment.** The current rules for § 1250 recapture only the additional depreciation that was reflected in the asset's basis and was allowed as a deduction provided that the TP's holding period for the asset is greater than one year. §§ 1250(a)(1), 1250(b)(1). For certain types of low-income housing, only a percentage of the property's additional depreciation is subject to recapture. As far as virtually all buildings and their structural components are concerned, for noncorporate TPs there will be no recapture on their disposition if the property was acquired after 1986 and if the TP's holding period is greater than one year. This is because virtually all buildings placed in service after 1986 cannot be depreciated on an accelerated method; they must be depreciated on the straight-line method. § 168(b)(3). Since, by definition, there can be no additional depreciation for a building that is depreciated on the straight-line method; the recapture rules will apply only to the disposition of buildings that were placed into service prior to 1987 unless the TP's holding period for a building that was placed in service after 1986 does not exceed one year. As noted below, a corporation can have recapture of depreciation when it disposes of a building or other section 1250 property.

If a TP's holding period for a building used in his business does not exceed one year, the building does not qualify as "property used in the trade or business" as that term is defined in § 1231(b)(1), and so the gain from the sale of that property is not section 1231 gain. Since the building is excluded from being a capital asset by § 1221(a)(2), gain from the sale of the building is ordinary income. In addition, but not in duplication, § 1250 will recapture any depreciation deductions that were allowed, but that will not affect the result in a sale or exchange since the TP will recognize ordinary income on all of his gain without regard to the application of § 1250. § 1250(a)(1)(A), (b)(1).

¶ 26.3330. **Corporate Disposition.** When a corporation disposes of section 1250 property, it will have recapture income equal to

20% of the excess of: (1) the amount of depreciation that would be recaptured under § 1245 if that provision applied to the disposition over (2) the amount treated as ordinary recapture income under § 1250. § 291(a)(1). This provision applies only to corporations.

¶ 26.4000.   SALE OF A BUSINESS. Where a TP (individual, corporation, or partnership) sells the assets of a business (as contrasted to the sale of the stock of a corporation or an interest in a partnership which owns and conducts a business), the purchase price must be allocated among all the assets of the business that were sold according to their respective fair market values.[33] Prior to 1986, when a buyer and seller dealt at arm's length, any reasonable allocation made by them in their sales agreement would usually be accepted by the Commissioner. As a consequence of the adoption of § 1060 in the Tax Reform Act of 1986, the purchase price is allocated among the assets of the business according to a formula that allocates to goodwill or going concern value any premium that the purchaser paid.

¶ 26.4100.   Gain and Loss. Once the price is allocated to each asset, the TP can determine the gain or loss on each asset and the character of that gain or loss. For example, the gain or loss on accounts receivable is ordinary income or loss; the gain on depreciable property will be ordinary income to the extent that §§ 1245, 1250 or 1239 (or § 291(a)(1) if the TP is a corporation) cause a recapture of depreciation; and the balance of such gain (if any) usually will be section 1231 gain.

¶ 26.4110.   Goodwill. Prior to the adoption in 1993 of § 197, the basis of goodwill could not be amortized, and gain recognized on the sale of goodwill was treated as capital gain. Where a TP who is engaged in a personal service business (such as a doctor, an accountant or a lawyer) sells his practice to another, or where such a TP accepts a payment from another to become the TP's partner, the Commissioner was reluctant to permit any amount of the payment to be attributed to the purchase of the TP's goodwill (which previously would have constituted capital gain to the TP). However, the Commissioner was unsuccessful in contending that no goodwill can be sold in such circumstances. Accordingly, the Commissioner has narrowed the area in which he makes this contention, but to date, the Commissioner has not prevailed even on this less ambitious proposal.

33.   *Williams v. McGowan*, 152 F.2d 570 (2d Cir. 1945).

Since goodwill acquired after August 10, 1993, in connection with the acquisition of assets constituting a trade or business (or a substantial portion thereof) can be amortized under § 197, the gain recognized on the disposition of such goodwill will be section 1231 gain (subject to the recapture of amortization rule of § 1245). Treas. Reg. § 1.197–2(g)(8). Perhaps, the change will induce the Commissioner to abandon entirely the effort to preclude the allocation of purchase price to goodwill.

¶ 26.4111. **Going Concern Value.** Going concern value is the increase in value of a group of assets due to their existence as integral parts of an ongoing business. While this might appear to be no more than an aspect of the goodwill of the business, the Sixth Circuit held that going concern value is an intangible asset that is separate and distinct from goodwill.[34] Accordingly, the Sixth Circuit held that the Tax Court's decision that a business had no goodwill but had going concern value was not inconsistent. The Sixth Circuit remanded the case to the Tax Court to explain the method that the Tax Court employed in calculating the going concern value. On remand, the Tax Court described the capitalization of earnings method that it employed.[35]

¶ 26.4120. **Covenant Not to Compete.** In connection with a sale of a closely held business, the vendor often will give a covenant not to compete to the purchaser; and in many cases, a specific amount of the consideration paid for the business will be allocated to the covenant not to compete. The payment received for giving the purchaser such a covenant constitutes ordinary income to the vendor. On the other hand, the amount paid by a purchaser for the vendor's covenant not to compete is amortizable over a 15–year period. § 197. In many cases, the granting of a covenant not to compete is merely an incident of the sale of the goodwill of the business, and the payment ostensibly given for the covenant should be treated as part of the payment for goodwill (which constitutes capital gain to the vendor and also is amortizable by the purchaser over a 15–year period). However, in many cases, the covenant not to compete has been bargained for separately and has independent significance to the parties; in such cases, the payment is ordinary income to the vendor. The designa-

---

34. *Concord Control v. Commissioner*, 615 F.2d 1153 (6th Cir. 1980).

35. *Concord Control v. Commissioner*, 78 T.C. 742 (1982), acq.

tion given to the transaction by the parties is entitled to great weight, but the courts may apply a "substance over form" rule in appropriate cases and thereby find that the reality of the transaction was different from the parties' description of it.[36]

Prior to the adoption of § 197, the issue of distinguishing the purchase of goodwill from a payment for a covenant not to compete often arose because the cost of the latter could be amortized while the former could not. Now that both can be amortized over a 15–year period, the issue is more likely to arise with the seller in determining whether the seller has ordinary income or capital gain.

¶ 26.4121.   Substance over Form Doctrine—Availability to Taxpayer.

While the government is free to challenge the form that the parties adopted for a transaction, a TP who was a party to the agreement that established the form of the transaction may encounter greater difficulty in seeking to have a court disregard the form that the TP himself chose even if it differs from the substance.[37] In *Proulx v. United States*,[38] the Court of Claims adopted the so-called *Danielson* approach and held that a TP cannot have the form of his transaction disregarded unless the TP can prove facts that would be admissible in an action between the parties to the agreement to alter the terms of the agreement or to show that the agreement is unenforceable because of fraud, duress, threats, mistake or undue influence.[39] This strong restriction on the TP's ability to repudiate the form of a transaction is sometimes referred to as the *Danielson* rule or approach.[40]

36. See *Schulz v. Commissioner*, 294 F.2d 52 (9th Cir. 1961); *O'Dell & Co. v. Commissioner*, 61 T.C. 461 (1974).

37. See *Bolger v. Commissioner*, 59 T.C. 760 (1973); *Coleman v. Commissioner*, 87 T.C. 178 (1986); *Bradley v. United States*, 730 F.2d 718, 720 (11th Cir. 1984); *Estate of Leavitt v. Commissioner*, 875 F.2d 420 (4th Cir. 1989); *Harris v. United States*, 902 F.2d 439, 443 (5th Cir. 1990).

38. 594 F.2d 832 (Ct. Cls. 1979).

39. See also *Commissioner v. Danielson*, 378 F.2d 771 (3d Cir. 1967) (en banc); *Plante v. Commissioner*, 168 F.3d 1279 (11th Cir. 1999).

40. See also *Spector v. Commissioner*, 641 F.2d 376 (5th Cir. 1981), in which the Fifth Circuit adopted the *Danielson* approach that was used in *Proulx*. *Spector* involved a partnership taxation issue.

In *Grojean v. Commissioner*,[41] Judge Posner, writing for the court, said that a TP cannot use the substance over form doctrine to change the nature of a transaction from the form that the TP had adopted. Judge Posner said that only the government can do that. The Seventh Circuit's position appears to be even stricter than the *Danielson* rule.

The Tax Court has imposed a "strong proof" requirement on TPs seeking to repudiate the substance of the allocation made in their agreement; this "strong proof" test is less demanding than the *Danielson* and *Proulx* rule.[42] The "strong proof" test requires a showing that the requested reallocation is based on the intent of the parties at the time that the contract was executed *and* that the requested reallocation has independent economic significance.[43]

The "strong proof" test applies only where a TP seeks to repudiate or alter the terms of his agreement; the test does not apply to a TP who urges a particular construction of ambiguous terms of an agreement.[44] In *Uri v. Commissioner*,[45] the Tenth Circuit stated this principle in very broad terms. The court stated that for tax purposes "[o]rdinarily, taxpayers are bound by the form of the transaction they have chosen. . . ."[46] While the court did use the word "ordinarily," the context of the court's opinion suggests that there will be few circumstances in which the court would permit a TP to repudiate the form in which he had previously cast a transaction.

¶ 26.4122. Duty of Consistency. The Tax Court and several courts of appeals have applied a duty of consistency rule (sometimes called "quasi-estoppel") under which a TP who reports a transaction to the government in one form will not be allowed to prevail on a contention that the transaction had a different substance from the form it took.[47] The purpose of the rule is to prevent a TP from benefitting in a later year

41. 248 F.3d 572 (7th Cir. 2001).

42. *Major v. Commissioner*, 76 T.C. 239 (1981); *Coleman v. Commissioner*, 87 T.C. 178 (1986).

43. *Major*, 76 T.C. at 247–49.

44. *Peterson Machine Tool v. Commissioner*, 79 T.C. 72 (1982).

45. 949 F.2d 371 (10th Cir. 1991).

46. 949 F.2d at 374–75, n. 4.

47. *See*, e.g., *Estate of Ashman v. Commissioner*, 231 F.3d 541 (9th Cir. 2000).

from an error or omission he made in an earlier year because the time to assess a tax for the earlier year has expired.[48] The Sixth Circuit's application of this rule is much narrower than the Tax Court's approach and imposes additional requirements for the rule to apply, including the requirement that the TP have knowingly made a representation to the government or concealed a material fact.[49]

The rule of consistency has been applied only to factual issues (or to issues of mixed fact and law) and does not apply to a situation where all relevant facts were disclosed, but the report of the transaction made an error in law.[50]

For a discussion of the rule of consistency in another context, see ¶ **5.5100**.

48. See *Estate of Posner v. Commissioner*, RIA TC Memo ¶ 2004–112.

49. *Banks v. Commissioner*, 345 F.3d 373 (6th Cir. 2003), rev'd on another issue, 543 U.S. 426 (2005).

50. See *Estate of Posner v. Commissioner*, Memo TC ¶ 2004–112; see also Raby and Raby, *Duty of Consistency: Facts versus Law*, 103 Tax Notes 1131 (2004).

CHAPTER TWENTY–SEVEN

ANTICIPATION OF INCOME

¶ 27.0000. ANTICIPATION OF FUTURE INCOME. Instead of assigning income to another person in the hope that the income will be taxed to the assignee, a TP may sell the right to income to a third party in an attempt to convert ordinary income to capital gains and to utilize his basis in the underlying property to offset some of the amount realized. The doctrine that has been employed to prevent that abuse is sometimes called the "anticipation of income" rule. While the rule is universally applied, the term "anticipation of income" is not often used to describe it. For convenience of reference, we will refer to it in this book as the "anticipation of income" rule.

¶ 27.1000. SALE OF INCOME–PRODUCING PROPERTY. Any item of property is capable of producing income. If the sale of all income-producing property were to constitute an anticipation of income and thereby cause ordinary income treatment, that would extend the rule too far and would virtually eliminate capital gain treatment. Consequently, the sale of all of the rights to an item of property will not be subject to that rule in most cases.

One circumstance in which the anticipation of income rule will apply is when the sale of an item of property included the right to receive income that had already been earned. In such circumstances, part of the purchase price will be treated as having been paid for that earned income and so will be separated and treated as ordinary income to the seller. Even in that latter case, the anticipation of income rule will not always apply. The income earned on the property generally has to have achieved an advanced stage for the rule to apply.

Another application of the anticipation of income doctrine arises when a TP sells an income interest in property and retains a residual interest in it. The amount received in that situation will be treated as ordinary income.

¶ 27.1100. Sale of Corporate Stock. Ordinarily, the sale of corporate stock will be income to the seller in the amount of his gain (the excess of the amount realized over the seller's basis); and any gain or loss recognized on the sale will be treated as a capital gain or loss.[1] There are a few statutory exceptions to that general rule. See §§ 306 and 1244. In the vast majority of cases, capital gain or loss treatment will prevail.

A problem arises when a dividend has been declared on the stock, and the right to receive that dividend passed to the purchaser. Corporate dividends are usually included in the recipient's gross income and treated as ordinary income. § 301(c). When a stock is sold after a dividend has been declared, the question arises as to whether the seller or the purchaser should be taxable on that dividend when paid. Before examining that issue, there are three significant dates concerning dividends that must be kept in focus.

The first date is the date on which the corporation declares that a dividend will be paid on the stock. That date is referred to as the "declaration date."

The declaration that a dividend will be paid typically will state that it will be paid to the person who, on a specific date, is listed on the corporation's records as the owner of the stock. That date is referred to as the "record date." The person who is listed as the owner of the stock on the record date is the one who is entitled to receive the declared dividend.

The third date is the date on which the dividend will actually be paid. That date can be referred to as the "payment date."

For example, X corporation declares on March 5, Year One, that it will pay a dividend of $2 per share to the record holder of stock on March 20, Year One, and the dividend will be paid on April 3, Year One. March 5, Year One, is the declaration date. March 20, Year One, is the record date. April 3, Year One, is the payment date.

It is possible for several of those dates to fall on the same day. For example, if X corporation declared a dividend of $2 per share on March 5, Year One, payable to holders of record on March 5, Year One, the declaration date and the record date would be the same day.

¶ 27.1110. **Significance of Record Date.** The record date usually is the crucial element in determining who is to be taxed on a dividend. If the transferor transfers the stock after the declaration date, but before the record date, the transferee will be the holder of the stock on the record date and so will be entitled to receive the dividend when paid. Consequently, the dividend will

---

1. See ¶ 25.3312.

be ordinary income to the transferee. Even if the purchase price represented an amount that is attributable to the anticipated dividend, the transferee will be taxable on the entire amount of the dividend. All of the purchase price is treated as paid for the stock and so none of it can offset the transferee's dividend income. The seller will treat the entire amount of the purchase price as the amount realized for the sale of the stock, and he will usually recognize capital gain or loss on his gain or loss on the sale. Treas. Reg. § 1.61–9(c).

If the sale of the stock takes place after the record date, the seller will be the holder of the stock on the record date; and so the seller will be the one who is entitled to receive the dividend. In that case, the dividend will be taxable to the seller when paid. Stock which is sold so that the seller retains the right to a declared dividend is referred to as sold "ex dividend."

But what is the tax consequence if the sale takes place after the record date but prior to the payment date and the seller transfers to the purchaser the right to the declared dividend so that the purchaser will actually collect the dividend? In that case, the seller will be treated as having sold the right to the declared dividend in addition to selling the stock. The purchase price will have to be allocated so that part of it will be for the sale of the stock and part of it will be for the right to the declared dividend.[2] The amount allocated to the purchase of the declared dividend will be ordinary income to the seller. When the purchaser collects that dividend, the purchaser will have ordinary dividend income to the extent that the amount of the dividend exceeds the portion of the purported purchase price that was allocated to the purchase of the dividend. Treas. Reg. § 1.61–9(c).

¶ 27.2000. ILLUSTRATIONS.

¶ 27.2100. **Illustration 1.** On July 10, X sold shares of stock of the M corporation to Y, who collected the dividends thereafter. At the time of the sale, there were no outstanding dividends that had been declared on the stock. Since X sold all of the interest in the stock, the amount realized by X on the sale less X's basis in the stock will be a capital gain. Dividends paid on the stock after the sale will be taxable to Y as ordinary income.

¶ 27.2200. **Illustration 2.** The same facts apply as in ¶ 27.2100 except that on June 14, M declared a cash dividend to shareholders of

2. Rev. Rul. 82–11.

record on July 8. The dividend was to be distributed on July 15. Since X sold the shares after the July 8 record date, X was entitled to receive the dividend that had been declared on June 14. Ordinarily, then, X would be taxed on that dividend. Treas. Reg. § 1.61–9(c). However, the rules of the stock exchange on which the stock was sold required that when X sells the stock on a date between the record date and the date of payment, X is required to execute an agreement assigning X's right to the dividend to Y (the purchaser). X did execute such an agreement; thus, Y collected the dividend from M when it was distributed on July 15. On similar facts, the Commissioner ruled in Rev. Rul. 82–11 that the price paid by Y to X must be allocated between a payment for the dividend and a payment for the stock. The portion of the payment that is allocated to the sale of the dividend was treated by the Commissioner, under the anticipation of income doctrine, as ordinary income to X. Surprisingly, the ruling also characterized that ordinary income as dividend income to X. The portion of the payment allocated to the sale of the stock will cause X to recognize capital gain or loss depending upon X's basis in the stock. In the facts of that ruling, the amount of the purchase price that the Commissioner allocated to the purchase of the dividend was equal to the entire amount of the dividend.

To the extent that the amount of Y's payment to X was allocated to the purchase of a right to the dividend, the dividend collected by Y on July 15 constitutes a return of Y's capital and is not included in Y's income. Note that any excess of the dividend that Y received over the amount that Y paid for the right to that dividend is ordinary dividend income to Y. In cases where the dividend that was purchased will be paid shortly after the purchase took place, there will be little or no excess since there will be only a small discount, if any.

If X had sold the stock on July 1 (after the declaration date but before the July 8 record date), the dividend would be payable to the purchaser (the holder on the July 8 record date). The purchaser ordinarily will be taxed on the dividend. Treas. Reg. § 1.61–9(c). X will not recognize any ordinary income.

¶ 27.3000. **RETENTION OF A RESIDUAL INTEREST.** A sale of a right to income from property in which the seller reserves a residual interest, no matter how small that interest might be, will be subject to the anticipation of income rule. The amount that the seller receives from the sale will be treated as ordinary income; the seller will not be permitted to use any of his basis in the property to treat part of the purchase price as a recovery of capital.[3] For example, if G owns stock in the X Corporation, and if G sold to L the right to dividends from the stock for the next 12 years, the entire amount that G received from L as payment for the right to the dividends will be ordinary income to G. None of G's basis in the stock can be used to reduce the amount of his gain, and G's basis in the stock will not be changed by the sale.

Since the landmark decision for the residual interest rule is the Supreme Court's decision in *Commissioner v. P.G. Lake, Inc.*,[4] let us examine that case.[5]

The principal issue in that case involved a transfer of an oil payment right to compensate an officer of the transferor for his services. This constituted a sale of the oil payment right to the officer. An oil payment right is the right to a specified amount of money to be paid out of a specified percentage of the oil produced or the proceeds from the sale of that oil. The transferor retained the right to the oil produced or sold after the transferee had received the full amount of his oil payment right. While the opinion in *Lake* refers to the substitute for ordinary income doctrine[6] in concluding that the transferor recognized ordinary income on the sale, the key to the decision in that case is that the seller retained a residual interest in the property it transferred to the officer. In footnote 5 of the Court's opinion, the Court quoted, with apparent approval, a 1950 ruling of the Commissioner which concluded that the sale of an oil payment right that extends over a period that is less than the life of the depletable interest from which it was carved will cause ordinary income to the seller; but the sale of an oil payment right that constitutes the entire depletable interest of the seller will cause capital gain to the seller. In other words, if the seller retains a residual interest, he will have ordinary income, but if he retains no residual interest he will have capital gain.

This residual interest rule is sometimes referred to as the "carved out interest" rule, but "residual interest rule" is the more precise term.

Eleven years after *Lake* was decided, Congress changed the tax treatment of the "sale" of a right to a production payment carved out of mineral property. Congress concluded that the purported sale of such rights substantively was not actually a sale but rather was equivalent to

3. *Commissioner v. P.G. Lake, Inc.*, 356 U.S. 260 (1958).

4. 356 U.S. 260 (1958).

5. *Lake* involved five consolidated cases. The discussion in the text deals with the facts of one of those cases, but the facts of that case are typical.

6. See ¶ **27.3100**.

the obtaining of a nonrecourse loan secured by the mineral rights. Congress added § 636 to the Code in 1969 to treat such transactions as nonrecourse loans. However, as the IRS has acknowledged, the principles of the *Lake* decision remains applicable to other circumstances in which the anticipation of income rule arises.[7]

¶ 27.3100. "Substitute for Ordinary Income" Doctrine or "In Lieu of Income" Test. Some courts have utilized a so-called "in lieu of" test or a "substitute for ordinary income" doctrine for applying the anticipation of income rule. The landmark case that adopted that doctrine is *Hort v. Commissioner*.[8] The doctrine purports to provide a standard for determining whether all or part of the amount received on a sale of a property interest is actually a substitute for all or some of the income that the underlying property will produce. To the extent that the payment received is deemed a substitute for ordinary income to be produced by the property, it will be taxed as ordinary income under the anticipation of income doctrine.

While many courts have purported to apply the substitute for ordinary income doctrine, it actually is completely useless in determining whether the anticipation of income rule is applicable to a specific set of facts. Perhaps, the substitute for ordinary income doctrine should be considered merely as a synonym for the anticipation of income rule; that is, it is a term to describe a consequence rather than a term for a test or standard for determining when that consequence takes place. Consider the following illustration, which is drawn from the *Hort* case.

¶ 27.3110. Illustration 1. *X* owns an office building. *Y* is the principal tenant under a lease expiring in ten years. *Y* desires to cancel the lease. *X* agrees to release *Y* from the lease in consideration of *Y*'s payment to *X* of $50,000. The entire $50,000 is ordinary income to *X;* it was received by *X* "in lieu of" the rent that *Y* otherwise would have had to pay.[9]

Why do we say that the in lieu of test is useless? The value of any property is the present value of the income stream that the property is deemed capable of producing. The outright sale of any

---

7. Field Service Advisory, 1996 WL 33320880 (1996).

8. 313 U.S. 28 (1941).

9. See *Hort v. Commissioner, supra*; see also Treas. Reg. § 1.61–8(b).

property (for example, corporate stock) can be seen as the sale of the income stream that that property will produce. So the purchase price for any property is a substitute for the income that the property can produce. Obviously, the fact that the payment represents a substitute for the future income that the property can produce does not prevent the seller from qualifying for capital gain treatment and from utilizing his basis in the property. If that were not so, there could be virtually no circumstances that qualify for capital gains treatment. Recognizing that the in lieu of test is too broad to be applied without modification, courts have applied standards to determine when the rule is to be applied.[10]

The better reason for treating X as having ordinary income on the $50,000 receipt in Illustration 1 is that X still owns the building and thus continues to own the residual interest that will produce the future income.

For example, as we will see, if a life income beneficiary sells her entire life income interest to an unrelated party, any gain or loss she recognizes will be a capital gain or loss.[11] The payment received clearly is given for the income that the trust will produce since that is the only interest that the seller has to sell. Nevertheless, since the seller did not retain any residual interest in the property, the anticipation of income rule does not apply.[12]

¶ 27.3120. Illustration 2. X owned an apartment building which was leased to Y for 15 years. X sold to Z for $30,000 his rights to receive annual rents from Y under the lease, but X retained his residuary interest in the building. X recognized $30,000 ordinary income from the "sale." The retention of any residuary interest by a seller will usually be sufficient to prevent the seller from enjoying capital gains treatment or utilizing his basis.[13]

¶ 27.3200. Sale of an Undivided Fractional Interest. If, instead of selling a right to income from property in which the seller retains a residual interest, what if the seller were to sell an undivided fraction of all of his interest in the property. In that latter case, the anticipation of income rule will not apply. The seller will not have

10. *See* ¶ 27.3310.

11. *See* ¶¶ 27.3300–27.3320.

12. For further exploration of this issue, see ¶ 27.3300.

13. *Commissioner v. P.G. Lake, Inc.*, 356 U.S. 260 (1958) (*Lake* is discussed in ¶ 27.3000, *supra*).

retained a residual interest in the property that he sold to the purchaser. This distinction is sometimes described by referring to the sale with a retained residual interest as a sale of a horizontal slice of the seller's property; whereas, the sale of an undivided fractional share of the property is described as a sale of a vertical slice of the seller's property.

¶ **27.3210. Illustration.** F owns a commercial building which is leased to N for 15 years. As noted above, if F sold to P the right to rents from the property for the remainder of the term of the lease, the anticipation of income rule would apply. Instead, F sells to P one-third of his interest in the property including one-third of his right to collect rent under the lease. The sale of that fractional interest is not substantively different from the situation where F sells all of his interest in the property since, in both situations, F retains no residual interest in the portion of the property sold to P. Consequently, the anticipation of income rule is not applicable.

¶ **27.3300. Sale of an Income Interest Where No Residual Interest Is Retained.** If a TP sells his entire interest in an item of property, or a fractional share of his entire interest, even if the TP's only interest is an income interest, the anticipation of income rule ordinarily will not apply.[14]

The landmark case for this proposition is *McAllister v. Commissioner*.[15] In that case, the TP inherited a life income interest in a trust. The TP sold her life income interest to the remainderman of the trust. The case came to the Second Circuit to resolve two issues: (1) in determining her gain or loss from the sale, should the TP be allowed to use the basis she acquired in the life income interest under the antecedent to § 1014 when she inherited that interest; and (2) should the gain or loss that the TP recognized from the sale of her life income interest be treated as a capital gain or loss. In a majority opinion, the Second Circuit answered both questions in the affirmative. The court held that TP could use her basis in the interest to measure her gain or loss, and any gain or loss she had was a capital gain or loss.

14. One possible exception to the treatment of a sale of a TP's entire interest arises when the TP's interest is a term interest in a trust when the amount of term remaining in the TP's interest is for a very short period. For example, if a TP who had a 20–year term interest sold it when there were only two months remaining in his interest, a court might be reluctant to allow capital gain treatment for the sale.

15. 157 F.2d 235 (2nd Cir. 1946), cert. denied, 330 U.S. 826 (1947). See also Douglas A. Kahn, *Gain From Sale Of An Income Interest In A Trust*, 30 VA TAX REV. 445 (2010).

Congress subsequently amended the Code to override the court's determination that a TP could use her basis in determining gain or loss on such sales. Subject to one exception, § 1001(e) disallows the use of basis on the sale of a term interest if the basis was acquired by §§ 1014, 1015, or 1041 (i.e., acquired from a decedent, or by gift, or from a spouse). The one exception to that rule is that the TP can use her basis if her sale of a term interest is part of a transaction in which the entire interest in the property is transferred to another person or persons. § 1001(e)(3).

Significantly, Congress did not pass any legislation altering the Second Circuit's decision that the TP's gain or loss on the sale of a life income interest is a capital gain or loss if the TP retains no residual interest. The Service has promulgated a Revenue Ruling adopting the *McAllister* view that the sale of a life income interest qualifies for capital gain treatment.[16] The congressional decision to overturn one of the two holdings of the *McAllister* court and to leave undisturbed the other holding of that decision constitutes an implicit approval of the second holding.

In a number of recent cases, courts have uniformly held that when the winner of a lottery that provides an annuity (i.e., the right to receive annual payments over a specified period of years) sells the right to subsequent annuity payments, the seller recognizes ordinary income. Those courts rested their decisions on the "substitute for ordinary income" doctrine.[17] In some of those cases, the sellers retained a residual interest in the annuity, and in some they did not. As we will see, the sellers will recognize ordinary income from such sales regardless of whether they retain a residual interest.

Several of the courts that imposed ordinary income treatment on the sale of the right to annuity payments questioned the current vitality of the *McAllister* decision on capital gains since it preceded Supreme Court cases adopting the substitute for ordinary income test.[18] That issue is discussed below.[19] For now, note that the substitute for ordinary income doctrine was first adopted by the Supreme Court in 1941 in *Hort v. Commissioner*,[20] which case predates *McAllister* and indeed was cited by the Second Circuit in its opinion in *McAllister*.

16. Rev. Rul. 72–243.
17. See ¶ **27.3100** for a discussion of that doctrine.
18. See, e.g., *Clopton v. Commissioner*, 87 T.C.M. 1217 (2004).
19. See ¶ **27.3310**.
20. See ¶ **27.3100**.

In *Lattera v. Commissioner*,[21] a case which dealt with the sale of the annuity payments, the Third Circuit suggested that *McAllister* was wrongly decided and is not good law today. The *Lattera* decision is worthy of some discussion.

¶ **27.3310.** **The *Lattera* Decision.** The facts of *Lattera* were that the TPs won a state lottery having a value of more than nine million dollars. The winnings were required to be paid in 26 annual installments. In other words, the TPs received an annuity payable over a period of 26 years. After receiving nine of the installments, the TPs sold their right to the remaining seventeen installments to a third party for a lump sum of over three million dollars. The TPs reported the sales price as a long-term capital gain, listing their basis in the right to the installment payments as zero. The Third Circuit sustained the Commissioner's determination that the amount the TPs received was ordinary income.

The result that the court reached in *Lattera* is correct, but its reasoning is faulty. While ostensibly relying on the substitute for ordinary income doctrine, the court correctly observed that the doctrine cannot be applied indiscriminately or else it would preclude capital gain treatment in virtually all situations. The court said that other standards had to be employed to determine when the substitute for ordinary income doctrine applied and when it did not. One fault with the Third Circuit's decision lies with its use of the substitute for ordinary income doctrine at all. Since, as the court acknowledged, virtually all sales involve a substitute for future income, the standards that the court says are to be used to distinguish when the doctrine applies are the only standards that matter. In other words, the substitute for ordinary income doctrine adds nothing to the analysis of the issue; the standards ostensibly used to determine whether that doctrine applies are the only standards to determine whether the anticipation of income rule applies. The in lieu of test has no useful function and constitutes a distraction.

The Third Circuit said that it was not prepared to set forth an exclusive list of the standards to be employed in determining whether the in lieu of test applied. It did, however, list three standards that can be used.

The first of the three standards that the court adopted is a resemblance test. The court listed a number of items that have

---

21.   437 F.3d 399 (3d Cir. 2006).

been treated as capital assets and a number that have not to see if the right to the installment payments looked more like one of the lists than the other. The court concluded that the resemblance test was of no help in that case because the right to the installment payments does not resemble items on either list.

The second standard is the well-established principle that if the seller of a right to future income (a carved out interest) retains a residual interest in that income or in the property that produces the income, the seller will recognize ordinary income on the sale.[22] Since the TPs in *Lattera* had sold all of the interest they had in the property, the residual interest rule did not apply. The court therefore turned to a third standard.

The third standard, like the resemblance test, requires an examination of the character of the property that was sold to determine whether it qualifies as a capital asset. This third standard, on which the court based its decision, rests on a distinction between "earned income" and the right to earn income. While an earned income distinction is proper if construed correctly, the court's construction and use of that standard makes no sense.

The court concluded that only if the transferee of the right to the income must do something further to earn the income can the seller have capital gain treatment. The court determined that if the mere ownership of property gives the owner the right to future income, then the sale of the right to that income will be treated as a sale of earned income and so be taxed as ordinary income. The court said that the right to the installments was earned by the TPs when they won the lottery; nothing further needed to be done; and so their sale of that right produced ordinary income.

One problem with the court's opinion is its construction of "earned income" for purposes of this issue. If the court's construction were adopted, the sale of a bond or stock would produce ordinary income. As the court itself noted, the sale of stocks and bonds typically produces capital gains. The court also noted that "a stock's value is the present discounted value of the company's future profits." Yet, on the sale of stock, the purchaser obtains the right to future income (dividends) solely by virtue of owning the stock; he need do nothing further to obtain the dividends. The same can be said about the sale of a bond. The tax treatment of

---

22. See ¶¶ **27.3000, 27.3110** and **27.3120** for a discussion of the residual interest issue.

the sale of those items cannot be reconciled with the construction of earned income that the court adopted.

Moreover, the court concluded that its application of the earned income distinction conflicts with the decision of the Second Circuit in the *McAllister* case on the capital gain issue. The court dismissed that decision in the following language: "We consider *McAllister* to be an aberration, and we do not find it persuasive in our decision in this case." The court ignored the significance of the fact that Congress changed the basis rule of the *McAllister* decision, but left unimpeded the part of that decision that adopted the capital gain rule. The court also ignored the fact that the Service has promulgated a Revenue Ruling adopting the *McAllister* view that such a sale produces capital gains.[23] If the court had construed the "earned income" distinction correctly, there would have been no conflict with the *McAllister* decision, and the court would not have had to try to repudiate that case.

The court's conclusion that the amount received for the sale of the right to the installment payments was ordinary income to the TPs is correct. The reason, however, is different from the rationale adopted by the court. When the TPs won the lottery, they received a property right that had a value. Why were they not taxed in that year for the present value of the right to those payments? The apparent answer is that the TPs likely are on the cash receipts and disbursements method of accounting, as most individuals are. While there are exceptions, an unfunded, nonnegotiable promise to make payments generally does not qualify as cash or its equivalent. The TPs' right to the installment payments was not taken into income in the year they won because of the accounting system they use. Their right to those annuity payments represented a kind of deferred income. As one student commentator put it, the transaction effectively was kept open until the payments were received.[24] The right to already earned but deferred income is not a capital asset, and so the sale of that right does not produce capital gain.

In applying the earned income test, the court should not have made its decision turn on the fact that the purchaser did not have to do anything to have the right to the future installment payments. Mere ownership of property is not an obstacle to capital gain treatment when the property itself will earn the income. A

23. Rev. Rul. 72–243.

24. Matthew S. Levine, Case Comment, *Lottery Winnings as Capital Gains*, 114 YALE L.J. 195 (2004).

bond will produce income because it represents a debt on which interest is payable. A share of stock represents ownership in a corporation that can produce income through the management of its business. The owner of the bond or stock does not have to do anything to receive that income, but that should not matter.

¶ 27.3320.   **Illustration 1.** *M* is the life income beneficiary of a trust which was established by her deceased husband's will. *M* sells her entire interest in the trust to *S* for $30,000. The entire $30,000 that M received is income to her because she is not permitted to use any of her basis in the term interest she sold. § 1001(e). M's gain however is treated as a capital gain under the *McAllister* decision. Note, that the Commissioner has ruled that he will follow the *McAllister* decision that such transactions are treated as the sale of a capital asset.[25] S is allowed to amortize the $30,000 he paid for the life income interest over M's estimated life expectancy. That deduction is a form of depreciation.

If M had sold one-third of her life income interest for $10,000, the entire $10,000 would be capital gain income to her. Her sale of an undivided fractional interest in her property will receive the same capital gain treatment as would be given to a sale of her entire interest since she did not retain a residual interest in the portion of the income interest she sold.[26]

¶ 27.3330.   **Illustration 2.** In Year One, D died and left property to a testamentary trust, the income from which is payable to J of 20 years, and then the trust corpus is to be distributed to M. In Year Three, J sold his remaining 17–year term interest in the trust to R for $45,000. Since J did not retain any residual interest in the trust, the $45,000 gain that J recognized on the sale will be capital gain under the *McAllister* rule.

If instead of making the Year Three sale, in Year Nineteen, J had sold his remaining 1–year term interest in the trust, that term might be regarded as too short a time period to qualify the sale for capital gain treatment. That issue is not resolved.

¶ 27.3400.   **Change of Timing of Recognition.** A TP might sell a right to income from his property for the purpose of manipulating

25.   Rev. Rul. 72–243.

26.   See ¶ 27.3200.

the timing of when the income is recognized. For example, in *Estate of Shoholm v. Commissioner*,[27] the TP had a large interest deduction in one year. In order to utilize those interest deductions, the TP "sold" his son the right to a dollar amount of future dividends from certain publicly held stock owned by the TP, and the son paid the TP $115,000 for that right. The TP claimed that the $115,000 was ordinary income to him in the year of sale and that the dividends purchased by the son were not taxable to TP when paid to the son. The Tax Court held that the purported sale was a sham; and, thus, treated the dividends as income to the TP when paid. The Tax Court's decision was reversed.[28] On facts somewhat similar to those in *Stranahan*, other courts have rejected the anticipation of income contention of the TP on the ground that the TP's purported sale of his right to income was a sham, and that the substance of the "sale" was a loan to the TP that was disguised as a sale.[29]

27.   30 T.C.M. 1070 (1971).

28.   *Estate of Stranahan v. Commissioner*, 472 F.2d 867 (6th Cir. 1973).

29.   See, e.g., *Mapco Inc. v. United States*, 556 F.2d 1107 (Ct. Cls. 1977); *Martin v. Commissioner*, 56 T.C. 1255, aff'd without opinion, 469 F.2d 1406 (5th Cir. 1972); *Hydrometals, Inc. v. Commissioner*, 31 T.C.M. 1260 (1972), aff'd per curiam, 485 F.2d 1236 (5th Cir. 1973).

PART F
AMT AND IRD

CHAPTER TWENTY–EIGHT

ALTERNATIVE MINIMUM TAX

¶ 28.0000. ALTERNATIVE MINIMUM TAX.

¶ 28.1000. PURPOSE OF THE MINIMUM TAX.

Some of the deductions and exclusions authorized by the Code do not relate to an accurate determination of net income as much as they serve programmatic goals that Congress wishes to accomplish. Congress felt that virtually all citizens should share the burdensome cost of maintaining a government to some minimum extent and, accordingly, that, a TP should not be permitted to enjoy an amount of tax advantages that is disproportionate to the TP's economic income. To that end, Congress imposed a special tax on those TPs who have what Congress deemed to be an excessive amount of certain specified tax benefits. This additional tax is referred to as the Alternative Minimum Tax (AMT).

As originally designed by Congress in 1969, the AMT reached only a relatively small number of TPs who were in the very highest tax brackets. For reasons attributable to changes in the tax law, including changes in the AMT itself, the number of individuals subject to the AMT has greatly increased since its original enactment; and the AMT now covers many middle income TPs.

If the AMT is applicable, it effectively disallows most tax credits and all or part of a number of deductions. For example, no deduction is allowed for most state and local taxes and for miscellaneous itemized deductions.[1] This denial of tax benefits together with a tax rate that is not that far removed from normal rates are major reasons that the AMT has become so pervasive.

An administrative cost of having an AMT is that many TPs will have to compute both the regular tax and the AMT to determine whether the AMT is applicable.

¶ 28.1100. Alternative Versus Add–On Minimum Tax.

The current tax system utilizes an alternative minimum tax (AMT) rather than an add-on minimum tax. An "add-on minimum tax" would

---

1. See ¶¶ **28.2230** and **28.2260**.

impose an additional tax (i.e., a surtax) on a TP who has an excessive amount of statutorily specified tax advantages. While an alternative minimum tax is similar, it is not the same. The "alternative minimum tax" that Congress adopted is determined by recomputing the TP's taxable income by making certain specified adjustments and additions and then reducing it by a specified exemption amount. The resulting income figure is referred to as the Alternative Minimum Taxable Income or AMTI. Specified tax rates are then applied to the AMTI, and a specially determined foreign tax credit is allowed. The resulting figure (the TP's "tentative minimum tax") is then reduced by the TP's regular tax, and only the difference (if any) is payable by the TP as an alternative minimum tax.[2] In essence, the TP is liable for whichever tax is greater—the tentative minimum tax or the regular tax.

¶ 28.1200. Exclusivity of the Alternative Minimum Tax. Immediately prior to the adoption of the Tax Reform Act of 1986, noncorporate TPs were subject to an alternative minimum tax, whereas corporations were subject to an add-on minimum tax. The Tax Reform Act of 1986 repealed the corporate add-on minimum tax, created a new alternative minimum tax on corporations, and expanded the scope of the alternative minimum tax on individuals. The rules regarding the alternative minimum tax are contained primarily in §§ 55–59. The alternative minimum tax for corporations is not discussed in this book. While the AMT also apples to estates and trusts, they are not discussed in this book. The AMT generally applies to estates and trusts in the same manner that it applies to individuals.

¶ 28.1300. Alternative Minimum Taxable Income (AMTI). The computation of an individual's alternative minimum tax for a taxable year begins by taking the individual's taxable income and then making a number of adjustments and additions to that figure. Most of the adjustments will be positive so that they will increase the figure, but there can be negative adjustments. After making the adjustments and additions to taxable income, the resulting figure is referred to as the "alternative minimum taxable income." § 55(b)(2). For convenience, the alternative minimum taxable income is sometimes referred to hereafter as "AMTI."

¶ 28.1310. "Adjustments" and "Tax Preferences." A TP's AMTI is determined: (a) by adjusting the amount of certain items that are taken into account in determining taxable income (such

2. See ¶¶ **28.1400–28.1440.**

adjustments are made by substituting a specially computed item for the figure that is used in computing the TP's taxable income), and (b) by adding the amount of certain tax benefits referred to as "items of tax preference" or TPI. § 55(b)(2). A "tax preference" item will be a positive figure—that is, it will always increase the amount of a TP's AMTI. On the other hand, while an "adjustment" to a TP's income usually is positive, some adjustments are negative (i.e., they reduce the amount of a TP's AMTI). It, therefore, is possible for an individual to have taxable income that is greater than his AMTI. The adjustments utilized in determining AMTI are set forth in §§ 56 and 58.[3] Items of tax preference (TPI), which are added to taxable income in determining AMTI are set forth in § 57.[4] The combination of adjustments and TPI additions is sometimes collectively referred to as the "Minimum Tax Income Alterations" or MTIA.[5]

¶ 28.1400. Determination of Alternative Minimum Tax (AMT). The next step in determining a TP's alternative minimum tax is to apply a specified rate to as much of the TP's AMTI for the taxable year as exceeds an exemption amount. § 55(b)(1). The amount of a TP's exemption amount depends upon the filing status of the TP. If the TP's AMTI exceeds a specified figure, the TP's exemption amount is phased out. § 55(d)(3). The applicable exemption amounts and their phase-outs are described below.[6]

¶ 28.1410. Taxable Excess. For a noncorporate TP, the excess of AMTI over the TP's exemption amount is referred to as the "taxable excess." § 55(b)(1)(A)(ii). The applicable exemption amounts and their phase-outs are described below.[7]

¶ 28.1420. Alternative Minimum Tax Rate and the Tentative Minimum Tax. The alternative minimum tax rate to be applied to the taxable excess is 26% for so much of the TP's taxable excess as does not exceed $175,000 ($87,500 for a married TP filing a separate return) and is 28% for so much of the TP's taxable excess as does exceed $175,000 (or $87,500 for a married TP filing a separate return). § 55(b)(1)(A)(i). The total amount of tax as so computed is then reduced by the TP's "alternative

3. Discussed in ¶¶ **28.2200–28.2290H**.
4. Discussed in ¶¶ **28.2100–28.2150**.
5. See ¶ **28.2000**.
6. See ¶¶ **28.4000–28.4300**.
7. See ¶¶ **28.4000–28.4300**.

minimum tax foreign tax credit,"[8] if any, and the resulting figure is referred to as the "tentative minimum tax" for that taxable year. § 55(b)(1)(A). No other credits are taken into account in determining the tentative minimum tax.

¶ 28.1430. **Alternative Minimum Tax.** The difference (if any) between the tentative minimum tax and the TP's "regular tax" constitutes the alternative minimum tax (AMT). § 55(a). The TP's "regular tax" is computed for this purpose as the amount of tax that would be owing if there were no AMT and if the only credits that were allowed were the foreign tax credit, the § 936 Puerto Rico and Possession tax credit, and the Puerto Rico Economic Activity credit. In effect, a TP pays either his normal tax liability or his tentative minimum tax, whichever is greater.

¶ 28.1440. **Net Capital Gains and Qualified Dividends.** Currently, under regular taxation, capital gains and qualified dividend income of individuals are taxed at preferential tax rates. The AMT applies the same preferential rates to those items. Although capital gains and dividends of an individual are included in AMTI, they are segregated and taxed separately at their normal preferential rates. § 55(b)(3). It is not clear at this writing whether qualified dividends will have a preferential tax rate for years beginning after 2012.

¶ 28.2000. **MINIMUM TAX INCOME ALTERATIONS (MTIA).** Section 55(b)(2) requires that certain "adjustments" and items of "tax preferences" must be considered in computing AMTI. "Adjustments" involve a substitution of a special alternative minimum tax treatment of an item for the regular tax treatment. If an item is characterized by the Code as a tax preference, the Code requires that the difference between the special alternative minimum tax treatment of that item and its regular tax treatment be added to AMTI. Both adjustments and tax preferences are sometimes collectively referred to as Minimum Tax Income Alterations or MTIA.

¶ 28.2100. **Tax Preference Items (TPI).** Section 57 lists the items of tax preference (TPI) that are included in the determination of a TP's AMTI. Currently, there are five items listed in § 57, one of which (depreciation and amortization) is now of diminished consequence in this context.[9]

---

8. See ¶ 28.5000.

9. Those items are described in ¶¶ 28.2110–28.2150.

¶ 28.2110. Percentage Depletion. The extent to which a TP's deduction for the percentage depletion of a property exceeds the TP's adjusted basis in that property constitutes a TPI. § 57(a)(1). However, this provision does not apply to the depletion deduction allowed by § 613A(c) for certain amounts of domestic crude oil and natural gas. Id.

¶ 28.2120. Intangible Drilling Costs. The cost of drilling for oil, gas and geothermal property typically is deductible in determining a TP's taxable income. Absent this special treatment, such costs would have to be capitalized and amortized on a straight-line method. If the additional deduction allowable because of the special treatment accorded to such intangible costs constitutes an excessively large percentage (i.e., more than 65%) of the TP's net income from that activity in a taxable year, a portion of the cost will constitute a TPI. The computation of this item is described in § 57(a)(2). This provision does not apply to costs incurred in drilling for what proves to be an unproductive well. § 57(a)(2)(B)(i). There is a special provision for the treatment of an independent producer of oil or gas. § 57(a)(2)(E).

¶ 28.2130. Accelerated Depreciation or Amortization of Certain Properties Placed in Service Prior to 1987. Depreciation or amortization for property placed in service by the TP after 1986 is not included in tax preference items, but a portion of such depreciation deductions may be included in MTIA as an "adjustment" required by § 56(a)(1).[10] While the adjustment required by § 56(a)(1) does not apply to property placed in service prior to 1987, a part of the accelerated depreciation or amortization deductions for certain properties is included in TPI under § 57(a)(6) to the same extent that such deductions would have been included in TPI under pre–1987 law. In other words, the pre–1987 treatment of accelerated depreciation and amortization continues to apply to property placed in service prior to 1987. Presumably, there currently are few assets that are subject to this provision.

¶ 28.2140. Tax–Exempt Interest. Interest on "specified private activity bonds," which is exempt from taxable income, is a TPI and so is included in AMTI. This provision does not apply if the bond was issued prior to August 8, 1986. § 57(a)(5)(C)(i). The amount of such tax exempt interest is reduced by the deductions that are not allowable in determining taxable income but which

10. See ¶¶ 28.2210–28.2211.

would have been allowable if such interest were included in taxable income. § 57(a)(5)(A). The term "specified private activity bonds" is defined in § 57(a)(5)(C). Tax-exempt interest on state or local bonds other than "specified private activity bonds" is not included in AMTI.

¶ **28.2150. Small Business Stock.** In general, § 1202 excludes from gross income 50% of the gain from the sale or exchange of "qualified small business stock" (defined in § 1202(c)) that was held for more than five years. Seven percent of the amount so excluded by § 1202 from gross income is a TPI and so is added in determining AMTI. § 57(a)(7). The percentage of the excluded amount that constitutes TPI is scheduled to be increased for years beginning after 2012.

¶ **28.2200. AMTI Adjustments.** In addition to increasing taxable income for TPI, as required by § 57, §§ 56 and 58 require that certain items be determined differently for purposes of computing a TP's AMTI than they are determined for purposes of computing a TP's taxable income. The differently computed items are substituted for the figures used for those items in determining taxable income. The recomputed items are sometimes referred to as "adjustments." § 55(b)(2)(A). Some adjustments apply only to noncorporate TPs; some apply only to corporations; and some apply to both. We will discuss only those adjustments that apply to noncorporate TPs regardless of whether they also apply to corporations.

¶ **28.2210. Depreciation.** As noted in ¶ **28.2130**, there is no "adjustment" for depreciation or amortization deductions allowable for property placed in service prior to 1987, but a portion of such deductions may be included in TPI and therefore added to the Minimum Tax Income Alterations. Depreciation deductions for most tangible property placed in service after 1986 are subject to adjustment in determining the AMTI. § 56(a)(1). As a consequence of a 1997 amendment, the adjustment rules for tangible property placed in service after 1998 are somewhat different from those that apply to property placed in service after 1986 but prior to 1999. We will restrict our examination to the rules for property placed in service after 1998.

¶ **28.2211. Tangible Property Placed in Service After 1998.** For tangible property placed in service after 1998, the recovery periods used for AMTI purposes are the same as those used for regular MACRS purposes (Modified Accelerated Cost Recovery System), so no adjustments are made for recovery period. If the property is depreciated on the straight line method for regular tax purposes, no adjustment is made for AMTI purposes. Consequently, no adjustments are made for the depreciation of buildings or of any property that the TP elected to depreciate on the straight line method. Also, no AMTI adjustment is made for property that is depreciated for regular tax purposes on the 150% declining balance method. The only tangible property for which AMTI adjustments must be made are those depreciated for regular tax purposes on the 200% declining balance method. The depreciation of such properties for AMTI purposes must be determined by utilizing the 150% declining balance method (switching to straight line at the optimum year), but using the same recovery period as is applied for regular tax purposes. § 56(a)(1)(A)(ii).

A number of tangible properties are excluded from AMTI adjustments. The several properties listed in § 168(f)(1)–(4) (for example, films, video tapes and sound recordings) are excluded from this AMTI provision, and so no adjustment is made to the depreciation allowed for regular tax purposes for those items. § 56(a)(1)(B). Also, no adjustments are made to property that is depreciated on a method other than MACRS. For example, property which is depreciated on the units of production method is not subject to AMTI adjustments.

In determining AMTI, the depreciation deduction, as determined by the method described above, is substituted for the depreciation deduction used in determining taxable income. In a given year, the substituted figure for a depreciable asset may be greater or less than the regular depreciation amount. In the later years of the recovery period of a depreciable asset, the AMTI depreciation may be greater than the regular depreciation amount. This can result in a TP's having higher taxable income than he has AMTI in a taxable year. If a TP has multiple items of depreciable property, some of which have positive adjustments and some of which have negative adjustments, the TP can net them and adjust AMTI by the net figure.

¶ 28.2220. Basis Adjustment. Since the depreciation deduction allowable for AMTI can be a different amount than the depreciation allowable for taxable income, in determining a TP's gain or loss on the sale of a depreciable item, the TP's adjusted basis may be different for AMTI purposes than the basis used for taxable income purposes. § 56(a)(6). Moreover, there are other expenditures connected to properties that are different for purposes of calculating AMTI than for taxable income. To reflect those differences, the TP will have a different adjusted basis in those properties for AMTI purposes than for taxable income computation purposes. § 56(a)(6), (b)(3). Accordingly, on the sale of such properties, the TP could have a different gain or loss for taxable income purposes than the TP will have for AMTI purposes. Some properties for which this can occur are: (a) depreciable property, (b) property with respect to which circulation or research and experimental expenditures were paid by an individual, (c) property with respect to which mine exploration or development expenditures were paid, (d) pollution control facilities, and (e) stock acquired pursuant to the exercise of an incentive stock option.

¶ 28.2230.   **Taxes.** No deduction is allowed for alternative minimum tax purposes for state, local and foreign taxes on income, sales, or on real or personal property. § 56(b)(1)(A)(ii). Such taxes are deductible for alternative minimum tax purposes, however, to the extent that they qualify as nonitemized deductions. § 56(b)(1)(A). Thus, *property* taxes are deductible for alternative minimum tax purposes only if they are incurred in connection with a trade or business in which the TP is self-employed or in connection with rental properties, and no *income taxes* can be deducted.[11] If a tax that is disallowed as a deduction by this provision is subsequently recovered by the TP, the recovery is excluded from the TP's AMTI. § 56(b)(1)(D).

¶ 28.2240.   **Medical Expenses.** Medical expenses may be deducted for alternative minimum tax purposes only to the extent they exceed 10% of the TP's adjusted gross income (AGI). § 56(b)(1)(B). For regular tax purposes, currently the floor on the deduction for medical expense is 7.5% of AGI; but that floor is scheduled to be increased to 10% of AGI for years beginning after 2012. That will bring the regular floor in line with the AMT floor. For any taxable year beginning after 2012 and before 2017, the 7.5% of AGI floor will apply if the TP or the TP's spouse has attained the age of 65 before the close of that year. § 213(f).

¶ 28.2250.   **Interest.** A TP may deduct "qualified housing interest" in computing AMTI. § 56(b)(1)(C), (e). In general, qualified housing interest is qualified residence interest (as defined in § 163(h)(3)) which is paid or accrued on a debt incurred to

---

11.   See Chapter **Seventeen**.

acquire, construct or substantially rehabilitate a TP's principal residence and one other personal use dwelling; and the term also includes interest resulting from refinancing such debt. § 56(e). Additionally, most other interest that is deductible for regular tax purposes is deductible for alternative minimum tax purposes. § 56(b)(1)(C).

¶ 28.2260. Miscellaneous Itemized Deductions. Miscellaneous itemized deductions [defined in § 67(b)] are not deductible in computing AMTI. § 56(b)(1)(A)(i).

> **¶ 28.2261. Other Itemized Deductions.** Itemized deductions, other than those that are listed herein, can be deducted in computing AMTI. The overall limitation of § 68 on itemized deductions does not apply to the AMTI. § 56(b)(1)(F).

¶ 28.2270. No Adjustments for Deductions Under § 179. A deduction allowed the TP under § 179 for the cost of acquiring certain business property does not cause any adjustment to be made for AMTI purposes.[12] Subject to a dollar limitation, § 179 permits a TP to expense the cost of certain tangible personalty that is acquired for business use. The § 179 deduction is sometimes referred to as "bonus depreciation."

¶ 28.2280. Use of the Completed Contract Method. TPs who use the completed contract method of accounting for long-term contracts in computing regular tax liability must substitute the percentage of completion method in determining AMTI. § 56(a)(3). This provision does not apply to a contract entered into prior to March 1, 1986.

¶ 28.2290. Mining Exploration and Development Costs. In computing deductions for alternative minimum tax purposes, mining exploration and development costs incurred after 1986 must be capitalized and amortized on a straight-line basis over ten years. § 56(a)(2).This provision does not apply to costs incurred in connection with an oil, gas, or geothermal well.

¶ 28.2290A. Certified Pollution Control Facilities. Amortization deductions on certified pollution control facilities [§ 169] placed into service after 1986 and before 1999 must be computed by using the alternative depreciation system set forth in § 168(g). Facilities placed in service after 1998 are depreciated under § 168 using the straight line method. § 56(a)(5).

---

12. S. Rept. 99–313 on the Tax Reform Act of 1986 at p. 522, n. 5.

¶ 28.2290B. Alternative Tax Net Operating Loss Deduction (ATNOL). A TP with a net operating loss for a year after 1986 must recompute the net operating loss for AMTI purposes by reducing it by the tax preference items and by taking into account the TP's alternative minimum tax adjustments. § 56(d)(2). The resulting amount is the TP's "alternative tax net operating loss" [ATNOL] and may be carried forward and back to offset income that would otherwise be subject to the alternative minimum tax. There is a cap on the amount of ATNOL that can be deducted in a taxable year. § 56(a)(4), (d)(1)(A).

¶ 28.2290C. Alcohol Fuel Credit. Sections 40(a) and 38(b)(3) allow a tax credit for the use of alcohol as a fuel. Section 87 requires that the amount of a TP's alcohol fuel credit be included in the TP's gross income. Since no such credit is allowed for alternative minimum tax purposes, it would be inappropriate to include the credit in a TP's AMTI. Accordingly, the § 87 inclusion of that credit in income does not apply in determining AMTI. § 56(a)(7).

¶ 28.2290D. Denial of Tax Shelter Farm Losses. In computing AMTI, no deduction is allowed for losses attributable to tax shelter farming activities. § 58(a). A disallowed loss is carried over to subsequent years. If the TP disposes of his entire interest in a tax shelter farm activity, all of the TP's losses attributable to that activity (including carryover losses) are deductible in computing AMTI. § 58(c)(2). Also, the amount of tax shelter farm loss that is disallowed by this provision is reduced by the amount (if any) by which the TP is insolvent at the end of the taxable year. § 58(c)(1).

¶ 28.2290E. Disallowance of Part of Passive Activity Losses (PAL). In general, the regular tax provisions regarding limitations on the deductibility of passive activity losses [§ 469] also apply for alternative minimum tax purposes.[13] However, for alternative minimum tax purposes, the amount of PAL that is subject to disallowance is determined after taking into account AMTI adjustments and TPI, and several provisions of § 469 are excluded. § 58(b). The PAL that is disallowed by this provision is reduced by the amount (if any) by which the TP is insolvent at the end of the taxable year. § 58(c)(1).

---

13. The passive activity loss (PAL) provisions are discussed in Chapter **Eighteen**.

¶ 28.2290F. Circulation, Research, and Experimental Expenditures. In computing the deduction for alternative minimum tax purposes for expenditures incurred after 1986 in circulating a newspaper or other periodical, such expenditures must be amortized on a straight-line basis over a three-year period. Research and experimental expenditures incurred after 1986 must be amortized on a straight-line basis over a ten-year period. § 56(b)(2). This provision does not apply to research and development expenses incurred in connection with an activity in which the TP materially participates. § 56(b)(2)(D).

¶ 28.2290G. Incentive Stock Options. The special tax treatment accorded by § 421 to an individual's purchase of stock at a bargain price pursuant to an incentive stock option does not apply in determining the individual's AMTI. § 56(b)(3). However, no AMT adjustment is required if the exercise of the option and disposition of the stock occur in the same year. Id.

¶ 28.2290H. Standard Deduction and Personal Exemption Deduction. The standard deduction and the personal exemption deduction [§§ 63(c), 151] are not deductible in computing the alternative minimum tax. § 56(b)(1)(E). The AMT provides its own set of exemption amounts.[14]

¶ 28.3000. EFFECT OF AMT ON CERTAIN NONREFUNDABLE CREDITS. The manner in which the AMT is computed is described at **¶¶ 28.1400–28.1440**. The provision for an AMT can have tax consequences even when the regular tax exceeds the tentative minimum tax so no alternative minimum tax is applicable. Certain personal nonrefundable tax credits, which would otherwise be available in determining a TP's normal tax liability, are limited so that they cannot exceed the difference between the amount of the TP's regular tax liability and his tentative minimum tax (computed without a reduction for the alternative minimum tax foreign tax credit). § 26(a)(1).

¶ 28.4000. EXEMPTION AMOUNTS. The alternative minimum tax rate is imposed on the TP's AMTI that exceeds specified exemption amounts. However, a TP's exemption amount will be phased-out, but not below zero, to the extent that TP's AMTI exceeds a specified amount. § 55(d).

¶ 28.4100. Married Individual Filing Jointly and Surviving Spouses. For the year 2011, the exemption amount is $74,450 less

14. See ¶¶ **28.4000–28.4300**.

25% of the amount by which AMTI exceeds $150,000. § 55(d)(1)(A), (3)(A) as amended by Section 201(a) of Public Law 111–312. The exemption amount is scheduled to be reduced for years beginning after 2011.

¶ 28.4200. Single Individual Other Than a Surviving Spouse. For the year 2011, the exemption amount is $48,450 less 25% of the amount by which AMTI exceeds $112,500. § 55(d)(1)(B), (3)(B). The exemption amount is scheduled to be reduced for years beginning after 2011.

¶ 28.4300. Married Individual Filing Separately. For the year 2011, the exemption amount is $37,225 less 25% of the amount by which AMTI exceeds $75,000. § 55(d)(1)(C), (3)(C). Moreover, the AMTI of a married individual who files a separate return is increased by the *lesser* of: (i) 25% of the excess of AMTI (determined without regard to this addition) over $223,900, or (ii) $37,225. § 55(d)(3). The purpose of making this addition to the individual's AMTI is to prevent married TPs from filing separately to minimize the phaseout of the exemption amount. The exemption amount is scheduled to be reduced for years beginning after 2011.

¶ 28.5000. ALTERNATIVE MINIMUM TAX FOREIGN TAX CREDIT (AMTFTC). A TP may offset his alternative minimum tax (computed without regard to this credit or the ATNOL deduction) by his alternative minimum tax foreign tax credit (AMTFTC). In general, the AMTFTC is computed in a manner that is similar to the computation of the regular tax foreign tax credit under § 27; but there are differences. § 59(a). Some of the differences are that in computing the AMTFTC, the AMTI of the TP is used instead of the TP's taxable income, and the tentative minimum tax (before deducting the AMTFTC) is the tax against which the credit is taken.

¶ 28.6000. MINIMUM TAX CREDIT. Many of the adjustments and TPI taken into account in determining AMTI deal with deferrals of income rather than exclusions. Congress wished to permit TPs to offset the alternative minimum tax paid on such deferrals against the greater regular tax incurred when the deferral expires. Accordingly, Congress provides that the alternative minimum tax paid in any year may be carried forward indefinitely as a credit against a TP's regular tax liability for a taxable year to the extent that the TP's regular tax (plus his personal nonrefundable credits) exceeds his tentative minimum tax for that year. § 53(c). This credit is referred to as the "minimum tax credit." The alternative minimum tax that can create a minimum tax credit is only that amount of the TP's alternative minimum tax that arises because of adjustments or TPI attributable to deferral items (such as depreciation deductions). § 55(d). The deferral amount of a year's alternative minimum tax is computed by subtracting from the TP's alternative minimum tax for that year the amount of alternative minimum tax the TP would have had in that year if the only applicable adjustments and TPI were non-deferral items. The difference is called the "adjusted net minimum tax." The minimum tax credit for a taxable year is the excess of adjusted net minimum taxes for prior years beginning after 1986 over the amount of minimum tax credits allowable for such prior years. § 53(b).

¶ 28.7000. **SPECIAL ELECTION FOR PROLONGED WRITE-OFFS OF CERTAIN EXPENDITURES.** A TP can prevent certain expenditures (including research and experimental expenditures, circulation expenditures, intangible drilling costs, and mine development and exploration expenditures) from being treated as tax preference items (TPI) or as adjustments by electing to amortize the expenditures (for all tax purposes) on a straight-line basis over a ten-year period (a three-year period in the case of circulation expenditures, and a 60–month period in the case of intangible drilling and development expenditures). § 59(e).

¶ 28.8000. **TAX BENEFIT REQUIREMENT.** Section 59(g) permits the Treasury to prescribe regulations under which items of tax preference will be properly adjusted when the tax treatment giving rise to such items will not result in a reduction of the TP's income tax liability.

CHAPTER TWENTY–NINE

INCOME IN RESPECT OF A DECEDENT (IRD)

¶ 29.0000.   INCOME IN RESPECT OF A DECEDENT (IRD).

¶ 29.1000.   DEFINITION OF "INCOME IN RESPECT OF A DE-CEDENT" (IRD). There is no statutory definition of "income in respect of a decedent," hereinafter referred to as "IRD." The term refers to items of income which a decedent earned or was entitled to before his death, but which were not received (if on the cash method of accounting) or did not accrue (if on the accrual method of accounting) until after his death. Treas. Reg. § 1.691(a)–1(b). In other words, although earned beforehand, the income was not recognized for tax purposes until after the decedent's death.

¶ 29.2000.   COMMON EXAMPLES OF IRD. Some common examples of IRD are:

(a) *Wages and Salaries, Generally.* Income from personal services of a cash method decedent (e.g., salaries, fees, bonuses and commissions, including renewal commissions of a deceased life insurance agent) which is payable for services performed during the decedent's life but which is not paid until after his death constitutes IRD. Treas. Reg. § 1.691(a)–2(b), Exs. (1) and (2).

(b) *Bonus Awards.* Payment of a postmortem bonus award is IRD if the payment of the bonus is included in gross income. See ¶ **6.4500**. If the decedent had a right or entitlement to have the bonus paid, it will be IRD when paid; but it is not necessary for there to be an actual legal right or entitlement for the payment to be income and therefore to constitute IRD. For example, in *Rollert Residuary Trust v. Commissioner,*[1] the courts held a postmortem bonus to be IRD in view of the employer's established practice of awarding bonuses and its tentative decision before decedent's death to assign funds to the bonus pool. Prior to the decedent's death, the company tentatively decided to award bonuses to all executive vice presidents, including the decedent, subject to forfeiture if, during a stated period, the

---

1.   80 T.C. 619 (1983), aff'd 752 F.2d 1128 (6th Cir. 1985).

employee failed to continue in the employ of the company or committed acts inimical to the company's interests. Those conditions terminated on the decedent's death. The bonus was awarded by the employer more than three months after the decedent died. While the employer was not committed to making the bonus at the time of decedent's death, the employer's consistent practice of paying bonuses in such cases was sufficient to classify the bonus as IRD. In affirming the Tax Court, the Sixth Circuit held that the test for IRD was the degree of likelihood at the time of the decedent's death that the bonus would be made rather than whether the decedent had a legal right to it.

(c) *Share of Partnership Income.* All payments coming within § 736(a), including a share of profits after death, made by a partnership to the estate or other beneficiary are IRD. A deceased partner's share of the income of the partnership which is attributable to the period ending with the date of death is IRD. § 753; Treas. Reg. § 1.753–1.

(d) *Income from Sale of Property.* When property is sold by the decedent prior to his death, any amount realized thereon after his death will constitute IRD. However, if a sale is not completed prior to death, income from a sale after death will not constitute IRD even when the decedent had executed a valid contract to sell prior to his death. Treas. Reg. § 1.691(a)–2(b), Exs. (4) and (5). If the decedent's gain from a sale was reported by the decedent on an installment method under § 453, the recipient of the installment obligation from the decedent, other than the obligor, will continue to report the gain on the same installment method. See ¶¶ **29.3000, 29.3430**.

(e) *Passive Income.*

> (i) *Interest Income.* When decedent was a cash method TP, uncollected interest earned on United States savings bonds is taxable as IRD when collected. Treas. Reg. § 1.691(a)–2(b), Ex. (3).

> (ii) *Dividend Income.* Dividends payable after death in accordance with decedent's ownership of stock at the record date for the dividend prior to his death are IRD.

¶ **29.3000. REPORTING OF IRD.** *Generally.* An item of IRD is reported as gross income in the year of collection by the decedent's estate or by the beneficiary or transferee who receives the item irrespective of whether they report their income on the cash or accrual method. § 691(a)(1), Treas. Reg. § 1.691(a)–2(a).

(a) *Installment Obligations.* When the decedent had been reporting gain on the installment method from a sale made while he was living, the estate or its beneficiary will likewise report it in the same way and such gain constitutes IRD. § 691(a)(4).

The transfer to the decedent's estate or beneficiary of an installment obligation for which the decedent had been reporting income on the installment method will not trigger immediate recognition of the remaining unrecognized income *unless the transferee was the obligor.* § 691(a)(2), (5). Further, a transfer of an installment obligation from the decedent's estate to a legatee (other than to a legatee who is the obligor of the debt instrument) is not a disposition that accelerates the recognition of the gain. § 453B(c); Treas. Reg. § 1.691(a)–4(b). The recipient (other than the obligor) of an installment obligation from the decedent will continue to report the income from payments on that obligation or its subsequent transfer on the installment method in the same proportion as income would have been reported by the decedent if he had continued to live. Treas. Reg. § 1.691(a)–5(a).

However, cancellation of the unpaid balance of the installment obligation on the decedent's death or a transfer of the obligation by the estate to the obligor will constitute a disposition that triggers the recognition of IRD by the estate, pursuant to § 691(a)(5)(A), in the amount by which the fair market value of the instrument exceeds the holder's basis § 691(a)(2), (4), (5)(A). The holder's basis will equal the basis that the decedent had in the instrument at the time of his death less any principal received from installment payments made after the decedent's death. If an installment obligation becomes unenforceable, it will be treated as cancelled. § 691(a)(5)(C).

Moreover, an installment obligation or other debt instrument may provide that it is cancelled on the death of the holder. An installment note that has such a provision is referred to as a "self-cancelling installment note" (SCIN) or a death-terminating note. The tax treatment of the cancellation at the decedent's death is determined by the application of the cancellation rules described above.

(b) *Contingent Claims.* Items to which the decedent had a contingent claim at the time of his death to the extent that such items would have constituted gross income to the decedent had he lived to collect it are IRD. Treas. Reg. § 1.691(a)–1(b).[2]

---

2. See *Rollert Residuary Trust v. Commissioner*, 80 T.C. 619 (1983), aff'd 752 F.2d 1128 (6th Cir. 1985).

¶ **29.3100.   Illustrations of IRD.**

¶ **29.3110.   Illustration 1.** A widow acquired by bequest from her deceased husband the right to receive renewal commissions on life insurance sold by him during his lifetime, which commissions were payable over a period of years. The widow died before the period expired. Those commissions paid to the widow prior to her death are IRD and are includable in her gross income. The widow's son inherited from her the right to receive the remaining commissions, and his collection of those commissions is also IRD and must be included in the son's gross income. Treas. Reg. § 1.691(a)–2(b), Ex. (2).

¶ **29.3120.   Illustration 2.** A decedent was entitled at the date of her death to a salary payment from her employer. Her estate collected the payment. The payment is IRD, and the estate must include it in gross income. See Treas. Reg. § 1.691(a)–2(b), Ex. (1). If the estate collected only one-third of the payments due and then distributed the balance of the claim to the decedent's sister (who was her beneficiary), the amounts subsequently collected by the sister are IRD and included in the sister's gross income. Id.

¶ **29.3200.   Characterization.** IRD retains the same character to the recipient that it would have had to the decedent had the decedent lived to collect it. § 691(a)(3). Note that if in the same year that the estate collected IRD, it distributed to a beneficiary of the estate an amount at least equal to that IRD (assuming that the estate had no other gross income that year and the distribution to the beneficiary constitutes a distribution of so-called "distributable net income"), the distribution to the beneficiary will be included in the beneficiary's income and will have the same character as the IRD had. § 662(b).

¶ **29.3300.   Basis.** Items of IRD do not acquire a new basis at death. § 1014(c). Thus, the decedent's basis (if any) carries over and no adjustments are made.

¶ **29.3400.   Disposition of Rights to IRD.**

¶ **29.3410.   General.** If the recipient of a right to receive IRD sells or otherwise transfers it to someone who is not required to treat the collection of the item as IRD of the decedent, the amount of the consideration, if any, received for the right or the fair market value of the right at the time of transfer, whichever is greater, is includable in the transferor's gross income. § 691(a)(2). Discussion of several circumstances where the transferee is required to treat the collection of the transferred item as IRD is set forth in ¶ **29.3430**.

¶ **29.3420. Illustration.** At date of death, D was entitled to a $60,000 salary payment to be made in six equal annual installments. His estate collected two installments, reported those installment payments as IRD, and then distributed the right to the remaining four installments to Smith, who was the residuary legatee of the estate. Smith collected the third installment, and he must report the amount collected as IRD. In an arms' length transaction, Smith sold his right to the remaining $30,000 of payments for its fair market value of $28,000. The $28,000 paid to Smith for the sale of the right to the remaining three installments is includable in his gross income at the date of sale. Since the sale was an arms' length transaction, it is presumed that the amount paid equals the fair market value of the instrument that was sold.

¶ **29.3430. Disposition Resulting from Decedent's Death.** On the disposition of a right to IRD, the transfer does not cause the transferor to recognize gross income if the transfer results from the decedent's death or the transfer is a distribution from a decedent's estate to a beneficiary unless the transfer was made to the obligor. In either of the above events, the transferee reports the IRD item as gross income when collected or transferred by that person. See ¶ **29.3000**.

¶ **29.4000. INCOME TAX DEDUCTIONS ALLOWED.**

¶ **29.4100. Deductions for Federal Estate Taxes Paid.** The tax law would be unduly harsh if items of IRD were taxed both for federal estate tax purposes as part of the decedent's gross estate and also for income tax purposes as gross income of the person who collected the IRD item after receiving it from the decedent. After all, had the decedent lived to include the items in his personal income tax return, the income tax paid would have reduced, on his subsequent death, the size of his gross estate and resulted in a smaller federal estate tax liability. However, IRD *is* subjected to both income tax and estate tax burdens.

To mitigate this double taxation of the same item, and to approximate the total amount of taxes (both income and estate tax) that would have been paid if the income item had been received by the decedent before his death, Congress enacted § 691(c) which allows an income tax deduction to a person who has IRD income for that item's allocable share of the amount of the decedent's federal estate tax that is attributable to the net value, for estate tax purposes, of the decedent's total amount of IRD. This deduction is not included in the computation of a TP's adjusted gross income (AGI)—i.e., it is an itemized deduction.[3] The significance of classifying a deduction as "an itemized deduction" is discussed in Chapter **Ten**. The deduction is *not* subject to the 2% of AGI floor that applies to some itemized deductions. § 67(b)(7). However, it is subject to the overall limitation on itemized deductions that is imposed by § 68.

While this item is an income tax deduction, it is sometimes called an "estate tax deduction" since the amount of the income tax deduction is determined by reference to the estate tax liability caused by the decedent's IRD. In determining the amount of the deduction, the decedent's estate tax is reduced by all credits allowed against that tax; the deduction is computed on the basis of the *net* estate tax. § 691(c)(2)(A). A similar deduction is allowed for IRD that was subjected to a generation-skipping tax. § 691(c)(3).

The reduction of the estate tax deduction that occurs when the overall limitation of § 68 is triggered runs afoul of the basic purpose for allowing the deduction—namely, to impose on IRD received after the decedent's death approximately the same amount of aggregate estate and income tax burden that would have been borne if the item had been received by the decedent during his life. There is no apparent reason for excluding high bracket TPs from the full benefit of that treatment.[4]

> **¶ 29.4110. Net Value of IRD.** The "net value" of IRD equals the total estate tax value of all § 691 income less the total amount of deductions that qualify as deductions in respect of a decedent under § 691(b). Treas. Reg. § 1.691(c)–1(a)(1). See **¶ 29.4200** for an explanation of what constitutes a "deduction in respect of a decedent."

> **¶ 29.4120. Computation of Estate Tax Deduction for IRD.** As noted above, an income tax deduction is permitted for the estate tax attributable to the inclusion of IRD in the decedent's gross estate. This income tax deduction is commonly referred to as an "estate tax deduction." See **¶ 29.4100**. The total amount of

---

3. See Rev. Rul. 78–203.

4. See Jeffrey H. Kahn, *Beyond the Little Dutch Boy: An Argument for Structural Change in Tax Deduction Classification*, 80 Wash. L. Rev. 1 (2005).

deductions allowable for the estate tax on all IRD items is the difference between: (a) the net estate tax actually payable, and (b) a recomputed net estate tax which is determined by excluding from the decedent's taxable estate the net value of all of the IRD items that were included in the decedent's gross estate. § 691(c)(2)(C). The meaning of "net value of IRD" is explained at ¶ **29.4110**. The recomputation of the decedent's taxable estate must take into account any estate tax deductions that are lost or changed as a consequence of excluding the net value of the IRD items from the decedent's taxable estate. The effect of this formula is that the estate tax that is deductible for income tax purposes is determined at the estate's highest marginal rates on the net value of the IRD. § 691(c)(2). The total estate tax deduction must then be allocated among the several items of IRD as described in ¶ **29.4130**.

¶ **29.4130. Collection of a Portion of the Decedent's Total IRD.** A person who receives only a portion of a decedent's total IRD is allowed a proportionate part of the estate tax deduction. The amount of a TP's deduction is the proportion of the death taxes attributable to the net value of all IRD items that the gross value for estate tax purposes of the IRD that is included in the TP's gross income bears to the gross value for estate tax purposes of all of the decedent's IRD. See Treas. Reg. § 1.691(c)–1(d), Ex. (1). Thus, although the total deduction for death taxes is based on the *net* value of the IRD, the apportionment of the deduction among items of IRD is based on the ratio that the *gross* estate tax value of each such item bears to the *gross* estate tax value of all such items. Id. However, if the amount included in a TP's gross income because of the collection of the IRD item is less than the gross estate tax value of that item, the proportion described above is based on the lower amount included in income rather than on the gross estate tax value of the item. Id., § 691(c)(1)(A).

¶ **29.4200. Deduction in Respect of a Decedent.** Since income earned by a decedent but recognized after his death may constitute IRD, a reasonable corollary would permit an income tax deduction to those who pay expenses incurred by the decedent if the decedent would have been entitled to a deduction had he lived. Congress adopted such a provision for certain deductions in § 691(b). Obligations incurred by a decedent prior to his death which were not properly allowable as deductions on the final income tax return for the decedent (or on any prior income tax return), but which would have qualified as deductions under §§ 162, 163, 164 or 212 if paid by

the decedent during his life, are allowed as deductions to the estate
or beneficiary who makes the payment in the year in which paid.
Similarly, a credit for foreign death taxes on IRD is allowed to the
estate or beneficiary liable for and making such payment, and a
depletion allowance under § 611 is allowed to the person who receives the income to which such depletion deduction relates.

¶ 29.4210.   **Restriction to Specified Deductions.** The deduction in respect of a decedent is allowed only for business expenses
deductible under § 162, non-business expenses deductible under
§ 212, interest charges (to the extent deductible under § 163),
taxes deductible under § 164, and depletion deductions (§ 611).
Note that not all interest expenses are deductible. Only the
recipient of the income to which a depletion deduction (under
§ 611) relates may take that deduction. Treas. Reg. § 1.691(b)–
1(b).

¶ 29.4220.   **Double Deductions Allowed.** Deductions in respect of a decedent are allowed both as an income tax deduction
to the one making the payment and as a federal estate tax
deduction as a claim against the estate under § 2053. § 642(g)
and Treas. Reg. § 1.642(g)–2. This is a rare situation in which the
same item is deductible both for income tax and estate tax
purposes.

TABLE OF CASES

References are to Pages.

859

TABLE OF INTERNAL REVENUE CODE SECTIONS

References are to Pages.

TABLE OF TREASURY REGULATIONS

References are to Pages.

TABLE OF REVENUE RULINGS

References are to Pages.

TABLE OF REVENUE PROCEDURES

References are to Pages.

TABLE OF PRIVATE LETTER RULINGS

References are to Pages.

TABLE OF TECHNICAL ADVICE MEMORANDUM

References are to Pages.

TABLE OF NOTICES

References are to Pages.

INDEX

References are to Pages

909